INTERNATIONAL LAW

INTERNATIONAL LAW

FOURTH EDITION

Charles G. Fenwick

Professor of Political Science
Bryn Mawr College, 1918-1940
Member of the Inter-American Juridical Committee, 1942-1947
Director, Department of Legal Affairs, Pan American Union, 1948-1962

NEW YORK
APPLETON-CENTURY-CROFTS
Division of Meredith Publishing Company

Copyright © 1965 by

MEREDITH PUBLISHING COMPANY

675-12

Library of Congress Card Number: 65-21405

PRINTED IN THE UNITED STATES OF AMERICA
E 31048

Preface

The first edition of the present volume, published in 1924, was dedicated:

> To those who gave their lives
> 1914-1918
> In the hope that new principles of justice might
> be found to govern the relations of states.

The second edition, published in 1934, saw that hope defeated, and could do no more than recite the failure of the United States to realize that it had a vital national interest in the maintenance of international law and order, and describe the resulting uncertainty of success of the new system of collective security established by the League of Nations. The third edition of 1948, prepared under the promise held out by the adoption of the Charter of the United Nations, seemed to mark the coming of a new era in which the agencies of international organization might effectively strengthen the rule of law and bring about higher standards of justice and cooperation for the common welfare.

Today the new era is still with us, but problems have arisen not contemplated in the Charter of 1945. The United States has, indeed, come to realize that it has a vital national interest in the maintenance of international law and order. But the conditions of law and order have fundamentally changed. With the invention of the atomic bomb collective security has given way to a new balance of power so acutely competitive as to merit the designation of a "cold war." A single state in possession of the bomb is now in a position to defy the community, and the only practical restraint upon it is the knowledge that the devastation it might be able to wreak upon its opponent by a surprise attack would be countered by equal devastation inflicted upon itself. Such a system, described as a "balance of terror," is obviously far from the conception of collective security that dominated the conference in San Francisco. For the moment the prospects are hopeful for a gradual lifting of the iron curtain that now divides the Communist and non-Communist worlds. But the cornerstone of law remains for the time in an unstable setting.

Other changes in international law since 1948 have been significant: the admission into the international community of new states for which the traditions of Western Europe command little authority; the psycho-

pathic reactions to colonialism; the impact upon law of the expansion of
activities into outer space; the progress of economic and social cooperation in raising standards of living; the political effects of the European
Common Market; and numerous other minor adjustments resulting from
the reaction of regional organization upon the universal system. But these
problems are relatively minor in the presence of the threat of the atomic
bomb.

As in the third edition, the experience of the author in inter-American
affairs has led to the introduction of numerous references to the law of
the American Republics as a regional group and to the practical applications of the inter-American security procedure, which has served as an
example to the United Nations of the possibilities of collective action on a
larger scale. The sharp abridgment of the chapters on the law of war and
of neutrality reflects the paradoxical situation in which the formal "state
of war" has lost its legal character, although the actual resort to force
in certain areas still continues.

No general expression of thanks can satisfy the debt which the author
owes to the many friends with whom he has collaborated for the past
forty years or more: some have passed on, others are still proclaiming the
ideal of a world of law and order and concentrating upon the practical
means of attaining it. Individual names will appear in the footnote references. Outstanding has been the help received from the contributions of
scholars to the successive issues of the *American Journal of International
Law*.

Once more the author would emphasize that the hope of peace lies in
the development and strengthening of the rule of law, which in its turn
must function not only as a restraint upon violence but as a continuing
search for higher standards of international justice. Functioning thus, the
rule of law becomes in a manner its own sanction, building up by its very
effectiveness a commanding interest in the maintenance of peaceful relations and a realization that conflicts of national claims can in many cases
be most equitably resolved by measures looking to the welfare of the
community as a whole.

C. G. F.

Contents

Chapter IV. THE DETERMINATION OF THE RULES OF INTERNATIONAL LAW

Chapter V. THE RELATION OF INTERNATIONAL LAW TO MUNICIPAL LAW

PART II. THE ORGANIZATION OF THE COMMUNITY OF NATIONS

Chapter VI. THE COMMUNITY OR "FAMILY OF NATIONS"

Chapter VII. ACQUISITION AND LOSS OF INTERNATIONAL PERSONALITY: SUCCESSION OF STATES

Chapter VIII. CONTINUITY OF INTERNATIONAL PERSONALITY: THE RECOGNITION OF NEW GOVERNMENTS

Chapter IX. THE UNITED NATIONS

PART III. THE SUBSTANTIVE RULES OF INTERNATIONAL LAW

Chapter XI. **THE GENERAL RIGHTS AND DUTIES OF STATES: THE PRINCIPLE OF EQUALITY**

Chapter XII. **THE RIGHT OF NATIONAL EXISTENCE: SELF-DEFENSE AND COOPERATIVE DEFENSE**

Chapter XIII. THE INDEPENDENCE OF STATES: GENERAL RIGHTS AND OBLIGATIONS OF JURISDICTION

Chapter XIV. THE INTERNATIONAL RESPONSIBILITY OF THE STATE FOR THE PROTECTION OF RESIDENT ALIENS

CONTENTS

Chapter XVII. JURISDICTIONAL COOPERATION BETWEEN STATES: EXTRADITION OF FUGITIVE CRIMINALS; LETTERS ROGATORY; COMITY

Chapter XVIII. JURISDICTION OVER TERRITORY: TITLES

✳Chapter XIX. JURISDICTION OVER TERRITORY: NATIONAL BOUNDARIES AND TERRITORIAL SEA

Chapter XX. RESTRICTIONS UPON JURISDICTION OVER TERRITORY: EASEMENTS AND SERVITUDES

✳ Chapter XXI. JURISDICTION OVER THE AIR ABOVE NATIONAL TERRITORY

Chapter XXII. THE HIGH SEAS

Chapter XXIV. THE AGENTS OF INTERNATIONAL INTERCOURSE

Chapter XXVII. FORCIBLE PROCEDURE BY METHODS FALLING SHORT OF WAR

Chapter XXVIII. FORCIBLE PROCEDURE BY WAR

Chapter XXIX. THE LAWS OF LAND AND AERIAL WARFARE

CONTENTS

Chapter XXXVI. INTERNATIONAL LAW: THE OLD AND THE NEW

APPENDICES

List of Works Referred to

The following list is limited to works appearing in footnotes in the text. While not a complete bibliography, it may be taken as a working library of the subject.

Académie de droit international: Recueil des Cours, 1923–1963, 108 vols. (Paris, 1925–1963).

ACADEMY OF SCIENCES OF THE U.S.S.R., INSTITUTE OF THE STATE AND LAW, *International Law* (Moscow).

ACCIOLY, H., *O reconhecimento da independência do Brasil* (Rio de Janeiro, 1927).

———, *Tratado de direito internacional público,* 2d ed., 3 vols. (Rio de Janeiro, 1956–1957).

———, *Actos internacionaes vigentes no Brasil,* 2d ed., 2 vols. (Rio de Janeiro, 1936–1937).

ALLEN, E. W., *The Position of Foreign States before National Courts Chiefly in Continental Europe* (New York, 1933).

ALVAREZ, A., *Le Droit international Américain* (Paris, 1910).

———, *The Monroe Doctrine: Its Importance in the International Life of the States of the New World* (New York, 1922).

———, *Le Continent américain et la codification du droit international* (Paris, 1938).

American Journal of International Law (New York, 1907–). Cited *Am. Journal.*

American Political Science Review (Baltimore, 1907–). Cited *Am. Pol. Sc. Rev.*

American State Papers, Class I, Foreign Relations, 1789–1828, 6 vols. (Washington, 1832–1859).

American White Book: European War, Nos. 1–4 (Washington, 1915–1918).

ANAND, R. P., *Compulsory Jurisdiction of the International Court of Justice* (Bombay and New York, 1961).

Annals of the American Academy of Political and Social Science (Philadelphia, 1890–).

Annuaire de l'Institut de droit international (1877–).

Annual Digest and Reports of Public International Law Cases, 9 vols., 1919–1942. 1919–1924, 2 vols. ed. by Sir J. F. Williams and H. Lauterpacht; 1925–1928, 2 vols. ed. by Sir A. D. McNair and H. Lauterpacht; 1929–1940, 5 vols. ed. by H. Lauterpacht (London, 1929–1942). Since 1950, *International Law Reports.*

Annual Register (London, 1863–).

ANZILOTTI, D., *Corso di diritto internazionale,* Vol. I, 3rd ed. (Rome, 1928). French trans. by G. Gidel, *Cours de droit international* (Paris, 1929).

ARECHAGA (H), E. J. DE, *Reconocimiento de Gobiernos* (Montevideo, 1947).
———, *Voting and the Handling of Disputes in the Security Council* (New York, 1950).
ASHER, R. E., AND OTHERS, *The United Nations and the Promotion of the General Welfare* (Washington, 1957).
AUSTIN, J., *Province of Jurisprudence Determined* (London, 1832).
AYALA, B. DE, *De jure et officiis bellicis et disciplina militari,* Vol. I, Latin text; Vol. II, English trans. by J. P. Bate (Washington, 1912).
AZCÁRATE, P. DE, *The League of Nations and National Minorities: An Experiment* (Washington, 1945).
AZUNI, D. A., *Sistema universale dei principii del diritto marittimo dell' Europa,* 1st ed. (Florence, 1795). French trans. of the 2d Italian ed. (Trieste, 1796), by J. M. Digeon.
BAILEY, T. A., *Diplomatic History of the American People,* 7th ed. (New York, 1964).
BAKER, P. J. N., *The Geneva Protocol for the Pacific Settlement of International Disputes* (London, 1925).
———, *The Mandates System* (London, 1930).
BAKER, R. S., *Woodrow Wilson and World Settlement,* 3 vols. (Garden City, 1922).
BALL, M. M., *The Problem of Inter-American Organization* (Stanford, 1944).
BARNES, H. E., see Merriam and Barnes.
BARNES, K., see Gregory and Barnes.
BARTLETT, R. J., ed., *The Record of American Diplomacy* (New York, 1947).
BATY, T., *International Law in South Africa* (London, 1900).
———, *International Law* (London, 1909).
BAU, M. J., *The Open Door Doctrine in Relation to China* (New York, 1923).
BAXTER, R. R., *The Law of International Waterways, with Particular Regard to Interoceanic Canals* (Cambridge, 1963).
BEALE, J. H., *A Treatise on the Conflict of Laws,* 3 vols. (New York, 1935).
BEARD, C. A., *The Open Door at Home* (New York, 1934).
———, see Ogg and Beard.
BELL, SIR CHARLES A., *Tibet, Past and Present* (London, 1926).
BELLI, P., *De re militari et bello tractatus,* Vol. I, Latin text; Vol. II, English trans. by H. C. Nuttig (Oxford, 1936).
BELLO, A., *Principios de Derecho Internacional,* new edition by C. M. Silva (Madrid, 1883); new edition by R. Caldera (Buenos Aires, 1946).
BEMIS, S. F., *A Diplomatic History of the United States,* rev. ed. (New York, 1942).
———, *The Latin American Policy of the United States* (New York, 1943).
———, *The United States as a World Power* (New York, 1955).
BENEŠ, E., *Les accords de Locarno* (Prague, 1925).
BENKERT, G. F., *The Thomistic Conception of an International Society* (Washington, 1942).
BENTON, E. J., *International Law and Diplomacy of the Spanish-American War* (Baltimore, 1908).
BENTWICH, N., *The Declaration of London* (London, 1911).

————, *The Mandates System* (London, 1930).

————, *The Religious Foundations of Internationalism* (London, 1933).

BERDAHL, C. A., *The Policy of the United States with Respect to the League of Nations* (Geneva, 1932).

BINGHAM, J. W., *The Report on the International Law of Pacific Fisheries* (London, 1938).

BISHOP, W. W., *International Law: Cases and Materials*, 2d ed. (Boston, 1962). Cited *Cases*.

BLACKSTONE, SIR W., *Commentaries on the Laws of England*, 2 vols. (Philadelphia, 1890).

BLUNTSCHLI, J. K., *Das moderne Völkerrecht der civilisirten Staaten als Rechtsbuch dargestellt*, 3d ed. (Nördlingen, 1878). French trans. by M. C. Lardy, *Le droit international codifié*, 3d ed. (Paris, 1881).

BONFILS, H., *Manuel de droit international public*, 7th ed., by P. Fauchille (Paris, 1914). For 8th ed., see Fauchille.

BORCHARD, E. M., *The Diplomatic Protection of Citizens Abroad, or the Law of International Claims* (New York, 1915).

BORDWELL, P., *The Law of War between Belligerents* (Chicago, 1908).

BOUCHEZ, L. J., *The Regime of Bays in International Law* (Leyden, 1964).

BOWETT, D. W., *Self-Defense in International Law* (New York, 1958).

————, *The Law of International Institutions* (London, 1963).

BRAILSFORD, H. N., *A League of Nations* (New York, 1917).

————, *The War of Steel and Gold*, 9th ed. rev. (London, 1917).

BRAY, F. E., see Hurst and Bray.

BREASTED, J. H., *Ancient Records of Egypt*, 5 vols. (Chicago, 1906–1907).

————, *The Conquest of Civilization* (New York, 1926).

BRIÈRE, Y. DE LA, *L'Organisation internationale du monde contemporain et la Papauté souveraine*, 2 vols. (Paris, 1924, 1927).

————, *Conception du droit international chez les théologiens Catholiques* (Paris, 1929).

————, *Le droit de juste guerre: Tradition théologique, Adaptations contemporaines* (Paris, 1938).

BRIERLY, J. L., *The Law of Nations*, 4th ed. (1949), 5th ed. (1955), 6th ed. (New York, 1963).

————, *The Outlook for International Law* (Oxford, 1944).

BRIGGS, H. W., *The Law of Nations: Cases, Documents and Notes*, 2d ed. (New York, 1952). Cited *Cases*.

British and Foreign State Papers, 1812– (London, 1832–).

British Year Book of International Law, 1920–1939; 1944– (London, 1920–1939; 1944–).

BRUNS, V., *Fontes juris gentium*, Series A, B (Berlin, 1931–).

BRYCE, VISCOUNT J., *The Holy Roman Empire*, new ed. (New York, 1911).

BUELL, R. L., *The Washington Conference* (New York, 1922).

————, *International Relations*, rev. ed. (New York, 1929).

BUSTAMANTE Y SIRVEN, A. S. DE, *The World Court* (New York, 1925).

————, *Derecho internacional público*, 5 vols. (Havana, 1933–1938). French trans. by P. Goulé, *Droit international public*, 5 vols. (Paris, 1934–1939).

BUTLER, C. H., *The Treaty-making Power of the United States* (New York, 1902).

BUTLER, SIR G., *A Handbook to the League of Nations*, 2d ed. (London, 1925).

———, AND MACCOBY, S., *The Development of International Law* (New York, 1928).

BUXTON, N., see Phillipson and Buxton.

BYNKERSHOEK, C. VAN, *De dominio maris*, Latin text, with English trans. by R. Van D. Magoffin (New York, 1923).

———, *Quaestionum juris publici libri duo*, Vol. I, Latin text; Vol. II, English trans. by T. Frank (Oxford, 1930).

———, *De foro legatorum*, Latin text, with English trans. by G. J. Laing (Oxford, 1939).

CADBURY, H. J., *National Ideals of the Old Testament* (New York, 1920).

CAICEDO CASTILLA, J. J., *Manual de derecho internacional privado*, 5th ed. (Bogotá, 1960).

CALLAHAN, J. M., *American Foreign Policy in Mexican Relations* (New York, 1932).

CALVO, C., *Le Droit international théorique et pratique*, 5th ed., 6 vols. (Paris, 1896).

CARDOZO, B. N., *The Growth of the Law* (New Haven, 1927).

CARPENTER, W. S., *Foundations of Modern Jurisprudence* (New York, 1958).

CARR, E. H., *The Twenty Years' Crisis 1919–1939* (New York and London, 1940).

———, *Conditions of Peace* (New York, 1942).

Case Against the Nazi War Criminals, The. Opening Statement for the United States of America by R. H. Jackson, and other Documents (New York, 1946).

CECIL, VISCOUNT (LORD ROBERT), *A Great Experiment* (New York, 1941).

CHADWICK, H. M., *The Nationalities of Europe and the Growth of National Ideologies* (London, 1945).

CHAMBERLAIN, J. P., *The Régime of the International Rivers: Danube and Rhine* (New York and London, 1923).

CHEN TI-CHIANG, *The International Law of Recognition* (London, 1951).

CHENG, B., *The Law of International Air Transport* (London, 1962).

———, *General Principles of Law as Applied by International Courts and Tribunals* (London, 1953).

CHESHIRE, G. C., *Private International Law*, 2d ed. (New York and London, 1938).

CHRÉTIEN, A., *Principes de droit international public* (Paris, 1893).

Claims Commission United States-Mexico: Opinions of the Commissioners (Washington, 1927, 1929, 1931).

CLARK, G., AND SOHN, L. B., *World Peace Through World Law* (Cambridge, Mass., 1958).

COBBAN, A., *National Self-Determination* (New York, 1945).

COBBETT, P., *Cases on International Law*, Vol. I, *Peace*, 5th ed., by F. T. Gray (London, 1931); Vol. II, *War and Neutrality*, 5th ed., by W. L. Walker (London, 1937).

Codification of International Law, Acts of the Conference for the, I, Plenary Meetings II, Minutes of the First Committee, Nationality (1930).

COHEN, M., ed., *Law and Politics in Space* (Montreal, 1963).

COKER, F. W., *Readings in Political Philosophy* (New York, 1914).

COLEGROVE, K., *International Control of Aviation,* World Peace Foundation Pamphlet (Boston, 1930).

COLOMBOS, C. J., *The International Law of the Sea,* 4th ed. (London, 1959).

Congressional Record (Washington, 1874–).

CONSENTINI, F., *Code international de la paix et de la guerre* (Berne, 1937).

Consular Regulations of the United States (Washington, 1932).

CORBETT, P. E., *Law and Society in the Relations of States* (New York, 1951).

COUDENHOVE-KALERGI, R. N., *Pan-Europe* (New York, 1926).

CRANDALL, S. B., *Treaties: Their Making and Enforcement,* 2d ed. (Washington, 1916).

CRESSON, W. P., *The Holy Alliance* (New York, 1922).

Criminal Code of the United States (Washington, 1911).

CROCKER, H. G., ed., *The Extent of the Marginal Sea* (Washington, 1919).

————, AND BAKER, J. R., see Baker and Crocker.

————, AND HENCKELS, see Henckels and Crocker.

CRUCHAGA-TOCORNAL, M., *Nociones de derecho internacional,* 3d ed., 2 vols. (Madrid, 1923). New ed., *Derecho Internacional,* Tomo I (Santiago, 1944).

CRUTTWELL, C. R. M. F., *A History of Peaceful Change in the Modern World* (New York and London, 1937).

CULBERTSON, W. S., *International Economic Policies* (New York, 1925).

DARBY, W. E., *International Arbitration, International Tribunals,* 4th ed. (London, 1904).

DAVENPORT, F. G., ed., *European Treaties Bearing on the History of the United States and Its Dependencies to 1648* (Washington, 1917).

DAVIS, G. B., *The Elements of International Law,* 4th ed. revised, by G. E. Sherman (New York, 1916).

DAWSON, C., *The Judgment of the Nations* (New York, 1942).

DEAK, F., see *Neutrality: Its History, Economics and Law.*

————, AND JESSUP, P. C., *A Collection of Neutrality Laws, Regulations and Treaties of Various Countries,* 2 vols. (Washington, 1939).

DELOS, J. T., *La société internationale et les principes du droit public* (Paris, 1929).

DE MURALT, R. W. G., *The Problem of State Succession with Regard to Treaties* (The Hague, 1954).

Department of State *Bulletin* (Washington, 1939–).

Department of State Publications, No. 1– (Washington, 1929–).

DE SMITH, S. A., *The New Commonwealth and its Constitutions* (London, 1964).

DESPAGNET, F., *Cours de droit international public,* 8th ed. revised, by C. de Boeck (Paris, 1910).

DE VISSCHER, C., *Belgium's Case: A Juridical Inquiry* (London, 1916).

————, *Theory and Reality in Public International Law* (Princeton, 1957).

Diario de la Conferencia Interamericana sobre Problemas de la Guerra y de la Paz (Mexico, 1945).

DICEY, A. V., *A Digest of the Law of England with Reference to the Conflict of Laws*, 5th ed., by A. B. Keith (London, 1932).

DICKINSON, E. D., *The Equality of States in International Law* (Cambridge, 1920).

Dictámenes jurídicos acerca del problema ecuatoriano-peruano dados por ilustres internacionalistas americanos (Quito, 1942).

Diplomatic Correspondence with Belligerents Relating to Neutral Rights and Duties, Department of State (Washington, 1915–1918). See *American White Book*.

Documents on Foreign Relations, 1938–1944, 6 vols. (Boston, 1939–1945).

Documents on International Affairs, 1928–, ed. by J. W. Wheeler-Bennett and others (London, 1929–).

DOMKE, M., *International Trade Arbitration* (New York, 1958).

DONALDSON, J., *International Economic Relations* (New York, 1928).

DUGUIT, L., *Traité de droit constitutionnel*, 2d ed., 5 vols. (Paris, 1922–1925).

DULLES, J. F., *War, Peace and Change* (New York and London, 1939).

DUNN, F. S., *The Practice and Procedure of International Conferences* (Baltimore, 1929).

———, *The Protection of Nationals* (Baltimore, 1932).

———, *The Diplomatic Protection of Americans in Mexico* (New York, 1933).

———, *Peaceful Change* (New York, 1937).

DUPUIS, C., *Le droit des gens et les rapports des grandes puissances avec les autres Etats avant le Pacte de la Societé des Nations* (Paris, 1921).

EAGLETON, C., *The Responsibility of States in International Law* (New York, 1928).

———, *International Government* (New York, 1932, 1948).

EAYRS, J., *The Commonwealth and Suez* (New York, 1963).

EDER, PHANOR J., *A Comparative Survey of Anglo-American and Latin-American Law* (New York, 1950).

EDMINSTER, L. R., see Wallace and Edminster.

EICHELBERGER, C. M., *United Nations: The First Fifteen Years* (New York, 1960).

EMENY, B., *The Strategy of Raw Materials* (New York, 1934).

———, see Simonds and Emeny.

ENGELBRECHT, H. C., AND HANIGHEN, F. C., *Merchants of Death: A Study of the International Armament Industry* (New York, 1934).

EPPSTEIN, J., *The Catholic Tradition of the Law of Nations* (Washington, 1935).

ESCARRA, J., *La Chine et le droit international* (Paris, 1931).

EVANS, L. B., *Cases on American Constitutional Law*, 7th ed. by C. G. Fenwick (Chicago, 1957).

Events Leading Up to World War II: 1931–1944 (Washington, 1944).

Everyman's United Nations, 7th ed. (New York, 1964).

FACHIRI, A. P., *The Permanent Court of International Justice*, 2d ed. (New York, 1932).

FAUCHILLE, P., *Traité de droit international public,* Tome I, I Partie (Paris, 1922); II Partie (1926); III Partie (1926); Tome II (1921).

FAWCETT, J. E. S., *The British Commonwealth in International Law* (London, 1963).

FAY, S. B., *Origins of the World War,* 2 vols. (New York, 1928).

FEIGHEL, I., *Nationalization: A Study in the Protection of Alien Property in International Law* (1959).

FEILCHENFELD, E. H., *Public Debts and State Succession* (New York, 1931).

FELLER, A. H., *The Mexican Claims Commission 1923–1934* (New York, 1935).

————, AND HUDSON, M. O., *A Collection of the Diplomatic and Consular Laws and Regulations of Various Countries,* 2 vols. (Washington, 1933).

FENWICK, C. G., *The Neutrality Laws of the United States* (Washington, 1913).

————, *Cases on International Law,* 2d ed. (Chicago, 1951).

————, *American Neutrality: Trial and Failure* (New York, 1940).

————, *The Organization of American States: The Inter-American Regional System* (Washington, 1963). Cited *OAS.*

FERGUSON, W. S., *Greek Imperialism* (Boston, 1913).

FERREIRA DE MELLO, R., *Tratado de Direito Diplomático,* 2 vols. (Rio de Janeiro, 1947).

FIELD, D. D., *Outlines of an International Code,* 2d ed. (New York, 1876).

FIGGIS, D., *The Irish Constitution* (Dublin, 1923).

————, *The Political Aspect of St. Augustin's "City of God"* (London and New York, 1921).

FINCH, G. A., *The Sources of Modern International Law* (Washington, 1937).

FIORE, P., *Trattato di diritto internazionale pubblico* (1865), 4th ed., 3 vols. (1904). French trans. of the 2d ed. by C. Antoine, *Nouveau droit international public,* 3 vols. (Paris, 1885–1886).

————, *Il diritto internazionale codificato e la sua sanzione giuridica,* 5th ed. (1915). English trans. by E. M. Borchard, *International Law Codified and Its Legal Sanction* (New York, 1918).

FLEMING, D. F., *The United States and the League of Nations, 1918–1920* (New York, 1932).

————, *The United States and World Organization, 1920–1933* (New York, 1938).

FLOURNOY, R. W., AND HUDSON, M. O., *A Collection of Nationality Laws of Various Countries, as Contained in Constitutions, Statutes and Treaties* (New York, 1929).

Fontes juris gentium, ed. by V. Bruns, Series A, B (Berlin, 1931–).

Foreign Affairs, Quarterly (New York, 1922–).

Foreign Policy Reports (New York, 1925–).

Foreign Relations of the United States, Papers Relating to (Washington, 1883–).

FOSTER, J. W., *The Practice of Diplomacy* (Boston, 1906).

————, *A Century of American Diplomacy* (Boston, 1911).

FRANK, T., *Roman Imperialism* (New York, 1914).

FREEMAN, A. V., *The International Responsibility of States for Denial of Justice* (London, New York, and Toronto, 1938).

FRIED, A. H., *The Restoration of Europe*, translated from the German by L. S. Gannett (New York, 1916).

FRIEDMANN, W., *The Changing Structure of International Law* (London, 1964).

FRIEDRICH, C. J., *Foreign Policy in the Making: The Search for a New Balance of Power* (New York, 1938).

FULLER, L. L., *The Morality of Law* (New Haven, 1964).

FULTON, T. W., *The Sovereignty of the Sea* (London, 1911).

GANJI, M., *International Protection of Human Rights* (New York, 1962).

GARCÍA-AMADOR, F. V., *The Exploitation and Conservation of the Resources of the Sea* (Leyden, 1959).

————, *Introducción al Estudio del Derecho Internacional Contemporaneo* (Madrid, 1959).

————, *Principios de Derecho Internacional que Rigen la Responsabilidad* (Madrid, 1963).

GARNER, J. W., *International Law and the World War*, 2 vols. (New York, 1920).

————, *Recent Developments in International Law* (Calcutta, 1925).

GENTILI, A., *Hispanicae advocationis libri duo*, Vol. I, Latin text; Vol. II, English trans. by F. F. Abbott (New York, 1921).

————, *De jure belli libri tres*, Vol. I, Latin text; Vol. II, English trans. by J. C. Rolfe (Washington, 1933).

GIBBON, E., *The History of the Decline and Fall of the Roman Empire*, with variorum notes, 7 vols. (London, 1884–1892).

GIDEL, G., *Le Droit international public de la mer*, 3 vols. (Paris, 1932–1934).

GIERKE, O. VON, *Natural Law and the Theory of Society, 1500–1800*, translated from original German by E. Barker (Cambridge, 1934).

GLUECK, S., *War Criminals, Their Prosecution and Punishment* (New York, 1944).

————, *The Nuremberg Trial and Aggressive War* (New York, 1946).

GOEBEL, J., JR., *The Struggle for the Falkland Islands* (New Haven, 1927).

GONELLA, G., *A World to Reconstruct: Pius XII on Peace and Reconstruction*. English trans. by T. L. Bouscaren (Milwaukee, 1944).

GOOCH, G. P., *History of Modern Europe 1878–1919* (New York, 1923).

GOODNOW, F. J., *China, an Analysis* (Baltimore, 1926).

GOODRICH, L. M., AND HAMBRO, E., *Charter of the United Nations: Commentary and Documents* (Boston, 1946, rev. ed., 1949).

————, AND SIMONS, A. P., *The United Nations and the Maintenance of Peace and Security* (Washington, 1955).

GOULD, W. L., *An Introduction to International Law* (New York, 1957).

GRAHAM, M. W., *The League of Nations and the Recognition of States* (Berkeley, 1933).

GREEN, L. C., *International Law Through the Cases* (New York, 1951).

GREENSPAN, M., *The Modern Law of Land Warfare* (Berkeley, 1959).

GREGORY, H. E., AND BARNES, K., *North Pacific Fisheries, with Special Reference to Alaska Salmon* (San Francisco, New York, and Honolulu, 1939).

GROTIUS, H., *De jure belli ac pacis*, Latin text with abridged English trans. by W. Wheewell, 3 vols. (Cambridge, 1853). Latin text (Washington, 1913); English trans. by F. W. Kelsey, H. A. Sanders, A. E. R. Boak, J. S. Reeves, and H. F. Wright, *The Law of War and Peace* (Oxford, 1925).

————, *Mare liberum* (1633). English trans. by R. Van D. Magoffin, *The Freedom of the Seas* (New York, 1916).

Grotius Society, Transactions (Proceedings) of the (London, 1916–).

Guatemala White Book, on the Belize Question (Guatemala, 1938).

GUTTERIDGE, H. C., *Comparative Law: An Introduction to the Comparative Method of Legal Study and Research* (Cambridge, 1946).

HABICHT, M., *Post-War Treaties for the Pacific Settlement of International Disputes* (Cambridge, 1931).

HACKETT, C. W., *The Mexican Revolution and the United States, 1910–1926* (Boston, World Peace Foundation, 1926).

HACKWORTH, G. H., *Digest of International Law,* 8 vols. (Washington, 1940–1944).

HAGUE ACADEMY OF INTERNATIONAL LAW, *Recueil des Cours.*

Hague Conventions and Declarations of 1899 and 1907, ed. by J. B. Scott (New York, 1915). Cited as *Hague Conventions.*

Hague Court Reports, ed. by J. B. Scott (New York, 1916); *Second Series* (1932).

Hague Peace Conferences, Proceedings of. Conference of 1899, trans. of official texts (New York, 1920); *Conference of 1907,* 3 vols. and index (New York, 1920, 1921).

HAINES, C. G., *European Integration* (Baltimore, 1957).

————, *The Revival of Natural Law Concepts* (Cambridge, Mass., 1930).

————, AND HOFFMANN, R. J. S., *The Origins and Background of the Second World War* (New York, 1947).

HALEY, A. G., *Space Law and Government* (New York, 1963).

HALL, H. DUNCAN, *Mandates, Dependencies and Trusteeships* (Washington, 1948).

HALL, W. E., *A Treatise on International Law,* 8th ed., by A. P. Higgins (Oxford, 1924).

HALLBERG, C. W., *The Suez Canal* (New York, 1931).

HALLSTEIN, W., *United Europe: Challenge and Opportunity* (Cambridge, 1962).

HALM, G. N., *International Monetary Cooperation* (Chapel Hill, 1945).

HAMBRO, E., *The Case Law of the International Court,* 2 vols. (Leiden, 1960).

HAMBRO, E., see Goodrich and Hambro.

HANIGHEN, F. C., see Engelbrecht and Hanighen.

HARCOURT, SIR W., *Letters by Historicus* (London and Cambridge, 1863).

HARLEY, J. E., *Documentary Textbook on the United Nations* (Los Angeles, 1947).

HARTLEY, L., *Atlantic Challenge* (New York, 1965).

Harvard Draft, see *Research in International Law.*

Harvard Law Review (Cambridge, Mass., 1887–).

HASKINS, C. H., AND LORD, R. H., *Some Problems of the Peace Conference* (Cambridge, 1920).

HAYES, C. J. H., *The Historical Evolution of Modern Nationalism* (New York, 1931).

————, *A Political and Social History of Modern Europe*, 2 vols. (New York, 1932).

HEATLEY, D. P., *Diplomacy and the Study of International Relations* (Oxford, 1919).

HEFFTER, A. W., *Das europäische Völkerrecht der Gegenwart auf den bisherigen Grundlagen* (1844); French trans. by J. Bergson, *Le Droit international de l'Europe*, 4th French ed., rev. by F. H. Geffcken (Paris, 1883).

HEMLEBEN, S. J., *Plans for World Peace through Six Centuries* (Chicago, 1943).

HERRING, H., *A History of Latin America*, 2d ed. (New York, 1961).

HERRIOT, E., *Europe* (Paris, 1930). English trans. by R. J. Dingle, *The United States of Europe* (New York, 1930).

HERSHEY, A. S., *The Essentials of International Public Law and Organization*, rev. ed. (New York, 1930).

HERTSLET, SIR E., *The Map of Europe by Treaty*, 4 vols. (London, 1875–1891).

HERVEY, J. G., *The Legal Effects of Recognition in International Law* (Philadelphia, 1928).

HIGGINS, A. P., *The Hague Peace Conferences* (Cambridge, 1909).

————, AND COLOMBOS, C. J., *The International Law of the Sea*, 4th ed. (London, New York, and Toronto, 1959).

HIGGINS, R., *The Development of International Law through the Political Organs of the United Nations* (Oxford, 1963).

HILL, D. J., *A History of Diplomacy in the International Development of Europe*, 3 vols. (New York, 1905–1914).

————, *The Rebuilding of Europe* (New York, 1917).

————, *American World Policies* (New York, 1920).

HILL, N. L., *The Public International Conference* (Baltimore, 1929).

————, *International Administration* (New York, 1931).

HINDMARSH, A. E., *Force in Peace: Force Short of War in International Relations* (Cambridge, 1933).

HOLDICH, SIR T. H., *Political Frontiers and Boundary Making* (London, 1916).

HOLLAND, T. E., *The Elements of Jurisprudence*, 10th ed. (Oxford, 1908).

————, *The European Concert in the Eastern Question* (Oxford, 1885).

————, *Studies in International Law* (Oxford, 1898).

HOPKINS, E. W., see Burnell and Hopkins.

HORNBECK, S. K., *China Today: Political* (Boston, 1927).

HOURANI, A. H., *Syria and Lebanon: A Political Essay* (London, Oxford, and New York, 1946).

HOWARD-ELLIS, C., *The Origin, Structure and Working of the League of Nations* (New York, 1928).

HUBER, M., *Die Gleichheit der Staaten* (Stuttgart, 1910).

HUBERICH, C. H., *The Law Relating to Trading with the Enemy* (New York, 1918).

HUDSON, M. O., *Cases and Other Materials on International Law*, 3d ed. (St. Paul, 1951).

——, *The Permanent Court of International Justice, 1920–1942* (New York, 1943).

——, *International Tribunals: Past and Future* (Washington, 1944).

——, ed., *International Legislation*, 9 vols. (Washington, 1931–1950).

——, ed., *World Court Reports*, 4 vols. (Washington, 1934–1943).

——, see Feller and Hudson.

——, see Flournoy and Hudson.

HUTCHINSON, P., *The United States of Europe* (New York, 1929).

HYDE, C. C., *International Law Chiefly as Interpreted and Applied by the United States*, 2d ed., 3 vols. (Boston, 1945). Cited as *International Law*.

IHERING, R. VON, *Der Zweck im Recht* (1877). English trans. by T. Husik, *Law as a Means to an End* (New York, 1924).

Institute of International Law, Resolutions of the. English trans., ed. by J. B. Scott (New York, 1916). Cited as *Resolutions*.

Instructions to Diplomatic Officers of the United States (Washington, 1927).

Instructions for the Government of the Armies of the United States in the Field (1863), by Francis Lieber, in Wilson and Tucker, *International Law*, 8th ed. Cited as *Instructions*.

Inter-American Juridical Committee, Recommendations and Reports, 1942–1944 (Rio de Janeiro, 1945).

——, *Atas da Comissão* (Rio de Janeiro, 1942–).

International Agencies in Which the United States Participates, Dept. of State Publication 2699 (Washington, 1946). Cited *International Agencies*.

International Commission of American Jurists: 1927 Meeting, 4 vols. (Rio de Janeiro, 1927–1929).

International Conciliation (New York, 1907–).

International Conferences of American States, 1889–1928 (Washington, 1931). First Supplement: 1933–1940 (Washington, 1940). Second Supplement: 1942–1954 (Washington, 1958).

International Control of Atomic Energy: Growth of a Policy. Department of State Publication No. 2702 (Washington, 1946).

International Labour Code 1939 (Montreal, 1941).

International Labour Conference, Conventions and Recommendations, 1919–1937 (Geneva, 1937).

International Labour Office, I.L.O. Year-Book (Geneva, 1930–).

International Law Association, Proceedings of the, Annual Reports (London, 1873–).

International Law of the Future: Postulates, Principles and Proposals (Washington, 1944).

International Organization (Boston, 1947–).

INTERNOSCIA, J., *New Code of International Law*. In English, French, and Italian (New York, 1910).

IRELAND, G., *Boundaries, Possessions and Conflicts in South America* (Cambridge, 1938).

———, *Boundaries, Possessions and Conflicts in Central and North America and the Caribbean* (Cambridge, 1941).

JACOBINI, H. B., *International Law: A Text* (Homewood, Ill., 1962).

JANOWSKY, O. I., *Nationalities and National Minorities* (New York, 1945).

JELLINEK, G., *Die Rechtliche Natur der Staatenverträge* (Vienna, 1880).

———, *Die Lehre von den Staatenverbindungen* (Vienna, 1882).

———, *Allemeine Staatslehre*, 1st ed. (1900). French trans. by G. Fardis, *L'Etat moderne et son droit*, 2 vols. (Paris, 1911–1913).

JENKS, C. W., *The Common Law of Mankind* (New York, 1958).

———, *The Proper Law of International Organizations* (New York, 1962).

———, *The Prospects of International Adjudication* (The Hague, 1964).

———, *International Immunities* (London, 1961).

JESSUP, P. C., *The Law of Territorial Waters and Maritime Jurisdiction* (New York, 1927).

———, *A Modern Law of Nations* (New York, 1948).

———, *Transnational Law* (New Haven, 1956).

———, see *Neutrality: Its History, Economics and Law.*

———, see Deak and Jessup.

———, AND TAUBENFELD, H. J., *Controls for Outer Space and the Antarctic Analogy* (New York, 1959).

JOLOWICZ, H. F., *Historical Introduction to the Study of Roman Law* (Cambridge, 1939).

JONES, C. L., *The Caribbean Since 1900* (New York, 1936).

JONES, S. B., *Boundary-Making* (Washington, 1945).

KAECKENBEECK, G., *International Rivers* (London, 1918).

KAPLAN, M. A., AND KATZENBACH, N. DE B., *The Political Foundations of International Law* (New York, 1961).

KAUFMANN, E., *Das Wesen des Völkerrechts und die clausula rebus sic stantibus* (Tübingen, 1911).

KEITH, A. B., *Theory of State Succession, with Special Reference to English and Colonial Law* (London, 1907).

———, *Responsible Government in the Dominions*, 2d ed., 3 vols. (Oxford, 1928).

———, see Dicey and Keith.

KELLOR, F., *American Arbitration* (New York, 1948).

KELSEN, H., *Law and Peace in International Relations* (Cambridge, 1942).

———, *Peace Through Law* (Chapel Hill, 1944).

———, *General Theory of Law and State* (Cambridge, 1945).

———, *Principles of International Law* (New York, 1952).

———, *The Communist Theory of Law* (London, 1955).

———, *Collective Security under International Law* (Washington, 1957).

———, *The Law of the United Nations* (New York, 1964).

KENT, J., *Commentaries on American Law*, 12th, 13th ed., by O. W. Holmes, Jr., and C. M. Barnes, 4 vols. (Boston, 1884).

KEYNES, J. M., *The Economic Consequences of the Peace* (New York, 1920).

KIRK, J., see Sharp and Kirk.

KLÜBER, J. L., *Droit des gens moderne de l'Europe*, rev. by M. A. Ott, 2d ed. (Paris, 1874).

KNIGHT, W. S. M., *The Life and Works of Hugo Grotius* (London, 1925).

KOHN, H., *The Idea of Nationalism* (New York, 1944).

———, *Nationalism: Its Meaning and History* (Princeton, 1955).

KOOIJMANS, P. H., *The Doctrine of the Legal Equality of States* (The Hague, 1964).

KUNZ, J. L., *The Changing Law of Nations: Essays on International Law* (Columbus, Ohio, 1965).

———, *Latin American Philosophy of Law in the Twentieth Century* (New York, 1950).

LADAS, S. P., *The International Protection of Industrial Property* (Cambridge, 1930).

LADOR-LEDERER, J. J., *International Non-Governmental Organizations and Economic Entities* (Leyden, 1963).

LA FONTAINE, H., *Pasicrisie internationale: Histoire documentaire des arbitrages internationaux* (Berne, 1902).

LA FOY, M., *The Chaco Dispute and the League of Nations* (Bryn Mawr, 1941).

LANGROD, G., *The International Civil Service* (The Hague, 1963).

LAPRADELLE, A., AND POLITIS, N., *Recueil des arbitrages internationaux*, Tome I, 1798–1855 (Paris, 1905); Tome II, 1856–1872 (Paris, 1924).

LARSON, A., *When Nations Disagree: A Handbook on Peace Through Law* (Baton Rouge, 1961).

LATANÉ, J. H., *A History of American Foreign Policy* (New York, 1927).

LAURENT, F., *Histoire du droit des gens et des relations internationales*, 2d ed., 14 vols. (Paris-Gand, 1879–1880).

LAUTERPACHT, H., *Private Law Sources and Analogies of International Law* (London, 1927).

———, *The Function of Law in the International Community* (Oxford, 1933).

———, *The Development of International Law by the Permanent Court of International Justice* (London and New York, 1934). *The Development of International Law by the International Court*, rev. ed. (London, 1958).

———, *Recognition in International Law* (Cambridge, 1947).

———, *International Law and Human Rights* (New York, 1950).

———, see *Annual Digest and Reports of Public International Law Cases*.

LAVES, W. H. C., AND THOMSON, C. A., *UNESCO: Purpose, Progress, Prospects* (Indiana Univ. Press, 1957).

LAWRENCE, T. J., *Principles of International Law*, 7th ed. revised, by P. H. Winfield (New York, 1923).

LAWSON, R. C., *International Regional Organizations* (New York, 1962).

———, *The Society of Nations* (New York, 1919).

League of Nations, Handbook of the, since 1920 (Boston, 1930).

League of Nations, Ten Years of World Co-operation (1930).

League of Nations Treaty Series (publication of treaties and international engagements registered with the Secretariat of the League of Nations), 204 vols. (Geneva, 1920–1944).

LEE, L. T., *Consular Law and Practice* (London, 1961).

LE FUR, L., *Précis de droit international public* (Paris, 1931).

———, *Le Saint-Siège et le droit des gens* (Paris, 1930).

LEGUM, C., *Pan-Africanism* (New York, 1962).

LEONHARD, A. L., *International Regulation of Fisheries* (Washington, 1944).

LE ROY, H. S., *Air Law: Outline and Guide to Law of Radio and Aeronautics*, rev. ed. (Washington, 1936).

LIEBER, F., see *Instructions*, etc.

LILLICH, R. B., *International Claims: Their Adjudication by National Commissions* (1962).

LIPSON, L., AND KATZENBACH, N. DE B., *Report to the National Aeronautics and Space Administration on the Law of Outer Space* (Chicago, 1961).

LISSITZYN, O. J., *International Air Transport and National Policy* (New York, 1942).

———, *The International Court of Justice: Its Role in the Maintenance of International Peace and Security* (New York, 1951).

LISZT, F. VON, *Das Völkerrecht systematisch dargestellt*, 12th ed. by M. Fleischmann (Berlin, 1925). French trans. of the 9th ed. (1913) by G. Gidel and L. Alcindor, *Le droit international* (Paris, 1927).

Lloyd's Reports of Prize Cases, 10 vols. (London, 1915–1922).

LOEWENSTEIN, K., *Political Reconstruction* (New York, 1946).

LORD, R. H., see Haskins and Lord.

LOUTER, J. DE, *Le droit international public positif*, 2 vols. (Oxford, 1920).

LYDE, L. W., *Some Frontiers of To-morrow* (London, 1915).

MACARTNEY, C. A., *National States and National Minorities* (New York, 1933).

McCLURE, W., *World Prosperity as Sought through the Economic Work of the League of Nations* (New York, 1933).

———, *World Legal Order: Possible Contributions by the People of the United States* (Chapel Hill, 1960).

MACCOBY, S., see Butler and Maccoby.

MACDONALD, W., *Select Charters Illustrative of American History, 1606–1775* (New York, 1910).

McDOUGAL, M. S., AND BURKE, W. T., *The Public Order of the Oceans* (New Haven, 1962).

———, AND ASSOCIATES, *Studies in World Public Order* (New Haven, 1960).

———, LASWELL, H. O., AND VLASIC, I. A., *Law and Public Order in Space* (New Haven, 1963).

———, AND FELICIANO, *Law and Minimum World Public Order* (New Haven, 1961).

MACIVER, R. M., *The Nations and the United Nations* (New York, 1959).

McKERNAN, L. W., see Baker and McKernan.

McNAIR, SIR A. D., *The Law of Treaties: British Practice and Opinions* (New York-Oxford, 1938).

———, *Legal Effects of War*, 3d ed. (Cambridge, 1948).

———, see *Annual Digest and Reports of Public International Law Cases*.

McNair, H. F., see Morse and McNair.

Madariaga, S. de, *Theory and Practice in International Relations* (Philadelphia, 1937).

———, *The World's Design* (London, 1938).

Madison, J., *The Debates in the Federal Convention of 1787*, ed. by G. Hunt and J. B. Scott (New York, 1920).

Maine, Sir H. S., *International Law*, 1st ed. (New York, 1888), 2d ed. (1894).

———, *Ancient Law*, Pollock's ed. (Oxford, 1906).

Malloy, W. M., *Treaties, Conventions, International Acts, Protocols and Agreements between the United States of America and Other Powers, 1776–1937*, 4 vols. (Washington, 1910–1938). Cited as *Treaties and Conventions*.

Mangone, G. J., *Elements of International Law: A Casebook* (Homewood, Ill., 1963).

Manning, W. R., *Arbitration Treaties among the American Nations to the Close of the Year 1910* (Washington, 1924).

Manual of the Laws of War on Land. See Oxford Manual.

Marburg, T., *Development of the League of Nations Idea*, ed. by J. H. Latané, 2 vols. (New York, 1932).

Marek, K., *Identity and Continuity of States in Public International Law* (New York, 1954).

Maritain, J., *Les droits de l'homme et la loi naturelle* (New York, 1942).

Martens, C. de, *Causes célèbres de droit des gens*, 2 vols. (Leipzig, 1827); 2d ed., 5 vols. (1858–1861). *Nouvelles causes célèbres*, 2 vols. (1843).

Martens, F. de, *Traité de droit international*, 3 vols., translated from the original Russian by A. Léo (Paris, 1883–1887).

Martens, G. F. von, *Précis du droit des gens moderne de l'Europe* (1788). Revised by Pinheiro-Ferreira and M. C. Vergé, 2d ed., 2 vols. (Paris, 1864).

———, *Nouveau recueil général de traités*, Troisième Série (1909–).

Masters, R. D., *International Law in National Courts* (New York, 1932).

———, *Handbook of International Organizations in the Americas* (Washington, 1945).

Masterson, W. E., *Jurisdiction in Marginal Seas* (New York, 1929).

Mattern, J., *The Employment of the Plebiscite in the Determination of Sovereignty* (Baltimore, 1921).

Mecham, J. L., *The United States and Inter-American Security, 1889–1960* (Austin, 1961).

Mérignhac, A., *Traité théorique et pratique de l'arbitrage international* (Paris, 1895).

Merriam, C. E., and Barnes, H. E., eds., *A History of Political Theories, Recent Times* (New York, 1924).

Miller, D. H., *The Drafting of the Covenant*, 2 vols. (New York, 1928).

———, *The Geneva Protocol* (New York, 1925).

———, *The Peace Pact of Paris* (New York, 1928).

———, ed., *Treaties and Other International Acts of the United States of America, 1776–1863*, 8 vols. (Washington, 1931–1942).

MIRKINE-GUÉTZÉVITCH, B., *Le droit constitutionnel dans ses rapports avec le droit international public* (Paris, 1934).
MITRANY, D., *The Problem of International Sanctions* (London, 1925).
Modern Theories of Law, ed. by W. I. Jennings (London, 1933).
MOON, P. T., *Imperialism and World Politics* (New York, 1926).
MOORE, B. T., *NATO and the Future of Europe* (New York, 1958).
MOORE, J. B., *A History and Digest of the International Arbitrations to Which the United States Has Been a Party*, 6 vols. (Washington, 1898). Cited as "Moore, Int. Arbitrations."
———, *A Digest of International Law*, 7 vols. and index vol. (Washington, 1906). Cited as Moore, *Digest*.
———, *Principles of American Diplomacy* (New York, 1918).
———, *International Adjudications, Ancient and Modern*, 6 vols. (New York, 1929–1933).
MORENO, I. R., *Lecciones de derecho internacional público*, 3 vols. (Buenos Aires, 1934–1935).
MORGENTHAU, H. J., *Politics among Nations*, 2d ed. (New York, 1954).
MORLEY, F., *The Society of Nations* (Washington, 1932).
MORSE, H. B., AND MCNAIR, H. F., *Far Eastern International Relations*, 2d ed. (Boston and New York, 1931).
MOUTON, M. W., *The Continental Shelf* (The Hague, 1952).
MUNRO, D. G., *Intervention and Dollar Diplomacy in the Caribbean 1900–1921* (Princeton, 1964).
MUNRO, F., See Stowell and Munro.
MURALT, R. W. G. DE, *The Problem of State Succession with Regard to Treaties* (The Hague, 1954).
MYERS, D. P., *Manual of Collections of Treaties and of Collections Relating to Treaties* (Cambridge, Mass., 1922).
———, *Origin and Conclusion of the Paris Pact* (Boston, 1929).
———, *Handbook of the League of Nations* (Boston, 1935).
MYRDAL, G., *Beyond the Welfare State* (New Haven, 1960).
Nazi Conspiracy and Aggression: Opinion and Judgment (Government Printing Office, Washington, 1947) (Same title, 8 vols., 1947).
Neutrality: Its History, Economics and Law, Vol. I: *The Origins*, by P. C. Jessup and F. Deak; Vol. II: *The Napoleonic Period*, by W. A. Phillips; Vol. III: *The World War Period*, by E. Turlington; Vol. IV: *Today and To-Morrow*, by P. C. Jessup (New York, 1935–1936).
Nielsen's Report, American and British Claims Arbitration under agreement of August 18, 1910, Report of F. K. Nielsen (Washington, 1926).
NORGAARD, C. A., *The Position of the Individual in International Law* (Copenhagen, 1962).
NORTHROP, F. S. C., *The Taming of the Nations: A Study of the Cultural Base of International Policy* (New York, 1952).
NUSSBAUM, A., *A Concise History of the Law of Nations*, rev. ed. (New York, 1954).
NYS, E., *Les Origines de droit international* (Paris, 1894).
———, *Etudes de droit international et de droit politique*, 2 vols. (Bruxelles-Paris, 1896–1901).

————, *Le Droit international,* 2d ed., 3 vols. (Brussels, 1912).

OBIETA, J. A., S. J., *The International Status of the Suez Canal* (The Hague, 1963).

O'CONNELL, D. P., *The Law of State Succession* (Cambridge, 1956).

OGILVIE, P. M., *International Waterways* (New York, 1920).

OPPENHEIM, L., *International Law,* 8th ed. by H. Lauterpacht, Vol. I (New York, 1955); 7th ed. of Vol. II by H. Lauterpacht (London, 1952).

O'ROURKE, V. A., *The Juristic Status of Egypt and the Sudan* (Baltimore, 1935).

PADELFORD, N. J., *International Law and Diplomacy in the Spanish Civil Strife* (New York, 1939).

PADELFORD, N. J., AND LINCOLN, G. A., *The Dynamics of International Politics* (New York, 1962).

PALMER, N. D., AND PERKINS, H. C., *International Relations: The World Community in Transition,* 2d ed. (Boston, 1957).

Pan American Union, Congress and Conferences Series (Washington).

Pan American Union, Law and Treaty Series (Washington).

Papers Relating to the Treaty of Washington, 6 vols. (Washington, 1872–1874).

PARDESSUS, J. M., *Collection des lois maritimes antérieures au XVIIe siècle,* 6 vols. (1828–1845).

PASQUAZI, J., *Ius Internationale Publicum,* Vol. I (Rome, 1935).

Peace and War: United States Foreign Policy, 1931–1941 (Washington, 1943).

Peaceful Change: An International Problem, ed. by C. A. W. Manning (New York, 1937).

PEASLEE, A. J., AND D. P. XYDIS, *International Governmental Organizations,* 2d ed., 2 vols. (The Hague, 1961). Cited Peaslee, *I.G.O.*

Penal Code of the United States, see *Criminal Code.*

PERKINS, D., *Hands Off: A History of the Monroe Doctrine* (Boston, 1941).

PERKINS, H. C., see Palmer and Perkins.

Permanent Court of International Justice: Publications of the Court. Series A, Judgments and Orders; *Series B,* Advisory Opinions; since 1931 *Series A/B,* Comprising Judgments and Orders and Advisory Opinions; *Series C,* Acts and Documents Relating to Judgments and Advisory Opinions; *Series D,* Acts and Documents Concerning the Organization of the Court; *Series E, Annual Reports* (Leyden, 1925–).

PESSÔA, E., *Projecto de código de direito internacional público* (Rio de Janeiro, 1911).

PHILLIMORE, R., *Commentaries upon International Law,* 3d ed., 4 vols. (London, 1879–1889).

PHILLIPS, W. A., *The Confederation of Europe* (New York, 1914).

————, See *Neutrality: Its History, Economics and Law.*

PHILLIPSON, C., *The International Law and Custom of Ancient Greece and Rome,* 2 vols. (London, 1911).

————, AND BUXTON, N., *The Question of the Bosporus and Dardanelles* (London, 1917).

PICCIOTTO, C. M., *The Relation of International Law to the Law of England and of the United States of America* (New York, 1915).

PIGGOT, SIR F. T., *The Freedom of the Seas* (Oxford, 1919).

PODESTÁ COSTA, L. A., *Derecho Internacional Público*, 2 vols. (Buenos Aires, 1955).

POLITIS, N., *La Justice internationale* (Paris, 1924).

———, *The New Aspects of International Law* (Washington, 1928).

———, *La neutralité et la paix* (Paris, 1935). English trans. by F. C. Macken, *Neutrality and Peace* (Washington, 1935).

———, see Lapradelle and Politis.

POLLOCK, SIR F., *The League of Nations*, 2d ed. (London, 1922).

POTTER, P. B., *An Introduction to the Study of International Organization*, 5th ed. (New York, 1948).

———, *The Freedom of the Seas in History, Law, and Politics* (New York, 1924).

POUND, R., *An Introduction to the Philosophy of Law* (New Haven, 1922).

———, *Interpretations of Legal History* (New York, 1923).

———, *The Spirit of the Common Law* (Boston, 1921).

PRADIER-FODÉRÉ, P. L. E., *Traité de droit international public européen et américain*, 8 vols. (Paris, 1885–1906).

PRATT, J. W., *History of the United States Foreign Policy* (New York, 1955).

Publications of the Permanent Court of International Justice, 1922– (Leyden, 1925–), see *Permanent Court of International Justice.*

PUENTE, J. I., *The Foreign Consul: His Juridical Status in the United States* (Chicago, 1926).

PUFENDORF, S., *De officio hominis et civis juxta legem naturalem libri duo*, Vol. I, Latin text; Vol. II, English trans. by F. G. Moore (New York, 1927).

———, *De jure naturae et gentium libri octo*, Vol. I, Latin text; Vol. II, English trans. by C. H. and W. A. Oldfather (Oxford, 1934).

QUINTANA, MORENO, AND SHAW, BELLINI, *Derecho Internacional Público* (Buenos Aires, 1950).

RACHEL, S., *De jure naturae et gentium dissertationes*, Vol. I, Latin text; Vol. II, English trans. by J. P. Bate (Washington, 1916).

RAJAN, M. S., *United Nations and Domestic Jurisdiction* (Bombay, 1958).

RALSTON, J. H., *International Arbitral Law and Procedure* (Boston, 1910).

———, *The Law and Procedure of International Tribunals*, rev. ed. (Stanford Univ., 1926), with *Supplement* (Stanford Univ., 1936).

———, *International Arbitration from Athens to Locarno* (Stanford Univ., 1929).

RAMUNDO, B. A., *The Socialist Theory of International Law* (Washington, 1964).

Recueil des Cours, see *Académie de droit international.*

REDSLOB, A., *Histoire des grands principes du droit des gens* (Paris, 1923).

REGOUT, R., *La doctrine de la guerre juste de Saint Augustin à nos jours* (Paris, 1935).

REID, H. D., *International Servitudes in Law and Practice* (Chicago, 1932).

REINSCH, P. S., *Public International Unions* (Boston, 1911).

Research in International Law: Nationality; Responsibility of States for Injuries to Aliens; Territorial Waters (Cambridge, Mass., 1929).

Research in International Law: Diplomatic Privileges and Immunities; Legal Position and Function of Consuls; Competence of Courts in Regard to Foreign States; Piracy; Piracy Laws of Various Countries (Cambridge, Mass., 1932).

Research in International Law: Extradition; Jurisdiction with Respect to Crime; Law of Treaties (Cambridge, 1935).

Research in International Law: Judicial Assistance; Rights and Duties of Neutral States in Naval and Aerial War; Rights and Duties of States in Case of Aggression (Cambridge, 1939).

REVES, E., *Anatomy of Peace* (New York, 1945).

Revue de droit international et de législation comparée (Brussels, 1869–).

RHODES, J. F., *History of the United States*, 8 vols. (New York, 1910–1919).

RICHARDSON, J. H., *Economic Disarmament* (London, 1931).

RICHES, C. A., *Majority Rule in International Organization* (Baltimore, 1940).

RIESENFELD, S. A., *Protection of Coastal Fisheries under International Law* (Washington, 1942).

RIPPY, J. F., *Latin America in World Politics*, 3d ed. (New York, 1938).

RIVIER, A., *Principes du droit des gens*, 2 vols. (1896).

ROBERTSON, A. H., *The Council of Europe: Its Structure, Functions and Achievement*, 2d ed. (New York, 1961).

———, *The Law of International Institutions in Europe* (New York, 1961).

ROBSON, W. A., *Civilization and the Growth of Law* (New York, 1935).

ROLING, B. V. A., *International Law in an Expanded World* (Amsterdam, 1960).

ROOT, E., *Addresses on International Subjects* (Cambridge, 1916).

ROSCOE, E. S., *Lord Stowell: His Life and the Development of English Prize Law* (Boston, 1916).

ROSE, J. H., *Nationality in Modern History* (New York, 1916).

ROSENNE, S., *The International Court of Justice* (Leiden, 1957).

———, *The World Court: What It Is and How It Works* (New York, 1962).

ROWE, L. S., *The Pan American Union and the Pan American Conferences* (Washington, 1940).

ROXBURGH, R. F., *International Conventions and Third States* (London, 1917).

Rules of Land Warfare, 1940: War Department Basic Field Manual (Washington, 1940).

RUSSELL, F. M., *Theories of International Relations* (New York and London, 1936).

RUSSELL, R. B., *A History of the United Nations Charter* (Washington, 1958).

SACK, A. N., *Les Effets des transformations des Etats sur leurs dettes publiques* (Paris, 1927).

SALTER, SIR ARTHUR, *The United States of Europe and other Papers* (New York, 1933).

SATOW, SIR E., *A Guide to Diplomatic Practice*, 1st ed., 2 vols. (New York, 1922); 4th ed. (New York, 1954).

SAYRE, F. B., *Experiments in International Administration* (New York, 1918).

———, *The Way Forward* (New York, 1939).

SCELLE, G., *La Société des Nations* (Paris, 1922).

———, *Précis de droit des gens*, 2 vols. (Paris, 1932–1934).

SCHIFFER, W., *The Legal Community of Mankind* (New York, 1954).

SCHMITT, B. E., *The Coming of the War: 1914,* 2 vols. (New York, 1930).

SCHÜCKING, W., *Der Staatenverband der Haager Konferenzen* (München and Leipzig, 1912). English trans. by C. G. Fenwick, *The International Union of the Hague Conferences* (Oxford, 1918).

SCHUMAN, F. L., *International Politics,* 5th ed. (New York, 1958).

SCHWARZENBERGER, G., *Power Politics: A Study of World Society,* 3d ed. (New York, 1964).

———, International Law, Vol. I, *International Law as Applied by International Courts and Tribunals* (London, 1945).

———, *Manual of International Law,* 4th ed., 2 vols. (London, 1960).

SCOTT, J. B., *The American Institute of International Law: Its Declaration of the Rights and Duties of Nations* (Washington, 1916).

———, *An International Court of Justice* (New York, 1916).

———, *The Status of the International Court of Justice* (New York, 1916).

———, ed., *The Hague Court Reports* (New York, 1916).

———, ed., *The Reports to the Hague Conferences of 1899 and 1907* (Oxford, 1917).

———, ed., *The Hague Conventions and Declarations of 1899 and 1907* (New York, 1918).

———, *The United States of America: a Study in International Organization* (New York, 1920).

———, ed., *Treaties for the Advancement of Peace* (New York, 1920).

———, *The Spanish Origin of International Law* (Washington, 1928).

———, *The Catholic Conception of International Law* (Washington, 1934).

———, *Law, The State and the International Community* (New York, 1939).

SECKLER-HUDSON, C., *Statelessness: With Special Reference to the United States* (Washington, 1943).

SEPULVEDA, C., *La Teoría y la Practica del Reconocimiento de Gobiernos* (Mexico, 1954).

SEYMOUR, C., *The Diplomatic Background of the War, 1870–1914* (New Haven, 1916).

———, *American Neutrality 1914–1917* (New Haven, 1935).

SHARP, W. R., *Field Administration in the United Nations System* (New York, 1961).

SHARP, W. R., AND KIRK, G., *Contemporary International Politics* (New York, 1940).

SHEA, D., *The Calvo Clause* (Minneapolis, 1955).

SHERIDAN, P. H., *Personal Memoirs* (New York, 1888).

SHERMAN, W. T., *Memoirs* (New York, 1875).

SHOTWELL, J. T., *War as an Instrument of National Policy* (New York, 1929).

SIMONDS, F. H., AND EMENY, B., *The Price of Peace* (New York-London, 1935).

———, *The Great Powers in World Politics,* rev. ed. (New York, 1937).

SINGH, N., *Nuclear Weapons and International Law* (New York, 1959).

SMITH, SIR F., *International Law,* 5th ed., by C. Phillipson (New York, 1918).

SMITH, H. A., *The Economic Uses of International Rivers* (London, 1931).

————, ed., *Great Britain and the Law of Nations*, Vol. I: *States* (London, 1932), Vol. II: *Territory* (Part I) (London, 1935).

————, *The Law and Custom of the Sea* (London, 1961).

SMITH, J. M. P., *The Moral Life of the Hebrews* (Chicago, 1923).

SNOW, A. H., *The Question of Aborigines in the Law and Practice of Nations* (New York, 1921).

SNYDER, L. L., *The War: A Concise History, 1939–1945* (New York, 1960).

SOHN, L. B., *Cases and Materials on World Law* (Brooklyn, 1950).

————, *Cases on United Nations Law* (1956).

SPAIGHT, J. M., *Air Power and War Rights*, 2d ed. (London, 1933).

SPIROPOULOS, J., *L'individu en droit international* (Paris, 1928).

————, *Théorie générale du droit international* (Paris, 1930).

STALEY, E., *Raw Materials in Peace and War* (New York, 1937).

————, *The Future of Undeveloped Countries* (New York, 1961).

STARKE, J. G., *An Introduction to International Law*, 5th ed. (London, 1963).

Statutes at Large of the United States, 1789– (Washington, 1855–).

STETTINIUS, E. R., JR., *Report to the President on the Results of the San Francisco Conference*, Department of State Publication 2349 (Washington, 1945).

STEWART, I., *Consular Privileges and Immunities* (New York, 1926).

STEWART, R. B., *Treaty Relations of the British Commonwealth of Nations* (New York, 1939).

STOKE, H. W., *The Foreign Relations of the Federal State* (Baltimore, 1931).

STONE, J., *International Guarantees of Minority Rights* (London, 1932).

————, *Legal Controls of International Conflict* (New York, 1954).

STOWELL, E. C., *Consular Cases and Opinions* (Washington, 1909).

————, *Intervention in International Law* (Washington, 1921).

————, *International Law* (New York, 1931).

STRAUSZ-HUPÉ, R., AND POSSONY, S. T., *International Relations*, 2d ed. (New York, 1954).

STROHL, M. P., *The International Law of Bays* (The Hague, 1963).

STRUPP, K., *Legal Machinery for Peaceful Change* (London, 1937).

STUART, G. H., *The International City of Tangier*, 2d ed. (Stanford Univ., 1955).

————, *American Diplomatic and Consular Practice* (New York, 1936).

————, *Latin America and the United States*, 3d ed. (New York and London, 1938).

STURZO, L., *The International Community and the Right of War*, trans. from Italian by B. B. Carter (New York, 1930).

————, *Church and State*, trans. from Italian by B. B. Carter (New York, 1939).

SUAREZ, F., *Tractatus de legibus ac deo legislatore*, 1st ed. (Coïmbra, 1612).

SVARLEIN, O., *An Introduction to the Law of Nations* (New York, 1955).

TEMPERLEY, H. W. V., ed., *A History of the Peace Conference of Paris*, 6 vols. (London, 1921–1924).

TEXTOR, J. W., *Synopsis juris gentium*, Vol. I, Latin text; Vol. II, English trans. by J. P. Bate (Washington, 1916).

THOMAS, A. VAN W., AND THOMAS, A. J., JR., *The Organization of American States* (Dallas, 1963).

———, *Non-Intervention: The Law and its Import in the Americas* (Dallas, 1956).

THOMASIUS, C., *Fundamenta juris naturae et gentium* (1705).

THOMMEN, J. K., *Legal Status of Government Merchant Ships in International Law* (The Hague, 1962).

TOBAR DONOSO, J., *La invasión peruana y el Protocolo de Rio* (Quito, 1945).

TOD, M. N., *International Arbitration amongst the Greeks* (Oxford, 1913).

TOMLINSON, J. D., *International Control of Radio Communications,* reprint (Ann Arbor, 1945).

TOSTAIN, L., *Le Traité politique du Latran et la personalité en droit international public* (Paris, 1930).

TOUT, T. F., *The Empire and the Papacy* (New York, 1898).

Treaties and Other International Acts of the United States of America, see Miller, D. H.

Treaties, Conventions, International Acts, Protocols and Agreements between the United States of America and Other Powers. Cited as *Treaties and Conventions.* See Malloy, W. M.

Treaties for the Advancement of Peace, ed. by J. B. Scott (New York, 1920).

Treaty for the Renunciation of War: Text of the treaty, notes exchanged, instruments of ratification and of adherence and other papers. Department of State Publication No. 468 (Washington, 1933).

Treaty Series (new treaties by number) (Department of State, Washington).

TREITSCHKE, H. VON, *Politics,* trans. from the German by B. Dugdale and T. De Bille, 2 vols. (New York, 1916).

Trial of Japanese War Criminals, Department of State Publication No. 2613 (Washington, 1946).

TRIEPEL, H., *Völkerrecht und Landesrecht* (Leipzig, 1899). French trans. by R. Brunet, *Droit international et droit interne* (Paris, 1920).

TUCKER, G. F., see Wilson and Tucker.

TUCKER, R. W., *The Law of War and Neutrality at Sea* (Washington, 1957).

TURLINGTON, E., see *Neutrality: Its History, Economics and Law.*

ULLMANN, E. VON, *Völkerrecht,* 2d ed. (Tübingen, 1908).

ULLOA, A., *Derecho Internacional público,* 4th ed., 2 vols. (Lima, 1957).

———, *Posición Internacional del Perú* (Lima, 1941).

United States Foreign Relations.

United Nations Conference on International Organization: Selected Documents, Department of State Publication No. 2490 (Washington, 1946).

United States Foreign Relations.

United States Treaties and Other International Agreements (Washington, 1950).

VÁLI, F. A., *Servitudes of International Law: A Study of Rights in Foreign Territory,* 2d ed. (London, 1958).

VAN ALSTYNE, R. W., *American Diplomacy in Action,* 2d ed. (Stanford University, 1947).

VANDENBOSCH, A., AND HOGAN, W. N., *The United Nations: Background, Organization, Functions, Activities* (New York, 1952).

————, *Toward World Order* (New York, 1963).

VANDERPOL, A., *La Doctrine scholastique du droit de guerre* (Paris, 1919).

VAN DYNE, F., *A Treatise on the Law of Naturalization of the United States* (Washington, 1907).

VATTEL, E. DE, *Le Droit des gens, ou Principes de la loi naturelle appliqués à la conduite et aux affaires des nations et des souverains,* Vols. I, II, French text; Vol. III, English trans. by C. G. Fenwick (Washington, 1916).

VERDROSS, A., *Völkerrecht* (Berlin, 1937).

VI(C)TORIA, F. DE, *De indis et de jure belli relectiones,* Latin text, with English trans. by J. P. Bate (Washington, 1917).

VINACKE, H. M., *International Organization* (New York, 1934).

————, *A History of the Far East in Modern Times,* 2d ed. (New York, 1936).

VINOGRADOFF, SIR P., *Historical Jurisprudence* (Oxford, 1923).

————, *Roman Law in Medieval Europe* (London, 1909).

VISWANATHA, S. V., *International Law in Ancient India* (New York, 1925).

VREELAND, H., *Hugo Grotius* (New York, 1917).

WALKER, T. A., *The Science of International Law* (London, 1893).

————, *A History of the Law of Nations,* Vol. I (Cambridge, 1899).

WALLACE, B. B., AND EDMINSTER, L. R., *International Control of Raw Materials* (Washington, 1930).

WALTERS, F. P., *A History of the League of Nations,* 2 vols. (New York, 1952).

WALTZ, W. E., *The Nationality of Married Women* (Urbana, Ill., 1938).

WAMBAUGH, S., *A Monograph on Plebiscites with a Collection of Official Documents* (New York, 1920).

————, *Plebiscites since the World War,* 2 vols. (Washington, 1933).

WARD, P. W., *Sovereignty—A Study of a Contemporary Political Notion* (London, 1928).

WEHBERG, H., *Das Problem eines internationalen Staatengerichtshofes,* English trans. by C. G. Fenwick, *The Problem of an International Court of Justice* (Oxford, 1918).

————, See Schücking and Wehberg.

WEIL, G. L., *The European Convention on Human Rights* (Leiden, 1963).

WEIS, P., *Nationality and Statelessness in International Law* (London, 1956).

WELLES, S., *Naboth's Vineyard: The Dominican Republic, 1844–1924* (New York, 1928).

WESTLAKE, J., *Chapters on the Principles of International Law* (Cambridge, 1894).

————, *International Law,* 2d ed., Part I, *Peace;* Part II, *War* (Cambridge, 1910–1913).

————, *A Treatise on Private International Law, with Principal Reference to Its Practice in England,* 7th ed. by N. Bentwich (London, 1925).

What Really Happened at Paris, ed. by E. M. House and C. Seymour (New York, 1921).

WHEARE, K. C., *The Constitutional Structure of the Commonwealth* (Oxford, 1960).

WHEATON, H., *Elements of International Law,* 1st ed. (1836); 8th ed., by

R. H. Dana, Jr. (Boston, 1866); 6th Eng. ed., by A. B. Keith (London, 1929).

————, *A History of the Law of Nations in Europe and America from the Earliest Times to The Treaty of Washington, 1842* (New York, 1845).

WHITE, G., *Nationalization of Foreign Property* (New York, 1961).

WHITEMAN, M. M., *Damages in International Law*, 3 vols. (Washington, 1937–1943).

————, *Digest of International Law*, Vol. 1, Vol. 2 (1963), Vol. 3 (1964).

WICQUEFORT, A. DE, *L'Ambassadeur et ses fonctions*, English trans. by J. Digby, *The Embassador and His Functions*, 2d ed. (London, 1740).

WILCOX, F. O., *The Ratification of International Conventions* (London-New York, 1936).

WILCOX, J. O., AND MARCY, C. M., *Proposals for Changes in the United Nations* (Washington, 1955).

WILLIAMS, B., *State Security and the League of Nations* (Baltimore, 1927).

WILLIAMS, B. H., *Economic Foreign Policy of the United States* (New York, 1929).

WILLIAMS, SIR J. F., *Chapters on Current International Law and the League of Nations* (New York, 1929).

————, see *Annual Digest and Reports of Public International Law Cases.*

WILLOUGHBY, W. W., *The Constitutional Law of the United States*, 2d ed., 3 vols. (New York, 1929).

————, *Foreign Rights and Interests in China* (Baltimore, 1920).

————, *The Sino-Japanese Controversy and the League of Nations* (Baltimore, 1935).

WILSON, G. G., *Handbook of International Law*, 2d ed. (St. Paul, 1927).

————, *International Law*, 9th ed. (New York, 1935). Earlier editions by G. G. Wilson and G. F. Tucker.

WOETZEL, R. K., *The Nuremberg Trials in International Law* (London, 1960).

WOLFF, C. VON, *Jus gentium methodo scientifica pertractatum*, Vol. I, Latin text; Vol. II, English trans. by J. H. Drake (Oxford, 1934).

WOLFF, M., *Private International Law*, 2d ed. (New York, 1950).

WOOLSEY, T. D., *Introduction to the Study of International Law*, 6th ed., by T. S. Woolsey (New York, 1891).

World Court Reports, see M. O. Hudson.

World Peace Foundation, Pamphlet Series, 1911–1917; League of Nations Series, Vol. I–Vol. XII (Boston, 1917–1929).

WORTLEY, B. A., *Expropriation in Public International Law* (Cambridge, England, 1959).

WRIGHT, Q., *The Enforcement of International Law through Municipal Law in the United States* (Urbana, Ill., 1916).

————, *Mandates under the League of Nations* (Chicago, 1930).

————, *The Causes of War and the Conditions of Peace* (London and New York, 1935).

————, *A Study of War*, 2 vols. (Chicago, 1942).

WRIGHT, R. F., *Medieval Internationalism* (London, 1930).

Yearbook of the United Nations, 1946–1947–.

YEPES, J. M., *La contribution de l'Amérique Latine au développement du droit international public et privé* (Paris, 1931).

――――, *Le Panaméricanisme au point de vue historique, juridique et politique* (Paris, 1936).

ZIMMERN, SIR A., *The Greek Commonwealth: Politics and Economics in Fifth Century Athens*, 2d ed. (Oxford, 1915).

――――, *The League of Nations and the Rule of Law, 1918–1935* (London and New York, 1936).

ZOLLMAN, C., *Law of the Air* (Milwaukee, 1927).

ZOUCHE, R., *Juris et judicii fecialis, sive, juris inter gentes, et quaestionum de eodem explicatio*, Vol. I, Latin text; Vol. II, English trans. by J. T. Brierly (Washington, 1911).

ZURCHER, A. J., *The Struggle to Unite Europe* (New York, 1958).

...

PART I

The Nature of International Law

CHAPTER I

The Historical Background
of International Law

A. URGENCY OF A RULE OF LAW BETWEEN NATIONS

The challenge to the statesmen of this generation is clearly the urgent need of establishing the rule of law between nations upon firmer foundations. It is a challenge directed, indeed, not only to those in positions of political authority, but to the public at large in every country; for the task of building an effective rule of law between nations has now become one in which every citizen must have concern, at the cost of the survival of civilization.

What, then, is the meaning in concrete terms of the *rule of law?* What are the defects of existing international law, what are the fundamental principles that must be reaffirmed? What are the practical steps to be taken to widen the areas of agreement among nations and to restrict the areas of conflict? Is there in any real sense a community of nations that has sufficient intrinsic unity to form the basis of a world of law and order? Can the conception of the "general welfare" be organized to the degree that it form what might be called the "hard core" of a legal system? Has the great body of the common interests of states come to take priority in fact as well as in principle over their mutual differences?

It is obvious that these broad questions are not academic ones, that the making of a world of law and order is not an act of creative imagination. For we are dealing with a community of states that have diverse historical backgrounds, states that have developed their own national unity under widely varying conditions, states that confront one another with different interpretations of what constitutes their national welfare in relation to the general welfare of the community as a whole. In the

3

background of the effort to coordinate national policies are traditions and ideologies which on occasion manifest themselves in acutely conflicting ways, at times to the point of attacking the fundamental conception of a law of nations.[1] To understand them is the first step towards bringing them under the control of a common law.

Historical background in relation to present policies. It is not, therefore, merely as a matter of historical research that the student is led to begin his inquiry into the nature of international law and the conditions of a stable world order by a survey of the political environment in which the conception of a community of states has developed through the centuries. He is forced to do so if he is to understand the elements entering into the law of today. Behind the legal traditions of Western Europe, which have been the chief influence in the development of international law, were the traditions of the Roman Law, and behind the Roman Law the traditions of Ancient Greece. Over and above these traditions Christianity proclaimed the ideal of a common spiritual brotherhood cutting across state lines and creating an allegiance rivaling that of temporal sovereigns. The law of Western Europe was bequeathed to its colonial descendants in America, and it may properly be said to have dominated the world of the nineteenth and early twentieth centuries.[2] Then, with the entry of the Near Eastern and Far Eastern states into the hitherto exclusive European community, followed in turn by former African colonies, new forces, new ideals, new policies have had to be taken into account and as far as possible assimilated with the principles and customs of the Western World. The upheaval resulting from the Second World War in a sense forced the assimilation, and the older members are now confronted with the problem of creating within the new larger community of nations a unity of principles and of concrete objectives out of which an effective rule of law may be developed.[3]

---

[1] In the third edition of the present volume the author spoke of the fact that international law was in a sense "an entailed inheritance," that it was "mortgaged" to its past. While the metaphors were graphic, they gave perhaps the impression that the nations of 1948 needed only to discard many of their inheritances, such as the conception of "sovereignty" in a world of interdependent states, and the way ahead would be clear. Unfortunately the "way ahead" appeared to be much clearer following the adoption of the Charter of the United Nations than it does today. Technology has outrun the progress of morality, and economic development has proceeded at such a fast pace that it has been impossible to adjust social relations to it.

[2] A study of the leading treatises of the late nineteenth and early twentieth centuries (Kent, Wheaton, Manning, Phillimore, Hall, Walker, Lawrence, and Woolsey) indicates no recognition of a necessity to take into account the law of any other part of the world. See pp. 66 ff.

[3] See Chap. IV, D; and a challenging study by Jenks, *The Common Law of Mankind.*

B. INTERNATIONAL RELATIONS IN ANCIENT TIMES

Oriental states. The story is a long one and only the most significant phases can be marked out.[4] The earliest traces of international law were naturally of a regional character, in the form of rules recognized by states in immediate contact with one another. Relations between states in the earliest historical times were maintained within relatively narrow geographical areas, and the points of contact between them were few. It would doubtless be too much to call these rules regional international law, so little had they the character of law at all. Treaties between the Egyptian Pharaohs and neighboring kings, entered into as far back as the fourteenth century B.C., provided for the recognition of their mutual sovereignty and equality, as well as for the extradition of political refugees and immigrants.[5] Similar treaties were entered into by David, Solomon, and later Hebrew kings with neighboring states, other than the seven nations marked for extermination; and instances are to be found showing a care for the faith of treaties and a recognition of the sanctity of the ambassadorial character.[6] But there was little to suggest that other states or their inhabitants had any rights as such. War was waged freely and hostilities were conducted without restraint. The description of the Assyrian coming down "like a wolf on the fold" applies equally to Babylonians, Medes and Persians, Phoenicians and Carthaginians; and even the Jews, in spite of their recognition of a higher moral law and in spite of the ideals of peace proclaimed by their prophets, rivaled their neighbors on occasion in the slaughter and extermination of the enemy.[7]

India and China. It is among the member states of the ancient Chinese and Indian empires that regional law began first to take more definite shape. Lofty precepts of universal conduct are to be found in the writings of the Chinese philosophers of the Golden Age; but their application appears to have been confined in practice to the separate states of the empire, the "world" as it was known to China.[8] So also in ancient India, the epic narratives and codes of law, in so far as they treat of obligations toward other states, were applicable chiefly to the

---

[4] Nussbaum's *Concise History of the Law of Nations* contains, in addition to descriptive material, a survey of the historiography of the subject, followed by an exhaustive bibliography.

[5] The original document of a treaty of alliance between Egypt and the Hittites may be found in Breasted, *Ancient Records of Egypt,* Vol. III, pp. 163 ff.

[6] See Walker, *A History of the Law of Nations,* pp. 31-36.

[7] For the war practices of the Hebrews, see Judges, Samuel, Kings, and other books of the Old Testament, *passim.* Also H. J. Cadbury, *National Ideals of the Old Testament.*

[8] See Russell, *Theories of International Relations,* Chap. II.

separate states within India itself; and even within that limited circle they appear to have been as often violated as observed.[9]

The Greek city-states. However, important as the precepts of the philosophers of China and of India were within their respective circles, they had no perceptible influence upon the body of law that came to be formulated in Western Europe in the seventeenth century and that dominated the international community at the beginning of the twentieth century. Far more highly developed than the regional law of China or of India was the bond of unity among the Greek city-states. Here it was that the first consciousness of a true community of interests developed, and with it a rudimentary form of international law. Within the narrow circle of the Hellenic world, city-state met city-state upon a basis of mutual recognition of independence and legal equality, modified, as in the world of the nineteenth century, by alliances of separate states, by religious and political leagues, and by the hegemony of successive individual states. A firm foundation for union was to be found in their common race, religion, language, and customs.[10] But it is one of the tragedies of history that these bonds which might have been expected to develop some form of Hellenic federation, or at least some form of mutual cooperation for the common welfare and for mutual defense against the common enemy, failed to do so. Greece fell a victim to the inability of its statesmen to extend their outlook, except upon rare occasions, beyond the range of their city-states.

This inability of Greek statesmen to develop a spirit of regional unity within the Hellenic circle was due to the strong sense of local patriotism developed within the city-states.[11] The very forces of creative imagination which led to the development of the highest civilization that the world had yet known led to concentration upon the national interests of the separate states. The emphasis upon the character of the individual man, upon "humanity," which made possible the leadership of Greece in the civilized world, which produced works of literature and of art that became a standard for subsequent generations, tended to create rival communities, isolated from one another by the intenseness of their loyalty to their own small circle. To the Greek city-state independence played the same part it has played in our own times. If they had had the word *sovereignty* they would have used it.

Owing to the peculiar city-state organization of ancient Greece, the system of international law developed there bears a closer relation to that of modern times than does the international law of any subsequent

---

[9] See Viswanatha, *International Law in Ancient India;* Bandyopadhyay, *International Law and Custom in Ancient India;* Russell, *op. cit.,* Chap. III.

[10] See Phillipson, *International Law and Custom of Ancient Greece and Rome,* Vol. I, Chaps. I, II. Nussbaum finds the relations of the Greek states to be rather "inter-municipal" than international. *Concise History of the Law of Nations,* pp. 9, 291 ff.

[11] Kohn, *The Idea of Nationalism,* pp. 50 ff.; Zimmern, *The Greek Commonwealth.*

period down to the year 1648.[12] Greeks were aliens in other cities but their own, but as aliens they possessed rights, based partly upon the universal law of hospitality and partly upon special treaty provisions. The right of asylum was regarded as of divine origin, and was particularly sacred in connection with Greek temples. Ambassadors were exceptionally privileged. Elaborate formalities attended their reception, their persons were regarded as inviolable, and severe punishment was meted out to those who maltreated them.[13] Arbitration was frequently resorted to for the settlement of disputes; and agreements in advance to submit disputes of a definite or of a general character to arbitration were to be found both in treaties of peace and in alliances between separate states. A treaty of alliance between Sparta and Argos in 418 B.C. stipulated that they would submit their differences to arbitration "on fair and equal terms, according to their ancestral customs." [14]

Failure of collective security. But while numerous rules of international law relating to minor interests were developed between the city-states, they failed in the essential task of developing a system of collective security for the maintenance of peace. Their religious leagues for the protection of the shrines of their gods, called *amphictyonies*, the most famous of which was the Amphictyonic League of Delphi, the shrine of Apollo, did not succeed in preventing wars between their members. At the very peak of the civilization of Athens, when Pericles was organizing the democracy of which he was so proud, he began to plan a policy of imperialism which denied to others the rights Athens claimed for herself. The Confederacy of Delos, which began as a union of free states, ended in the establishment of the Athenian Empire; and the empire led in the end to the Peloponnesian War. Athenian ambition had disturbed the balance of power; and the Spartans, whose national profession was war, proclaimed that they were fighting for the liberty of Hellas.[15]

An elaborate code, based upon the universal law and supported by treaties, governed the conduct of hostilities, prescribing many rules in mitigation of the severity of interstate conflicts.[16] But in actual practice the laws of war were as little able to restrain the Greeks as to restrain belligerents in more modern times. The deliberate massacre by the

[12] Phillipson, *op. cit.*, Vol. I, Chaps. VII, VIII.

[13] *Ibid.*, Vol. I, Chaps. XIII-XV.

[14] Thucydides, Vol. V, p. 79; quoted in full by Phillipson, *op. cit.*, Vol. II, pp. 61, 62. See on the subject of arbitration in Ancient Greece, Tod, *International Arbitration amongst the Greeks*, Chap. II; Ralston, *International Arbitration from Athens to Locarno.*

[15] See, in general, Phillipson, *op. cit.*, Vol. II, Chap. XVIII; Zimmern, *The Greek Commonwealth;* Ferguson, *Greek Imperialism;* Laurent, *Histoire du Droit des Gens et des Relations Internationales*, Vol. II; A. E. R. Boak, "Greek Interstate Associations and the League of Nations," *Am. Journal*, Vol. 15 (1921), p. 375.

[16] Phillipson, *op. cit.*, Vol. II, Chap. XXIII.

Lacedemonians of the Platean garrison that had capitulated is a notable instance.[17] In the classic drama of Sophocles, Antigone appealed to the higher law of the gods in justification of her offense; but her plea went unheeded. The doctrine of reprisals, so familiar an excuse for the violation of the laws of war down to the latest times, played its part in justifying acts of cruelty in flagrant contravention of the higher law.[18] Toward those outside the Hellenic circle the rules of the universal law, being applicable to men as men, were equally binding, but equally violated in practice. Paradoxically enough, it was a "barbarian," Xerxes, who respected the universal law when it was suggested to him that he should retaliate upon the Athenians and the Spartans for the murder of the Persian envoys. His reply was that they had violated the law of all mankind, and that he would not do that very thing which he blamed in them.[19]

If the Greeks were unable to develop a system of collective security against the aggression of one member of their group against another, they were equally unable to combine for collective defense against the "barbarians" outside the Hellenic circle. Leagues were formed for defense against the invader, but they rarely held together. Sparta arrived too late to assist the Athenians at Marathon; the Spartan troops stood almost alone, with their backs to the wall, at Thermopylae. Happily, in spite of numerous invasions, the Persians never succeeded in imposing their rule upon the divided city-states; and it remained for Alexander the Great, himself a Greek, to force union upon them at the price of the independence they so jealously cherished. Greece had now a mission to civilize the world by drawing upon the inspiration of those whose genius had thrived in the earlier days of freedom.

Rome as a city-state. Considered with respect to the development of the conception of a community of states, the history of Rome may be divided into two periods. In the first, Rome was a city-state among other city-states, and its relations with them bear a close comparison with those of the Greek city-states. Down to the beginning of the third century B.C. Rome recognized the existence of other independent communities and maintained relations with them on the basis of formal treaties of alliance. While she dominated her Latin and Italian allies and subsequently absorbed them, she nevertheless regarded herself bound by legal obligations towards them. Numerous institutions and practices attest to the possession by Rome of a sense of legal rights and duties existing in a community of distinct juridical units.[20]

After the Second Punic War, which came to an end in 201 B.C., Rome

17 Thucydides, Vol. III, pp. 52 ff.
18 Phillipson, op. cit., Vol. II, Chap. XXIV.
19 Herodotus, vii, 136; quoted by Phillipson, op. cit., Vol. I, p. 60.
20 Phillipson, op. cit., Vol. I, pp. 107-108. The author contests the views of those who hold that Rome recognized no such rights and obligations.

entered upon a phase of her history during which she proclaimed herself mistress of the world. From now on her relations with other states were no longer on a basis of mutual independence and equality. The law between them was no longer one of mutual agreement set forth in treaties, but the will of Rome imposed upon subject peoples. Hence the term *international law* ceased to be applicable to the relations of Rome either with her former allies within the peninsula or with the numerous states and tribes surrounding the Mediterranean Sea that had now been brought under subjection. Such rights as Rome recognized on the part of the various subject peoples conquered by her armies were rights of her own granting, administered by her appointed officials, to be enjoyed so long as Rome found it expedient not to revoke them.

But if in point of law the subject peoples brought under the domination of Rome had no rights in their own name, the system of constitutional law enforced by Rome had many of the elements of a federal state. The form of colonial government applied by Rome to the provinces was far from being an arbitrary one. Order was brought into the relations of peoples hitherto perpetually at war; the provinces learned the art of self-government within the limitations fixed by Rome; while the states not formally constituted as provinces were, although subject to Rome, sufficiently autonomous to enjoy their own laws and civil governments. Subjugation did not mean assimilation.[21]

"Pax Romana." With the accession of Octavian as "Imperator" in 31 B.C. the world of the Roman Empire entered upon a long period of almost unbroken peace. The occasional wars upon the fringes of the empire did not disturb the normal administration of the central government. But that a system of government applicable to peoples of such varied character and distributed over so wide an area should hold together indefinitely was not to be expected under the conditions of communication of the time. The fact that it held together for so long gave opportunity for the development of ideals of universalism which were to have a lasting effect upon the history of the world. If in the end the material empire was to fall apart by reason of corruption at the administrative center of the system, the ideal of unity which it embodied remained for more than a thousand years the symbol of law and order, and, to a degree, of peace and justice.

It was from the Greeks whom Rome had conquered that the philosophical basis of universality came. While in the later days of the Republic the *praetor peregrinus* was developing rules of law applicable to those who were denied the privileges of Roman citizenship and was thus laying the foundations of a universal law, Roman philosophers were absorbing the teachings of Stoicism and coming to believe that empire

[21] See Tenney Frank, *Roman Imperialism;* Breasted, *The Conquest of Civilization,* Part V, "The Roman Empire."

and mankind were interchangeable terms. The world, such as they knew it, was a unit, a *civitas gentium*, even though the *gentes* were subject peoples. The extension of Roman citizenship to the provinces fitted in with the conception of a common brotherhood of peoples. *Pax Romana* gave of itself a unity to the nations at peace. If Rome conceived it her mission to bring the world by force of arms under a common rule of law, she herself set in motion the forces which were in time to give precedence to law over force.[22]

Decline of the Roman Empire.   The period of the decline and fall of the Roman Empire was marked by a general loosening of the bonds which held the various dependencies of Rome together. Constitutional law failed before the provinces had as yet sufficiently established themselves as semi-independent units of law and administration to make international law possible. Had the Roman system been a federal one, with representation of the provinces in the government of the empire, it is possible that the corruption of the central source of authority from within might not have disintegrated the entire system. As it was, when the bond of a common dependence upon Rome was broken, there was no sense of a community of interest on the part of the provinces, and there was no working machinery of government that might have led them to maintain the unity of the empire for their mutual defense. The result was that invading hordes which had never been part of the recognized constitutional system of Rome broke through the defenses of the colonial outposts and occupied the law-giving seat of the empire. Each of the local centers of the empire was thrown upon its own defenses, and within each of them internal strife added to the demoralization caused by the overthrow of the central authority. The influence of Christianity was still largely in the field of personal morality. Justinian attempted to revive the authority of Rome by his codification of its system of law; but principles of law, lacking the support of an adequate organization, were not of themselves sufficient to bring about the necessary unity.[23]

C. THE HOLY ROMAN EMPIRE

The year 800 A.D., which saw the coronation of Charlemagne as Emperor of the West by Pope Leo III, opened a new era in the history of international relations. The plan was conceived of reviving the ideal of an ordered world by bringing to the support of the empire the new bond of the Christian faith. Throughout the Dark Ages of the barbarian

---

[22] See Scott, *Law, the State, and the International Community*, Vol. I, Chaps. VII–IX.

[23] Gibbon's description in his *Decline and Fall of the Roman Empire* is familiar to every student. Montesquieu's *Considérations sur les causes de la grandeur des Romains et leur décadence*, published in 1734, is still inspiring reading, even though new facts have been discovered since then.

invasions men looked back to Rome as the symbol of law and order, and it was felt that if peace among the nations was to be established at all, it must be upon the basis of a single unifying authority. But Christianity had in the meantime entered its claims to the spiritual allegiance of the Western World, and its official head, the pope, was able to promise the new emperor effective aid in accomplishing a task at which others before him had failed. The whole organized influence of the Church, cutting across national lines, was to help establish the reign of law upon which the salvation of society depended. The emperor was to wield the temporal sword which would reduce rebellious individuals to obedience to the actual precepts of the law. The pope was to hold the spiritual sword which would enforce the observance of those common principles of morality which lay behind the law. Thus was formed the Holy Roman Empire, within which peace through law was to be maintained by the cooperation of the temporal and spiritual authorities.[24]

Effects of the feudal system. In this reorganization of the old empire on a new basis there was even less room for the existence of an international law in the modern form than there was during the reign of Augustus. For the Roman system of colonial administration was replaced by the feudal system, which practically eliminated the corporate personality of the individual state by identifying political authority with land tenure. The internal organization of the state was fundamentally altered by reducing the individual to a position of immediate dependence upon his overlord, to whom he owed personal allegiance, whereas before he had been bound by the more comprehensive and abstract law of the state. The state thus ceased to be based upon a community of interest between citizens and became a successive series of personal relations to the feudal lord. Territorial sovereignty accompanied the feudal tie. The result was that the centralization of the authority of the empire in the hands of the emperor amounted to no more than an acknowledgment of personal homage. There was no community of feeling between the separate feudal states, just as there was none between the vassals of different lords. A common law of nations was as impossible as a common law of the state. If the emperors, by reason of their exalted position, from time to time acted as arbitrators between kings and princes, in so doing they were exercising their personal influence rather than performing recognized legal functions attendant upon the prerogative of their office.[25]

Influence of the Church. But what the empire lacked in cohesiveness the Church of Rome undertook to supply. Both directly and indirectly it

---

[24] Bryce's *The Holy Roman Empire* is still the standard work. See also Tout, *Empire and Papacy;* Walker, *History of the Law of Nations,* pp. 79 ff.; Nussbaum, *op. cit.,* Chap. II, "The Middle Ages—West."

[25] On the general subject, see Vinogradoff, *Roman Law in Medieval Europe.*

sought to lay a restraining hand upon the centrifugal forces which manifested themselves within the first century after the founding of the empire. On the one hand the pope, as spiritual head of Christendom, undertook to pass judgment upon the conduct of princes no less than upon that of individuals. Since sovereignty was a personal relationship between vassal and lord, it was possible in cases of misconduct to threaten rulers with deposition, and even to depose them by releasing vassals from their oath of allegiance, the binding force of which was moral rather than political. The same spiritual authority enabled the pope to offer his good offices and mediation and to act as arbitrator in disputes between princes. This latter function was one of the highest importance, and the record of arbitral cases decided either by the popes themselves or under their influence is one of the brighter pages of an era in which petty dynastic wars were all too frequent.[26]

Formation of national states.   The ideal was that of a world state, but neither emperor nor pope could effectively compel obedience, and the authority of each was greatly weakened by conflicts of jurisdiction between them. On all sides the units of the empire were beginning to assert their independence of control, so that the successive triumphs of Pope Gregory VII over Henry IV and of Boniface VIII over Philip the Fair, instead of strengthening the spiritual sword of the empire, merely weakened its temporal one. Dante's plea, in his *De Monarchia*, for a single world rule for all peoples, which argued both on theoretical and practical grounds, fell upon deaf ears.[27] The Holy Roman Empire was past saving. Dubois, Dante's contemporary, understood better the tendencies of the times. Advocating a plan for the pacification and unification of Europe as the condition for a successful crusade to regain the Holy Land, he proposed not a revival of the empire, but a Christian commonwealth (*respublica*) functioning through a congress composed of sovereign and independent states.[28]

But if Dante's plan failed to recognize the force of the new nationalism that was developing within the empire, Dubois' plan called for a greater moral unity than was to be found among the princes who were asserting their independence of the empire. Territorial sovereignty was replacing

---

[26] Nys, *Les Origines*, Chaps. V, XI; Moore, *International Arbitrations*, Vol. V, Appendix III, translating from Mérignhac, *Traité théorique et pratique de l'arbitrage international;* B. Goyau, "L'Eglise catholique et le droit des gens," *Recueil des Cours*, Vol. 6 (1925-I), p. 127. For the objectives of the "Truce of God," see Walker, *History*, Vol. I, p. 85; Goyau, *op. cit.*, p. 150; L. Quidde, "Histoire de la paix publique en Allemagne au Moyen Age," *Recueil des Cours*, Vol. 28 (1929-III), pp. 453, 476.

To be distinguished from the Truce of God was the "Peace of God," which consisted in a series of decrees issued by the Church proclaiming an unlimited state of peace.

[27] Russell, *op. cit.*, p. 99; Scott, *Law, the State, and the International Community*, Vol. I, Chap. XV.

[28] Russell, *op. cit.*, p. 105; Hemleben, *Plans for World Peace*, Chap. I.

feudalism in the internal organization of the state. But it was a territorial sovereignty which was not as yet accompanied by any corporate consciousness on the part of the peoples of the separate states which might have put some restraint upon the ambitions of their rulers. Dynastic claims continued to be a disrupting force. The Hundred Years' War between England and France would alone have made a federation of European states impossible; while France and Spain on their part engaged in a struggle which attacked the very heart of the empire and made mockery of its tradition of unity. A few independent city-states arose: Genoa, Venice, and others in the Mediterranean; Florence, Siena, and others in northern Italy; the members of the Hanseatic League along the shores of the Baltic. But they were too remote from one another and too weak individually to have any appreciable influence upon the organization of Europe as a whole.[29]

The loss of spiritual unity. Parallel with the development of a self-conscious nationalism, which marked the close of the Middle Ages, came the repudiation of the spiritual authority of the Church both in its external activities as an organized institution and in its assertion of the principle of Christian unity under a common head. The Renaissance had awakened men's imaginations, and it was to be expected that authority and law should seem of secondary importance in the presence of the new world of philosophic, literary, and scientific ideas that were being discussed on all sides. The Reformation gave further expression to the sense of independent self-determination that had already begun to assert itself; and so close was the connection between church and state that revolt against ecclesiastical authority inevitably carried with it an affirmation of absolutism on the part of the state.[30]

The Thirty Years' War. The old order in Europe was dead, but a new order had not yet come into being. States were sovereign and independent units; but there was no bond of unity among them. For a time Europe drifted in a condition of helpless anarchy; each nation's

[29] An important body of international private law developed during this period in the form of collections of maritime customs setting forth the rights and duties of merchants and ship owners of different countries in their dealings with one another. Among these codes were the Rhodian Laws, of uncertain origin, possibly dating back as far as the seventh century; the Tabula Amalfitana of the eleventh century; the Laws of Oleron of the twelfth century; the Laws of Wisby, dating from the thirteenth or fourteenth century; and in particular the *Consolato del Mare* of the fourteenth century. See Pardessus, *Collection de lois maritimes antérieures au XVIII siècle;* Azuni, *Droit maritime de l'Europe.* Pardessus and Azuni are at odds with respect to the origin and content of the famous *Consolato del Mare.* Azuni ascribes it (pp. 414 ff.) to a compilation made in Pisa, which was formally blessed by the pope in 1075. Pardessus, refuting Azuni's evidence, ascribes it to a collection made in Barcelona, written in a Romance dialect, under the title *Consulat de la Mer,* and published in the fourteenth century. For the text see Pardessus, *op. cit.,* Tome I, Chap. XII.

[30] See on this point Sturzo, *Church and State,* Chap. VII; Schiffer, *The Legal Community of Mankind.*

hand was against its neighbor, and no state was certain of its legal status in the community. The Thirty Years' War, beginning in 1618, was a confused struggle in which religious and political objectives were inextricably bound up. At the first a domestic struggle within the German states, the war drew into its vortex one state after another which had originally no part in the dispute. The emperor must not be allowed to threaten their security by becoming again the dominant power in Europe. To that end Catholic France was willing to take sides with Protestant forces in Germany. Finally, when the participants had exhausted their resources, the war was terminated by the Peace of Westphalia of 1648, consisting of the two treaties of Osnabrück and Münster, to which all of the leading Christian states of Europe were parties, although England and Poland were not represented in the negotiations.[31]

D. THE PEACE OF WESTPHALIA AND THE SOVEREIGNTY OF STATES

The negotiations at Osnabrück and Münster mark the first of the great conferences which were henceforth to determine from time to time the law of the international community and the political relations of its members. Two new states, Holland and the Swiss Confederation, were formally recognized as independent. France, Spain, Portugal, and the Italian cities and duchies had been so long emancipated from the empire that it was not thought necessary to give even formal confirmation of their status. The individual German states, some 350 in number, continued under a confederation with the emperor at its head; but since, with but one restriction, they were empowered to contract treaties with one another and with foreign powers, they became practically sovereign in their foreign relations as well as absolute rulers within their own domains. The emperor and the Imperial Diet remained, but so far shorn of power as to influence but little the politics of Europe.

The balance of power. Henceforth the international community was to consist of coequal members individually independent of any higher authority. The principle of territorial sovereignty was definitely established in both political and religious matters. Individual sovereigns were supreme in the exercise of spiritual control except in so far as religious toleration had been guaranteed to the three principal confessions.[32] A balance of power both within the empire and between the empire and its neighbors had been set up by which the dominance of any single state might be prevented in the future. Finally, a legal sanction was given to the settlement by the provision of both treaties to the effect that

[31] Russia had not yet been recognized as a European power. Turkey was also outside the pale.

[32] Namely, Catholic, Lutheran, and Calvinist. Hill calls attention to the "essentially political character of the religious settlement" in *History of Diplomacy*, Vol. II, p. 602.

"all and each of the contracting parties of this treaty shall be held to defend and maintain all and each of the dispositions of this peace, against whomsoever it may be, without distinction of religion." [33] The Peace of Westphalia thus marked the beginning of a new era in international relations—a statutory landmark in the public law of Europe.[34]

But the balance of power set up by the Peace of Westphalia soon proved unstable. The principle itself proclaimed the lack of unity within the group of signatory states. No organization had been established to give effect to the common will expressed in the two treaties. No new central authority replaced the old order of emperor and pope. Theories of sovereignty had been advanced to justify the unification of the state under a single ruler; but the process of unification stopped with the national state. The same principle that was used to make the monarch supreme within his territorial boundaries was used to make him independent of control by any authority outside his boundaries.[35] The faith of treaties was the one cohesive element in the relations of states. But what force could the faith of treaties have when there was no sense of moral obligation to the community as a whole and when each state, by the very definition of its sovereignty, was the ultimate arbiter of its rights and duties?

Period from 1648 to the French Revolution. Under such circumstances the principle of the balance of power degenerated into a confused struggle of rival dynasties and irresponsible rulers. In the absence of an organization competent to maintain law and order, security for the individual states could only be obtained by the formation of alliances to offset any attempt to overthrow the existing political equilibrium. Third states, having no direct interest of their own in a particular controversy, found it a matter of self-protection to intervene when it appeared that the victory of one of the parties might give to it a dominant position.[36] During the second half of the seventeenth century the dynastic claims of Louis XIV led to a series of wars in which one power after another intervened to prevent the undue extension of French control. The Peace of Utrecht of 1713, which ended the War of the Spanish Succession, had definitely in view the balance of power and gave what were thought to be new sanctions to it. By the Treaty of Nystad of 1721, which marked the transfer to Russia of the Baltic provinces of Sweden, Russia formally entered the family of nations, and by reason of the strength of her army and the domestic reforms of Peter the Great, Russia was promptly rec-

[33] Treaty of Osnabrück, Art. XVII, §§ 5-7; Treaty of Münster, §§ 116-117.

[34] Hill, *op. cit.*, Vol. II, pp. 599 ff.; Redslob, *Histoire des grands principes du droit des gens*, § 38. Compare L. Gross, "The Peace of Westphalia, 1648-1948," *Am. Journal*, Vol. 42 (1948), p. 20, where the principles of the Peace are followed through three centuries.

[35] See p. 34, note 6.

[36] See Butler and Maccoby, *Development of International Law*, pp. 61 ff.

ognized as a leading power. In 1740 Frederick the Great began the series of aggressions which were to make the name of Prussia feared throughout Europe. In 1772 came the first of the partitions of Poland, marking the decline of a great power which, at the time of the Peace of Westphalia, extended from the Baltic to the Black Sea. A second partition followed in 1793 and a third in 1795, the latter terminating Poland's existence as a member of the international community. These partitions were open and gross violations of the basic principles of international law; but inasmuch as they did not seriously affect the balance of power there was no one to be found strong enough and willing to undertake the defense of the victim. In the meantime the Treaty of Versailles of 1783 marked the recognition of the independence of the new American Republic, which in entering the family of nations was destined to make important contributions of its own to the development of international law.

Period from 1789 to 1815. With the outbreak of the French Revolution the problem of the balance of power again preoccupied the attention of Europe. The attitude of the leaders of the Revolution was at first strikingly progressive. The National Assembly declared in 1790 that the French nation renounced wars of conquest and would never use force against the liberty of any people. This was followed, however, in November, 1792, by an announcement from the National Convention that France was ready to come to the aid of all peoples who might wish to recover their liberty, and by a more drastic decree in December to the effect that the French nation would treat as enemies every people who, refusing liberty and equality or renouncing them, might wish to retain, recall, or treat with a prince or the privileged classes. The decrees of 1792 thus paralleled in their method, though not in their objects, the dynastic interventions of the absolute monarchs.[37] The radical doctrines of the revolution and the imprisonment of the king brought about the intervention of outside powers. The emperor of Austria declared in 1791 that it was necessary "to save all Europe from revolt and anarchy," and in 1792 the Duke of Brunswick, at the head of the allied armies of Austria and Prussia, invaded France. His defeat at Valmy gave encouragement to the belief that the propaganda of revolution by force of arms might be successfully carried out, as expressed in the December decree.[38] Equally unsuccessful was the intervention of the larger coalition in 1794-1795. But the powers were still unwilling to give recogni-

---

[37] For the texts of the various decrees, see Anderson, *Constitutions and Documents.*
[38] It is of interest to note that the draft Declaration of the Rights of Nations, which the Abbé Grégoire had been entrusted to prepare as an appendix to the Declaration of the Rights of Man, was rejected by the Convention in 1795 when the republic was about to enter upon new wars. For the text of Abbé Grégoire's plan, see Nys, *Etudes de droit international et de droit public,* Vol. I, p. 395.

tion to a state which in its government defied the political traditions of the rest of Europe.

The Napoleonic era. From having been on the defensive, the new republic now became conscious of its strength, and with Napoleon at the head of its armies the war was carried into the enemy's territory. Dynasties were overthrown, new states created, alliances contracted, and the boundaries of France extended. The balance of power was completely unsettled, and international law seemed in danger of becoming once more the will of a supreme monarch. But the power of a single state, supported by artificial alliances, was unable to hold out against the successive coalitions formed to check its menacing control. Napoleon fell in 1814, though not before Europe had been shaken to its foundations. Old conceptions of absolute monarchy had been questioned and new ideals of democracy spread abroad. The feudal system with its patrimonial conception of sovereignty had disappeared. A new code of law had been published which guaranteed the social equalities won by the Revolution. The old territorial landmarks had been shifted, and nationalism as a bond of statehood had gained both in Germany and Italy a hold upon the imagination of the people. The opportunity of reorganizing Europe upon a more stable basis was at hand if statesmen could be found to undertake the task.

E. THE CONGRESS OF VIENNA AND ITS AFTERMATH

The Congress of Vienna, meeting from September 1814 to June 1815, assumed, like the congresses of Osnabrück and Münster, what was practically the role of a great law-making body.[39] It formed new states by the union of Sweden and Norway and of Holland and Belgium, and it confirmed the action of Napoleon in consolidating the numerous German states and formed them into a loose confederation of thirty-nine members. Its chief object, however, was the restoration of the balance of power in Europe which had been so greatly unsettled. The leading powers had announced in the Treaty of Paris of May 30, 1814, that it was their desire "to put an end to the long disturbance of Europe and to the suffering of the people by a stable peace based upon a just division of forces between the powers and carrying with it a guarantee of its permanence." But the purpose thus announced was completely frustrated by the reactionary principles which dominated the congress. The decisions taken by it proved to be the occasion throughout the nineteenth century of new wars to undo the plans so carefully made. Domestic revolution followed in the wake of the restoration of the

[39] For a survey of the work of the Congress as an "Experiment in Mechanism," see Butler and Maccoby, *Development of International Law*, Chap. XI.

deposed monarchs, and wars of liberation followed the suppression of aspirations for national union.

The Holy Alliance. While the Treaty of Vienna was being drawn up, three of the leading powers, Russia, Prussia, and Austria, acting upon the initiative of the Czar Alexander, formed the Holy Alliance, whose name was destined to serve for more than a century as a symbol of the forces of despotism in combination to suppress democratic movements. As a matter of historical fact the alliance proposed by the Czar was nothing more than a personal union of sovereigns, whose proclaimed purpose was to apply the principles of Christian morality in the administration of their domestic affairs as well as in the conduct of their international relations. It was in that sense that the alliance was subsequently joined by most of the European states, Great Britain by exception holding aloof, not because of its objectives, but because of the personal character of the alliance.[40] In contrast with this idealistic alliance there was renewed in 1815 the the Quadruple Alliance which had been formed the year before to resist Napoleon. Russia, Prussia, Austria, and Great Britain pledged themselves "to hold periodical meetings for the consideration of important common interests, and to concert measures for the peace and welfare of the peoples." Thus was formed an inner circle or directorate of states which, without openly repudiating the principle of the equality of the members of the international community, assumed quasi-legislative powers and undertook the direction of the affairs of Europe as a whole.[41]

The Quadruple Alliance, or Tetrarchy, of 1815 became by the accession of France the Quintuple Alliance, or Pentarchy, of 1818. At the Congress of Aix-la-Chapelle in 1818 a declaration was signed in which the assembled powers recognized the law of nations as the basis of international relations and pledged themselves to act in the future according to its rules. But at the Congress of Troppau in 1820 the alliance, reduced by the defection of Great Britain and France to three members, was led to announce the fatal principle of armed intervention. The famous Troppau Protocol declared that "states which have undergone a change of government due to revolution, the results of which threaten other states, *ipso facto* cease to be members of the European [Holy] Alliance, and remain excluded from it until their situation gives guarantees for legal order and stability"; and the three allies bound themselves, if im-

[40] See Phillips, *The Confederacy of Europe;* Hayes, *A Political and Social History of Modern Europe,* Vol. II, pp. 11 ff.; Moore, *Digest,* Vol. VI, pp. 374 ff. For the text of the Alliance, see *Br. and For. State Papers,* Vol. III, p. 211.

[41] It is important to distinguish sharply between the Holy Alliance as a personal union of the rulers of European states, the Quadruple Alliance which defeated Napoleon and dominated the Congress of Vienna, and the Triple Alliance which, speaking in the name of the Holy Alliance, announced the policy of intervention at the Congress of Troppau.

mediate danger threatened other states in consequence of such changes, to resort if necessary to arms to bring back the guilty state into the bosom of the Great Alliance.[42] This was an attack upon the fundamental principles of the independence and equality of states, and it reduced the established traditions of international law to the arbitrary will of a small group of absolute monarchs. In the popular mind the Holy Alliance became associated with the declaration of the three powers at Troppau and their subsequent measures to give effect to it, and the alliance has accordingly had to bear the reproach of liberals ever since. Speaking strictly, the Holy Alliance in its original form was not so much a treaty as a declaration of faith, binding its members to no specific action.

The Monroe Doctrine. The effects of the Protocol of Troppau upon the development of international law were far-reaching. Intervention in Naples and Spain passed without protest. But when the alliance proceeded to offer support to Spain in a war to reconquer her colonies in America which had declared their independence, the United States saw that its own interests were deeply involved. President Monroe was thus led to deliver, on December 2, 1823, the message in which the American continent was marked off as a field within which distinct principles of international law were henceforth to apply. The Monroe Doctrine first declared that the American continents were no longer open to colonization by European powers. It then announced that the United States would consider any attempt on the part of the Allied Powers "to extend their system" to the Western Hemisphere as dangerous to its peace and safety. While disclaiming any intention on the part of the United States to interfere with the existing colonies or dependencies of Europe, the message announced that in respect to the new governments which had declared and maintained their independence and whose independence had been duly recognized by the United States, any interposition for the purpose of oppressing them or controlling in any way their destiny would be regarded as the "manifestation of an unfriendly disposition towards the United States." This assumption by the United States of a form of guardianship over the states of the Western Hemisphere as a means of defense of its own national security had not only far-reaching political effects, but it laid the foundation for the development of a regional system within the larger community of nations.[43]

The balance of power. Throughout the nineteenth century the maintenance of the balance of power continued to be the determining policy

[42] See Hayes, *op. cit.* Vol. II, pp. 13 ff.

[43] Bemis, *The Latin American Policy of the United States,* Chaps. IV, V; Perkins, *Hands Off: A History of the Monroe Doctrine,* Chap. II; Cresson, *The Holy Alliance: The European Background of the Monroe Doctrine;* Alvarez, *The Monroe Doctrine: Its Importance in the International Life of the States of the New World.*

in the relations of the leading powers. Indeed, with the increasing substitution of constitutional governments for irresponsible monarchs the balance of power came to acquire almost the character of an absolute principle. Alliances were balanced against alliances, and the art of diplomacy consisted in forestalling the designs of other states and in taking measures today which would prevent situations of danger in some distant future. War was the accepted instrument of national policy. Governments respected the morals of their peoples by being careful to proclaim that their wars were wars of self-defense. But under the existing system it was impossible to distinguish between defense and attack, since defense consisted in attacking by way of anticipating the attack of another.[44]

In 1853 the balance of power was upset by the attack of Russia upon Turkey; and Great Britain, France, and Sardinia came to the rescue of the failing Ottoman Empire. By the Peace of Paris of 1856 Turkey was formally admitted to membership in the society of nations; and the emancipation of the Balkan states had to await such time as it could be accomplished without enhancing the prestige of Russia. Again in 1877 Russia unsettled the balance of power by the defeat of Turkey and the subsequent Peace of San Stefano; but this time it was possible without war to check the threatened dominance of Russia in the Near East. The Congress of Berlin of 1878, while liberating Rumania and Serbia, left Bulgaria a vassal state until such time as the make-weight of Turkey in the balance of power was no longer needed.[45]

Alliances and counteralliances. In the meantime the political equilibrium of Central and Western Europe was in need of readjustment. The unification of Italy had been accomplished in 1870 and there was a new Great Power to be reckoned with. The German Confederation created by the Congress of Vienna had been broken up in 1866, and a federation of North German states under the leadership of Prussia had been formed. France, fearing the power of the new federation, had insisted in 1870 that a Hohenzollern should not sit upon the throne of Spain. The defeat of France and the federation of both North and South German states shifted the weights in the scale in favor of Germany. In 1879 Germany formed with Austria the Dual Alliance, which by the accession of Italy in 1884 became the formidable Triple Alliance. For a time the weight was heavily on one side. Then France formed with Russia in 1891-1895 the Dual Alliance, and the balance was for the

[44] On the general subject of the maintenance of peace by a balance of power, see Wright, *A Study of War*, Vol. II, pp. 743 ff. and references there cited; Dupuis, *Le principe d'équilibre et le concert européen*. For the relation between the principle of the balance of power and the subtle question of the right of self-defense as affected by the growing armaments of a neighboring state, see below, p. 275.

[45] For a survey of this period, see Holland, *European Concert in the Eastern Question*; Redslob, *Histoire des grands principes*, §§ 85-92.

time being restored. Soon, however, the growing power of the German Empire brought Great Britain to take sides with France and Russia. The Triple Entente was formed, characterized by the uncertainty of Britain's commitments. Thus the balance of power held unsteadily, until a rude jolt by Austria-Hungary in 1914 made the whole system collapse.[46]

The Concert of Europe. But while the unstable political structure of the international community remained unchanged during the nineteenth century, other forces were at work to create a growing sense of unity that gave promise at times of being strong enough to prevent the political system from moving to its inevitable breakdown. The Treaty of Vienna made provision that no change in the *status quo* should take place without consultation between the signatory powers, and each of them was given the right to propose a conference if conditions should arise calling for one. While the first effects of this "conference system" were unfortunate due to the initiative of the three absolute monarchies, Russia, Prussia, and Austria, it later came slowly to be an instrument of constructive changes in the relations of the European states, at that time the center of the international community. Conference succeeded conference, and the agreements which generally accompanied them were in the nature of legislative enactments within the sphere of their application. On occasion the Concert of Europe, as it was called, took joint action to put an end to abuses and to correct political situations involving danger to the peace. Thus Greece was recognized as independent in 1827, Belgium was separated from Holland in 1831 and neutralized, the conferences at Paris in 1856 and at Berlin in 1878 began the emancipation of the Balkan states, and the congress at Berlin in 1885 came to an agreement upon the partition of Africa.[47]

F. THE DEVELOPMENT OF LAW BY CONVENTIONS

Economic and social interests. In addition to these and other political conferences numerous international conferences met from time to time for the regulation of economic and social interests. Special "unions" were formed for the permanent administration of particular interests of a continuing character.[48] Problems of international public health, public morals, public safety were dealt with in a constructive manner, as if the nations were indeed a true international community. Statesmen and publicists in different countries began to have visions of a world of law

[46] The story of this period is told in numerous volumes. See, in particular, Gooch, *History of Modern Europe;* Hayes, *History of Modern Europe;* Seymour, *Diplomatic Background of the War, 1870-1914;* Schuman, *International Politics.*

[47] On the conference system, see Potter, *International Organization,* Part VI; Vinacke, *International Organization;* Dunn, *The Practice and Procedure of International Conferences;* Hill, *The Public International Conference.*

[48] See below, Chap. XXV.

and order based upon the voluntary cooperation of sovereign and independent states which had come to recognize so vast a body of common interests.

The Hague Conference of 1899. The turn of the twentieth century brought to a head the paradox of an international community whose unstable political structure made war almost inevitable while the economic and social interests of states were making more evident each year the fact of their interdependence. On May 18, 1899, the first of the two great peace conferences met at The Hague upon invitation of the Czar of Russia. The primary object was to promote a general limitation of armaments. No one pointed out that this could not be done without the establishment of some system of collective security, without the assumption by the whole community of a collective responsibility for the protection of its members when deprived of the protection their armaments were supposed to give. Instead the conference, dismissing summarily the problem of a limitation of armaments, sought to promote the general peace by encouraging resort to arbitration for the settlement of international disputes and by drawing up rules and regulations for the conduct of war. The Convention for the Pacific Settlement of International Disputes recognized arbitration as "the most effective, and at the same time the most equitable, means of settling disputes which diplomacy has failed to settle"; but it imposed no degree of obligation upon the parties to follow the proposed procedure. The conventions relative to the laws of war did not encroach upon the sovereign right of the individual state to resort to war as an instrument of national policy. Important, therefore, as was the conference in demonstrating the possibilities of law-making by common consent, it failed to strengthen the political structure of the international community.[49]

The Conference of 1907. The failure of the Second International Peace Conference, which met at The Hague on June 15, 1907, was all the more complete, since in the interval of eight years the need of strengthening the political structure of the international community had become all the more urgent. This time the Latin American states sent delegations, raising the number of states represented from twenty-six, at the Conference of 1899, to forty-four, which included practically the entire family of nations. As a law-making body the second conference did not differ essentially from the first, but the number and scope of the conventions adopted gave it a greater importance. The procedure of inquiry and of arbitration was improved, but the conference could come no nearer than in 1899 to an agreement upon even a limited obligation to arbitrate. The Final Act of the conference did no more than express its unanimous acceptance of "the principle of compulsory arbitration,"

---

[49] In excluding all of the American republics except the United States and Mexico, the Conference deliberately limited its possibilities of worldwide influence.

and it added irony to evasion in announcing that the assembled states had "succeeded in the course of this long collaboration in evolving a very lofty conception of the common welfare of humanity."

The Declaration of London. It is significant that of the thirteen conventions adopted by the peace conference of 1907 eleven related to the conduct of the next war.[50] The code of warfare on land, adopted in 1899, was revised, and it was supplemented by conventions dealing with various aspects of maritime war—the status of merchant ships at the outbreak of hostilities, the conversion of merchant ships into warships, the laying of submarine contact mines, bombardment by naval forces, the adaptation of the principles of the Geneva Convention to maritime war, and the other lesser matters. Conventions were adopted dealing with the rights and duties of neutrals in naval warfare; and provision was made for the establishment of an International Prize Court. The conference failed, however, to agree upon the principles of law to be applied by the Prize Court; and in consequence the London Naval Conference met the following year. The Declaration of London, signed on February 26, 1909, at the close of the conference, covered the chief points in dispute between belligerents and neutral states. So sharp, however, were the conflicting interests of the leading powers that the Declaration failed of ratification, and the subjects with which it dealt were left to be decided on the basis of the earlier uncertain customary law.[51]

Defects of the law. The failure of the Hague conferences lay not merely in the inability of the delegates to realize that, with the new instruments available to belligerents, war had reached the point where it was beyond effective regulation or control. It was rather their acceptance of the inevitability of war that left them out of touch with the changing conditions of international intercourse. No effort was made to organize the international community for the maintenance of law and order; to substitute the judgment of the community for the judgment of the individual state in a conflict of claims; to provide for the defense of the individual state by the collective power of the community. War was accepted as a legal procedure; and states not parties to the controversy prepared to stand aside as neutrals without concern for issues of right and wrong between the belligerents. Strangely enough, few statesmen showed signs of dissatisfaction with the situation.[52]

[50] For a study of the work of the Hague peace conferences see, Higgins, *Hague Peace Conferences;* Scott, *Hague Peace Conferences of 1899 and 1907.* For the texts of the conventions adopted at the two conferences, see Higgins, *op. cit.;* Scott, *The Hague Conventions and Declarations.*

[51] For the text of the Declaration of London, see Higgins, *op. cit.,* p. 540; Scott, ed., *The Declaration of London.* It should be noted that the smaller states were not invited to the conference, and that if the Declaration had come into force they would have been obliged either to accept it or to appeal as best they might to the uncertain customary law.

[52] See below, Chap. XXVIII.

Thus things stood when Austria-Hungary, driven to strong measures of self-help by the assassination of the Archduke Ferdinand in 1914, sent its peremptory ultimatum to Serbia. The negotiations preceding the outbreak of the First World War clearly indicate that none of the powers involved actually wanted war, certainly not a war on the scale of the one that developed. But Russia felt called upon to come to the aid of Serbia, Germany came to the aid of Austria-Hungary, and France to the aid of Russia. Under the political system of the time none of them could yield without loss of prestige and disturbance of the balance of power. There was no established machinery of consultation available by which the parties might have been brought together and confronted collectively with their respective demands. The system of occasional general conferences was not designed to meet cases of emergency. War came largely because the international community was not adequately organized to prevent it.[53]

G. EFFECT OF THE WORLD WAR

The war of 1914 had scarcely begun before it became clear that its effects upon the existing international law would be far-reaching. The violation by Germany, on plea of military necessity, of the treaty of 1839 by which Belgium was permanently neutralized showed that even the fundamental doctrine of the faith of treaties could not stand the pressure of alleged national self-preservation in a war between the guarantors of the treaty. The rigorous measures attending the invasion and occupation of Belgium made a mockery of the agreements reached at the Second Hague Conference. New and more drastic rules of contraband and blockade were put forth by Great Britain, with corresponding protest from neutrals. Belligerent merchant ships were sunk by German submarines without warning. New instruments of combat, such as poisonous gases, were devised; aerial warfare put an end to the rules regulating the bombing of unfortified towns; and intimidation was resorted to as a means of breaking the spirit of the civilian population. The entrance of the United States into the conflict was marked by an announcement that the old law of neutrality was at an end and that henceforth the nations must assume a collective responsibility for the peace of the world. New principles of international law were announced by President Wilson as properly forming the basis upon which a permanent peace might be concluded.[54] In the popular mind the term *international law* as relating to the existing rules and their imperfect

[53] The events immediately leading up to the war are well set forth in Fay, *Origins of the World War;* and in Schmitt, *The Coming of the War, 1914.*

[54] See under appropriate headings, pp. 429, 511. For a critical forecast of what a League of Nations might accomplish, see Brailsford, *A League of Nations.*

sanction was a term that no longer bore any relation to the realities or to the needs of international life.

H. COVENANT OF THE LEAGUE OF NATIONS

The Treaty of Versailles concluded between the Allied and Associated Powers and Germany, and signed on June 28, 1919, contained among its specific provisions numerous modifications of international law, in addition to including as its first twenty-six articles the fundamental agreements of the Covenant of the League of Nations.[55] The significance of the Covenant of the League of Nations lay both in the changes which it effected in the organization of the community of nations and in the amendments introduced into the substantive as well as the procedural parts of international law. The system of the balance of power was impliedly, if not formally, repudiated in the collective responsibility assumed by all the members of the League for the future peace of the world, and neutrality as an attitude of legal indifference to war on the part of third states came to an end. Qualified guarantees were given by the League to its individual members in respect to the enjoyment of their independence and territorial sovereignty. Provision was made for a degree of compulsory arbitration in the settlement of disputes and for the future creation of a Permanent Court of International Justice. Constructive provisions were laid down for the administration under mandates of backward and undeveloped countries, and general principles were adopted looking to greater social and economic cooperation. In a separate section of the treaty, Part XIII, an International Labor Organization was established for the improvement of labor conditions in all countries.[56]

Changes in the structure of the international community. Aside from the Covenant of the League of Nations, the several treaties of peace effected fundamental changes in the structure of the society of nations and in the relations of its component parts. The boundaries of France were enlarged by the annexation of Alsace-Lorraine, while those of Belgium received a slight increase by the cession of Moresnet, Eupen, and Malmédy. To Denmark was ceded the northern part of Schleswig, and to Italy South Tyrol, Istria, and a strip of the Adriatic coastline. Rumania was enlarged by the annexation of Bessarabia, Transylvania, and part of the Hungarian plain. A number of new states were created. Albania advanced from a condition of wardship under the Great Powers

[55] The Covenant also appeared as the first twenty-six articles of the treaties of St. Germain, Trianon, and Neuilly, between the Allied and Associated Powers and Austria, Hungary, and Bulgaria respectively. The United States signed all four of the treaties, but did not ratify them. China did not sign the Treaty of Versailles.

[56] Walters, *History of the League of Nations.*

to the status of an independent state. Poland was formed from territory taken from Germany, Austria, and Russia, while Czechoslovakia was formed of Austrian and Hungarian territory. Yugoslavia was constituted out of the existing states of Serbia and Montenegro and cessions from Austria and Hungary; while Finland, Estonia, Latvia, and Lithuania were formed of territory taken from Russia. The Arabian state of Hedjaz was carved out of Turkey. Danzig was made a free city under the protection of the League of Nations. The German colonies were apportioned among the victors under a system of mandates superintended by the League of Nations. In addition, many constructive provisions were inserted in the several treaties looking to the protection of minorities, the facilitation of international transportation, and the protection of international social interests.[57]

Period from 1919-1939. With the establishment of the League of Nations, followed by the creation of the Permanent Court of International Justice which came into existence on December 16, 1920, the scope of international law expanded. Questions that had been political before the adoption of the Covenant now became juridical. The members of the League abandoned much of their former sovereign right to be the judges in their own case, in spite of certain loopholes that were left in the obligations of peaceful settlement imposed by the Covenant. The right to resort to war for the enforcement of claims was correspondingly reduced. Individual members of the League were no longer dependent solely upon their own armaments for defense. "Collective security," a new principle in international law, came to be regarded as the cornerstone of the Covenant. In spite of the refusal of the United States to become a member of the League and in spite of the disabilities imposed upon Germany, Russia, and other states, the membership of the League was large enough to encourage efforts on the part of its members to strengthen the provisions of the Covenant where there were weak spots in the security system.[58] The Locarno Agreements of 1925 supplemented the obligations of the Covenant by creating for the small circle of the signatory states more definite pledges of nonaggression and peaceful procedure in the settlement of conflicting claims.[59] Germany was admitted to membership in 1926 and at the same time given a seat upon the Council of the League. At the close of the first decade of the

[57] For a survey of the political effects of the several peace treaties, see Temperley, *History of the Peace Conference of Paris,* Vols. II, IV; Hazen, *Europe Since 1815,* rev. ed., Vol. II; Hayes, *A Political and Social History of Modern Europe,* Vol. II; Bowman, *The New World;* Haskins and Lord, *Some Problems of the Peace Conference;* Schuman, *International Politics;* Buell, *International Relations.*

[58] For the important Geneva Protocol, signed in 1924 but left unratified by the leading signatories, see Miller, *The Geneva Protocol;* Noel Baker, *The Geneva Protocol;* Sharp and Kirk, *Contemporary International Politics,* Vol. XXIII.

[59] For the texts of the agreements, see *League of Nations Treaty Series,* Vol. LIV.

League's existence it could be said that the new organization gave promise of being able to fulfil the objective set forth in the preamble of the Covenant, "to promote international cooperation and to achieve international peace and security." The United States, while still avoiding membership, took the lead in securing the adoption of the Pact of Paris of 1928, which supplemented the obligations of the Covenant by proclaiming the renunciation of war as an instrument of national policy and the agreement of the contracting parties that the settlement or solution of all disputes or conflicts of whatever nature or origin should never be sought except by pacific means.[60]

The breakdown in the new juridical structure began with the invasion of Manchuria by Japan in 1931. China was a member of the League and as such was entitled by Article 10 of the Covenant to be protected in its territorial integrity and its existing political independence by the other members of the League. But the leading members of the League were unwilling to resort to force or to other effective sanctions. The United States, acting in pursuance of the Nine Power Treaty of 1922, announced its refusal to recognize any situation brought about by means contrary to the provisions of the Pact of Paris, and the Assembly of the League took similar action upon its own account two months later; but the sanction was too weak to restrain Japan.[61] In 1933, when Bolivia and Paraguay drifted into open war, the League of Nations subordinated its procedure to the inter-American regional system, but the latter was not sufficiently well organized to control the situation until the parties mutually exhausted themselves.[62] In 1935 Italy followed the lead of Japan and attacked Ethiopia. This time the League voted economic sanctions; but these proving ineffective, the guarantees of Article 10 were allowed to lapse.[63] In the spring of 1938 Austria was invaded by Germany and annexed to the Reich, with only the pretense of a plebiscite.[64] In the fall of 1938 Great Britain and France, acting outside the provisions of the Covenant of the League, acquiesced in the cession of the Sudeten area of Czechoslovakia to Germany.[65] In the spring of 1939 Germany converted Bohemia and Moravia into a "protectorate" and set

[60] The legal scope of the Pact is examined on p. 278.

[61] See the report of the Lytton Commission of Inquiry, *League of Nations Publications,* Political, 1932, Vol. VII, p. 12. Also, Vinacke, *History of the Far East in Modern Times,* 2nd ed., 1936; *Peace and War: United States Foreign Policy, 1931-1941,* pp. 4-8, 155-161.

[62] See Hackworth, *Digest,* Vol. VI, pp. 41 ff. See below, p. 413.

[63] For details, see J. H. Spencer, "The Italian-Ethiopian Dispute and the League of Nations," *Am. Journal,* Vol. 31 (1937), p. 614; Mandelstam, *Le Conflict Italo-Ethiopien devant la Société des Nations.*

[64] See Schuschnigg, *My Austria;* Gedye, *Betrayal in Central Europe.*

[65] See Gedye, *op. cit.;* Armstrong, *When There Is No Peace;* Q. Wright, "The Munich Settlement and International Law," *Am. Journal,* Vol. 33 (1939), p. 12.

up Slovakia as a separate state.[66] There was now no question of action by the League of Nations as a body. The withdrawal of Japan, Italy, and Germany had been followed by that of other states which were convinced that the League could no longer serve its original purposes. The United States, while deprecating acts of aggression and urging methods of peaceful settlement, was not prepared to pledge its military forces on the side of law and order.[67] The time had come when Great Britain and France must now in their own national interest restrain the aggressor, or it would be too late to do so. On August 23 Russia entered into a pact of nonaggression with Germany in direct violation of its obligations under Article 10 of the Covenant.[68] Poland became the focal point of resistance, and war began on September 1.

I. THE SECOND WORLD WAR

The United States declared its neutrality on September 3, but within two months the neutrality act of 1937 was modified so as to permit the sale of arms and ammunition, indicating clearly that the United States wanted to give to Great Britain and to France such practical assistance as it might within the technical limits of neutrality.[69] The twenty-one American states made a joint declaration of their neutrality and established a "security zone" around the American continent.[70] But international law, and with it neutrality, soon lost all meaning. Russia established protectorates over Estonia, Latvia, and Lithuania; and on November 30 invaded Finland without other justification than national policy.[71] In April, 1940, Germany invaded Norway and a month later Holland and Belgium. On the eve of the defeat of France, Italy entered the war on June 10, 1940. The United States, realizing the danger to itself in the triumph of aggression, transferred fifty destroyers to Great Britain in exchange for naval bases.[72] In March, 1941, Congress passed the Lend-Lease Act, and the United States was definitely enlisted on the side of the Allied Powers, although still technically neutral.[73]

---

[66] The condemnation by the United States of the "acts of wanton lawlessness and of arbitrary force" may be found in *Peace and War*, No. 126; the denunciation of Prime Minister Chamberlain in *British War Blue Book*, misc. No. 9 (1939), pp. 12 ff. France and Russia also protested the illegality of the act.

[67] For the several statements of President Roosevelt on behalf of peace and his successive appeals to Germany and Italy, see *Events Leading Up To World War II*, pp. 175 ff.; *Peace and War*, Nos. 128, 137, 139.

[68] For the text of the Pact, see Dept. of State *Bulletin*, Vol. I, p. 172; Sharp and Kirk, *op. cit.*, p. 806; Snyder, *The War: A Concise History 1939-1945*.

[69] For the text of the Act see *Peace and War*, No. 145.

[70] *International Conferences of American States*, 1933-1940, pp. 326, 334.

[71] See *Events Leading Up to World War II*, pp. 218 ff., and references there given.

[72] See *Peace and War*, Nos. 179, 180.

[73] For the text of the Act, see *ibid.*, No. 200.

Proposals for a new security system. On August 14, 1941, the Atlantic Charter was proclaimed in which the President of the United States and the Prime Minister of Great Britain agreed upon a series of "common principles" upon which they hoped to see a future peace established "after the final destruction of the Nazi tyranny." These principles contemplated the establishment "of a wider and permanent system of general security." [74] After the entrance of the United States into the war the principles of the Atlantic Charter were incorporated into the Declaration by United Nations. [75] In October, 1943, the Foreign Ministers of the United States, Great Britain, and Russia met in Moscow and adopted a series of declarations the first of which proclaimed that they recognized the necessity of establishing at the earliest practicable date "a general international organization, based on the principle of the sovereign equality of all peace-loving states, and open to membership by all such states, large and small, for the maintenance of peace and security." [76] A year later a conference of the three powers, held at Dumbarton Oaks in Washington, made public a series of "proposals for the establishment of a general international organization," which were then submitted to the members of the United Nations for their observations. [77] Early in February, 1945, a conference of the "Big Three" met at Yalta in the Crimea, and among other decisions it agreed that a conference of the United Nations should meet at San Francisco on April 25, 1945, to prepare the charter of an organization along the lines proposed at Dumbarton Oaks. [78] The Conference at San Francisco met as planned, and, after making substantial modifications in the original proposals, adopted the "Charter of the United Nations" on June 26, 1945. [79] The Charter was thereupon submitted to the signatory states for formal ratification in accordance with their respective constitutional procedures. [80] Annexed to the Charter was the Statute of the International

[74] For the text of the Charter, see Appendix A.
[75] *Ibid.*, No. 274.
[76] Dept. of State *Bulletin*, Vol. IX, p. 309.
[77] *Ibid.*, Vol. XI, pp. 368 ff.
[78] *Ibid.*, Vol. XII, p. 214.
[79] *Ibid.*, Vol. XII, pp. 1119 ff.
[80] The United States was the first of the signatory states to ratify the Charter, by proclamation of the President on August 8, 1945. The Charter came into effect on October 24, 1945, upon the deposit of the ratifications of twenty-nine states, including the five states named in Article 110 of the Charter and a majority of the other signatory states. The opening sessions of the General Assembly and of the Security Council were held in London on January 10 and 17, 1946, respectively. Some three months later, on April 8, the Assembly of the League of Nations held its twenty-first and closing session; and on April 18, 1946, delegates from thirty-four states answered "Yes" to a roll call on a motion providing that "With effect from the day following the closing of the present session of the Assembly, the League of Nations will cease to exist except for the sole purpose of liquidation."

Court of Justice, based upon the statute of the existing Permanent Court of International Justice and forming an integral part of the Charter.[81]

Charter of the United Nations. With the establishment of the United Nations the period of historical background comes to an end; and subsequent developments in respect to the authority of international law as a rule of conduct and the substantive content of the law will be examined under appropriate headings in the separate chapters to follow. While national traditions and ideological policies are in even sharper conflict, they may best be examined in relation to the Charter of the United Nations and the principles accepted as obligatory by the international community at the time of the adoption of the Charter. International law is expanding from the law of a closed circle of states of European tradition to a universal system embracing all nations. New principles are being recognized, and established principles are being given new applications. The process is a dynamic one, and the succeeding chapters will mark its progress and examine the political, economic, and social forces guiding its development.

[81] In accordance with the terms of the Statute, the General Assembly and the Security Council held separate elections for the members of the court on February 6, 1946. The opening session of the new court was held at The Hague on April 18, 1946.

CHAPTER II

The Nature and Scope of International Law

A. DEFINITION OF INTERNATIONAL LAW

International law may be defined in broad terms as the body of general principles and specific rules which are binding upon the members of the international community in their mutual relations.[1]

Problems presented. What is the juridical nature of this system of law which purports to govern the relations of states? How closely does it correspond to the conception of "law" as it has developed within the boundaries of the individual state? Upon what basis of theory and of

---

[1] The older writers, holding strictly to rules of obligation between states as such, defined international law in terms of the sources from which they believed the law to be derived, stressing reason and justice and custom. Modern writers are tending to include the wider range of rules actually in force if not of legal obligation, operating on the basis of mutual cooperation rather than of rigid obligation.

Compare:

Wheaton: "International law, as understood among civilized nations, may be defined as consisting of those rules of conduct which reason deduces, as consonant to justice, from the nature of the society existing among independent nations; with such definitions and modifications as may be established by general consent." *Elements of International Law* (1836), p. 14.

Sir Henry Maine: "The Law of Nations is a complex system, composed of various ingredients. It consists of general principles of right and justice, equally suited to the conduct of individuals in a state of natural equity, and to the relations and conduct of nations, of a collection of usages, customs and opinions, the growth of civilization and commerce; and a code of positive law." *International Law* (1883), p. 33.

McDougal: ". . . international law [may] be regarded not as mere rules but the effective operation of international organizations and their subordinate agencies." *Studies in World Order,* p. 170.

Jenks: "International law can no longer be reasonably or adequately defined or described in the traditional manner as the law governing the mutual relations, and in particular delimiting the jurisdiction of states. The law governing the relations between states is one, but only one, major division of the contemporary law." *The Common Law of Mankind,* p. 1.

fact do its principles and rules rest? How are they interpreted and
applied when the conflicting claims of states are presented for determination? How are they enforced when violated by states defiant of their
obligations? What is it that gives to the community of states those elements of moral and material unity without which no principles and
rules could have the authority of law? What are the new dimensions of
the law that have been brought about by the recent admission of new
states into the international community, by the creation of new regional
groups, and by the establishment of new international agencies to
promote the economic, social, and cultural interests of the nations? [2]

International law in transition. It is not to be expected that definite
and conclusive answers can be given to these and other questions. For
it is clear that international law is in a state of transition. Many principles which held good at the beginning of the twentieth century, or
indeed which held good during the period between the First and
Second World Wars, are no longer valid. Generalizations which were
then possible must now be qualified; categorical statements must be
modified. After a second world war of unparalleled devastation international law began and is now undergoing a process of reconstruction
in which statesmen and scholars are seeking to determine what new
principles and what new forms of organization are required to bring
order out of conflicting policies and to make peace and justice prevail.
The inquiry leads not only to an examination of the nature of international law as at present understood, but still further to an examination of the law as it must develop, *de lege ferenda,* if it is to attain the
objectives now contemplated. If at times we speak of the "new law"
dating from 1945 in contrast with the "old law" before 1945, it is important to keep the contrast confined to certain limited areas of the law.
Much of the substantive body of the old law is equally valid in principle
under the new, although the application of a particular principle may
have changed to meet new circumstances.

B. BASIS OF INTERNATIONAL LAW

The basis of international law is the simple fact of the interdependence
of states. In their formal relations states are the persons governed by
international law, the subjects in whom adhere the rights and duties
that constitute the body of the law.[3] But states are not juridical abstrac-

---

[2] Jessup, *Transnational Law,* uses the term to include "all law which regulates
actions or events that transcend national frontiers," p. 2. De Visscher introduces a
critical element into his definition of law, calling for an examination of: "the degree
in which its content corresponds to social needs, and the accuracy of its formal expression compared with the practice of states." *Theory and Reality in Public International Law,* p. 133.

[3] For a discussion of the sense in which individuals may be said to be subjects of
international law, see pp. 147 ff.

tions; they are corporate groups made up of individual human beings with common moral and material interests transcending territorial boundaries. Hence the same forces that have driven individual men to unite in civil society, to organize separate national groups, have driven states to recognize the need of developing a law to govern their mutual relations. As mutual defense against aggression has been the dominant element in the law of the state, so it has become the dominant element in modern international law. But side by side with this primary condition of civilization, other forces, moral and material, have cut across state lines and have created a higher unity which even the rigid organization of the national state has been forced to acknowledge. International law is thus based ultimately upon the realization by states that in spite of their national divergencies they have certain common ideals and common moral and material interests which give to their collective group the character of a community.

A community of states. This conception of a "community," a "society," a "family of nations" is deeply rooted in the traditions of the Western World. We have seen the struggle which took place at different epochs between the idealistic conception of a community of states, a commonwealth of mankind, and the political forces of dynastic ambition and imperialistic state policy. The struggle continued, under varying forms, into the twentieth century. On the eve of the First World War the community of nations had still not taken on the character of a juridical institution.[4] Rather it was a loose union of sovereign states each of which appeared to be more conscious of its separate national interests than of its duties as a member of a corporate body. The medieval conception of a Christian community of nations had long since given way to the rising tide of nationalism with its emphasis upon sovereignty and the dominance of rights over duties. Neither the First nor the Second Hague Conference was able to get beyond the negative task of regulating the conditions of armed conflict, which carried with it the acceptance of the probability, if not the inevitability of war. The League of Nations was designed to give to the international community the organization it had hitherto lacked. But it failed to obtain the support of the United States, and it failed to develop within the circle of its own members the conception of a dominant community interest prevailing over separate national interests. The Charter of the United Nations was adopted with the same general objective, but the presence in the international community of states dominated by ideological con-

---

[4] Alfred Zimmern, writing in 1936, went so far as to say that the rules of international law, as they existed previous to 1914, were, with a few exceptions, "not the outcome of the experience of a world society. They were simply the result of the contacts between a number of self-regarding political units—stars whose courses, as they moved majestically through a neutral firmament, crossed one another from time to time." *The League of Nations and the Rule of Law*, p. 98.

ceptions completely at variance with the traditional principles of Western
Europe and America soon divided the community into two rival communities: the one seeking to maintain its inheritance of independent
states constituting interdependent members of an international community, and the other seeking to create a new monolithic community
controlled by a single exclusive party enforcing its will upon separate
states held together by an ideology of commanding authority.

The doctrine of sovereignty. What is the meaning of the principle
of the "sovereignty of states" which appears to contradict the conception of a community of states, suggesting that the state itself is above
the law? In its extreme form the doctrine implied a half century ago
the complete freedom of the state from the control of any higher power
claiming authority to regulate its acts. It was a doctrine of legal anarchy,
which fastened its hold upon governments and in the name of maintaining the independence of states denied their responsibility to the community as a whole and left sovereign weak states at the mercy of the
sovereign strong. Only historical tradition could account for the support
given to the doctrine by jurists long after it had lost its original justification and had become a ready argument to justify arbitrary conduct.[5]

Scope of the doctrine. The doctrine of sovereignty began as a principle of national unity. Kings were seeking to develop strong national
states and to bring under their centralized control the various elements
of local authority. It was part of the same political process that, in asserting their supremacy within the state, princes should assert that
they were independent of control by any higher authority outside the
state; for under the conditions of the times any higher authority would
have meant the authority of some other emperor or king. Thus sovereignty
came to be synonymous with independence; and the paradox was
presented of a community of sovereign rulers who were not only "above
the law" within their own countries but in some mystical way "above
the law" in their mutual relations.[6]

In time, when the individual sovereign lost his personal rights as a

[5] The literature of the subject is extensive. See Wright, *A Study of War,* Vol. II,
Chap. XXIV, "Sovereignty and War"; Russell, *Theories of International Relations,*
p. 540; and see below, Chap. XXVIII.

[6] Bodin, writing in 1576 in *Six livres de la République,* used the term sovereignty
(*majestas*) to express "a power supreme over citizens and subjects, itself above the
law, *summa in cives ac subditos legisbusque soluta potestas.*" Coker, *Readings in
Political Philosophy,* p. 374. Grotius used it in the same sense in *De jure belli ac
pacis,* Bk. I, Chap. III, § VI; but the term had then come to imply an independence
of external control as well as supremacy within the state. See *Ibid.,* § XXI. Thereafter the term came into general use as negativing the overlordship of one state by
another. See Vattel, *Droit des Gens,* Eng. trans., Bk. I, §§ 4-12. By the nineteenth
century the term was further extended to suggest the independent position of the
individual state with respect to the community of nations as a whole. See Schwarzenberger, *Power Politics,* pp. 84 ff.

ruler, the "sovereign people" took over his authority, and the "sovereign state" asserted its independent position in the international community. Sovereign states were obviously not above the law, such as it was, which they had inherited through the centuries; but they had the veto power against any extensions of the law which might encroach upon their reserved sphere of sovereign rights; and they explicitly resisted the authority of the international community as a whole either to establish institutions for the interpretation of the law in cases of controversy or for the enforcement of the law in cases of its violation.

C. THE BINDING FORCE OF INTERNATIONAL LAW

How was it that the body of principles and rules which constitute international law came to acquire the binding force of law in an international community of sovereign states? In the absence of any form of international legislature, competent to enact law after the manner of the legislatures of democratic states, international law was said to be based upon the "consent" of states, upon their individual acceptance of its principles and rules. A rule of conduct became law when it was accepted as having binding force between the parties. No difficulty was found in respect to formal treaties and conventions; for these obviously expressed the consent of the parties to the agreement. In contrast with this "direct" consent, there was offered the fiction of "implied consent" to account for the acceptance of the great body of general principles and specific rules that had come to form the body of customary law.

The theory of consent as the basis of law. To the great majority of writers this "consent theory" seemed to offer the simplest explanation of the binding force of international law.[7] States were sovereign; but a sovereign state could, in the very exercise of its sovereignty, agree to observe certain rules of conduct. These rules of conduct constituted international law, and that was enough.

A number of writers, however, pressed the inquiry further. If the rules of international law were based upon consent, what was it that gave to consent its binding character? What was there to prevent a sovereign state from withdrawing its consent when new circumstances arose to make it no longer desirable to abide by the particular rule? A few writers

[7] Obviously what was meant, and still is meant when consent is said to be the basis of the law, was consent given in advance of the application of the rule to a given controversy. Such was the meaning of the Permanent Court of International Justice when it generalized in the *Lotus* Case that "International Law governs relations between independent States. The rules of law binding upon States emanate from their own free will as expressed in conventions or by usages generally accepted as expressing principles of law and established in order to regulate the relations between coexisting independent communities or with a view to the achievement of common aims."

of the more extreme German tradition frankly accepted the consequences of withdrawal of consent, holding that the sovereign state should be the ultimate arbiter of its destiny and the ultimate source of its international obligations.[8] International law was a *subjective* law; its binding force depended upon mutuality of interest, which could only be maintained by altering from time to time such rules as it might be no longer to the interest of the parties to observe.

Pacta sunt servanda.   Other writers, unwilling to recognize international law as having a purely subjective character, sought to give a certain finality to consent by bringing into play the principle of the good faith of treaties, *pacta sunt servanda.* Consent once given created a rule of law, which thereupon ceased to be subject to repeal by the individual state. But this raised the further question as to the source of the principle of the obligatory character of agreements, especially in the case of the large body of customary international law to which states could only be said to have given their "implied" consent.[9]

As a matter of fact the theory that international law is based upon the consent of states, taken in the sense of their individual consent, is simply inadequate to explain the assumptions upon which governments appear to have acted from the beginning of international law. Whatever the position taken by writers, governments have always looked upon international law as having an objective character, as being binding because it was "the law," not because states found it to their convenience to observe it. If governments have not undertaken to formulate any logical justification of the law, it has been because none seemed to be needed. Law was the alternative to anarchy; that was justification enough for it.

Necessity of law.   Within recent years it has come to be realized that the search for a separate basis for international law, as distinct from that of municipal law, is not only illogical but socially harmful.[10] Law within the individual state is not a mere accident of historical development; it is an essential element of human association. Man, as Aristotle put it, is by his very nature a social being; and he is by his very nature in need of law. *Ubi societas, ibi jus.* In like manner, under the conditions of modern times, the state, notwithstanding its corporate character, has become itself "a social being" in relation to other members of the international community. The time was when philosophers might properly describe the state as the "perfect society," the society

[8] See p. 68, where the writings of the German jurists are discussed from the point of view of the science of international law.

[9] See p. 88.

[10] The subject is exhaustively discussed by Lauterpacht, *The Function of Law in the International Community,* pp. 399 ff.

within whose circle man might fulfil all of his needs.[11] That time is now past. The interdependence of states is a fact; a community of interests between states exists in as real a sense as a community of interests between individual men. The need of law between state and state is as great, although less obviously so, as the need of law between man and man. The prevention of war, the regulation of conflicting claims, the promotion of the general welfare of the group are conditions which create a moral and material unity among the nations in the same manner that they create a moral and material unity between individuals within the state. The fact that nations have these common interests constitutes an actual community of states, and at the same time imperatively demands a rule of law; so that international law may be said to be based upon the very necessity for its existence, upon the very human beings in constant contact with one another under the conditions of the present day.[12] Beyond that all discussion of its philosophical basis is academic.

D. INTERNATIONAL LEGISLATION

International law consists of general principles and concrete rules. Many of its principles and rules, being derived from the dictates of "right reason" and from the usages and customs of states, have never been in any sense "enacted." As late as the seventeenth century international law was largely drawn from the writings of theologians and jurists who sought to interpret the existing practice of nations in the light of general principles of justice which they believed to be binding

[11] Aristotle, having in mind the city-states of his time, gave the definition: "The state is the perfect natural society"; and St. Thomas and later theologians echoed the conception. Pasquazi repeats it in 1935, "Status sunt coetus perfecti, scilicet in suo ordine supremi et independentes," although his later discussion makes it clear that states are far from the "perfect groups" which his definition suggests. *Ius internationale publicum*, p. 43.

[12] Phillimore expressed it well in a treatise the opening chapters of which reflect the Christian interpretation of the natural law: "To move, and live, and have its being in the great community of nations, is as much the normal condition of a single nation, as to live in a social state is the normal condition of a single man. From the nature of states, as from the nature of individuals, certain rights and obligations towards each other necessarily spring; these are defined and governed by certain laws." *Commentaries upon International Law*, 3rd ed., Vol. I, p. 3.

More recently Brierly has observed: "The subjection of states to law needs no special philosophical explanation other than that by which we explain the subjection of individuals to the law of the state; the differences between that law and international law are important, as we have seen, but they do not lie in metaphysics nor in any mystical qualities of an entity called state sovereignty." *Law of Nations*, Vol. II, § 2.

On the general subject, see L. Le Fur, "La théorie du droit naturel," *Recueil des Cours*, Vol. 18 (1927-III), pp. 263 ff.; Spiropoulos, *Théorie Générale du Droit International*, §§ 5-8; Delos, *La Société Internationale et les Principes du Droit Public*, Chap. III.

between nations as between man and man. It has been common to describe this formulation of general principles and of specific rules as "customary law," and it bears some analogy to the common law of Great Britain and the United States as being the combined expression of common conceptions of justice and of practical rules for the adjustment of conflicting claims.

Law-making treaties.   Beginning with the great treaties of Osnabrück and Münster of 1648 new rules of international law came into being as the result of what have been called "law-making treaties." To speak of these treaties as "international legislation" is perhaps giving to the agreements of a small group of powers too universal a character. But while the various conferences and congresses during the two hundred years succeeding the Peace of Westphalia were not in any sense open meetings of the whole community of nations, they prescribed rules which, by reason of the influence of the parties, became in time the law for Europe and for the world. During the last quarter of the nineteenth century the great conventions which established the Red Cross organization, the Telegraph Union, the Universal Postal Union, and other institutions could be said to be the initial steps in a process of "international legislation," which took definite shape at the Hague Conferences of 1899 and 1907. But while these conventions bore an analogy to the statutes of municipal law, they were only binding upon the signatory powers, so that the process of law-making by general convention differed in that respect from laws enacted by national legislatures by majority vote and binding upon majority and minority alike.[13]

Development after 1919.   The establishment of the League of Nations gave a great impulse to the development of international legislation by means of law-making conventions. While the Assembly of the League was without competence to legislate in the strict sense, it frequently acted itself as an international conference by drawing up and opening for signature a number of international treaties and conventions, such as the Convention on Traffic in Women and Children of 1921, the Slavery Convention of 1926, and the General Act for the Pacific Settlement of Disputes in 1928. At the same time the Assembly of the League initiated the holding of international conferences at which a wide variety of international conventions were opened for signature. The measures taken for the promotion of the codification of international law must also be included as among the legislative activities of the League of Nations. The establishment of the Secretariat of the League of Nations had made it possible to coordinate the activities of many of the international agencies already in existence and to create additional agencies to meet the new needs of international cooperation.

[13] See p. 94, where multilateral treaties as a source of international law are examined in detail.

The result was that multipartite law-making conventions doubled and tripled in extent, until the new conventional law exceeded many times in bulk the older customary law.[14]

Limited scope of international law. While the legislative machinery of the international community during the period following the First World War was far from adequate, being dependent upon the uncertainty of ratification by the separate states, it was not defective machinery which prevented the adoption of an effective body of law. The necessity of unanimity in the adoption of international agreements, while a technical obstacle to the development of international law by offering possibilities of obstruction by the smaller powers, rarely defeated an object desired by the leading powers. The obstruction came from the fact that the leading powers themselves were unwilling to submit their rivalries to a rule of law. Each state insisted upon being free to determine its own line of conduct. Side by side with the actual economic interdependence of states created by the complex web of international commerce and finance there existed a condition of economic competition in which the struggle for control over the raw materials of industry, for the trade of foreign markets, for concessions in undeveloped countries, and for other special advantages defied regulation.[15] Within these fields international relations were practically lawless; and it was to be expected that states which found themselves at a disadvantage in the struggle should resort to whatever ways and means were available to defeat their competitors. International law contained not even the most elementary rule against unfair trade practices. Such efforts as were made from time to time to bring order out of economic anarchy were doomed to failure by reason of the inability of the parties to find their national interest in the common welfare of the whole community.

Subjects outside the law. It was these "gaps" in international law that constituted the fundamental weakness of its substantive rules and which caused the ultimate breakdown of its procedural system. It was of relatively little consequence that a vast body of lesser international interests had been brought within the law, and that the rules relating to them were on the whole faithfully observed; as much so, indeed, as were the municipal laws of the separate states. Looked at superficially, these rules constituted an impressive body of law in every practical

[14] See Hudson, *International Legislation*, Vols. I-VI (1920-1937), with the subtitle: "A Collection of Multipartite International Instruments of General Interest, beginning with the Covenant of the League of Nations." See Chap. XXV of the present work.

[15] See Brailsford, *War of Steel and Gold,* a pioneer study; Simonds and Emeny, *Economic Nationalism;* Richardson, *Economic Disarmament;* Beard, *The Open Door at Home;* Staley, *Raw Materials in Peace and War; World Economy in Transition;* Sharp and Kirk, *Contemporary International Politics,* Part III, "The Economics of World Politics."

sense. They regulated the status of aliens resident in foreign countries, they fixed the privileges of national vessels in foreign ports, they secured the free navigation of international rivers, straits, and oceanic canals, they secured the extradition of fugitive criminals, they regulated the use of the high seas, they prescribed the immunities of diplomatic agents, and they provided for the administration of international economic and social relations. But upon closer examination it was not difficult to see that the interests regulated by these rules were not the determining factors of national policy, they were not the "vital national interests" which states withheld from agreements to arbitrate, they were not the "matters of policy," the decision of which states reserved for themselves individually. The façade of the international system was imposing, but the foundations were weak. How far the "gaps" in the law that were left open between the First and the Second World Wars are now being filled by the impulse given to law-making treaties resulting from the numerous specialized agencies of the United Nations is a matter of current record.[16] Already many "matters of policy," such as the competitive struggle for the raw materials of industry, are being brought under partial control; and the independence of former Asian and African colonies has removed the struggle from the arena of the colonial powers to the open markets of the world. Doubtless the emerging breakdown of economic barriers would offer greater promise of closing the gaps if the new problem of conflicting ideologies were not such a pressing one.

8. INTERPRETATION OF INTERNATIONAL LAW
IN CASES OF CONFLICTING CLAIMS

If the substantive body of international law was deficient by comparison with the comprehensiveness of municipal law, the judicial machinery for the interpretation and application of the law in the case of conflicting claims was equally deficient, with far graver consequences. Down to the eve of the First World War little progress had been made in establishing the responsibility of the international community as a whole for the settlement of disputes by peaceful procedures.[17] When questions arose between two states as to the law applicable to a claim made by one of them against the other, negotiations took place between their foreign offices in much the same manner that a dispute between

[16] See Chap. XXV. Details of the activities of the specialized agencies or, as they are now described, the organizations "related" to the United Nations, may be found in the *Yearbooks of the United Nations,* and in summary form in *Everyman's United Nations,* editions 1959, 1964.

[17] The inability of the Hague Peace Conference of 1907 to get beyond pious *voeux* in respect to compulsory arbitration represents the dominance of the conception of "sovereignty" even while the assembled powers were proclaiming, in the Preamble of the Convention for the Pacific Settlement of International Disputes, "the solidarity uniting the members of the society of civilized nations." *Hague Conventions,* p. 41.

two individuals might be discussed by their respective attorneys. If an agreement was reached, whether by compromise or by concession, the issue was disposed of without more ado. In the event of the failure of direct negotiations, resort might be had to arbitration tribunals if the contending parties were in agreement to follow that procedure. Numerous treaties had been entered into for the peaceful settlement of international disputes, but one and all contained exceptions which made it possible for the parties to evade the obligation of peaceful settlement if they wished to do so.[18] Failing settlement of the dispute by such optional methods, each party might insist upon the correctness of its own interpretation of the law, and when further negotiations resulted in a deadlock the last resort might be a declaration of war on the part of the claimant state or the sullen acquiescence of the weaker party in the position taken by the stronger. When the final test came, each nation was the judge in its own case.[19]

Restraints upon arbitrary judgments. With the establishment of the League of Nations in 1920, the earlier rule of the individual interpretation of rights and duties began to give way to the principle that the community of nations had henceforth a responsibility of its own in the peaceful settlement of disputes, and that it could make its collective judgment prevail as against the arbitrary judgment of the individual state. The requirement that the vote of the Council must be unanimous if it was to have the effect of restraining a state from having recourse to war was, however, in point of law a serious limitation upon the obligation of the individual members of the League to submit their disputes to pacific settlement, although the effect of the limitation was modified by the fact that the League had still the right to regard a threat to the peace as a matter of concern to its members collectively and the right to take any action which might be deemed effectual to safeguard the peace.[20] While the signatories of the Protocol of the Permanent Court of International Justice gave the Court no authoritative jurisdiction over international controversies, a large number of states signed the Optional Clause conferring a limited jurisdiction upon the Court. The signatories of the Kellogg Pact agreed in general terms that they would never seek the settlement of their disputes by other than pacific means. Thus on the eve of the Second World War it could be said that the old rule of arbitrary individual judgment could no longer be asserted as an attribute of sovereignty. If there was yet lacking an

[18] See below, pp. 617 ff.

[19] Statesmen had little or no shame in admitting the fact. See *Final Act* of the Second International Peace Conference, below, p. 616.

[20] The lengthy discussions of the problem by scholars of the post First World War period represented an effort to build up a constitutional law for the League of Nations comparable to the effort now being made to build up a constitutional law for the United Nations.

international tribunal entrusted with the function of applying the principles of international law to all cases without exception, it was equally true that each nation was no longer in point of law the judge in its own case.[21]

F. THE ENFORCEMENT OF INTERNATIONAL LAW

More serious than the lack of adequate legislative and judicial machinery was the lack of adequate means for the proper enforcement of international law against individual members of the international community refusing to abide by their obligations. Down to the eve of the First World War the international community had not yet come to recognize in any degree its collective responsibility for the maintenance of peace.[22] Under municipal law no right, whether of person or of property, is so sacred as to warrant a resort to violence against the person of another, save only in cases of resistance to illegal violence. Self-help is so narrowly restricted as to be practically nonexistent. Under international law, until recent years, the right of self-help was claimed by states as one of the essential attributes of sovereignty. In matters arising out of the normal intercourse of states, where no grave issues were at stake, the public opinion of the nations as a body, based upon their realization of the necessity of a rule of law, proved an adequate sanction both to prevent arbitrary assertions of national claims and to secure the observance of rights generally recognized.[23] When, however, issues arose which involved interests believed by a nation to be vital to its welfare, not only did it assert the right to be the judge in its own case, but in the absence of an international executive agency it undertook on its own account the defense of the claims it was making. Forcible measures falling short of war might prove sufficient; but, failing these, war might be resorted to as the ultimate means of self-help; and, since it was regarded at international law as a legal remedy, the

[21] See Chap. XXVI, where methods of peaceful procedure are discussed in detail.

[22] Again the proclamation of "the solidarity uniting the members of the society of civilized nations," made at the Second Hague Conference, and the refusal of the assembled powers to accept any collective responsibility for the maintenance of peace, stand out in grim contrast.

[23] The emphasis put by statesmen upon public opinion as a sanction of international law reads strangely today. See, for example, Elihu Root, "The Sanction of International Law," *Am. Journal*, Vol. 2 (1908), p. 451: "The most certain way to promote obedience to the law of nations and to substitute the power of opinion for the power of armies and navies is, on the one hand, to foster that 'decent respect to the opinions of mankind' which found place in the great Declaration of 1776, and on the other hand, to spread among the people of every country a just appreciation of international rights and duties and a knowledge of the principles and rules of international law to which national conduct ought to conform; so that the general opinion, whose approval or condemnation supplies the sanction for the law, may be sound and just and worthy of respect."

results secured by it were recognized by the international community as a final settlement on the case.

War as a sanction of international law. War, entered upon at the decision of the claimant and waged by its own armed force, thus became the supreme sanction of international law, the *ultima ratio*, the last argument in the controversy. So clearly was the right to make war recognized that the possession of that right was made one of the principal tests whether or not a particular state could be said to be a "sovereign state." [24] Whatever moralists might say as to the paradox that disputes over points of law should be decided by the superior force of one or other of the claimants, governments had no doubts in the matter. Third states not original parties to the dispute reserved, it is true, the right to intervene in the quarrel if their own particular interests became involved; but if this were not the case they promptly declared their neutrality and thus washed their hands of any responsibility for the outcome of the conflict.[25] As neutrals they were called upon to treat both belligerents alike, irrespective of the fact that one of them might be an aggressor and the other the victim of an unjust attack. Such impartiality was a rigid duty of the neutral state, and only on condition of observing it could the neutral remain aloof from the conflict. At times, as during the First World War, the extravagant demands of one or other of the belligerents led the neutral state to take part in the war. But in such cases the neutral acted primarily in defense of its own national interests and not in defense of the principle of international law and order.[26] Upon the defeat of one or other of the contending parties a treaty of peace was drawn up, and the conditions laid down in it were recognized by all parties, belligerents and neutrals alike, as a final settlement of the case. Might literally made right.[27]

Aggression as a form of self-defense. Such a system, which left the defense of a nation's rights to its own unaided strength, had little relation to abstract justice. The very existence of a nation might be at stake, and it would have only its own resources to fall back upon. The inevita-

[24] The chief test of the distinction between a sovereign and a semisovereign state was whether the latter had "the right to declare war." Not having that right a state could not claim first rank. See p. 126.

[25] Such was the character of the Neutrality Proclamation of the United States in 1914. Doubtless President Wilson went to extremes in urging the American people to be "neutral even in thought." See below, pp. 718, 746.

[26] It was only after President Wilson called upon Congress to declare war in answer to the German submarine attacks upon American shipping that a more idealistic motive was brought forward. See Seymour, *American Neutrality, 1914-1917;* Fenwick, *American Neutrality: Trial and Failure,* pp. 14 ff.

[27] See in this connection, *conquest* as a title to territory, p. 424. In point of law a treaty of peace, representing the terms imposed by the victor upon the vanquished, was supposed to be as binding as any other treaty, notwithstanding the element of coercion attending it, which, under municipal law, would invalidate a contract.

ble result was that the defense of the state became the primary object
of foreign policy. Unwilling or unable to organize for their mutual
protection, the leading nations of Western Europe entered during the
nineteenth century upon a system of competitive armaments which
brought them as a group to a condition of ill-disguised anarchy. Alliances were formed to strengthen the position of weaker nations, and
these were in turn met by counteralliances of opposing groups. The
unstable equilibrium thus resulting reacted upon the normal claims of
states and led to more aggressive assertions of national rights. At times
states believed it necessary to protect themselves against possible future
attack by themselves attacking first. What seemed an aggressive act
might thus be self-defense by way of anticipation. The dominant conception of national law, that the protection of the rights of the individual
citizen is to be obtained by the cooperative action of the community in
establishing common agencies of justice, simply did not enter into the
code of international law.

G. THE AUSTINIAN THEORY OF LAW

The character of international law on the eve of the First World War
can perhaps best be understood in the light of the question which
scholars of that period debated at length: Considering the divergencies
of international law from the municipal law of individual states, could
the term "law" properly be applied to international law? On the one
hand there were those who, following the rigidly legalistic position
taken by the British jurist John Austin,[28] held that the term "law"
should be limited to rules of conduct enacted by a determinate legislative authority and enforced by physical sanctions. Law was "a command," it implied a political superior and political inferiors. International law, lacking this characteristic of "positive law," had been rele-
gated by Austin to the domain of ethics or "positive morality," differing
in importance, but not in nature, from the social conventions sanctioned
by public opinion. Jurists of the Austinian tradition felt that there was
nothing to gain in pretending that it was anything more.

The school of historical jurisprudence. On the other hand by far
the greater number of jurists and writers argued that the definition of
law adopted by Austin, while true to the form of enacted law characteristic of modern times, was not true to the earlier forms of customary
law. Citing the historical researches of the German jurist Savigny and
of Sir Henry Maine they pointed out that long before enacted laws

---

[28] In his *Province of Jurisprudence Determined*, published in 1832, Austin endeavored to place the law upon a more scientific basis by classifying the various
rules of conduct to which the term *law* was applied, with the object of distinguishing
laws which had a definite origin and a definite obligation attached to them, described as "laws proper," from others indefinite in origin and obligation, described
as "laws improper."

took their place upon the statute books communities were ruled by customs and usages which enjoyed the full force of law as rules of conduct. Primitive law, it was said, was custom, and custom is a law in itself: its own legislature and its own sanction. Instances were to be found, as among the German tribes described by Tacitus and among the East Indian village communities, where the only rule of conduct known was the will of the community evidenced in the tribal or village customs of immemorial origin. The true test of law was, they held, the fact of its recognition as a binding rule and of its observance as such; and by this test the rules of international law might justly be called law.[29]

The controversy turned, thus, upon the definition of "law" accepted by the particular writer. A narrow definition, following the more rigid conception of modern municipal law, would deny a legal character to the rules of international law; a broader definition, taking into account the historical development of municipal law, would include international law as law. In strict legalistic terms there was an obvious difference between law enacted, interpreted, and enforced by a determinate political authority, and law embodied in custom and treaty, interpreted by the parties to the case, and enforced by the sanction of public opinion or by individual appeal to the sword. On the other hand, it was felt that the adoption of a narrow and what was believed to be an arbitrary definition of law, so as to deny to the rules of international law a legal character, would have an unfortunate effect upon the respect in which the rules of international law might otherwise be held and would lead the nations to set aside their obligations with an even lighter hand. What the controversy failed to bring out was the fact that while international law operated effectively, whether as "positive law" or as "positive morality," within a limited field of international relations, it did not operate in respect to the vital issue of national security or in respect to the fundamental economic issues upon which the leading nations believed their prosperity to depend. It was the restricted scope of international law, or, more strictly speaking, the wide area assigned to the free decision of the individual state, that constituted at the time its essential weakness.

[29] The argument is elaborately set forth in Walker, *History of the Law of Nations*, Chap. I. See also Hall's acute analysis of the problem, *International Law*, Introductory Chapter. For comment upon the contributions of Savigny and Sir Henry Maine, see J. B. Scott, "The Legal Nature of International Law," *Am. Journal*, Vol. 1 (1907), p. 831.

Among those who maintained the position that international law was true law, some held that a physical sanction need not necessarily be vested in a central authority but might take the form of self-help, as in the case of early Anglo-Saxon law. Other writers held that a physical sanction was not an essential element, but rather a mere accident, of law; it was a means to secure observance, but not the only means. The approval or disapproval of certain acts by the community might be, under certain circumstances, an adequate sanction.

H. THE LEAGUE OF NATIONS AND THE RULE OF LAW

Thus things stood on the eve of the First World War. The war had not been long in progress, however, before statesmen and jurists in Great Britain, the United States, and other countries began to discuss ways and means by which future wars might be prevented through the collective action of law-abiding states.[30] At the close of the war the principle of collective security was incorporated into the Covenant of the League of Nations, Article 10 of which pledged the members of the League "to respect and preserve as against external aggression the territorial integrity and existing political independence of all Members of the League." This was a definite guarantee of mutual protection against acts of aggression, and the principle it laid down was of far-reaching importance, in spite of the inadequate means provided for its effective application. Article 11 provided that "any war or threat of war, whether immediately affecting any of the Members of the League or not, is hereby declared a matter of concern to the whole League." Wars and threats of war had always been a matter of concern to the nations individually; they were here declared to be a matter of concern to the nations in their organized capacity as members of the League. While self-help was not absolutely barred by subsequent articles of the Covenant, it was narrowly restricted, and provision was made by Article 16 that any member of the League which resorted to war in disregard of its obligations should "*ipso facto* be deemed to have committed an act of war against all other Members of the League," with the certain effect of the application of an economic boycott and the possible effect of armed intervention.[31]

Reasons for the failure of the League. The reasons for the failure of the League of Nations to attain its objective of international peace by means of the system of collective security were many and varied. Lack of universality of membership was doubtless the principal reason. But even with universality of membership the League would doubtless have failed had its leading members not understood more clearly that the maintenance of law and order in the community was a matter of vital national interest to each individual state, and that the promotion of justice and the removal of the causes of war must go side by side with the prevention of violence. These were essential conditions of the suc-

---

[30] See, in particular, the program of the League to Enforce Peace, established in 1916; Marburg, *Development of the League of Nations Idea*, as indexed. In Great Britain the League of Nations Union was the leading influence. See Lord Robert Cecil, *A Great Experiment*.

[31] On the League of Nations as a system of collective security, see Morley, *The Society of Nations;* Eagleton, *World Government;* Zimmern, *The League of Nations and the Rule of Law;* League of Nations Secretariat, *Ten Years of World Coöperation;* Howard-Ellis, *The Origin, Structure and Working of the League of Nations;* Walters, *History of the League of Nations.*

cess of the League; but they called for a combination of moral idealism and practical realism to which public opinion in the leading states had not yet attained. When the test came statesmen took too narrow a view of their national security and too limited a view of their economic prosperity. They drifted into war, not because the great majority wanted war, but because they lacked the farsightedness and the will to take the necessary measures to anticipate the aggressors who did want it.[32] The United States, standing outside the League, witnessed its slow disintegration without realizing that its own vital national interests were involved, and that a general breakdown of law and order would inevitably make itself felt even in the geographically isolated Western Hemisphere.[33]

I. ESSENTIAL PRINCIPLES OF LAW

Charter of the United Nations. It is clear that the development of international law into a stronger legal system, competent to maintain peace and to promote justice in the relations of states, lies on the one hand in the acceptance of certain fundamental principles not hitherto adequately recognized, and on the other hand in a more effective organization of the international community. To that end the Charter of the United Nations is directed, and it is to be expected that whatever practical advances may be made in the development of international law in the immediate future will be made within the circle of the United Nations. The principle of the collective responsibility of the United Nations for the protection of each of its members against acts of aggression is now accepted in more explicit form, and the United States, which had not accepted the principle as set forth in the Covenant of the League of Nations, is now a leading member of the organization. Neutrality, in the sense of an attitude of legal indifference to the rights or wrongs of a particular controversy and a refusal to take sides between an aggressor and the victim of aggression, is now no longer possible. The obligation to settle disputes by pacific means in one form or another is now absolute, allowing for no exceptions or qualifications. The members of the United Nations pledge themselves to cooperate in the solution of problems of an economic, social, and humanitarian character, and to promote respect for and observance of human rights and fundamental freedoms for all.[34]

[32] See, in particular, *Problems of Peace*, Tenth Series, *Anarchy or World Order*, where the views of a number of jurists are set forth; Q. Wright, *A Study of War*, Vol. II, p. 1060, "The League's Decline"; Madariaga, *Theory and Practice in International Relations*.

[33] For the relations of the United States towards the League, see Fleming, *The United States and the League of Nations, 1918-1920; The United States and World Organization, 1920-1933;* Berdahl, *The Policy of the United States with Respect to the League of Nations*.

[34] For details, see Chap. IX.

In respect to the machinery for the attainment of the ends of the United Nations, the Charter introduces on the one hand more comprehensive provisions for the pacific settlement of disputes and on the other hand more effective measures for the enforcement of the law against possible aggressors. The Security Council has the right to intervene between the parties to a controversy in order to bring them to agree upon terms of settlement, and at the same time it may upon its own initiative decide what measures must be taken to maintain the peace, including the use of the armed forces which the members of the United Nations have placed at its disposal. Both functions of the Security Council are, however, subject to the veto power of any one of the five permanent members; [35] and if the veto power should be exercised the whole machinery comes to a stop, leaving only the traditional right of self-defense with the danger of resort to open war. While all members of the United Nations are *ipso facto* parties of the Statute of the International Court of Justice, their acceptance of its jurisdiction even in legal disputes is still optional. In respect to the adoption of new rules of law the powers of the General Assembly are limited to recommendations only, and it will continue to be necessary to have recourse to multipartite conventions subject to the individual ratification of the separate states.

The Charter and the doctrine of sovereignty. It is obvious that the term "sovereignty" has now lost the meaning attributed to it at the beginning of the twentieth century. States may still be described as "sovereign states," but their sovereignty is sovereignty under the law to which they have bound themselves by the Charter; or better, perhaps, it is sovereignty in the fields of national or domestic jurisdiction that lie outside the newer areas controlled by international law.[36] The Charter does, indeed, proclaim as the first of its Principles that "the Organization is based on the principle of the sovereign equality of all its Members"; but this means no more than formal legal equality in the fields in which the Charter operates. The term may continue to be used, but it must be understood in a manner consistent with the maintenance of law and order in the international community.[37] States have now abandoned their former right to be the judges in their own case and the right to take the law into their own hands; they have now recog-

---

[35] For the question of the veto power of the five permanent members of the Security Council, see p. 214.

[36] It is of interest that the Latin American states put even more emphasis upon sovereignty than other members of the old League of Nations, doubtless as a means of offsetting the possible arbitrary conduct of a powerful member of their group.

[37] The situation is admirably presented in Lauterpacht, *The Development of International Law by the International Court,* Part V, § A, "Restraints upon Claims of Sovereignty."

nized the higher right of the international community, acting through its appropriate organs, to protect the peace of the community and to remove the causes of dissent that lead to acts of violence. An individual state may, indeed, defy the law; it may refuse to cooperate in putting the procedures of pacific settlement into effect; but it can not offer in justification of its conduct any legal claim of "sovereign right."

It is a political question whether the Charter of the United Nations has created a sufficiently close organization to make the attainment of its objectives possible. From many quarters it has been argued that the United Nations may find it necessary to approximate more nearly to a federal union in order to meet the necessities of the time.[38] That is a question outside the range of present law. For the immediate future the members of the United Nations retain a certain reserved sphere of rights upon which the organization may not encroach. The jurist can only note that the older conception of sovereignty has now been abandoned, but that at the same time any further extensions of the authority of the United Nations are subject to the traditional rule of the approval of each separate state. For the moment the problem is not whether the United Nations can attain its objectives better by developing a closer form of union, but rather whether the rival communities into which the organization is now divided can find a basis of common interests which will enable them to adjust their conflicting views of the nature of international law and of the principles by which peace and economic and social justice may be most efficiently secured.

J. INTERNATIONAL LAW NOT STATIC BUT DYNAMIC

Underlying the Purposes and Principles of the Charter is the conception of the necessity of adapting the rules of international law to the changing conditions of international life. No legal system can be effective which limits its activities to the mere prevention of violence. It must seek to establish order in the community; it must set up a standard of justice which represents what the community believes to be the most equitable basis of economic and social life in the community. In accordance with this standard of justice the rights of individual members of the community must be judged not solely on the ground of possession, but on the ground of compatibility with the higher interests of the com-

---

[38] See, for example, Reves, *The Anatomy of Peace; contra*, P. M. Brown, "World Law," *Am. Journal*, Vol. 40 (1946), p. 159; *pro*, United World Federalists. The present tendency is rather in the direction of amending the Charter so as to make it a more effective instrument within its accepted legal character. See Goodrich and Simmons, *The United Nations and the Maintenance of Peace and Security.*

munity as a whole.[39] International law, like national law, must be a dynamic system if it is to fulfil its high purpose.[40] The international community must from time to time reaffirm its principles, clarifying them in the light of the objectives to be attained; it must from time to time define its objectives anew, taking into account the needs of its member states and the practical ways and means available for meeting them. Just as in determining the relation of the state to the international community a balance must be sought between national sovereignty and the authority of international law, so in the development of the law itself a balance must be sought between stability and justice. International law must be fixed enough to assure the continuity of rights and duties; it must be elastic enough to meet the changing conditions of international life and intercourse.[41]

International law and international ethics. Jurists of the nineteenth century and of the opening years of this century sought to draw a distinction between international law and the moral standards which constitute the science of ethics. The effort was not in all cases made in the interest of releasing the state from the obligations of the moral law. Many authors sought merely to segregate the two fields of obligation, and to speak of international *law* as including rules which were actually recognized and obeyed in the relations of states in much the same way that the law of the state is recognized and obeyed by the citizen body,

[39] This is a high standard and there are many who believe that it cannot be attained in a union of "sovereign states." One of the most effective, if exaggerated, criticisms of the security system established by the League of Nations was the assertion that it guaranteed the continued existence of the *status quo* in favor of certain privileged states. The leading members of the League, having appropriated the richest parts of the earth, were solely concerned, it was asserted, in securing a collective guarantee of their existing possessions. The "have-not" states could, therefore, the argument ran, accept the guarantees of Article 10 of the Covenant only by abandoning all hope of improving their economic position except in so far as the good will of the "haves" might consent to make concessions out of their more abundant resources.

[40] The literature of the problem is extensive. See, in particular, Dunn, *Peaceful Change*, which approaches the subject within the traditional procedures; Dulles, *War, Peace and Change*; Williams, *International Change and International Peace*; J. L. Kunz, "The Law of Nations, Static and Dynamic," *Am. Journal*, Vol. 27 (1933), p. 630; "The Problem of Revision in International Law," *ibid.*, Vol. 33 (1939), p. 33; Manning, ed., *Peaceful Change: An International Problem*; Strupp, *Legal Machinery for Peaceful Change*; Cruttwell, *A History of Peaceful Change in the Modern World*; MacLean, *A Dynamic World Order*.

[41] The analogies of municipal law are applicable here. See Cardozo, *The Growth of the Law*, quoting Pound, *Interpretations of Legal History:* " 'Law must be stable, and yet it cannot stand still.' Here is the great antinomy confronting us at every turn. Rest and motion, unrelieved and unchecked, are equally destructive. The law, like human kind, if life is to continue, must find some path of compromise. Two distinct tendencies, pulling in different directions, must be harnessed together and made to work in unison." P. 2. Compare also P. C. Jessup, "Diversity and Uniformity in the Law of Nations," *Am. Journal*, Vol. 58 (1964), p. 341.

and to speak of international *ethics*, or international morality, as including those principles of justice to which the rules of international law should conform whether they actually did so or not. This was done, it was said, in the interest of putting international law upon a more "scientific" basis and freeing it from the uncertainties which had attended it in the past. The attempted distinction between law and morality failed, however, in consequence of the inherent defects in the existing system of international law. Nations, like individuals, will always appeal to a "higher law" when a particular rule appears to them to work injustice; [42] and while the appeal may at times be arbitrary and purely argumentative, it may at other times, and certainly has in fact on a number of occasions, represented the need for a change in the law. But apart from this, there was the stern fact that international law of that time accepted the right of a state to use force to support its claims and recognized the legal character of the settlement imposed by the strong upon the weak. That the weak should appeal to fundamental principles of justice was to be expected, and these were identical with morality in its broadest sense.

A commonwealth of nations. The most urgent need of the immediate future is the creation of a stronger sense of unity within the universal community of states. How can the two present contending communities, the one making its appeal to the development of the individual man, the personality of the human being as such, the primary right of liberty and free will within and under restraints established by the community; and the other calling for the subordination of the individual to the state in the interest of the collectivity as determined by self-appointed leaders—how can the two contending communities find a basis of cooperation? How can the religious traditions of the Western World be brought to bear upon international conduct so as to moderate the materialistic conception of society which seeks its objectives without concern for the moral values that alone can make democracy an effective form of cooperation among free human beings? [43] Moralists have stressed that the same principles of moral conduct apply to states in their corporate character that apply to the individual men who compose the group, that there is but one standard of moral conduct be-

---

[42] An interesting historical illustration is to be found in Mr. Adams' appeal to "moral obligation" in correspondence with the British Foreign Minister during the American Civil War. *Fontes juris gentium,* Series B, § I, Tome I, p. 118.

[43] An adequate selection of references is difficult to make. See, in particular, Dawson, *The Judgment of the Nations;* Gonella, *A World to Reconstruct;* Maritain, *Les Droits de l'Homme et la Loi Naturelle;* Curtis, *Civitas Dei;* Bentwich, *The Religious Foundations of Internationalism;* Max Huber, "Some Observations upon the Christian Understanding of International Law," in *The Universal Church and the World of Nations.*

tween nation and nation and between man and man.[44] However inadequately put into practice, the conception now finds itself challenged by an ideology that is impatient with a system which, it is alleged, results in privileged and underprivileged classes, justifying revolution as the only means of breaking the control of the system and bringing about the changes desired. The so-called "peaceful coexistence" of the two contending groups has continued year after year on the basis of a balance of power. Whether the fear of mutual extinction by the newly discovered instruments of warfare may prove to have a constructive character, compelling the search for new methods of cooperation, is a question of commanding importance. International law will cease to have any meaning if the energies and resources of the two states are primarily directed to anticipating annihilation by the other.

Three conditions appear essential to the survival of the international community and to the maintenance of international law as the rule of conduct between states. The United Nations, using the processes of cooperation made available to them by the Charter, must seek to create so large a body of common international interests as to make the conflicts of policy between the contending groups diminish to the point where a true collective security system may be effective. At the same time each separate state must not only refrain from the use of force against other states, but must respect their national personality and their desire to follow their own national traditions and develop their national character, subject to no other control than the general rules of international law to which all are subject. Above all, the channels of communication must be kept open between states, so that the people of each country may be able to know the true attitude of other peoples and may be able to discover the character and scope of their common interests.[45] These conditions met, international law may be allowed to develop progressively, without forcing upon it a federal character before sufficient mutual confidence has developed to make such a plan workable.

[44] See J. B. Scott, "A Single Standard of Morality for the Individual and the State," *Proceedings,* Am. Soc. Int. Law, 1932, p. 10; Schwarzenberger, *Power Politics,* Chap. XIV; Fuller, *The Morality of Law.* Phillimore quotes Sir James Mackintosh, *Discourse on the Law of Nature and Nations,* as follows: "The duties of men, of subjects, of princes, of lawgivers, of magistrates, and of *States,* are all parts of one consistent system of universal morality. Between the most abstract and elementary maxim of moral philosophy, and the most complicated controversies of civil or public law, there subsists a connection. The principle of justice, deeply rooted in the nature and interest of man, pervades the whole system, and is discoverable in every part of it, even to its minutest ramification in a legal formality, or in the construction of an article in a treaty." *Commentaries on International Law,* 3rd ed., Vol. I, p. 28.

[45] See on this point C. G. Fenwick, "The Problem of Moral Disarmament," *Am. Journal,* Vol. 41 (1947), p. 112.

CHAPTER **III**

The Science of International Law

A. MEANING OF THE TITLE "SCIENCE OF INTERNATIONAL LAW"

The term "science" as applied to international law may be taken in the sense of a systematic classification of the principles and rules of international law, accompanied by an analysis of their origin and nature and their place in the general field of juridical relations. The term "international jurisprudence" might perhaps equally well describe the scientific study of international law and the attempt to relate the principles and rules governing the relations of states to those of public and private law within the individual state. From what sources, theoretical and practical, has international law been drawn? How far has it been influenced by prevailing religious and philosophical conceptions both of the nature of man and of the nature of the state? What is the ultimate basis of legal obligations between state and state? Are the rights and duties which international law recognizes in the relations between states fundamentally analogous to those of municipal law, or are there such essential differences between the two systems as to give to international law a specific character of its own? To some extent these problems have of necessity been anticipated in the survey of the nature and scope of international law. They may now be examined more carefully in the light of the teachings of the leading jurists whose works have had a commanding influence upon the development of the law.[1]

[1] The literature of the science of international law has become more and more extensive during the past three decades when jurists have come to realize the urgent necessity of developing an international law adequate to keep the peace. For an analysis of the problems presented, see Lauterpacht, *The Function of Law in the International Community*, Chaps. I, XX.

B. THE INFLUENCE OF THE CONCEPTION OF THE NATURAL LAW

The importance of the role played by the "natural law" in the early development of international law can scarcely be exaggerated. From the days of Ancient Greece down to the sixteenth and seventeenth centuries the conception of a higher law than the will of the individual state, a law binding upon men because they were men, a law drawing its authority not from specific agreements between states but from the very nature of the human beings who composed the individual state exercised a far-reaching influence upon the great jurists who from time to time undertook to formulate the law of nations.[2] In spite of its vague character, in spite of the difficulty jurists might have in reducing abstract principles to concrete rules of conduct, and in spite of disputes between them as to the actual content of the natural law, the general recognition that there was such a law, whatever its precise content, gave a common purpose to juristic thought and laid the foundations of the more modern science of international law. Due to the misconceptions of Vattel and other writers of the eighteenth and early nineteenth centuries, the conception of the natural law ceased to play a constructive role in the development of international law, and became a justification of extreme and illogical views of sovereignty. In consequence the conception came to be discarded in the nineteenth century as mere legal fiction, unnecessary and unscientific.[3] In the middle of the twentieth century the older natural law reappears as the general principles of morality, of equity, of justice, and of reason.[4]

The natural law of the Ancient Greeks. It is to the Greek city-states and to their great philosophers that we must look for the earliest affirmation of this "higher law" and for the most emphatic recognition of its authority. The "laws of the Hellenes," as they were called, consisted partly of customs based upon natural or universal law and partly of express conventions between the separate city-states. The former were derived from "a natural and universal principle of right and wrong, independent of any mutual intercourse or compact," which Aristotle observed to be recognized by all men.[5] A mystical quality was given to this

[2] For a general survey, see Lauterpacht, *An International Bill of the Rights of Man,* Pt. I, "The Law of Nature, the Law of Nations, and the Rights of Man"; Gierke, *Natural Law and the Theory of Society, 1500-1800* (trans. by Barker); Robson, *Civilization and the Growth of Law;* Haines, *The Revival of Natural Law Concepts;* L. Le Fur, "La Théorie du droit naturel depuis le XVIIe Siècle et la doctrine moderne," *Recueil des Cours,* Vol. 18 (1927-III), p. 263; Kent, *Commentaries,* Vol. I, Pt. I, Lecture I.

[3] See pp. 63 ff.

[4] See pp. 78 ff.

[5] See Phillipson, *International Law and Custom of Ancient Greece and Rome,* Vol. I, p. 53. Roscoe Pound brings out the fact that to the Greeks the "natural" object was that which most completely expressed the idea of the thing, the perfect object.

law of man's nature by the Stoics, who conceived it to be immanent, immutable, and eternal, giving rise to an absolute right to which man-made law must of necessity conform.[6] Being the embodiment of reason in relation to the very nature of man it must obviously apply to men collectively as to men individually. International law was thus not so much a law *between* states as a law *above* states.

The *jus gentium* of Roman tribunals. More practical and doubtless more significant was the contribution of the Roman jurists to the development of international law. The tribunals of the republic, as well as those of the empire later, exercised jurisdiction over tribes and peoples of the widest variety. The civil law of Rome applied to citizens only. Foreigners who came to Rome in large numbers were subject to the jurisdiction of the *praetor peregrinus,* and disputes between them, as well as disputes between foreigners and Romans, were settled by the application of the common elements of justice to be found in the customs and usages of the various tribes.[7] A law common to all nations, a *jus gentium,* was thus developed. It was in its origin a law to be applied to the citizens of different states and therefore a system of international private rather than public law. In time the principles of the *jus gentium* came to be associated and even identified with the *jus naturale,* which like the universal law of the Greeks, was a law based upon the rational nature of man. While Cicero and Seneca, as statesmen, found in the universalism of the Stoics a moral justification for the empire Rome had created, the jurists found in the conception of a fundamental natural justice a principle by which they might coordinate the variety of customs and laws with which they were confronted and bring them into some degree of unity. It was argued that principles of justice found to be acknowledged by all states must presumably have their foundation in nature itself. On the other hand the more abstract *jus naturale* came to serve as an ideal to which reference might be made when the more practical rules of the *jus gentium* appeared to be inadequate.[8]

The association of *jus gentium* with *jus naturale* led in turn to the enlargement of the *jus gentium* by the addition of rules governing the relationships between states themselves. Disputes between states within the empire were referred to Rome, and in so far as they involved ques-

---

"Hence the natural law was that which expressed perfectly the idea of law and a rule of natural law was one which expressed perfectly the idea of law applied to the subject in question; the one which gave to that subject its perfect development." *Introduction to the Philosophy of Law,* pp. 31 ff.

[6] The contribution of the Stoics to the development of the idea of a universal society of mankind was far-reaching. See, in particular, Scott, *Law, the State, and the Int. Community,* Vol. I, pp. 92 ff.; Russell, *Theories of International Relations,* pp. 81 ff.

[7] Maine, *Ancient Law,* Pollock's ed., p. 52.

[8] See Phillipson, *op. cit.,* pp. 92, 93; Jolowicz, *Historical Introduction to Roman Law,* pp. 100 ff.; Scott, *op. cit.,* Vol. I, Chap. VII.

tions of personal or property rights analogous to the rights of individuals, it was but natural to apply to their solution the rules of the *jus gentium*. The law of *alluvium*, the right to occupy land that was *res nullius*, absolute title to property, contract rights, and other parts of the private law were thus adjusted to form a code of international or rather of supranational law. By Justinian's time it had come to be the practice to state first the provisions of the natural law and then to define and limit them by the provisions of the *jus gentium*.[9] The *jus gentium*, what lawyers today might call the "positive law," took priority, but its interpretation was softened by reference to the ideal rule.

C. THE INFLUENCE OF CHRISTIAN TEACHINGS

Under the influence of Christian teaching the theory of the natural law as applied by the Roman jurists to the relations of their subject peoples underwent a fundamental transformation. Obviously for the Christian, the law of God took priority over human law. For that principle Christians must be prepared to die when the conflict between divine and human law was clear and unmistakable. But with the spread of Christianity the Church Fathers were presented with many embarrassing problems in their effort to reduce the high principles of Christianity to a working rule of conduct. Man, said St. Augustine, being subject to sin, must submit himself to the temporal state and fulfil the duties which it imposed upon him; but at the same time the Christian was a citizen of a spiritual community, and as such bound by the obligations of the divine law.[10] How were these two jurisdictions, the temporal and the spiritual, to be reconciled? It was a political as well as a religious problem, a problem of civil law and a problem of moral conscience. The attempt to solve it preoccupied theologian and jurist during the succeeding centuries, and with but slight variation of the terms it continues to challenge the theologian and jurist of the present day.[11]

Restraints upon war. The vital problem of the years following the fall of the Roman Empire was to put a restraint upon war. With the establishment of feudalism, states were no longer organized peoples but rather the territorial domains of ruling dynasties. International law was a law between princes, or rather a law *above* princes, in so far as they could be brought to observe the rules laid down for them by the doctors

[9] By Justinian's time law had become "a universal system in which the distinction between *ius civile* and *ius gentium* has become of purely historical and theoretical interest." For there was no room for the distinction in a society where, in effect, every free man was a citizen. Jolowicz, *op. cit.*, p. 518.

[10] See Scott, *op. cit.*, Vol. I, Chap. XI, "St. Augustine"; Figgis, *The Political Aspect of St. Augustine's "City of God."*

[11] See Benkert, *The Thomistic Conception of an International Society;* de la Brière, *Conception du droit international chez les théologiens Catholique;* Eppstein, *The Catholic Tradition of the Law of Nations;* Bentwich, *The Religious Foundations of Internationalism.*

of the Church. Was it lawful for a Christian prince to make war? Having gone to war, what measures of force were permitted against the enemy, and what were the terms that might be imposed upon him when defeated? The first of the two questions was the more important one. It involved juridical issues relating to the title of the prince and to the substantive rights of his people, as well as moral and practical issues relating to the procedures of peaceful settlement available and the possibility of obtaining the compliance of the opposing party with them. Princes had not yet learned to claim the later rights of "sovereignty."

The doctrine of a just war. As far back as the early fifth century St. Augustine laid the foundations of the doctrine of a just war.[12] Succeeding theologians and canonists sought to define it more exactly and apply it to the circumstances of their time. In the thirteenth century the greatest of the theologians, St. Thomas Aquinas, gave more logical form to the doctrine; and there was little to add to his analysis when, three hundred years later, Vitoria and the Spanish theologians sought to interpret it in terms of the problems of the newly discovered Western Hemisphere. War, said St. Augustine, was permissible to the Christian when resorted to in a just cause, in defense of the state against external enemies and in punishment of wrongdoing. Moreover, war must be declared by the competent authority; and when so declared the responsibility for the justice of the war rested with the ruler, not with the individual soldier; soldiers were in such cases not murderers but ministers of the law.[13] St. Thomas, elaborating upon these principles, pointed out that war must not only be waged in a just cause but the intention of the ruler must be a right intention. Even if the other conditions of a just war were present, it would not do for the ruler to wage war from wrong motives.[14]

Influence of Justinian's Code. In the meantime, while moral standards were being proclaimed for the guidance of the individual ruler, other forces were at work to broaden the juristic bases of the relations between feudal princes. The codification of Roman Law under Justinian in the sixth century had enhanced its prestige and extended its influence. Just as the earlier Roman jurists had applied the principles of the *jus gentium* to the relations of states within the Roman Empire, so in later centuries it was natural that conflicts of right within the more loosely organized Holy Roman Empire should be referred to the Justinian Code. The

[12] The literature of the theory of a just war is extensive. See, in particular, Vanderpol, *La doctrine scholastique du droit de guerre;* Regout, *La doctrine de la guerre juste de Saint Augustin à nos jours;* Eppstein, *op. cit.,* Pt. II, "The Ethics of War"; J. von Elbe, "The Evolution of the Concept of the Just War," *Am. Journal,* Vol. 33 (1939), p. 685; de la Brière, *Le droit de juste guerre: Tradition théologique, Adaptations contemporaines* (1938).

[13] *Contra Faustum;* Eppstein, *op. cit.,* p. 68.

[14] *Summa: Secunda Secundae,* Quaestio XL (de Bello); Eppstein, *op. cit.,* p. 83; Regout, *op. cit.,* pp. 79 ff.; Vanderpol, *op. cit.,* §§ 211 ff.

Corpus Juris Civilis was found to contain many principles of law for the solution of the claims of one prince against another.[15]

Influence of the Canon Law. Of less direct effect upon the development of international law, but not without important indirect influence, was the growth of the separate and distinct system of the Canon Law. The treatise published by Gratian at Bologna in 1148 (1144?), known as the *Decretum,* and supplemented by the Decretals of Gregory IX and similar decretals of later popes, came to be known under the general term of *Corpus Juris Canonici.* Although the Canon Law dealt primarily with problems relating to the organization of the Church and although it was administered in separate ecclesiastical courts, it discussed many political questions from the point of view of general morality and Christian tradition, and it kept before men's minds the ideal of a general rule of conduct transcending the local laws of the separate communities.[16]

Predecessors of Grotius. During the anarchy of the centuries following upon the disintegration of the Holy Roman Empire and the weakening of the moral authority of the papacy, the tradition of a common law of the nations had never been wholly forgotten. The Renaissance widened men's intellectual horizon, and the discovery of the New World stimulated the imagination of philosophers as well as of explorers. Vitoria, a Spanish theologian, in lectures published in 1557 after his death, sought to apply the principles of international morality to the problem of the native races of the Western Hemisphere. In another and earlier treatise he formulated, in clearer terms than had yet been done, the principle that the nations of the world constituted a community, based both upon natural reason and upon social intercourse.[17] The Spanish Jesuit, Suarez, in a classic passage of his treatise *De legibus ac Deo legislatore,* published in 1612, insisted clearly that the states of the world, although independent in their national life, were nevertheless members of the human race and as such subject to a law of conduct: a law based, he said, chiefly upon natural reason, but also in part upon

---

[15] See Scott, *op. cit.,* Vol. I, Chap. XVII, "The Survival and Influence of Roman Law and Jurisprudence"; Vinogradoff, *Roman Law in Medieval Europe;* R. F. Wright, *Medieval Internationalism.* Compare the innumerable citations of the Corpus Juris, chiefly of the Digest, in Grotius, *De Jure belli ac pacis, passim.*

[16] Scott, *op. cit.,* Vol. I, Chap. XII, "Now Gratian's object was nothing less than the preparation of 'a law book for the Church that should be parallel with the Corpus Juris Civilis,'" quoting Figgis, *op. cit.*

[17] *De indis et de jure belli relectiones,* text of 1696, and translation by J. P. Bate, Carnegie Institution of Washington, 1917, where the spelling Victoria is preferred. For an appraisal of Vitoria's contribution to the development of international law, see Scott, *The Spanish Origin of International Law,* Pt. I: "Francisco de Vitoria and his Law of Nations"; *The Catholic Conception of International Law,* Chap. I; H. Wright, *Catholic Founders of Modern International Law;* C. B. Trelles, "Francisco de Vitoria et l'école moderne du droit international," *Recueil des Cours,* Vol. 17 (1927-II), pp. 113-342.

human custom.[18] The Italian jurist Gentili, professor of civil law at Oxford, published in 1598 a treatise, *De jure belli libri tres*, in which, without discarding natural reason and natural law, he sought to find historical and legal precedents to regulate the conduct of nations.[19] The honor was reserved, however, to Hugo van Groot, better known as Grotius, to publish in 1625 a more formal treatise, *De jure belli ac pacis*, which was the first to obtain a hearing outside the schools and which won for its author the title of the Father of International Law.[20]

D. THE GROTIAN SYSTEM

Grotius followed the classical tradition in making the natural law the basis of his system. The "natural law," as he defined it, was "the dictate of right reason which points out that a given act, because of its opposition to or conformity with man's rational nature, is either morally wrong or morally necessary, and accordingly forbidden or commanded by God, the author of nature." [21] Since nations formed a society similar in its nature to the community of citizens, they too were bound by the dictates of the natural law. What these dictates were might be discovered in either of two ways: by arguing *a priori* that a given act was or was not in accordance with the fundamental moral principles without which human society could not exist; and on the other hand by arguing *a posteriori* that principles of conduct accepted by all or by the more civilized peoples, affirmed as certain by many men at different times and in different places, must have their origin in the natural law. In addition to the natural law Grotius recognized a "voluntary" law of nations based upon their free consent, whether explicit, as expressed in treaties and conventions, or implicit, as expressed in usages and customs. To this law he gave, somewhat incorrectly, the name *jus gentium*.[22] In so far

[18] The passage is quoted, in Latin, by Walker, *History of the Law of Nations*, pp. 155-156; and in English by Eppstein, *The Catholic Tradition of the Law of Nations*, p. 265. For a study of the influence of Suarez upon the development of international law, see the two volumes by Scott referred to in note 17; Regout, *op. cit.*, pp. 206, 210; C. B. Trelles, *Recueil des Cours*, Vol. 43 (1933-I), p. 389.

[19] *Classics of International Law* series, 1933. Other predecessors of Grotius include Legnano, *De bello, de represaliis et de duello*, circa 1390; Belli, *De re militari et bello tractatus*, 1563; Ayala, *De jure et officiis bellicis et disciplina militari*, 1582. For a recent critical study, see L. Erlich, "The Development of International Law as a Science," *Recueil des Cours* (1962-I), p. 177.

[20] The edition of 1646, photographically reproduced, was published by the Carnegie Institution of Washington in 1913. A standard translation, though abridged, is that of Whewell (Cambridge, 1853). A new translation by Kelsey, *et al.*, *The Law of War and Peace*, appeared in the *Classics of International Law* series in 1925.

[21] Bk. I, Chap. I, § X. For an analysis of the work, see Walker, *History of the Law of Nations*, Vol. I, pp. 285 ff.

[22] *Ibid.*, § XIV. Vitoria appears to have used the term in the same sense a century earlier. The new usage was destined to become the accepted one, and in due time "law of nations" and "international law" came to be interchangeable.

as it conformed to the dictates of right reason, the voluntary law might be said to blend with the natural law and be indeed the expression of it. Should there be a conflict between the two, the law of nature was to prevail as being the fundamental law, the authority of which could not be contravened by the practice of nations.[23]

Evidences of the natural law. Upon these foundations Grotius proceeded to take up, one by one, the questions that had been the preoccupation of theologians and jurists from the time of St. Augustine. Can war ever be just, and if so, who has the power to make war? What are the grounds of a just war? What is permissible in the conduct of war? To the solution of these questions Grotius brought a wealth of learning which is astounding to the modern reader. To Grotius himself the principles of the natural law, if one paid strict heed to them, were "clear and evident of themselves, almost as much so as things perceived by the physical senses." [24] But the existence of this law had to be proved to others; and in order to do so Grotius had recourse to the testimony of the philosophers, historians, poets, and statesmen of all ages. This was what gave authority to his exposition and converted his treatise from an academic discussion of abstract principles to a concrete statement of what was right and what was wrong in the conduct of states. The modern critic may readily find obscurities in the inferences which Grotius drew from the natural law, may easily contest the logic of some of the analogies which he found between the civil law and the rights and duties of states. But Grotius was engaged in a constructive task. Had he been content to do no more than record the customary law, as came to be the practice of the writers of the nineteenth century, the record would have contributed little to the development of international law. It was the very fact that the conduct of the times was lawless and unrestrained that led Grotius to appeal to a higher law of natural justice superior to the arbitrary conduct manifested in the existing practices of the nations. The success of this appeal was seen in the general acclaim with which his volume was received. Practical statesmen felt the need of putting some restraint upon the barbarous practices of the times, and were ready to accept the statement of lawful and unlawful conduct laid down by Grotius without giving more than a formal adherence to the doctrinal basis upon which it was constructed.

The substantive law. In Book II, dealing with the grounds of a just war, Grotius gave a new direction to juristic thought. Here is the substantive part of the law which earlier writers had largely overlooked.[25]

---

[23] *Ibid.*, Prolegomena, § 9.

[24] *Ibid.*, Prolegomena, § 39.

[25] An exception must be made of Gentili, see p. 51, who also sought to give to the moral principles of the theologians a specific legal content, so as to reduce the law as far as possible from abstract principles to concrete rules.

Successive chapters deal with the defense of self and of property; titles to property, original and acquired; the obligations of ownership; promises, contracts, and oaths; treaties and sponsions; the obligation to repair injuries, the right of legation, punishment for wrong done, and related subjects. It is this analysis of the rights and duties of states, in an attempt to decide when one state has a just claim against another, that constitutes the main contribution of Grotius to the science of international law. The *De jure belli ac pacis* is not merely an effort to put restraints upon the conduct of war, to which Book III of the treatise is devoted; it is an effort, guided by moral idealism and an exhaustive knowledge of the civil law, to determine specifically the rights and duties of states as the basis of peaceful relations between them. Grotius was not the first to discuss the many particular problems that fill the pages of his great treatise; but he was the first to bring all of them together in systematic form, and to combine in a single coordinated treatise the most progressive thought of the century in which he lived.[26]

Richard Zouche. Two years after the Peace of Westphalia a second, though much smaller, treatise was published which deserves a place among the important influences determining the development of the science of international law. Richard Zouche, who held the chair of civil law at Oxford, published in 1650 a manual of international law in which the term *jus inter gentes* was substituted for the *jus gentium* of Grotius, and stress was laid upon custom as a source of international law.[27] By reason of his more concrete point of view Zouche is regarded by some writers as the founder of what is called the "positive" or "historical" school of international law. But Zouche was still a citizen of the seventeenth century and influenced by its need for a higher standard of conduct than could be found in the common practices of the nations. Hence he defines *jus inter gentes* as "the law which is accepted among most nations by customs in harmony with reason," [28] and he does not hesitate to lay down dogmatic rules for which the incidents cited are rather examples than evidence.

[26] For a study of the influence of Grotius upon contemporary and later thought, see Vreeland, *Hugo Grotius;* Knight, *Life and Works of Hugo Grotius;* J. B. Scott, Introduction to translation in *Classics of International Law; Transactions of the Grotius Society,* pp. 1-29 (1943), *passim; Am. Journal,* Vol. 19 (1925), pp. 1, 12, 118, 251, 461, 685; W. Van der Vlugt, "L'Oeuvre de Grotius et son influence sur le développement du droit international," *Recueil des Cours,* Vol. 7 (1925-II), p. 399; H. Lauterpacht, "The Grotian Tradition in International Law," *British Year Book,* 1946, p. 1. The Dutch scholar Ter Meulen has published a *Concise Bibliography of Hugo Grotius.*

[27] A photographic reproduction of the text of 1650, *Juris et judicii fecialis, sive, juris inter gentes, et quaestionum de eodem explicatio,* edited by T. E. Holland, with translation by J. L. Brierly, was published by the Carnegie Institution of Washington, 1911, *Classics of International Law.*

[28] *Op. cit.,* p. 1.

E. SCHOOLS OF INTERNATIONAL LAW

Largely under the influence of the great treatise of Grotius and stimulated by the growing intercourse between nations and the need of more specific rules of international conduct, the science of international law developed rapidly during the succeeding centuries. Three main tendencies may be observed, which have led historians to classify the various writers into separate groups, sometimes described as schools of thought. The term "schools," however, suggests a greater unity than has actually existed within any of the several traditions. Some writers have sought to build up the theory of the law; others have laid chief stress upon the actual conduct of nations; but a great middle group has insisted that the most practical approach to the law involved of necessity some theory of international ethics, following in that respect in the footsteps of Grotius, although not having consciously before them the teachings of the master.

The Naturalists. The peculiar conception of the law of nature developed by the English philosopher Hobbes in his treatise on *The Great Leviathan,* published in 1651, had a far-reaching effect upon the science of international law, although the main interest of Hobbes was to formulate a defense of absolutism within the state. Man is antisocial, not social as in the Stoic and Christian tradition. Living in a state of nature in which he is "nasty and brutish," man is at war with every other man, until at last, driven by the instinct of self-preservation, man is led to form a compact with other men and surrender his natural rights to the authority of Leviathan, the embodiment of the separate wills of those who made the compact. There being no similar compact between nations, they, like individuals before being coerced by a superior authority, were "with respect to each other in a state of nature, which is a state of war." [29] The law of nature was thus divorced from theology. The divorce made it possible for states to assert their sovereignty in more absolute form; but at the same time it destroyed the conception of a higher law and made their conduct a matter to be determined by their own free agreement.

While following in the tradition of Hobbes in divorcing the natural law from theology, Samuel Pufendorf, a university professor first at Heidelberg and later at Lund in Sweden, conceived a new natural law of his own. In a work published in 1672, *De jure naturae et gentium,* Pufendorf conceived of a state of nature whose fundamental law was the obligation of man to promote sociability with his fellow men.[30]

[29] *Leviathan,* Chap. XIII.

[30] *De jure naturae et gentium libri octo, Classics of International Law.* An abridged edition of the larger work was prepared by Pufendorf himself under the title, *De officio hominis et civis juxta legem naturalem,* translated by F. G. Moore, *Classics of International Law,* with introduction by W. Schucking.

Whatever acts had that effect were laws of nature. The standard of international conduct was to be determined not by custom and treaty but by the natural law evidenced by the application of reason to international relations. While historians have placed Pufendorf at the head of the Philosophic or Pure Law of Nature School, there are few distinguished names among his followers; [31] and even those who have placed chief emphasis upon the philosophical basis of international law, as James Lorimer in his *Institutes of the Law of Nations*, published in 1883-84, have had ideas of their own as to the higher law from which international obligations are derived.[32]

The Grotians. A group of writers, designated as "Grotians," have been said to "stand midway" between the Naturalists and the later group known as Positivists. But Vattel, the leading writer of this school, was far from being true to Grotius either in respect to his conception of the natural law or in respect to the conclusions which might be drawn from the natural law. Owing to the practical use made of his treatise by statesmen, the name of Emer de Vattel came to be better known in the world of international relations than that of Grotius himself. Seeing the need in his day of a new treatise on the law of nations he believed it more expedient to popularize a volume published in 1749 by the German philosopher Wolff, entitled *Jus gentium*.[33] But in doing so Vattel expressly rejected the conception which Wolff had advanced of a *Civitas gentium maxima*, a great republic or commonwealth of the nations, a world-state having authority over its component members. Rather he preferred to relate international obligations to the theory of primitive society which had become the popular source of the rights and duties of individual men. His work, published in 1758, bore the title *Le Droit des gens*, with the subtitle, "Principes de la loi naturelle, appliqués à la conduite et aux affaires des nations et des souverains." [34]

The law of nature applied to nations. Vattel began with a recognition of the state as a corporate person having an understanding and will of its own and susceptible at once of obligations and of rights. He then argued, following the accepted theory of primitive society, that

[31] The leading names are Christian Thomasius, *Fundamenta juris naturae et gentium*, 1705; Jean Barbeyrac, Jean Jacques Burlamaqui, Thomas Rutherforth, and James Lorimer.

[32] The influence of Lorimer was significant. He was one of the few writers to foresee the need of international legislative, judicial, and executive institutions as essential conditions for the maintenance of peace. His conception of the moral basis of international law was in line with present-day conceptions of the inadequacy of the appeal to utilitarian motives.

[33] *Jus gentium methodo scientifica pertractatum*. The volume forms the ninth and last of a larger treatise on *Jus naturae*.

[34] The text of the edition of 1758, photographically reproduced, edited by A. de Lapradelle, with English translation by C. G. Fenwick, was published by the Carnegie Institution of Washington, 1916, *Classics of International Law*.

"as men are subject to the laws of nature, and as their union in civil society cannot exempt them from the obligation of observing those laws, since in that union they remain none the less men, the whole nation, whose common will is but the outcome of the united wills of the citizens, remains subject to the laws of nature and is bound to respect them in all its undertakings." [35] But the laws of nature could not be applied to nations without taking into account the changes called for by the fact that nations, not individuals, were the subjects of the law. It was this adaptation of the law of nature to nations which constituted what Vattel believed to be Wolff's contribution to a system of international law, and which constituted in turn Vattel's own contribution.

How was this adaptation to be effected? How was the law of nature to be interpreted when applied to *states* as subjects of the law? On the one hand there were certain matters in which right and wrong stood out clearly, so that there could be no doubt as to the principle of law involved. To such rules Vattel gave the name of the "necessary (or natural) law of nations." [36] These rules might be insisted upon by states, and the violation of them justified measures of self-help. On the other hand, in the absence of a supreme authority capable of deciding between nation and nation, there were cases in which the application of the law of nature was not clear. In these cases each nation must be allowed its own interpretation of the law of nature, with the result that the precepts of the law might be evaded by a nation, yet without the commission of a positive injury against the other party, giving rise to a demand for redress. This was the field of the "voluntary law of nations," a lower plane of imperfect rights, in which the precepts of the law of nature were accommodated to the duties of the state to itself.[37] In addition to the necessary and the voluntary law of nations Vattel recognized the existence of treaties in the form of "conventional law," and the existence of usages which constituted "customary law." But there must be no conflict between either conventional or customary law and the necessary law, since nothing could obligate a nation to violate the law of nature.[38]

The system proposed by Vattel is elaborate and complex, but it is important because of the great influence exercised by him upon the subsequent development of international law. The practical conclusions which he reached and the liberal and humanitarian spirit of his discussions won for him a wide hearing. Few, however, of the statesmen and

[35] *Ibid.*, Introduction, § 5. The student will note that Vattel's law of nature differs fundamentally from the Christian conception of the natural law, founded not upon contract but upon the application of the law of God to human relations. See note 2 of this chapter.

[36] *Ibid.*, Introduction, § 7.

[37] *Ibid.*, § 21.

[38] *Ibid.*, §§ 24-26.

jurists who quoted his authority in later years concerned themselves with his mistaken premises or foresaw the dangerous consequences of his enthronement of the sovereignty and independence of states. With Vattel passed the long established distinction between a just and an unjust war. The old standards established by the *necessary law* were still there, but by the *voluntary law* each prince must be allowed to be the judge in his own case and the community must accept his decision on the assumption that he knows what is best for his own interests. Thus a liberty, denied by the law of nature to individual citizens, was reserved by Vattel to states, by taking into account the changes in the natural law when applied to them. Even absolute governments could accept Vattel's liberal principles when so carefully adjusted to their convenience.[39]

The Positivists. A third group of writers has been classified as Positivists, or the Positive School. Zouche had led the way in 1650 by placing emphasis upon the customs of nations and concerning himself with practice rather than with theory. It was to be expected that with the growing intercourse of states and the greater stability in international relations that followed the Peace of Westphalia there should be increased interest in the substantive body of international law. Bynkershoek, a Dutch publicist, writing between 1702 and 1737, substituted *reason* for the law of nature, and held that reason and usage constituted the two sources of international law.[40] Permanent usage would appear to embody the dictates of reason; it represented the collective reason of successive generations and of various nations; and in consequence it imposed a reciprocal obligation as if such usage were based upon mutual consent.[41] In this way Bynkershoek was enabled to appeal directly to custom in support of certain claims, and he even went so far as to assert in one place that there was no law of nations except between those who voluntarily submitted to it by tacit agreement.[42] John Jacob Moser, a voluminous German writer of the middle of the eighteenth century, pointed the way to the more modern conception of international law by concerning himself solely with the accumulation of treaties and usages which, in the form of precedents, gave a positive character to

[39] For further details of Vattel's system and an estimate of the extent of his influence upon writers and upon governments, see the introduction, by A. de Lapradelle, in the edition published by the Carnegie Institution of Washington, 1916. The fact that Vattel's fundamental principle of the right of each nation to be the judge in its own case was unsound does not mean that the general moral basis upon which his system was constructed did not contribute greatly to the improvement of international standards of conduct. See on this point, C. G. Fenwick, "The Authority of Vattel," *Am. Pol. Science Review,* Vol. VII, p. 395; Vol. VIII, p. 375.

[40] *Quaestionum juris publici libri duo,* Lib. I, Cap. 10, *Classics of International Law.*

[41] *De foro legatorum,* Cap. III, § 10, *Classics of International Law.*

[42] *Ibid.,* Cap. XIX, § 6.

international law.[43] A similar service was performed by George Friedrich de Martens, professor at Göttingen, whose *Précis du droit des gens moderne de l'Europe* appeared in 1788.[44]

F. MODERN TREATISES

British. During the course of the nineteenth century and the opening years of the twentieth the progress of international law was marked by the increasing and finally predominating influence of the Positive School. Usage and custom, now grown large in bulk, preoccupied the attention of jurists; but many of them still referred to the older law of nature, or to its modern counterpart *reason,* as the ultimate test of international obligations. In Great Britain Sir William Scott, afterward Lord Stowell, as judge in the British High Court of Admiralty, gave to the law of prize in time of war the definiteness of a positive system and incidentally delivered valuable dicta upon other branches of the law.[45] Manning, in *Commentaries on the Law of Nations,* published in 1839, followed the old classification of the "natural" and the "positive" law of nations, and after the true Grotian tradition said that "customary law should be tested by the law of nature." [46] Phillimore, whose *Commentaries on International Law* were first published in 1854, spoke of custom and usage as outwardly expressing "the consent of nations to things which are *naturally,* that is by the law of God, binding upon them." [47] Hall, whose text on *International Law,* published in 1880, is accounted one of the best reasoned of the modern treatises, was strictly positive in adopting "the existing rules" actually in force between nations as the "sole standard of conduct or law of present authority"; [48] but he included among those rules broad general principles founded on an assumption as to the nature of states. Walker followed with his *Science of International Law,* published in 1893, and his *History of the Law of Nations,* Volume I, published in 1899, both of which gave a vigorous impulse to the study of international law in university circles. Lawrence's text, published in 1895, sought to lay emphasis upon the great ethical principles underlying international law and at the same time the dependence of the law upon the hard facts of history.[49] Westlake's

[43] Nys considers him, by reason of his historical labors, as worthy to be regarded as one of the "founders of international law." *Le Droit international,* Vol. I, p. 258.

[44] The publication of Martens' volume on the eve of the French Revolution makes it a landmark of progress up to the time of that great crisis.

[45] For the influence of this great jurist, see Roscoe, *Lord Stowell: His Life and the Development of English Prize Law.*

[46] Pp. 57, 69.

[47] Preface, p. v; Phillimore's conception of the natural law is perhaps nearer to that of the Schoolmen than any modern writer since Grotius.

[48] Introductory Chapter.

[49] *Principles of International Law,* 1st ed. (1895); 4th ed. (1910).

carefully reasoned treatise had a wide influence,[50] and Oppenheim's comprehensive range of learning gave to his work an outstanding position among scholars.[51]

United States. In the United States the judicial decisions of Chief Justice Marshall in respect to the law of prize played a part similar to those of Sir William Scott.[52] In 1826 James Kent, the first of American publicists to attempt a connected statement of the rules of international law, laid stress upon the consent of nations as furnishing the only positive basis of international law.[53] Henry Wheaton, whose *Elements of International Law*, published in 1836, exercised an important influence both in Great Britain and in the United States, followed more closely the Grotian tradition, giving due place to deductions from general principles.[54] In 1860 Theodore D. Woolsey published his *Introduction to the Study of International Law;* and Francis Lieber [55] and Richard H. Dana [56] made important contributions to the codification of the laws of war and to the rights and duties of neutral states. In 1887 General George B. Davis published his *Elements of International Law*, a text in which the laws of war and neutrality figured prominently. Wilson and Tucker's text [57] first published in 1901, was destined to be widely used, as was Hershey's text published in 1912,[58] and Stockton's *Outlines of International Law*, published in 1914. The most important work of the period was Moore's *Digest of International Law*,[59] published

[50] *International Law*, Pt. I, 2nd ed. (1910); Pt. II, 2nd ed. (1913); also his *Collected Papers on Public International Law*. See A. P. Higgins, *Recueil des Cours*, Vol. 40 (1932-II), p. 5.

[51] *International Law*, 1st ed. (1905-1906). Oppenheim, although of German birth and education, wrote his important treatise while a professor at the London School of Economics and at Cambridge University, and he is therefore classed here among British writers. For an appreciation of his scientific attainments, see *British Year Book, 1920-21*, pp. 1-9; *Am. Journal*, Vol. 14 (1920), p. 229.

[52] See Craigmyle, *John Marshall in Diplomacy and in Law;* Ziegler, *The International Law of John Marshall*.

[53] *Commentaries on American Law*, Vol. I.

[54] Compare Wheaton's definition of international law, in the present work, Chap. II, note 1. Wheaton's *History of the Law of Nations* was also a significant contribution.

[55] *Miscellaneous Writings*, 2 vols. (1881). See also *Instructions for the Government of the Armies of the United States in the Field*, below, p. 657, note 30.

[56] Dana's edition of Wheaton, published in 1866 at the close of the American Civil War, contains elaborate notes on the law of neutrality, equal almost to an original work. It was republished in 1936, with notes by G. G. Wilson.

[57] *International Law*, 7th ed. (1917). The editions of 1922 and 1935 appear under Wilson's name only.

[58] *Essentials of International Law*, revised ed. (1927).

[59] The work in seven volumes and index, while based upon an earlier *Digest* by Francis Wharton (3 vols., 1886), contains so large a body of original research study as to constitute an independent undertaking. It must be noted, however, that on many points the *Digest* represents the American interpretation of international law rather than a statement of rules universally accepted.

in 1906, which set forth in a wide variety of documents the international practice of the United States. James Brown Scott's *Hague Conferences of 1899 and 1907* proved to be the first of a long series of publications devoted chiefly to the development of judicial procedure for the settlement of international disputes and to the promotion of inter-American juridical relations.[60]

German. German writers of the nineteenth century showed a predominantly positive conception of international law. Klüber, who published in 1819 a volume in French entitled *Droit des gens moderne de l'Europe,* was still influenced by the theory of the natural law to the extent of having recourse to it to fill the gaps in the positive law and to give unity to its principles.[61] Heffter, whose volume *Das europäische Völkerrecht der Gegenwart* appeared in 1844, was more positive in his attitude, discarding metaphysical speculation and seeking merely to present a clear and precise picture of the actual customs and treaties in force between nations.[62] Bluntschli, in the introduction to his *Code,* published in 1868, stated that it was his intention "to formulate clearly the existing ideas of the civilized world." [63] Toward the close of the century special interest was shown in the philosophical basis of international law, the influence of the Hegelian conception of the nature of the state being strongly felt. If the state is the highest expression of human freedom, as Hegel contended, how can the state itself be subject to law? Jellinek [64] and Ihering [65] proposed the theory of self-limitation. International law, it was argued, was based upon the free consent of states. Consent, given implicitly by custom and expressly by treaty, constituted the basis of international law. But the consent thus given was not final. If the state should find that the obligations thus assumed were inconsistent with its highest interests it could as a matter of law disengage itself from them, although as a practical matter it would not be expedient to do so.

In an important work published in 1899 Triepel sought to offset the doctrine of self-limitation by taking as the basis of international law the formal agreement of states creating a common will, which thence-

---

[60] See G. A. Finch, "James Brown Scott, 1866-1943," in *Am. Journal,* Vol. 38 (1944), p. 183.

[61] Preface, Chap. I, § 5. Additional value attaches to Klüber's work by reason of its being representative of progressive thought at the time of the Congress of Vienna.

[62] 4th ed., in French translation, edited by Geffken (1883). Rivier commends Heffter as the best survey of the entire subject. Holtzendorf, *Handbuch,* Vol. I.

[63] *Das moderne Völkerrecht der civilisirten Staaten als Rechtsbuch dargestellt,* 3rd ed. (1878).

[64] *Die rechtliche Natur der Staatenverträge* (1880); *Die Lehre von der Staatenverbindungen; Allgemeine Staatslehre* (1900).

[65] *Der Zweck im Recht* (1880), Eng. trans. by I. Husick.

forth constituted a binding rule of law.[66] In sharp contrast Kaufmann reasserted once more in extreme form the theory of the supremacy of the state over its own self-imposed obligations. His monograph on *The Nature of International Law and the Clause rebus sic stantibus*, published in 1911, expressly rejected the suggestion of binding rules of international law and frankly proposed as the basis of international relations the competitive struggle of states according to the principle that might makes right.[67] These extreme positions, however, were not reflected in such textbooks as those of von Liszt [68] and von Ullman, [69] who took the moderately positive position common to Swiss, Dutch, Scandinavian, and Russian publicists.[70]

Continental European and Latin American. By contrast, writers of the Latin tradition, French, Spanish, Italian, and Latin American, showed a tendency to refer to theories of absolute right derived from the natural law as the ultimate source of international obligation. Many of them, notably Pradier-Fodéré, Bonfils, and Despagnet accumulated a wealth of incidents and cases to illustrate the practical application of abstract principles.[71] In Latin America the Venezuelan-Chilean publicist Andrés Bello published in 1832 a pioneer treatise, entitled *Principios de derecho internacional*, based upon his experience as secretary of various Venezuelan legations and as Foreign Minister of Chile.[72] The important treatise by Calvo, the distinguished Argentine jurist, first published in Spanish in 1868 and later in French, combined theory and practice in due proportion.[73] The volume by the Chilean publicist, Alvarez, *Le droit international américain*, published in 1910, represented an attempt

[66] *Völkerrecht und Landesrecht,* translated into French by R. Brunet, *Droit international et droit interne.*

[67] *Das Wesen des Völkerrechts und die clausula rebus sic stantibus.* See also his "Règles générales du droit de la paix," *Recueil des Cours*, Vol. 54 (1935-IV), p. 313. Compare Hold-Ferneck's *Lehrbuch*, 1930. See below, note 89.

[68] *Das Völkerrecht systematisch dargestellt,* 6th ed. (1910).

[69] *Völkerrecht,* 2nd ed. (1908).

[70] Outstanding names are those of Rivier, *Principes du droit des gens*, 2 vols. (1896); de Louter, *Het Stellig Volkenrecht*, 2 vols. (1910), translated, with modifications, into French by the author under the title *Droit international public positif* (1920); Kleen, *Lois et usages de la neutralité*, 2 vols. (1889-1900); Martens, *Traité de droit international*, 3 vols. (1883-1887), translated from the original Russian.

[71] Pradier-Fodéré's treatise in 8 volumes, *Traité de droit international public*, was perhaps the most important contribution. Bonfils' *Manuel de droit international public*, first published in 1894, was destined to go through many editions. Despagnet, *Cours de droit international public;* Chrétien, *Principes de droit international public;* and Mérignhac also made significant contributions. Anzilotti, *Corso di diritto internazionale* (1912), adopted, however, a positive attitude.

[72] 1st edition 1832. Calvo, *Droit international*, Vol. I, p. 109, speaks of Bello as a "precursor of Wheaton," but as a matter of fact both authors drew their inspiration from European sources.

[73] *Le Droit international théorique et pratique*, 5th ed. in 6 vols. (1896). For the application of the famous "Calvo Doctrine," see below, p. 341.

to delimit a field of inter-American relations in which special rules of law were held to apply; it was the forerunner of many subsequent studies.[74]

Results of the positive attitude towards international law. The development of international law during this period from a theoretical science, based upon abstract reasoning, into a practical science, based upon ascertainable facts of international usage, had the effect of making the law at once more definite and less elastic. On the one hand, a clear-cut separation was made between what *was* the law, in the sense of rules actually observed, and what under other conditions *might* or *should* be the law according to the conception of international justice held by the individual writer. The plain record of international practice furnished a definite starting point in the settlement of many international controversies. The precision of the law within one field led to its extension into other fields. New and closer relationships were being developed between the nations, calling for a more specific understanding of the force to be attributed to usage and precedent and for a wider application of general treaties and conventions.[75]

On the other hand the science of international law lost almost entirely its critical and constructive character. Writers were more intent upon weighing conclusions from facts than upon criticizing either the facts themselves or the political and economic basis upon which they rested. There was a strong tendency on the part of publicists to rally to the defense of national interests and to be advocates rather than judges in the interpretation of disputed points. Cases were sometimes quoted as arguments rather than as evidence. It was not thought consistent with scientific method to point out the wide gaps in the law or the defects of its underlying principles. War, as we have seen, was a legalized institution, and jurists accepted it as such and sought only to limit its excesses and to regulate its effects. Neutrality was regarded as the normal attitude of states not directly interested in the issues between the parties in conflict. The progress in the development of what might be called the architectural details of international law was so striking that few jurists concerned themselves with the foundations of the edifice. The constructive work of international organization and the establishment of an effective machinery of international government were regarded by most

[74] A critical bibliography of the more important works on international law may be found in Nys, *Le Droit international*, Vol. I, pp. 251-328. A briefer survey may be found in Oppenheim, *Int. Law*, Vol. I, §§ 52-62. On the general characteristics of the Latin writers, see H. Lauterpacht, "The So-called Anglo-American and Continental Schools of Thought in International Law," *British Year Book*, Vol. XII (1931), p. 31.

[75] Hall's treatise, perhaps, presents this approach to the law most effectively. *International Law*, Introductory Chapter.

writers as beyond the scope of legal study. International jurisprudence remained largely a neglected field.[76]

G. DEVELOPMENT 1920-1945

The disillusionment in respect to the value of the existing rules of international law which attended the outbreak of the World War in 1914 was followed by a time of earnest endeavor on the part of scholars both in belligerent and in neutral countries to discover the causes for the collapse of the existing system and to devise remedies for the future. The attention of publicists was given to constructive plans for the re-establishment and development of international law at the close of the war. A new international law was visualized under which war was to be outlawed as a means of procedure and a general association of the nations formed to maintain peace.[77]

These hopes and plans found their concrete realization, if not their fulfilment, in the establishment of the League of Nations in 1920, and in the elaborate series of supplementary agreements which followed upon the adoption of the Covenant. The leading foreign scholars with few exceptions supported the League as containing the best promise of the future, and their writings reflected their interest in its successful operation.[78] Studies and commentaries upon the Covenant appeared in large numbers, analyzing the legal relationships created by the League and examining the practical problems arising in connection with its functions. Opinion among scholars and publicists in the United States was divided, a majority favoring the adherence of the United States to the League and a minority opposing such action either because of the con-

[76] See on this point, "International Law and the Judicial Determination of Important Issues," in Lauterpacht, *The Function of Law in the International Community*, p. 169, where the Italian jurist Anzilotti is quoted as follows: "The interests protected by international law are not those which are of major weight in the life of states. It is sufficient to think of the great political and economic rivalries to which no juridical formula applies, in order to realize the truth of this statement. International law develops its true function in a sphere considerably circumscribed and modest, not in that in which there move the great conflicts of interests which induce states to stake their very existence in order to make them prevail." The great jurist might at least have added some expression of regret that this should be so.

[77] The literature is extensive, including such volumes as Fried, *The Restoration of Europe* (1916); Brailsford, *A League of Nations* (1917); Hill, *The Rebuilding of Europe* (1917); Minor, *A Republic of Nations* (1918); Dickinson, *The Choice before Us* (1918); Lawrence, *The Society of Nations* (1919); Notter, *The Origins of the Foreign Policy of Woodrow Wilson*, shows the influences brought to bear upon the President.

[78] Here also the literature is extensive. See, in particular, Oppenheim, *A League of Nations* (1919); Pollock, *The League of Nations*, 2nd ed. (1922); Scelle, *La Société des Nations* (1922); Schücking and Wehberg, *Die Satzung des Völkerbundes*, 3rd ed. (1931); Redslob, *Théorie de la Société des Nations* (1927); Gonsiorowski, *Société des Nations et problème de la paix* (1927).

nection of the Covenant with the Treaty of Versailles, or because of the inadequacy of the powers of the League to accomplish its purposes, or because of defects in the organization and functions of the League which were thought to involve the United States too intimately in the political life of Europe.[79] Latin American scholars, on the whole, followed the lead of their governments in upholding the League.

General treatises. Apart from its development in connection with the League of Nations the science of international law made great progress during the years immediately following the close of the war. A large number of general surveys of the law appeared, some of them mere compendia for the use of students, but others showing originality in the analysis of principles and in the classification of material. In the United States C. C. Hyde's *International Law, Chiefly as Interpreted and Applied by the United States* was an exhaustive study within the more limited field expressed by its title. Hackworth's *Digest of International Law,* appearing in successive volumes from 1940 to 1944, followed the lead of Moore's *Digest* of 1906 in stating the official position of the government upon questions of international law arising in the course of the international relations of the United States.[80] In Great Britain distinguished scholars undertook to revise the standard texts of Wheaton, Hall, and Oppenheim, with additions almost equivalent to new works.[81] Brierly contributed a brief volume justifying attention by its penetrating study of the origin and character of international law.[82] In continental Europe Anzilotti's treatise was perhaps the most acute analysis of the law;[83] but significant general texts were also published by Strupp,[84] Scelle,[85] Spiropoulos,[86] Politis,[87] Le Fur,[88] and others.[89]

[79] See, for example, Hill, *American World Policies* (1920); Snow, *The American Philosophy of Government* (1921); Brown, *International Society* (1923); Morley, *The Society of Nations* (1932).

[80] A new *Digest* by M. M. Whiteman is in course of publication, Vols. 1, 2 (1963).

[81] Wheaton, 6th Eng. ed. by A. Berriedale Keith, 2 vols. (1929); Hall, 8th ed. by A. P. Higgins (1924); Oppenheim, 5th ed. by H. Lauterpacht (1935, 1937); 6th ed., Vol. II (1940); 7th ed., Vols. I, II (1952); 8th ed.; Vol. I (1955).

[82] *The Law of Nations,* 5th ed. (1955).

[83] *Corso di diritto internazionale,* Vol. I, 3rd ed. (1928). French translation by Gidel (1929).

[84] *Eléments du droit international public,* 3 vols. (1930); "Les règles générales du droit de la paix," *Recueil des Cours,* Vol. 47 (1934-I), p. 263.

[85] *Précis de droit des gens,* 2 vols. (1932-34); "Règles générales du droit de la paix," *Recueil des Cours,* Vol. 46 (1933-IV), p. 331.

[86] *Théorie générale du droit international* (1930).

[87] *Les nouvelles tendances du droit international* (1927).

[88] *Précis de droit international public* (1931); "Règles générales du droit de la paix," *Recueil des Cours,* Vol. 54 (1935-IV), p. 5.

[89] Hatschek's abridged volume, translated into English under the title, *Outline of International Law* (1930), was a typical statement of the "coordination theory," that international law is based upon the voluntary acceptance of its obligations by equal sovereign states. Hold-Ferneck's *Lehrbuch des Völkerrechts* (1930) was an extreme statement of the doctrine of self-limitation, the voluntary acceptance of legal obliga-

In Latin America a number of important treatises appeared reflecting at once the independence of juridical thought in the Western Hemisphere and the recognition of the necessity of developing rules of law to meet the special conditions with which the American states were confronted. Outstanding among them was the treatise of the Cuban jurist, Bustamante, [90] the treatise of Accioly [91] of Brazil, the treatises of Ruiz-Moreno,[92] Antokoletz [93] and Podestá Costa [94] of Argentina, the treatise of Cruchaga Tocornal [95] of Chile, and the treatise of Ulloa [96] of Peru. In general these treatises were conservative in character, following the traditional classifications of subject matter, but recognizing the necessity of adapting the traditional law to the functions and activities of the League of Nations and of the Permanent Court of International Justice.

Monographs: field of theory. In addition to general texts numerous monographs appeared dealing with all branches of the law, theoretical and practical. An important study in the general theory of the law was contributed by Lauterpacht who, in his *Function of Law in the International Community*, published in 1933, sought to lay a broader base for the jurisdiction of the Permanent Court of International Justice by examining "some of the persistent problems of legal philosophy, such as the place of law in society, the nature of the judicial function, the problem of judicial discretion, and the antinomies of stability and change." [97] The Dutch jurist Krabbe reaffirmed his earlier position in respect to the supremacy of international law, the obligatory character

---

tions. "There does not exist, and there can not exist, a rule of international law prescribing that a new state must observe the rules of international law. On the contrary, it is a matter of free choice on the part of the new state to decide whether or not to subject itself to international law. In consequence international law only binds states which submit themselves to it voluntarily." I Teil, p. 177. Cavaglieri's *Corso di diritto internazionale*, 2nd ed. (1932) made the rule *pacta sunt servanda* the ultimate source of international obligation. By contrast, Pasquazi's *Ius internationale publicum* adhered rigidly to the traditional doctrine of a natural law of nations.

[90] *Derecho internacional público*, 5 vols. (1933-1938); French translation by Goulé.

[91] *Tratado de direito internacional público* (1933). French translation, revised (1941-1942); Spanish translation, revised (1945-1946); 2nd ed. (1956-1957).

[92] *Lecciones de derecho internacional público* (1934-1935).

[93] *Tratado de derecho internacional público*, 2nd ed. (1928).

[94] *Manual de derecho internacional público* (1943); *Derecho internacional público*, 2 vols. (1955).

[95] *Nociones de derecho internacional*, 3rd ed. (1923). New ed. *Derecho internacional*, Vol. I (1944).

[96] *Derecho internacional público*, 2nd ed., Vol. I (1938); 4th ed. (1957).

[97] See, in particular, Pt. VI, "The Limits of the Rule of Law," where the author analyzes the nature of international law in the light of contemporary theories. Note also Lauterpacht's *Development of International Law by the Permanent Court of International Justice;* and *The Development of International Law by the International Court* (1958).

of which, like that of national law, he found to be based "in the juridical conscience of man." [98] Duguit carried his earlier attack upon the sovereignty of the state to the point of holding that "the subjects of international law are not states, but the individual members of states." [99] Le Fur stated in strong terms the *monistic* position that national law and international law were of the same fundamental character: "International law is only a special form of the law of nature; it is only the last development of law, its extension to a wider group, the international community." [100] In the United States Roscoe Pound carried into the field of international law his philosophy of law as having a social function, implying the necessity of adapting the law to the changing needs of the international community.[101]

Significant also was the contribution of the Vienna School to the development of the theory of international law. Kelsen sought to establish a "pure science of law" by distinguishing sharply between positive law and natural law or "transcendental" justice. Positive law is the rule that must be obeyed. It rests upon a fundamental assumption that certain acts are lawful because they are done under the authority of the constitution. This "basic norm" makes it possible to determine thereupon what are the rules of law in force as distinct from those which ought to be in force. Law is not a deduction from an immutable principle of justice; it is something more realistic and relative. A rule becomes law by reason of the power of the state to make it obligatory. State and law are identical because the state is merely the expression of a legal system. In international relations the basic norm or assumption is that custom has the creative force to make rules of law. "Customary international law, developed on the basis of this norm, is the first stage within the international legal order." Then come treaties deriving their force from the rule of customary law *pacta sunt servanda;* then come rules created by international organs, such as the Permanent Court, themselves created by treaties. The primacy of international law is taken as a working hypothesis, without denying the alternative possibility of the primacy of national law. Acting on the first assumption, the sovereignty of the

[98] H. Krabbe, "L'Idée moderne de l'Etat," *Recueil des Cours,* Vol. 13 (1926-III), pp. 513 ff.

[99] *Traité de droit constitutionnel,* 3rd ed. (1927), pp. 720 ff. See also H. Laski, "M. Duguit's Conception of the State," in *Modern Theories of Law.*

[100] *Revue de droit international et de législation comparée* (1925), pp. 67-68, and his later *Précis de droit international public.* See also Politis, "Le problème des limitations de la souveraineté," *Recueil des Cours,* Vol. 6 (1925-I), pp. 5, 40.

[101] See R. Pound, "Philosophical Theory and International Law," in *Bibliotheca Visseriana,* Vol. I (1923); also his *Interpretations of Legal History; An Introduction to the Philosophy of Law; The Spirit of the Common Law.*

By contrast the Soviet Union subordinated international law to economic policies. Taracuzio, *The Soviet Union and International Law.*

state is subordinated to the legal order of the *civitas maxima* of the international community.[102]

In contrast with Kelsen, Verdross insisted upon the universality and objectivity of the fundamental conception of justice, in spite of subjective variations in the application of the principle in different historical periods. This higher "natural law," represented by the general principles of law common to civilized states, must be resorted to as a means of supplementing the inadequacies of the positive law and testing the value of conflicting usages.[103] In like manner Kunz, speaking in the realm of pure theory, maintained the primacy of international law, insisting that it was the only hypothesis upon which a unitary legal system could be scientifically conceived. International law is a "primitive" law, and as such predominantly static. It must become dynamic if it is to survive.[104] Erlich defines the present (1962) stage of international law as "neo-positivism," indicating that while the positivists relied upon treaties and custom as a science of international law, the scholar of today relies also upon judicial precedent and inferences drawn from the general principles of law. De Visscher emphasizes the necessity of keeping law in touch with reality and of balancing the social and political factors in its development.[105]

The theories of the Vienna School gave rise to renewed discussion of the unity of the two systems of law, international and national. The Dualistic theory, as stated by Triepel and Anzilotti, for example, had taken strong root during the years preceding the First World War when positivism was the dominant attitude, and international law was a law of "coordination," an agreement of sovereign states to be bound by given rules. The new Monist School, of which Kelsen was the leading exponent, found the two kinds of law to be of the same essential nature, based upon the inherent logic of a legal system as well as upon the same

---

[102] See *General Theory of Law and State; Law and Peace in International Relations.* A critical study of Kelsen's theories may be found in Lauterpacht, "Kelsen's Pure Science of Law," in *Modern Theories of Law,* Vol. VII. For the relation between Kelsen's theory and the earlier positivism of Austin, see Lauterpacht, *The Function of Law in the International Community,* pp. 402 ff.

[103] The theories of Verdross may be found in Pt. I of his general treatise *Völkerrecht,* and in "Le fondement du droit international" in *Recueil des Cours,* Vol. 16 (1927-I), p. 251; "Règles générales du droit international de la paix," *ibid.,* Vol. 30 (1929-V), p. 275; "On the Concept of International Law," *Am. Journal,* Vol. 43 (1949), p. 435.

[104] See J. L. Kunz, "On the Theoretical Basis of the Law of Nations," *Transactions of the Grotius Society,* Vol. 10 (1924), pp. 115-142; "La primauté du droit des gens," *Revue de droit international et de lég. comp.,* Tome VI (1925), pp. 556-598; "The Law of Nations, Static and Dynamic," in *Am. Journal,* Vol. 27 (1933), p. 630.

[105] "The Development of International Law as a Science." *Recueil des Cours,* Vol. 105 (1926-I), p. 177; De Visscher, *Theory and Reality in Public International Law.*

fundamental needs of man, although these were differently phrased according to the approach of the particular writer to the problem.[106]

Field of substantive law. In the field of substantive law, dealing with the rights and duties of states in their normal relations, the list of monographs was long and imposing. The theory of state succession, the equality of states, the responsibility of the state for injuries to aliens, territorial waters, treaties, diplomatic privileges and immunities were but a few of the titles.[107] Studies equal in length to monographs appeared in the *Recueil des Cours* of the Academy of International Law at The Hague. Leading articles in the *American Journal of International Law*, in the *British Year Book of International Law*, and in the French, German, Italian, and other reviews were frequently original contributions to the development of specific topics. Inter-American law, described as "American International Law," was the object of numerous studies, among which those of A. Alvarez of Chile were conspicuous.[108] Never before had so much attention been given to regulating the details of international intercourse. Had the means been available for coordinating the work of scholars in many different countries the progress of the work of codification would have been greatly simplified, limited, however, as it was by the political conditions of the time.

International organization. In the general field of international organization a number of volumes appeared which sought to strengthen the authority of the League of Nations and to point out the conditions under which it might hope to attain its objectives. The term "international government" came into use to describe the necessity of more effective measures to maintain peace and to promote the general welfare of the international community.[109] International administration was the object of a number of special studies. A series of volumes, under the title, *International Legislation*, edited by Manley O. Hudson, brought together the imposing array of multipartite treaties concluded since 1919.[110] In the field of international procedure Manley O. Hudson's

[106] See J. G. Starke, "Monism and Dualism in the Theory of International Law," *Brit. Year Book of International Law*, 1936, pp. 66-81. See also, Scelle, *Précis de droit des gens*, Première Partie, pp. 27 ff., "Sociétés internationales et droit des gens." The student will observe that the new positivism of Kelsen is fundamentally different from the positivism of the late nineteenth century. Compare J. L. Kunz, "Natural-Law Thinking in the Modern Science of International Law," *Am. Journal*, Vol. 55 (1961), p. 951; and Fuller, *The Morality of Law*.

[107] For authors and their works see the respective chapter heads of this book.

[108] See, in particular, Alvarez, *Le droit international américain; La codification du droit international;* Yepes, *La contribution de l'Amérique Latine au développement du droit international; Le Panaméricanisme au point de vue historique, juridique et politique.*

[109] See Eagleton, *International Government* (1932); Mower, *International Government* (1931); Potter, *Introduction to the Study of International Organization* (1922-1935); Politis, *Les nouvelles tendances du droit international* (1927).

[110] See also M. O. Hudson and M. H. Frost, "Multipartite International Instruments of Legislative Effect," *Am. Journal*, Vol. 22 (1928), Supp., pp. 90-108.

studies in the organization and jurisdiction of the Permanent Court of International Justice, together with the works of Politis, Francqueville, Fachiri, Bustamante, and others did much to clarify the questions presented by the judicial settlement of international disputes.[111] In both Great Britain and the United States much stress was laid upon the study of "cases," meaning the decisions of national and international courts, as the material for a study of the development of international law by judicial interpretation. The *Case Books* published in the United States were limited for the most part to the decisions of British and American courts; [112] but the *Annual Digest and Reports of Public International Law Cases,* published in Great Britain, made available summaries of recent decisions of the courts of the leading countries.[113]

In the field of the laws of war a number of studies appeared in the United States seeking, if not to justify, at least to place upon a legal basis the special position of a country not a member of the League of Nations when confronted with action by the League under Article 16 of the Covenant.[114] Later, as the possibility of war in Europe came nearer, attention was given to the clarification of the position of the neutral state in relation to the established rights and duties of neutrality.[115] The series of "neutrality acts" passed by the Congress of the United States between 1935 and 1939 gave rise to a voluminous literature in which national policy and the obligations of international law were at issue.[116] By contrast with these more controversial studies, Quincy Wright's encyclopedic treatise, entitled *A Study of War,* was a comprehensive

[111] Hudson, *The Permanent Court of International Justice, 1920-1942;* Politis, *La Justice Internationale* (1926); Francqueville, *L'Oeuvre de la Cour Permanente de Justice Internationale* (1928); Fachiri, *The Permanent Court of International Justice,* 2nd ed. (1932); Bustamante, *The World Court* (1925).

[112] See Hudson, *Cases and other Materials on International Law,* 2nd ed. (1936); Scott and Jaeger, *Cases on International Law* (1937); Dickinson, *A Selection of Cases and Other Readings on the Law of Nations* (1929); Fenwick, *Cases on International Law,* 2nd ed. (1951); Briggs, *The Law of Nations: Cases, Documents and Notes,* 2nd ed. (1952); Pfankuchen, *A Documentary Textbook in International Law;* Bishop, *International Law: Cases and Materials,* 2nd ed. (1962); Green, *International Law through the Cases* (1951).

[113] 9 vols., 1919-1942. (Now published as *International Law Reports.*)

[114] See Q. Wright and C. Eagleton, "Neutrality and Neutral Rights following the Pact of Paris for the Renunciation of War," *Proceedings,* Am. Soc. Int. Law, 1930, pp. 79, 87; C. Warren, P. C. Jessup, J. L. Kunz, M. O. Hudson, E. D. Dickinson, H. L. Stimson, *et al.,* in *Proceedings,* Am. Soc. Int. Law, 1933, pp. 128, 134; 1935, pp. 36, 42, 45, 121. See also Harvard Draft, *Rights and Duties of States in Case of Aggression,* Am. *Journal,* Vol. 33 (1939), Supp., p. 821.

[115] See, in particular, Harvard Research in International Law: *Rights and Duties of Neutral States in Naval and Aerial War* and *Rights and Duties of States in Case of Aggression,* P. C. Jessup, Reporter (1939); *Neutrality, Its History, Economics and Law,* 4 vols. (1935-1936).

[116] See, in particular, Borchard and Lage, *Neutrality for the United States,* advocating rigid maintenance of neutrality; Fenwick, *American Neutrality: Trial and Failure,* urging recognition of the national interest of the United States in the maintenance of international law and order.

history of war, an analysis of its causes and effects, and an examination of methods of control over war, touching in the course of its discussions many of the leading problems of international law as well as those of political science, economics, and sociology.[117]

The outbreak of war in 1939 further stimulated the activities of scholars in countries sufficiently remote from the scene of hostilities to permit a scientific approach to the law. The chief concern of jurists was to establish the legal basis upon which a new and stronger international organization might be built with power to protect the peace and with more adequate functions for the promotion of international justice. Numerous studies appeared, dealing with all phases of the problem and suggesting that the range of international law must be greatly widened after the war if the contemplated organization was to be adequate to fulfil its purposes. Outstanding among these studies was "The International Law of the Future: Postulates, Principles and Proposals," prepared by a group of North American jurists.[118] The official formulation in Washington of the Dumbarton Oaks Proposals led to a careful and exhaustive analysis of the Proposals, indicating a widespread desire to profit by the experience of the League of Nations and give to the international community the organization needed to restore law and order and to develop the international cooperation necessary to insure a stable peace.[119]

H. DEVELOPMENT SINCE 1945

It was to be expected that the first effort of scholars in the postwar period would be to analyze the Charter of the United Nations and examine on the one hand its contribution to the urgently needed system of collective security and on the other hand its promise of filling the gaps in international law that had been left open during the period between the two World Wars. Outstanding was a volume by Sohn, *Cases and Materials on World Law,* which sought to gather together the materials forming "the basis of the constitutional law of the world community"; and which included not only the decisions of international courts but other documents illustrating the application of legal principles to particular issues and demonstrating that international organization had now become an integral part of international law.[120] Dealing

[117] 2 vols. (1942). For a review of this important work, see *Am. Journal,* Vol. 37 (1943), p. 174.

[118] Original confidential copies distributed by Manley O. Hudson. See, also, among numerous others, the elaborate studies conducted by the Commission to Study the Organization of Peace; and P. E. Corbett, "World Order—an Agenda for Lawyers," *Am. Journal,* Vol. 37 (1943), p. 207.

[119] See H. Kelsen, "The Old and the New League: The Covenant and the Dumbarton Oaks Proposals," *Am. Journal,* Vol. 39 (1945), pp. 45-83; Inter-American Juridical Committee, *Recommendations and Reports,* p. 137.

[120] Followed by a second volume, *Cases on United Nations Law* (1956).

more specifically with the United Nations was a volume by Vandenbosch and Hogan presenting a picture of the complex factors involved in the processes and practices of international organization, looking to the ultimate aim of collective security.[121]

Emphasis was put upon the decisions of the International Court of Justice as showing the possibilities of the development of international law through the peaceful settlement of international disputes. Schwarzenberger led off with Volume I of a general treatise on *International Law*, "International Law as Applied by International Courts and Tribunals," seeking to build up rules of international law by the inductive method. But contrast his study of *Power Politics*, emphasizing "power" as the dominant factor in international relations. A volume by Edvard Hambro, the *Case Law of the International Court*, offered a classification of the decisions of the court according to the established headings of international law; [122] and this was followed by Lauterpacht's *The Development of International Law by the International Court*, analyzing more critically the law behind the cases and the procedure and effectiveness of the action of the Court.[123]

In the meantime it had become clear that the Charter of the United Nations must be amended if the organization was to meet the responsibilities thrust upon it by the successive vetoes of the Soviet Union in the field of collective security. Clark and Sohn proposed amendments modifying the Security Council and the General Assembly, providing for disarmament by stages, and the establishment of an international peace force and other agencies to strengthen the authority of the United Nations in the enforcement of the law.[124]

Side by side with studies of the United Nations and the International Court of Justice were studies provoked as it were by the "cold war." A new international law was needed, a law adequate to meet the changing conditions of the international community, a law representing a sociological approach to vital human problems. Constructive ideas were called for to bring "traditional" international law into touch with the realities of a larger and more closely integrated world. Jessup's *A Modern Law of Nations* laid emphasis upon the need of extending the law into new fields, particularly into the field of the protection of fundamental human rights and the recognition of the responsibility of the whole com-

---

[121] *The United Nations: Background, Organization, Functions, Activities* (1952), followed by *Toward World Order* (1963).

[122] Subtitle, "A Repertoire of the Judgments, Advisory Opinions and Orders of the Permanent Court of International Justice and of the International Court of Justice" (1952).

[123] Revised edition (1958) of an earlier volume (1934).

[124] *World Peace through World Law*. For comment see Chap. IX of this work, "The United Nations."

munity for the observance of the law.[125] This was followed by a provocative little volume, *Transnational Law*, pointing out the gaps in the traditional law and showing the multiplicity of human relationships that call for regulation by informal arrangements at lower levels, both studies involving proposals *de lege ferenda*.[126] Equally constructive, but with greater emphasis upon sociological objectives and values, was the volume by McDougal and associates, *Studies in World Public Order*, "postulating as its overriding goal the dignity of man in an increasingly universal public order," with an introductory inquiry into diverse systems of public order.[127] Reaching still further into the creative field came a volume by Jenks, *The Common Law of Mankind*, surveying the "progress toward universality" during the past hundred years and the emergence of a formal universal order, which was, however, still at an early stage of its development.[128]

Paralleling the contributions of individual scholars, but dealing with more specific problems of international law, has been the work of the International Law Commission of the United Nations, which year after year has presented reports on topics ranging from the "Draft Declaration of Rights and Duties of States" to the "Regime of the High Seas and the Law of Treaties." [129] Similar reports on inter-American regional topics have come from the Inter-American Council of Jurists and its permanent committee, the Inter-American Juridical Committee.[130] The emphasis placed by the International Commission of Jurists, a nongovernmental association of lawyers seeking the protection of human rights, upon the "Rule of Law" has had a far-reaching effect upon the legal profession, leading both to conferences of bar associations and of individual lawyers and to the expansion of the teaching of international law in American

---

[125] Compare W. Friedmann, "Some Impacts of Social Organization on International Law," *Am. Journal*, Vol. 50 (1956), p. 475; and Padelford and Lincoln, *The Dynamics of International Politics*. See also Friedmann, *The Changing Structure of International Law*.

[126] Compare also, "Diversity and Uniformity in the Law of Nations," *Am. Journal*, Vol. 58 (1964), p. 341.

[127] With a notable chapter on "Perspectives for an International Law of Human Dignity." Compare De Visscher's volume, *Theory and Reality in Public International Law*, where the emphasis is upon the sociological applications of the law; and Kaplan and Katzenbach, *The Political Foundations of International Law*, which deals constructively with what are described as "the interlocking patterns of international politics and law."

[128] The volume is reviewed at length in McDougal, *op. cit.*, p. 1020. For critical and constructive comment on the contrast between the old, "Classic," and "new" international law, see J. L. Kunz, "The Changing Science of International Law," *Am. Journal*, Vol. 56 (1962), p. 488.

[129] See the successive issues of the *U.N. Yearbooks*, as indexed under "International Law Commission."

[130] See pp. 102 ff. of the present work; also as indexed in Fenwick, *OAS*.

law schools in the form of "International Legal Studies." [131] Notable also have been the contributions of the Institute of International Law, the International Law Association, the American Society of International Law, and other similar groups of scholars and jurists.[132]

Marking the new extension of international activities into the field of economic and social relations have been numerous studies and reports coming from the specialized agencies of the United Nations, whose conclusions, although not law in themselves, constitute the necessary basis on which treaties and other lesser agreements can be put into effect. Almost every phase of human interest has been brought within the range of the activities of these specialized agencies.[133]

Supplementing the scientific studies of the International Commission of Jurists and other organized groups of lawyers has been what might be called the "field work" of the Special Committee on World Peace through Law of the American Bar Association.[134] With peace as its ultimate objective and law as the means to that end, the Committee has held a succession of continental conferences of private individual lawyers, emphasizing the procedures for the settlement of international disputes and the legal issues arising in current international relations, and seeking the collaboration of the legal profession with governments in the drafting of treaties and the development of a more effective international legal system.[135] In the more limited inter-American field, the program of the Inter-American Institute of International Legal Studies seeks to bring about the cooperation of jurists and teachers in increasing the availability of source materials and in developing standards of academic teaching in colleges and universities.[136]

Conflicting ideologies. Side by side with these developments in the field of what might be called the traditional or "classical" international

[131] Although a nongovernmental organization, the International Commission of Jurists has consultive status, Category "B," with the United Nations Economic and Social Council. *Cuba and the Rule of Law* and *Spain and the Rule of Law* represent typical studies.

[132] Specific references will appear under the particular topics to which the contributions relate.

[133] See the annual *U.N. Yearbooks;* and Chap. XXV of this work. A brief analysis of the new fields of international law may be found in L. B. Sohn, "The Many Faces of International Law," *Am. Journal,* Vol. 57 (1963), p. 868.

[134] Under the direction of Charles S. Rhyne, former president, American Bar Association. See "The Athens Conference on World Peace through Law," *Am. Journal,* Vol. 58 (1964), p. 138.

[135] Each continental conference has been accompanied by working papers in the form of an agenda for the conference. The world conference, held at Athens, 1963, concentrated upon strengthening the United Nations and the development of the procedures for the settlement of international disputes.

[136] See "Inter-American Institute for International Legal Studies," *Am. Journal,* Vol. 58 (1964), p. 122. Compare also Gutteridge, *Comparative Law: An Introduction to the Comparative Method of Legal Study and Research.*

law of the Western World has been the challenge of the new conceptions of international law coming first from the Soviet Union and later from the newly emancipated colonies and protectorates of Asia and of Africa. In spite of its acceptance of the Charter of the United Nations the Soviet Union soon showed that its interpretation of the principles of the Charter differed widely, at times fundamentally, from the interpretation of Western Europe. A rule of law, it was argued, was but a means to an end, and the end justified interpretations of the law that appeared to the Western World to be open violations of it. The ideological conception of Marxist-Leninist Communism, creating the necessity of the extension of Communism to other countries by direct or indirect means, made mutual respect for the "sovereign equality" of states, as declared in the Charter, impossible of observance; and even the acceptance of the principle of "coexistence" still left international law subordinate to the national law of dialectical materialism. Instead of being a higher law to which national law must conform, international law became a law of convenience, to be followed so long as national policies found it in their interest to do so. Even treaties were, on occasion, of doubtful binding force.[137]

It would appear that the rigidity of the Soviet conceptions of international law, as manifested in the immediate post-World War II period, is moderating; and it may be that as respect for the fundamental rights of the individual increase, respect will also increase for the equally fundamental right of self-determination by states now held as satellites. If and when these conditions are met, the ideological conflict will lose much of its significance.

In the case of the newly emancipated colonies and protectorates of Asia and Africa the resistance to the established law of the Western World has taken the more limited form of opposing all legal and practical elements associated with colonialism, including the exploitation of natural resources and the economic servitudes to which they consider that they were subjected when under foreign control. To a lesser and more subtle degree the religious philosophy of Buddhism in its various manifestations may have weakened the recognition of legal obligations in the more

[137] For a critical estimate of the attitude of the Soviet Union toward traditional international law, see M. Chakste, "Soviet Concepts of the State, International Law and Sovereignty," Am. Journal, Vol. 43 (1949), p. 21; W. W. Kulski, "The Soviet Interpretation of International Law," Am. Journal, Vol. 49 (1955), p. 518; E. McWhinney, "Peaceful Coexistence and Soviet Western International Law," Am. Journal, Vol. 56 (1962), p. 951; Kelsen, The Communist Theory of Law; Proceedings, Am. Soc. of Int. Law (1963), "Law and Conflict: Changing Patterns and Contemporary Challenges." A publication of the Academy of Sciences of the U.S.S.R., International Law, offered as a textbook for use in law schools, presents what might be described as an unofficial understanding of the law. Compare I. Lapenna, "International Law Viewed through Soviet Eyes," Yearbook of World Affairs (1961), pp. 204-232.

rigid form of treaties; but this appears to be lessening with the increasing contacts with the Western World.[138]

Collateral impact of modern technology. That the far-reaching scientific discoveries and inventions of recent years should have their effect upon rules of international law, as upon those of national law, was to be expected. National law on its part has found relatively little difficulty in modifying the rules of contract and of tort to meet the impact. But in the field of international law, where agreements are reached with greater difficulty, requiring the consent of governments with different national traditions, it has been more difficult to meet the new conditions, and on one issue of vital importance a solution is still being sought. Broadcasting is in process of regulation, or at least is not beyond it; the discharge of missiles into outer space gives promise of being brought under control; photographic inspections from beyond atmospheric limits may, like the satellites themselves, not be regarded as violating the national sovereignty of the air; but as yet the nations are still struggling with the control of the atomic bomb upon which the fundamental problem of national security depends. A generation ago the protection of the individual state by the collective action of the community was politically feasible even in spite of a recalcitrant member of the community. Today a single state in possession of the bomb can defy the community, and for the time the sole restraint upon it is the knowledge that its act might be suicidal. Law must develop faster than in the past if it is to control instruments of destruction so powerful in the hands of a state which might take the risk of its own defeat in the elimination of another.

[138] See R. P. Anand, "Role of the New Asian-African Countries in the Present International Legal Order," *Am. Journal,* Vol. 56 (1962), p. 383; M. Khadduri, "Islam and the Modern Law of Nations," *Am. Journal,* Vol. 50 (1956), p. 358; "Diverse Systems of World Public Order Today," *Proceedings,* Am. Soc. of Int. Law (1959); O. Lissitzyn, "International Law in a Divided World," *Int. Conciliation,* No. 542 (March, 1963); Roling, *International Law in an Expanded World.*

CHAPTER IV

The Determination of the Rules
of International Law

A. DIFFICULTIES OF THE PROBLEM

From the study of the general character of international law it is clear that it will frequently be difficult to determine the specific rule of international law applicable to a particular relation between states. It was said some years ago that the nations should proceed forthwith to draw up in detail the rules of international law; and having done so, they should thereafter be prepared to submit controversies as to their respective rights and duties to an international court and abide by its decisions. But the undertaking is far from being as simple as it might appear. Assuming that no more were attempted than to codify the existing rules of international law, apart from the merits of a particular rule as a standard of international conduct, the task would be a formidable one.[1] Paradoxically enough, it will be found that it is upon relatively minor matters that the rules of international law are fairly clear and definite. It is in respect to general principles and their more immediate corollaries that the area of disagreement exists.

B. SOURCES OF INTERNATIONAL LAW

It is common among jurists to speak of two main sources of international law, custom and conventions or treaties. The term *sources* has been used by writers in a number of senses. Some writers have interpreted the term to include the *causes* of international law, that is, the forces in international relations that have led to the establishment of the law, the social and economic conditions out of which the necessity of a law has arisen. Others have regarded as sources of international law certain historical facts, long-established usages and formal treaties, which have appeared to embody the consent of particular nations to be bound by a

---

[1] Codification, as a technical problem, is discussed on pp. 97 ff.

given rule. Again, a third group of writers have interpreted the word *sources* as meaning the *evidences* which bear witness to the existence of certain rules, the declarations or pronouncements or official documents which indicate that nations have recognized an obligation to do or not do certain things. While the term should be more properly applied to the historical facts which embody the recognition by states of the existence of rules of law, its use in the sense of evidences is readily explainable by the character of customary law.[2]

C. GENERAL PRINCIPLES OF RIGHT AND WRONG

When it is said that custom is one of the two sources of international law, and until the twentieth century the most important source of international law, custom must be understood to include the long-standing recognition of certain general principles as well as the established usages to which the word *custom* would seem more appropriately to apply. As we have seen, the earlier writers who sought to formulate rules of international law would have felt that they had done a poor service if they had limited their efforts to discovering what were the actual practices of nations. It was precisely because the usages of the time were contrary to what might be expected of Christian nations that Grotius made his appeal to the higher law of nature; a law to be deduced from general principles of morality, confirmed, it might be, by the practice of states, but valid whether so confirmed or not. This higher law was none other than the expression of that supreme rule of international conduct that nations, as aggregates of individual men, are bound by the same laws that govern men in their relations in civil society. Gradually these fundamental principles took more definite shape, and from constant reaffirmation under the practical conditions of international life they became more and more specific, with the result that, as sources of international law, they lost much of their *a priori* character and became tangible standards of international conduct.[3]

Transition from principle to practice. At precisely what stage it could be said that the concrete application of a general principle acquires more authority than the principle itself in its abstract form it would be difficult in many cases to determine. The principle of the good faith of treaties is constantly reaffirmed in its abstract form; it is a fundamental

---

[2] On the general subject of the sources of international law, see Finch, *The Sources of Modern International Law;* Lauterpacht, *Private Law Sources and Analogies of International Law;* Whiteman, *Digest,* Vol. I, pp. 66-103.

[3] Brierly includes "reason" as a source of international law, explaining as follows: "Reason in this connection does not mean the unassisted reasoning powers of any intelligent man, but a 'judicial' reason, which means that a principle to cover the new situation is discovered by applying methods of reasoning which lawyers everywhere accept as valid; for example, the consideration of precedents, the finding of analogies, the disengagement from accidental circumstances of the principles underlying the rules of law already established." *The Law of Nations,* p. 45.

postulate of international society; but in the course of time the rule has become associated in practical diplomatic intercourse with a number of precedents showing how the rule has been applied under practical conditions; and these precedents, in the form of customary interpretations of the principle, may perhaps be more authoritative in a particular case than the principle itself. So also the broad principle of the sanctity of the ambassadorial character came in time to be reduced from its abstract form to a number of concrete rules covering the different relations of the ambassador to the state to which he is accredited; rules which in case of a controversy would take priority over the general principle. A forced entrance of the premises of an embassy by officers of the local government would be judged today by an appeal to fixed custom rather than to the abstract principle.

In general the abstract principle will give way, perhaps it would be better to say, will be interpreted in the light of the specific rule which by time and practice has come to be regarded as the correct application of the general principle. When, in 1862, during the American Civil War, Mr. Adams appealed to Earl Russell, asserting that: "international law represents only the conscience of the peoples composing the civilized nations of the world, desirous, in the absence of any tribunal strong enough to enforce its decrees, to substitute in the place of the sword, a mode of determining differences, that has its only obligation in a general acknowledgment of certain abstract notions of right and wrong," the British Prime Minister met the appeal by pointing to customary rules of neutrality which clearly represented the accepted understanding of what was right and what was wrong under the circumstances.[4] When, again, counsel for the United States before the Bering Sea Arbitration Tribunal appealed to the "great book of the law of nature" in justification of the claims made by the United States, the ironical request of British counsel for a citation of chapter and page of the book expressed the necessary subordination of the law of nature, as interpreted by the individual claimant, to the definite rules of customary law that had developed in respect to jurisdiction over the high seas. Perhaps the customary law was wrong in point of common justice; but however that might be, it represented what nations had agreed was the correct interpretation of the general principle, and which must therefore prevail until a new rule might be adopted.[5] In like manner a principle of broader

[4] *Fontes juris gentium,* Series B, § I, Tome I, p. 113.

[5] The point was forcibly argued by Lord Stowell in the case of the *Flad Oyen,* 1 C. Rob. 135 (1799), involving the validity of the judgment of a French prize court sitting in a neutral country: "Now, it having been the constant usage, that the tribunals of the law of nations in these matters may exercise their functions within the belligerent country; if it was proved to me in the clearest manner, that on mere general theory such a tribunal might act in the neutral country, I must take my stand on the ancient and universal practice of mankind, and say that as far as that practice has gone I am willing to go, and where it has thought proper to stop, there I must stop likewise."

application, such as the territorial jurisdiction of states, must yield to one of narrower application, such as the obligation of the state to protect the life and property of aliens, which represents a qualification and restriction of the broad principle under the working conditions of international life. On the other hand, principles must prevail over practice when practice cannot be shown to be of generally acknowledged obligation.

General principles as a separate source of law. In view of the constant appeal of governments to general principles where the alleged rule of custom is not clear, it would make for greater clarity if the general principles of morality, of equity, of justice were set apart as a distinct source of international law; and if the term *custom* were limited to practices which have grown up between states and have come to be accepted as binding by the mere fact of persistent usage over a long period of time. But the separation between general principles and established usages as distinct sources of the law cannot be too rigidly made. Argument from general principles has so often been matched by argument from fixed practice that in one sense it might be said that the two processes have come from opposite directions to meet each other. It was the significant characteristic of the development of international law during the nineteenth century that jurists came to make usage and custom the starting point in the determination of the law, and the inductive method largely succeeded to the deductive. To the "Positivist" the rules of customary law represented the definite consent of states to be obligated by a particular rule; to the jurist of the Grotian School they represented inferences from fundamental principles which must be regarded as correct by the fact of being generally accepted.

In spite of differences of opinion among the jurists who formulated the Statute of the Permanent Court of International Justice it was finally decided to include "the general principles of law recognized by civilized nations" among the sources of international law to be applied by the Court; and the same source is recognized in Article 38 of the Statute of the International Court of Justice. During the intervening years scholars have sought to interpret the meaning of the term, and the Court itself has contributed its own interpretation. The fundamental principles of morality and justice, as Grotius and the Schoolmen before him understood them, are clearly included; but beyond them are the more specific principles to be found in the civil law codes and in the Anglo-Saxon common law of judicial precedents; and the further question then arises who is to determine when these principles are sufficiently "recognized" to be cited in support of a decision that is to commend itself as just in a particular controversy.[6] Obviously we are presented here

[6] The subject is critically examined in Lauterpacht, *The Development of Law by the International Court*, Chap. 9, "Judicial Legislation through Application of General Principles of Law." See also, Verdross, *Annuaire de L'Institut*, 1932, pp. 283 ff.;

with a problem that can only be solved step by step as the Court applies certain principles believed by it to be "general principles of law" and the application appears to be acceptable in the judgment of governments and jurists. In the Corfu Channel case, decided in 1949, the Court referred to "certain general and well recognized principles" as obligatory upon the Albanian authorities:

elementary considerations of humanity even more exacting in peace than in war; the principle of the freedom of maritime communication, and every State's obligation not to allow knowingly its territory to be used for acts contrary to the rights of other States.

In the earlier *Lotus* case, decided in 1927, in which the effect of the Treaty of Peace of Lausanne upon the status of Turkey was involved, the Court held that it could not construe the "principles of international law" otherwise than as meaning: ". . . the principles which are in force between all independent nations and which therefore apply equally to all the contracting parties." [7]

D. CUSTOM AS A SOURCE OF INTERNATIONAL LAW

Turning from general principles to customary law in the more limited sense of established usages which have come to be regarded as having an obligatory character, we find ourselves in the presence of a vast body of detailed rules which, until the turn of the twentieth century, constituted the chief body of international law. Many of these rules, such as those relating to maritime warfare, had their origin in the practice of a single state which was able to impose its will until the rule came to be accepted by other states without protest. Other rules, notably those relating to commerce, had their origin in the voluntary practice of a small group of states, and, being found useful and convenient, were gradually accepted by other states until the established practice became a binding rule. Customary law was thus almost of its very nature an uncertain law. Upon matters of obvious convenience there was less difficulty in determining the existence of a well-established usage and in reading into it the force of an obligatory custom. But in other cases, where there were conflicting interests, there was ample room for controversies between foreign offices. The question was, at what point in its development from particular to general usage could a practice be said to have hardened

---

1934, pp. 490 ff.; 1937, pp. 183 ff.; *Recueil des Cours,* Vol. 52 (1935-II); Jenks, *The Common Law of Mankind;* Cheng, *General Principles of Law as Applied by International Courts and Tribunals;* R. B. Schlesinger, "Research on the General Principles of Law Recognized by Civilized Nations," *Am. Journal,* Vol. 51 (1957), p. 734; W. Friedmann, "The Uses of 'General Principles' in the Development of International Law," *Ibid.,* Vol. 57 (1963), p. 279.

[7] See below, p. 324.

into custom? In the absence of an international court competent to decide according to precedent, governments were often at a loss to agree upon the number of reiterated acts which might be held to constitute regular observance, or upon the frequency of the affirmation of a particular principle necessary to show general acceptance. The small number of cases in which the facts presented were substantially the same added to the difficulty of deducing a common rule to cover the special situation.[8]

A second and more serious defect of customary law was the fact that by reason of its slow growth it could not keep pace with the changing relations of states. International law thus in many important features lagged far behind the newer phases of international relations brought about in the nineteenth century by the improvement in the means of communication between state and state and by the increasing complexity of international finance and trade. The customary law of neutrality was regularly violated in its existing form before the need of changes in the law was recognized. Moreover, customary law, being based upon precedent, was unable to fill up the gaps in international law as these were disclosed by the development of clearer conceptions of international justice. Many of the important reforms of the law came about by the action of a single state or group of states asserting claims not previously admitted and maintaining them in the face of opposition, until at last inherent justice and moral pressure succeeded in winning general recognition of the claims as legal rights.[9]

Evidences of customary law. The peculiar character of customary law, based upon the recognition of an obligation as manifested in repeated acts and professions, made it necessary to examine carefully the evidences which bore witness to the recognition by states of a particular rule, so much so that the evidences of customary law became scarcely distinguishable from the customs themselves which made up the law. Obviously the primary evidences should have been the documents of the foreign offices of the several states containing the record of international practice and the negotiations attending the settlement of international disputes.[10] But these not being generally accessible, it was left to jurists and scholars to compile the rules of international law from such historical materials as might be available to them. So important were the works of jurists in the earlier stages of international law that a number of them might properly be classed as secondary sources of the law. As we have seen, the great treatise of Grotius would have fallen short

[8] Compare, for example, the conflicting decisions of the British High Court of Admiralty and of the Supreme Court of the United States in the matter of the exemption of enemy fishing boats from capture in time of war. See below, p. 703.

[9] The right of expatriation, asserted by states in favor of their naturalized citizens, is a notable instance. See below, p. 308.

[10] See p. 93.

both of the author's high purpose and of the world's needs had he been content to do no more than record the actual practices of the nations. The urgent task, as he felt, was not to set forth the uncertain and unjust usages of the time, but to lay down better rules of conduct based upon inferences from moral principles acknowledged in the abstract but consistently violated; and his appeal from existing practice to the ideal conduct was so forcible that his words became authoritative and statesmen relied upon his judgments as the correct inference from accepted general principles. The treatise published by Vattel in 1758 won for itself the approval of statesmen as a correct statement both of abstract rules and of concrete practices; it became the reference work of foreign offices and was quoted with finality in diplomatic negotiations and in the decisions of national courts.[11]

Works of publicists as evidences.   Since the eighteenth century the works of publicists have been limited more strictly to evidences of international law. These writers, said Wheaton, writing in 1836, "are witnesses of the sentiments and usages of civilized nations, and the weight of their testimony increases every time that their authority is invoked by statesmen, and every year that passes without the rules laid down in their works being impugned by the avowal of contrary principles." [12] A sentence from the opinion of the Supreme Court of the United States in the case of the *Paquete Habana* [13] has become almost classical. The question at issue was the legality of the capture during the Spanish-American War of certain enemy fishing-vessels which it was alleged were exempt from capture by international custom. After an elaborate review of international practice in favor of such exemption and of the authorities supporting it, Justice Gray, referring to the works of jurists and commentators as witnessing the customs and usages of civilized nations, explained that:

Such works are resorted to by judicial tribunals, not for the speculations of their authors concerning what the law ought to be, but for trustworthy evidence of what the law really is.

The works of great writers must, however, be used with the caution that they have often failed to distinguish sharply enough between rules that have been generally adopted by the nations as a body and those to which two or more nations, their own included, have given their consent. Moreover, many writers have been inclined to adopt the role of advocates in the endeavor to show that the practice of their own country was the correct rule of law on controversial questions. At the present day, however, increasingly high standards of scholarship have now given us a collection of texts and monographs in which the student may

---

[11] See above, pp. 63 ff.
[12] *Elements of International Law,* § 15.
[13] 175 U.S. 677, 700 (1900). Fenwick, *Cases,* p. 12.

find the law stated with every effort on the part of the author to be strictly historical and impartial.

Decisions of international courts. Other evidences of international law, to be used with even greater caution than the works of great writers, are the decisions of international and national courts. In the case of the former, it must be observed that their jurisdiction, being purely voluntary, has in many instances arisen out of an agreement, known as a *compromis*, entered into by the parties defining the issue and at times laying down the principles by which it is to be decided.[14] In consequence, the decisions of international arbitration courts do not always, even in intent, represent the application of the rules of customary international law. Moreover, arbitration courts are not bound by the decisions of former courts as precedents, although the cases submitted to arbitration in the past have related to so wide a range of subjects that there has been little opportunity of testing the weight that might normally have been attributed to previous decisions. Decisions of the International Court of Justice, like those of its predecessor the Permanent Court of International Justice, have no binding force except between the parties and in respect to the particular case before the court. On the other hand the Court is specifically instructed to decide cases before it in accordance with international law as established by various evidences enumerated in the Statute;[15] so that its decisions, like those of its predecessor, are becoming influential precedents for future decisions, and will be in their turn not merely evidences of the correct interpretation of the law but authoritative sources of it.[16]

Decisions of national courts. With respect to the judgments of national courts, and in particular of national prize-courts, it is important to observe that they represent merely the decisions of domestic tribunals upon the points of law involved, and even when not controlled by enactments of the national legislature they tend to reflect the local interpretation of general principles. But in so far as national courts undertake to establish the true rule of international law to be applied to the case before them, their method of reasoning and their display of historical learning will have the same value as evidence of the law, and a corresponding influence upon the development of it, as the works of

[14] See, for example, the Three Rules of the Treaty of Washington, adopted in 1871 for the guidance of the Geneva Arbitration Tribunal. See below, p. 745.

[15] See below, p. 621.

[16] The subject is exhaustively treated in Lauterpacht, *The Function of Law in the International Community, passim,* and in *The Development of International Law by the Permanent Court of International Justice,* followed by *The Development of International Law by the International Court.* See also Sohn, *Cases and Materials on World Law* (1950), and *Cases on United Nations Law* (1956); Hambro, *The Case Law of the International Court* (1952), 2 vols. (1960-1961); Schwarzenberger, *International Law,* Vol. I, *International Law as Applied by International Courts and Tribunals.*

international jurists above mentioned. In the case of Thirty Hogsheads of Sugar v. Boyle,[17] Chief Justice Marshall laid down the rule that

the decisions of the courts of every country, so far as they are founded upon a law common to every country, will be received, not as authority, but with respect. The decisions of the courts of every country show how the Law of Nations, in the given case, is understood in that country, and will be considered in adopting the rule which is to prevail in this.

Sir William Scott, in the leading case of the *Maria*,[18] laid down as the true rule for the judgments of national prize-courts that it was the duty of the court

not to deliver occasional and shifting opinions to serve present purposes of national interest, but to administer with indifference that justice which the Law of Nations holds out, without distinction, to independent states, some happening to be neutral, and some belligerent: the seat of judicial authority is indeed locally here, in the belligerent country, according to the known law and practice of nations, but the law itself has no locality.

Again, in the case of the *Recovery*,[19] it was said that "it is to be recollected that this is a Court of the Law of Nations, though sitting here under the authority of the king of Great Britain. It belongs to other nations as well as to our own; and what foreigners have a right to demand from it is the administration of the Law of Nations simply."

Nevertheless, in spite of these high ideals of the duty of national prize-courts, one has only to compare the British law of prize with the claims of France and Holland at a given period to find that what is laid down by the British courts as international law is frequently the British interpretation of that law.[20] A similar bias, dictated by the emergency of the occasion, is to be observed in the decisions of the American courts in cases arising out of captures for carriage of contraband and breach of blockade during the American Civil War.[21] On the other hand, the decisions of national courts are facts, positive in character and forming a definite starting point from which rules of law may develop and have in the past developed. Their influence has in many cases been decisive in determining the policy of the home government, overruling all but the affirmative commands of the national legislature. Moreover, where

[17] 9 Cranch 191, 198 (1815). Fenwick, *Cases*, p. 21.
[18] 1 C. Rob. 340 (1799). Fenwick, *Cases*, p. 821.
[19] 6 C. Rob. 341 (1807).
[20] "It has been found, however," says Hyde, "that even when not restrained by the tenor of local statutory or other regulations, the natural prejudices of the most enlightened and scrupulous tribunal established under belligerent authority tend to weaken its impartiality and to diminish foreign respect for its conclusions." *International Law*, Vol. I, § 3. It is this limited application of judicial decisions that constitutes one of the serious objections to the teaching of international law by the exclusive use of the "case system."
[21] See below, pp. 733 ff.

founded upon what are believed by the national court to be general principles of justice as well as concrete rules of international law, these decisions have frequently been persuasive with foreign courts as evidence of the rule which it has not been possible to discover from general practice. This reciprocal influence of foreign judgments has undoubtedly tended to strengthen the general sense of a higher law pervading the international community as a whole. If international law should become ultimately a part of the law of each separate state, on a par with legislative enactments, the decisions of national courts may be expected to exercise an important influence upon the development of international law.[22] Especially is this likely if in time states should agree to permit an appeal from national courts to an international court of justice, when questions of international law are at issue.

Official documents. Within recent years it has become the practice for governments to publish volumes of official documents, such as *Papers Relating to the Foreign Relations of the United States,* containing correspondence with foreign nations, as well as decrees, proclamations, special instructions to the various branches of the government, and other acts bearing upon international relations.[23] Moore's *Digest of International Law,* published in 1906, one of the most valuable collections, was selected from the archives of the United States Department of State. During the First World War a number of governments began the practice of issuing official "white," "blue," "red," and other colored "books" containing diplomatic correspondence and governmental decrees and pronouncements. Hackworth's *Digest of International Law,* compiled in the tradition of Moore's *Digest,* made clear both the interpretation by the United States of general principles as well as the body of established usages which the United States had come to regard as having the character of international obligations.[24] In pursuance of its task of encouraging the progressive development of international law and its codification, the General Assembly of the United Nations, upon recommendation of the International Law Commission, authorized the Secretariat to prepare and distribute groups of publications which would make the evidence of customary international law more readily available, and at the same

---

[22] On the general subject, see Lauterpacht, "Decisions of Municipal Courts as a Source of International Law," *British Year Book* (1929), p. 65, not including, however, the decisions of prize courts; Wright, *The Enforcement of International Law through Municipal Law in the United States.* Art. 38 of the Statute of the International Court of Justice authorizes the Court to apply the judicial decisions of national courts as "subsidiary means for the determination of rules of law." See also the case of the *Lotus,* p. 324 of the present work.

[23] The series, beginning in 1870, is now down to 1945. It succeeded to the earlier *Am. State Papers, Foreign Relations. British and Foreign State Papers,* issued by the Foreign Office of Great Britain, reached a total of 137 volumes in 1939.

[24] Vols. I-VIII (1940-1944). It is now being continued by Whiteman, *Digest of International Law,* Vols. 1, 2, 3 (1963-1965).

time call to the attention of the governments the desirability of their publishing digests of their diplomatic correspondence.[25]

E. TREATIES AS A SOURCE OF INTERNATIONAL LAW

In contrast to general principles and to customary law, a third source of international law, now become of dominant importance, is to be found in the various treaties which embody the express consent of the nations to the rule or rules laid down in the treaty. It must be noted, however, that treaties are sources of international law only when adopted by the nations as a body. Treaties between two individual states are law as between the parties, but can obviously create no obligations on the part of other states. They have been called, for want of a better name, "particular international law." They are no more than contracts between two parties looking to their separate interests, as in the case of private contracts between citizens under municipal law. If, however, similar bilateral agreements are entered into by all the states of the world taken two by two, as in the case of extradition treaties, a point may be reached where such treaties become practically equivalent to a source of international law.

"**Law-making treaties.**" Distinct in character are the so-called "law-making treaties," entered into by a smaller or larger group of states acting in their common interest and later acquiesced in by other states or formally adhered to under a clause in the treaty inviting such adherence. The Peace of Westphalia of 1648 laid the foundations of the modern system of sovereign states. The Congress of Vienna assumed, as we have seen, the role of a great law-making body; and a number of agreements resulting from its deliberations, such as the internationalization of the Rhine and the classification of diplomatic officers, became in time the law of all Europe.[26] So also, the Declaration of Paris of 1856, originally the law merely between the limited group of signatory states, became subsequently the law of all nations in respect to privateering and certain rights of neutrals in time of maritime war.[27] The Geneva Red Cross Convention of 1864 is a similar instance of a treaty adopted by a group of powers and later adhered to by practically all states. Such treaties become a true source of international law when, and only when, the subsequent accession of a large number of states has changed the limited agreement to a general one.

Later in the nineteenth century began the series of general international conventions adopted by congresses and conferences which met to provide for the administration of certain common economic and social

[25] See *Ways and Means of Making the Evidence of Customary International Law More Readily Available*, Memorandum of the International Law Commission, 1949.

[26] See above, pp. 17 ff.

[27] See below, p. 695.

interests that had come to be recognized as calling for definite regulation.[28] Instead of seeking to regulate the conflicting claims of particular nations these conventions were concerned with the promotion of the public welfare of the whole international community. In certain cases they created "unions," or special associations of the contracting parties for the furtherance of the particular object of the agreement.[29] Conspicuous among these conventions were the Universal Postal Convention of 1874, the Convention for the Protection of Industrial Property of 1883, the Convention for the Suppression of the African Slave Trade of 1890, the International Sanitary Conventions of 1903 and 1913, the Agreements for the Suppression of the White Slave Traffic of 1904 and 1910, and the White Phosphorus Convention and the Convention Prohibiting Night Work of Women of 1906.

Conventions of the Hague Peace Conferences. The meeting of the First Hague Conference in 1899 [30] gave a more definite and recognized position to treaties as a direct, if not immediate, source of international law. At this conference important agreements, technically called "conventions," were entered into which gave universal application to certain existing usages of limited practice, abolished certain others, prescribed new rules of international conduct, defined rights, and imposed definite obligations. The Hague Conference of 1907, attended by practically the entire body of states recognized in that day, went still further in concluding general conventions, although, as in the case of the conference of 1899, the agreements related for the most part to the conduct of war. Several qualifications must, however, be made in respect to the Hague conventions as sources of international law: first they became binding only upon ratification by the several states acting individually; second, the condition attached to them, to the effect that they might be at any time denounced by those party to them upon giving due notice, made it impossible from the start to consider them as settled law; and third, certain of them were not to be binding even between the powers that had signed and ratified them in case third states, not parties to the convention, became involved.[31] It must be noted also that many of the provisions of the Hague conventions merely codified existing custom; and in consequence the rule so codified continued to be binding as customary law, even where the formal convention failed of ratification or where it came to be denounced after having been ratified.

---

[28] See Chap. XXV.

[29] See below, p. 587.

[30] With the exception of the United States and Mexico, the American republics were not represented.

[31] The failure, for example, of Serbia to ratify the several Hague conventions of 1907 relating to the conduct of war had the effect, in 1914, of rendering the conventions technically not binding upon the other belligerents who had ratified them. See below, p. 652.

Increase of multipartite treaties since 1920. With the establishment of the League of Nations in 1920 a great impulse was given to the promotion of common international interests by means of general international conventions, more accurately described as multipartite treaties. The Covenant of the League was itself a law-making treaty of first importance, prescribing new principles of international law and creating obligations for its members of a character hitherto not within the general scope of the law.[32] Conferences and congresses dealing with economic and social interests began to multiply in number, and for a time it appeared as if they might create such a large body of common interests as to offset the nationalistic tendencies in Central Europe.[33] With the establishment of the United Nations, the various "specialized agencies" were brought into relationship with the United Nations, and multipartite treaties are now the primary instrument of the development of international law.[34] The term "international legislation," used to describe them, rates them as in substance equivalent to the enactments of an international legislature, however different in point of form. At the same time the resolutions of the General Assembly, although not reaching treaty form, have come to acquire an increasingly authoritative character, still limited technically to recommendations, but actually regarded as practical conditions of cooperation in the policies of the organization.[35] The case of the resolution "Uniting for Peace" stands out conspicuously.[36] Mention has already been made of the importance of the resolutions and decisions of the numerous nongovernmental organizations, which, although lacking in obligatory character, have substantial effect in determining the policies of governments, *e.g.* the resolutions of the Institute of International Law, the International Law Association, and the more recent International Commission of Lawyers.

F. RESOLUTIONS OF INTERNATIONAL CONFERENCES

In addition to formal multipartite treaties as a source of international law mention must be made of the resolutions and declarations of international conferences, and particularly of the inter-American regional conferences and consultative meetings.[37] Jurists are not yet in accord as to the legal force of these declarations and resolutions. Inasmuch as

[32] See above, p. 25.

[33] Walters, *History of the League of Nations.*

[34] See Chap. XXV, "International Cooperation for the Promotion of Economic and Social Interests."

[35] See below, p. 214.

[36] See below, p. 222.

[37] The difficulty of obtaining ratification of formal conventions led the Lima Conference of 1938 to formulate not only its lesser agreements but its more important ones in the form of resolutions or declarations. Compare, in point of content, the Declaration of Lima with the Convention for the Maintenance, Preservation and Reestablishment of Peace, adopted at Buenos Aires in 1936.

they do not call for ratification by the regular constitutional procedure for treaties, they may seem to create purely moral obligations, similar to declarations of intention under the private law of contracts. On the other hand they have in many cases been regarded *de facto* as creating binding obligations, so that a state neglecting to comply with them may be called to account by the other parties to the declaration. Such, for example, was the attitude of the great majority of the American republics in respect to the obligations created by a number of the resolutions adopted at the Meeting of Foreign Ministers at Rio de Janeiro in 1942.[38] In 1945 the American states assembled at the Conference on Problems of War and Peace spoke of having been incorporating certain principles into their international law since 1890 "by means of conventions, resolutions and declarations." [39]

G. CODIFICATION OF INTERNATIONAL LAW

Senses in which the term is used. The term "code" has been used historically to cover a wide variety of rearrangements and restatements of the rules of law.[40] In the case of international law codification has taken three more or less distinct forms: (1) an attempt to state in systematic form the rules actually in force between states; (2) the compilation of the rules in force, modified by such amendments as have been regarded as necessary to bring the existing law into closer touch with the needs of the times and the standards of just and humane conduct; and (3) the complete reconstruction of the whole system of existing law based upon new principles and conforming to ideal standards of conduct. Few of the proposed codes have adhered to the first form. For international law has been so obviously defective in many of its branches that it would be difficult for the compiler of the code to escape the desire to improve upon existing conditions. At the same time, in view of the uncertain character of a number of the older rules of customary law, it has not been possible to draw a sharp line between rules actually in force and rules which the compiler has believed should be in force.

[38] Note, in particular, the resolution (I) on Breaking of Diplomatic Relations and the resolution (XVII) on Subversive Activities. C. G. Fenwick, "The Third Meeting of Ministers of Foreign Affairs at Rio de Janeiro," *Am. Journal,* Vol. 36 (1942), pp. 169 ff.

[39] Resolution VIII, "Reciprocal Assistance and American Solidarity." *Int. Conferences,* 1942-1954, p. 66.

[40] The literature of the subject is extensive. See, on the general subject, Alvarez, *La codification du droit international* (1912); Politis, *Les nouvelles tendances du droit international,* pp. 193 ff.; P. J. N. Baker, "The Codification of International Law," in *British Year Book,* V (1924), p. 38; addresses by J. W. Garner, A. S. de Bustamante, G. Wickersham, and others, *Proceedings,* Am. Soc. Int. Law, 1926, pp. 27, 108, 121; M. O. Hudson, "The Progressive Codification of International Law," *Am. Journal,* Vol. 20 (1926), p. 655; C. de Visscher, "La codification du droit international," *Recueil des Cours,* Vol. 6 (1925-I), p. 329; United Nations Documents, *Am. Journal,* Vol. 41 (1947), Supp., p. 29.

It should also be observed that in a number of cases the more idealistic codes have proved to be practical anticipations of the future.

A distinction should be made between codes formulated by individual jurists, or by private groups of jurists, and codes formulated by international conferences called for the specific purpose of formulating codes to be submitted to the separate states for their ratification. In many cases codes formulated by private groups, such as the Institute of International Law, have later been taken as the bases of international conventions, and have thus exercised an important influence upon the development of the law.[41]

Codification by individual writers.   In substance, if not in form and arrangement, the various texts and treatises on international law might fairly be brought under the head of codes. The older treatises of Grotius and of Vattel undertook to present both principles and practice in an orderly and logical form, and, as has been seen, their influence extended far beyond the original authority of the rules they set forth.[42] In like manner most of the more recent treatises on international law represent an attempt to set forth existing practice in a systematic arrangement. The more original of them, such as the treatises of Phillimore, Hall, Heffter, Rivier, and Nys, might, in respect to classification of subject matter and analysis of general practice, be regarded as informal codifications of the law.[43] The specific rules they set forth might readily, if the authors had so chosen, have been presented in more systematic form, accompanied by a commentary showing the origin of the rule and the extent of its practical application.

Formal codes.   Among writers who presented their subject in the strict form of a code the project of the Swiss-German jurist, Bluntschli, is outstanding.[44] This code, drawn up in 862 articles, followed the traditions of codification both in content and in form. Bluntschli announced that it was his intention "to formulate clearly the existing ideas of the civilized world." [45] Unhappily in his day this included the principle that "when controversies can not be settled by peaceful adjustment, and when arbitration appears to be impracticable, the injured state has the right to take the law into its own hands." An attempt at codification in the broader sense is to be seen in the *Draft Outlines of an International*

---

[41] In fact, with the exception of the studies undertaken by the Codification Committee of the League of Nations, the important work of codification has always been done by private bodies in advance of the meeting of the international conference.

[42] See above, pp. 59 ff.

[43] Art. 38 of the Statute of the International Court of Justice instructs the Court to apply, under restrictions as to the force of precedents, "judicial decisions and the teachings of the most highly qualified publicists of the various nations, as subsidiary means for the determination of rules of law."

[44] *Das moderne Völkerrecht der civilisirten Staaten, als Rechtsbuch dargestellt,* 3rd ed. (1878). French trans., *Le droit international codifié,* 3rd ed. (1881).

[45] Introduction, § 2.

Code, published by David Dudley Field in 1872 in the form of an international statute of 1,008 articles, supplemented with notes explaining and justifying the rules laid down.[46] More progressive than either of these was the code published first in 1890 by the Italian jurist Pasquale Fiori, under the title *Il diritto internazionali codificato e la sua sanzione giuridica.*[47] The fifth edition, published in 1915, embraced 1,985 articles covering the whole field of international law.[48] Internoscia's code, published in New York in 1910, was similarly progressive in character.[49] The code published at Rio de Janeiro, in Portuguese, by the Brazilian jurist Epitácio Pessôa, was significant not only because of its scientific character but because of its attempt to relate inter-American law to general international law.[50]

Codification of the laws of war. The American Civil War marked the beginning of a long succession of efforts to codify the laws of war. In 1863 Francis Lieber prepared, at the request of President Lincoln, a draft code of the laws of war on land, which was officially published under the title, *Instructions for the Government of the Armies of the United States in the Field.*[51] The following year, in 1864, a conference of the representatives of twelve powers met at Geneva and sought to bring together the best existing practice on the subject of measures for the relief of the wounded on the field of battle and the immunities of noncombatants engaged in caring for them, resulting in the adoption of the first Red Cross Convention.[52] Later amendments to this convention were adopted in 1868, but they failed of ratification. In 1874 the representatives of the leading powers met at Brussels, at the invitation of the Czar of Russia, to undertake a draft code of the laws of war on land. The conference drew freely upon the draft prepared by Francis

---

[46] The code was the contribution of the author to the work of a committee of the British Association for the Promotion of Social Science, which had been appointed to draw up a complete code of international law. In the preface to the first edition the author states that "the scheme embraced not only a codification of existing rules of international law, but the suggestion of such modifications and improvements as the more matured civilization of the present age should seem to require."

[47] 5th ed. (1915). Translated into English by E. M. Borchard (1918).

[48] The author describes his purpose as being "to set forth international law, taking into account the existing law and such rules as may be capable of becoming law." Borchard's trans., p. 78.

[49] *New Code of International Law.* The code was published in three languages, English, French, and Italian, in parallel columns.

[50] *Projecto de Codigo de Direito Internacional Público* (1911). Senhor Pessôa was subsequently President of Brazil, 1919-1922. For a resume of his contributions to the science of international law, see J. B. Scott, "The Gradual and Progressive Codification of International Law," *Am. Journal,* Vol. 21 (1927), pp. 417, 443.

[51] For the text of the Instructions, see Wilson, *International Law,* 8th ed., Appendix I. References to specific articles of the Instructions will be found under the laws of war.

[52] For the text of the Red Cross Convention, see Higgins, *The Hague Peace Conferences,* p. 8.

Lieber, but its code of some sixty articles, known as the Declaration of Brussels, failed of ratification.[53]

Private organizations now took up the work, and in 1880 the Institute of International Law published a *Manual of the Laws of War on Land*.[54] Numerous lesser attempts followed, but it was not until 1899 that the group of powers assembled at the Hague "International Peace Conference" succeeded in drafting the Convention Respecting the Laws and Customs of War on Land.[55] The Hague Conference of 1907 carried on the work of codification, extending it to include the rights and duties of neutral powers and persons in maritime war. At the same time the Conference adopted a number of other conventions relative to the conduct of hostilities and the mutual relations of the belligerents.[56] By this time, however, the humanitarian aspect of the codification of the laws of war had become subordinated to the political; and the leading military and naval powers were primarily concerned with adopting rules from which they might derive a relative advantage in the coming war which they looked upon as inevitable. The London Naval Conference of 1908-1909 undertook the more difficult task of the codification of the "generally recognized principles of international law" in respect to maritime war; but here the conflict of interests was irreconcilable.[57] When war actually came only the fundamentally humanitarian provisions of the Hague codes survived, and even these could not stand the strain of new instruments of warfare.

Codification under auspices of the League of Nations. The years following the First World War and the establishment of the League of Nations witnessed a concentration of effort upon the codification of various branches of the substantive law.[58] A new direction was given to codification by the Committee of Experts for the Progressive Codification of International Law appointed by the Council of the League of Nations in pursuance of a resolution of the Assembly of September 22, 1924. This committee submitted a series of questionnaires to the several governments, as a result of which seven subjects were submitted as "ripe" for codification.[59] At its meeting in September, 1927, the Assembly of the League of Nations adopted a resolution deciding to submit for

[53] For the text of the declaration, see Higgins, *op. cit.*, p. 273.

[54] See the *Annuaire* of the Institute; also *Resolutions of the Institute of International Law*, edited by J. B. Scott (1916).

[55] For the text of the convention, see Scott, *Hague Conventions and Declarations*, p. 100.

[56] For the texts, see *ibid.*, pp. 41 ff.

[57] For the text, see Higgins, *op. cit.*, p. 540; Charles, *Treaties*, p. 266. The Declaration failed of ratification. See above, p. 23.

[58] The Washington Conference of 1921-1922 went beyond its primary task of agreeing upon a limitation of armaments by drawing up rules of warfare restricting the use of poisonous gases and the methods of submarine warfare; but its labors in this field must be classed rather as new legislation than as the codification of existing law.

[59] *Am. Journal*, Vol. 22 (1928), Special Supp., p. 4.

examination to a first Codification Conference the questions of Nationality, Territorial Waters, and Responsibility of States for Damage Done in Their Territory to the Person or Property of Foreigners.[60] A preparatory committee was appointed to prepare bases of discussion for the conference. The conference itself met at The Hague in March-April, 1930, and succeeded in drawing up a Convention on Nationality which was signed by thirty-one states.[61] The two other questions were left for future consideration.[62]

Codification by scientific associations. Paralleling the work of the League of Nations were the efforts of numerous scientific bodies, among which may be mentioned the Institute of International Law, the International Law Association, and a group known as Research in International Law, working under the direction of Manley O. Hudson. The Institute of International Law made notable contributions in almost every branch of the law: the status of aliens, denial of justice, competence of courts in regard to foreign states, navigation, nationality, treaties, diplomatic privileges, the laws of war and of neutrality, and numerous other topics.[63] The International Law Association prepared projects both in the field of substantive and of procedural law.[64] Its most notable contribution, the so-called "Budapest Articles of Interpretation of the Pact of Paris," fell outside the strict field of codification.[65] Research in International Law prepared a series of draft codes upon a number of topics considered ripe for codification, collaborating as far as possible with the work of the League of Nations. The codes prepared by the Harvard Research were accompanied by elaborate commentaries explaining the relation of the proposed rule to the existing law and justifying the position taken by the group.[66]

[60] *Am. Journal,* Vol. 22 (1928), Special Supp., p. 231.

[61] For the text of the convention, see *Am. Journal,* Vol. 24 (1930), Supp., pp. 192 ff. For a discussion of the convention, see below, pp. 311 ff.

[62] On the question of codification in connection with the work of the League of Nations, see M. O. Hudson, "The First Conference for the Codification of International Law," *Am. Journal,* Vol. 24 (1930), p. 447. For adverse criticism, see J. L. Brierly, "The Future of Codification," *British Year Book,* Vol. XII (1931), p. 1.

[63] *Annuaire de l'Institut de Droit International.* The Institute was founded in 1873 at Ghent, in Belgium; it meets periodically and its codification projects are to be found in the successive issues of the *Annuaire.* See J. B. Scott, "The Institute of International Law," *Am. Journal,* Vol. 21 (1927), pp. 716 ff.

[64] The Association was founded in 1873 under the title Association for the Reform and Codification of the Law of Nations.

[65] See below, p. 278.

[66] Taken as a whole, the work of Harvard Research was the most important contribution to the codification of international law during the period between the two world wars. The codes related to Nationality, Responsibility of States for Damage Done in their Territory to the Person or Property of Foreigners, Territorial Waters, Diplomatic Privileges and Immunities, Legal Position and Functions of Consuls, Competence of Courts in Regard to Foreign States, Piracy, Law of Extradition, Jurisdiction with Respect to Crime, Law of Treaties, Rights and Duties of Neutral States in Naval and Aerial War, and Rights and Duties of States in Case of Aggression.

During this period the older conception of codification as a systematic presentation of the whole body of international law was abandoned, and it came to be generally recognized by scholars that the work of codification must be carried out topic by topic if it was to make any significant contribution to the development of international law. At the same time it had come to be realized that until the problem of collective security could be solved there were many fields of international relations which could not be brought for the time within the framework of rigid rules of law. The uncertainty as to the success of the system of collective security established by the League of Nations also explains how scientific bodies could devote so much of their attention to codes of land and maritime warfare.[67] Harvard Research, finding it impossible to secure agreement among its members in respect to a proposed codification of the traditional law of neutrality, compromised by preparing two codes, one on the Rights and Duties of Neutral States in Naval and Aerial War and a second on Rights and Duties of States in Case of Aggression.[68] Both were doomed to witness a war in which rules of law hitherto believed to impose restraints upon belligerents were swept away by a tidal wave of fanatical lawlessness unknown in modern times.

Codification of inter-American law. The inter-American community, from the time of its first organization as a regional group, has manifested a special interest in the work of codifying international law and has established special agencies to that end. As early as the conference held at Mexico City in 1901-1902, a convention was signed providing for the formation of codes on public and private international law.[69] The Conference of 1906 assigned the work of codification to an International Commission of Jurists, to be composed of one member from each of the signatory states.[70] Distinct from this commission was the unofficial group of jurists who, in 1915, formed the American Institute of International Law.[71] The Institute, although unofficial in character, cooperated closely with the steps taken by the several inter-American conferences. Its first code was published in Washington in 1916 under the title "Declaration of the Rights and Duties of Nations." [72] In 1924,

[67] See the drafts prepared by the Institute of International Law and the International Law Association, as well as the drafts prepared by the Commission of Jurists which met at The Hague in 1922-1923 in pursuance of a resolution of the Washington Conference on the Limitation of Armament.

[68] The second of the two codes was an ingenious attempt to reconcile neutrality with the principle of collective security.

[69] *International Conferences of American States,* 1889-1928, p. 69.

[70] *Ibid.,* p. 144.

[71] The organization of this body and its objectives are described in *The American Institute of International Law: Its Declaration of the Rights and Duties of Nations.*

[72] For the text of the Declaration, see *op. cit.,* p. 87.

the Institute, acting upon invitation of the Governing Board of the Pan American Union, submitted a series of thirty "projects of conventions," which were in turn transmitted to the International Commission of Jurists. The Commission, meeting in Rio de Janeiro in 1927, elaborated a series of twelve "projects of international public law," unofficially designated as "American international law." [73] These projects were presented to the International Conference of American States which met at Havana in 1928, and seven of them were adopted as conventions. These dealt respectively with the following topics: (1) The Status of Aliens, (2) Duties of Neutral States in the Event of Civil Strife, (3) Treaties, (4) Diplomatic Functionaries, (5) Consular Agents, (6) Maritime Neutrality, and (7) Asylum. [74]

Thereafter the American states sought to promote the work of codification by creating new agencies: the Permanent Committees of Rio de Janeiro, Havana, and Montevideo, [75] the Committee of Experts, consisting of seven jurists, and a new International Conference of American Jurists to be endowed with plenipotentiary powers. [76] Upon the outbreak of war in 1939 the Inter-American Neutrality Committee was created, and in 1940 it was assigned the function of preparing a draft convention which was to cover "all the principles and rules generally recognized in international law in matters of neutrality." [77] In 1942, after the entrance of the United States into the war, the Inter-American Juridical Committee, successor to the Neutrality Committee, was called upon "to develop and coordinate the work of codifying international law, without prejudice to the duties entrusted to other existing organizations." [78] Three years later, the Conference on Problems of War and Peace, meeting at Mexico City, sought to organize the work of codification more effectively by recommending to the American Governments that the Inter-American Juridical Committee be entrusted with "the

[73] For the texts of the projects, see *Am. Journal,* Vol. 22 (1928), Supp., pp. 234 ff.

[74] *Int. Conferences of Am. States,* 1889-1928, pp. 415-436; *Am. Journal,* Vol. 22 (1928), Supp., pp. 136 ff. The Conference at Havana also adopted a Convention on Private International Law, to which the Bustamante Code was attached. Conventions were also adopted at the Montevideo Conference of 1933, dealing with nationality, the nationality of married women, extradition, and political asylum. *Int. Conferences,* 1933-1940, pp. 106 ff.

[75] *Ibid.,* Resolution, "Future Codification of International Law," p. 439.

[76] *Int. Conferences of Am. States,* 1933-1940, "Methods of Codification of International Law," p. 84.

[77] Second Meeting of Ministers of Foreign Affairs, at Havana, 1940. *Int. Conferences,* p. 349.

[78] In pursuance of the functions thus assigned to it the Juridical Committee made a "Recommendation on a Reorganization of the Agencies Engaged in the Codification of International Law," accompanied by a report analyzing the existing agencies and their respective functions. *Recommendations and Reports,* p. 104.

functions of a central agency for the codification of public international law." [79]

The International Law Commission. The Charter of the United Nations makes provision that the General Assembly shall initiate studies and make recommendations for the purpose of "promoting international cooperation in the political field and encouraging the development of international law and its codification." The General Assembly established the International Law Commission, consisting at first of fifteen members and enlarged to twenty-one in 1956, the members serving not as representatives of governments but in their individual capacities as experts in international law. [80] The work of the Commission has been extensive, including among its draft projects and recommendations a declaration on the rights and duties of states, a code of offenses against the peace and security of mankind, reservations to multilateral conventions, the elimination or reduction of future statelessness, ways and means for making the evidence of customary international law more readily available, diplomatic intercourse and immunities, and an elaborate report on the law of the sea in time of peace. The Statutes of the International Law Commission interpret the "progressive development of international law" as relating to the preparation of draft conventions "on subjects which have not yet been regulated by international law or in regard to which the law has not yet been sufficiently developed in the practice of states"; while "codification" describes "the more precise formulation and systematization of rules of international law in fields where there already has been extensive State practice, precedent, and doctrine." [81] The draft project laying the basis for the Convention on the Territorial Sea, adopted by the Geneva Conference on the Law of the Sea in 1958, is perhaps the best example of codification in the strict sense.

---

[79] *Final Act,* Resolution XXV, "Reorganization of the Agencies Engaged in the Codification of International Law."

The literature of the codification of international law in America is extensive. See, in particular, the works of Alejandro Alvarez, *Le nouveau droit international public et sa codification en Amérique* (1924); *La reconstruction du droit international et sa codification en Amérique; Le continent américain et la codification du droit international;* and numerous articles in current periodicals; Urrutia, *Le continent américain et le droit international* (1928). For a survey of the codification of international law in the Inter-American System, see the *Outline* prepared by Division of the Development and Codification of International Law of the United Nations, *Am. Journal,* Vol. 41 (1947), Supp., p. 116; Fenwick, *OAS,* Chap. VIII.

[80] On the organization and activities of the International Law Commission, see the *U.N. Yearbooks,* accompanied by the *Annual Reports* of the Commission itself. Also, in summary, *Everyman's United Nations,* 1964. See also Whiteman, *Digest,* Vol. 1, pp. 171 ff.

[81] Compare H. Lauterpacht, "Codification and Development of International Law," *Am. Journal,* Vol. 49 (1955), p. 16; R. Y. Jennings, "The Progressive Development of International Law and its Codification," *British Year Book,* 1947, p. 301.

Paralleling the work of the International Law Commission of the United Nations has been the work of the Inter-American Council of Jurists assisted by its "permanent committee," the Inter-American Juridical Committee. The Charter of the Organization of American States makes the same distinction between the development and the codification of international law as is made in the Charter of the United Nations, but in practice it has been recognized that the two tasks complement each other and have an organic relationship. While efforts to codify the law of the recognition of *de facto* governments failed, as did similar efforts to codify the law of the responsibility of the state, agreement was reached upon a Convention on Territorial Asylum and a Convention on Diplomatic Asylum, and important reports were issued on extradition, reservations to multilateral treaties, and topics of private international law.[82]

Future of codification. It is clear that the technical work of codification and the development of international law in the various fields in which national interests are in conflict depends and will continue to depend upon the degree of mutual confidence that exists in the international community. A few of the lesser interests of the nations may yield to agreements of codification, but until collective security can be attained and the issue of national defense loses something of its dominant character, governments will doubtless continue to hesitate to commit themselves to treaty obligations which they believe may limit their freedom of action in unforeseen ways. Progress for the present will more likely be in the direction of agreements in noncontroversial economic and social fields, leaving political issues to be settled item by item as the particular problem arises, in other words by a procedure that would fall under the "development" rather than the codification of the law.

It was to be expected that the successive decisions of the Permanent Court of International Justice and of its successor the International Court of Justice would have a significant influence upon the development of international law, in spite of the fact that the Statutes of both Courts provide that their decisions have no binding force except between the parties and in respect to the particular case. The fact that a decision cannot be cited as a binding precedent does not prevent it from entering into the general body of "evidence of a general practice accepted as law" and thus forming "subsidiary means for the determination of rules of law," in the terms of Article 38 of the two Statutes.[83] Thus the

---

[82] See Fenwick, *OAS*, Chap. VIII; Whiteman, *Digest,* Vol. 1, pp. 140 ff., where individual topics are listed.

[83] See Lauterpacht, *The Development of International Law by the Permanent Court of International Justice;* and *The Development of International Law by the International Court;* Schwarzenberger, *International Law,* Vol. I, *International Law as Applied by International Courts and Tribunals; The Case Law of the International Court.*

decision of the International Court in the Fisheries Case had an acknowledged effect, even to the point of the phrases used, upon the adoption of the provisions of the Convention on the Territorial Sea in respect to the marginal sea.[84]

[84] See below, pp. 453 ff.

CHAPTER V

The Relation of International Law
to Municipal Law

A. DIFFERENT SPHERES IN WHICH INTERNATIONAL
LAW AND MUNICIPAL LAW OPERATE

International law is, in its formal aspects, a law governing the relations of states. Its precepts, whether in the form of customary law or of treaties and conventions, are addressed directly to states.[1] But the international community possesses no executive organ competent to act by its own agents for the enforcement of its rules; it has no judicial organ with authority in its own name to apply the rules of law to specific cases.[2] Hence if the rules of international law are to be put into effect they must be put into effect through the governmental organs of the separate states. Each separate state, however, has its own national constitution, and its own internal system of legislative, executive, and judicial powers which function in accordance with the provisions of the constitution. What, then, is the relation within a given state between the two systems of law? If, in principle, international law must of necessity take priority over the law of the individual state, how is this priority actually made effective in case of a conflict between international law and the provisions of the constitution of the state, or between international law and the authority and functions of the various agencies of the national government? More specifically, how far, if at all, has international law been incorporated into national law so as to insure its ap-

[1] For a discussion of the position maintained by a number of jurists that individuals may to a certain extent be subjects of international law, see below, pp. 147 ff.

[2] Except to the limited extent of the authority of the Security Council of the United Nations to prevent the use of force in the settlement of disputes. See below, p. 214.

plication in the ordinary course of the activities of the government of the particular state? [3]

Areas of conflict. The problem would not be a difficult one if the rules of international law were precise and definite on all points, so that it might be at all times possible to say just where the rights of a state and its corresponding duties begin and end. But this is not to be expected in international law when even in the constitutional law of federal states there are constant conflicts of jurisdiction between the central government and the local governments of the members of the union. In the practical relations of states the areas of conflict between international law and municipal law are largely in matters of jurisdiction.[4] A state, for example, has a primary right to exercise jurisdiction over all persons within its territorial boundaries, whether citizens or aliens; it has also a duty to protect aliens in accordance with the standards of international law. In the event of the passage by the legislature of a state of a law confiscating the property of aliens, the executive officers of the state would obviously be bound to execute the national law in spite of the fact that they might believe it to be in violation of international law; and the courts of the state would equally be bound to deny redress to the alien even if they too were convinced that the act of the legislature controvened the rights of the alien under international law. In both cases there would be a conflict between international and municipal law; and while the executive and judicial agencies of the state would be justified in their conduct by constitutional law, the state itself, as a corporate person, would remain bound by the international obligation. Similar situations might arise if the legislature of the state were to extend the provisions of the criminal law over a wider area of the marginal sea than is recognized by international law as coming within the protective jurisdiction of the state.[5]

---

[3] For a discussion of the general connection between the two branches of law, see Wright, *The Enforcement of International Law through Municipal Law in the United States* (1916); "International Law in Its Relation to Constitutional Law," *Am. Journal,* Vol. 17 (1923), p. 234; E. D. Dickinson, "Changing Concepts and the Doctrine of Incorporation," *ibid.,* Vol. 26 (1932), p. 239; Masters, *International Law in National Courts* (1932); Picciotto, *The Relation of International Law to the Law of England and of the United States of America;* B. Mirkine-Guétzévitch, *Le Droit constitutionnel dans ses rapports avec le droit international public;* Triepel, *Völkerrecht und Landesrecht,* trans. into French by Brunet as *Droit International et droit interne.* For the relation of the subject to the monistic and dualistic theories of the nature of international law, see above, pp. 74 ff.

[4] See, for example, the case of the *Lotus* (p. 324) where the exercise of territorial jurisdiction claimed by Turkey came in conflict with jurisdiction claimed by France over the officer of a French vessel.

[5] It should be observed that in the number of cases in which the courts of the United States have applied the provisions of acts of Congress in derogation of either general international law or specific treaty obligations, they have not been unmindful of the wrongful conduct of the legislative branch of the government; but they have recognized that it was not their function to afford redress for the breach of interna-

In like manner, if for want of action by the national legislature, the executive department or the courts are unable to exert the necessary control over individuals to prevent them from committing acts for which the state will be held responsible, there is no alternative but for the executive and judicial agencies to stand by and witness the violation of international law, admitting, it may be, their responsibility to the foreign state, but unable to act for want of constitutional power.[6] In the United States, under a federal constitution, it has more than once happened that the executive department was unable to make a specific form of redress to a foreign state because of alleged lack of constitutional power to coerce the agencies of an individual state of the Union.[7]

Obligations under treaties. The international obligations of a state under treaties and conventions frequently give rise to conflicts between international and national law. Obviously a treaty, duly ratified in accordance with constitutional procedures, becomes a binding obligation upon a state.[8] But suppose that the treaty can only be made effective by the passage of a legislative act, and the legislative branch of the government refuses to pass the act. What is the standing of the treaty before the executive department of the state and before the national courts? Or suppose that subsequent to the ratification of the treaty the legislature of the state should pass a law in contravention of its terms. Must the executive and the judicial departments give effect to the treaty or to the legislative act in violation of it?

In all of these cases there is no question of the duty of the state in respect to other states. The international obligation remains, whatever be the conduct of the agencies of the government as determined by the constitution of the state. International law is binding upon the state as a corporate person, and no provision of the national constitution or act of

---

tional law. That must be effected through diplomatic channels. See Whitney v. Robertson, 124 U.S. 190 (1888), citing Taylor v. Morton, 2 Curtis, 454 (1855). Hudson, *Cases,* p. 898; Fenwick, *Cases,* p. 604; Bishop, *Cases,* p. 150.

[6] It must be confessed that the too free use of the British and American phrase that "international law is part of the law of the land" has led to some confusion of thought. At the present day, acts of the British Parliament and acts of the United States Congress unquestionably take priority over international law in so far as the domestic administration of the two countries is concerned.

[7] See p. 339. The Constitution of the United States is perhaps unique in permitting the possibility of a situation where the Federal Government may be unable on occasion to fulfil its international obligations by reason of lack of power to coerce individuals over whom the separate state governments of the Union have primary jurisdiction. For the practice of the Latin American states, see J. B. Moore and G. G. Wilson, addresses on "The Relation of International Law to National Law in the American Republics," *Proceedings,* Am. Soc. of Int. Law, 1915, pp. 11, 23.

[8] The Constitution of the United States, Art. VI, provides: "This Constitution, and the laws of the United States which shall be made in pursuance thereof; and all treaties made, or which shall be made, under the authority of the United States, shall be the supreme law of the land." For the situation in France, see A. Mestre, *Recueil des Cours,* Vol. 38 (1931-IV), p. 237.

the national legislature or decree of the executive or judicial agencies can change the force of its provisions in so far as the legal relations of the state toward other states are concerned.[9] The foreign state which finds itself injured in consequence of positive acts of governmental officers, or in consequence of their inability to act, can always press its claims through diplomatic channels and hold the delinquent government to account. The problem before us is rather one of the adaptation of national law to international law, of the ways and means by which international law may be incorporated into the law of the state, so as to avoid controversies between states and the necessity of resorting to diplomatic negotiations for their settlement.

B. ENFORCEMENT OF INTERNATIONAL LAW BY MUNICIPAL LAW

But while in the case of a direct conflict between national and international law, the rule of national law will of necessity take priority until changed to conform to the international obligations of the state, there are numerous cases in which the provisions of the national constitution or the provisions of a particular legislative act are not so explicit but that they may be interpreted so as to enable the executive and the judicial agencies of the state to act in accordance with the obligations of international law. It is within this doubtful field that the executive and the judicial agencies of the different states have been free to act according to their own conceptions of the validity of the alleged international obligation, some states going further than others in their readiness to recognize the obligatory force of international law. A study of some of these reactions will throw light upon the problem of bringing municipal law more into line with international law in the future.

Practice of Great Britain. In Great Britain, doubtless owing to the

---

[9] This is a well-established principle, although frequently misunderstood. In reply to an assertion of the Cuban Government that it was legally unable to arbitrate certain claims of the British and other governments because to do so would infringe constitutional provisions limiting the liabilities of Cuba, the Department of State of the United States replied that "a government is not permitted to set up, as a final answer to demands for the performance of international obligations, provisions of its municipal law, either constitutional or statutory." Hackworth, *Digest,* Vol. I, p. 28. Schwarzenberger lists seven cases in support of his statement that the rule that municipal law which is contrary to international law can not be pleaded before an international court as an excuse for the nonfulfilment by a state of its obligations under international law has been affirmed and elaborated by the Permanent Court of International Justice "into one of the corner-stones of its jurisprudence." *International Law,* Vol. I, p. 21. In commenting upon the judgment of the Permanent Court regarding *Certain German Interests in Polish Upper Silesia,* Series A, No. 7, the author observes: "This means that the Court does not see any difference in kind between legislative and judicial activities of a State and its administrative and purely political acts. They are no more and no less than sets of facts which either are compatible with international law or, if not, involve State responsibility under international law. International law provides its own and exclusive standards by which all these various activities are to be measured." P. 20.

authority of the common law as a rule of precedent, international law
was early said to be incorporated into the body of municipal law. Blackstone, the legal authority of his time, asserted in 1765 that the law of
nations "is here adopted in its full extent by the common law, and is
held to be a part of the law of the land." [10] In the case of Triquet v.
Bath,[11] decided in 1764, in which the privileges of foreign ministers and
their domestic servants were at issue, Lord Mansfield quoted from an
earlier case (Buvot v. Barbuit) the opinion of Lord Talbot to the effect
"that the law of nations, in its full extent, was part of the law of England," and that an act of Parliament (7 Ann., c. 12) merely provided
summary jurisdiction where ordinary jurisdiction would otherwise have
been exercised. But in this case there was no conflict between the two
systems, but rather a question which of two municipal procedures was
applicable to the case. By contrast, in the case of Queen v. Keyn,[12] the
court held by a bare majority that it could not, in the absence of an
act of Parliament extending its jurisdiction over crimes committed in
the maritime belt, sustain the conviction for manslaughter of a German
captain whose ship had come into collision with a British ship, resulting
in the death of a passenger. The immediate issue in this case, however,
was not the authority of international law, but the jurisdiction of the
court over the marginal sea.[13]

The question of the authority of international law before the British
courts was raised again in 1905 in the case of West Rand Central Gold
Mining Company v. Rex.[14] Here the court, while dismissing the contention of the petitioners that Great Britain, as the conquering country,
was bound to fulfil the obligations of the Transvaal Government to the
company resulting from the confiscation of its property, found it desirable to add "a word of explanation and comment" upon the proposition that international law formed part of the law of England. It was
true, said the court, that whatever had received the common consent
of civilized nations must have received the assent of England, and that
as international law it would be acknowledged and applied by the
courts when occasions arose calling for its application. The court said:

But any doctrine so invoked, must be one really accepted as binding between
nations, and the international law sought to be applied must, like anything
else, be proved by satisfactory evidence, which must show either that the

---

[10] *Commentaries on the Laws of England*, Bk. IV, Chap. 5.
[11] 3 Burr. 1478 (1764). Fenwick, *Cases*, p. 36.
[12] L. R. 2 Ex. Div. 43 (1874). Fenwick, *Cases*, p. 529.
[13] For comment, see Picciotto, *Relation of Int. Law to the Law of England*, pp. 86 ff.
The decision was followed by the passage in 1878 of the Territorial Waters Jurisdiction Act, conferring jurisdiction upon the courts for the future. See below, p. 444.
[14] L. R. 2 K. B. 391 (1905). Fenwick, *Cases*, pp. 38, 131; Hudson, *Cases*, p. 723;
Briggs, *Cases*, p. 218.

particular proposition put forward has been recognized and acted upon by our country, or that it is of such a nature, and has been so widely and generally accepted, that it can hardly be supposed that any civilized state would repudiate it. The mere opinions of jurists, however eminent and learned, that it ought to be so recognized, are not in themselves sufficient. They must have received the express sanction of international agreement, or gradually have grown to be part of international law by their frequent practical recognition in dealings between various nations.[15]

A year later, however, a Scottish court treated the authority of international law with much less courtesy. Mortensen, the master of a Norwegian vessel, was convicted for acts, in violation of an act of Parliament, committed in Moray Firth outside the three-mile limit.[16] The court had no alternative but to apply the act of Parliament:

In this Court we have nothing to do with the question of whether the legislature has or has not done what foreign powers may consider a usurpation in a question with them. Neither are we a tribunal sitting to decide whether an act of the legislature is *ultra vires* as in contravention of generally acknowledged principles of international law.

But having thus disposed of the conflict between international law and municipal law, the Court went on to observe:

It is a trite observation that there is no such thing as a standard of international law, extraneous to the domestic law of a kingdom, to which appeal may be made. International law, so far as this Court is concerned, is the body of doctrine regarding the international rights and duties of States which has been adopted and made part of the law of Scotland.[17]

Upon protest, however, from Norway the British Foreign Office released the prisoners and interpreted the act of Parliament as applying only to British subjects.

Practice of the United States.   In the United States the necessary adjustment of municipal law to meet the obligations of international law has been passed upon in numerous judicial decisions and has been the object of a considerable body of statutory legislation.[18] In the first place the courts have undertaken, even in the absence of special legislation conferring jurisdiction upon them, to apply the rules of international

[15] For comment upon this much discussed case, see Scott, "The Legal Nature of International Law," *Am. Journal,* Vol. 1 (1907), pp. 855 ff.

[16] Mortensen v. Peters, 14 Scots L. J. R. 227 (1906). Fenwick, *Cases,* p. 42; Bishop, *Cases,* p. 78; Briggs, *Cases,* p. 52.

[17] The decision was the cause of much unfavorable comment from scholars who looked upon it as reflecting upon the authority of international law. The *obiter dicta* were unfortunate, but the conclusion reached by the court was sound. Compare a similar attitude on the part of the court in *The Over The Top* case where a British vessel was seized outside the three-mile limit. Hackworth, *Digest,* Vol. I, p. 26.

[18] The subject is treated in detail in Wright, *The Enforcement of International Law through Municipal Law in the United States.*

law in proper cases presented to them. In the case of the *Nereide*,[19] Chief Justice Marshall declared that the court, until an act of Congress should be passed, was "bound by the law of nations, which is a part of the law of the land"; and in an earlier case, Murray v. The Charming Betsy,[20] the chief justice went so far as to say that the interpretation of an act of Congress should never be such as to violate the law of nations if any other possible construction remained. An even more explicit affirmation of the implied adoption of international law is contained in the case of the *Paquete Habana*,[21] decided in 1899, in which the court declared that

international law is part of our law, and must be ascertained and administered by the courts of justice of appropriate jurisdiction, as often as questions of right depending upon it are duly presented for their determination.

After a review of the precedents and authorities on the subject the court found evidence, independently of any express treaty or act of municipal law, of the existence of a customary rule of international law

that coast fishing vessels, with their implements and supplies, cargoes and crews, unarmed and honestly pursuing their peaceful calling of catching and bringing in fresh fish, are exempt from capture as prize of war.

In contrast with these decisions the Supreme Court of the United States has had no hesitation in recognizing the priority of legislative enactments when passed not only in contravention of established custom but even of the provisions of a specific treaty. In the Head Money Cases [22] the Court, meeting the objection to the validity of a tax on immigrants as being in violation of "numerous treaties of our government with friendly nations," observed that:

A treaty, then, is a law of the land as an act of Congress is, whenever its provisions prescribe a rule by which the rights of the private citizen or subject may be determined. And when such rights are of a nature to be enforced in a court of justice, that court resorts to the treaty for a rule of decision for the case before it as it would to a statute.

Nevertheless, added the Court:

so far as a treaty made by the United States with any foreign nation can become the subject of judicial cognizance in the courts of this country, it is subject to such acts as Congress may pass for its enforcement, modification, or repeal.

[19] 9 Cranch 388 (1815). See below, p. 732.
[20] 2 Cranch 64 (1804). Scott and Jaeger, *Cases,* p. 161.
[21] 175 U.S. 677 (1900). Fenwick, *Cases,* p. 17; Bishop, *Cases,* p. 24; Briggs, *Cases,* p. 30. The principle was carried so far in the Sabbatino case as to lead the court to apply the "act of state" doctrine in the face of clear evidence of the illegality of the act of the Cuban government. See below, p. 347.
[22] 112 U.S. 580 (1884). Fenwick, *Cases,* p. 45.

In the case of Cunard Steamship v. Mellon,[23] involving the application of the Eighteenth Amendment and the National Prohibition Act of 1919 to foreign vessels in port, the Court was unwilling to read into the law an exception in favor of such vessels in spite of the established custom, recognized in a dissenting opinion, against interference by the local government with the internal affairs of the vessel.

Legislative measures. In addition to jurisdiction assumed by the courts in cases involving questions of international law, there exists in the United States, as in Great Britain and other countries, a large body of legislation directed explicitly to the enforcement of the obligations of international law. While leaving the executive department free to exercise discretion in the determination of what are known as "political questions," Congress has undertaken in other cases to guide the hands of the President and the administrative departments. Moreover, acting in pursuance of authority expressly conferred by the Constitution,[24] Congress has enacted penal laws prohibiting citizens and others from committing within the territory of the United States acts for which the nation would be held responsible as a violation of an international duty. Prominent among such statutes were the neutrality laws passed in 1793 and 1818, defining in detail the acts which, if done by individuals upon the soil of the country, would in the judgment of the United States compromise its position as a neutral state.[25] The British Foreign Enlistment Acts of 1819 and 1870 were similar illustrations of legislation in fulfilment of international obligations calling for positive legislation.

Practice of other states. The position taken by Great Britain and the United States in respect to the relation of international law to municipal law has been described by certain writers as the "Anglo-Saxon" attitude in contradistinction to the "Continental" attitude. But the contrast between the two attitudes has been less sharp in practice than in theory.[26] Much confusion has been caused by the failure to distinguish sharply between the international responsibility of the state for the fulfilment of its obligations under international law and the powers of the legis-

---

[23] 262 U.S. 100 (1923). Fenwick, *Cases,* p. 354; Hudson, *Cases,* p. 615; Bishop, *Cases,* p. 505. The decision was generally regarded at the time as an unduly rigid interpretation of the law.

[24] Art. I, § 8: [The Congress shall have the power] "to define and punish piracies and felonies committed on the high seas, and offenses against the law of nations."

[25] See below, p. 743. The acts passed from 1935-1939 were understood to be in excess of the strict obligations of neutrality, just as the act of 1818 fell short of them during the war from 1914-1917.

In contrast, note the alleged inability on occasion of the United States to fulfil its international obligations by reason of lack of power on the part of the Federal Government to coerce individuals over whom the separate state governments of the Union had primary jurisdiction. See below, p. 339.

[26] See Antokoletz, *Tratado de derecho internacional público,* Primera Parte, pp. 58 ff.; Accioly, *Tratado* (Spanish ed.), Vol. 1, pp. 16 ff.; Moreno, *Derecho Internacional Público,* Vol. I, pp. 39 ff.

lative, judicial, and administrative agencies of the state under its national constitution. The violations of international law during the First World War led to an effort to incorporate international law more fully into the municipal law of each state; but in the absence of a more definite and specific body of law little progress was made beyond broad statements of principle. It is significant that the Weimar Constitution, adopted by the German Republic on August 11, 1919, and the Austrian Constitution of 1920 both expressly provided that the generally recognized rules of international law should be constituent parts of their federal law,[27] and the provisions of the Weimar Constitution were repeated in the German Federal Republic Constitution of 1949. But while these provisions might seem to give a broad recognition to the doctrine that the obligations of international law must be "transformed" into municipal obligations, neither in Germany nor in Austria nor in any other of the leading countries of Europe or of America was the principle accepted that the courts of the state should give priority to the rules of international law under all circumstances. Distinctions and qualifications were invariably made which reduced the general principle to a conditional rule.[28]

Latin American states. Among the Latin American states the relations of international law to municipal law have been the subject of much controversy, and it has been said that the Latin American States are followers of the "Continental" attitude.[29] But again the contrast becomes less sharp upon close examination, and indeed it disappears altogether at times. In 1916 the American Institute of International Law, in its Declaration of the Rights and Duties of Nations, laid down, among others, the principle that:

International law is at one and the same time both national and international: national in the sense that it is the law of the land and applicable as such to the decision of all questions involving its principles; international in the sense that it is the law of the society of nations and applicable as such to all questions between and among the members of the society of nations involving its principles.[30]

[27] Reichsverfassung [German], Art. 4; Bundesverfassung [Austrian], Art. 8. For comment on Art. 4 of the Weimar Constitution, see Fleischmann, in Anschütz and Thoma, *Handbook des Deutschen Staatsrechtes,* Vol. I, p. 220: "The rule of international law is in this way transformed into a law of the Reich. The individual finds himself directly bound and authorized by this rule."

[28] See Masters, *op. cit.,* Chaps. I-VII. Inferences with respect to the relation of international law to the law of the land in the Soviet Union may readily be drawn from the attitude of the Soviet Union to international law in general. For the attitude of some of the newer states, see R. R. Wilson, "International Law and New National Constitutions," *Am. Journal,* Vol. 58 (1964), p. 432.

[29] See Antokoletz, *Derecho Internacional Público,* Primera Parte, p. 59.

[30] Art. VI. For the text of the Declaration, see *Am. Journal,* Vol. 10 (1916), p. 124. For comment, see E. Root, "The Declaration of the Rights and Duties of Nations," *ibid.,* p. 211.

But the principle was so broadly stated as to be of little practical value. In 1927 the International Commission of Jurists, meeting in Rio de Janeiro, adopted a more cautious resolution to the effect that: "International positive law forms part of the legislation of each state, and, as such, it must, in respect to matters coming within its scope and in conformity with prescriptions of the constitution of each state, be put into effect by the national authorities." [31] The first official pronouncement of the inter-American community is to be found in Resolution XIII of the Conference on Problems of War and Peace, 1945, entitled "Incorporation of International Law into Municipal Law," in which the Conference proclaimed "the need for all States to strive toward the incorporation of the essential principles of international law into their constitutions and other municipal law." The Charter of 1948, of treaty obligation, reaffirms as the first of its principles that "International law is the standard of conduct of States in their reciprocal relations," leaving open the decision of what constitutes international law in a particular case.[32]

A number of the American states have from time to time entered into their Constitutions the specific provision that "international law is part of the law of the land"; but in every case it is either understood or explicitly affirmed that the general principle is subject to qualifications similar to those recognized by Great Britain and the United States.[33]

C. SPECIFIC APPLICATIONS OF THE GENERAL RULE

The confusion attending the conflicting views of the relation of international law to municipal law may perhaps be reduced somewhat by enumerating some of the specific aspects of the problem and by submitting propositions corresponding to each, in part *de lege ferenda:*

1. As a general principle international law unquestionably takes priority over national law. Unless this general principle is accepted, international law has no meaning.[34] But the acceptance of the proposition

---

[31] Project No. 1, "Fundamental Bases of International Law," Art. 2. For the text, see *Am. Journal,* Vol. 22 (1928), Spec. Supp., p. 238.

[32] For the two texts, see *Int. Conferences,* 1942-1954, pp. 76, 178.

[33] See Antokoletz, *op. cit.,* where citations are given from the constitutions of a number of the American states. Art. 31 of the Argentine Constitution follows closely the provision of the United States Constitution, Art. VI, pt. 2, in providing that "This Constitution, the national laws passed by the Congress in pursuance of it, and treaties with foreign nations are the supreme law of the Nation"; but legislation relating to the jurisdiction of the national courts fixes the following order of precedence: the constitution, laws passed by the national congress, treaties, the laws of the provinces, and the "principles of international law." The constitution of Venezuela provides that "international law is part of the law of the land, but its provisions may not be invoked when opposed to the Constitution or the laws of the Republic."

[34] That is, no more meaning than the German writers of the late nineteenth century were willing to concede to it as a voluntary expression of rules which a state might normally be expected to observe. See above, p. 68.

still leaves open the practical question as to the ways and means by which its priority may be given practical application.

2. It is to be assumed that a treaty, duly signed and ratified, is in accord with the national constitution.[35] Otherwise the state would be guilty of bad faith in ratifying it. The assumption, however, is not final. If the plenipotentiaries of the state exceeded their powers, or if the ratifying agency was unaware of constitutional restrictions, the treaty is not law; but the state must immediately call the attention of the other party to the fact and must ask release from obligations entered into in violation of its constitution.[36] Undue delay in so doing would give rise to bad faith and would negative the right to request release from the obligations of the treaty.

3. A treaty duly signed and ratified becomes automatically part of the "law of the land," taking priority over all laws antecedent to its adoption.[37] It is the duty of the national courts to enforce the provisions of the treaty in cases calling for their application.

4. Legislation passed or administrative action taken subsequent to the adoption of the treaty and in violation of its provisions is invalid, and should be declared so by the appropriate agency of the national government.[38] In like manner, in doubtful cases where the national legislation or administrative ruling is open to different interpretations, the courts of the state will give the benefit of the doubt to the provisions of the treaty.

5. Treaties which can only be put into effect by the passage of a legislative act, such as treaties calling for appropriations by the national legislature, give rise to an international obligation on the part of the national legislature to pass the required act.[39] The provisions of the national constitution with respect to the ratification of treaties should be extended to include this obligation on the part of the national legislature.

6. The separate members of a federal state are automatically bound by the provisions of treaties entered into by the national government.[40]

[35] Treaties of peace are not included here. They form a separate class, not to be judged by the ordinary law governing voluntary agreements.

[36] On this controversial point, see Chap. XXIII, dealing with the law of treaty obligations.

[37] With emphasis upon the word *antecedent*, this rule is required by good faith, and constitutional provisions which give priority to national laws must be understood as relating to laws passed after the ratification of the treaty.

[38] This rule is at present *de lege ferenda*, not holding good in the United States, Argentina, and other countries.

[39] The obligation of the Congress of the United States under such circumstances has been widely discussed. See below, p. 521.

[40] The Constitution of the United States, Art. VI, pt. 2, after making treaties a part of the supreme law of the land (see note 8), provides "and the judges in every State shall be bound thereby, any thing in the constitution or laws of any State to the contrary notwithstanding."

Existing legislation contrary to the provisions of the treaty becomes invalid, and legislation necessary to put the treaty into effect becomes a legal obligation.

7. The specific rules of customary international law are no less binding upon the state than are the provisions of treaties, but in view of the uncertainty attending them the judicial agencies can only be expected to apply them subject to the interpretation given them by the national legislature and the administrative department of the government.[41] Where there is no conflicting legislation or administrative decision, the judicial agencies will apply the rule of customary law in accordance with their judgment of its binding character.[42] On its part the legislative body is equally under an obligation to enact the laws necessary to give practical effect to rules of international customary law.

8. In cases where there is no treaty provision and no specific rule of customary law the decision of questions of international law is to be made by the national courts in accordance with the general principles of justice which are traditional within the international community.[43] In such cases the national courts may be expected to follow legislative enactments or administrative decisions establishing the proper application of the general principle.

9. The resolutions of international conferences, duly signed by plenipotentiary delegates appointed by the state, have the full force of legal obligations. They are to be distinguished from treaty obligations not by the extent of their binding character but by the latitude of interpretation given to the individual state by the terms of the resolution.[44]

10. The responsibility of the state for the observance of its international obligations is to be determined, in relation to other states, by the action of the Executive Department entrusted by the constitution with negotiations with other states. The international conduct of the state is not to be judged in the first instance by the enactments of the legislature nor by the decisions of the national courts, although these may be facts upon which claims brought by foreign states may be based.[45]

[41] Compare the decision in Cunard Steamship Co. v. Mellon, p. 377, where the court refused to read into the law an exemption which would have maintained the traditional rule of international law.

[42] See the case of the *Paquete Habana,* p. 92. See, in this connection, C. C. Hyde, "The Supreme Court of the United States as an expositor of international law," in *British Year Book,* Vol. XVIII (1938), p. 1.

[43] Numerous dicta of Sir William Scott and Chief Justice Marshall dealing with questions of prize law have long since been incorporated into the body of international law.

[44] This proposition is highly controversial, a number of Latin American jurists maintaining that such resolutions create only a moral obligation. See below, p. 231.

[45] See Chap XIV, in connection with the responsibility of the state for the protection of aliens.

PART **II**

The Organization of the
Community of Nations

CHAPTER VI

The Community or "Family of Nations"

A. HISTORICAL CONCEPTION OF A COMMUNITY OF NATIONS

The conception of a community of nations was, as we have seen, deeply rooted in the traditions of the European states at the time when international law came to assume its modern shape. It is true that the conception was largely a moral one, and that it was not reflected in institutions which might have given it legal character. Neither the *jus gentium* of Justinian's Code nor the *jus naturale* of the Schoolmen, however they might imply a bond of unity among the different states, called for any form of organization by which the law might be given practical application to the relations of states. But with the great diplomatic gatherings of Osnabrück and Münster came the first of the international conferences which were to herald the development of a rudimentary and imperfect international organization.[1] Thenceforth a new "family of nations" began to take shape, more concrete and definite than the universal society of the Stoics and of the early Church Fathers, or the *civitas maxima* of Vitoria and Suarez, but not as yet possessed of agencies or machinery of government through which the authority of the community might have been made effective. Upon the leading powers of the community devolved the duty of asserting principles of law and maintaining them against the lawbreaker.[2] When they themselves were at war the law was in abeyance.

Growth of the community. Beginning with the small group of Christian European states which were parties to the Peace of Westphalia, and which might be called the charter members of the international

---

[1] Compare Oppenheim's elaborate description of what constitutes a "community." *International Law*, Vol. I, § 7.

[2] For the role of the Great Powers in the development of international law, see below, p. 265.

community, the narrow circle was soon widened by the addition to it of other European states. The Muscovite Empire of Russia, hitherto a stranger, was admitted in 1721. The new American Republic, born of revolution, was admitted in 1783. The following century witnessed a vast increase in membership by the accession of the Central and South American states, which had grown out of the colonial settlements of two of the older powers. In 1856, by the Treaty of Paris, the first non-Christian state, the Ottoman Empire, was admitted "to participate in the public law and concert of Europe." [3] The accession of the Balkan states followed in due course. By the close of the century Japan was admitted, together with other non-Christian states, such as Persia, China, and Siam, whose status in the community was, however, like that of Turkey, subject to certain claims of extraterritorial jurisdiction. The century closed with the meeting of the First Hague Conference, and its limited membership may be taken as a reflection of the dominant position of the Great Powers and their small regard for the legal equality of the Latin American and Far Eastern states whose political and economic power appeared to make them a negligible factor in international relations. Throughout the nineteenth century the Great Powers had constituted themselves, as we have seen, as a sort of self-appointed executive committee of the family of nations, meeting from time to time, as at the Congress of Vienna in 1815, at the Congress of Paris in 1854-1856, and at the Congress of Berlin in 1885, to reorganize the political system when collective decisions were called for.[4]

B. LEGAL CHARACTER OF THE COMMUNITY

What was the legal character of the international community at this stage of its growth? Had it any corporate personality, any identity in international law apart from that of its individual members? Statesmen were little concerned with the problem, but it would seem that in their use of the term "community" they had the conception of a body of states accepting the rules of international law and maintaining diplomatic relations with one another on that basis. When recognition was accorded to a new state, it was regarded as *ipso facto* assuming the obligations of membership in the community, and the new state did not for a moment think of picking and choosing which of the generally

[3] Treaty of Paris, Art. 7. Five of the leading European Powers: France, Austria, Great Britain, Prussia, and Russia, together with Sardinia, were parties to the treaty, a landmark in the history of international relations.

[4] The limited circle of the international community even so late as fifty years ago was described as consisting "for all practical purposes simply of the separate sovereignties of those sixty independent states, linked together only by the slender threads of diplomatic relations and of bilateral agreements." Sir Humphrey Waldock, "General Course on Public International Law," *Recueil des Cours* (1962-II), p. 1.

observed rules of international law it was willing to abide by. Secretary Webster observed in 1842 that:

Every nation, on being received, at her own request, into the circle of civilized governments, must understand that she not only attains rights of sovereignty and the dignity of national character, but that she binds herself also to the strict and faithful observance of all those principles, laws, and usages which have obtained currency among civilized states, and which have for their object the mitigation of the miseries of war.[5]

The Hague Peace Conferences. It is difficult at this date to understand how the select group of nations that met at the Hague Conference of 1899 could have failed to realize the need for a more permanent organization of the international community. But in this respect the Conference did no more than follow the traditions of the nineteenth century, meeting the problems before it, but not looking beyond them. The Second Hague Conference, meeting in 1907, did, indeed, voice the desirability of calling a third conference to complete its unfinished work, and publicists became enthusiastic over what appeared to be the beginning of an organized world.[6] But beyond the creation of the Permanent Court of Arbitration no steps were taken to meet constructively the political and economic rivalries of the nations or to develop controls for the unstable balance of power. Peace was said to be desirable, but in such abstract form as not to call for constructive measures. A recognition of the collective responsibility of the community for the maintenance of peace found no place among the conventions regulating the laws of war.[7]

The establishment of the League of Nations in 1920 gave to its constituent members a definite legal character and corporate personality. But while the founders of the League clearly expected it to become in time a universal body, the permanent absence of the United States and the temporary absence of other states created a situation in which the older community of nations still remained theoretically intact; and there were now, in a sense, two international communities existing side by side, creating numerous complications, legal as well as practical.[8] This illogical and paradoxical situation came to an end with the estab-

[5] Letter to the United States Minister to Mexico, April 15, 1842. Moore, *Digest,* Vol. I, p. 10. Webster's "circle of civilized governments" might be described as the community of nations which exists by the implied agreement of its members to uphold certain principles and rules.

[6] Professor Schücking went so far as to find in the Hague Conferences the elements of a federal union. See *The International Union of the Hague Conferences,* translated from *Der Staatenverband der Haager Konferenzen* (1912).

[7] Curiously enough, no provision was made that the Third Hague Conference, scheduled for 1914, should meet in an emergency threatening the peace.

[8] See on this point J. L. Kunz, "The Law of Nations, Static and Dynamic," *Am. Journal,* Vol. 27 (1933), p. 630; J. B. Moore, "The New Isolation," *ibid.,* p. 607.

lishment of the new organization of the United Nations, which gave to
the international community the unity it lacked under the League of
Nations; and there could thenceforth be no doubt that it had full corporate capacity and definite legal personality.[9]

C. STATES AS PERSONS OF INTERNATIONAL LAW

Side by side with the development of the conception of an international "community" was the development of the conception of a "state"
as a member of the community. Theoretically a state was a permanently
organized political society, occupying a fixed territory and enjoying
within the boundaries of that territory freedom from control by any
other state. During the nineteenth century the alternative term "nation"
was frequently used to describe a body of people more or less of the
same race, language, religion, and historical traditions; and taken in
that sense it was clear that nation and state do not necessarily coincide.[10]
Poland, for example, ceased to be a state, in the sense of international
law, after the third partition in 1795, although the Polish nation survived. Italy was a "nation" long before Italian unity was achieved in
1870. The problem of "nationalities," as it was presented in the nineteenth century, was the problem of making "nation" and "state" coincide;
and many statesmen were led to believe that it held the key to international peace. Now that the term "nation" has been taken over by the
United Nations, following the tradition of the League of Nations, the
two terms have become synonymous, and the problem of nationalities
has taken new form and substance.

Corporate character of states.   What is it that gives juristic character
to the "state" so that it can be marked off as having separate legal
unity and corporate personality and as such claim admission to membership in the international community? Clearly we are confronted with a
practical political problem as well as with a theoretical one. Political
scientists, speaking of the state as an abstract institution, tell us that it is
a "natural" association of persons bound together by bonds of a common race, language, religion, and historical traditions. Few states in
the concrete possess the national unity which the definition suggests.
The United States secured recognition as a separate state although not
differing in any of those respects from the mother country. As will be
seen later, in examining state by state the membership of the United
Nations, states are organized groups that have succeeded in maintaining
a separate legal personality by demonstrated political power or that
have been recognized as political units by a former colonial power and

---

[9] See below, p. 210.
[10] On the general subject of nation and nationalism see Kohn, *The Idea of Nationalism;* Hayes, *The Historical Evolution of Modern Nationalism;* Rose, *Nationality in
Modern History;* Cobban, *National Self-Determination.*

accepted as such by the international community without serious inquiry into the four theoretical elements of race, language, religion, and historical traditions. Membership in the United Nations is open to all "peace-loving states," with no definition of what constitutes a "state" other than the condition, as determined by the General Assembly upon recommendation of the Security Council, of being an organized group willing and able to carry out the obligations of the Charter.[11]

Necessity of a fixed territory. The necessity of a fixed territory determining the area over which the state is to exercise jurisdiction is a practical condition of statehood. But the size of the territory varies widely, and it has no effect upon the legal personality of the state, except in the few cases, such as Monaco and San Marino, where the state is diminutive.

Degrees of political independence. A more subtle condition of being a "state" was the necessity of being free from control by another state, so that it might be responsible before the world for its own acts and have what was called "the capacity to enter into relations with other states." Here international law of the nineteenth and early twentieth centuries was not clear, there being a standard classification of "sovereign" and "less-than-sovereign" states, leaving it an open, or rather a political question, whether a less-than-sovereign state, a "dependent state," could be admitted to share in any degree the privileges of membership in the international community.[12] In many cases the dependent state, such as Egypt in relation to Turkey in 1914, was one which had been previously outside the international community, but had come under the control of a more powerful state which exercised a greater or lesser degree of supervision over its foreign policy as well as over its domestic administration.

D. "SOVEREIGN STATES"

Meaning of "sovereignty." What then was a "sovereign state" which held a position of distinction in the international community? After centuries of use the meaning of the term "sovereignty" is still lacking in scientific precision, and its use is attended with many inconsistencies. In the technical usage of the past a sovereign state was one which exercised undivided authority over all persons and property within its borders and was independent of direct control by any other power. Attached to sovereignty were a number of concrete immunities and privileges, which writers of that date liked to describe as "the marks of

[11] See p. 207. The recent formation and dissolution of federal unions in the Near East and in Africa show the divergence between the ideal "state" of political science and the de facto states that have emerged from different political backgrounds.

[12] Mere colonies, it should be noted, were completely out of the picture. They had no rights before the law.

sovereignty." Sovereign states were by international custom entitled to the privilege of sending diplomatic representatives to other states and of receiving diplomatic representatives from them in return. They concluded in their own name treaties with one another looking to the advancement of their mutual interests; they enjoyed immunity from being sued in the courts of other states; and they met at international conferences on a basis of formal equality. Whatever rights were conferred by international law they enjoyed to the fullest degree, without the intermediation of any third party; whatever duties were imposed by international law were borne by them in their own person. One of the outstanding characteristics of sovereignty during the nineteenth century, "the right to make war" has happily now ceased to figure as such. The other "marks" still hold good.

Many jurists have urged that the term "sovereignty" should be discarded, as being out of harmony with the actual facts of international intercourse.[13] It is only by a fiction that sovereignty can be kept compatible with the numerous restrictions upon a state's freedom of conduct which arise as a direct consequence of the binding character of the rules of international law. To say that a state is "sovereign" when its conduct is restricted at almost every turn by rules of law is to use the term in a highly technical sense, far removed from its original meaning. Nevertheless that technical sense is still adhered to tenaciously. For it has come to represent the repudiation of the right of a stronger state to intervene in the affairs of a weaker state; it has come to represent the will on the part of the smaller states to exist as separate and independent members of the community; and as used in adjectival form in the Charter of the United Nations, where the principle is proclaimed of the "sovereign equality" of the members of the new organization, it has come to imply that states are not yet ready to submit themselves to anything in the nature of a federal or supergovernment which could act by virtue of its own resolutions and determine the conduct of states without previous reference of the measure to them for their separate approval.

Such is the sovereign state, the full member of the community of nations. It remains now to examine the cases of a number of states, which, while technically sovereign, have nevertheless been subject to certain restrictions upon their freedom of conduct not voluntarily as-

---

[13] The literature of the subject is extensive. See, in particular, Lauterpacht, *The Function of Law in the International Community;* Russell, *Theories of International Relations,* Chap. XXIII; Ward, *Sovereignty—A Study of a Contemporary Political Notion;* J. W. Garner, "Limitations on National Sovereignty in International Relations," *Am. Pol. Science Review,* Vol. XIX (1925), pp. 1-24; F. W. Coker and E. M. Borchard in *History of Political Theories: Recent Times,* Chaps. III, IV; N. Politis, "Le problème des limitations de la souveraineté," *Recueil des Cours,* Vol. 6 (1925-I), p. 5.

sumed by them and not common to other states. These cases are part of the recent history of international law; and while the conditions to which they gave rise have in large part ceased to exist the cases themselves are still of importance as marking a phase in the development of international law, the effects of which are still to be felt in some degree.

Neutralized states. Next after the sovereign state came, in the days when war was a legal procedure, the status of the neutralized state upon which the status of permanent neutrality was imposed by a group of the Great Powers. In accordance with the formal treaty of neutralization the neutral state agreed on its part to refrain from participating directly or indirectly in a future war, and the Great Powers on their part agreed to respect the fixed status of the neutral state; so that neutralization treaties to that extent represented reciprocal obligations. The neutralization of Switzerland was effected by an article of the Final Act of the Congress of Vienna of 1815, that of Belgium by the Treaties of London of 1831 and 1839, and that of Luxemburg by the Treaty of 1867.[14] Three cases of lesser importance involved the Ionian Islands, the Congo Free State, and the Aaland Islands.

Did the "collective guarantee" carry with it an individual obligation of the guarantors to act alone in case the other guarantors failed to act collectively? Great Britain so interpreted the obligation in respect to Belgium in 1914 in the negotiations immediately preceding the declaration of war against Germany on August 4, 1914. The German Government on its part did not disown the obligations of the treaty, in spite of the reference of the chancellor to it as a "scrap of paper," but regarded the obligation impossible of observance in the presence of a "state of necessity," alleging the danger of a later violation by France. At the close of the war the King of Belgium declared that the restrictions imposed by the treaty were at an end. But with the threat of another war on the horizon Belgium obtained a joint pledge from Great Britain and France in 1937, and a similar individual pledge from Germany. Notwithstanding the German pledge Belgium was invaded by the Axis air forces on May 10, 1940, without having received even an ultimatum or other warning.[15]

The neutrality of Switzerland was respected during the First World War, and upon its special request Switzerland was permitted to become a member of the League of Nations without assuming the obligation, under the provisions of Article 16, to take part in a war in defense of the Covenant. The neutrality of Switzerland was again respected during the Second World War, obviously, however, not in consequence of

[14] For the texts of the treaties relating to Switzerland and Belgium, see Hertslet, *Map of Europe by Treaty*, Vol. I, pp. 208, 370, 996.

[15] See De Visscher, *Belgium's Case: A Judicial Inquiry*, where the treaties of 1831 and 1839 are discussed in detail; Hackworth, *Digest*, Vol. I, pp. 69 ff., for the pledges of 1937; Snyder, *The War, 1939-1945*, p. 83.

mere treaty pledges. Luxemburg likewise decided to maintain its status of permanent neutrality after the First World War, only to be invaded by Germany on May 10, 1940.

It should be observed that states not parties to a neutralization treaty were under no legal obligation to come to the defense of a neutralized state. Thus the government of the United States, although a party to the Hague Convention, did not feel called upon to protest either in 1914 or in 1940 when the neutrality of Belgium was violated, however strongly public opinion in the United States felt in the matter.[16] In like manner a state, taking on its own account a position of neutrality in a war between two or more other states, could not call for legal help in the event that one or other of the belligerents might violate its neutrality. The violation by Germany of the neutrality of Holland and of Denmark in 1940 thus evoked no obligation on the part of the United States to come to their defense.

States admitted into the community of nations under conditions. In addition to neutralized states international law of the nineteenth century recognized as technically sovereign a number of states which, for one reason or another, were admitted into the community subject to fixed conditions. These states contracted at the time of their entrance into the international community that they would observe certain rules prescribed for them by certain of the older members of the community. Since the contract took the form of a treaty, which by legal fiction was voluntarily entered into, and since the obligations imposed were in general not different from the normal conduct to be expected of a civilized state, no derogation from the full international personality of the state was implied. The Treaty of Berlin of 1878,[17] in recognizing the independence of Montenegro, imposed special obligations upon the state in respect to religious and racial toleration, limitation of fortifications, sanitary police administration by Austria-Hungary along the coast, and freedom of transit across Montenegro for the subjects of other states. Similar restrictions were laid upon the new states of Serbia and Rumania. By the same Treaty of Berlin, Bulgaria was created an autonomous and tributary principality under the suzerainty of the Sultan, being subjected to restrictions similar to those imposed upon Serbia. However, it soon threw off the yoke of a "vassal state," and in 1899 delegates from Bulgaria were admitted to the Hague Peace Conference. The declaration of independence on October 5, 1908, by which Bulgaria formally severed the bond of vassalage, did no more than give a new legal character to a situation already definitely maintained.

[16] Compare the Neutrality Proclamation of the United States in 1939, declaring that the country was "on terms of friendship and amity with the contending powers." See below, p. 724.

[17] For the text of this important treaty, see *British and Foreign State Papers,* Vol. 69, p. 749.

Provisions of the treaties of 1919. The precedents established by the Treaty of Berlin were followed at the Peace Conference of 1919 in the creation of the new states of Poland, Czechoslovakia, and Yugoslavia. Poland was obligated by the Treaty of Versailles (Art. 93) to conclude a separate treaty with the Principal Allied and Associated Powers containing provisions which they might deem necessary "to protect the interests of inhabitants of Poland who differ from the majority of the population in race, language, or religion." The treaty contemplated was concluded June 28, 1919, and was placed under the guarantee of the League of Nations. Further, Poland agreed to embody in a similar treaty with the same powers "such provisions as they might deem necessary to protect freedom of transit and equitable treatment of the commerce of all nations." Similar agreements were entered into by Czechoslovakia, Yugoslavia, and Rumania by the Treaty of St. Germain. Supplementing these measures of the Peace Conference, the Assembly of the League of Nations adopted in 1920 a recommendation that "in the event of Albania, the Baltic and Caucasian states being admitted to the League," the latter should take the necessary measures to enforce the provisions of the minorities treaties.[18]

The emancipation of Cuba. The emancipation of Cuba as an independent state under the protection of the United States was without precedent in international law. On April 20, 1898, Congress adopted a joint resolution recognizing the independence of Cuba and demanding that the Spanish Government relinquish its authority over the island. By the Treaty of Paris Spain gave up its claim of sovereignty over Cuba, leaving the United States in military occupation. On March 2, 1901, an act of Congress authorized the President to leave the government and control of Cuba to its people upon their acceptance of certain conditions embodied subsequently in the "Platt Amendment." The conditions placed restrictions upon the financial and treaty-making powers of the new state, imposed minor administrative obligations, and provided for a right of intervention on the part of the United States for "the maintenance of a government adequate for the protection of life, property, and individual liberty." These conditions were accepted by Cuba and incorporated into a treaty between the two countries under date of May 22, 1903. Since the procedure was observed of a voluntary contractual acceptance on the part of Cuba of the conditions imposed, international law saw in the conditions merely a renunciation by Cuba of the exercise of certain powers, not an infringement of the new state's legal sovereignty or of its equal standing in the family of nations. No funda-

---

[18] On the general subject, see H. Rosting, "Protection of Minorities by the League of Nations," *Am. Journal*, Vol. 17 (1923), p. 641; Temperley, *History of the Peace Conference of Paris*, Vol. V, Chap. II, "The Treaties for the Protection of Minorities"; Azcarate, *The League of Nations and National Minorities*.

mental change in Cuba's position took place, therefore, when by the Washington Treaty of 1934 the Platt Amendment was formally "abrogated." [19]

Restrictions not affecting sovereignty. Panama, Haiti, and the Dominican Republic were, like Cuba, subject for a time to limitations upon the exercise of certain powers of sovereignty, while retaining their technical sovereignty and their full membership in the community of states. By a treaty entered into in 1903, the United States guaranteed the independence of Panama and at the same time obtained a lease in perpetuity of the Canal Zone, which carried with it the exclusive control incident to sovereignty. A right of intervention on the part of the United States was also provided for in order to enforce compliance with sanitary measures to be taken in the cities of Panama and Colon, not included in the grant, and to maintain order in them if necessary. By a treaty signed in Washington, March 2, 1936, the right of the United States to intervene in the cities of Panama and Colon and the territory adjacent thereto for the purpose of maintaining order was abrogated, removing the one restriction upon the sovereignty of Panama which had been regarded as carrying with it implications in derogation of the equality of sovereign states.[20]

By the treaty of February 8, 1907, the Dominican Republic agreed to receive assistance from the United States with the object of enabling it to pay off its public debt. Provision was made for the appointment by the United States of a receiver-general of Dominican customs, and restrictions were placed upon the right of the Dominican Government to increase the public debt. In 1916 Dominican territory was occupied by a United States naval force in consequence of the failure of the Republic to observe the terms of the treaty. The occupation continued until 1924 when a convention was signed in which the United States disclaimed any intention of attacking the sovereignty and independence of the Dominican nation. At the same time an agreement was made for a continuation of the period of receivership and for the exercise by the United States of the necessary military control which the receivership might call for. This second convention was replaced in 1940 by a Treaty of Special Assistance, by the provisions of which the Dominican Republic resumed the collection of its revenues, but agreed to deposit them in a bank selected by mutual agreement between the parties, the funds to be

[19] For the text of the treaty, see *Am. Journal,* Vol. 28 (1934), Supp., p. 97. See also Hyde, *International Law,* Vol. I, pp. 56 ff.; Bustamante, *Droit International Public,* Vol. I, p. 243.

[20] For the text of the treaty, see *Am. Journal,* Vol. 34 (1940), Supp., p. 139. For comment, see N. J. Padelford, "American Rights in the Panama Canal," *Am. Journal,* Vol. 34 (1940), pp. 416, 601. A later treaty of 1955 bore no relation to the question of sovereignty.

disbursed under an arrangement which would secure the necessary payments on the public debt.[21]

The treaty of September 16, 1915, between the United States and Haiti was directed towards the stabilization of its finances and the maintenance of law and order, the government of Haiti agreeing that, should the necessity occur, "the United States will lend an efficient aid for the preservation of Haitian independence and the maintenance of a government adequate for the protection of life, property, and individual liberty." In 1933 a new agreement was signed, providing for the withdrawal of the military forces of the United States and for a new financial arrangement for the disposition of the outstanding Haitian bonds. This agreement was in turn superseded by the agreement of September 13, 1941, which modified the earlier financial control and removed the restrictions which the government of Haiti believed to be an infringement upon its sovereignty.[22]

Nicaragua. The convention between the United States and Nicaragua, of August 5, 1914, by which the United States acquired in perpetuity a right to construct and operate an interoceanic canal across the territory of that state, provided that the particular territory leased and the naval base accompanying it should be "subject exclusively to the laws and sovereign authority of the United States."[23] No infringement of the sovereignty of Nicaragua was to be inferred from the terms of the treaty.

The Philippine Republic. In 1898, by the treaty of Paris, the United States acquired from Spain sovereignty over the Philippine Islands. The government of the Islands was reorganized in 1902, and under successive governors-general efforts were made to give the islands experience in self-government. In 1934 the Congress of the United States adopted the Tydings-McDuffie Act, in accordance with which a transitional government with the title "The Philippine Commonwealth," was established for ten years, after which the islands were to be given full independence. On July 4, 1946, the Philippine Commonwealth acquired independent statehood under the name "The Republic of the Philippines."[24] Even before acquiring the technical status of a sovereign state

[21] The financial story appears in a treatise by the Dominican jurist, Sanchez, *Curso de derecho público*, pp. 43 ff.; the political story in Welles, *Naboth's Vineyard: The Dominican Republic, 1844-1924*.

[22] For the text of the treaty, see *Documents on Am. For. Relations*, Vol. IV, p. 415. For a general survey of the relations of the United States with Cuba, Panama, the Dominican Republic, and Haiti, see Jones, *The Caribbean Since 1900;* Calcott, *The Caribbean Policy of the United States, 1890-1920;* Millspaugh, *Haiti under American Control;* Munro, *Intervention and Dollar Diplomacy in the Caribbean, 1900-1921.*

[23] For the text of the treaty, see *Am. Journal*, Vol. 10 (1916), Supp., p. 258.

[24] The proclamation issued by the President of the United States on July 4, 1946, concludes as follows: "On behalf of the United States of America, I do hereby recognize the independence of the Philippines as a separate and self-governing nation and acknowledge the authority and control over the same of the government instituted by

the Philippine Commonwealth signed the Charter of the United Nations as an original member.

Irish Free State (Eire). The manner in which the Irish Free State acquired international status was unique. The Free State came into legal being by the conclusion of the treaty of December 6, 1921,[25] between the British Government on the one hand and representatives of the Irish Sinn Fein on the other, the latter having at international law no *de jure* standing until the negotiations preceding the treaty. On January 8, 1922, the treaty was ratified by the Dail Eireann, whereupon Ireland, south of the treaty line separating it from Northern Ireland, became the "Irish Free State." A subsequent act of Parliament embodying the treaty gave to the new "state" the same constitutional status "in the community of nations known as the British Empire" as was held by the British self-governing dominions, naming Canada as the dominion whose relations to the Imperial Parliament were to be paralleled by those of the Free State. Having adopted a constitution and organized its government, the Free State was admitted to membership in the League of Nations in September, 1923, and was elected to the Council of the League of Nations in 1930. A new constitution adopted in 1937 changed the name of the Free State to "Éire, or, in the English language, Ireland," and at the same time omitted all reference to membership in the British Commonwealth of Nations. Ireland remained neutral during the Second World War, and in consequence it was not invited to participate in the conference at San Francisco and to become a signatory of the Charter of the United Nations.

Vatican and diminutive states. The breach in the Porta Pia on September 20, 1870, followed by the annexation of Rome to the Kingdom of Italy, raised a question with jurists whether the papacy, whose temporal power had been exercised more than 1100 years, could any longer be counted among the states of international law. Could there be a state without territory? Could the pope remain a sovereign merely by reason of the continuity of his spiritual jurisdiction after his temporal authority over a definite area of land had come to an end? What legal character in respect to international law could be attributed to diplomatic relationships still maintained by the papacy with a number of governments? Jurists of the Positive School, basing their judgment upon a strict inter-

---

the people thereof, under the constitution now in force." Department of State *Bulletin*, Vol. XV, p. 66. See also, E. W. Mill, "The New Republic of the Philippines," *ibid.*, p. 475.

[25] Technically known as "Articles of Agreement for a Treaty" and the "Scheduled Treaty." For the text, see *Annual Register*, 1921, p. 86. A survey of the historical development of the Free State may be found in Irish Free State v. Guaranty Deposit Co., 129 Misc. Rep. (N. Y. 1927), p. 551. Fenwick, *Cases*, p. 139. See also, Figgis, *The Irish Constitution*.

pretation of facts, held that the papacy had since 1870 lost all international character whatever. On the other hand certain writers of the Latin tradition saw in the minimum of territory left to the pope by the Italian Law of Guarantees and in the worldwide spiritual authority exercised by him a sufficient basis for a claim of sovereignty in the technical sense. Other writers compromised upon a "quasi-international" status, a "special" or "particular" sovereignty, a nonterritorial corporate personality different from that of other states, but nevertheless interternational in character.

The treaty signed on February 11, 1929, between Italy and the Vatican created the "City of the Vatican," over which the Holy See was recognized as having full proprietary and exclusive domain and sovereign jurisdiction. The right of the pope to send and receive diplomatic officers was recognized, and their immunity was provided for. The Vatican agreed to extradite fugitive criminals to Italy without awaiting formal requests for such action; and the Italian Government undertook to exercise criminal jurisdiction over offenses committed within the Vatican City. The Vatican stated unilaterally that it wished to remain outside the temporal rivalry of other states and apart from the international congresses convened for such purposes, except in cases where the parties to a conflict unanimously might appeal to its mission of peace. In time of war the Vatican City was to be neutral and inviolable. This position of neutrality was maintained during the Second World War, and the inviolability of the Vatican City was respected by all of the belligerents.

The treaty of 1929 thus created a new international person, of a unique and exceptional character. The Vatican City fits into none of the established categories of states, and the attribution to it of "sovereignty" must be made in a sense different from that in which it is applied to other states. It represents in a community of national states an institution organized primarily for international objects, whose legal personality is marked by a few acres of territory and a handful of subjects, but whose worldwide interests and activities are such as to make it in a sense an "international state." [26]

In a group somewhat apart are certain diminutive states which may properly claim to possess full international personality, yet which by reason of their small size have never taken a formal position in the family of nations. Liechtenstein appears to be a sovereign state, although it was refused admission into the League of Nations in 1921 on the

[26] For the text of the treaty of 1929, see *Am. Journal*, Vol. 23 (1929), Supp., pp. 187 ff. The "City" covers an area of about 103 acres. On the status of the Vatican City, see De la Brière, *L'Organization internationale du monde contemporain et la Papauté Souverain;* Le Fur, *Le Saint Siège et le droit des gens;* J. L. Kunz, "The Status of the Holy See in International Law," *Am. Journal*, Vol. 46 (1952), p. 308.

INTERNATIONAL LAW

ground that it did not appear to be in a position to carry out its obligations under the Covenant, and although it was not invited to sign the Charter of the United Nations. Monaco would appear to be an autonomous state under the protection of France; San Marino an autonomous state under the protection of Italy; and Andorra an autonomous state under the joint protectorate of France and the Bishop of Urgel on behalf of Spain.[27]

E. LIMITED OR QUALIFIED MEMBERSHIP IN THE COMMUNITY OF NATIONS BEFORE 1945

Dependent and vassal states. In addition to states having full membership in the community of nations international law of the nineteenth and early twentieth century recognized a number of states which could claim but limited or qualified membership, described as "semi-sovereign states" or better merely as "dependent states." The term "vassal states," derived from the relationship of vassal and suzerain under the feudal system of the Middle Ages, was applied to subject provinces which had succeeded in emancipating themselves from the control of an alien government in respect to the management of their domestic affairs while still subject to the suzerain state in respect to their foreign affairs. From 1829 to 1878 Rumania, then consisting of the separate provinces of Moldavia and Wallachia, was a vassal state subject to the suzerainty of Turkey, under the guardianship first of Russia and then, after 1856, of the Great Powers. Serbia's position during the same period closely approximated that of Rumania. Both became fully sovereign states by decision of the Congress of Berlin of 1878. Crete obtained the status of vassal by decision of the same Congress. Subsequently, by Article 4 of the Treaty of London of 1913 Crete was ceded to Greece. Bulgaria likewise was recognized as a vassal state by the Treaty of Berlin, but the

---

[27] Monaco's fortunes have shifted from being a protectorate of Spain (1523-1641), of France (1641-1814), and of Sardinia, to the status of a sovereign state by reason of the failure of Italy to keep the protectorate alive. By the treaty with France of July 17, 1918, France is to defend the independence and sovereignty of Monaco and to be consulted by Monaco in matters of foreign relations, and in the event of a vacancy in the Crown of Monaco the territory is to form an autonomous state under the protectorate of France. In 1934 the Supreme Court of the United States heard a petition of Monaco, asking leave to bring suit against the State of Mississippi, although the request was denied on ground of immunity from suit. Fenwick, *Cases*, p. 326. For the status of Monaco, see Hackworth, *Digest*, Vol. I, p. 78.

To speak of San Marino as a "sovereign state" when its total area is only 38 square miles seems to strain the imagination.

Andorra, although measuring only 190 square miles, has an impressive history, going back to 1278 and even to the time of Charlemagne, who is said to have established it as a buffer state against the Moors.

bond of vassalage was so nominal between 1878 and 1908 as to make it possible for Bulgaria to claim a position of full membership in the community of nations.[28]

Egypt. Egypt went through a variety of dependent stages. In 1840 it was recognized as a vassal of Turkey under the guardianship of the signatories of the London Convention. Subsequently its powers in foreign affairs were enlarged by Turkish firmans to the extent of enabling the khedive to contract loans and to enter into commercial treaties with foreign states. By 1883 the earlier guardianship of the Great Powers had been left in the hands of Great Britain, whose control over the country increased to such an extent that Egypt became a *de facto* British protectorate under the merely nominal suzerainty of the sultan. In November, 1914, Great Britain proclaimed a formal protectorate over the country, and the khedive assumed the title of sultan as indicating the termination of the state of vassalage. On February 28, 1922, the independence of Egypt was formally acknowledged by Great Britain, subject to certain reservations to be agreed to by Egypt. By the Treaty of Alliance of August 26, 1936, Egypt was recognized by Great Britain "as a sovereign independent State." While the treaty provided for the termination of the British occupation of the country, it was agreed, in view of the fact that the Suez Canal, while an integral part of Egypt, was an essential means of communication between the different parts of the British Empire, that Egypt would authorize Great Britain "to station forces in Egyptian territory in the vicinity of the Canal" in order to insure its defense in cooperation with the Egyptian forces. Egypt became a member of the League of Nations in 1937; and in 1945 it was one of the signatories of the Charter of the United Nations.[29]

The Transvaal. The Transvaal (South African Republic) and the Orange Free State appear to have been vassal states of Great Britain between 1881 and 1901 when they were conquered by their suzerain, only to be included later in the Union of South Africa, which became independent in 1910 and one of the original signatories of the Charter of the United Nations in 1945.[30]

Tibet. After a period of nominal Chinese suzerainty during the eighteenth century in which Tibet was practically autonomous, Chinese Communist troops invaded the country, and in 1951 a treaty was signed

[28] See, in general, Hayes, *A Political and Social History of Modern Europe,* Vol. II, pp. 11 ff.

[29] See M. O. Hudson, "Admission of Egypt to Membership in the League of Nations," *Am. Journal,* Vol. 31 (1937), p. 681. For the *condominium* exercised by Great Britain and Egypt over the Sudan, see O'Rourke, *Juristic Status of Egypt and the Sudan;* Hackworth, *Digest,* Vol. I, p. 57.

[30] For the problems arising in the relations between the Union and the British Commonwealth in connection with the mandate of South-West Africa, see p. 245.

recognizing the status of dependency, but confirming the autonomy of the country. Revolts followed the systematic oppression by Communist China, and in 1959 Tibet was again invaded and its autonomy completely suppressed.[31]

Outer Mongolia. Outer Mongolia came upon the international stage with the fall of the Manchu dynasty in China in 1911. The Mongol princes declared their independence, and a treaty was signed between Mongolia and Russia in 1912 by which the latter undertook to assist Mongolia in maintaining its autonomy. The following year China declared its recognition of Outer Mongolia as autonomous, and Russia recognized it as part of the territory of China and under Chinese suzerainty. This status was confirmed by a treaty of 1915, to which Outer Mongolia was a party. The independence of Outer Mongolia was, however, annulled by China in 1919, following the Russian Revolution. After claims and counterclaims between China and Russia a treaty was signed in 1924 by which Russia (U.S.S.R.) recognized Outer Mongolia as "an integral part of the Republic of China" and declared its respect of China's sovereignty over the country. In 1936 Russia entered into an agreement with the Mongolian People's Republic, under which title Outer Mongolia had been exercising its autonomy, providing for mutual support in the event of an attack by any third party. China protested the agreement as a violation of the treaty of 1924. By notes exchanged on August 14, 1945, between China and Russia, China recognized the independence of Outer Mongolia, which thereupon became one of the republics of the U.S.S.R.[32]

Protectorates. The term "protectorate" has, like "vassal state," been loosely used in international law and in the recent past covered a wide variety of dependent states, some of which possessed an unquestioned, if not definitely ascertainable, degree of international personality, while others possessed none at all. In general the protectorate was a state which by formal treaty placed itself under the protection of a stronger state, surrendering to the latter control over its foreign relations while retaining a large measure of control over its domestic government. It was distinguished from the vassal state not by reason of the degree of autonomy which it possessed, which might often be less than that of the vassal state, but by reason of the relationship to one or more of the Great Powers whose democratic constitutions would appear to forbid the conception of bonds of vassalage. In other cases where the protectorate enjoyed a degree of independence prior to the treaty, its status repre-

[31] See Bell, *Tibet, Past and Present;* Whiteman, *Digest,* Vol. 1, p. 455, citing the report of the International Commission of Jurists, *The Question of Tibet and the Rule of Law;* Tieh-Tseng Li, "The Legal Position of Tibet," *Am. Journal,* Vol. 50 (1956), p. 394.

[32] For the texts of the notes, see *Am. Journal,* Vol. 40 (1946), Supp., p. 54. Mongolia applied for membership in the United Nations in 1946, but failed of recommendation by the Council until 1961.

sented in theory a voluntary act of subordination to the protecting state by contrast with the concession of autonomy made by the suzerain state to the vassal state; so that a presumption of freedom, when not bound by the treaty, rested with the protectorate. A distinction should be made between protectorates under the guardianship of a single state and protectorates under the guardianship of the Great Powers as a body.

The Ionian Islands. In 1815, by a treaty between Great Britain, Austria, Prussia, and Russia, The Ionian Islands, previously subject to Turkey, were made a "single, free, and independent state" under the protection of the British Crown. Conditions were imposed in the form of the razing of fortifications and the supervision of the internal organization of the islands by the guardian state. The protectorate came to an end in 1863 when the islands were united to Greece, at which time they were made permanently neutral.[33]

Samos. A similar fate befell Samos, an autonomous principality of the Porte after 1832, until annexed to Greece in 1914.

Morocco. Morocco came under the guardianship of the Great Powers in 1906, when the general act of the Algeciras Conference recognized the independence and integrity of the country and undertook to provide for the reform of its domestic government and the regulation of its economic development. Measures were taken to organize a Moroccan police and to suppress illicit trade in arms; the construction of public works was to be carried out on a basis of equality in respect to the participation of foreign powers; and provision was made for equal commercial facilities in Morocco for all nations. This international guardianship practically came to an end in 1911, when an agreement was entered into between France and Germany by which Germany renounced all political interests in Morocco and agreed to the establishment of a French protectorate. As a result of the Protectorate Treaty between France and the Sultan in 1912, and of subsequent conventions between France and Spain in 1912, and between France, Great Britain, and Spain in 1923 and 1928, Morocco was divided into three zones: the French zone in which the Sultan resided, the much smaller Spanish zone, and the diminutive neutralized zone of Tangier. Independence came by a French-Moroccan Joint Declaration of March 2, 1956, uniting all three zones.[34]

The Tangier zone. Tangier first came to have a separate international status when the Sultan of Morocco made it the "diplomatic capital" in order to avoid the necessity of permitting the representatives of foreign

[33] Hertslet, *Map of Europe*, Vol. I, p. 337; Martens, *Nouv. rec.*, Vol. II, p. 663. In illustration of the distinct international personality of the islands under the protectorate, it was held in the case of the *Leucade* [2 Spinks 212 (1855)] that the fact that the protecting power was at war did not involve the islands in war in the absence of a clear intention on the part of Great Britain to declare war on their behalf.

[34] See Whiteman, *Digest*, Vol. 1, p. 338; *U.N. Yearbook*, 1956, p. 110.

powers to reside at Fez. Thereafter the interested foreign powers first came to acquire rights of sanitary control over the city, and later, by successive treaties entered into with Morocco, rights of guardianship and political administration. The Statute of Tangier, signed December 18, 1923, between Great Britain, France, and Spain, while recognizing the sovereign rights of the Sultan, made provision for the establishment of a Commission of Control, an international legislative assembly and an international administration.[35] In 1940 Spain occupied the zone in violation of the provisions of the Statute, taking over all of the functions of the administration except the mixed courts. In 1945 Great Britain, France, the United States, and the Soviet Union came to an agreement calling upon the Spanish Government to evacuate the zone and providing for the reestablishment of the international regime. In 1956 the zone was formally ceded to Morocco.

Albania. In 1912 an effort was made by the Great Powers to emancipate Albania from the control of Turkey. The following year the control of the Great Powers was confirmed by the Treaty of London; and by the decision of a Conference of Ambassadors, July 29, 1913, Albania was constituted a sovereign and independent state and its neutrality was guaranteed by the six powers. In 1917 a provisional government was set up, and this body acquired a *de jure* character when on December 17, 1920, Albania was admitted as a member of the League of Nations. As a condition of its admission Albania was obliged to make a declaration pledging the application in its domestic law of the general principles of the minority treaties accepted by the succession states. On April 7, 1939, Albania was invaded by Italian troops upon the alleged ground of reestablishing order and justice, and shortly after, the country was formally annexed to Italy.[36] At the close of the war the sovereignty of Albania was restored under Russian control; but Albania was refused admission as a member of the United Nations until 1955.

Ethiopia. In 1906 Great Britain, France, and Italy agreed among themselves to respect and protect the integrity of Ethiopia, while at the same time taking steps to adjust in an equitable manner their respective interests in the country. Not being itself a party to the treaty, and being powerless to assert an independent position, Ethiopia was thus reduced to a state of involuntary wardship. This part of the mutual self-denying ordinance came impliedly to an end in September, 1923, when Ethiopia was admitted as a member of the League of Nations. As a condition of its admission Ethiopia was obliged to sign a declaration agreeing to the gradual abolition of slavery and the prohibition of the traffic in arms

[35] For the text of the statute, as amended by the Protocol signed at Paris, July 25, 1928, see *Am. Journal*, Vol. 23 (1929), Supp., p. 235.

[36] The refusal of the United States to recognize the annexation raised a number of interesting legal issues. See Whiteman, *Digest*, Vol. 1, p. 373.

with African tribes. In October, 1935, Italian forces invaded Ethiopia, alleging the unwillingness of the Emperor, Haile Selassie, to make adequate satisfaction for the Wal-Wal incident. Ethiopia appealed to the League of Nations, but the sanctions imposed by the League proved ineffective and the country was formally annexed to Italy. Following the reconquest of Ethiopia by British troops in 1941, Haile Selassie was restored to the throne, and in 1945 Ethiopia signed the Charter of the United Nations as a fully sovereign member of the international community.[37]

Administered provinces. In addition to vassal states and protectorates there have been territories possessing so intangible a degree of international personality as to reach almost the vanishing point. The term "administered province" has been used to describe territory nominally subject to the sovereignty of one state while actually under the administrative control of another. By the Berlin Treaty of 1878 Bosnia and Herzegovina, while remaining subject to the sovereignty of Turkey, were to be "occupied and administered" by Austria-Hungary, which continued to exercise a sort of mandate over them until they were annexed by unilateral act in 1908. Great Britain, under agreement with Turkey, exercised a similar administrative control over Cyprus from 1878 until the annexation of the island in 1914. A self-assumed administrative mandate over Cuba was exercised by the United States from 1898 to 1903. Puerto Rico, transferred to the United States from Spain by the Treaty of Paris in 1898, was administered by the United States under an organic law of 1900 until the Constitution of the Commonwealth was proclaimed in 1952. The relations of Puerto Rico with the United States are set forth in a "compact" known as the Puerto Rican Federal Relations Act.[38] Following the unconditional surrender of Germany in 1945 and the extinction of the Nazi Government, the Allied Declaration of June 5 created a temporary administration, taking over all of the powers possessed by the German Government, without, however, affecting the latent sovereignty of the occupied state.[39]

F. MANDATES OF THE LEAGUE OF NATIONS

During the half century and more preceding the establishment of the League of Nations, the states of the Near and the Far East had come under a greater or lesser degree of control by one or other of the Great Powers. India had become incorporated in the British Empire; Siam, although independent, was subject to claims of extraterritorial jurisdiction; Cambodia, Laos, and Vietnam were under a French protectorate;

[37] For the special position of Ethiopia in the League of Nations, see *Am. Journal,* Vol. 18 (1924), pp. 442 ff., and Vol. 30 (1936), Supp., p. 19.

[38] Whiteman, *Digest,* Vol. 1, p. 392.

[39] Whiteman, *Digest,* Vol. 1, p. 911.

Indonesia under the control of Holland; the Philippines had passed from Spanish control to that of the United States; and Goa and other minor territories to the control of Portugal.

In like manner Central and Southern Africa had been apportioned among the Great Powers in accordance with the provisions of the Final Act of the Congress of Berlin of 1885, which prescribed the establishment of local governments and other measures for the maintenance of law and order. The agreements with the native chiefs by which these protectorates were established were little more than a cover for the later conversion of the territory into a "colonial protectorate." No suggestion of preparation for later self-government was to be found.

Obligations of the mandatory. The system of mandates established by Article 22 of the Covenant of the League of Nations represented an attempt to apply a form of international guardianship to certain colonies and territories which "as a consequence of the late war have ceased to be under the sovereignty of the States which formerly governed them and which are inhabited by peoples not yet able to stand by themselves under the strenuous conditions of the modern world." The system was thus limited to the colonies and territories of Germany and Turkey, and it did not extend to colonies and territories of the Allied and Associated Powers. The principle upon which the system proceeded was that "the well-being and development of such peoples form a sacred trust of civilization" and that securities for the performance of this trust should be embodied in the Covenant of the League. The tutelage of these peoples was to be entrusted to "advanced nations," which "by reason of their resources, their experience or their geographical position can best undertake this responsibility, and who are willing to accept it, and that this tutelage should be exercised by them as Mandatories on behalf of the League." [40]

Syria, Iraq, Palestine, Transjordan. Three distinct groups of such territories were marked off. The first group consisted of certain communities, formerly subject provinces of Turkey, which had reached a stage of development at which their existence as independent nations could be provisionally recognized, subject to a temporary regime of administrative assistance from a mandatory state. The mandate for Syria was accepted by France in 1920 and confirmed by the League of Nations in 1922. Subsequently the territory was divided into the Syrian Republic and the Lebanon Republic, separate constitutions for the two states being presented by France to the League in 1930. In 1933 France and

[40] A study of the origins of the system of mandates may be found in Wright, *Mandates under the League of Nations*, where an exhaustive bibliography is given. See also Bentwich, *The Mandates System*; Millot, *Les mandats internationaux*; Van Rees, *Les mandats internationaux*; M. C. Mills, "The Mandatory System," *Am. Journal*, Vol. 17 (1923), p. 50; Hall, *Mandates, Dependencies and Trusteeships*; Whiteman, *Digest*, Vol. 1, p. 598.

Syria signed a treaty of alliance contemplating the ultimate termination of the mandate and the admission of Syria into the League of Nations. The mandate for Iraq (Mesopotamia) was assigned to Great Britain; but before a text for the mandate was drafted the situation was modified by the conclusion in 1922 and 1926 of treaties of alliance between Great Britain and Iraq in which the former recognized the latter as a sovereign and independent state and undertook to exercise for twenty-five years a supervisory control accepted by the League as the equivalent of a mandate. The proposal of Great Britain that Iraq should be admitted to membership in the League of Nations was subsequently accepted, and Iraq became a member in 1932. The mandate for Palestine was also allotted to Great Britain, and it originally covered Transjordan as well. The latter was, however, separately organized by a treaty of February 20, 1928, which contemplated its admission into the League of Nations as an independent state.

The second group of territories under mandate, designated by the Council of the League as Class B mandates, included certain former colonies of Germany which were administered by the mandatory state under a separate form of government. But it is doubtful whether these territories could claim any degree of international personality. They included the British Cameroons, British Togoland, and Tanganyika under British mandate, the French Cameroons and French Togoland under French mandate, and Ruanda Urundi under Belgian mandate. The third group, designated as Class C, were administered as integral portions of the territory of the mandatory state and had no international status whatever. South-West Africa was assigned to the Union of South Africa; Samoa to New Zealand; Nauru to Great Britain, Australia, and New Zealand jointly; other Pacific Islands south of the equator to Australia; and Pacific Islands north of the equator to Japan.

G. TRUSTEESHIP SYSTEM OF THE UNITED NATIONS

The system of international trusteeship established by Chapters XII-XIII of the Charter of the United Nations is more comprehensive than the system of mandates under the Covenant of the League of Nations. Article 75 establishes an "international trusteeship system" for the administration of such territories as may subsequently be placed under the system by individual agreements with respect to each territory so placed. Article 76 sets forth the basic objectives of the trusteeship system: the furtherance of peace and security, the promotion of the political, economic, and social advancement of the people of the territory and their progressive development towards self-government or independence according to the circumstances of each territory, the encouragement of respect for human rights and fundamental freedoms, and the ensuring of equal treatment in social, economic, and commercial matters for all members of the United Nations and for their nationals. Article 77 makes the trusteeship system applicable, by means of special agreements, to territories now held under mandate, to territories which may be detached from enemy states as a result of the war, and to territories voluntarily placed under the system by states responsible for their administration. Articles 86 and 87 make provision for a Trusteeship Council which is to exercise administrative functions under the authority of the General Assembly with respect to nonstrategic areas and under the authority of the Security Council with respect to strategic areas, in the latter case without prejudice to security considerations.[41]

Although no explicit obligation was imposed by the Charter upon the mandatory states to transfer their mandates to the trusteeship system it is clear that the transfer was implied, and all but one of them promptly declared their intention to do so, except in the single case of the Union of South Africa which sought to incorporate its mandate of South-West Africa into its own territory.

In 1949 the General Assembly asked the International Court of Justice for an advisory opinion on the international status of South-West Africa, to clarify the situation resulting from the refusal of the Union of South Africa to comply with the resolution of the Assembly to place the territory under the Trusteeship System. In its refusal the Union took the position that its original mandate had lapsed with the dissolution of the League of Nations, thus terminating any international obligations of the Union. The opinion of the Court was to the effect that the Union still had obligations if not technically under the mandate, and that the Union was not competent to modify the status of the territory except with the consent of the United Nations, and that under the provisions of the Charter the Assembly was competent to exercise supervisory functions formerly exercised by the League of Nations.[42] Four years later the Court held, on request of the Assembly, that a rule drafted by the Assembly to give effect to its supervisory functions was a correct interpretation of its advisory opinion of 1950.

H. NON-SELF-GOVERNING TERRITORIES

In addition to the provisions of the Charter looking to the protection of territories placed under the trusteeship system, Article 73 embodies a "declaration" regarding all non-self-governing territories, in accordance with which the members of the United Nations responsible

[41] The *U.N. Yearbooks* (1946-1962) give regular reports of the administering authorities on the operation of the system. For a general survey, see Whiteman, *Digest*, Vol. 1, p. 731.

[42] *U.N. Yearbook*, 1950, p. 806. On July 18, 1947, the United States entered into a trusteeship agreement for the former Japanese-mandated Pacific Islands, including the Marshalls, the Carolines, and the Marianas. Whiteman, *Digest*, Vol. 1, pp. 769 ff. For the problem of South-West Africa, *ibid.*, pp. 485, 706.

for the administration of "territories whose peoples have not yet attained a full measure of self-government" accept as a sacred trust the obligation to promote the well being of the inhabitants of these territories. The declaration has proved to be even more far-reaching than contemplated, constituting a standard of colonial administration, although not creating a council or other machinery for its supervision. The scope of the obligations includes not only the provision: "To ensure the political, economic, social, and educational advancement of the inhabitants, with due regard to their culture, and to insure their just treatment and protection against abuses," but the more important provision: "To develop self-government, and assist the peoples in developing their own free political institutions according to the particular circumstances of each territory and the stage of advancement of its peoples." With almost dramatic reaction to this second provision one colony after another, British, French, Dutch, and Portuguese made a bid for independence, some forming separate independent states, others federating or being incorporated in existing states of related nationality. By 1960, colonialism was on the wane, except in cases such as the scattered islands of the Pacific, where independence is not a practical solution.[43]

I. MEMBERSHIP OF THE UNITED NATIONS

It was to be expected that with the establishment of the United Nations states of previously limited or restricted membership would seek formal admission into the reorganized community of nations. The Atlantic Charter had proclaimed respect for the right of all peoples to choose the form of government under which they would live; and the Charter had declared the same objective as one of its "purposes." The trusteeship system, as we have seen, specifically declared as one of its basic objectives the progressive development of the people of the trust territories towards self-government or independence as the particular circumstances might indicate as appropriate; and the Declaration regarding non-self-governing territories included the same objective, if phrased rather in terms of self-government than of possible independence.

Admitted with other sovereign states to membership of the United Nations as original signatories were not only Ethiopia, reconquered from Italy; but Iran, previously a member of the League of Nations; Iraq, Lebanon, and Syria, released from their status as mandates; the Philippines, in advance of its attainment of independence in 1946; and Saudi Arabia, already recognized as independent in 1931 when it bore the name of the Kingdom of Hejaz and Nejd.

In addition, two original signatories, the Byelorussian and the Ukrainian Soviet Socialist Republics, not sovereign states and possessing no

[43] *U.N. Yearbooks* give regular information on the particular territories. *U.N. Yearbook*, 1962, pp. 407 ff.

previous international personality, but given a sort of fictional independence to satisfy the desire of the Soviet Union for larger representation, were also admitted as original signatories of the Charter.[44]

Afghanistan, already recognized as an independent state and a member of the League of Nations, was admitted to membership in 1946; as were Iceland, declared independent of Denmark in 1944; Thailand, formerly Siam, a sovereign state and a member of the League of Nations; and Sweden as of right. Pakistan, separated from India by the Independence Act of 1947, was admitted in the same year, accompanied by Yemen, recognized as independent by Great Britain in 1934. Burma, declared independent by Great Britain in 1947, was admitted in 1948. Indonesia fought its way to independence from Holland and was admitted to membership in 1950. Israel was admitted in 1949 while hostilities between the new state and Egypt were still in progress.[45]

The new state of Pakistan was the result of the division of India between the Moslem and the Hindu religious groups following the declaration of the independence of India by the All-India Congress on January 22, 1947. In June of that year Great Britain submitted a plan by which the two religious groups might partition the country on the basis of dominion status within the British Commonwealth of Nations. Pakistan, the Moslem area, became an independent state in its own national character; while Hindustan is considered legally identical with the pre-independent state of India. Controversy continues with respect to the two states of Kashmir and Jannu, claimed by both India and Pakistan.[46]

The problem of Israel presented difficulty, due to the strong racial hostility between Jews and Arabs. Before the mandate had been assigned to Great Britain, the so-called "Balfour Declaration" of 1917 had been accepted by the other Allied Powers in favor of a national home for the Jewish people, consistently with respect for the civil and religious rights of non-Jewish communities in Palestine. In 1947 Great Britain submitted the question of Palestine to the United Nations; and the General Assembly, acting upon a report of its special commission, partitioned Palestine into two independent states, Jewish and Arabic (Jordan) and a zone comprising the city of Jerusalem. On May 14, 1948, upon expiration of the British mandate, the new state of Israel was proclaimed. Hostilities followed between Egypt and Israel, calling for the intervention of the General Assembly. Israel was admitted to membership in

[44] *U.N. Yearbook*, 1946-1947, p. 863. For the decision made at the Yalta Conference to accord membership to the two Soviet Republics, see Whiteman, *Digest*, Vol. 1, p. 406.

[45] *U.N. Yearbook*, 1946-1947, p. 122; 1948-1949, p. 373. The relations between Israel and its neighbors continue to be acute. For a report of the special United Nations Conciliation Commission, see *U.N. Yearbook*, 1962, pp. 135 ff.

[46] See, on the problem as a whole, Whiteman, *Digest*, Vol. 1, pp. 415, 505; *U.N. Yearbook*, 1962, p. 128, surveys the situation as of the current issue.

the United Nations in 1949. The sovereignty of the Gaza Strip remains undetermined.[47]

In 1955 nine European states whose sovereignty was not in question but whose political relations following the war had given rise to controversy, Albania, Austria, Bulgaria, Finland, Hungary, Italy, Portugal, Rumania, and Spain, were admitted to membership as the result of a "package deal," along with six Near and Far Eastern states: Cambodia and Laos, declared independent by France in 1945 and members of the French Community (Union); Ceylon, declared independent by Great Britain in 1947, and a member of the Commonwealth; Jordan, formerly part of the Palestine mandate and independent in 1946; Libya, declared independent by Italy in 1946; Nepal, long independent, but not in contact with the Western World until the 1920's. Ireland also, although a member of the League of Nations since 1923, but not invited to become an original signatory by reason of having remained neutral during the Second World War, and Spain, delayed because of opposition to the Franco government, were admitted. Austria was admitted following the treaty of May 15, 1955, between the Big Four and the Soviet Union by which Austria was "re-established as a sovereign, independent and democratic state." [48]

Three North African states were admitted as members in 1956: the Sudan, released from the condominium of Great Britain and Egypt; Morocco, recognized by France as independent in the same year, thus terminating the protectorate established by the Treaty of Fez of 1912; and Tunisia, released from a French protectorate established by a treaty of 1881. These were followed in 1957 by Ghana, formerly the British protectorate under the name of Gold Coast; the Federation of Malaya, a group of British protected states recognized as independent in 1957; and Japan, delayed for political reasons.[49]

In 1958 only Guinea was admitted, a former French Overseas Territory and a part of French West Africa, having achieved independence by rejecting the new Constitution of the French Fifth Republic.[50]

In 1960 a large number of African states won their independence and were admitted to membership of the United Nations almost automatically. Thirteen of them were former French dependencies, colonies, or trust territories: Central African Republic, Chad, Republic of the Congo (Brazzaville), Dahomey, Gabon Republic, Ivory Coast, Cameroon, Malagasy Republic (Madagascar), Mali, Republic of the Niger, Senegal,

---

[47] See Whiteman, *Digest*, Vol. 1, p. 225; and for the special status (*Corpus separatum*) of Jerusalem, p. 593.

[48] *U.N. Yearbook*, 1955; Whiteman, *Digest*, Vol. 1, pp. 284 ff.

[49] *U.N. Yearbooks*, 1956, 1957. In 1957 Viet Nam was proposed for membership, but the Soviet veto defeated the proposal; this resulted in a vote of regret by the General Assembly.

[50] *U.N. Yearbook*, 1958.

Togo, and Upper Volta, all of them, except Togo, becoming members of the French Community. Other new states, former British dependencies or trust territories, were admitted: Cyprus, Ghana, Nigeria, and Somalia. Also in 1960 the former Belgian Congo became a member, under the title Republic of the Congo (Leopoldville).[51]

The year 1961 saw the admission of three more African states: the Islamic Republic of Mauritania, attaining its independence the year before and becoming a member of the French Community; and Sierra Leone and Tanganyika, former British colonies, becoming members of the Commonwealth of Nations. In addition, the Mongolian Peoples Republic (Outer Mongolia), becoming nominally independent as a result of the Chinese-Russian treaty of 1945, was admitted. The representative of China had opposed the admission of Mongolia on grounds of his delegation's conviction that the country was still a colony of the Soviet Union, and Morocco opposed the admission of Mauritania as being historically and ethnically a part of the territory of Morocco.[52]

In 1962 six new states were admitted. Algeria presented a special problem. Originally an independent state, it became a protectorate of France in 1830, remaining such until 1881 when it was incorporated into France as an Overseas Department. As a result of civil war between Algerian nationalists and French colonists, General de Gaulle proposed self-determination; and on July 1, 1962, Algeria chose independence and was admitted as a member of the U.N. on October 8. Burundi and Rwanda, formerly the Belgian colony of Ruanda-Urundi, were admitted as separate members. Jamaica and Trinidad-Tobago, recognized by Great Britain as independent in August, 1962, were also admitted as separate members, together with Uganda, a former British protectorate, independent as of October 9, 1962; all three became at the same time members of the British Commonwealth. Western Samoa, a mandate of New Zealand and a United Nations trust territory in 1947, became independent on January 1, 1962, and remains closely associated with New Zealand.[53]

On September 16, 1963, the Federation of Malaya, which had been admitted as a member of the United Nations in 1957, was enlarged into the Federation of Malaysia by the inclusion of Singapore, Sarawak, and North Borneo (Sabah). Neighboring states, Indonesia and the Philippines, contested the formation of the new Federation.[54] Kuwait, independent in 1961, was admitted to membership in 1963.

On December 10 Zanzibar became independent, and on December 12 Kenya, the former British colony which only a few years before had been the scene of savage Mau Mau attacks, also became an independent

[51] U.N. Yearbook, 1960, p. 198.
[52] U.N. Yearbook, 1961, pp. 166 ff.
[53] U.N. Yearbook, 1962, p. 150.
[54] Dept. of State Bulletin, October 7, 1963, February 18, 1964; United Nations Review, October, 1963.

nation. The Federation and Kenya were admitted as members of the United Nations in the same month.[55] On April 27, 1964, Tanganyika and Zanzibar united to form the "United Republic of Tanganyika and Zanzibar." On October 24, 1964, Northern Rhodesia became the independent republic of Zambia.

Where, or perhaps how, are states to be classified which, while nominally sovereign and full members of the United Nations, are in fact under the control of another state and are popularly to be described as "satellites" of the state controlling them? Such is the relation of Poland, Hungary, Rumania, Bulgaria, and Czechoslovakia to the Soviet Union. So also, for the moment, is the status of Cuba; although in this last case the control of the Soviet Union was established at the invitation of the Cuban Government. The release of the satellite states is obviously a political issue, conditioned by the ideology of the dominant power. Albania's pro-Communist status is for the time uncertain.[56]

J. POSITION OF INDIVIDUALS IN INTERNATIONAL LAW

If international law is a law between sovereign states, have individuals, citizens of the various states, any standing before the law? Have they rights and duties which can properly be said to be international rights and duties? Are individuals "subjects" of the law as well as states, although in a more restricted degree, or are they merely "objects" of the law? The problem is a complicated one, due to the failure at times to distinguish between the substantive and the procedural law, and to the fact that the terms "subjects" and "objects" have been carried over from municipal law to international law without always taking into account the differences in the practical application of the terms.

Subjects and objects of the law. "Subjects," as the term is used in general jurisprudence, are the persons to whom the law attributes rights and duties; "objects" are the things in respect to which rights are held and duties imposed.[57] Individuals are the primary persons of municipal law, because in them inhere the rights which the state was created to protect and upon them devolve the correlative duties to respect the rights

[55] *United Nations Review,* January, 1964.

[56] The test of "satellite" status would appear to be the absence of free elections and the denial of fundamental human rights. The existence of such status is obviously not confined to the Eastern European states, but the name is confined to them because of their previous free status.

[57] Holland, *Elements of Jurisprudence,* Chap. VIII. The meaning of "subjects" in relation to international law is analyzed in Spiropoulos, *L'Individu en droit international,* where it is said, p. 32: "A subject of the law is one to whom the rules of a juridical system are immediately addressed, that is to say, one who is directly qualified or obligated by the rules of a juridical system." To the same effect Kelsen, *General Theory of Law and State,* p. 343. But many writers use the terms "subjects," "persons," "international personality" without careful distinctions, with the result that some writers may be cited on both sides of the controversy.

of other individuals. Groups of persons may be given by the state a corporate character, a moral personality; but such character is in most cases artificial and transient, and the state may terminate the existence of such persons when they have ceased to fulfil their purpose.

When Grotius wrote his famous treatise in 1625 states had not yet taken on the attributes of absolute sovereignty which came to characterize them a century later. International law was still based upon the law of nature, the law derived from the very nature of man as a moral being, binding equally upon Christian princes as upon their individual subjects. But with the substitution of the personality and sovereignty of the state for the personality and sovereignty of the prince, the rights of the individual ceased to be a determining factor in the making of the law, and publicists concentrated their attention upon the rights and duties of the state as a corporate person, in which the personality of the individual was almost wholly lost. Paradoxically enough, even democratic states were so intent upon their domestic sovereignty that, with a few exceptions, they abandoned the conception of rights of the individual transcending national boundaries.[58] In an age of national expansion and sharp rivalry governments gave little thought to the promotion of humanitarian interests, except in so far as backward peoples might be brought under their control by the assumption of what they chose to consider "the white man's burden."

The formal relations of states. Considering the question from the point of view of the formal relations of states, it would appear that the position taken by those jurists who consider states only as the subjects of international law is difficult to contest. It is states which meet at international conferences and congresses to determine the rules which are to govern their respective claims and to provide ways and means of international cooperation. The delegates to such conferences speak in the name of their respective states, and the decisions they take bind the state in its corporate capacity. It is states and states only that may be members of the United Nations, and it is states only that may be parties in cases before the International Court of Justice. It is states which maintain diplomatic representatives at their respective capitals and which negotiate with one another for the protection of their national interests. It is states which enter into treaties, bilateral or multilateral, creating new rights and duties superseding existing law. It is to his state that the individual must turn for protection when he is the victim of a denial of justice in a foreign country. By the law of war, as applied in 1914 and in 1939, the enemy character attaching to each of the belligerent states descended to each and every citizen of the state, whatever his personal

[58] Perhaps the most notable of these exceptions was the assertion by the Congress of the United States in 1868 that "the right of expatriation is a natural and inherent right of all people." See below, p. 308.

sentiments might be with respect to the justice of the conflict in which his state was engaged.

View that states only are subjects of the law. In the presence of these facts of international intercourse the majority of writers until of recent years have held that individuals were not *subjects* of international law but rather *objects* of the law.[59] Apparent exceptions have been explained by saying that it is a mere convenience that the language of diplomatic correspondence relating to the protection of citizens in other countries gives the impression at times that the claim is made in the name of the individual. The fact that individuals have on occasion been permitted to appear before international courts is likewise put down as a mere matter of convenience. It is the state of which the individual is a national which must ultimately assure the payment of the claim. The duties which international law appeared to ascribe to individuals, as for example by the former laws of war and of neutrality, were in reality not duties which the individual owed to international law itself, but rather they were the conditions under which the state of which he was a national was entitled to protect him against one or other of the belligerents.[60]

View that individuals are subjects of the law. On the other hand a number of jurists, looking behind the formalities of international procedure, insist that it is the individual who is the primary unit of society, international as well as national. The existing states of the world are but "artificial bodies," formed by the chance of historical circumstances. Each of them possesses a corporate character not by reason of any inherent right, but merely because it represents the desire of a particular group of individuals to unite for the protection of their fundamental and

[59] The case was, perhaps, most effectively stated in Oppenheim, *International Law*, Vol. I, § 13 (1928): "Subjects of the rights and duties arising from the Law of Nations are States solely and exclusively. . . . Therefore, all rights which might necessarily have to be granted to an individual human being according to the Law of Nations are not international rights, but rights granted by Municipal Law in accordance with a duty imposed upon the State concerned by International Law." See §§ 288, 293, 344.

Compare Sir J. F. Williams, *Chapters on Current International Law*, pp. 5 ff., where it is argued that, "A legal system cannot be said to recognize rights as belonging to persons, when it does not allow those persons to deal with those rights," having in mind the fact that the individual can only secure his alleged rights by having recourse to the state of which he is a national. Equally definitive is Sir Frederick Smith, *International Law*, 5th ed., p. 53: "States and states alone enjoy a *locus standi* in the law of nations; they are the only wearers of international personality."

[60] Westlake states this aspect of the problem as follows: "Where international law allows a state to have direct relations with a private person not its own subject, it is only by virtue of a rule prevailing between states that this is so." After giving examples, he observes: "These considerations furnish the answer to a question which is sometimes asked, whether private persons can be the subjects of international law. It would be pedantic to deny that the pirate and the blockade-runner are subjects of international law, but it is only by virtue of rules prevailing between states that they are so." *Chapters on the Principles of International Law*, pp. 1-2.

inalienable rights as individuals and for the promotion of their mutual interests. The state is, indeed, "natural to man," in the classic words of Aristotle; but it is natural only because it fulfils certain fundamental needs of man's nature, because it is a means for the development of the individual man in association with his fellows.[61] Its corporate unity gives it no such sacred character as to justify the assertion by it of rights in its own name which might violate the fundamental rights of its individual citizens or which might prevent or obstruct the normal intercourse of the citizens of one state with those of another. The state exists for man, not man for the state. Governments, says the Declaration of Independence, exist by the consent of the governed; they are therefore but the agents of the people, acting under their control and obedient to their injunctions. Under such circumstances to say that individuals are merely *objects* of the law is to assign rights to the state which are in contradiction with the principles upon which the constitutional law of all democratic states rests. Individuals are, indeed, not members of the international community; but that is not conclusive of the issue. A federal state can be a union of separate states without thereby denying to individuals rights under federal law.

If the formal relations of states proceed, as a matter of fact, upon the basis of their corporate character, this can be said to be a mere historical circumstance, a practical necessity, due to the difficulty of organizing an international community of individuals. Individuals, therefore, are the true subjects of international law, and states are only the agents through which they act in default of more convenient means of giving effect to their common interests.

Variations in the views of jurists.   The argument is obviously a highly theoretical one, and it is clearly directed against the absolutism of the sovereign state, whether as impeding the progress of international government or as resisting the extension of international law into new fields.[62] The fundamental thesis has been stated in a variety of ways, and there are perhaps as many expressions of it as there are writers on the subject.[63] Some are content to assert merely that individuals are *also*

[61] See p. 54. The student will distinguish sharply between the state in the abstract and the particular states that have taken shape as the result of political and economic factors, many of which can scarcely be described as "natural" expressions of man's need for social life.

[62] It is to be expected that those who have been most determined in their attacks upon the sovereignty of the state (see p. 125) should also be the ones to assert the place of the individual as a subject of international law. Duguit, for example, is consistent throughout his writings in denying the one and upholding the other. See H. J. Laski, "M. Duguit's Conception of the State," in *Modern Theories of Law*. See also Laski, *Studies in the Problem of Sovereignty*.

[63] The Italian jurist Fiore is conspicuous among the earlier proponents of the more extreme view. Man possesses rights *jure suo;* he must be considered as "a person of the *Magna civitas";* he has international rights because he is a human being, and he carries these rights with him wherever he goes. *Diritto internazionale codificato*

subjects of international law; and that it is possible for them to be subjects of the law without at the same time being members of the international community, which is clearly limited to states as such.[64]
Reference is made to the fact that many branches of the law have little or
no direct reference to the interests of states as such. The rights and
duties of aliens in the state of their domicile, the privileges of foreign
ships in national ports, the navigation of the high seas, for example, all
deal with what individuals, not states, may do under certain contin-
gencies. The law regulating these matters is, indeed, a law between
states, but in its practical application the individual is regularly treated
as if the right claimed were his own personal right.[65] The trials of war
criminals at Nuremberg suggest that individuals may also be made
directly responsible for acts in violation of international law.

The welfare of man as man. More effective, however, is the argument that the international community has come to realize more and
more of recent years that the welfare of the individual is a matter of
concern irrespective of the particular state of which he happens to be a
national, and that measures must be taken to improve his condition and

---

(Borchard's trans.), Bk. I, Title XXIII. Before Fiore, Heffter had asserted that the
fundamental human rights of man made him one of the "immediate subjects of present international law." *La droit international public de l'Europe*, 1866 ed., p. 31.
See also pp. 115-118 for a detailed exposition of these fundamental human rights.
Bluntschli foresaw a future in which international law might protect the rights of
man in the same way in which federal states did so when one of their members violated them. *Das moderne Völkerrecht*, 3rd ed., p. 20.

[64] For more recent statements of the view that individuals are subjects of the law,
see Lauterpacht, *Private Law Sources and Analogies of International Law*, where the
question is treated in connection with his theories of the objective character of international law; F. S. Dunn, *Proceedings*, Am. Soc. of Int. Law, 1935, pp. 14 ff.: "The
very basis on which international law was erected was the universal moral order
of the Christian Church, which in turn rested solidly on the concept of the worth
and dignity of the individual. . . . To give personality to the state rather than to
the individual is perhaps a harmless bit of anthropomorphism in normal times, but in
the present crisis there is great danger that it will be misunderstood." P. M. Brown,
referring to plans for the establishment of a "world assembly," asserted that "The
most serious error committed by the defenders of international law has been the
parrot-like reaffirmation that it applies only between sovereign states." *Am. Journal*,
Vol. 40 (1946), p. 160.

See also Scelle, *Précis de droit des gens;* Politis, *The New Tendencies in International Law;* H. Aufricht, "Personality in International Law," *Am. Pol. Science Rev.*,
Vol. XXXVII (1943), pp. 217-243, where a general survey of the problem is given;
Jessup, *A Modern Law of Nations*, Chap. II, where extensive references are given
and international law is defined as a "law applicable to states in their mutual relations
and to individuals in their relations with states." Compare also M. St. Korowicz, "The
Problem of the International Personality of Individuals," *Am. Journal*, Vol. 50
(1956), p. 533.

[65] The importance of the appearance of individuals before international courts is
stressed by a number of writers. E. I. Hambro, *Proceedings*, Am. Soc. of Int. Law,
1941, pp. 26 ff., speaks of the access of individuals to international courts as "a
symptom of a tendency to create a real international society," and as "a part of the
tendency to curtail the all important sovereignty of the national state."

to raise his standard of living not immediately in the interest of the state of which he is a national but in his own interest as a human being. The various sanitary conventions that have been adopted have had in contemplation not merely the protection of the health of one state against the contagion of disease in another, but the humanitarian object of preserving the health of individuals as human beings.[66] In like manner measures that have been adopted for the protection of public morals have had a humanitarian rather than a merely protective purpose. The International Labor Organization has demonstrated the concern of its members not only for the welfare of the worker as a citizen of a particular state but the worker as a human being whatever his nationality or racial group.[67] The fact that the draft conventions of the organization call for ratification by the separate states relates to the administration of the measures proposed, not to the humanitarian objectives of the measures themselves.

The recognition of fundamental human rights. But it is in the field of the recognition of fundamental human rights that the individual has come of recent years to be a subject rather than an object of the law. The "Four Freedoms" proclaimed by President Roosevelt in his message to Congress in 1941 were directed towards the individual human being as such, apart from his membership in a particular state.[68] The Declaration by United Nations, signed on January 1, 1942, proclaimed that the protection of human rights in all countries was one of the results which it was hoped might be obtained from victory over the Axis Powers.[69] The Conference on Problems of War and Peace, held in Mexico City in 1945, declared the support of the American Republics of a system of international protection of the essential rights of man, and it made provision for the preparation of a Declaration of the International Rights and Duties of Man to be attached to the new organic pact of the Inter-American System.[70] In more specific terms, and having in mind the

[66] See p. 595, where the various conventions are set forth in detail.

[67] The constitution of the International Labor Organization, however, lays stress upon the relations between states, proclaiming that "peace can be established only if it is based upon social justice," and that "the failure of any nation to adopt humane conditions of labor is an obstacle in the way of other nations which desire to improve the conditions in their own countries."

[68] "We look forward," said the President, "to a world founded upon four essential human freedoms," freedom of speech and of expression, freedom of worship, freedom from want, and freedom from fear, each of them to be enjoyed "everywhere in the world."

[69] For the text of the Declaration, see Dept. of State *Bulletin*, January 3, 1942, p. 3. The Declaration confirmed the Atlantic Charter which had expressed the hope that a peace might be established "which will afford assurance that all men in all the lands may live out their lives in freedom from fear and want."

[70] Resolution IX, No. 9; Resolution XL, "International Protection of the Essential Rights of Man." In pursuance of the latter resolution the Inter-American Juridical Committee prepared a draft Declaration of the International Rights and Duties of Man.

creation of the conditions necessary for peaceful relations, the Charter of the United Nations declared that the organization would promote "universal respect for, and observance of, human rights and fundamental freedoms for all without distinction as to race, sex, language, or religion"; and the members pledged themselves individually to take joint and separate action in cooperation with the organization to achieve that purpose. At the same time both the General Assembly and the Economic and Social Council were called upon to make recommendations for the advancement of human rights, and the Council was specifically instructed to set up a commission for the promotion of human rights.[71]

Acting in pursuance of these provisions the General Assembly, upon recommendation of its special commission, adopted on December 10, 1948, a Universal Declaration of Human Rights setting forth in thirty articles basic rights and fundamental freedoms to which all men and women everywhere in the world are entitled, "a common standard of achievement for all peoples and all nations." [72] In view, however, of a belief that the cause of human rights would be promoted by an obligation of binding force, the General Assembly made provision in 1951 for two separate conventions, a Covenant on Political and Civil Rights, embracing the traditional rights recognized in the Western World, and a Covenant on Economic, Social, and Cultural Rights, including provisions looking to raising standards of living, protecting labor, promoting education, and in other ways advancing the general welfare.[73] Greater difficulty was experienced in drafting this second instrument in view of the fact that it does not lend itself readily to enforcement in the traditions of the Western World.

Side by side with the activities of the United Nations in the field of human rights has been the action of the American States under the Bogotá Charter of 1948. Accompanying the Charter was a Declaration of the Rights and Duties of Man, including both the traditional privileges of a bill of rights and the economic and social provisions common to recent Latin American constitutions.[74] But again, as in the case of the United Nations, it was believed that a formal contractual agreement was necessary; and in response to a resolution of the Fifth Meeting of Consultation, the Inter-American Council of Jurists prepared a draft convention enumerating the rights to be protected and the functions of an Inter-American Court of Human Rights, to be submitted to the Eleventh Conference.[75]

[71] Preamble; Article 1, 3; Article 13, 1b; Article 55, c; Article 62, 2; Article 68.
[72] For the text of the Declaration, see *Am. Journal*, Vol. 43 (1949), Supp., p. 127.
[73] *U.N. Yearbook on Human Rights*, 1951, 1952.
[74] *Int. Conferences of Am. States*, 1942-1954, p. 263.
[75] Resolution XX, "Human Rights," *Final Act* of the Fourth Meeting of the Inter-American Council of Jurists, *I.C.J. Reports*, 1959, p. 47.

Of similar regional significance is the European Convention on Human
Rights signed on November 4, 1950, by the members of the Council of
Europe, which, although limited in membership, contains provisions for
the "collective enforcement of certain Rights stated in the Universal
Declaration." The obligations of the Convention are, therefore, both
legal and specific; and as measures of enforcement the Convention
created a European Commission on Human Rights and a European
Court of Human Rights.[76]

Account must also be taken of the fact that in the peace treaties
signed by the Allied Powers with Italy, Hungary, Rumania, Bulgaria,
and Finland at the close of the Second World War, provision was made
that the former Axis partners should take all measures to secure to all
persons under their jurisdiction the enjoyment of human rights and
fundamental freedoms, although no special provision was made for
recourse, by an individual alleging violation of the provisions, to procedure before the United Nations.[77]

In the presence of these facts it would seem unreal to say that individuals are not in some degree subjects of international law. While the
procedures for the protection of the rights assigned to the individual are
as yet in large part a matter of domestic law, the obligations assumed
by the parties under the existing treaties and resolutions are influenced
by decisions of the commissions entrusted with their supervision, before
which the individual may appear and state his case. The individual is
clearly to that extent a subject of international law.

[76] For the text of the Convention, see *Am. Journal,* Vol. 45 (1951), Supp., p. 24.
[77] For the provisions of the minorities treaties, see below, pp. 128, 316.

CHAPTER VII

Acquisition and Loss

of International Personality:

Succession of States

A. ACQUISITION OF INTERNATIONAL PERSONALITY

The procedure of recognition.   We have seen above that the modern international community of sovereign and independent states began with the small exclusive group of European powers which were maintaining diplomatic relations at the time international law began to take shape about the middle of the seventeenth century, and which might be described as the "charter members" of the international community.[1] Thereafter new states were admitted into the community one by one as the charter members found it convenient to widen their circle; each state, upon its admission, acquiring the rights of membership and assuming its obligations.[2]

What were the conditions upon which the older members of the community might agree to accept these new members into their exclusive circle? What principles were applied to determine whether the applicants were competent to exercise the rights and able and willing to fulfil the duties of membership in the community? Was it possible to fix with any degree of legal accuracy at what point a "people" might be said to have taken on the characteristics of a state? The questions were difficult ones, and jurists as well as governments were embarrassed to find an answer.[3]

---

[1] See above, p. 121.

[2] Compare Secretary Webster's statement in 1842, cited above, p. 123.

[3] Attention is called in Chap. VIII to the necessity of distinguishing sharply between the recognition of new states and the recognition of new governments. Certain of the principles regulating the two procedures are the same, but their application is different and the results are wholly unlike.

On the general subject of the recognition of new states, see Moore, *Digest*, Vol. I, §§ 28-42; Hackworth, *Digest*, Vol. I, §§ 35-46; Whiteman, *Digest*, Vol. 2, pp. 1-133;

A half century ago the procedure of "recognition" played an important role in the development of international law. It might be defined as the formal acknowledgment by an existing member or by existing members of the international community that a state or a political group hitherto not holding membership in the community was now entitled to it, and, as an incident of membership, entitled to all of the rights and privileges of other members of the community. Therein lay its importance in the days before the formal organization of the community. Recognition by Great Britain, by the United States, or other of the Great Powers might mean life or death to a people declaring their independence as a separate state. Apart from the Monroe Doctrine, the recognition by the United States of the Latin American states in the 1820's undoubtedly strengthened their claim to statehood; and while recognition by a particular state could confer no more than the individual state had to give, recognition by a leading power had normally the effect of leading lesser powers to take similar action. On occasion the Great Powers acted collectively; but the general practice was individual, and each state was free to act or not to act, according to its judgment of the situation.

What was the legal effect of recognition in respect to the state recognized? Jurists were not in agreement, some holding that a new state became a member of the international community *ipso facto,* and that recognition was, therefore, merely a "declaratory" act; others holding that recognition was constitutive in character, that is, it gave international personality to the new state and thus brought it within the rights and obligations of international law.[4] Obviously there were conditions attending recognition: did the new state meet the prerequisites of statehood, so as to be able to assert its rights and fulfil its obligations? Clearly enough, every group of people calling itself a state could not expect to be taken into the international community on the strength of a mere declaration of independence.

Forms of recognition. Recognition was said to be express when a definite and explicit statement was made to that effect; it was tacit or

---

Hyde, *Int. Law,* Vol. I, §§ 35-42; Fauchille, *Traité de droit international public,* Tome I, Nos. 199-204; Kunz, *Die Anerkennung von Staaten und Regierungen im Völkerrecht;* H. Kelsen, "Recognition in International Law," *Am. Journal,* Vol. 35 (1941), p. 605; Lauterpacht, *Recognition in International Law* (1947); Marek, *Identity and Continuity of States in Public International Law.*

[4] See, on this point, Lauterpacht, *Recognition in International Law,* pp. 87 ff.; J. L. Kunz, "Critical Remarks on Lauterpacht's 'Recognition in International Law,'" *Am. Journal,* Vol. 43 (1950), p. 713; H. Briggs, "Recognition of States: Some Reflections on Doctrine and Practice," *ibid.,* Vol. 42 (1948), p. 113. The Convention on the Rights and Duties of States, adopted at the Seventh Conference of American States at Montevideo in 1933, proclaims the Latin American position in strong terms: "The political existence of the state is independent of recognition by the other states." *Int. Conferences,* 1933-1940, p. 121. But the statement still left open the question of the *de facto* existence of the state.

"implicit" when the older member entered into official intercourse with the new member by sending diplomatic representatives to it, concluding treaties with it, acknowledging its flag or otherwise entering into formal relations with it. Political conditions were the determining factor in the choice of one or the other method of recognition.[5]

Admission of states outside the European community. As applied to states already long in existence but not as yet within the circle of the international community, recognition gave rise to little controversy. Russia's position was so well established in 1721 that the procedure attending its admission into the family of nations by the Treaty of Nystad in 1721 could scarcely be described as "recognition."[6] The admission, however, of non-Christian states presented difficulties. In general it might be said that their admission was determined by the decision of the leading states as to the possibility of the performance by the particular non-Christian state of the duties prescribed by international law. The Barbary Pirates, as they were called, while given some degree of official recognition of their legal personality during the eighteenth and early nineteenth centuries by the conclusion of treaties with them, failed to improve their conduct sufficiently to be admitted into the family of nations before they lost their personality altogether.[7] Turkey was the first non-Christian state to be admitted, being made a party to the treaty of Paris of 1856 at the close of the Crimean War. But long before its admission treaties had been entered into with the Ottoman Empire, so that the term "recognition" seems hardly applicable to the statement of the Paris Conference that Turkey was thereupon admitted "to participate in the public law and concert of Europe."[8] Its capital was moved from Constantinople to Ankara in 1923.

Japan entered into official relations with the Western World in 1854 and 1858, when treaties were signed with the United States, Great Britain, and other states, opening certain ports and granting commercial privileges. It was not, however, until 1895 that the empire, having demon-

---

[5] For a list of the various forms of recognition used by the United States, see Hackworth, *Digest*, Vol. I, pp. 166 ff.; Hyde, *International Law*, Vol. I, p. 49; Whiteman, *Digest*, Vol. 2, p. 48.

[6] Following the demonstration of its military strength by the defeat of Sweden, Russia took at once the position of a Great Power.

[7] See the decision in the case of *The Helena*, 4 C. Rob. 4 (1801), in which the court, in determining the validity of the title to a vessel captured by the Dey of Algiers and subsequently sold, held that the title could not be annulled on ground of the original "piratical seizure." Although the Algerine's notions of justice to be observed between nations, said the court, "differ from those which we entertain, we do not, on that account, venture to call in question their public acts." An extraordinary decision, reflecting the policy of appeasement of that day.

[8] The admission of Turkey was doubtless not so much an acknowledgment of its capacity to fulfil the obligations of membership as the result of the necessity of an agreement among the Great Powers concerning the future of that country and of its vassals.

strated its military power by its defeat of China, won an acknowledged place in the circle of the Great Powers. No formal "recognition" was needed to establish its claim to the full rights and privileges of membership in the international community.[9] The admission of China, Persia, and Siam, likewise partial for some years previous, became complete at the time of their attendance at the Hague Conference of 1907.[10] Recognition seems, however, applicable to the case of Ethiopia, which became a member of the international community by its admission to the League of Nations in 1923.[11] Afghanistan was recognized as independent by Great Britain in 1919, and in 1921 an Afghan mission was received by the President of the United States; an act which was later interpreted as recognition of the regime of King Amanullah.[12] In 1931, upon receiving a request for recognition from the Foreign Office of the Kingdom of Hejaz and Nejd, the United States inquired whether that government was prepared to enter into a treaty of friendship, commerce, and navigation, and upon receiving an affirmative answer extended "full recognition" to it.[13] The name of the kingdom was changed to Saudi Arabia in 1932, and the new member of the international community participated in the Conference of San Francisco and signed the Charter of the United Nations.

The creation of new states by the process of the voluntary subdivision of an existing state or the voluntary federation of a number of existing states in like manner raised no controversial problems of recognition. The North German Federation of 1866 was recognized without hesitation and the new state admitted as a matter of course to the place hitherto occupied by the Germanic Confederation of 1815.[14] In like manner the recognition of the short-lived Central American Federation of 1921 was automatic, all of its separate members having been sovereign states before the formation of the Federation.[15] The separation of Sweden and Norway in 1905 raised no problem in respect to the separate recognition of the two states. The dissolution of the union of Austria and Hungary in October,

[9] A. Pearce Higgins, however, speaks of the Anglo-Japanese treaty of 1902 as setting "the final seal on the recognition of the latter Empire." Hall, *International Law,* 8th ed. by Higgins, p. 49.

[10] On the question of the admission of China, see Bau, *The Foreign Relations of China;* Escarra, *La Chine et le droit international;* Morse and McNair, *Far Eastern International Relations.*

[11] On the admission of Ethiopia to the League of Nations, see the report of the Council of the League of Nations and the declaration made by Ethiopia, *Am. Journal,* Vol. 30 (1936), Supp., p. 19. See also, M. O. Hudson, "Membership in the League of Nations," *ibid.,* Vol. 18 (1924), p. 444.

[12] See Hackworth, *Digest,* Vol. I, p. 195. Afghanistan was admitted into the League of Nations on September 27, 1934.

[13] Hackworth, *Digest,* Vol. I, pp. 218 ff.

[14] Recognition by the United States was given by a formal letter addressed by President Grant to Emperor William. Moore, *Digest,* Vol. I, p. 137. The subject, however, is classified by Moore under "Recognition of New Governments."

[15] For the text of the Pact of Union, see *Am. Journal,* Vol. 15 (1921), Supp., p. 328.

1918, was confirmed by the terms of the peace treaties entered into at the close of the war. Recognition of Austria and Hungary as separate and independent states followed as a matter of course.[16]

From time to time certain of the leading powers voluntarily conferred the privileges of statehood upon hitherto dependent parts of their colonial domain, or upon protectorates hitherto without international personality. In such cases recognition by other states of the international personality of the new state generally followed in due time the lead of the mother country. The formal recognition of the separate international personalities of the members of the British Commonwealth of Nations took place at the time of their admission as individual members of the League of Nations.[17] Egypt, a protectorate since 1914, was declared independent by Great Britain in 1922, and was recognized by the United States and other powers shortly after.[18]

On occasion one or another of the leading powers undertook to adopt a backward community not hitherto possessing even an inchoative personality, as in the case of Liberia by the United States and the Congo Free State by Belgium. The recognition of the new state by other states in such cases was dependent upon the progress of the new state in its political and economic relations under the guiding hand of its guardian. Liberia, adopted by the United States in 1847, remained outside the circle of the international community until 1920 when, under the patronage of President Wilson, it was admitted into the League of Nations.[19] The Congo Free State, created by Belgium in 1885, failed to obtain recognition as an independent state, and it had no farewells to make when it was annexed by Belgium in 1908.[20]

Recognition of revolting territories: the principle of self-determination. The real problem of recognition arose when a subject people sought to throw off the yoke of an alien oppressor, or when a colony or other part of an existing state sought to break off from the mother country and take an independent position in the international community. In 1776 when the United States of America declared their independence of Great Britain there was no accepted rule of international law by which the right of a colony to self-determination might be judged;

[16] See note 61. Diplomatic relations between the United States and Austria were simply "resumed." See Hackworth, *Digest,* Vol. I, p. 284.

[17] For the character of the members of the British Commonwealth as sovereign states, see below, pp. 243 ff.

[18] See above, p. 135.

[19] For the special problems presented by Liberia, see Azikiwe, *Liberia in World Politics.* Liberia was one of the original signatories of the Charter of the United Nations.

[20] On the subject of the Congo Free State, see J. S. Reeves, "The Origin of the Congo Free State," *Am. Journal,* Vol. 3 (1909), p. 99. For a historical survey of the Free State, see Thomson, *Fondation de l'Etat Indépendant du Congo.* For its status, see above, p. 145.

rather, the rule of international law was that the mother country had absolute right to determine the form of government to be put into effect in the colony, and any interference on the part of other states was regarded as unwarranted intervention in the domestic affairs of the mother country. The United States appealed to fundamental principles, to self-evident truths, that men were endowed with certain inalienable rights, that governments derived their just powers from the consent of the governed; but the appeal did not come within the rules of the international law which the British courts then proclaimed to be part of the law of the land.[21]

Emancipation by successful revolt. But legal title was one thing and facts were another. The practical question was, had the contest between the rebellious colony and the parent state reached a point where the latter had apparently abandoned all effort to reduce the insurgent colony to submission or gave no promise of being able to do so? Up to that time the province in revolt was left to fight its way into the international community as best it could. Having proved its ability to survive it was ready for recognition by such powers as might find it to their interest to begin official relations with it. Premature recognition of the independence of a revolutionary state would obviously be regarded by the parent state as an interference with its legal right to retain control over its subjects. The recognition of the United States of America by France in 1778 was unquestionably premature, and it was presently followed by a declaration of war by Great Britain against France.[22] Until the mother country itself recognized the independence of its former colony, third states took a risk, small or great as the case might be, in doing so. The recognition of the independence of the South American states by the United States in 1822, and by Great Britain in 1825, was justified by the facts, Spain having lost practically its last foothold on the continent.[23]

[21] The right of a state to determine whether its particular colonies or dependencies are ready for self-government or independence came practically to an end with the establishment of mandates and of trust territories; but it is still technically a domestic question for a few smaller areas which are admittedly unable to stand alone.

[22] The declaration of war was, of course, anticipated by France, and the recognition cannot be said to have been given upon juridical grounds. See Bemis, *Diplomatic History of the United States*, Chap. II.

[23] See Moore, *Digest*, Vol. I, §§ 28-36. The long struggle of the Spanish American states for independence must explain the insistence with which Latin American jurists hold that "the political existence of the state is independent of recognition by the other states," in the words of the Montevideo Convention of 1933. The Convention goes on to assert that "even before recognition the state has the right to defend its integrity and independence, to provide for its conservation and prosperity, and consequently to organize itself as it sees fit, to legislate upon its interests, administer its services, and to define the jurisdiction and competence of its courts." *Int. Conferences of American States*, 1933-1940, p. 122. Accioly well observes that while the doctrine that recognition is declaratory in effect rather than constitutive is more correct, as a matter of fact what is recognized is something which already exists. *Tratado*

But in any case Spain was clearly in no position to resent effectively the acts of recognition. The independence of Brazil was declared on September 7, 1822, and within less than two years the United States had given recognition to the new empire. But in this case the mother country, Portugal, made little effort to subdue the new state.[24]

The principle of nationalities.   A new impulse was given to the principle of self-determination during the second half of the nineteenth century by the struggle of the Italian states to attain freedom and national unity. Mazzini, Mancini, and other Italian jurists and patriots developed the "principle of nationalities," in accordance with which peoples of the same race, language, religion, and culture were to be united under common institutions and common laws. A generation of struggle was, however, required to unify Italy under the leadership of Sardinia; and it was only with the aid of Napoleon III that the yoke of Austria was at last thrown off. On March 17, 1861, the new "Kingdom of Italy" was proclaimed; but it was not until the occupation of Rome on September 20, 1870, that unity was finally attained. Recognition of the Kingdom of Italy was promptly given by Great Britain, France, Prussia, and Austria.[25]

The revolt of Greece and the Balkan peoples.   In the meantime the "call of humanity," inspired in part by the romantic aspect of the effort of the Greeks to throw off the yoke of the Ottoman Empire which they had borne since the fall of Constantinople in 1453, led the Great Powers to intervene in the struggle and to assure the independence of the country in 1827. The cry of the Serbs and the Rumanians was next heard, and after a period of guardianship both peoples were given independence in 1878.[26] Turkey was now disintegrating, and the appeal of its remaining subject peoples for independence would have found an even readier response had the Great Powers themselves not been engaged in the contest for the balance of power.

But self-determination in the abstract had not yet been accepted as a principle of international law. The Declaration of Independence had,

---

de Derecho Internacional, Vol. I, p. 144, quoting R. Erich, *Recueil des Cours,* Vol. 13 (1926-III), p. 431.

With respect to the question whether recognition is constitutive or merely declaratory, see Anzilotti, *Cours de droit international,* p. 160, who maintains that recognition is constitutive; and Fauchille, *Traité,* Première Partie, No. 199. See also Lauterpacht, *Recognition in International Law.*

[24] Moore, *Digest,* Vol. I, § 36. For details, see Accioly, *O reconhecimento da independencia do Brasil.* In consequence of the ready acceptance by Portugal of the loss of its former colony the relations between the two states have always been of the friendliest character.

[25] See, on the principle of nationalities, Hayes, *The Historical Evolution of Modern Nationalism;* Kohn, *Prophets and Peoples,* "Mazzini"; Chadwick, *The Nationalities of Europe and the Growth of National Ideologies;* Cobban, *National Self-Determination.*

[26] See above, p. 134.

indeed, proclaimed it in the broadest terms, and the Latin American states had followed the example in their separate constitutions. But it was still a conflict between the abstract right to demand and the power of the dominant state to refuse. Texas won its own self-determination by force when it seceded from Mexico in 1836, as the Latin American states had done from Spain a decade or more earlier.[27] But it took the dramatic incident of the sinking of the *Maine* to lead the United States to come to the aid of the Cuban people in 1898; [28] and it took the power and the national interests of the United States to confirm the self-determination of Panama in 1903.[29] Doubtless Albania would have failed in its struggle for self-determination had not the Great Powers come to its rescue in 1913 following the war between the Balkan states and Turkey in 1913.[30]

Effect of the World War, 1914-1918. It was only with the outbreak of the First World War that the principle of self-determination can be said to have made any effective progress. The subject nationalities of Central Europe saw the opportunity to obtain their independence if the polyglot empire of Austria-Hungary were defeated, while the revolution in Russia held out the hope of the liberation of peoples whose desire for freedom had hitherto not been pressed upon the attention of the international community.

President Wilson, in proclaiming on January 8, 1918, his Fourteen Points of a just peace, specified the return of Alsace-Lorraine to France, the readjustment of the frontiers of Italy "along clearly recognizable lines of nationality," the creation of an independent Polish state, and the autonomous development of the peoples of Austria-Hungary and of the nationalities under Turkish rule.[31] The recognition by the United States on September 3, 1918, of the Czechoslovak National Council as being "a *de facto* belligerent government clothed with proper authority to direct the military and political affairs of the Czecho-Slovaks" was made while the territory of the new state was still under the actual control of Austria-Hungary.[32] In the case of Poland, Germany and Austria-Hungary anticipated the movement for liberation by proclaiming the independence of the country in 1916, while the Russian Cadet Government had likewise recognized in 1917 that the creation of an independent

[27] See above, p. 160.

[28] See Moore, *Digest*, Vol. VI, p. 226. While the Joint Resolution of Congress preceded the Treaty of Peace with Spain, it was clearly made in anticipation of it.

[29] The case for self-determination on the part of Panama was a weak one, and the United States must be held to have been the responsible party. See Moore, *Digest*, Vol. III, p. 71.

[30] Hackworth, *Digest*, Vol. I, p. 196, explains the delay in granting recognition by the United States.

[31] See Nos. 9-13 of the "Fourteen Points." Ogg and Beard, *National Governments and the World War*, p. 565; Latané, *History of American Foreign Policy*, p. 606.

[32] See *Am. Journal*, Vol. 13 (1919), p. 93; Hackworth, *Digest*, Vol. I, p. 203.

Poland must be one of the conditions of a just peace.[33] When, on January 22, 1919, the United States gave full recognition to the Polish Provisional Government the communication described the new state as entering "upon a new cycle of independent life." [34]

As a result of the revolution in Russia, Finland proclaimed its independence on December 4, 1917. Denmark promptly recognized the new state, but other powers preferred to await the formation of a stable constitutional government; and it was not until May 3, 1919, that the United States and Great Britain decided to recognize "the independence of Finland and the *de facto* Government." [35] By contrast, the United States declined at first to recognize the Baltic states, believing that "friendship and honor" required that all decisions with respect to the sovereignty and territory of Russia should be held in abeyance until a "restored, free, and united Russia" would again take its place with other free nations in upholding peace and orderly justice. When, however, it appeared that there was no disposition on the part of the Bolsheviks to reconquer the three provinces, the United States on July 28, 1922, extended recognition to "the Governments of Esthonia, Latvia, and Lithuania." [36] Recognition had already been granted by the principal governments of Europe. Early in 1920 the Supreme Council of the Allied Powers agreed to recognize the *de facto* government of Armenia, and a mandate for the country was offered to the United States. This being declined, Armenia was annexed by the Soviet Union and became later a component part of the Transcaucasian Socialist Federated Soviet Republic, itself a part of the U.S.S.R.[37]

Effect of the system of mandates. But new winds had begun to blow with the establishment of the League of Nations in 1920, and the system of mandates pointed in the direction of self-determination for "certain communities formerly belonging to the Turkish Empire," whose independence could be provisionally recognized subject to assistance by a mandatory until such time as they were able to stand alone.[38] On this basis four Near Eastern territories were emancipated: Iraq was recognized by the United States as an independent state by the signature in 1930 of a tripartite convention with that country and Great Britain, although it was still at the time under British mandate. Syria and Lebanon, under French mandate, were not given formal recognition until

[33] Hackworth, *Digest*, Vol. I, pp. 214-215.
[34] *Ibid.*, p. 217.
[35] *Ibid.*, pp. 209 ff.
[36] *Ibid.*, pp. 199 ff.
[37] *Ibid.*, p. 222. On May 24, 1920, President Wilson formally requested the advice and consent of the Congress to acceptance of the proposed mandate. The Congress, however, respectfully declined to grant to the executive the power to accept it. *Ibid.*, p. 106.
[38] Covenant, Art. 22.

invited to send delegations to the San Francisco Conference and to become signatories of the Charter of the United Nations. Transjordan became an independent state by the Treaty of Alliance, which Great Britain signed with the former mandate on March 22, 1946. In 1948, upon expiration of the British mandate, the independence of Israel was proclaimed.[39]

Provisions of the Atlantic Charter. Forecasting the provisions of the Charter of the United Nations, the Atlantic Charter of 1941 declared the desire of the United States and Great Britain "to see no territorial changes that do not accord with the freely expressed wishes of the peoples concerned"; and that they respect "the right of all peoples to choose the form of government under which they will live." Unhappily the further wish "to see sovereign rights and self-government restored to those who have been forcibly deprived of them" was defeated by political conditions too strong to be resisted, the annexation by the Soviet Union of Lithuania, Latvia, and Esthonia, and the occupation of Poland.[40]

Provisions of the Charter of the United Nations. With the adoption of the Charter of the United Nations it would appear that the existing practice of recognition of new states by individual members of the community practically came to an end. The Charter states among its "Purposes" the development of friendly relations among nations based on respect for the principle of equal rights and self-determination of peoples; and the trusteeship system clearly contemplated, as we have seen, the progressive development of the people of the trust territories towards self-government or independence as the particular circumstances might warrant.[41] But more important still, the provisions for membership give to the Security Council and the General Assembly the decision whether the particular state seeking membership is or is not a "peace-loving" state able and willing to carry out the obligations of the Charter.[42] Here we have for the first time a collective decision equivalent to the former collective recognition of statehood. The old procedure of individual recognition would now be meaningless, except when it might occur in anticipation of the collective action of the United Nations.

The problem is clearly not one to which rigid rules can be applied.[43]

---

[39] For details, see *U.N. Yearbook,* 1948-1949, pp. 373, 395.

[40] For the text of the Declaration of United Nations embodying the Atlantic Charter, see Dept. of State *Bulletin,* Vol. XII, p. 576; *Am. Journal,* Vol. 36 (1942), Supp., p. 191.

[41] Art. 1 (2); Art. 55.

[42] Art. 4.

[43] Whiteman, *Digest,* Vol. 2, lists alphabetically the separate cases of fifty-five states recognized by the United States, beginning with Algeria in 1962 and ending with Yemen in 1946. On the general subject, see a critical study by Lowenstein, *Political Reconstruction,* Chaps. I-IV, where the theoretical and practical aspects of the problem are examined in detail. Compare, also, the admission of the same states as members of the United Nations, see below, Chap. VI.

Time will be required to create national unity among many of the recently emancipated peoples whose historical traditions have set class against class along religious, economic, and more recently along ideological lines. Is there hope of reconciling the two Chinas, the two Koreas, North and South Viet Nam? Can the new federations, for example, the Malayan Federation, hold together? Will the new African states maintain separate nationality, or are we to expect federal unions or regional organizations? Whatever the form taken by independent or confederated groups, it will be for the United Nations to decide the issue of nationality in accordance with the principles laid down in the Charter. The decision will obviously be at times along political lines, as in the case of the succession of the Federation of Malaysia to the Federation of Malaya.

Two cases of what might be described as "restored identity" are worth noting, although the transition from extinction to new life was effected without difficulty. In 1935 Ethiopia, conquered by Italy during the period of Nazi high fever, lost its international personality *de facto*, only to have it restored *de jure* when the country was reconquered by Great Britain in 1941. In 1938 Austria was coerced into forming an *Anschluss* with Germany and lost its international personality; but with the defeat of Germany the Austrian State Treaty was signed at Vienna in 1955 by representatives of the Soviet Union, the United Kingdom, the United States, France, and Austria.

B. RECOGNITION OF BELLIGERENCY

During the first quarter of the nineteenth century, when so many of the American states were fighting for their independence, the problem was presented whether political groups, in revolt against the state of which they were legally a part, might be entitled to be recognized as lawful belligerents even though they might not have demonstrated such a degree of control over the particular area of territory as to justify their recognition as having the status of *de jure* statehood.[44] Great Britain and the United States were both put under the necessity of formulating specific rules of international law in justification of an attitude toward the revolting colonies which was based upon fundamental principles of humanity and self-protection. It was impossible to regard such colonies, organized as separate states and conducting a war in behalf of political freedom, as mere groups of rebels against their law-

---

[44] On the subject of the recognition of belligerency, see Hall, *International Law*, § 5; Wilson, *Insurgency Lectures;* R. R. Wilson, "Recognition of Insurgency and Belligerency," *Proceedings,* Am. Soc. Int. Law, 1937, pp. 136 ff.; J. W. Garner, "Recognition of Belligerency," *Am. Journal,* Vol. 32 (1938), pp. 106 ff.; Hackworth, *Digest,* Vol. I, pp. 318 ff. The student should observe the distinction between the recognition of insurgent communities seeking to establish a separate state and the recognition of insurgent groups seeking to control an existing government.

ful government, devoid of rights under international law. In consequence, it came to be held that where a *de facto* political organization had been set up, giving promise of being able to maintain itself and conducting military and naval operations in accordance with the laws of war, and where, on the other hand, the parent state was exercising the belligerent rights of visit and search and of blockade, the situation must be recognized as one of public war.[45]

Effects of recognition. The effect of this recognition by third states of belligerent rights on the part of insurrectionists was to confer upon them a *de facto* international character in respect to the rights and duties of legal warfare. These included the right of admission of ships of the insurgents into the ports of the recognizing state, the right to borrow money on the credit of the *de facto* state, and principally the right of visit and search at sea, the confiscation of contraband goods, and the maintenance of blockade. The accompanying responsibilities could, of course, only be made good if the insurrection ultimately succeeded. At the same time, the act of recognition imposed upon third states the obligations of formal neutrality between the contending parties. Since both consequences were burdensome to the state giving recognition, its action was, as a rule, dictated either by sympathy with the rebellion or by the necessity of warning its citizens against the exercise of the rights of war by the *de jure* or the *de facto* state and protecting them against illegal acts of either belligerent.[46]

Controversies as to the time of recognition. Precipitate action on the part of third states in recognizing the *de facto* status of belligerent communities was naturally regarded as an unfriendly act by the parent state; but as in the case of the recognition of actual statehood it was difficult to determine the precise moment in advance of which recognition would be premature. The action of the United States in recognizing the belligerency of the South American states during the first quarter of the nineteenth century was regarded by Spain and the Holy Alliance as premature; but it was founded upon a fair basis of fact, and it would seem to have been equally as justifiable from the point of view of *de facto* conditions as was the recognition of statehood which followed later.[47] By contrast, the justification of the recognition of the belligerency of the Greek patriots in 1827 must, like the subsequent recognition of the independence of Greece, be seen to rest rather upon humanitarian grounds than upon the actual status of the revolutionists.[48]

An exceptional case, which caused an acute controversy between the

[45] See Moore, *Digest,* Vol. I, §§ 59-71, where the story of the Latin American states is given. See above, pp. 160 ff.
[46] See the opinion of the Solicitor of the Department of State, November 18, 1909. Hackworth, *Digest,* Vol. I, p. 321.
[47] See Moore, *Digest,* Vol. I, § 56.
[48] See above, p. 161.

United States and Great Britain, was the recognition by the latter of the belligerency of the Confederate States of America in 1861. Great Britain argued that its proclamation of neutrality, which recognized the Confederates as belligerents, followed both the proclamation of President Davis announcing the purpose of the *de facto* Confederate Government to exercise the rights of a belligerent and the proclamation of President Lincoln announcing the blockade of the Southern coasts. Inasmuch as British shipping interests were seriously affected by both proclamations, the British Government maintained that its act of recognition was not premature.[49] On the other hand, the United States insisted, first, that the rebellion of the Southern states did not amount to a state of war, and, later, that even if a state of war existed there was no necessity for the action of the British Government. It is now generally conceded that the position taken by Secretary Seward was an extreme one, and that the *de facto* status of the Confederate States justified the treatment of their forces as belligerents.[50]

Recognition of insurgency.   Recognition of the status of belligerency implied the existence of an organized political group *de facto* in control of certain territory but not yet having such an assured status as to warrant recognition as a new state. But what if the revolutionists were unable to control any large area of territory yet were sufficiently well organized to offer effective resistance to the mother country? Were they to be treated as mere outlaws and pirates, having no rights either in relation to their own government or in relation to third states? The situation was peculiar to the American continent, and the conception of a "status of insurgency" was invented to meet it.[51] The United States, seeking to prevent its citizens from taking part in expeditions and in other ways giving aid to the insurgents in violation of its neutrality laws, found it necessary to interpret the hostilities conducted by the insurgents as "war" against the mother country. At the same time recognition of insurgency was the expression of a belief on the part of the recognizing power on the one hand that the insurgents should not be executed as rebels if captured by the mother country and on the other hand that the insurgents should be entitled to prevent the access of supplies to the mother country from neutral states without, however, going so far as to exercise the right of visit and search at sea. In 1895 President Cleveland recognized the insurgency of the Cuban revolutionists and enjoined

[49] The argument is presented at length in Hall, *International Law*, 8th ed., § 5, p. 43.

[50] The controversy fills a large place in the literature of international law following 1861. See Moore, *Digest*, Vol. I, § 66; *Papers Relating to the Treaty of Washington*, Vol. I, pp. 19-46; Dana's Wheaton, *International Law*, ed. by Wilson, p. 29, note 15; Bemis, *Diplomatic History*, Chap. XXI.

[51] The term *insurgents* is also applied to groups in revolt against the government of the state, whose objective is to obtain control of the government and not to form a separate state. See below, p. 203.

the observance of the neutrality laws.[52] During the following year, in the case of the *Three Friends*,[53] the Supreme Court upheld the distinction "between recognition of belligerency and recognition of a condition of political revolt" and condemned, under the terms of the act of 1818, a vessel which had been fitted out and armed in the United States on behalf of Cuban insurgents unrecognized as belligerents. It does not appear likely that the circumstances which gave rise to the doctrine of the status of insurgency are likely to arise again; but the principle upon which the doctrine was based may not be without application in analogous cases.

C. EFFECT OF CHANGES OF POPULATION AND TERRITORIAL AREA

To what extent, if any, do changes in territorial area and in the size of its population affect the corporate character of the state as an international person? In general it may be said that the international personality of the state is not affected by accessions or losses of territory, with corresponding increase and decrease of its population, provided the changes are not so radical as to affect the central organization of the state or to deprive the state of that nucleus of territory in which the organization of the state has had its governmental seat.[54] The United States of America began as a group of thirteen states lying along the Atlantic seaboard, with an area of unoccupied territory extending northwest into the interior of the continent. By the purchase of Louisiana in 1803 and the purchase of Florida in 1819, by the incorporation of the independent state of Texas in 1845, by the cessions from Mexico in 1848, and by the purchase of Alaska in 1867, vast new areas of territory were added to the Union; but the United States remained the same person in law that it was, or rather *they* were, in 1783.[55]

The case of Sardinia is remarkable in that during the years from 1859 to 1870 it annexed new territory larger than its original area, changed its legal name to "Kingdom of Italy," and transferred its seat of government to Rome which was previously outside its territory.[56] The corporate personality of Great Britain, of France, and of Italy remained unaffected by their large territorial annexations in Asia and in Africa. Rumania doubled its size as a result of accessions of territory from Hungary and Russia after the First World War without question of its continuing

[52] Moore, *Digest*, Vol. I, § 74.

[53] 166 U.S. 1 (1897).

[54] The attention of the student is once more called to the distinction between "the state" as an abstract conception, natural to man because essential to the fulfilment of his human needs, and the state as a specific corporate person, whose personality may change *de facto* while it retains its formal juridical character.

[55] The *de facto* transition of the United States from a federation to a federal state is marked by the gradual use of a singular rather than a plural verb.

[56] Hall, *International Law*, 8th ed., p. 21, note 1.

identity. In the case of the Serb-Croat-Slovene State (later Yugoslavia) not only was new territory annexed from adjacent states, but a separate international person, Montenegro, was incorporated, without affecting the identity of the original Serbia.[57]

In spite of the partitions of Poland in 1772 and 1793 the state retained its legal personality until the final partition of 1795. Heavy losses of territory by Turkey in 1856 and in 1878, and again in 1911-1913, had no effect upon its legal identity. Nor would the corporate identity of the United States have been affected had the Confederate States succeeded in winning their independence in 1861-1865.[58] As a result of the First World War Turkey lost such great areas of territory that the delegates from Angora at the Conference of Lausanne in 1923 argued that the former Ottoman Empire had ceased to exist and a new international person had come into existence.[59] This position, however, was subsequently repudiated by the arbitrator on appeal from a decision of the commission charged with the distribution of the Ottoman debt.[60] While the losses incurred by Germany and Russia in 1918-1922 had no effect upon their legal personality, the more serious losses incurred by Austria led it to claim that continuity with the former Austrian Empire had been broken and that the new Austria was but one of a number of states formed out of the former monarchy.[61]

D. EXTINCTION OR LOSS OF INTERNATIONAL PERSONALITY

By voluntary act. Once international personality has been acquired by a state, it is lost only by the extinction of the state. Mere nonrecognition of its government does not put an end to its legal rights, although they may be unenforceable for the time being.[62] Extinction marks the end of the state itself. Occasionally it has occurred by voluntary act of the state itself, as when a federation breaks up into a number of separate states or a number of separate states unite to form a federation.[63] Each of the three divisions of Colombia required separate recognition by the United States when that state broke up in 1829-1830 into Venezuela, Ecuador, and New Granada, although it would seem that Colombia itself retained its original international personality under the name of New Granada, which was subsequently changed back to Colombia.[64]

---

[57] This, however, is disputed. See Feilchenfeld, *Public Debts and State Succession*, p. 566.

[58] Upon the suppression of the *de facto* Confederate Government it was held by the courts of the United States, as a point of constitutional law, that the seceding states had never been legally out of the Union. Keith v. Clark, 97 U.S. 454 (1878).

[59] Feilchenfeld, *op. cit.*, p. 435.

[60] *Annual Digest*, 1925-1926, p. 78.

[61] Feilchenfeld, *op. cit.*, p. 436.

[62] See below, p. 180, where the continuity of state personality is discussed.

[63] See below, p. 242.

[64] Moore, *Digest*, Vol. 1, § 36.

The independent "Lone Star" state of Texas voluntarily extinguished itself when it became one of the United States in 1845.[65] Montenegro was absorbed in Yugoslavia in 1919, although the voluntary character of its act might be questioned. Query, did Syria and Egypt each extinguish itself when they formed in 1958 the short-lived United Arab Republic, reducing by one the number of United Nations members? Egypt still retains the name after the dissolution of the union, as if in anticipation of new members. The same question may be raised for the union of Tanganyika and Zanzibar.

By forcible annexation. On the other hand extinction might occur against the will of the state as the result of conquest or annexation by another state; and in this case the state might not even retain any part of its former legal character. Poland disappeared as an international person in 1795.[66] The Transvaal lost its character as a semi-independent state in 1901, acquiring, however, shortly after, a constitutional position in the Union of South Africa. Korea, having received recognition of its independence of China in 1895, became a prize of war between Russia and Japan in 1905 and was formally annexed by Japan in 1910, losing thereby even the autonomy proclaimed in the Treaty of Portsmouth.[67] Ethiopia was annexed by Italy in 1936; but in this case the annexation, being in violation of the Stimson Doctrine and the principle announced by the Assembly of the League of Nations, was not recognized by other states, so that it cannot be said that Ethiopia became extinct as a result of the annexation. Austria was annexed to Germany by the *Anschluss* of March 11, 1938; but the annexation was not recognized by other states. In like manner Czechoslovakia can be said to have retained its international personality in spite of the partitioning of the country by Germany in 1939. So also the international personality of Poland survived the partitioning of the country by Germany and Russia in 1939; and the international personality of Albania survived its annexation by Italy in 1940. By contrast Lithuania, Latvia, and Esthonia lost their separate international personalities upon their annexation by the U.S.S.R. in 1940, the international community having made no protest or otherwise indicated its refusal to recognize the Soviet decrees.[68]

---

[65] *Ibid.*, Vol. I, p. 453. The annexation took effect not by treaty but by a joint resolution of Congress of March 1, 1845.

[66] But not the Polish "nation," in the sense attributed to that word by European writers of the nineteenth century.

[67] Hackworth, *Digest,* Vol. I, p. 84. For the reconstruction of Korea as an independent state, see below, p. 294.

[68] The violation of the provisions of the Atlantic Charter in the case of the Baltic states was obvious; but political considerations led to temporary acquiescence in the *fait accompli.* See, however, the statement of Undersecretary of State, Sumner Welles, July 23, 1940. Dept. of State *Bulletin,* Vol. III, p. 48.

For the doctrine of the nonrecognition of territorial acquisitions brought about by force, see below, p. 424, note 87.

The sovereignty of Ethiopia was restored following the expulsion of Italian troops

Partial extinction. It is a question whether a state may retain its international personality in part when, having been an independent state, it unites with another state or states to form a federal union. Under the old law, when coercion could create legal relations, Algeria became a protectorate of France from 1830-1881, retaining some measure of international personality until its incorporation in France itself by becoming an Overseas Department; and so also Morocco during the period of the guardianship of the Great Powers, 1906-1911. Whether the incorporation of a state or states into a confederation, as distinct from a federal union, is accompanied by a loss of international personality depends upon the closeness of the confederation. The thirteen individual states of the United States sought to retain each its "sovereignty and independence" under the Articles of Confederation of 1781; but in as much as their separate personalities had never been recognized by other states before the adoption of the Constitution of 1789, their disappearance as international persons was not noticed by the international community.[69] The five members of the Central American Federation retained their international personalities during its short-lived existence from 1921-1923, as they now retain their separate personalities in the existing Organization of Central American States.

Whether coercive or voluntary, the extinction of the state as an international person puts an end to its own international rights and obligations. All treaties concluded by it become as legal contracts null and void. All its rights at international law cease to be enforceable in its own name; none of its obligations can be pressed against it as a legal person. Its former rights must henceforth be asserted, if asserted at all, and its obligations must be met, if met at all, by the state which has absorbed it.[70] This may prove inconvenient to other members of the

by the British in 1943. See p. 165. Notwithstanding the plebiscite taken in Austria following the occupation by German troops, the Joint Declaration Regarding Austria made on October 30, 1943, at the close of the Moscow Conference declared that "the annexation imposed upon Austria" by Germany was null and void. Compare J. L. Kunz, "Identity of States under International Law," *Am. Journal,* Vol. 49 (1955), p. 68.

[69] The union under the Articles of Confederation had been proclaimed to be "perpetual"; but this provision of the Articles was violated without compunction when conditions made it necessary to form "a more perfect union." The status of the individual states of the "United States" during the period between the Declaration of Independence in 1776 and the adoption of the Articles of Confederation in 1781 has never been decided; but the conditions which once gave it urgency have long since ceased to exist.

[70] Hence the decision in the case of Terlinden v. Ames, 184 U.S. 270 (1902), holding that a treaty of extradition entered into by the United States with Prussia in 1852 continued to bind Prussia as a member of the German Empire, proceeded upon a wrong basis. "It does not," said the court, "necessarily follow [from the fact of the formation of the German Empire] that the Kingdom of Prussia lost its identity as such, or that treaties theretofore entered into by it could not be performed either in the name of its King or that of the German Emperor." Prussia actually became extinct. The question should have been decided on the point of the succession of the German Empire to the rights and obligations of Prussia.

international community; but international law has not as yet recognized any right on their part to protest.

E. SUCCESSION OF STATES

Closely associated with the special problems connected with the acquisition and loss of international personality is the difficult and as yet largely unsettled problem of the extent to which one state succeeds to the rights and obligations of another in cases of change of jurisdiction over a given area of territory. Succession between states must be sharply distinguished from a mere "succession of governments," where a succeeding *de jure* government is obliged to assume responsibility for the acts of a preceding government, *de jure* or *de facto*.[71] It involves the substitution of a new sovereign over the territory in question, and it calls for the determination not of the *de jure* character of the sovereign, which is a different question, but of the right of the new sovereign to assert the claims of the former sovereign in respect to the particular area of territory and the duty to meet its obligations.[72]

The idea of a succession of international persons was introduced into international law by Grotius as a corollary of the rule of Roman civil law by which an heir became the substitute in law of the deceased person and was clothed with the latter's rights and obligations.[73] But in consequence of the peculiar circumstances arising from the corporate personality of the state, the rule of law laid down by Grotius proved impossible of strict application; and down to the present day there has been no general agreement as to whether a true legal succession takes place or, if not, what practical rules of succession are to be inferred from precedents offered by the actual usage of states. The matter has been largely determined by treaties which indicate certain tendencies without, however, establishing fixed rules of law.[74]

---

[71] Confusion is sometimes caused by the parallel treatment of the different principles applicable to the two cases. Compare Smith, *Great Britain and the Law of Nations*, Vol. I, Chap. V, "Succession of States and Governments."

[72] On the general subject of the succession of states, see Moore, *Digest*, Vol. I, §§ 92-99; Hackworth, *Digest*, Vol. I, pp. 524 ff.; Keith, *Theory of State Succession;* Feilchenfeld, *Public Debts and State Succession;* Kunz, "Identity of States under International Law," *Am. Journal*, Vol. 49 (1955), p. 68; Whiteman, *Digest*, Vol. 2, p. 754; Marek, *Identity and Continuity of States in Public International Law;* O'Connell, *The Law of State Succession;* de Muralt, *The Problem of State Succession with Regard to Treaties.*

[73] *De jure belli ac pacis*, Eng. trans., Bk. II, Chap. XIV, § XI; also Bk. II, Chap. IX, § XII. The theories of Grotius and of his successors are discussed in Feilchenfeld, *Public Debts and State Succession*, Chap. II.

[74] Oppenheim, while rejecting a *"general* succession" according to what he describes as the "common doctrine" of writers, insists that succession does actually occur in specific cases which should be discussed singly. *Int. Law*, Vol. I, § 81. Brierly questions whether, in view of the complexities of the subject, the problems raised by it "are made easier by speaking, as many writers do, of a doctrine of state 'succession.'" *Law of Nations*, 2nd ed., 1936, p. 86.

Universal succession. Succession is said to be *universal* when one state completely absorbs the international personality of another state and thereby becomes the sole representative at law of the rights and obligations of the latter state. Universal succession may take place as the result of the annexation of the extinct state by conquest or other forcible means, as in the case of the South African Republic in 1901 or that of Korea in 1910; or it may take place as the result of the incorporation of the extinct state into a larger federal union. The division of a state into separate states, as in the case of Norway and Sweden in 1905, may also give rise to universal succession, but in this case there are as many successors at law as there are separate states. An exceptional case was that of the United Arab Republic, consisting of the separate states of Egypt and of Syria, which on February 24, 1958, informed the Secretary-General of the United Nations that the Union would henceforth be a single member of the United Nations, and that all international treaties and agreements concluded by Egypt or Syria with other countries would remain valid within the limits prescribed in those documents and in accordance with the principles of international law.[75] In 1961 Syria resumed its status as an independent state, but the United Arab Republic continued as a member of the United Nations.

Partial succession. On the other hand, succession is said to be *partial* when an existing state takes over, whether by forced or voluntary cession, the sovereignty of a portion of territory formerly belonging to another state, as in the case of the annexation of California by the United States in 1847; or again when a new state is formed by breaking off from a larger state, as in the case of the United States in 1776; or when a state previously a member of a federal state or of a confederation, or previously a protectorate of another state, as in the case of Algeria in 1962, obtains its complete independence. In such cases the problem presented is the distribution between the two parties—the one acquiring and the other losing sovereignty over the territory—of the rights and obligations attached to it.

Conditions of universal succession. Where the succession is *universal*, a distinction must be made between rights and obligations associated with the international personality of the extinct state, and rights which have become vested in the territory of the state, together with obligations created by treaties or contracts already executed in whole or in part. In the former class are the rights and obligations arising from political treaties, such as treaties of alliance, which relate to the future policy of the state under a given set of conditions. These are abrogated upon the extinction of the state which concluded them. In the same class are the rights and obligations arising from treaties of commerce and navigation and of extradition, which, though relating to

[75] *U.N. Yearbook*, 1958, p. 106.

matters of more general interest, nevertheless represent a give-and-take between the parties based upon their character as international persons.[76] On the other hand, rights which have become vested in the extinct state pass by succession to the annexing state. Among such rights are the title to the public property of the extinct state in third states, credits owing by third states or their citizens to the extinct state, easements possessed by the extinct state in respect to the public or private property of third states, etc. In the case of United States v. Prioleau,[77] decided in 1865, it was held that upon the extinction of the *de facto* Confederate States, cotton owned by them passed of right to the United States, but that the latter took the property subject to the obligations of the Confederate Government to a British citizen, Prioleau.[78]

Contractual obligations of the extinct state. The assumption by the annexing state of the obligations of the extinct state created by executed treaties or contracts is subject to exceptions which make the validity of a general rule of succession somewhat doubtful. Servitudes, *i.e.*, obligations to permit a third state to enjoy an easement in respect to territory, such as a right of transit through the territory, coastal fishing rights, etc., undoubtedly must be taken over by the successor.[79] Contractual obligations with third states or with their citizens, such as concessions for the development of mines or railways, have generally been assumed by the annexing state.[80] The case with respect to debts contracted by the extinct state is not so clear. In general they have been taken over, but there are many precedents to the contrary. The United States took

[76] These treaties may continue temporarily by implied consent, but they may be canceled at the option of either of the parties.

[77] 2 H. and M. (1865). Fenwick, *Cases*, p. 128; Hudson, *Cases*, p. 757.

[78] See also the case of the United States v. Smith, 1 Hughes, Rep. 347 (U.S. Circuit Court, 1877), in which it was held that a debt owed to the Confederate Government passed by right of conquest to the United States. In an earlier case before a British Court, United States v. MacRae, L. R. 8 Eq. 69 (1869), the court held that the United States was entitled, as successor to the Confederate Government, to an account of money and goods held by an agent of the Confederate Government, but would have to have the account taken as between the Confederate Government and the agent, which the United States was unwilling to do.

A unique instance of the extinction of a *de facto* state, the "Republic of Ireland," which not being held *de facto* could leave no successor, is to be found in the case of the Irish Free State v. Guaranty Safe Deposit Co., 129 Misc. Rep. 551, 222 N. Y. S. 182 (1927), involving an attempt by the Free State to obtain funds collected on behalf of the "Republic." The court refused to recognize the succession, and ordered distribution of the funds to the original subscribers. Fenwick, *Cases*, p. 139; Hudson, *Cases*, p. 760.

[79] A close analogy is here found with the covenants running with the land in the common law of Great Britain and the United States, following the principle *res transit cum onere.*

[80] See F. B. Sayre, "Change of Sovereignty and Concessions," *Am. Journal*, Vol. 12 (1918), p. 705. Obligations in tort need not, however, be assumed. See United States and Great Britain, Robert E. Brown Claim, Special Arbitration Tribunal, Fenwick, *Cases*, p. 136; Briggs, *Cases*, p. 215.

over the debts of its member states in 1790.[81] By contrast, the United
States refused in 1845 to permit the debts and liabilities of the annexed
Republic of Texas to become a charge upon itself, although provision
was made for the payment of the same by Texas from the sale of public
lands.[82] Italy assumed part of the papal debt in 1864, while Prussia
took over the debts of the annexed German states in 1866. In the case
of the West Rand Central Gold Mining Co. v. Rex,[83] the British court
refused to hear the suit, brought by a citizen of the annexed Transvaal
Republic, based upon funds confiscated by the Republic during the
war. Had the plaintiff been the citizen of a third state his claim might
perhaps have been successfully pressed through the mediation of his
government, notwithstanding the fact that the money confiscated had
been used by the Transvaal Government for the prosecution of the war.[84]

Conditions of partial succession. Where the succession is partial, the
same distinction is drawn between rights and obligations of a character
personal to the state losing the territory and rights and obligations of a
local nature associated with the physical property of the territory. If an
existing state takes over territory by way of forced or voluntary cession
from another, it does not succeed to rights and obligations connected
with the political treaties entered into by the former sovereign. On the
other hand, it does succeed to vested local rights such as the ownership
of public property and possibly, but doubtfully, easements, such as
special rights of navigation or rights of way. Corresponding local obligations must be assumed. It is not always clear, however, what obligations are local as distinct from personal obligations of the former
sovereign. In the case of United States v. Percheman,[85] decided in 1833,
the court held that a title to land under a grant from Spain prior to the
sale of Florida must be respected by the United States even if the treaty
of 1818 had not contained a stipulation to that effect. In the case of the
Eastern Extension, Australasia and China Telegraph Co.,[86] however, the
court held that the concession granted by the Government of Spain to
the company was "a personal one" which need not be assumed by the
United States upon taking over the Philippine Islands. On the other
hand, in the case of Vilas v. City of Manila,[87] involving the liability of

[81] For details, see Channing, *History of the United States,* Vol. IV, pp. 70-79.
[82] Moore, *Digest,* Vol. I, pp. 343 ff.
[83] L. R. 2 K. B. 391 (1905). Fenwick, *Cases,* pp. 38, 131; Hudson, *Cases,* p. 723;
Briggs, *Cases,* p. 218.
[84] The opinions of the respective justices hearing the case constitute an exhaustive
survey of the principles alleged to be involved in the case. The decision has been
sharply criticized by British as well as other writers. See Oppenheim, *International
Law,* Vol. I, § 82.
[85] 7 Peters 51 (1833). Fenwick, *Cases,* p. 153.
[86] 48 Ct. of Claims, 33 (1912). Fenwick, *Cases,* p. 263; Briggs, *Cases,* p. 33. Sustained in 251 U.S. 355 (1920).
[87] 220 U.S. 345 (1911). Fenwick, *Cases,* p. 150.

the city for obligations incurred before its cession to the United States, the court held that, while there was a "total abrogation" of the former political relations of the city, the "great body of municipal law which regulates private and domestic rights continues in force until abrogated or changed by the new ruler."

In the matter of succession to debts it is likewise not clear which debts are local as distinct from the general public debt of the ceding state. There are a number of cases in which the public debt of the state ceding the territory has been ratably divided between itself and the ceded territory, the latter portion being assumed by the successor; but there would appear to be no legal obligation in the matter.[88] The United States recognized no obligation to take over any part of the Mexican public debt because of the cession of California in 1848. On the other hand, debts contracted for the benefit of local improvements and, it may be, secured by local revenues must be taken over. In 1898 the United States refused to take over, on behalf of Cuba, the debt settled upon Cuba by Spain before the war, arguing that the debt had not been created by Cuba as a province or incurred by Spain for the benefit of Cuba.[89] Nor was the Philippine debt assumed, although under the terms of the Treaty of Peace a sum approximating the debt was paid for the cession of the islands.

Rights and obligations of a new state. Where a new state is formed by breaking off from an old one, its position in respect to succession parallels in general that of the state obtaining territory by annexation. Political treaties of the old state do not bind it. Local property rights are taken over. Local easements may or may not pass according to their vested character. The United States claimed in 1818 that fishing rights along the coasts of Newfoundland were merely confirmed, not granted, by the treaty of peace of 1783, since it already had title to them as successor to the rights of the original colonies. But this claim could not be successfully maintained, and the new treaty of 1818 made specific reference to a "liberty" to fish, instead of the imprescriptible *right* that had been claimed.[90] Local obligations, contracted with direct reference to the territory, must be assumed. Local debts must also be taken over. Precedents exist in favor of a ratable apportionment of the general public debt of the old state; but there would appear to be no fixed rule in the matter.[91] Belgium was made to pay a portion of the Netherlands debt by the treaty of 1839, and Montenegro, Serbia, and Bulgaria were made to take over part of the general debt of Turkey in 1878; but in

[88] The subject of succession to public debts in all its aspects is exhaustively treated in A. N. Sack, *Les effets des transformations des Etats sur leur dettes publiques;* and in Feilchenfeld, *op. cit.*

[89] Moore, *Digest,* Vol. I, § 97.

[90] Moore, *Digest,* Vol. I, §§ 163-64. See below, p. 478.

[91] See Feilchenfeld, *op. cit.*, Chaps. XXX, XXXI; Sack, *op. cit.*, pp. 219 ff.

both instances external pressure was brought to bear upon the new states.

Provisions of the treaties of 1919. By the terms of the Treaty of Versailles the powers to which German territory was ceded acquired all property belonging to the German Empire and to the German states, and in return were obligated to pay to the Reparations Commission the value of such acquisitions as fixed by the commission.[92] An exception was made in favor of the free acquisition by Poland of former German state property in Poland. Moreover, the "succession states" undertook to pay a portion of both the debt of the German Empire and the debt of the German state to which the territory belonged, as those debts stood on August 1, 1914, the amount in each case being determined by the Reparations Commission.[93] An exception was made in the case of Alsace-Lorraine on the ground that Germany had refused in 1871 to undertake any portion of the French debt. A further exception was made in the case of Poland in respect to that portion of the German debt attributable to the measures taken by the German and Prussian governments for the German colonization of Poland.[94] Similar provisions were contained in the Treaties of St. Germain and Trianon in respect to the succession of the new states of Czechoslovakia and the Serb-Croat-Slovene State (later Yugoslavia) to the rights and obligations of the former Austrian and Hungarian states.[95] By the Treaty of Lausanne, July 24, 1923, the Ottoman public debt was apportioned between the new Turkey and its detached parts. Protocol XII annexed to the treaty required the succeeding states to maintain prewar concessions granted by Turkey.[96]

Status of inhabitants of transferred territory. The status of the inhabitants of territory passing from one state to another is, in general, a problem of domestic law, but it may take on an international character when a multilateral treaty makes specific provision for the treatment of the inhabitants of the ceded areas. As a rule, treaties of cession contain special stipulations with respect to the collective naturalization of the inhabitants of the transferred territory, or at least their continued enjoyment of the rights of person and property enjoyed by them as citizens of the ceding state;[97] but such stipulations relate to the law of treaties, not to that of succession. In so far as citizens of third states happen to be resident in the transferred territory their status is properly a matter of concern to their home governments. In such cases the third state may intervene to protect them; but in so doing it appeals, not to

[92] Art. 256. *Am. Journal,* Vol. 13 (1919), Supp., p. 281.
[93] Art. 254.
[94] Art. 255.
[95] *Am. Journal,* Vol. 14 (1920), Supp., pp. 84 ff. (Austria); Vol. 15, Supp., pp. 66 ff. (Hungary).
[96] See Feilchenfeld, *op. cit.,* pp. 443 ff., 468 ff.
[97] See below, pp. 427 ff.

the obligations of the annexing state as successor to the ceding state, but to the general obligation of all states to accord just treatment to aliens.[98]

Problems of succession multiplied following the Second World War. Was the Bonn Republic successor to the former Germany? What treaty obligations, if any, passed to the German Democratic Republic under Soviet control? Did Ethiopia recover its full treaty rights when released from Italian sovereignty? If the second Austrian Republic of 1945 is not identical with the Austria under the Constitution of 1929, are its treaty rights and obligations affected? On what basis could the former treaties of India devolve upon the separate states of India and Pakistan following the territorial division in 1947?[99] Added to these and others involving members of the international community before 1945 have been the innumerable problems arising from the new states of Asia and of Africa, emancipated from colonial control. Some of these have inherited rights and obligations from their former sovereigns, and others secured them by special treaty. Morocco, for example, assumed in 1956 the obligations resulting from the treaties concluded by France in the name of Morocco; and the Philippines similarly took over the obligations assumed by the United States under the treaties with Spain of 1898 and 1900.[100]

[98] See p. 329. Compare the advisory opinion rendered by the Permanent Court of International Justice on September 10, 1923, upon questions relating to the property rights of settlers of German origin in the territory ceded by Germany to Poland. *Advisory Opinions*, Series B, No. 6. M. O. Hudson, "The Second Year of the Permanent Court of International Justice," *Am. Journal*, Vol. 18 (1924), p. 13.

[99] See, for a wide range of cases, O'Connell, *The Law of State Succession;* Marek, *Identity and Continuity of States in Public International Law.*

[100] Whiteman, *Digest,* Vol. 2, pp. 810 ff., lists them one by one, analyzing the special problems of each.

CHAPTER VIII

Continuity of International Personality:

The Recognition of New Governments

A. DISTINCTION BETWEEN RECOGNITION OF NEW GOVERNMENTS AND RECOGNITION OF NEW STATES

The important and highly controversial problem of the recognition of new governments is to be sharply distinguished from the problem of the recognition of new states. The two problems have frequently, indeed generally, been treated as if they were parts of a single problem, governed by the same general principles.[1] Incidents and judicial decisions relating to the recognition of new states have been cited as if they bore upon the recognition of new governments, and vice versa. The result has been to add unnecessarily to the confusion attending the application of the principles governing the two problems, neither of which has as yet been brought, in all of its phases, within clear and definite rules of law.[2]

As we have seen, the recognition of new states necessarily involves the recognition of the particular government which happens to be in control of the state at the time of recognition;[3] and this is perhaps an excuse for treating the two procedures as if they involved the same issues. But while in actual fact the tests applied to determine whether recognition

---

[1] So in Hackworth, *Digest*, Vol. I, §§ 30-34. H. Kelsen goes so far as not only to combine the two subjects as a matter of convenience, but to justify the combination as "essentially the same problem," arguing that a state must have a government if it is a state at all. "Recognition in International Law," *Am. Journal*, Vol. 35 (1941), pp. 605, 614.

[2] On the general subject of the recognition of new governments, see Moore, *Digest*, Vol. I, §§ 43 ff.; Hackworth, *Digest*, Vol. I, §§ 47 ff.; Whiteman, *Digest*, Vol. 2, §§ 61-65; Hyde, *International Law*, Vol. I, §§ 43-46 B; Goebel, *The Recognition Policy of the United States;* Jaffe, *Judicial Aspects of Foreign Relations*, Chap. 2; Hervey, *Legal Effects of Recognition in International Law;* Lauterpacht, *Recognition in International Law* (1947); Arechaga, *Reconocimiento de Gobiernos* (1947).

[3] See Chap. VII.

is to be granted appear to be much the same in the two cases, the conclusions to be drawn are fundamentally different. The recognition of new states bears upon the admission of a new political group to membership in the international community; it involves a decision as to the stability of the new political group as a corporate body and its ability to maintain itself as a separate and distinct international person. If in the course of determining this issue it becomes necessary to decide whether a particular government claiming to represent the political group seeking recognition as a state is actually entitled to represent it, that is a collateral issue distinct from the right of the political group to be an international person.

B. CONTINUITY OF INTERNATIONAL PERSONALITY

Once its identity as an international person has been fixed and its position in the international community established, the state continues to be the same corporate person whatever changes may take place in its internal organization and government. This continuity of the legal personality of the state may withstand the most radical transformations in its constitution. During the years from 1791 to 1875 France passed through a succession of constitutional changes, from monarchy to republic and from republic to empire, then back again to monarchy, empire, and republic. But throughout all these changes France remained France, one and the same international person, having the same rights at international law and subject to the same obligations. In the case of the *Sapphire*,[4] decided in 1871, it was held by the Supreme Court of the United States that the deposition of Napoleon in no way affected a suit brought in the name of the Emperor to obtain damages for losses to a French transport injured in collision with the American ship *Sapphire*.[5] So also the radical transformation in the constitution of Russia, its transition from an empire into a federation (R.S.F.S.R.) and in turn into a larger union (U.S.S.R.) had no effect upon the corporate character of Russia as a state; and there was no question at any time of Russia's position as a member of the international community, whether or not other members of the community were willing to maintain relations with the government in control of the country.[6]

---

[4] 11 Wallace, 164 (1870). Fenwick, *Cases,* p. 92; Bishop, *Cases,* p. 243.

[5] "The next question," said the court, "is, whether the suit has become abated by the recent deposition of the Emperor Napoleon. We think it has not. The reigning sovereign represents the national sovereignty, and that sovereignty is continuous and perpetual, residing in the proper successors of the sovereign for the time being. Napoleon was the owner of the *Euryale,* not as an individual, but as sovereign of France. This is substantially averred in the libel. On his deposition the sovereignty does not change, but merely the person or persons in whom it resides." *Ibid., loc. cit.*

[6] See below, p. 190.

C. PRINCIPLES GOVERNING RECOGNITION OF NEW GOVERNMENTS

It has long been accepted as a fundamental principle of international law that every people has the right to choose its own form of government. In no other respect is the internal independence of the state more manifest than in its right to determine its constitutional organization and to select the public officials under whom the constitution is to be put into practical effect. A government coming into power through normal constitutional procedures is regularly regarded as expressing the popular will. The actual fact that it may have been elected by only a majority of the voters is subordinated to, or rather absorbed in, the legal fact that it represents the results of certain constitutional procedures which the whole body of the people have agreed in advance to accept as expressing their collective will. The free expression of public opinion under a democratic government is implied.

When, therefore, changes take place in the government of a state in accordance with constitutional procedures, there is no question of the "recognition" of the new governmental officials by other states. The succession is direct and automatic. In such cases there is, strictly speaking, no "new" government. Republicans may oust Democrats, Conservatives may oust Labor; but in respect to other states the government is, for international purposes, the same government; and the only formality which the diplomatic representatives of other states observe is that of attending the inauguration of the head of the government in countries in which there is an elective head.[7]

Problem arises when constitutional procedures violated. But the forcible overthrow of an existing government, or the accession to power of a new government by a procedure not provided for by the constitution of the state, or it may be the continuance in power of an existing government in violation of constitutional procedures, raises at once the issue with third states whether the new government, claiming the right to represent the state in its international relations, is in fact competent to do so. Does it actually represent the will of the people, so that other states may enter into relations with it for which it would be just to hold the state as a corporate body legally responsible? Clearly this can only be determined by certain objective tests. Has the new government *de*

----

[7] The formalities attending the assumption of office by such new governments are sometimes described as "recognition," but they are not in any case part of the controversial problem of recognition. Occasionally foreign governments find it convenient to overlook minor constitutional irregularities of succession, as when a government continues itself in power by unconstitutional means, as in the case of President Vargas of Brazil in 1937, or when the coercion used in obtaining the resignation of a government is not too violent, as in the case of the same president in 1945.

facto control over the administrative agencies of the state? Does it appear to have the support of a substantial body of public opinion? Is there an absence of resistance to its authority which would indicate the acquiescence of the people, if not their formal approval? International law has never regarded the constitution of a state as so sacred that the people of the state may not change it by unconstitutional methods, or acquiesce in changes brought about by a minority resorting to violence. An inflexible constitution might readily present a practical situation in which only a revolution could succeed in breaking the hold of a small minority in possession of the reins of government. On the other hand a majority of the people might readily acquiesce in the establishment of an unconstitutional government by a minority when the conduct of the new government was such as to make the upholding of the constitution not worth the price of a civil war.[8]

Objective test of *de facto* character. In view of these various possibilities international law has developed the first of its two rules of recognition, that a new government coming into power by means not provided for in the constitution of the state should be recognized when it can meet the objective test of being a *de facto* government. A *de facto* government is understood to be one in actual control of the governmental machinery of the state and exercising its authority without substantial opposition.[9] It is said to possess the quality of "stability," taken in a broad sense. The decision of third states as to this point has naturally been influenced by the political conditions prevailing in the country in which the revolution has broken out. In countries normally stable even a radical change in the structure of the state may take place without giving rise to doubts as to the representative character of the

[8] Whether the alleged "right of revolution" is as sacred a right as it is sometimes alleged to be is another question, and obviously a political one. But it is at least clear from a study of the domestic revolutions of recent years that it would be wholly impracticable to propose as a rule of international law that the strict observance of constitutional procedures should be a condition of recognition.

[9] The objective test is sometimes divided into two parts: (1) control over the machinery of government and (2) the acquiescence of public opinion or the absence of organized resistance. In a memorandum of March 28, 1913, prepared by the Assistant Secretary of State, Adee, with reference to the recognition of the Government of the Republic of China, it was said: ". . . ever since the American Revolution entrance upon diplomatic intercourse with foreign states has been *de facto,* dependent upon the existence of three conditions of fact: the control of the administrative machinery of the state; the general acquiescence of its people; and the ability and willingness of their government to discharge international and conventional obligations. The form of government has not been a conditional factor in such recognition; in other words, the *de jure* element of legitimacy of title has been left aside, probably because liable to involve dynastic or constitutional questions hardly within our competency to adjudicate, especially so when the organic form of government has been changed, as by revolution, from a monarchy to a commonwealth or vice versa. The general practice in such cases has been to satisfy ourselves that the change was effective and to enter into relation with the authority in *de facto* possession." Hackworth, *Digest,* Vol. I, pp. 175-176.

new regime. The transition of France from an empire to a republic in 1870 during the course of the Franco-Prussian War was recognized promptly by the leading powers in spite of the exceptional circumstances.[10] In like manner the overthrow of the empire in Brazil in 1889 by a "bloodless revolution" was followed by immediate recognition by the United States of the provisional government, and by formal recognition of it when it was clear that a majority of the people supported the new government.[11] By contrast, in 1903, when King Alexander and other members of the royal Obrenovitch family were assassinated in Serbia, there was some hesitancy in recognizing King Peter I; but the apparent acceptance by the people of Serbia of the new Karageorgevich dynasty finally overcame the scruples of the reluctant states. In the case of the revolution in Portugal in 1910, there was delay in according recognition, due in part perhaps to sympathy with the monarchy; but by the time of the adoption of the new constitution in August, 1911, there could no longer be question as to the stability of the new government.[12] In 1930 the revolutionary government of President Vargas of Brazil was recognized by the United States within three weeks of his accession to office after the deposition of President Washington Luiz. In 1959 the revolutionary government of Fidel Castro in Cuba was recognized by the United States within six days of his coming into power. In 1962 the constitutional government of Peru and in 1963 the constitutional governments of the Dominican Republic and of Honduras were overthrown by military *coups d'etat;* but while recognition by the United States was delayed for a time, it was duly granted when there appeared to be no counterreaction.[13]

On occasion the United States has overlooked elements of force behind the scenes and not felt called upon to extend formal recognition to new governments actually installed by a *coup d'etat.* In 1945 President Vargas of Brazil was forced by army leaders to resign; but inasmuch as constitutional procedures were followed in the election of his successor, the Department of State held that the question of recognition did not arise.[14] So also in 1964, when President Goulart of Brazil fled the coun-

---

[10] On the part of the United States, President Grant promptly telegraphed his congratulations as soon as he had "learned that a republican body had been proclaimed at Paris, and that the people of France has acquiesced in the change." Moore, *Digest,* Vol. I, § 43.

[11] Ibid., § 55. For the attitude of other powers, see Accioly, *Tratado,* Vol. I, No. 214.

[12] See Hackworth, *Digest,* Vol. I, pp. 291-292.

[13] Whiteman, *Digest,* Vol. 2, pp. 266 ff., where numerous other cases and documents are given. On October 3, 1963, the delegations of Venezuela and Costa Rica called for a Meeting of Consultation under the Charter of the OAS to consider what collective attitude should be taken, but no decision was reached. See "The Recognition of *de facto* governments: Is there a Basis for Inter-American Collective Action?" *Am. Journal,* Vol. 58 (1964), p. 109.

[14] Whiteman, *Digest,* Vol. 2, p. 264.

try, the action of the Congress in swearing in a provisional president and proceeding thereupon to follow constitutional procedures in the election of a permanent president, appeared to call for no more than a telegram congratulating the Brazilian people for resolving their difficulties within the "framework of constitutional democracy."

Whether a totalitarian dictatorship, coming into power by methods of violence and maintaining itself in power by suppression of the fundamental liberties of the people, could be regarded as having the "stability" required for recognition is a question with which international law has not as yet concerned itself. Thus far international law has not looked beyond the fact of apparent acquiescence of the people in the new government, without reference to possible intimidation. Nor has international law as yet made inquiry into the representative character of a government which, having entered into power in accordance with constitutional procedures, proceeds to overturn the constitution and establish a totalitarian dictatorship. No question was raised by foreign states in 1933 when the Nazi Party, called by President Hindenburg to take over the government, proceeded to do so in ways which practically constituted a domestic revolution. In like manner the overthrow of the Brazilian Constitution of 1934 by President Vargas in 1937 raised no question with foreign states of his representative character, although the regime which he established was, in terms of constitutional procedures, a new government, notwithstanding the fact that all of its members remained in their previous posts.

The question of stability may on occasion call for delay in recognizing a new government, especially as the government recently overthrown may give signs of rallying its forces and threatening to recover its control. During such an interim period recognition is generally given *de facto*, that is, relations will be maintained with the new government on a working basis without formally acknowledging it as speaking in the name of the state. Recognition *de jure*, however, appears to be final. What if the new government should repudiate the promises that secured its support by public opinion and its formal recognition by other governments, as Fidel Castro did in 1959 within six months of taking power? In such cases the practice is to break relations with such a government, not to deny its character as representative of the state. In like manner a dictator, once duly recognized, may maintain a stable government by methods in violation of fundamental human rights, as in the case of Rafael Trujillo in the Dominican Republic, yet still retain his representative character, as *de jure* spokesman of his people.

Subjective test of willingness to fulfil obligations. In addition to the objective test of the *de facto* character of the new government, international law has developed a second test of a much more subtle character. Is the new government prepared to carry out the obligations of the state under international law? In point of abstract principle there would seem to be but one answer. Obviously any government holding itself out as the representative of the state and accepted as such by other states is bound to observe the rules of international law and to abide by the treaty obligations of the state. For the state itself undergoes no change because of a mere change in the governing body which represents it. The continuity of the state as an international person remains, as has been seen, unaffected by the fall of one government and the succession of another. Hence when a new government comes into power it is bound to carry out the obligations of the state by the very fact that it pretends to be the government of the state. The new government takes over these obligations not in a strict sense as successor to the government which has been overthrown but in its own character as representative of the state in its relations with other states.[15]

But international practice has not been satisfied with this abstract principle of the representative character of a new government. The fact that the new government has come into power in violation of the procedures established by the constitution of the state might be expected to raise the question whether it might not attach as little importance to the international obligations of the state as it had already shown for the constitutional procedures established for the succession of governments, especially in the case where obligations contracted by the preceding government may have led to its overthrow. In the case of states normally stable and characterized by their respect for democratic institutions the question might be raised only to be dismissed. But in the case of states which have been subject to frequent revolutions and in which revolutions have been accompanied by dictatorships which by their very nature have thrown doubt upon their representative character, the inquiry into the intention of the new government to respect the international obligations of the state has become an accepted feature of the procedure of recognition. New revolutionary governments of this type have on their part frequently made a bid for recognition by publicly proclaiming their intention to observe the international obligations of the state, referring at times specifically to treaties and contracts.[16]

In spite of acknowledged abuses that have occurred from time to time, to which reference will be made later, this "subjective" test, as it has

---

[15] The general rules of international law obviously bind the state as a state. Treaty obligations in like manner bind the state, not merely the government which contracts them. Compare the attitude of Secretary of State Jefferson in 1793 with respect to the binding character of the treaty of alliance entered into with France in 1778. Latané, *A History of American Foreign Policy*, p. 83.

[16] For instances, see Hackworth, *Digest*, Vol. I, pp. 223 ff.

been called, has been accepted by jurists with practical unanimity.[17]
The fact that third states may at times take it for granted that the new
government will observe the obligations of the state does not make that
condition any the less a part of the procedure of recognition. More
often, however, a declaration to that effect is specifically required; although, as has been said, new governments frequently anticipate the
requirement by making a proclamation upon their own initiative.

Difficulties in its application. The practical problem arises at times
in connection with the observance of the general rules of international
law and at times in connection with specific treaty obligations. In respect to the general rules of international law controversies have arisen
as to the application of a broad principle to certain concrete facts, such
as the right of a state, as an exercise of internal sovereignty, to expro-
priate the property of aliens under conditions alleged to amount to
confiscation.[18] In respect to specific treaty obligations, controversies
have arisen as to whether certain so-called "treaties of peace" should
continue to bind the state when the preceding government which entered into them was said to be acting under compulsion. In both cases
third states have at times been unwilling to give formal recognition to
a new government without first receiving assurances that its advent to
power would not mean a repudiation of the particular rule of law in
which they had an interest or the specific treaty which they have wanted
to maintain in force. The abuses by more powerful states of the procedure of recognition have been due in large part to the fact that
recognition has regularly been given by each state upon its own account
and in accordance with its own judgment of its rights in the case.

The General Assembly of the United Nations, confronted with the

[17] Fauchille's statement may be taken as expressing the opinion of continental
European scholars: "The one thing which States should take into account in the
matter of recognizing the government of another state is that it should in fact be
obeyed by the country which it undertakes to rule, that it has the power, and that it
offers satisfactory guarantees for the fulfilment of its international obligations." *Traité
de droit int. public*, Tome I, première partie, § 205 (2), p. 321.

Latin American writers handle the subject cautiously. Professor Podestá Costa, of
Argentina, published in 1926 his *Ensayo sobre las luchas civiles y el derecho internacional* in which the objective and subjective conditions of recognition are set forth in
clear and definite terms. The Brazilian jurist, Accioly, accepts the subjective test without question, *Tratado*, Vol. I, Nos. 205, 213. Judge Bustamante, of Cuba, quotes approvingly an article of Secretary Stimson in which the objective and subjective tests
are both set forth, although at the same time he finds merit in the Estrada Doctrine
(see below, p. 196) as avoiding the appearance of "qualifying" the right of
states to change their form of government. *Droit International Public, Tome* I, pp.
231, 237. Compare Ulloa, the Peruvian jurist, who, although accepting the Estrada
Doctrine, points out that the maintenance or withdrawal of diplomatic representatives tends to weaken [desvirtuar] the principle it proposes. *Derecho internacional
público*, Tome I, p. 103. Sepulveda, *La Theoria y la Practica del Reconocimiento de
Gobiernos.*

[18] As in the case of the controversy with Mexico following the adoption of the
constitution of 1917. See below, pp. 345 ff.

problem in 1950, adopted a resolution recommending a novel procedure by which whenever more than one authority claimed to be the government entitled to represent a member state in the United Nations and the question became a subject of controversy, the question should be considered in the light of the Purposes and Principles of the Charter and the circumstances of each case.[19]

D. SPECIFIC APPLICATIONS OF GENERAL PRINCIPLES

The French Revolution.   The French Revolution of 1789-1793 shook the European community of nations to its foundations. The announcement by the National Convention in 1792 that France was ready to come to the aid of all peoples who might wish to recover their liberty appeared to the monarchies of the time as an open declaration of war upon them.[20] To expect them to recognize the new government and thus encourage the spread of revolutionary principles was obviously out of the question. By contrast, Jefferson, as Secretary of State of a country born of revolution, waived aside the doctrines of the Revolution and confined himself to the objective test of the *de facto* character of the new government. His reply on November 7, 1792, to the American minister at Paris has become classic: "It accords with our principles to acknowledge any Government to be rightful which is formed by the will of the nation, substantially declared."[21] Again, on March 12, 1793, Jefferson declared:

We surely can not deny to any nation that right whereon our own Government is founded—that every one may govern itself according to whatever form it pleases, and change these forms at its own will; and that it may transact its business with foreign nations through whatever organ it thinks proper, whether king, convention, assembly, committee, president, or anything else it may choose. The will of the nation is the only thing essential to be regarded.[22]

Jefferson took it for granted that the new revolutionary government would observe the international obligations of France; he was not aware of, or at any rate did not take account of, the repudiation by the National Convention of the fundamental principle of the independence of states in respect to their domestic organization; or perhaps he was not prepared to defend autocratic government even if the principles of international law of that day respected it.

Consistently with the principles proclaimed by Jefferson, the United States promptly recognized Napoleon as Emperor in 1804 and Louis

---

[19] *U.N. Yearbook*, 1950, pp. 429, 435.
[20] Burke's *Reflections on the Revolution in France* well expresses the ultraconservative attitude in regard to the fundamental opposition of the principles of the Revolution to the established principles of international law and morality.
[21] Moore, *Digest*, Vol. I, § 43, p. 120.
[22] *Ibid.*, p. 120.

XVIII as King in 1814.[23] No question was made of their intention in either case to observe the rules of international law. When, in 1848, the legitimate government of Louis Philippe was overthrown and a provisional government of the French Republic was established, the American Secretary of State, James Buchanan, sent instructions repeating the principles of Jefferson:

In its intercourse with foreign nations the Government of the United States has, from its origin, always recognized *de facto* governments. We recognize the right of all nations to create and re-form their political institutions according to their own will and pleasure. We do not go behind the existing Government to involve ourselves in the question of legitimacy. It is sufficient for us to know that a government exists capable of maintaining itself; and then its recognition on our part inevitably follows.[24]

When, three years later, by a *coup d'état*, Louis Napoleon established the Second Empire, recognition followed with equal promptness. "While we deeply regret the overthrow of popular institutions," wrote Secretary Webster to the American Minister at Paris, "yet our ancient ally has still our good wishes for her prosperity and happiness, and we are bound to leave to her the choice of means for the promotion of those ends." [25]

Latin American revolutions. During the course of the nineteenth century the numerous revolutions both in Europe and in Latin America led to the extension of Jefferson's original rule to include regularly an inquiry into the ability and willingness of new revolutionary governments to abide by the obligations of international law. Drastic changes in dynastic succession added to the necessity of clarifying the attitude of new governments. On February 19, 1831, the Great Powers proclaimed in the Protocol of London that "treaties do not lose their binding force whatever changes may take place in the internal organization of peoples." [26] In 1851 when Napoleon III established the Second Empire, he declared his intention to respect existing treaties. In like manner the Provisional Government of France, in 1870, following the abdication of the Emperor, made a similar declaration. In Latin America the practice of requiring a statement of the intention of a new government to observe the obligations of the state developed naturally from the fact that the recognition of new states had always involved both an inquiry into the *de facto* character of the political community holding itself out as a state as well as an inquiry into the intention of the new state to accept the obligations of a member of the international community.[27] In as much as the intentions of the state could only be known

23 *Ibid.*, p. 122.
24 *Ibid.*, p. 124.
25 *Ibid.*, p. 126.
26 *British and Foreign State Papers*, Vol. 18, p. 780.
27 See above, p. 123.

through the declarations of the government which represented it, it came to be the custom to extend to new revolutionary governments arising within established states the same conditions that had previously been applied to the state itself upon seeking admission into the international community.

The transition from emphasis upon the *de facto* character of the new government to emphasis upon its intention to abide by the obligations of the state under international law is clearly marked in the instructions of the Department of State of the United States to the American minister in Mexico at the time General Porfirio Diaz announced himself provisional president of Mexico in 1876. In view of disturbances occurring on the Rio Grande border, the instructions said that although the United States was accustomed to accept and recognize the results of a popular choice in Mexico and not to scrutinize closely the regularity or irregularity of the methods by which those results were brought about, it would in the particular instance "wait before recognizing General Diaz as President of Mexico until it shall be assured that his election is approved by the Mexican people, and that his administration is possessed of stability to endure and of disposition to comply with the rules of international comity and the obligations of treaties." [28]

This inquiry by the United States into the disposition of the new government to comply with the obligations of the state continued during the last quarter of the nineteenth century, and by the first decade of the twentieth it had become a fixed element of the recognition policy of the United States. Great Britain pursued a similar policy, putting stress upon the fulfilment of treaty obligations. Gradually the practice became well established, that a new *de facto* government should announce publicly its intention to carry out the obligations of the state under international law. Had the matter stopped there, the question of recognition would probably not have become so highly controversial an issue among the American states. But the rapid succession of revolutionary dictatorships in a number of the Latin American countries made it difficult at times to avoid extending the subjective test to the policies of the new government as well as to its obligations under international law. Pledges were exacted from revolutionary governments as the price of recognition, and these were given at times without due regard for the interests of the state; so that when new revolutions brought other governments into power it was to be expected that they would regard the promises made by their predecessors as personal obligations of the deposed dictator rather than as obligations binding upon the state itself. On the other hand new governments, not as yet *de facto*, sometimes received support from the United States in anticipation of policies to be followed by them looking to the maintenance of law and order and to

[28] Moore, *Digest,* § 51.

the furtherance of the interests which the United States sought to protect.[29]

Recognition becomes a form of intervention. The procedure of recognition thus became a form of intervention; and being put into effect by the arbitrary decision of the United States it gave rise to criticism even in countries where the relative stability of governments made the application of the policy to themselves not to be considered. From the point of view of the United States the action taken was justified by the general right to protect its citizens and their property against the excesses of revolutionary factions; but it became difficult at times to distinguish the defense of legitimate rights from the promotion of economic interests. A constructive solution of the problem would have called for the adoption of more definite rules of international law in respect to the protection of aliens and to the obligations of the state in the matter of public contracts with foreign companies. But international law had not yet developed that far. The result was that the United States acted for itself, according to the sense of justice of its government at the time. On occasion the United States, before granting recognition to a new revolutionary government, insisted upon assurances from it of its intention to protect American interests in the country, indicating specific measures to be taken.[30] In 1904 President Roosevelt announced the necessity of exercising "an international police power" in certain flagrant cases of instability and disorder.[31] The two policies were parts of a whole.

The Soviet Government of Russia. The case of the Soviet Government of Russia [32] from 1917 to 1933 illustrates the application of the subjective test of recognition to its fullest extent. When the revolution broke out in 1917 recognition was withheld by the United States and other powers at the start partly because of uncertainty as to the tenure of the new government and partly because of its desertion of the Allied cause by the conclusion of a treaty of peace with Germany. At the close of the war recognition was still refused, chiefly upon grounds of the Bolshevik political principles, though it was insisted in certain quarters that the despotic character of the Soviet rule made it questionable whether its apparently firm tenure really represented the will of the Russian people. Even provisional recognition was denied by most of the powers. But as time went by and the government of the Soviets appeared to be

[29] It has been the wide latitude of judgment exercised by the individual state in deciding to grant or to withhold recognition that has made the decision a "political" rather than a legal question, in spite of the fact that there has been general agreement upon the legal principles governing the procedure.

[30] Hackworth cites the case of the Dominican Republic in 1903 and that of Haiti in 1911. See *Proceedings*, Am. Soc. Int. Law, 1931, p. 122.

[31] See below, pp. 282 ff.

[32] Technically, the Union of Soviet Socialist Republics (U.S.S.R.), of which Russia (the Russian Socialist Federated Soviet Republic, R.S.F.S.R.) is but one member.

definitely in control, the leading states began one by one to accord recognition: Great Britain, France, and Italy all in 1924. Germany had already entered into a treaty of mutual nonaggression which carried with it implied recognition. By contrast, the United States not only withheld recognition during the early years of Soviet control but consistently maintained the same policy during more than fifteen years. Successive Secretaries of State emphasized the failure of the Soviet Government to live up to the obligations of international law; [33] and they thus shifted the basis of recognition from the *de facto* character of the Soviet Government to the actual conduct of the Government in its international relations. The resulting situation in which one of the important states of the world was not maintaining official relations with the United States while recognized diplomatically by other states was an anomaly in international law, and it compelled the maintenance of indirect and unofficial relations of a somewhat paradoxical character. When recognition was finally given, on November 16, 1933, it was accompanied by an exchange of notes in which the Soviet Government undertook "to respect scrupulously the indisputable right of the United States to order its own life within its own jurisdiction in its own way and to refrain from interfering in any manner in the internal affairs of the United States, its territories or possessions." Moreover, the Soviet Government agreed to grant American nationals the free exercise of religious worship in Russia and to conclude a consular treaty giving to American nationals rights of legal protection "not less favorable" than those enjoyed by nationals of the most-favored nation.[34]

The failure of the United States to recognize the *de facto* government

[33] In justification of the policy of the United States Secretary Hughes, on March 21, 1923, stated that "The fundamental question in the recognition of a government is whether it shows ability and a disposition to discharge international obligations. Stability, of course, is important; stability is essential. Some speak as though stability was all that was necessary. What, however, would avail mere stability if it were stability in the prosecution of a policy of repudiation and confiscation? In the case of Russia we have a very easy test of a matter of fundamental importance, and that is of good faith in the discharge of international obligations. I say that good faith is a matter of essential importance because words are easily spoken. Of what avail is it to speak of assurances, if valid obligations and rights are repudiated and property is confiscated?" *Am. Journal*, Vol. 17 (1923), p. 296. For the earlier statements of Secretary Colby, August 10 and 18, 1920, see Hyde, *International Law*, Vol. I, § 45. Subsequent statements of Secretary Hughes on July 25, 1923, and December 18, 1923, again emphasized the necessity of the fulfilment of the "obligations of intercourse" as a condition of recognition; Russia had failed to accord to the persons and property of foreigners the degree of protection required by international law, it had failed to respect the international obligations of preceding governments, and it had failed, by its propaganda of Communism, to respect the right of other nations to conduct their internal affairs without interference by other states. See G. H. Hackworth, "The Policy of the United States in Recognizing New Governments during the Past Twenty-five Years," *Proceedings*, Am. Soc. of Int. Law, 1931, p. 120.

[34] For the text of the Russian note, see Hackworth, *Digest*, Vol. I, p. 304. Further details of relations between the two governments may be found on pp. 298 ff.

of Russia over so long a period raised a number of special problems with respect to the standing of an unrecognized government before the courts of the United States in suits involving property rights. Should the mere fact of nonrecognition operate to defeat the rights of a government which had been recognized by other states and whose *de facto* control over its territory could not be questioned? One court took the position that the government of Russia, though unrecognized, was immune from suit in its corporate capacity at the instance of a plaintiff who asserted its existence as a government and sought to hold it to account for governmental acts within its territorial jurisdiction.[35] On the other hand the same court also held that the Russian Government had no standing to sue in the courts of the United States until recognition was accorded.[36] In view, however, of the maintenance by the United States of diplomatic relations with representatives of the short-lived Kerensky Government which succeeded the Constitutional Democratic (Cadet) Government of 1917, the courts felt obliged to permit those representatives, as late as 1927, to sue in the name of Russia and to recover damages for losses accruing to the Government of the Czar in 1916.[37]

The case of Spain. Upon the deposition of the monarch in Spain in 1931 the United States, following the lead of Great Britain, promptly recognized the provisional government, with Zamora as President, having previously received assurances from the minister of finance that the new government would respect the financial engagements entered into by the monarchy.[38] When, however, civil war broke out in Spain in 1936 a different situation was presented. The ideological division between the opposing forces was deepened by foreign intervention, Germany and Italy taking sides with General Franco and Russia giving aid to the *de jure* Republican (Loyalist) Government. Germany and Italy, therefore, formally recognized Franco in November, 1936, even before Madrid was captured. Austria and Hungary followed soon after. It was not, however, until April 1, 1939, that the United States recognized the *de facto* character of the new government by a proclamation announcing the end of the civil war and revoking the embargo on arms. At the

[35] Wulfsohn v. Russian Socialist Federated Soviet Republic, 234 N.Y. 372 (1923). Fenwick, *Cases,* p. 95; Hudson, *Cases,* p. 112.

[36] Russian Socialist Federated Soviet Republic v. Cibrario, 25 N.Y. 255 (1923). Fenwick, *Cases,* p. 97; Hudson, *Cases,* p. 114. For the contrast between Anglo-American and Continental practice, see Lauterpacht, *Recognition in International Law,* pp. 145 ff.

[37] Lehigh Valley Railroad Co. v. State of Russia, 21 F. (2d) 396 (1927). Fenwick, *Cases,* p. 646; Hudson, *Cases,* p. 118; Briggs, *Cases,* p. 194. Only the barest technical justification can be found for the fact that for a number of years the United States maintained diplomatic relations with a holdover appointee of the Kerensky Government who did not represent even an organized minority party in Russia.

[38] See Hackworth, *Digest,* Vol. I, p. 295.

same time steps were taken to renew formal diplomatic relations which had been suspended during the civil war.[39]

E. DEVELOPMENT OF AN INTER-AMERICAN POLICY

Nonrecognition as a means to discourage revolutions: the Tobar Doctrine. In the year 1907 the governments of the five Central American republics signed a treaty agreeing not to recognize "any other government which may come into power in any of the five republics as a consequence of a *coup d'etat,* or of a revolution against the recognized government, so long as the freely elected representatives of the people thereof have not constitutionally reorganized the country." [40] The public approval by the Foreign Minister of Ecuador of the principle contained in the treaty led to its designation as the "Tobar Doctrine," Señor Tobar going so far as to recognize a right of intervention in this indirect way in the internal dissensions of the American states. Few jurists in other Latin American states, however, were ready to accept the new principle. The provisions of the treaty of 1907 were repeated in the General Treaty of Peace and Amity signed by the five Central American republics in 1923, and new provisions were added seeking to prevent what might be called the dynastic succession of dictators. This second treaty was subsequently denounced by two of the parties. During the period of its validity, however, the United States adjusted its policy of recognition so as to be in accord with it.[41]

The Mexican controversy. The principle contained in the Tobar Doctrine was taken up by President Wilson in 1913 and given new application and enlarged scope. President Madero of Mexico, duly elected in accordance with constitutional processes in 1911, had been overthrown by General Huerta and had been killed while being taken into custody. Could the United States recognize the new government under such circumstances? President Wilson refused to do so. "We can have no sympathy," said the President, "with those who seek to seize the power of government to advance their own personal interests or ambition. We are the friends of peace, but we know that there can be no lasting or stable peace in such circumstances." [42] Later in the same year Secretary Bryan was even more explicit:

---

[39] *Ibid.,* p. 297. For the resolution of the General Assembly of the United Nations in 1946 calling upon the members to withdraw their diplomatic representatives from Spain, see below, p. 576.

[40] For the text of the treaty, see Malloy, *Treaties and Conventions,* Vol. II, p. 2397; Hackworth, *Digest,* Vol. I, p. 186.

[41] For the text of Article II of the treaty, see Hackworth, *Digest,* Vol. I, p. 188. For comment, see C. P. Anderson, "Our Policy of Non-Recognition in Central America," *Am. Journal,* Vol. 25 (1931), p. 298.

[42] See Hackworth, *Digest,* Vol. I, pp. 181, 259.

The purpose of the United States is solely and singly to secure peace and order in Central America by seeing to it that the processes of self-government there are not interrupted or set aside. Usurpations like that of General Huerta menace the peace and development of America as nothing else could. They not only render the development of ordered self-government impossible; they also tend to set law entirely aside, to put the lives and fortunes of citizens and foreigners alike in constant jeopardy, to invalidate contracts and concessions in any way the usurper may devise for his own profit and to impair both the national credit and all the foundations of business, domestic or foreign. It is the purpose of the United States therefore to discredit and defeat such usurpations whenever they occur.[43]

The communication was confidential, but it contained a clear threat of intervention, which was borne out by the events that followed.

In spite of this determined stand, the United States was compelled to deal with Huerta indirectly as the head of a *de facto* government, and in the matter of the Tampico incident [44] the American State Department demanded from Huerta an apology in the name of Mexico while still denying him a *de jure* official character. After the fall of Huerta the government of President Carranza was recognized, first as *de facto* in 1915, and later as *de jure* in 1917. Three years later Carranza was himself driven from office, and after an interval of transitional government President Obregon was duly elected and took office January 1, 1921. The United States, however, withheld recognition pending reassurances as to the protection of American interests in Mexico, which appeared to be threatened by Article 27 of the Constitution of 1917.[45] After long negotiations during the spring of 1923 the Mexican Government was finally

[43] *Ibid.* Some years later this "Wilsonian Policy" of inquiry into the constitutionality of the *de facto* government was formally abandoned by the United States. On February 6, 1931, Secretary Stimson, in an address before the Council on Foreign Relations in New York City declared: "The present administration has refused to follow the policy of Mr. Wilson and has followed consistently the former practice of this Government since the days of Jefferson. As soon as it was reported to us, through our diplomatic representatives, that the new governments in Bolivia, Peru, Argentina, Brazil, and Panama were in control of the administrative machinery of the state, with the apparent general acquiescence of their people, and that they were willing and apparently able to discharge their international and conventional obligations, they were recognized by our Government. And, in view of the economic depression, with the consequent need for prompt measures of financial stabilization, we did this with as little delay as possible in order to give those sorely pressed countries the quickest possible opportunities for recovering their economic poise. Such has been our policy in all cases where international practice was not affected or controlled by preëxisting treaty." *Ibid.*, pp. 185-186.

[44] See below, pp. 292, 642.

[45] Art. 27 provides that "the ownership of lands and waters comprised within the limits of the national territory is vested originally in the Nation, which has had, and has, the right to transmit title thereof to private persons, thereby constituting private property." Further, the ownership of all minerals, solid mineral fuels, and petroleum is vested directly in the nation. For the full text, see *Annals of the Am. Academy of Political and Social Science*, Supplement, May, 1917, pp. 15-25.

recognized on August 31, 1923.[46] Recognition was attended by an implied promise on the part of Mexico to follow the interpretations placed by the Mexican commission upon legislation respecting agrarian and petroleum rights under the constitution of 1917. These interpretations were reported by the American commission as adequately protecting the rights of American citizens owning land or holding concessions in Mexico.[47] The recognition, if not technically *conditional*, was clearly *sub modo*, that is, attended by understandings as to the principles which were to govern the future relations of the two countries in respect to the questions in controversy.

Attempt at codification of the law. In view of the numerous controversies that had arisen in connection with the procedure of recognition, the subject clearly called for codification if the legal elements of the problem could be detached from the political. The Executive Committee of the American Institute of International Law, meeting at Havana in 1925, adopted a draft convention on the Recognition of States and Governments in which it was laid down that "every abnormally constituted government may be recognized if it is capable of maintaining order and tranquillity and is disposed to fulfil the international obligations of the nation." [48] In 1927, the International Commission of American Jurists, meeting in Rio de Janeiro and acting upon the projects submitted to it by the American Institute, approved a new draft convention, Article 6 of which described the recognition of a government as having for its object "the commencement of diplomatic relations with such Government, or the normal continuation of relations previously existing." Article 8 provided:

A Government is to be recognized whenever it fulfills the following conditions: (1) Effective authority with a probability of stability and consolidation, the orders of which, particularly as regards taxes and military service, are accepted by the inhabitants. (2) Capacity to discharge pre-existing international obligations, to contract others, and to respect the principles established by international law.[49]

[46] See Hackworth, *Digest*, Vol. I, pp. 261 ff.

[47] Recognition took the form of an announcement on the part of the American Department of State that, in view of the reports of their respective commissions, the two countries had resolved to renew diplomatic relations. The earlier proposal, objectionable to Mexico, of recognition in the form of a treaty containing the desired guarantees, was abandoned, Mexico regarding it as conditional recognition which it held to be in derogation of the sovereignty of the state.

[48] Art. 5. For the text of the draft convention, see *Am. Journal*, Vol. 20 (1926), Special Supp., p. 310.

[49] For the text of the draft, see *Am. Journal*, Vol. 22 (1928), Special Supp., p. 240. The reporter of the subcommission, Sr. Podestá Costa, commented at length upon the purpose of Article 8, applying his well-known doctrine of the distinction between the objective and the subjective tests of recognition. *Comisión Internacional de Jurisconsultos Americanos*, Reunión de 1927, Vol. II, pp. 138 ff., Ministerio de Relaciones Exteriores del Brasil, in Spanish.

The draft of the International Commission of Jurists was submitted to the Sixth International Conference of American States meeting at Havana in 1928, but no action was taken upon it.

The Estrada Doctrine. In direct opposition to the position taken by the International Commission of American Jurists the Foreign Minister of Mexico, Señor Estrada, put forward in 1930 a doctrine of recognition which has since been associated with his name. Influenced doubtless by the long controversy between Mexico and the United States, Señor Estrada proposed the outright repudiation of the practice of recognition "which allows foreign governments to pass upon the legitimacy or illegitimacy of the regime existing in another country." It should, he declared, be considered as "an insulting practice and one which, in addition to the fact that it offends the sovereignty of other nations, implies that judgment of some sort may be passed upon the internal affairs of those nations by other governments." The announcement was then made that in the future the Mexican Government would confine itself to the maintenance or withdrawal, as it might deem desirable, of its diplomatic agents, and to the continued acceptance, as it might deem advisable, of the accredited diplomatic agents of the countries in question; "and in so doing it does not pronounce judgment, either precipitately or a posteriori, regarding the right of foreign nations to accept, maintain or replace their governments or authorities." [50]

In spite of its mistaken interpretation of the practice of recognition as involving an inquiry into the legitimacy of the new government, when the inquiry is actually into its representative character, and in spite of the fact that the principles of the doctrine appeared to be contradicted by the alternative procedure of maintaining or withdrawing diplomatic agents, the Estrada Doctrine has since entered into much of the discussion of the problem of recognition in Latin America. If interpreted as seeking the elimination of the subjective test of the ability and willingness of a new government to observe the international obligations of the state, so that recognition would be accorded to, or rather diplomatic relations would be maintained uninterrupted with, a *de facto* government on the assumption that as a government it must of necessity carry out the international obligations of the state, the doctrine is not far removed from the earlier statements of the policy of the United States where the entire emphasis was put upon the *de facto* character of the government.[51] On the other hand, as a matter of practice, new governments,

[50] The doctrine was stated in the form of a note addressed by the Mexican Minister to the diplomatic representatives of Mexico in foreign countries. For the text, see *Am. Journal,* Vol 25 (1931), Supp., p. 203.

[51] For comments upon the Estrada Doctrine, see P. C. Jessup, *Am. Journal,* Vol. 25 (1931), p. 719; Accioly, *Tratado,* Vol. I, No. 212; Ulloa, *Derecho Internacional Público,* p. 103; Bustamante, *op. cit.,* Vol. I, p. 237; Whiteman, *Digest,* Vol. 2, pp. 84 ff.

coming into power in the American states, have never made any difficulty in proclaiming their intention to observe the obligations of international law, one of which is the observance of the good faith of treaties.[52]

The Montevideo Resolution of 1943. The "subversive activities" carried on by enemy agents after the entrance of the United States and other American states into the war in 1941-1942 gave a new direction to the policy of nonrecognition. On December 24, 1943, the Emergency Advisory Committee for Political Defense, which had been set up at Montevideo for the purpose of studying and coordinating measures for the prevention of the subversive activities of non-American nationals, adopted a resolution recommending to the American governments which had declared war upon the Axis Powers or which had broken relations with them that they not recognize during the existing world conflict a new government established by force before consulting with one another in order to determine whether the new government was complying with inter-American commitments for the defense of the continent and exchanging information relative to the circumstances which led to the establishment of the new government.[53] The recommendation that an inquiry should be made into the circumstances under which the new government came into power was a novelty in inter-American practice, and the explanation of it is to be found in the reference made by the Committee for Political Defense to the danger that totalitarian elements or Axis sympathizers might overthrow a government by force in order to prevent fulfilment of inter-American agreements for defense. The proposal of the Committee was received with hesitation by a number of governments, which pointed out that there was danger of "intervention" if the procedure of consultation and common action were to be extended beyond the existing conditions.[54]

[52] The practice was followed, for example, by the *de facto* governments of Argentina, Brazil, Peru, and Bolivia in 1930. See Hackworth, *Digest,* Vol. I, p. 223. A more recent illustration is to be found in the note of the Brazilian Minister of Foreign Affairs on October 30, 1945, informing the American Ambassador that President Vargas had resigned and had been substituted by the President of the Federal Supreme Tribunal, Dr. Linhares. "There is order throughout the country, over which the authority of the new Government is freely exercised," said the Minister. "The Government will respect the principles which have always guided the foreign policy of Brazil." In reply the American Ambassador took cognizance of the change and looked forward to continuance of the existing friendly relations between the two countries. It is of interest to observe that the American Government overlooked the coercion put upon President Vargas to resign and regarded the succession as within the Brazilian Constitution. Dept. of State *Bulletin,* Vol. XIII, p. 870.

[53] Department of State *Bulletin,* Vol. X, p. 20. For the application of the resolution by the United States to the Farrell government of Argentina, see *ibid.,* p. 225; Vol. XI, pp. 107, 158.

[54] For comment upon the conditions attending the resolution, see C. G. Fenwick, "The Recognition of New Governments Instituted by Force," *Am. Journal,* Vol. 38 (1944), p. 448.

The project of Guatemala. The recommendation of the Committee for Political Defense in 1943 and the subsequent negotiations attending the application of the recommendation to the situation in Argentina were followed by a number of proposals looking to the denial of recognition to "anti-democratic" governments, on the ground that such governments inevitably tend to deny the fundamental rights of their peoples and thus to constitute an indirect menace to the general peace. At the Conference on Problems of War and Peace a project was introduced by the Government of Guatemala reciting the dangers to the unity and solidarity of the American states arising from totalitarian dictatorships and proposing that the American states should deny recognition to and refuse to maintain relations with "anti-democratic regimes." [55] The project was referred to the Inter-American Juridical Committee, which entered a report against its adoption, chiefly on ground of the uncertainty attaching to the term "anti-democratic regimes." [56]

In striking contrast to the Guatemalan project, however, was a project presented to the same conference by the delegation of Ecuador, which reverted to the Estrada Doctrine, asserting in its preamble that the right to change governments belonged to domestic questions and that any effort on the part of foreign states to exercise moral coercion in such cases was a violation of the principle of nonintervention. The resolution then proposed that the procedure of recognition should be abolished, and that it should be the rule that the establishment of a new government was not to affect the continuity of diplomatic relations.[57] The project gave no indication as to the basis upon which a decision was to be reached as to whether a particular government was or was not a *de facto* government, and it would appear that a decision on that point would involve the very inquiry into domestic conditions which it was the purpose of the project to avoid.

But the subject would not rest; and the Conference at Bogotá in 1948, unable to agree upon the actual conditions of recognition, adopted a resolution declaring that continuity of diplomatic relations was desirable and that the right of maintaining, suspending, or renewing diplomatic relations should not be used as a means of obtaining unjustified ad-

[55] For the text of the project, see *Diário de la Conferencia Interamericana sobre Problemas de la Guerra y de la Paz,* p. 130. The resolution itself read as follows: "(1) To recommend to the American Republics that they refrain from granting recognition to and maintaining relations with anti-democratic régimes which, in the future, may establish themselves in any of the countries of the continent; and in particular with régimes which may result from a coup d'état against legitimately established governments of a democratic character. (2) To recommend, as a specific rule for characterizing such régimes, the extent to which the popular will in the particular country may have contributed to their establishment, according to the free judgment of each state."

[56] *Recomendaciones e Informes, 1945-1947,* p. 115.

[57] For the text of the project, see *Diario de la Conferencia,* p. 129.

vantages under international law. Again in 1950 the newly created Inter-American Council of Jurists took up the subject, having before it a draft convention prepared by the Juridical Committee along the lines of the draft of the International Commission of Jurists of 1927. But the Council failed to reach agreement "on essential points," as did the Council at its meeting at Buenos Aires, in 1953. The connection of the topic with the principle of nonintervention was clearly too close.[58]

Points at issue. The correction of the abuses to which the procedure of recognition has on occasion given rise would seem to lie not in substituting for the traditional practice of recognition something which would be practically equivalent to it, but in clarifying the principles upon which recognition should be based and in restraining the arbitrary conduct of individual governments by resorting to the practice of consultation proposed by the Montevideo Resolution. The conception set forth in the Estrada Doctrine, that any inquiry by third states into the character of a revolutionary government is unwarranted, is based upon a misunderstanding of the practical purpose of recognition. It is not third states that create the conditions calling for recognition. It is the new government itself which, by abandoning constitutional procedures, raises the question of its right to be the representative of the state; and the answer to this question cannot be given without some form of inquiry into the domestic conditions which throw light upon its representative character. No act of "intervention" is to be seen in an inquiry thus forced upon third states. Moreover, in the interest of international justice it would seem that a revolutionary government should not have the right immediately upon assuming office, and irrespective of its representative character, to pledge the good faith of the state and create contractual obligations for which the state itself would be responsible. Nor would there seem to be any attack upon the sovereignty of the state if third states were, on occasion, to hesitate to accept as spokesman for the state a government which had come into power by deeds of violence so shocking as to raise doubts whether it could be counted upon to observe the good faith of treaties or any other obligations of international law that might happen to run counter to its immediate interests.[59]

---

[58] See Fenwick, *The Organization of American States*, pp. 298 ff. The delegate of the United States at the meeting of the Council of Jurists in 1950 took the position that the subject did not admit of a juridical decision, being essentially of a political character.

[59] Compare the objectives of the note addressed to the foreign offices of the American Republics on November 22, 1945, by the Foreign Minister of Uruguay, Sr. Larreta, affirming the "parallelism between democracy and peace" and calling for "collective multilateral action" against the notorious and repeated violation by any republic of the elementary rights of man or the nonfulfilment of obligations which entitle the state to be a member of the international community. See Dept. of State *Bulletin,* Vol. XIII, p. 864.

F. SPECIAL CASE OF CHINA

The case of the People's Republic of China is a difficult one, partly resulting from the ideological principles of the Communist Government and partly from the territorial issue of Formosa. The Nationalist forces, under the leadership of Chiang Kai-shek, had been represented at San Francisco and had been an original signatory of the Charter of the United Nations. Then in 1948, defeated by the Communists on the mainland, the Nationalists took refuge on the island of Formosa. But to whom did Formosa belong? The island had been taken from China by Japan after defeat in the war of 1895. Then, itself defeated in 1945, Japan agreed to the terms of the Cairo Conference of 1943 by which the United States, Great Britain, and China declared that it was their purpose that Manchuria, Formosa, and the Pescadores should be "restored to the Republic of China." But what was the "Republic of China" to which Formosa was to be restored? Was it the Communist People's Republic at Peking or the Republic of China at Taipei, Taiwan (Formosa)? The United States recognized the Formosa Government in 1949 as the legal government of China and consistently refused to accept the Communist Government of Peking as representing China in the United Nations. There were thus practically two governments of China, one recognized as the *de jure* government at Peking, the other as the *de jure* government at Taiwan. Were there two Chinas? Not for those states which had recognized the People's Republic at Peking, nor for the United States which had recognized the Chinese Republic at Taipei. The issue came regularly before the United Nations after 1949, but as of 1964 the United States was still able to prevent a vote which might have been favorable to Communist China.[60]

G. RECOGNITION OF ABSENTEE GOVERNMENTS

Problems arising out of the World War. The territorial annexations carried out by Germany and Italy in the years preceding the outbreak of war in 1939, together with the annexations of enemy territory and occupations of neutral territory by Germany, Italy, and the Soviet Union during the war, led to the recognition by Great Britain and other powers of numerous "absentee governments." In some cases, such as those of Ethiopia, Czechoslovakia, Poland, and the Baltic states, the recognition

---

[60] The story is a long and involved one. For the position taken by the United States in refusing to recognize the government of Communist China at Peking, see Dept. of State *Bulletin*, Vol. 39 (1958), p. 385; and Bishop, *Cases*, p. 298.

See also Wright, "The Chinese Recognition Problem," *Am. Journal*, Vol. 49 (1955), p. 320; D. P. O'Connell, "The Status of Formosa and the Chinese Recognition Problem," *ibid.*, Vol. 50 (1956), p. 405; J. P. Jain, "The Legal Status of Formosa," *ibid.*, Vol. 57 (1963), p. 25; Whiteman, *Digest*, Vol. 1, p. 272; Vol. 2, p. 90, where details are given of official statements.

of the absentee governments was in fact the recognition of the continued existence of the state itself which the absentee government represented. In other cases, such as those of Norway, Holland, Belgium, Yugoslavia, and Greece, the recognition of the absentee government was based upon a repudiation of the *de facto* governments of the particular countries which had been set up in them by the military power of the enemy army of occupation. New questions of international law were thus presented, involving the extent to which the *de jure* absentee government could speak in the name of its country while under occupation by the enemy. While it cannot be said that new rules of international law were developed in respect to the status of such absentee governments, the practice of the leading governments shows the effort made to protect the rights of the people of the occupied state while dealing with the absentee government as the temporary expression of the popular will.[61]

Case of the Spanish Republican Government. The recognition by certain countries of the Spanish Republican Government in exile during the period of the Franco regime in Spain represented a novel practice in international relations; and it cannot be said to have had either logic or convenience to support it. Individual countries are free not to recognize a *de facto* government no matter how well established, just as they are free at any time to break relations with it. But except in cases of military occupation by enemy forces, the recognition of governments in exile as *de jure,* on the ground that the elements they claim to represent are denied the freedom to express themselves in national elections, is a form of intervention which could only be justified if applied universally to all countries denying freedom of speech and of expression.

H. QUALIFIED OR PROVISIONAL RECOGNITION

In view of the uncertainties which have attended at times the application of the objective and subjective tests upon which recognition is made contingent, it has been the practice of governments to maintain relations with a new revolutionary government on the basis and to the extent of its actual control of the administrative services of the country. This form of qualified or provisional recognition, sometimes described as *de facto* recognition, makes it possible to continue without interruption the ordinary business relations between the two countries and to obtain protection for life and property when circumstances may arise making it necessary to appeal for special protection. In this way goods may be imported into and exported from the country, the postal and telegraphic services may be used and other activities of daily life carried on without raising

[61] See F. E. Oppenheimer, "Governments and Authorities in Exile," *Am. Journal,* Vol. 36 (1942), p. 568; Chen, *The International Law of Recognition.* At the meeting of Foreign Ministers in Rio de Janeiro in 1942, a recommendation (XXXVIII) was adopted calling upon the American republics to continue their relations with the absentee governments of the occupied countries.

the question whether the new government is entitled to speak in the name of the state in its international relations.[62] The diplomatic representatives of foreign states remain as a rule at their posts.

Retroactive effect of formal recognition. Formal recognition, if ultimately given to a government under which the affairs of ordinary business have been thus transacted for a longer or shorter period of time, is retroactive in effect and operates to validate the actions and conduct of the new government from the commencement of its existence. In the case of Underhill v. Hernandez,[63] involving an action for damages brought by Underhill against a Venezuelan officer in command of revolutionary forces which were later recognized as the legitimate government, the court held that: "If the party seeking to dislodge the existing government succeeds, and the independence of the government it has set up is recognized, then the acts of such government, from the commencement of its existence, are regarded as those of an independent nation." In the case of Oetjen v. Central Leather Co.[64] the court upheld the validity of a title to hides maintained by persons who had purchased them at a confiscation sale ordered by General Villa, commanding the forces of General Carranza, whose government was subsequently recognized by the United States. In the case of Republic of China v. Merchants' Fire Assurance Corporation of New York [65] the court held that while a mere *de facto* government might not sue in the name of the state in the courts of the United States, the recognition of such government by the United States would operate to validate a suit already begun. During the regime of a *de facto* government, acts of subordinate administrative officials may be regarded by a nonrecognizing state as normally valid governmental acts for which the succeeding *de jure* government will be held accountable.[66] As has been said, the routine business of the embassy and consulates of a nonrecognizing government

[62] The subject is treated at length in Hackworth, *Digest*, Vol. I, p. 53, under the title "Acts falling short of recognition." Podestá Costa makes the distinction between the informal (*oficiosas*) relations maintained during the period before recognition is given and the official (*oficiais*) relations which follow recognition. *Ensayo*, pp. 52 ff.; *Manual de derecho internacional*, p. 67. Compare the terms of the resolution adopted by the Institute of International Law at Brussels in 1936.

[63] 168 U.S. 250 (1897). Fenwick, *Cases*, p. 120; Briggs, *Cases*, p. 392; Hudson, *Cases*, p. 696.

[64] 246 U.S. 297 (1918). Fenwick, *Cases*, p. 123; Bishop, *Cases*, p. 309; Hudson, *Cases*, p. 142. For comment on this case and parallel cases, see Harvey, *Legal Effects of Recognition in Int. Law*, Chap. V.

[65] 20 F. (2d) 278 (1929). Fenwick, *Cases*, p. 102; Bishop, *Cases*, p. 290; Briggs, *Cases*, p. 133; Hudson, *Cases*, p. 85.

[66] The responsibility of the succeeding *de jure* government extends also to tortious acts of the unrecognized *de facto* government. See the award rendered in the Tinoco Arbitration between Great Britain and Costa Rica, contrary to the contention of Costa Rica that a government could not be considered *de facto* when not established in accordance with the Constitution. Fenwick, *Cases*, p. 111; Bishop, *Cases*, p. 330; Briggs, *Cases*, p. 197.

will as a rule continue to be transacted, on the theory that such relations are relations with the state in its abstract character as distinguished from the particular persons pretending to represent it.[67] Special difficulties arise when a *de facto* government has been recognized by one or more states and not by others; and the success of particular claims arising from acts of the *de facto* government may depend upon the nationality of the claimant and the recognition policy of his government.

Recognition of insurgent governments. In a number of cases the United States has applied to conflicts between a *de jure* government and revolutionary parties within the state the principle of "recognition of insurgency" applied to revolting groups seeking to create an independent state. The purpose of such recognition has been to enable the United States to put into effect its neutrality laws or to be in a position to demand from the insurgents the protection of the lives and property of its citizens, or, it may be, to define the extent to which it will acquiesce in the exercise of belligerent rights by the insurgents. During the revolution in Chile in 1891 the United States applied its neutrality laws to the extent of demanding from the insurgent Congressionalist Party the surrender of a vessel, the *Itata*, which had obtained supplies of arms in the United States. Compensation was subsequently made by the United States for the violation of Chilean territory involved in the pursuit of the vessel on the high seas and the demand for the surrender of the vessel in Chilean waters.[68]

On the other hand some of the leading powers have at times refused to allow insurgents to interrupt their commerce with the country when the circumstances did not appear to justify the full exercise by the insurgents of belligerent rights. During the Brazilian revolution of 1893 the United States instructed its minister to warn the commander of the insurgents in the harbor of Rio de Janeiro that American vessels must be free to load and unload their cargoes without interference by the insurgents, provided they did not cross the actual lines of fire. Similar orders were issued by the English, French, German, and other naval commanders present, who in addition notified the insurgent commander that force would be used by them to prevent a bombardment of the city.[69]

[67] See Hackworth, *Digest,* Vol. I, pp. 327 ff.
[68] Moore, *International Arbitrations,* Vol. III, p. 3067; Scott and Jaeger, *Cases,* p. 365. See also, *United States* v. *Trumbull,* 48 Fed. Rep. 99 (1891).
[69] Moore, *Digest,* Vol. I, § 70.

CHAPTER IX

The United Nations

A. ORIGIN OF THE UNITED NATIONS

The organization of the United Nations had its more immediate origin in the Declaration on General Security adopted at the Moscow Conference of October, 1943.[1] The Atlantic Charter had already referred to the "establishment of a wider and permanent system of general security," [2] pending which the aggressor nations must be disarmed; and this reference obtained the approval of some forty-five nations upon the adoption of the Declaration of United Nations on January 1, 1942. The Moscow Declaration contained a more specific pledge, that the four governments participating in the conference recognized "the necessity of establishing at the earliest practicable date a general international organization, based on the principle of the sovereign equality of all peace-loving states, and open to membership by all such states, large and small, for the maintenance of international peace and security."

Following up this pledge, delegates of Great Britain, the United States, and the Soviet Union met at Dumbarton Oaks in Washington, August 21 to September 28, 1944, and adopted proposals for the establishment of a general international organization, which came to be known as "The Dumbarton Oaks Proposals." [3] A second meeting took place between representatives of Great Britain, the United States, and China. The pro-

---

[1] For the text of the Declaration, see *Am. Journal,* Vol. 38 (1944), p. 5.

[2] For the text of the Atlantic Charter, see *ibid.,* Vol. 35 (1941), p. 191.

[3] For the text of the Proposals, see *ibid.,* Vol. 39 (1945), p. 42. The draft submitted by the delegates of the United States to the meeting at Dumbarton Oaks was the result of long study in which a number of private organizations took part. See Reports of the Commission for the Study of the Organization of Peace, Parts I-IV; *The International Law of the Future: Postulates, Principles and Proposals.* See also, *Design for a Charter of the General International Organization,* M. O. Hudson, *Am. Journal,* Vol. 38 (1944), p. 711, and *ibid.,* Supp., p. 216.

posals were then submitted to the four governments for their approval, and were subsequently communicated to other states which had signed the Declaration by United Nations.[4] On April 25, 1945, the United Nations Conference on International Organization met at San Francisco, and on June 26, after two months of labor, the states represented at the Conference adopted the "Charter of the United Nations" as a formal international treaty. On October 25, 1945, upon ratification of the Charter by twenty-nine of the signatories, including the five permanent members of the Security Council, the United Nations became a legal reality. At the time of the holding of the first meeting of the General Assembly in January, 1946, there were fifty-one members.[5]

B. THE CHARTER

Preamble. The Preamble of the United Nations opens with words modeled upon the opening words of the Constitution of the United States: "WE THE PEOPLES OF THE UNITED NATIONS." [6] No special juridical character, however, is to be attached to the phrase, in as much as the various delegations were appointed by their respective governments, a number of which could with difficulty be said to be the legal equivalent of "the people." Nor is any special juridical character to be attached to the various obligations proclaimed in the Preamble, since these are set forth in more specific terms in the opening articles of the Charter itself.

Purposes and principles. The purposes of the United Nations are set forth in Article 1 under four heads: (1) To maintain peace and security, which is to be attained by "collective measures" to prevent acts of ag-

[4] Many of the Latin American states commented at length upon the Proposals, and the Inter-American Juridical Committee analyzed them chapter by chapter, in both cases with noticeable effect, especially upon the provisions for regional arrangements. See below, p. 222.

[5] The literature of the Charter and of the activities of the United Nations has become voluminous. Outstanding are the *Yearbooks* of the United Nations, which not only survey the events of the year but in many cases give the background of issues and events. *Everyman's United Nations,* published in frequently revised editions, gives a convenient summary of leading problems and accomplishments. The *Annual Reports of the Secretary General* are briefer summaries of the *Yearbooks* with emphasis upon the functions of the Secretary General. *The United Nations Review* is an official monthly publication from the U.N. Office of Public Information. Stettinius, *Report to the President,* gives the background of the Charter and prints the text of the Charter side by side with the Dumbarton Oaks Proposals. The committee reports and discussions may be found in Department of State Publications No. 2490, *The United Nations Conference on International Organization: Selected Documents.*

For a general survey, see Goodrich and Hambro, *Charter of the United Nations: Commentary and Documents;* Vandenbosch and Hogan, *The United Nations* and *Toward World Order;* Kelsen, *Law of the United Nations; U.N. Yearbook,* 1946-1947, pp. 1-43.

[6] The parallel was not accurate and the meaning of "We, the people" in the Constitution of the United States was misunderstood. For the discussion in Committee, Subcommittee, and Commission, see *United Nations Conference,* pp. 488, 492, 532. Sentiment appears to have prevailed over legal precision.

gression and by bringing about the peaceful settlement of international disputes; (2) To develop friendly relations "based on respect for the principle of equal rights and self-determination of peoples"; [7] (3) To achieve cooperation in solving international problems "of an economic, social, cultural, or humanitarian character" and in promoting "respect for human rights and for fundamental freedoms"; and (4) To be a center for harmonizing the actions of nations in the attainment of these common ends. The only new item here is the inclusion of the promotion of respect for human rights and fundamental freedoms among the objectives of cooperation, that problem having hitherto been left to the individual states. [8]

The principles set forth in Article 2 bear chiefly upon the first of the purposes of the United Nations, the maintenance of peace and security. The members of the organization pledge themselves to settle their disputes by peaceful means; they agree to refrain from the use of force against the territorial integrity or political independence of any state; and they pledge themselves to give every assistance to the United Nations in measures taken for the maintenance of peace and to refrain from giving assistance to any state against which the United Nations is taking preventive or enforcement action. Lest there be any misunderstanding as to the effect of these principles upon the fundamental relationships of the members of the United Nations under existing international law, the list of principles begins with the statement that "The Organization is based on the principle of the sovereign equality of all its members." [9] This principle is further strengthened by the provision of the last paragraph of the Article, which provides that "Nothing contained in the present Charter shall authorize the United Nations to intervene in matters which are essentially within the domestic jurisdiction of any state or shall require the members to submit such matters to settlement"; but this far-reaching provision is qualified to the extent that it shall not prejudice the application of enforcement measures under Chapter VII.

Even with the exception of enforcement measures under Chapter VII the provision of Article 2 (7) is a highly debatable one, and it was adopted only after long discussion and the compromise of conflicting

[7] See below, pp. 223, 597.

[8] See p. 597. The conception of an "International Bill of Rights" was not new, but it had never before taken shape in an official international document.

[9] Whether the principle of "the sovereign equality" of the members of the United Nations is the same as the principle of "the sovereignty and equality" of the members is more than a matter of words. But for the present it is only of academic interest.

The term "sovereign equality" was interpreted at the Conference to include: (1) that states are juridically equal; (2) that each state enjoys the rights inherent in full sovereignty; (3) that the personality of the state is respected, as well as its territorial integrity and political independence; (4) that the state should, under international order, comply faithfully with its international duties and obligations. See *United Nations Conference*, pp. 483, 497, 548.

opinions.[10] The Covenant of the League of Nations had contained a corresponding provision, but it was limited to the settlement of disputes before the Council: "If the dispute between the parties is claimed by one of them, and is found by the Council, to arise out of a matter which by international law is solely within the domestic jurisdiction of that party, the Council shall so report, and shall make no recommendation as to its settlement." [11] The provision of the Charter is much broader, applying to all of the activities of the United Nations and its organs, except in respect to the specified enforcement measures. No specific provision is included to determine which questions are "essentially" domestic. Questions are at times claimed by a state to be domestic but may not be considered so by the Security Council or the General Assembly, a notable instance being the claim of South Africa that its *apartheid* policy was a domestic question and the refusal of the General Assembly to consider it so.[12]

C. MEMBERSHIP OF THE UNITED NATIONS

The Charter of the United Nations makes a distinction between original members of the United Nations and states subsequently admitted to membership. Original members are states which, having participated in the Conference at San Francisco or having previously signed the Declaration by United Nations of January 1, 1942, have signed and ratified the Charter. Provision is made that membership shall be open to all other "peace-loving states" which accept the obligations of the Charter and which, in the judgment of the organization, are able and willing to carry out these obligations. The determination of these conditions is to be by decision of the General Assembly upon recommendation of the Security Council. Membership in the organization is thus qualified and limited, and it is therefore not necessarily coterminous with the membership in the community or family of nations, although the Charter clearly anticipated that in due time all states would become members of the organization, as has, with a few exceptions, proved to be the case.[13]

Scope of the term "peace-loving." The term "peace-loving," as applied to states seeking membership in the United Nations, soon proved

---

[10] See Stettinius, *Report*, pp. 42-45; Goodrich and Hambro, *op. cit.*, p. 72; Vandenbosch and Hogan, *The United Nations*, pp. 103-105; Kelsen, *Law of the United Nations*; Rajan, *United Nations and Domestic Jurisdiction*.

[11] Art. 15 (8).

[12] For a detailed discussion of the cases before the Council, see Rajan, *op. cit.*, Chap. IV; *Everyman's United Nations*, 1964, p. 130; Vandenbosch and Hogan, *Toward World Order*, pp. 118-134.

[13] The question of the basis of membership in the United Nations was widely discussed both before and during the San Francisco Conference. The draft project known as *The International Law of the Future* proposed that "The Community of States should be organized on a universal basis. All States which exist or which may come into existence in the future should be included."

to have political connotations. Was Austria peace-loving while still awaiting a treaty of peace? Were Ireland, Portugal, and Jordan peace-loving
when the Soviet Union had no diplomatic relations with them? The
Soviet Union would vote for Italy and Finland if Bulgaria, Hungary,
and Rumania were also admitted. The situation had become one of
judging an applicant not on the basis of its being "peace-loving," but
on the basis of political affiliations. In consequence, on November 17,
1947, the General Assembly requested the International Court of Justice
to give an advisory opinion on whether a member of the United Nations
might make its consent to the admission of a new member dependent on
conditions not expressly provided in the Charter—in particular whether
it could make its consent subject to the condition that other states be
admitted at the same time.[14] The reply of the Court was to the effect
that the conditions laid down in the Charter were exhaustive and that
any attempt to make the admission of one state dependent upon that of
another would prevent the exercise of the free judgment implied in
Article 4.[15] When the Soviet Union refused to accept the opinion, the
General Assembly requested of the Court in 1949 an opinion as to
whether the General Assembly could proceed to admit states on the
basis of seven votes of the Security Council. But to this question, the
Court replied definitely in the negative.[16]

Suspension and expulsion of members. The provisions of the Charter
in accordance with which membership in the organization is separate
and distinct from membership in the community of nations are accompanied by provisions for the suspension from the exercise of the
rights and privileges of membership in the case of members against
which preventive or enforcement action has been taken by the Security
Council.[17] Suspension is effected by action of the General Assembly
upon the recommendation of the Security Council. The exercise of
rights and privileges which have been suspended may be restored by
the Security Council. Moreover, it is further provided that a member
which has "persistently violated" the principles contained in the Charter
may be expelled from the organization by the General Assembly upon
recommendation of the Security Council. This is a far-reaching provision, inasmuch as the principles set forth in Article 2 are phrased in
general terms, leaving much latitude of interpretation. Protection against
abuse of the provision, however, is to be found in the voting majorities
necessary in the Security Council and in the General Assembly.[18]

---

[14] *U.N. Yearbook,* 1947-1948, p. 796.
[15] *Ibid.,* p. 797; *I.C.J. Reports,* 1948, p. 57.
[16] *U.N. Yearbook,* 1950, p. 409; *I.C.J. Reports,* 1950, p. 4.
[17] Art. 5.
[18] The provisions for the expulsion of members met with sharp opposition from a
number of the delegations at San Francisco. Mere suspension would still leave the
member subject to the obligations of the Charter, whereas expulsion would leave

In contrast with the Charter of the United Nations, the Charter of the Organization of American States, while permitting denunciation by a member, contains no provision for expulsion. In consequence, while a two-thirds majority voted to exclude "the present Government of Cuba" from participation in the inter-American system, a number of states voted against the resolution on grounds of lack of a provision in the Charter authorizing expulsion, citing the parallel of the United Nations Charter.[19]

Withdrawal of members. The important question whether a member of the United Nations is free to withdraw from the organization upon its own initiative is left unanswered by the Charter. The Covenant of the League of Nations had made provision for the withdrawal of a member after two years' notice of its intention to do so; and it was further provided that while amendments to the Covenant were not binding upon a particular member which signified its dissent from the amendment, in such case it should cease to be a member of the League.[20] At the San Francisco Conference a number of delegations sought to prohibit withdrawal absolutely; others sought to permit withdrawal in the event of the adoption of amendments which they found it impossible to accept; others held that in the latter case the right of withdrawal could be implied from the kind of organization that was being established.[21] It was finally agreed that no express provision should be made in the Charter either to permit or to prohibit withdrawal from the organization, and a formal statement was made to that effect by the committee. The statement recognizes that "exceptional circumstances" might make a member feel constrained to withdraw. On the other hand withdrawal or some other form of dissolution would be obviously inevitable if the organization "was revealed to be unable to maintain peace or could do so only at the expense of law and justice." [22] More serious from a legal standpoint is the right of withdrawal recognized in the event of the adoption of amendments to the Charter in which the particular state has not concurred and which it finds itself unable to accept, or in the

---

to the state complete freedom of action, and measures to control its conduct would have to be taken outside the framework of the Charter. Moreover the necessity of expulsion in a particular case would suggest that the organization did not have within itself the means to secure the observance of its obligations. See *United Nations Conference,* pp. 507, 527.

[19] Fenwick, *OAS,* p. 84; *Am. Journal,* Vol. 56 (1962), p. 610.

[20] Covenant, Arts. 1 (3), 26.

[21] See Stettinius, *Report,* pp. 47-49. Goodrich and Hambro, *Charter of the United Nations,* pp. 86-89.

[22] Stettinius, *Report,* p. 48. For committee reports and discussions at the Conference, see *United Nations Conference,* pp. 506, 525, 578, 595. In a letter of January 20, 1965, Indonesia announced its intention to withdraw from the United Nations, the withdrawal to take effect March 1. The reason given was the appointment of Malaysia as a nonpermanent member of the Security Council. *United Nations Monthly Chronicle,* February, 1965.

event that an amendment duly adopted fails to secure the ratification necessary to bring the amendment into effect.[23]

D. LEGAL CHARACTER OF THE UNITED NATIONS

Analogy of the League of Nations. What is the legal character of the international organization of the United Nations? Does it fit into any of the established classifications of composite states familiar to political science—confederation, federation, or federal state? The question is now academic, but it was of concern to scholars in the early days of the United Nations; and light may be thrown upon it by the discussions attending the establishment of the League of Nations which, by reason of its novelty in international relations, immediately challenged the attention of scholars to determine its specific character as an organization.[24]

Opponents of the League of Nations described it as a "superstate," implying that states which became members of the League would lose thereupon their sovereignty and independence. The term "superstate" was a novelty in jurisprudence, but it readily took on a popular connotation as describing a sort of federal state in which the central agency of government had the authority to act in its own name without the necessity of referring its decisions to its individual members for their separate approval. In this sense the League of Nations was so obviously not a superstate as to reduce the charge to mere political obstructionism. For while the obligations assumed by membership in the League imposed restraints upon states in the sense that international law in general imposes restraints upon them, yet the necessity of unanimity in all important decisions of the Council and Assembly of the League precluded the possibility of a decision being taken by the League contrary to the will of any one of its members.[25]

A confederation? In its general structure the League of Nations might well have been described as a "confederation," although dif-

[23] These serious structural weaknesses in the Charter are to be explained by the paradoxical circumstances under which it was drawn up: the general recognition of the need of creating an organization while public opinion in certain countries was still influenced by the disastrous effects of the war, and on the other hand the mutual lack of confidence in an organization established under conditions of urgency which precluded clarification of certain basic issues.

[24] On this general subject, see Oppenheim, *International Law*, 4th ed., § 167c; Corbett, *British Year Book*, 1924, pp. 119 ff.; Schücking and Wehberg, *Die Satzung des Völkerbundes*, 3rd ed., pp. 83 ff.; Williams, *Chapters on Current International Law*, Chap. XV; Ray, *Commentaire*, pp. 56 ff.; Redslob, *Théorie de la Société des Nations*. The high hopes held out by the League explain the keen interest of European political scientists in determining its legal character.

[25] At the opening session of the Assembly in September, 1920, the President of Switzerland, as host, felt it necessary to "affirm once more that the League of Nations is not and never will be a superstate which will absorb the sovereignty of states or reduce them to tutelage." A little more reduction of the sovereignty of certain states between 1931 and 1939 might have saved the League.

ferent in specific character from any of those known to history. A confederation, taken in its broadest sense, is a loose union of states which associate themselves for certain specific purposes without depriving themselves of a latent "sovereignty and independence" characteristic of distinct international personalities. Leading British, French, and German scholars found no difficulty in classifying the League as a confederation.[26] On the other hand a number of the delegates to Geneva were so anxious to overcome popular opposition to a strong central organization that they explained the League as being not essentially different from the earlier international "unions" of strictly limited objectives.[27] The League was thus said to be no more than an organ through which the community of nations undertook to perform certain functions; it was a piece of machinery for the conduct of business regarded as the common interest of the members of the League; and the two chief parts of this machinery, the Council and the Assembly of the League, were composed of delegates who rendered their decisions as the representatives of their respective states and who had no standing except as such representatives.

If it was no more than political obstructionism to describe the League of Nations as a "superstate," it would be even more so to designate the United Nations as such. Not only was the suggestion of that characterization pointedly denied by leading statesmen who took part in the framing of the Charter, but, as if to close discussion upon the subject, Article 2 of the Charter proclaims that "The Organization is based on the principle of the sovereign equality of all its Members." It may be left to students of political science to determine into what classification of composite states the United Nations fits, confederation or other; or to regard it as a wholly new international person, an organization unique in character, performing functions that are vital to the maintenance of law and order in the community. What the future holds remains for statesmen to determine in the light of experience.[28]

Corporate character of the United Nations. Like its predecessor the League of Nations, the United Nations has a definite legal personality, a corporate character of its own apart from that of its individual members. It can take title to property in its own name; it can enter into contracts as a corporate body and acquire rights and assume obligations; it can administer public international services and act as trustee for dependent international persons. Article 104 of the Charter provides that

[26] Brierly, Higgins, and McNair, for example, with Corbett of Canada. In Germany, Schücking and Wehberg, Liszt, Strupp; in Austria, Verdross.

[27] Among others, Lord Robert Cecil, one of the founders of the League, went out of his way to depreciate its legal character. See *Journal Officiel* (1923), p. 938; (1924), p. 329.

[28] Compare Clark and Sohn, *World Peace through World Law*, where the problem of the revision of the Charter is examined. See below, p. 225.

"The Organization shall enjoy in the territory of each of its Members such legal capacity as may be necessary for the exercise of its functions and the fulfillment of its purposes"; and Article 105 includes "such privileges and immunities as are necessary for the fulfillment of its purposes," and it extends the privileges and immunities to the representatives of the members and officials of the Organization in so far as is necessary for the independent exercise of their functions.[29]

Following the decision to make New York the headquarters of the United Nations an agreement was entered into with the United States, on June 26, 1947, in accordance with which the headquarters district is under the control and authority of the United Nations, and federal, state, and local laws must yield to regulations established by the United Nations.[30] At the same time, in 1945, Congress passed the International Organization Immunities Act giving to public international organizations in large part the privileges and immunities accorded to foreign embassies and diplomatic officers.[31]

The unhappy assassination of Count Folke Bernadotte and others serving the United Nations in Palestine led to a request by the General Assembly for an advisory opinion of the International Court, given in 1949, on the question of reparation for injury suffered in the service of the United Nations. The opinion of the Court was unanimous: the United Nations was "an international person," having the capacity to bring a claim for damages caused to itself or to any of its agents, and making unnecessary a claim by the national state of the agent. In the efficient performance of its missions the United Nations must be able to provide its agents with adequate protection. The functions assigned to the Organization, said the Court, "have clothed it with the competence required to enable those functions to be effectively discharged." [32]

E. PRINCIPAL AND SUBSIDIARY ORGANS

The Charter of the United Nations makes a distinction between the "principal organs" of the organization and other "subsidiary organs" which it may be found necessary to establish.[33] Listed as principal organs are the General Assembly, the Security Council, the Economic and Social Council, the Trusteeship Council, the International Court of Justice, and the Secretariat. The subsidiary organs are not specified,

[29] See J. L. Kunz, "Privileges and Immunities of International Organizations," Am. Journal, Vol. 41 (1947), p. 828.

[30] U.N. Treaty Series, Vol. XI, p. 11.

[31] See L. Preuss, "The International Organization Immunities Act," Am. Journal, Vol. 40 (1946), p. 332.

[32] I.C.J. Reports, 1949, p. 179; U.N. Yearbook, 1948-1949, p. 936. Q. Wright, "Responsibility for Injuries to United Nations Officials"; and "The Jural Personality of the United Nations," Am. Journal, Vol. 43 (1949), pp. 95, 509.

[33] Art. 7.

provision merely being made that such organs are to be established as may be found necessary. They are not to be confused with the various specialized agencies established by intergovernmental agreement and dealing with economic, social, cultural, educational, health, and related matters, which are to be brought into relationship with the United Nations.[34] These latter are organized under their separate constitutions; whereas the subsidiary organs are established by the Security Council or by the General Assembly. The Economic and Social Council has also the right to set up such commissions as may be required for the performance of its functions.[35] Provision is made in the Charter that no restrictions are to be placed on the eligibility of men and women alike to participate in any capacity and under conditions of equality in either the principal or subsidiary organs.[36]

The General Assembly. The Charter describes the General Assembly as consisting "of all of the Members of the United Nations," each member, however, being limited to five representatives.[37] Provision is made for regular annual sessions, and for such special sessions as occasion may require, these last being convoked by the Secretary-General at the request of the Security Council or of a majority of the members of the General Assembly. As in the case of the Assembly of the League of Nations, the principle of the equality of states is maintained in the provision that each member of the General Assembly shall have one vote; [38] so that the number of representatives is merely a matter of convenience to facilitate membership in the various committees and to permit wider contacts. The rule of unanimity followed by the Assembly of the League of Nations has, however, been abandoned. The Charter makes a distinction between "important questions," in respect to which decisions are to be made by a two-thirds majority of the members present and voting, and "other questions," in respect to which decisions are to be made by a majority vote. A number of "important questions" are listed, and new questions may be added to the list by a majority vote. The experience of the League of Nations appears to be responsible for the provision which deprives a member of a vote in the General Assembly if in arrears in respect to the contributions due from it.[39] The General Assembly adopts

[34] Art. 57. See below, p. 218.

[35] Arts. 22, 29, 68. The Atomic Energy Commission, for example, was set up by the General Assembly, the Balkan Investigation Commission by the Security Council, and the Human Rights Commission by the Economic and Social Council.

[36] Art. 8.

[37] Art. 9.

[38] Art. 18. For comment upon the principle of "one state one vote," see L. B. Sohn, "Multiple Representation in International Assemblies," *Am. Journal,* Vol. 40 (1946), pp. 71, 98.

[39] This issue dominated the nineteenth meeting of the General Assembly when the Soviet Union refused to contribute to the expenses of the police action in the Congo in 1960, which the International Court of Justice had held fell properly within the terms of Article 19 of the Charter. *U.N. Yearbook,* 1962, p. 551.

its own rules of procedure, elects a president for each session, and may establish such subsidiary organs as it deems necessary for the performance of its functions.[40]

While the decisions of the General Assembly, whether in respect to "important questions" or others in respect to which a majority vote is sufficient, have merely the legal force of recommendations, there is no question but they have great weight, at times practically the weight of binding obligations. On occasion, as in the case of the resolution, "Uniting for Peace," adopted in 1950, in the event of the failure of the Security Council to exercise its responsibility for the maintenance of peace, the General Assembly went so far as to assume authority to recommend the use of armed force to maintain peace and security.[41]

The Security Council. In contrast with the General Assembly the Security Council of the United Nations is restricted in membership. It consists of eleven members, five of whom are permanent members, and the other six nonpermanent members. The five permanent members are named in the Charter, being the Republic of China, France, the Union of Soviet Socialist Republics, the United Kingdom of Great Britain and Northern Ireland, and the United States of America. The six nonpermanent members are elected by the General Assembly, which is instructed by the Charter to take into account the contribution of the members to the maintenance of international peace and security and to the other purposes of the organization, and also equitable geographical distribution.[42] The terms of the elected members are for two years, with one-half of the members retiring each year. Retiring members are not eligible for reelection. In contrast to the larger representation allowed to members of the General Assembly, each member of the Security Council is limited to one representative.

Voting provisions. Article 27 of the Charter, dealing with the provisions for voting, was the subject of sharp differences of opinion at San Francisco. The conference that met at Dumbarton Oaks had been unable to come to an agreement upon the subject. The Security Council was to be given primary responsibility for the maintenance of peace and security, involving as an ultimate possibility the use of force against an aggressor state. Must important decisions in this matter be by unanimous vote? And if not by unanimous vote of the eleven members of the Security Council, then must the majority include in any case the unanimous vote of the five permanent members? A unanimous vote of the five permanent members, if unanimity were limited to them, would

[40] Arts. 21, 22.
[41] See p. 222; and compare L. B. Sloan, "The Binding Force of a 'Recommendation' of the General Assembly of the U.N.," *British Year Book*, 1948, p. 1.
[42] An amendment is pending to increase the membership of the Council from 11 to 15 members.

mean that each of them would have a right of veto against the enforcement of the law in its own case. A member of the so-called "Big Five" could thus sit in judgment upon other states and enforce the law against them, but would be itself above the law. The problem thus involved a conflict between the principle of the "sovereign equality" of all of the members of the United Nations and the practical situation created by an attempt to enforce the law against a state under conditions which would amount to a major war.[43]

The Yalta formula. Two months before the Conference at San Francisco, President Roosevelt, Prime Minister Churchill, and Marshal Stalin met in the Crimea and agreed upon what came to be known as the "Yalta voting formula." This formula provided for a system of qualified majority voting, in accordance with which votes were in all cases to be taken by a majority of seven. But a distinction was made between "procedural matters" and "all other matters." In respect to procedural matters decisions were to be made by the vote of any seven members. In respect to all other matters the vote of the seven members was to include the concurring votes of the permanent members, except that in decisions under Chapter VIII, Section A of the Dumbarton Oaks Proposals, dealing with the pacific settlement of disputes, and in decisions under Chapter VIII, Section C, Paragraph 1, dealing with the settlement of local disputes through regional arrangements or by regional agencies, a party to a dispute must abstain from voting. This formula was officially interpreted as making a distinction between the "quasi-judicial function" of promoting the pacific settlement of disputes and the "political function" of taking action for the maintenance of peace and security.[44]

The Yalta formula, after long controversy as to its application in certain specific cases, finally came to be adopted as Article 27 of the Charter. A joint statement of the Sponsoring Powers interpreted "procedural matters" to be those on which decisions of the Council did not involve its taking "direct measures" in connection with the settlement of a dispute or the adjustment of a situation likely to lead to a dispute. Where such direct measures were involved the decision would be governed by a "qualified vote," *i.e.* the five permanent members must concur in the majority of seven, the preliminary question whether a particular matter

[43] The Addis Ababa Conference of 1962 contested the fairness of the "gentlemen's agreement" of 1946 for the distribution of seats on the Security Council, insisting that Africa, as a geographical region, should have representation in proportion to its growing importance. An increase in the size of the Council would require an amendment to the Charter.

[44] See statement by Secretary Stettinius, released March 5, 1945. Dept. of State *Bulletin*, Vol. XII, p. 396. For comment see G. A. Finch, "International Law in the United Nations Organization," *Am. Journal*, Vol. 39 (1945), pp. 28, 37.

came or not under the head of "procedural" being decided, however, by a qualified vote.[45]

The procedure of the Security Council differs from that of the General Assembly in that the Council must be so organized as to "function continuously," and for this purpose each member must be represented at all times at the seat of the organization. Meetings of the Council may be held at other places than at the seat of the organization if the Council finds it expedient to do so. Provision is further made that members of the United Nations which are not members of the Council may participate, without vote, in the discussion of questions before the Council when the latter considers that the interests of that member are specially affected; and also that members and states which are not members of the United Nations may participate, without vote, in the discussions of the Council in relation to a dispute to which the said member or state is a party.[46]

The Economic and Social Council. Subordinate to the General Assembly and acting as its agent in the discharge of certain of its functions is the Economic and Social Council. The Economic and Social Council is elected by the General Assembly, but once elected it exercises its functions more or less independently. It consists of eighteen members, elected in groups of six, one-third retiring each year. It is not a policy-forming body, but rather a special committee designed to promote and to carry on the practical work of international economic and social cooperation without detracting from the ultimate responsibility of the General Assembly in the matter.[47]

The Trusteeship Council. The Trusteeship Council is, like the Economic and Social Council, a special committee operating under the

[45] See Stettinius, *Report*, pp. 73 ff.; Goodrich and Hambro, *op. cit.*, p. 124; *United Nations Conference*, pp. 739, 746, 801, 811. Within less than a year of the adoption of the Charter it became obvious that the veto power was being used for purposes far beyond those contemplated in the joint statement, as for example, the use of the veto in respect to applications for membership in the United Nations. For the position of the United States on the veto question, see statement of Senator Connally, November 15, 1946. Dept. of State *Bulletin*, Vol. XV, p. 987. The problem is analyzed by Jiménez de Aréchaga, *Voting and the Handling of Disputes in the Security Council*.

W. E. Rappard, "The United Nations as Viewed from Geneva," *Am. Pol. Science Review*, Vol. XL (1946), p. 545, observes that the Charter "much as it speaks of the 'sovereign equality of states,' violates that principle to a degree unknown in all previous annals of international law. . . . It, in fact, places the five Great Powers above the law laid down for the others."

[46] Arts. 28, 31, 32.

[47] Art. 61. In advance of the session of 1963, the Economic and Social Council adopted a motion calling upon the General Assembly to increase the membership of the Council (ECOSOC) and to insure the adequate membership of Africa. An amendment is pending to increase the membership from 18 to 27 members.

authority of the General Assembly and responsible directly to it.[48] Its membership is in part fixed by the Charter and in part elected by the General Assembly. It consists of members of the United Nations which are administering trust territories, those of the five permanent members of the Council which are not administering trust territories, and as many other members to be elected by the General Assembly as are necessary to insure that the total membership is equally divided between those members of the United Nations which administer trust territories and those which do not.[49] Each member of the Council is to have one vote, and decisions may be taken by a majority of members present and voting.

The International Court of Justice. A separate chapter of the Charter deals with the International Court of Justice. It is declared that the Court shall be "the principal judicial organ of the United Nations," and that the Statute of the Court is to form an integral part of the Charter.[50] The decision of the San Francisco Conference to set up a new court, rather than to continue the existing Permanent Court of International Justice, was reached only after long debate. The Dumbarton Oaks Proposals had left open the question, merely suggesting that if the existing statute were continued modifications would be in order, or that if a new statute were prepared it should be based upon the Statute of the Permanent Court.[51] The Committee of Jurists which met in Washington in advance of the Conference at San Francisco prepared a draft which was applicable under either alternative. The final decision was in favor of a new court, bearing a modified name and functioning in accordance with a statute which is proclaimed to be based upon the Statute of the Permanent Court.[52] The Charter specifically declares that all members of the United Nations are *ipso facto* parties to the Statute of the International Court.[53] The declaration in the Charter that the Court is to be the "principal judicial organ" of the United Nations is supplemented by a special article providing that the members of the United Nations are not precluded from entrusting the solution of their differences to "other tribunals," by virtue of agreements already in existence or which might be concluded in the future.[54]

The Secretariat. The Secretariat of the United Nations consists of

[48] Art. 85.
[49] Art. 86.
[50] Art. 92. For the organization and functions of the Court, see below, pp. 627 ff.
[51] Proposals, Chap. VII, pp. 1-3. See Stettinius, *Report*, p. 137.
[52] For the text of the Statute, see Appendix D.
[53] Art. 93.
[54] Art. 95. See Goodrich and Hambro, *op. cit.*, p. 257; *United Nations Conference*, pp. 837-902. The decisions and advisory opinions of the Court appear under the separate issues involved.

the Secretary-General and "such staff as the organization may require." [55]
The Secretary-General is appointed by the General Assembly upon recommendation of the Security Council, and he is the chief administrative
officer of the organization, acting in that capacity at all meetings of the
General Assembly and of the Security Council and at meetings of the
two auxiliary organs, the Economic and Social Council and the Trusteeship Council.[56] A special political function is assigned to him in the
provision that he may bring to the attention of the Security Council any
matter which in his opinion may threaten the maintenance of peace and
security. The staff of the Secretariat is appointed by the Secretary-General under regulations established by the General Assembly; and it
is specifically provided in the Charter that neither the Secretary-General
nor the staff are to seek or to receive instructions from any government
or from any authority external to the organization. In this respect the
provisions of the Charter draw upon the experience of the Secretariat
of the League of Nations, as also in respect to the other conditions
prescribed for the employment of the staff, looking to the establishment
of a true international civil service.[57]

Specialized agencies. The Charter recognizes the existence of the
numerous institutions, intergovernmental and private, which are engaged
in the promotion of various economic and social interests common to all
of the members of the international community.[58] Provision is made that
these "specialized international agencies," as they are called, shall be
brought into relationship with the United Nations through special agreements to be negotiated between them and the Economic and Social
Council, subject to the approval of the General Assembly.[59] The United
Nations will make recommendations for the coordination of the policies
and activities of these specialized agencies; and where appropriate the
organization will initiate negotiations among the states concerned for
the creation of any new specialized agencies required for the accomplishment of the economic and social purposes set forth in the Charter as the
objectives of the organization.[60]

[55] Arts. 97-101.

[56] The importance of the role of the Secretary-General has increased with the
years, due in part to the personality of the holder of the office. See O. Schachter,
"Dag Hammarskjold and the Relation of Law to Politics," *Am. Journal,* Vol. 56
(1962), p. 1; E. Stein, "Mr. Hammarskjold, the Charter Law and the Future Role
of the United Nations Secretary General," *ibid.,* p. 9. For a broader study, see
O. Schachter, "The Development of International Law through the Legal Opinions
of the United Nations Secretariat," *British Year Book,* 1948, p. 91.

[57] Art. 101. See Ranshofen-Wertheimer, *The International Secretariat: A Great
Experiment in International Administration.*

[58] For a study of the activities of these various bodies, see Chap. XXV.

[59] Arts. 57, 63. See G. Pollaczek, "The United Nations and Specialized Agencies,"
Am. Journal, Vol. 40 (1946), p. 592.

[60] Arts. 59, 63. Outstanding among the specialized agencies are UNESCO (The
United Nations Educational, Scientific and Cultural Organization) and FAO (The
Food and Agriculture Organization).

In the light of these provisions it would appear that the function of the United Nations is to direct and coordinate the activities of these agencies rather than to bring them under the immediate control of the Economic and Social Council. Provision is made that the Council may make arrangements for representatives of these agencies to participate, without vote, in its deliberations and in those of the commissions established by it; and on the other hand it may make arrangements for its own representatives to participate in the deliberations of the specialized agencies.[61] Coordination is thus to be obtained by reciprocal consultation and agreement, and it would appear to be the object of the Charter to obtain the advantages of a decentralized administration without the duplication of effort and conflict of objectives which has in greater or less degree marked their activities in the past.

Provision is also made in the Charter for arrangements for consultation between the Economic and Social Council and nongovernmental or private organizations which are engaged in activities coming within the competence of the Council. In the case of national organizations, the arrangements for consultation are to be made after consultation with the member of the United Nations under whose domestic jurisdiction the particular national organization functions.[62]

F. FUNCTIONS OF THE UNITED NATIONS

In accordance with the terms of Article 1, dealing with the purposes of the United Nations, the functions of the organization fall within two general groups: those dealing with the maintenance of peace and security and those dealing with the promotion of international cooperation in the different fields of political, economic, and social interests. The peaceful settlement of disputes and the enforcement of law and order stand out prominently because of the critical conditions under which the organization was established. But the promotion of the common political, economic, and social interests of the members may well come to be the dominant feature of the organization. Indeed, the chief hope for the success of the organization appears to lie in this possibility.

The maintenance of peace and security. The immediate and most urgent, and in that sense the primary objective of international, as of municipal law, must, as has been repeatedly emphasized, consist in the prevention of acts of violence. Without that condition all progress in cooperation for the promotion of common interests must remain at a standstill. Upon the Security Council falls the primary responsibility for the maintenance of peace and security; and the members of the United Nations which are not members of the Security Council agree that the latter, in carrying out its duties in this respect, acts on their behalf.[63]

[61] Art. 70.
[62] Art. 71.
[63] As specifically stated in Art. 24.

The Charter meets the problem of peace and security first by detailed provisions for the pacific settlement of disputes, and secondly by equally detailed provisions for action by the Security Council in the event of threats to or breaches of the peace. The parties to any dispute, the continuance of which is likely to endanger the peace, agree first of all to seek a solution by one or other of the various procedures available.[64] On its part the Security Council has the right to investigate any dispute in order to determine whether its continuance is likely to endanger the peace; and it has also the right, at any stage of a dispute, to recommend appropriate procedures or methods of settlement.[65] In the event of a failure of the parties to a dispute to settle it by any of the various peaceful procedures, they agree to refer it to the Security Council; and the Security Council may, if it considers that the continuance of the dispute is likely to endanger the peace, intervene and either recommend appropriate procedures or such terms of settlement as it may consider appropriate under the circumstances.[66]

Measures of enforcement. Failing a settlement of the dispute between the parties it remains for the Security Council to determine whether the situation constitutes a threat to the peace, and if so, what measures must be taken to maintain the peace. Provisional measures may be agreed upon and the Security Council may call upon the parties to comply with them. These failing, the Security Council may decide upon measures not involving the use of armed force; but if these should prove inadequate the Security Council may then "take such action by air, sea or land forces as may be necessary to maintain or to restore international peace and security." In this latter case the members of the United Nations agree to make available to the Security Council, on its call and in accordance with a special agreement or agreements, the armed forces, assistance, and facilities necessary to maintain the peace. The agreements referred to are to govern the specific details of the forces, assistance, and facilities to be provided; and they are to be negotiated as soon as possible on the

[64] Art. 33. This article supplements the principles of Art. 2, pledging the members of the United Nations to refrain from the use of force and to resort to peaceful methods of settlement.

Brazil appears to be the first state to incorporate the obligations of the Charter in this respect into its constitutional law. Art. 4 of the Constitution of September 18, 1946, reads: "Brazil shall resort to war only in case of the inapplicability or of the failure of arbitration or other peaceful methods for the settlement of controversies, determined by an international security organization in which it participates; and in no case shall it enter upon a war of conquest, directly or indirectly, whether alone or in alliance with another state."

[65] Arts. 34, 36.

[66] Art. 37. Goodrich and Hambro, pp. 140-154. See also, C. Eagleton, "The Jurisdiction of the Security Council over Disputes," *Am. Journal*, Vol. 40 (1946), p. 513.

The student may compare the provisions of Arts. 12, 13, and 15 of the Covenant of the League of Nations looking to the settlement of disputes between the members of the League, in particular in respect to the "gap" in Art. 15.

initiative of the Security Council, and when so negotiated they shall be subject to ratification by the signatory states in accordance with their respective constitutional procedures. National air force contingents are to be held immediately available for urgent military measures.[67]

As it has happened, the agreements referred to in the Charter have failed to materialize. In 1950, when the Council voted to assist the Republic of Korea in defending itself against an attack by North Korean forces, it did so in the form of a recommendation to the members of the United Nations to provide the necessary forces, at the same time requesting them to act under the unified command of the United States.[68] In 1956, when hostilities between Israel and Egypt broke out over the Suez Canal, the General Assembly passed a resolution requesting the Secretary-General to submit a plan for a United Nations Emergency Force, which assisted in maintaining the cease-fire agreement between the parties.[69] In 1960, the Security Council adopted a resolution sending United Nations troops to maintain order in the Congo (Leopoldville) when the Katanga province resisted incorporation into the new state.[70] In the spring of 1964 hostilities between the Greek and Moslem Cypriots emphasized once more the urgent need of a permanent United Nations force that could be dispatched to the scene without delay.

Military Staff Committee. A novel feature of the enforcement provisions of the Charter is the creation of a Military Staff Committee which is to advise and assist the Security Council on all questions relating to the armed forces placed at the disposal of the latter. It consists of the chiefs of staff of the permanent members of the Security Council, although other members of the United Nations may be invited to sit with it when the efficient discharge of the Committee's responsibilities so requires. The Committee is given power to establish regional subcommittees, subject to the approval of the Security Council and after consultation with appropriate regional agencies.

While the general obligations of all of the members of the United Nations in respect to enforcement measures are the same, provision is made that the Security Council may determine in each instance which particular states are to carry out its decisions. Action may be taken directly or through an international agency of which the states are members. Finally, the Charter reserves to the members of the United Nations "the inherent right of individual or collective self-defense" if an armed attack should occur against them, until such time as the Security Council has taken the necessary measures to maintain peace and

[67] Arts. 39-42, 43.
[68] *U.N. Yearbook,* 1950, pp. 220 ff.
[69] *U.N. Yearbook,* 1956, pp. 19-67, Resolution November 2, 1956. On November 4 a second resolution made provision for an international "police force."
[70] *U.N. Yearbook,* 1960, p. 97.

security. Any measures so taken must be reported to the Security Council, and must not in any way limit or qualify its responsibility to take such action as it may deem necessary.[71]

While the Charter confers upon the Security Council the "primary responsibility for the maintenance of international peace and security," the General Assembly has also a general responsibility for the maintenance of peace and security, modified only by the provisions of Article 12. Acting on this basis, the General Assembly, confronted with the situation in Korea, adopted a resolution, November 3, 1950, "Uniting for Peace," to the effect that if the Security Council, because of lack of unanimity among the permanent members, should fail to exercise its primary responsibility for the maintenance of peace and security, the General Assembly should consider the matter immediately with a view to making recommendations to members for collective measures, including the use of armed force when necessary. At the same time, a Peace Observation Commission was established to report on the situation in any area of tension likely to endanger the peace.[72]

Regional arrangements. A significant feature of the Charter is the series of articles providing for "regional arrangements." [73] These were due chiefly to the desire of the American Republics to maintain their inter-American system which had demonstrated its usefulness in preserving the peace of the Western Hemisphere. The problem was, how to integrate regional systems with the universal system, so as not to weaken in any way the overall authority of the world organization, and yet at the same time to encourage recourse to regional agencies for the pacific settlement of disputes and to make use of regional agencies for enforcement action. The fact that the Conference on Problems of War and Peace, held at Mexico City shortly before the opening of the Conference at San Francisco, adopted a temporary plan of inter-American collective security, known as the "Act of Chapultepec," gave to the delegates of the American Republics a special interest in the maintenance of their inter-American system.[74] As finally adopted after a number of amendments to the Dumbarton Oaks Proposals, the Charter recognizes the existence of regional arrangements or agencies for the maintenance of peace, provided that they are consistent with the purposes and principles of the United Nations. The members of regional groups are to make every effort to settle local disputes through regional agencies. On its part the Security Council shall encourage such re-

[71] Arts. 48, 51.

[72] For a discussion of the technical points at issue, see Kelsen, *Recent Trends in the Law of the United Nations*, Chap. 4; L. H. Woolsey, "The Uniting for Peace Resolution of the United Nations," *Am. Journal*, Vol. 45 (1951), p. 129. For the text of the Resolution "Uniting for Peace," see *Am. Journal*, Vol. 45 (1951), Supp., p. 1.

[73] Chap. VIII, Arts. 52-54.

[74] *Int. Conferences*, 1942-1954, p. 66.

gional efforts, and shall, where appropriate, utilize regional arrangements or agencies for enforcement action. The regional groups themselves, however, may not take enforcement action without the authorization of the Security Council, except in the cases of self-defense provided for in Article 51; [75] and the Security Council shall at all times be kept fully informed of activities undertaken or in contemplation by regional groups for the maintenance of international peace and security.

International cooperation in the political field. The promotion by the United Nations of the common political, economic, and social interests of its members is assigned by the Charter to the General Assembly. The three groups of interests are, however, not sharply defined. The Assembly is called upon to initiate studies and to make recommendations for the purpose of promoting international cooperation in the political field and encouraging the progressive development of international law and its codification, and for promoting cooperation in the economic, social, cultural, educational, and health fields, and assisting in the realization of human rights and fundamental freedoms.[76] From the context in which it is used it would appear that "international cooperation in the political field" relates to the regulation of those various conflicts of interest which have not yet been brought under general rules of law. "The progressive development of international law" clearly indicates the extension of existing rules of law into these new fields, while the "codification" of international law is apparently to be understood in the usual sense of the more precise definition of existing law, modified by such new rules as may be necessary to adapt the existing law to changing conditions.

Cooperation in the economic and social fields. International cooperation in the economic, social, and other related fields is referred to in general terms in the chapter (IV) dealing with the General Assembly and again, more specifically, in the chapter (IX) dealing with "International economic and social cooperation." Here the primary condition is laid down that such cooperation shall be directed to the maintenance of peaceful and friendly relations among nations "based on respect for the principle of equal rights and self-determination of peoples." The condition is a broad one, and it is to be assumed that it reaffirms both the principle of the "sovereign equality of states" proclaimed in Article 2 and the principle of nonintervention "in matters which are essentially within the domestic jurisdiction of any state." Responsibility for the discharge of functions relating to the fields of economic and social cooperation is, as has been seen, vested in the General Assembly, and, under its authority, in the Economic and Social Council.

[75] The case of Cuba in October, 1962, clearly came under that head. See p. 279. The various regional groups are discussed in detail in Chap. X.
[76] Art. 13.

The functions of the Economic and Social Council parallel those of the General Assembly in respect to the initiation of studies and reports and the making of recommendations. Specific provision is made that the Council may prepare draft conventions for submission to the General Assembly, and that it may call international conferences on matters falling within its competence. The preparation of these draft conventions is further evidence that the recommendations of the General Assembly are not to have the force of law-making agreements, but that in all matters which involve the assumption of new legal obligations the procedure will be followed of submitting the proposed agreement to the ratification of the members of the United Nations in their character as separate states.[77]

Supervision of administration of trust territories. The functions of the United Nations with regard to the trusteeship agreements, to be entered into for all areas not designated as "strategic," are to be exercised by the General Assembly, which is to be assisted by the Trusteeship Council operating under its authority. Detailed provisions are set forth in the Charter with respect to the various trusteeship agreements, the territories to be placed under the trusteeship system, the manner of their administration, and the duties of the administering authority. Both the General Assembly and the Council are authorized to supervise the administration of the trust territories; while the Council is called upon to formulate questionnaires on the status of the inhabitants of each trust territory, upon the basis of which the administering authorities are to make annual reports to the General Assembly for the trust territories within the competence of the Assembly.[78]

G. RELATIONS BETWEEN THE UNITED NATIONS AND ITS MEMBERS

A separate chapter of the Charter deals with a number of miscellaneous relations between the members and the organization.[79] In the first place provision is made for the registration of treaties with the Secretariat. Instead of the provision in the Covenant of the League of Nations that a treaty should not be binding unless so registered, the Charter provides that a party to a treaty or agreement that has not been registered may not "invoke that treaty or agreement before any organ of the United Nations." Secondly, in the event of a conflict be-

[77] No provision is made in the Charter for determining the number of ratifications necessary to bring a particular convention into effect, thus leaving the Assembly free to decide that question according to the particular character of the convention.

[78] Arts. 75-91. On the general subject, see Stettinius, *Report*, pp. 125 ff.; R. J. Bunche, "Trusteeship and Non-Self-Governing Territories in the Charter of the United Nations," Dept. of State *Bulletin*, Vol. XIII, p. 1037; E. H. Armstrong and W. F. Cargo, "The Inauguration of the Trusteeship System of the United Nations," Dept. of State *Bulletin*, Vol. XVI, p. 511. The annual *Yearbooks* give a detailed report of the operation of the Trusteeship System.

[79] Arts. 102-105.

tween the obligations of members under the Charter and their obligations under any other international agreement, the obligations of the Charter are to prevail. Thirdly, the organization is to enjoy in the territory of each of its members "such legal capacity as may be necessary for the exercise of its functions and the fulfilment of its purposes," as well as such privileges and immunities as are necessary for the fulfilment of its purposes, the latter provision being extended to the representatives of the different members and to the officials of the organization.[80]

H. AMENDMENTS TO THE CHARTER

The procedure provided in the Charter for the adoption of amendments differs in a number of important respects from that of the Covenant of the League of Nations.[81] The unanimity rule of the Covenant was abandoned in respect to the adoption of amendments, and provision was made for adoption by vote of two-thirds of the members of the General Assembly, which may not necessarily include the votes of the members of the Security Council. Amendments take effect when ratified by two-thirds of the members, including all the permanent members of the Security Council. Unlike the provisions of the Covenant, under the terms of the Charter no explicit provision is made for dissent, with consequent cessation of membership, and the right of veto upon amendments is reserved to the permanent members of the Security Council instead of the entire membership of the Council, as in the case of the Covenant.

General revision of the Charter. A unique feature of the Charter is the provision for its revision by a General Conference of the members of the organization. This provision (Article 109) was inserted in order to meet the belief of some of the delegates to the San Francisco Conference that the difficulty of establishing an international organization under the circumstances then existing made it desirable to reexamine it as a whole at a later date in the light of experience that might be gained in its operation. The Assembly may call such a Conference upon vote of two-thirds of its members and by a vote of any seven members of the Council. Alterations in the Charter must be voted by two-thirds of the members of the Conference, and when so adopted they must be submitted for ratification under the same conditions as amendments adopted by the Assembly itself. In order to meet the desire of certain delegations to fix a specific date for the calling of a conference to revise the Charter, provision was made that if such a conference should not be held before the tenth annual session of the Assembly, a proposal to call

[80] See L. Preuss, "Immunity of Officers and Employees of the United Nations for Official Acts: The Ranallo Case," *Am. Journal,* Vol. 41 (1947), p. 555.
[81] Art. 108.

it should be placed on the agenda of the Assembly and the decision to call it should be by a majority vote instead of the two-thirds vote required on other occasions.

Long before the Tenth Session of the General Assembly was due in 1955, the question of revision was discussed both officially at the United Nations and unofficially by individual scholars and private organizations, the General Assembly itself instructing the Secretary-General to make preliminary studies. The United States Senate established a special subcommittee under its Foreign Relations Committee, and the Secretary of State testified before the Committee on the more important revisions which were of concern to the United States. The Tenth Session appointed a Committee on Arrangements for a Conference for the Purpose of Reviewing the Charter, which after consultation with the Secretary-General, would report to the Twelfth Session in 1957; which in turn voted to continue the work of the Committee until "auspicious international circumstances" created an appropriate time. Urgent as was the need of revision, it was clear that the issue would involve sharp controversy which might weaken rather than strengthen the organization.[82]

Withdrawal in protest against amendments.   What if an amendment, adopted and ratified as prescribed, should seem to a particular member to be contrary to the fundamental principles of the Charter or to increase its obligations in a manner which it believes to be contrary to its fundamental interests? As has been seen, the Charter contains no provision for the withdrawal of members; but in compensation for the omission of such a provision an "interpretative statement" was adopted by the San Francisco Conference in accordance with which it was formally agreed that if a member "because of exceptional circumstances feels constrained to withdraw, and leave the burden of maintaining peace and security on the other Members, it is not the purpose of the Organization to compel that Member to continue its cooperation in the Organization."[83] This general principle is given specific application in relation to amendments to the Charter by the further statement: "Nor would a Member be bound to remain in the Organization if its rights and obligations as such were changed by Charter amendment in which it has not concurred and which it finds itself unable to accept, or if an amendment duly accepted by the necessary majority in the Assembly or in a general conference fails to secure the ratification necessary to

[82] The subject is exhaustively treated in Clark and Sohn, *World Peace Through World Law*, where the articles of the Charter and the proposed revisions are printed in parallel columns, followed by explanation of the changes and critical comment. Seven Annexes discuss the fundamental conditions necessary to the maintenance of an effective rule of world law. See *U.N. Yearbook,* 1962, p. 152, for the resolution of the General Assembly in that year.

[83] Stettinius, *Report,* pp. 48, 171. See note 22 of this chapter.

bring such amendment into effect." The second half of this statement on amendments is difficult to justify, since the failure of an amendment would not change the conditions under which the obligations of the Charter were originally accepted.[84]

[84] For the committee reports and discussions at San Francisco, see *United Nations Conference,* pp. 506, 525.

CHAPTER X

International Regional
and Specialized Organizations

A. ORGANIZATION OF AMERICAN STATES

It is for the historian to weigh the various interests on the basis of which the regional organization bearing the name of "The International Union of the American Republics" and now called the "Organization of American States" has developed.[1] The roots of "continental solidarity," as it is called, go deep into the past. Common doctrines of revolutionary rights, justifying their emancipation from the control of their several mother countries, were the earliest, and are still doubtless the strongest, tradition among the American states. Common constitutional structures of government have also played their part, and common conceptions of liberty and democracy in the relation of the individual to the state.[2] Commercial interests have increased steadily decade after decade. Idealism has not been wanting, particularly of recent years, a conception of the moral duties of Christian states and of the common social interests of a community of good neighbors.[3] Paradoxically enough, geographical propinquity has doubtless been the weakest of the factors of unity, except in so far as the isolated location of the hemisphere as a whole

---

[1] For a general survey of the inter-American regional system before and after the adoption of its present organization, see Fenwick, *The Organization of American States;* Thomas and Thomas, *The Organization of American States;* Mecham, *The United States and Inter-American Security;* Bemis, *Latin American Policy of the United States;* Herring, *A History of Latin America.*

[2] Many of the early Latin American constitutions were modeled upon that of the United States, in spite of the fact that conditions were not always suited to a federal government.

[3] Compare, among numerous other documents, the Preamble of the Declaration of Lima of 1938 and the declaration at Panama in 1939 on Maintenance of International Activities in Accordance with Christian Morality. *Int. Conferences of American States,* 1933-1940, pp. 308, 332.

has served as a basis for the appeal to common political, economic, and social interests.

Juridical character of the organization. In spite of the close co-operation of the American states during more than half a century, it was only when confronted with the larger organization of the United Nations that they sought to give to their organization a more precise juridical character. In 1890, at the first conference held in Washington, a resolution was adopted that an association should be formed under the title of "The International Union of the American Republics," the object of which was the prompt collection and distribution of commercial information.[4] Beyond that "Union" it was not felt necessary to go. Successive conferences extended the cooperation of the American states into new fields and enlarged the functions of the original Commercial Bureau, giving it the name of "Pan American Union." But not until the Conference on Problems of War and Peace, held at Mexico City in 1945, was it found advisable to draw up a formal document to replace the unwritten constitution that had developed during the course of more than fifty years. The Charter of the United Nations was about to be adopted at San Francisco, and it was clear that if the American states were to maintain their character as a regional group they must define more specifically the legal character of the inter-American community and the scope of its powers and functions. The result was the formulation of an "Organic Pact," abandoning the earlier conception of a "Union" and describing the proposed regional group as "The Inter-American System." [5]

First, however, came the adoption of the Treaty of Reciprocal Assistance, signed at Rio de Janeiro, September 2, 1947, creating a formal regional security system as the keystone of the arch of continental unity. Article 3 of the treaty creates an immediate obligation of mutual assistance in the event of armed attack, and Article 6 an obligation to take such action as the organ of consultation may determine is necessary in the event of an act of aggression short of an armed attack or other situation creating a threat to the peace. Decisions are taken by a two-thirds vote, which is binding on all the members, except that no state is obligated to use armed force without its consent.[6]

A year later, at the Conference at Bogotá in 1948, the Charter of the Organization of American States was adopted, giving to the existing Union of American Republics a more specific character, setting forth in detail the principles by which the Organization was to be guided, the objectives which it proposed to pursue, and the various organs or

---

[4] *Int. Conferences*, 1889-1928, p. 36.

[5] For the text of the decisions at Mexico City in 1945, see *Int. Conferences*, 1942-1954, p. 69. For comment, see Fenwick, *OAS*, pp. 69 ff.

[6] For details of the treaty, see Fenwick, *OAS*, pp. 231 ff.; Thomas, *The OAS*, pp. 249 ff.

agencies by which it intended to carry out its activities. Behind the Charter was the long tradition of inter-American cooperation which the crisis of the postwar period made it possible to galvanize into a formal legal document.[7] The Charter took effect on December 13, 1951, upon ratification by two-thirds of the signatory states; but by a special provision of the Bogotá Conference, its provisions were recognized as *de facto* and effective immediately.

Basic principles. The basic principles of the inter-American system had already been proclaimed in numerous declarations and resolutions, so that the Charter of 1948 could declare that it was merely "reaffirming" them.[8] Foremost among these principles is that of the sovereignty and equality of the American states, emphasizing the separate and independent personality of each of them without regard to territorial size or degree of material progress. The principle of nonintervention follows from that of sovereignty and equality; and concern for its observance is manifested in numerous treaties and resolutions. The good faith of treaties has received special emphasis, largely in consequence of the desire to give finality to boundary controversies. The repudiation of the use of force and the nonrecognition of territorial transfers made under coercion are in line with the general development of international law, as is the principle that all disputes between states must be settled by peaceful procedures. In 1936 the principle of the collective responsibility of all of the American states for the protection of any one of them against attack by a non-American state had been asserted; in Havana in 1940, it had been more specifically defined; in Mexico City in 1945, it was extended to include mutual protection in the event of an attack by an American state as well as by a non-American one; and it was given specific and definite form by the Treaty of Reciprocal Assistance.

Policy-forming organs. The sole policy-forming organ of the American states was, until the year 1938, the International Conference of American States, the first conference being held in Washington in 1889-1890.[9] Supplementing the regular scheduled conferences, special conferences met at Buenos Aires in 1936 and at Mexico City in 1945. In 1938, at the conference at Lima, Peru, a new organ was created in the form of a meeting of foreign ministers to be called in the event of threats to the peace. This new "Organ of Consultation," as it came to be called, met in Panama in 1939, at Havana in 1940, and again at Rio de Janeiro in 1942, to meet problems arising from the war; and later, on a number of occasions to meet threats to the peace and urgent prob-

---

[7] For details of the Charter, see Fenwick, *OAS*, pp. 80 ff., Thomas, *The OAS*, pp. 35 ff. For the text of the Charter, see Fenwick, *op. cit.*, p. 547.

[8] Charter, Art. 5. See Thomas and Thomas, Book III, "The Principles of the OAS."

[9] The Final Acts of these and later conferences are available in collected form in *Int. Conferences of Am. States,* 1889-1928; 1933-1940; 1942-1954.

lems of common interest. Both conferences and meetings of consultation function according to the principle of the full juridical equality of all of the American states, each state having one vote and no distinction being made between large and small powers. The Charter declares the Conference to be "the supreme organ of the Organization," deciding the general action and policy of the Organization and determining the structure and functions of its organs. But in fact, the Meetings of Consultation are equally authoritative within the limits specifically assigned to their competence.

In addition to the functions of the Meeting of Foreign Ministers, described as the "Organ of Consultation" under the Rio Treaty, the Charter of the Organization provides that a Meeting of Consultation shall be held "in order to consider problems of an urgent nature and of common interest to the American States," a wider jurisdiction than that assigned by the Rio Treaty, and intended to meet in cases where the threat to the peace was less imminent than in Article 6 of the Rio Treaty. In spite of the fact that the Council of the Organization is composed of representatives of the member states, with the rank of ambassador, the conference at Bogotá in 1948 was unwilling to entrust such competence to the Council. By contrast, however, taking into account the time necessary to assemble a Meeting of Foreign Ministers, the Council was given competence to act "provisionally" as Organ of Consultation in cases arising under the Rio Treaty.[10]

Forms of agreement. From the time of the first inter-American conference in 1889-1890 the American states have found it convenient to promote their various interests not merely by formal treaties, but also by means of numerous declarations, resolutions, and recommendations. The character of these agreements, other than treaties, has been much debated; but it would seem clear that certain of them are to be regarded as definite juridical commitments, creating legal obligations even though not subject to formal ratification. The Preamble of the Resolution (VIII) on Reciprocal Assistance and American Solidarity, known as the "Act of Chapultepec," adopted at the Conference on Problems of War and Peace held at Mexico City in 1945, in setting forth a list of fundamental principles of international law, proclaimed that the American states had been incorporating these principles in their international law since 1890 "by means of conventions, resolutions and declarations." No distinction was made in respect to the juridical character of the agreements in which the various principles had been incorporated.[11]

Resolutions have been resorted to for agreements to follow a general or a specific line of conduct believed to be in the common interest of all. In emergencies they have been used as a substitute for treaties, as

[10] See Fenwick, *op. cit.,* p. 88; Thomas and Thomas, *op. cit.,* pp. 86 ff.
[11] Fenwick, *op. cit.,* p. 155.

in the case of the resolution, known as the Act of Habana, adopted in 1940 pending ratification of a convention covering the same subject. Certain resolutions, such as those of 1902 and 1910, establishing the Pan American Union, have practical, if not technical, juridical character. On the other hand recommendations are what their name implies, the expression of policies which it is believed desirable to follow but in respect to which the American states do not wish to impose an obligation.

Pan American Union. The administrative machinery of the Organization is somewhat complicated. First of the organs is the Council, a sort of executive committee which carries out the special duties assigned to it by conferences or meetings of consultation as well as specific administrative duties; then come three "organs" of the Council: the Economic and Social Council, the Council of Jurists, and the Cultural Council; then the general secretariat, given the name of Pan American Union and described as "the central and permanent organ of the Organization," with its technical and informational departments and offices. The functions of the Union are of the most varied character, ranging from the preparation of the agenda of inter-American conferences and consultative meetings to the publication of reports upon the activities of inter-American agencies and documents and other material bearing upon every phase of the political, economic, social, and cultural relations of the community. It is the custodian of the documents of the conferences and consultative meetings, and it is the depository of the instruments of ratification of inter-American agreements.[12] In addition there are the intergovernmental "Specialized Organizations" which have specific functions with respect to technical matters. To these must be added the special agencies created from time to time for specific purposes, such as the Inter-American Peace Committee, the Commission on Human Rights, and the Special Consultative Committee on Security.[13]

Specialized organizations or agencies. During the years preceding the adoption of the Charter of 1948, the American republics had found it convenient to create by multilateral agreements a number of specialized organizations of a more or less permanent character, having specific functions with respect to technical matters of common interest. The Charter, while recognizing the technical autonomy of these organizations, makes provision for their integration within the Organization. Standards have been established to that end, and special agreements have been entered into with them by the Council of the Organization. As of December 31, 1964, six agencies had been brought within the class of specialized organizations: The Pan American Institute of Geography and History, the inter-American Institute of Agri-

---

[12] For a survey of the activities of the Pan American Union, see *ibid.*, p. 98, and Chaps. VIII-XI.
[13] Fenwick, *op. cit.*, p. 106.

cultural Sciences, the Inter-American Children's Institute, the Inter-American Commission of Women, the Pan American Health Organization, and the Inter-American Indian Institute. The Charter makes provision for establishing cooperative relations with international agencies having similar objectives, as illustrated in the case of the Pan American Health Organization which is the regional branch of the World Health Organization.[14]

Procedures for the peaceful settlement of inter-American disputes. Beginning with the conference of 1889-1890 the American states have sought to adopt treaty after treaty looking to the peaceful settlement of international disputes. Notable was the Gondra Treaty of 1923 calling for investigation and report on all disputes without exception, and the Washington treaties of arbitration and of conciliation of 1928-1929. The Lima Conference of 1938 made provision for the coordination of the various procedures into a single instrument; and at the Bogotá Conference of 1948 the "Pact of Bogotá" was adopted replacing eight agreements. In view, however, of the competence of the Organ of Consultation to meet disputes arising under the Treaty of Reciprocal Assistance, recourse to the traditional procedures of pacific settlement has ceased to play as important a role as in past years.[15]

Relations with the United Nations. The adoption of the Charter of the United Nations brought about important changes in the inter-American regional system. Already, in contemplation of the proposed general organization for the maintenance of peace and security, the American states had at Mexico City extended their system of mutual protection against attacks from without the continent to the possible attack of one American state against another, and they had provided sanctions for the purpose of meeting acts of aggression. At one extreme was the desire of a majority of the Latin American delegations at San Francisco to continue to function independently of the Security Council; at the other extreme was the view that the Security Council should have the right to intervene in all regional settlements. The Conference finally adopted an intermediate solution of limited intervention, in accordance with which the primary responsibility for the pacific settlement of disputes rests upon regional agencies or arrangements, and only in the event of a failure of regional procedures of settlement is the controversy to be referred to the Security Council. The Security Council, however, has at all times the right to investigate any dispute, or any situation which may lead to international friction or give rise to a dispute. In the event that enforcement action is necessary, the regional agency must first obtain the authorization of the Security Council. At the same time, on the basis of Article 51 of the Charter of the United Nations, the American

14 *Ibid.*, p. 103.
15 *Ibid.*, pp. 171 ff.; Thomas and Thomas, *op. cit.*, p. 277.

states have the inherent right of collective as well as individual self-defense in the event of an armed attack against a member of their group until such time as the Security Council has taken the measures necessary to maintain international peace and security.[16]

B. EUROPEAN REGIONAL GROUPS

Proposed European Federal Union. The conception of a federal union of European states has its origins far back in European history. Until the nineteenth century it might be said that European union and the organization of the international community were identical aspirations, in some cases utopian, in others highly practical. The meetings of the Hague Peace Conferences of 1899 and 1907, however, marked definitely the end of European domination; while the establishment of the League of Nations in 1920 put an end to the system of the balance of power which had so long dominated the political life of Europe. The question of a regional organization of Europe now became feasible, and a number of concrete plans were presented looking to that objective.

On May 17, 1930, the Foreign Minister of France, M. Briand, addressed to the twenty-six governments of Europe a Memorandum on the Organization of a Regime of European Federal Union. The objective of the proposal was said to be an association which would devote its collective effort to the pacific organization of Europe by means of regular meetings for the examination in common of problems primarily of concern to the peoples of Europe. A representative European conference was to be held, composed of all the European governments which were members of the League of Nations. An executive organ in the form of a permanent political committee was to be constituted which would undertake to develop the basis of the future Federal European Union; and an administrative secretariat was to be established for the execution of the decisions taken.

The replies of the twenty-six governments were embodied in a report submitted to a meeting of the representatives of the European states held at Geneva on September 8, 1930. There was general agreement upon the principle of the proposed organization. Shortly after, the Assembly of the League of Nations appointed a Commission of Enquiry for European Union, which was to report to the next Assembly. With the death, however, of the German Chancellor Stresemann and that of Briand himself, the proposed plan failed to materialize.[17]

NATO. With the close of the Second World War the conception of European regional union took on a radically different shape from that

---

[16] Fenwick, *op. cit.,* pp. 515 ff.; Thomas and Thomas, *op. cit.,* p. 249.

[17] On the Briand and other plans of the period, see Coudenhove-Kalergi, *Pan-Europe;* Herriot, *United States of Europe;* Hutchinson, *The United States of Europe;* Salter, *The United States of Europe and Other Papers.*

contemplated by M. Briand. The aggressive diplomacy of the Soviet Union made it clear that the collective security system of the United Nations could not be relied upon. An Anglo-French alliance, the Treaty of Dunkirk of 1947, was succeeded in 1948 by the so-called Western European Union, a treaty of economic, social, and cultural collaboration and collective self-defense, called the Pact of Brussels, based upon Article 51 of the Charter; and this treaty was in turn followed by the North Atlantic Treaty Organization, NATO, signed in Washington, April 4, 1949. This agreement, drafted along the lines of the Inter-American Treaty of Reciprocal Assistance, is a true regional security agreement, making an attack upon one an attack upon all, but qualifying the obligation of mutual assistance by the phrase, "such action as it deems necessary." [18]

The original parties were twelve in number, later extended to fourteen by the accession of Greece and Turkey in 1951 and to fifteen by the accession of the German Federal Republic in 1954. While its primary purpose is that of mutual or regional military defense, it seeks to maintain and develop the individual and collective capacity of the parties to resist attack, and to that end the parties are to consult together whenever, in the opinion of any of them, the territorial integrity, political independence, or security of any of the parties is threatened. What distinguishes NATO from a mere military alliance is the political as well as military scope of the annual Parliamentarians' Conference.

Council of Europe. In the meantime, efforts to coordinate economic and social interests and to promote cultural exchange continued along with military defense, and in 1949 ten nations signed a statute constituting the Council of Europe. While primarily a consultative body, making recommendations to the member states, the Council has initiated a number of social and cultural measures, notably the European Convention on Human Rights. Its internal organization consists of a committee of ministers, a consultative assembly, and a secretariat; and it is of particular interest that the delegates to the Assembly, the "deliberative organ," speak and vote as individuals, not as representatives of their governments. The opening words of the preamble are inspiring:

Convinced that the pursuit of peace based upon justice and international cooperation is vital for the preservation of human society and civilization;

[18] On the general subject of European regional groups, see Haines, *European Integration;* Zurcher, *The Struggle to United Europe;* Haas, *The Uniting of Europe.* On NATO in particular, Moore, *NATO and the Future of Europe;* Dean Rusk, "The State of the North Atlantic Alliance," Dept. of State *Bulletin,* August 5, 1963; T. V. Kalijarvi and F. O. Wilcox, "The Organizational Framework of the North Atlantic Treaty," *Am. Journal,* Vol. 44 (1950), p. 155. For the text of the treaty, Peaslee, *Int. Intergovernmental Organizations,* Vol. II, p. 1614. For the text of the Agreement between the Parties Regarding the Status of their Armed Forces, *Am. Journal,* Vol. 48 (1954), p. 83. For comment see R. R. Baxter, "Jurisdiction over Visiting Forces and the Development of International Law," *Proceedings,* Am. Society of Int. Law, 1953, p. 174. See also Hartley, *Atlantic Challenge.*

Reaffirming their devotion to the spiritual and moral values which are the common heritage of their peoples and the true source of individual freedom, political liberty, and the rule of law, principles which form the basis of all genuine democracy. . . .[19]

European Coal and Steel Community. Side by side with the measures having military defense primarily as their objective were the plans of the small group of six states which, on the basis of the Schuman Plan, decided to pool their resources for the production of coal and steel as the first step towards a larger plan of economic and political unity. The Treaty Establishing the Coal and Steel Community was signed on April 18, 1951, by Belgium, France, the German Federal Republic, Italy, Luxemburg, and the Netherlands. The institutions of the Community consist of a High Authority, a Common Assembly, a Special Council of Ministers, and a Court of Justice. It is significant that the members of the High Authority are chosen for their competence and are not instructed by their governments, and their decisions are not subject to subsequent ratification by their governments. The function of the Court is to "ensure the rule of law in the interpretation and application" of the treaty, its jurisdiction extending to appeals by a member state for the annulment of decisions and recommendations of the High Authority.[20]

European Economic Community (the Common Market). Outstanding among the economic regional groups is the European Economic Community, created by a treaty signed at Rome on March 25, 1957, which is popularly known as the Common Market Treaty. Here the same six states that began with common policies in coal and steel production went on to establish not only free trade within their common market, but the free movement of persons and capital as well as goods, looking step by step from common economic and social policies to ultimate political unity, the initial steps to a supranational government. European states may apply to be members, but the vote of the Council must be unanimous, which made possible the rejection in 1962 of the British application by the negative vote of France. By contrast, provision is made for bringing into association with the Community the non-European countries and territories that have special relations with Belgium, France, Italy, and the Netherlands. The Community operates through an Assembly holding annual sessions, a Council, a technical commission at the service of the Council, and a Court of Justice.[21]

The European Atomic Energy Community (EURATOM), created by

---

[19] Robertson, *The Council of Europe: Its Structure, Functions, and Achievements.* For the text of the Statute, Peaslee, *op. cit.,* Vol. I, p. 344.

[20] Mason, *The European Coal and Steel Community.* For the text of the agreement, see Peaslee, *op. cit.,* Vol. I, p. 464.

[21] See Deniau, *The Common Market.* For the text of the treaty, Peaslee, *op. cit.,* Vol. I, p. 524.

a treaty signed at Rome on the same day as the Common Market Treaty, represents an attempt on the part of the members to anticipate the need of atomic energy to replace the shortage of fuel supplies. Its general objectives are similar to those of the Common Market, with emphasis upon the establishment of agencies of investigation and development of nuclear industries. A commission established by the treaty has far-reaching powers of control, looking for sources of fissionable materials both within and without the Community. In addition to its special commission, EURATOM is served by the organs of the Coal and Steel Community and the Economic Community.[22]

C. THE ARAB LEAGUE

The conception of Arabian unity centers historically around the figure of Mohammed Ali, who became Pasha of Egypt in 1805. But a century passed without significant progress being made. Arab nationalists hoped to profit by the defeat of Turkey in the First World War to establish unity; but the peace treaties divided up the "Fertile Crescent" into five mandates. Then one by one these mandated territories were given independence; and during the Second World War Egypt took the lead in negotiations to put into effect a specific plan for unity.[23]

On March 22, 1945, a pact was signed at Cairo by seven Arab states, creating the League of Arab States.[24] Five of its members (Egypt, Iraq, Lebanon, Saudi Arabia, and Syria) were about to take part in the drafting of the Charter of the United Nations at San Francisco in 1945 as independent states. Yemen was an independent state, only recently having entered into the international community. Transjordan was still a British mandate, to be given its independence by Great Britain in 1946. Membership in the League was limited to "independent Arab States," and another six later joined: Libya (1953), Sudan (1956), Morocco and Tunisia (1958), Kuwait (1961), and Algeria (1962).

The pact of 1945 has two main objectives: to strengthen the relations between the Arab states in order to maintain their independence and promote their general interests, and to bring about the close cooperation of the members in various fields of economic and social interest enumerated in the pact. The chief organ of the League is a Council composed of all the members of the League, in which each state has a single vote. This Council, meeting in ordinary session twice a year, is to have

[22] For the text of the treaty, Peaslee, op. cit., Vol. I, p. 403. The activities of the Community as a regional agency must be distinguished from those of the International Atomic Energy Agency, one of the specialized agencies of the United Nations.

[23] See M. Khadduri, "The Arab-League as a Regional Arrangement." Am. Journal, Vol. 40 (1946), p. 756, where bibliographical references may be found.

[24] For the text of the pact, see Am. Journal, Vol. 39 (1945), p. 266; Peaslee, op. cit., Vol. II, p. 1600.

both legislative and executive functions within the scope of the powers of the League; and it is instructed to set up special commissions which are to determine the principles and the extent of cooperation in respect to the particular subject. Proposals are to take the form of draft conventions, to be submitted by the Council to the separate states for ratification. Recourse to force between the member states is prohibited; and provision is made that in case of aggression against any member of the League, the Council shall be immediately convoked and shall determine the measures to be taken to repel the aggression. The permanent seat of the Council is at Cairo, Egypt. Accompanying the pact and contemplating more effective provisions for resistance to aggression was a Joint Defense and Economic Cooperation Treaty between the states of the Arab League, declaring the principle that an attack upon one would be considered as an attack upon all, and indicating the conformity of the procedure with Article 51 of the Charter of the United Nations.[25]

D. SEATO; CENTO

Although not strictly regional in its geographic membership, the Southeast Asia Treaty Organization is sufficiently regional in its collective defense purposes that it falls properly within the general classification of regional organizations. In 1947 the six powers with problems of colonial administration calling for cooperation (Australia, France, the Netherlands, New Zealand, United Kingdom, and the United States) entered into an agreement establishing the South Pacific Commission, following to some extent the model of the Caribbean Commission in its concern for the peoples of non-self-governing territories. The Commission, having twelve members, is a consultative and advisory body making recommendations covering a wide field of economic and social interests, and its activities are recognized as highly effective in developing local cooperative agencies.

But the war in Korea made it clear that a strong defense force was needed to meet the Communist threat to the whole Southeast area, and on September 8, 1954, the Southeast Asia Collective Defense Treaty was signed at Manila. While collective defense is the primary purpose of the treaty, the organization (SEATO) fails to impose the specific obligations of NATO, and important Southeast Asian states, i.e. India, Burma, Ceylon, and others have refused to participate. Accompanying the treaty was an Understanding of the United States and a Protocol, to the effect that the commitment of the United States in the event of armed attack was to apply only to Communist aggression. A special feature of SEATO is the combination of Western members (United States, Great Britain, and France) with Far Eastern and South Pacific states (Australia, New Zealand, Pakistan, the Philippines, and Thailand)

[25] See Macdonald, *The League of Arab States*.

as original signatories, with South Vietnam, Cambodia, and Laos being designated as within the terms of the defense and the economic provisions of the treaty.

The organs of SEATO consist of a Council, established to consider matters concerning the implementation of the treaty, a Secretariat with permanent headquarters at Bangkok, and an Economic Committee with a regional agrarian research program designed "to promote economic progress and social well-being and to further the individual and collective efforts of governments towards these ends." [26]

In like manner CENTO, the Baghdad Pact of Mutual Cooperation between Iraq and Turkey of 1955, to which the United Kingdom, Pakistan, and Iran subsequently adhered, followed by an Agreement of Cooperation between the United States and Turkey, is more than a military alliance, having economic objectives looking to raising standards of living in the member countries in respect to agricultural development, trade, and communicating highways. Iraq subsequently withdrew as a result of criticism from members of the Arab League. Perhaps, like SEATO, CENTO might be better classified as an agency of economic cooperation, except for its primary political objective.[27]

E. UNION OF AFRICAN STATES AND MALAGASY

As early as 1950 the four African colonial powers (United Kingdom, France, Belgium, and Portugal) together with South Africa and the Federation of Rhodesia and Nyasaland, created a Commission for Technical Cooperation in Africa South of the Sahara (CCTA), which met in regular technical conferences to make recommendations with respect to economic and social problems. The informal arrangement of 1950 was followed in 1954 by an international agreement along the same lines, which, however, did not become effective until May 30, 1958, when a number of African states joined the organization.

With independence came a variety of efforts on the part of the former African colonies to establish regional groups as well as bilateral federations. On September 12, 1961, twelve of the former French African territories entered into an agreement to form the Union of African States and Malagasy (UAM), the Charter of which describes its purpose as being:

to organize cooperation among members in all aspects of foreign policy in order to strengthen their solidarity, assure their collective security, aid their development, and maintain peace in Africa, Malagasy, and the world.

A Conference of Heads of State and Government meets in regular session twice yearly to determine general policy, and it also appoints

[26] See M. L. Thomas, "A Critical Appraisal of SEATO," *Western Political Quarterly*, 1957. For the text of the treaty, Peaslee, *op. cit.*, Vol. II, p. 1750.

[27] For the text of the pact, see Peaslee, *op. cit.*, Vol. I, p. 260.

the administrative Secretary-General whose headquarters are at Cotonou.[28]

F. CASABLANCA GROUP

Functioning separately but along the same lines as UAM, is the Casablanca Group, consisting of Ghana, Guinea, Mali, Morocco, the United Arab Republic, and Algeria, which adopted its African Charter of Casablanca on January 7, 1961. The group puts emphasis on defense, having an African Command Supreme Council and a permanent military staff; but it has also political, economic, and social objectives for which the Charter provides separate committees. An African Consultative Assembly was contemplated as soon as conditions might permit.[29]

G. ORGANIZATION OF AFRICAN UNITY

Still another regional group, wider in scope than either the UAM or the Casablanca group, is the Organization of African Unity, the Charter of which was signed at Addis Ababa on May 25, 1963. The objectives of the Organization follow the lines of other regional groups: to promote unity and solidarity, to raise standards of living, to defend their independence, and to eradicate all forms of colonialism from Africa. The organs, or "institutions" as they are called, consist of an Assembly of Heads of State and Government, a Council of Ministers, a General Secretariat, and a Commission of Mediation, Conciliation, and Arbitration. All of the African states, thirty-two in number at the time, signed the Charter, Egypt signing as the United Arab Republic.[30]

H. ORGANIZATION OF CENTRAL AMERICAN STATES

The idea of Central American unity took shape as early as 1823 when a congress of the five states declared the former provinces to be free and independent states, confederated into a single nation. But in spite of successive efforts to federate during the nineteenth and particularly the early twentieth century, it was not until after the adoption of the Charter of the Organization of American States in 1948 that the Central American states signed on October 14, 1951, their own Charter of San Salvador, establishing a regional organization rather than carrying out the earlier projects of federal union.[31]

ODECA, as the Organization of Central American States is called in Spanish, appears to be a regional group within the larger regional

[28] The future of this and other Central African regional groups is uncertain. See, on the general subject, "Political and Regional Groupings in Africa," *International Organization*, Vol. 16 (1962), pp. 426 ff.

[29] *Ibid.*, p. 437.

[30] For the text of the Charter, see *Am. Journal*, Vol. 58 (1964), p. 873. Thirty-four states were represented at the conference in Cairo in 1964. See B. Boutros Ghali, "The Addis Ababa Charter," *International Conciliation*, No. 546.

[31] See Fenwick, *OAS*, pp. 131 ff.; Peaslee, *op. cit.*, Vol. II, p. 1662.

group of the Organization of American States (OAS). There is, however, actually no such legal relationship as the American states bear to the United Nations, for the reason that the dominant objective of the Central American group is not collective defense, but rather economic, social, and cultural cooperation, looking, in the vague terms of the Charter, to ultimate political union. Apart from the occasional Meeting of Presidents the "princpial organ" of the Organization is the Meeting of Ministers of Foreign Affairs, held in one city or another by rotation among the members. The secretariat of the Organization, described as the Central American Bureau, is permanently located at San Salvador. A significant feature of the Charter is the provision for meetings of ministers in charge of the different departments of the governments, and the additional provision for an economic council responsible to the Conference of Foreign Ministers, the emphasis clearly being upon activities in the fields of economic and social interests.

Supplementing the Charter, and signed in 1960, was the General Treaty on Economic Integration which established the Central American Common Market. A new, revised Charter was adopted December 12, 1962.[32]

I. CARIBBEAN ORGANIZATION

The leasing by the United States of naval bases in six British Caribbean possessions led to the establishment in 1942 of the Anglo-American Caribbean Commission for economic and social cooperation as well as naval defense. This was followed in 1946 by a more formal organization, the Caribbean Commission, which included France and the Netherlands, its general objectives being to diversify economies and raise living standards. As the years passed it was realized that it would be desirable to have the direct participation of the territories themselves, with the result that on June 21, 1960, the four powers signed the Agreement and Statute for the Establishment of the Caribbean Organization. Declared to be eligible were the territories of the four signatories of the Agreement, France, however, representing three territories that were Departments of the Republic. The Organization is unique in the provision for membership of territories not as yet having attained full self-government.[33]

J. SPECIAL TYPES OF UNIONS

Confederations. The term "confederation" has been used historically to describe a variety of loose unions of separate states which have asso-

[32] S. Engel, "The New Charter of the Organization of Central American States," *Am. Journal,* Vol. 58 (1964), p. 127, where the text of the new Charter is given.

[33] For the text of the agreement, see Peaslee, *op. cit.,* Vol. I, p. 123; Dept. of State *Bulletin,* July 11, 1960, p. 68. The Virgin Islands and Puerto Rico were declared to be eligible members.

ciated for certain specific political or economic purposes without surrendering their formal sovereignty and independence. But the term
must not be interpreted too strictly. Vattel, writing in 1758, insisted
that confederations, such as the United Provinces of the Netherlands
and the Swiss Confederation, did not "impair the sovereignty of the
individual members," owing to the voluntary character of the union.
But the facts appear to have been against him in so far as international
law recognized the governmental organs of the confederacy as speaking for the component members. Under the Articles of Confederation
of 1781-1789, the states of the United States, in spite of the explicit retention by each state of its "sovereignty, freedom, and independence,"
lost their international personality, as did the individual states of the
Southern Confederacy during its short-lived existence. The German
Confederation of 1815-1866 left to the individual states the right to
enter into treaties not in conflict with the treaties of the confederation,
to maintain diplomatic representation with other states, and to enter
into alliances not prejudicial to the confederation; and to that extent they
enjoyed a degree of international personality. The members of the Swiss
Confederation have, in spite of the name, lost all element of whatever
original sovereignty they possessed at the time of the recognition of
the Confederation in 1648 by the Peace of Westphalia.[34]

"Real unions." A special form of confederation is the "real union,"
which exists when two or more severally sovereign states have the same
monarch and for international purposes act as one state. The potential
international personality retained by the individual states in such unions
is to be seen in the peaceful dissolution of Norway and Sweden by the
Treaty of Karlstad in 1905. By the act of separation Norway automatically became a member of the family of nations without the necessity
of the usual formality of recognition. The real union of Austria-Hungary,
formed in 1867, was dissolved under stress of defeat in war in 1918.
The union between Denmark and Iceland between 1918 and 1944 was
probably a real union, although the right retained by Denmark to attend
to Iceland's foreign affairs gave to the latter something of the character
of a protectorate. On April 10, 1940, following the invasion of Denmark
by Germany, Iceland suspended the exercise of royal power by the
King of Denmark; and on June 17, 1944, the independence of the Republic of Iceland was formally proclaimed, the country being at the
time occupied by British and American troops.[35]

[34] Most confederations have been short-lived, due to their inherent instability, the
Swiss Confederation being an exception more in name than in fact. Recent African
confederations appear to be in a state of transition.
[35] The occupation of Iceland during the war was justified by the United States as
necessary "to insure the safety of the Western Hemisphere." Dept. of State *Bulletin*,
Vol. V, p. 15. Iceland became a member of the United Nations in 1946. For the
temporary "real union" of Italy and Albania, see Whiteman, *Digest*, Vol. 1, p. 373.

Federal states. Closer than the union of states in a confederation is the union between the members of a federal state. Here the federal state appears as a composite person, responsible at international law for the conduct of the members of the union and competent to speak in their collective name. Such was the effect of the Constitution of the United States of 1789, under which the identity of the members continued only as a matter of constitutional law. The States retained their separate and independent autonomy in respect to the sphere of self-government reserved to them under the Constitution; they delegated to the Federal Government full control of their external affairs.[36]

British Commonwealth of Nations. The international status of the members of the British Commonwealth of Nations is anomalous and cannot be fitted into any of the traditional categories previously recognized by international law. Until 1919 Canada, Australia, New Zealand, and South Africa were technically parts of the British Empire. As a practical matter, however, these colonies had attained a degree of independence in the control of their foreign as well as of their domestic affairs which placed them in the category of the more advanced protectorates. Their status as international persons was given definite recognition at international law when the four dominions were made, each in its own name, signatories of the Treaty of Versailles and became in their separate personalities original members of the League of Nations. With them as a signatory of the treaty and member of the League was included India, which consisted of the native states (protectorates having almost complete internal autonomy) and of British India, which was given a limited measure of self-government under the Government of India Act of 1919.

The limited degree of international personality explicitly recognized as belonging to the British self-governing dominions by the fact of their admission into the League of Nations was given sharper definition by the Imperial Conference of 1926, at which a report was adopted defining the "group of self-governing communities composed of Great Britain and the Dominions," henceforth to be known as the British Commonwealth of Nations.[37] The individual members of the Commonwealth thus obtained a formal position of equality within a group which was itself part of the separate international person known as the British Empire.

---

[36] In the leading case of State of Texas v. White, 7 Wallace 700 (1868) (Fenwick, *Cases,* p. 56), the court held that Texas continued to be a legal member of the Union in spite of its decrees of secession and its period of forcible resistance to the Government of the Union. "The Constitution," said the court, "looks to an indestructible Union, composed of indestructible States."

[37] "They are autonomous communities within the British Empire, equal in status, in no way subordinate to one another in any aspect of their domestic or external affairs, though united by a common allegiance to the Crown, and freely associated as members of the British Commonwealth of Nations." For the complete text of the Report, see *Am. Journal,* Vol. 21 (1927), Supp., p. 21.

Great Britain itself is thus a member of the Commonwealth and the international representative of the larger unit of the Empire.

By the Statute of Westminster of November, 1931,[38] the Dominion parliaments were largely emancipated from the restrictions limiting their legislative competence, so that the duty thenceforth devolved directly upon them of bringing their legislation into harmony with international conventions. Thereafter the "autonomous communities" proceeded to appoint diplomatic representatives to a number of the leading states and to negotiate treaties in their own separate interest, using at times the British Crown as the formal signatory of the treaty. The Imperial Conferences became more and more gatherings of states cooperating freely in their common interest, adopting measures having the practical effect of law, and formulating plans to meet the political and economic situations with which the Commonwealth was confronted. When, in 1939, Great Britain was led to declare war upon Germany in defense of Poland, all of the members of the Commonwealth except Eire promptly responded with separate declarations of war in their own names.

The secession of Ireland from its earlier status as a member of the Commonwealth came about with the enactment in 1948 of the Republic of Ireland Act, repealing the Act of 1936 restricting the external relations of Ireland and proclaiming the State the "Republic of Ireland." This was followed in 1949 by an act formally recognizing that Eire had ceased to be "a part of His Majesty's Dominions." Thenceforth Ireland ceased to be legally a member of the Commonwealth, although by a special provision of the law Ireland was held not to be "a foreign country" for the purposes of any law of the United Kingdom.[39]

The political upheaval in the colonial world following the Second World War expanded the narrow circle of the Commonwealth, and one by one the former colonies of the British Crown were recognized as independent and admitted as members of the Commonwealth. In addition to the members of more strictly British origin, i.e. Canada, Australia, New Zealand, there are the Caribbean members, Jamaica and Trinidad-Tobago; the African members, Ghana (the Gold Coast), admitted in 1957, Nigeria, admitted in 1960, Sierra Leone, admitted in 1961, Tanganyika, Uganda, Zanzibar, and Kenya; the Eastern Mediterranean member, Cyprus; the Asian members, India, Pakistan, Ceylon, and the Federation of Malaysia. In 1947 India, hitherto a part of the

---

[38] For the text of the Statute, see Peaslee, op. cit., Vol. I, p. 313. The literature of the status of the members of the British Commonwealth is extensive. See in particular Keith, The Sovereignty of the British Dominions; The Dominions as Sovereign States; Baker, The Present Juridical Status of the British Dominions in International Law; Toynbee, British Commonwealth Relations; Wheare, The Constitutional Structure of the Commonwealth; Fawcett, The British Commonwealth in International Law.

[39] See Whiteman, Digest, Vol. 1, pp. 510 ff. A survey of the historical development of the Free State may be found in Irish Free State v. Guaranty Deposit Co., 129 Misc. Rep. N.Y. 1927, 551. Fenwick, Cases, p. 139.

Empire, was partitioned into two independent Dominions, completely free of control by the British Parliament but united by a common allegiance to the Crown. The partition was on the basis of the divergencies between the two leading religious groups, Hindu and Moslem, it being left to them to decide whether a unified India was possible.[40]

In 1960-1961 a crisis arose when the Union of South Africa seceded from the Commonwealth, and the discussions attending the secession brought to the forefront the legal character of the Commonwealth. South Africa had made application at the Prime Ministers' Conference in that year for continued membership in the Commonwealth as a republic. But the strong opposition manifested to the *apartheid* policy of the government led the Prime Minister of the Union to withdraw the application. The general policy of the Ministers' Conference was described as recognizing the right of the individual members of the Commonwealth to manage their own domestic affairs, but that there were certain standards of human rights and human freedom that constituted implied conditions of membership.[41]

In view of the increase in the membership of the Commonwealth and the diversity of national policies resulting from the emancipation of colonies of different traditions, observers foresee that the Commonwealth will develop along loose juridical lines, having as its underlying unity a certain loyalty to the British Crown as expressing British traditions of law and government and relying upon common economic and social interests to form whatever legal ties may from time to time be needed. The Queen is described officially as "Head of the Commonwealth"; and the single political organ is the annual Conference of Prime Ministers. While the decisions taken at the Commonwealth conferences are informal agreements rather than legal commitments, they appear to be sufficiently concrete to have a definite effect upon conduct, as in the case of the agreement between India and Pakistan in 1964 to undertake summit talks on Kashmir, and the agreement to support Malaysia in its resistance to Indonesian aggression. Conference decisions were influential in bringing about the establishment of the Republic of Cyprus in 1960, together with the treaties of guarantee and of alliance associated with it.[42]

French Community. In 1959 a new form of union, approximating a confederation, yet possessing the closer characteristics of a federal state, came into being with the establishment of the French Community, consisting of the mother country (the French Republic), the Overseas Departments, the Overseas Territories, and the autonomous Member States. The President of the French Republic is President of

---

[40] Whiteman, *Digest,* Vol. 1, pp. 489 ff.; Peaslee, *Constitutions,* p. 218.
[41] Whiteman, *Digest,* Vol. 1, pp. 484 ff.
[42] *Ibid.,* pp. 476 ff., 525 ff.

the Community, and the organs of the Community consist of an Executive Council, a Senate, and a Court of Arbitration. The extensive powers of the President over foreign policy, defense, and economic and financial affairs are in sharp contrast with the limited "common allegiance to the Crown" in the British Commonwealth.[43]

K. INTERNATIONAL SPECIALIZED AGENCIES

Closely associated with regional groups are the international unions and specialized agencies or organizations that have been formed for the promotion of specific objectives of an economic or social character. With the growth of international commerce and particularly of international communications during the second half of the nineteenth century, the need of creating international agencies for the administration of matters of common interest to all states became more and more apparent. Conferences and congresses, such as the Congress of Vienna in 1815 and the Congress of Paris in 1856, called to meet situations of emergency, were familiar forms of group action; but their activities were limited as a rule to political decisions in which only a small number of the leading powers were recognized as having an interest. The new need was not the regulation of conflicting interests but the promotion of common interests; and in the absence of a general international organization the simplest method of meeting these interests appeared to be the formation of special groups of states operating under agreements directed to the particular end in view. These groups were of the widest variety, the more important of them being designated as "unions," with their membership open to all states having an interest in the objectives sought. Between 1865, when the Telegraphic Union was established, and the eve of the Second World War, some forty-five such associations were established, the original name "union" being replaced at times by the name of the bureau maintained by the group. More recently the name "union" has been abandoned in favor of the term "organization." The Charter of the United Nations now makes provision for bringing these "specialized agencies," as they are described, into relationship with the United Nations; but even when this has been accomplished they will still retain a semi-autonomous character and they may be expected to continue to play an active part in the administrative work of the international community.[44]

---

[43] For details of membership and constitutional provisions, *ibid.*, p. 544; Peaslee, *Int. Gov. Org.*, Vol. I, p. 683.

[44] On the general subject of international unions, see Reinsch, *Public International Unions* (1911); Woolf, *International Government* (1916); Sayre, *Experiments in International Administration* (1919); Eagleton, *International Government*, Chap. IX; Hill, *International Administration;* Potter, *Introduction to the Study of International Organization,* Chap. VIII; Vinacke, *International Organization,* Chap. XIV. On the question of membership, see H. Aufricht, "Principles and Practices of Recognition by International Organizations," *Am. Journal,* Vol. 43 (1949), p. 679. For the various unions and organizations, Chap. XXV.

Legal character of international unions. The public, as distinct from private, international union owes its legal existence to the terms of the treaty or convention creating it. It draws its authority, therefore, not from the general rules of international law but from the specific agreement of the parties to the treaty; and there is no question of its claiming rights or exercising functions beyond the strict terms of the agreement. The treaty is in a sense its constitution or charter, differing from the charters and constitutions of associations operating under municipal law in that it is not controlled by any higher authority than the members themselves of the union. This basic treaty is, like other treaties, subject to amendment; and it is the constant adoption of amendments, whether of the treaty itself or of the regulations attached to it, which gives to the union the dynamic character of a living institution. From time to time the union, instead of amending its basic treaty, may set it aside entirely in favor of a new one. The Universal Postal Union has followed the practice of amending previous conventions by substituting a new convention containing the desired revisions, as at London in 1929, at Cairo in 1934, and at Buenos Aires in 1939.

Organization of unions. The outstanding characteristic of the international union is the permanent organization which it creates for the accomplishment of the particular objectives of the union. While unions are of the widest variety and there is no special type of organization, in general there is a periodic conference or congress which determines the policies of the union and which may be said to be its legislative organ; and there is an administrative bureau or commission which carries out the policies adopted by the general conference and performs the specific functions set forth in the basic treaty.

Control of policies and activities. The periodic conference or congress which meets from time to time is representative of the entire membership of the union. In the case of the Congress of the Universal Postal Union, which meets every five years, each country is represented by one or more delegates but has one vote only. A special feature of the Union is that it includes in its membership "countries" which are not technically states but merely colonial dependencies. In the case of the Telecommunications Union, under the Madrid Convention of 1932, there are two kinds of conferences, the one a conference of plenipotentiaries which has the power to revise the basic convention, the other an administrative conference of delegates having power to revise the regulations only. The conference of plenipotentiaries meets at a date fixed by the preceding conference or upon special call by twenty governments. The administrative conference determines for itself the place and time of the following meeting.

The International Labor Organization. The International Labor Organization (ILO), created by Part XIII of the Treaty of Versailles in 1920, marks the beginning of the coordination of the separate agencies of limited membership with the larger international organization. Provision was made in the treaty creating the League of Nations that "the original members of the League of Nations shall be the original members of this organization, and hereafter membership of the League of Nations shall carry with it membership of the said organization." But in spite of this close connection with the League, the International Labor Organization maintained its separate legal personality and survived the extinction of the League on April 18, 1946. On May 30, 1946, the Chairman of the Governing Body of the ILO signed with the President of the Economic and Social Council of the United Nations a draft agreement with the object of bringing the ILO into relationship with the United Nations as a "specialized agency." The agreement was subsequently approved by the General Assembly; and by a protocol signed December 20, 1946, the ILO became the first of the autonomous groups to be "brought into relationship with the United Nations" under the terms of Article 57 of the Charter.[45]

Specialized agencies of the United Nations. In accordance with the terms of Article 57 of the Charter the specialized agencies that are to be "brought into relationship with the United Nations" are those "established by intergovernmental agreement and having wide international responsibilities" in economic, social, cultural, educational, health, and related fields. Relationship is established by individual agreements between the agency and the United Nations on the basis of recommendations from the Economic and Social Council to the General Assembly. On its part the Council is called upon to coordinate the activities of the specialized agencies, with the object of adjusting the overlapping of functions that naturally follows from agencies dealing with different aspects of the same general problem.

Agreements with fifteen specialized agencies have come into force, seven dealing with economic and financial problems: the International Bank for Reconstruction and Development, the International Monetary Fund, the International Finance Corporation, the International Development Association, the International Monetary Fund; also the Food and Agriculture Organization and the General Agreement on Tariffs and Trade; three dealing with social and cultural problems: the International Labor Organization, the United Nations Educational, Scientific and Cultural Organization, and the World Health Organization; and five dealing with scientific and technical problems with obvious economic and social correlations: the International Civil Aviation Organization, the Universal Postal Union, the International Telecommunication Union, the World Meteorological Organization, and the Intergovernmental Maritime Consultative Organization. The International Atomic Energy Agency,

[45] For a general study of the work of the International Labor Organization, see *I.L.O. Year Books; U.N. Yearbooks;* Peaslee, *op. cit.*, Vol. II, p. 1248.

although not a specialized agency, is an autonomous intergovernmental organization having working relations with the United Nations, having been established to further the peaceful uses of atomic energy.[46]

The internal structure of the specialized agencies varies with the agency, but all follow a more or less general pattern. In the case of the ILO there is a general conference of representatives of the member states and an International Labor Office operating under the control of a governing body which names the director, supervises the work of the office, prepares the agenda of the Conference, conducts investigations, and makes studies through its own separate committees. The governing body is unique in its inclusion of representatives both of employers and of labor. In like manner the Food and Agriculture Organization works through a conference, a council, and a staff headed by a director general. The organization of the financial agencies consists of a board of governors, executive directors, a managing director or president, and the usual staff.

L. NONGOVERNMENTAL ORGANIZATIONS

Side by side with the earlier unions there developed a wide range of semipublic or "private international organizations" having interests and objectives of an international character but organized by private persons or associations. The term "nongovernmental organizations" (NGOs) has come to be applied to them, and although still private their activities are recognized by the Economic and Social Council as of international interest; and a number of them, described as Class A, have been given consultative status, and others, Class B, a more limited relationship due to the restricted field in which they function. Outstanding among the ten or more organizations in Class A are the International Chamber of Commerce and the Inter-Parliamentary Union.[47]

[46] Details of the activities of these agencies "related to the United Nations" may be found in the U.N. Yearbooks; and in Peaslee, op. cit. See Chap. XXV of the present work.

[47] U.N. Yearbook, 1962, pp. 383 ff.; Lador-Lederer, International Non-Governmental Organizations and Economic Entities.

PART **III**

The Substantive Rules of
International Law

CHAPTER XI

The General Rights and Duties of States:

The Principle of Equality

A. CHARACTER OF INTERNATIONAL RIGHTS

Turning from the organization of the international community to an examination of the rights and duties of its members, we are confronted once more with a number of doctrinal problems resulting from the attempt of jurists, and at times of governments, to apply to states the principles of conduct recognized as applicable between man and man within the state.[1] The fact that the older writers on international law, Grotius, Zouche, Pufendorf, Vattel drew so heavily upon general moral principles and upon the specific rules of the civil law had the natural effect of developing a tendency to classify the rights and duties of states in terms of the classifications of municipal law.[2] But the older writers themselves were not in accord as to the basic conceptions upon which they proceeded; so that it is not surprising that later writers, following in their footsteps, should manifest the widest divergencies in their approach to the problem.

The doctrine of fundamental rights. Two main approaches to the problem of the classification of the rights of states may be indicated, reflecting more or less the attitude of the particular writer towards the nature of international law. The great majority of writers, following the classification of Vattel and other jurists of the "state of nature" tradition, laid down certain rights of states which were regarded as fundamental,

---

[1] See above, p. 59.

[2] The student may be reminded of the title of Vattel's treatise which exercised so great an influence upon later writers: "The Law of Nations, or the Principles of Natural Law applied to the Conduct and to the Affairs of Nations and of Sovereigns." See above, p. 63. The relations between the two branches of law are admirably treated in Lauterpacht, *Private Law Sources and Analogies of International Law.*

essential, and absolute; [3] in addition to which were other rights of a secondary, derived, or relative character. Fundamental rights were rights which were said to be inherent in the very nature of the state, the primary conditions of the existence of a state, derived, if they could be said to be derived at all, by direct inference from that "sovereignty and independence" which constituted the cornerstone of the whole edifice of international law. Different lists of these fundamental rights of states appeared in the various treatises, some writers listing distinct fundamental rights: the right to existence, to independence, to equality, to respect, to territory; and others deriving the various fundamental rights from the primary right of existence.[4] Constructive thinkers made their own classifications.

Conception of rights as absolute. Within the above group a number of writers showed a tendency to ascribe to the fundamental rights of states an absolute character, regarding them as having the same final and inalienable character as the rights of man as a citizen of the individual state. Close analogies were drawn by certain of these writers between the rights of man and the rights of the state, just as if the corporate personality of the state were something as sacred as the natural person of the individual human being.[5] Strangely enough, this

[3] Compare, in respect to the rights of individuals, the classical words of the Declaration of Independence of the United States: "We hold these truths to be self-evident, that all men are created equal, that they are endowed by their Creator with certain inalienable Rights, that among these are Life, Liberty and the Pursuit of Happiness." But the transfer of these rights from man to the state as a corporate group presents another question.

[4] Rivier, the Swiss publicist, writing in 1896, states the conception of fundamental rights most effectively: "These rights of self-preservation, respect, independence, and mutual commerce, which can all be carried back to a single right of self-preservation, are founded on the very notion of the state as a person of the law of nations. They form the statutory basis of the law of nations, and the common constitution of our political civilization. The recognition of a state as a subject of the law of nations implies *ipso jure* the recognition of its legal possession of these rights. They are called the essential, or fundamental, primordial, absolute, permanent rights, in opposition to those arising from tacit conventions, which are sometimes described as hypothetical or conditional, relative, accidental rights. The authorities differ in referring to one or another of them the specific legal rights which are their manifestations. Those differences are scarcely more than external; there is agreement at bottom. Every act which violates an essential right is a breach of the law of nations, an international crime or misdemeanor. The state injured has the right to demand reparation and satisfaction, and to compel the offending or responsible state to give it." *Principes du droit des gens,* Vol. I, p. 257. For a survey of the various lists of fundamental rights adopted by different writers, see Fauchille, *Droit international public,* Vol. I, Part 1, pp. 395 ff.

[5] This character of finality and absoluteness marks the Declaration of the Rights and Duties of Nations [*Am. Journal,* Vol. 10 (1916), p. 124] adopted by the American Institute of International Law on January 6, 1916, at its meeting in Washington:

"I. Every nation has the right to exist, and to protect and to conserve its existence; but this right neither implies the right nor justifies the act of the state to protect itself or to conserve its existence by the commission of unlawful acts against innocent and unoffending states.

"II. Every nation has the right to independence in the sense that it has a right to the pursuit of happiness and is free to develop itself without interference or control attitude was manifested by writers who would have been far from ascribing to the state an absolutism in relation to its own citizens. Their desire appeared rather to be to protect the weaker states against the dominance of the great powers, and their belief was that by asserting certain rights of states as absolute, there would be less danger of encroachment upon them.[6]

Postulates of existing law. Other writers, while adhering to the tradition of the fundamental rights of states, took a more realistic view of them, looking upon them merely as the assumptions or postulates which during the past three hundred years had come to be regarded as essential conditions of membership in the international community. By custom states had come to be regarded as possessing these rights, and in consequence they were part of the international law of the time. But there was no reason to assign to them any absolute or inherent character.[7]

---

from other states, provided that in so doing it does not interfere with or violate the rights of other states.

"III. Every nation is in law and before law the equal of every other nation belonging to the society of nations, and all nations have the right to claim and according to the Declaration of Independence of the United States, 'to assume, among the powers of the earth, the separate and equal station to which the laws of nature and nature's God entitle them.'

"IV. Every nation has the right to territory within defined boundaries and to exercise exclusive jurisdiction over its territory, and all persons whether native or foreign found therein.

"V. Every nation entitled to a right by the law of nations is entitled to have that right respected and protected by all other nations, for right and duty are correlative, and the right of one is the duty of all to observe.

"VI. International law is at one and the same time both national and international: national in the sense that it is the law of the land and applicable as such to the decision of all questions involving its principles; international in the sense that it is the law of the society of nations and applicable as such to all questions between and among the members of the society of nations involving its principles."

See J. B. Scott, *The American Institute of International Law: Its Declaration of the Rights and Duties of Nations.*

[6] Such was clearly the intention of the Declaration issued by the American Institute of International Law.

[7] Westlake's attack was perhaps the most effective: "Natural persons may have inherent rights, that is, rights to be ordinarily enjoyed within the definition given to them by the law of the land, but which are so sacred as in extreme cases to warrant revolutionary resistance if that law does not adequately recognize them. The right of association is one of them, but it is one over which the laws of all countries find it necessary to exercise a very real control, so much greater is the power of an association for evil than that of its individual members. But states are nothing more than associations of natural persons, acting too outside the salutary control of national law. Surely then the natural right of association is pushed to an intolerable extent when men are deemed to be empowered by it to give absolute rights to their creations in the international world; for instance, to give to a state an absolute right of self-preservation, in circumstances analogous to those which would justify a well ordered state in dissolving an association which had been erected within it. Surely also it is a logical error to assume, because states are moral persons and therefore capable of rights equally with natural individuals, that they must have the same rights as natural individuals." From Westlake, *International Law*, Part I, p. 307 (Cambridge University Press, England). By permission of The Macmillan Company, publishers, N. Y.

The state was made for man, not man for the state. So long as international law continued to be a law of sovereign states, obviously the traditional rights of sovereign states must accompany them. But there was no absolute necessity that international law should be for all time a law of sovereign states. It might some day be the law of a sovereign community of states. States in general had their justification in the fact that the people composing them found in them an expression of their sense of national unity and a means of promoting their common interests. But there was nothing final or absolute in the corporate character of a particular state. If the people of two or more states might find in a federal union a better expression of their sense of unity and a better means of promoting their common interests, the federal state might absorb the former individual states without violating any inherent rights of the latter. Conceivably, if with less probability, the whole body of individual states might form an international federal union without thereby violating any fundamental principles of international law.[8]

Rights dependent upon recognition. To a third group of writers the whole question of fundamental and accidental, of absolute and relative, of primary and secondary rights seemed irrelevant. Jurists of the so-called "positive" tradition, looking only to the facts of international life and to the members of the international community as they found them, saw no reason for introducing doctrinal conceptions into their discussions of current practice. Rights were rights if they were recognized as such, and a state could claim only what custom had established or what specific treaties had prescribed. Consent was the basis of international law; and if the members of the international community had shown their acquiescence or their direct agreement in respect to the assertion of certain rights by states, that was enough. Besides, it was hard at times to distinguish between a fundamental right and a nonfundamental right. Much better was it simply to discuss the accepted rights of states, classifying them according to the convenience of the subject matter, not according to any alleged intrinsic character.[9]

The practice of governments was, on the whole, more pragmatic than the attitude of the jurists. In general, smaller states laid more insistence upon fundamental rights, due, as has been suggested, to a desire to

[8] The question is obviously closely related to the problem of the limitations of sovereignty. See p. 125. It was not that the writers of the nineteenth century wished to close the door against any fundamental change in international organization, but simply that, with a few exceptions, they did not have the imagination to look beyond the existing system.

[9] Oppenheim, although not taking a rigidly "positivist" position, agreed with those who asked "that the fundamental rights of States should totally disappear from the treatises on the Law of Nations." *International Law*, Vol. I, § 112. Compare Kelsen's conclusion that "The so-called fundamental rights and duties of States are rights and duties of the States only in so far as they are stipulated by general international law, which has the character of customary law." *General Theory of Law and State*, p. 249.

protect themselves against the encroachments of the larger states. But even the larger states had recourse at times to arguments based upon fundamental rights, when the subject at issue appeared to them to be of sufficient importance. Vattel's distinction between "perfect" and "imperfect rights," although abandoned in respect to its terminology, long kept a practical hold upon governments. Fundamental rights were rights worth fighting for, rights with respect to which a state could not make concessions without sacrificing its position in the international community.[10] Other rights could be the subject of concessions; disputes concerning them could be arbitrated, if need be, without loss of prestige. Violations of them could be submitted to without raising any question of the legal personality of the state. Whether fundamental rights were actually involved in the various claims of "vital interests" made by states was, so far as governments regarded it, a matter that could be left to the jurists for discussion within their academic circles.

B. DECLARATIONS OF FUNDAMENTAL RIGHTS

It was within the inter-American regional community that a first effort was made to proclaim a general declaration of the rights of states corresponding roughly to the historical declarations of the rights of man. The Declaration of the Rights and Duties of Nations, adopted by the American Institute of International Law in 1916,[11] was followed by a project entitled "Fundamental Rights and Duties of American Republics," prepared for submission to the International Commission of Jurists which met in Rio de Janeiro in 1927.[12] Upon the basis of this project the Commission of Jurists submitted to the Habana Conference of 1928 a draft treaty on "States, their existence, equality and recognition"; but the proposed treaty was defeated by reason of the opposition of the United States to the absolute form of the doctrine of nonintervention which it incorporated.[13]

The Montevideo Convention. The first official action was taken at the Montevideo Conference of 1933. A Convention on Rights and Duties of States was adopted [14] in which the signatory states agreed, subject to various qualifications and limitations, that the political existence of the state was independent of recognition,[15] that states were juridically

[10] For an analysis of the broad scope given by governments to the right of self-preservation, see below, p. 275.

[11] For the text of the Declaration, see note 5.

[12] See *Am. Journal,* Vol. 20 (1926), Spec. Supp., p. 313.

[13] See Bemis, *Latin American Policy of the United States,* Chapter XIV. For the text of the project, see *Am. Journal,* Vol. 22 (1928), Spec. Supp., p. 240.

[14] *International Conferences of American States,* 1933-1940, p. 121.

[15] The meaning of this article (3) is somewhat elusive. It represents an effort to defy the procedure of recognition prevailing at the time of the establishment of the American states, but in doing so it confuses international and constitutional law. See p. 160, note 23.

equal,[16] that the fundamental rights of states were not susceptible of being affected in any manner whatsoever,[17] that the recognition of a state merely signified the acceptance of its personality,[18] that no state had the right to intervene in the internal or external affairs of another,[19] that nationals and foreigners were under the same protection of the law and that foreigners might not claim rights other or more extensive than those of nationals,[20] that disputes should be settled by pacific methods, and that territorial acquisitions or special advantages obtained by force should not be recognized.[21] A number of these principles were reaffirmed at the Conference at Buenos Aires in 1936,[22] and again at the Conference at Lima in 1938.[23] In 1945, at the Conference on Problems of War and Peace held at Mexico City, a resolution was adopted calling for the preparation of a "Declaration of the Rights and Duties of States" to be annexed, together with a "Declaration of the International Rights and Duties of Man," to the new charter of the Pan American System.[24]

The Charter of the United Nations, while not formulating a code of the rights and duties of its members, enumerates in its opening articles a succession of principles that might be included under that head. It is declared that "The Organization is based on the principle of the sovereign equality of all its Members." They have the duty to "fulfill in

[16] See below, p. 260.

[17] This article (5) must be interpreted to mean that states possess certain fundamental rights simply because they are states. Otherwise it is in flat contradiction with the whole conception of international law.

[18] This article (6), like Article 3 above, appears to be a challenge to states which might attempt to attach conditions to their recognition. It is difficult to attach any practical meaning to it under the conditions of 1933.

[19] This article marks the triumph of the opponents of Secretary Hughes in 1928. See Bemis, op. cit., Chap. XV. For an analysis of the doctrine of nonintervention, see pp. 285 ff.

[20] This article (9) raises the controversial problem whether there is an international standard of justice. See p. 331.

[21] This article (11) is related to the Stimson Doctrine of 1931 and to the action of the Washington Conference of 1932, but its phrasing suggests an attempt to check still further the interventionist policy of the United States.

In signing, and again in ratifying the Montevideo Convention, the United States entered a reservation to the effect that the United States Government had made sufficiently clear since March 4 of that year that it supported the general principle of nonintervention, but that it was desirable to prepare "interpretations and definitions of these fundamental terms" if differences of opinion in their application were to be avoided. International Conferences of American States, 1933-1940, pp. 123-124.

[22] See Resolution XXVII, Declaration of Principles of Inter-American Solidarity and Cooperation, op. cit., p. 160.

[23] See Resolution CIX, Declaration of the Principles of the Solidarity of America, op. cit., p. 308.

[24] See Resolution IX, Reorganiaztion, Consolidation and Strengthening of the Inter-American System. A tentative Draft Declaration of the Rights and Duties of American States was submitted by the Pan American Union to the American governments for their approval on July 17, 1946.

good faith" the obligations assumed by them in the Charter; to settle disputes by peaceful means; to refrain from the threat or use of force in their mutual relations; and to assist the United Nations in any action taken in accordance with the Charter. Each of these duties is obviously attended by corresponding rights in respect to other states.[25]

At its first session in 1949 the International Law Commission drafted a Declaration on Rights and Duties of States, consisting of fourteen articles formulated in the light of new developments of international law and in harmony with the Charter of the United Nations. Four of the articles listed the basic rights of the states and ten articles the basic duties. The General Assembly commended the draft and transmitted it to the member states for consideration. No further action was taken by the Assembly, and interest appears to be transferred to the topic "Principles of International Law Concerning Friendly Relations and Cooperation among States in accordance with the United Nations Charter," a preliminary draft of which was adopted by the General Assembly on December 18, 1962.[26]

More detailed are the rights and duties of the twenty-one members of the Organization of American States. Chapter II of the Charter reaffirms twelve "Principles" governing the conduct of members of the Organization, and Chapter III sets forth a succession of "Fundamental Rights and Duties of States," which repeat in part principles proclaimed in earlier documents and specify in more detail certain concrete applications of the law, such as the general prohibition of intervention and the exception to it in the case of measures taken to maintain peace and security.[27]

C. RIGHTS AND DUTIES CORRELATIVE

In international law, as in municipal law, rights and duties are correlative, that is, the right of one state implies a corresponding duty on the part of other states to respect it. In the various conflicts of claims between states arising from their efforts to give practical application to fundamental principles, it has been found desirable to state the rule of law at times in terms of the right of the claimant, at other times in terms of the duty of the state against which the claim is made.[28] It is to be expected that rights should receive more emphasis than duties, and that states should seek to exercise their rights without due consideration for

[25] Art. 2.

[26] *U.N. Yearbook,* 1948, p. 445, where the text of the draft is given. See also, R. Alfaro, "Rights and Duties of States," *Recueil des Cours,* 1959. For the text of 1962, see *U.N. Yearbook,* 1962, p. 494.

[27] Charter of the Organization of American States, Arts. 5-19. Fenwick, *OAS,* pp. 549-551.

[28] For example, the *right* of a state to control immigration into its territory, and the *duty* of the state to give due protection to resident aliens. Compare the Draft of the International Law Commission above.

the exercise of a similar right on the part of other states. The adjustment of these conflicting rights and their correlative duties is obviously the primary function of international law, which becomes practically effective to the extent to which it can reduce abstract principles to concrete rules of conduct.

Relation of the individual state to the international community. Until of recent years it was the practice of jurists to discuss the rights and duties of states in terms of the relation of one state to another. Little account was taken of the relation of the individual state to the community of states as a whole, whether in respect to the rights of the community of states to maintain the peace and to promote the general welfare, or in respect to the duties of the individual state to cooperate with the community in the maintenance of law and order. The provisions of the Charter of the United Nations, such as those set forth in Article 2, clearly contemplate rights and duties of this second kind; and in consequence they call for a reexamination of the traditional rights and duties of states, and of the limitations and restrictions which must be put upon them in the interest of the welfare of the community as a whole.[29]

D. THE EQUALITY OF STATES

It has long been the practice of writers to list the "right of equality" as one of the fundamental rights of states. Strictly speaking, the equality of states is not so much a separate right in itself as it is a characteristic of the whole system of international rights and duties, and it can best be considered in that connection. There can be little doubt but that in view of the innumerable affirmations of the equality of states, notably by the American states,[30] culminating in the formal proclamation of the principle of the "sovereign equality" of the members of the United Nations, the principle of equality is now firmly established in international law. But there is little agreement among jurists as to the basis upon which the principle rests, or upon the scope of its application, or upon

---

[29] The analogies of national law are here applicable, *private* law dealing with the relations between individual citizens and *public* law dealing with the organization of the government and the relation of the individual to the state.

[30] The Latin American states have been particularly insistent upon the principle of the equality of states, clearly in answer to the claim of the United States before 1933 of a right to "interpose" in the internal affairs of smaller states in order to restore law and order. Article 4 of the Montevideo Convention on Rights and Duties of States asserts: "States are juridically equal, enjoy the same rights, and have equal capacity in their exercise. The rights of each one do not depend upon the power which it possesses to assure its exercise, but upon the simple fact of its existence as a person under international law." Each succeeding declaration of rights (see p. 259) reaffirms the principle in one form or another.

the inferences that may be drawn from it in the practical relations of states.[31]

The influence of Vattel. The principle of the sovereignty and independence of states, which found its first legal expression in the Treaty of Westphalia, while not inevitably necessitating an international community in which each state was the legal equal of every other,[32] would doubtless in time have led to that conclusion. Where no common superior was recognized it would naturally follow that all were upon an equal footing. But Vattel soon came and struck the keynote. Writing in 1758 under the influence of the prevailing theory of a state of nature, Vattel laid down the rule that since men were by nature equal, so nations, composed of men, were also by nature equal. "A dwarf is as much a man as a giant is; a small Republic is no less a sovereign State than the most powerful Kingdom." [33] However faulty the logic of the argument, it was destined to become a classic, regarded almost with veneration by smaller states which sought to find in it protection against more powerful states, whose very power tended to be a justification for arbitrary conduct. The larger states accepted the principle in its broad form, but were little troubled by it when it ran counter to policies of aggression.

Divergent views of modern jurists. Jurists, seeking to reconcile theory with practice, took the most divergent positions. Some attacked the principle as being an outworn tradition which had come to be an obstacle to international progress.[34] Others, too realistic to accept a legal principle so obviously in contradiction with the facts of international life, sought to draw distinctions between legal and political equality, and thus to save the principle without the inconsistencies attaching to it.[35] On the other hand many jurists strenuously upheld the principle, believing that it embodied an essential condition of a just international order, a condition as vital as that of the liberty of the individual under a modern democratic constitution.[36] The confusion in doctrine arose because writers frequently discussed different practical applications of the principle as if they had equal bearing upon the principle itself.

[31] The divergent views of modern publicists are presented at length in Dickinson, *The Equality of States in International Law*, Chap. IV. See also Goebel, *The Equality of States;* and compare Kooijmans, *The Doctrine of the Legal Equality of States*.

[32] Dickinson points out that the frequently repeated statement that Grotius was responsible for the formulation of the principle of the equality of states is unfounded.

[33] *Droit des gens*, Eng. trans., Introduction, §§ 18-21. Vattel merely rephrases the principle proclaimed by Wolff.

[34] See P. J. Baker, "The Doctrine of Legal Equality of States," *British Year Book*, 1923-1924, pp. 1-20.

[35] See Dickinson, *op. cit.*, Chap. IV.

[36] Notably Latin American jurists, as illustrated in the Declaration of the American Institute of International Law.

E. APPLICATIONS OF THE PRINCIPLE

Three main applications of the principle of equality may be discussed in turn. The first relates to the substance of the rights possessed by states and is described in the statements that "all states have the same rights and the same obligations," or again that "all states are equal before the law." The second application relates to the protection given by international law to substantive rights, and it calls for equal respect by all states for the recognized rights of each and for the equal application of the rules of procedure which international law affords for the settlement of disputes and for the maintenance of just claims. The third application of the principle relates to the part played by states in the adoption of new rules of law which are to determine their future rights and duties. By keeping these three aspects of equality separate it becomes possible to discern somewhat more clearly the essential features of the present international situation.

Equality of substantive rights.   The application of the rule of equality to the substantive rights of states calls for distinctions which, if somewhat subtle, are familiar in their application to the rights of citizens under municipal law. States can be said to have "the same rights and the same obligations" when one and all are able to appeal under the law to the same general rules of conduct for the determination of the claims they may make or that may be made against them. They are "equal before the law" because the law makes no discrimination among them.[37] What one may claim another may claim; what one must do another must do. Thus every state has the same "right" to national security and the same obligation to respect the security of another; every state has the same "right" to independence, that is, to determine domestic and foreign policies without interference and to exercise jurisdiction within fixed boundaries, and the same obligation to refrain from interfering or "intervening" in the domestic affairs of another state; every state has the same right to purchase and sell territory, to use freely the high seas, to send and receive diplomatic agents, and to negotiate agreements which may be mutually satisfactory. In the case of the Schooner *Exchange* v. McFaddon,[38] Chief Justice Marshall referred to the "perfect equality and absolute independence of sovereigns" as one of the reasons leading them to waive the exercise of their exclusive territorial jurisdiction in the case of public vessels of another state in their ports. At the same

---

[37] Dickinson, however, is of the opinion that the expression *equality before the law* should properly be applied to the *protection* of rights rather than to the substance of rights. See p. 263.

[38] 7 Cranch 116 (1812). Fenwick, *Cases,* p. 363; Bishop, *Cases,* p. 551; Briggs, *Cases,* p. 413.

time it is recognized that particular states may bind themselves by treaty to refrain from exercising a specific "right," but that in so doing they do not give up the right itself.[39]

Equal legal capacities and unequal physical capacities.   This equality of substantive rights appears to lose some of its significance when account is taken of the unequal physical capacities of different states. The distinction observable in municipal law between a right considered as a legal power to act and the specific or concrete claims to particular material objects resulting from the exercise of that power is applicable also to international law. Municipal law recognizes that persons of unequal physical and mental abilities have the same primary rights to the enjoyment of life, liberty, and property, notwithstanding the fact that in the one case the natural and inherent limitations of personal capacity may make the exercise of those rights far less significant in results than in the other. Equality of opportunity is dependent, in respect to its substantial results, upon the physical capacity of the individual; liberty of contract is practically restricted by economic and social conditions. So in international law states of varying size, strength, and resources are held to possess certain fundamental rights in common, in spite of manifest divergences in the objects over which those rights are exercised.[40] The test of legal equality would seem to be that no obstacle be placed by the law in the way of the exercise of the powers or faculties recognized by the law as belonging to all members of the community alike. Obstacles resulting from the physical incapacities of the individual state are not regarded as incompatible with equality of legal status. Legal equality in international law, as in municipal law, is thus consistent with inequality in the actual sphere of control within which rights of the same nature are operative.

Equality in respect to the protection of rights.   But equality of substantive rights might have only a very abstract character unless it were accompanied by the equal protection of rights before the law. It was here, however, that international law was so signally defective in the years preceding the First World War. In principle the sanctions of international law held good for the protection of the weak as well as of the

[39] It is by the convenient legal fiction that a state may, without loss of technical "sovereignty," transfer to another state the exercise of certain of the normal rights of sovereignty or, it may be, restrict itself in respect to the exercise of those rights in favor of another state, that the principle of equality is maintained where the facts seem to deny it. Many states are under special treaty restrictions not applicable to all members of the international community, but their general status of equality is not affected by these restrictions. See p. 125.

[40] For example, a state with poor material resources may not be able to offer inducements for reciprocal trade favors in a commercial treaty. Note, however, the assertion in Article 4 of the Montevideo Convention that "States are juridically equal, enjoy the same rights, and have equal capacity in their exercise."

strong. But what if the best sanctions of the law were inadequate, and the injured state was left to its own limited resources to defend itself against attack or to maintain its claims against a more powerful state. In the absence of an international executive agency competent to protect the rights of weak states, the nineteenth and early twentieth centuries witnessed numerous cases of high-handed action on the part of strong states which at times reduced the principle of equal rights to an empty formula. The violation of the neutrality of China during the Russo-Japanese war was passed over by international public opinion as being of relatively little consequence. Nor was any protection offered by international law to Korea in 1910, when that state was deprived of its very existence as an international person. The contradiction between legal principle and hard fact was so manifest that realists before 1914 readily drew the conclusion that the whole business of equality was a legal paradox.[41]

Equality in respect to the adoption of new rules of law. The third aspect of equality relates to the part played by states in the adoption of new rules of law. In the case of the *Antelope*,[42] Chief Justice Marshall held that the slave trade, being lawful at international law, could not be declared to be piracy by one nation so as to limit the rights of others. "No principle of general law is more universally acknowledged, than the perfect equality of nations. Russia and Geneva have equal rights. It results from this equality that no one can rightfully impose a rule on another." A similar decision had been given some years earlier by the British High Court of Admiralty in the case of the French vessel *Le Louis*,[43] when Sir William Scott referred to the "perfect equality and entire independence of all distinct states" as being the great foundation of public law. In the case of the *Scotia* the court affirmed explicitly that "no single nation can change the law of the sea. That law is of universal obligation, and no statute of one or two nations can create obligations for the world. Like all the laws of nations, it rests upon the common consent of civilized communities." [44] The doctrine of these cases is still good law, in so far as it is limited strictly to the assumption of new obligations by treaty or convention. But new conditions are now coming to create new forms of obligation, and the rigid rule of treaties no longer applies to them.

---

[41] Dickinson, *op. cit.*, p. 4. It was the existence of implicitly accepted facts contradicting the formally acknowledged principle of equality that led certain writers to deny the validity of the legal rule. Whether such facts reduce the legal rule to a "mere fiction" must be determined by the number and seriousness of the violations of the law. Compare the question whether a domestic statute, violated on occasion with impunity, ceases to be "the law."

[42] 10 Wheaton 66 (1825). Fenwick, *Cases,* p. 86.

[43] 2 Dodson 210 (1817). Fenwick, *Cases,* pp. 84, 408.

[44] 14 Wallace 170 (1871). Fenwick, *Cases,* p. 11; Briggs, *Cases,* p. 25.

F. PRIMACY OF THE GREAT POWERS

Such are the three main applications of the principle of equality in point of legal principle. Obviously the effective enjoyment of equal rights depends upon the development of the law of the community in which the rights are recognized.

Under the constitutional law of highly developed states the fundamental rights of the individual, being common to the whole group, are protected in spite of inequalities of physical and mental capacity. In international law the protection has been less effective, due partly to the unequal size and resources of the individual states and partly to the historical development of communities that only of recent years have come to realize their common interests and the underlying human relationships of their peoples.

The primacy of the Great Powers was, therefore, a natural consequence of the development of international law in an era in which the conception of a community of states was limited to the relatively small European area, and within that area to the larger members of the group. During the nineteenth century the Great Powers, while recognizing the equality of states in the abstract, found no difficulty in settling concrete problems in which their common interests were more directly involved by meeting in groups apart and there taking decisions which had the force of law in the case before them. The Congress of Vienna in 1815 played the part of a supreme political authority in rearranging the map of Europe at the close of the Napoleonic regime. The Congress of Paris in 1856 exercised limited legislative functions in respect to new rules of war at sea. The Congresses of Berlin in 1878 and 1885 acted as *de facto* executive and judicial bodies in respect to the reconstruction of the Balkan states and the partition of Africa. The Conference of Algeciras in 1906 disposed of the problem of Morocco. The London Conference of Ambassadors intervened in the Balkan situation of 1913 and undertook the emancipation of Albania.[45]

Its legal effects. The primacy of the Great Powers, exercised under varying circumstances through more than a century, had in 1914 become, by force of established custom, an accepted fact of international relations. It had been exercised chiefly as a means of supplementing the deficiencies of international law in respect of legislative, executive, and judicial agencies. While the decisions taken at the several congresses and conferences were not binding upon third states, it was practically inevitable that other members of the international community should give their implicit assent to them by reason of the power and prestige

---

[45] The primacy of the Great Powers during the nineteenth and early twentieth centuries is exhaustively studied in Dupuis, *Le droit des gens et les rapports des grandes puissances avec les autres Etats avant le pacte de la Société des Nations.*

of the states which laid down the new rule or created the new political situation. Thus the Great Powers succeeded in forming a self-constituted governing body whose decrees had behind them a force adequate to secure their observance pending such time as the accomplished fact might come to be part of the established order of things.[46]

Procedure at the Hague Conferences.   The calling of the Hague Peace Conferences of 1899 and 1907 brought the question of the equality of states into the foreground of international controversy. Without questioning the right of each single state not to be bound by the action of the others, the leading powers at the conferences found themselves in the position of being unable to formulate new rules of conduct without taking into account the views of states whose interests they believed to be relatively inconsiderable. The principle of equality was strictly adhered to in the formal organization of the conferences. Each state enjoyed the right to be represented on the various commissions and subcommissions, and a rule was adopted that no convention should be recommended for adoption by the conference unless there was unanimity in the commission in favor of it.[47] The votes taken in plenary session proceeded in complete conformity with the formal equality of the powers represented. States refrained from signing particular conventions or signed with reservations or omitted ratification after having signed. The result of this procedure was conspicuously manifested in the defeat of the project for the Judicial Arbitration Court, which, though favored in principle by practically all of the powers, failed of adoption by reason of the opposition of the smaller states to a court not constituted on the basis of the equality of all sovereign states.[48]

G. ORGANIZATION OF THE LEAGUE OF NATIONS

In the organization of the League of Nations a compromise was effected by which the principle of equality was set aside in one branch

---

[46] Many writers, perhaps a majority of them, denied that the primacy of the Great Powers had any legal basis whatever, maintaining that it constituted nothing more than a political inequality. But if international law be tested by facts as well as by theories, it would seem that some measure of legal validity must be accorded to a continuous and successful maintenance by the Great Powers of their paramount influence. See Lawrence, *Principles of International Law*, § 114; Dickinson, *op. cit.*, Chap. IV. The negative side of the case was presented by Professor Huber, of the University of Zurich, in *Die Gleichheit der Staaten*.

[47] The leading powers succeeded, however, in obtaining control, through an appointed chairman of each committee, of the "committees of examination" in which much of the detailed work of the conference was done. Note should also be made of the rule of "quasi-unanimity," by which a smaller power refrained from voting when a resolution to which it was opposed was presented for adoption.

[48] See p. 617. The difficulties encountered by the Great Powers at the Hague Conferences in legislating for the advancement of their predominant interests resulted in the limitation of the membership of the succeeding London Naval Conference to the states more immediately interested in the regulation of maritime warfare. See p. 23.

of the governing body of the League and adhered to in the other.[49] The Covenant of the League recognized in the composition of the Council the dominant position of the five Great Powers surviving the larger group of 1914.[50] No distinction, however, was made among these five, although in point of numbers, wealth, and extent of territory there were more marked divergences between the United States or Great Britain and Italy than between Italy and many of the lesser powers. In the composition of the Assembly of the League the principle of equality was retained, each member being entitled to one vote and as many as three representatives. Decisions of the Assembly, except in a few cases specially provided for, required the agreement of all the members of the League represented at each meeting. The expenses of the permanent Secretariat were, however, borne by the members of the League in accordance with a scale of allocation adopted by the Assembly on the basis of capacity to contribute. Amendments to the Covenant took effect when ratified by a majority of the Assembly, provided the majority included all the members of the Council; but no such amendments bound members dissenting from them, in case of which dissent the said states ceased to be members of the League.

But while the Covenant of the League respected the principle that all of its members were equal before the law it failed because of inherent weakness to give to its members the equal protection of their rights as sovereign states. In 1931 Japan invaded Manchuria and the League found it impossible to take action under Article 10 of the Covenant.[51] The United States, standing aloof from the League, could do no more than reprimand Japan and refuse to recognize territorial conquests. Four years later Italy successfully attacked and annexed Ethiopia;[52] and the League stood by helpless when Austria and Czechoslovakia were annexed by Germany.[53] When in 1939 Germany invaded Poland, the Pledges of Article 10 of the Covenant had already become meaningless. The Great Powers were divided and in the absence of unity among them the rest of the community reacted as it had done in 1914.

[49] The student may compare the method followed by the convention at Philadelphia which framed the Constitution of the United States. A reconciliation between the larger and the smaller states was effected by creating an *upper* house on the basis of equality and a *lower* house on the basis of relative population, the arrangement being known as the "Connecticut Compromise." See Scott, *The United States of America: a Study in International Organization,* pp. 179-187, citing Madison's *Notes of the Proceedings of the Federal Convention.*

[50] These included the United States, the British Empire, France, Italy, and Japan. Art. 4, Covenant of the League of Nations. Germany was subsequently admitted to permanent membership on the Council in 1926.

[51] See above, p. 27.

[52] See above, p. 27.

[53] Churchill, *The Gathering Storm,* pp. 259 ff.

H. PROVISIONS OF THE CHARTER OF THE UNITED NATIONS

With the establishment of the United Nations the principle of equality before the law, of equal rights and duties, found full recognition, the Organization being "based on the principle of the sovereign equality of all its members." The Security Council may, indeed, take into account the practical ability of members to carry out its decisions in respect to the maintenance of peace and security, but this is not to be regarded as affecting equality before the law any more than the corresponding obligations of municipal law where physical capacities are unequal.[54]

With respect, however, to the equal protection of the law the United Nations has grave failures on its record. The unity of the five leading powers, the permanent members of the Security Council, broke down almost from the start. Lithuania, Latvia, and Esthonia had already lost their independence before the principle of "sovereign equality" was proclaimed. Albania, Bulgaria, Hungary, Poland, and Rumania lost their autonomy and became satellites of the Soviet Union. Germany, Austria, and Italy, as former enemy states, were subjected to special measures to prevent renewal of aggressive policies. By contrast, the attack upon South Korea put collective security in motion, and the General Assembly, by the "Uniting for Peace" resolution, undertook to protect the integrity of the country, even if with inadequate results.[55] In like manner the intervention of the United Nations in the organization of an emergency force to restrain hostilities in the conflict between Great Britain, France, Israel, and Egypt resulting from the nationalization by Egypt of the Suez Canal might well be interpreted as being in fulfilment of the articles of the Charter looking to the protection of the weak against the strong.[56]

Adoption of new rules of law. How far has the principle of equality been applied in respect to the adoption of new rules of law? Here we are confronted with a situation that is political rather than legal, so complex at times that politics, law, and logic are in conflict. It is clear that the dominant position of the five permanent members of the Security Council gives them individually the power to defeat decisions which might have the effect of creating situations out of which new rules of law might develop. The veto power is, indeed, a negative one, but indirectly it may have positive results and bring the international community on occasion to a deadlock and prevent constructive action. Thus while the Security Council can not make new rules of law and can only maintain security and peace on the basis of existing law, its

[54] Charter, Arts. 43-48.
[55] See below, p. 294.
[56] See below, pp. 472 ff.

decisions may create new political relations and invalidate or make ineffective the enforcement of established obligations.[57]

By contrast, the General Assembly may make recommendations covering a wide variety of political, economic, and social interests; and while these recommendations do not create new legal obligations they do have strong persuasive force. In the areas described in Article 18 the decisions of the Assembly by a two-thirds majority are definitive, creating obligations for the minority that may have opposed them. The principle of the equality of states in the adoption of new rules of law still holds for treaties and conventions sponsored by the General Assembly, as in the case of the Conference on the Law of the Sea; but within the United Nations as a organized community the old rule of unanimity no longer holds. A two-thirds vote to admit a new member to the United Nations makes it necessary for all members of the minority to accept the new member with the usual privileges and immunities. A decision, such as that of the "Uniting for Peace" resolution supplementing the decision of the Council on June 27, 1950, clearly affected the relations of states voting against the resolution. Such it is, and should be, any principle of sovereign equality to the contrary, if an organization as large in number and as varied in the character of its members is to function with any degree of practical effectiveness.[58]

But in a world of states large and small, the principle of equality can work in reverse gear and can make it possible for a minority, organized along racial or ideological lines, to impose its will upon a majority. While each state has but one vote, there are wide variations in population, economic power, and technical skill; so that it is theoretically possible for a minority in terms of population, but voting by states, to impose its will upon the majority in terms of population and create obligations which only the latter would have the resources to carry out. This is an unlikely contingency, but one justifying consideration of the possibility of a weighted representation in the General Assembly.[59]

Experience has shown, however, that while not qualifying their adherence to the principle of equality, the smaller states with lesser resources and more limited economic and political power have on the whole recognized their relatively weaker position and adjusted their voting power to the hard facts, content to be able to prevent the im-

[57] See p. 214; and compare Arechaga, *Voting and the Handling of Disputes in the Security Council*, Chap. VI.

[58] Compare the proposed "legislative powers" assigned to the General Assembly in respect to disarmament and related matters in Clark and Sohn, *World Peace Through World Law*, pp. 30 ff. Also, H. Weinschel, "The Doctrine of the Equality of States and its Recent Modifications," *Am. Journal*, Vol. 46 (1951), p. 417; and above, p. 213.

[59] See Wilcox and Marcy, *Proposals for Changes in the United Nations*, pp. 344-373; Vandenbosch and Hogan, *Toward World Order*, p. 103.

position of new legal obligations upon themselves while recognizing that the General Assembly must not defeat the effectiveness of its own resolutions by imposing undue burdens or creating unreasonable difficulties for the larger powers who might happen to be in the minority.[60]

A different procedure is followed in the decisions taken by the numerous administrative unions created during the past hundred years beginning with the establishment of the Telegraphic Union in 1865, followed by the Metric Union of 1875 and the Universal Postal Union. Here the principle of the equality of states has had to yield to the necessity of performing with efficiency functions of a service character, not involving the assumption of final and definitive legal obligations. In like manner the specialized agencies of the United Nations have their separate types of voting procedure, whether by simple majorities or by weighted representation where, as in the case of the International Bank for Reconstruction and Development, and the International Monetary Fund, members are given votes in proportion to their contribution to the resources of the agency.[61]

[60] Compare the equality of states in the voting system of the Conferences and Meetings of Consultation under the Charter of the Organization of American States. where the equality is legally absolute.

[61] See Chap. XXV, where the specialized agencies are discussed in detail.

CHAPTER XII

The Right of National Existence:

Self-Defense and Cooperative Defense

A. NATURE AND SCOPE OF THE "RIGHT OF EXISTENCE"

International law is, as we have seen, based upon the assumption of a body of states possessing certain fundamental rights; and the Charter of the United Nations confirms the established tradition. It is now in order to examine the specific character of these rights, and to inquire how far their abstract character is borne out by the facts of international life. To what extent are these rights assured to the individual state as a member of the international community, so that the actual enjoyment of the particular right corresponds to the content assigned to it by international law? [1]

The primary right of a state is clearly the integrity of its personality as a state, since the existence of the state is the necessary condition of any other rights that it may claim. For that reason the science of international law has concentrated upon this "right of national existence," and a number of jurists have made it the source of all other rights. Governments, being less concerned with theory, have asserted the right in terms of the practical situations confronting them, designating it by various names in accordance with the circumstances. At times it is described as "national security," or as "the right of self-preservation," or the "right of self-defense," "the fundamental law," "the first law of nature" to which all other laws are subordinate. [2]

[1] It is this lack of critical inquiry into the actual as distinguished from the theoretical rights of states that characterized so many of the older treatises on international law, which recite the rights of states without inquiry into the extent to which they were actually observed.

[2] In a letter of Secretary Seward to Mr. Adams in 1861, it is said: "They [the positions assumed by the United States] are simply the suggestions of the instinct of self-defense, the primary law of human action, not more the law of individual than of national life." *Fontes juris gentium,* Series B, Sec. I, Tome I, p. 317. See Chap. XI, note 4.

Principle versus fact. On the eve of the First World War there was, therefore, no question but that, in theory, all states possessed in equal degree the right of existence. The existence of each was as inviolable as that of any other. Each had the same right to maintain its corporate personality, to protect and conserve all the elements of its national life, to do, as Vattel had put it a century and a half earlier, whatever was necessary for its self-preservation.[3] But as a practical matter the continued existence of a state, or at least the continued integrity of its territory, depended upon its own ability to protect itself in a community of fellow states some of which were all too ready to solve their controversies with other states by an appeal to the sword and to retain by right of conquest whatever might fall to their lot in the established trial by battle. There being no organization of the community for mutual protection, each state had to look to its own security and had to build up around itself such defenses as its resources permitted. In consequence the right of existence on the part of weaker states was often precarious, and on occasion no more than a legal fiction. Poland, divided within itself, fell a prey to ambitious neighbors in 1772-1795. Hanover was annexed by Prussia in 1864. Korea was taken over by Japan in 1910. Whatever jurists might say as to the abstract right of existence, the actual enjoyment of the right was largely conditioned upon the physical power of the individual state to meet attacks upon it. As a rule, however, war resulted not in the complete annihilation of the defeated state, but in the annexation of larger or smaller parts of its territories, as in the transfer of Alsace-Lorraine from France to Germany in 1871.

B. SELF-DEFENSE AGAINST DIRECT ATTACK

Under this system of self-defense as the ultimate guarantee of security, it followed almost of necessity that the distinction between acts of aggression and acts of defense ceased to have any real meaning.[4] General principles might limit self-defense to resistance to attack; practical considerations frequently made it necessary for a state to anticipate the attack of another state by itself striking first. Thus an act of aggression of the most flagrant character might, in the eye of the state committing it, take on a defensive character and be no more than a wise measure of precaution against the future.[5] This interpretation of self-defense was, as will appear later, capable of being extended into the most remote fields; but even when limited to the issue of immediate danger of attack it made it impossible to determine which of two states first set in motion

[3] *Droit des gens,* Chap. II, § 18.

[4] It is still difficult to distinguish them, but much less so than in the days before 1920. See Bowett, *Self-Defense in International Law.*

[5] Napoleon at the gates of Moscow in 1812 seems to have regarded his attack upon Russia as a defensive war.

the forces, or created the conditions, which gave to the other the right of self-defense. Germany, for example, might maintain that mobilization by Russia in July, 1914, created the immediate necessity of self-defense; Russia might maintain that Germany "began the war" by its formal declaration of hostilities. There was no legal answer to the question of responsibility, and the conclusions of the Commission on the Responsibility of the Authors of the War, established at Paris in 1919, must be looked upon as a political rather than a judicial decision.[6]

Self-defense in time of war. Since war itself was normally an act of alleged self-defense, it happened on occasion that in the course of a war a belligerent might be led to violate the rights of third states, neutral to the conflict, under plea of military necessity. In 1807 the British Government, having reason to believe that France and Russia would coerce Denmark to join in the war then under way, or that in any case Denmark would be unable to resist the seizure of its fleet by Napoleon, called upon Denmark to deliver up the fleet under a promise that it would be restored at the end of the war; and when Denmark refused to accede to this demand, the British Government undertook to shell the port of Copenhagen and seize the fleet.[7] The more serious step of the invasion of Korea by Japan during the war with Russia in 1904 to prevent its coming under the control of the enemy was justified by Japan on similar principles of self-defense.[8]

German invasion of Belgium in 1914. The violation of the neutrality of Belgium by Germany in 1914 furnishes an extreme instance of this form of alleged self-defense. The act must be judged both by the obligations of the treaty of 1839 and by the provisions of general international law. The breach of the treaty of 1839 was without doubt the more serious offense, in that it involved a greater degree of bad faith, since the treaty had been entered into in anticipation of just such circumstances as induced the German Government to repudiate it. But independently of the treaty there was the customary law of neutrality, possessing, in addition to the authority of long usage, the formal sanction of the Hague Convention Relating to the Rights and Duties of Neutral Powers in War on Land.[9] As overruling both these forms of obligation, Germany set forth the principle of necessity based upon the primary right of self-preservation.[10] A more ruthless German Government did not concern

---

[6] For the report of the Commission, see *Am. Journal,* Vol. 14 (1920), p. 95.

[7] The act has been variously commented upon by writers, some, as Hall and Westlake, excusing it, others condemning it, and again others finding extenuating circumstances. See Stowell, *Intervention in International Law,* pp. 409 ff.

[8] The justification may be examined in the light of the subsequent fate of Korea.

[9] See below, p. 718.

[10] The statement of the chancellor, Von Bethmann-Hollweg, has become historical. Speaking before the Reichstag on August 4, he said: "Gentlemen, we are now in a state of necessity, and necessity knows no law! Our troops have occupied Luxemburg, and perhaps are already on Belgian soil. Gentlemen, that is contrary to the dictates

itself to placate the public opinion of neutral nations when it decided to strike at the enemy more effectively by first invading Norway, Denmark, Holland, Belgium, and Luxemburg in 1940. The attack by Russia upon Finland in 1939 appears to fall within this class of measures of defense, Finland being the innocent victim of Russia's desire to anticipate an attack by Germany notwithstanding the recently signed pact of non-aggression between the two countries.

Defense against irresponsible groups. If the right of self-defense against direct attack justified immediate recourse to whatever measures of resistance might be available to the state attacked, it was also recognized that a state would be equally justified in taking such measures as the occasion might require to defend itself against armed bands of irresponsible individuals who might happen to cross the border and commit acts of depredation. Cases of this kind occurred quite frequently during the nineteenth century, and they would doubtless have attracted little notice but for the fact that the political relations between the two countries were already somewhat strained, so that the measures of defense taken against the irresponsible groups appeared to be in excess of the necessities of the situation. Could a state, in anticipation of such an attack, or in punishment of its commission, invade the territory of its neighbor? Two conditions were said to attend the exercise of this form of self-defense: first, that the necessity of self-defense should be of the very gravest character; and second, that the state whose territory was violated should be either unwilling or unable itself to prevent the commission of the threatened act. In 1837, during the progress of a rebellion in Canada, the Canadian Government, in order to anticipate an attack upon its territory by insurgents established upon an island in the Niagara River through which ran the boundary line between Canada and the United States, despatched a force across the river to a point on the American side from which the insurgents were obtaining supplies, and captured and destroyed a small boat, called the *Caroline,* killing two of the crew in the act.[11] In answer to the protest of the American Gov-

---

of international law. It is true that the French Government has declared at Brussels that France is willing to respect the neutrality of Belgium as long as her opponent respects it. We knew, however, that France stood ready for the invasion. France could wait, but we could not wait. A French movement upon our flank upon the lower Rhine might have been disastrous. So we were compelled to override the just protest of the Luxemburg and Belgian Governments. The wrong—I speak openly—that we are committing we will endeavor to make good as soon as our military goal has been reached. Anybody who is threatened, as we are threatened, and is fighting for his highest possessions, can have only one thought—how he is to hack his way through." Stowell, *Diplomacy of the War of 1914,* p. 445, note 2. The justification offered must be weighed in the balance of general public morality rather than in that of strict law. For a discussion of the views of German publicists, see De Visscher, *Belgium's Case: A Juridical Inquiry.*

[11] Moore, *Digest,* Vol. II, § 217.

ernment against this invasion of its territory, Great Britain put forth in justification the imperative needs of self-defense, which required immediate action.[12] In 1916, following a raid upon American territory by Francisco Villa and a body of insurgents, a column of American troops was despatched in hot pursuit. General Huerta, the *de facto* president of Mexico, was notified of the act; but no pretense was made of awaiting his permission, on the ground that the very inability of Huerta to suppress the insurgents justified the action taken by the United States. After spending several months in an unsuccessful attempt to locate the bandits, the American troops were withdrawn.[13]

C. SELF-DEFENSE AGAINST INDIRECT MENACE OF ATTACK

Just as the system under which each state was responsible for its own defense made it necessary at times for a state, in the presence of an impending threat of attack, to anticipate the attack by itself striking first, so it led naturally to the formulation of national policies which took a long-range view of the defense of the state and sought to forestall conditions which, if allowed to develop, might become in time a source of danger. In some cases the possibility of future attack was so remote as to have been meaningless had there been in existence an international organization capable of protecting its individual members should the contemplated danger prove to be a reality. But failing such an organization it became the most vital problem of statesmanship to look to the future and to study the political activities of other states in order to discover in them any possible elements of danger. The underlying principle, as Secretary Root put it on the eve of the First World War, was "the right of every sovereign state to protect itself by preventing a condition of affairs in which it will be too late to protect itself." [14]

Menace of armaments of neighboring states. The most important question of the nineteenth century in this field was to determine how far a nation might build up within and around itself military and naval defenses as a barrier against possible future attacks, and at what point

[12] Webster's statement that the necessity of self-defense in such cases should be "instant, overwhelming, and leaving no choice of means, and no moment for deliberation" has become historical, although doubtless not tenable in its literal form.

[13] For a discussion of principles, see A. S. Hershey, "Incursions into Mexico and the Doctrine of Hot Pursuit," *Am. Journal,* Vol. 13 (1919), p. 557.

[14] "It is well understood," said Senator Root in 1914, "that the exercise of the right of self-protection may and frequently does extend in its effect beyond the limits of the territorial jurisdiction of the state exercising it. The strongest example probably would be the mobilization of an army by another power immediately across the frontier. Every act done by the other Power may be within its own territory. Yet the country threatened by the state of facts is justified in protecting itself by immediate war. The most common exercise of the right of self-protection outside of a state's own territory and in time of peace is the interposition of objection to the occupation of territory, of points of strategic military or maritime advantage, or to indirect accomplishment of this effect by dynastic arrangement." *Am. Journal,* Vol. 8 (1914), p. 427.

a neighboring state was justified in regarding such armaments as constituting impending danger of attack. Defensive armaments have an equal value for offensive purposes, and it was obviously impossible for one state to take the word of its neighbor that elaborate preparations for self-defense contained no concealed intention of aggression. The problem was an old one. Grotius vigorously denounced the "intolerable doctrine of some writers, that by the law of nations we may rightly take arms against a power which is increasing, and may increase so as to be dangerous." [15] Equity, he held, was entirely opposed to the idea that the possibility of being attacked gives us the right to attack on our part; it was only when there was just ground of war on other counts that the growing strength of a rival might properly influence a decision to make war. Vattel rendered a similar decision upon the abstract question, with the even more ambiguous qualification that evidences of injustice or ambition on the part of a neighbor whose power was growing, indicated by the slightest wrong inflicted upon another state, were sufficient to justify anticipating his probable designs.[16] Such were the theories of the jurists. But in the meantime practical statesmen, as Vattel himself confessed, paid but little attention to their teachings, and confined themselves to the formation of treaties of alliance and of guarantee and to the maintenance of the political equilibrium of Europe.

The balance of power. The doctrine of the necessity of a balance of power between the leading states as the basis of mutual self-protection dominated the international relations of the nineteenth century. Vattel had regarded it as an essential condition of the maintenance of order and the preservation of liberty within the European system. By the balance of power, he wrote, is meant "an arrangement of affairs so that no state shall be in a position to have absolute mastery and dominate over others." The Congress of Vienna in 1815 rearranged the map of Europe with that object in view. The Crimean War of 1854 was undertaken by Great Britain and France from a conviction that the protection of the Ottoman Empire within its existing boundaries was of vital importance for the maintenance of the balance of power among the states of Europe. The Congress of Berlin in 1878 felt the necessity of keeping the dying Sultanate in existence as a check upon Russia. The culmination was reached in the delicately adjusted balance between the Triple Alliance of Germany, Austria-Hungary, and Italy, and the Dual Alliance of France and Russia, the latter subsequently enlarged into a Triple Entente by the qualified accession of Great Britain. Stripped of their trappings, these alliances were based upon the fundamental law of self-defense under a system of international relations in which each state was left to shift for itself, choose helpers where it could get them,

---

[15] De jure belli ac pacis, Eng. trans., Bk. II, Chap. I, § XVII.
[16] Droit des gens, Eng. trans., Bk. III, §§ 42-46.

watch with a suspicious eye the slightest rise and fall of the political balance, and be ready to strike, as Germany did in 1914, when it appeared prudent to prevent in advance a possible future disaster.[17] Taken thus, self-defense had obviously no legal limitations.

Self-defense in relation to the League of Nations. The establishment of the League of Nations in 1920 might have been expected to have far-reaching effects upon the practical application of the right of self-defense. The guarantee of mutual defense contained in Article 10 of the Covenant seemed to assure to the weak as well as to the strong the protection of an organized community. The provisions of Article 11 making war and the threat of war the common concern of the whole League promised to give rise to a sense of collective responsibility which would put an end to the paradoxical situation of great powers remaining neutral in the presence of acts of aggression. The procedures of peaceful settlement came close to making all war illegal, while the provision for the application of sanctions contained in Article 16 would have reduced the necessity of self-defense to the narrowest limitations.[18]

But it was one thing to proclaim principles of cooperative defense and another thing to create confidence in their observance. The test came when the effort was made to bring about the reduction of armaments contemplated in Article 8 of the Covenant. Obviously unless some system of pooled armaments could be adopted, or some fixed ratios of separate national armaments established, the system of collective security could not be expected to replace individual self-defense for those powers which were in a position to maintain elaborate armaments. The Washington Conference of 1921-1922 sought to bring about mutual reductions according to definitely assigned ratios applicable to the powers participating in the Conference. But the reductions agreed upon merely eliminated competition in particular classes of ships without modifying the existing function of armaments as instruments of individual self-defense rather than of general cooperative defense.[19] Collective security was obviously a condition precedent to disarmament, as emphasized so frequently at Geneva in the discussions of the League.[20] But on the other hand a limitation of armaments was an equally necessary condition precedent to collective security. The inability of the leading powers to put the two

---

[17] On the subject of the balance of power in recent years, see Friedrich, *Foreign Policy in the Making: The Search for a New Balance of Power.*

[18] The so-called loophole left in Article 15 of the Covenant would have been of little actual importance if the members of the League had been able to maintain a united front in upholding the other principles of the Covenant. Article 11 practically closed the opening. See below, p. 620.

[19] See, on this point, "Conference on the Limitation of Armaments: Report of the American Delegation," *Am. Journal,* Vol. 16 (1922), p. 159.

[20] See Zimmern, *The League of Nations and the Rule of Law;* League of Nations, *Ten Years of World Coöperation,* Chap. II, "The Organization of Peace and Disarmament"; Geneva Institute, *Anarchy or World Order.*

measures into effect simultaneously left the problem of competitive armaments in relation to national self-defense practically where it was at the beginning of the twentieth century.

The Pact of Paris. The question of the right of self-defense entered into the negotiations attending the conclusion of the Treaty for the Renunciation of War signed at Paris in 1928. The Pact of Paris, known popularly as the Kellogg-Briand Pact, sought to substitute for the more specific commitments of the Covenant of the League of Nations a broad general condemnation of recourse to war for the solution of international controversies and a renunciation of war "as an instrument of national policy." [21] The text of the treaty made no reference to the right of self-defense; but a qualification to that effect was set forth in identical notes of June 23, 1928, addressed by Secretary Kellogg to the states invited to sign the document. "There is nothing," said the notes, "in the American draft of an anti-war treaty which restricts or impairs in any way the right of self-defense. That right is inherent in every sovereign state and is implicit in every treaty. Every nation is free at all times and regardless of treaty provisions to defend its territory from attack or invasion and it alone is competent to decide whether circumstances require recourse to war in self-defense." The qualification was a broad one, and it was not clear whether self-defense, as interpreted by each nation for itself, could be kept within the strict limits of a direct attack upon the territory of the state, limits corresponding roughly to those imposed upon the right of self-defense under municipal law.[22] No provision was made for a collective decision of the signatories in respect to the facts of a particular case.

During the years between the adoption of the Pact of Paris and the outbreak of the Second World War numerous efforts were made to draw a working distinction between wars of aggression and wars of self-defense. After the outbreak of the Second World War, when plans for a more effective international organization were being studied, it was clear that the right of self-defense had still to be recognized, but that it should be held within rigid limits. Article 51 of the Charter of the United Nations provides that nothing in the Charter shall impair the "inherent right of individual or collective self-defense" if an armed attack occurs against a member of the United Nations. The term "collective self-defense" is novel, being inserted with the object of assuring the maintenance of the inter-American regional system and the policy of hemi-

[21] See Miller, *The Peace Pact of Paris*, pp. 213 ff.; Q. Wright, "The Meaning of the Pact of Paris," *Am. Journal*, Vol. 27 (1933), p. 39.

[22] The danger that the qualification might be abused was pointed out at the time of the negotiations attending the treaty; but the American Secretary of State thought that it was not "in the interest of peace that a treaty should stipulate a juristic conception of self-defense." Yet it is only juristic conceptions that can in the end establish law between states.

spheric defense set forth in the Act of Habana of 1940 and in the Act of Chapultepec of 1945.[23] It is clear, however, that both of the cases contemplated by the Charter have in mind self-defense of the most restricted character, since self-defense is limited to armed attacks, and it is expressly provided that the measures thus taken shall be immediately reported to the Security Council and shall be permissible only until the Security Council has taken the measures necessary to maintain international peace and security.

NATO and other defense groups. It was to be expected that the recognition of so fundamental a principle would give rise to an effort on the part of scholars to define to some degree the application of the principle, and on the part of statesmen to plan how collective self-defense might be made effective if the need for it should arise. The American states were the first to act, the Treaty of Reciprocal Assistance being signed on September 2, 1947, at Rio de Janeiro, followed by the North Atlantic Treaty Organization (NATO) in 1949, the Warsaw Pact in 1955, the Southeast Asia Treaty Organization (SEATO) of 1955, and other lesser regional agreements. Obviously these regional agreements must be studied in relation to the collective security system established by the Charter of the United Nations, which lost its effectiveness when the invention of the atomic bomb made it possible for a single state, armed with the bomb, to challenge the decisions of the organized community.[24]

The issue of self-defense under Article 51 of the Charter arose in acute form in connection with the missile bases under construction by Soviet engineers in Cuba in October, 1962, discovered by aerial reconnaissance by the United States. The establishment of these bases with atomic warheads available, would have made the cities of the Atlantic coast of the United States vulnerable to attack at the decision of one who had denounced the United States as responsible for the economic ills under which Cuba was suffering. President Kennedy, interpreting the bases as a threat to the security of the country, called upon the Soviet Union to remove them. Query, might the existence of the bases have been interpreted as a constructive "armed attack" to bring the case more directly under Article 51? [25]

[23] See Fenwick, *OAS*, pp. 73, 230.

[24] For comment upon the scope of Art. 51 of the Charter, see Goodrich and Hambro, *Charter of the United Nations*, pp. 51 ff.; H. Kelsen, "Collective Security and Collective Self-Defense under the Charter of the United Nations," *Am. Journal*, Vol. 42 (1948), p. 20; J. L. Kunz, "Individual and Collective Self-Defense in Article 51 of the Charter of the United Nations," *ibid.*, Vol. 41 (1947), p. 872; Bowett, *Collective Self-Defense under the Charter of the United Nations.*

[25] See Q. Wright, "The Cuban Quarantine," *Am. Journal*, Vol. 57 (1963), p. 546, in criticism of the quarantine on the ground that it was an illegal exercise of the right of self-defense as defined in the U.N. Charter; and also accompanying editorials in defense of the quarantine, *ibid.*, pp. 373, 588, 592, 597.

D. THE MONROE DOCTRINE AS A POLICY OF SELF-DEFENSE

The right of self-defense against indirect or future menace of attack was the principle underlying the assertion of the Monroe Doctrine, both in its original unilateral form and in its more recent derivative form of continental defense. Sympathy with the struggle of the Spanish American states for independence undoubtedly played a part in determining the stand taken by the United States, and the commercial interests of the country were not overlooked. But more important in the mind of President Monroe and his advisers was the fact that the extension to the American hemisphere of the system represented by the Triple Alliance would be "dangerous to our peace and safety." To the United States of 1823 its isolated geographical situation was an asset of the greatest value for national protection, and hence it became a matter of urgent self-defense to forestall the reestablishment upon the American continent of powers whose presence would entail for the United States the burden of defensive armaments and a possible entanglement in conflicting alliances. The American continents were, said President Monroe, "henceforth not to be considered as subjects for future colonization by any European powers." That disposed of the possibility of further efforts to secure a foothold upon the continent on the ground of its being unoccupied territory. At the same time while disclaiming any intention to interfere with "the existing colonies or dependencies of any European power," President Monroe made it clear that in the case of those governments which had declared their independence and maintained it and whose independence had been acknowledged by the United States "we could not view any interposition for the purpose of oppressing them, or controlling in any other manner their destiny, by any European power in any other light than as the manifestation of an unfriendly disposition towards the United States." [26]

Throughout the rest of the nineteenth century the Monroe Doctrine continued to be regarded by the United States as a bulwark of national defense, although a number of the applications of the doctrine appeared to other states to have a somewhat remote connection with the original purpose of the Doctrine. The most direct challenge came from France in 1863 when an attempt was made by Louis Napoleon to impose a monarchical government upon Mexico.[27] Spain challenged the Doctrine by annexing Santo Domingo in 1861 and by threats against the territorial integrity of Peru in 1864.[28] In each case the challenge was successfully

[26] For the text of that part of President Monroe's address to Congress, December 3, 1823, in which the Doctrine is stated, see Moore, *Digest*, Vol. VI, p. 401. For a history of the Doctrine, see *ibid.*, Vol. VI, §§ 927-969; Bemis, *The Latin American Policy of the United States*, Nos. IV-VII; Perkins, *Hands Off*.

[27] For details, see Perkins, *Hands Off*, Chap. IV.

[28] Perkins, *op. cit.*, Chap. IV.

met. Great Britain was believed to be challenging the Doctrine in 1895 by refusing to arbitrate a boundary dispute with Venezuela; and the American Secretary of State was led to make the bold assertion that "the United States is practically sovereign on this continent, and its fiat is law upon the subjects to which it confines its interposition." [29] Great Britain, Germany, and Italy raised the issue of the Doctrine in 1902 by the use of armed force to collect debts from Venezuela. The claims were arbitrated, and only in Germany was there manifest any disposition to challenge the Doctrine itself.[30] In 1912 the United States imposed a formal interdiction against the suggested lease of Magdalena Bay by Mexico to Japan.[31]

Its indirect recognition by international law. In view of the discussions attending the application of the Monroe Doctrine in the Venezuelan controversy of 1895, the United States was led to enter a reservation to the Convention for the Pacific Settlement of International Disputes, adopted at The Hague in 1899, disclaiming any intention of departing from its traditional policy of noninterference in the political affairs of foreign states or from its traditional attitude towards purely American questions.[32] This reservation was interpreted by President Roosevelt as an acquiescence of the other powers in the Monroe Doctrine; and it was repeated at the time of signing the revised convention at The Hague in 1907. The negative policy of noninterference in European political affairs, which was a regular accompaniment of the Monroe Doctrine, obviously raised no question of conflicting international rights and needed no acquiescence from other states.[33] On the other hand the positive features of the Doctrine, the ban against territorial encroachments upon the Central and South American states was a standing restriction upon the freedom of action of European states in dealing with those states. Whether their silence in overlooking the reservation attached to the Hague Convention could be properly interpreted as acquiescence was an open question.[34]

[29] Moore, *Digest*, Vol. VI, p. 553. Perkins, *op. cit.*, Chap. V.

[30] See Rippy, *Latin America in World Politics*, Vol. XI; and for a critical estimate of the alleged ultimatum to Germany, Perkins, *op. cit.*, Chap. VI.

[31] Hackworth, *Digest*, p. 437.

[32] Moore, *Digest*, Vol. VI, p. 594. For comment, see Perkins, *op. cit.*, p. 202.

[33] The policy of isolation, as a measure of self-protection, dates from Washington's farewell address of September 17, 1796. Its connection with the Monroe Doctrine is accidental rather than essential, so that occasional departures from it, as in the signature of the General Act of the Algeciras Conference of 1906, in no way weakened the assertion of the Monroe Doctrine. Compare, however, the alleged connection of the two policies, in the Senate debates attending the rejection of the Treaty of Versailles, 1919-1920.

[34] In 1914 Senator Root stated that "the doctrine is not international law, but it rests upon the right of self-protection and that right is recognized by international law." *Am. Journal*, Vol. 8 (1914), p. 427. Again, in 1923, Secretary Hughes asserted that the doctrine "is not a part of international law, maintained by the consent of civilized powers and alterable only at their will." *Am. Journal*, Vol. 17 (1923), p. 611.

Relation to the guarantees of the Covenant of the League of Nations.
The drafting of the Covenant of the League of Nations in 1919 raised
the question of the effect of the obligations assumed under Articles
10-16 upon the Monroe Doctrine. On the one hand it was argued that
the guarantees contained in the Covenant amounted to a worldwide
adoption of the Monroe Doctrine and that therefore there was no incompatibility between them and the Doctrine. Against this position it
was claimed that under the Covenant the United States would give up
its right of individual action in circumstances calling for the application
of the Monroe Doctrine, while European powers would acquire a joint
right to take the collective action contemplated by the Covenant. In
deference to these objections the draft Covenant was amended so as to
provide (Article 21) that "nothing in this Covenant shall be deemed
to affect the validity of international engagements, such as treaties of
arbitration or regional understandings like the Monroe doctrine, for securing the maintenance of peace." Whether this article, conceding to the
United States a privileged position in respect to questions affecting the
American continent, could have been reconciled with other provisions of
the Covenant (Articles 10, 11, 16) was never determined in consequence
of the failure of the United States to join the League.[35]

The continentalization of the Monroe Doctrine. Down to the year
1936 the Monroe Doctrine had always been regarded by the United
States as its own distinctive national policy, as a sacred national heritage
which it was hoped that other nations would respect, but which the
United States was prepared to maintain and defend against all the world.
The unilateral character of the Doctrine, however, did not prevent it
from being regarded by the other American states during the greater
part of the nineteenth century as their own shield of defense.[36] Doubts
of the altruistic intentions of the United States came later; and when at
the opening of the twentieth century President Roosevelt announced

---

In both these cases, however, stress was being laid upon the fact that the Monroe
Doctrine originated as a policy of self-defense and continued to be maintained by the
United States without assistance from other states. Such, however, has been the case
with many rules of international law which, beginning as assertions of individual
claims, have in time been acquiesced in by other states.

[35] It should be observed that in Mexico's note of acceptance, September 11, 1931,
of the invitation of the League of Nations to become a member, it was stated that
Mexico "has never recognized the regional understanding mentioned in Article 21
of the Covenant"; but the Assembly of the League, in declaring Mexico a member on
September 12, was able to note the fact that Mexico "agrees without reservation to
enter the League on the terms announced." For comment, see M. O. Hudson, "Mexico's Admission to Membership in the League of Nations," and P. M. Brown, "Mexico
and the Monroe Doctrine," *Am. Journal,* Vol. 26 (1932), pp. 114, 117. For the general question of the relation of the Monroe Doctrine to the provisions of the Covenant
of the League, see Ray, *Commentaire,* pp. 571 ff.; Perkins, *Hands Off,* Chap. VIII,
which gives the reaction in the United States to the problem.

[36] See Alvarez, *The Monroe Doctrine,* Chaps. VII, IX.

the principle of an "international police power" as a means of putting an end to conditions which might lead to intervention by European powers, the new corollary to the Monroe Doctrine came to be regarded by other American states as a form of intervention equally if not more objectionable than the intervention it was intended to prevent.[37] During the decade succeeding the establishment of the League of Nations the refusal of the United States to accept the obligations of the Covenant was accompanied by renewed assertions of the unilateral character of the Monroe Doctrine. Secretary Hughes stated in 1923 that "as the policy embodied in the Monroe Doctrine is distinctively the policy of the United States, the Government of the United States reserves to itself its definition, interpretation, and application." [38]

The following decade, however, this exclusive attitude was abandoned, and in 1936, at Buenos Aires, and again in 1938 at Lima, the United States, aided by Brazil and other American states, succeeded in converting the unilateral policy into a multilateral one, supported by all of the American republics. The Convention of 1936 provided in broad terms that "in the event that the peace of the American Republics is menaced," there should be consultation for the purpose of finding methods of peaceful cooperation.[39] The Declaration of Lima of 1938 was more specific, setting forth the principles of "continental solidarity" and reaffirming the determination of the American republics to defend them "against all foreign intervention or activity that may threaten them." [40] Two years later, at the Meeting of Foreign Ministers at Havana in 1940, the continentalization of the Monroe Doctrine reached its most explicit form in a declaration "that any attempt on the part of a non-American State against the integrity or inviolability of the territory, the sovereignty or the political independence of an American State shall be considered as an act of aggression against the States which sign this declaration." [41] The Convention on the Provisional Administration of European Colonies and Possessions in the Americas, signed at the same meeting, announced the refusal of the American states to recognize any transfer of the sovereignty or control over any of the territories from one non-American state to another and the right of the American states "as an international community" to take the territories under their provisional administra-

[37] Criticism was, however, slow in developing, and it does not appear that the intervention in the Dominican Republic in 1904 met with any open opposition. See Bemis, *Latin American Policy of the United States,* Chap. VII.

[38] See *Am. Journal,* Vol. 17 (1923), pp. 611, 616.

[39] *International Conferences of American States,* 1933-1940, p. 188. For comment see C. G. Fenwick, "The Inter-American Conference for the Maintenance of Peace," *Am. Journal,* Vol. 31 (1937), p. 201.

[40] *International Conferences,* 1933-1940, p. 308. For comment, see C. G. Fenwick, "The Monroe Doctrine and the Declaration of Lima," *Am. Journal,* Vol. 33 (1939), p. 257.

[41] *International Conferences,* 1933-1940, p. 360.

tion.[42] The provisions of the Havana declaration on reciprocal assistance were repeated in the Act of Chapultepec of 1945.[43]

Provisions of the Charter of the United Nations. One of the most important and difficult problems confronting the Conference at San Francisco which drafted the Charter of the United Nations was the position of regional organizations, such as the Union of American States, in relation to the world organization. In respect to the question of continental defense against an attack by a non-American power, the new Charter goes beyond the Dumbarton Oaks Proposals, Article 51 recognizing "the inherent right of individual or collective self-defense if an armed attack occurs against a Member of the United Nations," although the right can only be exercised until such time as the Security Council has taken the measures necessary to maintain international peace and security. The Charter thus respects both the original Monroe Doctrine and its continentalized form to the extent which is compatible with a universal system of collective security.[44] The Treaty of Rio de Janeiro of 1947 merely confirms the coordination of the regional and the universal systems.[45]

E. PARALLEL DOCTRINES OF OTHER STATES

Doctrines of self-defense parallel to the Monroe Doctrine were to be found in the foreign policies of a number of the leading states. With the building of the Suez Canal, Great Britain came to regard the passage to India by way of the Mediterranean and the Suez Canal as an essential link in the chain of empire communications and was prompt to oppose the threatened establishment of Russian and German naval bases in the immediate neighborhood.[46] Further, in the reply of the British Foreign Office to the communication of Secretary Kellogg submitting the draft treaty for the renunciation of war it was explicitly stated as a condition to the acceptance of the treaty by Great Britain that "there are certain regions of the world the welfare and integrity of which constitute a

[42] *Ibid.*, p. 373.

[43] *Ibid.*, p. 66.

[44] For comment, see Fenwick, *OAS*, pp. 521 ff.

[45] For the text of the Treaty, see Appendix E.

[46] "The objection of England in 1911 to the occupation of a naval station by Germany on the coast of Morocco; the objection of the European Powers generally to the vast force of Russia extending its territory to the Mediterranean; the revision of the Treaty of San Stefano by the Treaty of Berlin; the establishment of buffer states; the objection to the succession of a German prince to the throne of Spain; the many forms of the Eastern question; the centuries of struggle to preserve the balance of power in Europe; all depend upon the very same principle which underlies the Monroe Doctrine, that is to say, upon the right of every sovereign state to protect itself by preventing a condition of affairs in which it will be too late to protect itself." Senator Root, "The Real Monroe Doctrine," *Am. Journal*, Vol. 8 (1914), p. 427. Compare Secretary Hughes' statement in 1923: "They [the American states] have, of course, corresponding rights of self-defense, but the right is individual to each." *Ibid.*, Vol. 17 (1923), p. 611.

special and vital interest for our peace and safety. His Majesty's Government have been at pains to make it clear in the past that interference with these regions cannot be suffered. Their protection against attack is to the British Empire a measure of self-defense." [47] France manifested from the opening of the twentieth century a serious concern that the communications with its African colonies be secured against danger of interruption in the event of war. Japan entered upon its war with Russia in 1904 upon grounds similar to those underlying the Monroe Doctrine, believing that the too near presence of Russia in the Liaotang Peninsula made more difficult the defense of the empire and its interests in Manchuria; and during the decade of the 1930's Japan sought to justify its action in China upon grounds related to self-defense.

F. INTERVENTION AS A MEASURE OF SELF-DEFENSE

One of the older and recurrent problems of international law before the more recent organization of the international community was determining under what circumstances a state might interfere in the internal or external affairs of another state, whether for the purpose of putting an end to conditions of misgovernment or for the purpose of forcing a change in the politics of the government in the interest of law and order in the community or of its own domestic peace. The problem might, indeed, be said to be as old as civilization itself, the Greek city-states and the Roman Empire being familiar with it. In more modern times it presented itself in the form of an alleged "right of intervention" asserted by the intervening state as a corollary of the broader right of self-defense. War was one form of defense. A state, finding conditions in a neighboring country a menace to its security, could declare war, and after defeating the offending state it could impose terms of peace which would prevent the recurrence of the offense. But war was a drastic remedy, and it had at times a way of getting out of hand. Much simpler was it, if the circumstances permitted, to attempt to obtain redress by overturning the offending government or by otherwise coercing it to modify its domestic or foreign policies. Obviously this could only be done if the intervening state was so much more powerful than the offending state that the latter would prefer to submit to the terms imposed upon it rather than accept the challenge of war and risk losing far more than would otherwise be demanded of it.

Intervention thus involved a conflict of two fundamental principles of international law, the right of self-defense on the part of the complainant state and the right of self-government or "independence" on the part of the state against which the complaint was brought. For the solution of the conflict international law had, at the time, no acceptable remedy. The intervening state alleged wrongful conduct on the part of its neighbor.

[47] Miller, *The Peace Pact of Paris*, p. 198.

The neighbor denied the charge and asserted the arbitrary and illegal interference with its domestic affairs. Each was the judge in its own case, and the international community had not yet reached a stage of organization at which it might have been possible to assert the obligation upon the parties of recourse to peaceful settlement.[48]

It was with the outbreak of the French Revolution that the conflict of the two principles of self-defense and independence began to take its modern shape. Austria and Prussia saw in the Revolution a threat to the peace of all Europe. They had the right, as they saw it, to intervene to prevent the spread of ideas which would incite all Europe to revolt and anarchy. France resisted and proclaimed in 1792 a practical declaration of war against the conservative world. At the close of the Napoleonic Wars the Congress of Vienna of 1815 boldly reorganized the domestic governments of France, Spain, and Portugal in the interest of a stable and conservative regime. In 1820 the Triple Alliance, acting in the name of the larger Holy Alliance, undertook at Troppau to excommunicate from the family of nations "states which have undergone a change in government due to revolution, the results of which threaten other states"; and they pledged themselves, if immediate danger threatened, to have recourse if necessary to arms "to bring back the guilty state into the bosom of the Great [Holy] Alliance." [49] On the basis of this principle Austria intervened to suppress uprisings in Italy in 1821, France intervened for a similar purpose in Spain in 1823, and plans were made to assist the Spanish Government in recovering its rebellious colonies.[50]

Intervention now succeeded to intervention, and it is difficult to classify the numerous cases which fill the pages of the history of Europe during the second and third quarters of the nineteenth century. Statesmen made no attempt to place their interventions upon a logical basis, or to draw a line between defense against the military power of a neighboring state and defense against domestic conditions within the state which might prove a source of danger at a later time. The widely varying

[48] See, on this conflict of general principles, Fenwick, "Intervention: Individual and Collective," Am. Journal, Vol. 39 (1945), p. 645.

For a compendium of instances of intervention, see Stowell, Intervention in International Law. On the law of the subject, see P. H. Winfield, "The History of Intervention in International Law," British Year Book, Vol. III (1922-1923), p. 130; "The Grounds of Intervention in International Law," ibid., Vol. V (1924), p. 149.

[49] For the text of the famous, or perhaps infamous, Troppau Protocol, see Phillips, The Confederation of Europe, p. 222. For the background, see Cresson, The Holy Alliance, p. 99.

A curious reversal of the policy of the Triple Alliance is now being witnessed in the efforts of the United States and other democratic states to resist the spread of Communism.

[50] It was in reaction against these plans that the Monroe Doctrine was proclaimed, a doctrine of "nonintervention" in the sense of opposing the intervention of the Triple Alliance in the relations between Spain and its rebellious colonies which had been recognized by the United States as independent.

circumstances of each case makes a critical estimate in terms of international law impossible. If the United States proclaimed the Monroe Doctrine in resistance to plans of intervention by the Triple Alliance to assist Spain in recovering its rebellious colonies, no criticism was forthcoming when the Great Powers intervened on successive occasions to liberate Greece and the Balkan states from the yoke of Turkey. When, in 1849, Russia responded to the call of Austria to assist it in suppressing the revolt in Hungary, the intervention was regarded as a question between the two countries with which other states, certainly not the United States, were not concerned. To intervene or not to intervene was a matter which each state decided for itself according to its military power and its national interests. The right of intervention and the obligation of nonintervention fell within the field of political action, and jurists could do little more than find justification for what governments were doing by referring to the necessity of a summary procedure which, as one jurist expressed it, "may sometimes snatch a remedy beyond the reach of law." [51]

Intervention on "grounds of humanity." Numerous interventions took place during the nineteenth century upon what were called in a broad way "grounds of humanity." The Ottoman Empire, seeking to retain its hold over its rebellious vassal states and subjects, resorted to methods of suppression which shocked the conscience of Europe. In 1827 the Great Powers jointly intervened to secure the independence of Greece, and the battle of Navarino may fairly be looked upon as the use of force by the community of nations, acting through the intervening powers, in the interest of law and justice. In spite of the admission of the Ottoman Empire to participate in the public law and concert of Europe in 1856, interventions again took place in 1860 to protect the Christians of Mount Lebanon, in 1878 to secure the deliverance of the Balkan states, and in 1891-1896 following massacres in Armenia and in Crete. Jurists discussed at length the possible technical grounds in justification of these interventions, since they constituted an interference in the domestic government of the misbehaving state and a violation of its right of independence.[52] The international community had not as yet developed any machinery for the assertion of its higher right to maintain law and order. But while differing as to the technical grounds of intervention, jurists found no difficulty in responding to the higher appeal of a common humanity,

[51] Sir William Harcourt, *Letters of Historicus*, p. 41.

The inability of the jurists to bring the subject of intervention within the law was due to the inherent lawlessness of the system of individual self-defense, in which each state was the judge of the extent to which its security was menaced and was free to take such action as its power might permit. The fact that at times a remedy was required "beyond the reach of the law" did not appear paradoxical to the jurists. They accepted the limitations of the law with complacency.

[52] See, for example, the discussion in *Am. Journal*, Vol. 6 (1912), p. 186; and compare Ganji, *International Protection of Human Rights* (1962).

and in conceding to a state the same right to protect the moral feelings of its people, shocked by the accounts of the massacres of their co-religionists, that it had to protect their material interests.

The removal of an international nuisance.   Intervention with the object of protecting the state against conditions of continued misgovernment in a neighboring state was strikingly illustrated in the declaration of war by the United States against Spain in 1898. International law had never explicitly recognized a right on the part of states similar to the common-law right of an individual to abate a nuisance. At the same time, in the absence of an international tribunal of compulsory jurisdiction, it was not possible for a nation to sue out a writ of injunction against a foreign state. In the judgment of the United States Government the condition of chronic rebellion in Cuba, accompanied by military repression of a particularly odious character, as well as by the failure to establish proper sanitary measures against the spread of yellow fever, constituted a continuous disturbance to the peace of the United States.[53] Whether war was the only available remedy was a question of public morality, not of positive law. The particular method of self-protection to be adopted under the circumstances was left by international law to the discretion of the injured party.

Conflicting views of jurists.   Corresponding to the widely divergent attitudes of governments was the complete lack of agreement among jurists down to the time of the First World War as to the legal nature of intervention or its moral justification. Some jurists approached it from the point of view of the state intervening as a measure of self-defense, others took the side of the state whose independence was being violated. British and American jurists showed a tendency to defend intervention, while most Continental and Latin American writers rejected the alleged right or limited it sharply.[54] The establishment of the League of Nations in 1920, in restricting the right of self-help and in setting up the judgment of the League as against the arbitrary decision of the individual

[53] See the address of President McKinley to Congress, April 11, 1898. Moore, *Digest,* § 909.

[54] The conflicting views of the jurists were reflected in the lack of agreement upon the very definition of intervention. In popular use the term "intervention" included the interference of a third state in a war between two states, the interference of foreign governments between parties to a civil war, and the interference of one government in the domestic or foreign affairs of another. To some writers the interference was only intervention when unwarranted; and this is doubtless the accepted attitude towards intervention at the present day. See Hyde, *Int. Law,* Vol. I, p. 246. But inasmuch as the rules of international law were ill defined in respect to measures of self-defense, what might be justifiable interference in the eyes of one state might be unwarranted interference in the eyes of another. Whether the consent of the existing government of a state would excuse intervention was, and still is, a matter of doubt, depending apparently upon whether the government represented the free choice of the people or was one maintaining itself in power by suppression of the opposition.

state, should have opened the way for the development of new rules of law. When, however, the League proved itself unable to restrain aggression, new and more drastic forms of intervention appeared, marking the beginning of the general breakdown of law and order.

The inter-American doctrine of nonintervention. In the Western Hemisphere the problem presented itself in a separate and distinct form. The United States, having intervened between Spain and Cuba, was led on to other forms of intervention in the interest of maintaining the principle of nonintervention. In 1904 President Roosevelt, confronted with the attempts of European states to collect debts due from American states by forcible methods, was led to announce the possible necessity on the part of the United States of exercising "an international police power." [55] Numerous interventions followed during the succeeding decades, many having little or no relation to the upholding of the Monroe Doctrine. Resistance in Latin America was general; but it was not until the Montevideo Conference of 1933 that the Latin American states were able to obtain from the United States a qualified acceptance of the principle of nonintervention.[56] The principle was accepted in more definite form at Buenos Aires in 1936,[57] and it has since become one of the fundamental principles of the inter-American system. The Charter of the Organization of American States of 1948 declares in the strongest terms that "No State or group of States has the right to intervene, directly or indirectly, for any reason whatever, in the internal or external affairs of any other State." Only one exception is recognized: that measures adopted for the maintenance of peace and security in accordance with existing treaties do not constitute a violation of the principle, referring obviously to the Treaty of Reciprocal Assistance signed at Rio de Janeiro the previous year.[58]

But so extreme a statement could not long hold against the necessity of taking measures to meet the threat of international Communism; and the resolution taken at Caracas in 1954 gave a new meaning to the provision of Article 6 of the Rio Treaty.[59] Query, would collective action taken to meet a threat to the peace resulting from the control of an

[55] For the text of President Roosevelt's pronouncement, made in the course of his Annual Message to Congress, December 6, 1904, see Moore, *Digest*, Vol. VI, p. 596.

[56] Convention on the Rights and Duties of States, *Int. Conferences of American States*, 1933-1940, p. 122.

[57] Additional Protocol relative to Non-Intervention, *ibid.*, p. 191. The Protocol adds the words, "directly or indirectly, or for whatever reason." The preamble of the Act of Chapultepec, as well as the Declaration of Mexico, 1945, reverted to the earlier form.

[58] Charter, Arts. 15-19.

[59] Resolution XCIII, "Declaration of Solidarity for the Preservation of the Political Integrity of the American States against the Intervention of International Communism." *Int. Conferences of American States*, 1942-1954, p. 433.

American state by a non-American state constitute a threat to the peace if the particular state were to invite and welcome such control, as in the case of Guatemala in 1954 and of Cuba in 1960? In 1961, following the assassination of the dictator Trujillo, the Government of the Dominican Republic needed assistance in stabilizing the conflicting forces. Was it intervention for the American States to offer assistance? In 1963, the Government of Haiti appeared to be on the verge of civil war. Would it have been intervention for the American States to invoke the Rio Treaty and consult as to measures that it might be necessary to take? On January 9 and 10 of 1964, a clash between Panamanians and the armed forces of the Canal Zone led to the convocation by the Organization of American States of the Organ of Consultation under the Rio Treaty in spite of the fact that the conditions laid down in Article 6 of the Treaty did not appear to have been met.[60] In July, 1964, the Ninth Meeting of Consultation of Foreign Ministers took place in Washington in response to evidence submitted by the Government of Venezuela that the subversive activities of the Cuban Government were a violation of the principle of nonintervention; and the Meeting reaffirmed the principle in the strongest terms. Collective intervention under Article 15 of the Charter does not, as we have seen, fall under the condemnation of intervention.

Intervention in time of civil war. Intervention in time of civil war has formed the subject of numerous controversies. The principle of the Troppau Protocol was used to justify the intervention of third states on the side of a "legitimate" government based upon dynastic succession. Might democratic governments advance a similar claim to aid rebels who were seeking to establish constitutional regimes based upon the will of the people? They were reluctant to do so. The question was presented in a new form when, with the establishment of constitutional regimes, a *de jure* government was confronted with rebellion based upon its alleged failure to observe constitutional guarantees, or perhaps based upon nothing more than a desire on the part of the rebels to obtain control of the public offices. In 1928 the American republics, after long experience in intervention in time of civil war, adopted at Havana a convention setting forth the rights and duties of third states in such cases.[61] It was agreed that third states should use all means at their disposal to prevent their inhabitants from participating in civil strife in neighboring states, that they should intern rebel forces crossing their boundaries, and that they should forbid the traffic in arms except when intended for the Government while the belligerency of the rebels had not been recognized. The Convention of 1928 was supplemented in 1957 by a Protocol

[60] See "Legal Aspects of the Panama Case," *Am. Journal,* Vol. 58 (1964), p. 436.
[61] Convention: Duties and Rights of States in the Event of Civil Strife, *Int. Conferences of American States,* 1889-1928, p. 435; Fenwick, *The OAS,* pp. 252 ff.

extending the obligations in the light of recent activities of refugees seeking to overturn the government in power.

The intervention of third states in the Civil War in Spain in 1936 came close to precipitating a general conflict.[62] Germany and Italy intervened on the side of General Franco, Russia on the side of the Loyalists, while Great Britain and France enacted embargo measures against both sides. A Non-Intervention Committee was set up in London, seeking to maintain neutrality between the two parties. The Council of the League of Nations adopted a resolution affirming the obligation of states to refrain from intervention in the internal affairs of another state; but no constructive rules of law were drawn up to govern similar cases in the future.[63] It remained uncertain whether aid to a *de jure* government could be said to be an illegal act, although its consequences might be aid by other states to the rebels and the danger of war.

Recent cases in the light of the Charter of the United Nations. The Charter of the United Nations, in imposing restrictions upon the arbitrary use of force, clearly condemns the traditional forms of intervention as measures of self-help. Even the collective intervention of the United Nations as a body is prohibited, "in matters which are essentially within the domestic jurisdiction of any state," exception being made of enforcement measures taken by the Security Council in accordance with the provisions of Chapter VII of the Charter. The scope of this provision has been a subject of controversy, and it is clear that it can only be interpreted in the light of successive cases coming before the Council. In 1945 the Soviet Union intervened in Iran by giving support to rebels in Azerbaijan; and the case was referred to the Security Council, which did not regard itself as intervening in the domestic affairs of Iran. In 1946 Great Britain and in 1947 Yugoslavia, Albania, and Bulgaria were alleged to have intervened in Greece, the former by assisting the government against guerrillas and the latter by assisting guerrillas against the government. The action of the United States in 1947 in making loans to Greece and Turkey was regarded by Soviet delegates to the United Nations as a form of intervention. The United States and Great Britain regarded the support given by the Soviet Union in 1947 to the Communist party in Hungary and other countries as an unwarranted interference in the domestic affairs of that state; and quite clearly the intervention of the Soviet Union in Hungary in 1956 was an outright violation of the prohibition. The intervention of the Soviet Union in Cuba in 1962, being with the consent of Cuba, raises a separate issue, as does the intervention of the United States in Viet Nam in 1965.

[62] See, on the legal aspects of the case, N. J. Padelford, "International Law and the Spanish Civil War," *Am. Journal,* Vol. 31 (1937), p. 226; *International Law and Diplomacy in the Spanish Civil Strife.*

[63] See Fenwick, "Can Civil Wars be brought under the control of International Law?" *Am. Journal,* Vol. 32 (1938), p. 538.

G. DEFENSE OF NATIONAL HONOR

It has been common with governments to regard an insult to the national honor as only less serious than a physical attack upon the state itself. The "right to respect," as it is called, has been classed among the fundamental rights of states because states have come to regard manifestations of respect for the national flag and for the higher officers of state as essential conditions of friendly relations. An affront to the honor of the state, an insult offered to the symbols through which its personality is expressed appears to imply an attack upon the position of the state in the international community, upon its equality with other sovereign states. The sharpest resentment, therefore, has always been shown in such cases, and at times the redress demanded has appeared to be out of all proportion to the offense.

The Tampico incident. In the great majority of instances insults offered to the dignity or national honor of a foreign state are not the deliberate act of the government of the state but rather the result of individual or mob violence beyond the power of the state to control, or they are the result of unauthorized acts on the part of subordinate officers of the state.[64] An instance in which the redress demanded for an insult to the national flag led to consequences far beyond the intrinsic character of the offense is to be seen in the Tampico incident between the United States and Mexico in 1914. After President Wilson had advocated a policy of patient waiting pending the restoration of stable political conditions in Mexico, he suddenly reversed his attitude in consequence of the temporary arrest of an American officer and crew in Tampico and appeared before Congress to ask its approval of drastic measures to be taken to demand redress for the insult offered to the American flag under whose protection the whaleboat had tied up at the wharf.[65] Congress thereupon acceded to the request of the President that he be permitted to "use the armed forces of the United States in such ways and to such an extent as may be necessary to obtain from General Huerta and his adherents the fullest recognition of the rights and dignity of the United States." [66] As a result Vera Cruz was occupied, and war would doubtless have resulted if the Mexican Government had been in a position to resist.

H. COOPERATIVE DEFENSE

Even before the establishment of the League of Nations in 1920 international law was not altogether without precedents exemplifying, if

[64] For the distinction between acts for which a state is directly responsible and those for which it can only be held indirectly responsible, see below, pp. 333 ff.

[65] The position taken by the President is summarized in his address before Congress, April 20, 1914. *Congressional Record*, Vol. 51, p. 6908.

[66] Resolution approved April 22, 1914. For the text of the resolution see Hyde, *Int. Law*, Vol. II, § 591.

not justifying, the common action of a group of states in self-defense against the lawless conduct of a particular state. Vattel had laid down the principle that "all nations may put down by force the open violation of the laws of the society which nature has established among them, or any direct attacks upon its welfare." [67] Even if a state's own security was not threatened, such acts, if allowed to go unpunished, might have the effect of undermining all law and reducing the whole international system to anarchy. The coalition formed against Napoleon in 1805 appears to have been influenced by such ideas, when it appeared that the rights of any state that stood in his way were being ruthlessly crushed underfoot. Doubtless the violation of the neutrality of Belgium by Germany in 1914 and the ruthless use of the submarine against neutral commerce contributed to the coalition of thirty-one Allied and Associated Powers to protect themselves against a lawless nation which, if victorious, might use its power to oppress them.[68] But such collective interventions, being put into effect after the commission of the unlawful act and being motivated by a variety of political interests on the part of the participants, could not be said to be acts of an organized community of nations.

System established by the League of Nations. The establishment of the League of Nations in 1920 marked the inauguration of a system of cooperative defense fundamentally at variance with the traditional systems of individual defense. The Covenant pledged the members of the League mutually to respect and to preserve as against external aggression their individual territorial integrity and existing political independence. It discarded the old law of neutrality by adopting the principle of the collective responsibility of all the members of the League for the maintenance of peace. It laid down requirements in respect to the pacific settlement of disputes that restricted within the narrowest limits the possibility of a resort to war in disregard of its covenants, and it held in the background the threat of combined military action.[69]

Problems presented by cooperative defense. The reasons for the failure of the system of cooperative defense established by the League lay partly in the absence of the United States and partly in the inability of the League to create the mutual confidence necessary to lead its members to abandon their old right of individual self-defense, with all its implications and connotations. The reduction of competitive armaments, which was an essential condition of mutual confidence, did not proceed in accordance with the original plans of the League; and it was clear that the stronger powers preferred for the time to rely upon their own

[67] *Droit des gens,* Eng. trans., Intro., § 22.

[68] See the address of President Wilson, April 6, 1917, calling upon the Congress of the United States to declare war against Germany.

[69] See *Ten Years of World Coöperation,* published by the Secretariat of the League of Nations, Chaps. I, II; Howard-Ellis, *The Origin, Structure and Working of the League of Nations;* Bassett, *The League of Nations.*

resources rather than to trust to the League with its diversified membership to live up to its pledges and to make its sanctions effective. Attempts to tighten the system failed for want of a realization by each state that its own national defense was intimately dependent upon the maintenance of international law and order. When the League proved unequal to the task of restraining the series of acts of aggression which began in 1931, its members looked once more to their own national defenses and began to shift for themselves as in the days before the establishment of the League. Plans of economic and social cooperation that might have alleviated conditions of tension slipped into the background when it appeared that changes in the *status quo* would be interpreted as concessions to aggression. In the end the security system failed because the law-abiding elements of the community lacked the necessary unity of purpose to organize their collective defense and to anticipate attack before the aggressors could gather sufficient strength to risk carrying their plans into execution.[70]

Provisions of the Charter of the United Nations. Taking its provisions at their face value, the Charter of the United Nations established a far stronger system of collective security than that of the Covenant of the League of Nations, imposing more rigid restrictions upon the use of force by individual states and providing for prompter action by the Security Council, which was given the primary responsibility for the maintenance of peace. But the Security Council ceased to be an effective agency when the Soviet Union put forward policies believed by the West to be at variance with the principles of the Charter, and when on occasion the delegate of the Soviet Union used the power of the veto to prevent remedial action by the Council. The invention of the atomic bomb, giving to the recalcitrant state possessing it the power to challenge the community as a whole, put an end to the collective security system of the United Nations before it had begun to function.[71] The result was the creation of the North Atlantic Treaty Organization (NATO), which sought to establish a system of cooperative defense within a more limited circle of states having common political principles.

Nevertheless, in spite of the practical breakdown of the collective security system of the United Nations, it proved possible for a smaller group to act collectively to restrain the invasion of the Republic of Korea by North Korean forces in 1950. Upon receiving word of the invasion, the Security Council on June 25 noted the fact of an armed attack and called for an immediate cessation of hostilities; and on June 27, it recommended that the members of the United Nations furnish such

[70] See, among numerous other commentaries, Sharp and Kirk, *Contemporary Int. Politics*, Parts V, VI; Schuman, *Int. Politics*, Chap. XV, "The Testing of the League"; Walters, *History of the League of Nations*.

[71] Compare, however, Kelsen, *Collective Security under International Law;* and compare Chap. XXIX, D.

assistance to the Republic of Korea as might be necessary to repel the armed attack; and in a resolution of July 7, the Council welcomed the support given to its earlier resolutions and recommended a unified command under the United States. The three resolutions were adopted in the absence of one of the permanent members of the Council, a fact which raised the question of the constitutionality of the resolutions.[72] But without being delayed by that issue, the forces of sixteen member states, under the unified command of the United States, carried on hostilities until an armistice agreement was signed on July 27, 1953. Efforts to agree upon a permanent solution of the Korean question failed at the Geneva Conference in 1958 and were still under way at the seventeenth session of the General Assembly of the United Nations in 1962.[73]

[72] The technical aspects of the subject are discussed in Kelsen, *Recent Trends in the Law of the United Nations,* Chap. 2, "The Action in Korea."

[73] *U.N. Yearbook,* 1962, pp. 117-124.

CHAPTER XIII

The Independence of States:

General Rights and Obligations

of Jurisdiction

A. THE "RIGHT OF INDEPENDENCE"

Second in importance only to the right of national existence, and indeed forming a natural corollary of it, is the right of independence. In accordance with this right a state claims to be free from control by any other state in the management of its domestic affairs and in the determination of its relations with other members of the international community. As in the case of the right of existence, the right of independence is one of the fundamental assumptions of international law, a postulate rather than a principle, an essential condition of international law as it has developed during the past three hundred years.[1] The fact that it is commonly discussed by jurists as separate and distinct from the primary right of existence is a matter of convenience of classification and treatment rather than of strict logic.

Internal independence. The right of independence has two distinct aspects: the one relating to the freedom of the state in the management of its domestic affairs, and the other relating to the freedom of the state in the relations which it maintains with other states. The former is known as the "internal independence" of the state, and it involves the supreme authority or jurisdiction of the state to control all persons or property within its territorial domain. In pursuance of this right a state adopts its national constitution, organizes its government, determines the personal and property rights of its citizens, fixes the conditions of the admission of aliens into its territory and their rights and duties under the law, and regulates in a thousand ways the economic and social activities of its people. In a broad way the right of internal independence creates a gen-

[1] See pp. 253 ff., where the general character of international rights is discussed.

eral presumption that the state is master within its own territory and has a primary claim to be free from interference by other states, save only insofar as it is bound by the general rules of international law or by specific treaty agreements. Until of recent years this right was conceived by governments in terms of the freedom of the state from control by any other state. It is only of recent years that jurists have come to relate the independence of the state to the supreme authority of the international community, and in that connection the right of internal independence might, perhaps, be more adequately described as the "right of national self-government." [2]

External independence. In contrast with internal independence, "external independence" connotes the supreme power of the state to determine the relations it desires to maintain with other states, without interference on the part of any third state. The absence of any such interference, or at least interference of legal right, is necessary to enable the state to act as a free agent in dealing with other states and to be in consequence responsible for the fulfilment of its obligations. In pursuance of its right of external independence a state enters into treaties of every sort with other states; it forms alliances for mutual defense or general covenants of collective defense; it establishes relations of special or general commercial intercourse; and it cooperates by means of multilateral conventions in the promotion of economic and social objects of common advantage to all. External independence is, as has been seen, a necessary condition of membership in the community of nations, being the principal test of the possession by a state of a separate international personality.[3]

B. INDEPENDENCE AND SOVEREIGNTY

It is obvious that these rights of internal and external independence are subject to the limitations imposed by international law, and that "independence" means only freedom from control by any other state, not freedom from the restrictions that are binding upon all states. The term "sovereignty" appears to be used interchangeably with independence, when it is desired to emphasize the independence of the state in resistance to threatened encroachments upon it. Sovereignty might be defined in this connection as the independent personality of the state in its relations with other members of the international community.[4]

[2] A generation ago the term "self-government" would have been said to be more applicable to the members of a federal union, such as that of the United States, than to the members of the international community.

[3] See above, pp. 125 ff.

[4] The use of the term "sovereignty" as expressing the independence of the state in relation to other states is to be distinguished from the derivative use of the term to describe the dominion of the state over certain territory, as when it is said that a state claims "sovereignty" over particular arctic regions.

Taken thus it is frequently associated with the equality of states in international law; and this usage, long familiar in the declarations and resolutions of inter-American conferences,[5] has now been confirmed by the provision of the Charter of the United Nations that the organization is based upon the principle of "the sovereign equality of all its Members."[6] A generation ago jurists were practically unanimous in the opinion that the term "sovereignty," which had so long been used by states to assert a complete freedom from control, a sort of final and absolute right of the state to determine the lawfulness of all acts done within its territory, should be discarded as inconsistent with international law.[7] If, however, the term is to continue in use in spite of the logical inconsistency of its literal acceptation, then it must be used with greater care than has been the case in the past. States can obviously not be above the law and at the same time subject to it.[8]

The limitations of independence. Every rule of international law is obviously a restriction upon the actual independence of the state. Every treaty entered into is obviously, to the extent of the obligations it entails, a restriction upon the freedom of the state in the particular field of activity covered by the treaty.[9] In addition to the special obligations of bilateral treaties every state is now a party to numerous multilateral treaties which impose upon it a wide variety of restrictions which, in their sum total, make the term "interdependence" seem a more fitting description of actual conditions.[10] In the field of *external* independence states have now, with the adoption of the Charter of the United Nations, assumed a general obligation to refrain from the use of force in their

[5] See, in particular, the Declaration of Principles of Inter-American Solidarity and Coöperation, adopted at Buenos Aires in 1936, and the Declaration of Lima of 1938. *International Conferences of American States*, 1933-1940, pp. 160, 308.

[6] Art. 2.

[7] See J. W. Garner, "Limitations on National Sovereignty in International Relations," *American Political Science Review*, Vol. XIX (1925), p. 1; Ward, *Sovereignty—A Study of a Contemporary Political Notion;* J. L. Brierly, *Recueil des Cours*, Vol. 23 (1928-III), pp. 467, 523.

[8] Nations can scarcely be blamed for holding on tenaciously to a term that ceases to correspond with the facts of life when even within the Union of the United States reference is frequently made to "the sovereign commonwealth" of Massachusetts, of Virginia, etc. The Articles of Confederation of 1781 made the loss of actual sovereignty easier by announcing in Article I that "the members of this Confederation retain their sovereignty." Succeeding articles then proceeded to transfer much of the sovereignty to the Confederation.

[9] The obligations imposed upon a state by treaties are said by certain writers not to be a limitation of "sovereignty" because they are deliberately accepted by states. See p. 255. But whatever the theoretical situation, a state is on the one hand less free after the treaty than before, in that it gives up the right to do certain things, and on the other hand it is actually more free, in that it can now do things it could not do before or is now protected from things it was not protected from before. In any case it is less "sovereign," whether or not less free.

[10] Justifying, for example, the title *Transnational Law*, used by Professor Jessup. Compare, also, Jenks, *The Common Law of Mankind*.

mutual relations and to resort to peaceful procedures for the settlement of their disputes.[11] In the field of *internal* independence the restrictions upon the freedom of the state are numerous and detailed, if of less intrinsic importance. A half century ago a state was free to treat its own citizen body as it pleased, and the community at large refrained from interfering except in those rare cases when the persecution of minorities shocked the somewhat hardened conscience of the leading powers. Today the United Nations recognize in their Charter the necessity of promoting universal respect for the observance of "human rights and fundamental freedoms," [12] although no provision is as yet contemplated for the enforcement of these rights by international machinery. International law has long imposed an obligation upon states to give due protection to the lives and property of persons of alien nationality who happen to be temporarily or permanently within their borders, to respect the privileges and immunities of the diplomatic representatives of foreign states, to prevent persons within their jurisdiction from committing armed attacks upon neighboring states, and in other ways to regulate their internal affairs so as not to disturb the peace or threaten the safety of neighboring states.[13]

Scope of domestic questions.   Where is the line to be drawn between the sphere of national self-government and the dominant authority of international law? The term "domestic questions" has been applied to those matters which are said to be subject to the final decision of the state in whose territory they arise; and we have seen how in drafting both the Covenant of the League of Nations and the Charter of the United Nations the leading states found it necessary to deny their respective councils jurisdiction in the settlement of international disputes when domestic questions were at issue.[14] The terms of the Charter are explicit:

Nothing contained in the present Charter shall authorize the United Nations to intervene in matters which are essentially within the domestic jurisdiction of the state or shall require the members to submit such matters to settlement under the present Charter; but this principle shall not prejudice the application of enforcement measures under Chapter VII.[15]

It is agreed that when there is a threat to the peace, a breach of the peace, or an act of aggression, that the Security Council may on this ground assume jurisdiction against any claim of a state that the question is a domestic one. But in many cases the line between the two may give rise to controversy. In its opinion in the Tunis-Morocco Nationality

[11] See above, p. 205.
[12] Charter of the United Nations, Art. 55.
[13] See below under separate titles.
[14] See p. 206.
[15] Art. 2 (7).

Decrees case, decided in 1923, the Permanent Court of International Justice spoke as follows:

The question whether a certain matter is or is not solely within the jurisdiction of a State is an essentially relative question; it depends upon the development of international relations. Thus, in the present state of international law, questions of nationality are, in the opinion of the Court, in principle within this reserved domain.

In view, however, of earlier treaties between the two parties, Great Britain and France, the Court held that the nationality decrees were not solely within the domestic jurisdiction of France.[16]

The mere fact, however, that the policy or conduct of a state is offensive or even hurtful to another state does not take the matter from the class of domestic questions. Control of immigration is admittedly a domestic question, although the legislation of the United States against the Japanese in 1906 and 1924 gave rise to controversy. For years the tariff policies of many countries were hurtful to the economic interests of other countries, but without giving rise to legal complaint when treaty rights were not involved.

The decisions of the Security Council may doubtlessly build up in time a body of precedents that may constitute a rule of law, but thus far the political elements of the particular cases presented to it have prevented the decisions of the Council from having the juridical authority that they might otherwise have. Query, was a domestic question at issue when Spain was refused admission to the United Nations in 1946 because of the political record of the Franco regime? [17] Was domestic jurisdiction involved when a political party in Czechoslovakia welcomed the intervention of the Soviet Union in 1948? [18] Was the claim of South Africa, in reply to the complaint of India before the Security Council in 1946, that the alleged discrimination against Indian nationals involved a matter of domestic jurisdiction, a conclusive answer? [19] In 1949 an effort was made to get the General Assembly to take action against Bulgaria, Hungary, and Rumania for violation of fundamental human rights stipulated in the peace treaties. But the International Court of Justice, to which the case was referred for an opinion, found no means of enforcing the obligation.[20] Nor could any action be taken in 1956 when Hungary was invaded by Soviet troops, the Soviet veto claiming domestic jurisdiction, and the General Assembly being limited to a resolution of condemnation.

[16] Advisory Opinions, Series B, No. 4; Fenwick, Cases, p. 171; Am. Journal, Vol. 18 (1924), p. 2; Bishop, Cases, p. 621; Briggs, Cases, p. 452.

[17] U.N. Yearbook, 1946-1947, pp. 66, 126.

[18] See "The Coup d'Etat in Prague," House Document, No. 154, Part I, 81st Congress, 1st Sess., Gov't Printing Office, 1949.

[19] U.N. Yearbook, 1946-1947, p. 144.

[20] I.C.J. Reports, 1950, p. 65; U.N. Yearbook, 1950, p. 385.

Paralleling the provisions of the Charter of the United Nations are the provisions of Article 15 of the Charter of the Organization of American States. Intervention "directly or indirectly, for any reason whatever, in the internal or external affairs of any other state" is forbidden; but Article 19 makes exception of "measures adopted for the maintenance of peace and security in accordance with existing treaties." There must, therefore, be a threat to the peace in the terms of the Treaty of Reciprocal Assistance; and the experience of the years has shown that a "threat to the peace" must involve some form of controversy with another country which might lead to hostilities, not a mere psychological disturbance of the peace by reason of the denial of fundamental rights or even of shocking cruelties inflicted by a dictator upon his own people.[21] Public opinion is moving in the direction of insisting upon the observance of the Universal Declaration of Human Rights, but as yet a formal convention on the subject awaits adoption.

C. JURISDICTION OVER NATIONALS

The determination of nationality. Since states are composite persons it is obvious that it must be a problem of first importance with them to be assured of the membership of their corporate body. The problem was one of relatively little consequence until the great movement of peoples began about the middle of the nineteenth century. Since then it has increased in complexity; and in spite of numerous efforts to codify the law of nationality there are still wide differences of opinion between governments both as to the basis of nationality and as to the correct solution of conflicting claims.[22]

The problem of nationality solves itself in the case of the great majority of the people who are born within the boundaries of a particular state and live out their lives within them. The conflicting claims of governments arise when a person moves from one state to another and each of the two states has, upon different grounds, a claim to his allegiance; so that in consequence of his dual nationality he becomes the subject of two sets of rights and obligations which are at certain points mutually exclusive. "Nationality" may thus be defined as the bond which unites a person to a given state, which constitutes his membership in the particular state, which gives him a claim to the protection of that state, and which subjects him to the obligations created by the laws of that

---

[21] Fenwick, *OAS*, p. 234.

[22] On the general subject of nationality, see *Research in International Law: Draft Conventions on Nationality, Responsibility of States, Territorial Waters* (1929); *Acts of the Conference for the Codification of International Law*, Vol. I, *Plenary Meetings*, Vol. II, *Minutes of the First Committee, Nationality* (1930); Flournoy and Hudson, *A Collection of Nationality Laws;* D. V. Sandifer, "A Comparative Study of Laws Relating to Nationality at Birth and to Loss of Nationality," *Am. Journal,* Vol. 29 (1935), p. 248. An elaborate bibliography may be found in Hyde, *Int. Law,* 2nd ed., Vol. II, p. 1064.

state. The term "national" has come into use of recent years in place of "citizen" or "subject," the term "citizen" not applying in some states to all members of the body politic and the term "subject" carrying with it traditions of monarchical rule.[23]

Nationality by birth. The law is well established that persons are nationals if born on the soil of the state and of parents who are themselves nationals of the state. This general rule covers, in most states, the large majority of the citizen body. Apart from this general rule, the practice of nations varies widely. Great Britain, the United States, and a number of Latin American states adhere primarily to the principle of *jus soli,* by which mere birth upon the soil is sufficient to confer nationality, irrespective of the nationality of the parents.[24] This principle was of feudal origin, and it originally prevailed in France and other Continental countries, which, however, in time abandoned it. By contrast with the *jus soli,* France (since the adoption of the *Code Napoléon*), Germany, and other European states adhere primarily to the civil law principle of *jus sanguinis,* by which the nationality of children follows that of their parents, irrespective of their place of birth.[25] It follows, therefore, that a conflict of jurisdiction may arise when a child is born on the soil of one state of parents who are citizens of another state. For example, a child born in the United States of French parents is an American citizen *jure soli,* but the child is at the same time a French citizen *jure sanguinis.* His effective citizenship will then depend upon the jurisdiction within which he happens to be. In the United States he is an American; in France, a Frenchman; in any other country he is both.[26]

[23] See Harvard Draft, p. 23.

[24] *Ibid.,* p. 37. For details, see Flournoy and Hudson, *op. cit., passim.*

The Fourteenth Amendment of the United States Constitution proclaims that "all persons born or naturalized in the United States, and subject to the jurisdiction thereof, are citizens of the United States and of the State wherein they reside." Prior to the Civil Rights Act of 1866, which preceded the adoption of the amendment, the American federal courts followed the principle as a rule of the common law.

The above provision of the Fourteenth Amendment was interpreted in the case of United States v. Wong Kim Ark, 169 U.S. 649 (1898), to confer citizenship upon the child of alien parents who were not themselves eligible to citizenship by naturalization, as being of Chinese descent. In commenting, *obiter,* upon the general principle of citizenship, the court said: "It is the inherent right of every independent nation to determine for itself, and according to its own Constitution and laws, what classes of persons shall be entitled to its citizenship." See Fenwick, *Cases,* p. 162; Hudson, *Cases,* p. 226. American Indians fall within a special class, being citizens through special statutory provisions.

[25] Harvard Draft, pp. 28-32.

[26] In the comment on Art. 3 of the Harvard Draft it is said: "From an examination of the nationality laws of the various states it appears that seventeen are based solely on *jus sanguinis,* two equally upon *jus soli* and *jus sanguinis,* twenty-five principally upon *jus sanguinis* but partly upon *jus soli,* and twenty-six principally upon *jus soli* and partly upon *jus sanguinis.* The nationality law of no country is based solely upon *jus soli.* A combination of the two systems is found in the laws of most countries."

Claims based upon both principles. Most states, however, hold in varying degree to both systems. Great Britain, before 1870, not only claimed the allegiance of the children born to aliens on the soil of the country, but that of children born to British citizens resident in other countries. The former claim has, since the Naturalization Act of 1870, been qualified to permit the children born of alien parents on the soil of the country to assume the nationality of their parents by a declaration of alienage made upon attaining majority. The United States in like manner has supported its claims *jure soli* by claims *jure sanguinis*. By a law of Congress, enacted in 1855,[27] all children born out of the jurisdiction of the United States, whose fathers were at the time of the children's birth citizens of the United States, were declared to be citizens of the United States; but the rights of citizenship were held not to descend to children whose fathers never resided in the United States.[28] Successive laws of 1907, 1934, 1940, and 1952 have fixed the conditions upon which children, born abroad, of citizens of the United States may acquire and retain citizenship of the United States.[29] Citizenship of the mother as well as of the father may descend to the child; but in cases where one of the parents is an alien the child must reside in the United States or its outlying possessions for a period or periods totaling five years between the ages of thirteen and twenty-one years. In France while the *jus sanguinis* constitutes the primary claim of allegiance, elements of the *jus soli* are to be found in the provision that any person born in France of alien parents and domiciled in France may by declaration become a Frenchman and automatically does so on attaining majority unless he formally refuses to do so.[30] In Brazil the *jus soli* constitutes the first basis of citizenship enumerated in the Constitution, then follows the *jus sanguinis* applied to children born abroad, provided the parents return to the country, in which case the child, upon attaining majority, must choose Brazilian nationality within four years.[31]

Conflicts of claims. The various conflicts resulting from the simultaneous presence of these basically different claims of allegiance are, as a practical matter, generally settled between states by deferring *jus sanguinis* to *jus soli* when the state asserting its primary claim of allegiance has at the same time *de facto* jurisdiction over the individual in question. The obligations of military service have frequently given rise

[27] Act of February 10, 1855; incorporated in Revised Statutes, § 1993.

[28] See Weedin v. Chin Bow, 274 U.S. 657 (1927). Hudson, *Cases,* p. 243; Fenwick, *Cases,* p. 190.

[29] See Flournoy and Hudson, *op. cit.* For the text of the act of 1940, see *Am. Journal,* Vol. 35 (1941), Supp., p. 79. For comment, see C. C. Hyde, Vol. 35 (1941), p. 314. For an analysis of the act of 1952, see Bishop, *Cases,* pp. 427 ff.

[30] Law of August 10, 1927. Flournoy and Hudson, *op. cit.,* p. 245. See also, decree-law, November 12, 1938.

[31] Art. 129, Constitution of 1946.

to controversies.[32] In the case of Frank Ghiloni the United States Department of State requested the Italian Government, in 1915, to release from compulsory military service a man born in the United States in 1885, whose father was at that time an Italian subject. Ghiloni had resided seventeen years in the United States before going to Italy in June, 1914, and it was held by the Department of State that such continued residence indicated that Ghiloni, although born with dual nationality, had elected American nationality. The Italian Government, however, refused to recognize the prior claim of the United States, although a third party, Austria-Hungary, on capturing Ghiloni in battle, acknowledged the justice of the claim and released the prisoner.[33] In the case of P. A. Le Long, the Department of State was presented in 1915 with an inquiry whether a person, born in the United States of a native French father, who had immigrated to the United States at twenty years of age, could be held liable for military service in case he should visit France during the progress of the war. In reply the Department of State, after citing the provisions of the French Civil Code, explained the legal status of Le Long as being one of dual nationality, and informed him that it could not therefore give him "any assurance that you would not be held liable for the performance of military service in France should you voluntarily place yourself within French jurisdiction." [34] At the Conference for the Codification of International Law held at The Hague in 1930, a Protocol was signed by a number of states providing that a person of dual nationality habitually resident in one of the two countries should be exempt from all military obligations in the other country.[35]

Questions of dual nationality frequently arise in connection with the presentation by one state of claims for redress for injuries received by one of its citizens in another state. International law recognizes in such

[32] See Harvard Draft, Art. 11, and Comment.
[33] Am. White Book, European War, Vol. III, pp. 373-387.
[34] See Hackworth, Digest, Vol. III, p. 359, where other similar cases are cited.

In the case of Ugo Da Prato, a native born citizen who went to Italy in 1912 to study architecture, the father, a native of Italy, had been naturalized in the United States before the birth of his son, and hence it did not appear to the Department of State that the son could be considered an Italian subject under Italian law. A request was therefore made for his immediate release from detention for military service. Am. White Book, Vol. II, p. 149; Hackworth, Digest, Vol. III, p. 352.

In 1938 the Department of State instructed the Embassy in Rome to request the release of Salvatore Scavuzzo from military service in Italy on the ground that he had habitually resided in the United States since birth, and that he had taken steps to return to the United States after he had been in Italy a little more than one year and when he was less than nineteen years of age, and that his departure from Italy within two years from the date of his arrival appeared to have been prevented by circumstances beyond his control. He was thereupon released by Italy on condition that he return to the United States within two months. Hackworth, Digest, Vol. III, p. 362.

[35] Protocol Relating to Military Obligations in Certain Cases of Double Nationality. Am. Journal, Vol. 24 (1930), Supp., p. 201. On the general subject, see P. Louis-Lucas, "Les conflits des nationalités," Recueil des Cours, Vol. 64 (1938-II), p. 5.

cases that the person in whose behalf a claim is made must be a citizen of the state making the claim; and at the same time no state is required to make redress if the person on whose behalf the claim is made is at the same time its own citizen. In the Canevaro case between Italy and Peru, decided in 1912, involving a claim of the Italian Government on behalf of three brothers Canevaro, the arbitral tribunal held that in view of the fact that the Government of Peru "has a right to consider him [Rafael Canevaro] a Peruvian citizen and to deny his status as an Italian claimant," judgment could be passed only in regard to his two brothers, who were accordingly awarded damages.[36]

D. NATIONALITY BY NATURALIZATION

In addition to nationality based upon birth, international law recognizes a nationality acquired by voluntary act, in accordance with which a person, born a citizen of one state, obtains the status of an adopted citizen of another state. The procedure by which such new nationality is acquired is known as *naturalization*, and it is a matter regulated by each state according to its own conception of the degree to which its national interests will be promoted by extending its citizenship to outsiders. In the United States the procedure of naturalization provided by the Nationality Act of 1940,[37] amending earlier acts, requires two distinct steps in the acquisition of citizenship. First, there must be a "declaration of intention" to become a citizen. This declaration, made under oath, contains a number of averments as to the bona fide intention of the applicant to become a citizen of the United States and to renounce his allegiance to any foreign state, as well as other statements bearing upon qualifications of the applicant for admission to citizenship. The second step consists in filing a petition, verified by affidavits of witnesses, setting forth that the applicant is not opposed to organized government and is not a believer in polygamy, that it is his intention to renounce his foreign allegiance and to reside permanently in the United States, and that he will support the Constitution of the United States.[38] The declaration of intention may be made at any time after the arrival of the alien in the United States; but two years must intervene between the declaration and the final admission to citizenship. Since there is a further requirement of five years' residence in the United States, it is immaterial, in point of the time of actual admission to citizenship, at what time

[36] Tribunal of the Permanent Court of Arbitration, 1912. Scott, *Hague Court Reports*, p. 284; Fenwick, *Cases*, p. 169; Bishop, *Cases*, p. 416; Briggs, *Cases*, p. 512.
[37] 54 *Stat.* 1137. For the text, see *Am. Journal*, Vol. 35 (1941), Supp., p. 79.
[38] The provisions in respect to opposition to organized government are set forth in great detail in Section 305, and they include persons who believe in or teach the overthrow by force of the Government of the United States, the duty of killing any officer of the Government because of his official character, the unlawful damage or destruction of property, or sabotage.

within the first three years of residence the applicant takes out his "first papers." [39] Naturalization was formerly limited by law to "free white persons" and "persons of African descent," and it was held by the courts that the former term excluded Chinese, Japanese, and other persons of the brown and yellow races.[40] The Act of 1940 declares that: "The right to become a naturalized citizen under the provisions of this Act shall extend only to white persons, persons of African nativity or descent, and descendants of races indigenous to the Western Hemisphere." This was amended in 1943 so as to include "Chinese persons and persons of Chinese descent." [41]

Cancellation of naturalization. International law leaves it to each state, in fixing the conditions of naturalization, to fix the conditions upon which it may be forfeited. But no obligation is placed upon the state whose citizenship is abandoned to reinstate the person whose naturalization is canceled in consequence of failure to observe the conditions attached to it. The United States Naturalization Act of 1906 provided that the acquisition by a naturalized citizen of a permanent residence abroad within five years after naturalization raised a presumption that the naturalization was procured fraudulently. The law of 1940 makes such permanent residence "*prima facie* evidence" of a lack of intention to become a permanent citizen.[42]

In the Nottebohm case, submitted to the International Court of Justice in 1951, Liechtenstein claimed damages against Guatemala for war measures taken by Guatemala against Nottebohm, alleged to be a citizen of Liechtenstein. The Court first held that it had jurisdiction in the case, since it had been seized of it before the expiration of Guatemala's acceptance of jurisdiction for a period of five years. Then, on the merits of the case, the Court held that the naturalization in Liechtenstein of Nottebohm, born in Germany, had no legal force which could offset the fact that he had been settled for thirty-four years in Guate-

---

[39] For an analysis of the provisions, see C. C. Hyde, *Am. Journal,* Vol. 35 (1941), pp. 314 ff.

[40] Act of February 18, 1875, amending Acts of 1802 and 1804. For the decisions of the courts, see Moore, *Digest,* Vol. III, § 383; Van Dyne, *Naturalization,* Chap. I. The question with respect to the admission of Japanese to naturalization was finally decided in the negative in the case of Ozawa v. United States, 260 U.S. 178 (1922). See *Am. Journal,* Vol. 17 (1923), pp. 151, 328. In the case of Morrison v. California, 291 U.S. 82 (1934), the court held that "men are not white if the strain of colored blood in them is a half or a quarter, or, not improbably, even less, the governing test . . . being that of common understanding." See Hackworth, *Digest,* Vol. III, p. 48.

[41] Act to Repeal the Chinese Exclusion Acts, December 17, 1943. *Am. Journal,* Vol. 38 (1944), Supp., p. 1. The Chinese quota was fixed by proclamation of the President at 105 yearly. Dept. of State *Bulletin,* Vol. X, p. 180. For the question of the collective naturalization of the inhabitants of territory transferred by one state to another, see Chap. XVIII, G.

[42] For details, see Hackworth, *Digest,* Vol. III, pp. 89 ff.

mala, which was the center of his business, interests, and activities. The claim was therefore held to be inadmissible.[43]

Conflicts of national claims and doctrine of indelible allegiance. The conflicts of national allegiance resulting from the respective claims over a particular person advanced on the one hand by the state of his birth or of his parentage and on the other hand by the state of his adoption by naturalization have been equally serious and much more frequent than the conflicts of allegiance arising from the dual claims based upon birth. During the early decades of its national life, the United States, following the doctrines of nationality held by Great Britain,[44] maintained through its courts the doctrine of "indelible allegiance." *Nemo potest exuere patriam.* Born a citizen of the United States, no one might transfer his allegiance to another state without the consent of the state which had first claim upon him. In Williams' Case,[45] decided in 1799, the defendant had been born in the United States and had, as he offered to prove, become naturalized in France in the year 1792, after which he accepted a commission in the French navy. Upon the subsequent arrest of the defendant in the United States upon a charge of violating the Neutrality Act of 1794, it was held by the United States District Court that Williams had no power to renounce his allegiance without the consent of the United States,[46] so that he was still subject to the law of the United States and might properly be punished for an offense committed against it.[47]

Expatriation and loss of nationality. But while the judicial department of the United States Government was asserting the doctrines of the common law, the executive department found it necessary to take a stand in favor of the right of a state to protect its naturalized citizens against the claims of the country of their native allegiance. The growing tide of immigration to the United States from Europe raised in an acute form the question how far the American Government might protect its naturalized citizens upon their return to the country of their birth. The factor of compulsory military service in the states of Continental Europe entered in to complicate the situation. In 1840 the American Minister to Prussia had refused to protect a naturalized citizen

[43] *I.C.J. Reports*, 1955, p. 4; Bishop, *Cases*, p. 401.

[44] See MacDonald's Case, Foster's Crown Law, 59 (1747), in which the court instructed the jury that, if the prisoner should be found to have been born in Great Britain, his long residence in France and his French commission should not constitute a defense to a charge of high treason for participation in war against his native country. Fenwick, *Cases*, p. 177.

[45] U. S. Circ. Ct. Dist. Conn. (1799). Fenwick, *Cases*, p. 178.

[46] An interesting application was made by the court of the contract theory of civil society, in accordance with which "one of the parties to this compact cannot dissolve it by his own act."

[47] The same position was reaffirmed in subsequent cases, *e.g.* Shanks v. Dupont, 3 Peters 242 (1830), until a new rule of statutory law was adopted.

who had been forced to enter the Prussian army upon his subsequent return to that country, holding that the "native domicile and national character" of Knoche reverted upon his return to the country of his birth.[48] But in 1845 Secretary Buchanan asserted the principle that the act of naturalization dissolved any former tie of allegiance; and in 1859, when Buchanan was President, the principle became a fixed policy. In the case of Christian Ernst [49] the Department of State insisted that a naturalized foreigner who returns to his native country "returns as an American citizen and in no other character," and that he might be protected by his adopted country against any attempt on the part of the country of his birth to punish him for an offense, such as the evasion of military service, which had not been committed before his immigration to the United States.

The Bancroft Treaties. In consequence of popular agitation brought on by the refusal of Great Britain to constitute mixed juries for the trial of naturalized American citizens implicated in the Fenian rebellion of 1867, Congress passed the act of July 27, 1868, which declared that "the right of expatriation is a natural and inherent right of all people," and that in consequence all naturalized citizens, being *ipso facto* absolved from their former allegiance, should receive in foreign countries the same protection of person and property that was accorded to native-born citizens.[50] This unilateral pronouncement, while competent to dictate the duties of the Department of State and the rule of decision in the federal courts, was obviously unable to introduce a general rule of international law. The act stood, therefore, merely as a declaration of American policy, considerably in advance of the views held by the states of Continental Europe. It was followed in 1868 by the conclusion with the North German Confederation and other German states of a group of treaties, known as the Bancroft Treaties, in which reciprocal recognition of naturalization was provided for when accompanied by an uninterrupted residence of five years. Similar treaties with Belgium, Sweden and Norway, Austria-Hungary, and other countries followed shortly after.[51]

In spite of the declaration by the American Congress that the right of expatriation was a "natural and inherent right of all people," the principle failed to gain general acceptance. The liberal movement of the

---

[48] Moore, *Digest,* Vol. III, p. 564.

[49] Moore, *Digest,* Vol. III, p. 573.

[50] 15 *Stat. at Large* 223; *Rev. Stat.,* §§ 1999-2001.

[51] For the texts of the treaties, see *Treaties and Conventions,* Vol. I, pp. 45, 80; Vol. II, pp. 1298, 1758. In accordance with the provisions of these treaties the naturalized citizen, on returning to the country of his birth, might still be held liable for an offense "punishable by the laws of his original country and committed before emigration," and the evasion of military service was later held to be included among such offenses.

late nineteenth century was succeeded by nationalist tendencies in many countries, which became even stronger in the decades between the two World Wars. The United States, Great Britain, Italy, and a majority of states accepted the fact of the naturalization of one of their citizens in a foreign country as an automatic release of the citizen from his former allegiance; but a number of other states, including France, Poland, and Russia, provided in their laws that naturalization did not cause loss of prior nationality unless the express consent of the state had been obtained or unless military service required by the law had been performed; other states again, including Austria, Sweden, and Japan, refused to naturalize aliens until they had obtained the consent of the state of which they were nationals.[52] The conflicting interests of states receiving immigrants and of states losing emigrants prevented the adoption of a uniform rule. The Hague Convention of 1930 failed to recognize expatriation as a fundamental right; and the establishment of totalitarian governments weakened the position of the individual in respect to the assertion of rights in his own name.[53]

In contrast with the inability of the Hague Conference of 1930 to secure a general agreement, the Inter-American Conference at Montevideo in 1933 adopted a Convention on Nationality of a progressive character, providing that naturalization carried with it the loss of nationality of origin and that naturalization, as well as the loss of it, affected the nationality only of the individual. Then, in 1948, the American Declaration of the Rights and Duties of Man included an article that every person has the right to change his nationality for that of any other country that is willing to grant its nationality to him.[54]

E. SPECIAL STATUS OF MARRIED WOMEN AND CHILDREN

By the common law of Great Britain and the United States the marriage of a woman to an alien did not operate to dissolve her native allegiance. In the case of Shanks v. Dupont, decided in 1830, it was held that an American woman who had married a British officer in 1781 and had moved to England in 1782 had not lost her citizenship by the fact of her marriage, although she had lost it by removal to Great

---

[52] The complexity of national legislation in the different countries may be seen in the Analysis of Laws given in Appendix No. 1 of the Harvard Draft. Article 13 of the Draft provides: "Except as otherwise provided in this convention, a state may naturalize a person who is a national of another state, and such person shall thereupon lose his prior nationality."

[53] The problem of "collective naturalization" presents distinct issues and it is so closely related to transfers of territory that it has been found advisable to discuss it in that connection. See below, pp. 427 ff.

[54] *Int. Conferences of Am. States*, 1933-1940, p. 108; *ibid.*, 1942-1954, p. 263.

Britain under the terms of the treaty of 1783.[55] This rule of the common law was modified by Great Britain in 1844 and again in 1870.[56] In the United States an act of Congress of 1855 followed the British law of 1844 in conferring citizenship upon an alien woman who should marry a citizen of the United States, but it remained unsettled whether by marriage to an alien an American woman lost her nationality.[57] In 1907 an act of Congress provided on the one hand that "any American woman who marries a foreigner shall take the nationality of her husband" and on the other hand that such a woman should resume her American citizenship upon the termination of the marriage relation, either by mere residence in the United States or by registration at a United States consulate.[58] The position thus taken by Great Britain and the United States had long been held by the majority of Continental and Latin American countries, the latter apparently influenced by the *Code Napoléon*.

The Cable Act.   The act of Congress known as the Cable Act,[59] approved September 22, 1922, marked a departure from both the policy of the United States and the general practice of other states. Adopted, it would appear, with the object of regulating the admission of women to suffrage by putting married women upon a footing independent of their husbands, it provided (1) that a woman should not acquire citizenship by marriage to a citizen of the United States or by the naturalization of her husband, but, if eligible to citizenship, must be personally naturalized under the conditions prescribed; (2) that a woman citizen of the United States should not cease to be a citizen by reason of marriage unless she made a formal renunciation of citizenship or unless she married an alien ineligible to citizenship. Women who had lost their citizenship by reason of marriage prior to the passage of the act might acquire citizenship by naturalization unless their husbands were in-

---

[55] 3 Peters 242 (1830). In reaching its conclusion on the first point the court relied upon the doctrine of "indelible allegiance." "Marriage with an alien, whether a friend or an enemy," said the court, "produces no dissolution of the native allegiance of the wife. It may change her civil rights, but it does not affect her political rights or privileges. The general doctrine is, that no persons can, by any act of their own, without the consent of the government, put off their allegiance and become aliens."

[56] First with respect to the marriage of an alien woman to a citizen and later with respect to the marriage of a British woman to an alien.

[57] See Van Dyne, *Citizenship of the United States*, § 55. Moore, *Digest*, Vol. III, § 408.

[58] 34 *Stat. at Large*, 1228. *U.S. Comp. Stat.*, 1918, § 3960. The constitutionality of the law was upheld in Mackenzie v. Hare, 239 U.S. 299 (1915), in which the court referred to the identity of husband and wife as "an ancient principle of our jurisprudence" and as having "purpose, if not necessity, in purely domestic policy" and "greater purpose and, it may be, necessity, in international policy." See Hudson, *Cases*, p. 297; Fenwick, *Cases*, p. 184. See also Hackworth, *Digest*, Vol. III, p. 251.

[59] *Stat. at Large*, 67th Congress, Vol. 42, No. 346. See also *Am. Journal*, Vol. 17 (1923), Supp., p. 52; Flournoy and Hudson, *op. cit.*, p. 608.

eligible.[60] The result, however, of the new legislation and of similar legislation in a number of other countries was that in certain cases married women lost the nationality of their native country without acquiring the nationality of their husbands, and in other cases objectionable situations of dual nationality were created. The conflict was between the principle of "family unity," adhered to by one group of states as the simplest rule, and the principle of the independent personal status of women irrespective of marriage.

The subject of the nationality of married women was taken up by the League of Nations Committee of Experts for the Progressive Codification of International Law, and a draft convention was submitted in 1926 which, *inter alia,* followed the rule providing that a married woman should not lose her original nationality unless by the law of her husband's state she acquired his nationality, and that if her husband's nationality changed during marriage she should not lose his former nationality without acquiring his new nationality.[61] The principle of the League Committee's draft was accepted at the Conference on the Codification of International Law held at The Hague in 1930, with the further provision that the naturalization of the husband during marriage should not involve a change in the nationality of the wife without her consent, and an added provision dealing with the recovery of the wife's nationality upon dissolution of the marriage.[62]

The Montevideo Convention. At the Seventh International Conference of American States, held at Montevideo in 1933, a Convention on the Nationality of Women was adopted, Article 1 of which provided: "There shall be no distinction based on sex as regards nationality, in their legislation or in their practice." [63] This was an agreement of far-reaching importance at the time, although limited to the states of the inter-American regional group. Later, the International Law Com-

---

[60] This last restriction was removed by an amendment of March 3, 1931. See also amendment of July 3, 1930, facilitating naturalization of native-born women who have lost citizenship by marriage prior to the Cable Act. See E. J. Hover, "Citizenship of Women in the United States," *Am. Journal,* Vol. 26 (1932), p. 700; Waltz, *The Nationality of Married Women.* Sections 310-312 of the Nationality Act of 1940 relaxed the requirements with respect to declaration of intention and period of residence.

[61] For the text, see *Am. Journal,* Vol. 23 (1929), Spec. Supp., p. 121. Compare Harvard Draft, Art. 19: "A woman who marries an alien shall, in the absence of a contrary election on her part, retain the nationality which she possessed before marriage, unless she becomes a national of the state of which her husband is a national and establishes or maintains a residence of a permanent character in the territory of that state."

[62] Convention on Certain Questions Relating to the Conflict of Nationality Laws, Arts. 8-11. *Am. Journal,* Vol. 24 (1930), Supp., p. 192. See also, A. N. Makarov, "La nationalité de la femme mariée," *Recueil des Cours,* Vol. 60 (1937-II), pp. 115-239.

[63] For the text, see *Int. Conferences of American States,* 1933-1940, p. 106.

mission at its first session in 1949 included the topic on its list selected for codification, together with that of statelessness; and at succeeding sessions in 1950 and 1951 the Commission undertook, at the request of the Economic and Social Council, to prepare drafts of conventions on both topics. A draft on the nationality of married persons was submitted to the Commission at its session in 1952, but the decision was reached that the question could only be considered as an integral part of the whole subject of nationality. In the meantime the Commission on the Status of Women, created by the General Assembly in 1946, drafted a Convention on the Nationality of Married Women, which was later approved by the General Assembly and opened for signature in 1957. It provides, *inter alia,* that neither the celebration nor the dissolution of marriage between a national and an alien shall have effect upon the nationality of the wife.[64]

Status of children. In states in which the rule of *jus soli* holds, exceptions of one kind or another are made in the case of children born to diplomatic officers and other public officials of foreign states. This general practice is confirmed by the Convention on Certain Questions relating to the Conflict of Nationality Laws adopted at The Hague in 1930. Special difficulties, due to the single operation of the principle of *jus sanguinis,* have arisen in connection with the nationality by birth of children of unknown parents and of foundlings and of children of illegitimate parentage, and numerous cases of statelessness have resulted.[65] The Hague Convention of 1930 provides that a child whose parents are both unknown shall have the nationality of the country of birth, that foundlings shall be presumed to have been born on the territory of the state in which they were found, and that in case an illegitimate child should lose its nationality of birth by reason of legitimation the loss should be conditional upon acquiring the nationality of another state.[66] The laws of most states provide that minor children acquire the new nationality of their parents when the latter are naturalized abroad, and this rule is accepted with qualification by the Hague Convention of 1930, with the provision that, in cases where the minor children do not acquire the nationality of their parents as a result of their parents' naturalization, they shall retain their existing nationality. Under the law of the United States a child acquiring citizenship by birth in the country may lose it if taken during minority to the country of its parents' origin where its parents resume their former allegiance; and in like manner it may lose citizenship acquired *jure sanguinis* when it fails to meet certain residence requirements, and it may lose citizenship acquired through

[64] As of October 31, 1964, the Convention had been ratified by twenty-nine states. For the political rights of women apart from nationality, see *Everyman's United Nations,* 7th ed., p. 321.

[65] See Harvard Draft, Arts. 7-9, and Comment.

[66] Arts. 12-16.

the naturalization of its parents when they become naturalized in another country and the child does not acquire residence in the United States upon attaining the age of twenty-three years.[67]

Query, if there were a convention between two countries governing the guardianship of infants and providing that, in the case of children of a nationality different from that of the state in which they resided, the national law of the child should be applied, would this convention remove the child from the general body of local law? In 1957, in proceedings brought by the Netherlands against Sweden, the International Court of Justice held that a Convention of 1902 to that effect had not been violated by a Swedish law on protective upbringing which involved compulsory education.[68]

F. STATELESSNESS

The problem of statelessness has become increasingly grave of recent years.[69] Not only have many persons become stateless by reason of the conflict of laws relating to nationality, or by reason of absence from their country, but many more have lost their nationality by reason of the deliberate act of the government of the state of their birth. Numerous Russians lost their nationality after the Revolution because they were unwilling to return to Russia or even to register themselves at a Russian consulate in the country of their residence. The Hague Convention on Certain Questions Relating to the Conflict of Nationality Laws, while recognizing in its preamble "that the ideal towards which the efforts of humanity should be directed in this domain is the abolition of all cases both of statelessness and of double nationality," contained few provisions that might have corrected the conditions leading to statelessness. Each state was left free to determine under its own law who were its nationals, and any question as to whether a person possessed the nationality of a particular state was to be determined in accordance

---

[67] On the first of these cases, see E. Borchard, *Am. Journal*, Vol. 30 (1936), p. 694. In the case of Perkins v. Elg. 307 U.S. 325 (1939), *Am. Journal*, Vol. 33 (1939), p. 773, it was held that Miss Elg, by returning to the United States upon attaining majority, had elected to retain her citizenship *jure soli*. On the loss of citizenship *jure sanguinis*, see Weedin v. Chin Bow, 274 U.S. 657 (1927), which turned upon an interpretation of a statute providing that citizenship acquired *jure sanguinis* should not "descend" to children whose fathers had never resided in the United States, the court holding that the residence of the father must commence before the birth of the son. Fenwick, *Cases*, p. 190. On loss of citizenship acquired by naturalization of parent, see Nationality Act of 1940, § 401.

[68] *I.C.J. Reports*, 1958, p. 55.

[69] On the general subject, see Seckler-Hudson, *Statelessness: With Special Reference to the United States;* J. P. A. François, "Le Problème des apatrides," *Recueil des Cours*, Vol. 53 (1935-III), pp. 287-375; L. W. Holborn, "The Legal Status of Political Refugees," *Am. Journal*, Vol. 32 (1938), p. 680; H. Fields, "Closing Immigration Throughout the World," *ibid.*, Vol. 26 (1932), p. 671; Weis, *Nationality and Statelessness in International Law* (1956).

with the law of that state.[70] Thus even had the convention been ratified by Germany there would have been nothing to prevent the denationalization and denaturalization of numerous persons on political grounds. As early as 1933 the Nazi Government revoked by collective decree the naturalization of all Jews who had been naturalized since August 1, 1914. Subsequent decrees authorized the denationalization of individual persons regarded as hostile to the Nazi regime. In 1935 decrees were issued distinguishing between citizens and nationals, and Jews were excluded from the first category. Finally in 1941 all Jews, without distinction, were denationalized. The result was to create a vast number of stateless persons, who, even when they were able to leave Germany, could not be assured of obtaining the nationality of the country of their refuge.[71]

It was to be expected, therefore, that the Commission on International Law would select the subject of nationality for codification, with chief attention to two problems: the nationality of married women and the elimination of statelessness. In respect to statelessness, at the request of the Economic and Social Council, the Commission prepared in 1953 two drafts, one on the elimination of statelessness and one on the reduction of statelessness, leaving it to the General Assembly to decide which one should be given preference. In 1959, an International Conference of Plenipotentiaries was held at Geneva, and in 1961 a second part of the Conference in New York, at which a Convention on the Reduction of Statelessness was opened for signature. By this Convention, both *jus sanguinis* and *jus soli* countries were required to grant nationality under certain circumstances to persons who would otherwise be stateless; and special provisions were adopted for persons who might lose their nationality by reason of a change in personal status.[72]

The problem of refugees.   Closely related to the problem of statelessness is the work of the United Nations High Commissioner for Refugees. Even before the adoption of the Charter in 1945, a Relief and Rehabilitation Administration was established (UNRRA) in 1943 which carried on relief activities until succeeded by the International Relief Organiza-

---

[70] Arts. 1, 2.

[71] In 1945, in its *Draft Declaration of the International Rights and Duties of Man*, the Inter-American Juridical Committee proposed, among other fundamental rights, the "Right to a Nationality," in the following terms: "Every person has the right to a nationality. No state may refuse to grant its nationality to persons born upon its soil of parents who are legitimately present in the country. No person may be deprived of his nationality of birth unless by his own free choice he acquires another nationality. Every person has the right to renounce the nationality of his birth, or a previously acquired nationality, upon acquiring the nationality of another state."

The denaturalization of persons upon grounds of religion or race must be distinguished from the cancellation of naturalization in consequence of disloyal acts. See Resolution XVII, on Subversive Activities, adopted at the Meeting of Foreign Ministers of the American Republics at Rio de Janeiro in 1942.

[72] *U.N. Yearbook*, 1961, p. 553.

tion (IRO) in 1946, which was in turn succeeded in 1951 by the Office of High Commissioner for Refugees under the direct responsibility of the General Assembly. The basic task of the Office is to organize, coordinate, and supervise international action on behalf of the refugees under its mandate, who, for fear of persecution on ground of race, religion, or political opinion, cannot return to their country of origin. In addition to earlier problems in Europe and Asia, new problems have arisen in Africa from the creation of new independent states.[73]

Nationality of business associations. The complex organization of the modern business association or corporation has made it difficult at times to determine the national character of such an association and has in consequence given rise to numerous controversies, particularly in respect to the status of such associations in time of war. The general principle holds that incorporated companies have the nationality of the state in which they are incorporated and unincorporated associations have the nationality of the state in which they are constituted or in which their governing body is normally located. The national character of the individual shareholders of a corporation does not normally affect the national character of the corporation itself, although it may be material in determining the nature of the activities of the corporation. In the case of Daimler Company v. Continental Tyre and Rubber Company,[74] the House of Lords held that a company incorporated in the United Kingdom might, in spite of its technical legal character, nevertheless assume an enemy character in time of war where its agents, as the persons *de facto* in control of its affairs, are resident in the enemy country or are acting under the instructions of enemy shareholders.[75] It may be observed that corporations, like natural persons, may have a dual or multiple nationality when the same persons are incorporated in different countries.

G. CONTROL OVER ACTS AND PROPERTY OF NATIONALS ABROAD

It is definitely accepted that the exercise of a state's jurisdiction over its citizens is strictly limited to territorial boundaries. Any attempt to extend the control of the state beyond those limits would be an encroachment upon the independence of another state and a serious infraction of international law. But this territorial restriction upon jurisdiction still leaves the state free to assert rights over its citizens which may be made effective if at any subsequent time they should return within the bound-

[73] For details of the recent activities of the Office, see *U.N. Yearbook*, 1961, pp. 331-342; 1962, pp. 354-361.

[74] [1916] 2 A. C. 307. Hudson, *Cases*, p. 311; Fenwick, *Cases*, p. 194.

[75] For criticism of the Daimler Case and discussion of the general subject, see A. D. McNair, "The National Character and Status of Corporations," *British Year Book, 1923-1924*, pp. 44-59; M. Travers, "La nationalité des sociétés commerciales," *Recueil des Cours*, Vol. 33 (1930-III), p. 5.

aries of the state. Hence while the enforcement of a particular law is a matter of actual physical control over the citizen within national boundaries, there is nothing to prevent the state, where there is no conflict of allegiances, from making claims of the widest variety upon its citizens and enforcing them in any way which does not involve the exercise of authority within the jurisdiction of another state.

In respect to the acts of citizens outside national boundaries the most frequent assertion of personal jurisdiction by the state is over the commission of crimes. The constitutional law of different states varies in this matter, some states asserting a right to punish their citizens for crimes wherever committed, other states, such as Great Britain and the United States, choosing to restrict their ordinary criminal jurisdiction to acts committed within their territorial boundaries. In the case of American Banana Co. v. United Fruit Co.,[76] decided in 1909, the Supreme Court of the United States refused to enforce the Sherman Anti-Trust Act against persons alleged to have violated the law in Panama and Costa Rica. On the other hand, it has been held constitutional for Congress to impose an income tax upon a citizen domiciled abroad in respect to real and personal property located abroad.[77] In the case of Blackmer v. United States,[78] it was further held that a citizen owes his government a duty to attend its courts and to give his testimony whenever properly summoned, and that a refusal to return from abroad to give such testimony may subject him to penalties of the law. No question of international law, said the court, arises with respect to such an exercise of authority.[79]

H. RESTRICTIONS UPON JURISDICTION OVER NATIONALS

Minorities treaties. The problems of territorial readjustment created by the First World War led to the imposition upon a number of states of special restrictions in the interest of protecting "minorities" which it was found impossible to eliminate in the redrawing of boundary lines. Precedent for these restrictions was found in the provisions of the Treaty of Berlin of 1878. In concluding treaties with Poland, Czechoslovakia, Yugoslavia, Rumania, Greece, Austria-Hungary, Bulgaria, and Turkey, the Principal Allied and Associated Powers stipulated that there should be just and equal treatment of their racial, religious, and linguistic minorities.[80] The scope of these separate treaty provisions was sub-

---

[76] 213 U.S. 347 (1909). Hudson, *Cases,* 1929 edit., p. 601.

[77] Cook v. Tait, 265 U.S. 47 (1924). Hudson, *Cases,* p. 555.

[78] 284 U.S. 421 (1932). Fenwick, *Cases,* p. 199; Briggs, *Cases,* p. 520; Hudson, *Cases,* p. 558.

[79] See Oppenheim, *International Law,* 4th ed., p. 281, as referred to by the court; 8th ed., p. 330.

[80] The texts of the first five treaties are to be found in the League of Nations *Treaty Series,* Nos. 6, 8, 13, 17, 20; for Austria, Treaty of St.-Germain, Arts. 64-69; for Hungary, Treaty of Trianon, Arts. 54-60; for Bulgaria, Treaty of Neuilly, Arts. 49-57; for Turkey, Treaty of Lausanne, Arts. 37-45.

stantially the same, provision being made for equality before the law and equality of civil and political rights for all nationals of whatever race, language, or religion, including freedom of organization for religious and educational purposes and opportunity of elementary education for children in their own languages in districts where the minority formed a considerable part of the population. The provisions of these minority treaties were held to constitute "obligations of international concern" and they were placed under the guarantee of the League of Nations, and the Council of the League was given authority to take action in regard to complaints of infractions of the treaties. A special procedure was devised by the League for dealing with petitions presented by minority groups. Moreover, disputes between the contracting states were to be referred to the Permanent Court of International Justice.[81]

The application of the provisions of these minorities treaties gave rise to numerous controversies in consequence of the sharp restriction they imposed upon the jurisdiction of the state subject to them. In an Advisory Opinion on the German Settlers in Poland,[82] given in 1923, the Permanent Court of International Justice defined the functions which minorities treaties were intended to fulfil, holding that the provisions of the minorities treaty guaranteed the same treatment and security "in law and in fact." This interpretation led the Court, in the Advisory Opinion on the Minority Schools in Albania,[83] given in 1935, to hold that an Albanian law abolishing private schools in that country was not justified by the fact that it constituted a general measure applicable to the majority as well as to the minority. "The idea," said the Court, "underlying the treaties for the protection of minorities is to secure for certain elements incorporated in a State, the population of which differs from them in race, language or religion, the possibility of living peaceably alongside that population and cooperating amicably with it, while at the same time preserving the characteristics which distinguish them from the majority, and satisfying the ensuing special needs."

While the protection of alien minorities in the countries in which they have had their historical and permanent residence met with a favorable response from the members of the League of Nations, the American states, recipients of various races emigrating from their home countries, have insisted strongly that such aliens should not be allowed to claim in their new homes the status of minorities. A declaration on "Foreign Minorities," announcing that policy, adopted at the Lima Conference of

[81] The literature of the subject of minorities under the protection of the League of Nations is extensive. See, in particular, Stone, *International Guarantees of Minority Rights;* Mair, *The Protection of Minorities; Ten Years of World Coöperation,* Chap. XI; Macartney, *National States and National Minorities;* Azcárate, *The League of Nations and National Minorities;* A. Mandelstam, "La protection des minorités," *Recueil des Cours,* Vol. 1 (1923), pp. 367-517; Janowsky, *Nationalities and National Minorities.*

[82] Series B, No. 6. Hudson, *World Court Reports,* Vol. I, p. 208.

[83] Series A/B, No. 64. *Ibid.,* Vol. III, p. 484.

1938, was reaffirmed at Rio de Janeiro in 1942 as a "principle of American public law," and again reaffirmed at the Conference at Mexico City in 1945.[84]

Treaties following the Second World War. The treaties between the Allied Powers and the satellite states following the Second World War contain broad provisions looking to the protection of all persons without distinction as to race, sex, language, or religion in respect to the enjoyment of human rights and fundamental freedoms. The treaties do not, however, make provision for the special ethnic privileges granted to minorities by the treaties following the First World War, no provision, for example, being made for conducting schools in the language of the minority or for permitting the use of the minority language before the courts.[85]

The obligations thus imposed, while restricting the jurisdiction of each of the states subject to them, and thus constituting a temporary inequality in their international status, may be expected to extend in due time to all states when the principle of respect for human rights and fundamental freedoms contained in Article 1 of the Charter of the United Nations takes shape in a general convention. It is not expected that such a convention will be considered as intervention on the part of the United Nations "in matters which are essentially within the domestic jurisdiction of any state," under the terms of Article 2.[86]

I. JURISDICTION OVER ALIENS

The presence of aliens within the territory of a state has become of recent years one of the most frequent occasions of international controversy. While on the one hand the rapid growth of international commercial relations in modern times has resulted in greatly increasing the number of aliens in certain states offering opportunities for labor and for business enterprise, on the other hand the enlargement of governmental functions and the changing social policies of certain states in

---

[84] For the Lima Declaration, see *Int. Conferences of American States,* 1933-1940, p. 256. For the Rio de Janeiro declaration, and the Mexico City resolution, see *ibid.,* 1942-1954, pp. 32, 103.

[85] See Treaty with Italy, Art. 15: "Italy shall take all measures necessary to secure to all persons under Italian jurisdiction, without distinction as to race, sex, language or religion, the enjoyment of human rights and of the fundamental freedoms, including freedom of expression, of press and publication, of religious worship, of political opinion and of public meeting." Similar provisions occur in the treaties with Bulgaria, Finland, Hungary, and Rumania.

The question whether the existing system of protecting minorities was the correct solution of the problem was widely discussed, some writers maintaining that it should be continued, others that it was essentially unsound. See J. L. Kunz, "The Future of International Law for the Protection of Minorities," *Am. Journal,* Vol. 39 (1945), p. 89.

[86] See above, p. 152.

respect to individual rights of person and of property have given rise
to new issues for the solution of which the precedents of the past have
proved inadequate. Here perhaps more than in any other field, international law is in a state of transition, and rules must be laid down
tentatively and generalizations made with reservations. A preliminary
issue concerns the right of the state to exclude aliens from its territorial
domain or to expel them when they have entered—questions not so much
of jurisdiction as of national independence in the larger sense.

The exclusion of aliens. It is a well-established general principle
that a state may forbid the entrance of aliens into its territory, or admit
them only in such cases as commend themselves to its judgment.[87] The
right of total exclusion is, however, more theoretical than real. As a
practical issue, no state can be assumed to be desirous of cutting itself
off from all intercourse with the outside world, unless, perhaps, obsessed
with an extreme ideological conception of impending conflict. When it
was asserted by the older jurists that there was a legal "right of intercourse" as between states, all that was meant, consistent with the law,
was that by custom some degree of commercial and social intercourse
had come to be regarded as a normal condition of modern international
life. This is quite a different matter from an obligation on the part of a
particular state to admit all or any of those who only come with the
intention of becoming permanent residents. The partial exclusion of
alien immigrants by the United States has been acquiesced in by other
states in so far as it has been applied to all alike. Total exclusion of
immigrants may at any time become a necessity for those states of the
Western Hemisphere which feel that the number of immigrants to their
territories has exceeded the capacity for beneficial assimilation. Under
such circumstances there would seem to be no doubt that the general
principle of the right of exclusion might be given practical application
without giving rise to legal grounds of protest from other states.

Discrimination against particular countries. The controversial issue,
however, has arisen in connection with the discrimination shown against
the citizens of particular states. Exclusion upon purely personal grounds,
such as was put into effect by the United States laws prior to 1921,[88]
being directed against the citizens of all states indiscriminately, presented
no international issue. The exclusion of certain types of immigrants, such
as idiots and paupers, was not contested, as being a purely domestic
question. The United States, however, undertook by successive acts of

[87] The rule was stated clearly by Vattel in 1758. *Droit des gens*, Eng. trans., Bk.
II, §§ 94, 100. The dictum in the case of Nishimura Ekiu v. United States, 142 U.S.
651 (1892), is often quoted: "It is an accepted maxim of international law, that
every sovereign nation has the power, as inherent in sovereignty, and essential to self-
preservation, to forbid the entrance of foreigners within its dominions, or to admit
them only in such cases and upon such conditions as it may see fit to prescribe."

[88] For the earlier laws, see Moore, *Digest*, Vol. IV, § 562.

Congress, beginning in 1882, wholly to exclude Chinese immigrants,[89] as well as the natives of other specified sections of the continent of Asia.[90] By a treaty of 1880 [91] China had agreed to the regulation or temporary suspension by the United States of Chinese immigration, but it was not until 1894 that China, by treaty, acquiesced in the absolute prohibition of the entrance of Chinese laborers into the United States for a period of ten years from the ratification of the treaty.[92] Agitation in the United States for the exclusion of Japanese immigrants resulted in the conclusion in 1907 of the Root-Takahira Agreement, known as the "gentleman's agreement," by which Japan undertook itself to prevent the immigration of Japanese laborers to the United States.[93] By an act of May 26, 1924, however, the Japanese were directly excluded under the head of persons "ineligible to citizenship." [94] It should be observed that in the cases both of China and of Japan the right of entry into the United States which the two states might have claimed for their citizens was merely an inferential right following from the principle of the equality of states. To exclude all aliens impartially raises no issue of discrimination; to exclude the citizens of a particular state denies to that state a right accorded to others. The exclusion of certain races as being unassimilable is, it would appear, a political rather than a legal question.

Quota laws. In more recent years the United States has put into effect a method of regulation known as the "quota system," the effects of which may be in fact discriminatory without thereby giving rise to valid legal protest. The Immigration Act of 1924, in undertaking to restrict immigration in a way designed to maintain the existing racial composition of the United States, affects adversely immigration from Southeastern Europe; but the discrimination is indirect and due to conditions which do not reflect upon the character of the immigrants from that particular area.[95] In Brazil the Constitutions of 1934 and 1937 both incorporated provisions for the quota system; [96] and subsequent decree-laws granted special privileges to Portuguese. Under the Constitution of 1946 the matter is left to be regulated by ordinary law.

The expulsion of aliens. The right of a state to expel aliens from its territories for reasons bearing upon the public welfare of the state is

---

[89] For the provisions of the several Acts, see *Treaty, Laws, and Rules Governing the Admission of Chinese,* Department of Labor, Bureau of Immigration, p. 1917.

[90] Act of February 5, 1917; 39 *Stat. at Large,* p. 875.

[91] *Treaties and Conventions,* Vol. I, p. 237. See the Chinese Exclusion Case, Chae Chan Ping v. United States, 130 U.S. 581 (1889) [Fenwick, *Cases,* p. 205; Hudson, *Cases,* p. 1041], where the exclusion act of 1888 was held to overrule existing treaties.

[92] *Treaties and Conventions,* Vol. I, p. 241.

[93] See Hackworth, *Digest,* Vol. III, p. 757.

[94] *Ibid.,* Vol. III, p. 761. For comment, see *Am. Journal,* Vol. 18 (1924), p. 520.

[95] See Hackworth, *Digest,* Vol. III, pp. 741 ff.; Hyde, *Int. Law,* Vol. I, § 60A; A. W. Parker, "United States Immigration Act of 1924," *Am. Journal,* Vol. 18 (1924), p. 738; Vol. 19, p. 23.

[96] See Accioly, *Tratado,* Vol. I, No. 697A.

well established; but in the exercise of this right there must be, as in the case of the admission of aliens, no discrimination against the citizens of a particular foreign state as such. It would appear that the foreign government has a right to inquire into the reason for the expulsion of its citizens.[97] Precedents exist, chiefly in the relations between the Great Powers and small and unstable states, showing the exaction by foreign governments of an indemnity for the arbitrary expulsion of their subjects. Great Britain obtained from Nicaragua in 1895 an indemnity for the expulsion of twelve British subjects who had been arrested and expelled for alleged participation in the Mosquito Rebellion. In the same Blue-fields Case the United States, relying chiefly upon the treaty of 1867, demanded that the two American prisoners be informed of the charges against them and of the evidence in support of the charges, admitting, however, the right of Nicaragua to expel them if the charges were true.[98] In 1920 the United States deported to Russia, on the ship *Buford*, a group of anarchists and radical socialists who had emigrated from that country to the United States and whose activities on behalf of their political principles were considered detrimental to the welfare of the United States.[99] In 1926 the Government of Panama decided to expel one R. O. Marsh and others on account of their subversive activities among the San Blas Indians, and the United States, upon receiving a request for its cooperation, saw no reason why Panama should not "handle the matter independently." A decree of expulsion was accordingly issued.[100]

Status of resident aliens. By international law, as has been seen, each state is left free to concede to aliens resident within its territory such measure of rights, apart from the protection of life and property, as it may see fit to confer upon them. Most states, however, in modern times have come to concede to aliens substantially the same civil privileges, as distinct from political rights, which are enjoyed by citizens of the state. These privileges include the right to hold, inherit, and transmit real property, the right to contract, the right to practice the professions and other licensed occupations, and the right of religious worship and of freedom of speech. The earlier *droit d'aubaine*, a relic of feudal times,

[97] See cases in Moore, *Digest*, Vol. IV, § 551. In Ben Tillett's case between Great Britain and Belgium the arbitrator held that Belgium was justified in the means taken to ensure the expulsion in 1896 of one who had come from England to foment a strike of dock workers. Hudson, *Cases*, p. 1056; Fenwick, *Cases*, p. 210.

[98] Moore, *Digest, loc. cit.* In 1888 the United States demanded an indemnity from Guatemala for the expulsion, by executive decree, before the completion of judicial process, of an American citizen, Hollander, who had been arrested upon a charge of malicious libel and forgery. *Ibid.* See also the decision in the Boffolo case before the Italian-Venezuelan Commission in 1903. Ralston, *Venezuelan Arbitrations*, p. 699.

[99] The deportations were in accordance with an act of May 10, 1920.

[100] See Hackworth, *Digest*, Vol. III, p. 698. On the general subject of expulsion, see C. J. B. de Boeck, "L'Expulsion et les difficultés internationales qu'en soulève la pratique," *Recueil des Cours*, Vol. 18 (1927-III), pp. 447-647.

in accordance with which the sovereign confiscated to the use of the state the movable and immovable property of deceased foreigners, had largely disappeared by the end of the eighteenth century.[101] Under the common law of Great Britain and of the United States an alien could take lands by purchase, *i.e.* by will or by deed, but not by descent, *i.e.* not by intestate succession; [102] but these restrictions have now been largely removed. In the United States the restrictions imposed by a number of the individual States of the Union have been rendered inoperative by treaties entered into by the United States with other countries.[103] In many countries aliens are forbidden to own land within a certain distance of the national boundaries. In Brazil and other countries aliens are forbidden to operate mines and water-power systems, concessions being granted only to nationals. The Brazilian Constitution of 1946 denies to aliens the right to own newspapers and radio stations, nor can aliens be shareholders of corporations conducting such enterprises; [104] but the restriction of the liberal professions to native Brazilians, prescribed by the Constitution of 1937, has now been abolished.

Discrimination against particular aliens. On rare occasions states have found it necessary to discriminate against the citizens of a particular state and to deny them privileges granted to other aliens. Such a case arose in 1906 when the city of San Francisco undertook to segregate Japanese students in separate schools. The United States argued, in answer to the protest of Japan, that there existed a reasonable basis for the alleged discrimination, and that the action taken did not necessarily reflect upon the character of the Japanese citizen and by inference upon the honor of Japan.[105] In 1913 a more acute issue arose in connection with the protest of Japan against the discriminatory character of California laws prohibiting aliens who were not "eligible to citizenship" from owning and transmitting real property, except in so far as the right was secured to them by treaty. Since Japanese citizens were unable to become naturalized, they were thus limited to the rights granted by a treaty of 1911, which fell short of the privileges enjoyed by other aliens. The United States urged in defense of the law that it was the result

[101] The practice was vigorously condemned by Vattel in *Droit des gens,* Eng. trans., Bk. II, § 112.

[102] See Fairfax's Devisee v. Hunter's Lessee, 7 Cranch 603 (1813).

[103] For instances, see Moore, *Digest,* Vol. IV, §§ 544-545. In the case of Traux v. Raich, 239 U.S. 33 (1915) [Fenwick, *Cases,* p. 214; Hudson, *Cases,* p. 1066], it was held as a point of constitutional law that a law of Arizona discriminating against aliens in respect to opportunities of employment was in violation of the Fourteenth Amendment. In Jordan v. Tashiro, 278 U.S. 123 (1928) [Hudson, *Cases,* p. 1070; Fenwick, *Cases,* p. 221], it was held that a treaty between the United States and Japan should be interpreted liberally so as to secure to the Japanese respondents the right to construct and operate a hospital.

[104] Art. 160.

[105] Hackworth, *Digest,* Vol. III, p. 755.

rather of local economic conditions than of direct racial discrimination; but Japan refused to acquiesce in the justice of the explanation.[106] Additional legislation was enacted by California in 1920, with fresh protest from Japan.[107]

Domiciled aliens. International law recognizes a distinction between the status of those aliens who are merely transient visitors in a foreign country and those who have established a permanent residence there with apparent intention of remaining indefinitely. Not only must domiciled aliens obey the local laws and pay the normal taxes imposed by the state, whether upon person or upon property; but should the necessity arise they may be called upon by the state to perform such public duties as police and militia service, as distinct from military service, as well as to submit to special measures, such as quarantine regulations, restricting their personal liberty and the enjoyment of their property in the interest of the public welfare. Domicile thus creates a sort of qualified or temporary allegiance.[108] A delicate question is presented when the state in which the alien is domiciled goes to war with the state of which he is citizen. In such a case, while the alien may not be drafted into military service, he is at the same time bound not to contribute by an overt act to the success of the state of his nationality; and he may be punished for high treason and may be subjected to other penalties imposed by state law upon such offense.[109]

J. LIMITATIONS UPON CRIMINAL JURISDICTION OVER ALIENS

We have seen that a state may exercise personal jurisdiction over its nationals for acts committed abroad and may make its jurisdiction effective when such nationals return again within the jurisdiction of the state. Can a similar jurisdiction be exercised with regard to an alien for an act committed abroad when such alien happens to come subsequently within the territorial jurisdiction of the state? The question has given rise to much controversy. Acts of the alien not directly injurious to the state or to its citizens may be excluded from consideration. What of acts such as forgery or treasonable plotting directly injurious to the state? Con-

---

[106] See *Am. Journal*, Vol. 8 (1914), p. 571. For the text of the California law, see *ibid.*, Supp., p. 177. For cases in illustration of the application of the law, see Hackworth, *Digest*, Vol. III, pp. 683 ff.

[107] See *Am. Journal*, Vol. 15 (1921), p. 55; Vol. 16 (1922), p. 420.

[108] See Carlisle v. United States, 16 Wallace 147 (1873), where the court held that certain domiciled aliens who had given aid and comfort to the Confederacy were guilty of high treason; and see the case of "Lord Haw Haw," below, p. 324.

[109] In the case of De Jager v. Attorney-General of Natal, L. R. App. Cas., 326 (1907), a British court held guilty of high treason a resident of Natal who during the occupation of that country by the Boer army served in its ranks. Hudson, *Cases*, p. 1060.

tinental jurists generally assert the right to punish in such cases.[110] What of acts which although committed abroad take effect within national territory? In a case in dispute between the United States and Mexico, the latter country attempted in 1886 to punish one Cutting for a libel published in a Texan newspaper against a Mexican citizen then in Mexico. While a demand by the United States for the release of Cutting was refused, the Mexican plaintiff withdrew his action and Cutting was released without criminal prosecution.[111] The case of the *Lotus*,[112] decided in 1927, brought this question of jurisdiction before the Permanent Court of International Justice and contributed much valuable discussion upon it. A French steamship, the *Lotus*, collided with a Turkish steamship, the *Boz-Kourt*, on the open sea with loss of life to Turkish citizens on the latter vessel. Upon the arrival of the *Lotus* at Constantinople, the French officer of the watch was prosecuted and sentenced to imprisonment. The resulting dispute between France and Turkey was referred to the Permanent Court, which held by a majority vote that the criminal proceedings instituted by Turkey were not in conflict with international law, since the act of the French officer "produced its effects on the Turkish vessel and consequently in a place assimilated to Turkish territory."

The conviction of William Joyce, popularly known as "Lord Haw Haw," by the British Government for high treason was upheld by the House of Lords in 1945.[113] Joyce, although born in the United States, resided in England between 1921 and 1939, at which time he applied for a passport, describing himself as a British subject born in Galway, Ireland. In September, 1939, he entered the service of the German Radio Company of Berlin as an announcer of British news. The House of Lords held that the accused while "not in law a British subject," yet in obtaining possession of a British passport, in which he described himself as a British subject, he had "by his own act . . . maintained the bond which while he was within the realm bound him to his Sovereign."

The Eichmann case. The trial of Adolf Eichmann before the Jerusalem District Court of Israel in 1961 involved the question of whether the abduction of the accused in violation of the jurisdiction of Argentina was contrary to international law, which would preclude the jurisdic-

---

[110] In a report presented to the League of Nations Codification Committee in 1926 the conclusion was reached that the diversity of practice among states was too great to permit the formulation of a general rule on the subject. *Am. Journal,* Vol. 20 (1926), Spec. Supp., pp. 253 ff. See also W. E. Beckett, "The Exercise of Criminal Jurisdiction over Foreigners," *British Year Book,* Vol. VI (1925), p. 44.

[111] Fenwick, *Cases,* p. 227, reproduced from Moore, *Report on Extraterritorial Crime and the Cutting Case.*

[112] Series A, No. 10. Fenwick, *Cases,* p. 232; Bishop, *Cases,* p. 443; Briggs, *Cases,* p. 3; Hudson, *Cases,* p. 677.

[113] Joyce v. Director of Public Prosecutions. House of Lords, December 18, 1945. *Am. Journal,* Vol. 40 (1946), p. 663.

tion of the Court to try the case, and whether the accused might be tried for acts outside the jurisdiction of Israel, committed against persons who were not Israeli citizens and in pursuance of orders of a foreign country. The Court held that the offenses were against the law of all mankind, thus conferring universality of jurisdiction; that the defense of "act of State" had been rejected by the Military Tribunal at Nuremberg; and that the violation of international law involved in the abduction of the accused was an offense between the two countries and did not limit the jurisdiction of the Court with respect to the individual abducted. The accused was sentenced to death.[114]

Special exemption of aliens from jurisdiction in non-Christian states. During the Middle Ages it was common for commercial towns to concede to foreign merchants the privilege of residing in separate parts of the town and being governed by their own domestic laws. This privilege died out in Europe with the growth of the principle of territorial sovereignty; but it continued to be recognized in Turkey, where, because of the religious character of the Mohammedan law, there were special reasons for permitting foreign residents to remain subject to the laws of their own country.[115] A system of "extraterritorial jurisdiction," based partly upon custom and partly upon treaties of unilateral obligation, known as "capitulations," was thus developed, in accordance with which cases relating to foreign citizens were tried before diplomatic or consular courts operating in accordance with the laws of the several states.[116] During the nineteenth century the system was extended to other non-Christian states whose customs and legal systems differed radically from those of Europe. Japan succeeded in releasing itself in 1899 from the limitations imposed upon its sovereignty by the exemption of aliens from its local jurisdiction. Upon the outbreak of war in 1914 Turkey announced the abrogation of the capitulations, which, it asserted, restricted its sovereignty. At the close of the war the capitulations were temporarily renewed; but by the Treaty of Lausanne of 1923 the contracting parties accepted their "complete abolition." [117] The United States acceded to the abolition in a separate treaty signed in 1931.[118] In Egypt a special system of Mixed Courts dealing with civil and commercial cases was established in 1876, in accordance with which the Egyptian Government appointed a body of judges partly native and

[114] For the text of the decision, see *Am. Journal*, Vol. 56 (1962), p. 805. For comment, H. Silving, "In re Eichmann: A Dilemma of Law and Morality," *Am. Journal*, Vol. 55 (1961), p. 307.

[115] For the historical background, see Brown, *Foreigners in Turkey: Their Juridical Status*, Chap. I. See also Dainese v. Hale, 91 U.S. 13 (1875); Hudson, *Cases*, p. 703.

[116] On the general subject of extraterritorial jurisdiction, see Brown, *op. cit.*, Chap. II; Hackworth, *Digest*, Vol. II, pp. 493 ff.; Hyde, *Int. Law*, Vol. II, pp. 849 ff., where an elaborate bibliography may be found.

[117] Art. 28, treaty of July 24, 1923.

[118] For the text, see *Am. Journal*, Vol. 28 (1934), Supp., p. 129.

partly foreign, the latter being nominated by the respective foreign
capitulatory governments and forming a majority of the court.[119] In
1937 a convention was signed at Montreux declaring the "Complete
abolition in all respects of capitulations in Egypt"; but at the same
time provision was made for a transition period of ten years during which
the Mixed Court of Appeal and the Mixed Tribunals were to be maintained.[120] Extraterritorial rights were terminated in Iran by unilateral
action of the government in 1927.[121] For many years China complained
of the abuses attending the enjoyment by foreigners of extraterritorial
rights; and at the close of the Washington Conference of 1921-1922 a
resolution was adopted by the participating powers looking to the promotion of legislative and judicial reforms in China which would warrant
them in relinquishing their rights.[122] It was not, however, until 1943
that the United States signed with China, at Washington, the Treaty for
the Relinquishment of Extraterritorial Rights, and on the same day a
treaty to the same effect was signed between Great Britain and China
at Chungking.[123]

K. THE CRIME OF GENOCIDE

The limitation imposed upon the jurisdiction of states by the Universal
Declaration of Human Rights and the collateral agreements associated
with it have already been described in connection with the status of the
individual as a subject of international law.[124] More in the nature of a
minority treaty, but looking not positively to the upholding of individual
fundamental human rights but rather negatively to the punishment of
criminal acts directed against a group, was the resolution taken by the
General Assembly at its first meeting in 1946. So shocked were the sig-

[119] For details, see Scott, *The Law Affecting Foreigners in Egypt*, rev. ed.; J. Y.
Brinton, "The Mixed Courts of Egypt," *Am. Journal*, Vol. 20 (1926), p. 670.
[120] For the text, see *Am. Journal*, Vol. 34 (1940), Supp., p. 201. In 1949 France
filed a complaint with the International Court of Justice against measures taken by
Egypt against French nationals alleged to be in violation of the Montreux Convention. The case was, however, removed from the Court's list upon notice subsequently
given to the Court by France to the effect that the measures complained of had been
withdrawn.
[121] See Hackworth, *Digest*, Vol. II, p. 532.
Extraterritorial rights enjoyed by the United States in Siam were surrendered by a
treaty of 1920. See F. B. Sayre, "The Passing of Extraterritoriality in Siam," *Am.
Journal*, Vol. 22 (1928), p. 70; Hackworth, *Digest*, Vol. II, p. 532.
For the abolition of capitulatory rights in Palestine, Syria, and Iraq, see Hackworth,
Digest, Vol. II, pp. 517 ff.
[122] See *Am. Journal*, Vol. 16 (1922), Supp., p. 76; H. S. Quigley, "Extraterritoriality in China," *Am. Journal*, Vol. 20 (1926), p. 46; M. Bishop, "American Extraterritorial Jurisdiction in China," *ibid.*, p. 281; Keeton, *The Development of Extraterritoriality in China*.
[123] For the text of the treaty with the United States, see Dept. of State *Bulletin*,
Vol. VIII, p. 238. For comment, see Q. Wright, "The End of Extraterritoriality in
China," *Am. Journal*, Vol. 37 (1943), p. 286.
[124] See above, p. 152.

natories of the Charter at the inhuman efforts of the Nazi Government during the war to exterminate the Jews that on December 10, 1946, the General Assembly, by unanimous resolution, declared that genocide was "a crime under international law" for which the perpetrators, whether private individuals or public officials, were punishable.[125] Two years later, on December 9, 1948, the General Assembly adopted the Convention on the Prevention and Punishment of the Crime of Genocide, defining what should constitute acts of genocide and providing procedure for their punishment.[126] The acts defined consist in killing or causing bodily harm or inflicting on the group conditions of life calculated to bring about its destruction; and it makes public officials as well as private persons punishable for the crime.

Severe as are the terms of the convention, perhaps because of their very severity, it entrusts the punishment primarily to the municipal courts of the countries concerned; but while the enforcement of the convention is thus weakened, any failure on the part of the country to prevent and suppress the acts may be reported to the International Court of Justice and, as in the case of the Universal Declaration of Human Rights, the intervention of the Court could not be considered as encroaching upon the domestic jurisdiction of the state concerned.[127]

---

[125] For the text of the resolution, see *Am. Journal,* Vol. 41 (1947), p. 145, with comment by R. Lemkin. For details of its adoption, see *U.N. Yearbook,* 1946-1947, p. 255.

[126] For the text of the convention, see *Am. Journal,* Vol. 45 (1951), Supp., p. 7.

[127] For comment on the convention, see G. A. Finch, "The Genocide Convention," and J. L. Kunz, "The United Nations Convention on Genocide," *Am. Journal,* Vol. 43 (1949), pp. 732, 738.

CHAPTER XIV

The International Responsibility

of the State for the Protection

of Resident Aliens

A. GENERAL PRINCIPLES

In no field of international law have more highly controversial questions arisen than in that which involves the relations between the state and citizens of foreign states.[1] These relations may be divided into two general classes: those of resident aliens who are living within the jurisdiction of the state and are exercising therein the normal commercial and social activities of citizens of the state itself; and on the other hand those of aliens with whom the state has entered into special contractual relations for the loan of money or for the performance of particular services. The two classes of cases present different legal issues, but it is common to group them together because of certain points of contact between them.[2]

---

[1] On the general subject of the responsibility of the state in relation to aliens, see Borchard, *Diplomatic Protection of Citizens Abroad;* "The 'Minimum Standard' of the Treatment of Aliens," *Proceedings,* Am. Soc. Int. Law, 1939, pp. 51 ff.; "The 'Committee of Experts' at the Lima Conference," *Am. Journal,* Vol. 33 (1939), pp. 269 ff.; Eagleton, *Responsibility of States in International Law;* Harvard Research, *Draft Conventions on Nationality, Responsibility of States, Territorial Waters;* Dunn, *The Protection of Nationals;* Freeman, *The International Responsibility of States for Denial of Justice;* Whiteman, *Damages in International Law;* Feller, *The Mexican Claims Commissions;* García-Amador, *Principios de Derecho Internacional que Rigen la Responsabilidad;* Jessup, *A Modern Law of Nations,* Chap. V; L. B. Sohn and R. R. Baxter, "Responsibility of States for Injuries to the Economic Interests of Aliens," *Am. Journal,* Vol. 55 (1961), p. 545, containing draft convention and explanatory introduction.

[2] The subject of the responsibility of the state in relation to aliens is frequently treated under the title of "International Claims," where the subject is approached from the point of view of the state making the claim on behalf of its citizen rather than from the point of view of the state against which the claim is brought. The rights of the former and the obligations of the latter are, however, obviously correlative.

Protection of resident aliens. The advantages as well as the needs of commercial and social intercourse have resulted in recent years in the presence in practically every state of a large number of aliens. We have seen that the state itself is the judge of the extent of the civil privileges which they may be permitted to enjoy in common with the citizens of the state, privileges which in general represent the purpose of their presence within the state.[3] But over and above these privileges there are certain fundamental rights of person and of property which accompany the individual alien wherever he goes as a part of his human inheritance.[4] The privileges may be revoked; but the fundamental rights remain. The question then arises, what is the scope of these fundamental rights, and what is the responsibility of the state to see that they are respected by its own officers and that they are protected against the illegal acts of in-dividuals? Putting the question in terms of the relations between states, under what circumstances may the state of which the alien is a national intervene in his behalf when it believes that his fundamental rights have not been duly respected and protected by the foreign state, and what measure of redress may it claim for him in the particular case? Is the redress qualified by the treatment accorded by the foreign state to its own citizens?

Normal position of the alien. Under ordinary conditions a citizen of one state coming within the jurisdiction of another state, whether as a transient visitor or as a more or less permanent resident, may make no claim to a favored status. His substantive rights are the rights of the citizens of the country, less those special civil and political rights reserved to citizens. His procedural rights are in like manner those of the citizens of the country. If a wrong is done to him he expects to ap-peal to the same law for redress and to have access to the same courts that are open to the nationals of the country. His rights of personal security and his personal liberty are as sacred as those of the citizen; his property rights, and his rights under contract, limited as they may be, are entitled to the same protection of the law. If his rights are violated he has access to the courts of the state for redress upon the same footing as if he were a citizen.[5] What if the law itself is flagrantly oppressive, or openly discriminatory against the alien, or is administered in an unjust manner? What if the redress to which he is entitled under the law when his rights are violated should be denied by a flagrantly unjust decision of the courts or by delays equivalent to an unjust decision? What if in being prosecuted for a violation of the law on his own part he is denied due process of law or given a sentence out of all proportion to the gravity

---

[3] See above, p. 318.

[4] See above, pp. 152 ff.

[5] The question of the exhaustion of local remedies has given rise to controversy. For comment, see D. R. Mummery, "The Content of the Duty to Exhaust Local Judicial Remedies," *Am. Journal,* Vol. 58 (1964), p. 389.

of the offense committed? In such cases of "denial of justice" the treatment of the alien ceases to be a question of municipal law, and it may become the occasion for the assertion by his home state of an international right to secure proper redress for him.[6]

"Denial of justice." The term "denial of justice" may be taken in a broad sense to indicate a failure on the part of the authorities of the government either to provide adequate means of redress to the alien when his substantive rights have been violated or, when the alien himself has violated the law, to observe due process of law in bringing him to trial and determining his guilt. But the term is not a strictly technical one, some writers limiting it to include acts of the judiciary only, or of the judiciary and of administrative officers, while others extend it to include all forms of internationally illegal treatment of aliens.[7] The definition of the Harvard Research Draft appears to exclude the violation of the substantive rights of the alien, but interprets broadly the violation of procedural rights: "A state is responsible if an injury to an alien results from a denial of justice. Denial of justice exists when there is a denial, unwarranted delay or obstruction of access to courts, gross deficiency in the administration of judicial or remedial process, failure to provide those guarantees which are generally considered indispensable to the proper administration of justice, or a manifestly unjust judgment. An error of a national court which does not produce manifest injustice is not a denial of justice." [8] The term is so well established that it would seem desirable to retain it and define it as above, rather than to avoid its use altogether.

An international standard of justice. The controversial aspect of the problem of the responsibility of the state in relation to aliens has arisen from the claim on the part of certain governments and jurists that the alien, coming into the state of his own free will, is entitled to no better treatment than that which is accorded to citizens of the state itself. This doctrine of "equality of treatment" does not mean that the alien is to share in all of the privileges of citizens, but merely that such rights as the law permits him to enjoy will be protected as would similar rights

[6] The term "diplomatic protection" is regularly used to indicate action on behalf of the alien by the state of which he is a national. Up to the time such action is taken the question is a domestic one between the alien and the state in which the injury takes place. The term "diplomatic intervention" is used by certain Latin American writers to describe the unlawful interference of a state on behalf of its citizens abroad.

[7] For the wide variety of meanings attached to the term "denial of justice," see Freeman, *op. cit.*, Chaps. V-VII; O. L. Lissitzyn, "The Meaning of the Term Denial of Justice in International Law," *Am. Journal*, Vol. 30 (1936), pp. 632 ff.; Hackworth, *Digest*, Vol. V, p. 526; Feller, *op. cit.*, p. 129; De Visscher, "Le deni de justice en droit international," *Recueil des Cours*, Vol. 52 (1935-II), p. 369.

[8] Harvard Draft Convention on Responsibility of States, Art. 9. It is assumed that this definition would include the decisions of administrative authorities in cases where there is no appeal to the courts.

of the citizen. But what if the protection afforded to the citizen himself is below the minimum standard of treatment to be expected of a civilized state? Some writers have gone so far as to deny that there is any such minimum or "international standard of justice"; holding that each state, in the exercise of its sovereign rights, is privileged to maintain its own methods of procedure. If they are observed, the alien can have no complaint and the state of which he is a national can have no ground of intervention in his behalf.

Latin American doctrine of "equality of treatment." This view has found expression particularly in Latin America, as an offset to what has been considered the "interventionist" policy of the United States.[9] The first International Conference of American States, held in Washington, 1889-1890, proclaimed the doctrine of equality in broad terms, recommending to the governments of the countries represented at the conference the adoption of the following rules as principles of American international law: "(1) Foreigners are entitled to enjoy all the civil rights enjoyed by natives; and they shall be accorded all the benefits of said rights in all that is essential as well as in the form or procedure, and the legal remedies incident thereto, absolutely in like manner as said natives. (2) A nation has not, nor recognizes in favor of foreigners, any other obligations or responsibilities than those which in favor of the natives are established, in like cases, by the constitution and the laws." [10] The delegation of the United States, submitting a minority report, voted against the recommendation.

The conflict of opinion manifested on this occasion by the United States and the other American states continued in succeeding conferences, notably at Montevideo in 1933. The Convention on the Rights and Duties of States adopted at that conference, after stating in Article 9 the established principle that "The jurisdiction of states within the limits of national territory applies to all the inhabitants," provides that: "Nationals and foreigners are under the same protection of the law and the national authorities and the foreigners may not claim rights other or more extensive than those of the nationals." [11] The convention was signed

[9] See C. G. Fenwick, "Intervention: Individual and Collective," *Am. Journal,* Vol. 39 (1945), p. 645.

In support of the principle of equality of treatment, see Yepes, *El panamericanismo y el derecho internacional.* See a recent manifestation in the form of the "Cardenas Doctrine," P. M. Brown, *Am. Journal,* Vol. 34 (1940), p. 300.

[10] *Int. Conferences of Am. States,* 1889-1928, Recommendation, "Claims and Diplomatic Intervention," p. 45; Fenwick, *OAS,* pp. 304 ff.

[11] *Ibid.,* 1933-1940, p. 121. Compare Resolution LXXIV of the same conference, on "International Responsibility of the State," by which the conference "reaffirms once more, as a principle of international law, the civil equality of the foreigner with the national as the maximum limit of protection to which he may aspire in the positive legislations of the states. *Ibid.,* p. 91.

by the United States, but with a reservation based upon the lack of time to prepare the necessary "interpretations and definitions" of the proposed doctrines and principles.[12]

The insistence of the United States and other governments that there is an international standard of justice is supported by the views not only of jurists of the United States, Great Britain, and other countries, but by the decisions of international arbitration tribunals. The following is a statement of Elihu Root, Secretary of State of the United States, in 1910:

There is a standard of justice, very simple, very fundamental, and of such general acceptance by all civilized countries as to form a part of the international law of the world. The condition upon which any country is entitled to measure the justice due from it to an alien by the justice which it accords to its own citizens is that its system of law and administration shall conform to this general standard.[13]

Compare it with the statement of the Brazilian jurist Hildebrando Accioly to the same effect:

In Brazil, as in the majority of civilized states, the question loses much of its importance, because the respective laws are so advanced that the equality of rights conceded to aliens represents sufficient protection for them. However, in countries in which the national legislation does not offer, in respect to life, liberty and property, the protection generally due to individuals according to the accepted principles of international law, the case is different and equality of treatment is not enough.[14]

In its opinion on the Neer Claim the General Claims Commission, representing the United States and Mexico, accepted the principle that the "propriety of governmental acts should be put to the test of international standards." The Commission went on to observe, however:

the treatment of an alien, in order to constitute an international delinquency, should amount to an outrage, to bad faith, to wilful neglect of duty, or to an insufficiency of governmental action so far short of international standards that every reasonable and impartial man would readily recognize its insufficiency.[15]

It is obvious that if this international standard is higher than that which is maintained by the government of a particular state the result will be to give to the alien a greater degree of protection than that enjoyed by the citizens of the country in question and thus put the alien in a privileged position. Of recent years the earlier opposition

---

[12] *Ibid.*, p. 123. For details, see *Report of the Delegates of the United States to the Seventh International Conference of American States*, pp. 170 ff.

[13] E. Root, "The Basis of Protection to Citizens Residing Abroad," *Proceedings*, Am. Society of Int. Law, 1910, p. 16.

[14] *Tratado de direito internacional público*, Vol. I, p. 370.

[15] *Opinions of the Commissioners*, 1927, p. 73.

of Latin American jurists to the recognition of an international standard has been to some degree modified by the successive declarations of fundamental human rights which have appeared to raise national standards to a level comparable to the international standard.[16] At the same time, by contrast, the wholesale confiscations of private property in a number of states, notably by the Castro Government of Cuba, have made it clear that national standards can not be taken as the final test of responsibility.

In the meantime efforts to bring about some measure of codification of the law have continued. The Pact of Bogotá, a coordinated peace treaty adopted in 1948 by the Ninth International Conference of American States, repeated the traditional Latin American position, prohibiting diplomatic intervention when aliens "have had available the means to place their case before competent domestic courts of the respective state," resulting in a reservation by the United States; [17] but the Economic Agreement adopted at the same Conference laid down the broad rule in respect to investments that "any expropriation shall be accompanied by payment of fair compensation in a prompt, adequate and effective manner." In 1953 the General Assembly of the United Nations called upon the International Law Commission to undertake the codification of the law governing state responsibility; and this in turn led the Tenth Inter-American Conference of 1954 to call upon the Inter-American Council of Jurists and the Juridical Committee to prepare a report "on the contribution the American Continent has made to the development and the codification of the principles of international law that govern the responsibility of the state." [18]

B. THE THEORY OF THE "RESPONSIBILITY OF THE STATE"

Proceeding on the assumption that there exists an international standard of justice in respect to the treatment to be accorded to the alien by the government of the state, the problem arises to determine under what circumstances and at what time the state becomes responsible for wrongs done to an alien? Is the responsibility absolute or relative, direct or indirect? With respect to wrongs committed against the alien by individuals, singly or in groups, scholars have discussed at length the question whether the state is responsible indirectly or vicariously for the acts of individuals within its jurisdiction, or whether the act of the individual merely "engages the responsibility of the state," that is to say, is the occasion for creating a situation out of which that responsibility

[16] See J. G. Laylin, "Developments in the Law of State Responsibility," reprint of address before the Inter-American Bar Association, Bogotá, 1961; García-Amador, *Estudio del Derecho Internacional Contemporaneo,* pp. 339 ff.

[17] *Int. Conferences of American States,* 1942-1954, p. 200.

[18] *Ibid.,* p. 442. See F. V. García-Amador, "State Responsibility in the Light of New Trends of International Law," *Am. Journal,* Vol. 49 (1955), p. 339.

may arise.[19] On the one hand we can say that the state is in general responsible for the maintenance of law and order, so that when violence takes place the state is indirectly responsible for the breach of the law. But since it is beyond the power of any state to prevent all acts of violence, and wholly impracticable for it to make redress from its own resources, the responsibility of the state can be considered as having been met when it affords proper means of redress for the wrong done. On the other hand we can say that the state is not in any way responsible for the mere commission of the wrong, and that its responsibility begins only when it fails to provide adequate means of redress.[20] The difference between the two positions is largely academic, since both sides are agreed that under ordinary circumstances the actual responsibility of the state is based upon some wrongful act on its part, or some failure to act where action should have been taken.[21] The phrase "responsibility of the state" in this connection may, therefore, be defined as the secondary obligation of the state to make reparation to another state for the failure to fulfil its primary obligation to afford the proper protection due to the alien.[22]

Relation between governmental officials and the state. With respect to wrongs to the alien committed by the officers of the government a different situation is presented. States are corporate persons, and they can only give expression to their corporate will through the acts of lawfully appointed officers. The responsibility of the state for the acts of these officers might, therefore, be described as the "law of agency in

[19] See, on this subject, Eagleton, *op. cit.*, pp. 76 ff.; Freeman, *op. cit.*, pp. 19 ff.

[20] Eagleton finds the second conception "most nearly in harmony with the practice of states to-day," arguing that "the state can not be regarded as an absolute guarantor of the proper conduct of all persons within its bounds." *Op. cit.*, p. 77.

[21] An interesting theory described as "community of fortune" was offered by the Argentine jurist, Podestá Costa, in 1922 to distinguish between the immediate (direct) and mediate (indirect) responsibility of the state. An alien, coming into a state, shares with the citizens of the state a common fortune, benefiting by the rights which they enjoy and burdened by the obligations to which they are subject. Only when something occurs to destroy this community of fortune does the right of diplomatic protection arise. If a state should deny to aliens the fundamental rights of man, its responsibility before its own law would then be converted into international responsibility.

[22] Following in the lead of Grotius, who wrote a chapter "On damage caused through injury, and the obligation arising therefrom" (Book II, Chap. XVII), many writers determine the responsibility of the state in terms of "fault" on its part. See Eagleton, *op. cit.*, p. 208, where the writer points out that, starting from the original proposition of Grotius, two paths have been followed: the one seeking to extend the field of responsibility by widening the definition of fault, the other seeking to eliminate the idea of fault and to make responsibility objective. The elusiveness of the idea of fault and the subtle distinction between actual and constructive fault would seem to make it a less satisfactory test than that of "denial of justice" and "due diligence," although both of these contain subjective as well as objective elements. Compare the observations of Anzilotti, *Cours de droit international*, p. 496.

international relations." [23] Not all officers of the state are, however, of the same degree. The executive head of the government and the national legislature are in most states the primary agents of the state for the determination of foreign policy and the performance of international obligations, so that their acts are acts of the state itself and the responsibility of the state for them is direct and immediate. The confiscations of the property of foreigners by the Cuban Government in 1959-1960 are obvious examples. In such a case, described as an "act of state," the courts of the United States, as in the Sabbatino case, will not so much as hear the complaint on its merits, but rather will leave the complainant to have recourse to the executive department of his government for such redress as may be obtainable. Equally direct, but less immediate, is the responsibility of the state for the acts of its higher administrative officers and of its judicial tribunals; but the state is always free to disclaim their acts and, although accepting responsibility for them, to clear itself of any imputation of international wrong. Minor public officers, local sheriffs, magistrates, and policemen are also agents of the state, but they are in many cases so remotely connected with the central government that it would seem more correct to say that the state is only indirectly responsible for their acts, that is to say, the responsibility of the state is engaged not because of the act itself but because of the failure of the state to punish the offender when the act has been committed. Where acts are done by minor officials, soldiers, and others under orders, as in the case of the shooting down of the American transport planes by Yugoslav airmen, or the shooting down of the U-2, the responsibility is thrown back upon the higher officers who ordered the men to act.[24]

C. ACTS OF INDIVIDUALS

Where the alien is injured by the unlawful act of an individual, there is complete agreement with respect to the first stage of the procedure to be followed. The alien, finding himself injured by breach of contract, tort, or any other civil offense, must have recourse to the local courts for redress.[25] Should these deny him redress, he must make his appeal to the higher courts in accordance with the provisions of municipal law. Normally the decision of the highest courts to which an appeal may be taken is final; but should the decision be so arbitrary or discriminatory

[23] The analogy breaks down on certain points, but is on the whole sufficiently close to be helpful.

[24] In this case the act was admittedly an act of state, not raising the question of responsibility on the part of the agents directly connected with it. See below, p. 347.

The plea of *respondeat superior* is, however, not good in the case of certain acts of a particularly barbarous character. See below, pp. 760 ff.

[25] See Freeman, *op. cit.*, Chap. XV, "Delegated Control: The 'Local Remedy' Rule and its Relation to Denial of Justice"; Eagleton, *op. cit.*, Chap. V.

as to constitute a clear "denial of justice," the state of which the alien is a national may then take up his case and intervene diplomatically in his behalf, in which event the question ceases to be merely a domestic one between the alien and the foreign government and becomes an international issue to be settled by the principles of international law.

If the alien should be the victim of a criminal act, the state must not only afford such redress as a suit for damages might obtain, but it must show due diligence in arresting and prosecuting the offender. Negligence on its part in this latter respect will give rise to a claim for compensation. In the Galván case [26] compensation was awarded by the General Claims Commission in favor of the widow of a Mexican killed in Texas on the ground that "there was a clear failure on the part of the authorities of the state of Texas" to act in conformity with "the general principle of international law requiring authorities to take proper measures to apprehend and punish a person who appears to be guilty of a crime against an alien." In the Janes case,[27] in which an American superintendent of mines in Mexico was murdered by a discharged employee, compensation was awarded to the widow on the ground that the local authorities failed to apprehend and punish the slayer under circumstances in which the negligence might be said to have amounted to indifference to the commission of the crime. In the Neer case, in which an American superintendent of a mine was killed by a body of armed men, compensation was refused on the ground that while in the opinion of the Commissioners "better methods" might have been used, the Mexican authorities had not shown "such lack of diligence or such lack of intelligent investigation" in apprehending and punishing the culprits as to render Mexico liable in the case.[28]

The claim of "denial of justice" appears more often in the case of aliens accused of criminal acts where there has been undue delay in bringing the accused to trial, evidence of cruel treatment while awaiting

[26] Mexico v. United States, *Opinions of the Commissioners* (1926), p. 408. Fenwick, *Cases,* p. 256.

[27] *Opinions of the Commissioners* (1927), p. 108. For comment, see Feller, *op. cit.,* p. 292.

[28] *Ibid.* (1927), p. 71. In the course of its opinion the Commission discusses the various interpretations of "denial of justice" and observes: "Without attempting to announce a precise formula, it is in the opinion of the Commission possible to go a little further than the authors quoted, and to hold—(first) that the propriety of governmental acts should be put to the test of international standards, and (second) that the treatment of an alien, in order to constitute an international delinquency, should amount to an outrage, to bad faith, to wilful neglect of duty, or to an insufficiency of governmental action so far short of international standards that every reasonable and impartial man would readily recognize its insufficiency. Whether the insufficiency proceeds from deficient execution of an intelligent law or from the fact that the laws of the country do not empower the authorities to measure up to international standards is immaterial."

trial, or a manifestly unjust sentence. In the Chattin case [29] compensation was awarded on ground of the irregularity of court proceedings following the arrest of Chattin for alleged embezzlement. "Irregularity of court proceedings," said the General Claims Commission, "is proven with reference to absence of proper investigations, insufficiency of confrontations, withholding from the accused the opportunity to know all of the charges brought against him, undue delay of the proceedings, making the hearings in open court a mere formality, and a continued absence of seriousness on the part of the Court." In the Dyches case [30] compensation was granted on the ground that, in spite of the fact that the Mexican Supreme Court of Justice had finally acquitted the accused, he had been imprisoned for two and a half years when only a minor offense was involved.

Acts of minor officials. Where the injury to the alien is the result of the act of some local officer, such as a sheriff, the redress of the wrong is expected to proceed with greater promptness and concern than otherwise, since a criminal act on the part of such a person is properly to be regarded as a more serious affront to the law, although not directly involving the responsibility of the state. Circumstances must determine whether the act of the petty officer was performed in pursuance of official duties, although in excess of the necessities of the situation. In the Way case,[31] in which an American superintendent was killed by persons acting under the instigation of the local mayor, it was found by the Commission that the mayor has issued a void warrant, "a warrant stating no charge," and had "directed the execution of that so-called warrant by armed men who killed a cultured and inoffensive man, who evidently had sought to avoid trouble with the Alcalde." An indemnity was awarded in favor of the claimants. In the case in which two Mexican students, Gomez and Rubio, were killed by sheriffs in the town of Ardmore, Oklahoma, in 1932, the sheriffs were acquitted by the state courts on the basis of their testimony that they shot in self-defense. The incident took place at midnight, and while both boys were alleged to have had revolvers it appeared that the sheriffs fired with unnecessary

---

[29] *Ibid.* (1927), p. 422. The case contains a detailed, if somewhat confusing, statement of the distinction between "indirect" and "direct" responsibility. See Feller, *op. cit.,* pp. 130, 143.

[30] *Ibid.* (1929), p. 193. The case contains an interesting discussion of the question whether a final decision of the highest court can redress an unjust decision of a lower court.

[31] *Ibid.* (1929), p. 94; *Am. Journal,* Vol. 23 (1929), p. 466. "It is believed to be a sound principle," said the Commission, "that, when misconduct on the part of persons concerned with the discharge of governmental functions, whatever their precise status may be under domestic law, results in a failure of a nation to live up to its obligations under international law, the delinquency on the part of such persons is a misfortune for which the nation must bear the responsibility." For comment, see Feller, *op. cit.,* p. 236.

haste. In view of the facts Congress made an appropriation for the payment of an indemnity to the families of the deceased "as an act of grace and without reference to the question of legal liability." [32]

D. ACTS OF MOB VIOLENCE

Outbreaks of mob violence resulting in injury to the alien raise regularly the question of prevention as well as of redress. While occasional outbreaks of mob violence may be expected in any state, and their mere occurrence is not of itself a ground of responsibility, the state is expected to use "due diligence" to prevent them. What constitutes "due diligence" is a question of time and circumstances. Attacks directed against aliens as such raise the question of prevention more acutely than if aliens as well as citizens are incidental victims of a riot. In the classic case of Don Pacifico, an English Jew whose house was attacked and burnt in consequence of efforts made by the Greek Government to prevent the national custom of burning Judas Iscariot in effigy on Easter Day, 1847, the British Government emphasized the lack of due diligence in preventing the outrage and insisted upon an indemnity. The failure of Pacifico to resort to the local courts was explained by the legal disabilities of Jews in Greece. An indemnity not being forthcoming the British Government resorted to reprisals.[33] On the occasion of the riots at Key West and New Orleans in 1851, following the execution of certain American filibusters in Cuba, Secretary Webster argued inconclusively that Spanish subjects were not entitled to compensation because Americans also had suffered, since in this instance the riots were directed primarily against the Spanish consul and his countrymen.[34] While the obligation to make compensation was denied in this case, compensation was in fact granted as an act of courtesy.

Again, the distance of the scene of the riot from the centers of governmental control is a factor qualifying "due diligence." In the case of the anti-Chinese riots at Rock Springs, Wyoming, in 1885, responsibility was denied on general principles and on the special grounds that the perpetrators of the offense were also aliens and that the remoteness of the locality made it difficult to maintain law and order.[35] In the case of

---

[32] Hackworth, *Digest*, Vol. V, p. 573; Whiteman, *Damages in International Law*, Vol. I, p. 750. In the case of James Pugh, an Irish Free State citizen who was killed on June 30, 1929, by two police agents in Colon, Republic of Panama, the arbitrator dismissed the claim for indemnity on the ground that Pugh "came to his death through his own fault, while attempting to resist lawful arrest and while engaged in unlawfully attacking police officers in the lawful discharge of their duties." *Am. Journal*, Vol. 36 (1942), p. 708.

[33] *Brit. and Foreign State Papers*, Vol. 39, p. 332; Moore, *Digest*, Vol. VI, p. 852; Vol. VII, p. 132.

[34] See Moore, *Digest*, Vol. VI, § 1023.

[35] *Ibid.*, Vol. VI, § 1025. The position taken by Secretary Bayard on this occasion has been generally condemned by American writers.

Henry Youmans and others, American citizens who were killed by a mob at Angangueo, Mexico, in 1880, troops which had been sent to disperse the mob joined with it on arriving at the scene and opened fire on the house in which the Americans were living. Compensation was granted on the ground that "it can not properly be said that adequate protection is afforded to foreigners in a case in which the proper agencies of the law to afford protection participate in murder." [36] In 1891 a number of Italians were lynched in New Orleans as a result of mob violence directed against the activities of the Mafia gang which had culminated in the murder of the chief of police. There was no question but that the local authorities were negligent in not preventing the attack of the mob upon the prison in which the Italians were held. Indemnity was demanded by Italy on the basis of an alleged violation of rights assured to the Italians by treaty. While it was impossible for Secretary Blaine to meet the insistence of the Italian Government that the guilty parties should be brought to trial, it was admitted that an indemnity was due, and this was duly paid the following year.[37]

Special protection due to foreign officers. The general duty of the state to use due diligence to prevent the commission of wrongful acts to the injury of aliens is increased when the alien happens to be an officer of a foreign state. As a rule the gravity of the case is determined by the rank of the foreign officer; but political conditions sometimes intervene to aggravate what would normally be minor offenses. A striking instance of the liability of a state to give special protection to the officers of a foreign state is shown in the peremptory demands made on August 29, 1923, by Italy upon Greece for redress for the murder of General Tellini and four other Italian members of the international commission surveying the boundary between Albania and Greece. The demands included formal apologies and a salute to the Italian flag, an inquiry into the circumstances of the murder, to be carried out upon the scene with the help of the Italian military attaché, capital punishment for the murderers, and an indemnity of fifty million lire to be paid within five days. In order to demonstrate the seriousness of the situation the Italian fleet attacked and seized Corfu on August 31 and held the island as security for the performance of the terms of the ultimatum. Greece thereupon applied both to the League of Nations and to the Conference of Ambassadors at Paris under whose direction the boundary commission was acting. Italy accepted the decision of this latter body, after having contested the jurisdiction of the League. Corfu was evacuated a month later.[38]

[36] *Opinions of the Commissioners* (1927), p. 150.

[37] Moore, *Digest*, Vol. VI, § 1026. See below, p. 356.

[38] The decision of the Conference of Ambassadors holding Greece delinquent appears to have been influenced by political considerations. The unqualified demand by Italy for an indemnity was first modified by the conference so as to require the deposit of the sum in a Swiss bank, leaving it to the Permanent Court of International

Case of Count Bernadotte. On September 17, 1948, Count Bernadotte, acting as mediator appointed by the Security Council of the United Nations in the hostilities between the Arab and the Jewish communities in Palestine, was assassinated in the Israel-held sector of Jerusalem, together with the Chief of the French Observers, Colonel André Sérat. The General Assembly, after obtaining from the International Court of Justice in 1949 an opinion that the United Nations was an "international person" and competent to demand reparation for damages to one of its agents, entered a claim by the Secretary General against the Israeli Government, based upon the liability of the Government for acts committed by irregular forces in territory under its control, and upon the failure of the Government to exercise due diligence under the circumstances. Both claims were duly paid by the Israeli Government, without, however, admitting the validity of the legal contentions made.[39]

E. ACTS OF INSURGENTS

The responsibility of the state for the acts of insurgents in cases in which the persons and property of aliens are involved is determined upon principles which vary somewhat from those governing the acts of mobs. The very existence of an organized rebellion raises a presumption of "due diligence" on the part of the state in suppressing it, since the government has an immediate interest in such open attacks upon its authority.[40] This presumption may become practically absolute when the state is confronted with such widespread revolt as to make it necessary to recognize the insurgents as belligerents.[41] In such cases, bordering on or actually constituting civil war, it may be not only impossible for the state to prevent the losses to foreigners incidental to the disorder, but impracticable, even if physically possible, to inflict punishment upon a whole section of the population when the rebellion has been suppressed. Under such circumstances can the state be held responsible for losses which may be suffered by aliens in common with the rest of the population in consequence of the insurgent movement or actual

---

Justice to assess the damages. Subsequently the Conference, finding Greece delinquent in its efforts to discover and punish the guilty parties, required payment forthwith of the money on deposit. The Council of the League, whose competence Italy had denied, was led to submit to a Special Committee of Jurists the inquiry, "In what circumstances, and to what extent, is the responsibility of a state involved by the commission of a political crime in its territory?" See Eagleton, *op. cit.*, pp. 187 ff.; Briggs, *Cases*, pp. 960 ff.; and p. 643 of the present work.

[39] *U.N. Yearbook*, 1948-1949, p. 936. See Q. Wright, "Responsibility for Injuries to United Nations Officials," *Am. Journal*, Vol. 43 (1949), p. 95.

[40] On the general subject, see Hyde, *Int. Law*, Vol. II, §§ 229B-302; Hackworth, *Digest*, Vol. V, p. 666; Eagleton, *op. cit.*, §§ 41-45; H. Silvanie, "Responsibility of States for Acts of Insurgent Governments," *Am. Journal*, Vol. 33 (1939), p. 78.

[41] Recognition of the insurgents by the *de jure* government as belligerents changes their character from that of rebels to that of legitimate combatants. Recognition by foreign states would give them a similar character at international law. See p. 203.

civil war, or for any special losses due to confiscation of property or to attacks upon the person or property of the alien due to the fact of alienage? Would the ultimate success of the revolution create a responsibility on the part of the new government which would not have existed if the revolution had been defeated and the *de jure* government remained in power? [42]

The Calvo Doctrine. The general principle that the state is not responsible for losses incurred by aliens in time of civil war became associated in Latin America with the name of the Argentine publicist Calvo, who argued in his treatise on international law [43] that a state could not accept responsibility for losses suffered by foreigners as the result of civil war or insurrection, on the ground that to admit responsibility in such cases would be to menace the independence of weaker states by subjecting them to the intervention of strong states, and would "establish an unjustifiable inequality between nationals and foreigners." [44] The United States, Great Britain, and other states have, however, been reluctant to accept the principle in so absolute a form. Their attitude has rather been to accept the principle in conditional form, that a state is not responsible for losses to aliens at the hands of revolutionists unless there has been negligence on the part of the government in suppressing the insurrection or want of due diligence in preventing the particular acts which have caused the injury. Their attitude has been further modified by the degree of stability in the government of the particular state. Owing to the frequency of domestic revolution in certain states, the presumption that the state is exercising its utmost efforts to suppress the rebellion is weakened by the fact that it is continually unable to do so and must in consequence accept a responsibility based, if not upon the lack of due diligence on the part of the *de jure* government, then upon the inherent weakness of the organization of the state. A distinction is thus made between a revolution in a state normally stable and a revolution in a state which is in a condition of more or less chronic domestic upheaval. The tests applied have thus in many cases been political rather than legal.[45]

[42] Hyde, *op. cit.*, and Hackworth, *op. cit.*, both quote with finality a statement from Ralston's Report on the Bolivar Railway Co. Case, to the effect that "The nation is responsible for the obligations of a successful revolution from its beginning, because, in theory, it represented ab initio a changing national will, crystallizing in the finally successful revolt."

[43] *Le Droit international théorique et pratique*, 5th ed., Tome I, liv. iii.

[44] *Ibid.*, § 1280. Quoted by Moore, *Digest*, Vol. VI, § 1044. The "Calvo Doctrine" is to be distinguished from the "Calvo Clause" in contracts between a government and aliens. See below, pp. 350 ff.

[45] See the annual message of President Roosevelt, December 6, 1904, and the special message of February 15, 1905. There are, in fact, two rules applied to civil war as well as to acts of mob violence. In the case of more stable governments the presumption is on the side of the state that it is doing all in its power to suppress the rebellion; in the case of less stable governments, the presumption is to the contrary.

In the Gelbtrunk case,[46] in which the property of an American citizen carrying on a mercantile business in El Salvador was looted by soldiers of the revolutionary army, indemnity was refused by the arbitrator on the ground that the alien coming into another state to carry on business is to be considered "as having cast in his lot with the subjects or citizens of the State in which he resides and carries on business," and that in this instance Gelbtrunk was not treated any less favorably than the citizens themselves. In the Sambiaggio case [47] between Italy and Venezuela, involving a claim by Sambiaggio, an Italian citizen resident in Venezuela, for losses sustained at the hands of revolutionists who failed of success, the arbitrator laid it down as a general rule that "the very existence of a flagrant revolution presupposes that a certain set of men have gone temporarily or permanently beyond the power of the authorities; and unless it clearly appear that the government has failed to use promptly and with appropriate force its constituted authority, it can not reasonably be said that it should be responsible for a condition of affairs created without its volition"; and he refused to discriminate against Venezuela on the ground that it was on a lower plane of civilization and as such responsible "in derogation of the general principles of international law." Nevertheless the arbitrator, while rejecting a general presumption of inferior status, was prepared to hold Venezuela responsible if the authorities "failed to exercise due diligence" to prevent damages from being inflicted by the revolutionists. No such failure being found, the claim was dismissed. In the Home Missionary Society case,[48] in which a claim was made by an American religious body for losses due to a rebellion in the British Protectorate of Sierra Leone, the arbitration tribunal dismissed the claim on the ground that "no government can be held responsible for the act of rebellious bodies of men committed in violation of its authority, where it is itself guilty of no breach of good faith, or of no negligence in suppressing insurrection." With respect to the place of the revolt the tribunal observed: "It is impossible to judge the system of police and protection of life and property in force in the savage regions of Africa by the standard of countries or cities which enjoy the social order, the respect for authority, and the settled administration of a high civilization."

[46] United States and Salvador, Claim of Rosa Gelbtrunk. *U.S. Foreign Relations,* 1902, p. 874; Fenwick, *Cases,* p. 258; Bishop, *Cases,* p. 665; Briggs, *Cases,* p. 713. In this case the arbitrator made a broad statement of the principle of equality of treatment, which was said to be "the well-established doctrine of international law." But later the arbitrator added: "It is, however, not to be assumed that this rule would apply in a case of mob violence which might, if due diligence had been used, have been prevented by civil authorities alone or by such authorities aided by an available military force. In such case of spoliation by a mob, especially when the disorder has arisen in hostility to foreigners, a different rule may prevail."

[47] Ralston, *Venezuelan Arbitrations of 1903,* p. 679; Briggs, *Cases,* p. 715.

[48] *Nielsen's Report,* p. 421; Fenwick, *Cases,* p. 260.

During the American "Civil War," as it is usually described, Secretary Seward, in correspondence with the resident French, Austrian, and British ministers, rejected the suggestion of responsibility of the United States for losses sustained by nationals of their respective states in consequence of military operations in the Confederate States.[49] But the war was rather a sectional war than a true civil war, in as much as the Confederate States were not seeking to get control of the United States Government, but to establish themselves as an independent state. It would seem more correct, therefore, to have decided the question of responsibility on the basis of the principles governing international war.[50]

Losses suffered in time of international war.   In the event of a formal war between two states there is no question of responsibility on the part of the state for losses suffered by aliens in common with the rest of the population, whether from acts of the enemy in occupation or from legitimate acts of the *de jure* government in conducting military operations. International law recognizes that in such cases the state is on the one hand powerless to prevent the acts of the enemy and is on the other hand too deeply committed to the necessity of self-preservation to be able to take into account the special interests of aliens who happen to be temporarily or permanently resident within its jurisdiction. In the Eastern Extension, Australasia and China Telegraph Co. case,[51] between Great Britain and the United States, involving a claim for losses resulting to a British corporation from the cutting of its submarine cables connecting Manila and Hongkong by the United States forces during the war with Spain in 1898, the arbitration tribunal to which the case was submitted disallowed the claim on the ground that to deprive the enemy of the means of communication was a "legitimate object of sea warfare," and that the lines of the company were located in Spanish territory and therefore subject to the risk of being treated in time of war as a Spanish public service.

F. RESPONSIBILITY FOR ACTS OF GOVERNMENTAL AUTHORITIES

Acts of state officers in violation of the rights of aliens fall into different classes according to the degree to which the officer may be taken as an agent of the state. We have seen that minor public officers may be so remotely connected with the central government that the latter should be held only indirectly responsible for their acts. On the other hand acts

---

[49] See Moore, *Digest*, § 1032. The fact that compensation was subsequently granted as a matter of grace did not amount to the recognition of a legal principle.

[50] It should be noted that the term "civil war" is used somewhat broadly in Latin America, so that Secretary Seward's policy in respect to the obligation of the United States to make compensation for injuries is cited by certain writers as a precedent for a similar refusal to make compensation for losses due to minor insurgent movements which involve no element of class struggle but are merely contests for political control of the government.

[51] *Nielsen's Report*, p. 73; Fenwick, *Cases*, p. 263; Briggs, *Cases*, p. 33.

of the judicial agencies of the state from the lowest courts to the highest are acts of state organs, and immediate responsibility attaches to them. Under modern constitutional governments the position of the courts within the state is a privileged one, and as a rule they can not be controlled by the executive department which is charged with the management of foreign affairs. Hence if a decision by the highest court of the state should result in a denial of justice to the alien, whether as plaintiff or as defendant in the case, the head of the state can not take action against the delinquent judges or secure a reversal of the decision, but can only accept responsibility for it and make such reparation as may be in order.[52]

A subtle question arises whether a mere error of judgment on the part of the court is sufficient to constitute "denial of justice." The subtlety consists in the fact that it is not easy at times to distinguish between an honest error of judgment, either in the interpretation of the law or in its application to the particular case before the court, and a decision clearly biased against the alien. For this reason it is generally said that only where the decision of the court is *manifestly* unjust can it be regarded as constituting the "denial of justice" for which redress must be made. In the case of the *Costa Rica Packet*,[53] the Australian master was arrested by order of a Dutch court in the Dutch East Indies for an offense which was later shown to have been committed outside Dutch territorial waters. The award of the arbitrator called upon Holland to pay damages; but the decision has been generally criticized.

Acts of national legislatures. Acts of the national legislature, being the law-making body of the state, are acts of the state itself, and the responsibility of the state for them is direct and immediate.[54] Where there is temporarily no national legislature and the president or other executive acts authoritatively, the same rule holds: the order or decree is an "act of state." In most cases the laws enacted by the national legislature do not become effective except through the executive act either of the head of the state or of higher administrative officials, so that the question of responsibility generally arises in that connection. Foreign states may, however, protest against legislation which threatens

---

[52] On this subject, see Borchard, *op. cit.*, pp. 195 ff.; Freeman, *op. cit.*, Chap. XII.

[53] Moore, *Arbitrations*, Vol. V, pp. 4948 ff. For other cases, see *Digest*, Vol. VI, §§ 1002.

[54] See, on the general subject, Eagleton, *op. cit.*, § 21, and authorities there cited; White, *Nationalization of Property;* Wortley, *Expropriation in Public International Law;* Feighel, *Nationalization: A Study in the Protection of Alien Property in International Law;* A. P. Fachiri, "Expropriation and International Law," *British Year Book*, 1925, p. 159; Sir J. F. Williams, "International Law and the Property of Aliens," *ibid.*, 1928, p. 1; M. Zander, "The Act of State Doctrine," *Am. Journal*, Vol. 53 (1959), p. 826; L. B. Sohn and R. R. Baxter, "Responsibility of States for Injury to the Economic Interests of Aliens," *Am. Journal*, Vol. 55 (1961), p. 545; M. Domke, "Foreign Nationalizations: Some Aspects of Contemporary International Law," *ibid.*, p. 585.

injury to their citizens without waiting for the actual execution of the law.[55]

Legislation which is discriminatory against the alien, whether in respect to his fundamental rights under international law or his acquired rights under national law, obviously constitutes a ground for protest by the state of which the alien is a national. The practical problem consists in determining where the line is to be drawn between discriminatory legislation, arbitrarily confiscating the property of aliens or denying them due process of law, and legislation which is enacted to meet what are alleged to be urgent national needs and which affects adversely the property of aliens and citizens alike.

Clearly no nation can be denied the right to put into effect a great national program of economic or social reform. An amendment to the United States Constitution, adopted in 1866, destroyed the property in Negro slaves of alien residents as well as of citizens.[56] Another amendment, the Eighteenth, adopted in 1920, rendered property used for the manufacture of intoxicating liquors practically valueless.[57] But in both cases the losses imposed by the law upon aliens were negligible compared to those imposed upon citizens; and in both cases alien owners of the property had due warning of its probable destruction. The controversial issue arises where the act of confiscation amounts to no more than the transfer to the state of property formerly owned by aliens, and the alien is deprived of his property for public purposes in the benefit of which he, as an alien, cannot share. In the years following the Bolshevik revolution of 1918 the United States refused to recognize the right of the new government to confiscate the property of American citizens and insisted upon "effective compensation" as a condition of recognition of the new regime.[58]

Controversies with Mexico. In 1925–1926 the United States protested vigorously against acts of the Mexican legislature embodying a program of "nationalization" of oil and other mineral deposits and large estates in land, in pursuance of provisions of the Mexican Constitution of 1917. It was argued by the United States that both laws were confiscatory and retroactive. The Petroleum Law provided for the compulsory exchange of a title to subsoil property in return for a government concession to use the property for a limited term of ten years; and the Alien Land Law put sharp restrictions upon ownership in respect to extent and dura-

[55] It would seem, however, that a protest against pending legislation, as distinct from enacted laws, is not permissible. See below, p. 561.

[56] The Amendment was preceded by the Emancipation Proclamation of 1863, adopted as a war measure.

[57] With reference to a law of the State of Kansas, passed in 1881, the Supreme Court of the United States decided [Mugler v. Kansas, 123 U.S. 623 (1887)] that the police power of the State could not be burdened with the necessity of making compensation in such cases. Evans, *Cases on Constitutional Law*, 7th ed., p. 779.

[58] Hackworth, *Digest*, Vol. I, p. 302. See above, pp. 190 ff.

tion. Both laws called for the renunciation by the alien owner of the right to resort to his own government for diplomatic protection.[59] Some ten years later a Mexican federal law of 1936 provided for the expropriation of private property of public utility as a measure for meeting "collective necessities." In the same year a presidential decree expropriated the properties of American and British oil companies because they were unwilling to accept the award of the Mexican Supreme Court in regard to inspection of their books and management by labor unions. The United States did not contest the right of expropriation by Mexico of foreign properties under eminent domain, but insisted that the exercise of this right should be accompanied by provision for just and prompt compensation. In the end settlements were effected not by an impartial arbitration tribunal or mixed claims commission but by diplomatic adjustment looking to political cooperation beyond the range of the specific issues involved.[60] The foreign officers of the two countries clashed almost directly with respect to the principles to be applied to the situation. The United States contended that "The taking of property without compensation is not expropriation. It is confiscation. It is no less confiscation because there may be an expressed intent to pay at some time in the future." [61] The Mexican Government replied that "there is in international law no rule universally accepted in theory nor carried out in practice, which makes obligatory the payment of immediate compensation nor even of deferred compensation, for expropriations of a general and impersonal character like those which Mexico has carried out for the purpose of redistribution of the land." [62]

In 1936 the Spanish Republican Government put into effect a "col-

---

[59] For the texts of the Mexican laws and a survey of the controversy, see Hackett, *The Mexican Revolution and the United States, 1910-1926.* See also Dunn, *Diplomatic Protection of Americans in Mexico,* Chaps. XI, XII. For a survey of the background of the controversy, see Callahan, *American Foreign Policy in Mexican Relations.*

[60] For comment upon the political aspects of the controversy, see Bemis, *Latin American Policy of the United States,* pp. 345 ff.

[61] Hackworth, *Digest,* Vol. III, p. 656.

[62] *Ibid.,* p. 657. Compare the exchange of notes between the two governments in respect to the expropriation by Mexico of agrarian properties owned by American citizens, in the course of which Secretary Hull observed: "The doctrine of equality of treatment, like that of just compensation, is of ancient origin. It appears in many constitutions, bills of rights and documents of international validity. The word has invariably referred to equality in lawful rights of the person and to protection in exercising such lawful rights. There is now announced by your Government the astonishing theory that this treasured and cherished principle of equality, designed to protect both human and property rights, is to be invoked, not in the protection of personal rights and liberties, but as a chief ground of depriving and stripping individuals of their conceded rights. It is contended, in a word, that it is wholly justifiable to deprive an individual of his rights if all other persons are equally deprived, and if no victim is allowed to escape. In the instant case it is contended that confiscation is so justified. The proposition scarcely requires answer." *Am. Journal,* Vol. 32 (1938), Supp., pp. 181, 198.

lectivization" plan as a result of which the distributing agency of an American company was threatened with complete loss. A warning was entered by the Department of State in which, without passing upon the validity of the collectivization decrees, it was stated that "prompt and full compensation" of American nationals would be expected for any losses suffered by them. Application of the collectivization decree to the agency in question was subsequently annulled.[63]

The Sabbatino Case. In the case of Banco Nacional de Cuba v. Sabbatino, decided by the United States Court of Appeals in 1962, the Government of Cuba claimed that it was entitled to the proceeds of a shipment of sugar on the ground of a law of August 6, 1960, ordering the nationalization of all property and enterprises owned by nationals of the United States or in which such nationals had a predominating interest. Sabbatino, acting as temporary receiver for a company organized under the laws of Cuba but whose shareholders were predominantly residents of the United States, claimed that the Cuban law was in violation of international law in failing to pay adequate compensation for property seized from a particular class of aliens in retaliation against their homeland and discriminating against them only. The Court held that the decree violated international law, and that the title of the Banco Nacional was invalid.[64] Upon appeal by the Banco Nacional to the Supreme Court of the United States, it was held, reversing the Court of Appeals, that "the Judicial Branch will not examine the validity of a taking of property within its own territory by a foreign sovereign government, extant and recognized by this country at the time of suit, in the absence of a treaty or other unambiguous agreement regarding controlling legal principles, even if the complaint alleges that the taking violates customary international law." The "act of state" doctrine was thus upheld in practically absolute form.[65]

Of recent years a special issue has arisen in connection with the right of sovereign ownership authorizing the state, in the name of urgent national needs, to take over natural resources and develop them for the benefit of its people, notwithstanding concessions for the development of the particular resources previously made to foreign investors under contracts specifying the period and scope of the concession. Is the title of the state as sovereign owner so supreme that any and every conflict-

[63] Ibid., p. 588.

[64] 307 F. 2d 845; 371 U.S. 907. See, for the text, Am. Journal, Vol. 56 (1962), p. 1085. For comment, J. R. Stevenson, "The Sabbatino Case—Three Steps Forward and Two Steps Back"; Am. Journal, Vol. 57 (1963), p. 97; "The State Department and Sabbatino—'Ev'n Victors are by Victories Undone'"; ibid., Vol. 58 (1964), p. 707; M. G. Cooper, "The Act of State Doctrine in the Light of the Sabbatino Case," ibid., Vol. 56 (1962), p. 143.

[65] 376 U.S. 398. Am. Journal, Vol. 58 (1964), p. 779. On October 7, 1964, by Public Law 88-633, Congress instructed the Supreme Court to decide similar cases in the future on their merits.

ing title of an alien individual or alien government is subordinate to it? Assuming that the state has inadequate financial means to exercise its right of eminent domain, may it nevertheless do so on grounds of an inalienable right? A resolution of the General Assembly of the United Nations of December 14, 1962, appeared to some governments to take such a position, leading to protest by the United States and other governments. Qualifications and checks were, however, entered in the resolution of the General Assembly. The preamble of the resolution, "Permanent Sovereignty over Natural Resources" emphasized the permanent sovereignty of the state over its natural wealth and resources "as a basic constituent of the right of self-determination," declaring that this sovereignty must be exercised in the interest of their national development, and that the import of the foreign capital required must be in conformity with the interests and well-being of the people and in no case constitute an infringement of national sovereignty. Subsequent articles make provision for appropriate compensation when expropriation is resorted to on grounds of public utility or national interest.[66]

Acts of administrative officials. The determination of the responsibility of the state for the acts of its administrative officers presents considerable difficulty. A decree of the president of the state is, as we have seen, an act of the state itself, and the responsibility of the state for it is direct and immediate. In like manner the acts of the highest administrative officers, against whose decisions there is no appeal, are also acts of the state itself. Below these highest officers, however, are numerous lesser officers whose acts raise questions of *agency* analogous to those of private law. Is the officer acting within the powers which belong to his office? If so, the state is clearly responsible for his act. What if he is acting *ultra vires?* Can the state evade responsibility by saying that the officer exceeded the instructions given him and therefore that his illegal act is no more than a tort committed by one person against another, for which a suit at law is the final remedy? Obviously a strict interpretation of the theory of *ultra vires* would result in having the state escape responsibility altogether. The very fact that the act of the administrative officer was wrongful would put it outside the scope of his authority. An administrative officer discriminates against an alien, resulting in heavy loss to him. Complaint is made, and the state replies that the officer was instructed not to discriminate, so that the remedy is against the officer personally, and if this brings nothing, then the alien must stand the loss.[67]

Few writers go so far. The majority make a distinction between the authority given to an officer to perform a certain class of acts and the ex-

---

[66] For the text of the resolution, see *Am. Journal*, Vol. 57 (1963), p. 710. For background, see J. N. Hyde, "Permanent Sovereignty over Natural Wealth and Resources," *Am. Journal*, Vol. 50 (1956), p. 854.

[67] See Eagleton, *op. cit.*, §§ 18, 59; Feller, *op. cit.*, pp. 130 ff.

press or implied instructions as to the proper exercise of the authority conferred. If the officer is acting within the general scope of his authority, while his act may not be attributable to the state, the state is responsible for it and must make compensation to the person wronged by it. Thus the state may be held responsible for the unlawful refusal of port authorities to clear a vessel, or for the damage done by one of its public ships to a foreign merchant vessel as the result of a collision, or for the unlawful capture of a neutral vessel in time of war. The international responsibility only arises, however, when the remedies provided by law have been exhausted, and when the state has failed to discipline the officer when discipline is called for. In view of the more rigid rules of military discipline the acts of officers of the army and navy raise the issue of responsibility more immediately than in the case of administrative officers of corresponding rank. On the other hand the acts of soldiers in their individual capacity are, like the acts of local officers, not to be attributed directly to the state, but only indirectly when the facts show that there has been want of due diligence in preventing the act or in punishing the offender.[68] In rare cases, where the act of the local officer or soldier is done under orders, the responsibility, as has been said, is thrown back upon the officer commanding the act. Where the command of the officer is given under direct orders of his government, as in the case of the shooting down of American transport plans crossing Yugoslav territory in 1946, the issue becomes no longer one of responsibility, but of the lawfulness of the act under the general rules of international law.

G. CONTRACTS BETWEEN THE STATE AND ALIENS

A special phase of the general obligation of the state to protect aliens in their persons and property is presented in the case of an alleged breach of a governmental contract with the alien. No question arises here of the responsibility of the state, since one of the parties to the contract is the government itself. Rather the issue is presented whether the state of which the alien is a citizen may take up his claim and press for payment when the courts of the other state have denied redress. On the whole, governments have been reluctant to intervene in support of claims of their citizens arising out of monetary transactions with foreign states. This attitude would appear to be based partly on the consideration that persons entering into such contracts do so with a knowledge of the risks involved and with expectation of correspondingly large returns upon their investment, and partly upon the ground that a state whose citizens engage in such ventures on a large scale would find its relations with foreign states embarrassed by the numerous appeals made to it by citizens to intervene on their behalf. Nevertheless, diplomatic interven-

[68] For illustrations, see Moore, *Digest*, Vol. VI, § 1009.

tions have taken place with sufficient frequency to indicate the necessity of clearer rules of law than those that exist at present.[69]

The action of the United States under the Marshall Plan in 1948, setting up a program of guarantees to American investors in the countries specified, fell, of course, outside the range of normal investments, and is to be looked upon as postwar emergency legislation, although numerous proposals to the same effect are under discussion.

In general the alien, believing himself to be the victim of breach of contract by a foreign government, must first exhaust such local remedies as are available to him. These failing him, he may seek to press his claim through the foreign office of his government. As classic instances of diplomatic intervention the following may be cited: In the Delagoa Bay case between the United States and Portugal,[70] involving the seizure by the Portuguese Government of a railway built by an American citizen, McMurdo, in Mozambique, an arbitration tribunal in 1900 awarded damages to the claimant on the ground that the concession had been unjustly annulled, the action of the Portuguese Government having been taken because of the nonfulfillment of conditions which were not in the original contract. In the El Triunfo case between the United States and El Salvador,[71] involving the cancellation of a franchise and the resulting destruction of a concession given to the El Triunfo Company, a local corporation whose stockholders were American citizens, a special arbitration tribunal awarded damages on the ground that the Government of Salvador had intervened in the case by its executive decrees, closing the port of El Triunfo and granting the franchise to strangers. In answer to the argument of Salvador that the company should first seek its remedy in the courts in connection with alleged fraudulent bankruptcy proceedings, the tribunal observed: "It is apparent in this case that an appeal to the courts for relief from the bankruptcy would have been in vain after the acts of the executive had destroyed the franchise." In 1911 the United States secured from Persia the full payment of the salary of Mr. Shuster, who had been arbitrarily expelled from the country before the expiration of his contract as treasurer-general.[72]

The Calvo Clause. In order to prevent appeals by aliens to their home governments for diplomatic intervention in behalf of their contract rights, a number of Latin American states during the latter part of the nineteenth century adopted a policy of writing into their contracts with aliens a clause, known as the "Calvo Clause," the general tenor of which

---

[69] On the general subject, see Eagleton, *op. cit.*, Chap. VII; Hyde, *Int. Law*, Vol. II, §§ 303-308; Hackworth, *Digest*, Vol. V, pp. 610 ff.

[70] Moore, *International Arbitrations*, Vol. II, pp. 1865 ff.; Whiteman, *Damages in International Law*, Vol. III, p. 1694.

[71] Salvador Commercial Co. v. Salvador. Special Arbitration Tribunal. *Foreign Relations of the United States*, 1902, pp. 838 ff.; Bishop, *Cases*, p. 672.

[72] C. L. Bouve, "Russia's Liability in Tort for Persia's Breach of Contract," *Am. Journal*, Vol. 6 (1912), p. 396.

was that the alien agreed that any disputes that might arise out of the contract were to be decided by the national courts in accordance with national law and were not to give rise to any international reclamation.[73] In some cases it was provided that the alien was to be "considered as a national" for the purposes of the contract. The question presented was, can an alien, by agreeing to renounce in advance an appeal to his government for protection, restrict in any degree the free action of his government to intervene in his behalf if it believes that a wrong has been done to him under the circumstances. No question is raised by the Calvo Clause in respect to the obligation of the alien to have recourse to national courts for redress before appealing to his government for protection, for that is an established rule of international law. Suppose, however, that there is a denial of justice by the national courts, and that the state of which the alien is a national believes the matter sufficiently grave to warrant its interposition. Is it precluded from doing so by the fact that the alien, its citizen, has deliberately waived his right to such protection?

The decisions of international arbitration tribunals and of mixed claims commissions upon the subject have been conflicting, some upholding the Calvo Clause as a bar to the interposition of the alien's government, others rejecting it on the ground that the act of the alien can not restrict the rights of his government under international law. In the Orinoco Steamship Co. case between the United States and Venezuela,[74] decided in 1903, involving a claim for losses sustained by the company due to requisition of its vessels during the revolution and to unlawful discrimination against it in the navigation of the river, the umpire upheld the Calvo Clause and decided that the parties, having chosen their court, must accept its decision as final. The United States protested the award of the commission as disregarding the terms of the protocol under which the case was submitted to the commission and as containing essential errors of law and fact. The validity of the award was subsequently submitted to arbitration before the Hague Permanent Court, which decided that the rejection of the claim by the umpire in the earlier case was unwarranted.

---

[73] On the general subject of the Calvo Clause, see Ralston, *Law and Procedure of International Tribunals,* Nos. 70-89; Borchard, *Diplomatic Protection,* §§ 371 ff.; Eagleton, *op. cit.,* § 49; Freeman, *op. cit.,* pp. 470 ff.; Hackworth, *Digest,* Vol. V, p. 635; Feller, *op. cit.,* Chap 10. In "Recent Aspects of the Calvo Doctrine and the Challenge to International Law," *Am. Journal,* Vol. 40 (1946), pp. 121-147, A. V. Freeman criticizes sharply the project submitted to the Inter-American Bar Association at Havana in 1944 by García Robles entitled "Diplomatic Protection, the Calvo Clause, and the Safeguard of the International Rights of Man." See also Shea, *The Calvo Clause.*

[74] Orinoco Steamship Co. (United States) v. Venezuela, 1903. Ralston, *International Arbitral Law and Procedure,* pp. 72 ff. See also the Orinoco Steamship Case before the Hague Permanent Court of Arbitration, 1910. Scott, *Hague Court Reports,* p. 226; Whiteman, *Damages in International Law,* Vol. II, p. 1134.

The North American Dredging Company case between the United States and Mexico,[75] decided in 1926, involved a claim for damages resulting from the alleged breach by Mexico of a contract with the company for dredging at the port of Salina Cruz. The contract contained a clause by which the contractor and persons working under him were to be "considered as Mexicans in all matters, within the Republic of Mexico, concerning the execution of such work and the fulfillment of this contract. . . . They are consequently deprived of any rights as aliens and under no conditions shall the intervention of foreign diplomatic agents be permitted, in any matter related to this contract." The Mixed Claims Commission held that under the rules of international law an alien might make such a promise; but at the same time that "he can not deprive the government of his nation of its undoubted right of applying international remedies to violations of international law committed to his damage." The Calvo Clause was interpreted as binding the claimant to be governed by the laws of Mexico, but, said the Commission, "this provision did not, and could not, deprive the claimant of his American citizenship and all that that implies. It did not take from him his undoubted right to apply to his own Government for protection if his resort to the Mexican tribunals or other authorities available to him resulted in a denial or delay of justice as that term is used in international law." The Commission, however, refused to consider the claim on the ground that the existence of the Calvo Clause in the contract made it necessary for the claimant to show denial of justice before the Commission could take jurisdiction.

In the International Fisheries Company case between the United States and Mexico,[76] decided in 1931, involving a claim based upon the cancellation of a contract, the same principles were applied as in the Dredging Company case; but the American Commissioner dissented on the ground that at the time the contract was canceled there was no remedy for the company under Mexican law. The concession, it was said, had been "canceled by a Mexican military leader who undertook to combine in himself the exercise of military, executive, legislative, and judicial power," and that in fact "no Federal courts functioned when General Carranza canceled the company's concession." [77]

---

[75] United States v. Mexico, General Claims Commission, 1926. Fenwick, *Cases,* p. 268; Hudson, *Cases,* p. 1109; Bishop, *Cases,* p. 710; Briggs, *Cases,* p. 640. For comment on the case, see Dunn, *Diplomatic Protection of Americans in Mexico,* pp. 406 ff.

[76] *Opinions of the Commissioners, 1931,* pp. 207 ff.

[77] *Ibid., loc. cit.* The dissenting opinion of Commissioner Nielsen criticizes sharply the decision of the Commission in the North American Dredging Co. case, asserting that such claims were within the competence of the Commission and that the Calvo Clause, not being a rule of international law, could not operate of itself to preclude consideration of the case. For citations, see Hackworth, *Digest,* Vol. V, p. 645.

H. PUBLIC BONDS

The obligation of a government towards aliens who are holders of its public bonds creates problems somewhat different from those arising from the obligation of a government towards aliens who have entered into special contractual relations with it.[78] Public bonds, being payable to bearer and being bought and sold on the open market, constitute a much looser contract than a bargain with a particular individual. They are a sort of impersonal contract by which the state pledges itself to all comers to meet the terms set forth in the bond. Those who buy the bonds do so on the principle of *caveat emptor*. Nevertheless, in view of the fact that the state which issues the bonds is in most cases immune from suit both in its own courts and in international courts, it is to be expected that holders of the bonds should call upon their respective governments for aid when there is default in payment of interest or principal. On their part governments have been less ready to intervene on behalf of their citizens than in cases of breach of special contract; but they claim a legal right to do so, and their action has in general been determined by circumstances indicating lack of good faith on the part of the debtor government, whether actual or constructive.

Discrimination by a state in favor of bond holders of one nationality against those of another would be an obvious ground for alleging lack of good faith. Thus when the Government of Portugal undertook in 1924 to pay interest on gold bonds in depreciated currency, but made an exception in favor of British holders resident in Great Britain, the United States protested against the "unwarranted discrimination." [79] A serious breach of good faith would consist in pledging certain revenues for payment of the bonds and then diverting the revenues to other uses. In like manner payment, whether of the principal of the bond or of interest, in depreciated paper when payment has been pledged in gold would be an obvious fraud on the holder of the bond. In the case of the Serbian Loans,[80] involving a dispute between France and Yugoslavia resulting from the intervention of France on behalf of French holders of Serbian bonds, which had been designated at the time of issue as gold loans or as being for a sum of gold francs, and which Serbia sought to pay off in current gold francs of lesser value, the Permanent Court of International Justice held that the bonds must be paid in the gold francs contemplated by the contract. A similar decision was rendered by the Permanent Court

---

[78] On the general subject of public bonds, see Borchard, *op. cit.*, §§ 116 ff.; "International Loans and International Law," *Proceedings*, Am. Soc. Int. Law, 1932, pp. 135 ff., and discussion following.

[79] Hackworth, *Digest*, Vol. V, p. 627.

[80] Permanent Court of International Justice, Judgment 14, July 12, 1929. Hudson, *World Court Reports*, Vol. II, p. 344. Hackworth, *Digest*, Vol. V, pp. 630 ff.

in a case involving the payment in gold of Brazilian Federal Loans issued in France.[81]

The proceedings instituted by France against the Government of Norway before the International Court of Justice in 1955, on the ground of failure to pay, in gold, bonds made payable in gold, failed to reach a decision on the merits because the French acceptance of the compulsory jurisdiction of the Court did not apply to disputes relating to matters essentially within the national jurisdiction; and the Court found that Norway was entitled to invoke the French declaration on ground of reciprocity. The Court therefore decided that it lacked jurisdiction.[82]

The Drago Doctrine. The question of the right of a state to resort to force to collect the claims of its citizens against foreign governments became an acute political issue at the opening of the twentieth century. In 1902, at the time of the blockade of Venezuela by the combined fleets of Great Britain, Germany, and Italy with the object of enforcing contractual and other claims against Venezuela, Dr. Drago, foreign minister of the Argentine Republic, formulated the doctrine, now known by his name, that "a public debt cannot give rise to the right of intervention, and much less to the occupation of the soil of any American nation by any European power." [83] The Drago Doctrine was thus advanced by its author as supplementary to the Monroe Doctrine. International attention was directed to the question during the next few years with the result that the subject was taken up at the Second Hague Conference in 1907; and a convention, known by the name of the United States delegate, General Porter, was adopted in which the contracting powers agreed "not to have recourse to armed force for the recovery of contract debts claimed from the Government of one country by the Government of another country as being due to its nationals." The agreement, however, was made subject to the condition that the debtor state should not refuse to reply to an offer of arbitration or, having accepted it, fail to abide by the award.[84]

The United States took a special interest in the problem of the forcible collection of contract debts in consequence of its connection with the

[81] *Ibid.,* Judgment 15. Hudson, *op. cit.,* Vol. II, p. 404. For comment, see Nussbaum, *Money in the Law,* pp. 378 ff.

[82] *U.N. Yearbook,* 1957, p. 359. *I.C.J. Reports,* 1957, p. 9.

[83] Note to the Argentine Minister at Washington, December 29, 1902. Moore, *Digest,* Vol. VI, p. 592. The Drago Doctrine fills a large place in the legal literature of Latin America. See, in particular, Moreno, *Derecho Int. Público,* pp. 207 ff.; Antokoletz, *Derecho Int. Público,* Segunda parte, No. 173; Accioly, *Tratado,* Vol. I, Nos. 384 ff.; A. Alvarez, "Latin America and International Law," *Am. Journal,* Vol. 3 (1909), pp. 269, 334; K. Strupp, "L'intervention en matière financière," *Recueil des Cours,* Vol. 8 (1925-III), pp. 5-123.

[84] The convention was signed with numerous reservations, entered principally by the Latin American states. See *Hague Conventions,* pp. 242 ff.; Higgins, *Hague Peace Conferences,* pp. 191 ff. Podestá Costa explains and justifies the objections raised against the convention. *Manual de derecho internacional público,* p. 208.

Monroe Doctrine. President Roosevelt acquiesced in the blockade of Venezuela by Great Britain, Germany, and Italy in 1902, only after receiving assurances that no occupation of territory was contemplated.[85] But the outcome of the blockade was not a happy one so far as international law was concerned. Venezuela agreed to submit the claims of all foreign nationals to arbitration by a series of mixed commissions. But the powers which had used force to secure the settlement insisted that their claims should receive priority. This particular question was then submitted to the decision of a special tribunal of the Hague Permanent Court of Arbitration, which, looking upon the forcible intervention of the three powers as accepted international practice, gave preference to their claims as against those of other states.[86] The tribunal appeared to regard its jurisdiction as strictly limited by certain facts recognized in the protocols which terminated the resort to force, and general principles of equity were sacrificed to meet a practical situation.[87]

Shortly after the settlement with Venezuela was effected under the coercion of the three European powers, President Roosevelt was confronted with a similar situation in the Dominican Republic. Seeing the Republic embarrassed by its foreign debts and in danger of having its ports occupied by the governments of its creditors, he concluded a treaty with it by which the United States agreed to undertake the adjustment of outstanding Dominican debts, domestic as well as foreign, and with that object to take charge of and administer the customhouses.[88] The proposed treaty was rejected by the Senate, but in 1907 a new treaty was negotiated providing for the issuance of new bonds and the appointment by the President of the United States of a receiver-general of customs.[89] In the message accompanying the earlier treaty, President Roosevelt explained the situation as presenting the alternative of the adoption of effective measures by the United States to see to the payment of the foreign debts of the Republic, or its acquiescence in the measures taken by foreign governments to safeguard the interests of their citizens, the latter choice implying the abandonment of the traditional policy of the Monroe Doctrine.[90] The old order has now changed, and similar unilateral intervention is now of historic interest only.

[85] See Moore, *Digest*, Vol. VI, pp. 969 ff. For further details see Latané, *American Foreign Policy*, pp. 490 ff.; Perkins, *Hands Off*, pp. 215 ff.; Bemis, *The Latin American Policy of the United States*, pp. 145 ff.

[86] Germany *et al.* v. Venezuela: Preferential Claims Case. Tribunal of the Permanent Court of Arbitration, 1904. Scott, *Hague Court Reports*, p. 56; Fenwick, *Cases*, p. 732.

[87] For brief critical comment, see Schwarzenberger, *International Law*, Vol. I, p. 239.

[88] See Hollander, "The Convention of 1907 between the United States and the Dominican Republic," *Am. Journal*, Vol. 1 (1907), p. 287.

[89] For the text of the treaty, see *Treaties and Conventions*, Vol. I, p. 418.

[90] For details of the situation, see Perkins, *op. cit.*, pp. 236 ff.; Bemis, *op. cit.*, pp. 154 ff.

I. SPECIAL SITUATION OF A FEDERAL GOVERNMENT

Responsibility in tort. Is the responsibility of a state in any way modified by the fact that a wrong done to an alien, whether by way of denial of justice or the repudiation of a contractual obligation, has been due to the act of one of the political subdivisions of the state or of a colony or other dependency of the state which does not conduct its foreign relations independently? [91] The question is one in which conditions of domestic constitutional law have embarrassed the practical application of the rules of international law; but there would seem to be but one answer to the legal proposition. In cases of tort, as distinct from breach of contract, the state must assume international responsibility for the act of its political subdivision or dependency, whatever be the internal constitutional relations between the bodies. In the United States, in consequence of the division of the powers of government between the national government and the several states of the union, a special difficulty has arisen in connection with the responsibility for international wrongs. The national government, notwithstanding its powers in respect to foreign affairs, has under the Constitution no direct control over the administration of justice by the several states. It can annul the legal effects of state law, but it can not compel the state to perform positive acts, such as the payment of indemnity for wrong done. At the same time, the states themselves, having no international personality, cannot be held directly accountable by the foreign state for delinquencies whether in the form of a positive act or of a neglect to act. The Constitution leaves a gap between the two jurisdictions.

On several occasions the United States, in confessing to foreign states its inability to furnish redress for the delinquent acts of officers of the state governments, has been effectively answered by the foreign state by showing that such constitutional inability did not affect the question of international responsibility. In the case of the riots at Denver, in 1880, in which a number of Chinese were killed, Secretary Evarts sought to evade responsibility, asserting that "the powers of direct intervention on the part of this government are limited by the Constitution of the United States"; but the Chinese Government was naturally unwilling to accept the excuse.[92] Again, on the occasion of the more serious anti-Chinese riots at Rock Springs, Wyoming, in 1885, Secretary Bayard attempted to extend the argument of Secretary Evarts to a federal territory. But the protest of the Chinese Government was logically unanswerable.[93] In the

---

[91] On the general subject, see Stoke, *Foreign Relations of the Federal State;* Hyde, *Int. Law,* Vol. II, § 291; Eagleton, *op. cit.,* p. 32.

[92] "So far as the arrest and punishment of the guilty parties was concerned," said the Secretary, "it is a matter which . . . belongs exclusively to the government and authorities of the State of Colorado." Moore, *Digest,* Vol. VI, § 1025.

[93] Moore, *Digest,* Vol. VI, § 1025. See above, p. 338.

case of the Mafia riots in New Orleans in 1891, Italy withdrew her minister in protest against the failure of the United States to take steps to prosecute the parties responsible for the lynching. But on this occasion the President recognized the responsibility of the federal government and not only paid an indemnity but proposed that Congress should make offenses against the treaty rights of foreigners cognizable in the federal courts.[94] In spite of inconsistencies in its own record, the United States has regularly refused to accept from other federal states a disclaimer of liability for the acts or omissions to act of political subdivisions of the federal state.[95]

Breaches of contract. Conceding responsibility in cases of tort or delict committed to the injury of an alien, is a federal government responsible for breach of contract between one of its subdivisions and a citizen of a foreign state? Is it responsible for a default in the payment of the principal or interest of municipal bonds? With respect to breach of contract it seems to be agreed that responsibility need only be assumed when there has been denial of justice, as in the case of contracts between an alien and a citizen. Those who enter into contracts with the semi-independent subdivisions of a federal state do so with knowledge of the fact that the state or province or city in question has no authority to pledge the credit of the federal government, and that if it fails to perform its part of the contract the only remedy will be to sue it for breach of the contract as an ordinary citizen or corporation would be sued.[96] In like manner an alien who buys a public bond issued by a political subdivision of a federal state does so with knowledge that the bond, unless otherwise stipulated, has only the credit of the particular city or other subdivision behind it. In both cases, however, where there is breach of contract or default in meeting the obligations of bond issues, responsibility would shift to the federal government if local remedies against the delinquent political subdivision should be unavailable, or if there should be denial of justice in the application of the law.

The United States has for many years rejected any suggestion that it should assume responsibility for the repudiated debts of certain of its member states. The position taken has been that these political subdivisions were beyond the control of the federal government, and that those who bought the bonds issued by them were aware of that fact. On the other hand foreign creditors have argued that the fact that the States of

---

[94] *Ibid.,* § 1026. Hackworth, *Digest,* Vol. V, pp. 593 ff.

[95] See Hackworth, *Digest,* Vol. V, pp. 593 ff. The Harvard Draft on *Responsibility of States,* Art. 3, provides: "A state is not relieved of responsibility because an injury to an alien is attributable to one of its political subdivisions, regardless of the extent to which the national government, according to its constitution, has control of the subdivision. . . ."

[96] The United States Constitution is exceptional in protecting its member States from suit by a foreign state. Counties and cities may, however, be sued.

the Union cannot be sued in the courts of the United States constitutes in itself a denial of justice for which the federal government should be responsible.[97] In the case of Monaco v. Mississippi,[98] involving a petition by the principality to be allowed to bring suit in the Supreme Court of the United States against the State of Mississippi upon bonds issued by the state, the court held Mississippi was equally immune from suit by the principality as by the individual owners of the bonds who had donated them to the principality. The decision left the international question unanswered. But in apparent recognition of the equities of the situation, the court went on to observe that: "The National Government, by virtue of its control of our foreign relations, is entitled to employ the resources of diplomatic negotiations and to effect such an international settlement as may be found to be appropriate, through treaty, agreement of arbitration or otherwise." [99]

J. TAXATION OF ALIENS

As a general principle states have the right, incident to their jurisdiction over persons and property within their boundaries, to tax resident aliens equally with citizens. Discriminatory taxation, formerly renounced specifically in treaties of amity and commerce, may now be said to be prohibited by international customary law. But international law has not as yet developed fixed rules with respect to the protection of the resident alien against double taxation.[100] A resident alien may be subjected to a tax not only upon real property and bonds and other securities held in the foreign state, but upon his entire income even though derived from sources outside the foreign state; while at the same time he is being taxed by his national state upon the same income. Inheritance taxes may be imposed upon securities present in a foreign country even though the same securities are being taxed in the country in which the transfer of the decedent's estate takes place. In the case of Burnet v. Brooks,[101] decided in 1933, involving the imposition of a federal estate tax upon securities which were owned by a British subject resident in Cuba at the time of his death, but which were physically present in

[97] On the question of the repudiated debts of the member States of the Union, see B. Randolph, "Foreign Bondholders and the Repudiated Debts of the Southern States," Am. Journal, Vol. 25 (1931), pp. 63 ff. See also Hackworth, Digest, Vol. V, p. 596, citing the refusal of the United States to accept responsibility for the repudiated debts of the State of Georgia.

[98] 292 U.S. 313 (1934). Fenwick, Cases, p. 326; Hudson, Cases, p. 507.

[99] For comment upon the case, see C. P. Anderson, Am. Journal, Vol. 28 (1934), p. 527; J. S. Reeves, ibid., p. 739.

[100] On the general subject, see Hyde, Int. Law, Vol. I, §§ 205-206A; Hackworth, Digest, Vol. III, p. 575; B. Griziotti, "L'imposition fiscale des étrangers," Recueil des Cours, Vol. 13 (1926-III), p. 5; E. Allix, "La condition des étrangers au point de vue fiscal," ibid., Vol. 61 (1937-III), p. 545.

[101] 288 U.S. 378 (1933). Fenwick, Cases, p. 278; Am. Journal, Vol. 27 (1933), p. 766.

New York City, the Supreme Court of the United States held that since the property in question was within the jurisdiction of the United States,

it was property within the reach of the power which the United States by virtue of its sovereignty could exercise as against other nations and their subjects without violating any established principle of international law. . . . As jurisdiction may exist in more than one government, that is, jurisdiction based on distinct grounds—the citizenship of the owner, his domicile, the source of income, the situs of the property—efforts have been made to preclude multiple taxation through the negotiation of appropriate international conventions. These endeavors, however, have proceeded upon express or implied recognition, and not in denial, of the sovereign taxing power as exerted by governments in the exercise of jurisdiction upon any one of these grounds.

In support of its conclusions the court cited the case of Winans v. Attorney-General, decided by the British House of Lords in 1910.

CHAPTER **XV**

Special Jurisdictional Obligations
Toward Foreign States

A. PREVENTION OF ACTS INJURIOUS TO FOREIGN STATES

The jurisdiction of a state over all persons and property within its national boundaries carries with it a wide variety of obligations towards foreign states in addition to the obligation to afford due protection to resident aliens. A number of these obligations call for the adoption of positive measures directed towards the prevention of acts injurious to foreign states. Others involve restrictions upon the application of domestic law to the person of visiting sovereigns, or to the property of a foreign state which happens to be temporarily within the national jurisdiction. Others, again, involve certain jurisdictional courtesies to foreign states which have in the course of time come to be regarded as quasi-legal obligations. In each case they involve corresponding rights on the part of the state whose interests are affected.

Invasions by armed bands. There is no question but that a state is under a general obligation to prevent the use of its territory by persons organized to commit hostile acts against a foreign state.[1] But the obligation is obviously modified by the practical possibility of doing so. No state can exercise such complete control over its territory as to prevent secret acts of small groups of persons. The rule has therefore developed that the responsibility of the state in such cases is measured by the degree of "due diligence" which it shows in carrying out its general obligation, due diligence being determined by the circumstances of the case. Thus a state must show due diligence in preventing the organization within its jurisdiction of military expeditions intended to effect an attack upon the territory of a friendly state. Following the American Civil War the

---

[1] On the general subject, see V. Pella, "La répression des crimes contre le personnalité de l'Etat," *Recueil des Cours,* Vol. 33 (1930-III), p. 677.

United States sought to hold Great Britain responsible for the attack in 1864 upon the town of St. Albans, Vermont, by a small party of persons acting in the interest of the Confederate States who had prepared their expedition upon Canadian soil. But the mixed commission, to which the claims were submitted in 1871, disallowed responsibility on the ground of the secrecy with which the enterprise had been planned. Again, Great Britain sought to hold the United States responsible for an attack by Fenians upon Canada and New Brunswick in 1866. In both cases strained political relations gave importance to relatively minor incidents.[2]

In 1916 the United States held the *de facto* government of Mexico responsible for the invasion of American territory by a band of brigands under the leadership of Francisco Villa.[3] In this case, however, American troops crossed the border in pursuit of the bandit; and an elaborate correspondence followed between the two governments with regard to reciprocal passage of troops across their respective borders in pursuit of similar lawless bands of armed men. No agreement being reached, Mexico protested against the pursuit by American troops, some two months later, of Mexican bandits who had raided another border town in Texas, arguing that it was the duty of the United States to protect its frontier adequately against such incursions. The United States replied that it was rather the duty of Mexico to prevent the incursions than the duty of the United States to guard against them. The inability of the Mexican Government to prevent the outrages might excuse the failure to do so, "but it only makes stronger the duty of the United States to prevent them [by pursuit], for if the Government of Mexico can not protect the lives and property of Americans exposed to attack from Mexicans, the Government of the United States is in duty bound, so far as it can, to do so." [4]

Military expeditions against a foreign state. The duty of a state to prevent the formation upon its soil of military expeditions against a foreign state has frequently been an issue in connection with neutrality in time of war, whether between two foreign states or between a foreign state and a rebellious colony or dependency. The so-called Neutrality Act, passed by the United States Congress in 1818, was adopted to meet the situation created by the attempt to use American soil as a base for military and naval expeditions in favor of the rebellious Spanish colonies in their wars of independence.[5] The British Foreign Enlistment Act of 1819 had the same object in view. The classic case of the *Alabama* Claims arose between the United States and Great Britain following the

---

[2] For the two incidents, see Moore, *Arbitrations,* Vol. IV, p. 4042; Moore, *Digest,* Vol. I, pp. 686 ff.

[3] For a discussion of the legal principles at issue, see A. S. Hershey, "Incursions into Mexico and the Doctrine of Hot Pursuit," *Am. Journal,* Vol. 13 (1919), p. 557.

[4] See Hackworth, *Digest,* Vol. II, pp. 291 ff.

[5] See below, p. 743.

American Civil War, in consequence of a demand by the United States for indemnity for losses suffered by it through the alleged failure of Great Britain to use "due diligence" to prevent the building and equipping in its ports of vessels to be used in the service of the Confederate States.[6]

Sale of arms. In 1912, the Congress of the United States, responding to frequent complaints by the Government of Mexico that arms sold in the open market of the United States came into the hands of hostile Indians, whether by indirect purchase or by smuggling across the border, adopted a joint resolution providing "That whenever the President shall find that in any American country conditions of domestic violence exist which are promoted by the use of arms or munitions of war procured from the United States, and shall make proclamation thereof, it shall be unlawful to export, except under such limitations and exceptions as the President shall prescribe, any arms or munitions of war from any place in the United States to such country until otherwise ordered by the President or by Congress." [7]

Numerous complaints were preferred by the Government of Mexico during the years of the Diaz regime of military expeditions formed in the United States with the object of overthrowing the regime. In answer, the United States admitted the obligation of using due diligence to prevent such expeditions, but pointed out the distinction which existed "on the one hand between the passage of men singly or in small groups across our frontier and into another country, or the sailing of individuals or small groups in the ordinary course of events from one of our ports, and on the other hand the departure from our territory of organized groups of men avowing the purpose of undertaking belligerent activities in foreign territory." [8]

In 1927, at the meeting of the International Commission of Jurists, a draft convention was adopted relative to the rights and duties of states in the event of civil war, which was subsequently adopted as a convention by the Habana Conference of 1928 and was ratified, among other states, by the United States and by Mexico. The convention provides, *inter alia*, that the contracting states must use the means at their disposal to prevent persons within their territory "from participating in, gathering

[6] See below, p. 745.

[7] The constitutionality of the prohibition was upheld by the Supreme Court in United States v. Chavez, 228 U.S. 525 (1913). See Hackworth, *Digest*, Vol. VII, p. 626. The arms embargo adopted at the time of the conflict between Bolivia and Paraguay in the Chaco in 1934 was based upon a similar conception of duty.

[8] See Hackworth, *Digest*, Vol. VII, pp. 335 ff. In accordance with the principle that a crime takes place where the criminal performs the last act on his part in consequence of which the crime takes place, the courts both of the United States and of Brazil took jurisdiction during the First World War over cases in which explosives were stored in belligerent ships while in port, with the intention that they should explode when the vessels were on the high seas. See Hackworth, *Digest*, pp. 335 ff.

elements, crossing the boundary or sailing from their territory for the purpose of starting or promoting civil strife"; they must disarm and intern rebel forces coming into their territory; they must forbid the traffic in arms except such as are intended for the government of the country when the belligerency of the rebels has not been recognized; and they must prevent equipment or arming of a vessel intended to operate in favor of the rebellion.[9]

Query, was the United States delinquent in its international duty in not preventing Cuban refugees in Miami from cooperating with other refugees in Central America in preparing the ill-fated expedition that landed at the Bay of Pigs in 1962? Did the fact that the Government of Cuba was at the time violating treaty obligations with the United States affect the failure of the United States to prevent the expedition? Was the violation of the fundamental human rights of non-Communist Cubans in Cuba, resulting in the enforced exile of the refugees, a threat to the peace of sufficient gravity to justify the United States in making no effort to prevent the departure of a military expedition in violation of the Havana Convention? [10]

On December 2, 1963, the Council of the Organization of American States, responding to a request of the Governments of Venezuela and Costa Rica, called a Meeting of Consultation under the Rio Treaty of Reciprocal Defense and acting provisionally as Organ of Consultation, appointed a committee to investigate charges that the Government of Cuba was secretly supplying arms to pro-Castro rebels in Venezuela and otherwise aiding in efforts to overthrow the government.[11]

Pollution of water and air. Is a state under an obligation to see that acts are not performed within its jurisdiction which have the effect of polluting the waters or the air of a neighboring state? The problem is a modern one, and it would seem that, in default of customary law upon the subject, it should be governed by general principles of justice and equity. In the case of Missouri v. Illinois,[12] involving a petition by Missouri for an injunction to prevent the discharge of sewage by the City of Chicago into a river which emptied into the Mississippi River, the Supreme Court of the United States, while denying the injunction on the ground that it was not shown that the pollution was of serious mag-

---

[9] *Int. Conferences of American States,* 1889-1928, p. 435. For the text of the draft of the Commission of Jurists, see *Am. Journal,* Vol. 22 (1928), Spec. Supp., p. 267.

[10] The questions are obviously closely related to the larger issue of the right of the United States to demand the removal of the missile bases on October 22, 1962. See L. C. Meeker, "Defensive Quarantine and the Law," *Am. Journal,* Vol. 57 (1963), p. 515, and accompanying articles.

[11] *Acta,* 3 de diciembre, 1963. The report of the committee fully justified the charges of Venezuela. *Acta,* 24 de febrero, 1964. The Meeting of Consultation was held on July 21, 1964, and sanctions were adopted against the Government of Cuba.

[12] 200 U.S. 496 (1906). Fenwick, *Cases,* p. 291; Hudson, *Cases,* p. 433.

nitude or that it had been clearly and fully proved, had no doubt with respect to the principles to be applied to the case. "The nuisance set forth in the bill," said the Court, "was one which would be of international importance—a visible change of a great river from a pure stream into a polluted and poisoned ditch. The only question presented was whether, as between the States of the Union, this court was competent to deal with a situation which, if it arose between independent sovereignties, might lead to war." [13] In the case of New Jersey v. City of New York,[14] involving a petition for an injunction to prevent the city from dumping sewage into the ocean adjacent to the shores of New Jersey, the Supreme Court held that the fact that the dumping took place on the high seas outside the territorial waters did not preclude the granting of an injunction when the property alleged to have been injured by the dumping was within the jurisdiction of the court.

In 1909 the United States and Great Britain concluded a treaty concerning the boundary waters between the United States and Canada, Article IV of which contains the provision that the waters defined in the treaty as boundary waters and waters flowing across the boundary "shall not be polluted on either side to the injury of health or property on the other." In 1918 the International Joint Commission provided for in the treaty found that the waters of the Detroit and Niagara Rivers were being polluted, and a draft treaty was prepared to carry out the recommendation of the Commission that no untreated sewage from cities or towns should be discharged into boundary waters.[15]

Query, whether an obligation on the part of the United States, under treaty, to deliver a fixed quantity of water of a river flowing from the United States into Mexico, would be violated if the water became salty from natural causes resulting from the use of the upper water of the river for purposes of irrigation? [16] The issue bears a close relation to the Lake Lanoux case, involving a claim by Spain against France by reason of the diversion of the waters of the lake as part of a hydroelectric project, the defense of France being upheld on the ground that there was no diminution of the flow into Spain. In this case there was no showing that the returned waters were polluted by reason of their use in France.[17]

Query, does the same principle apply to pollution of the air? In the

[13] The Court observed further that "It may be imagined that a nuisance might be created by a State upon a navigable river like the Danube, which would amount to a *casus belli* for a State lower down, unless removed."

[14] 283 U.S. 473 (1931).

[15] Hackworth, *Digest*, Vol. II, p. 342.

[16] See below, p. 464, under the title "Flow of Rivers." For a critical study, see A. P. Lester, "River Pollution in International Law," *Am. Journal*, Vol. 57 (1963), p. 828.

[17] *Am. Journal*, Vol. 53 (1959), p. 156; Whiteman, *Digest*, Vol. 3, p. 1066. See also below, p. 465, note 30, where the issue is raised in connection with easements and servitudes.

Trail Smelter Arbitration, held under an agreement between the United States and Canada for the settlement of a complaint by the United States that fumes discharged from the smelter of a mining company at Trail in British Columbia were injurious to the State of Washington, the tribunal held in 1941 that damages were due, on the principle which it considered as valid in international as in national law, *sic utere tuo ut alienum non laedas.*[18] The same principle had been applied in 1907 by the Supreme Court of the United States in a case between the State of Georgia and the Tennessee Copper Co. holding that "it is a fair and reasonable demand on the part of a sovereign that the air over its territory should not be polluted on a great scale by sulphurous acid gas. . . ."[19] Query, would the principle hold equally well for the explosion of a hydrogen bomb over the Pacific Ocean, the fallout from which was alleged to have injurious effects upon neighboring territory?

Counterfeiting foreign currency. Is a state under an obligation to prevent persons within its jurisdiction from counterfeiting the coin or securities of a foreign state? In the case of Emperor of Austria v. Day and Kossuth,[20] the British Court of Appeal in Chancery sustained a decree to prevent the further printing and to secure the delivery of notes intended by Kossuth to be circulated as money in Hungary. In the case of United States v. Arjona,[21] the Supreme Court of the United States found, as a point of constitutional law, that the power given to Congress to punish "offenses against the law of nations" covered the offense of counterfeiting a foreign bank note in the United States. In deciding the case the court laid down the general principle that the law of nations requires every national government to use due diligence to prevent the commission within its dominion of a wrong to another nation or its people.

In 1913 the Government of Brazil appealed to the United States to punish persons who were counterfeiting Brazilian money and securities. In reply the United States pointed out that its laws already provided for the punishment of such offenses when committed within its jurisdiction, but that in view of the fact that the territorial theory of crime prevailed in the United States it was not possible to prosecute persons who had committed the offense in Brazil.[22] On its part the United States complained to foreign governments on a number of occasions that advertise-

[18] Hackworth, *Digest,* Vol. II, pp. 344 ff.

[19] 206 U.S. 230 (1907). See M. S. McDougal, "The Hydrogen Bomb Tests and the International Law of the Sea," *Am. Journal,* Vol. 49 (1955), p. 357, where justification is offered on grounds of self-defense.

[20] 3 De Gex, Fisher, and Jones, 217 (1861). Fenwick, *Cases,* pp. 282, 286; Briggs, *Cases,* p. 408; Hudson, *Cases,* p. 497. The case was not strictly one of counterfeiting, for Kossuth was seeking to introduce into Hungary notes signed by himself which would be payable only in the event of a successful revolution.

[21] 120 U.S. 479 (1887). Fenwick, *Cases,* p. 288.

[22] Hackworth, *Digest,* Vol. II, p. 350.

ments were being circulated on which were printed a facsimile reproduction of American dollar certificates.[23] An International Convention on the Suppression of Counterfeiting Currency was adopted in 1929, in which elaborate provisions are laid down for the suppression of that offense.[24]

Slander and libel against foreign governments. Is a state under an obligation to prevent persons within its jurisdiction from uttering slanderous remarks or publishing libelous statements against a foreign government? The protection given to freedom of speech in the constitutions of democratic states has made it difficult to restrain the acts of private individuals. The acts of public officers, however, may be restrained, if not subjected to criminal prosecution. In 1931 the Secretary of State of the United States formally apologized to "Mr. Mussolini and to the Italian people" for remarks reflecting upon the Italian Prime Minister made in a public address by a major-general of the United States Marine Corps. The offending officer was placed under arrest, pending court-martial.[25] In like manner Secretary Hull apologized in 1937 for remarks about the German Government made by the mayor of New York. But by contrast Secretary Hull explained to the German ambassador in 1935, on the occasion of the designation by Magistrate Brodsky of the swastika emblem as a "pirate flag," that "State and municipal officials are not instrumentalities of the Federal government." [26]

Libelous statements in newspapers and other publications under direct government control present a distinct question. Propaganda directed against a foreign government, imputing obviously false motives to it, might reasonably be regarded as an offense against the state whose government is thus attacked, all the more so if there is no free press to correct the official propaganda. In like manner radio broadcasts, controlled by government agencies, which systematically misrepresent the policies of other governments, constitute a just ground of complaint on their part. Carried to an extreme degree such official propaganda might, indeed, be regarded as an act of aggression in itself, in that it creates the conditions that might well lead to a military conflict. Fear and distrust are the most powerful solvents of obligations to refrain from the use of force; and fear and distrust are promoted in direct proportion to the

---

[23] *Ibid.*, pp. 351 ff.

[24] Hudson, *International Legislation*, Vol. IV, p. 2692.

[25] E. C. Stowell, "The General Smedley D. Butler Incident," *Am. Journal*, Vol. 25 (1931), p. 321.

[26] Hackworth, *Digest*, Vol. II, p. 145. For the apology made by Secretary Hull for the attack upon the German flag flying over the consulate in San Francisco in 1941, see *Documents on Am. Foreign Relations*, Vol. III, p. 420.

On the question of the alleged defamation of Mexico by the Hearst newspapers in 1927, see E. D. Dickinson, *Am. Journal*, Vol. 22 (1928), p. 840. On the responsibility of states for international propaganda, see V. Van Dyke, *ibid.*, Vol. 34 (1940), p. 58.

degree to which peoples are intellectually isolated from one another. It would seem, therefore, that it has now become a jurisdictional obligation of every government not only to refrain on its own part from deliberate misrepresentation of the policies of other states, but to keep open the channels of communication and information, so that its people may be able to maintain those contacts with other peoples which are the normal correctives of official propaganda.[27]

But the obligation is one which it would be difficult, if not impossible, to enforce under particular circumstances. Haiti, acting in accordance with the procedures of the Organization of American States, succeeded in 1949 in calling the Dominican Republic to account for permitting the use of its radio and other facilities by a former Haitian official for the purpose of agitating in favor of the overthrow of the Haitian Government.[28] On the other hand the press of the Soviet Union, under state control, consistently misrepresents the policies of the United States and other capitalist countries; and doubtless the Soviet Union, with its ideological preconceptions, may make a corresponding claim against the press of the United States, which, however, is not subject to state control. Freedom of the press would thus appear to be an essential condition of the friendly relations of states, and it is recognized as such in the objectives of UNESCO. Whether the denial of freedom of communication is a violation of international law by inference from general principles is controversial.[29]

B. ACTS OF STATE OFFICERS OUTSIDE NATIONAL JURISDICTION

The principles of state responsibility which apply to acts of officers of the state committed within the jurisdiction of the state apply equally to the acts of state officers committed on the high seas or on foreign territory. For the most part cases involving such acts are committed in time of war when the exigencies of war lead to the commission of offenses which the officer would not be tempted to commit in time of peace. In 1864, during the American Civil War, a Federal warship captured the Confederate cruiser, *Florida,* in the territorial waters of Brazil. Due apology was made, the United States stating that the capture was "an unauthorized, unlawful and indefensible exercise of the naval force of the United States, within a foreign country, in defiance of its established and duly recognized government." [30] In like manner Germany made

[27] See, on this point, C. G. Fenwick, "The Problem of Moral Disarmament," *Am. Journal,* Vol. 41 (1947), p. 112.

[28] Fenwick, *OAS,* p. 199.

[29] See the conflicting views of Q. Wright, C. G. Fenwick, and others in "Freedom of Communication across National Frontiers," *Proceedings,* Am. Society of Int. Law, 1950, pp. 95 ff.; J. B. Whitton, "The United Nations Conference on Freedom of Information and the Movement against International Propaganda," *Am. Journal,* Vol. 42 (1948), p. 73.

[30] Moore, *Digest,* Vol. VII, pp. 1090 ff. See below, p. 729.

apology to Brazil for the "transgression of orders" by officers of a public ship, the *Panther,* who had violated the territorial sovereignty of Brazil by invading private homes in their search for a deserter.[31] The occasional acts of minor officials to the direct injury of a foreign state differ only in the gravity of the offense from the acts of higher officers. The state is responsible for them as being the acts of its agents; but the redress is likely to be less formal.

In contrast with such cases calling for an apology, it may happen that the act when originally committed by the officer was unauthorized, yet the state may subsequently approve and ratify it, and thus take upon itself direct responsibility for it. In such cases the act becomes "an act of state" and the officer committing it is relieved from civil and criminal prosecution in the foreign country where the act was committed, should the latter happen to have control of his person. This assumption of responsibility was undertaken by Great Britain in 1837 in the case of McLeod, the leader of a Canadian force which crossed the Niagara River and committed hostilities on the American side.[32] In the case of People v. McLeod, the Supreme Court of the State of New York rejected the plea of "act of state" in answer to a criminal indictment of McLeod for his illegal acts, and it remanded the prisoner for trial, at which, however, he was acquitted.[33]

C. JURISDICTIONAL IMMUNITIES OF FOREIGN STATES

Personal immunity of foreign sovereigns. The principle that a state can not be sued in the courts of a foreign state is a long-standing rule of customary international law. In the classic case of the schooner *Exchange,* Chief Justice Marshall observed that the "perfect equality and absolute independence of sovereigns" had "given rise to a class of cases in which every sovereign is understood to waive the exercise of a part of that complete exclusive territorial jurisdiction which has been stated to be the attribute of every nation." [34] In earlier times, before the general establishment of democratic states, the principle was identified with the personal immunity of a foreign sovereign from suit; but the two forms of immunity are now distinct. At the present day a foreign sovereign, whether he is in constitutional law the actual head of the

---

[31] See Accioly, *Tratado,* Vol. I, No. 431; Vol. II, No. 1059.

[32] Moore, *Digest,* Vol. II, § 217. See p. 274.

[33] 25 Wendell, 483 (1841). Hudson, *Cases,* p. 686. The decision was sharply criticized by Secretary Webster, and as a result of it Congress passed a law, August 29, 1842, authorizing the federal courts to issue writs of habeas corpus in cases where a citizen of a foreign state, domiciled therein, is in custody for acts alleged to have been committed by authority of the foreign state.

[34] The Schooner *Exchange* v. McFaddon, 7 Cranch 116 (1812). Fenwick, *Cases,* p. 363; Bishop, *Cases,* p. 551; Hudson, *Cases,* p. 524. See below, p. 384.

The immunities of diplomatic officers, which logically might be considered in this connection, are treated under the general rules applying to those agents. See below, p. 561.

state or only the nominal head, enjoys when temporarily present in a foreign state a personal immunity from suit which is regarded as an essential condition of friendly international intercourse. He may not be made a party defendant to a suit under any circumstances. The president of a republic, who is technically not a sovereign, enjoys the same immunities. A special inviolability attaches to the person of a foreign sovereign, and an attack upon him is regarded as a particularly grave offense. The immunity of the foreign sovereign extends not only to exemption from criminal prosecution, whatever be the character of his acts, but also to exemption from civil suit *in personam* arising out of contracts entered into with private persons or torts committed against them.

Applications of the principle have been numerous. In the leading British case of Mighell v. Sultan of Johore,[35] decided in 1893, the plaintiff brought suit for breach of promise of marriage against the defendant, who had been known to the plaintiff as a private citizen under the assumed name of Albert Baker and who had in that character made the alleged promise of marriage. Upon being sued, the defendant disclosed his real character as sultan of the independent state of Johore in the Malay Peninsula, whereupon the court dismissed the proceedings for want of jurisdiction. A similar decision was reached in Statham v. Statham and the Gaekwar of Baroda,[36] involving a suit against the Gaekwar as co-respondent in proceedings for divorce, where the British court examined the status of the Gaekwar and found that his position as reigning sovereign entitled him to immunity from suit.

In addition to his personal immunity from suit a foreign sovereign or head of state may not be made a party defendant to a suit against him as representative of his state. In the case of De Haber v. Queen of Portugal,[37] decided in 1851, an action of debt was brought against the Queen, in her public capacity, for money wrongfully paid over to the Portuguese Government. On appeal the court made an absolute rule for a prohibition of the suit, on the ground that "to cite a foreign potentate in a municipal court, for any complaint against him in his public capacity, is contrary to the law of nations, and an insult which he is entitled to resent." [38]

---

[35] L. R. (1894), 1 Q. B. Div. 149. Hudson, *Cases*, p. 504.

[36] Probate 92 (1912). Hudson, *Cases*, p. 67.

[37] L. R. (1851), 17 Q. B. Div., 196. Fenwick, *Cases*, p. 295.

[38] During the Second World War numerous conflicts of jurisdiction arose as a result of the presence of foreign troops in friendly territory. Acts committed by these troops within the area of their encampment were in principle left to the jurisdiction of the foreign state. What if the act committed within the encampment should take effect outside of it? In the case where an American soldier, standing at the gate of "Camp Admiral Ingram," shot and killed a Brazilian citizen, the Brazilian Federal Supreme Court, on November 22, 1944, decided in favor of the jurisdiction of the United States to try the case. See H. Accioly, "Conflito de jurisdições em materia penal internacional," *Boletim da Sociedade Brasileira de Direito Internacional*, 1945, No. 2, p. 96. Accioly criticizes the decision, holding that jurisdiction was with the Brazilian courts.

Immunity of state-owned property. A direct suit against a foreign sovereign being out of the question, the practical question of the immunity from suit of a foreign state in its corporate capacity, as distinct from the personal capacity of its sovereign, arises in connection with personal and real property owned by the foreign state which, but for such ownership, would normally fall within the jurisdiction of the local courts.[39] In general the rule is well established that all such property is immune from suit. Whether the property be personal or real makes no difference in respect to the immunity.[40] Nor is it of consequence whether the property is of a governmental character, such as a consulate, or of a nongovernmental character, such as goods purchased by the foreign government or funds deposited in trust companies. In the case of Vavasseur v. Krupp,[41] decided in 1878, an injunction had been obtained by Vavasseur to prevent the defendants from delivering to a Japanese vessel of war certain shells bought by the Mikado in Germany, which it was alleged had been manufactured in infringement of the plaintiff's patent. On appeal, the higher court set aside the injunction on the ground that, even if there was an infringement of the patent, the Mikado could not be sued for it. The court held that it had no jurisdiction "to interfere with the property of a foreign sovereign, more especially with what we call the public property of the state of which he is sovereign as distinguished from that which may be his own property." In the case of Hassard v. United States of Mexico,[42] decided in 1899, a New York State court vacated an attachment which had been obtained against personal property of the Mexican Government with the object of satisfying in that way certain claims against the Government having no connection with the title of the Mexican Government to the property.

Jurisdiction by consent. Jurisdiction may, however, be assumed by the local courts over the property of a foreign state when the latter has consented to the exercise of such jurisdiction. The question then arises, what constitutes "consent"? Must it be express, or may it be implied from the nature of the suit? [43] Consent is implied where a state voluntarily appears in court as plaintiff for the purpose of obtaining a remedy,

[39] State-owned ships, public and private, are excluded from present consideration, being treated below, Chap. XVI.

[40] The question of the *title* of a foreign state to certain property may, however, be brought before the local court. Compare *Harvard Draft, Competence of Courts in Regard to Foreign States*, Art. 9. *Am. Journal*, Vol. 26 (1932), Supp., p. 572.

[41] L.R. (1878), 9 Ch. Div. 351. Fenwick, *Cases*, p. 297; Hudson, *Cases*, p. 511.

[42] 29 Misc. Rep. (1899). Fenwick, *Cases*, p. 300. For more recent cases involving suits by the American Bondholders Committee to obtain an accounting of funds claimed by the Government of Mexico to be its property, see Hackworth, *Digest*, Vol. II, pp. 394 ff.

[43] A British court was unwilling to see "consent" in a contract between a foreign state and a citizen where immunity from suit was expressly waived, such consent not being between the foreign state and the court. Duff Development Co. v. Government of Kelantan, L.R. (1924), Appeal Cases, 797. Hudson, *Cases*, p. 540.

and in such event the defendant may file a set-off or counterclaim or may take other proceedings to bring all the facts before the court. In the case of Kingdom of Norway v. Federal Sugar Refining Co.,[44] involving a suit by the plaintiff for the recovery of money paid in excess of the original contract price of the sugar, the court denied the motion of the Kingdom of Norway to restrict the answer and counterclaim of the defendant. But the counterclaim must arise out of the same action and must not relate to another and distinct matter. In the case of South African Republic v. Compagnie Franco-Belge,[45] decided in 1897, the court held that the Republic, in coming before the court as plaintiff, had not submitted to the general jurisdiction of the court "so as to be capable of being caught and sued here in respect of any matter which would be a proper subject of litigation between them if the two parties were private individuals, both resident in this country, and subject to the jurisdiction of its courts." [46]

D. PRIVILEGE OF FOREIGN STATE TO BRING SUIT

While foreign states are immune from suits brought against them without their consent, they have on the other hand the privilege of themselves instituting proceedings in the local courts. Here the problems presented are less difficult. It appears to be agreed that a foreign state, in exercising its privilege to sue, undertakes the observance of the proper forms of procedure. The privilege of suit, however, carries with it the implied consent to submit to the jurisdiction of the court in respect to a counterclaim arising out of the same cause, referred to above. But in exercising its privilege of suit a foreign state may not sue to enforce its penal or revenue laws. In the case of Queen of Holland (Married Woman) v. Drukker,[47] decided in 1928, the plaintiff entered a claim as creditor of the estate in England of a deceased Dutch subject, the basis of the claim being a succession tax imposed by Dutch law on estates of Dutch nationals. The Court of Chancery held that there was "a well recognized rule, which has been enforced for at least 200 years or thereabouts, under which these Courts will not collect the taxes of foreign

[44] 286 Fed. Rep. 188 (1923). Fenwick, *Cases*, p. 301; Hudson, *Cases*, p. 543.

[45] L.R. (1898), 1 Ch. Div. 190.

[46] A similar conclusion was reached by the court in Kingdom of Rumania v. Guaranty Trust Co., 250 Fed. Rep. 341 (1918), where the court observed that the action by the plaintiff to recover a debt owed to it by the defendant "was not a waiver of its immunity as a sovereign state to be sued by other parties. If this be not so, the immunity can be frittered away either by interpleader or attachment in any case when a foreign sovereign undertakes to collect a debt owed it."

Upon the general subject, see *Harvard Draft, Competence of Courts*, and bibliography on p. 466; E. D. Dickinson, "Waiver of State Immunity," *Am. Journal*, Vol. 19 (1925), p. 555; E. M. Borchard, "Theories of Governmental Responsibility in Tort," *Columbia Law Review*, Vol. XXVIII (1928), pp. 577, 734; Allen, *The Position of Foreign States before National Courts*.

[47] L.R. (1928), 1 Ch. Div. 877. Hudson, *Cases*, p. 501.

States for the benefit of the sovereigns of those foreign States; and this is one of those actions which these Courts will not entertain. . . . The statement of claim must therefore be struck out and the action dismissed; and, as the sovereign State has submitted to the jurisdiction by coming here, I am in a position to order the sovereign State to pay the costs of the action."

E. CODIFICATION OF THE LAW

For many years the need has been apparent of a more uniform rule in respect to the immunity from jurisdiction of foreign states in respect to commercial property and commercial relations which, but for the interest of the foreign state, would fall under the ordinary jurisdiction of the local courts. The subject was considered by the Institute of International Law at its meeting in 1891, and a series of articles was adopted under the head, "Competence of Courts in Suits against Foreign States or Sovereigns," [48] Article IX of which recognized six kinds of actions against a foreign state in which jurisdiction might be taken. In 1927 the report of the subcommittee of the League of Nations Committee of Experts pointed out the confusion existing upon the subject and the need of agreement upon it; [49] and in the same year the International Commission of Jurists at its meeting at Rio de Janeiro included some rules on immunity in its Project of an International Law of Procedure.[50] The Harvard Draft of 1932 contains a complete convention on the subject, and it seeks not only to reflect "existing practices and points of view" but constructive rules *de lege ferenda*.[51] In view of the increasing tendency toward public ownership and toward public administration through the use of subsidiary corporations, it is particularly urgent that uniform rules be adopted which will protect the interests of private individuals having just claims against the foreign state in respect to such business relations.

[48] *Resolutions,* p. 90.
[49] *Am. Journal,* Vol. 22 (1928), Spec. Supp., pp. 117 ff.
[50] *Ibid.,* pp. 310 ff.
[51] *Am. Journal,* Vol. 26 (1932), Supp., p. 474.

CHAPTER XVI

Jurisdiction Over Private and Public Vessels

A. JURISDICTION OUTSIDE TERRITORIAL LIMITS

International law recognizes in certain cases the right of a state to extend its effective jurisdiction beyond its territorial limits. Since the relationship between the state and its citizens is a personal one, the allegiance of the citizen is due to the state, in whatever part of the world the citizen may happen to be. It is true that a state cannot hold its citizen to the observance of its laws while he is within the jurisdiction of another state; but it may, if it so chooses, call him to account when he returns again within its jurisdiction. On the other hand, if the citizen is on board a vessel flying the flag of the state on the high seas, the state may place him in the same legal position as if he were on the soil of the state itself, and may apply its domestic laws, both civil and criminal, to whatever acts he performs or whatever circumstances attend them. It is in respect to jurisdiction over merchant vessels that the extension of the territorial jurisdiction of the state finds its most significant application.[1]

B. THE NATIONAL CHARACTER OF MERCHANT VESSELS

International law has no rules regulating the conditions under which vessels are entitled to fly the flag of a particular state and are accordingly invested with a degree of the national character possessed by citizens of the state. Each individual state fixes its own conditions of registration,

---

[1] On the general subject of jurisdiction over public and private vessels, see Jessup, *Law of Territorial Waters and Maritime Jurisdiction;* Rienow, *The Test of the Nationality of a Merchant Vessel;* Higgins and Colombos, *The International Law of the Sea;* A. H. Charteris, "The Legal Position of Merchantmen in Foreign Ports and National Waters," *British Year Book,* 1920-1921, pp. 45-96; P. Fedozzi, "La condition juridique des navires de commerce," *Recueil des Cours,* Vol. 10 (1925-V), pp. 5-221.

and there is no uniformity in respect to them. Some states refuse to permit the registration of vessels not owned in whole by citizens of the state. Other states admit to registration vessels owned only in part by citizens of the state or even vessels owned by foreigners. All that international law has prescribed is that some one state must authorize the vessel to use its flag, provide it with the proper "ship's papers," and thereupon exercise in respect to the vessel the degree of jurisdiction permitted by the law. The vessel itself, when registered, becomes by law of most states invested with the character of a legal person against which civil and criminal suit may be brought. In addition, its national character determines the territorial location of acts done on board it.

An unregistered vessel over which no state claimed jurisdiction would be without legal rights, and if it managed to leave its first port could not gain admission to a second. Prior to the year 1920 no state without a seacoast had attempted to register vessels and have a maritime flag. The Treaty of Versailles, Article 273, and the Treaty of St. Germain, Article 225, made provision for the recognition of the flag of Allied and Associated Powers having no seacoast, while a Declaration adopted at Barcelona in 1921 extended such recognition to all states parties to the Declaration.[2] The Geneva Convention on the High Seas of 1958 provides in successive articles that states having no seacoast shall have free access to the sea; that every state, whether coastal or not, has the right to sail ships under its flag on the high seas; and that each state shall fix the conditions for the grant of its nationality to ships and for the right to fly its flag. The Convention also provides that ships shall sail under the flag of one state only; and that a ship which sails under the flags of two or more states, using them according to convenience, loses nationality with respect to other states.[3]

Theoretical basis of jurisdiction over merchant vessels. A theory put forth in the eighteenth century in explanation of the jurisdiction exercised by a state over vessels flying its flag won sufficient acceptance to lay claim for a time to be regarded as a principle of international law. Vessels were held to be floating portions of the territory of the state; they were extensions or prolongations of the home state, and hence what took place upon them was regarded as taking place upon the soil of the state. This fiction of the "exterritoriality" of vessels, while it found expression in earlier decisions of British and American courts,[4] has been

[2] For the text of the Barcelona Declaration see Hudson, *International Legislation*, Vol. I, p. 622.

[3] Arts. 3-6.

[4] The theory was forcibly expressed in 1842 in a letter written by Webster as Secretary of State to the British Foreign Minister in answer to the assertion by Great Britain of a right of impressment through the visit and search of American vessels. "Every merchant vessel on the seas," said Webster, "is rightfully considered as part of the territory of the country to which it belongs." Moore, *Digest*, Vol. II, § 320. Webster's letter is quoted at length in United States v. Rodgers [150 U.S. 249 (1893); Hudson, *Cases*, p. 410], in which the court specifically reaffirms the theory.

rejected by most modern writers on the ground that it is inconsistent with other relations affecting the vessel both on the high seas and in foreign ports, and it was explicitly rejected in the decision of Cunard Steamship Co. v. Mellon, 262 U. S. 100 (1923),[5] where the court dismissed the suggestion that a merchant ship is a part of the territory of the country whose flag it flies as being "a figure of speech—a metaphor." The jurisdiction arises, said the court, "out of the nationality of the ship as established by her domicile, registry, and use of the flag, and partakes more of the characteristics of personal than of territorial sovereignty." A better basis of jurisdiction might be found in the fact that the jurisdiction of the flag state has been acquiesced in by other states simply as a matter of mutual convenience. Let the state which for the promotion of its overseas commerce gives the protection of its flag to its citizens who engage in that venture be also the state whose law controls acts done on board the vessel.[6] Thus, by regarding the jurisdiction of the flag state as qualified rather than absolute, it is easier to reconcile with it the jurisdiction possessed by other states over the vessel when it is temporarily in their ports, as well as the belligerent right of visit and search on the high seas when the flag of the vessel is neutral in time of war.

Exceptions to the general principle. The jurisdiction of a state over its merchant vessels on the high seas is subject to a number of exceptions. In the first place, the customary laws of war give to a belligerent the right of visit and search of all vessels in the enforcement of the rules of contraband and blockade.[7] In this connection it should be noted that the United States vigorously contested during the Napoleonic wars the attempt on the part of Great Britain to enforce on board American vessels the British municipal law of allegiance.[8] In his war message of June 1, 1812, President Madison asserted that on the high seas no laws

[5] Fenwick, *Cases,* p. 354; Bishop, *Cases,* p. 505. See below, p. 443, note 23.

[6] The Harvard *Draft Convention on Jurisdiction with Respect to Crime* adopts the rule (Art. 4) that "A State has jurisdiction with respect to any crime committed in whole or in part upon a public or private ship or aircraft which has its national character." In like manner the Harvard *Draft Convention on Extradition* proposes the rule (Art. 3, c) that "For the purposes of this article public and private vessels and aircraft of a State, which have its national character, are assimilated to a State's territory; but while a private vessel is within the territorial waters of another State, or while a private aircraft is on or over the land or territorial waters of another State, acts committed upon such vessel or aircraft are also committed within the territory of the other State."

[7] See below, pp. 733 ff., although these rules have now become obsolete.

[8] The British Government did not assert that its men-of-war might search a neutral vessel for the express purpose of finding seamen of British nationality, but it did claim—and the distinction was without practical difference—that if in the exercise of the belligerent right of visit and search for contraband, British seamen were found on board, they might be impressed into the British navy. On the other hand, the United States, by successive secretaries of state, insisted during the long period of the controversy, from 1792 to 1842, that such searches were open to the gravest objections, and that, in the language of Jefferson, "the simplest rule will be that the vessel being American shall be evidence that the seamen on board are such." Moore, *Digest,* Vol. II, § 317.

should operate except "the law of nations [*i.e.* the traditional law of contraband and blockade] and the laws of the country to which the vessels belong."[9] In the second place, in the exercise of the right of self-protection against piracy, states have the right, put into effect by their public ships, to approach all merchant vessels, whatever their ostensible nationality, with the object of verifying their flag and, in case the circumstances are suspicious, to visit and search the vessel to obtain more conclusive evidence of its character.[10] In the third place, international conventions have been entered into providing for a limited right of visit and search for the suppression of the slave trade.[11] Lastly, a state has the right in self-defense to seize a vessel flying the flag of another state under circumstances indicating that the vessel either is fraudulently registered or is being used by insurgents and rebels as a means of attack upon the state. Had the action of Spain in 1873 in the case of the *Virginius* [12] extended no further than the mere capture of the vessel and the imprisonment of its crew of filibusterers, there would have been no international ground of offense against the state of the vessel's flag.

C. JURISDICTION OVER MERCHANT VESSELS IN FOREIGN PORTS

When merchant vessels leave the high seas and enter foreign ports, the jurisdiction of their national state comes into conflict with the jurisdiction of the foreign state.[13] This conflict has been adjusted, by custom and treaty, so as to permit the exercise of a limited jurisdiction by the flag state in respect to matters of internal discipline, without encroaching upon the ultimate right of the territorial state. "It is a part of the law of civilized nations," said the court in Wildenhus's Case, decided in 1887,[14] "that when a merchant vessel of one country enters the ports of another for the purposes of trade, it subjects itself to the law of the place to which it goes, unless by treaty or otherwise the two countries have come to some different understanding or agreement." No very definite line, however, has been drawn between matters relating to the internal discipline of the vessel and matters disturbing the peace of the port. Some states interpret the term "internal order of the vessel" broadly. The Supreme Court of Mexico held in 1876 that the murder of a Frenchman by another Frenchman on board a French vessel in a Mexican port did not necessarily disturb the peace of the port.[15] In contrast, the attitude of the American courts is shown in the case of Wildenhus, cited above

[9] See Moore, *Principles of American Diplomacy*, p. 275.

[10] See below, p. 505.

[11] See below, pp. 508 ff.

[12] For details of the case, see Moore, *Digest*, Vol. II, § 309, p. 899.

[13] See A. H. Charteris, "The Legal Position of Merchantmen in Foreign Ports and National Waters," *British Year Book*, 1920-1921, pp. 45-96.

[14] Mali v. Keeper of the Common Jail, 120 U.S. 1 (1887). Fenwick, *Cases*, p. 345; Bishop, *Cases*, p. 501; Briggs, *Cases*, p. 341.

[15] Case of Antoni (*l'Anemone*). Hudson, *Cases*, p. 601.

in this connection, in which the Belgian consul asked for a writ of habeas corpus on behalf of Wildenhus, who had committed murder on board a Belgian steamer in the port of Jersey City. The court held that the crime was of such a nature as by its very commission to "disturb tranquillity and public order on shore or in the port," so that it must be regarded as falling within the exceptional cases provided for in the treaty of 1880, in which the local authority might interfere.[16]

Stores of intoxicating liquors. A novel ground for interference by the local government in the internal discipline of foreign ships in port was presented in 1920 by the Eighteenth Amendment of the United States Constitution, with its supplementary enforcement legislation, known as the Volstead Act. The amendment prohibited the manufacture, sale, transportation, importation, or exportation of intoxicating liquors within, into, or from the United States and all territory subject to its jurisdiction.[17] The enforcement act contained more specific provisions to the same effect and prescribed that the act should be "liberally construed to the end that the use of intoxicating liquor as a beverage may be prevented." Following the passage of the law a number of steamship companies sued for an injunction to prevent the application of the law to supplies of liquor carried by their ships for the consumption of passengers and crew. In the case of Cunard Steamship Company v. Mellon,[18] the Supreme Court of the United States held, first, that the amendment "could be made to cover both domestic and foreign merchant ships when within the territorial waters of the United States"; secondly, that the amendment did intend such an effect. The jurisdiction of a nation within its own territory, said the court, is necessarily exclusive and absolute, and any exception to such jurisdiction must arise from the consent of the nation itself. No such exception was to be found in the terms of the amendment, and none could be "reasonably regarded as implied." The sole exception recognized by the law was that of "liquor in transit through the Panama Canal or on the Panama railroad." [19]

16 For further cases, see Jessup, *op. cit.*, pp. 144 ff. In 1898 the Institute of International Law attempted to secure greater uniformity in the law by formulating a series of "Regulations concerning the legal status of ships and their crews in foreign ports." See *Resolutions*, p. 143. Compare Article 18, Harvard *Draft Convention on Territorial Waters.*

17 The amendment provided: "After one year from the ratification of this Article the manufacture, sale, or transportation of intoxicating liquors within, the importation thereof into, or the exportation thereof from the United States and all territory subject to the jurisdiction thereof for beverage purposes is hereby prohibited."

18 262 U.S. 100 (1923). Fenwick, *Cases*, p. 354; Bishop, *Cases*, p. 505; Hudson, *Cases*, p. 615.

19 In a dissenting opinion Justice Sutherland urged that while there was no question as to the power of Congress to do what the court held had been done, "due regard for the principles of international comity, which exist between friendly nations, in my opinion, forbids the construction of the 18th Amendment and of the act which the present decision advances." The affair was the object of sharp controversy, and the decision of the court gave rise to much criticism. See T. S. Woolsey, *Am. Journal*, Vol. 17 (1923), p. 504.

The enforcement of the law, in accordance with this decision of the Supreme Court, against the steamship *Baltic* in June, 1923, while calling forth protest from individual members of Parliament, was acquiesced in by the British Government as offering "no grounds for protest." [20] Subsequently, by a treaty, signed in 1924, Great Britain obtained exemption from such seizures on condition of permitting the seizure within an hour's run from shore of "rum-runners" flying the British flag.

In spite of the annoyance to foreign vessels in port attending the enforcement by the United States of the La Follette Seaman's Act of 1920, the Supreme Court held the provisions of the act were not limited to American seamen and that the jurisdiction of the government over foreign vessels in port gave authority to Congress to enact the legislation protecting seamen on such vessels notwithstanding the interference with contracts entered into in other countries.[21]

Civil suits against foreign vessels in port. Merchant vessels in foreign ports are not exempt from civil suit *in rem* brought by a citizen of the foreign state, nor are the officers or crew of the vessel exempt from civil suit *in personam* or from criminal prosecution by the foreign government for acts in contravention of the laws of the state. But the jurisdiction of the foreign state does not generally extend so far as to interfere with personal and property rights on board the vessel as regulated by the law of the flag state. In the case of the *Creole*,[22] submitted to arbitration by the United States and Great Britain in 1853, it was held by the arbitrator that the authorities of Nassau, in liberating a number of slaves who had revolted against the officers of the ship and had put in at the port of Nassau, had acted "in violation of the established law of nations," and that the claimants were "justly entitled to compensation for their losses."

The authority of the foreign consul to take cognizance of cases arising between the captain and crew of the vessel is wholly dependent upon treaty provisions. In the case of Dainese v. Hale,[23] the Supreme Court of the United States laid down the rule that "it may now be considered as generally true, that, for any judicial powers which may be vested in the consuls accredited to any nation, we must look to the express provisions of the treaties entered into with that nation, and to the laws of the States which the consuls represent."

Concurrent jurisdiction of several states. It will be observed that, in consequence of the territorial and personal grounds upon which jurisdiction is assumed over the conduct of individual persons, the same act

---

[20] See statement of Prime Minister Baldwin in Parliament, June 25, 1923.

[21] Strathearn Steamship Co. v. Dillon, 252 U.S. 348 (1920). Fenwick, *Cases,* p. 351; Hudson, *Cases,* p. 611.

[22] Moore, *International Arbitrations,* Vol. IV, p. 4375; *Digest,* Vol. II, p. 358; Fenwick, *Cases,* p. 342.

[23] 91 U.S. 13 (1875). Hudson, *Cases,* p. 703.

committed on board a vessel may be at once subject to the jurisdiction of a number of states: to the state whose flag the vessel flies, to the state within whose territorial waters the vessel happens to be, and to the state to which the individual owes allegiance. The jurisdiction of any one of these states can, of course, only be exercised singly, with due respect to the prior rights of the state within whose territory the individual happens to be at the time. In the case of Regina v. Anderson,[24] an American citizen was convicted by a criminal court of Great Britain for murder committed on board a British vessel in French waters. The court held that "although the prisoner was subject to the American jurisprudence as an American citizen, and to the law of France as having committed an offense within the territory of France, yet he must also be considered as subject to the jurisdiction of British law, which extends to the protection of British vessels, though in ports belonging to another country."

In 1934 the chief officer of an American ship, the *Exchange*, was killed on board the ship by the chief engineer, De Mott, while it was in the port of Messina, Italy. The Department of State instructed the American Embassy to ascertain whether the Italian Government would be willing to surrender De Mott if arrangements could be made for his trial in the United States, since there was concurrent jurisdiction in the case. But the Italian Foreign Office replied that, as the crime had taken place in Italian territorial waters, the Italian courts had jurisdiction of the case, and that in consequence De Mott must be tried in Italy and undergo sentence there if found guilty.[25]

Jurisdiction over cases of collision on the high seas. In two matters of slight intrinsic importance international law has worked out a system of concurrent jurisdiction which is of considerable historical interest and

[24] 11 Cox C.C. 198 (1868). Fenwick, *Cases*, p. 332; Bishop, *Cases*, p. 477; Briggs, *Cases*, p. 333.

In the case of United States v. Santos Flores, 289 U.S. 137 (1933), the court held that an American citizen who committed a crime while on board an American vessel in foreign territorial waters was subject to the concurrent jurisdiction of both states and might be tried in the United States on being brought back within its territory.

[25] Hackworth, *Digest*, Vol. II, p. 216. It should be observed that while a state may exercise, or forgo exercising, jurisdiction over offenses committed on board a merchant vessel in its territorial waters, it is not at liberty to try persons on board such foreign vessels for offenses committed on the high seas. Hence the British Government disavowed the action of the local authorities at Calcutta in trying one Anderson for a crime committed upon an American merchant vessel on the high seas. Wharton, *Digest*, Vol. I, p. 123. A unique illustration of the passage of a merchant vessel from the law of one state into that of another is furnished by the case of Regina v. Lesley, Bell's Crown Cases, 220 (1860), in which it was held that the master of a British vessel might, upon his arrival in Great Britain, be prosecuted for false imprisonment for the act of forcibly transporting banished Chileans, although the act of the defendant in contracting with the Chilean Government to transport them was justifiable in its inception, having been done within Chilean territorial waters. Fenwick, *Cases*, p. 336; Hudson, *Cases*, p. 590; Bishop, *Cases*, p. 478.

which presents an instructive analogy for the development of international judicial institutions. In cases of collision on the high seas the courts of a number of the leading states undertake to assume jurisdiction in suits *in rem* brought by the injured party against the alleged guilty vessel of whatever nationality. The same custom holds where proceedings are instituted for salvage for the rescue of shipwrecked vessels. When the defendant vessel is sued in the courts of the state whose flag it flies, no question of jurisdiction can be raised. Practice is not uniform, however, in cases in which a vessel flies a foreign flag or in which the parties are both citizens of the same foreign state. In the case of the *Scotia*,[26] decided in 1872, the courts of the United States assumed jurisdiction in a suit brought by an American sailing vessel against a British steamer for damages resulting from the loss of the vessel in a collision on the high seas. In the case of the *Belgenland*,[27] decided in 1885, jurisdiction was exercised in a similar suit for damages brought by the captain of a Norwegian bark, the *Luna,* against a Belgian steamer.[28] The basis upon which jurisdiction was assumed in these and other cases was the necessity of doing present justice to the injured party, who, if unable to sue in the nearest port, might have to go to the ends of the earth to seek his remedy. In 1952, an International Convention on Certain Rules concerning Civil Jurisdiction in Matters of Collision was signed at Brussels; it limited actions for collisions between seagoing vessels, or between seagoing vessels and inland navigation craft to three specific jurisdictions:

(a) Either before the court where the defendant has his habitual residence or a place of business;

(b) or before the court of the place where arrest has been effected of the defendant ship or of any other ship belonging to the defendant which can be lawfully arrested, or where arrest could have been effected and bail or other security has been furnished;

(c) or before the court of the place of collision when the collision has occurred within the limits of a port or in inland waters.

The parties retain, however, the right to bring an action in any other place by agreement. A separate convention dealing with Certain Rules Relating to Penal Jurisdiction was signed at the same time providing that criminal or disciplinary proceedings may be instituted only before

[26] 14 Wallace 170 (1872). Fenwick, *Cases,* p. 11; Hudson, *Cases,* p. 667; Briggs, *Cases,* p. 25.

[27] 114 U.S. 355 (1885). Fenwick, *Cases,* p. 360.

[28] In presenting its opinion the court cited an earlier British case, that of the *Johann Friedrich,* 1 W. Rob. 35, decided in 1839, in which the High Court of Admiralty entertained jurisdiction in a suit brought by the owner of a Danish ship against a Bremen ship.

the judicial or administrative authorities of the state the flag of which the ship was flying at the time of the collision.[29]

Jurisdiction in suits for salvage. The jurisdiction exercised over foreign vessels in cases of salvage is based upon the same principle, that the question involved is one *communis juris*. In the case of the *Two Friends*,[30] the British Court of Admiralty, in 1799, entertained jurisdiction in a suit for salvage brought against an American ship which had been captured by the French and afterward rescued by the crew, who, however, were British subjects by birth. In explaining the basis of the jurisdiction taken, the court said that "salvage is a question of *jus gentium*," and it could "see no reason why one country should be afraid to trust to the equity of the courts of another on such a question of such a nature, so to be determined." In a similar suit for salvage brought in a port of the United States by a British ship against a French ship,[31] the Supreme Court of the United States held that "where such controversies are *communis juris, i.e.*, where they arise under the common law of nations, special grounds should appear to induce the court to deny its aid to a foreign suitor when it has jurisdiction of the ship or party charged." On the other hand, in the case of the *Reliance*,[32] decided in 1848, a federal district court, while reiterating that salvage was "essentially a question of the *jus gentium*," held that the doctrine that jurisdiction may be assumed in cases involving foreigners was not "peremptory," and it refused to hear the case before it on the ground that the suit was brought by British libellants against goods destined to a British port under circumstances which could best be passed upon in a British port.

Basis of jurisdiction. The jurisdiction assumed by national courts in these cases is partly due to the fact that by long custom there has grown up a body of maritime common law to be applied with even justice whatever the nationality of the parties to the case. In the presence of this common law of the sea, states have been willing to recognize the exercise of a reciprocal jurisdiction in cases not otherwise properly before the court. It is in this light that a question, otherwise one of private law only, becomes one of public international law. The content of this common law traces its origin back to the early Rhodian law, to the Amalfitan table, to the ordinances of the Hanseatic League, and to other early codes of international private law. "Whatever may have been its origin," said the court in the case of the *Scotia*,[33] "whether in the usages of navigation or in the ordinances of maritime states, or in both, it has

---

[29] For the texts of the two conventions, see *Am. Journal*, Vol. 53 (1959), p. 532.
[30] 1 C. Rob. 271.
[31] Mason v. Le Blaireau, 2 Cranch 240 (1804).
[32] 1 Abbott's Adm. Rep. 317. *Fed. Cas.* No. 10, 521.
[33] See note 26 of this chapter.

become the law of the sea only by the concurrent sanction of those nations who may be said to constitute the commercial world."

Efforts have been made from time to time to secure the adoption of a
general international convention upon these subjects. In 1889 a maritime
conference held at Washington recommended to the states represented
the adoption by each state individually of a common body of rules for
preventing collisions at sea.[34] A later International Maritime Conference,
which met at Brussels in 1909, endorsed a draft convention concerning
collisions for separate national adoption.[35] The Convention on Safety of
Life at Sea, signed at London in 1929, calls for the adoption by national
legislation of revised Regulations for Preventing Collisions at Sea.[36]

Asylum on foreign merchant ships.   Foreign merchant ships, not being
exempt except by comity from the jurisdiction of the state in whose
ports they drop anchor, may not be made an asylum for fugitive criminals or political refugees. It has been questioned, however, whether a
foreign merchant ship is so far under the jurisdiction of the state as to
give the local authorities the right to enter upon the vessel and arrest a
passenger who, as a political refugee, has taken passage upon the vessel
in the port of a third state. Calvo relates the case of one Sotelo, a political
refugee who took passage in 1840 on board a French vessel at one
Spanish port and was arrested upon the arrival of the vessel at a second
Spanish port. Diplomatic correspondence between the two countries
established the complete right of Spain to execute its laws within its
territorial jurisdiction without disrespect to the foreign flag.[37] In the
case of Gomez (Gámez), a political refugee from Nicaragua who took
passage on board a United States steamship in the harbor of San José
de Guatemala in 1885, and whose arrest was sought by the local authorities when the vessel stopped en route at a port of Nicaragua, the Department of State refused to support the action of the captain in declining
to deliver the passenger. "It is clear," said Secretary Bayard, "that Mr.
Gomez voluntarily entered the jurisdiction of a country whose laws he
had violated. Under the circumstances it was plainly the duty of the
captain of the *Honduras* to deliver him up to the local authorities upon
their request." [38] In a later case involving a political refugee from Hon-

[34] Compare the rules formulated by the Institute of International Law in 1888.
Resolutions, p. 83.

[35] For the text of the draft, see *Am. Journal*, Vol. 4 (1910), Supp., p. 115. For
comment, *ibid.*, Vol. 4, p. 412.

[36] Hudson, *International Legislation*, Vol. IV, p. 2825. The convention came into
force January 1, 1933. On March 19, 1943, a Treaty on International Commercial
Navigation Law was signed at Montevideo, Chapter II of which deals with collisions
and Chapter III with assistance and salvage.

[37] *Droit international*, 4th ed., Vol. I, p. 569.

[38] *U. S. For. Rel.* (1885), p. 82. Compare, however, the attitude of Secretary Blaine
in the Barrundia case, contesting the right of the Government of Guatemala to demand the surrender of a fugitive under similar circumstances. See Moore, *Digest*,
Vol. II, § 307.

duras named Bonilla, Secretary Gresham, while admitting the right of the local authorities to demand the surrender of a passenger, instructed the American minister to protest against the act of the commander of the port in firing upon the vessel because the captain refused to surrender the refugee.[39]

D. STATUS OF FOREIGN PUBLIC VESSELS IN NATIONAL PORTS

The relation between a state and its public vessels is closer and more direct than that between the state and privately owned vessels flying its flag and subject to its jurisdiction. Certain public vessels, such as men-of-war or naval auxiliaries, are immediately identified with the personality of the state. The fiction of "exterritoriality" is borne out in the actual position they enjoy, if not in legal theory. Both on the high seas and in foreign ports they are for all practical purposes "floating portions" of the territory of their state. They may not, as neutrals, be visited, searched, or detained by belligerent warships in the enforcement of the law of contraband and blockade. When in foreign territorial waters they are completely exempt from local jurisdiction, in respect not only to the internal discipline of the ship but even to crimes committed on board ship by persons not members of the crew or committed in the port itself by one who has taken refuge on board. In the latter case the commander may agree to surrender the offenders; but should he refuse to do so the foreign state must secure redress, if any, through diplomatic channels. By reason of their territorial character, public vessels in foreign ports have frequently been made an asylum for political refugees, particularly in times of revolutionary disturbances in Central and South American countries. States have the right to refuse permission to foreign warships to enter their ports; but having admitted them they must, even in cases of misconduct on their part, resort to diplomatic, rather than local judicial, procedure against them.[40]

In contrast with public warships and their auxiliaries are the public ships engaged in various administrative services of the state. Certain of these services are traditional governmental services, such as the geodetic

---

[39] *Ibid.* For the question of asylum on foreign warships, see p. 387 of the present work.

[40] This fiction of "exterritoriality" was strongly contested by the British House of Lords in a case, *Chung Chi Cheung*, [1939], A. C. 160, *Am. Journal*, Vol. 33 (1939), p. 376, arising out of a murder committed on board a Chinese public armed ship at that time in British territorial waters. The decision, however, involved merely the right of the accused to be tried by the British Court of Hong Kong, where he was put ashore for hospital treatment. In the course of his judgment Lord Atkin observed: "Their Lordships have no hesitation in rejecting the doctrine of exterritoriality expressed in the words of Mr. Oppenheim, which regards the public ship 'as a floating portion of the flag state.' However the doctrine of exterritoriality is expressed, it is a fiction, and legal fictions have a tendency to pass beyond their appointed bounds and to harden into dangerous facts." Brierly's interpretation of the law is cited with approval. *Law of Nations*, p. 192.

survey and the postal service; others are normal commercial activities once generally left to private initiative and only in comparatively recent times undertaken by the state, whether in competition with similar activities of its citizens or as a governmental monopoly closed to individual enterprise. While these vessels, by reason of the fact of public ownership, are when on the high seas identified with the state as closely as are other public vessels, a number of problems have been raised as to their status when they are within the territorial jurisdiction of foreign states.

Exemption of public vessels from civil suit. The question whether public warships in foreign ports are subject to civil suit *in rem* has been passed upon by British and American courts in several important cases. In the case of the French man-of-war *Exchange*,[41] a vessel owned by an American citizen had been seized by Napoleon in 1810 and commissioned as a public vessel of France. In a suit brought by the original owners against the vessel upon its arrival in the port of Philadelphia, the Supreme Court, after a lengthy review of the law which has become classic, held that the public character of the vessel exempted it from the jurisdiction of the American courts. The decision is paralleled by that of the British High Court of Admiralty in the case of the *Constitution*,[42] in which the court refused to issue a warrant, served by a British steam tug, for payment of salvage for the rescue of the ship when stranded on the English coast. Greater difficulty was experienced by the British courts in reaching the conclusion that public vessels other than warships should be exempt from local jurisdiction. In the case of the *Parlement Belge*[43] the Court of Appeals reversed the judgment of the High Court of Admiralty and held that a publicly owned vessel of the state of Belgium, used as a mail packet as well as for general commercial purposes, was exempt from suit *in rem* for damages arising out of a collision. The court held that even though an action *in rem* were an action against the property only, suit could not be brought; but it went on to show that in an action *in rem* the owner of the property is indirectly impleaded and that "to implead an independent sovereign in such a way is to call upon him to sacrifice either his property or his independence."

Difficulties attending such exemption. The exemption granted to the *Parlement Belge* proved to have created an embarrassing precedent. The

---

[41] Schooner *Exchange* v. McFaddon, 7 Cranch 116 (1812). Fenwick, *Cases,* p. 363; Hudson, *Cases,* p. 524; Bishop, *Cases,* p. 551; Briggs, *Cases,* p. 413. The jurisdiction of a state over foreign vessels within its territorial waters other than ports does not differ in principles from the jurisdiction of the state over the same vessels within its national ports. See L. T. Lee, "Jurisdiction over Foreign Merchant Ships in the Territorial Sea," *Am. Journal,* Vol. 55 (1961), p. 77.

[42] L. R. 4 P. D. 39 (1879). Fenwick, *Cases,* p. 368.

[43] L. R. 5 P. D. 197 (1880). Fenwick, *Cases,* p. 370.

outbreak of war in 1914 resulted in extending widely the practice of states in taking over privately owned vessels into the public service as naval auxiliaries, and at the same time it created conditions which led a number of states to take over the ownership and operation of merchant vessels engaged in ordinary trade. In the case of the *Porto Alexandre*,[44] involving the salvaging of a trading vessel owned by the state of Portugal, the British court called attention to the fact that, now that "the fashion of nationalization is in the air" and states are trading with public ships, "if these national ships wander about without liabilities, many trading affairs will become difficult." Nevertheless the court felt that, owing to the precedent of the *Parlement Belge*, the remedy was not with the courts. The American courts have on several occasions held foreign public ships immune from suit *in rem*, even though used for mere commercial purposes. In the case of Berizzi Brothers Co. v. Steamship *Pesaro* [45] the Supreme Court dismissed a libel against the *Pesaro*, which was engaged in ordinary trade but owned and operated by the Italian Government. The court said,

We think the principles are applicable alike to all ships held and used by a government for a public purpose, and that when, for the purpose of advancing the trade of its people or providing revenue for its treasury, a government acquires, mans, and operates ships in the carrying trade, they are public ships in the same sense that ships of war are. We know of no international usage which regards the maintenance and advancement of the economic welfare of a people in time of peace as any less a public purpose than the maintenance and training of a naval force.

The difficult problems presented by the demand for the exemption from the local jurisdiction of public commercial vessels have led to various efforts to secure a greater degree of uniformity in respect to their status. Finally, in 1926, at the International Maritime Conference at Brussels, a Convention for the Unification of Certain Rules relating to the Immunity of State-owned Vessels was signed by twenty-one states. It provided that, with the exception of ships of war and other vessels used exclusively on governmental service, seagoing vessels owned or operated by states and cargoes owned by states should be subject "to the same rules of liability and to the same obligations as those applicable to private vessels, cargoes and equipments," and that in the case of vessels used on noncommercial governmental service claimants

---

[44] 36 Times L. R. 66 (1919). *Am. Journal*, Vol. 14 (1920), p. 273; Fenwick, *Cases*, p. 375.

[45] 271 U.S. 562 (1926). Fenwick, *Cases*, p. 377; Bishop, *Cases*, p. 556; Hudson, *Cases*, p. 530.

should have the right of taking proceedings in the competent tribunal of the state owning or operating the vessel.[46]

Spanish Civil War cases. But the United States did not become a party to the Brussels Convention, and in consequence, in a case involving the *Navemar*, requisitioned by the Spanish Republican Government in 1936 from a private owner, the Court recognized the right of the Spanish Ambassador to intervene in a suit brought in New York by the original owners, declaring that:

Admittedly a vessel of a friendly government in its possession and service is a public vessel, even though engaged in the carriage of merchandise for hire, and as such is immune from suit in the courts of admiralty of the United States.

To the same effect, the British House of Lords held in the case of the *Cristina*, a Spanish vessel requisitioned by the Government from a private owner in 1937, that the rule was that the courts of a country

will not implead a foreign sovereign, that is, they will not by their process make him against his will a party to legal proceedings, whether the proceedings involve process against his person or seek to recover from him specific property or damages.[47]

The immunity from suit of a vessel owned by a foreign government is allowed, however, only in cases where the vessel is in the possession and service of the foreign government. In the case of Republic of Mexico v. Hoffman, the Supreme Court of the United States was unwilling to extend immunity to a Mexican vessel, the *Baja California*, in a suit filed against it for collision damage, on the ground that it was operated in freight service by a private Mexican company under a five-year contract.[48]

---

[46] For the text of the convention, see Hudson, *International Legislation*, Vol. III (1837). Prior to the meeting of the conference at Brussels a subcommittee of the League of Nations Committee of Experts presented a report on the "Legal Status of Government Ships Employed in Commerce" which considered it both "desirable and practicable" to regulate the subject by way of convention. *Am. Journal*, Vol. 20 (1926), Spec. Supp., pp. 260 ff. See, on the general subject, J. W. Garner, "Immunities of State-owned Ships Employed in Commerce," *British Year Book*, Vol. VI (1925), p. 128; *Harvard Draft, Competence of Courts*; F. R. Sanborn, "The Immunity of Government-Owned Merchant Vessels," *Am. Journal*, Vol. 39 (1945), p. 794; Thommen, *Legal Status of Government Merchant Ships in International Law*.

[47] For the case of the *Navemar*, 303 U.S. (1938) 68, see *Am. Journal*, Vol. 32 (1938), p. 381. For editorial comment, see C. C. Hyde, *Am. Journal*, Vol. 33 (1939), p. 530. For the case of the *Cristina* (1938), see *Am. Journal*, Vol. 32 (1938), p. 824. For comment, see L. Preuss, *Am. Journal*, Vol. 35 (1941), p. 263.

[48] 324 U.S. 30 (1945). For comment upon an earlier case, Ex parte Peru, 318 U.S. 578 (1943), in which immunity was granted on the basis of a declaration of the Department of State, see P. C. Jessup, "Has the Supreme Court abdicated one of its functions?" *Am. Journal*, Vol. 40 (1946), p. 168.

Following the signature of the Brussels Convention the regional group of American states, in conference at Buenos Aires in 1936, adopted a resolution recommending adherence to the Convention, but without effect. Years later, in 1959, the Inter-American Council of Jurists adopted a resolution declaring that the principles of the Brussels Convention and of the Protocol of 1934 had received both scientific and official recognition and had "the commendable characteristics of universality and unification," so that there was no need of promoting uniformity on the American regional level, other than by a general ratification of the Brussels Convention.[49]

Asylum on foreign warships. The exemption from the territorial jurisdiction of a state accorded to foreign warships lying in its harbors has, as in the case of legations, led to the granting of asylum upon them to fugitives from justice. This practice, however, is not so direct a limitation upon the sovereignty of the state; and while asylum is no longer granted to ordinary criminals, it is still granted quite frequently to political refugees. In view, however, of the serious objections attending it, the United States has on its part discouraged the granting of asylum by its warships. In the Regulations of the United States Navy issued in 1913 it was laid down that "the right of asylum for political or other refugees has no foundation in international law." [50] While it is recognized in the Regulations that usage sanctions the granting of asylum in countries subject to frequent revolutions, it is directed that even in such cases asylum should be granted only in extreme cases, as to refugees from mob violence. At the Sixth International Conference of American States, held at Havana in 1928, a convention was signed forbidding the granting of asylum on warships, as in legations, military camps, and military aircraft, to persons accused of or condemned for crime, but laying down conditions under which asylum might be granted to political offenders. The United States, in signing the convention, refused to recognize "as part of international law, the so-called doctrine of asylum." [51]

[49] Resolution IX, "Immunity of State-Owned Vessels," *Final Act*, P.A.U., 1959.
[50] *U.S. Navy Regulations and Naval Instructions*, 1913, Art. R-1649.
[51] For the text of the convention, see *Am. Journal*, Vol. 20 (1928), Supp., p. 158. See below, pp. 566 ff., where asylum in embassies and legations is discussed.

CHAPTER XVII

Jurisdictional Cooperation Between States:

Extradition of Fugitive Criminals;

Letters Rogatory; Comity

A. LEGAL BASIS OF EXTRADITION

The jurisdiction of a state over all persons within its territorial boundaries and its right in consequence to punish them for violation of its laws is frequently defeated for the time being by the escape of an offender into the jurisdiction of a neighboring state. So strictly is the independence and sovereignty of states interpreted that not even the repression of the most outrageous crimes will warrant the exercise by one state of the slightest act of jurisdictional authority within the territory of another state.[1] Under these circumstances a mutual interest in the maintenance of law and order and the administration of justice has led nations to cooperate with one another by surrendering fugitive criminals to the state in which the crime was committed. This surrender, in compliance with a formal demand, and in accordance with the conditions attached to the general obligation assumed in the treaty agreement, is known as "extradition."

As early as 1625 Grotius recognized the social necessity, and hence the *duty* under the natural law, that a state either punish such fugitive criminals itself or else surrender them to the state whose laws were immediately concerned in bringing the offender to justice.[2] This moral

---

[1] In the famous Savarkar case the French Government construed its territorial integrity so strictly as to demand that the prisoner, who had escaped from a British vessel while in the port of Marseilles and had been caught and returned to the vessel with the unauthorized assistance of the local police, should be returned to France and a formal demand made for his extradition. The British Government declined to surrender the prisoner. Upon reference of the dispute to the Permanent Court of Arbitration, it was decided that, while there were irregularities in the recapture of the prisoner at Marseilles, there was no rule of international law imposing an obligation to return him. *Hague Court Reports*, p. 275. Fenwick, *Cases*, p. 420; Hudson, *Cases*, p. 969.

[2] *De jure belli ac pacis*, Eng. trans., Bk. II, Chap. XXI, § IV.

duty of extradition did not, however, become a legal obligation until states began to enter into special treaties providing for the surrender of particular fugitives, although apart from these treaty arrangements states frequently surrendered fugitives by voluntary act. The earlier treaties provided chiefly for the surrender of *political* fugitives; but by the time Vattel published his treatise in 1758,[3] ordinary criminals were also surrendered upon specific demand. In the second half of the nineteenth century the urgent need of offsetting the greater facilities for the escape of criminals provided by modern methods of transportation led to the conclusion of extradition treaties of a more general nature, covering stipulated crimes and applicable to any offenders; and by the opening decade of the twentieth century the scope of these treaties had widened greatly. Numerous as they have become, however, extradition treaties continue to be bilateral in character, and there is a noticeable lack of uniformity in their provisions and in their interpretation. The surrender of fugitive criminals in the absence of treaty provisions still takes place on occasion, but in such cases the act is one not of legal obligation, but of international comity.[4]

B. CONDITIONS ATTACHED TO TREATIES OF EXTRADITION: SPECIFIED OFFENSES

Since extradition is effected as the result of the provisions of treaties entered into by the nations two by two, it is impossible to formulate any general rule of international law upon the subject. It is, however, possible to bring together the provisions common to the treaties of the leading states and to point out the more important conditions attached to the practice of extradition. The United States has concluded in the course of its history a great number of treaties of extradition, which, in their wide variety, illustrate the common as well as the exceptional practice of nations. The list of offenses for which extradition will be granted includes not only the more serious crimes which are felonies at common law but others which are either felonies by statute or merely misdemeanors. The treaty with France of 1909, replacing earlier treaties, in-

[3] *Droit des gens,* Eng. trans., Bk. II, § 76.

[4] On the general subject of extradition, see Harvard Research, *Draft Convention on Extradition,* with bibliography. Moore, *Digest,* Vol. IV, §§ 579-622; Hackworth, *Digest,* Vol. IV, pp. 1-241.

In the United States the Supreme Court has held that it is not within the power of the Executive Department to surrender a fugitive in the absence of a treaty or a law of Congress. On January 20, 1947, the Department of State informed the Soviet Embassy in Washington that it would not be possible to comply with the Embassy's request to turn over to the Soviet authorities a former employee accused of embezzling state funds in Mexico. "It is a well-established principle of international law," said the Department, "that no right to extradition exists apart from treaty. No extradition treaty exists between the United States and the Soviet Union." Dept. of State *Bulletin,* Vol. XVI, p. 213.

cludes such crimes as forgery, fraud by a guardian or trustee, perjury, kidnapping, and mutiny on the high seas. In general, the crime must be one with respect to which there is a general agreement among civilized nations as to definition,[5] the kind and amount of evidence to be adduced as proof, and the punishment assigned to the offense.[6] Requests for the extradition of fugitive criminals are presented through the diplomatic representatives resident in the foreign state. Upon receiving the request the foreign government institutes a judicial investigation to determine whether there is sufficient evidence, in accordance with the local law, to warrant apprehension of the fugitive. If, as a result of this investigation, there is prima facie evidence of guilt, the fugitive is thereupon surrendered. Pending the presentation of a formal request for extradition, application may be made by the foreign state by telegraph for the arrest and detention of a fugitive for a period not exceeding forty days.[7] When the fugitive is returned he must be tried for the offense mentioned in the request for his extradition, and for no other, not even for a lesser offense included in the more serious one specified.[8]

So insistent have nations been at times with respect to the observance of the principle of trial for specified offenses recognized as such by both countries as to give the impression of greater concern for the protection of the fugitive criminal than for the local community whose law has been violated. In 1910 one Nalbandian was indicted for murder in Massachusetts and fled to his native state, Bulgaria. Bulgaria cooperated by surrendering him even in the absence of a treaty of extradition. When, however, the agents of the State Department asked permission of Rumania for the transit of the prisoner through that country, the request was refused on the ground that, even though there had been a treaty of extradition between the United States and Rumania, the penalty for murder in the United States was death, and Rumania would have been obliged to require that the United States should not exact the death penalty.[9] In 1928 the United States requested the extradition of H. M. Blackmer on the ground of "false swearing"; but the French court advised against granting the request, on the ground that the punishment for the offenses differed in the two countries and that the corrective, as opposed to criminal, penalty imposed by France had been barred by prescription.[10] In the notorious case of Samuel Insull, the Chicago banker, whose ex-

[5] The specific offenses included in the general definition of a crime are, as a rule, determined by the law of the place where the offense was committed. See Factor v. Laubenheimer, below.

[6] See Art. I, treaty of 1909 between the United States and France. *Treaties and Conventions*, Vol. III, p. 2580.

[7] *Ibid.*, Art. IV.

[8] See United States v. Rauscher, below, p. 391.

[9] Stowell and Munro, *International Cases*, Vol. I, pp. 403-408.

[10] Court of Paris, Chamber of Indictments. Hudson, *Cases*, p. 953.

tradition from Greece was requested by the United States for the offense of "embezzlement and larceny," the Greek court twice held that the alleged deliberate intention on the part of Insull to evade the United States Bankruptcy Act in the concealment or transfer of assets had not been proved, and accordingly it released the prisoner.[11] In consequence, the United States, deeming the Greek court to have exceeded its proper function, immediately gave notice to Greece that the recently concluded treaty of extradition would be terminated in accordance with its provisions.

In illustration of the principle that the fugitive must be tried for the offense mentioned in the request for his extradition, Great Britain inquired whether the United States would agree that a certain Winslow,[12] whose extradition had been requested by the United States in 1876, should only be tried for the crimes specified. The United States maintained that, in the absence of restrictive terms in the treaty of 1842, there was nothing to prohibit trial for another offense. As a result the prisoner was released, and the treaty was temporarily suspended. Years later the British contention was sustained by the Supreme Court of the United States in the case of United States v. Rauscher,[13] decided in 1886, where the court ordered the release of a prisoner who had been extradited from Great Britain upon a charge of murder, but who had been tried in a lower court upon a charge of inflicting cruel and unusual punishment, the latter offense, however, not being specified as extraditable under the treaty.

In the case of Factor v. Laubenheimer,[14] involving an application for the extradition of Factor based upon a charge that he had received certain sums of money in London "knowing the same to have been fraudulently obtained," the District Court of Illinois ordered the petitioner released from custody on the ground that the offense was not within the terms of the applicable treaties because it was not an offense against the laws of Illinois, the state in which Factor was apprehended and held. On appeal, the Federal Court of Appeals held that the crime *was* an offense against the law of Illinois. The Supreme Court then affirmed the decision, holding that the terms of the treaty of 1842 with

---

[11] As it turned out, the extradition of Insull was later effected from Turkey when the ship *Maiotis*, which he had chartered, put in at the port of Istanbul, on its way somewhere. An item of additional interest in the case was the claim of Insull before the Greek court that he had taken refuge in Greece before the treaty under which the United States demanded his extradition had come into effect, due to delay in the exchange of ratifications. On this point the Greek court held that the accused could not invoke the principle of nonretroactivity as a bar to his extradition.

For comment on the case, see C. C. Hyde, "The Extradition Case of Samuel Insull, Sr. in Relation to Greece," *Am. Journal*, Vol. 28 (1934), p. 307.

[12] Moore, *Digest*, Vol. IV, § 596.

[13] 119 U.S. 407. Fenwick, *Cases*, p. 425; Hudson, *Cases*, p. 956.

[14] 290 U.S. 276 (1933). Fenwick, *Cases*, p. 430; Briggs, *Cases*, p. 580.

Great Britain did not require that the offense charged must be a crime under the law of the state where the fugitive is found. The court chose to give a liberal interpretation to the treaty, stating that, "Considerations which should govern the diplomatic relations between nations, and the good faith of treaties, as well, require that their obligations should be liberally construed so as to effect the apparent intention of the parties to secure equality and reciprocity between them." [15]

In view of the obstacles to extradition resulting from the conflicting interpretations of criminal offenses, jurists have suggested that in the adoption of a general convention upon the subject the usual list of crimes should be replaced by a comprehensive clause covering offenses of a certain gravity as indicated by the penalty imposed for their commission. The Montevideo Convention of 1933 contained a clause designating the act as one for which "a minimum penalty of imprisonment for one year" might be imposed.[16] The Harvard Research *Draft Convention on Extradition* offers a general formula of extraditable acts, being those "for which the law of the requesting State, in force when the act was committed, provides a possible penalty of death or deprivation of liberty for a period of two years or more" and for which the law in force in that part of the state in which the offender was apprehended provides a similar penalty applicable if the act had been committed there.[17]

Extradition of citizens. The unwillingness of most states to surrender their own citizens when fugitives from justice has frequently operated to obstruct the orderly administration of criminal law. Continental countries, such as Italy and France, and many of the Latin American states follow the rule of criminal law in accordance with which a crime committed by one of their citizens in any part of the world is a crime against their own law as well as against the local law of the place in which the crime is committed. Hence it is possible for these states to bring to justice before their own courts a fugitive of their own nationality without the necessity of surrendering him to a foreign state for trial; and they do not consider it necessary to vindicate the law of the foreign state by the trial of the offender in the place where the crime was committed.[18] On the other hand Great Britain and the United States, following the traditions of the common law, hold that crimes must be tried at the place where they are committed and that their criminal courts have no juris-

[15] For comment on the case see M. O. Hudson, "The Factor Case and Double Criminality in Extradition," *Am. Journal,* Vol. 28 (1934), p. 274; E. M. Borchard, *ibid.,* p. 742.

[16] For the text of the convention, see *Am. Journal,* Vol. 28 (1934), Supp., p. 65.

[17] For the text of the Harvard Draft, see *Am. Journal,* Vol. 29 (1935), Supp., p. 21.

[18] It is difficult to determine the motives of the policy of these states. If it be to assure that the accused national obtain a just trial, that might be had by getting the diplomatic representative of the country to attend the trial as an observer. To suggest lack of confidence in the local courts would be to contradict their theory that the alien, in going to a foreign country, must submit himself to the local law.

diction over offenses committed outside the territorial boundaries of the state. Hence if a fugitive criminal, one of their own citizens, is not extradited, he escapes punishment altogether.[19]

The question of reciprocity. The lack of reciprocity here between states following the common law and those following the civil law has given rise to numerous diplomatic negotiations in which neither side was wholly logical or consistent. In Charlton's case,[20] decided in 1913, the Supreme Court of the United States affirmed the judgment of a district court which had dismissed a petition for a writ of habeas corpus in behalf of an American citizen who had murdered his wife in Italy and had escaped to the United States. It was objected against the extradition of the prisoner that under the treaty with Italy neither party was bound to deliver up its own citizens and that, inasmuch as Italy by domestic law forbade extradition of her own citizens, the treaty lacked mutuality and therefore, as regarded the case in question, had been abrogated. The court recognized that the lack of mutuality rendered the treaty voidable, but held that in view of the character of American criminal law the Department of State was entitled to recognize the treaty as binding. Charlton was thereupon extradited. More recently, the United States Secretary of State refused to grant the extradition of an American citizen at the request of the Mexican Government, stating that "the true basis of action under extradition treaties should be reciprocity" and referring to the "long-existing practice" on the part of Mexico of refusing to extradite Mexican citizens.[21] In 1936 the Supreme Court of the United States, in the case of Valentine v. United States ex rel. Neidecker,[22] construed strictly the powers of the Executive Department, holding that the treaty of 1909 with France, which provided that "Neither of the contracting parties shall be bound to deliver up its own citizens or subjects under the stipulations of this convention," did not contain a grant of power to surrender a citizen of the United States in the discretion of the Executive.[23]

[19] There is, of course, no reason at international law why the United States or Great Britain should not give jurisdiction to their criminal courts to try citizens for offenses committed outside the jurisdiction of the state. They are free to do so if they find it desirable to depart from their traditional conception of the territorial nature of criminal acts.

[20] Charlton v. Kelly, 229 U.S. 447 (1913). Hudson, *Cases,* p. 949; Fenwick, *Cases,* p. 439; Bishop, *Cases,* p. 190.

[21] Hackworth, *Digest,* Vol. IV, p. 61. Query, what has the United States to gain in giving asylum to criminals in such cases? Is "reciprocity" the true basis of extradition?

[22] 229 U.S. 5 (1936). *Am. Journal,* Vol. 31 (1937), p. 134.

[23] While the issue before the court was primarily a constitutional one, the strict construction put by the court upon the statute and the treaty throws light upon the conception of extradition in international relations. For editorial comment upon the case, see J. W. Garner, *Am. Journal,* Vol. 30 (1936), p. 480; A. K. Kuhn, *ibid.,* Vol. 31 (1937), p. 476.

Obligation to prosecute citizens not extradited. In consequence of the miscarriages of justice resulting from the principle of reciprocity the Montevideo Convention on Extradition made provision that, while each state might decide whether to extradite one of its citizens, it was under an obligation, if it did not surrender the fugitive, to prosecute him for the crime of which he was accused when the crime met certain established conditions.[24] The Harvard Research *Draft Convention on Extradition* provides, "A requested State shall not decline to extradite a person claimed because such person is a national of the requested State." It was recognized, however, that this rule might be unacceptable to certain states, and provision was made for a reservation by which a state might decline to extradite on ground of nationality, but that in such case "the requested state shall have a duty to prosecute the person claimed for the act for which his extradition is sought." [25]

Political offenses regularly excepted. It is not difficult to understand why, if it be a condition of extradition that the offense should be one with respect to which there is a general agreement among states as to definition and punishment, treaties of extradition should regularly make exception of political offenses. The provision of the treaty of 1909 between the United States and France is typical: "A fugitive must not be surrendered if the offense in respect to which his surrender is demanded be of a political character." [26] This exception had its origin in the natural unwillingness of more democratic governments in the latter half of the nineteenth century to surrender political refugees whose offenses against established autocratic governments in many cases excited the sympathy of the country of their asylum. It has proved difficult, however, to draw a clear distinction between political and ordinary offenses. Are all attacks upon an established government political offenses, whether committed by liberals against an autocratic government or by radicals against a liberal government? May the same act bear a different character if committed by an individual singly or as a member of a group? There are many cases in which political object and personal motive are inextricably tangled. Moreover, there are the so-called "relative political offenses," *délits complexes,* which are at the same time political acts and ordinary crimes. In 1890, in the case of a Swiss refugee, Castioni,[27] who had taken part in an uprising against the local cantonal authorities and had killed a government official in an attack upon the municipal palace, the British court ordered the release of the prisoner on the ground that the offense was political. To exclude extradition under the terms of the act, said the court, it must at least be shown that

[24] Article 2. *Am. Journal,* Vol. 28 (1934), Supp., p. 65.

[25] Article 7; Schedule A, Reservation No. 3. *Ibid.,* Vol. 29 (1935), Supp., pp. 123, 236.

[26] Article VI. *Treaties and Conventions,* Vol. III, p. 2580.

[27] 1 Q. B. Div. 149 (1890). Fenwick, *Cases,* p. 450; Hudson, *Cases,* p. 942.

the act was an overt one, done in the furtherance of a political rising, "a dispute between two parties in the state as to which is to have the government in its hands." In contrast with this decision, the same British court rendered an opinion in 1894 [28] delivering up to France the anarchist Meunier, who had caused the explosion of a bomb in a Paris café and another explosion in a government barracks. The court repeated the principle that "in order to constitute an offense of a political character, there must be two or more parties in the state, each seeking to impose the government of their own choice on the other." The party with which the accused was identified, said the court, "is the enemy of all governments. Their efforts are directed primarily against the general body of citizens."

Limitation of political offenses. The sympathy of liberal governments with political refugees received a sharp check as the result of the numerous assassinations of rulers during the second half of the nineteenth century. Murder committed in the course of a political uprising was obviously different from the futile murder of the head of a state by an irresponsible individual. In 1856, in the presence of the inability of the Belgian court to extradite Jacquin, who had attempted to murder Napoleon III, Belgium enacted the so-called *attentat* clause, providing that the murder of the head of a foreign state, or of a member of his family, should not be considered a political crime. Following the assassination of President Garfield, the United States incorporated into its treaty with Belgium in 1882 the clause that "an attempt against the life of the head of a foreign government, or against that of any member of his family, when such attempt comprises the act either of murder or assassination or of poisoning, shall not be considered a political offense or an act connected with such an offense." [29] The Montevideo Convention on Extradition of 1933 makes exception of offenses "of a political nature or of a character related thereto," but in turn excepts from such offenses, "An attempt against the life or person of the chief of state or members of his family. . . ." [30]

Specification of political offenses. The Harvard Research Draft Convention on Extradition attempted to define more specifically the meaning and application of "political offense." After recognizing that a requested state may decline to extradite a person whose extradition is sought either for an act which constitutes such an offense or with the object of prosecuting him for such an offense, it continues: "As it is used in this Convention, the term 'political offense' includes treason, sedition and espionage, whether committed by one or more persons; it includes any offenses connected with the activities of an organized group directed

[28] 2 Q. B. Div. 415. Fenwick, *Cases,* p. 455.
[29] *Treaties and Conventions,* Vol. I, p. 100.
[30] Art. 3(e).

against the security or governmental system of the requesting State; and it does not exclude other offenses having a political objective." [31] The Draft recognizes that extradition may in like manner be declined for military offenses, defining a "military offense" as one "punishable only as a violation of a military law or regulation" and which would not be punishable as a violation of a civil law if the military law or regulation did not exist. The Draft also admits the possibility of a reservation as to "fiscal offenses," defining them as offenses "in connection with the customs or revenue law of a State, and not involving misuse of public funds." [32]

Attempted extradition of the ex-Kaiser. A unique extradition case for which there was no precedent in international law was presented on January 15, 1920, when the Supreme Council, representing the Allied and Associated Powers, addressed an official demand to the Government of Holland calling upon it "to deliver into their hands William Hohenzollern, former emperor of Germany, in order that he may be put on trial." The demand for extradition had its origin in Article 227 of the Treaty of Versailles, which stated that "the Allied and Associated Powers publicly arraign William II of Hohenzollern, formerly German Emperor, for a supreme offense against international morality and the sanctity of treaties." Provision was made for a special tribunal to try the accused. In its decision the tribunal was to be "guided by the highest motives of international policy, with a view to vindicating the solemn obligations of international undertakings and the validity of international morality." [33] A request for the surrender of the emperor was to be addressed to the Government of Holland.

In its reply the Dutch Government called attention to the fact that Holland was not a party to the Treaty of Versailles, and that in consequence the case must be judged by the municipal law of the state and its national traditions. The decision reached was that neither "the constituent laws of the kingdom, which are based upon the principles of law universally recognized, nor the agelong tradition which has made this country always a ground of refuge for the vanquished in international conflicts" permitted the Government of Holland to accede to the request made upon it. [34]

Extradition of the Nazi leaders. Anticipating the possibility that the Axis leaders might attempt to escape from Germany and take refuge in

[31] Art. 5.

[32] Art. 6, Reservation No. 2. For comment, see Draft, *op. cit.*, pp. 119, 228.

[33] See below, p. 758.

[34] New York *Times*, January 22, 1920. The most that Holland would promise was that "in the free exercise of Dutch sovereignty" it would take all necessary effective measures of precaution to prevent the return of the Kaiser to Germany, and that it would subject his freedom to the necessary restrictions to accomplish that object. A summary of the facts, and argument upon them, may be found in "The trial of the Kaiser," by J. B. Scott, in *What Really Happened at Paris,* ed. by E. M. House and C. Seymour.

a neutral country, President Roosevelt, in a statement of July 30, 1943, expressed the hope that "no neutral will permit its territory to be used as a place of refuge or otherwise assist such persons in any effort to escape their just deserts." [35] Six of the leading neutral governments replied to the statement, assuring the United States that they would not permit war criminals to take refuge in their countries; although there were doubts on the part of some states as to the legal basis upon which the fugitives might be denied asylum.[36] The Tripartite Conference, in its "Declaration of German Atrocities," signed at Moscow on October 30, 1943, announced that the three Allied Powers would pursue the guilty persons "to the uttermost ends of the earth and will deliver them to their accusers in order that justice may be done." [37] As it turned out, the question of extradition did not arise, the leading members of the Nazi Party being captured in belligerent territory.[38]

C. NEED OF A UNIFORM RULE

In view of the inconveniences attending the negotiation of bilateral treaties of such wide variety, attempts were made in the latter part of the nineteenth century, when constitutional government was in the ascendant, to formulate a uniform rule for general adoption. In 1880 the Institute of International Law adopted at Oxford a series of twenty-six rules governing the whole subject of extradition, three articles of which related to political offenses.[39] These last were modified at the meeting at Geneva in 1892, when four new articles were adopted.[40] Extradition was held to be inadmissible not only for purely political crimes but also for acts of a mixed character called "relative political offenses," except where the crime was one "of great gravity from the point of view of morality and of common law." Acts committed in the course of insurrection or civil war were not extraditable unless they were "acts of odious barbarity or vandalism forbidden by the laws of war," and then only when the civil war was at an end. An important exception was made of "criminal acts directed against the bases of all social organization, and not only against a certain state or a certain form of government," which were not to be considered political offenses.

In 1926 the League of Nations Committee of Experts pronounced itself against the codification of the law of extradition under existing conditions, the report of the subcommittee pointing out the "sacrifices" that would be demanded from states adhering strictly to the territorial basis

[35] Dept. of State *Bulletin,* Vol. IX, p. 62.
[36] *Ibid.,* Vol. XI, p. 339; Vol. XII, p. 190.
[37] *Am. Journal,* Vol. 38 (1944), Supp., p. 7.
[38] For the trial and conviction of the Nazi leaders, see below, p. 760.
[39] *Resolutions,* p. 42, Arts. 13-15.
[40] *Ibid.,* p. 102.

of jurisdiction and from those claiming nonterritorial jurisdiction.[41] Badly needed as was a general convention on the subject, as a substitute for the thousand and more bilateral treaties required to meet the international need, it appeared that the divergencies in the national law and policy of the different countries were too great to be overcome.[42] In 1935 a Draft Convention prepared by Harvard Research offered a constructive treatment of the subject; but no action was taken upon it.[43] Even among the American states the same difficulties were confronted.[44] The Conference at Caracas in 1954 realized that, in adopting its two draft conventions on territorial asylum and on diplomatic asylum, the provision conceding to the state granting asylum the competence to determine the political character of the refugee made the right to request extradition an "indispensable complement of the right of asylum," as being "the only legal means for rectifying an erroneous determination of the nature of the offense by the state offering asylum." [45] But this called for an agreement upon an extradition treaty, leaving the matter still in the stage of draft conventions, with the United States prominent among others taking exception to particular articles.

Case of Pérez Jiménez.   A marked exception to the general practice is to be seen in the 1963 extradition by the United States to Venezuela of the former President of that country, Marcos Pérez Jiménez. On the basis of a treaty of 1922, a district judge, acting as extradition magistrate, found that the evidence presented by Venezuela showed probable cause to believe the accused guilty of the crimes of embezzlement, breach of trust, and receiving money unlawfully obtained. The decision was challenged by Pérez Jiménez in habeas corpus proceedings, but upheld by the Court of Appeals, and certiorari was refused by the Supreme Court. In view of the political status of Pérez Jiménez, Venezuela agreed that security measures would be taken to protect him and that, in accordance with the treaty, he would be tried only for the offenses for which extradition was granted.[46]

D. LETTERS ROGATORY

For many years the courts of justice of different states have followed the practice of aiding in the administration of justice in their several

[41] *Am. Journal,* Vol. 20 (1926), Spec. Supp., pp. 242, 257.

[42] The student may make profitable comparison with the single clause of the Constitution of the United States (Art. IV, Sec. 2, Clause 2), providing for "interstate rendition"; and its interpretation in Kentucky v. Dennison, 24 Howard 66 (1860).

[43] For the text, see *Am. Journal,* Vol. 29 (1935), Supp., p. 21.

[44] A regional convention was adopted by the American States at Montevideo in 1933, but only five governments ratified it without reservations. *Int. Conferences, 1933-1940,* p. 110. For the reservations made by the United States, see *ibid.,* p. 114.

[45] Resolution CVII, "Extradition," *Int. Conferences, 1942-1954,* p. 444.

[46] Dept. of State *Bulletin,* September 2, 1963; *Am. Journal,* Vol. 58 (1964), p. 105.

countries by compelling persons within their jurisdiction to appear and give their depositions to be used as testimony in a foreign country. The request from the foreign court for such depositions is made in the form of a writ or "letter rogatory" informing the local court of the action that is pending and of the testimony that is desired "in the furtherance of justice" and promising reciprocity. So well established has the practice of responding to letters rogatory become that it may be said to approximate closely to a rule of customary international law.[47]

Comity in matters of jurisdiction. By custom, which may now be said to have obtained a degree of legal validity, many states have adopted into their judicial systems a body of rules in accordance with which the laws and judicial decrees of foreign countries are applied to the decision of cases involving acts done in a foreign country or property located therein. Such cases may arise between two citizens of the state, or between a citizen of the state and a domiciled alien. This body of rules is known as "private international law" or "conflict of laws," and its precise content is a matter of domestic law laid down by the judicial tribunals or the legislatures of the respective states. The element of international law present is not to be found in the specific rules applied to these cases, which are strictly national in their authority and relate to the acts of individuals, not of states, but is to be found in the general practice of the nations in giving a greater or less degree of validity to the legislation of other states under the particular circumstances. In the case of Hilton v. Guyot,[48] involving a suit by Guyot against Hilton upon a judgment recovered in a French court, decided in 1895, the United States Supreme Court went so far as to say that

international law in its widest and most comprehensive sense—including not only questions of right between nations, . . . but also questions arising under what is usually called private international law, or the conflict of laws, and concerning the rights of persons within the territory and dominion of one nation, by reason of acts, private or public, done within the dominions of another nation—is part of our law. . . .

and must be administered by the courts of justice in cases duly presented to them. The basis of these rules is the "comity of nations," not the

---

[47] For a sample letter rogatory addressed to France in relation to H. M. Blackmer, see Hudson, *Cases*, p. 972. On the general subject of letters rogatory in connection with "judicial cooperation" see Report of the Sub-Committee of the League of Nations Committee of Experts for the Progressive Codification of International Law, *Am. Journal*, Vol. 22 (1928), Spec. Supp., pp. 47 ff. For the refusal of a Federal District Court of the United States to execute letters rogatory from a court of Mexico City which sought to require the personal appearance of the defendant, see Fenwick, *Cases*, p. 457.

[48] 159 U.S. 113 (1895). Fenwick, *Cases*, p. 459; Hudson, *Cases*, p. 985; Briggs, *Cases*, p. 398.

extraterritorial validity of the law of the foreign state. Comity, as explained by the Supreme Court in the same case, is in the legal sense

neither a matter of absolute obligation on the one hand, nor of mere courtesy and good will, upon the other. But it is the recognition which one nation allows within its territory to the legislative, executive, or judicial acts of another nation, having due regard both to international duty and convenience, and to the rights of its own citizens or of other persons who are under the protection of its laws.[49]

The practice of nations varies in the matter, however, and it is doubtful whether many states push the idea of comity to the same extent as was done in the case just cited.

Scope of international private law.   The detailed rules which make up the body of private international law are outside the scope of a volume on international law. In general, however, they embrace questions relating to marriages contracted or divorces granted under the laws of a foreign state,[50] title to real or personal property located in a foreign state or the transfer of such property by devise or descent, the validity of wills made in a foreign state, the legal capacity of parties contracting under the laws of a foreign state, the enforcement of foreign judgments, and related questions.[51] It must be noted that as a condition of the enforcement of foreign judgments national courts require the fulfillment of certain conditions as to the jurisdiction of the foreign tribunal over the parties and the subject matter of the case as well as to the substantial justice of the proceedings. In addition, some states require a reciprocal recognition of their own judgments on the part of the foreign state. In the case of Hilton v. Guyot above cited, the Supreme Court refused to give full credit and conclusive effect to the judgment of the French court, on the ground that judgments of American courts were reviewable upon their merits in the French courts.[52]

[49] *Comity* is used here in a narrower sense, which is properly only one aspect of the general rule of courtesy falling short of legal obligation.

[50] The refusal of the French tribunals, under the influence of political pressure from the chief executive, to recognize the validity of the marriage of Jerome Bonaparte to Miss Patterson, contracted under the laws of the United States but without observing the forms required by French law, has obtained a place in history by reason of the parties to the case, not by reason of the problem presented. See Dana, note 55 to Wheaton, *Elements of International Law,* 1866 ed., § 93.

[51] For a bibliography of the subject and a survey of its nature and history, see Beale, *A Treatise on the Conflict of Laws,* Vol. I, Pt. I (1916); Westlake, *A Treatise on Private International Law, with Principal Reference to Its Practice in England,* 7th ed. (1925); Dicey, *A Digest of the Law of England with Reference to the Conflict of Laws,* 5th ed., edited by Keith (1932); Cheshire, *Private International Law,* 4th ed. (1952); Wolff, *Private International Law.*

[52] "In holding," said the court, "such a judgment, for want of reciprocity not to be conclusive evidence of the merits of the claim we do not proceed upon any theory of retaliation upon one person by reason of injustice done to another; but upon the broad ground that international law is founded upon mutuality and reciprocity. . . ."

Conventions regulating the conflict of laws. The desirability of obtaining a greater degree of uniformity in their mutual recognition of foreign laws and judgments has influenced the leading states of Europe on a number of occasions to enter into international conventions dealing with the conflict of laws.[53] In 1928 the Sixth International Conference of American States adopted at Havana a Convention on Private International Law, accepting the Bustamante Code which had been presented to the conference by the International Commission of Jurists.[54] The Code covers international civil law, commercial law, penal law, and the law of procedure.[55] In 1948 the Charter of the Organization of American States called upon its newly created Inter-American Council of Jurists to promote the development of public and private international law and to study the possibility of attaining uniformity in the legislation of the various American countries in so far as it might appear desirable. The two problems of codifying private international law and attaining uniformity of legislation are distinct, the one bearing upon the procedures followed by national courts in seeking to give effect to rights acquired under the law of a foreign state, and the other bearing upon the formulation of agreements to adopt common principles and rules in relation to matters of private law. In both fields the American states have carried on the work begun in 1928 and made significant progress.[56]

[53] See Research in International Law (Harvard Law School, 1932), No. 6, "Competence of Courts in Regard to Foreign States," *Am. Journal*, Vol. 23 (1929), Spec. Supp.

[54] *Int. Conferences of Am. States*, 1889-1928, p. 443.

[55] See *Am. Journal*, Vol. 22 (1928), Spec. Supp., pp. 234, 273. For the question of the revision of the Bustamante Code, see Fenwick, *OAS*, p. 342; K. H. Nadelmann, "The Question of the Revision of the Bustamante Code," *Am. Journal*, Vol. 57 (1963), p. 384. An instructive analogy might be drawn between the efforts of the leading states to secure greater uniformity in the recognition of their respective laws and the constructive action taken under more favorable conditions by the Philadelphia Convention of 1787 in introducing into the Constitution of the United States the clause stipulating that "full faith and credit shall be given in each state to the public acts, records, and judicial proceedings of every other state" (Art. IV, Sec. I). An instructive comparison between Anglo-Saxon and Latin American law may be found in Eder, *A Comparative Survey of Anglo-American and Latin-American Law*.

[56] For details, see Fenwick, *OAS*, pp. 346 ff.

CHAPTER **XVIII**

Jurisdiction Over Territory: Titles

A. JURISDICTION OVER TERRITORY AS DISTINCT FROM PERSONS

For purposes of scientific treatment the jurisdiction of a state over the persons within its territory may be distinguished from the jurisdiction of the state over the territory itself. As a practical matter the two forms of state authority, or the two methods by which the state gives effect to its right of independence, are on many points legally indistinguishable. Both the citizen body and the territorial domain of the state are essential elements of its corporate character. The membership of the former is, in general, determined by the fixed boundaries of the latter. The exercise of effective control over individual citizens is dependent upon their presence upon the territory of the state. Aliens who owe no formal allegiance to the state come under the authority of its laws by entering within its physical limits. Jurisdiction over persons, therefore, necessarily raises the collateral question of jurisdiction over territory, whether the connection between the two be close or remote. Nevertheless it is a convenient and not wholly arbitrary rule of international jurisprudence to regard the territory of the state as something distinct from the state itself, and to treat it as if it were national property possessed by the state in much the same way that property in land is held by individual citizens within the state.[1]

Nature of territorial jurisdiction. The jurisdiction of a state over its territory must, as a matter of constitutional law, be distinguished from property rights in the land itself. In feudal times the exercise of sovereignty was coincident with the ultimate ownership by the king of the land included within the boundaries of the state. The sovereignty of the

[1] The subject is critically examined in G. Schwarzenberger, "Title to Territory: Response to a Challenge," *Am. Journal,* Vol. 51 (1957), p. 308.

king thus implied a property right in the land as well as a personal right to the allegiance of the tenant. Vattel, writing in 1758, thought it necessary even in his day to denounce the view of certain writers who regarded the prince as the real owner (*propriétaire*) of the empire and in whose eyes "the kingdom is the inheritance of the prince, in the same manner as his fields and his flocks." In modern times the state appears as a corporate person distinct from the person of its ruler; it possesses an ultimate authority within its territorial borders without being the actual owner of the land itself. It may, indeed, own definite portions of the territory in its capacity as a public corporation, in which case it exercises over the particular area both territorial jurisdiction and the rights of private ownership. Or again the state may possess a right of eminent domain by which it has the power to withdraw a given area of land from private use for purposes of state. But these are exceptional cases, leaving the general rule intact that the territorial jurisdiction of the state is, in point of constitutional law, a right of political control, of ultimate authority, not a right of property. It is an *imperium* as distinct from a *dominium* in the sense of Roman Law.[2]

Sovereignty and ownership. This distinction has, however, not yet been fully recognized by international law. The reason is twofold. Until of recent years international law dealt only with the relations of states and did not take cognizance of the constitutional relations between the individual state and its citizens except in so far as these were indirectly presented in connection with claims asserted by the state itself. Since the members of the state were not recognized by international law in their individual capacity, any rights which belonged to them must, as Hall expressed it, "be clothed in the garb of state rights before they can be put forward internationally."[3] When, therefore, a state asserted its right to sovereignty over a disputed area of territory, the claim differed in no appreciable way from the assertion of a right of complete ownership, and its merits were determined by the same rules of law, whether the state did or did not happen to be the actual owner of the land from the point of view of constitutional law.

In the second place, owing to the fact that at the time Grotius wrote the conception of the sovereignty of the state as distinct from the ownership of the property of the state was not clearly understood, it seemed both logical and convenient to transfer to international law the traditional rules of the Roman Law with regard to the rights of property between individuals. These rules remain to this day the basis of the territorial rights of states, in spite of the fact that many of them are applied with difficulty to the concrete situations of international life. The attempt, for

---

[2] See Oppenheim, *International Law*, Vol. I, § 158. For the more recent issue of "sovereignty over natural resources," see above, p. 347.

[3] *International Law*, § 9. On this contentious point, see above, p. 149.

example, to apply the rules of the Roman Law to international problems, such as the acquisition of unoccupied territory in the New World, led to numerous disputes, for the solution of which the principles of the Roman Law were entirely inadequate.[4]

B. ACQUISITION OF TITLE TO TERRITORY

Title to territory has been obtained by states either through the acquisition of land not hitherto belonging to any other state or through the transfer of land from one state owner to another.[5] The former method confers an original title, the latter a derivative title. Jurists have differed as to the number and character of the titles to property, but in actual practice the following titles appear to be recognized by states: occupation, accretion, prescription, voluntary cession, conquest, treaties of peace, and assimilation.

Title by occupation. Occupation has been both in legal theory and in practical usage the most important mode of acquiring territory as between states. Grotius referred to it as "the only natural and original mode of acquisition." [6] To him, as to Vattel,[7] occupation represented a tacit form of agreement by which the division of lands among the peoples of the earth was brought about, once they came to realize that their original common ownership was inadequate to meet their needs. Thus arose the rights of property between nations, which in the due course of time became absolute by prescription. This theory, however, of the primitive settlement of states is only of academic interest at the present day. Occupation as a title to territory obtained its important place in international law in connection with the claims of existing European states to acquisitions of territory in the New World opened up by explorers after the discovery of the American continent in the fifteenth century; and it continued to be an acute issue until the definitive partition of Africa toward the close of the nineteenth century. The problem presented was, upon what grounds might the claims put forward by European states to the ownership of territory in unoccupied lands be adjudged valid? The question raised issues both as to the law and as to the facts, and in both respects there was ample ground for controversy. For the law was in the making, and it had no more than the opinions of jurists behind it; while the facts were often difficult to ascertain, even where there was a desire for justice on both sides.

Discovery does not give valid title. Not until the eighteenth century

---

[4] Compare Lauterpacht, *Private Law Sources and Analogies of International Law*, pp. 91 ff.

[5] The term *title* has long been in use by statesmen and writers to describe rights or legal claims to territory. See, *e.g.* Moore, *Digest*, Vol. I, §§ 80, 81. On the general subject, see Hill, *Claims to Territory in International Law and Relations*.

[6] *De jure belli ac pacis*, Eng. trans., Bk. II, Chap. III, § IV; Chap. II, §§ II, V.

[7] *Droit des gens*, Eng. trans., Bk. I, § 207.

did discovery as a basis of title to unappropriated lands cease to be asserted as sufficient of itself to give validity.[8] The two preceding centuries, being an age of discovery, furnish numerous instances of claims based upon nothing more than the fact that a single navigator landed upon the soil and in the name of his sovereign "took possession" of it. Extravagant claims met, however, with equally sweeping denials. The famous bull, *Inter cœtera,* issued by Alexander VI on May 4, 1493, suggesting a division of the New World between Spain and Portugal by a line drawn 100 leagues west of the Azores and Cape Verde Islands,[9] was not taken seriously by the competitors of the two favored states. Spain, England, and France each claimed the coast of America north of the Gulf of Mexico, on the basis of first discovery by a vessel flying their national flag.[10] By the time of Vattel the rule appears to have been recognized that mere discovery could give no more than a temporary inchoate title, which would lapse unless followed within reasonable time by an effective possession. "Navigators," said Vattel, "setting out upon voyages of discovery and bearing with them a commission from their sovereign, when coming across islands or other uninhabited lands, have taken possession of them in the name of their nation; and this title has usually been respected, provided actual possession has followed shortly after." [11] In a case before the Supreme Court of the United States in 1823, Chief Justice Marshall doubtless went too far in declaring that "discovery gave title to the government by whose subjects, or by whose authority, it was made, against all other European governments." [12] He entered, however, the qualification that the "title might be consummated by possession."

Conditions of occupation. By "occupation," in international law, is meant the settlement by a state of territory hitherto unappropriated, with the object of incorporating the territory into the national domain and exercising sovereignty over it.[13] The territory thus appropriated must be,

[8] See, in general, Lindley, *The Acquisition and Government of Backward Territory in International Law,* Chap. XVIII.

[9] The bull marking off the line of demarcation was withdrawn the same year in favor of another which left the parties to their original rights. The Treaty of Tordesillas was thereupon concluded between them, June 7, 1494, moving the line to 370 leagues west of the Cape Verde Islands. See *Cambridge Modern History,* Vol. I, pp. 23-24; Hyde, *Int. Law,* Vol. I, p. 165, note 1. For the text of the bull, see Davenport, *European Treaties Bearing on the History of the United States and Its Dependencies to 1648.*

[10] In the charter given by the British Crown to the London Company in 1609 the grant of land was made to extend "up into the land, throughout from sea to sea, west and northwest," beyond the limits of known discovery. A similar grant of territory without known limits was made in the charter obtained by the Plymouth Company in 1620. See MacDonald, *Select Charters,* pp. 11, 23.

[11] *Droit des gens,* Eng. trans., Vol. I, § 207.

[12] Johnson and Graham's Lessee v. M'Intosh, 8 Wheaton 543 (1823). Fenwick, *Cases,* p. 466.

[13] See Lindley, *op. cit.,* Chap. XIX.

in law, *res nullius,* which is interpreted as requiring not that the territory be uninhabited, but that it be not already occupied by a people or state whose political organization is such as to cause its prior rights of occupancy to be recognized. Until of recent years no line was drawn by international law between the civilized and uncivilized peoples whose prior sovereignty would or would not be recognized under the circumstances. But, in general, international law did not recognize the title of wandering tribes or even of settled peoples whose civilization was regarded as below the European standard. Vattel's theoretical justification may be open to question, but he correctly stated the law when he said that the uncertain occupancy by wandering tribes of the vast regions of the New World "cannot be held as a real and lawful taking of possession; and when the Nations of Europe, which are too confined at home, come upon lands which the savages have no special need of and are making no present and continuous use of, they may lawfully take possession of them and establish colonies in them." [14] In the case of Johnson and Graham's Lessee v. M'Intosh,[15] the Supreme Court of the United States was presented with a claim to land, based upon grants made by certain Indian tribes, which conflicted with the claims of Virginia under her charter of 1609. The court held that such rights as were possessed by the Indians at the time of their grant were no more than rights of occupancy left in their enjoyment after the discovery and annexation of the territory by the British Crown. "While the different nations of Europe respected the rights of the natives, as occupants," said the court, "they asserted the ultimate dominion to be in themselves; and claimed and exercised, as a consequence of this ultimate dominion, a power to grant the soil, while yet in possession of the natives." The court found no difficulty in conceding a like validity to similar titles of Holland and of Portugal, as well as to that of Spain in respect to Mexico, in spite of the superior civilization of the Aztec natives.

Necessity of actual settlement.   In addition to a formal expression of the intention of a state to take possession of unappropriated territory, there must be an actual settlement upon the land if the inchoate title conferred by discovery is to be made final and definitive so as to secure the respect of other states. The particular form which the settlement must take to keep alive the title asserted by the state was obviously in the early days a matter too dependent upon local conditions to make possible the development of a definite rule. Considerable time was allowed to elapse between the formal act of annexation and actual establishment of military garrisons or colonies. The long period between the annexation of North America to the British Crown and the founding of the Virginia and New England colonies would have invalidated the

[14] *Droit des gens,* Eng. trans., Vol. I, § 209.
[15] 8 Wheaton 543 (1823). Fenwick, *Cases,* p. 466.

title in a later century. Likewise the temporary abandonment of a settlement was judged more leniently in the seventeenth century, owing to the greater difficulty attending colonial establishments. The dispute between the United States and Spain to determine the boundary between the newly acquired Louisiana Territory and the Spanish possessions in Mexico is illustrative of the conditions under which an accepted principle of law had to be applied to uncertain facts. The United States, as successor to the French title, claimed the Rio Grande as the western boundary on the ground of a French settlement in the Bay of Espíritu Santo in 1685. Spain claimed title by prior discovery of the coast of Texas in the sixteenth century, followed by a permanent settlement on the coast in 1689 after the French settlement had been abandoned.[16] Under the circumstances, a decision on the legal rights of the parties would have been impossible, although the claim of Spain appears to have been the better founded. As part of the price for the purchase of East Florida in 1819 the United States abandoned its claim.[17]

In the controversy between the United States and the Netherlands over the sovereignty of the Island of Palmas (Miangas), claimed by the United States to have been obtained by cession from Spain in 1898,[18] the Tribunal of the Permanent Court of Arbitration held that, even conceding that the original discovery by Spain constituted a valid title at the time, it could not without any subsequent act prevail against the principle that had come to be accepted since the beginning of the nineteenth century that "an inchoate title of discovery must be completed within a reasonable period by the effective occupation of the region claimed to be discovered." As regards the question whether a rule of law which controlled rights in the sixteenth century should continue to control them in the nineteenth, the tribunal made a distinction between "the creation of rights and the existence of rights." "The same principle," the tribunal said, "which subjects the act creative of a right to the law in force at the time the right arises, demands that the existence of the right, in other words its continued manifestation, shall follow the conditions required by the evolution of law." [19]

Loss of title by abandonment of territory. The case of the Falkland [Malvinas] Islands presented difficulties as to both the law and the facts. Both Spain and Great Britain asserted title by discovery, the former through Vespucius, the latter through Drake and Hawkins. The

---

[16] For further details, see Hall, *International Law*, § 33.

[17] Art. III, treaty of February 22, 1819 (*Treaties and Conventions*, Vol. II, p. 1651). See also Hill, *Leading American Treaties*, Chap. VIII.

[18] Tribunal of the Permanent Court of Arbitration, 1928. *Hague Court Reports* (Second Series), pp. 83 ff.; Fenwick, *Cases*, p. 470; Hudson, *Cases*, p. 361; Bishop, *Cases*, p. 345; Briggs, *Cases*, p. 239.

[19] The same principle of *inter-temporal* law was applied in the Grisbadarna arbitration between Norway and Sweden in 1909. See Schwarzenberger, *Int. Law*, Vol. I, pp. 10, 137.

first settlement appears to have been made in 1764 in the name of France, whose rights were transferred to Spain in 1767. In the meantime formal possession was taken of the islands in the name of Great Britain in 1765. In 1771 the islands were left by Spain in British possession without a reservation as to the right of sovereignty. Three years later the British in turn withdrew their forces after leaving "marks and signals" of possession. Occupation by Spain ensued until 1810, followed by occupation by the Government of Buenos Aires until the latter withdrew under pressure from the British in 1833, since which time the British have remained in actual possession and thus acquired a prescriptive title which, however, Argentina still contests. The Argentine claim rests mainly upon the long abandonment of the Islands by Great Britain between 1774 and 1810. Title by prescription is rejected on ground of the coercion involved.[20]

Other instances of claims based upon abandonment may be cited as follows: In the case of the island of Santa Lucia in the Caribbean, a British colony had been massacred by the Carib Indians in 1640, and no further attempt was made to occupy the island. In 1650 the French occupied it as unappropriated territory.[21] In the Delagoa Bay case the French Government, as arbitrator between Great Britain and Portugal, assigned to the latter country in 1875 certain territory which had been occupied by Portugal intermittently since the sixteenth century, but which had been abandoned temporarily in 1823, at which time the native chiefs asserted their independence and ceded the lands to Great Britain.[22] In 1896 Great Britain renounced its claims over Trinity Island (Ilha da Trindade) and formally recognized the sovereignty of Brazil. The island, situated 700 miles from the Brazilian State of Espirito Santo, was discovered by the Portuguese but not effectively occupied. After being occupied and abandoned by the British and the Portuguese, an occupation was attempted by Great Britain in 1895, against the protest of Brazil. Great Britain claimed title on ground of the annulment of former titles by disuse. Brazil justified the lack of effective occupation on ground of the physical character of the island. Portugal offered its good offices as mediator, and found that the temporary abandonment of the island was offset by repeated assertions by Brazil of intention to retain title.[23]

Extent of the area of occupation. The chief ground of international

---

[20] See Goebel, *The Struggle for the Falkland Islands*. A summary of the Argentine case may be found in Podestá Costa, *Manual de Derecho Internacional Público*, No. 65; Moreno, *Derecho Int. Público*, Tomo II, p. 182; Antokoletz, *Derecho Int. Público*, Tercera Parte, p. 133. The islands are also known as Malvinas Islands.

[21] Hall, *International Law*, § 34.

[22] See Hall, *International Law*, § 34; for the text of the award, see Moore, *Arbitrations*, Vol. V, p. 4984.

[23] Moore, *Digest*, Vol. I, p. 299; Accioly, *Tratado de Derecho Internacional Público*, Vol. II, p. 196.

dispute in connection with the occupation of unappropriated territory has been to determine how far a settlement upon the outer fringe of annexed territory should be regarded as the possession required to confirm title to the whole.[24] Obviously it was not possible in most cases for states to do more than establish settlements at one point or another along the seacoasts of a continent or large island. Yet for the future protection of their settlements, as well as for their subsequent expansion, it was necessary that large stretches of inland territory should be brought within the control of the same state. Mention has been made of the claims indirectly made by the British Crown in the charters granted in 1609 and 1620 to the London and Plymouth companies to the inland territory "from sea to sea." [25] By the eighteenth century these sweeping claims were reduced to narrower limits, and Great Britain was content in 1765 to accept the Mississippi River as a western boundary. The United States did not feel called upon, however, to exercise similar self-restraint at a later date.[26]

The Oregon boundary dispute. The crest of the watershed came to be regarded as a natural inland boundary, so as to include, together with the land actually settled, the basins of the smaller rivers emptying along the coast. Such was the claim pressed by the United States against Spain in 1805 in connection with the boundaries of the Louisiana Purchase.[27] If, however, a river extended far back into the land, including, together with its branches, a wide area of unsettled territory, the question whether a settlement on the coast at the mouth of the river should give title to the entire basin was more doubtful. In the long controversy between Great Britain and the United States over the Oregon boundary, the United States claimed the territory lying between 42° and 54° 40', north latitude, on the ground of prior discovery and prior settlement, as well as on the ground of succession to Spanish rights by discovery. Great Britain denied both claims on point of fact. On the point of law, the two countries differed as to the doctrines of "continuity" and "contiguity." The United States was undoubtedly without justification in law in claiming, as heir to British claims, territory "extending westward from her settlements (on the Atlantic) to the Pacific Ocean." [28] Nor can a valid defense be made for the claim to the entire region drained by the Columbia River, which in its many branches extended far into the interior and embraced territory in no sense necessary to the protection of the settlements at the mouth of the river. In truth, existing legal prin-

---

[24] The problem has no analogies in municipal law, under which actual possession is a prerequisite of such titles as "squatter's rights." Compare, however, the "staking-out" of claims, where land is granted by a government to new settlers.

[25] See above, p. 405, note 10.

[26] See p. 461.

[27] See Moore, *Digest,* Vol. I, § 81.

[28] See *ibid.,* where the claims of Secretary Calhoun in 1844 are given.

ciples were quite inadequate to settle the claims made by either side; so that the compromise upon the line of 49°, laid down in the treaty of 1846, must be looked upon as an "amicable composition" of a dispute which no international court could have settled on a basis of strict law.[29] Beyond the rule that occupation should extend as far as it was actually made effective, it was impossible for international law to go; the "constructive occupation" of territory not actually occupied presented facts too uncertain for customary law to act upon.

Later law of occupation. But at the time of the partition of Africa in the last quarter of the nineteenth century new principles of law came to the front. International law, in general, had grown greatly within the century preceding, and the nations were on the whole more desirous of making their colonial undertakings conform to accepted law. The old formalities attending discovery and annexation gave way to a definite notification by the occupying power of its intention to take over the territory. Article 34 of the Final Act of the Berlin Conference of 1885 [30] provided that any power which should thenceforth take possession of territory upon the coasts of the African continent should accompany the act "with a notification addressed to the other signatory Powers of the present Act," in order that they might, if need be, make good any claims of their own. In addition to the necessity of confirming by occupation and settlement the inchoate title acquired by notification of intention to occupy, it was now required that the power taking possession of territory should set up a local government capable of maintaining order. Article 35 of the Berlin convention imposed upon the signatory powers the obligation to assure in their territories "the existence of an authority sufficient to cause acquired rights to be respected, and as the case may be, liberty of commerce and of transit under the conditions agreed upon." [31] The provisions of the Berlin convention showed the desirability of formulating a general rule of international law upon the subject. In consequence, the question was taken up by the Institute of International Law, which offered in 1888 a "Draft of an International Declaration Regarding Occupation of Territories." The draft proposed that the taking of possession should be carried out "by the establishment of a responsible local power, provided with sufficient means to maintain order and assure the regular exercise of its authority within the limits of the occupied territory." It was further proposed that, in the notification given of taking

---

[29] For the text of the Oregon Treaty, see *Treaties and Conventions*, Vol. I, p. 656. The final settlement of the controversy may be found in Moore, *Arbitrations*, Vol. I, pp. 196 ff.

[30] *Br. and For. State Papers*, Vol. LXVI, p. 4.

[31] The provisions of the Berlin convention relating to the administration of the territories of Central Africa in the interest of the welfare of the native tribes may be studied in connection with the system of mandates established by the Covenant of the League of Nations. See above, p. 139.

possession, a statement should be made of the approximate limits of the occupied territory.[32]

Colonial protectorates. A characteristic feature of the occupation of the African continent was the large number of agreements entered into with the native chiefs by states seeking to obtain a prior right of control over territory which at the time they were unable to occupy effectively. These treaties were not, however, regarded as in the class of agreements with independent states having international validity. They were rather administrative acts on the part of the European power, having for their object to disguise the ultimate intention of obtaining sovereign control over the territory. The "colonial protectorate" [33] which they established made it possible to overcome more easily the opposition of the natives, and at the same time to serve notice upon other powers that the territories in question were already in process of being occupied.[34] In the Island of Palmas arbitration case [35] the tribunal found that while contracts between a state, or a company such as the Dutch East India Company, and native princes or chiefs of peoples not recognized as members of the community of nations were not in the international sense valid legal agreements, they were "not wholly void of indirect effects on situations governed by international law" and constituted "facts of which that law must in certain circumstances take account." "Thus," said the tribunal, "suzerainty over the native state becomes the basis of territorial sovereignty as towards other members of the community of nations." [36]

Delimitation of the hinterland. Mindful, doubtless, of the difficulties experienced on the American continent in delimiting the area of occupation, the European powers interested in acquiring territory in Africa found it desirable to enter into separate conventions, marking off the frontiers of their respective claims and stipulating that within the defined areas each should respect the exclusive rights of the other. These zones of territory, more or less contiguous to actual settlements along the

---

[32] *Resolutions,* p. 86.

[33] To be distinguished from "colonial protectorates" are the protectorates in which the native ruler is left in the exercise of a limited sovereignty subject to the guardianship, particularly in foreign affairs, of the protecting states. See pp. 136 ff.

[34] In its constructive proposals adopted in 1888 the Institute of International Law recommended (Art. 2) that the same rules with respect to notification and local administration adopted for territory formally occupied should be made applicable to these protectorates as well. *Resolutions,* p. 86.

[35] See above, p. 407.

[36] It may be observed that these colonial protectorates mark an advance over the practice recorded in Johnson and Graham's Lessee v. M'Intosh (p. 406), which denied to the native inhabitants not merely sovereignty over the territory they occupied but even rights of private property in the soil. The student of American constitutional law may make comparison between these agreements with native chiefs and the succession of treaties entered into by the United States Government with the several Indian tribes during the gradual westward progress of the settlement of the country. See Snow, *The Question of Aborigines,* Chap. III.

coast, were designated as "hinterland," and, inasmuch as they were not "occupied" in the technical sense, they came to be spoken of as "spheres of influence" or "spheres of interest." [37] In the treaty of 1885 between Great Britain and Germany each state engaged not to make acquisitions of territory or to accept protectorates on the one or the other side of the conventional line adopted in the hinterland of the western coast.[38] A second convention, entered into in 1890, delimited the frontiers of the hinterland of the eastern coast. In 1890 a dispute broke out between Portugal and Great Britain as the result of an endeavor on the part of the former to link together its eastern and its western African possessions. Claim was made to the territory adjoining Portuguese East Africa on the ground of cession from a native chief and of effective occupation and to the adjoining western territory on the ground of prior discovery and the doctrine of "contiguity." Great Britain contested the claim on the basis of the exploration of the British South Africa Company; and the matter was finally adjusted by the treaty of 1891, leaving the disputed territory in the hands of Great Britain.[39] By the close of the nineteenth century bilateral agreements between Great Britain, France, Italy, Germany, and Portugal had definitely settled the interior boundaries of their respective colonial possessions. It should be observed, however, that these treaties were legally binding only upon the parties to them, third states being free to set up separate claims to the particular territory. In the course of time the acquiescence of third states was to be implied, while acts of effective occupation came to confirm title by the rules of customary law.

Recent territorial disputes: Eastern Greenland. In the dispute between Denmark and Norway over Eastern Greenland, Norway had published a proclamation on July 10, 1931, declaring that it had occupied certain territories of Eastern Greenland. These territories were believed by Norway to be *terra nullius,* but were held by Denmark to be subject to Danish sovereignty, which, it was claimed, had been continuously and peacefully exercised over a long period of time and had not been contested by any other power. Moreover, Norway had, it was claimed, recognized Danish sovereignty by various treaties. Suit was brought by Denmark before the Permanent Court of International Justice under the Optional Clause, and it was held by the court, April 5, 1933, that Denmark "possessed valid title to the sovereignty over all Greenland." [40] The

---

[37] These "spheres of influence" or "spheres of interest," which look to an ultimate annexation of the territory thus marked off, are to be distinguished from such spheres of influence as were defined by Great Britain and Russia in the treaty of 1907 for their respective exploitations in Persia. See p. 589. In the latter case the object was more economic than political and apparently did not contemplate ultimate annexation.

[38] See Lindley, *op. cit.,* p. 210.

[39] *Ibid.,* p. 211.

[40] *Publications of the Court,* Series A/B, Fasc. No. 53. Fenwick, *Cases,* p. 476; Bishop, *Cases,* p. 107.

fact that there had been little exercise of sovereign rights by Denmark over Eastern Greenland was offset by the fact that no other state could make out a superior claim.[41]

Clipperton Island; Letitia. In the Clipperton Island dispute between France and Mexico, decided in 1931, the arbitrator held that the island, an uninhabited coral reef some 670 miles off the western coast of Mexico, had been acquired by France in 1858 and that, since there was no reason to conclude that France had any intention of abandoning the island, an abandonment could not be implied from failure to exercise authority in a positive way considering the character of the territory.[42] In the Letitia dispute between Colombia and Peru, a settlement agreed upon in 1922 was reopened by Peru on grounds extraneous to the interpretation of the treaty, questioning the expediency of the situation created by the treaty. The dispute was finally settled by a commission of three members designated under an agreement between the disputants and the President of the Council of the League of Nations. Peruvian forces evacuated the area, which passed under the administrative control of the commission. The award resulted in a Protocol signed at Rio de Janeiro on May 24, 1934, in which the earlier boundary treaty of 1922 was reaffirmed as "one of the juridical ties" binding the two countries.[43]

The Gran Chaco. More serious was the dispute between Bolivia and Paraguay over their boundaries in the Gran Chaco, which, after minor acts of hostility over several years, finally broke into open war in 1933. The legal issues were difficult of determination, bearing primarily upon the lines of Spanish colonial administrative divisions, the evidence of which was ambiguous due to the geographical errors of early maps. Efforts were made both by the League of Nations and by the American republics to effect a settlement; [44] but it was not until 1935 that the belligerents agreed to end hostilities and submit the dispute to the arbitral award of six American states. A Peace Conference met at Buenos Aires in that year, and on July 21, 1938, a Treaty of Peace, Friendship and Boundaries was signed between the two countries, leav-

[41] For the background of the case, see L. Preuss, "The Dispute between Denmark and Norway over the Sovereignty of East Greenland," *Am. Journal,* Vol. 26 (1932), p. 469. The dispute raised interesting questions in connection with the discovery and claims of title to polar areas where "occupation" is impossible in any real sense. See below, pp. 417 ff.

[42] For the text of the decision, see *Am. Journal,* Vol. 26 (1932), p. 390. For comment, *ibid.,* Vol. 27 (1933), p. 130. The legal status of the island at the time France took possession was held to be *territorium nullius,* and the court found that the continuous assertion of title by France was as sufficient "occupation" as the character of the island called for.

[43] See L. H. Woolsey, "The Letitia Dispute between Colombia and Peru," *Am. Journal,* Vol. 27 (1933), pp. 317, 525; Vol. 29 (1935), p. 94; Hackworth, *Digest,* Vol. I, p. 752; Ireland, *Boundaries, Possessions and Conflicts in South America,* pp. 196 ff.

[44] See Report of the League of Nations Commission on the Chaco Dispute, *Am. Journal,* Vol. 28 (1934), Supp., p. 137; La Foy, *The Chaco Dispute and the League of Nations.*

ing the boundary line to be determined by the arbitrators according to the directions laid down.[45]

Ecuador and Peru. The controversy between Ecuador and Peru over the title to territory originally forming part of colonial provinces lasted for more than a hundred years, and after successive efforts at arbitration and mediation had failed was finally settled by a Protocol of Peace, Friendship and Boundaries signed at Rio de Janeiro, January 29, 1942.[46] The area involved in the controversy measured some 45,000 square miles of land, running roughly from the undisputed eastern boundary of Ecuador back, in the shape of a wedge, to the lowlands leading to the Amazon basin. The legal points at issue were highly complicated. Peru, being in possession of the greater part of the territory most of the time, claimed the provinces on the basis of an original act of self-determination on their part, supported by the rule of *uti possidetis*. The question was, therefore, Peru held, not one of title to the territory but merely of boundaries.[47] Ecuador claimed on the basis of a treaty of 1829 between Peru and Colombia, to which Ecuador succeeded when it became an independent state in 1830, as well as on the basis of a protocol of 1830; and it rejected the application of the principle of prescription on the ground that it had continuously asserted its claim to the territory throughout the whole period.[48] The protocol of 1942 assigned the greater part of the disputed area to Peru; and the acceptance of the settlement by Ecuador might be said to represent the contribution of that country to the cause of inter-American unity in time of great danger.[49] In spite, however, of the ratification of the treaty by the Ecuadorean legislature within the prescribed period of thirty days, the government of Ecuador subsequently repudiated the Protocol on ground of coercion.

Belize. Still outstanding is the dispute between Guatemala and Great Britain over the title to Belize, or British Honduras. Originally settled by buccaneers, Belize was transformed into a British colony in spite of the opposition of Spain and later of Guatemala. By a treaty of

[45] For the text of the treaty, see *Am. Journal*, Vol. 32 (1938), Supp., p. 139. The award of the arbitrators was announced on October 10, 1938. For the text, see *ibid.*, Vol. 33 (1939), p. 180. For a survey of the case, see *Documents on Am. Foreign Relations*, 1938-1939, pp. 72 ff.; L. H. Woolsey, editorials in *Am. Journal*, Vol. 23 (1929), p. 110; Vol. 24 (1930), pp. 122, 573; Vol. 26 (1932), p. 796; Vol. 28 (1934), p. 724; Vol. 33 (1939), p. 126; Ireland, *op. cit.*, pp. 66-95.

[46] For the text of the protocol, see Dept. of State *Bulletin*, Vol. VI, p. 195. For background, see L. H. Woolsey, "Dispute over Oriente Territory," *Am. Journal*, Vol. 25 (1931), p. 330; Vol. 31 (1937), p. 97. The controversy was reopened by Ecuador in 1960. See Whiteman, *Digest*, Vol. 3, p. 676.

[47] A detailed statement of the Peruvian case may be found in Ulloa, *Posición Internacional del Perú.*

[48] For the case of Ecuador, see Tobar Donoso, *La invasión peruana y el Protocolo de Río.* Also, *Dictámenes Jurídicos acerca del problema ecuatoriano-peruano dados por ilustres internacionalistas americanos.*

[49] See statement of the Acting Secretary of State, Sumner Welles, Dept. of State *Bulletin*, Vol. VI, p. 194.

1859 Guatemala recognized the sovereignty of Great Britain over the territory; but by the same treaty Great Britain was obligated to build a road from the Atlantic Coast to Guatemala City. The juridical issue, therefore, is not the effect of territorial occupation, but the construction of the treaty of 1859, whether the failure of Great Britain to build the road caused the whole treaty to lapse and with it the recognition by Guatemala of the sovereignty of Great Britain over the territory.[50]

In 1946 Great Britain offered to have the matter determined by the International Court of Justice, but Guatemala refused to accept the offer unless the case would be decided not as a strictly legal issue but *ex aequo et bono*, that is, on the basis of other nonlegal considerations. This condition being unacceptable to Great Britain the controversy remains open, Great Britain continuing in active possession, and Guatemala continuing to refer to "Belice" as part of the national territory.

Other disputes. The long controversy between Honduras and Nicaragua over the eastern boundary between the two countries was finally settled by a decision of the International Court of Justice in 1960. The issue was the validity of an award of the King of Spain in 1906, assigning the area north of the Segovia, or Coco, River to Honduras. Nicaragua claimed that the award was not within the terms of reference of the Bonilla-Gámez Treaty of 1894 submitting the controversy to arbitration. The International Court found that the award was valid and binding and that Nicaragua was under an obligation to give effect to it.[51] Nicaragua accepted the decision and cooperated in giving effect to it.

A controversy of exceptional interest between Cambodia and Thailand, involving the boundary line between the two countries and the territorial sovereignty over the area in which the Temple of Preah Vihear was located, was submitted to the International Court of Justice in 1959. In 1962, the Court decided, on the basis of a map prepared by a boundary commission in 1907, that the Temple was situated in territory under the sovereignty of Cambodia.[52]

The dispute between Venezuela and Great Britain involving the boundary line between Venezuela and British Guiana, in which the United States became involved by reason of the Monroe Doctrine, was

---

[50] For a summary of the issues involved in the dispute, see J. L. Kunz, *Am. Journal*, Vol. 40 (1946), p. 383. The case of Guatemala is presented in *Guatemalan White Book*, and that of Great Britain in D. A. G. Waddell, "Developments in the Belize Question, 1946-1960," *Am. Journal*, Vol. 55 (1961), p. 459. See also W. M. Clegern, "New Light on the Belize Dispute," *Am. Journal*, Vol. 52 (1958), p. 280; Garcia Bauer, *La Controversia sobre el Territorio de Belice.*

[51] *I.C.J. Reports* (1960), p. 192. *Am. Journal*, Vol. 55 (1961), p. 478. For brief background, C. G. Fenwick, "The Honduras-Nicaragua Boundary Dispute," *Am. Journal*, Vol. 51 (1957), p. 761.

[52] *I.C.J. Reports* (1962), p. 6. *Am. Journal*, Vol. 56 (1962), p. 1033; G. Weissberg, "Maps as Evidence in International Boundary Disputes," *Am. Journal*, Vol. 57 (1963), p. 792.

INTERNATIONAL LAW

submitted to arbitration in 1897; and an award was handed down in 1899 granting the larger part of the area to Great Britain, but assigning the mouth of the Orinoco River and part of its headwaters to Venezuela. The award was accepted at the time as definitive, but contested later by Venezuela on the ground of the discovery of evidence that the award was the result of a "political deal." [53]

A unique case, which one might expect to have been settled not years but centuries ago, was submitted to the International Court of Justice in 1951 when the United Kingdom, on the basis of a special agreement with the French Government, requested the Court to determine whether the sovereignty over two small groups of islets and rocks in the British Channel, the Minquiers and the Ecrehos, belonged to the United Kingdom or to France. The judgment of the Court in favor of the sovereignty of the United Kingdom, in so far as the islets and rocks were capable of appropriation, was based upon documents showing their relationship with the Island of Jersey in respect to local administration, an item of which was jurisdiction in the cases of wrecks.[54]

Equally difficult to believe is that certain parcels of land lying between Belgium and the Netherlands should have remained so long of uncertain sovereignty. In 1957, by special agreement between the two states, the International Court was asked to determine which of the two states had sovereignty over certain parcels of land, of some fourteen hectares, situated in the frontier region of Baarle Nassau and Baarle-Duc. The controversy arose in connection with an error in a boundary convention of 1843; and while the decision of the Court in favor of Belgium was said to be perpetuating "a geographic anomaly," the Court felt that it could itself do no more than clear the way for a revision of the treaty.[55]

Titles in the Arctic and Antarctic regions. It is only of recent years that the claims of different states to sovereignty over the various areas of the north and south polar regions have raised serious international problems.[56] With the nineteenth century began a series of planned expeditions of discovery, and by the close of the third decade of the present century both polar regions had been carefully surveyed and

[53] See O. Schoenrich, "The Venezuelan-British Guiana Boundary Dispute," *Am. Journal,* Vol. 43 (1949), p. 523; *U.N. Yearbook,* 1962, p. 112. For background, see W. C. Dennis, "The Venezuelan-British Guiana Boundary Arbitration of 1899," *Am. Journal,* Vol. 43 (1949), p. 720, written in the interest of raising standards of arbitration.

[54] *I.C.J. Reports,* 1953, p. 47; *Am. Journal,* Vol. 48 (1954), p. 316.

[55] *I.C.J. Reports,* 1959, p. 209; L. Gross, "The Jurisprudence of the World Court: Thirty-Eighth Year," *Am. Journal,* Vol. 57 (1963), p. 771.

[56] For a general survey of the subject, see Smedal, *Acquisition of Sovereignty over Polar Areas;* Balch, "The Arctic and Antarctic Regions and the Law of Nations," *Am. Journal,* Vol. 4 (1910), p. 265; R. D. Hayton, "The Antarctic Settlement of 1959," *Am. Journal,* Vol. 54 (1960), p. 349.

mapped. Parts of both regions had been from time to time claimed by the discoverers in the name of their respective states. So long as the polar regions were uninhabitable areas of ice and nothing more, the claims of the different states were not taken too seriously. But with the coming of long-range airships and with the realization that valuable minerals might be found in the polar regions the question of sovereignty became of importance. Query, whether under any circumstances discovery alone can be sufficient to give title? And if discovery alone be not sufficient, can title be claimed on the basis of geographical continuity or contiguity? [57] Does the fact that the continental tableland of the claimant state extends northward or southward into the polar regions give validity to its claim of sovereignty over uninhabitable areas? Does the fact that the territory of the claimant state lies geographically nearer to certain parts of the polar regions add weight to its claim of sovereignty?

In the light of recent developments it is clear that the earlier view advanced by certain writers that the Arctic and the Antarctic regions should be regarded as *res communis,* open like the high seas to the use of all nations and not subject to the sovereignty of any of them, is not a practical solution.[58] The elaborate network of weather stations already established in the different sectors and the air bases built and projected constitute a new form of "occupation," far short of that required to give title in habitable parts of the globe, but sufficient to make it necessary to come to a more definite agreement as to the status of the polar areas than has as yet been reached.

The north polar regions. In the case of the north polar regions five countries, the Soviet Union, Norway, Denmark, Canada, and the United States have laid claims to "sectors," each having as its base the continental tableland of the claimant and as its apex the Pole itself.[59] The Soviet sector is the largest, the Canadian sector the next largest. The Danish sector is based upon Greenland and Iceland, the United States

---

[57] "Continuity" is said to relate to the geographical extension of the continental tableland. "Contiguity" relates to the geographical nearness of the continental state to the particular polar area. But the terms are not always used in these precise senses.

In 1924 Secretary Hughes stated that, "It is the opinion of the Department that the discovery of lands unknown to civilization, even when coupled with a formal taking of possession, does not support a valid claim of sovereignty unless the discovery is followed by an actual settlement of the discovered country. In the absence of an act of Congress assertative in a domestic sense of dominion over Wilkes Land this Department would be reluctant to declare that the United States possessed a right of sovereignty over that territory." Hackworth, *Digest,* Vol. I, p. 399.

[58] See R. D. Hayton, "Polar Problems and International Law," *Am. Journal,* Vol. 52 (1958), p. 746; W. W. Mouton, "The International Regime of the Polar Regions," *Recueil des Cours,* 1962-III.

[59] The Pole itself is merely a geodetic point in the seas underneath a moving cover of ice. Admiral Peary's presentation of the Pole to President Taft in 1909 was no more than a dramatic gesture.

sector upon Alaska. Within the Soviet sector lie Nansen Land, claimed by Norway, Wrangel Island, claimed by the United States, and other claims, the validity of which has not yet been definitely established. The strategic importance of these sectors is now recognized. All of the great northern land masses come together within the area of the arctic circle. The shortest air routes between the industrial centers of the leading nations cross the arctic area. From the point of view of military defense the arctic regions have become a new frontier for every country of the northern hemisphere.

Spitzbergen. Until 1914 Spitzbergen was regarded as "terra nullius." In that year an international conference met to consider the government of the archipelago and plans were submitted for an international administration. After the war a treaty was signed at Paris, in 1920, by which the United States, Great Britain, and other powers recognized "the full and absolute sovereignty of Norway" over the archipelago. The islands were demilitarized, and provision was made for equality among the parties in respect to freedom of access for commercial and other purposes.[60]

The south polar regions. In the south polar regions there are numerous conflicting claims.[61] Chile has applied the sector principle, supported by the principle of contiguity, as the basis of a claim lying between 53° W and 90°.[62] Great Britain claims a sector known as the Falkland Islands Dependency; a claim which, however, is contested by Argentina.[63] In 1924, when the Norwegian minister announced that the lands discovered by Amundsen would be taken possession of in the name of the King of Norway, the American Secretary of State replied that the Government of the United States "cannot admit that such taking of possession as a discoverer by Mr. Amundsen of areas explored by him

[60] For the text of the treaty see Hudson, *Int. Legislation*, Vol. I, p. 436. Article 8 reads: "Norway undertakes to provide for the territories specified in Article 1 mining regulations which . . . shall exclude all privileges, monopolies, or favors for the benefit of the State or of the nationals of any one of the High Contracting Parties, including Norway. . . ."

[61] See J. S. Reeves, "Antarctic Sectors," *Am. Journal*, Vol. 33 (1939), p. 519; R. D. Hayton, "The 'American' Antarctic," *Am. Journal*, Vol. 52 (1956), p. 583.

[62] A decree of the Foreign Office of November 6, 1940, proclaims: "Forman la *Antartica Chilena* o Territorio Chileno Antartico, todas las tierras, islas, islotes, arrecifes, glaciares (pack-ice), y demas, conocidos y por conocerse, y el mar territorial respectivo, existentes dentro de los limites del casquete constituido por los meridianos 53° longitud Oeste de Greenwich y 90° longitud Oeste de Greenwich." República de Chile: *Memoria del Ministério de Relaciones Exteriores y Comércio, Correspondiente al ano 1940*, pp. 440 ff.

[63] For a list of the areas claimed by Great Britain, see Hackworth, *Digest*, Vol. I, pp. 455 ff. Argentina, contesting the claim of Great Britain to the Falkland Islands, contests the antarctic sector based upon it. For the Argentine decree of October 9, 1946, see *Am. Journal*, Vol. 41 (1947), p. 117 and Supp., p. 11.

could establish the basis of rights of sovereignty in the Polar regions." [64]
The United States on its part reiterated in connection with the discoveries
of Admiral Byrd that it could not admit "that sovereignty accrues from
mere discovery unaccompanied by occupancy and use." Great Britain,
however, asserted in 1934 sovereignty over sectors on the Pacific and
Indian Ocean sides of the Pole known as the New Zealand and Australian
Dependencies; while France claims an area known as Adelie Land. Norwegian claims were extended in 1939, covering an area of about one-fifth
of the continent.[65] In 1955 Great Britain filed with the International
Court of Justice two applications, one against Argentina and the other
against Chile, contending encroachment by the two states upon territories claimed to be under British sovereignty. But the Court found that
neither state had accepted the jurisdiction of the Court and ordered the
cases to be removed from the list.[66]

The Antarctic Conference. In 1959 a Conference on Antarctica met
in Washington, and on December 1, twelve states signed the Antarctic
Treaty. While the treaty makes no effort to reconcile and delimit the
respective claims of the parties, it does establish the principle that "it
is in the interest of all mankind that Antarctica shall continue forever
to be used exclusively for peaceful purposes and shall not become the
scene or object of international discord." Military bases are prohibited,
as well as the testing of any type of weapons. Freedom of scientific information and cooperation to that end, as applied during the International Geophysical Year of 1958, is to continue; and scientific personnel
and scientific observations are to be exchanged between expeditions and
stations.[67]

C. TITLE BY ACCRETION

Accretion as a mode of acquiring title to territory is of ancient lineage
but of little practical consequence. It may be defined as the slow addition
made to land by the action of rivers flowing past it or by the action of
the ocean on the coast. The rules which govern it were taken from the

[64] See Hackworth, Vol. I, p. 399. In 1929, at the time of Admiral Byrd's aerial ex-
plorations in the Antarctic, the Norwegian Government referred to the fact that
certain areas had already been "taken possession of" by Amundsen in the name of the
King of Norway but explained that it did not "claim sovereignty to the territories"
on that basis, but that it considered "that the said discovery and annexation constitute
a valid basis for a claim of priority to acquire such territories whenever the requirements of international law as to effective occupation of a new territory shall have
been fulfilled." *Ibid.*, pp. 453-460.

[65] *Ibid.*, pp. 459, 460.

[66] *I.C.J. Reports*, 1956, p. 15. For background, C. H. M. Waldock, "Disputed
Sovereignty in the Falkland Islands Dependencies," *British Year Book*, 1948, p. 311.

[67] See R. D. Hayton, "The Antarctic Settlement of 1959," *Am. Journal*, Vol. 54
(1960), p. 349. For the text of the treaty, see *ibid.*, p. 476.

Roman Law by Grotius [68] and his followers and have remained practically unmodified to this day. The principle of *accessio cedat principali, i.e.* a thing that is added follows the fortune of the principal thing, governs all the different forms which accretion takes. The addition may take the form of alluvion, which is the imperceptible increase which the material deposited by the waters of a river or by the ocean adds to the banks or shores. It may also take the form of a delta, which is a triangular island built up at the mouth of a river by the gradual deposit of silt; or again, it may take the form of islands built up in the bed of a river. In each case the addition becomes the property of the owner of the mainland, though a difficulty may arise where the river forms the boundary between two states.[69]

Where islands are built up within the maritime belt of a state, they have the effect of extending the maritime belt to an equal distance beyond the newly acquired territory, with corresponding extension of the jurisdiction of the state. This rule was applied by the British Court of Admiralty in the decision of the case of the *Anna*,[70] a Spanish vessel captured by a British privateer near the mouth of the Mississippi River during the war between the two countries in 1805. The question presented to the court was whether the capture had been made within the territorial jurisdiction of the United States. The capture had been made outside the three-mile limit if measured from the Balise, a fort on the extreme point of the mainland, but within the maritime belt if measured from some little mud islands composed of earth and of driftwood "which form a kind of portico to the main-land." The court was of the opinion "that the right of territory is to be reckoned from those islands."

D. TITLE BY PRESCRIPTION

Prescription in international law may be defined as the acquisition of territory by an adverse holding continued through a long term of years. It presumes the existence, at least in theory, of an earlier title held by another. If the earlier title is an uncertain one, the adverse holding may be *bona fide* in its origin; if it is clear and definite, the adverse holding will be *mala fide* in its origin. In both cases the new title is acquired on the ground of a presumed abandonment of the territory by the original owner, so that the rules relating to prescription are closely related to those governing "occupation." Prescription in international law, as supported by Grotius and writers of the Grotian tradition, differs from the usucaption and prescription of the Roman Law in having no fixed period at the end of which the title of the original holder may be presumed to

[68] See *De jure belli ac pacis,* Eng. trans., Bk. II, Chap. VIII.

[69] See p. 440, where the subject is treated at greater length in connection with boundaries, particularly the boundary of the Rio Grande.

[70] C. Rob. 373 (1805). Fenwick, *Cases,* p. 482.

have been abandoned. Grotius had in mind uninterrupted possession "going beyond memory," [71] whereas Vattel was ready to recognize adverse possession as giving title if the owner had neglected his right or been silent about it during "a considerable number of years." [72] The question of the time required to create a presumption of abandonment presented serious difficulties in the eighteenth century, and Vattel was so conscious of them that he laid stress upon the great advantage it would be "if neighboring nations would come to an agreement on the subject by means of treaties." [73] Other writers deny altogether the possibility of acquiring title by prescription; [74] but in so doing they would appear not to be stating law but to be defending morality against the facts of international life. There is, further, the academic question whether prescription is an original or a derivative mode of acquisition, some writers classifying it as derivative on the ground that it is a title to property which previously belonged to another, others classifying it as an original mode of acquisition on the ground that title is not derived from the former owner directly but from certain facts created by the presumed abandonment of the territory by the former owner.[75] The bearing of the question upon the realities of international life will appear presently.

Part played by prescription in international law. There can be no doubt that from one point of view the recognition of title by prescription is as important in international law as it is in the municipal law of the several states. Grotius saw clearly that if controversies concerning kingdoms and their boundaries were not extinguished by lapse of time wars would be perpetuated and therefore that it was "for the good of human society that governments should at some time be placed beyond the risk and doubt of controversy." [76] Vattel became eloquent upon the necessity "for the sake of the peace and welfare of the human race . . . that sovereigns be not easily troubled in their possession and that after a great number of years, if their title has not been contested during all that time, it should be regarded as valid and indefeasible." [77] The Supreme Court of the United States, applying international law to a dispute between Rhode Island and Massachusetts, laid it down that "for the security of rights, whether of states or of individuals, long possession

---

[71] *De jure belli ac pacis*, Eng. trans., Bk. II, Chap. IV, §§ I, VII, IX.

[72] *Droit de gens*, Eng. trans., Bk. II, § 142.

[73] *Ibid.*, § 151.

[74] Notably, among the older writers, G. F. von Martens, *Précis du droit des gens*, §§ 70-71 and among the more recent, Von Ullmann, *Völkerrecht*, § 92.

[75] The student of the common law may make comparison with the legal fiction invented by English jurists that a title by prescription to incorporeal hereditaments rested upon an original grant.

[76] Bk. II, Chap. IV, § VIII.

[77] Bk. II, § 147.

under a claim of title is protected." [78] In the Island of Palmas case [79] the tribunal accepted the principle that "the actual continuous and peaceful display of state functions is in case of dispute the sound and natural criterium of territorial sovereignty," and it found that the evidence showed that the Netherlands had been exercising undisputed sovereignty over the island for more than 200 years.

Had prescription been limited to territory held in distant and hitherto unoccupied parts of the world where the original title was doubtful, title acquired by prescription might have been permitted to obtain legal validity without debate of any consequence. When, however, prescription was put forth as a desirable means of securing stability in international affairs by putting an end to the claims of a dismembered state, such as Poland, or by confirming the title of, for example, Austria to its Italian possessions or to the provinces of Bohemia and Moravia, it was met by an indignant denial, and it found itself confronted with the new doctrine of nationality, which swept aside old titles in international law with the same revolutionary hand that had swept aside the existing titles to land in France in 1793. Long-continued possession by a powerful state seemed no ground of title to subject peoples whose silent acquiescence in their dispossession had been due chiefly to fear of contesting the will of a stronger power. It would appear, therefore, that prescription in international law could only play the effective part of quieting possession that it has played in municipal law, provided there were in existence a higher authority, having jurisdiction over such cases, to which the dispossessed party could make appeal. In the absence of such an authority, time, aided by force, might do no more than mark the perpetuation of injustice. [80]

E. TITLE BY VOLUNTARY CESSION

Title by cession in international law corresponds in a general way to title by deed of transfer in municipal law. Cession may be defined as the formal transfer from one state to another of the sovereignty over a definite area of territory. It is usually carried out by means of a treaty between the two parties, defining the territory to be transferred and fixing the conditions under which the transfer is to take place. These con-

[78] 4 Howard 591, 639 (1846). Fenwick, *Cases*, p. 484. See also Maryland v. West Virginia, 217 U.S. 1 (1910), *ibid.*, p. 456; and Virginia v. Tennessee, 148 U.S. 503 (1893), Evans-Fenwick, *Cases on Constitutional Law*, 7th ed., p. 674. In the above cases, the doctrine of prescription was applied to boundaries originally fixed by agreement but subsequently giving rise to question as to their validity. The principle of prescription and acquiescence was reaffirmed by the Supreme Court in Arkansas v. Tennessee, 311 U.S. (1940), *Am. Journal*, Vol. 35 (1941), p. 154.

[79] See above, p. 407.

[80] Account must, of course, be taken of the difference between prescription as applied to territories in which there are subject nationalities and prescription as applied to territory where no issue of self-determination is presented.

ditions vary widely, and they may include such matters as the status of the inhabitants of the territory under the sovereignty of the new owner, the adjustment of the public debt of the ceded territory, the creation of servitudes upon the territory in favor of the ceding state, and other like stipulations. Whether these conditions are to be regarded as personal obligations assumed by the assignee state or as covenants running with the land, following the distinction made by the common law, is of only incidental interest in international law, since there is no difference of procedure for a suit *in rem* and a suit *in personam*. It is important, moreover, not to confuse the international law of cession with the provisions of the domestic constitutional law of the assignor or of the assignee state. As far as international law was concerned it was, for example, a point of no consequence whether the acquisition of the Philippines and of Puerto Rico by the United States brought those territories under the protection of the law of the Constitution.[81] International law recognized the transfer of sovereignty; constitutional law determined whether the new territory should or should not enjoy certain privileges under the constitution of the state acquiring title.

Forms of cession. The treaty by which transfer of sovereignty is effected may take one or another of several forms. The simplest of these, in point of law, is the *treaty of sale,* which has figured so prominently in the history of the United States. The Louisiana Purchase of 1803, the Florida Purchase of 1819, the Gadsden Purchase of 1853, the Alaska Purchase of 1867, and more recently the purchase of the Danish West Indies in 1916, in addition to several lesser purchases, make the record of the United States, in respect to expansion by purchase of territory, unique in the history of international law. A second form of transfer is the *exchange* of one area of territory for another, of which there are recent instances in the cession by Rumania to Russia in 1878 of a part of Bessarabia lying north of the Danube in exchange for the Dobrudja south of the Danube, and in the cession by Great Britain to Germany in 1890 of the island of Helgoland in exchange for territory adjoining German East Africa.

In addition to these normal business transactions may be mentioned such cases, rare in modern times, as the transfer of the Congo Free State in 1908 to Belgium by devise of King Leopold, who at the time of his death was sovereign of the Congo in his personal capacity as distinct from his position as king of Belgium.[82] Here also may be mentioned the occasional *free gifts* made by one state to another, such as the cession in

[81] For the status of these territories following their cession by Spain, see Willoughby, *Constitutional Law,* 2nd ed., Vol. I, Chap. XXX, and judicial decisions there cited. For their present status see Chap. VI of the present work.

[82] See Martens, *Nouv. Rec. Gén.,* 3rd Series, Vol. ii, pp. 101 ff.; Reeves, "Origin of the Congo Free State from the Standpoint of International Law," *Am. Journal,* Vol. 3 (1909), p. 99.

1850 of a portion of the Horse-Shoe Reef in Lake Erie by Great Britain to the United States on condition that the latter would erect upon it a lighthouse for the benefit of the navigation of both countries.[83] Austria's gift of Lombardy to France in 1859 and of Venice to the same power in 1866 were, it should be noted, merely disguised methods of avoiding a direct transfer to Sardinia. The provision of the Treaty of Berlin of 1878 that Bosnia and Herzegovina were to be occupied and administered by Austria-Hungary was merely a disguised cession. The nominal sovereignty of Turkey came to an end by unilateral proclamation of Austria-Hungary in 1908.

On occasion transfers of territory actually made under duress will take on the disguise of a purchase, as in the case of the payment by the United States to Mexico in 1848 of the sum of fifteen millions of dollars "in consideration of the extension acquired by the boundaries of the United States, as defined in the 5th Article of the present treaty"; [84] and again in the case of the payment to Spain of the sum of twenty millions of dollars for the Philippine Islands, which, had the United States chosen to exercise the traditional rights of conquest, could quite as easily have been taken over without payment, as was Puerto Rico.

F. TITLE BY FORCED CESSION: CONQUEST

Title by conquest has of recent years come to be used in the same sense as title by cession made under duress, and it may perhaps be desirable to accept the term in its larger signification. Writers on international law formerly reserved the term *conquest* for those cases in which the territory of an enemy state was effectively occupied in time of war and then retained at the close of the war without confirmation by the treaty of peace or other formal document. Conquest was thus an inchoate title, made perfect either by the complete subjugation of the state or by its silent acquiescence in the fact that the conquered territory had passed under the control of its former enemy. In the first case the extinction of the former sovereign left the territory, by a legal fiction, *res nullius;* in the second case the rule of prescription operated, based upon the presumed abandonment of the territory by its former owner. Title by conquest in this more restricted sense, common enough when Grotius and Vattel wrote, had disappeared by the close of the nineteenth century; a curious survival, however, appearing in the abandonment by Turkey in 1912 of Tripoli and Cyrenaica and the subsequent annexation of the territories by Italy. No reference was made to the cession of the two provinces in the formal treaty of peace between Italy and Turkey at Lausanne on October 18, 1912.[85] Conquest accompanied by subjuga-

---

[83] Moore, *Digest,* Vol. I, p. 554.
[84] Art. XII. See *Treaties and Conventions,* Vol. I, p. 1107.
[85] See "Peace between Italy and Turkey," *Am. Journal,* Vol. 7 (1913), p. 155.

tion appeared to have come to an end with the annexation by Great Britain of the territory of the Boer Republics in 1900, only to be revived temporarily by Italy in 1936 when Ethiopia was defeated and formally annexed to the new Italian Empire.

Cession by "treaties of peace." Taken in the larger sense of cession under duress, "conquest" played the leading role in the transfer of territory during the nineteenth century. Until the adoption of the Covenant of the League of Nations in 1920 war was a legal method of procedure, and the fact that the defeated state was often coerced into making cessions of territory in the "treaty of peace" did not affect their legal character. The enforced transfer of Alsace-Lorraine to Germany by the Treaty of Frankfort of 1871 was a "legal" act as international law was understood at the time, as was the subsequent transfer of the same territories by Germany to France by the Treaty of Versailles of 1919.[86] Title by a treaty of peace was thus a valid legal title, and was recognized by third states as such. All that the defeated state could do under the circumstances was to await its time when a change in the political situation might give it the opportunity of making war upon a different issue, and then, if victorious, recover its former territory by a new "treaty of peace."

Repudiation of conquest as giving legal title. With the adoption of the Covenant of the League of Nations in 1920 and with the formal renunciation of war as an instrument of national policy by the Kellogg Pact conquest lost its validity as a legal title to territory. In 1932, in the presence of the invasion of Manchuria by Japan, Secretary Stimson gave the impulse to a long series of denunciations of the acquisition of territory by force, whether accompanied or not by the formal acquiescence of the former sovereign.[87] In 1932, having before them the hostilities between Bolivia and Paraguay in the Gran Chaco, the nineteen other American Republics addressed to the two states a Declaration of Principles announcing that "they will not recognize any territorial arrangement of this controversy which has not been obtained by peaceful means nor the validity of territorial acquisitions which may be obtained

---

[86] The contrast between the two transfers appears in the insistence of President Wilson that "the wrong done to France by Prussia in 1871 in the matter of Alsace-Lorraine, which has unsettled the peace of the world for nearly fifty years, should be righted, in order that peace may once more be made secure in the interests of all." Point VIII of the Fourteen Points. *Am. Journal*, Vol. 13 (1919), p. 161.

[87] For the text of the statement of Secretary Stimson, January 7, 1932, see League of Nations, *Official Journal*, Spec. Supp. No. 101, p. 155. For comment, see Q. Wright, *Am. Journal*, Vol. 26 (1932), p. 342; F. A. Middlebush, *Proceedings*, Am. Soc. Int. Law, 1933, p. 40. On March 11 the Assembly of the League of Nations endorsed the principle and gave it a collective character: "The Assembly . . . declares that it is incumbent upon the members of the League of Nations not to recognize any situation, treaty, or agreement which may be brought about by means contrary to the Covenant of the League of Nations or the Pact of Paris."

through occupation or conquest by force of arms." [88] Similar declarations were made at the Conferences of Montevideo in 1933, of Buenos Aires in 1936, and of Lima in 1938.[89] In 1940 the Meeting of Foreign Ministers of the American Republics at Havana, confronted with the conquests of the Axis Powers in Europe, proclaimed that "force can not constitute the basis of rights, and they condemn all violence whether under the form of conquest, of stipulations which may have been imposed by the belligerents in the clauses of treaty, or by any other process." [90] The condemnation was repeated in the Declaration of Mexico adopted at the Conference of 1945 and again, more forcibly, in Articles 5, 16, and 17 of the Charter of the Organization of American States.

The Atlantic Charter. On August 14, 1941, President Roosevelt and Prime Minister Churchill signed the Atlantic Charter proclaiming as representatives of their respective countries that among other principles of national policy upon which they based their hopes for a better future for the world, "First, Their countries seek no aggrandizement, territorial or other." The incorporation of the Charter in the Declaration by United Nations of January 1, 1942, gave to the principle an international character; and the Charter of the United Nations closed the issue by declaring as one of its principles that "All members shall refrain in their international relations from the threat or use of force against the territorial integrity or political independence of any state." Query, whether the acquisitions of territory by the Soviet Union, by Poland (acquisition balancing loss), by Yugoslavia, and by France in the several treaties of peace can be brought within the principle of "no aggrandizement"? The question, while primarily political, is not without its bearing upon the good faith of international declarations.

Into what classification will fall the case of Goa, the Portuguese territory taken over by India on December 18, 1961, without forcible resistance by Portugal? The case came before the Security Council the following day, but the veto of the Soviet Union defeated the resolution of the United States and other members calling for the withdrawal of Indian forces and for a peaceful settlement of the controversy. With Goa were associated two other adjacent territories, Damao and Diu. The defense of India was that colonialism had been condemned by the General Assembly and that the matter was within the domestic jurisdiction of India as it concerned colonial territories forming integral

---

[88] See Report of the League of Nations Commission, *Am. Journal,* Vol. 28 (1934), Supp., pp. 137, 168.

[89] *Int. Conferences of American States,* 1933-1940, pp. 122, 160, 254. See also the Anti-War Treaty of 1933, *ibid.,* p. 496.

[90] *Ibid.,* p. 373, Convention on the Provisional Administration of European Colonies and Possessions in the Americas.

parts of India. The decision of the Council was clearly a political one.[91] In the earlier Right of Passage Case, involving the Portuguese enclaves of Nagar-Aveli and Dadra, the International Court of Justice had recognized the Portuguese title to the enclaves, but refused to condemn the denial of access to them when India occupied them on ground of disorders arising from the demand for self-determination by the people of the enclaves.[92]

G. THE PLEBISCITE AS A CONDITION OF TRANSFER

The growth of democratic government during the second half of the nineteenth century introduced a new issue into the rules governing the cession of territory. Hitherto it had been the custom for one state to transfer territory to another without question as to the wishes of the inhabitants of the ceded lands. A number of writers had, indeed, laid down the principle that transfers of territory should be made to depend upon the approval of the inhabitants. Grotius relied upon the contract theory of the state in asserting that "in the alienation of a part of a sovereign state it is, moreover, required that the part which is to be alienated must give its consent." [93] Vattel argued on the same basis that a nation "has no right to barter away their [its members'] allegiance and their liberty for certain advantages which it hopes for in return." [94] But both writers were laying down theoretical doctrines rather than stating customary law. The American Declaration of Independence announced the doctrine of the right of a people to determine its own form of government,[95] and the success of the revolution based upon that doctrine prepared the ground for the subsequent extension of the idea to an analogous field. It was the French Revolution, however, that gave the first definite expression to the principle that, consistently with the new doctrine of popular sovereignty, wars of conquest should be abandoned, and the consent of the people of a territory should be obtained to their transfer from one sovereignty to another.[96] Several minor transfers of territory were shortly afterward made in accordance with the new principle.

Practice during the nineteenth century. In the second decade of the

[91] See Q. Wright, "The Goa Incident," *Am. Journal,* Vol. 56 (1962), p. 617, and references there given.

[92] Right of Passage over Indian Territory, *I.C.J. Reports,* p. 6; *Am. Journal,* Vol. 54 (1960), p. 673.

[93] *De jure belli ac pacis,* Eng. trans., Book II, Chap. VI, § IV.

[94] *Droit des gens,* Eng. trans., Book I, § 263.

[95] The student will note that the Declaration of Independence asserted both a right of self-government on the part of the people of the state as a whole and a right on the part of a particular group or community of people to sever themselves under certain circumstances from the larger state of which they constituted a part. This latter right might be exercised even by colonies of the same race, language, and legal traditions as those of the mother country.

[96] Wambaugh, *Monograph on Plebiscites,* p. 177.

nineteenth century a new impulse was given to the theory by the development of nationalism in general, and in particular by the wars for the unification of Italy. Plebiscites were taken in 1848 in Lombardy, Venetia,
and other Italian duchies, which formally annexed their territories to
Sardinia while remaining under *de facto* Austrian control. Further
plebiscites were taken in 1860 in other Italian provinces liberated in the
war of 1859. Napoleon III, a warm advocate of the doctrine of nationality, applied the plebiscite to the annexation of Savoy and Nice to
France in 1860. Three years later Great Britain agreed to cede the Ionian
Islands to Greece on condition of a vote of approval by a legislative
assembly of the islands especially elected for the purpose. In the Treaty
of Prague following the "Seven Weeks' War," the transfer of Northern
Schleswig to Prussia was made conditional upon a free vote of the inhabitants, a condition, however, which was canceled by the treaty of
Vienna of 1878. In the treaty of 1867 between the United States and
Denmark provision was made for the cession of the Danish West Indies
subject to an affirmative vote on the part of the inhabitants. The plebiscite
provided for was duly taken, but in spite of its favorable results the
treaty failed of ratification by the United States.[97]

But side by side with these cases were others in which the principle
of the plebiscite was equally applicable but in which there was no
thought on the part of the annexing state of applying it. The failure of
Prussia to carry out the provisions of the Treaty of Prague, and in particular the annexation of Alsace-Lorraine in 1871 over the protests of its
inhabitants, gave a distinct setback to the principle. After 1871 the few
minor instances of its application were more than counterbalanced by
the conspicuous neglect of it in other cases.

It cannot be said, therefore, that at the opening of the World War the
isolated cases of the taking of a plebiscite had had the effect of establishing a rule of customary international law. That it was a recom-
mendable practice to resort to the plebiscite where the circumstances
permitted was the most that might be inferred from the actual practice
of the nations. Certain publicists and writers, particularly of the French
and Italian schools, asserted dogmatically that the principle was part
of international law, but their appeal to the natural and inalienable
rights of man could not change a rule fixed by the hard facts of international life. British and American writers, consistently with the practice
of their governments, gave little weight to the theory. There was a tone
of finality in the statement of Hall that "the principle that the wishes of
a population are to be consulted when the territory which they inhabit
is ceded, has not been adopted into international law, and cannot be
adopted into it until title by conquest has disappeared."[98] German

[97] For a summary of these and other proposed and actual applications of the
plebiscite, see Wambaugh, *op. cit.*, pp. 33 ff.
[98] *International Law*, § 9.

writers, having in mind apparently a justification of the expansion of Prussia by right of conquest, attacked the theory as wrong in principle and worthless in practice.[99]

Plebiscites attending the transfer of territory in 1919. A new impulse to the doctrine of the right of self-determination was given by the United States on the eve of its entrance into the World War. On January 22, 1917, President Wilson laid before the Senate, as one of the conditions of cooperation by the United States in the establishment of an international league to guarantee peace, the principle that "no peace can last, or ought to last, which does not recognize and accept the principle that governments derive all their just powers from the consent of the governed, and that no right anywhere exists to hand peoples about from sovereignty to sovereignty as if they were property." [100] A year later, in the enumeration of the Fourteen Points forming the basis of a durable peace, the same principle of self-determination was reiterated in more definite form as applying specifically to the subject nationalities of the enemy powers.[101] Again, on July 4, 1918, the President demanded "the settlement of every question, whether of territory, of sovereignty, of economic arrangement, or of political relationship, upon the basis of the free acceptance of that settlement by the people immediately concerned." [102]

These principles were recognized by the Conference at Paris in 1918-1919 as properly governing the determination of new boundary lines, although the application of the principles was defeated at several points by the intrusion of political interests. The new states of Czechoslovakia, Poland, and Yugoslavia were established on the basis of nationality, the assumption being that the wishes of the inhabitants would coincide with their national origin.[103] Doubtful boundaries were determined in a few cases by plebiscites, as in the case of the boundaries between Poland and Germany in Upper Silesia and in certain sections of the boundary with East Prussia.[104] The retention by Belgium of the districts of Eupen and Malmédy was made dependent upon the decision of the League of

[99] A summary of the opposing views of publicists with respect to the application of the plebiscite to transfers of territory may be found in Wambaugh, *op. cit.*, pp. 21-33.

[100] For the text, see *Congressional Record*, Vol. 54, p. 1743.

[101] Address of January 8, 1918, before the Congress, *Am. Journal*, Vol. 13 (1919), p. 161.

[102] That President Wilson recognized the practical difficulties in the way of the application of the principle may be seen in his statement that "All well-defined national aspirations shall be accorded the utmost satisfaction that can be accorded them without introducing new or perpetuating old elements of discord and antagonism that would be likely in time to break the peace of Europe and consequently of the world." Hackworth, *Digest*, Vol. I, p. 424.

[103] See Haskins and Lord, *Some Problems of the Peace Conference.*

[104] Arts. 88, 94-97. For a study of the difficulties attending the determination of the Upper Silesian boundary, see G. A. Finch, "Upper Silesia," *Am. Journal*, Vol. 16 (1922), p. 75. For the final settlement, see treaty of May 15, 1922, between Poland and Germany.

Nations following a plebiscite taken in the territory.[105] The Saar Basin was put under the League of Nations as trustee, with the provision that at the end of fifteen years a plebiscite should be taken to indicate the sovereignty under which the inhabitants desired to be placed.[106] The boundary between Germany and Denmark was fixed by dividing the disputed area of Northern Schleswig into two zones and providing for a separate plebiscite to be taken in each zone.[107] The wishes of the people of Alsace-Lorraine were taken for granted.[108] By contrast, the desire of Italy for a strategic boundary led to the annexation of parts of the Tyrol which were admittedly Austrian in nationality.[109]

Treaties of 1947. None of the transfers of territory following the Second World War contain provisions for plebiscites to determine the wishes of the inhabitants. The annexation by the Soviet Union of the eastern part of Poland was accepted at the Yalta Conference of 1945 as no more than a return to the proposed Curzon Line of 1919.[110] The partition of East Prussia would obviously not have been possible if a plebiscite had been taken.[111] The transfer of Venezia Giulia by Italy to Yugoslavia was in like manner carried out as a penalty rather than as a measure of self-determination.[112] The transfer of Bessarabia to the Soviet Union passed almost unnoticed by the other members of the Allied Powers.[113]

Individual option of inhabitants. Although unwilling to make cessions of territory conditional upon a plebiscite of the inhabitants, states have in many cases during the past century stipulated in treaties of cession that the inhabitants of the territory should have the option of

[105] Treaty of Versailles, Art. 34. The plebiscite was rather a "public expression of opinion" than a secret vote. The final decision in favor of the transfer was made by the League of Nations, and it included Prussian Moresnet.

[106] Art. 49. In 1935 the plebiscite was taken and the territory was annexed to Germany. See Wambaugh, *The Saar Plebiscite.*

[107] Arts. 109-111.

[108] The treaty, Section V, recognizes the "moral obligation" to redress the wrong done to France contrary to the wishes of the population of Alsace-Lorraine, "which were separated from their country in spite of the solemn protest of their representatives at the Assembly of Bordeaux."

[109] See Treaty of Saint Germain, Art. 27, p. 2. The frontier then established remained unchanged after the Second World War. Peace treaty with Italy, Art. 1. An agreement concluded between the two interested states on September 5, 1946, now protects the ethnical character of the Austrian element of the former South Tyrol. Annex IV to the treaty.

[110] For the text of the Yalta agreement, see *Am. Journal,* Vol. 39 (1945), Supp., pp. 103, 107.

[111] The partition was arranged for provisionally at the Potsdam Conference, Communiqué of August 2, 1945, leaving the "final delimitation" to await the peace settlement. *Ibid.,* p. 254.

[112] Peace treaty with Italy, Art. 3.

[113] Peace treaty with Rumania, Art. 1, anticipated by the bilateral agreement between Rumania and the Soviet Union, June 28, 1940. The plebiscite taken in the territories ceded by Italy to France in 1947 was by virtue of provisions of the new French Constitution.

retaining their old allegiance instead of automatically acquiring the allegiance of the state annexing the territory.[114] Provision for such an election was made with respect to Mexicans residing in the territory ceded to the United States in 1848, with respect to Russian subjects residing in Alaska in 1867, and with respect to Spanish subjects "natives of the Peninsula" residing in the Philippines and Puerto Rico in 1898,[115] natives of the islands themselves not being given the option. The treaty with Denmark of August 4, 1916, providing for the cession of the Danish West Indies, contained liberal provisions for the option of change of allegiance, without prejudice to the property rights of those electing to retain Danish citizenship, whether or not continuing in residence in the islands.[116] The practice of other nations has varied according to the circumstances. The older rule, dating back to the seventeenth century, of requiring persons wishing to retain their old nationality to emigrate within a given period, was frequently applied in the nineteenth century. In the case of the cession of Alsace-Lorraine by the Treaty of Frankfort, May 10, 1871, residents wishing to retain their French nationality were given until October 1, 1872, within which to transfer their domicile to French soil, and they were at the same time required to dispose of real property located in the annexed provinces.[117]

Provisions of the peace treaties of 1919. The provisions of the several treaties concluding the First World War were, with the exception of the Treaty of Lausanne, on the whole, more liberal. The Treaty of Versailles provided for the automatic transfer of nationality in the case of persons continuing to reside in the territories transferred to Belgium, Poland, and Czechoslovakia.[118] Persons who wished to retain their former nationality might, however, elect to do so within a period of two years, in which case they must transfer their residence to Germany, although they might retain their immovable property in the ceded territory. A similar provision regulated the status of former German nationals resident in the Free City of Danzig. More elaborate rules, of a unique character, were prescribed for the national status of the in-

[114] In the absence of special exceptions the transfer of territory after the First World War was accompanied by a "collective naturalization" of the inhabitants. See Moore, *Digest*, Vol. III, § 379; *Harvard Draft, Nationality*, Art. 18, and comment. Among the five peace treaties of 1947 only that with Italy provides for the collective naturalization of Italians resident in the transferred territory, subject to the right of option. Art. 19.

The property rights of persons remaining in the territory were sometimes protected by treaty. In the case of United States v. Percheman, decided in 1833, the Supreme Court of the United States held that "security to private property" would be assured by "the laws and usages of nations." Fenwick, *Cases*, p. 153.

[115] Treaty of Guadalupe Hidalgo, Art. VIII; Treaty of Washington, Art. III; Treaty of Paris, Art. IX.

[116] *Treaties and Conventions*, Vol. III, p. 2558.

[117] Art. 2. Hertslet, *Map of Europe by Treaty*, Vol. III, p. 1954.

[118] Arts. 36, 84, 91.

habitants of Alsace-Lorraine.[119] With these provisions must be associated the special treaties entered into for the protection of minorities.

Compulsory transfer under the Treaty of Lausanne. Unique provisions, almost without precedent in modern history, were contained in the Convention Concerning the Exchange of Greek and Turkish Populations, concluded as a supplement to the Treaty of Lausanne on July 24, 1923. While persons of alien races other than Greek and Turkish were left undisturbed and were offered protection under the minorities provisions of the main treaty, it was provided in the special convention that there should be a compulsory transfer to Greece of Turkish nationals of the Greek Orthodox religion and the transfer to Turkey of the Moslem inhabitants of Greek territory.[120] The exchange of populations was, however, to be carried out without prejudice to the property or monetary assets of the transferred inhabitants, with the exception of immovable property, which was to be liquidated by a mixed commission. Reciprocal acquisition by the transferred persons of a new Greek or Turkish nationality was provided for.[121]

Reacting against the spirit of racialism developed by the Nazi Government of Germany preceding the war and doubtless embittered by the devastation resulting from the German invasion, the Government of Poland undertook to expel large numbers of Germans from the German territory assigned to Poland by the Potsdam Conference of 1945.[122] In like manner Czechoslovakia expelled large numbers of Germans from the Sudetenland which was reannexed to Czechoslovakia at the close of the war.[123] In both cases action was taken before the treaty of peace was drawn up. No option clauses are contained in the treaties with Hungary, Rumania, Bulgaria, and Finland. The Treaty with Italy, however, stipulates that the government of the state to which former Italian territory is transferred shall adopt legislation by which persons whose language is Italian shall be entitled to opt for Italian citizenship; but in such cases the state to which the territory is transferred "may require those who take advantage of the option to move to Italy within

[119] Art. 53 and annex. On the general subject, see C. L. Gettys, "Effect of Changes of Sovereignty on Nationality," *Am. Journal,* Vol. 21 (1927), p. 268.

[120] For an interpretation of certain clauses of the convention, see Advisory Opinion of the Permanent Court of International Justice, Exchange of Greek and Turkish Populations, February 21, 1925. *Publications of the Court,* Series B, No. 10. Hudson, *World Court Reports,* Vol. I, p. 421.

[121] For the text of the convention, see *Am. Journal,* Vol. 18 (1924), Supp., pp. 54, 84. See S. Séfériades, "L'échange des populations," *Recueil des Cours,* Vol. 24 (1928-IV), p. 311.

[122] Potsdam Communiqué, Vol. XIII, "Orderly Transfers of German Populations," *Am. Journal,* Vol. 39 (1945), Supp., p. 256.

[123] *Ibid.* For a survey of the numerous enforced transfers of populations, see Schechtman, *European Population Transfers 1939-45.*

a year from the date when the option was exercised." [124] Similar provisions are contained in the Permanent Statute of the Free Territory of Trieste.[125]

H. ASSIMILATION UNDER PRESSURE

The term "assimilation," or better "assimilation under pressure," may be used to describe those cases in which weaker states have been absorbed by stronger ones without war or other forms of open violence, but nevertheless contrary to the principle of self-determination.

In 1910, by a formal treaty between the two countries, Korea, after passing through the transitional condition of a protectorate, became merged in Japan and simply disappeared from the international community.[126] In 1938 Austria annexed itself to Germany under circumstances clearly indicating coercion, the German army being in occupation of the country. The approval of the annexation by a subsequent plebiscite was in like manner an act done under coercion.[127] In 1939 Lithuania, Latvia, and Esthonia entered into "treaties of nonaggression" with the Soviet Union, ceding to the latter military bases. The following year, under pressure from the Soviet Union, new governments were formed in the three countries under the control of a representative of the Soviet Commissariat of Foreign Affairs and in the presence of Russian troops. Elections were then held for national assemblies, each of which voted unanimously to join the Soviet Union. On August 7 the Supreme Soviet of the USSR voted to admit them into the Union, and on August 25, 1940, the separate independence of the three Baltic states came to an end.[128]

I. LEASES

Within recent years states have frequently resorted to long-term leases as a means of securing control of territory without prejudicing the formal sovereignty of the lessor state. Thus, in 1898 when the war with Japan had shown its government to be helpless in the presence of force, China leased Port Arthur and Talien-wan (Dalny) to Russia for a term of twenty-five years, with a possible further extension by common agreement. Germany obtained a lease of Kiao-chau for a term of ninety-nine years; Great Britain a lease of Wei-hai-wei for twenty-five years, and a

[124] Treaty with Italy, Art. 19.

[125] *Ibid.*, Annex VI, Art. 6 (3).

[126] See above, p. 170, "Extinction of States."

[127] The plebiscite took place on April 10, 1938, just a month after the occupation of Austria by German troops.

[128] With respect to the elections Molotov observed that the people of the three states had "voted solidly" for their incorporation in the Soviet Union, from which they had been "forcibly torn" by "Western imperialist power." *Int. Conciliation,* 1943, p. 94.

lease of territory opposite Hongkong for ninety-nine years; and France a lease of Kwang-chau-wan.[129] These leases differed in several respects from the leases familiar to municipal law. Apart from the element of coercion in their negotiation, it would seem that the sovereignty of the lessor state over the territory was more nominal than real. When at the close of the Russo-Japanese War in 1905 Russia agreed in the Treaty of Portsmouth to "transfer and assign" to Japan the lease of Port Arthur and Dalny, China, as landlord, was not consulted as to the new tenant. Article 156 of the Treaty of Versailles provided for the transfer by Germany to Japan of "all her rights, title, and privileges" which were acquired from China in 1898 and subsequently. China protested against the transfer and refused to sign the Treaty of Versailles in consequence. Subsequently the transfer was nullified by the treaty concluded between China and Japan, February 4, 1922, at the close of the Conference on the Limitation of Armaments at Washington, in accordance with which Japan agreed to restore the territory to China.[130] At the same time Great Britain announced its readiness to surrender under suitable conditions the lease of Wei-hai-wei, while France repeated an earlier declaration of its readiness to surrender the lease of Kwang-chau-wan *pari passu* with the surrender of the leases held by the other powers.[131]

Lease of the Panama Canal Zone. The term "lease" is not mentioned in the treaty of 1903 by which "the Republic of Panama grants to the United States in perpetuity the use, occupation and control" of the zone of land and adjacent territory for the construction of an interoceanic canal. Technically, Panama retained sovereignty over the territory, although it was expressly provided that the United States should be allowed to exercise over the territory "all the rights, power, and authority" which it would possess if it were sovereign. In compensation for the rights acquired, the United States agreed to make both a cash payment and a smaller annual payment during the life of the convention.[132] The lease of Guantánamo and Bahia Honda from Cuba presented fewer administrative complications. The treaty of 1903 defining the relations between the United States and Cuba provided that, in order to enable the United States to maintain the independence of Cuba and to protect the people of the island, as well as to further the island's own defense, Cuba should sell or lease to the United States lands necessary for coaling or naval stations. The lease of the two areas was thereupon effected by means of an executive agreement defining the territory leased, fol-

[129] The Chinese leases are discussed in detail in Willoughby, *Foreign Rights and Interests in China,* Chap. VIII.

[130] For the text of the agreement, see *Am. Journal,* Vol. 16 (1922), Supp., p. 84.

[131] Willoughby, *China at the Conference,* Chap. XIV.

[132] *Treaties and Conventions,* Vol. II, p. 1349. For later amendments of the treaty of 1903, see "Easements and Servitudes," below, p. 476.

lowed by a second agreement fixing the conditions of the lease.[133] In 1914 the United States, by the Bryan-Chamorro Treaty, leased the Great Corn and Little Corn Islands in the Caribbean Sea from Nicaragua for ninety-nine years.[134] The validity of the lease was contested by Costa Rica and Salvador in suits against Nicaragua before the Central American Court of Justice, which pronounced against Nicaragua but found itself unable to declare the treaty void in view of the fact that the United States was not a party to the suits.[135]

On September 2, 1940, by notes exchanged between the two governments, Great Britain agreed to lease to the United States a number of naval and air bases in the Caribbean Sea and adjacent waters, in exchange for the transfer of certain overage American destroyers.[136] The leases were made effective by a subsequent agreement of March 27, 1941. By this latter agreement the United States acquired the right to use and operate the bases for a period of ninety-nine years.[137]

[133] *Ibid.*, Vol. I, pp. 358, 360, 362.

[134] *Treaties and Conventions,* Vol. III, p. 2740. For details, see Hackworth, *Digest,* Vol. I, pp. 702 ff. Proprietary rights were also granted for the construction of a canal.

[135] See *Am. Journal,* Vol. II (1917), pp. 181, 674, and comment by P. M. Brown, *ibid.,* p. 156.

[136] For the text of the agreement, see *Am. Journal,* Vol. 34 (1940), Supp., p. 184; Dept. of State *Bulletin,* Vol. III, p. 199.

[137] *Am. Journal,* Vol. 35 (1941), Supp., p. 134; Dept. of State *Bulletin,* Vol. IV, p. 387. The leases marked the transition by the United States from the status of technical neutrality to that of practical assistance short of war. See below, p. 726.

CHAPTER XIX

Jurisdiction Over Territory: National Boundaries and Territorial Sea

A. SOURCES OF THE LAW

The extent of a state's territorial domain is determined by definite boundary lines, which mark at once the limits of the property rights of the state and of its jurisdiction over persons. In the determination of these boundary lines, as in the case of the acquisition of title to the territory itself, international law has drawn heavily upon the *jus gentium* of the Roman Law. So close did the analogy between states as corporate persons and the individual citizens of the state seem to be to the early writers that wherever there was doubt as to a particular boundary line they did not hesitate to decide the case according to the time-honored principles of the civil law.[1] The comparison between the two legal systems is instructive; but here, as elsewhere, the practice of states must interpret the meaning of abstract principles.[2] It should be noted, however, that neither in municipal nor in international law have boundary lines been fixed upon any general principle of the common welfare of the group as opposed to the personal interests of the individual owner. In municipal law the disadvantages of the late comer as against the first comer, of the landless as against the landed interests, are largely offset by the highways of common property which everywhere intersect private property; whereas in international law boundaries have a distinct strategic value for political and economic purposes. These latter aspects of boundary lines will appear more clearly in connection with easements

[1] See Lauterpacht, *Private Law Sources and Analogies of International Law*, pp. 91 ff.
[2] See above, p. 85.

and servitudes. For the moment only the technical aspects will be presented.[3]

B. DETERMINATION OF BOUNDARY LINES

The existing boundary lines of European states have been determined for the most part by definite international conventions. Many of these conventions have been in the form of treaties of peace following wars of conquest or wars with disputed territory as their object; others have been in the form of voluntary agreements by which an amicable settlement of boundaries has been brought about. Since 1648 the map of Europe has been redrawn many times, whether by such general treaties as those of Westphalia in 1648, Vienna in 1815, the peace treaties of 1919 and of 1947, or by more restricted agreements between smaller groups of states. In many instances these conventional agreements merely confirmed old lines fixed by prescription which, as was observed in connection with the occupation of territory, is the original ground of title. Other European boundaries are purely prescriptive, and it would be difficult to find the international document, if any, in which they were originally laid out. The boundary lines of the Western hemisphere have been determined partly by prescription at the time of the occupation of the territory by the colonizing states of Europe and partly by conventions entered into at the time of the establishment of the independence of former colonies or by subsequent treaties of cession. The boundaries of Africa are almost wholly conventional, following earlier prescriptive titles; those of Asia are partly conventional and partly prescriptive.

"Natural" and artificial boundaries. It is common for writers to distinguish between natural and artificial boundaries, the former consisting of mountains, rivers, etc., while the latter consist of the geographic lines of longitude and latitude. The distinction is, however, apt to be misleading, since it suggests that qualities which really belong to the mere surveyor's lines of demarcation are to be attributed to boundaries as political lines of separation. The regional movements of civilization have not in fact conformed themselves in all cases to the physical contour of nature. As an abstract proposition it may well be questioned, for example, whether rivers are a "natural" boundary line, since they separate by political barriers groups which by the laws of economic life are "naturally" drawn together. Care should be taken, moreover, to test both by positive law and by constructive politics other misleading senses

[3] On the general subject of boundaries and territorial waters, see Gidel, Le droit international public de la mer, Tome III, "La mer territorial et la zone contigue"; Jessup, The Law of Territorial Waters and Maritime Jurisdiction; Masterson, Jurisdiction in Marginal Seas; Mouton, The Continental Shelf; C. J. Colombos, The International Law of the Sea; Jones, Boundary Making; Holdich, Political Frontiers and Boundary Making; Boggs, International Boundaries; J. S. Reeves, "International Boundaries," Am. Journal, Vol. 38 (1944), p. 533.

in which the term "natural boundaries" is used. Mountains which have
a strategic value for purposes of defense have been called, as in the case
of the Tyrolese Alps, a "natural" frontier, although it may happen that
in accepting them as a conventional boundary, as was done by the Treaty
of St. Germain in 1919, violence is done to those other frontiers, also said
to be "natural," which include members of the same race and language.
If by *natural* should be meant "desirable from an economic or social
point of view," many of the present boundaries of states are admittedly
unnatural, whatever natural landmarks there may be to designate
them.[4]

C. THE WATER DIVIDE AS A BOUNDARY

In the technical delimitation of boundary lines certain rules have been
worked out which may be regarded as the prescriptive or customary law
of the subject holding good in the absence of treaty stipulations. When
a range of hills forms the boundary, the water divide or watershed
constitutes the frontier line. This line, in undefined form, is frequently
provided for in treaties, leaving to boundary commissions the more exact
survey. The chief difficulty in the delimitation of such boundaries has
arisen from the fact that the water divide is sometimes not identical with
the highest crest of the range. This issue arose, for example, in connection with the Northeastern Boundary Dispute between the United States
and Great Britain,[5] and more recently between Chile and the Argentine
Republic in connection with the watershed of the Andes.[6]

D. RIVERS AS BOUNDARIES: THE THALWEG

As a matter of geographic convenience, and in certain cases because
of their strategic value as natural barriers, rivers have frequently been
incorporated into the boundary lines of states. In the delimitation of
the dividing line formed by a boundary river, the older rule laid down
by Grotius and endorsed by Vattel was that the line followed the middle
of the stream. This rule came to be modified at the beginning of the
nineteenth century by substituting in the case of navigable rivers the
middle of the main channel or strongest current downstream, technically
known as the "thalweg." [7] The advantages of the latter rule were that
the boundary line followed more closely the chief thoroughfare of commerce and was at the same time less subject to change than the middle

---

[4] For a discussion of boundary lines from the point of view of a "practical delimitation as opposed to sociological theories, see Holdich, *op. cit.*, Chap. II. For an
opposing view, see Lyde, *Some Frontiers of To-morrow*, Chap. II.

[5] See Moore, *Arbitrations*, Vol. I, pp. 65-161.

[6] *Ibid.*, Vol. V, pp. 4854 ff.

[7] The derivation of this term is discussed by Westlake, *Int. Law*, 2nd ed., Vol. I,
p. 144.

line between bank and bank. In the various boundary treaties of the United States involving rivers, the terms used to describe the boundary have not been uniform, and several international disputes have arisen in consequence. The treaty of 1783 with Great Britain referred to the "middle" of boundary rivers; [8] the treaty of 1795 with Spain to the "middle" of one river and to the "middle of the channel" of another. In other treaties it is provided that the boundary shall follow the "middle of the main channel" or, in the more recent treaty of 1908 with Great Britain, "the center of the main channel or thalweg." [9]

New Jersey v. Delaware. In the case of New Jersey v. Delaware,[10] decided in 1934, the Supreme Court of the United States applied what it believed to be the principles of international law to the settlement of the boundary in the lower Delaware River and in the bay between the two states. Said the court,

International law today divides the river boundaries between states by the middle of the main channel, when there is one, and not by the geographical center, half way between the banks. . . . It applies the same doctrine, now known as the doctrine of the *Thalweg*, to estuaries and bays in which the dominant sailing channel can be followed to the sea. . . . The *Thalweg*, or downway, is the track taken by boats in their course down the stream, which is that of the strongest current. . . . The underlying rationale of the doctrine of the *Thalweg* is one of equality and justice. . . . If the dividing line were to be placed in the center of the stream rather than in the center of the channel, the whole track of navigation might be thrown within the territory of one state to the exclusion of the other. . . . If the boundary be taken to be the *Thalweg*, it will follow the course furrowed by the vessels of the world.

The decision with respect to the boundary of the lower river was in favor of the claim of the State of New Jersey.[11]

In some European treaties an effort has been made to give a greater degree of stability to river boundary lines by locating the thalweg definitely by means of fixed points which were to constitute permanent landmarks for the future. In the Treaty of Versailles of 1919 provision was made that the principal channel of navigable rivers should be the dividing line; but it was further provided that it should be left to the several boundary commissioners appointed by the treaty to determine whether the boundary line should follow subsequent changes of the

[8] Art. II. See *Treaties and Conventions,* Vol. I, p. 586.
[9] Arts. II, IV. See *Treaties and Conventions,* Vol. II, p. 1640.
[10] 291 U.S. 361 (1934). Fenwick, *Cases,* p. 575; Briggs, *Cases,* p. 253; Hudson, *Cases,* p. 445. The opinion of the Court contains valuable historical material.
[11] The boundary of an upper section of the river was set forth in an early colonial grant, and the award was in favor of the State of Delaware.

channel or should be definitely fixed by the position of the channel at the time.[12]

Effect of erosion and avulsion. The gradual shifting of the thalweg from one side to the other by reason of imperceptible erosion or accretion of the banks of the river has, as a general rule, the effect of changing the boundary to a corresponding degree. If, however, the river should, by the process known as "avulsion," suddenly become diverted from its regular channel, the boundary line remains where it was before the change. This general rule, borrowed from the civil law, would seem to be ill adapted to the relations between states.[13] Its application to the settlement of the dispute between the United States and Mexico in connection with the boundaries of the Rio Grande presented grave inconveniences. A boundary convention of 1884 had made provision for the shifting of the boundary line following the mid-channel when due to slow erosion without abandonment of the river bed. A controversy developed with respect to the sovereignty over a tract of land known as "El Chamizal," lying between El Paso and Juarez. The United States claimed that the

---

[12] The student will find a wealth of illustrative material in the numerous boundary disputes between the several states of the United States. In such cases the federal Supreme Court, having obligatory jurisdiction over the parties, has attempted to apply the principles of international law to the relations of the members of the federal union. While the decisions rendered are not precedents for the establishment of a rule of international law, since the parties involved are not technically "states" and the law applied is constitutional law, nevertheless they are valuable practical applications of rules deemed by the court to be good international law. In the case of Handly's Lessee v. Anthony, 5 Wheaton 374 (1820), Fenwick, *Cases*, p. 506, the court dealt with the exceptional case in which a state, in making a cession of territory lying on the further side of a river (the Ohio), retains ownership of the whole river, so as to make the further shore the boundary line between the two states. The same rule governed the later case of Indiana v. Kentucky, 136 U.S. 479 (1889). See also Vermont v. New Hampshire, 289 U.S. 593 (1933), in which the court held that the boundary between the two states was the low-water mark on the Vermont side, not the top of the bank as claimed by New Hampshire. In the case of Iowa v. Illinois, 147 U.S. 1 (1893), Fenwick, *Cases*, p. 511; Hudson, *Cases*, p. 449; the court held that by international law, as shown in the usage of European states, the terms "middle of the stream" and "mid-channel" were synonymous; but this interpretation has been contested as incorrect. The case of Washington v. Oregon, 211 U.S. 127 (1908), dealt with the problem of a river (the Columbia) having two channels, each of which was at different times the main channel. See Scott, *Judicial Settlement of Controversies between States of the American Union,* under index title "Boundaries." Also, Hyde, *International Law,* Vol. I, § 138, notes.

[13] The loss to a riparian state of a part of the river as a boundary line might be expected to be far more serious than a similar loss to an individual under the civil law. A more reasonable rule would call for the retention of the river as a boundary, subject to the necessity on the part of the state which acquires the territory of making compensation to private owners for property losses due to the change of sovereignty over the area. Each case, however, should be settled on its merits, in accordance with principles of equity, rather than by the application of the rigid rule of the civil law.

The discussion of the subject by Grotius and by Vattel throws light upon the practical problems of their day. See *De jure belli ac pacis,* Book II, Chap. VIII, §§ XII ff.; *Droit des gens,* Book I, § 270.

tract had been formed by the process of slow erosion and accretion. Mexico contended that it had been formed by avulsion. By a convention of 1910 the controversy was submitted to arbitration, and the Commission held that part of the tract came within the provisions of the treaty of 1884 with respect to "slow and gradual erosion," but that another part which resulted from "the great flood of 1864" did not come within the provisions of the treaty and should, therefore, be assigned to Mexico. The American Commissioner dissented from the award.[14] Years later, on July 18, 1963, the Presidents of the United States and of Mexico announced an agreement to conclude a convention for the settlement of the dispute, which, having as its objective the restoration of the Rio Grande as the boundary between the two countries, would transfer to Mexico some 437 acres of territory, partly adjacent to El Paso, Texas, and Mexico would transfer a smaller area to the United States. At the same time a new channel would be dug for the river so as to restore in part the old boundary of 1864, the cost of the new channel being divided equally between the two countries.[15]

In the case of Arkansas v. Tennessee,[16] in its latest phase, the Supreme Court of the United States held in 1940 that while the rule of the thalweg rested upon equitable considerations and was intended "to safeguard to each State equality of access and right of navigation in the stream," yet the rule yielded to the doctrine that a boundary was unaltered by an avulsion. This doctrine, however, in turn became inapplicable "when it is established that there has been acquiescence in a long-continued and uninterrupted assertion of dominion and jurisdiction over a given area. Here that fact [in respect to a portion of the bed of the Mississippi River] has been established and the original rule of the thalweg no longer applies."

Dividing line upon bridges. The convenience of making the mid-channel of a river the dividing line between two riparian states has not necessarily led to the adoption of a corresponding boundary line overhead where bridges span the river. European treaties of the nineteenth century generally fixed upon the middle of the bridge as the dividing

[14] For the text of the convention, see *Treaties and Conventions*, Vol. III, p. 2729. For the text of the award, see *Am. Journal*, Vol. 5 (1911), p. 785. Hudson, *Cases*, p. 457. A summary of the case is given in Hackworth, *Digest*, Vol. I, pp. 411 ff. For the reasons set forth in the opinion of the American Commissioner and of the American agent, the United States notified Mexico that it did not accept the award as valid or binding.

[15] For the Memorandum submitted to the two Presidents by their respective Foreign Offices, see Whiteman, *Digest*, Vol. 3, p. 680. The Convention was formally ratified by the United States and entered into force January 14, 1964. For the text of the Convention, see *Am. Journal*, Vol. 58 (1964), p. 336; Whiteman, *op. cit.*, p. 689.

[16] 311 U.S. 1 (1940). *Am. Journal*, Vol. 35 (1941), p. 154. The doctrine of avulsion is discussed at length in the earlier case of Nebraska v. Iowa, 143 U.S. 359 (1892), dealing with changes in the bed of the Missouri River. Fenwick, *Cases*, p. 520; Hudson, *Cases*, p. 453.

line, irrespective of the channel underneath. Such was the provision made in the declaration of 1861 with respect to the jurisdictional limits of France and Baden on bridges crossing the Rhine.[17] The problem of the joint construction and maintenance of the bridge apparently dictated the choice of a different boundary line in the one case from that in the other. By contrast, the United States and Mexico found it more convenient to provide, as stipulated in the convention of 1884, that in the event of the building of an international bridge across the Rio Grande or the Rio Colorado the dividing line of jurisdiction should be determined by a point immediately over the main channel, which line, however, should remain fixed notwithstanding subsequent changes in the channel.[18]

E. BOUNDARY STRAITS AND LAKES

Straits forming the boundary between two states are governed by the same general rules that apply to boundary rivers. Too few precedents exist to determine whether the middle of the strait or the middle of the main channel, if there be one, constitutes the dividing line; but it is generally asserted by authors that, by logical inference from the case of rivers, the latter rule should prevail.[19] In the case of lakes which are incorporated into the boundary between two states, the dividing line, in the absence of special provisions to the contrary, follows the middle of the lake. In the treaty of 1783 with Great Britain the boundary line between the United States and Canada was fixed by a line running through the middle of Lakes Superior, Huron, Ontario, and Erie and their connecting links.[20] In the case of Lake Constance, which forms a corner boundary between Germany, Austria, and Switzerland, the three boundaries meet at a surveyor's point on the waters of the lake.

F. THE MARITIME BOUNDARY: THE MARGINAL SEA

Much more difficult of determination than the boundary line formed by a river, strait, or lake is the maritime boundary marking the limits of the territorial domain of the state when terminating at the high seas. The problem presents several distinct aspects, the first relating to the general claim by states of jurisdiction over the marginal sea bordering their coasts, the others relating to more specific claims of jurisdiction over gulfs and bays along the coast and over straits connecting the high seas on either side of a state's territory.

The "marine league" or "three-mile limit." That the territorial juris-

---

[17] De Clercq, *Treaties*, Vol. VIII, p. 160; quoted by Hyde, *op. cit.*, Vol. I, § 140.
[18] Art. IV. See *Treaties and Conventions*, Vol. I, p. 1159.
[19] Compare Art. 6 of the Amended Draft Convention of the League of Nations Committee of Experts and Art. 9 of Harvard Draft on *Territorial Waters*, pp. 281, 366.
[20] Art. II. See *Treaties and Conventions*, Vol. I, p. 586.

diction of a state should extend beyond the low-water mark along its coasts seemed to the early writers on international law a logical necessity of self-defense. At the same time it formed the rational basis of a claim to the exclusive enjoyment of local fisheries and other similar advantages. Setting aside the extravagant claims made by certain maritime states to jurisdiction over wide areas of the high seas adjacent to their coasts,[21] we find that by the middle of the eighteenth century the maritime boundary of a state was coming to be accepted as extending out from the shore to the limit of the carrying range of a cannon-shot. This strip of marginal sea, or maritime belt, represented the area over which a state might exercise effective control and in that sense "occupy" the area as a ground for the assertion of sovereignty over it. The Dutch publicist Bynkershoek, writing in 1702, stated the rule in terms which later were accepted as authoritative.[22] At about the same time the maritime boundary began to be more clearly defined in terms of a fixed three-mile limit corresponding approximately to the range of cannon-shot at that day, and it became thereafter known as the "marine league." During the nineteenth century this more specific maritime boundary became accepted by a number of the leading powers, particularly by Great Britain and the United States, as marking the extreme limit of territorial sovereignty.[23] Other maritime states, however, claimed wider areas of marginal sea, Russia twelve marine miles, Sweden and Norway four miles, Spain and Portugal six, and Mexico nine miles. At the Hague Conference of 1930 a concerted effort was made to reconcile these differences, but no agreement could be reached upon a fixed distance; nor could the Conference of the United Nations held at Geneva in 1958 come to an agreement on the subject. Proposals to maintain the traditional three-mile limit were defeated, as were proposals to extend the marginal sea to twelve miles; and the final report of the Conference noted that international practice was not uniform and that many states

[21] See Chap. XXII, "The High Seas."

[22] *De dominio maris,* Eng. trans., Chap. 2. "Wherefore on the whole it seems a better rule that the control of the land [over the sea] extends as far as cannon will carry (*quousque tormenta exploduntur*); for that is as far as we seem to have both command and possession. I am speaking, however, of our times, in which we use those engines of war; otherwise I should have to say in general terms that the control from the land ends where the power of men's weapons ends (*potestatem terrae finiri ubi finitur armorum vis*)." For "control of the land" might be substituted "territorial jurisdiction." Bynkershoek's rule reappears in his *Quaestionum juris publici libri duo,* Lib. I, Cap. 8, published in 1737.

[23] The rule is stated with unwarranted finality in Cunard Steamship Co. v. Mellon, 262 U.S. 100 (1923): "It is now settled in the United States and recognized elsewhere that the territory subject to its jurisdiction includes the land areas under its dominion and control, the ports, harbors, bays, and other inclosed arms of the sea along its coast, and a marginal belt of the sea extending from the coast line outward a marine league, or three geographic miles." Fenwick, *Cases,* p. 354; Bishop, *Cases,* p. 505; Hudson, *Cases,* p. 615. Compare Harvard Research, *Draft Convention on Territorial Waters,* Art. 2 and Comment.

had fixed a greater breadth than three miles which, however, was not recognized by others.[24]

A second attempt was made at the Geneva Conference on the Law of the Sea of 1960, at which the United States, the United Kingdom, and Canada offered a compromise proposal which could have extended the territorial sea to six miles with an additional six-mile zone giving to the coastal state the same rights in respect of fishing and the exploitation of the living resources of the sea as it had in its territorial sea. But it proved impossible, by one vote, to secure the necessary two-thirds vote for the adoption of the proposal.[25]

Exclusive jurisdiction of the state. Within the limits of the marginal sea, whatever its exact width, the jurisdiction of the state is as exclusive as is its jurisdiction over the land itself. The right of innocent passage granted to foreign states, and the privileges granted to public ships in port and in part to private ships, are concessions which leave the general principle of sovereignty intact. In the much discussed case of Queen v. Keyn,[26] the captain of a German steamer, the *Franconia*, was convicted by a lower British court of manslaughter for the death of a passenger caused by a collision that took place within three miles of the British coast. The higher court dismissed the case on the ground that, although the exercise by states of jurisdiction over the marine league was evidenced by the practice of nations and by the statements of writers of authority, yet Parliament had not actually extended the criminal jurisdiction of the courts over the territorial waters in question. It should be observed that the case raised no question as to the sovereign right of Great Britain to exercise jurisdiction through its own appropriate agencies; and the decision was promptly followed by the passage of an act of Parliament of 1878 clothing the courts with the requisite authority to hear such cases in the future.

In consequence of the extension of the jurisdiction of the state over the marginal sea, no other state may commit acts within that area which are regarded as in violation of the territorial sovereignty of the state. In the case of the *Itata*,[27] a transport that was being used in the service of

[24] See A. H. Dean, "The Geneva Conference on the Law of the Sea: What was Accomplished," *Am. Journal,* Vol. 52 (1958), pp. 607, 614. For the corresponding efforts of the Inter-American Council of Jurists to agree upon a definite width, see Fenwick, *OAS*, p. 314. The conclusions of the Hague Conference of 1930 may be found in *Am. Journal,* Vol. 24 (1930), Supp., pp. 234 ff.

[25] See A. H. Dean, "The Second Geneva Conference on the Law of the Sea: The Fight for the Freedom of the Seas," *Am. Journal,* Vol. 54 (1960), p. 751.

[26] I. L. R. 2 Exch. Div. 63 (1876). Fenwick, *Cases,* p. 529. In the case of Manchester v. Massachusetts, 139 U.S. 240 (1891), the Supreme Court of the United States held as a point of constitutional law that the territorial jurisdiction of Massachusetts was that of an independent nation and that the State could define its sea boundaries so as to include Buzzard's Bay within them.

[27] South American Steamship Co. v. United States, Moore, *Arbitrations,* Vol. III, p. 3067.

Chilean insurgents was, on the ground of alleged violation of the neutrality laws of the United States, pursued by an American cruiser into the harbor of Iquique, Chile, and there captured without resistance. Chile protested against the violation of its sovereignty and demanded redress. The case was arbitrated and an award was rendered holding the United States liable for damages.[28]

In time of war belligerents may not commit acts of hostility within the maritime belt of a neutral state. Hence not only may battles not take place between warships of the contending states, but the pursuit of a belligerent merchant ship or of an offending neutral ship may not be continued once the three-mile limit has been crossed. The scuttling of the German cruiser, *Graf Spee*, in Uruguayan territorial waters was a clear violation of the sovereignty of Uruguay, although that state made no official protest against the act.[29]

The further extension of the marine league: measures to prevent smuggling. Both Great Britain and the United States were, however, early forced to take into account the necessity of extending what came to be called a "protective jurisdiction" over a wider area than the three-mile belt, chiefly in connection with the enforcement of customs duties. The British Hovering Acts of 1736 and 1784, passed with the object of preventing smuggling, forbade the transshipment of foreign goods within four leagues of the coast.[30] In 1799 Congress passed an act, directing officers of United States revenue cutters to board vessels arriving within four leagues of the coast, and to visit and search them to determine the character of their cargo. It was further provided that if any part of the cargo should be unladen within four leagues of the coast or transferred to another vessel without a permit, the masters of the respective vessels should be guilty of a penal offense.[31] Since the act of 1799 refrained from authorizing the seizure of the vessel while still beyond the three-mile limit, the question of a right of seizure was not put at issue. Two early cases are quoted as affirming and denying respectively the existence of such a right. In the case of Church v. Hubbart,[32] the Supreme Court

---

[28] For the issue as to the violation of the neutrality laws, see United States v. Trumbull, 49 Fed. 99 (1891); United States v. The *Itata*, 56 Fed. 505 (1893). Scott and Jaeger, *Cases,* p. 365.

[29] See below, p. 730.

[30] A detailed survey of British legislation may be found in Masterson, *Jurisdiction in Marginal Seas,* Part I; Jessup, *Law of Territorial Waters and Maritime Jurisdiction,* Chap. I.

[31] *Rev. Stat.,* §§ 2760, 2867, 2868. *U. S. Comp. Stat.,* §§ 8459½ b. (52), pp. 5555, 5556; Masterson, *op. cit.,* Part III. The acquiescence of foreign powers in the enforcement of hovering laws has generally been put down by writers to "comity" as distinct from law, and this was the position taken by Secretary Fish in 1873. Oppenheim (*Int. Law,* Vol. I, § 190) holds that such measures had, by long usage, received the sanction of customary law.

[32] 2 Cranch 187 (1804). Fenwick, *Cases,* p. 544; Hudson, *Cases,* p. 627; Briggs, *Cases,* p. 356.

of the United States was unwilling to pronounce void the seizure for illicit trade of an American trader by a Portuguese cruiser at four leagues from the coast of Brazil, holding that a state's "power to secure itself from injury may certainly be exercised beyond the limits of its territory." But in the later case of Rose v. Himely,[33] the same court held that the seizure under municipal law of an American vessel by a French privateer beyond the limits of the territorial jurisdiction for illicit trade with rebels was not warranted by the law of nations.[34] The circumstances of the latter case gave it at the time the more conclusive character, and it was supported by the subsequent attitude of the Department of State.[35]

Issues raised by the Eighteenth Amendment. For a brief period between the adoption of the Eighteenth Amendment, prohibiting the manufacture and sale of intoxicating liquors, in 1919, and the repeal of the Amendment in 1933, the United States found itself in the presence of a formidable "rum-fleet" which stationed itself outside the three-mile limit and delivered its forbidden wares to swift motorboats which put out from the shore. The enforcement of the Volstead Act led to the seizure of a number of foreign vessels unloading their goods within four leagues of the coast, as in the case of the *Henry L. Marshall*, which was captured while delivering its cargo by prearrangement to small boats belonging to others.[36]

Beginning in 1924 a number of treaties were negotiated between the United States and foreign powers providing for an extension of jurisdiction beyond the three-mile limit. The treaty with Great Britain, signed January 23, 1924, provided that, without departing from the principle that three miles from low-water mark constituted the proper limits of territorial waters, the United States might search and seize British vessels attempting to commit offenses against its liquor laws within the distance from the coast that might be traversed in one hour by the vessel suspected of endeavoring to commit the offense. In return for this concession the United States agreed to refrain from enforcing its liquor laws against

---

[33] 4 Cranch 241 (1808). Dickinson, *Cases*, p. 502.

[34] "It is conceded," said the court, "that the legislation of every country is territorial; that beyond its own territory, it can only affect its own subjects or citizens. It is not easy to conceive a power to execute a municipal law, or to enforce obedience to that law without the circle in which that law operates. A power to seize for the infraction of a law is derived from the sovereign, and must be exercised, it would seem, within those limits which circumscribe the sovereign power. The rights of war may be exercised on the high seas, because war is carried on upon the high seas; but the pacific rights of sovereignty must be exercised within the territory of the sovereign. If these propositions be true, a seizure of a person not a subject, or of a vessel not belonging to a subject, made on the high seas for the breach of a municipal regulation, is an act which the sovereign cannot authorize."

[35] The consistent position of the United States Department of State may be found in Moore, *Digest*, Vol. I, §§ 145-151. See also Woolsey's Memorandum, *Foreign Relations* (1912), pp. 1289 ff., where the conflicting decisions of municipal and international arbitration courts are given.

[36] 292 Fed. Rep. 486 (1923). Jessup, *op. cit.*, p. 247; Masterson, *op cit.*, p. 222.

British vessels in port, provided the intoxicating liquors were kept under seal while the vessel was within territorial waters.[37] The treaties with France, Italy, Norway, and certain other states omitted the provision with respect to the three-mile limit and reserved the respective "rights and claims" of the parties with respect to the extent of their territorial jurisdiction, without prejudice to the provision permitting seizure within an hour's run from shore.[38] In the case of Ford v. United States,[39] a British vessel, the *Quadra,* had been seized on the high seas off the coast of the United States and persons aboard her had been prosecuted for a conspiracy to violate both the National Prohibition Act and the Tariff Act of 1922. The convictions were upheld on the ground that when the vessel lost its immunity from seizure by reason of the treaty of 1924 the persons on board also lost their immunity and that a conspiracy to violate the laws of the United States might be committed by persons corporeally out of the jurisdiction of the United States.

The repeal of the Eighteenth Amendment brought to an end the special problem of preventing "rum-running," but the general problem of the enforcement of customs duties continued. In 1935 the American Congress abandoned the earlier limitation of four leagues and made provision that whenever the President found that any vessels were hovering "within any area on the high seas adjacent to but outside customs waters," and the unlawful removal of merchandise was being occasioned or threatened, he should declare the area "a customs enforcement area" and thereupon customs officers might go aboard the vessels and bring them to port.[40]

Finally, at the United Nations Conference on the Law of the Sea, held at Geneva in 1958, the Convention on the Territorial Sea and the Contiguous Zone, in spite of the inability of the members to agree, as we have seen, upon the breadth of the territorial sea, included an article permitting the coastal state to exercise within twelve miles the control necessary to prevent infringement of its customs and other regulations within its territory or territorial sea.[41]

Extension of jurisdiction over the continental shelf. The proclamation of the President with respect to the natural resources of the subsoil and sea bed of the continental shelf, and the accompanying proclamation with respect to coastal fisheries in certain areas of the high seas, both under date of September 28, 1945, marked a radical development

[37] For the text of the treaty, see *U. S. Treaty Series,* No. 685; *Am. Journal,* Vol. 18 (1924), Supp., p. 127.

[38] See Jessup, *op. cit.,* pp. 289 ff.; Masterson, *op. cit.,* pp. 352 ff.

[39] 273 U.S. 593 (1927). Fenwick, *Cases,* p. 551. For additional cases illustrating the application of the law, see Hackworth, *Digest,* Vol. I, pp. 678 ff.

[40] For the text of the act, see *Am. Journal,* Vol. 31 (1937), Supp., p. 183.

[41] Art. 24. For the text of the Convention, see *Am. Journal,* Vol. 52 (1958), p. 834. For the extravagant claims of some of the Latin American states bordering on the Pacific, see Fenwick, *OAS,* pp. 314 ff.

of the policy of the United States in respect to jurisdiction over the marginal sea.[42] The first of the two proclamations called attention to the need for new sources of petroleum and other minerals, to the belief that such resources underlie many parts of the continental shelf off the coast of the United States, and to the view of the United States that "the exercise of jurisdiction over the natural resources of the subsoil and sea bed of the continental shelf by the contiguous nation is reasonable and just." [43] It then announced as "the policy" of the United States to regard these resources "as appertaining to the United States, subject to its jurisdiction and control." In cases where the continental shelf extended to the shores of another state, or was shared with an adjacent state, the boundary was to be determined by the United States and the state concerned "in accordance with equitable principles." The proclamation then stated that: "The character as high seas of the waters above the continental shelf and the right to their free and unimpeded navigation are in no way thus affected." [44]

Other countries followed suit, accompanied by vigorous debate and discussion by scholars. The question finally came up before the Geneva Conference on the Law of the Sea, and a Convention on the Continental Shelf was adopted, which defined the continental shelf as "the seabed and subsoil of the submarine areas adjacent to the coast but outside the area of the territorial sea, to a depth of 200 metres or, beyond that limit, to where the depth of the superjacent waters admits of the exploitation of the natural resources of the said areas." Over the continental shelf the coastal state exercises sovereign rights for the purpose of exploring it and exploiting its natural resources, including mineral and other non-living resources together with living organisms belonging to sedentary species which are immobile on or under the sea bed, this latter excluding such crustaceans as shrimp, but including oyster beds and pearl fisheries.

[42] For the texts of the two proclamations, see Am. Journal, Vol. 40 (1946), pp. 45, 46. For a critical examination of the two proclamations in relation to the existing rules of international law, see E. Borchard, "Resources of the Continental Shelf," Am. Journal, Vol. 40 (1946), p. 53; J. L. Kunz, "The Continental Shelf and International Law: Confusion and Abuse," ibid., Vol. 50 (1956), p. 828; H. Lauterpacht, "Sovereignty over Submarine Areas," British Year Book, Vol. XXVII (1950).

[43] No specific water depth was fixed as determining the extent of the continental shelf, but it was understood that a depth of some 600 feet was contemplated.

The preamble of the proclamation argues further that the exercise of jurisdiction is reasonable and just "since the effectiveness of measures to utilize or conserve these resources would be contingent upon coöperation and protection from the shore, since the continental shelf may be regarded as an extension of the land-mass of the coastal nation and thus naturally appurtenant to it, since these resources frequently form a seaward extension of a pool or deposit lying within the territory, and since self-protection compels the coastal nation to keep close watch over activities off its shores which are of the nature necessary for utilization of these resources."

[44] The proclamation nowhere asserts the extension of territorial jurisdiction over the waters above the continental shelf, the "jurisdiction and control" being merely with respect to the subsoil and sea bed resources.

The rights of the coastal state over the continental shelf do not affect the legal status of the superjacent waters as high seas.[45]

Conservation areas for fisheries. The proclamation with respect to coastal fisheries called attention to "the inadequacy of present arrangements for the protection and perpetuation of the fishery resources" contiguous to the coasts of the United States and to the need of "improving the jurisdictional basis for conservation measures and international cooperation in this field." In consequence the Government of the United States "regards it as proper to establish conservation zones" in such contiguous areas. These zones were to be "explicitly bounded," whether by unilateral action of the United States in the case of fisheries maintained by nationals alone, or by agreement with other states in the case of fisheries maintained jointly by nationals of the United States and nationals of other states. The character of the conservation areas "as high seas" and the right to their free and unimpeded navigation remained, as in the case of the natural resources of the continental shelf, unaffected.[46]

By the time of the Geneva Conference on the Law of the Sea the conservation of the natural resources of the sea, long a subject of conflicting national interest particularly for the Latin American states along the western coast of the hemisphere, had come to be closely associated with the extension of territorial waters. Obviously if limits were to be put to extensions of territorial waters, some protection must be given to fishing rights in the open sea adjacent to territorial waters, apart from the general interest of all states in the conservation of so important a supply of food. Here the Conference was singularly successful in the adoption of the Convention on Fishing and Conservation of the Living Resources of the High Seas. The Preamble of the Convention lays stress upon the danger that the development of modern techniques may result in overexploitation of the living resources of the sea, and upon the need of international cooperation in solving the problems presented. Article 1, while recognizing the broad general right of all states to fish on the high seas, imposes the duty upon all states of adopting individually or in cooperation with others the necessary measures of conservation so as to render possible "the optimum sustainable yield from those resources so as to secure a maximum supply of food and other marine products." Succeeding articles impose specific duties of cooperation, giving to coastal

---

[45] For the text of the Convention, see *Am. Journal*, Vol. 52 (1958), p. 858. For comment, M. M. Whiteman, "Conference on the Law of the Sea: Convention on the Continental Shelf," *ibid.*, p. 629; R. Young, "Sedentary Fisheries and the Convention on the Continental Shelf," *Am. Journal*, Vol. 55 (1961), p. 359.

[46] The pearl fisheries around Ceylon extend from six to twenty-one miles from the coast, and they have been recognized by other nations as the exclusive property of the rulers of the island, although in this case prescription would appear to play a distinctive part. See, also, the various treaties regulating access to oyster beds outside the territorial waters of Great Britain, France, and Ireland. See below, p. 500.

states a special status as to the seas adjacent to them and a prior right in the establishment of conservation measures. In view of the conflicts to be expected in the application of conservation measures, Article 9 of the Convention establishes an arbitration procedure with a special arbitral commission of five members.[47]

In addition to the formal Convention adopted by the Conference, a number of separate resolutions were adopted looking to the prevention of conflicts between the coastal state claiming special rights in fishing areas adjacent to territorial waters and other states engaged in fishing on the high seas. Taking into account the conclusions reached at the International Technical Conference on the Conservation of the Living Resources of the Sea held at Rome in 1955, the Conference recommended that the states concerned should cooperate in establishing the necessary conservation regime through the medium of organizations covering particular areas of the high seas or species of living marine resources. Another resolution requested states to prescribe methods for the capture and killing of marine life, especially of whales and seals, which would spare them suffering as far as possible. A separate resolution called upon states fishing in areas adjacent to territorial seas to take into account, when conservation measures should become necessary, the possible dependence of the coastal state upon the fishery concerned. Another resolution called upon the General Assembly to arrange for a study of the juridical regime of historic waters, which had not been included in the agenda of the Conference.[48]

The doctrine of "hot pursuit." Legally distinct from the extension of national jurisdiction out upon the high seas is the old and well-established doctrine of "hot pursuit," in accordance with which a vessel which has committed an offense within territorial waters may be forthwith pursued upon the high seas and there captured. The reason for the rule appears to be that pursuit under such circumstances is, as Hall expresses it, "a continuation of an act of jurisdiction which has been begun or which but for the accident of immediate escape would have been begun within the territory itself and that it is necessary to permit it in order to enable the territorial jurisdiction to be efficiently exercised." [49] In the case of The Ship *North* v. The King,[50] the Supreme Court of Canada quoted with approval the above statement by Hall and condemned a vessel which had been fishing within three miles of the coast of British Columbia and which had been subsequently pursued and apprehended

---

[47] For the text of the Convention, see *Am. Journal*, Vol. 52 (1958), p. 851. For comment, see A. H. Dean, "The Geneva Conference on the Law of the Sea," *ibid.*, p. 607.

[48] For the texts of the resolutions, see *ibid.*, p. 865.

[49] *International Law*, § 80. See also Jessup, *op. cit.*, pp. 106 ff., and compare Art. 21, Harvard Research, *Draft Convention on Territorial Waters*, and Comment.

[50] 37 Canada Sup. Ct. Reports, p. 385. Hudson, *Cases*, p. 643.

on the high seas. In the case of the *I'm Alone,* a Canadian vessel engaged in rum-running appears to have been from ten to fifteen miles from shore when first sighted, and was pursued for two days by a patrol boat which was later joined by a second patrol boat. Upon refusal of the *I'm Alone* to heave to when overtaken, she was fired upon and sunk on March 22, 1929, being then some 250 miles out on the high seas.[51] The circumstances under which the vessel was fired upon aroused public feeling in Canada and led to the arbitration of the dispute before a mixed commission. The commission was unable to agree upon the point of law whether a pursuit, in order to come within the doctrine of "hot pursuit," must be begun within territorial waters or merely within the "hour's sailing distance" recognized by the treaty of 1924. Damages were, however, awarded for what was recognized as the unlawful sinking of the vessel.[52]

G. BAYS AND GULFS

Thus far the maritime boundary has been considered as following the sinuosities of the coast at a uniform distance from the shore. The delimitation of the boundary becomes more difficult, and in certain places is still a matter of controversy when bays, gulfs, and other indentations in the coastline are met with. That the maritime boundary in such cases should not have been readily determinable was a natural result of complex geographical and economic conditions. The logical application of the rule of the marine league would have left within the territorial jurisdiction of the state all bays and gulfs inside of a line drawn from shore to shore at points six miles apart, since such a line could not be crossed by the maritime boundary without bringing it within less than three miles of the coast on either side. On the other hand, certain bays, considerably wider than six miles at their entrance, were of such a configuration, deep out of all proportion to their width, as to bring them naturally under the control of the state in possession of the territory on both sides of the bay. In consequence a number of states have laid special claim to complete territorial jurisdiction over certain of their bays and gulfs of this character, and it would seem that their claims have obtained legal validity by reason of the long-continued acquiescence of other states. Each case must be judged on its merits, and no general rule can be laid down other than the rule that if the bay exceeds six miles in width a special prescriptive title must be advanced to bring it within the territorial jurisdiction of the state.

Prescriptive rights to territorial bays. The Delaware and Chesapeake Bays, the one ten, the other nine and one-half miles wide at its entrance,

[51] For the facts of the case, see Hackworth, *Digest,* Vol. II, p. 703, where the correspondence between the two governments is given.

[52] For a summary of the arbitral award, see *ibid.,* p. 706; Fenwick, *Cases,* p. 559. For editorial comment upon the case, see W. C. Dennis, "The Sinking of the *I'm Alone,*" *Am. Journal,* Vol. 23 (1929), p. 351.

are by prescriptive right within the exclusive territorial jurisdiction of the United States. In 1793 the Attorney-General rendered an opinion that, in consequence of the proprietorship of the United States of the lands on both sides of the Delaware, the bay was territorial, so that the capture of the British ship *Grange* by a French man-of-war within the waters of the bay was a violation of the neutrality of the United States.[53] A corresponding decision in respect to the Chesapeake Bay was rendered in 1885 by the Court of Commissioners of Alabama Claims, which held that the *Alleganean*,[54] a vessel which had been captured in 1862 within the waters of the Chesapeake Bay by officers of the Confederate navy, was not captured on the "high seas."

Similar claims, legal by prescription, with respect to Conception Bay in Newfoundland were advanced by the British Privy Council in a suit brought in 1877 by the Direct United States Cable Company against the Anglo-American Telegraph Company.[55] In the case of Mortensen v. Peters,[56] the master of a Norwegian vessel was convicted for acts in violation of municipal law committed in Moray Firth outside the three-mile limit. In this instance the bay was seventy-four and one-half miles wide between the designated headlands, but the court had no alternative other than to follow an Act of Parliament assuming territorial sovereignty over the firth. Norway protested against the arrest of its citizens upon the high seas; whereupon the British Foreign Office released the prisoners and interpreted the Act of Parliament as applying only to British subjects.[57] In 1917 the Central American Court of Justice, in a suit brought by El Salvador and Costa Rica against Nicaragua, held that the Gulf of Fonseca must be regarded as "an historic bay possessed of the characteristics of a closed sea" and therefore part of the territories of the three states bordering it.[58] By contrast a United States-British Claims Commission held in 1853, in the case of the schooner *Washington*, that the Bay of Fundy was not a British bay nor a "bay" at all within the meaning of the word as used in the treaties of 1783 and 1818;[59] and in the case of the *Fagernes*,[60] decided in 1927, the British court followed an instruction from the Home Secretary that a collision taking place in the Bristol Channel at a point where the Channel was twenty miles wide was not within British territorial jurisdiction.

[53] See Moore, *Digest*, Vol. I, § 153.
[54] See Moore, *Arbitrations*, Vol. IV, p. 4332.
[55] L. R. 2 App. Cases, p. 394. Moore, *Digest*, Vol. I, p. 740.
[56] 14 Scots L. T. R. 227 (1906). Fenwick, *Cases*, p. 42; Bishop, *Cases*, p. 78; Briggs, *Cases*, p. 52.
[57] See Jessup, *op. cit.*, pp. 430 ff.
[58] Jessup, *op. cit.*, pp. 398 ff. See above, p. 435.
[59] Fenwick, *Cases*, p. 563; Hudson, *Cases*, p. 404.
[60] [1927] Probate 311. Fenwick, *Cases*, p. 569; Hudson, *Cases*, p. 486. In this case, however, the court expressed an opinion contrary to that of the Home Secretary, although deciding the case according to the instruction, which it regarded as conclusive.

North Atlantic Fisheries case. The problem as to what should constitute a bay figured prominently in the North Atlantic Fisheries Arbitration of 1910. Mixed questions of customary law and the interpretation of treaty obligations were presented. By the treaty of 1818 the United States renounced the liberty to fish within "three marine miles of any of the coasts, bays, creeks, or harbours" of Newfoundland, Labrador, and adjoining British coasts not included within the limits earlier specified in the treaty.[61] This provision was interpreted by counsel for the United States as referring to territorial waters within a line measured from low-water mark following all the indentations of the coast. This interpretation was, however, rejected by the arbitration tribunal as not expressing the intention of the governments negotiating the treaty of 1818, at which time there were precedents for considering bays exceeding six miles in width as territorial. The award provided that the line should follow the sinuosities of the coast, except that in the case of bays the three marine miles were to be "measured from a straight line across the body of water at the place where it ceases to have the configuration and characteristics of a bay." [62] Owing to the vagueness of this definition of a bay, a number of bays were specifically provided for, while in the case of others the rule, already adopted by the North Sea Convention of 1882, was put into effect, that the three-mile limit of exclusion should be measured from a straight line drawn from point to point where the bay was ten miles in width.

In the Anglo-Norwegian Fisheries case, decided by the International Court of Justice in 1951, the United Kingdom claimed that a Norwegian decree of 1935 had closed areas off the Norwegian coast which under international law were high seas open to the fishing vessels of all nations. The decree had adopted the method of straight lines which, it was claimed by Great Britain, delimited basins that did not have the character of a bay and included coastal archipelagoes. The Court held that both the method used by Norway in the decree for the delimitation of the zones and the actual base lines that had been fixed were not contrary to international law. "Where a coast is deeply indented and cut into," said the Court ". . . the base line becomes independent of the low-water mark," which can no longer be regarded as the rule requiring the coast line to be followed in all of its sinuosities.[63]

The Zuider Zee is admittedly, by prescriptive right, a Dutch territorial sea; and Holland remains free to attempt to exclude its waters and convert it into land territory.[64] On the other hand the Gulf of California, 103 miles in width and 565 miles in depth is not regarded by the United

[61] Art. I. See *Treaties and Conventions,* Vol. I, p. 631.

[62] For details of the award, see Scott, *Hague Court Reports,* pp. 141 ff.; Fenwick, *Cases,* p. 565; Briggs, *Cases,* pp. 284, 313; Hudson, *Cases,* p. 406.

[63] *I.C.J. Reports,* 1951, p. 116; *Am. Journal,* Vol. 46 (1952), p. 348.

[64] Jessup, *op. cit.,* p. 438.

States as within the territorial waters of Mexico.[65] It is a matter of controversy whether the Gulf of Finland is to be regarded as territorial.[66] The status of Hudson Bay is in like manner a matter of controversy. The Canadian Parliament claimed the bay as territorial in a Fisheries Act of 1904; but the claim has not been generally admitted.[67]

Conventional agreements. In a number of cases states have entered into treaties regulating fishing rights within particular bays. An Anglo-French fishery treaty of 1867 reserved exclusive fishing rights in bays the entrance of which was not more than ten miles in width; and in 1882 a general convention, concluded at The Hague between the six interested powers, adopted the same rule with respect to exclusive fishing rights in the bays along the coasts of the North Sea.[68] A treaty between Spain and Portugal in 1885 fixed upon twelve miles as marking the area of exclusive rights,[69] while a treaty of 1907 between Russia and Japan adopted the rule of reserving rights in certain bays whose depth was three times as great as their width at entrance.[70]

The determination of what constitutes a territorial bay, like the width of the marginal sea, long called for international agreement. As early as 1894 the Institute of International Law proposed a general twelve-mile entrance rule. The Harvard Research Draft Convention on Territorial Waters proposed in 1929 that "The seaward limit of a bay or river-mouth the entrance to which does not exceed ten miles in width is a line drawn across the entrance." Where the entrance exceeds ten miles the line is to be drawn across the bay or river mouth where the width of one or the other first narrows to ten miles. The Hague Codification Conference of 1930 was unable to reach an agreement upon this as upon other aspects of the general problem of territorial waters.[71]

Decisions of the Conference on the Law of the Sea. It was to be expected, therefore, that the Geneva Conference on the Law of the Sea would undertake to reach some conclusions on the subject, and while it did not attempt to enumerate the historic bays of the world, it did clarify the base lines from which the territorial sea might be measured, and the

---

[65] See Hackworth, *Digest*, Vol. I, p. 708.

[66] See Jessup, *op. cit.*, p. 397.

[67] See T. W. Balch, "Is Hudson Bay a Closed or an Open Sea?" *Am. Journal*, Vol. 6 (1912), pp. 409-459; Vol. 7 (1913), pp. 546-565. For general comment on the territoriality of bays, see Sir C. Hurst, "The Territoriality of Bays," *British Year Book*, 1922-1923, p. 42.

[68] Martens, *Nouv. rec. gén.*, Vol. XX, p. 466; 2nd series IX, p. 556.

[69] *Ibid.*, Vol. XIV, p. 77.

[70] *Am. Journal*, Vol. 2 (1908), Supp., p. 274.

[71] The student of constitutional law may compare such cases as that of the ship *Rex*, involving the prosecution by the State of California of persons maintaining a gambling ship anchored in Santa Monica Bay beyond the three-mile limit measured from the shore. The court held the waters of the bay to be territorial waters, with jurisdiction extending three miles beyond a line drawn from headland to headland. See *Am. Journal*, Vol. 34 (1940), p. 143.

area that might be included in bays, outside of which would be the high seas. With the decision of the International Court of Justice in the Fisheries Case before it, the Conference first set forth in Article 4 of the Convention on the Territorial Sea what should be, in general, the geographical circumstances under which base lines might not follow the sinuosities of the coast in fixing the limit of the territorial sea. Using substantially the language of the Fisheries Case Article 4 permits, in cases where the coastline is deeply indented or there is a fringe of islands along the coast, "the method of straight base lines joining appropriate points" to be employed in drawing the base line from which the breadth of the territorial sea is measured. Such base lines must not depart to any appreciable extent from the general direction of the coast, and, while no maximum length was fixed, the general principle constitutes a restriction. An exceptional provision allows a state, such as Norway, in determining base lines to take account of "economic interests peculiar to the region concerned," so as to include in territorial waters fishing grounds sanctioned as exclusive areas by long usage.[72]

Definition of a bay. Having excluded from the category of "bays" the minor indentations following the sinuosities of the coast, the Convention proceeded to define a bay as "a well-marked indentation whose penetration is in such proportion to the width of its mouth as to contain landlocked waters and constitute more than a mere curvature of the coast." A maximum distance of twenty-four miles was fixed as the closing line to be drawn between the low-water marks of the natural entrance to the bay.[73]

H. TERRITORIAL STRAITS

Where the maritime boundary comes into contact with a strait separating the territory of a single state, it is governed by the same principles that control bays and gulfs. In general, if the strait is less than six miles in width its waters are territorial waters subject to the exclusive jurisdiction of the state; although in a number of cases custom has given a prescriptive title to territorial sovereignty over straits greater than six miles in width.[74] The Great Belt of Denmark, being of an average width of ten miles, is part of the territory of Denmark, so that the two parts of the state, east and west of the Belt, form continuous territory. So also the Bosporus and the Dardanelles are territorial waters of Turkey; while the Strait of Kertch, connecting the Sea of Azov with the Black Sea, is Russian. The United States and Canada claim territorial sovereignty, divided by the middle boundary line, over the Strait of

[72] For the text of Art. 4 of the Convention, see *Am. Journal,* Vol. 52 (1958), p. 835. For comment by A. H. Dean, *ibid.,* p. 616.

[73] It should be noted that the provisions of Art. 7 relate only to bays the coasts of which belong to a single state, thus excluding the Gulf of Aqaba.

[74] Compare Art. 8, *Harvard Draft,* and Comment.

Juan de Fuca, which has an average width of fifteen miles. Chile claims territorial jurisdiction over the Straits of Magellan. It should be noted that the question of territorial jurisdiction over straits is closely associated with the more important question of the servitudes upon such waters by which freedom of navigation is secured for the commerce of all nations.[75] Consequently in certain cases, such as those of Long Island Sound and the Strait of Solent, where the strait does not form an international highway, third states have been indifferent to the assertion of territorial claims by the state in possession of the land on both sides.

An acute situation arose in 1946 when two British cruisers were fired upon by Albanian shore batteries while passing through the Straits of Corfu which divide the island of Corfu on the west and Greece and Albania on the east. At points the Straits are less than six miles wide, and at these points both riparian states claimed territorial waters to the middle line, Albania claiming the necessity of prior consent to passage through the Straits. Great Britain, without obtaining authorization, sent warships through the Straits prepared to resist attack. The warships struck mines laid in the Albanian waters, and thereupon Great Britain sued Albania for damage before the International Court of Justice. The Court held that it was in accordance with international custom

that States in time of peace have a right to send their warships through straits used for international navigation between two parts of the high seas without previous authorization of a coastal State, provided that the passage is innocent. . . .

The Court imposed damages against Albania for the initial firing upon the British ships, but not for the losses sustained by the mines, on the ground that the passage in that case was not innocent, but rather there was a violation of Albanian sovereignty.[76]

Status of the Gulf of Aqaba. An equally acute controversy arose in 1954 between Israel and Egypt when the latter, alleging the continuation of a state of war between the two countries, closed to Israeli shipping the Strait of Tiran leading from the Gulf of Aqaba to the Red Sea. The Gulf of Aqaba is located at the northern end of the Red Sea, and both Israel and Jordan have small strips of land bordering on it. Israel claimed that the Gulf should be free and open to all shipping and contested the Egyptian contention that the Armistice of 1949 did not put an end to a state of war.[77]

In its sessions preparatory to the meeting of the Conference on the Law of the Sea, the International Law Commission, following the deci-

[75] See below, p. 469.

[76] See *I.C.J. Reports*, Vol. 4, p. 22; *Am. Journal*, Vol. 44 (1950), p. 1.

[77] See C. B. Selak, Jr., "A Consideration of the Legal Status of the Gulf of Aqaba," *Am. Journal*, Vol. 52 (1958), p. 660.

sion of the International Court in the Corfu case, qualified the general rule of freedom of transit through straits by limiting it to straits normally used for international navigation "in line with the emphasis of the Court upon the geographical situation" of the strait. But the Conference went beyond the Commission's draft, dropping the word "normally" and including access to national waters. Article 16 (4) of the Convention on the Territorial Sea provides:

There shall be no suspension of the innocent passage of foreign ships through straits which are used for international navigation between one part of the high seas and another part of the high seas or the territorial sea of a foreign state.

The rule appears to be applicable to the Israeli-Arab controversy.[78]

[78] For the text, see *Am. Journal,* Vol. 52 (1958), p. 834. For comment, see A. H. Dean, *ibid.,* p. 621.

CHAPTER XX

Restrictions Upon Jurisdiction Over Territory:
Easements and Servitudes

A. SERVITUDES DEFINED

Thus far the jurisdiction of a state over territory has been discussed as if it implied a right of absolute political control, whether over land, water, or air. This is, in fact, the normal situation. Territorial sovereignty or jurisdiction carries with it a presumption of exclusive rights of use and disposal of the object over which sovereignty is exercised. Nevertheless, by exception, the jurisdiction of a state over its territory may be subject to restrictions in favor of other states without encroachment upon the formal sovereignty of the state whose jurisdiction is thus restricted. These restrictions upon territorial jurisdiction have, by the analogy of similar restrictions long known to municipal law, been designated as "servitudes"; and they may be defined as obligations on the part of the state in possession of the territory to permit a certain use to be made of it by or in favor of another state or states. Some of these servitudes are customary, established as a result of long-continued usage; others are conventional, created by express agreement between the parties. The corresponding right on the part of the other state to make such use of the territory of the first state may, for convenience, be designated as an "easement"; [1] but it should be noted that the latter term has not yet found its way into international law. The term "servitude" and the object indicated by it have now obtained recognition in international law; but there is still no general agreement as to the restrictions that may properly be designated as servitudes or as to the

---

[1] The term "easement" is, in municipal jurisprudence, more strictly limited to the special group of servitudes granting rights of way, the use of water, etc. Holland, *Jurisprudence*, 8th ed., p. 196. A broader meaning is, however, attached in common legal use.

legal character of the limitations they impose upon the state subject to them.[2]

Legal nature of servitudes. To what extent do servitudes limit, if at all, the formal sovereignty of the state subject to them? Do the privileges they grant to other states imply a corresponding limitation upon the jurisdiction of the state in the area involved, or are they to be strictly construed so as to impose only those limitations without which the particular privilege could not be enjoyed? In the Northeastern Fisheries Arbitration the United States attempted to set forth the conception of a servitude as carrying with it a right of administrative control on the part of the state in whose favor it existed. But the argument was rejected by the arbitration tribunal as contrary to the modern principle of sovereignty.[3] As a general rule a servitude is an obligation attached to the territory as such, giving rise to a corresponding right *in rem*, so that the transfer of the territory from one state to another must be made subject to the rights of the third state.[4] For the same reason servitudes are generally perpetual obligations. It may be convenient to note the distinction made in municipal jurisprudence between a "real" servitude, which is a burden imposed upon a piece of land not for the benefit of any individual as such, but for the benefit of another adjoining piece of land, and a "personal" servitude, which is a burden imposed upon movable as well as immovable property for the benefit of a particular individual.[5] It would seem that a lease of land, such as the lease of Guantánamo from Cuba by the United States, or the lease of the Canal Zone from Panama,[6] is properly not to be classed as a servitude, since the lessor state loses possession and use of the land by the lease, although it retains formal sovereignty over it.

B. GENERAL SERVITUDES: SERVITUDES UPON RIVERS

The Rhine and the Danube. Until the nineteenth century navigable rivers as highways of commerce were almost without exception subject to the complete territorial jurisdiction of the single state in possession of both banks, or of the two states in possession of the opposite banks. Grotius argued on abstract principles in favor of freedom of navigation for all states on rivers as well as on the high seas.[7] Vattel, however, while

[2] The whole question of servitudes is contentious. See, in general, Reid, *International Servitudes in Law and Practice*, Part I; P. B. Potter, "The Doctrine of Servitudes," *Am. Journal*, Vol. 9 (1915), p. 627; J. B. Scott, ed., *International Servitudes*; Lauterpacht, *Private Law Sources and Analogies of International Law*, pp. 119 ff.; Váli, *Servitudes of International Law*; Oppenheim, 8th ed., §§ 203 ff.

[3] See Award, *sub* Question I. Scott, *Hague Court Reports*, pp. 141, 156. Below, p. 478.

[4] See Oppenheim, *International Law*, Vol. I, § 207.

[5] See Holland, *Jurisprudence*, 8th ed., pp. 194 ff.

[6] See above, p. 434.

[7] *De jure belli ac pacis*. Eng. trans., Bk. II, Chap. II, § XIII. On the special topic see Reid, *op. cit.*, Chap. XIV.

asserting a right of innocent passage for third states upon territorial rivers, designates the right as an "imperfect" one which for "good reasons" might be denied by the riparian owner or owners.[8]. It was not until the Treaty of Paris in 1814, and the Final Act of the Congress of Vienna in 1815, that these theoretical rights of mankind were translated into definite legal rights in respect to particular rivers. The Rhine and the Scheldt had been proclaimed by the Treaty of Paris to be open to navigation from the point at which they became navigable to the sea; and this freedom was confirmed by the Treaty of Vienna and extended to the Main, the Moselle, and the Meuse from the point where each of them became navigable to its mouth.[9] A commission was appointed to act in the name of the riparian states in the execution of the provisions relating to the navigation of the rivers. The articles of this agreement, while apparently opening the rivers designated to the commerce of all nations, were at times narrowly interpreted as conferring common rights of navigation only upon the riparian states. In 1856, following the Crimean War, the Treaty of Paris applied to the Danube the principles laid down by the Congress of Vienna, and a second international commission was created to prepare and administer regulations for the navigation of the river.[10] A new treaty was entered into in 1883, creating the famous Mixed Commission of the Danube, an administrative body of a unique character in that it appeared to possess a degree of international personality, having the power to reach decisions by a majority vote and to impose and enforce penalties for the violation of its regulations.[11] Following the separation of Belgium from Holland in 1831, the Scheldt, which had been internationalized in 1815, became nationalized to the extent of a concession by the Treaty of London of 1839 to Holland to levy tonnage duties upon vessels coming to and leaving Belgian ports. These tolls were, however, abolished in 1863 by means of a treaty between the two states providing for their capitalization at a fixed sum.[12]

---

[8] *Droit de gens,* Eng. trans., Bk. II, §§ 123, 127, 129.

[9] Arts. CVIII-CXVI. See *Br. and For. State Papers,* Vol. II, pp. 7, 52-53; Martens, *Nouv. rec.,* Vol. II, p. 427; Hertslet, *Map of Europe by Treaty,* Vol. I, p. 208. On the general subject of international rivers, see Chamberlain, *The Régime of the International Rivers: Danube and Rhine;* Ogilvie, *International Waterways;* C. Dupuis, "Liberté des voies de communications," *Recueil des Cours,* Vol. 2 (1924-I), pp. 128, 219.

[10] Arts. XV-XVIII. See *Br. and For. State Papers,* Vol. XLVI, pp. 8, 12; Martens, *Nouv. rec. gén.,* Vol. XV, p. 776; Hertslet, *op. cit.,* Vol. II, p. 1250.

[11] *Br. and For. State Papers,* Vol. LXXIV, p. 20; Hertslet, Vol. IV, p. 3104; Sayre, *Experiments in Int. Administration,* Chap. IV. See also Arts. LII, LIII of the Treaty of Berlin of 1878, relating to the navigation of the Danube and to its neutralization in time of war.

[12] *Brit. and For. State Papers,* Vol. LIII, pp. 8, 15. Following the treaty the United States entered into a separate convention with Belgium for the extinguishment of the Scheldt dues. See *Treaties and Conventions,* Vol. I, p. 75, where the text of the Netherlands-Belgium treaty is also given.

North American rivers. Beginning in the second half of the nine-teenth century, rapid progress was made in opening up to the commerce of the world the boundary rivers of North and South America. The controversy over the navigation of the Mississippi began with a demand on the part of the United States in 1792 for a joint right of navigation with Spain, then in possession of both banks at the mouth of the river. The demand was met by the treaty of 1795,[13] the relevant article of which lapsed when the river became nationalized by the subsequent acquisition by the United States of Louisiana and the Floridas.[14] After persistent efforts on the part of the United States, and in return for the concession of special privileges to British subjects in respect to the navigation of Lake Michigan, the navigation of the St. Lawrence was finally opened to the vessels of the United States by the Reciprocity Treaty of 1854.[15] The treaty terminated upon notice given by the United States in 1866, and a new agreement was reached in the Treaty of Washington of 1871, which provided that the river, from the point where it ceased to be the international boundary, should "forever remain free and open for the purposes of commerce to the citizens of the United States." At the same time it was provided that the Yukon, Porcupine, and Stikine rivers in Alaska should be open to the commerce of British subjects.[16] A more recent boundary convention of January 11, 1909, opened up to the joint use of the citizens of both countries all the navigable waters forming part of the boundary between the United States and Canada.[17] The Rio Grande, on becoming a boundary river after the admission of Texas into the Union in 1845, was by customary law open to the vessels of both countries; but a special agreement with Mexico was necessary to permit the United States to obtain access to the Gulf of California through the waters of the lower Colorado River.[18] It should be noted that the nego-tiations preceding the opening of these and other rivers, although at-tended in some cases by an assertion of rights under international law, resulted in the conclusion of definite contractual agreements which avoid

[13] The king of Spain agreed that the navigation of the river "shall be free only to his subjects and the citizens of the United States, unless he should extend this privi-lege to the subjects of other powers by special convention." Art. IV; *Treaties and Conventions*, Vol. II, p. 1640.

[14] It is of interest that the United States had agreed with Great Britain, by Art. VIII of the treaty of 1782-1783, that the Mississippi, "from its source to the ocean, shall forever remain free and open to the subjects of Great Britain and the citizens of the United States." The right thus acknowledged to Great Britain was, however, based upon an inaccurate assumption that the river had its source in British territory, and it accordingly was lost when the mistake was discovered in the subsequent survey of the boundary. See Moore, *Digest*, Vol. I, § 130.

[15] Art. IV. See *Treaties and Conventions*, Vol. I, p. 668.

[16] Art. XXVI. See *Treaties and Conventions*, Vol. I, p. 700.

[17] *Ibid.*, Vol. III, p. 2607. For the problem of the Great Lakes-St. Lawrence Sea-way, see Hackworth, *Digest*, Vol. I, p. 605; Whiteman, *Digest*, Vol. 3, p. 909.

[18] Art. IV, treaty of 1848. See *ibid.*, Vol. I, p. 1107.

mention of general principles and confine the privileges granted to the citizens of the contracting states.[19]

South American and African rivers. The opening of the important South American rivers to international commerce was accomplished upon a more liberal basis. Their geographical location rendered them particularly susceptible to the claim of common rights of navigation for a number of states. In 1852 the Argentine Confederation opened the Paraná and the Uruguay not only to the navigation of the riparian states, but to the merchant vessels of other nations as well. In 1858 Bolivia, being in possession only of the upper waters of the Amazon and La Plata rivers, announced in a treaty with the United States that it was ready to regard them as "highways or channels opened by nature for the commerce of all nations." [20] Brazil resisted for some time the pressure brought to bear upon it, but in 1867 the government by unilateral decree opened the Amazon to the vessels of all nations.[21] Shortly after, in 1869, by unilateral decree Venezuela opened the Orinoco River and its branches to the commerce of all nations, although several restrictions upon international commerce were later imposed.[22] The important African rivers, the Congo and the Niger, were by the Final Act of the Berlin Conference of 1885 opened to the free navigation of "the merchant ships of all nations equally," not only in respect to ships coming from the open sea but in respect to the coasting trade as well, and at the same time the provisions of the treaty were announced as henceforth forming "a part of the international law." [23]

In 1963 seven of the nine riparian states of the Niger River, now independent, met at Niamey, the capital of the Republic of Niger, and adopted a draft convention, with annexed statute, to replace the Treaty of Berlin and the Convention of St. Germain-en-Laye of 1919 as the governing instruments for the regime of the river.[24]

Provisions of the peace treaties of 1919; new international rivers. In the Treaty of Versailles an effort was made to grant to Poland and Czechoslovakia advantages of navigation which would facilitate their access to the ocean.[25] But the servitudes created were not limited to these two states. The Elbe and the Ultava, connecting Prague with the sea, the Oder from the point of its confluence with the Oppa, the Niemen

---

[19] The practice of the United States is summarized by Hyde, *Int. Law*, Vol. I, § 165. Compare R. E. Bacon, "British and American Policy and the Right of Fluvial Navigation," *British Year Book*, Vol. XIII (1932), p. 76.

[20] Art. XXVI. See *Treaties and Conventions*, Vol. I, p. 113.

[21] Moore, *Digest*, Vol. I, § 131.

[22] Moore, *Arbitrations*, Vol. II, p. 1696; *Digest*, Vol. I, § 131.

[23] Preamble; Arts. II, XIII-XXXV. See *Br. and For. State Papers*, Vol. LXXVI, p. 4.

[24] T. O. Elias, "The Berlin Treaty and the River Niger Commission," *Am. Journal*, Vol. 57 (1963), p. 873.

[25] Arts. 331 ff.

from Grodno to the sea, the Danube from Ulm, as well as "all navigable ports of these river systems which naturally provide more than one state with access to the sea," together with lateral canals and channels forming connecting links, were declared to be international, *i.e.* open to the vessels of all nations upon a footing of equality with the vessels of the riparian state. A special concession was made to vessels of the Allied and Associated Powers of the right to enjoy in German ports and on inland navigation routes the same privileges enjoyed by German vessels in respect to the transportation of both goods and passengers. A temporary administration of the new international waterways was provided for, to be followed by the adoption of a general convention which was to be submitted to the League of Nations for approval. Separate international commissions were also created for the administration of the regulations governing the navigation of the designated rivers.[26] Special provisions were adopted enlarging the personnel and powers of the Rhine Central Commission, as well as regulating the hydrotechnical use of the waters of the Rhine and the conditions under which a Rhine-Danube and a Rhine-Meuse navigable waterway might be constructed.

The new Danube Statute of 1921 proclaimed that navigation on the Danube was "unrestricted and open to all flags on a footing of complete equality over the whole navigable course of the river, that is to say, between Ulm and the Black Sea." The existing European Commission of the Danube was continued, its jurisdiction extending over that part of the river known as the "maritime Danube," from Braila to the Black Sea; and a new "International Commission" was created with jurisdiction over the navigable fluvial Danube between Braila and Ulm.[27] Special provision was made for the settlement of disputes between the Commissions and the separate riparian states, with the right of appeal to the Permanent Court of International Justice in certain cases.[28]

The Barcelona Convention. More comprehensive in its provisions was the reciprocal servitude of free navigation created by the General

[26] For the International Commission of the Elbe, see Convention Instituting the Statute of Navigation of the Elbe, February 22, 1922. *Am. Journal,* Vol. 17 (1923), Supp., p. 227. For the International Commission of the Oder, see Hudson, *World Court Reports,* Vol. II, p. 609, where the judgment of the Permanent Court of International Justice in respect to the jurisdiction of the Commission may be found.

[27] For the text of the Statute, see *Am. Journal,* Vol. 17 (1923), p. 13. See, in general, Chamberlain, *op. cit.,* pp. 47 ff.; L. B. Wehle, "International Administration of European Inland Waterways," *Am. Journal,* Vol. 40 (1946), pp. 100, 107; J. Blociszewski, "Le Régime international du Danube," *Recueil des Cours,* Vol. 11 (1926-I), pp. 257-339.

[28] In an Advisory Opinion (B 14) given in 1927, the Permanent Court of International Justice held that the European Commission had not only technical powers to keep the navigation of the Danube open but judicial powers as well, in order to enable it to impose effective sanctions for the enforcement of its decisions. Hudson, *World Court Reports,* Vol. II, p. 140. See, however, in this connection, the agreement of 1933. Hudson, *Int. Legislation,* Vol. VI, p. 364.

Convention and Statute on the Régime of Navigable Waterways of International Concern, signed at Barcelona in 1921, by which the contracting powers agreed mutually to accord "free exercise of navigation" on those parts of navigable waterways under their sovereignty specified in the convention. An additional protocol, signed the same day, provided that, on condition of reciprocity, all their navigable waterways or all their "naturally navigable" waterways might be opened to commerce.

In the treaties following the Second World War the satellite states bordering the Danube agreed individually that "Navigation on the Danube shall be free and open for the nationals, vessels of commerce, and goods of all states, on a footing of equality in regard to port and navigation charges and conditions for merchant shipping. The foregoing shall not apply to traffic between ports of the same state." [29] Nothing was said with respect to the continuance of the functions of the European Commission and the International Commission.

The flow of rivers. It is doubtful whether international law can be said to have recognized any servitude corresponding to that existing in civil and common law in the form of a right to the uninterrupted flow of streams and rivers. Conscious of the possession of the traditional rights of sovereignty, states in possession of the upper waters of a river have not recognized any general obligation to refrain from diverting its waters and thereby denying to the states in possession of the lower waters the benefits of its full flow. Such restrictions as have been recognized have been in every case the result of treaty stipulations. The controversy between the United States and Mexico over the diversion by the former of the upper waters of the Rio Grande for purposes of irrigation was settled in 1906 by the conclusion of a treaty for the equitable distribution of the waters of the river. The United States agreed to deliver to Mexico annually a specified number of cubic feet at a given point on the river, distributing the delivery through the year according to a fixed schedule.

On February 3, 1944, a new treaty was signed guaranteeing delivery by the United States to Mexico of 1,500,000 acre-feet of the waters of the Colorado River from any and all sources. No specifications were entered as to the quality of the water. On the basis of the treaty Mexico developed the once-barren Mexicale Valley into a fertile agricultural area. Then in 1961 the United States began operating irrigation pumps at the Welton-Mohawk reclamation area east of Yuma, Arizona, the effect of which was to raise the saline content of the water to the point where cotton and other crops in the Mexicale area were said to be killed, leading to protest from Mexico and raising the question whether,

---

[29] For the Barcelona Convention, see Hudson, *Int. Legislation,* Vol. I, p. 638; *Am. Journal,* Vol. 15 (1921), Supp., p. 151. For the agreements of 1948, see J. L. Kunz, "The Danube Regime and the Belgrade Conference," *Am. Journal,* Vol. 43 (1949), p. 104; W. L. Griffin, "The Use of Waters of International Drainage Basins under Customary International Law," *Am. Journal,* Vol. 53 (1959), p. 50.

in the absence of specifications as to the quality of the water to be delivered, the United States was violating the obligations of the treaty.[30]

An important convention was concluded between the United States and Great Britain in 1909 regulating the use of the boundary waters between the United States and Canada. It was provided that each state, while retaining jurisdiction over the waters on its side of the line, should grant to parties on the other side of the line, if injured by any interference or diversion of waters, the same rights and legal remedies as if the injury took place on the first side. Moreover, the parties agreed not to obstruct or divert the waters in the future without the approval of an international joint commission established by the convention, a majority of whose members should have power to render a decision.[31]

Special provisions with respect to the diversion of the upper waters of the Rhine were inserted in the Treaty of Versailles of 1919. France was given the right to take water from the Rhine to feed navigation and irrigation canals or for any other purposes, and was to have exclusive right to the power derived from hydrostatic works ("works of regulation") on the river, subject to a fixed payment to Germany in money or

[30] For the text of the treaty, accompanied by an historical survey, see *Documents on Am. Foreign Relations*, Vol. VI, p. 547. For comment, see F. B. Clayton, "United States-Mexican Water Treaty," Dept. of State *Bulletin*, Vol. XII, p. 71. In December, 1961, an agreement was reached which, by modifying the schedule of water deliveries during the winter months, it was hoped would meet the situation. Dept. of State *Bulletin*, January 22, 1962, p. 144; April 16, 1962, p. 650; D. C. Piper, "A Justiciable Controversy concerning Water Rights," *Am. Journal*, Vol. 56 (1962), p. 1019.

In the Lake Lanoux case between France and Spain, involving the diversion by France of water flowing from the lake so as to serve hydraulic purposes and its subsequent diversion, by tunnel, back into the river flowing into Spain, the arbitration tribunal held that the consent of Spain was not necessary to the diversion because there was no diminution of the final flow into Spain. See J. G. Laylin and R. L. Bianchi, "The Role of Adjudication in International River Disputes: The Lake Lanoux Case," *Am. Journal*, Vol. 53 (1959), p. 30. For problems relating to the Columbia, Indus, and Nile rivers, see *Proceedings*, Am. Society of Int. Law, 1960, pp. 120 ff.

[31] *Treaties and Conventions*, Vol. III, p. 2607. For the application of this treaty in the controversy between Canada and the United States over the level of the Great Lakes, see below, p. 467.

The student of United States constitutional law may compare profitably the decision of the Supreme Court in the case of Kansas v. Colorado, 206 U.S. 46 (1907), in which the court held, in a suit brought by Kansas to restrain Colorado from diverting the waters of the Arkansas River for irrigation purposes, that the diversion was not sufficient in amount to injure perceptibly property lying along the lower valley. For a summary of the case, see Scott, *Judicial Settlement of Controversies between States of the American Union*, pp. 431 ff. In the case of Wyoming v. Colorado, 259 U.S. 419 (1922), dealing with the diversion by Colorado of the upper waters of the Laramie River, the court enjoined the defendant from diverting more than a fixed number of acre-feet of water per year. Fenwick, *Cases*, p. 589. Compare also the decisions in Connecticut v. Massachusetts, 282 U.S. 660 (1931); New Jersey v. New York, 283 U.S. 336 (1931); and Arizona v. California, 283 U.S. 423 (1931). Fenwick, *Cases*, p. 600.

water-power. The same rights were to be accorded on demand to Switzerland in respect to that portion of the river along its boundary.[32]

In connection with the transfer by Italy to France of the plateau of Mont Cenis and of the Tenda-Briga district, France is required to supply to Italy adequate quantities of water for hydroelectric purposes as well as of electricity. In connection with the transfer by Italy to Yugoslavia of a part of Gorizia, the obligation was imposed upon the two parties to supply water mutually from adjacent water systems.

In 1937 the Permanent Court of International Justice, in the case of the Diversion of Water from the Meuse, between Belgium and the Netherlands, interpreted a treaty of 1863 between the two states so as to accomplish what the court believed to be the original purpose of the treaty, an equitable diversion of the waters of the river through certain canals in Belgium with least disturbance to other uses of the river.[33]

The Lauca River controversy.   The controversy between Bolivia and Chile over the diversion of the waters of the Lauca River follows the lines of numerous cases in public as well as in private law. The river rises on the eastern slope of the Andes and flows from Chile into Bolivia. In 1962 Chile opened a canal at the upper waters of the river, diverting some of the water westward into arid Chilean land for irrigation purposes. Bolivia brought its case before the Council of the Organization of American States on April 17, 1962, alleging aggression on the part of Chile on the ground that the diversion was made without its consent, and that it was having injurious effects upon the established humanitarian uses of the river in Bolivian territory. Chile contested on the ground that it had announced its intention in 1939 to use part of the upper waters for irrigation purposes in the valley of Azapa, and that Bolivia had consistently refused to cooperate in arriving at a settlement. Bolivia on its part claimed that at no time had Chile made the formal announcement called for by the Montevideo Declaration and that its consent had never been given to the diversion.[34]

C. BAYS AND GULFS, LAKES AND LANDLOCKED SEAS

Territorial bays do not appear to be subject to any general servitude in favor of third states. But in so far as passage through them may be a

[32] Art. 358. In connection with the constructive development of the law, it may be observed that the Institute of International Law, at its meeting at Madrid in 1911, adopted a draft code covering the regulation of international streams and rivers from the point of view of available water-power for industrial and agricultural purposes. *Resolutions*, p. 168. On the general subject, see Smith, *The Economic Uses of International Rivers*.

[33] Publication of the Court, Series A/B, No. 70. For comment, see M. O. Hudson, *Am. Journal*, Vol. 31 (1937), p. 14; Vol. 32 (1938), Part I.

[34] For the Bolivian position, see *La Desviacion del Rio Lauca*, Ministerio de Relaciones y Culto (1962). The Chilean position is presented in *La Cuestion del Rio Lauca*, Ministerio de Relaciones Exteriores (1963).

condition of access to ports of the territorial state, foreign vessels enjoy the same privilege, or perhaps limited right, to their use which they enjoy in respect to admission to the port itself. While no question of a right of passage on the part of third states has arisen in connection with inland lakes, such as Lake Michigan,[35] and landlocked seas, such as the Sea of Azov, which are wholly surrounded by the territory of a single state, if such a lake or sea should form the boundary between two or more states, as in the case of Lake Constance, the territorial waters of each of the riparian states are subject to a servitude permitting innocent passage on the part of the other riparian states. The coasting trade, from port to port of one of the riparian states, is, however, generally reserved to the vessels of the respective states. Four of the five Great Lakes, *i.e.* Superior, Huron, Erie, and Ontario, although not absolutely landlocked, being connected with the sea by artificial waterways, are regarded in international law as such and are subject to the exclusive territorial jurisdiction of the two states whose boundary runs through them. Each state enjoys a right of use of the lakes in their entirety for purposes of navigation, while fishing rights on either side of the water boundary are reserved to the respective countries. In the case of United States v. Rodgers,[36] the Supreme Court held that a crime committed upon an American vessel in the Detroit River connecting Lakes Huron and Erie was committed upon the "high seas" within the scope of that term as used in Revised Statutes § 5346, defining the places within which federal criminal jurisdiction should be operative. There was, however, no suggestion in the decision that the waters in question were not subject to the territorial jurisdiction of Great Britain and the United States exclusively.

With respect to the right of riparian states to the natural level of a lake or inland sea, the principle appears to be the same as that governing the flow of rivers, namely that no one of the riparian states may utilize the water of the lake so as to lower its level substantially to the injury of the other states. In 1925 the Supreme Court of the United States issued an injunction against the Sanitary District of Chicago, restricting the diversion of the waters of Lake Michigan and requiring the construction of a sanitary waste disposal system which would permit the enforcement of a sharper restriction at a later date.[37] In a series of separate suits brought by Wisconsin, Michigan, and other states against Illinois,[38] decided in 1929, the Supreme Court of the United States held that the complainants were entitled to an injunction to stop the diversion of

[35] By special agreement between the United States and Great Britain, Art. I of the convention of January 11, 1909, a right of navigation on Lake Michigan was granted to Canadian inhabitants and their vessels. *Treaties and Conventions,* Vol. III, p. 2607.

[36] 750 U.S. 249 (1893). Hudson, *Cases,* p. 419; Moore, *Digest,* Vol. I, p. 670.

[37] Sanitary District of Chicago v. United States, 266 U.S. 405 (1925).

[38] 278 U.S. 367 (1929). Fenwick, *Cases,* p. 595.

water caused by the drainage canal which had the effect of lowering their levels on the Great Lakes, except for the small part necessary to keep up navigation in the Chicago River.[39]

A special problem is presented when a lake or sea is not wholly land-locked, being connected with the open sea by a narrow navigable strait. Where, as in the case of the Sea of Azov, the body of water is wholly surrounded by the territory of a single state, it remains in the class of inland lakes. But where it is surrounded by the territory of more than one state, practice would appear to indicate that the lake or sea is not only open to the commerce of the states bordering its shores, but is open to the commerce of other nations as well. At the same time, it apparently loses its territorial character. When Russia obtained a foothold upon the shores of the Black Sea in 1774, not only was the former exclusive juris-diction of Turkey shared by Russia but the territorial waters of both powers were, by a series of treaties, opened to third states for purposes of commerce and trade.[40] By 1878, when Rumania and Bulgaria also became riparian states, the Black Sea came to be regarded as part of the "open sea." [41] In spite of occasional efforts on the part of the riparian powers to close it to foreign warships in time of war, the Baltic has re-mained an open sea.

The marginal sea. There is a well-established servitude imposed upon the marginal sea along the coast of maritime states, by which the ships of every nation enjoy a right of innocent passage through such ter-ritorial waters. The enjoyment of this right may be conditioned upon the observance of special regulations laid down by the littoral state for the protection of navigation and the execution of municipal laws relating to customs, quarantine, and other local interests. There was a difference of opinion among writers as to whether the marginal sea was formerly open to the innocent passage of foreign warships.[42] The Geneva Conven-tion on the Territorial Sea, in recognizing the right of innocent passage through the territorial sea by the "ships of all states," whether for the purpose of traversing without entering or for the purpose of entering

[39] In keeping with the principles of equity relief the decree was framed so as to allow the Sanitary District a reasonable time within which to provide another means of disposing of the sewage. For the point of view of the interests of Canada in the diversion, see H. A. Smith, "The Chicago Diversion," *British Year Book,* Vol. X (1929), p. 144.

[40] The limitation imposed by the Great Powers upon Russia in 1856, forbidding the admission of vessels of war into the Black Sea, is to be classed as a special rather than as a general negative servitude. The terms of the treaty were general, but they were in reality directed principally against Russia. See Treaty of Paris, Art. XI. Hertslet, *op. cit.,* Vol. II, p. 1250.

[41] For the changes in the status of the Black Sea after the Treaty of Paris of 1856, see Oppenheim, *International Law,* Vol. I, § 181.

[42] Oppenheim, *International Law,* Vol. I, § 188. Art. 14, *Harvard Draft, Terri-torial Waters,* lays down the right of innocent passage through the marginal sea, but limits it to commercial vessels. *Am. Journal,* Vol. 24 (1930), Supp., p. 239.

or leaving, includes a special article applicable to warships, providing that they must comply with the regulations of the coastal state or else be required to leave.[43]

D. STRAITS AND CANALS

Straits connecting territorial bays and seas with the open sea are governed by the same rule as the territorial bay itself. There is, therefore, no definite servitude imposed upon the Strait of Kertch, connecting the Sea of Azov with the Black Sea, nor upon the Strait of Juan de Fuca connecting Puget Sound with the ocean, although in the latter case the boundary between the United States and Canada runs through the strait.[44] The only problems of any considerable difficulty are those that have arisen in connection with straits connecting one open sea with another. By immemorial custom, sanctioned by a succession of treaties, the powers of Europe acquiesced in the collection by Denmark of tolls levied upon vessels passing through the Danish Sound and the two other narrow passages connecting the North Sea with the Baltic. In 1853 the United States announced its purpose to press to a conclusion its earlier protest against the collection of these Sound Dues, with the result that in 1857 they were abolished by Denmark in consideration of the payment by the parties interested of a total sum equivalent to the capitalization of the cost to Denmark of maintaining lights and buoys for the safe navigation of the waters in question.[45] Perhaps the best precedent illustrating the easement of innocent passage enjoyed by all states through straits connecting open seas is to be seen in the declaration of Chile and the Argentine Republic in 1881, following the protest of the United States in 1879 that it would not tolerate exclusive claims by any nation whatsoever to the Straits of Magellan and would hold responsible any government that undertook to lay any impost or check on United States commerce through the straits. The treaty of 1881 between the two states provides that "Magellan's Straits are neutralized forever, and free navigation is guaranteed to the flags of all nations." [46]

The Dardanelles and the Bosporus. The status of the Dardanelles and the Bosporus has been regulated by a series of international conventions

[43] Arts. 14-23.

[44] On the general subject, see Baxter, *The Law of International Waterways, with Particular Regard to Interoceanic Canals.*

[45] Moore, *Digest,* Vol. I, § 134.

[46] *Ibid., loc. cit.* The use of the term "neutralized" in this connection apparently indicates no more than an intention on the part of the contracting powers to warn third states against the commission of hostilities within the said waters. Warships are allowed free passage upon implied acceptance of the condition that no act of hostility be performed. The phrase "neutralized and internationalized" better describes the situation. In the case of the *Bangor* (1916) Probate 181, the British court held, *obiter,* that Chile might regard the waters as strictly territorial in time of war, but that a capture within such waters was valid as between the belligerents. Fenwick, *Cases,* p. 573; Hudson, *Cases,* p. 402.

having principally in view the political object of maintaining the integrity of Turkey but incidentally the economic object of opening the straits to the merchant marine of all nations.[47] These bodies of water were the arena of sharp diplomatic conflicts during the nineteenth century, Russia seeking to control them in the alleged interest of self-defense and commercial freedom and Great Britain, supported by other Great Powers, seeking to check the threatened advance of Russia toward Constantinople and the dominance by that country of the Balkan states and the eastern Mediterranean. The successive agreements concluded by the Great Powers must be read in connection with the status imposed at the same time upon the Black Sea.[48]

International conventions. As early as 1809 Great Britain, in concluding with Turkey the Treaty of the Dardanelles, recognized the "ancient rule of the Ottoman Empire" excluding foreign ships of war from the straits. More formal recognition of the same rule was accorded by the signatory powers of the Convention of London in 1841. At the close of the Crimean War the Treaty of Paris in 1856 revised the convention of 1841,[49] expressly confirming the right of the sultan to exclude warships from the straits, but permitting the passage of light cruisers put at the service of the foreign embassies or engaged in protecting the freedom of navigation of the Danube. In consequence of the repudiation by Russia in 1870 of the binding force of the Treaty of Paris in respect to the exclusion of Russian warships from the Black Sea, the Treaty of London in 1871, while continuing the general exclusion of warships from the straits, gave power to the sultan to make an exception in time of peace in favor of the vessels of war of friendly and allied powers, if necessary to secure the execution of the terms of the treaty of 1856.

The Straits Conventions of 1923 and 1936. Accompanying the treaty of peace between the Allied and Associated Powers and Turkey, a separate Straits Convention was signed on July 24, 1923, at Lausanne, in which the contracting parties proclaimed "the principle of freedom of transit and of navigation by sea and by air" through the Straits. The new convention abandoned the principle of excluding warships in favor of the principle of admitting all ships alike on condition of observing the restrictions laid down in the convention. The convention created along both shores of the Dardanelles and the Bosporus "demilitarized zones" within which no fortifications or military establishments could be maintained. For the execution of the provisions of the convention a special international Straits Commission was constituted at Constantinople to

---

[47] The historical evolution of the status of the straits is given in Phillipson and Buxton, *The Question of the Bosporus and Dardanelles*, Part II; H. N. Howard, "Problem of the Turkish Straits," Dept. of State *Bulletin*, Vol. XV, p. 790.

[48] See p. 468, note 40.

[49] Art. 10 and the annexed Straits Convention.

exercise its functions under the auspices of the League of Nations and render an annual report to that body.[50]

The Lausanne Convention was followed by the Montreux Convention of 1936, in accordance with which the supervision and control of the international commission were set aside in favor of exclusive Turkish sovereignty, and Turkey was given the right to remilitarize the Straits.[51] "The principle of freedom of transit and navigation by sea in the Straits" was recognized and affirmed. Elaborate provisions were laid down with respect to the passage of merchant vessels and warships both in time of peace and in time of war. Turkey was given the right, when it considered itself "threatened with imminence of war," to require that merchant vessels enter the Straits by day, and that their transit must be by a route indicated by the Turkish authorities. In time of peace the maximum tonnage of foreign naval forces, except Black Sea powers, in transit must not exceed 15,000 tons. In time of war, belligerent warships must not pass through the Straits except when acting in accordance with the collective security provisions of the Covenant of the League of Nations, or of a mutual assistance treaty, to which Turkey was a party, concluded in accordance with the Covenant. If Turkey should be a belligerent, or consider itself threatened with imminent danger of war, the passage of warships through the Straits was to be left "entirely to the discretion of the Turkish Government." The functions of the International Commission established by the Lausanne Convention were transferred to the Turkish Government.[52]

Straits of Corfu. On October 22, 1946, two British destroyers were struck by mines while in innocent passage through the Straits of Corfu. Great Britain thereupon undertook to send mine sweepers into the Straits, in accordance with a decision of the International Mine Sweeping Commission. Albania protested against the "premeditated violation of its sovereignty." After sharp diplomatic correspondence between the two countries the case was referred to the Security Council of the United Nations, which held by a majority vote, on March 25, 1947, that Albania must have known of the presence of the mines, implying responsibility. The Soviet Union, by its veto, made the vote of the majority ineffective. Great Britain then proposed that the case be referred to the International Court of Justice. Albania, after agreeing to appear before the Court, raised a question of jurisdiction on the ground of the unilateral applica-

[50] For the text of the treaty see 28 *League of Nations Treaty Series,* p. 115; *Am. Journal,* Vol. 18 (1924), Supp., p. 53; Hudson, *Int. Legislation,* Vol. II, p. 1028. For comment upon the convention see E. Turlington, "The Settlement of Lausanne," *Am. Journal,* Vol. 18 (1924), pp. 696, 702.

[51] For the text of the convention, see *Am. Journal,* Vol. 31 (1937), Supp., p. 1. For the text of the Protocol on remilitarization, *ibid.,* p. 16.

[52] For comment upon the Montreux Convention, see H. N. Howard, Dept. of State *Bulletin,* Vol. XV, p. 435; C. G. Fenwick, *Am. Journal,* Vol. 30 (1936), p. 701.

tion of Great Britain, which was, however, rejected by the Court. On the merits of the case the Court held that the Peoples Republic of Albania was responsible under international law for the explosions and for the damage and loss of human life that resulted therefrom. Compensation was subsequently assessed and paid by Albania. In respect, however, to the acts of the British Navy in sending the mine sweepers into the Straits, the Court held that the United Kingdom had violated the sovereignty of Albania, although no further satisfaction was due other than the declaration of the Court to that effect.[53]

Interoceanic canals. Canals, being artificial waterways, built at the cost of the owner, are not subject to the servitude of innocent use as are natural straits. Those which are purely internal in character, such as the Chesapeake and Ohio Canal, the Erie Canal, and the numerous canals of Holland, Belgium, and France, connecting bodies of water one or both of which are not open to the commerce of other nations than the state through whose territory they are built, raise no issues of international law. They are in the class of rivers, such as the Mississippi, whose navigation is the exclusive right of the territorial sovereign. When, however, the canal connects two open seas, the state in possession of it may decide, for reasons of its own, financial or otherwise, to open the canal to the commerce of other nations upon payment of fixed tolls and subject to such other conditions as the state may find it necessary to prescribe. The Kiel, or Emperor William, Canal, connecting the Baltic with the North Sea, having been constructed primarily for strategic purposes, was nevertheless thrown open by Germany from 1896 to 1914 to the commerce of other nations. But this was no more than a voluntary concession on the part of Germany, which retained the right to withdraw the canal from international use at any time. In like manner the Corinth Canal, connecting the Gulf of Corinth with the Gulf of Aegina, has been opened by Greece to general commerce; but no obligation has been assumed to maintain it open or to administer it with reference to the interests of any other nation than the owner.

The Suez Canal. On the other hand, the two most important interoceanic canals, the Suez and Panama canals, have been subjected by the states in control of them to a sort of self-imposed servitude, in consequence of which the states of the world at large enjoy a privilege, closely approximating to a legal right, of innocent use, subject to definite conditions laid down in a formal international document. The fortunes of the Suez Canal have been varied. Originally built in 1869 under a concession from the khedive of Egypt obtained by a French stock com-

---

[53] *I.C.J. Reports* (1949), p. 4; *Am. Journal*, Vol. 44 (1950), p. 1; Fenwick, *Cases*, pp. 310, 575; Briggs, *Cases*, p. 291.

pany under the direction of Ferdinand de Lesseps, it came partly under the control of Great Britain when that country purchased, in 1875, the shares of the khedive and later came all but nominally under its control when Great Britain assumed a veiled protectorate over Egypt after 1883. Great Britain then proposed, in consequence of difficulties arising during the revolt of Arabi Pasha, that the canal be neutralized; but it was not until October 29, 1888, that the Convention of Constantinople was finally signed by Great Britain, France, Germany, Italy, Austria-Hungary, Russia, Spain, Holland, and Turkey.[54] The convention represented a definite agreement on the part of the signatory powers that the canal should be open in time of peace as well as of war to the merchantmen and men-of-war of all nations; and, further, that in order to ensure such use, especially on the part of men-of-war, the canal should be under all circumstances, even if Turkey were at war, immune from the commission of hostilities, being treated strictly as if neutral territory. No permanent fortifications were to be erected; but the territorial sovereign, the sultan or the khedive, could take such police measures as might be necessary to defend Egypt and to maintain public order.

In 1936, in the Treaty of Alliance between Great Britain and Egypt by which the independence of the latter state was formally acknowledged, it was agreed that until such time as the parties might agree that the Egyptian army was in a position to protect the liberty of the navigation of the canal, Great Britain might station forces in the vicinity of the canal.[55] Following the evacuation of British troops from the Suez Canal zone by agreement with Egypt in 1954, Egypt proclaimed the nationalization of the Suez Canal Company and placed the administration of the Canal in the hands of an Egyptian operating authority. Consultations were held in London regarding the control of the Canal and the compensation to be paid to the stockholders. But in the meantime Israeli troops invaded the Egyptian territory in violation of the armistice of 1949 on the ground that Israeli vessels had been denied the use of the Canal because of the state of war between the two countries. Great Britain and France intervened with their armed forces in order to safeguard the use of the Canal. The United States, opposing the use of force, pressed the case before the Security Council, but to no effect. The General Assembly then established a United Nations Emergency Force aiming at the cessation of hostilities, and it called upon Great Britain, France, and Israel to withdraw their troops. Egypt sank ships in the canal, closing it to navigation.

[54] Br. and For. State Papers, Vol. LXXIX, p. 18; Am. Journal, Vol. 3 (1909), Supp., p. 123.
[55] See Am. Journal, Vol. 31 (1937), Supp., pp. 77, 88, 92. For comment, see J. Y. Brinton, "The Transition Period in Egypt," ibid., Vol. 34 (1940), p. 208.

On April 24, 1957, the Egyptian Government delivered a formal communication to the Secretary-General of the United Nations, stating:

It remains the unaltered policy and firm purpose of the Government of Egypt to respect the terms and the spirit of the Constantinople Convention of 1888 and the rights and obligations arising therefrom . . .

To afford and maintain free and uninterrupted navigation for all nations, within the limits of and in accordance with the provisions of the Constantinople Convention of 1888.

Later items of the Declaration deal with tolls, operation and management, the Canal Code, and compensation and claims.[56]

The Panama Canal. The international status of the Panama Canal is governed by the provisions of the Hay-Pauncefote Treaty between the United States and Great Britain, signed November 18, 1901.[57] This treaty supersedes the earlier Clayton-Bulwer Treaty of 1850,[58] by which the same parties agreed that neither should ever obtain for itself any exclusive control over the proposed canal by erecting fortifications near it or by occupying or assuming dominion over the adjoining country. The canal, when built, was to be protected by the contracting parties, who guaranteed its "neutrality," so that it might "forever be open and free." Other states were to be invited to join "a work of such general interest and importance," which would be maintained "for the benefit of mankind, on equal terms to all." It was not, however, found feasible to build a canal under the conditions of joint control thus contemplated. The new treaty of 1901 was therefore entered into, permitting the construction, as well as the regulation and management of the canal, under the single auspices of the United States, without, however, impairing the "general principle of neutralization" established in the convention of 1850. Certain definite rules were thereupon adopted "as the basis of the neutralization of such ship canal," corresponding substantially to those embodied in the Suez Convention of 1888. These rules contemplate two distinct objects: (1) the opening of the canal to the common use of the vessels of commerce and of war of all nations on terms of equality and (2) the protection of the canal against the commission of acts of hostility by belligerents in time of war or its use by belligerents for

[56] For the text of the Declaration, see *Am. Journal*, Vol. 51 (1957), p. 673. For comment on the case, see Q. Wright, "Intervention, 1956," *ibid.*, p. 257; T. T. F. Huang, "Some International and Legal Aspects of the Suez Canal Question," *ibid.*, p. 277. For related documents, including Heads of Agreement between the Government of the United Arab Republic and the Suez Stockholders, *ibid.*, Vol. 54 (1960), pp. 493-518.

[57] *Treaties and Conventions*, Vol. I, p. 782. On the general subject of the Panama Canal, see Padelford, *The Panama Canal in Peace and War;* also *Am. Journal*, Vol. 34 (1940), pp. 416, 601.

[58] *Ibid.*, Vol. I, p. 659.

strategic purposes. In respect to both these objects difficulties have arisen as to the obligations assumed by the United States and Great Britain and indirectly by other states.[59]

The question of tolls. The controversy between the United States and Great Britain over the right of the former to exempt its merchant vessels from payment of tolls in passing through the canal is primarily a question relating to interpretation of treaty obligations and will be examined later in that connection.[60] The only point in the controversy relative to the international status of the canal is the question whether third states not parties to the treaty have acquired any rights in the case. In this connection it is important to note that the agreement on the part of the United States and Great Britain, in the earlier Clayton-Bulwer Treaty, to invite all other states to enter into stipulations similar to those entered into between the immediate contracting parties finds no place in the later Hay-Pauncefote Treaty. Nevertheless, it would appear that the "general principle" of neutralization embodied in both treaties implies the recognition of a self-imposed obligation on the part of the United States not to discriminate against vessels of any nations in respect to the conditions or charges of traffic. This self-imposed obligation or servitude may with some justice be said to have obtained by lapse of time a degree of prescriptive legal obligation. Acting in good faith under it, third states have entered upon commercial undertakings which have contributed, by payment of tolls, to the cost of maintenance of the canal and which have thus created in some degree a consideration for an implied contract.[61]

The status of the Panama Canal in time of war. Following the construction of the Panama Canal the question of its status in time of war was widely discussed. In accordance with the general principle of neutralization, it was agreed that the canal should be open to vessels of the belligerents in time of war, upon the condition of their observance of the regulations attached to its use. What, however, if the United States should be a belligerent? In such event it was not to be expected that an artificial waterway, so vulnerable in its construction, should be open to enemy warships. Under such circumstances, did the United States have the right to fortify the canal? The question was answered by the

---

[59] It should be observed that the subsequent acquisition by the United States from the Republic of Panama of a "grant in perpetuity" of the use, occupation, and control of the Canal Zone, equivalent to practical sovereignty, did not in any way modify the provisions of the treaty, since it was expressly provided (Art. IV) that no change of the territorial sovereignty of the Canal Zone should affect the general principle of neutralization.

[60] See below, p. 536.

[61] With the passage of time a question which was of importance a generation ago has now become of historical interest only.

United States in the affirmative, and fortifications were erected in 1912.[62]

During both World Wars belligerent warships passed freely through the canal during the years in which the United States was neutral. Few German warships, however, were able to make use of it, for reasons apart from the neutralized character of the canal. During the period in which the United States was a belligerent the canal and the adjacent waters were closed to enemy ships.[63]

By the treaty of 1936 between the United States and Panama,[64] amending and supplementing the treaty of 1903,[65] the United States, as lessor of the canal zone, transferred to Panama "jurisdiction" over a corridor connecting the city of Colon on the Atlantic with other territory of Panama. The corridor transferred was made subject to the negative servitude that no other construction was to take place within the corridor than that relating to the construction of a highway and to the installation of electric power, telephone, and telegraph lines. On the other hand a positive servitude was imposed by virtue of which the United States was to enjoy at all times "the right of unimpeded transit across the said corridor at any point, and of travel along the corridor . . ." An easement in favor of the United States was thus attached to the easement granted to Panama; or considered from the point of view of the obligations assumed, a servitude was imposed upon a servitude.[66]

A later treaty of 1955 modified the treaty of 1936 by increasing the annuity to be paid for the lease of the zone, modifying the dual wage system, and permitting Panama to tax Panamanian workers in the Canal Zone.[67]

The Kiel Canal under the treaty of 1919. At the Peace Conference at Paris in 1919 the powers took advantage of the opportunity to impose a definite international status upon the Kiel Canal, the administration of which had hitherto been conducted by Germany as a purely domestic concern. The Treaty of Versailles provided that "the Kiel Canal and its approaches shall be maintained free and open to the vessels of com-

[62] For a discussion of the question of the legal right and practical expediency of fortifying the Panama Canal, see *Am. Journal,* Vol. 3 (1909), pp. 354, 885; Vol. 4 (1910), p. 314; Vol. 5 (1911), pp. 298, 615, 620. Hackworth, *Digest,* Vol. II, pp. 791 ff. So far as Panama was concerned, the right to fortify had been granted by the treaty of 1903.

[63] Hackworth, *Digest,* Vol. II, p. 787.

[64] For the text of the treaty, see *Am. Journal,* Vol. 34 (1940), Supp., p. 139. Ratifications of the treaty were exchanged on July 27, 1939.

[65] See above, p. 434.

[66] For comment upon the treaty of 1936, see N. J. Padelford, *Am. Journal,* Vol. 34 (1940), pp. 416, 601; Hackworth, *Digest,* Vol. II, pp. 798-810.

[67] For comment upon the treaty, see Fenwick, "The Treaty of 1955 between the United States and Panama," *Am. Journal,* Vol. 49 (1955), p. 543. Negotiations for a revision of the treaty situation were begun in 1964 following the clash in the Canal Zone, January 9-10.

merce and of war of all nations at peace with Germany on terms of entire equality." [68] Further provision was made that the nationals, property, and vessels of all powers should be treated in respect to charges and facilities of traffic upon a footing of equality with the nationals, property, and vessels of Germany. Only such tolls might be levied as were intended to cover in an equitable manner the cost of maintaining the canal in a navigable condition. Germany was left responsible for maintenance of satisfactory conditions of navigation; but provision was made that in the event of a violation, or dispute as to the interpretation, of the articles of the treaty, the plaintiff state might make complaint, first to a local authority set up by Germany at Kiel and then, if necessary, to the court instituted for that purpose by the League of Nations. In the case of the *Wimbledon*,[69] the Permanent Court of International Justice, at the instance of a suit brought against Germany by France, Great Britain, Italy, and Japan, decided on April 17, 1923, that the action of the German Government in excluding, in pursuance of its neutrality regulations, a British steamer laden with munitions for Poland from the use of the Kiel Canal was in violation of the obligations assumed under Article 380 of the Treaty of Versailles. The argument made by Germany that such passage was inconsistent with its obligations of neutrality was overruled by citation of the precedents of the Suez and Panama canals.

E. LAND TERRITORY NOT SUBJECT TO GENERAL SERVITUDES

Such are the principal general servitudes, based in part upon international custom and in part upon specific conventions. Whether the principle of restricting territorial sovereignty in favor of the general needs of the international community can logically and advantageously be carried still further is a problem of constructive, rather than of positive, international law. It may be noted, however, that there is no recognition of any general principle of servitudes upon land territory. When, for example, the United States was seeking in 1901-1903 to obtain possession of a part of the Isthmus of Panama for the building of a canal, there was no legal obligation on the part of the state of Colombia to yield to the interests of the world at large in permitting the development, whether by the United States or by any group of nations, of the artificial highway which Colombia itself appeared unwilling or unable to build. The community of nations had no recognized right of eminent domain similar to that possessed by the individual state when taking over the property of individuals for public use.

---

[68] Art. 380.
[69] Publications of the Court, Series A, No. 1. Hudson, *World Court Reports*, Vol. I, p. 163; Fenwick, *Cases*, p. 577; Hudson, *Cases*, p. 474. For comment, see M. O. Hudson, *Am. Journal*, Vol. 18 (1926), p. 10.

F. SPECIAL SERVITUDES

Special servitudes, generally designated merely as servitudes, are such as are imposed upon a state in favor of another particular state or states. While they are of less intrinsic importance than general servitudes, nevertheless they merit attention because they permit a contrast between the actual restrictions to which the territorial sovereignty of states has been subjected from time to time and the theoretical doctrines of its absolute character. Moreover, they suggest in certain cases the possibilities of constructive international legislation through the conversion of a special servitude in favor of a single state into a general servitude in favor of the community of nations as a whole.

Special servitudes were common in the seventeenth and eighteenth centuries, being a heritage from the feudal relations of the Middle Ages; but with the growth of a more rigid conception of territorial sovereignty they became much less frequent. For the most part they are created by definite treaty stipulations. This is always the case when the servitude is of a negative character, consisting in an obligation on the part of the state to refrain from exercising its territorial jurisdiction in specified ways. When, however, the servitude is a positive one, consisting in an obligation to permit another state, known as the "dominant" state, to perform certain acts upon the territory of the "servient" state subject to the servitude, it is possible that, as in the case of general servitudes, the obligation may be created by prescription. More commonly, however, it rests upon treaty agreement. As was observed in connection with general servitudes, international usage is not clear as to the precise legal character of special servitudes, authorities differing upon such points as the extent to which they are inherent in the territory, the effect upon them of transfers of territory from one state to another, and their permanence in the event of war between the parties.[70]

Positive servitudes: the North Atlantic Coast Fisheries case. Positive servitudes have been created for a wide variety of objects. Some are economic in character, involving, for example, a right on the part of the dominant state to fish in the territorial waters of the servient state or a right to build or operate a railway through the servient state. The obligations imposed upon British territorial waters by the treaty of 1783,[71] recognizing the right of the people of the United States to fish upon the Grand Banks and in the Gulf of St. Lawrence and granting the liberty to fish on the coast of Newfoundland and on other coasts, bays, and creeks of British territorial waters in America, proved to be the occasion of a long controversy. The parties disputed whether the intervening War of 1812 extinguished the obligations imposed by the treaty

[70] See, in particular, A. D. McNair, *British Year Book,* 1925, pp. 111-127.
[71] Art. III. See *Treaties and Conventions,* Vol. I, p. 580.

of 1783.[72] A new treaty was entered into in 1818, followed by fresh disputes and later treaties of 1854, 1871, and 1885.[73] The points at issue were finally decided by arbitration in 1910, the tribunal rendering an award in favor of Great Britain on the principal points.[74] The tribunal discussed at length the legal character of servitudes, with the result that not only was the contention of the United States rejected, that a servitude existed in the particular case, but the whole doctrine of servitudes was dismissed as being inconsistent with modern political theory, owing to the "essential sovereignty and independence" required by the constitution of the modern state.[75]

Railways. The grant by a state to a foreign power of the right to build and operate a railway through its territories is conspicuously illustrated in the case of China. By successive agreements in 1896 and 1898 the Peking Government granted to Russia and to Germany the right to build and operate railways in Manchuria and Shantung respectively.[76] Japan succeeded to the rights of Russia in 1905 and took possession of Germany's rights in 1914. By agreements reached in 1915 and 1918, China granted to Japan Germany's rights of control over the Shantung Railway running from Tsing-tao to Tsinan-fu. This servitude, however, being a serious encroachment upon the territorial independence of China as well as a continuous interference with her administration of the province, was renounced by Japan in the treaty signed by the two states on February 4, 1922, at the close of the Washington Conference on the Limitation of Armaments.[77]

Rights of way. Distinct from corporeal property rights are the incorporeal rights of way which have been occasionally granted for the transit of persons or of goods across the land territory of the particular state. In 1871 the United States granted to Great Britain freedom of transit, in the form of an exemption from payment of customs dues, for goods arriving at certain United States ports and destined for British

[72] Moore, *Digest*, Vol. I, § 163.

[73] *Treaties and Conventions*, Vol. I, pp. 631, 668, 700, 729.

[74] Scott, *Hague Court Reports*, pp. 141-225; Wilson, *Hague Arbitration Cases*, p. 134; *Am. Journal*, Vol. 4 (1910), p. 948. Fenwick, *Cases*, p. 583; Hudson, *Cases*, p. 468; Briggs, *Cases*, pp. 284, 313.

[75] The decision was reached on the assumption that a servitude by its nature involved a grant of sovereignty over the territory to the extent required by the servitude. For the argument that this assumption was based upon theory rather than upon practical conditions, see Oppenheim, *International Law*, Vol. I, § 203. The student may compare the Northeastern Fisheries case with the similar right to fish on the banks of Newfoundland granted in favor of France by the Treaty of Utrecht of 1713. The original right was confirmed and modified by subsequent treaties but continued to remain a source of controversy until finally abandoned by France in 1904. See Fauchille, *Droit international*, No. 342.

[76] Willoughby, *Foreign Rights and Interests in China*, p. 371.

[77] Willoughby, *China at the Conference*, pp. 391, 395. *Am. Journal*, Vol. 16 (1922), Supp., p. 84. For other instances, see Reid, *op. cit.*, Chap. XI.

North American possessions.[78] In 1903 Panama by treaty gave to the
United States a monopoly in perpetuity for the construction of a canal
across its territory.[79] Again in 1914 Nicaragua granted to the United
States for the sum of $3,000,000 the exclusive proprietary rights neces-
sary for the construction of an interoceanic canal across Nicaraguan territory.[80] When the opportunity presented itself to the Allied and Associated Powers at Paris in 1919 to introduce into international law a
principle, long approved in the abstract and now of urgent necessity
in the concrete, the obligation was imposed upon Germany and upon
Austria to grant freedom of transit through their respective territories,
by rail as well as by water, to the persons, goods, vessels, and wagons
coming from or going to the territory of any of the Allied and Associated
Powers. Special provision was made for the exemption of such traffic
from payment of customs duties, from undue charges on transport, or
from any discrimination in the charges and conditions of transport.[81] In
1921 a Conference on Freedom of Communications and Transit met at
Barcelona and opened for signature the Convention on Freedom of
Transit, with its annexed Statute which provides for measures to facilitate "traffic in transit" by the removal of obstructions and discriminations.[82]

By treaty between the United States and Panama a right of way, described as a corridor, is granted to Panama across the Canal Zone,
subject, as above noted, to a right of way on the part of the United
States.

Negative servitudes. Negative servitudes appear to be confined to
political and military objectives. The obligation not to fortify a particular
town was frequently a condition of peace treaties in the seventeenth
and eighteenth centuries. France was forbidden by the Treaty of
Utrecht in 1713 to rebuild the fortifications of Dunkirk. The Treaty of
Paris in 1814 required that Antwerp should never become a military
port. The Treaty of London in 1831 exacted the demolishing of several
Belgian fortresses. In 1856 the Treaty of Paris required Russia to demolish fortresses upon the shores of the Black Sea and not to maintain
a navy in those waters; but this servitude, forced upon Russia against
its will, was thrown off when two of the coercing parties, France and
Prussia, were at war in 1870. The convention of London in 1867 stipulated that the fortifications of the city of Luxemburg should be demolished. The same treaty provided that, for the protection of the Swiss

---

[78] *Treaties and Conventions,* Vol. I, p. 700. See Hyde, *Int. Law,* Vol. I, § 195.

[79] *Treaties and Conventions,* Vol. II, p. 1349. See above, p. 477.

[80] *Treaties and Conventions,* Vol. III, p. 2740. *Am. Journal,* Vol. 10 (1916), Supp.,
p. 258.

[81] Arts. 321-326.

[82] See below, pp. 587 ff.

canton of Basle, the Alsatian town of Hüningen should never be fortified; and this servitude passed with the territory when Alsace was transferred to Germany in 1871.[83] By the Treaty of Portsmouth in 1905 Russia and Japan obligated themselves not to construct upon their respective possessions on the island of Sakhalin or the adjacent islands any fortifications or other similar military works.[84]

Of exceptional importance were the negative servitudes imposed upon Germany by the Treaty of Versailles in 1919. By the terms of the treaty "all fortified works, fortresses and field works, situated in German territory to the west of a line drawn fifty kilometers to the east of the Rhine, shall be disarmed and dismantled." The construction of new fortifications of whatever kind was forbidden in the above zone. When on March 7, 1936, Germany proceeded to militarize the zone, the justification given was the violation by France of the Locarno Pact which had reaffirmed the demilitarization provisions of the Treaty of Versailles. The alleged violation of the Locarno Pact was the conclusion of the Franco-Soviet Mutual Assistance Pact of May 2, 1936.[85] Nothing was said by Germany of the violation of the provisions of the Treaty of Versailles.

An interesting servitude of a nonmilitary character was that imposed by the treaty between Italy and the Holy See in 1929, by which the Holy See agreed that the Piazza di San Pedro, although forming part of the Vatican City, should be policed by the Italian authorities, but that the jurisdiction of these authorities should not extend beyond the foot of the steps leading to the Basilica. Several other reciprocal servitudes were imposed, one of which requires that the Italian Government must not permit the construction of new buildings overlooking the Vatican, and another of which makes the treasures of art and science of the Vatican accessible to scholars and visitors.[86]

Demilitarization provisions of the treaties of 1947. The treaties following the Second World War contain numerous provisions looking to total or partial demilitarization, whether of the territory of certain countries as a whole or of specified areas. The Aaland Islands are to continue demilitarized, as under the agreement of 1922 between Sweden and Finland.[87] The provisions of the convention of 1923 with respect to the northern boundary of Greece are supplemented by a servitude imposed

[83] For details of these and other lesser servitudes, see Vali, *op. cit.*

[84] Art. IX. For the text of the treaty, see *Am. Journal,* Vol. 1 (1907), Supp., p. 17.

[85] *Survey of International Affairs,* 1936, p. 252, "The German Military Reoccupation of the Rhineland and the Subsequent Negotiations between the Locarno Powers," where the subject is exhaustively treated. The justification offered was obviously no more than a pretense to cover a predetermined act.

[86] For the text of the treaty, see *Am. Journal,* Vol. 23 (1929), Supp., p. 187. See above, p. 133.

[87] Treaty with Finland, Art. 5. See R. Erich, "La question des zones démilitarizées," *Recueil des Cours,* Vol. 26 (1929-I), pp. 591, 632.

upon Bulgaria not to construct "permanent fortifications where weapons capable of firing into Greek territory can be emplaced.[88] A similar servitude is imposed upon Italy with respect to the frontier with France and the frontier with Yugoslavia; and at the same time Italy must destroy existing fortifications within a distance of twenty kilometers.[89] The island of Pelagosa, ceded by Italy to Yugoslavia, is to remain demilitarized. The Dodecanese Islands, ceded to Greece, are to be demilitarized, as are other Italian islands in the Adriatic and Mediterranean Seas. Italy is also prohibited from establishing naval bases along the Adriatic coast in the vicinity of the Free Territory of Trieste.[90] Trieste itself is completely demilitarized and declared neutral.[91] The eastern part of the Apulian Peninsula, Sardinia, and Sicily are also subject to various forms of demilitarization.[92]

More comprehensive than these local restrictions are the general provisions in the treaties with the satellite states in accordance with which, "The maintenance of land and air armaments and fortifications shall be closely restricted to meeting tasks of an internal character and the local defense of frontiers." [93]

[88] Treaty with Bulgaria, Art. 12.
[89] Treaty with Italy, Arts. 47 (4), 48 (4).
[90] Ibid., Arts. 11 (2), 14 (2), 48 (5), 49.
[91] Ibid., Annex VI, Art. 3.
[92] Ibid., Arts. 48 (6), p. 50.
[93] Treaty with Hungary, Art. 12; with Bulgaria, Art. 9; with Rumania, Art. 11; with Finland, Art. 13.

CHAPTER **XXI**

Jurisdiction Over the Air Above
National Territory

A. LAW OF AERIAL NAVIGATION: GENERAL PRINCIPLES

At the beginning of the twentieth century states were presented with the problem of regulating the navigation of the air spaces above their territory by balloons and more particularly by the newly invented airplanes. There being no customary law on the subject, jurists led the way in an attempt to formulate the principles of aerial jurisdiction by resorting to the analogies of the jurisdiction of states over land and territorial waters. But in so doing the widest diversity of views was manifested.[1] In the first place there was the older view, based upon a pre-airship tradition, of the complete freedom of the air spaces, analogous to the freedom of the high seas. Secondly, there was the more practical view that while a state might claim territorial rights in a lower zone of air, some thousand feet above the ground, it could not claim sovereignty in the higher air spaces which, like the high seas beyond the marginal sea, remained open to free navigation.[2] Again, certain jurists argued that the entire air space above the territory of a state should be regarded as under its territorial jurisdiction but subject to a servitude of innocent passage in favor of other states. Lastly, it was asserted that states had complete sovereignty over the air spaces above their territory without any restrictions, following the principle of the common law, *cujus est solum ejus est usque ad coelum.*[3] Failing various efforts of scientific associations, notably the Institute of

[1] For a summary of the opposing views of publicists, see Hazeltine, *Law of the Air,* Lect. I; Fauchille, *Droit international public,* Vol. I, Nos. 531 ff.; Garner, *Recent Developments in International Law,* Lect. IV.

[2] For an exposition of this view, see Fauchille, *loc. cit.,* and Garner, *loc. cit.* See, also, on the general subject, Spaight, *Aircraft in Peace and the Law;* Zollman, *Law of the Air;* Le Roy, *Air Law;* Hyde, *Int. Law,* Vol. I, §§ 188-191C.

[3] See Blackstone, *Commentaries,* Bk. II, p. 18. Fauchille contests the alleged derivation of the principle from the Roman Law. *Op. cit., loc. cit.*

International Law at its meetings in 1910 and 1911 [4] and the International Law Association at its meeting in 1913,[5] to secure the adoption of a constructive program of legislation, it remained for the World War of 1914 to settle the question of jurisdiction in terms of the extreme claims of sovereignty.

Effect of the First World War. Upon the outbreak of the war the belligerent states immediately asserted full jurisdiction over the air above their territory as a measure of national defense. At the same time adjacent neutral states, solicitous not to be wanting in fulfillment of the obligations of neutrality, refused to belligerent airships a right of passage across their territories, thus making the use of the air space conform to that of the land beneath it rather than to that of the marginal sea or of international straits.[6] The Dutch and Swiss governments were particularly alert to prevent the passage of Allied and German planes across their territories. By the close of the war the jurisdiction of a state over the air space above its territory appeared to be settled in favor of the assertion of complete sovereignty, but the question whether innocent passage for the ships of other states should be regarded as a right or conceded by treaty as a privilege still awaited decision.[7]

The Aerial Navigation Convention of 1919. On October 13, 1919, the Aerial Navigation or International Flying Convention was signed at Paris, bringing the whole subject under international treaty law.[8] The convention, however, dealt only with times of peace, and did not restrict in any way the right of belligerents or of neutrals to assume full control over their air spaces for purposes of national defense in time of war. The primary question of jurisdiction was settled by the recognition that "every Power has complete and exclusive sovereignty over the air space above its territory," including adjacent territorial waters. But at the same time each state undertook in time of peace to accord freedom of innocent passage above its territory and territorial waters to the aircraft of the contracting states without distinction of nationality, provided the conditions established in the convention were observed. Special provisions were laid down with respect to the courses to be followed when

[4] *Resolutions*, p. 171, and report of Fauchille on p. 243.

[5] *Proceedings*, 28th Conf., pp. 222-245.

[6] A suggestive contrast is presented between the use of the Panama Canal by belligerent men-of-war and the denial of the use of the air spaces over the canal to belligerent airships. The Proclamation of the President relative to the neutrality of the Canal Zone, September 5, 1939, prescribed that "No belligerent aircraft shall be navigated to, within, or through the air spaces above the territory or waters of the Canal Zone." *Am. Journal*, Vol. 34 (1940), Supp., p. 28.

[7] See M. O. Hudson, "Aviation and International Law," *Am. Journal*, Vol. 24 (1930), p. 238.

[8] For the text of the convention, see *L. of N. Treaty Series*, Vol. XI, p. 173; Hudson, *Int. Legislation*, Vol. I, p. 359; *Am. Journal*, Vol. 17 (1923), Supp., p. 195. The convention was signed by the United States, but not ratified. See Hackworth, *Digest*, Vol. IV, p. 363.

such freedom of passage was resorted to. The nationality of aircraft was to be determined according to their ownership and registration, registration being restricted to nationals of the state or to incorporated national companies. In order to secure observance of the conditions of navigation, only aircraft of the contracting states were to be permitted freedom of innocent passage; and, as an additional means of protecting the safety of aerial navigation, a technical minimum standard of competence of officers and crew was provided for in an annex, further requirements being left to the individual states.[9]

Commission for Air Navigation. The convention further made provision for the creation of a permanent International Commission for Air Navigation (C.I.N.A.), organized so as to secure preponderant voting power to the five Great Powers as against all contracting states, and placed under the direction of the League of Nations. The commission was empowered to receive and act upon proposals for amending the convention or any of its annexes, and it was called upon to collect information with respect to air navigation and publish official maps and prepare opinions. Disagreements relating to the interpretation of the convention were to be referred to the Permanent Court of International Justice, but the commission itself was given authority to decide by a majority vote disputes concerning the technical regulations.[10] A special difficulty foreseen by the convention was the prevention of customs fraud. Provision was made that aircraft must depart only from and alight only in specially designated "customs aërodromes"; frontiers must be crossed at points indicated on aeronautical maps; and there was to be examination of the aircraft's papers after the manner of the examination of a merchant vessel's papers in port.[11] In 1929 a conference of signatory states, called by the International Commission, met at Warsaw and adopted resolutions embodying a draft protocol of amendments to the convention,[12] the chief object of which was to modify certain clauses and thus remove

[9] Arts. 11-14. An earlier draft of the convention, elaborated during the Paris Conference of 1919, applied to airships the rules governing jurisdiction over merchant vessels in territorial waters. Provision was made (Art. 23) that "the legal relations entered into between persons on board an airship in flight are governed by the law of the nationality of the aircraft," an exception being made in the case of offenses committed against a national of the territorial sovereign when the offense was followed by a landing upon the territory. See A. K. Kuhn, "International Aerial Navigation and the Peace Conference," *Am. Journal*, Vol. 14 (1920), p. 369.

[10] Art. 37. Attention may be called to the unique method of representation of the member states in the new union as originally provided. The five leading powers were to have each two representatives; other states, including the British self-governing dominions, each one representative. Votes were to be cast by states, but the votes of the five leading powers were overweighted, so as to give them as a whole a majority of one over the total number of votes of the other contracting parties. See Art. 34.

[11] The right of adherence to the convention was confined to members of the League of Nations and other states admitted by a three-fourths majority vote.

[12] For the text, see Hudson, *op. cit.*, Vol. I, p. 384.

the objections of certain states which had not as yet ratified or adhered to the convention.[13]

The Havana Convention of 1928. In 1928 the Sixth International Conference of American States incorporated in its Final Act a Convention on Commercial Aviation,[14] which repeated the principle of the Paris Convention of 1919 in respect to sovereignty over the air space and the mutual agreement "to accord freedom of innocent passage" and in other respects followed closely the lines of the more general convention. Without setting up a commission corresponding to the International Commission, it created obligations to cooperate in the distribution of meteorological information, in the establishment of a uniform system of signals, and in the promotion of uniform laws and regulations governing aerial navigation.

Neither the provisions of the Paris Convention of 1919 nor their administration proved equal to the necessities of the situation. The commercial service of airplanes had increased enormously, and serious abuses developed in respect to the observance of the conditions of navigation which the International Air Commission was unable to correct. There was lack of uniformity in the regulations of the service and failure to impose adequate standards of airworthiness of planes and competency of pilots. The failure of the United States to support the convention limited the authority of the commission, so that its activities were confined chiefly to Europe. A general reform was in order, if the political conditions of the time had permitted it. The chief obstacles lay in the sharp political rivalries of the nations and in the desire of the leading powers to have a free hand in the manufacture of new planes and in the development of new techniques of navigation. War came before agreement could be reached.[15]

The Chicago Civil Aviation Conference. The war was still in progress when the International Civil Aviation Conference met at Chicago on

[13] The failure of the United States to ratify the Convention of 1919 must be ascribed partly to political motives. It may be noted, however, that the Air Commerce Act of 1926 (44 *U.S. Statutes at Large* 572) provided for reciprocity of treatment (Sec. 6) by permitting the Secretary of Commerce to authorize aircraft registered under the laws of a foreign nation to fly over the United States if the foreign nation granted a similar privilege to United States aircraft. See, however, on this point, B. Lee, "Freedom of the Air in the United States," *Am. Journal,* Vol. 25 (1931), p. 238.

[14] For the text see *Int. Conferences of American States,* 1889-1928, p. 385; Hudson, *Int. Legislation,* Vol. IV, p. 2354; *Am. Journal,* Vol. 22 (1928), Supp., p. 124.

[15] See Colegrove, *International Control of Aviation;* Le Roy, *Air Law;* Puffer, *Air Transportation;* Lissitzyn, *International Air Transport and National Policy;* D. Goedhuis, "Civil Aviation after the War," *Am. Journal,* Vol. 36 (1942), p. 596; M. O. Hudson, "Aviation and International Law," *ibid.,* Vol. 24 (1930), p. 228.

For the work of the Comité International Technique d'Experts Juridiques Aériens, CITEJA, engaged in drafting projects of conventions on matters of private air law, see S. Latchford, "Pending Projects of the International Technical Committee of Aerial Legal Experts," *Am. Journal,* Vol. 40 (1946), p. 280.

November 1, 1944, with the representatives of fifty-four nations present. Sharp conflicts of interest developed between the leading powers, and it proved impossible to reach agreement upon all of the points at issue.[16] The Conference closed with the signature of a convention and three separate agreements, as well as a number of resolutions and recommendations.[17] The Convention on International Civil Aviation, described as the "constitution for the postwar global air world," is a comprehensive agreement covering all phases of civil aviation, leaving open, however, the regulation of scheduled air services covered by separate agreements.[18] State aircraft are specifically excluded from the terms of the convention. Article 1 proclaims that "the contracting States recognize that every State has complete and exclusive sovereignty over the air space above its territory." Aircraft not engaged in scheduled international air services have the right to make flights into or in transit nonstop across the territory of contracting states and to make stops for nontraffic purposes, without the necessity of obtaining prior permission and subject to the right of the state flown over to require landing. The right of each state to monopolize cabotage is recognized. Aircraft have the nationality of the state in which they are registered, and no aircraft may be validly registered in more than one state. Each state may designate the route to be followed within its territory by any international air service and the airports which any such service may use.

The Convention creates the International Civil Aviation Organization (ICAO), which is made up of an Assembly, a Council and such other bodies as may be necessary. The objectives of the organization are to develop the principles and techniques of international air navigation and to foster the development of international air transport. The Assembly is composed of representatives of all of the contracting states, which vote upon the basis of equality. The Council is a permanent body, responsible to the Assembly and composed of twenty-one states elected by the Assembly. In addition, there is an Air Navigation Commission composed of twelve members appointed by the Council.[19]

[16] See J. P. van Zandt, "The Chicago Civil Aviation Conference," *Foreign Policy Reports*, February 15, 1945; S. Latchford, Dept. of State *Bulletin*, Vol. XII, p. 411.

[17] For the text of the convention and the separate agreements, see *Final Act and Related Documents of the International Civil Aviation Conference*, Dept. of State Publication, No. 2282.

[18] The Convention came into effect on April 4, 1947. The number of separate agreements concluded by the United States is large. For a description of them, see J. D. Walstrom, "Bilateral Air-Transport Agreements Concluded by the United States," Dept. of State *Bulletin*, Vol. 15, p. 1126.

[19] In view of the fact that a considerable time was expected to elapse before the convention could be ratified, a separate Interim Agreement on International Civil Aviation was adopted, the provisions of which followed closely those set forth in the main convention. This agreement, setting up the Provisional International Civil Aviation Organization (PICAO), came into effect June 7, 1945.

The Air Services Transit Agreement.   In addition to the main convention, separate transit and transport agreements were signed. The International Air Services Transit Agreement, known as the "Two-Freedoms
Document," provides that in respect of scheduled international air services each contracting state grants to the other contracting states (1) the
privilege to fly across its territory without landing and (2) the privilege
to land for nontraffic purposes.[20] A contracting state has, however, the
right to require that airlines of another contracting state stopping for
nontraffic purposes must offer reasonable commercial service at the
points at which such stops are made. Just and reasonable charges may
be made for the use of airports and other facilities. A provision of great
practical importance gives to each contracting state the right to call upon
the Council of the ICAO to examine a situation which is causing injustice
or hardship to it; and the Council may make suitable recommendations
and, if necessary, call upon the Assembly to support them by suspension of the offending member from its rights and privileges under the
agreement.[21]

The Air Transport Agreement.   The International Air Transport Agreement, described as the "Five Freedoms Document," provides for the
reciprocal grant by each contracting state not only of the two freedoms
of the Transit Agreement but (3) the privilege to put down passengers,
mail, and cargo taken on in the territory of the state whose nationality
the aircraft possesses; (4) the privilege to take on passengers, mail, and
cargo destined to such territory; and (5) the privilege to take on passengers, mail, and cargo destined for the territory of any other contracting state, and the privilege to put down passengers, mail, and cargo
coming from any such territory. The grant of the above privileges is,
however, limited to "through services on a route constituting a reasonably
direct line out from and back to the homeland of the State whose
nationality the aircraft possesses." [22]

Right of innocent passage in time of distress.   While the principle of
the "complete and exclusive sovereignty" of the separate states over the
air space above their territories has been repeatedly affirmed, it would
seem that even in the absence of conventional agreements the aircraft
of one state have a right of innocent passage over the territory of other
states when under stress of weather conditions they are obliged to

---

[20] For the text of the "Two Freedoms Document," see *Am. Journal,* Vol. 39 (1945),
Supp., p. 135.

[21] These are far-reaching provisions and they show the recognition on the part of
the contracting states of the need of discipline in the observance of the spirit as well
as the letter of the agreement.

[22] For the text of the "Five Freedoms Document," see *Am. Journal,* Vol. 39
(1945), Supp., p. 139. For an analysis, Cheng, *The Law of International Air Transport* (1962).

deviate from their course.[23] On August 9, 1946, a United States airplane, while in regular flight from Vienna to Udine, encountered bad weather and while attempting to find its bearings was attacked by Yugoslav fighters and forced to crash land. The United States protested, inquiring whether the usual courtesies, including the right of innocent passage, could not be expected from the Yugoslav Government under such conditions.[24] Before an answer was received, an unarmed American transport plane was shot down by Yugoslav aircraft on August 19, resulting in the death of the pilot and crew. In answer to a second protest the Government of Yugoslavia expressed regrets that the pilots lost their lives when the plane "crashed after disobeying signals to land." Marshal Tito then stated that planes would not be fired upon in the future, but that they should be invited to land, and if they refused to do so their identity should be taken so that "any necessary steps could be undertaken through appropriate channels." The United States claimed indemnification for the loss of lives and property.[25]

Other cases occurred in which planes of the United States lost their way and were forced to land, as on Hungarian territory in 1951, or were fired upon when on routine patrol, as by Czechoslovakian military aircraft in 1953, or were attacked over neutral territory, as by Soviet aircraft in 1952; but no judicial settlement could be reached because the International Court had no jurisdiction to entertain the claims.[26] In 1955 an Israeli plane was shot down over Bulgarian territory, causing the death of the crew and fifty-one passengers; but again the Court found itself without jurisdiction.[27] In 1958 and again in 1960 and 1964, when United States planes missed their course and were shot down over East Germany, the United States called for the return of the pilots, but made no formal claim against the Soviet Union.

Case of the U-2. More serious is the violation of the air space of a particular state when the airplane is in the service of a state and is deliberately seeking such information about military bases and installations as may be obtainable by long-range photography. In 1960, the U-2, an American plane flying at high altitude over the Soviet Union, was shot down by Soviet fire and the pilot arrested on criminal charges. The Soviet Government condemned the flight before the Security Council

[23] It is of interest to note that in the relations of the States of the United States the courts have broken with Blackstone's maxim of a property right *usque ad coelum*. See cases cited in P. C. Jessup, "International Law and Totalitarian War," *Am. Journal*, Vol. 35 (1941), p. 329. Compare, however, the observations of Hyde, *Int. Law*, Vol. I, §§ 188, 191 C.

[24] Dept. of State *Bulletin*, Vol. XV, p. 415.

[25] *Ibid.*, pp. 501, 505.

[26] *U.N. Yearbooks*, 1951, 1952, 1953.

[27] L. Gross, "The Jurisprudence of the World Court: Thirty-eighth Year (1959)," *Am. Journal*, Vol. 57 (1963), p. 758.

as an act of "aggression," and the United States defended it as a necessary measure of self-defense against a surprise attack by atomic missiles. The violation of Soviet territory was obvious, whether justified or not under the circumstances.[28]

Equally in violation of the sovereignty of the air spaces of Cuba were the regular flights of United States observation planes seeking to discover possible evasions by Cuba of the agreement of the United States with the Soviet Union, in October, 1962, that the missile bases in Cuba would be demolished and that inspectors from the United Nations would supervise the execution of the agreement. Query, in view of the refusal of the Cuban Government to permit inspection by a United Nations commission, was the right of self-defense an adequate justification on the part of the United States of the violation of Cuban air spaces? Query, would photographs taken by satellites flying through the outer spaces be any less a technical violation of the sovereignty of the state beneath?

B. LAW OF OUTER SPACE

The launching by the Soviet Union of the artificial satellite Sputnik in October, 1957, gave a realistic forecast of the uses of outer space. The old rule that the territory of the state extended *usque ad coelum,* above and beyond any possible use of the air space, was now antiquated. Here was a man-made instrument circling over any and all countries, beyond the reach of any of them except possibly through electronic control by the state launching the satellite. Was it violating the sovereignty of the states over which it passed? Or was it, like a vessel on the high seas, outside the jurisdiction of states other than the one whose flag it flew, the only difference being that if it should descend upon the territory of another state than the one that started it there might be a claim for damages? [29]

In 1959 the United Nations Committee on the Peaceful Uses of Outer Space reported that a comprehensive code on the subject was not practical or desirable at the present stage of knowledge and development; but that, with the peaceful uses of outer space in mind, the outer space should be freely available for exploration and use, as appeared to be accepted during the discussions of the preceding International Geophysical Year. That the possible uses of satellites for peaceful purposes were far-reaching no one doubted: observations of the weather and the development of means to control it; television relays; the study and application of solar energy; the impact of micrometeorites; the forms

[28] See *U.N. Yearbook,* 1960, p. 40; Q. Wright, "Legal Aspects of the U-2 Incident," *Am. Journal,* Vol. 54 (1960), p. 836; O. Lissitzyn, "Some Legal Implications of the U-2 and RB-47 Incidents," *ibid.,* Vol. 56 (1962), p. 135.

[29] The literature of the subject has become extensive. See, in particular, McDougal, Laswell, and Vlasic, *Law and Public Order in Space;* Haley, *Space Law and Government.*

of cosmic radiation; and manned flights to the moon. A new world had opened up, but as yet it was too soon to bring it within rigid rules of law.[30] Three years later, however, lengthy discussions took place in the Assembly on a variety of proposals put before the Outer Space Committee, with lists of general principles governing the exploration and use of outer space, the United States, among others, submitting its own declaration of principles.[31]

Beyond peaceful uses there lay the wide field of military uses both for offense and for defense. Here it was clear that there was the most urgent need for legal control and yet the least hope of obtaining agreement upon it. Already ballistic missiles had penetrated outer space, but here the area of the flight was limited. An outright prohibition of the use of satellites for atomic warfare was urgently needed, but it could only be made effective with the closest degree of inspection of satellite bases.[32]

C. THE LAW OF RADIO COMMUNICATION

The invention of the means of transmitting messages by wireless telegraphy gave rise at the beginning of the century to the same discussion of general principles of jurisdiction created by the invention of airships, but the question of sovereignty was not raised in so acute a form as in the case of air navigation. At the meeting of the Institute of International Law at Ghent in 1906 the principle was laid down that "the air is free. States have over it, in time of peace and in time of war, only the rights necessary for their preservation." [33] The legal problem of jurisdiction was, however, subordinate to the practical problems on the one hand of devising ways and means by which some measure of control could be exercised when the emergency called for it, and on the other hand of framing administrative regulations to prevent in normal times the conflict of one system of transmission with another and to secure the social benefits of the new method of communication. This last object was the one first provided for.

Conventions of 1906 and 1912. In 1906 an International Wireless Telegraph Convention was signed at Berlin.[34] In this convention the signatory powers provided for the reciprocal exchange of wireless telegrams by their coastal stations and stations on shipboard without distinc-

[30] Report of July 14, 1959 (A-4141). See also J. C. Cooper, *et al.*, *Proceedings*, Am. Soc. Int. Law, 1956, pp. 85-115; M. S. McDougal and L. Lipson, "Perspectives for a Law of Outer Space," *Am. Journal*, Vol. 52 (1958), p. 407.

[31] *U.N. Yearbook*, 1962, pp. 37 ff.; *Am. Journal*, Vol. 58 (1964), p. 472; J. Simsarian, "Outer Space Cooperation in the United Nations," *Am. Journal*, Vol. 57 (1963), p. 854.

[32] See R. D. Crane, "Soviet Attitude toward International Space Law," *Am. Journal*, Vol. 56 (1962), p. 685.

[33] Scott, *Resolutions of the Institute of International Law*, p. 164.

[34] *Treaties and Conventions*, Vol. III, p. 2889. The United States signed the treaty, but ratifications were not exchanged until 1912.

tion of the particular wireless system adopted by such stations. Coast stations were obligated to give absolute priority to calls of distress from ships, to answer such calls with similar priority, and to take such other action as might be required. Provision was made for the connection of the coastal stations with the telegraph system by special wires so as to facilitate the forwarding of messages. A supplementary agreement made provision for a similar reciprocal exchange between ships at sea which possessed wireless installations.[35] The convention of 1906 was superseded by the International Wireless Convention signed in London on July 5, 1912, by the representatives of forty-three governments,[36] to which was annexed a series of "service regulations" dealing with the organization of radio stations and the conditions and methods of transmitting messages.[37] The convention of 1912, however, failed to meet the question of the obligation of a state to permit the free passage across its territory of waves coming from foreign wireless stations.[38]

The Washington Convention of 1927. In 1927 the International Radiotelegraph Conference met at Washington, and on November 25 the International Radio Convention, with its annexed General Regulations, was signed by the delegates of seventy-eight governments.[39] The convention was chiefly significant for the extension of its provisions to all radio communication stations established or operated by the contracting governments and "open to the international service of public correspondence." Provisions were inserted to protect as far as possible the secrecy of radio correspondence. The contracting governments agreed to propose to their respective legislatures the legislation necessary to enforce the observance of the provisions agreed upon, reserving, however, to each government "entire freedom" with relation to the organization and character of the service of its radio stations provided they conformed to the regulations prescribed when carrying on "an international service of public correspondence." [40] An International Technical Consulting Commission on Radio Communication was established for the purpose of

[35] *Ibid.*, Vol. III, p. 2896.

[36] *Ibid.*, Vol. III, p. 3048.

[37] With the experience of the *Titanic* disaster in mind special emphasis was laid upon giving absolute priority to distress calls. See Report of the American Delegation, Hackworth, *Digest*, Vol. IV, p. 277.

[38] In 1912, the Institute of International Law, at its meeting at Madrid, laid down the principle that a state does not have the right "to prevent the simple passage of wave lengths over its territory." *Annuaire*, 1912. The principle was reiterated at the Lausanne meeting of 1927, but it proved difficult to get it accepted in such categorical form.

[39] For the text of the convention, see *Treaties and Conventions*, Vol. IV, p. 5031; Hudson, *Int. Legislation*, Vol. III, p. 2197. The governments included those of a number of dependent states, such as French Indo-China, Eritrea, and Tripolitania, represented as having been signatories of the convention of 1912.

[40] For details of the conference and its problems, see I. Stewart, "The International Radiotelegraph Conference of Washington," *Am. Journal*, Vol. 22 (1928), p. 28; Hackworth, *Digest*, Vol. IV, p. 278.

studying technical questions pertaining to radio communications. The General Regulations attached to the convention prescribed, among other things, that no private radio transmission stations should be established without special governmental license, and they classified radio emissions and provided for the allocation and use of frequencies and types of emission.[41]

The Telecommunication Convention of 1932. The International Telegraph Conference which met at Paris in 1925 and the Radiotelegraph Conference which met in Washington in 1927 both adopted resolutions in favor of combining the two organizations. The combination was effected by the Madrid Telecommunication Convention of 1932, which created a new International Telecommunication Union.[42] "Telecommunication" was defined as: "Any telegraph or telephone communication of signs, signals, writings, images, and sounds of any nature, by wire, radio, or other systems or processes of electric or visual (semaphore) signalling." [43] Separate sets of telegraph, telephone, and radio regulations were drawn up; and provision was made that the terms of the convention should bind the contracting states only with respect to the services governed by the Regulations which they had accepted.[44] Provision was made for Consulting Committees for the purpose of studying questions relating to telecommunication services. A central office, called the Bureau of the International Telecommunication Union, was established at Bern under the supervision of the Swiss Government.[45] The governments pledge themselves to take all measures possible, compatible with the system used, to insure the secrecy of international correspondence. All radio stations, regardless of their purpose, must be operated in such a manner as not to interfere with the radio services or communications of any of the other contracting governments or of the agencies authorized by them. States participating in the mobile service are obliged to give priority to distress calls and immediately to take such action as the circumstances may require.

[41] For a discussion of the Commission and its problems, see I. Stewart, *Am. Journal*, Vol. 25 (1931), p. 684; Schmeckebier, *International Organizations in which the United States Participates*, pp. 331-335.

[42] For the text of the convention, see *Treaties and Conventions*, Vol. IV, p. 5379; Hudson, *Int. Legislation*, Vol. VI, p. 109. For a brief survey of the development and present status of the Union, see *International Agencies in which the United States Participates*, p. 264.

[43] The definition of terms is given in an Annex to the Convention. The term "telecommunication" was adopted as best expressing all the services covered by the convention.

[44] Art. 2, § 3. The United States ratified the General Radio Regulations, but not the Additional Regulations. It did not ratify the Telegraph or the Telephone Regulations. See excerpts from the Report of the American Delegation to the Conference, Hackworth, *Digest*, Vol. IV, p. 280.

[45] The new Bureau took the place of the International Bureau of the Telegraph Union established at Bern in 1869.

Two separate conferences of the Union convened at Cairo in 1938, the Telegraph and Telephone Conference and the Radio Conference, each seeking to revise the regulations adopted at Madrid in 1932. Outstanding among the acts of the Radio Conference was the adoption of a plan for radio channels for intercontinental air routes.[46] On September 2, 1947, a new Telecommunications Convention and accompanying Regulations were signed at Atlantic City, superseding previous agreements; and on the basis of new measures taking into account the advances in the techniques of telecommunications the United Nations entered into an agreement with the Union by which it became a specialized agency of the United Nations. A new convention, adopted at Buenos Aires in 1952, gave special facilities to the services of the United Nations, and again a new convention adopted at Geneva in 1959 carried forward the technical activities of the General Secretariat of the Union (ITU). An International Radio Consultative Committee is engaged in technical research, and an International Frequency Registration Board deals with the difficult task of assigning and registering frequencies.[47]

In accordance with the provisions of the Madrid Convention contemplating the conclusion of regional agreements, the American States adopted the Inter-American Radiocommunications Convention at Havana in 1937 and the Telecommunications Convention at Rio de Janeiro in 1945.[48] The purpose of these conventions was to make provision for periodic conferences at which solutions might be found for regional problems arising in the field of radio communications. An Inter-American Radio Office was established, with headquarters in the city of Havana. In addition to this wider agreement a more limited North American Regional Broadcasting Agreement was signed at Havana in 1937,[49] and a still more limited Regional Radio Convention including the Central American States, Panama, and the Canal Zone.[50] Successive radio conferences continued to be held, but the problem of adjustment proved to be a difficult one. A Meeting of Experts on Telecommunications met in Washington in 1962 and prepared an elaborate report on the role of regional telecommunications under the international system, and draft statutes were prepared for the establishment of an Inter-American Telecommunications Commission.[51]

Distinct from the problem of communications is the problem of regulat-

---

[46] As at Madrid in 1932, the United States signed only the General Radio Regulations. *Treaty Series,* No. 948. See Hackworth, *Digest,* Vol. IV, p. 285; F. C. de Wolf, "The Cairo Telecommunication Conferences," *Am. Journal,* Vol. 32 (1938), p. 562.

[47] *U.N. Yearbook,* 1962, p. 625.

[48] For the text of the Havana convention, see *Am. Journal,* Vol. 35 (1941), Supp., p. 56. For comment on the convention of 1945, see Dept. of State *Bulletin,* Vol. XIII, p. 735.

[49] Hudson, *Int. Legislation,* Vol. VII, p. 962.

[50] *Am. Journal,* Vol. 35 (1941), Supp., p. 71.

[51] *Official Documents,* Ser. H/X3.

ing radio broadcasting, the primary object of which is to protect the broadcasts of one state from interference by the broadcast stations of an adjacent state. But in spite of agreements which have facilitated broadcasting in the inter-American field, it can not be said that in the larger international field it has been possible to establish the fundamental principles upon which the use of the radio for purposes of broadcasts should be based. Other issues are involved than the mere technical adjustment of frequencies and types of emission. States which deny freedom of information to their peoples may be expected to resist the passage of wave lengths over their territory. Hostile propaganda against a foreign state may be expected to provoke a different reaction from other states when the broadcasts come from government controlled stations. On the other hand the international community as a whole has an interest in the use of the radio as a means of promoting mutual understanding and extending the range of general education.

Query, is the maintenance of open channels of communication between state and state an international obligation or merely a matter of national policy? Associated with this issue is the question of whether a state can be called upon to prohibit systematic and hostile propaganda against another state with the intent to provoke rebellion against the established government. The first issue involves the maintenance of principles of the Charter of the United Nations, to which no sanction is attached; the second involves a conflict with freedom of speech under national constitutions. Both issues remain *de lege ferenda*.[52]

[52] See J. B. Whitton, "The United Nations Conference on Freedom of Information and the Movement against International Propaganda," *Am. Journal*. Vol. 43 (1949), p. 73; "Radio Propaganda—A Modest Proposal," *ibid.*, Vol. 52 (1958), p. 739; Fenwick, "The Problem of Moral Disarmament," *ibid.*, Vol. 41 (1947), p. 112; "Freedom of Communication across National Boundaries," *ibid.*, Vol. 44 (1950), p. 562; "Proposed Control over the Radio as an Inter-American Duty in Cases of Civil Strife," *ibid.*, Vol. 48 (1954), p. 289; and see above, p. 366.

CHAPTER XXII

The High Seas

A. THE HIGH SEAS OPEN TO THE USE OF ALL NATIONS

Outside the territorial waters of the several states, as circumscribed by the maritime belt following the sinuosities of the coast, lie the high seas.[1] These bodies of water, embracing the several oceans; the arms or branches of those oceans, such as the Mediterranean Sea, the North, the Baltic, the Caribbean, and the Black seas; bays and gulfs too wide at their mouths to be territorial, such as the bays of Biscay and Bengal; and connecting seas, such as the Sea of Marmora and the Red Sea, are open to all nations alike for purposes of navigation, of deep-sea fishing, and of submarine cable communication. Upon the high seas no state may claim rights of jurisdiction other than over ships flying its national flag; and on these the basis of control is personal rather than territorial.

Early claims to exclusive jurisdiction. The principle that the high seas are open and free to the use of all nations was not recognized in its full extent until the first quarter of the nineteenth century.[2] The early Roman jurists looked upon the sea, as upon the air, as common to all mankind. But with the development of commerce in the later Middle Ages, maritime states began to claim dominion over parts of the open sea adjacent to their territories. The Adriatic Sea was claimed by Venice and the Ligurian Sea by Genoa. The Baltic Sea was shared by Sweden

---

[1] The use of the term "high seas" in international law is to be distinguished from its use in the admiralty jurisdiction of the United States. See, for example, United States v. Rodgers, above, p. 467.

[2] On the general subject of the high seas, see Fulton, *Sovereignty of the Sea;* Potter, *Freedom of the Seas;* Piggott, *The Freedom of the Seas;* Gidel, *Le droit international public de la mer,* Vol. I, "Introduction—La Haute Mer"; Hackworth, *Digest,* Vol. II, pp. 651 ff.; McDougal and Burke, *The Public Order of the Oceans* (1962); Colombos, *The International Law of the Sea.*

and Denmark. England not only claimed sovereignty over the Narrow Seas and the North Sea, but staked out the Atlantic Ocean itself by a line drawn from Cape Finisterre in Spain around the British Isles to Stadland in Norway. These claims reached the height of their extravagance when Portugal and Spain, in dispute as to the extent of their territorial possessions in the Atlantic and the Pacific, entered into the Treaty of Tordesillas in 1494, delimiting their boundaries of discovery in the New World by a line drawn 370 leagues west of the Cape Verde Islands, Spain receiving the lands west of the line and Portugal those to the east.[3] Thereupon Portugal claimed sovereignty over the Indian Ocean and the south Atlantic, and Spain over the Pacific and the Gulf of Mexico. Some of these claims to exclusive jurisdiction were acquiesced in by other powers. England on its part succeeded, by the power of its navy, in compelling foreign fishing vessels to take out licenses to fish in the North Sea,[4] while foreign vessels entering the waters claimed by England as territorial were obliged to strike their topsails and take in their flags in recognition of its sovereign jurisdiction. On the other hand, the excessive pretensions of Spain and Portugal were stoutly resisted by England, as illustrated in the famous statement of Queen Elizabeth, who, untroubled by the inconsistency of English claims, informed the Spanish ambassador that "the use of the sea and air is common to all; neither can a title to the ocean belong to any people or private persons, forasmuch as neither nature nor public use and custom permitteth any possession thereof." [5] On the whole but little law was recognized in the matter. Each state asserted such claims as seemed warranted in its own eyes and obtained recognition of them in proportion to its power to defend them.

Conflicting doctrines of writers. Naturally the conflicting claims of states gave rise to a corresponding doctrinal controversy. To Grotius belongs the distinction of making the first effective plea for a larger freedom of the seas. His pamphlet *Mare liberum* [6] appeared in 1609 in defense of the right of the Dutch to navigate the Indian Ocean, claimed by Portugal to be its exclusive territorial waters. His argument was based upon *a priori* principles derived from the Roman Law, that the sea could not in fact be "occupied" as in the case of land and therefore must have been intended by nature to be free to all. Moreover, the sea, being inexhaustible in use, was not in principle susceptible of occupation, which was necessary in the case of things the utility of which could only be conserved if they became private property. These arguments are somewhat qualified in the *De jure belli ac pacis* [7] of 1625.

Grotius was answered by a number of advocates of territorial claims.

[3] See above, p. 405.
[4] See Hall, *International Law,* § 40.
[5] *Ibid.*
[6] Eng. trans., *The Freedom of the Seas,* by R. Van D. Magoffin.
[7] Bk. II, Chap. III, §§ VIII-XIV.

Notes of Gentilis in defense of Spanish claims were published posthumously in 1613 under the title *Hispanicae advocationis libri duo*.[8] John Selden replied in 1618 with his *Mare clausum*,[9] controverting theories of natural law with the bald fact that parts of the sea had actually been appropriated by England. In 1653 Sir John Burroughs published a further defense of British claims under the title *The Sovereignty of the British Seas*, while Paolo Sarpi defended the claims of Venice in a volume published in 1676.[10] For the time being Grotius appeared to be in the minority; but by the eighteenth century new writers came to his support, notably Bynkershoek, whose work, *De dominio maris*, was published in 1702.[11] Bynkershoek recognized, however, the fact that the seas could be effectively occupied to the extent of the maritime belt measured by the range of a cannon-shot.[12] Vattel repeated in 1758 [13] the a priori arguments of Grotius, and his principles found a ready hearing among the writers of the early nineteenth century.

Modern practice of states. Side by side with the change of doctrine came a change of practice.[14] The right of free navigation won general acceptance by the close of the seventeenth century, but it continued for more than a century to be attended by the necessity of saluting the British flag when vessels entered the waters regarded by that government as the "British Seas." This last survival was, however, tacitly abandoned after its vigorous reassertion in 1805.[15] Fishing rights came later, Denmark abandoning its claims to the regions of Greenland and Iceland and Great Britain abandoning its claims to the German Ocean. A last attempt on the part of Russia in 1821 to assert a claim to the exclusive sovereignty of Bering Sea by prohibiting foreign ships from approaching within 100 Italian miles of the shores of Alaska was resisted by the United States and other powers and was promptly abandoned by conventions concluded in 1824 and 1825.[16] At the present day general practice recognizes the high seas as open and free to the use of all nations beyond the strict limits of the marginal sea surrounding the several maritime states. The Convention on the High Seas, signed at Geneva, April 29, 1958, at the close of the United Nations Conference on the Law of the Sea, proclaims its provisions as "generally declaratory of established principles of international law," the term "high seas"

[8] See F. F. Abbott, "Alberico Gentili and His *Advocatio Hispanica*," *Am. Journal,* Vol. 10 (1916), p. 737.

[9] The volume was not printed until 1635.

[10] For details, see Fulton, *Sovereignty of the Sea.*

[11] Eng. trans. by R. Van D. Magoffin in *Classics of International Law* series.

[12] See above, p. 443.

[13] *Droit des gens,* Eng. trans., Bk. I, §§ 279 ff.

[14] On the later history of the "freedom of the seas," see in particular Gidel, *Le Droit international public de la mer,* Vol. I, Part I.

[15] See Hall, *International Law,* § 40.

[16] Moore, *Digest of Int. Law,* Vol. I, pp. 890 ff.

being defined as "all parts of the sea that are not included in the territorial sea or in the internal waters of a state." The end of the former exclusive claims is definitely marked by the provision that "The high seas being open to all nations, no state may validly purport to subject any part of them to its sovereignty." [17]

A significant feature of the Convention is the provision that states having no seacoast should have free access to the sea in order that they enjoy the freedom of the seas on equal terms with coastal states. To this end, the states lying between the inland state and the sea are called upon to accord to the inland state free transit through their territory and equal treatment in their ports. On its part, the inland state has the same right to sail ships under its flag as have coastal states.[18]

B. THE LAW OF THE SEA

The law of the sea in respect to the protection of navigation has already been discussed in part in connection with the jurisdiction of states over vessels flying the national flag. Order is maintained on the high seas as between individuals by subjecting the internal discipline of each vessel to the law of the state whose flag it flies, irrespective of the nationality of the parties involved in the case.[19] Each state determines for itself the conditions under which it will admit merchant vessels to its registry; and once a vessel is authorized to fly the flag of a particular state, no other state may question its right to sail the seas or interfere in any way with its movements.[20] On the other hand, the maintenance of order on the high seas as between national vessels is secured by general regulations to prevent collisions and by special regulations governing fishing vessels in parts of the sea where the need of such regulations has been felt.

Regulations to prevent collisions. While no single code of navigation for the prevention of collisions has yet been adopted, the urgent need of common action in this matter has led the individual maritime states to adopt identical municipal regulations with respect to lights and signals, the law of the road, piloting, and courses. Great Britain led the way with a "Commercial Code of Signals for the Use of All Nations," published in 1857, which was subsequently adopted by all maritime states. In 1888 the Institute of International Law drew up a "Draft of Uniform Law for Marine Collisions," and this was followed in 1889 by another draft convention prepared by a maritime conference of the leading states assembled at Washington. Action by the separate states was delayed, however, and a new conference met at Brussels in 1909. The

---

[17] Arts. 1, 2. *Am. Journal,* Vol. 52 (1958), p. 842.
[18] Arts. 3, 4.
[19] Art. 5, Convention on the High Seas. See above, pp. 374 ff.
[20] Convention on the High Seas, Art. 6.

draft conventions prepared by this last body dealt with limitations upon
the liability of ship owners, maritime mortgages and privileged liens, and
reparation for injuries resulting from collisions.[21] They were endorsed
the following year and recommended to the several states for separate
adoption as national law. In 1929, a new Convention on Safety of Life
at Sea was adopted at London, replacing the earlier convention of 1914.
Annex II to the Convention contains revised regulations for preventing
collisions at sea.[22] The Convention adopted at Geneva in 1958 requires
states to take measures for ships under its flag to insure safety at sea in
accordance with accepted international standards, limiting penal and
disciplinary proceedings to the flag state in cases of collision, and requiring the master of a ship to render assistance in so far as possible to
persons and ships in distress at sea.[23]

Control of pollution. Complaints have long been made, as in the
case of New Jersey against New York, by coastal states of the pollution
of the seas adjacent to their shores; and in response to them, the
Geneva Convention provides that every state shall draw up regulations
to prevent pollution of the seas by the discharge of oil from ships or
pipelines or resulting from the exploitation of the seabed and its subsoil, as well as pollution from the dumping of radioactive waste, subject
to the regulations formulated by the competent international organizations.[24]

C. REGULATION OF FISHING ON THE HIGH SEAS

Before the recent action aimed at the adoption of a general international convention for the regulation of fishing on the high seas, special
cases arose where joint action was called for by states interested in
protecting the fisheries and the fishing vessels in a particular part of the
sea adjacent to their coasts. One of the first and most important conventions adopted with this object in view was the Hague Convention of
1882 for the Regulation of the Police of the Fisheries in the North Sea
outside Territorial Waters. This agreement made provision for the
registration of fishing vessels and for a special emblem to be borne by
them, while specific rules were laid down for the avoidance of conflicts
between vessels of different nationalities. An exceptional provision, of

---

[21] The text of the conventions may be found in *Am. Journal*, Vol. 4 (1910), Supp.,
p. 115.

[22] For the text of the Convention, see Hudson, *Int. Legislation*, Vol. IV, p. 2825.
    The question of the jurisdiction taken by national courts in cases of collision is dis-
cussed above, on p. 379. See in particular the case of the *Scotia*, 14 Wallace 170
(1871), where the universal obligation of established maritime usages is emphasized.
Fenwick, *Cases*, p. 18; Hudson, *Cases*, p. 667.

[23] Arts. 10-12.

[24] Geneva Convention, Arts. 24, 25. See above, p. 498.

great collateral importance, is the authorization of the cruisers of the signatory powers to exercise a reciprocal right of visit, search, and seizure of the vessels of their several flags for the enforcement of the rules laid down.[25] A second general convention adopted in 1887 was directed toward the abolition of the liquor traffic among fishermen in the North Sea.[26]

The Bering Sea Seal Fisheries case. The controversy between the United States and Great Britain over the seal fisheries in the waters adjacent to Bering Sea was perhaps too exceptional in respect to the issues raised to form a precedent of importance. The outcome of the resort to arbitration shows, however, the possibilities of international regulation of an industry at once domestic and international. In 1886 and 1887 United States police cruisers seized certain British Columbian vessels for violation of regulations made by the United States for the protection of the seal fisheries. The seizures were upheld by the United States courts, which relied upon the theory that the waters of Bering Sea were a closed territorial sea.[27] The dispute was submitted to arbitration by a treaty of 1892, which called upon the arbitrators not only to render an award on the merits of the case but to frame regulations which might be concurrently adopted for the protection of the seals.[28] In presenting its case the United States, while not claiming exclusive jurisdiction over Bering Sea, relied upon rights, inherited from Russia, by which jurisdiction might be exercised to the extent of protecting the seals when absent from their breeding places on American territory in search of food on the high seas. This claim of a property right in the seals, which might be protected in the open sea as well as on the Pribilof Islands themselves, was rejected by the arbitration tribunal.[29] The tribunal, however, drew up a series of regulations for the protection of the seals, to be adopted by the parties to the case and such other maritime powers as might agree to them. The failure of this effort to protect the seals from threatened extinction led the United States to call, in 1911, the Pelagic Sealing Conference, which met in Washington and drew up a convention provid-

[25] *Br. and For. St. Papers,* Vol. LXXIII, p. 39. The agreement of 1901 between Great Britain and Denmark for the regulation of the fisheries in the waters adjacent to the Faeroe Islands and to Iceland follows the lines of the North Sea convention of 1882. See Martens, *Nouv. rec. gén.,* 2e sér., Vol. XXXIII, p. 268.

[26] *Ibid.,* Vol. LXXIX, p. 894. For other treaties looking primarily to the conservation of natural resources, see below, pp. 502 ff.

[27] Moore, *Digest,* Vol. I, § 172.

[28] For the text of the convention, see *Treaties and Conventions,* Vol. I, p. 746. The scope of the regulations was at issue in the case of the *Wanderer.* See Hudson, *Cases,* p. 647; Fenwick, *Cases,* p. 415.

[29] For the text of the award, see Moore, *Arbitrations,* Vol. I, p. 910; *Am. Journal,* Vol. 6 (1912), p. 233; Fenwick, *Cases,* p. 412. For comment upon the case, see W. Williams, "Reminiscences of the Bering Sea Arbitration," *Am. Journal,* Vol. 37 (1943), p. 562.

ing for a closed season and other supplementary measures.[30] The convention expired in 1941, and it was not until 1957 that a new convention was adopted, *ad interim,* pending research into the habits of the seals.

The halibut and salmon fisheries.   The regulation of the halibut and sockeye salmon fisheries off the western coasts of the United States and Canada presented legal problems of the same general character as the regulation of seal fisheries.[31] Earlier conceptions of the freedom of the high seas had made it impossible for the states most interested in the conservation of these fisheries to suppress practices which might lead to their extermination. Each state was free to prosecute its own citizens, but was unable to apply its protective legislation to the vessels of foreign states. In due time the two states most interested in the North Pacific fisheries were able to come to an agreement upon their regulation. The Convention, signed in 1923, for the Preservation of the Halibut Fisheries of the North Pacific Ocean and Bering Sea, was superseded by a new convention of 1930, and this was in turn superseded by the convention of January 29, 1937, which was followed by Regulations drawn up by the International Fisheries Commission. Closed areas and closed seasons are provided for; and either party has the right to seize persons or vessels violating the regulations and deliver them to the country of their nationality for trial. The Convention for the Protection of Sockeye Salmon Fisheries, signed between the United States and Canada May 26, 1930, provides that the two parties shall share equally in the fishery; and the special Fisheries Commission established by the convention is given legislative powers with respect to closed seasons, as well as administrative functions.[32]

The Convention for the Regulation of Whaling, opened for signature by the League of Nations at Geneva in 1931, represented a series of cooperative measures to conserve certain kinds of whales which were in danger of becoming extinct.[33] While the provisions of the convention were made applicable to "all the waters of the world, including both the high seas and territorial and national waters," punishment of infractions

---

[30] *Treaties and Conventions,* Vol. III, p. 2966. For the act of Congress of 1912, see *Am. Journal,* Vol. 7 (1913), p. 140. Four states were parties to the Pelagic Sealing Convention.

[31] On the special subject of the regulation of the North Pacific fisheries, see Leonhard, *International Regulation of Fisheries;* Bingham, *Report on the International Law of Pacific Coastal Fisheries;* Riesenfeld, *Protection of Coastal Fisheries under International Law;* Gregory and Barnes, *North Pacific Fisheries, with Special Reference to Alaska Salmon;* G. Ireland, "The North Pacific Fisheries," *Am. Journal,* Vol. 36 (1942), p. 400; A. P. Daggett, "The Regulation of Maritime Fisheries by Treaty," *ibid.,* Vol. 28 (1934), p. 693.

[32] For the texts of the several conventions, see *Am. Journal,* Vol. 19 (1925), Supp., p. 106; *ibid.,* Vol. 25 (1931), Supp., p. 108; *ibid.,* Vol. 32 (1938), Supp., p. 71; *ibid.,* Vol. 35 (1941), Supp., p. 184; *ibid.,* Vol. 32 (1938), Supp., p. 65.

[33] For the text of the convention, see *Treaties and Conventions,* Vol. IV, p. 5372.

of the measures prescribed was left to the contracting parties within the limits of their respective jurisdictions. A later agreement of 1937, signed at the close of the International Whaling Conference in London, supplemented the convention of 1931 by provisions looking to the protection not only of baleen but of other whales as well, fixing closed seasons and closed areas and restricting the use of factory ships.[34] In 1946 an International Whaling Conference met in Washington and a new convention was signed by the delegates of thirteen governments, setting forth detailed regulations aimed at preserving and developing the world's existing whale resources. Provision was made for the establishment of an International Whaling Commission which might eventually be brought within the framework of the United Nations as a specialized agency.[35]

Supplementing its agreements on the territorial sea and the high seas, the Geneva Conference of 1958 adopted a separate Convention on Fishing and Conservation of the Living Resources of the High Seas, defining "conservation" as "the aggregate of the measures rendering possible the optimum sustainable yield from those resources so as to secure a maximum supply of food and other marine products." Separate resolutions were directed to particular conservation measures, one on Humane Killing of Marine Life, referring especially to whales and seals, which were to be spared suffering to the greatest extent possible.[36]

Control of resources of the continental shelf. In the chapter dealing with territorial waters, attention was called to the proclamation of the President of the United States, under date of September 28, 1945, in accordance with which the United States claims jurisdiction and control over the natural resources of the subsoil and seabed of the continental shelf beneath the high seas but contiguous to the coasts of the United States.[37] On the same date a similar proclamation was issued announcing the policy of establishing conservation zones in those areas of the high seas contiguous to the coasts of the United States where fishing activities have been or in the future may be developed and maintained on a substantial scale. The controversial phases of the problem have now been regulated by the Geneva Conventions on the territorial sea and on fishing (which define the areas involved and the extent of the rights of the coastal state), and more specifically by the separate Convention on the Continental Shelf.[38]

[34] For the text of the agreement, see Hudson, *Int. Legislation*, Vol. VII, p. 754. For comment, see L. L. Leonard, "Recent Negotiations toward the International Regulation of Whaling," *Am. Journal*, Vol. 35 (1941), p. 90.
[35] Convention for the Regulation of Whaling, December 2, 1946. See Dept. of State *Bulletin*, Vol. XV, p. 1101.
[36] For the texts, see *Am. Journal*, Vol. 52 (1958), pp. 865 ff.
[37] See above, p. 447.
[38] Convention on the Continental Shelf, *Am. Journal*, Vol. 52 (1958), p. 858.

D. REGULATION OF SUBMARINE CABLES

While the terminal points of submarine cables rest upon the territory of a particular state and are therefore subject to its immediate control, the greater part of their length rests upon an ocean bed open for the use of all who desire to lay such lines of communication. Hence there arose the need for joint action on the part of interested powers, both to regulate the placing of cables and to prevent injury to them on the part of irresponsible individuals. In 1884 a conference of twenty-six states met at Paris and adopted an International Convention for the Protection of Submarine Telegraph Cables.[39] The importance of this convention lies not merely in the fact that it provides for the administrative regulation of what might be called an "international public utility," but in the fact that the signatory powers undertook to punish the negligent breaking or damaging of a cable by the prosecution of offenders in their national courts and, in order to facilitate such protective measures, agreed to permit their men-of-war to stop and verify the nationality of merchantmen of all nations which were suspected of having infringed the regulations of the treaty.

The Geneva Convention on the High Seas, in laying down the general provision that all states shall be entitled to lay submarine cables and pipelines on the bed of the high seas, imposes specific obligations with respect to the laying of the cables, the protection to be given them, the punishment of deliberate injury to them, and the compensation due to the owners of adjacent cables or of ships whose gear has been sacrificed to avoid injuring them.[40]

E. CONCURRENT JURISDICTION ON THE HIGH SEAS

The suppression of piracy. The suppression of robbery on the high seas has never been disputed as a legal act of national self-defense. Pirates, by custom of immemorial origin, have been *hostes humani generis*.[41] Grotius pointed out, with references to the law of ancient Rome, that a body of pirates did not constitute a state and that the laws of war did not apply to their acts, as they would if done under the authority of an organized state.[42] Pirates, therefore, having cut themselves off from organized society for purposes of crime, are outside the pale of international law. As no state was responsible for their acts, so on the other hand no state might claim an infringement of its rights if persons, nominally its citizens, were captured in the act of robbery on the

[39] For the text of the convention, see *Treaties and Conventions,* Vol. II, 1949.
[40] Arts. 26-29.
[41] On the general subject of piracy, see Moore, *Digest,* Vol. II, § 311; Hackworth, *Digest,* Vol. II, pp. 681-695; Harvard Research, *Draft Convention on Piracy,* with bibliography.
[42] *De jure belli ac pacis,* Eng. trans., Bk. III, Chap. III, § 11.

high seas and summarily executed by the captors or condemned by the courts of the captors' state. The crime is in most cases a capital one, but the precise punishment for it depends upon the municipal law of the state exercising jurisdiction.[43] In the effort to suppress piracy, the public vessels of a state have the right to stop and visit a suspicious vessel for the purpose of verifying her papers and the flag she is flying, subject, however, to payment of damages in case the suspicion should prove to be unfounded. In the case of the *Marianna Flora* [44] the Supreme Court held that no damages were due to a Portuguese vessel which had been approached by an American armed schooner under circumstances justifying inquiry, although as a result of the approach an engagement took place and the Portuguese vessel was silenced by the guns of the American vessel and thereupon brought into port and libeled for alleged piratical conduct.

Piracy and privateers. One of the chief problems of modern international law presented by the suppression of piracy arose in connection with the practices of maritime war. Until the latter part of the nineteenth century belligerents were in the habit of arming private ships with the object of preying upon the merchant vessels of the enemy. These "privateers," operating under a commission or letter of marque from the belligerent government,[45] were distinguished from pirates in that their acts of depredation were not committed with intent to rob (*animo furandi*), and at the same time the vessels were responsible for their conduct to the state which had commissioned them. Obviously there was room for many abuses. Irresponsible persons obtained commissions and carried on their depredations without due regard for the laws of war. It was a clear case of piracy if the same commander obtained a commission from both belligerents with the object of making indiscriminate captures. A more debatable question was whether it was lawful for the citizen of a neutral state to take a letter of marque from one or other of the belligerents. France maintained the negative in its war with Mexico in 1839, and President Polk suggested in 1846 that the bearers of commissions issued by the Mexican Government in blank and sold to foreigners might be regarded by the criminal courts as pirates.[46] With the Declaration of Paris of 1856, by which privateering was abolished, the confusion of privateering with piracy ceased to be a practical problem.

Status of vessels in the service of insurgents. It is now largely of historic interest to analyze the cases in which commissions issued by insurgent bodies were recognized as authorizing captures on the high

---

[43] The *Harvard Draft, Piracy* (1932), calls attention to the wide variations in respect to the definition of piracy and the "important difference between piracy in the sense of the law of nations and piracy under municipal law" (p. 749).

[44] 11 Wheaton 1 (1826). Scott, *Cases*, p. 1009; Fenwick, *Cases*, p. 390.

[45] See below, p. 695.

[46] See Hall, *International Law*, § 81.

seas, the general practice being not to regard the captures as piratical if limited to the property of the state against which the insurgents were in revolt. But recognition of the insurgents as belligerents was essential. In United States v. Smith,[47] the court held that the defendant Smith, who with other members of the crew of a vessel commissioned by the Government of Buenos Aires, then at war with Spain, mutinied and after seizing another vessel in the same port proceeded, without any commission or other authority, to plunder and rob a Spanish vessel on the high seas, was guilty of piracy "as defined by the law of nations" and might be punished by the courts of the United States in accordance with the act of Congress of 1819. The defendant and his associates, said the court, were "freebooters upon the sea, not under the acknowledged authority, or deriving protection from the flag or commission of any government." In the case of the Magellan Pirates,[48] involving the capture of a British and of an American merchant vessel by persons in revolt against the Government of Chile, the British court held that even if the acts of the defendants were acts of insurgents, which was not the case, their acts would have been "piratical" as having no connection with the insurrection and being mere acts of "wanton cruelty, in the murder of foreign subjects and in the indiscriminate plunder of their property."

In the case of certain Spanish insurgents, who in 1873, having seized Spanish warships in the harbor of Cartagena, were conducting operations in the Mediterranean and who had been denounced by the Spanish Government as "pirates," Great Britain, France, and Germany decided not to consider them as pirates provided the insurgent vessels did not interfere with their own neutral commerce.[49] When, however, the Peruvian vessel *Huascar*, having been seized by revolutionists, undertook to requisition coal from neutral British vessels and to take from another British vessel two Peruvian officers on board, a British admiral in command of the English squadron in the Pacific regarded the acts of the *Huascar* as piratical and fired upon her.[50]

The position taken by the United States District Court in 1885 in the case of the *Ambrose Light* [51] gave rise to considerable controversy. In that case a vessel duly commissioned by Colombian insurgents was seized by an American gunboat and brought into the port of New York for condemnation. No proof was shown of any intention on the part of the vessel to commit hostilities other than such as might be incident to the struggle against the established government. The court held that the precedents all went to show "that recognition by at least some established

[47] 5 Wheaton 153 (1820). Fenwick, *Cases,* p. 394.
[48] 1 Spinks 81 (1853). Fenwick, *Cases,* p. 396.
[49] Hall, *International Law,* § 82, taken from Calvo, *Droit International,* §§ 1146-1148.
[50] Moore, *Digest,* Vol. II, § 331.
[51] 25 Fed. Rep. 408 (1885). Fenwick, *Cases,* p. 400; Hudson, *Cases,* p. 187.

government of a 'state of war,' or of the belligerent rights of insurgents, is necessary to prevent their cruisers from being held legally piratical by the courts of other nations injuriously affected"; so that the public vessels of all nations had "the right to seize as piratical" vessels operating under commissions regarded as void.[52]

"Rum-runners" and "high-jackers." A novel form of piracy was presented during the period of the operation of the National Prohibition Act, passed by the United States Congress in 1920. The eastern coast of the United States was beset with "rum-runners" engaged in the business of smuggling intoxicating liquors into the United States in violation of the law. These rum-runners, being outside the protection of the law in respect to their illegal activities, were in turn preyed upon by "high-jackers" operating within and outside territorial waters. Query, were the high-jackers "pirates," who might be captured and brought to trial by any foreign public vessel that might happen to be passing? [53]

Submarines as "pirates." In consequence of the failure by German submarines upon a number of occasions during the First World War to observe the laws of war in respect to making provision for the safety of passengers and crew before destroying enemy merchant vessels, a treaty was signed at the Washington Conference on the Limitation of Armaments prescribing rules for the use of the submarine in time of war. Article III of the treaty provided that any person in the service of any power "who shall violate any of those rules, whether or not such person is under orders of a governmental superior, shall be deemed to have violated the laws of war and shall be liable to trial and punishment as if for an act of piracy and may be brought to trial before the civil or military authorities of any Power within the jurisdiction of which he may be found." The treaty, however, never came into effect.[54]

"Piracy" during the Spanish Civil War. During the Spanish Civil War the operations of submarines of undeclared nationality against not only the commerce of the Republican Government but also against the private and public vessels of neutral states led to calling of a conference at Nyon, France, where an "Arrangement" was signed on September 14, 1937, by a number of powers with shipping interests in the Mediterranean to treat as "acts of piracy" attacks by submarines against merchant ships not belonging to either of the conflicting parties in Spain. The Mediterranean area was divided into zones to be patrolled by the

---

[52] The vessel was subsequently released on the ground that the Secretary of State had impliedly recognized a state of war. See Moore, *Digest*, Vol. II, p. 1098.

[53] See E. D. Dickinson, "Is the Crime of Piracy Obsolete," *Harvard Law Review*, Vol. XXXVIII (1925), p. 334.

[54] For the text of the treaty, see *Treaties and Conventions*, Vol. III, p. 3116; *Am. Journal*, Vol. 16 (1922), Supp., p. 57. The treaty obviously extended the term "piracy" far beyond its traditional meaning, whether or not the condemnation of the individual offenders was otherwise justifiable.

participating states; and it was provided that any submarine which might attack a ship in a manner contrary to the rules of international law should be counterattacked and, if possible, destroyed.[55]

The Geneva Convention on the High Seas defines piracy in broad terms to include "any illegal acts of violence, detention or any act of depredation committed for private ends by the crew or the passengers of a private ship or a private aircraft whether on the high seas or in any place outside territorial jurisdiction." Vessels of all other states may seize a pirate ship and arrest the persons on board, leaving it to the courts of the state which carried out the seizure to decide upon the penalties to be imposed.[56]

Query, was it an act of "piracy" when a Portuguese national, seeking to overthrow the government in Lisbon, seized in 1961 a private ship, the *Santa Maria*, and sought to sail it to Angola? Violence was used in overcoming the crew to the extent that it resulted in the death of the Third Officer, but the passengers were molested only in so far as they were left uncertain as to their fate. Should the leader of the movement, Captain Galvão, have been tried for piracy when the vessel, unable to reach its destination, arrived in a Brazilian port? [57]

The suppression of the slave trade. When in the opening decades of the nineteenth century the growth of public sentiment against the slave trade led several of the Great Powers to extend the legal definition of piracy so as to include the slave trade, two international problems were presented. So long as the statutory definition of piracy had kept within the definition of customary international law, the exercise of jurisdiction over the nationals of a foreign state who were brought before the courts for trial presented no difficulty. Might the courts of a state now apply the new statutory definition of piracy to acts committed on the high seas by the citizens of a second state when they had been arrested and brought to a port of the first state for trial? And, secondly, might the public vessels of a state visit and search vessels flying the flag of other states under circumstances raising the suspicion that they were engaged in the slave trade? In answer to the first question the British High Court of Admiralty, in a classic decision rendered in 1817 in the case of the French vessel *Le Louis*,[58] held that the fact that the municipal laws both of Great Britain and of France had made the slave trade unlawful did not render the act piracy at international law. Moreover, the right of

[55] See R. Genet, "The Charge of Piracy in the Spanish Civil War," *Am. Journal,* Vol. 32 (1938), p. 253; N. J. Padelford, "Foreign Shipping during the Spanish Civil War," *Am. Journal, ibid.,* p. 264. For other problems of the Spanish Civil War, see Padelford, *International Law and Diplomacy in the Spanish Civil Strife.*

[56] Arts. 14-22.

[57] See "Piracy in the Caribbean," *Am. Journal,* Vol. 55 (1961), p. 426; L. C. Green, "Rebels or Pirates," *British Year Book,* 1961, p. 496 (the latter contesting the assertion of piracy).

[58] 2 Dodson, 210 (1817). Fenwick, *Cases,* p. 408; Hudson, *Cases,* p. 659.

visit and search, being a grave encroachment upon the equality and independence of states, could not be extended by implication to new cases not recognized by international law. Hence it followed that the resistance offered by the vessel to capture, and the circumstance of her being actually engaged in the slave traffic, could not be made a ground of condemnation. The position taken by the British court was made the basis of a similar decision by the United States Supreme Court in the case of the *Antelope*,[59] in which the court ordered the release of a Spanish vessel captured by an American cruiser, notwithstanding the fact that in 1820 Congress had passed an act declaring the slave trade to be piracy.[60]

International cooperation. The inadequacy of existing international law to meet the growing demand for the suppression of the slave trade led Great Britain, as chief protagonist, to bring the question before the Congress of Vienna in the hope of securing collective action on the part of the Great Powers. Eight of the powers signed a statement "declaring in the face of Europe that, regarding the universal abolition of the trade in negroes as a measure particularly worthy of their attention," they were animated by a sincere desire to put a stop to it when the interests of their subjects permitted, and would negotiate later with regard to the time at which it should stop.[61] Efforts were made subsequently by Great Britain to secure a general agreement permitting a reciprocal right of search of ships suspected of slave trading; but several of the powers, including the United States, regarded the right of search as derogatory to their sovereignty and likely to have unfortunate consequences.[62] Great Britain then sought to conclude separate treaties with individual powers and by 1850 had secured treaties with a large number of states, as well as a special treaty of 1841 with the five leading powers. The United States, however, refused to cooperate except by such police measures as did not involve the search of American vessels. To permit the right of search would, in the view of the United States, subject American commerce "to the risk of constant and harassing vexations." [63] The immunity of its merchant vessels on the high seas from detention or search by any

[59] 10 Wheaton 66 (1825). Fenwick, *Cases*, p. 86.

[60] "If," said Chief Justice Marshall, "we resort to this standard [usages, national acts, and general assent on the part of the leading nations] as the test of international law the question . . . is decided in favor of the legality of the trade. . . . As no nation can prescribe a rule for others, none can make a law of nations; and this traffic remains lawful to those whose governments have not forbidden it." The decisions in both these leading cases contain oft-quoted dicta with regard to the equality of sovereign states. See above, pp. 262 ff. It may be noted that the decision of a United States federal court in the case of *La Jeune Eugénie* [2 Mason's Reports 409 (1822); Fenwick, *Cases*, p. 1], contrary to the principle followed in the case of the *Antelope*, called for the subsequent payment of damages by the United States.

[61] Art. 118, No. 15, Final Act, June 9, 1815.

[62] Moore, *Digest*, Vol. II, § 310.

[63] Message of President Tyler, February 27, 1843. *Ibid.*, p. 930.

other than American public vessels was regarded as an attribute of
sovereignty which the United States could not abandon. When, however,
Great Britain had given up the claim to a right of visit and search based
upon customary law, the United States finally agreed, in 1862, to a treaty
permitting a right of detention, search, and seizure within a restricted
area off the coasts of Africa and Cuba.[64]

The convention of 1885. Cooperative action by the Great Powers as
a body was not secured until the meeting of the Congress of Berlin in
1885, at the close of which fourteen states, including the United States,
signed a convention pledging themselves "to strive for the suppression
of slavery and especially of the negro slave trade," while the powers
exercising sovereignty in the Congo declared that the Congo territories
should not serve either as a market or as a way of transit for the slaves
of any race; and they engaged severally to put an end to the commerce.[65] More definite and comprehensive international legislation was,
however, still needed; and in response to public agitation the same group
of powers met at Brussels in 1889 and signed in 1890 a General Act
providing for a limited right of visit and search, and for concerted police
measures for the suppression of the traffic. At the same time it was agreed
to create special consular courts for the investigation and trial of offenders
and an international maritime bureau for the collection of information
facilitating the repression of the trade within the defined zone.[66] The
provisions of the conventions of 1885 and 1890 were revised by the treaty
of St. Germain-en-Laye, September 10, 1919, by which the signatory
states agreed to endeavor to secure "the complete suppression of slavery
in all its forms and of the slave trade by land and sea." [67] By the Slavery
Convention, signed at Geneva, September 25, 1926,[68] the contracting
powers agreed, "each in respect of the territories placed under its
sovereignty" to prevent and suppress the slave trade and to bring about
as soon as possible the complete abolition of slavery in all its forms.
Lastly, the Geneva Convention of 1958 calls upon all states to adopt
effective measures to prevent and punish the transport of slaves in ships
authorized to fly its flag, and to prevent the unlawful use of its flag for
that purpose. Any slave taking refuge on board any ship, whatever its
flag, shall *ipso facto* be free.[69]

---

[64] It is instructive to observe the connection between the opposition of the United
States to visit and search of American vessels for the purpose of suppressing the slave
trade and the earlier controversy with Great Britain over the visit and search of
American vessels by British men-of-war with the object of impressing sailors of Brit-
ish birth into the service of the British navy. See Moore, *Principles of American
Diplomacy*, Chap. III.

[65] Art. IX, treaty of February 26, 1885.

[66] *Treaties and Conventions*, Vol. II, p. 1964.

[67] Hudson, *International Legislation*, Vol. I, p. 343.

[68] *Ibid.*, Vol. III, p. 2010.

[69] Art. 13.

F. FREEDOM OF THE SEAS IN TIME OF WAR

By long custom international law of the year 1914 had come to recognize sharp restrictions upon the normal freedom of the seas in the event of war between two maritime states. Neutral states, not parties to the conflict, were called upon to submit to the visit and search of their merchant vessels by the public vessels of the belligerent states with the object of ascertaining the nationality of the vessel and the character and destination of its cargo. Moreover, the right of belligerents to engage in battle on the high seas might seriously inconvenience neutral vessels whose course led them through those waters. At the same time belligerents exercised an authority to extend the area of maritime jurisdiction by marking off zones of offense and defense, in some cases planted with mines, into which neutrals entered at their own risk. Neutral states were thus obliged to subordinate their normal rights upon the high seas to the prosecution of a war in the making of which they had no part and with which, furthermore, they had no legal right to interfere notwithstanding the consequences to themselves. As for the belligerents, they obviously sacrificed the enjoyment of their rights of navigation, fishing, and communication in so far as either could succeed in doing injury to the other; while the entire merchant marine of both states, although privately owned by individual noncombatant citizens, was by the law of maritime war subject to capture and confiscation by the enemy.[70]

Freedom of the seas as a condition of peace. A new aspect of the freedom of the seas came to the front during the First World War. Both combatant groups, confronted with new conditions, found it necessary to stretch the rules of maritime warfare beyond the accepted interpretations of the past. As a neutral, the United States suffered both from the application of the law of contraband and blockade by one belligerent and from the ruthless offensive measures of the other belligerent. American commerce, even that carried on with the neutral nations of Europe, was for the time completely demoralized. At the same time Great Britain, although having fought scarcely a single sea battle, had captured or driven to cover the entire merchant marine of the enemy. It was under these circumstances that President Wilson made his address before the Senate on January 22, 1917, laying down the conditions under which he considered it possible that the United States might cooperate with other nations in establishing an international authority to guarantee peace, and stating that "the freedom of the seas is the *sine qua non* of peace, equality, and coöperation." [71] Again, in his inaugural address of March 5, the President enumerated among "the principles of a liberated mankind" which the United States would stand for, whether in war or in peace,

---

[70] See Chaps. XXX, XXXIII.
[71] *Official Statements of War Aims and Peace Proposals,* p. 53.

"that the seas should be equally free and safe for the use of all peoples, under rules set up by common agreement and consent, and that so far as practicable they should be accessible to all upon equal terms." [72] This plea for a new freedom of the seas thereafter played a prominent part in the discussions in America and in Europe of the constructive basis of international peace. The second of the "Fourteen Points" repeated the principle in the form of "absolute freedom of navigation upon the seas, outside territorial waters, alike in peace and in war, except as the seas might be closed in whole or in part by international action for the enforcement of international covenants." [73]

Relation of freedom of the seas to international sanctions. Jurists and the public alike disagreed, however, as to the meaning to be attached to the "freedom of the seas" as a principle of international law.[74] In time of peace the seas had long been free, so that any change in the law in that respect would seem to have been uncalled for. Was it to be understood that the principle would require of belligerents in a future war that they must forgo the right to capture contraband and maintain blockades as well as refrain from the various uses of the submarine that had been denounced by the United States as lawless? The answer was not clear.[75] In consequence when it was proposed that the principles of the Fourteen Points should be incorporated into the terms of the armistice of November 11, 1918, Great Britain and the other Allied Powers reserved a right to further interpretation of the second point bearing upon the freedom of the seas. The interpretation was never given.

The second of the Fourteen Points recognized the exception that the seas might be closed in whole or in part "by international action for the enforcement of international covenants." If that implied that individual

[72] With these statements must be associated the frequent mention of the "freedom of the seas" in unofficial German discussions of the terms of peace, and in particular the address of Von Bethmann-Hollweg before the Reichstag on November 9, 1916, in which, after pledging Germany's cooperation in peaceful arrangements to prevent war, the chancellor said: "Then the principles of justice and free development, not only on the Continent but also on the seas, must be made valid." See on this subject Nippold, *Development of International Law after the World War*, pp. 149-186. See also A. S. Hershey, "The German Conception of the Freedom of the Seas," *Am. Journal*, Vol. 13 (1919), p. 206.

[73] For the text of the Fourteen Points, see *Am. Journal*, Vol. 13 (1919), p. 161.

[74] See Potter, *Freedom of the Seas;* Garner, "The Freedom of the Seas," *Am. Journal*, Vol. 23 (1929), p. 363; C. Dupuis, "Liberté des voies de communication," *Recueil des Cours*, Vol. 2 (1924-I), pp. 129, 135.

[75] Even in President Wilson's own mind there appears to have been a transition from mere restrictions upon belligerents in respect to the capture of private property at sea to the elimination of war itself. In this light may be read his statement on January 22, 1917, that "no doubt a somewhat radical reconstruction of many of the rules of international practice hitherto thought to be established may be necessary in order to make the seas indeed free and common in practically all circumstances for the use of mankind." *Official Statements, loc. cit.* See, on this aspect of the subject, Potter, *op. cit.*, Chap. XII, in particular, pp. 242-247, where the relation of the freedom of the seas to the general problem of international organization is discussed.

belligerents were no longer at liberty to close the seas by arbitrary resort to war, what did it mean with respect to states which, not being members of the League of Nations, might not be willing to participate in such "international action"? What if the League should take collective action against a state violating the Covenant and should find that its measures, such as the enforcement of a naval blockade, brought it into conflict with the "rights" of neutrals under the old law of neutrality? It was a situation which President Wilson had not contemplated; but the absence of the United States from the League made it a reality.[76] Could the League, enforcing sanctions against an aggressor, claim under such circumstances any greater rights against neutrals than individual belligerents had claimed in the past when fighting "private" wars? Conceding the right of the United States to remain neutral, would the United States perhaps waive some part of its rights under the old law in the interest of maintaining the peace and order of the international community? A definite answer to the questions was evaded; and when a war of the old type broke out in 1939 the seas became even less free than they were in 1914.

The Atlantic Charter.   The seventh principle of the Atlantic Charter, which became a rule of international law when incorporated into the Declaration by United Nations, expressed the desire of the signatories that the peace to be established after victory would be one which "should enable all men to traverse the high seas and oceans without hindrance." [77] No explanation was ever forthcoming to clarify what the framers of the Charter had in mind; but it is to be assumed that they looked forward, as President Wilson did, to the protection of the peace by the collective action of the international community and to the denial to an aggressor of the right to interrupt the use of the seas by the traditional belligerent measures of the past.

With the adoption of the Charter of the United Nations, it would appear that the "freedom of the seas" in respect to the restrictions formerly imposed by belligerents in time of war ceased to have any meaning, unless a situation should arise in which the Security Council of the United Nations would impose sanctions upon a state guilty of aggression. To date no such situation has arisen. Perhaps the quarantine imposed by President Kennedy on October 22, 1962, might come under the head of a restriction upon the freedom of the seas, justified by the traditional measures of defense short of war, in accordance with the right of self-defense recognized by Article 51 of the Charter.[78]

[76] See Chap. XXXII, "The Relation of Neutral States to Belligerents."
[77] For the text of the Charter, see Appendix B.
[78] See above, p. 279.

CHAPTER XXIII

International Treaties and Other Agreements

A. FUNCTION OF TREATIES IN INTERNATIONAL LAW

From the time of Grotius down to recent years it has been the practice of writers to draw heavily upon the rules of the civil law regulating contracts between individuals in developing rules of international law governing the contractual relations between states. The reasons for resort to the analogies between the two forms of agreement are obvious enough. For the promises and the contracts of more or less absolute monarchs of the period of Grotius and Vattel were scarcely to be distinguished in their essence from similar obligations assumed by individuals, and the same fundamental principles of the natural law appeared to be equally applicable to both. With the coming of constitutional governments the analogies between the private contracts of individuals and agreements between states gradually became less close; but many of the rules of international law derived from those analogies continued to be quoted as authoritative when in fact the reason for their validity had ceased to exist.[1]

The scope of bilateral treaties. In considering the legal character of

[1] On the general subject of treaties, see McNair, *The Law of Treaties. British Practice and Opinions;* also his "Functions and Differing Legal Character of Treaties," *British Year Book,* Vol. XI (1930), p. 100; Crandall, *Treaties, Their Making and Enforcement;* Harvard Research, *Draft Convention on the Law of Treaties, Am. Journal,* Vol. 29 (1935), Supp., p. 655, where an elaborate bibliography may be found; *United Nations: Report of the International Law Commission,* April 24 through June 29, 1962, where draft articles of a proposed convention are set forth. *Am. Journal,* Vol. 57 (1963), p. 241. The International Law Commission of the United Nations has had the question of treaties under consideration since it was selected by the Committee for codification in 1949. Successive reports have been submitted; and in 1962 draft articles were adopted and circulated among the governments. See *U.N. Yearbook,* 1962, p. 480.

international agreements and the function they perform in modern international law, it is important to observe the distinction between bilateral and multilateral treaties. Many bilateral treaties still bear the closest analogy to the private contracts of individual citizens.[2] When two states seek to promote interests peculiar to themselves which it would be impossible or inexpedient to regulate by a general rule of law, such as the development of the St. Lawrence Waterway, their agreement may be a purely personal one, raising no issues of international law and involving in no way the interests of the international community. A treaty providing for the cession of territory, such as the sale of Louisiana by France to the United States in 1803, may differ in no substantial way from a deed of sale executed between two individual citizens of the same state. Again, the treaty of 1818, by which Great Britain granted to the United States special fishing rights on the banks of Newfoundland, was closely analogous to the creation of a similar servitude—for example, *profits à prendre*—under the rules of the common law. These treaties, being strictly private contracts, are not in themselves sources of international law, although controversies as to their interpretation may raise points of law implied in the conclusion of the contract.

Other bilateral treaties may take on a wider scope and enter the field which, in municipal law, would be occupied by legislative enactments and executive functions. Individual citizens, confronted with conflicting claims of interest to which the existing rules of law are inadequate, turn to the national legislature of the state for the enactment of a general rule governing the particular field. States themselves, not having recourse to an international legislature, have been obliged to do for themselves, two by two or in small groups, what the community as a whole has been unable to do. Hence the multiplicity of bilateral treaties dealing with matters which, in municipal law, would fall within the jurisdiction of the legislative or executive departments of the government. Fugitive criminals should obviously be sent back for trial to the country whose law they have violated. But because of differences in the criminal law of separate states, and particularly differences in the conception of political as distinct from strictly criminal offenses, states have thus far been unable to conclude a general international convention on the subject of extradition, to replace the innumerable bilateral treaties that clutter up the files of foreign offices and give rise to equally innumerable divergencies of interpretation.[3] In like manner the numerous bilateral treaties of amity, commerce, and navigation represent an attempt on the part of states to establish relations with other states in respect to interests which it has not yet been found possible to bring under a single rule of international law.

[2] See Lauterpacht, *Private Law Sources and Analogies of International Law.*
[3] For the efforts made to codify the law of extradition, see below, p. 397.

Multilateral law-making treaties. By contrast with these bilateral treaties, there are two groups of general or multilateral treaties, which have been called "law-making" treaties and which, although differing in many respects from the statutes of municipal law, do in fact express the common will of the parties upon the subjects of the treaty. Certain of these treaties have dealt with the political interests of states and have attempted to adjust conflicts of claims by defining rights and duties and laying down new principles of international law. Of such character was the important Final Act of the Congress of Vienna of 1815 which, because of the dominant position of the signatory powers, became in time the law for all Europe and, in part, for the world at large. The Declaration of Paris of 1856, concluded between a small group of states, likewise became by the adhesion of other states a general law-making treaty. The Hague Conventions of 1899 and 1907 became law-making treaties between the states ratifying them. The Covenant of the League of Nations was in like manner a great law-making treaty, in spite of the indefinite character of certain of its obligations.[4] The Pact of Paris created new rights and obligations and extended the range of both substantive and procedural law.[5] The Charter of the United Nations now replaces the Covenant of the League of Nations as the outstanding international legislative document.

In addition to the more formal law-making treaties of universal application mention must be made of the successive "declarations" of inter-American conferences and meetings of foreign ministers, in accordance with which principles of inter-American law have been from time to time proclaimed.[6] These declarations are regarded by the American Republics as having the force of law within their regional group.[7] They mark a distinct contribution of the inter-American community to the development of regional law, giving expression as they do to what has been called "the juridical conscience of America," or, in Anglo-Saxon terms, "international common law."

Far more numerous, if intrinsically less important than treaties relating to the field of political interests, are the multipartite treaties dealing

[4] Art. 10 of the Covenant marked, perhaps, the greatest step forward in international law taken up to that time. That it failed to accomplish its purpose was not due to the intrinsic weakness of the principle it involved.

[5] See below, p. 625.

[6] Of such character, for example, among others was the Declaration of Principles of Inter-American Solidarity and Coöperation, adopted at Buenos Aires in 1936, the Declaration of American Principles, adopted at Lima in 1938, and the Declaration of Mexico, adopted at Mexico City in 1945.

[7] In the Preamble of the Act of Chapultepec, adopted at the Conference on Problems of War and Peace at Mexico City in 1945, it is said that "The American States have been incorporating in their international law, since 1890, by means of conventions, resolutions and declarations, the following principles . . ." No distinction is made with respect to the juridical character of principles incorporated in treaties or those incorporated in resolutions and declarations.

with the economic and social interests of states.[8] These agreements do not in general define the rights and duties of the parties in respect to some preexisting matter of dispute. Rather they propose a common object to be attained by mutual cooperation, and they usually set up administrative agencies for the execution of the provisions agreed upon. Within recent years they have come to include an ever wider range of interests, and they are comparable in international law to the legislation of national governments in the broad field of "social justice."

Meaning of the term "law-making." The term "law-making" applied by jurists to these multipartite conventions must, however, be understood in a descriptive and analogical rather than in a strictly legal sense. They approximate to statutory legislation, but they differ from it in several important respects. In the first place the plenipotentiaries who attend the conferences and congresses at which such conventions are drawn up have in spite of their titles no delegated powers enabling them to take final decisions in respect to the subject before them, and they have no collective authority enabling them to control the acts of states not members of the conference or, if members, not wishing to be bound by the decision taken. Hence the conventions come into force only upon the subsequent ratifications of the states which choose to act upon them, leaving other states free to remain outside the agreement and be governed by the former law, if any. In the second place the force of the conventions is qualified by the fact that, as generally provided, an individual signatory power may, upon giving due notice, denounce the convention and thereby release itself from the obligations it has assumed.[9] Nevertheless it seems appropriate to use the term "law-making," or the alternative term "legislative," [10] in regard to such agreements. For they do actually have the effect of creating new legal relationships and at times of setting up new machinery for the continuous administration of the affairs covered by the agreement.

B. BINDING FORCE OF TREATIES

The oldest and doubtless the most fundamental rule of international law is that of the sanctity of treaty obligations. That good faith should be kept between states in respect to their contractual agreements has been from the earliest times regarded not merely as a matter of legal duty between the parties to the treaty, but as a matter of common concern to the whole community of states.[11] To the Greeks the rule of good

[8] The scope of these conventions is surveyed in a subsequent chapter, XXV.

[9] Denunciation, however, is less likely in the case of treaties dealing with economic and social interests than in the case of treaties dealing with political interests.

[10] "The term *international legislation* would seem to describe quite usefully both the process and the product of the conscious effort to make additions to, or changes in, the law of nations." Hudson, *International Legislation*, Vol. I, § xiii.

[11] See Phillipson, *International Law of Ancient Greece and Rome*, Vol. I, Chaps. XIII-XV.

faith was part of the universal law. To the Romans it was part of the *jus gentium* common to every tribe and people. *Pacta sunt servanda.*[12] Philosophers, theologians, and jurists have recognized with unanimity that unless the pledged word of a state could be relied upon the relations of the entire international community would be imperiled and law itself would disappear.[13]

But when this broad principle has been laid down, many embarrassing questions have arisen as to its particular application in specific cases. What if the good faith of the state has been pledged by a monarch or dictator whose right to speak in the name of the state is morally unfounded even if legally valid? What if a state has been intimidated into signing a treaty by threats of violence by the other party, or as a result of defeat in war? What if, during the passage of years, the conditions under which the treaty was entered into should change so fundamentally as to make it doubtful whether the terms of the treaty are any longer in line with the original intention of the parties? All of these questions call for careful examination. While they do not challenge the principle of good faith directly, they do so indirectly through exposure of certain fundamental weaknesses of international law, of which unscrupulous governments have at times been ready to take advantage.[14]

C. CLASSIFICATION OF TREATIES

International law knows no formal classification of treaties. Like the contracts of municipal law, treaties are of the widest variety, dealing with the whole range of interests of international life. Methods of classification have at times been suggested by publicists in the interest of scientific precision and clearness, and several of them are helpful as throwing light upon the legal character of the engagement entered into. Thus the distinction between *unilateral* and *bilateral* treaties indicates whether the obligation is binding upon one party only or upon both parties. Unilateral in substance, if not in form, was the treaty between the United States and Cuba in 1903. The distinction between *bipartite* and *multipartite* bears merely upon the number of parties to the treaty, not upon its legal character. The distinction between *simple*

[12] Cicero, in his *De Officiis*, § iii, no. 24, puts the question "Pacta et promissa semperne servanda sint?" and answers it in words that might be read with profit at the present day.

[13] Compare the impressive appeal made by Grotius, *De jure belli ac pacis*, Eng. trans., Bk. III, Chap. XXV: "For not only is each separate state held together by good faith, but also that greater society of which states are the members. Aristotle speaks truly when he says that if good faith has been taken away, 'all intercourse between men becomes impossible.'" To the same effect the statement of Secretary Hull, July 16, 1937. Hackworth, *Digest*, Vol. V, p. 164.

[14] See on the general subject, J. L. Kunz, "The Meaning and the Range of the Norm *pacta sunt servanda*," *Am. Journal*. Vol. 39 (1945), p. 180; Harvard Research, *Draft Convention on Treaties*, Art. 20 and Comment.

and *conditional* treaties bears upon the absolute or qualified character of the obligation assumed, as in the case of a treaty of guarantee. More important is the distinction between *executed* and *executory* treaties. Executed treaties, also known as transitory or dispositive treaties, deal with single acts which are to be performed forthwith and which, when performed, dispose of the matter once and for all. Of such character are boundary conventions and treaties of cession, which closely approximate to deeds of transfer and other executed contracts of municipal law. On the other hand, executory treaties are continuous, dealing with acts which are to be performed regularly whenever the occasion for them is present or with exceptional acts which must be performed when the particular conditions specified in the treaty come about. Such are treaties of commerce and of extradition and the numerous treaties establishing administrative agencies, which set up continuous relations between the parties for the life of the treaty. Such also are treaties of alliance, which may operate over a long period of years without once calling for performance. The classification of treaties according to their objects, distinguishing between political, social, and economic objects, has little or no bearing upon the legal nature of the obligations assumed, although it is a convenient method for a descriptive treatment of the substance of the treaty.[15]

D. FORMATION OF TREATIES: CAPACITY OF THE PARTIES

International law has long recognized as one of the distinguishing tests of international personality that the state possessing it should be able to contract freely with other states. At the same time, however, international law has recognized that a sovereign state, a state which held full membership in the international community, could as a matter of fact bind itself by a treaty with one state not to enter into certain treaties with other states which might bring about the conditions which the first treaty sought to prevent. Such restrictions are a clear notice to third states that the state subject to them is not competent to enter into the particular treaty; or that if legally competent to do so from the point of view of international law, it could not do so without breach of faith to another state. By the treaty of 1839 Belgium obligated itself to observe toward all other states the neutrality imposed upon it by the powers which guaranteed to it that status. Treaties of alliance were thus barred to Belgium during the period of neutralization. Again, in the treaty of 1903 with the United States by which Cuba formally acquired independence, the new republic agreed not to enter into any treaty with a foreign state which would have the effect of impairing its independence or of authorizing any foreign power to obtain a lodgment in or control

[15] The distinction between executed and executory treaties was in former times of special importance in connection with the effect of war upon treaties. See p. 765.

over the island.[16] If in both cases the control of the state over its foreign
affairs seemed to be seriously restricted, the improbability that it would
desire to take the action contemplated reduced the restriction to relative
insignificance. Restrictions of this character are not regarded as affecting
the sovereignty of the state or as qualifying its capacity to contract in
other matters. The same is to be said of the numerous restrictions imposed upon the treaty-making power of Germany by the Treaty of
Versailles of 1919.[17] By the treaty of St. Germain, Austria was forbidden to alienate its independence except with the consent of the
Council of the League of Nations.

In the peace treaties following the Second World War no restrictions
were put upon the treaty-making powers of the satellite states; but the
Free Territory of Trieste was put under the obligation not to make or
discuss any military arrangements or undertakings with any state.[18]

Treaties with dependent states. In contrast with the above instances
where the legal capacity to contract was left untouched but the scope
of its practical application was restricted, there were the various treaties
entered into between fully sovereign states and states whose legal position in the community of nations was of a doubtful character. In the
case of the native tribes of Africa or of the smaller islands of the Pacific,
the agreements were not regarded as creating the rights and obligations
of the international law of treaties, due to lack of capacity to contract
on the part of the native princes or chiefs. In the Island of Palmas case [19]
the arbitrator reached that conclusion with respect to treaties between
the Dutch East India Company and the native chieftains of the adjacent
islands. More difficult situations were presented where the contracting
state had some standing in international law but an undetermined one,
as in the case of vassal states such as Bulgaria and Egypt in the latter
part of the nineteenth century, or in the case of backward states such as
Abyssinia before its admission into the League of Nations. On the other
hand no difficulty was experienced in connection with treaties made
with the British self-governing dominions, in spite of the indirect forms
of negotiation and signature. Canada's treaty-making power, for example, passed through several stages. After 1884 Canada had the right
to negotiate commercial treaties with foreign nations, but its agent acted
for that purpose through the channels of the British Foreign Office.
Later, Canada's representative negotiated alone but signed in conjunc-
tion with the British ambassador. Still later, the Halibut Fisheries Treaty

[16] See pp. 129 ff., where the later treaty of 1934 is referred to.
[17] Arts. 282-295. Germany was required to abrogate certain treaties, to continue
others in force, and to conclude new treaties of a stipulated character.
[18] Treaty with Italy, Annex VI, Art. 3.
[19] Tribunal of the Permanent Court of Arbitration, 1928. *Hague Court Reports*
(Second Series), pp. 83 ff. Fenwick, *Cases,* p. 470; Hudson, *Cases,* pp. 41, 361. See
above, p. 422.

of 1923 was signed by the Canadian minister alone, he acting on that occasion as the representative of the British Crown and holding full powers from it. The treaty was officially described, however, as having been entered into by the United States with "Great Britain." [20] Since the establishment of the British Commonwealth of Nations the members contract by their own agents and in their own names.

The right of the members of a confederation to enter into treaties with foreign nations is a matter of constitutional rather than of international law. The member states of Switzerland are competent, under the constitution of that country, to enter into treaties with foreign powers with respect to local matters. In such cases the particular foreign power may be expected to take notice of the constitutional limitation upon the capacity of the canton to contract.

Constitutional limitations. May the capacity of a sovereign state to contract be limited by its own constitution, so that other states are held to notice of any restrictions which it may impose? [21] The question has been discussed at length in the United States where the Constitution assigns a wide field of reserved powers to the member states of the union.[22] In theory it would seem reasonable that foreign states, contracting with the United States, should be held to a knowledge of any express prohibitions of the Constitution against the adoption of the provisions in question.[23] But this is an academic issue, since it is not to be expected that the Senate, in giving its advice and consent to the ratification of the treaty by a two-thirds vote, would overlook an express prohibition of the Constitution. Suppose, however, that, in a matter in respect to which the Constitution contained no express provisions, the President, after receiving the advice and consent of the Senate, should

[20] Even at that time the formality that the treaty had been entered into with "Great Britain" was sharply criticized. See A. L. Lowell, "The Treaty-Making Power of Canada," *Foreign Affairs,* September 15, 1923, pp. 12-22. Since then the situation has changed, and the Government of Canada now signs treaties in the name of "His Majesty, for the Dominion of Canada," as in the case of the Halibut Fisheries Treaty of 1930. See R. B. Stewart, *Treaty Relations of the British Commonwealth of Nations;* McNair, *op. cit.,* pp. 68 ff.

[21] The question is to be distinguished from that of the observance of constitutional provisions in respect to the ratification of a treaty, which relates to the powers of state agents, not to the capacity of the state to contract.

[22] Instances of conflicts between the treaty-making power and the Constitution may be found in Moore, *Digest,* Vol. V, §§ 735-736. The scope of the treaty-making power in the United States is discussed at length in Missouri v. Holland, 252 U.S. 416 (1920), upholding, against the plea by Missouri of an invasion of its state rights, an act of Congress enforcing the Migratory Bird Treaty Act of 1918. Fenwick, *Cases,* p. 608; Bishop, *Cases,* p. 89; Briggs, *Cases,* p. 872; Hudson, *Cases,* p. 850. See also Cook v. United States, 288 U.S. 102 (1933), in which the court construed an act of Congress of 1930 in the light of the treaty of 1924 between the United States and Great Britain. Fenwick, *Cases,* p. 613; Hudson, *Cases,* p. 637.

[23] The subject is discussed at length in Hyde, *Int. Law chiefly as Interpreted and Applied by the United States,* Vol. II, pp. 138 ff., where an elaborate bibliography is given.

ratify a treaty, and that subsequent to ratification the Supreme Court
of the United States should declare the provisions of the treaty to be
contrary to the Constitution, would the treaty become invalid in consequence? [24] A case has not actually arisen in more than one hundred
and seventy years of practice, so that the issue is academic, as in the case
of the supposed violation of express provisions of the Constitution.[25] If,
however, it should arise it would seem that the answer should be that
foreign states are entitled to take the approval of the Senate and the
subsequent ratification of the treaty by the President as a final decision
in respect to the constitutionality of the treaty.[26] Proceedings for the
abrogation of the treaty would then be in order, assuming that no other
way could be found of meeting the constitutional requirements; and it
is not to be believed that under the conditions of the present day the
other party would decline to adjust the situation upon an equitable basis.

Powers of state agents. Prior to the development of modern constitutional governments, there was a clear rule of international law that
the agents delegated by their governments to negotiate a treaty must
have "full powers" to conclude a binding agreement. Since the decision
of the monarch was final in point of domestic law, it was only necessary
for him to authorize his agent to act in his name, and upon the signature
of the latter the agreement became binding forthwith. Moreover, communication being slow, it was impossible for the agent to be in close
touch with his government. For this reason it became necessary to confide in his skill as a negotiator and to accept as final the best bargain he
could succeed in making. The works of the writers of the eighteenth
century are consequently preoccupied with questions of the due authorization of diplomatic agents, and of the results which should follow in

[24] Few states are in the embarrassing position of the United States where the final
word in the determination of the constitutionality of a treaty rests with a body which
took no part in the negotiation of the treaty or in its subsequent approval. But, as
observed, the embarrassment is theoretical rather than practical.

[25] Hyde accepts the test of the existence of "an international relationship" as determining the constitutionality of a treaty, quoting Secretary of State Hughes as follows: "The normal scope of the power [to make a treaty] can be found in the
appropriate object of the power. The power is to deal with foreign nations with regard to matters of international concern. . . . This is a sovereign nation; from my
point of view the nation has the power to make any agreement whatever in a constitutional manner that relates to the conduct of our international relations unless there
can be found some express prohibition in the Constitution, and I am not aware of any
which would in any way detract from the power as I have defined it in connection
with our relations with other governments." Acting on this principle Secretary Hughes
was unwilling to accept the Bustamante Code of Private International Law proposed
at the Havana Conference of 1928, believing it "inadvisable to attempt to press the
treaty-making power in such a novel exercise." Compare the ratification by the United
States of the Migratory Bird Treaty, note 22 of this chapter.

[26] The necessity of this rule may best be seen by contemplating the alternative,
that foreign states could not rely upon the treaty until a test case had been presented
to the Supreme Court.

case an agent had exceeded his powers.[27] Cases might arise where an agent pledged his government to acts so clearly detrimental to the state that good faith did not require the acceptance of the terms. Or again, an agreement might be concluded by an agent in excess of the powers entrusted to him, and on the strength of it acts might be performed by the other party to the advantage of the state before it could repudiate the act of its agent. What were the obligations of the state benefiting by such an agreement? It was clear that restitution must be made, and as far as possible conditions must be put back where they were before.[28] In many instances this presented serious practical difficulties, especially in the case where the agreement was made between military commanders in the field.[29] These and other rules of the older law have now little more than historical interest, since international law at the present day recognizes that treaties become binding not upon the signature of the diplomatic agents who have concluded them but upon subsequent exchange of ratifications of the agreement by the governments of the states parties to the treaty.

Ratification of treaties. Formal ratification has now become an accepted part of the procedure of treaty-making, and international law clearly recognizes that there is no legal ground of complaint by one party if the other should subsequently repudiate the agreement signed in its behalf by its agent.[30] The constitutional procedures of the different states vary widely in respect to the conditions of ratification. Ratification itself is an executive act, performed by the head of the state, announcing the formal acceptance of the treaty.[31] But before the head of the state can take such action many constitutions require the consent of one or both branches of the legislature. In the United States the ad-

---

[27] See, for example, Vattel, *Droit des gens,* Bk. II, §§ 207, 212, where numerous phases of the law of his time are discussed.

[28] Compare the rules laid down by Grotius, Bk. II, Chap. XV, § XVI, and Vattel, Bk. II, § 209, for the agreement known as *sponsio* made by a public official in excess of authority conferred or upon his own personal responsibility.

[29] The classic case is that of the agreement between the Roman consuls and the Samnites at the Caudine Forks, 321 B.C. See Vattel, *loc. cit.* See below, p. 690.

[30] The doctrine of the older writers that ratification could not be legally or morally refused has long since been abandoned. Vattel, *Droit des gens,* Bk. II, § 156, marks the transition to the later doctrine. In the case of the *Eliza Ann,* 1 Dodson 244 (1813), Sir William Scott found the practice of ratification well established. Fenwick, *Cases,* p. 736; Hudson, *Cases,* p. 857.

The modern rule is specifically laid down in the Convention on Treaties, adopted at Havana in 1928, Art. 5: "Treaties are obligatory only after ratification by the contracting States, even though this condition is not stipulated in the full powers of the negotiators or does not appear in the treaty itself." Hudson, *Int. Legislation,* Vol. IV, p. 2380.

[31] Ratification is often popularly used to indicate the approval of one or both bodies of the legislature; but strictly taken, it is an executive act. On the general subject, see Wilcox, *The Ratification of International Conventions.*

vice and consent of a two-thirds majority of the Senate is required.[32] In Great Britain it has become customary for the Cabinet before ratifying a treaty in the name of the Crown in Council to submit the treaty to Parliament for approval. In Brazil, under the constitution of 1946, the President has the power to enter into treaties *ad referendum* of the Congress, which must "decide definitively" upon them;[33] and a similar rule prevails in the other American states, it being the general practice to require the approval of both houses of the Congress.[34]

Effect of failure to observe constitutional procedures. What is the validity of a treaty which has been ratified by the head of the state without submission to the legislature in accordance with the provisions of the Constitution? A number of authors have held that foreign governments are justified in considering the act of the head of the state as definitive, leaving it to constitutional law to determine whether he has acted within the scope of his powers.[35] Constitutional processes, they hold, vary in the different states; and it is sufficient that the head of the state shall declare that they have been fulfilled to consider them as fulfilled. The majority of writers, however, maintain that foreign governments should be held to a knowledge of the constitutional prerequisites of ratification in each country with which they are dealing; and they insist that a treaty which has been ratified without the proper observance of these requirements is *ipso facto* invalid, whatever the proclamation of the head of the state may assert in that respect.[36]

While the doctrine of the necessity of the observance of constitutional procedures makes a strong appeal on ground of democratic principles, it is open to serious inconveniences. In general it would seem but just and equitable that a treaty entered into by a government should represent the will of the people, in so far as that can be determined by the vote

[32] Art. II, § 2: The President "shall have the power, by and with the advice and consent of the Senate, to make treaties, provided two thirds of the Senators present concur."

[33] Article 87, VII.

[34] See, for Argentina, Antokoletz, *Tratado,* Tercera parte, p. 267.

[35] The subject is carefully treated in the Harvard Draft, Comment on Art. 21. Anzilotti, Cavaglieri, Verdross, and Basdevant, and in the United States Willoughby, are cited as supporting the position that the declaration of the head of the state that a treaty has been concluded in accordance with the requirements of the constitution is conclusive as to the facts.

[36] The Harvard Draft cites, among others, Strupp, Schücking, C. De Visscher, Mirkine-Guetzévitch, Hyde, Hall, and McNair. The Harvard Draft itself, Art. 21, proposes: "A State is not bound by a treaty made on its behalf by an organ or authority not competent under its law to conclude the treaty; however, a State may be responsible for an injury resulting to another State from reasonable reliance by the latter upon a representation that such organ or authority was competent to conclude the treaty." The Convention on Treaties, signed at Havana in 1928, is indecisive on the point, merely providing that: "Treaties will be concluded by the competent authorities of the States or by their representatives, according to their respective internal law."

of the legislative body. Otherwise there will be a tendency to repudiate the treaty if at a later date it should become burdensome. But what if the constitution of the state be temporarily in suspense? What if the head of the state has assumed the legislative power and is governing the state under "decree-laws"? Are treaty negotiations to be discontinued with such a government, even though normal diplomatic relations are being maintained with it? Or are foreign states to consider themselves free to treat with such a totalitarian ruler and to look upon the acquiescence of the people in his dictatorial rule as approval of his personal decisions in the determination of the foreign policies of his country? Obviously each state, in treating with him, should take into account the circumstances and decide for itself whether, as a practical matter, apart from legal obligations, it is safe to take his word as the word of the state which he pretends to represent.[37] After assuming power as a "liberal," Fidel Castro first postponed elections, and subsequently not only withdrew his promise of them but proceeded to suppress fundamental human rights. Under the circumstances, no treaty with him could be considered on general principles of justice and morality as binding upon the Cuban people; and governments that still maintained relations with him did so at a risk. But international law left with each state the decision in the matter.[38]

In the case of multilateral treaties greater difficulties are to be experienced. For each exchange of full powers at the time of signing the treaty must be attended by an inquiry into the existing constitutional situation in each of the fifty or more states parties to the treaty; and under the changing conditions of the present day it may not be easy in certain cases to obtain precise answers. Doubtless no little embarrassment would have been created at San Francisco in 1945 if it had been understood that the United States, before accepting the ratifications of the signatories of the Charter of the United Nations for deposit, would find it necessary to decide whether the ratifications of each of the signatories was in accord with the constitutional procedures of the particular states.[39] Account should also be taken of the fact that in a number of states with one-party governments the approval of a treaty by the legislative body would have no significance beyond the approval of the executive power.[40]

It is suggested as the correct rule, *de lege ferenda*, that when the national legislature, by reason of the suspension of the constitution, is

[37] At this point the issue is closely connected with the problem of the recognition of new governments. See Chap. VIII.

[38] As it happens, international law has no procedure for withdrawing recognition *de jure*, once it has been granted, no matter how unrepresentative a particular government may be. See "Recognition *de facto:* In Reverse Gear," *Am. Journal,* Vol. 58 (1964), p. 965.

[39] The number at that time of constitutions in suspense or nonexistent must have almost equaled the number in effect.

[40] As in the case of the Soviet Union and of Yugoslavia.

unable to give its approval to a treaty, the ratification of the head of the state should be regarded as temporary and conditional, pending the reestablishment of the constitution and the subsequent approval by the legislature of the agreement. The mere fact of the suspension of constitutional procedures does not of itself suggest that the act of the head of the state may not represent the people of the state. But it raises the issue; and it suggests that temporary and conditional ratification would be the more equitable rule. The same is to be said of agreements with totalitarian governments, in which the free expression of public opinion is suppressed. There may be no other alternative than to contract with them as if they represented the public opinion of the state. But the international community should not be surprised if succeeding governments should take somewhat lightly the obligations of their predecessors.[41]

Retroactive effect of ratification. Does a treaty, when ratified, operate retroactively, so as to take effect as from the date of signature? The earlier rule, taken over by the United States courts, that a treaty had such retroactive effect has been widely questioned. In the case of Haver v. Yaker [42] the Supreme Court of the United States stated that the rule did not apply where the treaty operated upon private rights, and held that the property of an intestate naturalized citizen should pass to his heir under the earlier law, to the exclusion of certain other alien heirs whose rights were recognized by a treaty signed prior to Yaker's death but not ratified until after his death. The Harvard Research Draft Convention on the Law of Treaties definitely abandoned the old rule, finding that the rule "has no support today [1935] among writers on international law outside the United States," and that it "also runs counter to considerations of convenience, logic and reason." [43]

Ratification with reservations. Since the signature of a treaty represents a meeting of minds of the several parties upon specific provisions involving reciprocal obligations, any changes or amendments inserted by one party as a condition of ratification must be accepted by the other party if the treaty is to come into legal effect.[44] Thus the amendments to the Treaty of Versailles proposed by members of the United States Senate, in the form of the "Lodge Reservations," would have required the acceptance of the other signatory powers before the ratification of

---

[41] See pp. 199 ff. in connection with the effect of changes in governments.

[42] 9 Wallace 32 (1869). Hudson, *Cases*, p. 865; Fenwick, *Cases*, p. 603.

[43] Art. 11, Comment, p. 811. For applications of the earlier rule, see Moore, *Digest*, Vol. V, p. 244.

[44] The Harvard Draft defines a reservation as follows: "As the term is used in this Convention, a 'reservation' is a formal declaration by which a State, when signing, ratifying or acceding to a treaty, specifies as a condition of its willingness to become a party to the treaty certain terms which will limit the effect of the treaty in so far as it may apply in the relations of that State with the other State or States which may be parties to the treaty." Art. 13.

the United States could have had legal effect.[45] In such cases the negotiations may be regarded as continuing up to the time of ratification, the effect of the original signature being thereby waived. Reservations may be made to multilateral treaties at the time of signing, at the time of ratification, or at the time of accession. In each case, if they are to be valid, they must be accepted by all states which up to that time have signed the treaty or acceded to it.[46]

Ratification with reservations must be distinguished from ratification "with the understanding" that a specific interpretation is to be placed upon certain doubtful terms of the treaty. It is a common practice of states to stipulate in advance, by means of such "understandings," the interpretation they place on particular clauses of the agreement. When these advance interpretations are acceptable to the other party, they remain as evidence of intent in case of subsequent disagreement, although perhaps not formally incorporated into the treaty. In the case of the Kellogg-Briand Pact of 1928 the "understandings" of the Senate were incorporated in a committee report so as not to have the effect of reservations.[47]

On occasion it has happened that the failure of one of the parties to a limited multilateral treaty to ratify it has thrown doubt upon the obligations of others which have already ratified it. Are they thereby released from their obligations? When Great Britain, France, and other states ratified the Treaty of Versailles and assumed the obligation, under Article 10 of the Covenant of the League of Nations, to uphold the principle of collective security, they did so in anticipation of the United States becoming a party to the obligation. Did the failure of the United States to ratify the treaty change fundamentally the conditions under which the provisions of the treaty were expected to operate?[48] No general rule can be laid down, and each case must be taken on its own merits.

The question of reservations to a multilateral treaty became a practical issue when the General Assembly of the United Nations, confronted in 1950 with the problem of reservations to the Convention for the Prevention and Punishment of the Crime of Genocide, requested the Inter-

[45] For the text of the Lodge Reservations, see Lodge, *The Senate and the League of Nations,* pp. 172 ff.; Fleming, *The United States and the League of Nations,* Chap. XVII.

[46] Compare the detailed provisions of Arts. 14-16, Harvard Draft, and see Comment.

[47] See Myers, *Origin and Conclusion of the Paris Pact,* p. 68; Hackworth, *Digest,* Vol. V, p. 144.

[48] The German Government argued to that effect with respect to the failure of the United States to ratify the Treaty of Versailles, claiming that the presence of the United States on the Council of the League of Nations would have resulted in bringing the terms of the treaty more into accord with the terms of the armistice.

national Court of Justice to give an advisory opinion on the effect of reservations to the Convention; and at the same time it called upon the International Law Commission to study the general question from the point of view of the codification and progressive development of international law.

Diverse answers were forthcoming. The International Court of Justice left the question in doubt, proposing that each party to the Convention consider the state making the reservation a party to it if the reservation appeared in its judgment to be "compatible with the object and purpose of the Convention," thus making the decision individual for the particular state.[49] The International Law Commission held to the existing practice of the General Secretariat, stating that a reservation, to be valid, must be acceptable to all of the contracting parties.[50] The General Assembly thereupon closed the issue by approving a resolution requesting the Secretary General to continue to act as depository of documents containing reservations "without passing upon the legal effect of such documents," and to communicate the documents relating to reservations to all States concerned, "leaving it to each State to draw the legal consequences from such communications."[51] Was the Gordian knot cut, or only tied tighter?

The same question was presented to the Inter-American Council of Jurists and to its permanent committee, the Inter-American Juridical Committee. Earlier Pan American rules had held that a multipartite treaty attended by reservations would not be in force between the ratifying state and other states not accepting the reservation; but that the state making the reservation should submit it in advance, so that the comments of other states might lead it to modify its reservation so as to make it acceptable. The Council of Jurists, with numerous drafts of its Permanent Committee before it, drew up in 1959 a series of rules to be submitted to the Eleventh Conference, calling for prior submission of reservations, but for maintenance of the existing rule that the treaty would not be in force between the state making a reservation and other states rejecting it.[52]

E. ACCEPTANCE UNDER DURESS

Under municipal law, whether the common law of Great Britain and the United States or the civil law of Continental states, contracts entered into under duress are not binding. To constitute a legal agreement there must be a free offer and a free acceptance. Duress, however, is with a few exceptions limited to physical coercion or intimidation, and

[49] *U.N. Yearbook,* 1951, p. 820.
[50] Report of the International Law Commission, 1951, pp. 3-8.
[51] *U.N. Yearbook,* 1951, p. 832.
[52] Fenwick, *OAS,* pp. 337-341.

it does not include such moral coercion as is involved in taking advantage of the financial embarrassment or other material distress of a rival. By contrast, international law, having no final court of obligatory appeal for the adjustment of contract obligations, not only has overlooked the duress incident to the economic pressure that may be brought to bear by a strong state against a weaker state, but has never questioned, until of recent years, the validity of other forms of duress, especially the duress incident to treaties of peace at the conclusion of a war which has left one party in a position to impose its will upon the other.

Violence or intimidation used against the person of the sovereign or of his diplomatic agent, as in the case of the pressure brought to bear by Napoleon against Charles IV and Prince Ferdinand of Spain in 1808, or possibly in the case of the pressure exerted against the King of Korea by Japan in 1905 to accept a protectorate, would, of course, invalidate the agreement signed under such duress.[53] But in other cases where the intimidation was not against the person of the negotiator but against the state itself, the effect of coercion was more difficult to determine. In 1915, when the Great Powers of Europe were involved in war, Japan forced China to conclude a number of conventions embodying what became popularly known as the "twenty-one demands." China at first refused to enter into the agreements, which constituted a direct encroachment upon its sovereignty and independence. Japan applied the pressure of an ultimatum, and the conventions were finally signed, with the omission, however, of Group V of the "demands." Asserting that it had acted under duress, China sought a revision of the treaties at the bar of the Peace Conference at Paris. Failing to obtain redress, China again presented its case before the Washington Conference of 1921-1922, the Chinese delegate urging that "in the common interests of the Powers as well as of China" the treaties be reconsidered and canceled.[54] But while some of the obnoxious provisions of the treaties and notes of 1915 were modified by the conclusion of new treaties between the group of

[53] Compare Harvard Draft, Art. 32: "As the term is used in this Convention, duress involves the employment of coercion directed against the persons signing a treaty on behalf of a State or against the persons engaged in ratifying or acceding to a treaty on behalf of a State. . . ."

[54] Willoughby, *China at the Conference*, pp. 174, 249. The issue was clearly presented when, on February 2, the Japanese delegation argued that "if it should once be recognized that rights solemnly granted by treaty may be revoked at any time on the ground that they were conceded against the spontaneous will of the grantor, an exceedingly dangerous precedent will be established." In reply the Chinese delegation pointed out "that a still more dangerous precedent will be established with consequences upon the stability of international relations which cannot be estimated if, without rebuke or protest from other Powers, one nation can obtain from a friendly but, in a military sense, weaker neighbor, and under circumstances such as attended the negotiation and signing of the Treaties of 1915, valuable concessions which were not in satisfaction of pending controversies and for which no quid pro quo was offered." *Ibid.*, pp. 251, 254.

powers assembled at the conference, they refused to consider the technical question of the binding force of the earlier treaties and notes; and at the conclusion of the conference China declared its reservation of the right to seek relief on all appropriate occasions from those portions of the treaties and notes which did not appear to have been expressly relinquished by the Japanese Government.[55] The agreement signed by President Hacha on March 14, 1939, incorporating Bohemia and Moravia into the German Reich was entered into under threat of the immediate destruction of Prague. It would appear that the treaties between the Soviet Union and Esthonia, Latvia, and Lithuania in the opening months of the Second World War were signed under pressure; but the ultimate absorption of the three states into the Soviet Union kept the issue from being raised.

Treaties of peace. It is in connection with treaties of peace, however, that the question of acceptance under duress has been an international problem of first importance. From the earliest days rulers defeated in war have been obliged to sign treaties of peace fixing the terms upon which the conqueror was willing to bring hostilities to an end. Grotius recognized the validity of such treaties, regarding them an exception to the general principle of "equality" in the making of treaties.[56] Vattel applied the principle of good faith to treaties of peace as to other treaties, arguing with much subtlety that they should be regarded as the prudent choice of the sovereign when his country is confronted with the alternative of complete destruction.[57] This conception of the "voluntary" character of peace treaties was taken up by later writers and became the standard argument in favor of considering these treaties as binding obligations. War, they reasoned, was a legal remedy for the redress of wrongs. The treaty of peace was the price paid by the defeated party in redress of the injury that led to the war.[58] That force and intimidation were actually present at the signing of the treaty was no more taken into consideration than was the fact that the state which won the war might not be the one deserving redress. The distinguished British jurist Hall laid down the rule in positive terms: "In international law force and intimidation are permitted means of obtaining redress for wrongs, and it is impossible to look upon permitted means as vitiating the agreement, made in consequence of their use, by which redress is provided for." [59]

---

[55] For the views of publicists, see addresses by MacMurray, Butler, Turlington, and others, *Proceedings,* Am. Soc. Int. Law, 1932, pp. 37 ff.

[56] *De jure belli ac pacis,* Bk. II, Chap. XII, § X.

[57] *Droit des gens,* Bk. IV, § 37.

[58] See Chap. XXXV, "The Termination of War."

[59] *Int. Law,* § 108. Compare the position taken by Lawrence, that the fact that treaties of peace "were extorted by force is no good plea for declining to be bound by them." *Principles of International Law,* § 134.

Doubtful applicability of the rule of good faith. That the general principle of the good faith of treaties should suffer from the paradoxical situations thus presented was natural. Much depended upon the intrinsic character of the treaty of peace. If it appeared to the international community to be a reasonably just settlement of the conditions which led to the war the treaty of peace could be expected to take on a definitive character and give rise to the obligation of good faith. If it appeared to be oppressive and flagrantly unjust, it could be expected to last only as long as the state which imposed it was in a position to enforce it.[60] Opinions differed, however, as to the justice or injustice of particular treaties. When Germany coerced France into signing the Treaty of Frankfort in 1871, the community of nations accepted the treaty as setting up a new legal situation, and questions relating to Alsace-Lorraine were thenceforth referred by third states to Germany precisely as if the two provinces had been voluntarily ceded by France. But it was too much to expect that France should regard itself as bound in good faith to abide by the conditions imposed upon it by the treaty. Had France at any time after 1871 believed itself to be in a position to repudiate the treaty, it is doubtful whether third states would have cast any reproach of bad faith against it for attempting to do so.[61] Appearances could be saved, if necessary, by finding other grounds of war, and then, if the outcome were successful, taking back what had been previously granted under duress. War could be entered upon more lightly in days when its destructive effects were largely confined to the field of battle; and the sovereignty of the state was rarely put at issue in the conflict. Thus the faithful execution of treaties of peace was adjusted to shifts in the balance of power, and the principle of good faith was maintained while being indirectly undermined.

The Treaty of Versailles. The paradox of applying the principle of good faith to treaties of peace signed under duress appeared conspicuously in the conclusion of the Treaty of Versailles. The most destructive war of modern times had come to an end, and the victors were deter-

[60] This, it should be observed, was the condition attached by Vattel to his subtle argument. See note 57. There was understood to be a certain equality between the belligerents and mutual respect for their respective sovereignties, even though one was the victor and the other the vanquished. "If ever the plea of constraint may be admitted," said Vattel, "it is against an agreement which does not merit the name of a treaty of peace, against a forced submission to terms which are equally contrary to justice and to all the duties of humanity. If an ambitious and unjust conqueror subdues a Nation, and forces it to accept hard, disgraceful, and unendurable terms of peace, necessity may constrain the Nation to submit to them. But this show of peace is not real peace; it is oppression, which the Nation endures so long as it lacks the means to free itself; it is a yoke which men of spirit will throw off upon the first favorable opportunity." *Droit des gens,* Eng. trans., Bk. IV, § 37.

[61] Compare the eighth of President Wilson's Fourteen Points: ". . . and the wrong done to France by Prussia in 1871 in the matter of Alsace-Lorraine, which has unsettled the peace of the world for nearly fifty years, should be righted."

mined that the party primarily responsible should pay for the damage done and should be subjected to conditions which it was hoped would prevent a repetition of the offense. The settlement took the form of a treaty, but a treaty not negotiated with the offending state but imposed upon it. In signing the treaty the German delegates, although representing elements believed to be opposed to the policies of the government which had brought on the war, entered a formal protest against its terms: "Yielding to overwhelming force, but without on that account abandoning its view in regard to the unheard-of injustice of the conditions of peace, the Government of the German Republic therefore declares that it is ready to accept and sign the conditions of peace imposed by the Allied and Associated Governments." [62] This was a clear warning that Germany merely accepted the treaty without acknowledging any obligation of good faith in the execution of it should the military pressure be at any time removed. When, on May 17, 1933, Chancellor Hitler demanded a general revision of the treaty, asserting that decisions had been taken "which, in their injustice and lack of logic, bore the seeds of fresh conflicts," [63] the issue of good faith did not enter into the discussions of the foreign offices of the leading powers. Statesmen and jurists looked only to the practical effects of the revision demanded.

Now that the use of force by individual states has lost its legal character, "treaties of peace" belong to the law of the past. Minor wars, particularly civil wars or wars of secession, may doubtless take place; but it is to be expected that the United Nations, acting under its responsibility for maintaining law and order, will refuse approval of agreements imposed on one or other of the parties in conflict or, it may be, will itself impose conditions of settlement. The decision of the United Nations in such cases might well be in the nature of a sentence imposed upon the party at fault rather than a treaty of peace under the old law. [64]

Effect of fraud.   The presence of fraud or misrepresentation in the making of a treaty would, of course, render it invalid, as in the case of contracts under municipal law. [65] This rule, deducible from the general principle of good faith, obviously relates, however, to the case of fraud as to the subject matter of the contract, not to fraud in respect to the motives leading to the conclusion of the contract. For example, in the negotiations preceding the conclusion of the Treaty of Portsmouth in 1905, both the Russian and Japanese delegates made every effort to conceal facts tending to indicate domestic political conditions requiring a termination of hostilities irrespective of the fortunes of war. There appear to be no modern instances in which fraud has been alleged as a

[62] Baker, *Woodrow Wilson and World Settlement*, Vol. II, p. 519.
[63] Royal Institute, *Documents*, 1933, p. 196.
[64] Compare *Harvard Draft*, Comment, pp. 1152 ff., and writers cited.
[65] Compare Harvard Draft, Art. 31.

ground of nullification of a treaty, due, doubtless, to precautions taken in the negotiation of treaties and to the publicity generally attending them.

F. TREATIES IN VIOLATION OF INTERNATIONAL LAW

Precedents are wanting to decide, other than by inference from general principles, whether a treaty would be void if in violation of the accepted rules of international law. Undoubtedly, if international law is law in any sense of the word, its rules must take precedence of any compact or contract between individual members of the international community. But when this has been said, there remains so much latitude of interpretation as respects the application of the rules of international law that contracts in violation of the general law may readily continue, and have in fact continued, to remain in force irrespective of their dubious character. Doubtless an agreement between two or more states to commit an international crime, such as the partition of Poland in 1774, would not be regarded by third states as giving rise to any degree of good faith which public opinion would wish to see respected if one or other of the conspirators should fail to keep the traditional "honor among thieves." Nevertheless, treaties of such a character have come in time to be accepted by third states as representing a state of fact, from which prescriptive rights have arisen, and to that extent public opinion of the international community has acquiesced in the original agreement and given it a qualified legal standing. On the other hand, an agreement between two states in violation of principles of international law, such as the freedom of the seas, in which third states had a direct and personal interest, would, it may be inferred, be promptly repudiated by them; and would not only be regarded as null and void, but be taken as an attack upon their rights even before any concrete act were performed in pursuance of the agreement.[66]

Treaties opposed to public morality. It was commonly said that treaties were not binding when their provisions were opposed to the principles of morality and justice.[67] But this statement meant nothing more than that international law included within its rules certain general principles drawn from the fundamental laws of human conduct and that if a treaty were obviously to run counter to these it would not be recognized by third states as having binding force. A rule, stated in such broad terms, could have little practical effectiveness. In 1907 Great Britain and Russia entered into an agreement by which, without the consent of Persia, they marked off for themselves spheres of interest in

[66] See Roxburgh, *International Conventions and Third States*, pp. 31 ff.

[67] See, for example, Oppenheim, *International Law*, Vol. I, § 505, where it is nevertheless admitted that "it cannot be denied that in the past many treaties stipulating immoral obligations have been concluded and executed, but this does not alter the fact that such treaties were legally [sic] not binding upon the contracting parties."

that country and each agreed to respect the other's interests within their respective spheres.[68] The treaty unquestionably constituted a serious encroachment upon the actual, if not the formal, sovereignty of Persia, and might from that point of view have been said to be contrary to international public policy, if not to international law proper. The domestic conditions of Persia were, however, such as to make it possible for the parties to the treaty to assert philanthropic motives, and as a matter of fact the public opinion of the international community concerned itself very little with the affair.

An unusual situation arose in 1960 between Ecuador and Peru over title to territory on the eastern range of the Andes. By the Protocol of 1942, signed during the Conference of Ministers of Foreign Affairs at Rio de Janeiro, Ecuador ceded the greater part of the disputed area to Peru, and the agreement had been duly ratified within the thirty days fixed by the Protocol. But though ratified, the Protocol was so bitterly resented that it became a permanent political issue which finally took shape in a reassertion of the issue of coercion in spite of the formal ratification of the agreement.[69]

G. REGISTRATION OF TREATIES

The first of President Wilson's "Fourteen Points" had a far-reaching effect upon the development of international law: "Open covenants of peace, openly arrived at, after which there shall be no private international understandings of any kind, but diplomacy shall proceed always frankly and in the public view." [70] In accordance with this principle the Covenant of the League of Nations made provision that "Every treaty or international engagement entered into hereafter by any Member of the League shall be forthwith registered with the Secretariat and shall as soon as possible be published by it. No such treaty or international engagement shall be binding until so registered." [71] In 1934 the United States, although not a member of the League, agreed to register its treaties in the same way. In the course of some twenty years over 4,500 treaties were registered with and published by the League Secretariat.[72] The Charter of the United Nations carried over the tradition of the League of Nations, changing, however, the provision that unregistered treaties should not be binding into a provision that unregistered treaties may not be invoked by a member before any organ of the United Na-

---

[68] For the text of the agreement, see *Am. Journal,* Vol. 1 (1907), Supp., p. 400.

[69] Fenwick, *OAS,* p. 313. See above, p. 414.

[70] For the background of President Wilson's demand for open covenants, see Baker, *Woodrow Wilson and World Settlement,* Vol. I, p. 38.

[71] For comment on Art. 18 of the Covenant, see Ray, *Commentaire,* pp. 545 ff.; Harvard Draft, Art. 17 and Comment; M. O. Hudson, *Am. Journal,* Vol. 19 (1925), p. 280.

[72] See *League of Nations Treaty Series,* 1920-1944.

tions.[73] Within the inter-American regional group the Habana Convention on Treaties, of 1928, provided that "Treaties shall be published immediately after exchange of ratifications. The failure to discharge this international duty shall affect neither the force of treaties nor the fulfilment of obligations stipulated therein." At the International Conference of American States at Lima in 1938 a resolution was taken to adopt the system of depositing treaties in the Pan American Union; and in execution of this resolution the Pan American Union inaugurated in 1939 the registration of treaties between the American states.[74]

H. INTERPRETATION OF TREATIES

Beginning with the treatise of Grotius, publicists have developed a large body of theoretical rules applicable to the interpretation of treaties. It is difficult, however, to assign any very definite legal validity to these rules on account of the limited number of precedents illustrating their application. The absence, until of recent years, of an international tribunal of obligatory jurisdiction left this branch of international contractual relations to be worked out in each case by the parties to the particular treaty, with the result that disputes have been settled on the basis of concession or compromise, as the case might be, rather than on the basis of general principle.[75] Nevertheless, the rules laid down by the publicists have acquired at least an inchoate legal value, inasmuch as formal deference has from time to time been paid to them, even when the actual settlement of the dispute was worked out along different lines. Hence it seems proper to enumerate the more important of these general principles, with qualifications and illustrations drawn from the relatively few cases of their application. The close parallel between the rules of interpretation in international law and the corresponding rules of municipal law arises not only from the tendency of the earlier publicists to formulate their rules of international law upon the familiar basis of civil and common-law jurisprudence, but from the fact that statesmen themselves, when at a loss to settle concrete cases, naturally fell back upon principles of interpretation with which they were already familiar in the law of private contracts.[76]

Clear and specific terms not open to interpretation.   The object of

---

[73] Art. 102. For comment, see Goodrich and Hambro, *Charter of the United Nations.*

[74] See M. O. Hudson, "Registration of Treaties by the Pan American Union," *Am. Journal,* Vol. 38 (1944), p. 99; Fenwick, *OAS,* pp. 330 ff.

[75] The large number of states that have made declarations under Art. 36 of the Statute of the International Court of Justice has now remedied this situation. See p. 621.

[76] See, on this point, Schwarzenberger, *Int. Law,* Vol. I, p. 193, where the principles of interpretation adopted by the Permanent Court of International Justice are set forth: "The Court has freely made use of methods customarily applied regarding the interpretation of contracts in the principal systems of municipal law."

interpretation is to discover the understanding of the parties at the time the contract was entered into, not the design or motives of one or either of them in entering into the agreement. The understanding, or meeting of minds, must obviously be gathered from the terms themselves. It is the terms of the treaty which take legal priority in determining the alleged intention of the parties. Hence it is laid down that where the terms are clear and specific, no proof of an intention contrary to them is admissible.[77] This rule found application in the dispute between Great Britain and the United States over the meaning of the clause of the Hay-Pauncefote Treaty of 1901 which provided that the Panama Canal should be "free and open to the vessels of commerce and of war of all nations observing these Rules, on terms of entire equality." [78] On the side of the United States, it was contended that the term "all nations" should not be held to include the United States, since that country was the builder and owner of the canal and could not have had the intention to give up the right of preferential treatment for its own ships, especially when such treatment did not actually alter the basis upon which tolls were to be levied upon the vessels of other states.[79] On the side of Great Britain, it was argued that the terms of the treaty were definite and explicit, and were at the same time in conformity with the conditions under which the contract was entered into and with the consideration which had induced the making of the contract.[80]

Terms in conflict with the object of the treaty. When, however, the words of a treaty, if literally interpreted, run counter to the treaty's manifest object, the literal sense of the terms must not be held to exclude the broader interpretation required to accomplish that object. The classic example quoted in this connection is the stipulation contained in the Treaty of Utrecht that the port and the fortifications of Dunkirk should be destroyed and never rebuilt. Literally taken, the terms of the treaty left it open to France to build another fortress at Mardyck, at a distance of three miles from Dunkirk; and this France proceeded to do. Great Britain, however, protested against this evasion of the reasonable sense to be attached to the treaty, and in the end France acquiesced in the justice of the protest and abandoned the plan.[81]

Intrinsic and extrinsic evidence. Where the language of the treaty is

[77] For comment upon the conditions of his time, see the elaborate rules laid down by Vattel in 1758. *Droit des gens,* Eng. trans., Bk. II, Chap. XVII.

[78] Art. III, § 1. *Treaties and Conventions,* Vol. I, p. 782.

[79] Memorandum of President Taft, August 24, 1912, accompanying the signature of the Panama Canal Act. See *Proceedings,* Am. Soc. Int. Law, 1913, p. 324. See also C. H. Stockton and others, "Does the Expression 'All Nations' in Article 3 of the Hay-Pauncefote Treaty Include the United States?" *ibid.,* pp. 93-150; *Analytical Index, Am. Journal,* 1907-1920, under the heading "Panama Canal,—Tolls Question."

[80] *Am. Journal,* Vol. 7 (1913), Supp., pp. 46, 48.

[81] *Ibid.* For a more recent instance, see G. A. Finch, "The Legality of the Occupation of the Ruhr Valley," *Am. Journal,* Vol. 17 (1923), p. 724.

doubtful, it has been laid down that the general sense of the words must take precedence of a technical sense, unless the latter conforms more to the character and circumstances of the agreement. Also, the sense must be adopted which yields a reasonable meaning to the treaty, which does not reduce it to an absurdity, and which does not bring it into conflict with the general rules of international law.[82] Supplementing this intrinsic evidence of the meaning of the treaty, external evidence has been regularly produced showing the intention of the parties at the time of the making of the contract. This intention may be gathered not only from statements made at the time, but from the circumstances leading up to the treaty, the objects sought by it, and the consideration given on both sides. Hall quotes the celebrated case of the dispute between Great Britain and Holland in 1756 as to the meaning of earlier treaties of guarantee by which each state guaranteed to the other all its rights and possessions in Europe against "all Kings, Princes, republics, and states," and specific assistance was promised if either party should "be attacked or molested by hostile act, or open war." Being called upon for help by Great Britain when at war with France, Holland urged an interpretation of the treaty as requiring assistance only in the event that Great Britain should be attacked without itself having been in the first instance the aggressor; otherwise the treaty would be in contravention of international law.[83] But in view of the absence of any clear distinction between aggressive and defensive wars in that day, the reservation by Holland of the right to interpret the words "attacked or molested by hostile act" reduced the obligation to a nullity.

Terms with different meanings.   An exceptional case is that of a treaty in which terms are used which have a different meaning in the legal usage of the two contracting parties. The rule laid down for such cases is that the terms are to be understood according to the usage of the state in which they are to take effect, and that, if they are to take effect in both states, they must be given their proper meaning in each state. Hall

[82] In the case of Geofroy v. Riggs, 133 U.S. 258 (1890), the court observed that "it is a general principle of construction with respect to treaties that they shall be liberally construed, so as to carry out the apparent intention of the parties to secure equality and reciprocity between them," the interpretation of the court being to include the District of Columbia in "States of the Union." Fenwick, *Cases*, p. 621. In Asakura v. Seattle, 265 U.S. 332 (1924), the court interpreted liberally a treaty between the United States and Japan so as to protect a Japanese national in a particular form of "trade." *Ibid.*, p. 576. In Factor v. Laubenheimer, 290 U.S. 276 (1933), the court construed liberally a treaty between the United States and Great Britain so as to permit the extradition of a fugitive criminal. "If a treaty fairly admits of two constructions," said the court, "one restricting the rights which may be claimed under it, and the other enlarging them, the more liberal construction is to be preferred." *Ibid.*, p. 393. See also the decision of the tribunal of the Permanent Court of Arbitration in the Japanese House Tax Case interpreting later treaties in the light of earlier treaties. Scott, *Hague Court Reports*, pp. 77-92.

[83] Hall, *International Law*, § 111. The student may compare the restrictive interpretation put by Italy in 1914 upon the terms of the Triple Alliance.

cites the case of the treaty of 1866 between Austria and Italy, in which the "inhabitants" of the ceded provinces were to be allowed the privilege of withdrawal from the territory. As the word had different signification under Austrian and Italian law, it was interpreted in the Austrian sense, since the territory was Austrian at the time of the signing of the treaty.[84]

Austro-German Customs Union case. An important dispute of recent years regarding the interpretation of treaties was that concerning the proposed customs union between Germany and Austria in accordance with the Protocol of March 19, 1931, between the two countries. By Article 88 of the Treaty of St. Germain of 1919 Austria had undertaken not to do any act which might directly or indirectly compromise its independence without the consent of the Council of the League of Nations, and by the Geneva Protocol of 1922 Austria had undertaken in addition to abstain from any economic or financial engagement calculated directly or indirectly to compromise its independence and not to grant to any state a "special régime or exclusive advantages calculated to threaten this independence." The announcement of the proposed union was followed by diplomatic protests that it would be in violation of Austria's treaty obligations; and upon motion of Great Britain the matter was brought before the Council of the League of Nations and referred by it to the Permanent Court of International Justice for an advisory opinion.[85] The court, by a vote of eight to seven, held that the proposed union was not incompatible with the Treaty of St. Germain, but was incompatible with the Geneva Protocol. Six of the eight judges believed the union also incompatible with the Treaty of St. Germain, while the seven dissenting judges held it not to be incompatible with either treaty.[86]

Most-favored-nation clauses. The interpretation of the "most-favored-nation" clause, frequently inserted in commercial treaties, has given rise to numerous controversies. The purpose of this clause is to provide for an equality of treatment in commercial relations on the part of a particular state toward other states and, with this in view, to provide that any subsequent privileges that may be granted to any one state shall be automatically extended to other states with which such treaties have been concluded. The operation of the clause is illustrated in the case of Santovincenzo v. Egan,[87] in which the court allowed Italy the benefit of a treaty between the United States and Persia providing that the estates of aliens dying intestate and without known relatives should escheat

[84] Hall, *International Law*, § 111.

[85] *Publications of the Court*, Series A/B, No. 41 (1931). Fenwick, *Cases*, p. 632.

[86] For comment on the case see E. M. Borchard, *Am. Journal*, Vol. 25 (1931), p. 711; M. O. Hudson and P. C. Jessup, *ibid.*, Vol. 26 (1932), pp. 9, 105; A. P. Fachiri, *British Year Book*, Vol. 13 (1932), p. 68. For recent cases in the diplomatic relations of the United States, see Hackworth, *Digest*, Vol. V, p. 222.

[87] 284 U.S. 30 (1931), p. 583. Fenwick, *Cases*, p. 631; Bishop, *Cases*, p. 172.

to the state of which they were nationals. Disputes have arisen, as between the United States and Great Britain, whether, after concluding such an agreement, a state is precluded from entering into individual arrangements with a third state known as "reciprocity treaties," by which particular privileges are granted in return for reciprocal concessions from the other party, the United States claiming that the latter agreements, being based upon special advantages, formed the consideration of a contract distinct from the mere general commercial treaty, and Great Britain denying their separate character.[88]

Arbitration of disputed interpretations.   In spite of the somewhat uncertain basis upon which rest the rules of interpretation above enumerated, nations have quite generally regarded disputes concerning the interpretation of treaties as peculiarly susceptible to arbitration. This has doubtless been because the issues in such cases are definite and concrete, and because, while the rules of general jurisprudence are not per se legally applicable, they nevertheless furnish a convenient standard by means of which the arbitration tribunal may be enabled to arrive at an equitable decision. In the Final Act of the Second Hague Peace Conference of 1907 the conference announced itself unanimous, not only in admitting the principle of compulsory arbitration, but in declaring that certain disputes, particularly those relating to the interpretation and application of international agreements, might be submitted to compulsory arbitration without any restriction.[89] The general arbitration treaties concluded by the United States in 1908, known as the Root treaties,[90] specifically provided that differences of a legal nature and those "relating to the interpretation of treaties existing between the two contracting parties" should, with certain exceptions, be referred to the Permanent Court of Arbitration. The Taft, or Knox, treaties of 1911 specified differences arising by virtue of claims made by one party against the other "under treaty or otherwise." [91] Article 13 of the

---

[88] For a historical review of the controversy between the United States and foreign states regarding the interpretation of the most-favored-nation clause, see Moore, *Digest,* Vol. V, § 765. In particular, see the case of Whitney v. Robertson, 124 U.S. 190 (1888), in which the court held that the most-favored-nation clause in a treaty with the Dominican Republic "was never designed to prevent special concessions, upon sufficient considerations. . . ." Fenwick, *Cases,* p. 628; Hudson, *Cases,* p. 898.

In 1923 the United States reversed its policy and adopted the unconditional form of the most-favored-nation clause. See Art. 7, treaty of December 8, 1923, with Germany. See Hackworth, *Digest,* Vol. V, pp. 269 ff.; Culbertson, *Int. Economic Policies,* p. 94; Williams, *Economic Foreign Policy of the United States,* Chap. XV; Hyde, *Int. Law,* Vol. II, § 536.

For a study of the Reciprocal Trade Agreements entered into in pursuance of the Act of 1934, see *Am. Journal, Analytical Index,* 1921-1940, under title United States, Trade Agreements Act.

[89] *Hague Conventions,* p. 27.

[90] See, for example, the treaty with Great Britain. *Treaties and Conventions,* Vol. I, p. 814.

[91] See Hackworth, *Digest,* Vol. VI, p. 65.

Covenant of the League of Nations referred to the interpretation of treaties as being among the disputes "which are generally suitable for submission to arbitration." The interpretation of treaties figured as the first of the several classes of disputes in respect to which arbitration was accepted as obligatory under the Optional Clause accompanying the Statute of the Permanent Court of International Justice,[92] and it continues to hold that place in the declaration of compulsory jurisdiction contemplated in the Statute of the International Court of Justice.

A typical dispute involving the interpretation of a treaty arose between Mexico and the United States in 1961 over the provision of the treaty of 1944 which called for the delivery of a fixed quantity of water of the Colorado River, but which did not specify the quality of the water. Was it implied that the water would be without saline content, although the effect of the interpretation would make it impossible for the United States to use its share of the water for irrigation in the drainage areas of the river? [93]

I. EFFECT OF TREATIES UPON THIRD STATES

International law has no clear rule for determining what indirect effect treaties concluded between two or more states may have upon third states not parties to the agreement.[94] Statements are made in positive terms in many of the treatises, but the conflicting views of the different writers indicate the absence of any accepted customary rule.[95] The following rules may, however, be laid down tentatively, as in harmony with such precedents as are to be found in the modern practice of states.

Many treaties have been concluded since the beginning of the nineteenth century which, by the clear expression of their terms, have been intended by the contracting parties to be beneficial to third states. Where such treaties, as in the case of the Congo Treaty of 1885 providing for the free navigation of the principal rivers of the Congo basin, contain an accession or adhesion clause, third states are at liberty to become parties to the original treaty, and by so doing they acquire legal contractual rights to what would have been otherwise no more than voluntarily conceded privileges. Third states not acceding to the treaty would seem to acquire no rights under it, contrary to the position assumed by the United States in 1888, when, without having adhered to the Congo Treaty, the Government claimed the undisturbed enjoyment of free navigation as a "right." [96]

[92] See C. C. Hyde, "The Interpretation of Treaties by the Permanent Court of International Justice," *Am. Journal,* Vol. 24 (1930), p. 1.

[93] See above, p. 364.

[94] See Harvard Draft, Art. 18, where numerous authorities are cited.

[95] A summary of the views of publicists may be found in Roxburgh, *International Conventions and Third States,* Chap. III.

[96] *U.S. For. Rel.* (1888), Vol. I, p. 38; quoted by Roxburgh, *op. cit.,* p. 50.

Treaties conferring privileges. Where a treaty confers privileges upon third states without the assumption of any obligations on their part, it is a matter to be determined by the circumstances of each case whether in the course of time the rule of prescription may not have the effect of extending the scope of the treaty so as to include states not originally parties to it. The treaty of 1881 between Argentina and Chile, neutralizing the Straits of Magellan, embodied a fundamental principle of international law and may be said to have represented not so much a grant of privileges as the recognition of natural rights.[97] Hence if the treaty were to be annulled the question of the rights of third states would be thrown back upon customary law. The Hay-Pauncefote Treaty of 1901 provided that "the canal shall be open and free to the vessels of commerce and of war of all nations observing these Rules, on terms of entire equality." This was a voluntary grant of privileges to third states, which at that time could have set up no legal claim had the treaty been dissolved by the contracting parties.[98] In 1912 the protests of Great Britain against the exemption of American vessels from payment of tolls at the canal were seconded by other states having maritime shipping interests, although the latter had under the law no rights in the case. It would seem, however, that third states might acquire prescriptive rights after a long period of use during which they might have adjusted their commerce to the facilities at first freely offered them.[99]

Has a state cause for redress when its interests are injuriously affected by treaties to which it is not a party? By analogy with municipal law the right of redress in such cases would seem to depend upon whether the injury is the result of a violation of a legal right, or is merely what is known in English common law as a *damnum sine injuria*, a loss which involves no legal wrong.

J. TERMINATION OF TREATIES: PERFORMANCE

International law recognizes a variety of ways in which agreements legally entered into may terminate or become extinct.[100] The most obvious of these is doubtless termination by performance of the acts called for by the treaty. An international contract of sale, such as the purchase of the Virgin Islands by the United States from Denmark, is discharged or satisfied, and in that sense terminated, when the object of the sale has been transferred and the price stipulated has been paid.

[97] See above, p. 455.

[98] Roxburgh (*op cit.*, pp. 63-68) points out that the clause here quoted was adopted by the Senate as a substitute for the clause in an earlier treaty which made provision for the separate adherence of third states.

[99] Query, have third states come to have rights under the treaty of 1903 between the United States and Panama? See "Legal Aspects of the Panama Case," *Am. Journal*, Vol. 58 (1964), p. 436.

[100] On the general subject see A. D. McNair, "La Terminaison et la dissolution des traités." *Recueil des Cours,* Vol. 22 (1928-II), p. 463.

Such executed treaties remain, however, on record as the evidence of a valid title on the part of the assignee to the territory or other object transferred by the treaty.

Expiration of treaties in accordance with terms. By contrast with executed treaties, executory treaties, which deal with acts to be performed on specified occasions, or under specified conditions, may either expire in accordance with their own provisions or be dissolved by act of the parties or by force of circumstances. In both instances it is possible that the original object of the treaty may not have been attained, or may have been attained only in part.

Expiration in accordance with the definite provisions of the treaty is characteristic of a large body of treaties, bipartite and multipartite. Treaties of commerce and navigation have for the most part been concluded for a definite period of years, following which the treaty is to continue operative until six months' or a year's notice has been given in advance. Other treaties may, at the close of the fixed period, be automatically renewed for a similar period unless denounced within a specified time. In other cases expiration of the treaty has been provided for upon the occurrence of certain conditions contemplated in the treaty.[101]

Dissolution by agreement. International law recognizes the possibility of the dissolution of a treaty by mutual consent of the parties in advance of the time set for the treaty's expiration or, if no time is set, in advance of the fulfillment of the object of the treaty. In such cases the treaty may be completely set aside, rescinded, or superseded by a new treaty more in accord with the existing wishes of the contracting parties, as in the case of the dissolution of the Clayton-Bulwer Treaty of 1850 in favor of the Hay-Pauncefote Treaty of 1901.[102] Dissolution by the unilateral act of one or other of the parties may take place in the case of commercial and other treaties after the definite period for which they were concluded has expired. It may also take place in connection with those general international conventions to which the great body of states are parties when provision is made, as is commonly done, for the withdrawal of individual signatory powers upon giving due notice. The greater number of the thirteen conventions adopted at the Second Hague Peace Conference of 1907, for example, were without time limit; but provision was made that in the event of one of the contracting parties denouncing the particular convention, the denunciation should be notified to the Dutch Government and should not take effect until the expiration of one year after the notification had been given. Two conventions were

---

[101] See Tobin, *The Termination of Multipartite Treaties;* Hackworth, *Digest,* Vol. V, §§ 505-512.

[102] See Art. I, Hay-Pauncefote Treaty. *Treaties and Conventions,* Vol. I, p. 782.

concluded for specific periods, after which, unless denounced, they were to continue in force.[103]

Dissolution by force of circumstances. Treaties are in some cases legally dissolved, or better, perhaps, rendered void, by force of circumstances over which one or both of the parties have no control. This may happen when the international personality of one of the contracting parties becomes extinct. Treaties between Korea and other states formally terminated upon the annexation of that kingdom to Japan. The question whether in such cases the obligations of the extinct state must be taken over by the successor belongs rather to the law of international succession than to the law of treaty obligations in the strict sense of the term.[104] In cases where a previously independent state becomes a member of a federation and in so doing loses to a greater or less degree control over its foreign affairs, international law regards the act of entering the federation as the legal extinction of its international personality, and its former obligations devolve upon the federal state by the law of succession, as in cases of complete extinction.[105] On the other hand, the enlargement of a federal state by the addition of new members might raise the question whether rights previously enjoyed by it should extend to the new members. In 1871 the United States customs officers declined to extend to British Columbia concessions granted by treaty to the Dominion of Canada before that province had been admitted into the Dominion; and their action was acknowledged by the law officers of the Crown as consistent with the obligations of the United States.[106] On rare occasions treaties become void by reason of physical impossibility of performance. Or again, the arising of conditions physically or morally incompatible with the fulfillment of the treaty would either render it void or at least suspend its operation until the conditions had changed.

Violation of treaty by one party. The violation of a treaty by one of the contracting parties makes it voidable, or subject to cancellation, by the other party. This general principle appears to be an accepted rule of international law, but its application to concrete cases has raised difficulties. If a treaty is violated by a state in a minor detail, it is not clear whether the other party has forthwith the right to cancel the treaty as a whole. A majority of publicists, arguing *a priori*, concede such a right,

[103] *Hague Conventions*, pp. 151, 188.

[104] See p. 172. The Harvard Draft deliberately avoids a decision of this question, as being beyond the scope of the Draft. Art. 27, Comment.

[105] In the case of the new Serb-Croat-Slovene State in 1919 (later Yugoslavia), it was disputed whether it was a mere expansion of Serbia, or an entirely new state not responsible for the treaties of Serbia. Art. 12 of the treaty concluded with the Serb-Croat-Slovene State, September 10, 1919, required, however, that the treaties of Serbia should "*ipso facto* be binding upon the Serb-Croat-Slovene State." *Am. Journal*, Vol. 14 (1920), Supp., p. 333.

[106] Moore, *Digest*, Vol. V, p. 352.

owing to the impossibility of distinguishing between essential and non-essential stipulations.[107] Hall offers the "main object of a treaty," rather than any distinction between principal and secondary articles, as a "test which shall enable a candid mind to judge whether the right of repudiating a treaty has arisen in a given case." A breach which is material to the main object, he holds, liberates the other party from its obligations.[108] It is not clear whether, if one of a group of states should violate even the essential provisions of a treaty, the other states would be released from their obligations toward one another. In any case the treaty is not *ipso facto* canceled. The violation by Austria in 1908 of the Treaty of Berlin of 1878, by the annexation of Bosnia and Herzegovina, left the treaty intact as respected other territorial arrangements in the former European possessions of Turkey; although Bulgaria, itself a party to the Treaty only by implied consent, made use of the same opportunity to throw off the condition of formal vassalage to Turkey imposed upon it by the treaty.[109]

Optional validity of a voidable treaty. The extradition of Charlton by the United States to Italy under the treaty of 1868, to be put on trial for the murder of his wife, was contested by Charlton [110] on the ground that Italy had violated the treaty by its refusal to extradite its own citizens. The treaty called for the extradition of "persons," which in the technical usage of the United States included citizens. Since the obligations of an extradition treaty are reciprocal, Italy's action abrogated the clause of the treaty by which the United States agreed to surrender American citizens. The court held, however, that even if the action of Italy constituted a violation of the treaty, which, in international law, would have justified the United States in denouncing the treaty as no longer obligatory, it did not automatically effect its cancellation. There was, said the court, no necessity that treaties of extradition be reciprocal, so that if the United States should choose to acquiesce in the position taken by Italy, consistently with the more comprehensive Italian criminal law, the treaty might legally remain binding, and the executive department be at liberty to surrender the fugitive.[111]

Treaties of guarantee. Prior to the establishment of the League of

[107] See Oppenheim, *International Law,* Vol. I, § 547. The Harvard Draft makes the question dependent upon the decision of "a competent international tribunal or authority." Art. 27 and Comment, where the whole subject is exhaustively discussed.

For the long controversy between the United States and France in 1798-1800 whether the violations by France of the obligations of existing treaties justified their unilateral annulment by the United States, see Moore, *Digest,* Vol. V, pp. 356 ff.; Harvard Draft, Art. 27, Comment.

[108] *Int. Law,* § 116.

[109] See above, p. 128.

[110] In the form of a petition for a writ of habeas corpus to secure the release of the petitioner from detention under an extradition warrant. See above, p. 393.

[111] Charlton v. Kelly, 229 U.S. 447 (1913). Hudson, *Cases,* p. 949; Fenwick, *Cases,* p. 439; Bishop, *Cases,* p. 190.

Nations in 1920 jurists discussed at length the scope of the obligations of treaties of guarantee. These treaties were concluded with the object of maintaining special political situations and creating a special sanction for the observance of the obligations entered upon. The guarantees of the neutrality of Switzerland and of Belgium were joint and several obligations of the parties to the treaties, and it would appear that each of them was separately bound to uphold their provisions in case of their violation. By contrast, the guarantee of the neutrality of Luxemburg was a collective guarantee of all the parties, in accordance with which they were to act in concert to uphold the treaty as against any state not a party to the treaty.[112]

With the adoption of the Covenant of the League of Nations, Article 10 became a collective guarantee entered upon by all of the members of the League to respect and preserve as against external aggression the territorial integrity and existing political independence of each of them. The practical application of the guarantee was, however, made to depend upon a decision of the Council of the League as to the means by which the obligation should be fulfilled, so that individual members were not expected to uphold the guarantee except in concert with others.[113] While the Charter of the United Nations contains no formal guarantee similar to that of Article 10 of the Covenant, it pledges its members to "join in affording mutual assistance in carrying out the measures decided upon by the Security Council" in cases of threats to the peace or acts of aggression. Again the guarantee is collective, not joint and several.[114]

K. EFFECT OF CHANGE OF CIRCUMSTANCES

The most difficult problem presented by international treaties, and the one in respect to which the fundamental principle of the faith of treaties has been put to its crucial test, is the question whether a state is released from its treaty obligations by reason of an essential change of the circumstances under which the treaty was concluded.[115] On this point international law gives but a vague and unsatisfactory answer. Publicists would appear to be correct in stating as a rule of positive law the general principle that all international contracts are entered into under certain implied conditions, which accompany the express conditions of the treaty and are equally part of the "valuable consideration"

[112] See above, p. 127.
[113] See pp. 293 ff.
[114] See p. 229. Compare the obligations assumed by the American States under the Treaty of Reciprocal Assistance of 1947. See p. 229.
[115] On the general subject, see Harvard Draft, Art. 28 and Comment, where numerous authorities are cited and their opinions discussed; Sir J. F. Williams, "The Permanence of Treaties," *Am. Journal,* Vol. 22 (1928), p. 89; H. Wehberg, "Pacta Sunt Servanda," *Am. Journal,* Vol. 53 (1959), p. 775.

which forms the essence of the contract.[116] Every contract, according to
the Roman Law, carried with it the implication *rebus sic stantibus*. But
when this is said, it remains to determine what are the implied conditions attending the making of a treaty. It is conceded that one of these
conditions is that the treaty be faithfully observed on both sides; another
is that the international personality and consequent freedom of will of
the parties shall remain unchanged; another is that the treaty must be
consistent with international law and with the moral standards of the
international community. Moreover, it would seem to be generally accepted that it is an implied condition of every treaty that it be morally
possible of fulfillment, which may be interpreted as meaning that a state
cannot be expected to sacrifice its very existence to uphold its treaty
obligations. "A treaty, therefore," says Hall, "becomes voidable so soon
as it is dangerous to the life or incompatible with the independence of
a state, provided that its injurious effects are not intended by the two
contracting parties at the time of its conclusion." [117] This rule is logically
deducible from the general principle that a state cannot be presumed to
have bargained away the very conditions of its continued existence as
an international person unless it has done so in clear and explicit terms.
Stated in this restrained manner the principle is scarcely open to question.

Views of publicists. But international practice records the breach of
treaty obligations in numerous cases in which the justification of an
essential change of conditions would appear to rest upon much less
solid ground. Not only in the name of the national existence of the state,
but in the name of its vital interests, its fundamental needs, its necessary
development, governments have declined to be bound by engagements
which would hamper them in the pursuit of these objects. And in so
doing they have had the support of publicists and writers, who have
risked stating a general principle on the matter. Grotius dismissed the
question with the observation that a change of circumstances did not
affect a promise unless it was "most patently clear" that the original
circumstances were part of the consideration of the contract.[118] Bynkershoek unhesitatingly rejected the suggestion of a unilateral repudiation
of treaty obligations.[119] Vattel, familiar with the subtleties and evasions
of statecraft, insisted that "only those circumstances because of which
the promise was made are essential to it; and it is only a change in those
circumstances which can lawfully hinder or suspend the effect of the

---

[116] Hall states the case as follows: "Neither party to a contract can make its binding effect dependent at his will upon conditions other than those contemplated at the
moment when the contract was entered into, and on the other hand a contract ceases
to be binding so soon as anything which formed an implied condition of its obligatory
force at the time of its conclusion is essentially altered." *Int. Law,* § 116.

[117] *Ibid., loc. cit.*

[118] *De jure belli ac pacis,* Eng. trans., Bk. II, Chap. XVI, § XXV.

[119] *Quaestionum juris publici libri duo,* Lib. II, Cap. X.

promise." [120] With the growth of nationalism in the nineteenth century the caution of the older writers was succeeded by a bolder attitude. Heffter [121] and Bluntschli [122] both opened the door to the repudiation of treaties on the ground that they conflicted with the "rights and welfare" of the people, or were incompatible with the development of the state. A later German writer, Treitschke, went to much greater length in asserting that no state need feel bound by treaties which pledged its future to another state; and, again, that when a state recognized that existing treaties "no longer express the actual political conditions" it might request the other party to cancel the treaty, and if the request were not granted it might declare war and thus test whether the relative strength of the parties had not changed since the original conclusion of the treaty.[123]

This loose interpretation of the binding force of treaty obligations was not confined to German writers whose attitude was doubtless influenced by the emergence of German national unity. Hautefeuille, writing in 1868, held that "a treaty containing the gratuitous cession or abandonment of an essential national right, such, for example, as part of its independence, is not obligatory." [124] Bonfils laid down as the accepted doctrine that "a treaty should without question come to an end when the causes which gave rise to it have disappeared. With the passage of time this treaty has become useless or hurtful, because the relations of the states have been modified; their respective situations have been influenced by changes in their economic and political interests." [125] Quoting Bynkershoek, he held that the treaty should be dissolved by mutual consent; but should this be refused, the resulting situation would inevitably be tense. Fiore, the Italian publicist, held that "all treaties are to be looked upon as null which are in any way opposed to the development of the free activity of a nation, or which hinder the exercise of its natural rights." [126] Oppenheim, writing at Cambridge in 1910, formulated the principle that when "the existence or the necessary development of a State stands in unavoidable conflict with such State's treaty obligations, the latter must give way, for self-preservation and development, in accordance with the growth and necessary requirements of the nation are the primary duties of every state." [127]

[120] *Droit des gens,* Eng. trans., Bk. II, § 296.
[121] *Völkerrecht,* § 98.
[122] *Das moderne Völkerrecht,* §§ 415, 456.
[123] *Politics,* Vol. I, p. 28; Vol. II, p. 597, trans. by Dugdale and De Bille.
[124] *Droits et devoirs des nations neutres,* cited by Hall, § 116.
[125] *Manuel de droit international public,* § 857.
[126] *Nouveau droit international,* Part I, Chap. IV. See the same author's *International Law Codified,* Borchard's trans., § 835. A strikingly low standard for an author upholding high moral principles in other fields.
[127] *International Law,* Vol. I, § 539. The fact that Oppenheim, in most respects so sound a writer, could make such a statement, and at Cambridge, shows the unstable foundations upon which the law of 1910 rested. In the Fourth Edition the word "necessary" was changed to "vital."

Instances of international practice. The classic instance during the nineteenth century of the repudiation of treaty obligations on ground of an essential change of circumstances was the action of Russia in 1870 in declaring itself no longer bound by that part of the Treaty of Paris of 1856 which related to the neutralization of the Black Sea and to the restriction imposed upon Russia in respect to keeping armed vessels in that sea. In addition to alleging a violation of the treaty on the part of the other signatory powers, Russia pointed out that a material change in the conditions contemplated by the treaty had been brought about by the subsequent union of the Danubian principalities, acquiesced in by the Great Powers, as well as by the changes in the conditions of naval warfare incident to the use of iron-clad vessels.[128] When, at the close of the Franco-Prussian War, the powers were able to meet in conference at London, Russia was allowed to have its way; but at the same time it was publicly rebuked for its conduct by the publication of a declaration to the effect that "it is an essential principle of the law of nations that no Power can liberate itself from the engagements of a treaty, nor modify the stipulations thereof, unless with the consent of the contracting powers, by means of an amicable arrangement." [129] This "principle" has occasioned much controversy. An examination of it suggests that it is either obvious, if it admits of qualifications,[130] or wholly at variance with international practice and morally untenable if it admits of no exceptions whatever.[131]

In 1915 Greece refused to be bound by the treaty concluded with Serbia in 1913 by which mutual aid was pledged in the event of either party's being attacked by any other Balkan state. Doubtless in this instance the fact that adherence to its obligations would have involved Greece in a war of unexpected proportions might reasonably be held to have amounted to an essential change of circumstances.[132]

In 1926 China notified Belgium that the exterritoriality treaty of 1865 would be regarded as nonoperative after a fixed date, although the treaty was unilateral and allowed only Belgium the right of denuncia-

[128] See Holland, *European Concert in the Eastern Question,* pp. 220-270.

[129] 61 *British and Foreign State Papers,* 1870-1871, p. 1198.

[130] Hall comments as follows: "The general correctness of the principle is indisputable, and in a declaration of the kind made it would have been impossible to enounce it with those qualifications which have been seen to be necessary in practice." *International Law,* § 116.

[131] Lawrence observes that the doctrine of the London conference "sounds well; but a little consideration will show that it is as untenable as the lax view that would allow any party to a treaty to violate it on the slightest pretext." *Principles,* § 134.

[132] For the documents in the case, see *Am. Journal,* Vol. 12 (1918), Supp., pp. 86 ff. Other instances of the application of the principle of *rebus sic stantibus* may be seen in the argument made by France before the Permanent Court of International Justice to the effect that treaties made by Great Britain with Tunis and Morocco had lapsed in consequence of the new legal and judicial regime set up by France in the two protectorates; in the argument made by Turkey in 1923 at Lausanne that the capitulations should be abolished; and in pleas by China for relief from the obligations of old treaties.

tion. The dispute went to the Permanent Court of International Justice, which, in an "Order" of January 28, 1927, upheld the Belgian contention.

In 1960, Fidel Castro, Foreign Minister of Cuba and spokesman of the Government, having come under the influence of international Communism, formally rejected the Treaty of Reciprocal Assistance, declaring it to be null and void because not entered into by the Revolution; he thus repudiating openly the principle of the succession of governments.

The revision of treaties. Jurists writing in the period between the two world wars recognized almost universally the necessity of making some practical provision for the revision of treaties.[133] If the sanctity of the rule of good faith was to be maintained it could only be maintained by not permitting the continuance of conditions which put too great a strain upon it. The two principles, *pacta sunt servanda* and *rebus sic stantibus* were not in such fundamental conflict that the recognition of the one must necessarily amount to a denial of the other. The task of the jurists was to reconcile them. Article 19 of the Covenant of the League of Nations formed a starting point. The Assembly of the League might "from time to time advise the reconsideration by Members of the League of treaties which have become inapplicable," as well as the consideration of international conditions whose continuance might endanger the peace of the world.[134] But action under the article was difficult to obtain. The fear that the reconsideration of treaties might weaken the whole structure of international law proved to be a strong deterrent to proposals of revision. The Habana Convention on Treaties, signed in 1928, instead of adopting provisions looking to the revision of treaties, laid down the rule that "No state can relieve itself of the obligations of a treaty or modify its stipulations except by the agreement, secured through peaceful means, of the other contracting parties." [135] But it was clear that in many cases the "other contracting parties" were more insistent upon maintaining their rights under the treaty than upon making concessions to the principle of justice.[136]

Harvard Research, in its Draft Convention on the Law of Treaties

[133] On the general subject see J. L. Kunz, "The Law of Nations, Static and Dynamic," *Am. Journal*, Vol. 27 (1933), p. 630; "Revision in International Law," *ibid.*, Vol. 33 (1939), p. 33.

[134] See Q. Wright, "Article 19 of the League Covenant and the Doctrine 'Rebus Sic Stantibus,'" *Proceedings*, Am. Soc. Int. Law, 1936, p. 55, and references there cited.

[135] *Int. Conferences of American States*, 1889-1928, p. 416. The article, 10, was taken over from Project No. 4 of the International Commission of Jurists which met in Rio de Janeiro in 1927. *Am. Journal*, Vol. 22 (1928), Spec. Supp., p. 244.

[136] In its revised text of the Reaffirmation of Fundamental Principles of International Law, submitted to the American governments in 1944, the Inter-American Juridical Committee recognized the necessity of the revision of a treaty "when, by reason of new circumstances, some modification of it may be necessary with the objective of improving the relations between the parties." But even this weak statement proved too strong for acceptance by a number of governments. *Recommendations and Reports*, 1942-1944, p. 26.

published in 1935, laid down the rule that "A treaty entered into with reference to the existence of a state of facts the continued existence of which was envisaged by the parties as a determining factor moving them to undertake the obligations stipulated, may be declared by a competent international tribunal or authority to have ceased to be binding, in the sense of calling for further performance, when that state of facts has been essentially changed." [137] Here the danger of the unilateral denunciation of treaties is recognized, but at the same time the necessity of revision is affirmed.

It is suggested that the problem is not one to be solved by the further extension of the jurisdiction of the International Court of Justice. For in most cases, as in the case of the Treaty of Versailles of 1919, it is not the interpretation of the treaty that is in question but the fairness of the obligations which the treaty clearly entails. It might, of course, be possible to give the court jurisdiction not only over the interpretation of the original meaning of treaties but over their application to the changing circumstances of the times. But this latter is properly a legislative function and one that would seem less suitable to a court of justice than to a law-making body.[138] Pending the establishment of such a body, international law must continue to witness the struggle of two conflicting principles: on the one hand the necessity of stability in international relations and on the other hand the demand for such changes in the legal situation created by past treaties as will meet the requirements of present justice.[139] If it can only lead to anarchy to permit the individual state to be the judge in its own case in passing upon the changed circumstances warranting repudiation of its contractual obligations, the alternative must be a resolute facing by the international community of

---

[137] Art. 28. In *The International Law of the Future: Postulates, Principles and Proposals*, the Permanent Court of International Justice was to have jurisdiction "to give a declaratory judgment that an executory treaty or engagement has ceased, in whole or in part, to be binding in the sense of calling for further performance, if it finds that the treaty or engagement was entered into with reference to the existence of a state of facts the continued existence of which was envisaged by the parties as a determining factor moving them to undertake the obligations stipulated and that this state of facts has essentially changed." Proposals, 20, 21. But this progressive principle failed to find a place in the Charter of the United Nations.

[138] The revision of treaties sought by the jurists was closely connected with the problem of "peaceful change," which presented the issue of readjusting established rights and obligations so as to be more in accord with justice under the changing conditions of international life. Many of the difficult situations in which certain states found themselves were due not to the obligations of outworn treaty provisions but to geographic and economic conditions which could only be modified by international legislation superseding the existing order in the name of the interests of the community as a whole.

[139] "Every system of law," observes Brierly, "has to steer a course between the two dangers of impairing the obligations of good faith by interfering with contractual engagements, and of enforcing oppressive or obsolete contracts." *Law of Nations*, 5th ed., p. 257.

its collective responsibility in the matter and its duty to extend the confines of the law to meet the economic and social conditions of each generation.[140] As it has become more and more an accepted function of national law to alter personal and property relations in the interest of the general welfare, so in international relations a way must be found to make obligation and justice coincide, with perhaps a margin on the side of obligation in the interest of that law and order which is the primary condition of justice.[141]

[140] Manley O. Hudson has offered the suggestion, *inter alia*, that "all international engagements calling for continuing performance should be limited to 19 years," applying Jefferson's limit of the possible foresight of man. See *Proceedings*, Am. Soc. Int. Law, 1932, p. 198.

[141] The subject is discussed in an illuminating way by Sir J. F. Williams in his *International Change and International Peace.* "The condition of the permanence of treaties," he observes (p. 76), "is that they should not exclude possibilities of peaceful modification, and contrariwise the condition of the possibility of peaceful modification is that treaties should be faithfully observed and that the world be not disturbed by constant efforts at their revision."

CHAPTER **XXIV**

The Agents of International Intercourse

A. HISTORICAL ORIGINS OF THE LAW

The law regulating the diplomatic intercourse between nations is one of the oldest parts of the general body of international law. Indeed, in some of its branches it antedates all other parts of that law. The records of ancient China, India, and Egypt show a respect for the person of ambassadors and for the sacred character of their office. The Greeks and Romans, while having no permanent embassies, recognized the right of sovereign states to send ambassadors, received their envoys with great respect, and accorded to the envoys a personal inviolability supported by the strongest sanctions. In Rome the principle of exterritoriality found definite, if only partial, recognition.[1]

After the fall of the Roman Empire and the establishment of the feudal system, ambassadors became rather the personal messengers of princes than the formal representatives of states. But with the development of the independent Italian states in the fourteenth century, embassies took on a more formal character, particularly in the case of the papal representatives sent out from the Holy See to the various secular courts. By the fifteenth century the permanent interrepresentation of states, in the form of resident embassies, made its appearance; and within two centuries an elaborate code of diplomatic procedure was built up.[2] Questions of precedence and of the personal inviolability of the ambassador occupied the attention of statesmen and writers and were the occasions of numerous disputes between states.[3] After the adoption in 1815 and 1818 of a

[1] For details, see Phillipson, *International Law and Custom of Ancient Greece and Rome,* Vol. I, Chap. XIII.

[2] Grotius gives an exceptionally interesting survey of the historical background. *De jure belli ac pacis,* Bk. II, Chap. XVIII, "On the Right of Legation."

[3] Vattel's long account gives a vivid picture of conditions in his day. *Droit des gens* (Eng. trans.), Bk. IV, Chaps. V-IX.

formal classification of diplomatic agents there were few important changes in the law. It was not until the Vienna Conference on Diplomatic Intercourse and Immunities of 1961 that a comprehensive agreement upon all phases of the subject was signed, although few of the established rules were more than clarified by the agreement.[4]

The Vienna Conference was called by the General Assembly of the United Nations, being attended by the governments of eighty-one states. The Conference had before it the reports of the International Law Commission as well as the observations of the governments on the drafts submitted to them; on April 18 it adopted the Vienna Convention on Diplomatic Relations together with an Optional Protocol concerning Acquisition of Nationality and an Optional Protocol concerning the Compulsory Settlement of Disputes.[5]

B. REPRESENTATIVE CHARACTER OF THE HEAD OF THE STATE

The law with respect to the representative character of the head of the state and of the various subordinate officers engaged in the administration of the foreign affairs of the state has undergone many changes of recent years, and it is still doubtful on a number of points. With respect to the head of the state the chief concern of the law at the beginning of the twentieth century was to distinguish between the authority of the titular head of the state and that of the actual responsible officer.[6] Constitutional law determined whether the titular head of the state, British King or French President, for example, enjoyed formal or actual powers of government; international law merely recorded that the titular head of the state had spoken or taken action. Ambassadors and ministers were sent and received in the name of the head of the state. International law took it for granted that the persons designated were the actual choice of the head of the state and that the policies they stood for were his policies. That was a matter of constitutional law over which international law had no control.

The problem of representation in constitutional governments became more complicated when the actual government failed at times to function in accordance with the constitution. Duly elected governments were

[4] For a study of the problems of modern diplomacy, see Foster, *The Practice of Diplomacy;* Satow, *Guide to Diplomatic Practice;* Stuart, *American Diplomatic and Consular Practice;* Genet, *Traité de diplomatie et de droit diplomatique;* Harvard Research, *Draft Convention on Diplomatic Privileges and Immunities;* Ferreira de Mello, *Tratado de Direito Diplomático.*

[5] For the texts adopted, see *Am. Journal,* Vol. 55 (1961), p. 1062. For explanatory comment, see E. L. Kerley, "Some Aspects of the Vienna Conference on Diplomatic Intercourse and Immunities," *Am. Journal,* Vol. 56 (1962), p. 88.

[6] The term "head of the state" must be taken in a formal rather than a legal sense. The Constitution of the United States, for example, following the principle of the separation of the powers of government, gives no such distinction to the position of the Executive; but he is permitted to assume it in view of his functions in the field of foreign affairs.

overthrown by military leaders who proclaimed themselves the heads of their respective states. Were they to be accepted as representing the state and entitled to speak in its name? International law did not inquire too closely into the legitimacy of the head of the state. The rules of recognition were content with ascertaining the stability of the new government and its intention to carry out its obligations as a member of the international community. That settled, the new head of the state spoke thereafter in a *de jure* capacity, irrespective of the extent of the support which he might have of public opinion in the country. His ambassadors and ministers were received in other countries with due honors, and the treaties they signed were signed in the name of the state.

How long this traditional rule can continue to hold is an open question when in recent outstanding cases the representative character, as head of the state, has been attributed to persons whose authority rested only upon their ability to suppress opposition. Did Trujillo, in the Dominican Republic, represent the people of his country in the long period of his dictatorial rule? Was Fidel Castro the head of the state of Cuba once he had suppressed fundamental liberties and invited the Soviet Union to take over the administration of the island? International law left it to other states to break relations with such a government, if they chose; if they did not so choose, they had no alternative but to receive ambassadors sent by it.[7]

The Minister of Foreign Affairs. In view of the established practice of modern governments of entrusting to the Minister of Foreign Affairs the actual conduct of the relations of the state with other states, international law recognizes his authority and, as in the case of the head of the state, makes no inquiry into his constitutional position. In general practice he is the responsible medium of communication with foreign states. Documents sent out in the name of the state are signed by him, and resident diplomatic officers conduct their negotiations with him.[8] International usage until of recent years prescribed that the foreign secretary of one state communicate with the foreign secretary of another state only through the medium of resident diplomatic agents, or on occasion through special envoys. But the facilities of radio communication have now made it possible for the foreign secretary of one state to speak to the people of another state over the head of their government.[9]

[7] Thus far no procedure has been developed for withdrawing recognition from a government once it has been recognized as *de jure,* and the procedure of breaking relations continues to be unilateral. See Chap. VIII.

[8] Details may be found in Satow, *op. cit.,* Vol. I, Chap. VII. The procedure followed by American diplomatic agents may be found in *Instructions to Diplomatic Officers of the United States* (1927).

[9] With this practice must be associated that of personal addresses by a chief of state or foreign minister before the congress of the country he has been invited to visit.

What is the still greater innovation is the practice of direct communication between the head of one state and that of another. Public addresses made by the President of the United States in Caracas or in Ottawa may well give a new direction to the foreign policy of the country. And on occasion, as between President Kennedy and Chairman Khrushchev over the missile bases in Cuba in October, 1962, an acute crisis may be settled without the foreign office of either country being directly involved. In anticipation of possible similar crises in the future, lines of direct communication have been established to overcome the delays of transmission.

C. THE "RIGHT OF REPRESENTATION"

The question whether states have a "right of representation," otherwise known as a "right of legation," was until of recent years, in the days when the members of the international community were concerned with points of prestige in their mutual relations, a subject of controversy among writers.[10] Later the question came to be merely whether a particular state enjoyed the requisite degree of independence to justify a claim to be represented in its own name. The line between sovereign and semisovereign states was never clearly drawn; and the leading powers used their judgment in determining when the time had come to recognize the independent status of the former colony or protectorate. Obviously much depended upon the attitude of the suzerain state. Great Britain looked on with approval when Canada and other "dominions" became members of the League of Nations and subsequently sent diplomatic representatives to Washington and other capitals. Whether they were sovereign or semisovereign states, or something else, was a matter of indifference under such circumstances. The Vienna Convention of 1961 solves the problem by the simple declaration that "The establishment of diplomatic relations between states, and of permanent diplomatic missions, takes place by mutual consent." [11]

On the other hand international law of the nineteenth century, seeking to determine the sovereign or nonsovereign character of a particular state, relied upon the fact of diplomatic representation as one of the evidences of sovereignty. In the case of the *Charkieh*,[12] involving a claim to the exemption of the ship from the jurisdiction of the court on ground of its ownership by a sovereign prince, the Khedive of Egypt, the court cited the fact that "no attempt appears to have been made on the part of the Pacha to exercise the principal attribute of sovereignty, namely, the *jus legationis*, to be represented by an ambassador or diplomatic

---

[10] See Satow, *op. cit.*, Vol. I, Chap. XII.
[11] Art. 2.
[12] L. R. 4 Adm. and Eccl. 59 (1873). Fenwick, *Cases*, p. 53.

agent at the court of foreign sovereigns," as proof that the Khedive was not the sovereign of an independent state.

Case of two conflicting governments. The question as to which of two or more contesting governments is entitled to exercise the right of representation is answered by the rules of international law concerning the recognition of new governments.[13] When a *de jure* government has been overturned by domestic revolution, the diplomatic representatives of the former government continue to exercise their functions, at least nominally, until the new *de facto* government has been formally recognized as *de jure*. Thereupon the foreign governments granting such recognition maintain relations only with diplomatic agents representing the new government. By reason of the lack of precedents, no rule exists covering the case of a diplomatic agent who, owing to the failure of foreign governments to recognize a new revolutionary government, continues to exercise his functions long after the government which sent him has ceased to exist. The official relations maintained by the United States with the Russian ambassador, Bakhmeteff, an appointee of the Lvoff Government, for a period of over four years, during which his representative character was repudiated by the *de facto* Bolshevik Government, was in conformity with technical rules, although, it would seem, in contradiction of the general principles of the law.[14]

Attention has already been called to the recognition during the Second World War by Great Britain and other allied states of the "governments in exile" of a number of the countries occupied by the armed forces of the Axis Powers.[15] The recognition of the representative character of these governments was clearly an emergency measure during the period of hostilities, and no inferences are to be drawn from it with respect to normal relations in time of peace. In like manner, the inclusion of Esthonia, Latvia, and Lithuania in the Diplomatic List of the United States does not represent the *de facto* situation in their respective countries, but rather the protest of the United States against their annexation by the Soviet Union in 1940 under guise of controlled elections.

D. CLASSIFICATION OF DIPLOMATIC AGENTS

The annals of the seventeenth and eighteenth centuries are full of conflicts between large and small states as to questions of precedence in diplomatic rank. In spite of the theoretical equality of sovereign states, the marked political inequalities, supported by the ambition of governments and the personal vanity of princes, brought about a constant

[13] For the general principles governing the recognition of new governments, see above, Chap. VIII.

[14] See letter of Mr. Bakhmeteff to Secretary Hughes, April 28, 1922, and reply of the Secretary, April 29, 1922. For editorial comment on the case, see *Am. Journal*, Vol. 16 (1922), p. 426.

[15] See pp. 200 ff.

struggle for the enhancement of national prestige by the relative position accorded to the diplomatic representatives of the state. The representatives themselves were not backward, on occasion, in asserting the dignity of their respective states as evidenced in the honors shown to their own persons.[16] The matter was further complicated by the different functions performed by diplomatic agents. The early ambassador of the fifteenth century not only conducted the business of his sovereign but represented his person as well. Shortly after, the practice developed of sending an agent, later known as *envoy* or *envoy extraordinary*, who carried on the affairs of his sovereign without representing his person. Again, there was the resident, ranking below the envoy, but otherwise performing much the same functions. Still again, there was the minister or minister plenipotentiary, whose representation of his sovereign was likewise below that of the ambassador.

At the Congress of Vienna, in 1815, an effort was made "to prevent in the future the inconveniences which have frequently occurred, and which may still occur, from the claims of precedence among the different diplomatic characters" by dividing them into "classes," as follows: (1) ambassadors, legates, or nuncios, who alone were allowed to represent the person of their sovereign; (2) envoys, ministers, or other persons accredited to sovereigns; (3) chargés d'affaires, accredited to ministers for foreign affairs.[17] A further rule was adopted at the Congress of Aix-la-Chapelle, in 1818, creating a fourth class of ministers resident, accredited, like envoys and ministers, to sovereigns, but of lower rank. Within this class the representatives of minor states found the less conspicuous place intended for them. The Vienna Convention divides the "heads of mission" into three classes, ambassadors and ministers being accredited to heads of state and chargés d'affaires being accredited to ministers of foreign affairs; but except as concerns precedence and etiquette there is no difference between them by reason of their class.

The earlier custom that the smaller states should not appoint representatives of the first class has now practically disappeared. The Vienna Convention does no more than state that the class to which the heads of their missions are to be assigned shall be agreed between states.[18] The group of foreign diplomats resident in each state forms collectively

[16] Wicquefort's treatise, *L'Ambassadeur et ses fonctions*, published in 1679 and translated into English by John Digby (*The Embassador and His Functions*), cites numerous instances of the competition between ambassadors concerning honors and rank. Bynkershoek, writing in 1721, gives evidence in his *De foro legatorum* of continued contests. But by 1758 Vattel was able to lay down more definite rules based upon accepted usage. See *Droit des gens*, Bk. IV, §§ 69-75.

[17] Satow, *op. cit.*, Vol. I, p. 244. See also "Instructions to Diplomatic Officers of the United States" (1927), in Feller and Hudson, *Diplomatic and Consular Laws and Regulations*, Vol. II, p. 1255.

[18] Art. 14. The Ivory Coast, Jamaica, Jordan, and Nepal, for example, are all represented in Washington by ambassadors.

what is known as the "diplomatic corps" and is presided over by the oldest ranking member, or "dean"; and while this loose organization has no corporate character in point of law, it has at times acted in concert where the emergency called for it, as at Peking in 1900 at the time of the Boxer riots.

Appointment of diplomatic representatives. International law contains no positive rules regarding the personal character or qualifications of the persons appointed by a state as its representatives abroad. States are not, however, so far free in the choice of their diplomatic agents as to have the right to send particular persons to a foreign government when, for good reason, the foreign government does not wish to receive them. The law draws no clear line between what are and what are not "good reasons" for refusing to receive a particular person, precedents being too few to permit the formulation of a customary rule. Political, social, and religious reasons have, on one occasion or another, been assigned. A conspicuous instance in the annals of the United States is that of Mr. Keiley, who, on being sent as minister to Italy in 1885, was refused reception on the ground that fourteen years earlier, at a public meeting in the United States, he had protested against Italy's annexation of the Papal States. Secretary Bayard recognized the "full and independent right" of Italy to decide the question of personal acceptability of an envoy from another government.[19] When, however, Mr. Keiley was accredited to Austria-Hungary, and that government requested that his nomination be withdrawn, stating that "the position of a foreign envoy wedded to a Jewess by civil marriage would be untenable and even impossible in Vienna," [20] President Cleveland refused to acquiesce in the reasons assigned, and in his annual message to Congress in 1885 asserted that he could not acquiesce without "violation of my oath of office and the precepts of the Constitution." When the Chinese Government refused to receive Mr. Blair as minister of the United States because as a senator he had participated in the enactment of the exclusion legislation, President Harrison felt justified in entering a public protest.[21]

Inquiry before appointment. In its correspondence over the Keiley case, the Austro-Hungarian Government called the attention of Secretary Bayard to "the generally existing diplomatic practice to ask previously to any nomination of a foreign minister the *agrément* (consent) of the government to which he is accredited." [22] Mr. Bayard rejected the validity, as well as the practicability, of the rule; but with the appointment of ambassadors in 1893 the Department of State acquiesced in the

[19] See Moore, *Digest,* Vol. IV, p. 480.
[20] *Ibid.,* p. 481.
[21] *Ibid.,* p. 484.
[22] *Ibid.,* p. 481.

practice of inquiring beforehand of foreign governments whether the proposed nominee of that rank would be *persona grata* to them. The Vienna Convention provides that the sending state must make certain the *agrément* of the receiving state has been given for the person it proposes to accredit as head of the mission to that state; the Convention also provides that the receiving state is not obliged to give reasons to the sending state for a refusal of *agrément*.[23]

Once appointed to his post, international law prescribes that the diplomatic agent shall be armed with certain documents which are the credentials of his office. A "letter of credence," addressed by the head of the state sending the public minister to the head of the foreign state, identifies the minister and designates his rank and the general object of his mission; at the same time, it asks that the minister be received favorably and that full credence be given to what he shall say on the part of his state. In the case of chargés d'affaires, the letter of credence is addressed by the foreign secretary of the one state to the foreign secretary of the other. Where the minister is sent to fill the regular post of permanent representative, his letter of credence generally constitutes his official authorization to perform the routine duties of his office. When, however, a diplomatic agent is sent to perform a particular task, usually the negotiation of a treaty or convention, or when the permanent minister is called upon to undertake similar duties, a document known as "full powers" is also given him, the object of which is to inform the foreign government of the authority conferred upon him by his government, and of the lengths to which he may go in negotiating in behalf of his government.

Credentials of office. In earlier times, before the practice of ratifying treaties came to be the accepted rule, it was a matter of consequence for foreign governments to ascertain accurately the scope of the powers of diplomatic agents sent to negotiate with them; but at the present day there is little room for mistake. When envoys or ministers are sent to general international conferences or congresses, the letter of credence is usually omitted, and full powers, or general full powers, alone are given. These are not presented to the government of the state in which the congress is held, but are mutually "exchanged" by the assembled delegates when the treaty or convention is about to be signed. In addition to the above documents, or letters patent, diplomatic agents also receive from their home governments general or special "instructions" for the conduct of the business entrusted to them; but these are of no concern to international law.

The reception of diplomatic agents. International practice contains a number of customary rules regulating the reception of diplomatic agents when they have arrived at the seat of the government to which

[23] Art. 4.

they are accredited. The Vienna Convention now specifies in detail the notification to be given to the Minister of Foreign Affairs of the receiving state of the appointment of members of the mission and their staff; the presentation of credentials; the rules of precedence; and the use of the flag of the sending state.[24]

E. FUNCTIONS OF DIPLOMATIC AGENTS

The functions or duties performed by diplomatic agents are primarily determined by the municipal law of their home states. Certain of these functions are purely domestic, in the sense that they do not bring the minister into contact with the foreign government. Such, for example, are the registrations of births, deaths, and marriages of citizens of the minister's home state. Again, other functions bring the minister into contact with the foreign government in an unofficial way only. Such is the duty imposed upon the minister by his government of observing and making reports upon political, commercial, and social conditions in the foreign country and, in particular, upon the attitude of the foreign government and of public opinion with respect to matters which might prove a cause of friction between the two countries. A third group of functions brings the minister into direct and official contact with the foreign government. The Vienna Convention adds the item of "promoting friendly relations between the sending state and the receiving state, developing their economic, cultural and scientific relations." [25]

Relations with the foreign office. The procedure to be followed in presenting demands for the extradition of fugitive criminals offers no difficulty, the burden being upon the home government to see that the proper evidence of guilt accompanies the demand. The issuance of passports to citizens of the minister's country merely requires an investigation of the actual nationality of the applicant. An important function of the public minister consists in affording protection to the person, property, and other interests of citizens of his home state. In such cases, where the injured individual has failed to secure redress through the intermediation of the consular representatives with the judicial or executive authorities of the local government, the diplomatic representative may take up the affair directly with the foreign office, and the matter is then disposed of according to the rules of international law. In no case may the diplomatic representative negotiate with any other officer of the local government.

Restraints upon public ministers. In pursuance of their function of observing the progress of events in the country to which they are accredited, public ministers are forbidden by international law to interfere, whether by word or deed, with the internal political affairs of the local

[24] Arts. 10, 13, 16-20.
[25] Art. 3.

government. Discussion of pending legislation is debarred, as are also controversial questions of party politics. In the United States criticism by a foreign diplomat of speeches made in the houses of Congress is a breach of rule which is likely to be sharply resented.[26] While minor infractions of these rules may be overlooked by the local government, more serious breaches may lead to a demand by the local government for the recall of the offender.[27] Diplomatic etiquette likewise forbids public ministers to correspond with the press upon matters which are the subject of official communication, or to publish a note or despatch from their home government before it has been received by the foreign government, or to publish correspondence with the foreign government without requesting its consent in advance. In like manner an embassy may not be used to maintain contacts with nationals of the foreign state in an effort to keep alive their loyalty and to organize them into "fifth columns" for the promotion of the interests of the foreign state, as happened in a number of Latin American countries during the Second World War. The Vienna Convention merely calls upon persons enjoying the privileges and immunities of a mission "to respect the laws and regulations of the receiving state" and not to "interfere in the internal affairs of that state"; and reference is made to "other rules of general international law" in prohibiting the use of the premises of the mission in a manner inconsistent with its functions.[28]

F. PRIVILEGES AND IMMUNITIES OF DIPLOMATIC AGENTS

By long custom, antedating perhaps all other rules of international law, the diplomatic agents sent by one state to another have been regarded as possessing a peculiarly sacred character, in consequence of which they have been accorded special privileges and immunities. The Ancient Greeks regarded an attack upon the person of an ambassador as an offense of the gravest nature. The writers of ancient Rome were unanimous in considering an injury to envoys as a deliberate infraction of the *jus gentium*.[29] Grotius wrote in 1625 that there were "two points with regard to ambassadors which are everywhere recognized as prescribed by the law of nations, first that they be admitted, and then that they

---

[26] On the other hand, in the name of freedom of speech, it appears that the most offensive remarks may be made by members of Congress, and by local officers of the state governments, without thereby giving rise to any right of protest by the representative in Washington of the foreign state.

[27] In the case of Ambassador Hanihara, who wrote to the State Department in April, 1924, pointing out the gravity of the pending legislation excluding Japanese from immigration into the United States and suggesting that it was likely to have "grave consequences," his government permitted him to return to explain his act, and a successor was appointed shortly after. See "The New Immigration Law and the Exclusion of Japanese," *Am. Journal*, Vol. 18 (1924), p. 518.

[28] Art. 41.

[29] See Phillipson, *op. cit.*, Vol. I, pp. 328 ff., 331.

be not violated." [30] The basis upon which this personal immunity rested was generally found in the principle that the ambassador personified the state or sovereign he represented. From this principle developed not only the custom of according special protection to the person of the ambassador but also a comprehensive exemption from the local jurisdiction. In explanation of the privileges and immunities thus granted, writers worked out the fiction of *exterritoriality*, which held that the ambassador and his suite, together with his residence and the surrounding property, were legally outside the territory of the state.[31] This fiction obtained for a time a foothold in international law, and served the useful purpose, on the one hand, of explaining the actual immunities granted to foreign representatives and, on the other hand, of emphasizing the sovereignty and equality of the several states. It was, however, open to the disadvantage not only of being a fiction but of permitting inferences more comprehensive than the position of the ambassador called for. The conception is abandoned in the Vienna Convention; which offers no theoretical basis for the privileges and immunities it grants.

Personal immunities.   Since the personal inviolability of public ministers is more sacred than that of the ordinary citizens of the state, international law not only regards an affront offered to a public minister by the government of the foreign state as calling for prompt apology and redress but requires that the local government prosecute with exceptional energy any assault upon the minister by private citizens.[32] In many states there are special municipal statutes providing for the punishment of offenses against public ministers. The laws of the United States impose a heavy penalty upon one who in any manner offers violence to the person of a public minister, "in violation of the law of nations." Even the outbreak of war between two countries does not lessen the obligation of the local government in this respect. When the residence of the British ambassador in Berlin was attacked on August 4, 1914, not only did the

---

[30] *De jure belli ac pacis,* Bk. II, Chap. XVIII, § III.

[31] Grotius, after discussing precedents, came to the "unqualified conclusion . . . that the rule has been accepted by the nations that the common custom, which makes a person who lives in foreign territory subject to that country, admits of an exception in the case of ambassadors. Ambassadors as if by a kind of fiction are considered to represent those who sent them; thus of a certain ambassador Cicero says: 'He had borne with him the majesty of the senate and the authority of the state.' In consequence, by a similar fiction, ambassadors were held to be outside the limits of the country to which they were accredited. For this reason they are not subject to the municipal law of the state within which they are living." *De jure belli ac pacis,* Eng. trans., Bk. II, Chap. XVIII, § IV, p. 5.

[32] In the case of Respublica v. De Longchamps [1 Dallas 111 (1784); Fenwick, *Cases,* p. 650], in which the defendant was convicted for having threatened to assault the secretary of the French legation, the court said: "The person of a public minister is sacred and inviolable. Whoever offers any violence to him, not only affronts the Sovereign he represents, but also hurts the common safety and well-being of nations; he is guilty of a crime against the whole world."

local police act promptly to suppress the mob, but the secretary for foreign affairs sent assurances of profound regret. The Vienna Convention lays down the imperative that "the premises of the mission shall be inviolable," and in a later article, "The person of a diplomatic agent shall be inviolable," without entering the customary exceptions that the minister must not have committed the first assault, nor have unnecessarily exposed himself to danger in time of riot or insurrection. The strong statement that "He shall not be liable to any form of arrest or detention," may be taken as implying such rare exceptions.[33]

Exemption from criminal jurisdiction.   In addition to enjoying special protection of their persons, public ministers are completely immune from the criminal jurisdiction of the state. Under no circumstances may they be prosecuted for offenses against law and order. But while international law exempts them from criminal suit, it requires of them a voluntary obedience to the municipal law of the foreign state, so that it would be good ground for remonstrance, and even for a demand upon their government for their recall, if continued breaches of the law were committed. Should a public minister resort to personal violence against another he may be restrained and, if necessary, temporarily detained and expelled from the country. Likewise should he conspire against the safety of the state, he may temporarily forfeit his personal freedom; but no further punishment, other than expulsion, may be inflicted upon him. The classic cases of conspiracy are those of Count Gyllenborg, the Swedish ambassador in London in 1717, who was arrested for complicity in a plot against George I, and of Prince Cellamare, the Spanish ambassador in Paris, who was arrested in 1718 for conspiring to overthrow the French regent.[34]

Exemption from civil jurisdiction.   The exemption of public ministers from the civil jurisdiction of the country is complete in so far as is necessary to secure to them the fullest freedom in the performance of their official duties. Grotius laid down the rule in positive terms: "For an ambassador ought to be free from all compulsion—such compulsion as affects things of which he has need, as well as that which touches his person, in order that he may have full security." [35] In Great Britain a statute of 1708 imposed heavy penalties upon any person who "shall presume to sue forth or prosecute" any writ or process against a public minister. The law was passed following the arrest for debt of the ambassador of Peter the Great and the demand of the latter for the drastic punishment of the offenders. In the United States a law of Congress declares any such judicial process null and void and pronounces the

---

[33] Arts. 22, 29-30.
[34] Satow, *op. cit.*, Vol. I, pp. 254, 256.
[35] *De jure belli ac pacis*, Eng. trans., Bk. II, Chap. XVIII, § IX.

person suing out the process to be "a violator of the Law of Nations, and a disturber of the public repose." [36] The exemption granted continues even to the time when, at the termination of his appointment, the minister is leaving the country and placing himself beyond the jurisdiction of the state over him as a private individual. The Vienna Convention confirms the existing custom in this respect.

Business activities of a minister. The immunity of a public minister from suit does not, however, extend to business activities of the minister which have no connection with his official duties. Consequently it is asserted that if a public minister undertakes to hold real property other than his official residence, suit may be brought *in rem* against the property; or that if the minister acts as guardian or trustee he may be sued in that capacity; or that if he engages in private business or takes part in a commercial venture he may be sued in connection with the undertaking. The Vienna Convention confirms these exceptions from immunity, provided, however, that the measures taken do not infringe upon "the inviolability of his person or of his residence"; but a later article provides that "A diplomatic agent shall not in the receiving state practice for personal profit any professional or commercial activity." [37]

Further personal immunities of a public minister consist in his exemption from the service of subpoena as a witness in court, in his exemption from income and other personal taxes, and in the now obsolete right of private worship in his domestic chapel in cases where freedom of public worship is not permitted. In certain cases public ministers have voluntarily appeared in court as witnesses, as happened when Señor Comancho, minister from Venezuela to the United States, appeared as one of the chief witnesses at the trial of the murderer of President Garfield.[38] The Vienna Convention confirms the immunity.

Special treaty immunities. With the privileges and immunities conferred upon diplomatic officers must be associated those attributed by special treaty agreements to certain public officials engaged in international activities. The Hague Convention for the Pacific Settlement of International Disputes gave to the members of an arbitration tribunal constituted under its provisions diplomatic privileges and immunities when in the performance of their duties and when outside their own country. Similar immunities were granted by the Covenant to representatives of members of the League of Nations and to officials of the League when engaged in the business of the League and, by the Statute of the Permanent Court of International Justice, to judges and deputy

---

[36] *Rev. Stat.,* §§ 4063-4064.

[37] Arts. 31, 42. For earlier British cases to the contrary, see Taylor v. Best, Moore, *Digest,* Vol. IV, p. 657; Magdalena Steam Navigation Co. v. Martin (1859), Fenwick, *Cases,* p. 655.

[38] Moore, *Digest,* Vol. IV, p. 644.

judges of the court.[39] Article 105 of the Charter of the United Nations provides that the organization itself, and the representatives of the members of the United Nations and officials of the organization, shall enjoy such privileges and immunities as are necessary for the independent exercise of their functions in connection with the organization.[40]

Immunity of official residence. The privileges conferred upon the public minister extend beyond his person to his official residence and to the members of his suite. The immunity of his official residence, or domicile, known as *franchise de l'hôtel,* was formerly much more absolute than at present and included a right of asylum now greatly restricted. In the seventeenth and eighteenth centuries the theory of the exterritorial character of an embassy led to an exaggerated conception of the rights attaching to it and to abuses against which Vattel felt it necessary to protest. Is the ambassador, he asked, to be allowed to avail himself of the immunity of his house so as to make of it "an asylum into which he will admit enemies of the sovereign and of the state, criminals of every sort, and thus protect them from the punishment which they deserve"? [41] Such conduct would, he asserted, be contrary to the purpose for which the ambassador was admitted into the state. While the theory of exterritoriality has been largely abandoned at the present day, the privileges attached to the minister's person are extended to his domicile, including outbuildings, carriages, and automobiles, and it may not be entered by the local police or other officers of justice or administration in the ordinary exercise of their duties.

Two practical problems are presented. What of crimes and other offenses against the local law that have been committed within the mission or by members of the mission who have taken refuge within it? In the case of Gallatin's coachman the British police authorities, in 1827, arrested the offender within the stable of the embassy for an assault committed outside the embassy; [42] but writers have found the action of the Foreign Office in supporting the police in this case to be contrary to the general practice of states. In the affair of Nikitchenkow in 1867, the French police were called in to arrest a Russian subject who had assaulted a member of the embassy within its precincts. The Russian ambassador demanded his extradition upon the ground that the offense had been committed upon Russian territory; but the French govern-

---

[39] Covenant, Art. 7; Statute, Art. 19.

[40] On December 29, 1945, the United States Congress passed a law extending privileges, exemptions, and immunities to international organizations and to the officers and employees thereof. Text in *Am. Journal,* Vol. 40 (1946), Supp., p. 85. For comment, see Preuss, "The International Organizations Immunities Act," *ibid.,* Vol. 40, p. 332; "Immunity of Officers and Employees of the United Nations for Official Acts: The Ranallo Case," *ibid.,* Vol. 41 (1947), p. 555.

[41] *Droit des gens,* Eng. trans., Bk. IV, § 118.

[42] Satow, *op. cit.,* Vol. I, p. 295.

ment refused to comply.[43] In this instance the Russian ambassador was attempting to extend the exterritorial theory beyond its customary application.

Asylum in foreign legations. The further question, to what extent a diplomatic mission possesses a "right of asylum" which may be taken advantage of by fugitives from justice not members of the mission, is still in part unsettled. In the first place it is agreed that, waiving cases of imminent danger, the local authorities, judicial or administrative, may not enter the premises of the mission or the residence of a member of the mission without the consent of the head of the mission or of the particular member. In 1836 a United States court considered it in violation of international law that a constable should enter the house of the secretary of the British legation and remove a fugitive slave.[44] This rule of customary law found expression in the Convention on Diplomatic Officers adopted at Havana in 1928,[45] and it is definitely laid down in Article 22 of the Vienna Convention. In the second place, little doubt seems to exist that, should persons guilty of ordinary crimes take refuge in a mission, they must be delivered up by the minister on request.[46] Pending such delivery the local authorities are free to surround the mission with troops if necessary and to take other precautions called for by the situation.

Political refugees. It is with respect to political refugees, however, that the chief problem has arisen. Even when the practice of giving asylum was at its height, it was still qualified by the condition that the foreign embassy must not become in any way a source of danger to the state. Vattel comments approvingly upon the decision of the Council of Castile in the case of the Duke of Ripperda, who, being accused of official misconduct, had taken refuge in the house of the British ambassador. It was decided that he might be taken from the embassy even by force, "since otherwise privileges whose object was to maintain a freer intercourse between sovereigns would on the contrary turn to the ruin and destruction of their authority." [47] During the nineteenth century the practice fell largely into disuse, except in the case of legations in

[43] Moore, *Digest,* Vol. II, p. 778, where the name is given as Nitchencoff.

[44] United States v. Jeffers, 4 Cranch, Circ. Ct. Rep. 704, Fed. Cases No. 15, 471. Scott and Jaeger, *Cases,* p. 497.

[45] Art. 16 of the Convention provides: "No judicial or administrative functionary or official of the State to which the diplomatic officer is accredited may enter the domicile of the latter, or of the mission, without his consent." For the text of the Convention, see *Int. Conferences of Am. States,* 1889-1928, p. 420; Hudson, *Int. Legislation,* Vol. IV, p. 2583; *Am. Journal,* Vol. 22 (1928), Supp., p. 142.

[46] Art. 17 of the Habana Convention supplements the protection given to the premises of the diplomatic mission by the provision that: "Diplomatic officers are obliged to deliver to the competent local authority that requests it any person accused or condemned for ordinary crimes, who may have taken refuge in the mission." Confirmed by Art. III of the Convention on Diplomatic Asylum of 1954.

[47] *Droit des gens,* Bk. IV, § 118; Martens, *Causes célèbres,* Vol. I, p. 178.

Central and South America, in parts of the Orient, and occasionally in states of Southeastern Europe. In 1875 Secretary Fish, in a letter to the Secretary of the Haitian legation at Washington, referred to the right to grant asylum to fugitives as "one of the still open questions of public law"; and he was frank enough to say that "the instability of the Governments in countries where the practice has been tolerated may in a great degree be imputed to such toleration." [48] In the Instructions issued by the United States Department of State to its diplomatic agents in 1885, attention was called to the fact that "exterritorial asylum has become so firmly established, that it is often invoked by unsuccessful insurgents," and notice was given that "this government does not sanction the usage, and enjoins upon its representatives in such countries the avoidance of all pretexts for its exercise." [49] An exception was, however, admitted to the extent of permitting temporary shelter to be given to persons whose lives might be threatened by mob violence as distinct from persons evading the pursuit of the legitimate agents of justice. The same notification was repeated in the Revised Instructions issued in 1897. In the Instructions issued in 1927, while it is admitted that in some countries where frequent revolutions occur the practice of extraterritorial asylum is "virtually recognized by the local government," it is said that this Government "does not look with favor on such usage" and wishes it limited to "temporary shelter" to a person in danger of mob violence or other illegal acts.[50] In 1928 a convention was adopted at Havana by the twenty-one American Republics defining the extent to which asylum might be given.[51] While it was to be denied to persons accused of common crimes and to deserters from the army and navy, it might be granted under certain circumstances, specified in part, to political offenders. The United States, in signing the convention, entered a reservation to the effect that it did not recognize the so-called "doctrine of asylum" as part of international law. The Montevideo Convention, signed five years later at the Seventh International Conference of American States, clarified the Convention of 1928 by providing that the decision as to the political nature of the offense as distinct from a common crime rested with the state granting asylum.[52]

[48] U.S. For. Rel., 1875, p. 343.

[49] Personal Instructions to the Diplomatic Agents of the United States in Foreign Countries (1885), Art. V.

[50] Quoted in Harvard Draft, p. 63. For the full text of the Instructions see Feller and Hudson, Diplomatic and Consular Laws and Regulations, Vol. II, p. 1253.

[51] For the text of the convention, see Hudson, Int. Legislation, Vol. IV, p. 2412; Int. Conferences of American States, 1889-1928, p. 434.

[52] Int. Conferences, 1933-1940, p. 116. The United States refrained from signing the Convention since it "does not recognize or subscribe to, as part of international law, the doctrine of asylum." In respect to the special policy of the United States towards asylum, see Moore, Digest, Vol. II, pp. 755 ff.; Hackworth, Digest, Vol. II, pp. 621, 624 (in embassies and legations), 633 (in consulates); Hyde, Int. Law,

In 1948 a *cause célèbre* arose between Peru and Colombia resulting from the grant of asylum by the Colombian Embassy in Lima to Raul Haya de la Torre, leader of the Aprista party, who was held responsible by Peru for a military rebellion. Peru, not having ratified the Montevideo Convention of 1933, disputed the right of Colombia to qualify Haya de la Torre as a political refugee and refused to grant a safe-conduct; and on October 15 the case was referred to the International Court of Justice. The Court, interpreting the Convention of 1928, decided on November 30, 1950, that Colombia, as the state granting asylum, was not competent to qualify the offense by a unilateral decision binding on Peru and was not entitled to claim from Peru the necessary safe-conduct to permit Haya de la Torre to leave the country in safety; but as against the counterclaim of Peru the Court held that the offense of military rebellion was not a common crime.[53] Colombia then asked for an interpretation of the judgment, but this was refused on technical grounds, leading Colombia to institute new proceedings to determine whether it was bound to deliver the refugee to Peru. The second judgment still left the case in suspense. The asylum had, indeed, been "irregularly granted" and should cease; but Colombia was not under an obligation to surrender the refugee. There was no contradiction between the two findings, said the Court, because surrender was not the only way of terminating asylum.[54] In the end, by negotiation between the parties, Haya de la Torre was permitted to leave the country in secret; only to return later and be a candidate in the presidential elections of 1962.

Are the premises of a diplomatic mission and of a consulate entitled to be protected against demonstrations of public opinion in the form of picketing? In 1938 the Congress of the United States passed a joint resolution making it a penal offense for persons to display banners or placards intended to intimidate, coerce, or bring into public odium any foreign government; or to commit certain specified offensive and intimidating acts within 500 feet of any building or premises within the District of Columbia used or occupied by any foreign government as an embassy, legation, consulate, or for other official purposes; or to con-

---

Vol. II, p. 443; B. Gilbert, "The Practice of Asylum in Legations and Consulates of the United States," *Am. Journal,* Vol. 3 (1909), p. 594.

The Foreign Service Regulations of July, 1939, provide as follows: "*Asylum.* A diplomatic representative or consular officer may not extend asylum to persons outside of his official or personal household." This is followed by a Note which provides: "*Involuntary refuge.* The extension of refuge to persons outside the official or personal household of a diplomatic or consular officer can only be justified on humanitarian grounds. Diplomatic and consular officers may afford refuge to uninvited fugitives whose lives are in imminent danger from mob violence, but only during the period active danger continues." Hackworth, *Digest,* Vol. II, pp. 623 ff.

[53] *I.C.J. Reports,* 1950, p. 266; *Am. Journal,* Vol. 45 (1951), p. 179.
[54] *I.C.J. Reports,* 1951, p. 71; *Am. Journal,* Vol. 45 (1951), p. 781.

gregate within 500 feet of such buildings or premises and refuse to disperse after ordered to do so by the police authorities.[55] The Vienna Convention imposes upon the receiving state "a special duty to take all appropriate steps to protect the premises of the mission against any intrusion or damage and to prevent any disturbance of the peace of the mission or impairment of its dignity." [56]

Exemption from taxation. Prior to the Vienna Convention, practice varied in respect to the extent of the exemption of the minister's residence from local taxation and of the minister and his staff from the payment of customs duties upon imported goods. Article 23 of the Convention now provides for the exemption "from all national, regional or municipal dues and taxes in respect of the premises of the mission, whether owned or leased"; and Article 36 grants exemption "from all customs duties, taxes and related charges," other than for special services, on articles for the official use of the mission and for the personal use of the agent or members of his household.

Immunities of a minister's retinue. The privileges and immunities granted to public ministers are extended in large part to the members of their retinue or suite. Those who are officially connected with the embassy or legation enjoy by old custom the same inviolability and personal exemptions as are enjoyed by the ambassador or minister himself. In the case of Heathfield v. Chilton [57] the court recognized that section of the law of 1708 which included the servants of a public minister in the exemption from the service of process as being equally part of the law of nations, but denied its application to the defendant as not actually being, as alleged, secretary to the minister of the bishop of Liège. In the case of Engelke v. Musmann, decided in 1928, diplomatic immunities were extended to a "consular secretary" in the employ of the German ambassador in spite of the character of the services he was performing.[58] In the class with official members of the minister's suite are to be placed couriers or despatch bearers, who not only must be granted immunity from local jurisdiction but must be afforded special protection and facilities in the exercise of their duties. The immunities granted to persons in the private employment of the minister and his official suite are, however, subject to qualifications. If citizens of the foreign state, they remain amenable to its laws. Otherwise they are exempt from local jurisdiction, but their exemption may be waived by the minister at his dis-

---

[55] For the text of the joint resolution, see *Am. Journal,* Vol. 32 (1938), Supp., p. 100. For comment upon the problem, see L. Preuss, "Protection of Foreign Diplomatic and Consular Premises against Picketing," *ibid.,* Vol. 31 (1937), p. 705; E. C. Stowell, *ibid.,* Vol. 32 (1938), p. 344.

[56] Art. 22.

[57] Court of King's Bench, 1767. 4 Burr. 2015. Fenwick, *Cases,* p. 654.

[58] (1928) A. C. 433. Hudson, *Cases,* p. 784; Fenwick, *Cases,* p. 697.

cretion. In the case of Triquet v. Bath,[59] decided three years before Heathfield v. Chilton by the same court, a bill brought by the county against the defendant was set aside upon satisfactory evidence that he was a bona fide domestic servant of the Bavarian minister. The exceptional case of Gallatin's coachman has already been referred to.

A minister's relatives. The dependent relatives of a public minister, living with him under his roof, share in his exemption from civil and criminal jurisdiction. Oppenheim rightly regards it as an obsolete precedent that Don Pantaleon Sa, a brother of the Portuguese ambassador in London and a member of his suite, was arrested, tried, and executed by order of Cromwell in 1653 for the murder of an English subject.[60] When Carlos Waddington, the son of the Chilean minister at Brussels, killed the secretary of the legation in 1906, the Belgian Government recognized his immunity from arrest and would not even accept the waiver of privilege offered by the minister until it had been confirmed by the Chilean Government.[61] As part of the immunity of the minister from the local jurisdiction, it is an established rule that children born to him while holding his official position are regarded as born upon the territory of his home state, and are subject to its allegiance *jure soli.*[62]

G. RIGHTS WITH RESPECT TO THIRD STATES

It is an old rule, deduced from the general principle of the recognized necessity of diplomatic intercourse between states, that public ministers have a "right of innocent passage" through the territory of third states, whether their mission has not yet begun or has officially terminated. What shall be regarded as "innocent passage" is, however, left to the decision of the third state. In 1854 Soulé, United States minister to Spain, was detained at Calais by the French Government in order, as it said, to determine whether he intended going direct to Madrid via Paris or planned to stop off in Paris, in which latter case the privilege of transit would be denied him. The circumstances were that the minister, a naturalized American citizen born in France, had rendered himself on a previous occasion obnoxious to the French Government.[63] In 1926 the United States declined to allow passage through its territory to the newly appointed Russian diplomatic representative to Mexico, Madame Kal-

---

[59] 3 Burr. 1478 (1764). Fenwick, *Cases,* p. 36; Bishop, *Cases,* p. 69.

[60] *International Law,* Vol. I, § 404.

[61] Oppenheim, *op. cit.,* Vol. I, § 404.

[62] The Fourteenth Amendment to the United States Constitution has this rule of international law in view when it provides that "all persons born or naturalized in the United States, and subject to the jurisdiction thereof, are citizens of the United States and of the State wherein they reside." The exemption is recognized in Art. 4 of the Hague Convention on Nationality. See also Harvard Draft, Art. 28, and Vienna Convention, Art. 37.

[63] Moore, *Digest,* Vol. IV, § 643.

lontai; but in this case personal grounds were involved.[64] The Vienna Convention appears to evade the issue by providing that if a diplomatic agent passes through or is in the territory of a third state "which has granted him a passport visa if such visa was necessary," he shall be accorded inviolability and such other immunities as may be required to insure his transit or return.[65] What if a visa should be required but refused to the particular diplomatic agent?

Innocent passage in time of war. It is in time of war, however, that the question of innocent passage presents special difficulty. An old precedent shows the third state arresting a minister sent by its enemy to a neutral state. On his way from France to Berlin in 1744 Maréchal de Belle Isle passed through the territory of Hanover, then at war with France, and was made prisoner by that state.[66] But it is doubtful whether that case carries any weight at the present day. On November 28, 1916, the British Government refused a safe-conduct to Count Tarnowski, newly appointed ambassador of Austria-Hungary to the United States, awaiting passage from Holland, the reason alleged being the fact that the count's predecessor had been engaged in plots against the Allies. The United States asked a reconsideration of the decision, pointing out that it was an inalienable right of sovereign states to exchange ambassadors and that third states, even in time of war, were not justified in denying that right. The safe-conduct was thereupon granted.[67]

Case of Mr. Washburne. International law is likewise not clear as to the rights of the diplomatic agents of a neutral state when the capital of the state to which they are accredited is occupied by the enemy. Their personal immunity in such case is clearly established, but it is doubtful whether they may claim any other privileges beyond the right to leave the country. In 1870, during the siege of Paris by the German troops, the American minister to France, Mr. Washburne, was refused permission to send a messenger with sealed despatches through the German lines to London. The United States protested, urging that the rights of legation "must be regarded as paramount to any belligerent right" and should not be curtailed unless there was reason to believe that they would be abused or unless some military necessity required it. The German Government finally made an exception in favor of the American minister in the form of a "privilege" of receiving closed despatches.[68]

---

[64] Department of State, Press Release, November 5, 1926.

[65] Art. 40.

[66] Vattel commented favorably upon the case and formulated a general rule on the subject. *Droit des gens,* Eng. trans., Bk. IV, § 85.

[67] Hackworth, *Digest,* Vol. IV, p. 462; Garner, *Int. Law and the World War,* Vol. I, p. 33, note. Public discussion of the incident compared it with the case of the *Trent* (see p. 738), but the latter presented substantially different circumstances.

[68] Moore, *Digest,* Vol. IV, § 675.

H. TERMINATION OF A DIPLOMATIC MISSION

Diplomatic missions, whether embassies or legations, do not, like governments, possess a corporate character in consequence of which they continue their legal existence in spite of changes in the personality of the head of the mission. On the contrary, letters of credence are personal documents, completely so in respect to the minister appointed, and to a degree in respect to the sovereign to whom he is accredited. Hence a diplomatic mission comes to a formal end with the death of the minister or with his recall by his home government, and a new letter of credence must be presented by his successor. On the other hand, there is no well-established rule to determine what changes in the foreign government bring the mission to a similar formal end. The death of the foreign sovereign generally calls for new letters of credence, although the rule has lost its meaning with the establishment of constitutional monarchies. The death of a foreign president leaves the minister's position unchanged, as does obviously a mere change of the incumbent of the office.

Effect of revolution. A more difficult question, to which precedent gives no definite answer, is the effect of constitutional changes in the government of the foreign state. A revolution, such as that in Portugal in 1910, by which a constitutional monarchy is overthrown and a republic set up in its place generally has the effect of suspending, not terminating, a diplomatic mission until such time as the government of the home state decides whether it will recognize the new government. During this *ad interim* period the public minister continues to enjoy his diplomatic privileges and immunities, although he maintains no formal relations with the *de facto* government. The United States minister to Russia continued at his post after March, 1917, until his home government decided that it could not recognize the Bolshevik Government set up in November, 1917, when he was recalled. In like manner the overthrow of a government by violence, when the constitutional form of the state is left intact, leads to a suspension of diplomatic relations, which may result, as in the case of the Mexican Government after the overthrow of Carranza in 1920, in the actual termination of the mission by a refusal on the part of the minister's home government to recognize the *de facto* revolutionary government.[69] Great Britain refused for a period of more than two years beginning in 1904 to renew diplomatic relations with Serbia as a form of protest against the overthrow of the Obrenovitch dynasty.[70]

Recall of offending minister. The general principle appears to be recognized that a state may for good and sufficient reason demand of

[69] See above, p. 194.
[70] See above, p. 183.

a foreign government that it recall an individual minister who has rendered himself *persona non grata;* but the law is not clear as to what circumstances shall give rise to good and sufficient reason. Consequently the minister's home government may inquire into the facts, and if it finds them inadequate it may either refuse to recall the minister or recall him and neglect to appoint a successor in his place. Should it decide not to recall him, it is open to the state to which he is accredited either to refuse to deal with him or to dismiss him from the country. Dismissal is an extreme measure, and, as there is no law governing its justice or injustice in a given case, it has more than once proved a cause of sharp friction between the two countries involved.

Circumstances justifying recall. The circumstances giving rise to a demand for the recall of a public minister have, as a rule, involved some interference on the part of the minister with the internal affairs of the country. The American demand for the recall of the French minister, Genêt, in 1793 was granted without demur by the French Government, which declared that his "proceedings and criminal manœuvres" were not authorized by his instructions.[71] On its part, however, the French Government made the recall of Genêt the occasion for a demand for the recall of the American minister at Paris, Gouverneur Morris, who had taken part in plots for the escape of the imprisoned king.[72] The recall of the Russian minister to the United States, Catacazy, in 1871, after he had indulged in personal criticism of President Grant, was demanded on the ground that his conduct was such as "materially to impair his usefulness to his own government and to render intercourse with him, for either business or social purposes, highly disagreeable." [73] In 1898, shortly before the outbreak of the Spanish-American War, the recall of the Spanish minister at Washington, de Lome, was asked for in consequence of the theft and publication of a private letter in which he had criticized President McKinley.[74] On September 9, 1915, the United States demanded the recall of the Austro-Hungarian ambassador Dumba on the ground of the "admitted purpose and intent of Mr. Dumba to cripple legitimate industries of the people of the United States and to interrupt their legitimate trade, and by reason of the flagrant violation of diplomatic propriety in employing an American citizen protected by an American passport as a secret bearer of official dispatches through the lines of the enemy of Austria-Hungary." [75] On December 4, 1915, the Department of State informed the German Government that the continued presence of Captain Boy-Ed, naval attaché, and Captain von Papen, military

---

[71] Moore, *Digest,* Vol. IV, p. 485.
[72] *Ibid.,* p. 572.
[73] *Ibid.,* p. 501.
[74] *Ibid.,* p. 507.
[75] *U. S. Foreign Relations,* 1915, Supp., p. 933; Hackworth, *Digest,* Vol. IV, p. 449.

attaché, was no longer desired.[76] It should be observed that an entirely different situation is presented when the recall of a minister is demanded, as in the case of the American minister to Brazil, Mr. Wise, in 1847, because of acts done by him under instructions from his government.[77] To accede to a demand for recall under such circumstances would be equivalent to a repudiation by the minister's government of its own conduct. The foreign government has only the choice of retaining or dismissing him.

Dismissal of diplomatic agent.   The extreme step of dismissing a public minister or of refusing further to deal with him when the demand for his recall has not been promptly complied with has been taken on several occasions by the United States upon grounds the adequacy of which has been much debated. In the early case, in 1806, of the Spanish minister Yrujo, who had been guilty of intemperate public utterances, the United States refused further dealings with him when his government failed to recall him upon request; but it allowed him to remain in the country.[78] In the case in 1809 of the British minister Jackson, who had insinuated that the Government of the United States had been guilty of duplicity in its negotiations with his predecessor, the Department of State refused forthwith to deal further with him; and he was subsequently recalled by his government.[79] In 1856, when the British Government refused to recall its minister, Crampton, on the ground that the charges that he had violated the neutrality laws of the United States were unfounded, the Department of State announced the determination of the President to "discontinue further intercourse" with him.[80] The dismissal of the British minister Lord Sackville by the United States in 1888, following a refusal of his government to recall him, met with general disapproval by writers on international law. His offense, only technically serious, was committed under circumstances which would doubtless have exonerated him had political conditions not called for his sacrifice.[81] A legal solution to the problem is now to be found in the simple provision of Article 9 of the Vienna Convention:

1. The receiving state may at any time and without having to explain its decision, notify the sending state that the head of the mission or any member of the diplomatic staff of the mission is not acceptable. In any such case, the sending state shall, as appropriate, either recall the person concerned or terminate his functions with the mission . . .

[76] U. S. Foreign Relations, 1915, Supp., p. 947; Hackworth, Digest, Vol. IV, p. 447.
[77] For the facts of the case, see Moore, Digest, Vol. IV, p. 495.
[78] Ibid., p. 508.
[79] Ibid., p. 511.
[80] Ibid., p. 533.
[81] Ibid., p. 536.

2. If the sending state refuses or fails within a reasonable period to carry out its obligations under paragraph 1 of this article, the receiving state may refuse to recognize the person concerned as a member of the mission.

Obviously any grossly unjustifiable notice would still give rise to offense; but this would be a matter beyond the reach of any specific provision of the law.

Breach of diplomatic relations. International law has no definite rules covering the circumstances under which a breach of diplomatic relations is justified. Where the breach is due to a revolutionary change in the government of the state to which the public minister is accredited, it generally takes the less conspicuous form of a failure to renew the credentials of the minister accredited to the previous government. The question is then subordinated to the decision of the minister's state to recognize the new *de facto* government.[82] The breach of diplomatic relations between Great Britain and Serbia following the dynastic changes of 1904 lasted for more than two years. The breach of diplomatic relations between the United States and Mexico following the overthrow of the Carranza regime lasted three years. In 1923 Soviet Russia broke off diplomatic relations with Switzerland by reason of the acquittal of a man alleged to have assassinated a Russian delegate to the Lausanne Conference; and in 1927 Great Britain broke off relations with the Soviet Union because of alleged military espionage and subversive activities. In 1935 the Government of Uruguay announced to the Soviet Minister its decision to suspend diplomatic relations between the two countries on the ground that the Soviet Legation at Montevideo was a center of the Communist activity which had just been responsible for bloodshed in Brazil. The Soviet Minister denied the charge, and shortly after the Soviet delegate at Geneva informed the Secretary General of the League of Nations that the resort by Uruguay to a rupture of diplomatic relations, instead of a proceeding in accordance with Article XII of the Covenant, was "a grave breach of one of the fundamental principles of the League." The Uruguayan delegate, Sr. Guani, rejected any connection between the maintenance of diplomatic relations and the obligations of Article XII, holding that the action was taken in self-defense and was not a question calling for "submission to an international court of law or to the Council of the League."[83]

A unique instance of collective action looking to the withdrawal of diplomatic representatives in the form of a protest against the character

---

[82] A mere breach of diplomatic relations, where there has been no change in the government of the offending state, does not signify withdrawal of recognition. Recognition once granted is definitive. See above, Chap. VIII.

[83] See C. C. Hyde, "Freedom to Withdraw Diplomatic Relations," *Am. Journal,* Vol. 30 (1936), p. 284.

of a foreign government is to be seen in the resolution of the General Assembly of the United Nations adopted on December 12, 1946, recommending "that all Members of the United Nations immediately recall from Madrid their ambassadors and ministers plenipotentiary accredited there." While the mere withdrawal of an ambassador or a minister would not ordinarily constitute a breach of diplomatic relations, the fact that in this case it was done not because of the character of the agent but because of the character of the government to which he was sent made the recall practically equivalent to a breach of relations, although the Assembly deliberately avoided phrasing its action as such. The resolution set forth the reasons for the recall as being "that the Franco Fascist Government of Spain, which was imposed by force upon the Spanish people with the aid of the Axis Powers and which gave material assistance to the Axis Powers in the war, does not represent the Spanish people, and by its continued control of Spain is making impossible the participation of the Spanish people with the peoples of the United Nations in international affairs." [84] A similar decision might well have been reached by the General Assembly in the case of Cuba when in 1960 the Prime Minister, in addition to repudiating pledges given to the Organization of American States by successive resolutions and declarations, also invited the Soviet Union to strengthen the armed forces of the country and thus prevent any popular outbreak against the dictatorship. While the United Nations failed to take action, the Organization of American States excluded "the present government of Cuba" from participation in the inter-American system.[85]

I. THE CONSULAR SERVICE: ORIGINS

While the status and functions of consular agents, as at present recognized, are of modern origin, the roots of the consular system extend far back beyond the establishment of permanent embassies. The Greek city-states developed an inchoate consular service differing from the modern system in that the consuls were citizens of the foreign state instead of the state whose interests they protected, but resembling the modern system in a number of other respects.[86] During the Middle Ages the practice grew up among the coast cities of the Mediterranean of appointing "maritime consuls" whose function it was to decide in their home ports disputes growing out of sea trade and who were in time led to go to foreign ports and set up a temporary residence there. On the other hand, at perhaps an even earlier period, the custom arose among

[84] For the text of the resolution, see Dept. of State *Bulletin*, Vol. XV, p. 1143.

A summary of the points of view of the delegates of the different countries may be found in United Nations *Weekly Bulletin*, Vol. I, No. 21, p. 21.

[85] See Fenwick, *OAS*, p. 84.

[86] See Phillipson, *International Law and Custom of Ancient Greece and Rome*, Vol. I, Chap VI.

the foreign merchants of maritime cities of electing one of their group to act as judge of their commercial disputes. In time these two sets of judges were fused, and states came not only to send out consuls to foreign countries, but to enter into treaties stipulating the protection to be afforded them and the functions they were to be permitted to perform. With the establishment of permanent embassies in the seventeenth century the functions of consuls were greatly reduced; and at the same time the strengthening of the conception of national sovereignty led to a refusal, except in Mohammedan countries, to permit them any longer to exercise civil and criminal jurisdiction over their countrymen.[87]

Legal status of consuls. Unlike diplomatic agents, consuls are not representatives of their state as such, they are not accredited to the foreign government but are merely custodians in the foreign country of such of their state's domestic interests as the latter has seen fit to confide to them. Fundamentally, therefore, their status is not an international but a national one. But inasmuch as they are appointed by their state, are recognized by the foreign states in which they reside as possessing an official character, and are permitted in that guise to perform certain functions otherwise belonging to officials of the foreign states, they have come to acquire a limited international status; and they are governed and protected by definite, if somewhat restricted, rules. Until the Conference at Vienna in 1963 the character and functions of consuls were regulated by separate treaties between their home state and the individual foreign states to which they were sent. Within the Union of American Republics, a Convention on Consular Agents had been adopted at Havana in 1928, creating definite rules of law for the regional group.[88]

Supplementing the work of the Vienna Conference on Diplomatic Intercourse and Immunities in 1961, a Conference on Consular Relations met at Vienna in 1963 and adopted a Convention on Consular Relations covering the whole field of status and activities, although a reserve was entered that the rules of customary law should continue to govern matters not expressly regulated by the Convention.[89]

While the functions of diplomatic and consular officers are essentially different and their legal character correspondingly distinct, a number of

[87] For a study of the character of the modern consular system, see Potter, *Introduction to the Study of Int. Organization*, 5th ed., Chap. VI, § A; Stowell, *Consular Cases and Opinions from the Decisions of the English and American Courts;* Harvard Draft, *Legal Position and Functions of Consuls,* Introductory Note; Stewart, *Consular Privileges and Immunities;* Puente, *The Foreign Consul: His Juridical Status in the United States;* Hackworth, *Digest,* Vol. IV, pp. 655-949; Hyde, *Int. Law,* Vol. II, §§ 460-488.

[88] For the text of the Convention, see *Int. Conferences,* 1889-1928, p. 424; Hudson, *Int. Legislation,* Vol. IV, p. 2394; *Am. Journal,* Vol. 22 (1928), Supp., p. 147.

[89] For the text of the Convention, see *Am. Journal,* Vol. 57 (1963), p. 995.

states have found it convenient to combine the two functions in the same person, so that diplomatic officers may in certain cases be vested with consular powers and consular officers with limited diplomatic functions. Such arrangements must, of course, be made in agreement with the state to which the officer is sent; and some confusion has arisen in the determination of the status of an officer when performing the two distinct sets of functions. In general it may be said that the formalities for admittance to the two offices must be separately complied with, the officer presenting his full powers as a diplomat and asking for his exequatur as a consul. In the United States, by act of Congress of 1924, as amended in 1931, it is provided that "Foreign Service officers may be commissioned as diplomatic or as consular officers or both: Provided. . . . That all official acts of such officers while serving under diplomatic or consular commissions in the Foreign Service shall be performed under their respective commissions as secretaries or as consular officers." The Vienna Convention sets forth the conditions under which a state having no diplomatic mission may, with the consent of the receiving state, authorize a consular officer to perform diplomatic acts, and, a new item, act as representative of the sending state to any intergovernmental organization.[90]

Grades of consuls. Since consuls have no representative character, international law does not concern itself with their various grades. Hence the questions of rank and precedence which have been raised with respect to public ministers do not concern consuls. As a matter of domestic administration, however, most large states adopt a classification which distinguishes between consuls-general (having supervision over a larger area), consuls, vice-consuls, and consular agents. One distinction, however, which formerly obtained some recognition at international law was that between *consules missi,* professional consuls, or "consuls of career" as they are now called, sent out by their government for the express purpose of attending to its interests and forbidden as a rule to engage in any other business, and *consules electi,* chosen by the state from among merchants resident in the foreign country and not necessarily citizens of the state they represent. The latter, when appointed at all, are of inferior rank; and they do not enjoy all of the privileges and immunities conceded to the former. The new Vienna Convention follows the customary classification.[91]

As in the case of diplomatic officers, it has now become an academic question whether a state is obliged to admit consuls from other states. The conditions of modern intercourse make their admission an implied

_____

[90] Art. 17. The combination of two services has obvious administrative advantages. On its part the United States, being notified of the appointment of foreign representatives in a similar dual capacity, accords them a formal reception in their diplomatic character and issues an exequatur to them in their consular capacity.

[91] Art. 9.

condition of membership in the international community. However, as in the case of diplomatic agents, a state may refuse to admit a particular individual whose conduct has given ground for belief that his presence in the country would be undesirable. No reasons need be assigned for so doing. In 1869 Great Britain refused to admit Major Haggerty, a naturalized American of Irish descent, because of his alleged connection with Fenian plots.[92] The admittance of a consul is accomplished by the presentation on his part of a patent or commission, in return for which he is furnished by the foreign state with an exequatur, which recognizes him as an official of his government and authorizes him to exercise the functions appropriate to his office. Should the conduct of the consul become obnoxious to the foreign state, it may request his home government to recall him; or if the matter be serious, it may forthwith withdraw his exequatur and thus leave him without authority to continue his functions. In 1856 the United States withdrew the exequaturs of three British consuls because of their alleged activities in recruiting men for the British army in the Crimea.[93] In 1861 Great Britain conceded the right of the United States to withdraw the exequatur of the British consul at Charleston, although in so doing it expressed the opinion that the authority had been exercised without sufficient grounds.[94]

Functions of consuls. While the various functions of consuls are primarily determined by the municipal law of the state appointing them, the exercise of many of their functions encroaches upon the jurisdiction of the local government and to that extent requires its consent. This consent is regularly given in the form of consular treaties or conventions, which specify the rights consuls are to enjoy and the functions they are to perform in the two countries respectively. The more important of these mutually recognized functions, now so generally provided for as to have become part of customary international law, relate to the merchant marine of the consul's home state and to the settlement of the estates of deceased persons. A typical consular convention, such as that between the United States and Sweden of June 1, 1910,[95] provides that the respective consuls shall have exclusive charge of the in-

---

[92] Hall, *International Law*, § 105.

[93] *Ibid.*

[94] Moore, *Digest,* Vol. V, § 700. Numerous later cases might be cited. See, for example, the controversy between the United States and Great Britain over the announcement by the latter of its intention to withdraw the exequaturs of two American consular officers at Neucastle-on-Tyne on grounds of alleged misuse of their office to divert traffic from British to American steamship lines. Hackworth, *Digest,* Vol. IV, pp. 677 ff.

For the demand of the United States in 1941 that German and Italian consular officers be withdrawn because of activities outside the scope of their legitimate duties, see *ibid.,* pp. 681 ff.

[95] *Treaties and Conventions,* Vol. III, p. 2846.

ternal order of the merchant vessels of their nation and shall alone take
cognizance of differences which may arise between captains and their
crews, except in cases where the differences are of a nature to disturb
the peace of the port. They shall also have authority to arrest deserters
from the vessels of their nation, shall settle damages suffered at sea by
such vessels, and shall superintend proceedings relative to the salvage
of vessels. The notarial powers of consuls consist in receiving the depositions of the captains and crews of vessels of their own country and
in authenticating deeds and testamentary dispositions of their countrymen. They may also appear personally on behalf of the absent heirs or
creditors of deceased nationals of their own state. In addition to these
functions, expressly stipulated in treaties, consuls are intrusted with
numerous duties relating to the commerce of their country with the
foreign state, such as the legalizing of ship's papers, the inspection of
invoices, and the collection of information regarding conditions of trade
and industry, as well as with the protection of citizens of their home
country when in distress. For these latter duties, however, no special
authorization of the foreign state is required, and they are governed by
domestic law only. The Vienna Convention lists the functions in elaborate detail.[96]

Privileges and immunities of consuls.   The long-established privileges
and immunities conceded by states to foreign diplomatic agents are not
enjoyed by consuls in like degree, there being no representative character attaching to their persons. Nevertheless, since consuls are public
officers of their states and are custodians of its material interests, it has
been customary for the state in which they perform their functions to
afford special protection to them and to regard their consular offices
and archives as possessing a certain degree of inviolability. An attack
upon a consulate by a mob in time of riot and disorder is regarded as a
serious affront to the state whose arms and national flag are displayed
upon the building, and redress is demanded much as if the consul were
a diplomatic agent. In 1919 when the American consular agent Jenkins
was kidnapped by bandits in Mexico, the Department of State advised
the Mexican Government that the United States expected that measures
would be taken to obtain the release of Jenkins even if it should become
necessary to pay the ransom demanded.[97] In addition to these somewhat

96 Art. 5. For earlier lists, see Harvard Draft, Art. 11, and Hackworth, *Digest,* Vol.
IV, pp. 806 ff.

97 For details, see Hyde, *Int. Law,* Vol. II, § 286. In the Francisco Mallén case,
involving a claim for indemnity for an attack upon the Mexican consul in El Paso,
Texas, the Commission was presented with the question whether consuls were entitled to a special protection of their persons, the answer of the Commission being in
the negative in respect to other prerogatives than those enjoyed by the citizens of the
state, but being in the affirmative if "special protection" meant that in executing the
ordinary laws of the country "the government should realize that foreign governments
are sensitive regarding the treatment accorded to their representatives, and that there-

vague customary privileges and immunities, numerous others have been stipulated for in consular treaties and conventions, with the result that there are wide variations in the practice of the several states. The Havana Convention of 1928 introduced a degree of uniformity into the practice of the American Republics, keeping on the whole within the range of general practice.[98] The Vienna Convention lists the privileges and immunities in detail.[99]

Amenability to criminal jurisdiction. As a general rule, consuls are subject to the civil and criminal jurisdiction of the foreign state. In respect to civil suit it was held in Barbuit's Case that a commercial agent of the king of Prussia in Great Britain was not entitled to the privileges of *jus gentium* belonging to ambassadors and was therefore not protected from civil suit by the municipal law, which the court held to be "only declaratory of the ancient universal *jus gentium*." [100] In the case of Viveash v. Becker,[101] decided in 1814, the British court refused to exempt a consul to the duke of Oldenburg from the necessity of giving bail bond when arrested for debt, the same distinction being adverted to between consuls and public ministers as was made in Barbuit's Case. In 1890 it was held by the Supreme Court of the United States, *In re* Biaz,[102] that a consul-general of Guatemala, who alleged that he was exercising the functions of a diplomatic officer, was not a public minister within the intent of statutes of the United States and could claim no exemption from civil suit. In the case of Fenton Textile Association v. Krassin,[103] the British court denied immunity from process to the defendant, an official agent of the Soviet Government appointed under the terms of a special trade agreement. His claim of a diplomatic character was rejected. In the case of Bigelow v. Princess Zazianoff,[104] involving a suit for damages brought by the Princess against Consul Bigelow

---

fore the government of the consul's residence should exercise greater vigilance in respect to their security and safety." Commissioner Nielsen denied, however, that there could be any element of "punitive damages" in the amount awarded. *Opinions of the Commissioners,* 1927, pp. 254, 264; *Am. Journal,* Vol. 21 (1927), pp. 803, 805.

[98] Hudson, *Int. Legislation,* Vol. IV, p. 2394. *Int. Conferences of American States,* 1889-1928, p. 424.

[99] Arts. 28-39.

[100] Buvot v. Barbuit, High Court of Chancery, 1737. Fenwick, *Cases,* p. 690; Hudson, *Cases,* p. 810. In the course of his opinion the Lord Chancellor said: "But what creates my difficulty is, that I do not think that he [Barbuit] is intrusted to transact affairs between the two crowns: the commission is, to assist his Prussian Majesty's subjects here in their commerce; and so is the allowance. Now this gives him no authority to intermeddle with the affairs of the King: which makes his employment to be in the nature of a consul."

[101] 3 M. & S. 284; Cobbett, *Cases,* Vol. I, p. 309.

[102] 135 U.S. 403 (1890). Fenwick, *Cases,* p. 693.

[103] 38 Times L. R. 259 (1921). Hudson, *Cases,* p. 787; Fenwick, *Cases,* p. 643.

[104] Court of Appeals of Paris, 1928. Fenwick, *Cases,* p. 699; Hudson, *Cases,* p. 817; *Am. Journal,* Vol. 23 (1929), p. 172.

for libelous statements in an American newspaper, the French court refused to admit Bigelow's plea to the jurisdiction of the court on the
ground that the alleged libel was connected with his official act of refusing a passport, holding that the statements were not a "necessary
and indispensable corollary" of the official act. The Vienna Convention
of 1963 is explicit in its provision that "Consular officers shall not be
liable to arrest or detention pending trial except in the case of a grave
crime and pursuant to a decision by the competent judicial authority,"
and in the case of criminal proceedings for lesser offenses special consideration is to be shown to the consul so as to hamper the exercise of
his consular functions as little as possible.[105]

But consuls are not on a par with diplomatic officers in respect to
general privileges and immunities. In the Kasenkina case, a writ of
habeas corpus was served on the Soviet Consul General in New York
in 1948 calling upon him to produce Mrs. Kasenkina in open court after
she had refused to return to the Soviet Union and was being held in
the Soviet Consulate. That same day Mrs. Kasenkina jumped from the
third floor of the Soviet Consulate and was seriously injured. The Department of State held that the Soviet Consul General was not entitled
to diplomatic immunity and that he was not privileged to insist upon
seeing Mrs. Kasenkina, against her will, while she was recovering from
her injuries in a public hospital. The consulates in New York and in
San Francisco were closed by the Soviet Union in protest.[106]

The general rule of the amenability of consuls to criminal jurisdiction
is sometimes modified to the extent of exempting them from prosecution
for minor offenses and, in other cases, of taking more moderate action
than would normally be taken. In 1868 the United States pressed for a
heavy indemnity from Peru for alleged illegal and hasty procedure in
the arrest of Consul Weile for participation in an assault.[107] When, however, a consul is guilty of grave offenses, he is subjected to regular
criminal prosecution and punished according to the law, as in the case
of the German consul-general at San Francisco, Franz Bopp, who was
convicted on January 10, 1917, of conspiring to destroy munitions and
sentenced to fine and imprisonment. The vice-consul and a consular
attaché were given life sentences.[108]

Liability to taxation. It is common to exempt consuls from direct
personal taxes, such as income taxes and taxes upon other personal property, but to subject them to the usual taxes upon real property and upon
the private business in which they may happen to be engaged. The
subject is governed by treaty stipulations, which have now become

[105] Art. 41.
[106] See L. Preuss, "Consular Immunities: The Kasenkina Case," *Am. Journal,* Vol.
43 (1949), p. 37; Bishop, *Cases,* p. 601.
[107] Stowell and Munro, *Cases,* Vol. I, p. 22.
[108] Hackworth, *Digest,* Vol. VII, p. 402.

sufficiently common and uniform to approximate to a general rule.[109] In a case relating to the consul of the elector of Hesse, the United States Department of State in 1856 announced the doctrine that consuls, provided they were not citizens of the United States, were "exempted from all public service, and from all taxes, imposts and contributions except such as they may have to pay on their property, or in consequence of their engaging in commercial pursuits." [110] It is also common to exempt consuls from the obligation of appearing in person as witnesses in court in civil cases. Where necessary, the consul's evidence may be taken in the form of a deposition at the consulate. In Dillon's Case,[111] involving a criminal prosecution, a conflict arose between a provision of the French-American treaty of 1853, giving to the respective consuls immunity from appearance as witnesses before the courts, and the provision of the United States Constitution giving to accused persons the right to be confronted with witnesses in open court. The result of controversy was, on the one hand, an apology on the part of the United States for its action in compelling the attendance of the consul in court, and, on the other hand, an unwillingness on its part to conclude treaties in the future exempting consuls from the duty of giving testimony in criminal cases. The Vienna Convention provides in broad terms that the members of a consular post may be called upon to attend as witnesses in the course of judicial or administrative proceedings, except in respect to matters connected with the exercise of their functions, with the qualification that the authority requiring the evidence of a consular officer avoid interference with the performance of his functions.[112]

Special status of consuls in the Orient. The function of exercising civil and criminal jurisdiction over their countrymen assigned to consuls in the Mohammedan countries of the Mediterranean during the fourteenth and fifteenth centuries continued to be exercised by them in those parts after having been taken from them in European countries. Treaties known as "capitulations" were entered into from time to time, extending the system to other non-Christian countries in the Near and Far East, and also enlarging the jurisdiction of the consuls and conferring upon them many of the privileges and immunities belonging to diplomatic agents. In consequence of the differences between the European and the Oriental systems of law, the right was secured by the leading powers to have their consuls exercise jurisdiction not only over cases between citizens of their own country but over *mixed cases* between

---

[109] See *ibid.*, Vol. IV, p. 774, where the provisions of the treaty of 1923 between the United States and Germany are cited. Compare Harvard Draft, Art. 24, and comment.

[110] Moore, *Digest*, Vol. V, § 715. The Vienna Convention of 1963 lists the exemptions in detail, Art. 49.

[111] *Ibid.*, § 714.

[112] Art. 44.

such citizens and natives of the non-Christian state. As the result of recent treaties these extraterritorial rights have now come practically to an end.

J. PRIVILEGES AND IMMUNITIES OF INTERNATIONAL ORGANIZATIONS

With the establishment of the League of Nations in 1920 the question arose of the privileges and immunities to be granted to representatives of the member states and to officials of the League itself. Article 7 of the Covenant provided that, when engaged on the business of the League, they were to enjoy diplomatic privileges and immunities. The Charter of the United Nations, after first providing that the Organization itself shall enjoy in the territory of each of its members such privileges and immunities as are necessary for the fulfillment of its purposes, extends to the individual representatives and to officials of the Organization such privileges and immunities as are necessary for the independent exercise of their functions in connection with the Organization. The following year the General Assembly approved the General Convention on the Privileges and Immunities of the United Nations, specifying in detail the privileges and immunities, but excluding the diplomatic privilege of exemption from customs duties on imported goods and excise and sales taxes.[113]

In 1948 the unhappy assassination of Count Folke Bernadotte in Palestine raised the question of whether the United Nations was competent to bring a claim against the responsible government for injury done to one of its agents. The General Assembly referred the question to the International Court of Justice for an advisory opinion, and the Court declared unanimously that the United Nations possessed the necessary judicial personality to give it competence to bring suit. A year later the Israeli government paid the claim, although protesting the principles of responsibility on which it was based.[114]

The distinction between diplomatic privileges and those of a mere employee of the United Nations appeared clearly in the refusal of the United States to set aside an indictment of one Gubitchev for conspiracy to violate the U.S. Espionage laws in 1949 on the ground that he "did not enter the United States as an emissary from the USSR," but merely sought employment in the Secretariat of the United Nations; and that as an employee of the United Nations he enjoyed "immunity from legal process only in relation to acts performed by him in his official capacity and falling within his functions as an official of the United Nations." [115]

---

113 See Bishop, *Cases,* p. 614; J. Kunz, "Privileges and Immunities of International Organizations," *Am. Journal,* Vol. 41 (1947), p. 828.

114 *I.C.J. Reports,* 1949, p. 174; *Am. Journal,* Vol. 43 (1949), p. 589. See above, where the legal personality of the United Nations is discussed, Chap. IX.

115 United States v. Coplon and Gubitchev, 84 F. Supp. 472 (S.D.N.Y. 1949); 88 F. Supp. 915 (S.D.N.Y. 1950).

CHAPTER **XXV**

International Cooperation for the Promotion
of Economic and Social Interests

A. RECENT GROWTH OF INTERNATIONAL COOPERATION: TWOFOLD FUNCTION OF LAW

Law between nations, as between the citizens of the more highly developed states, performs a twofold function. In the first place it determines the legal relation of states to the community of which they are members and their respective relations to one another within that community. This is the older function of international law, and in accordance with it we have the whole system of personal status and of rights and duties discussed in the preceding chapters. In the second place international law performs the function of promoting common interests, in respect to which there is not so much a conflict of rights as a need of cooperative action to bring about an orderly regulation of matters of mutual benefit to all. This second function of international law has been of relatively late manifestation; but having once come into being it has grown with striking rapidity and has within recent years come to occupy a significant place in the foreign relations of states, paralleling the adjustment of mutual rights and duties.[1]

Machinery of international legislation. The legislative function is performed by multipartite treaties. Since no international conference has ever been given the authority to act directly on behalf of the mem-

[1] For a general survey of this branch of the law, see *U.N. Yearbooks* under the head, "Economic and Social Questions," "Intergovernmental Organizations"; Jessup, *A Modern Law of Nations;* Vandenbosch and Hogan, *Toward World Order,* Chap. 12; Asher, *et al., The United Nations and the Promotion of the General Welfare;* Dept. of State, *International Organizations in which the United States Participates;* P. C. Jessup, *et al., International Regulation of Economic and Social Questions* (containing a reprint of J. P. Chamberlain, *International Organization*); Higgins, *The Development of International Law through the Political Organs of the United Nations;* Union of International Associations, *Yearbook of International Organizations.*

bers of the international community, it is necessary for states, when seeking to promote common interests by cooperative action, to draw up general treaties, commonly described as "conventions," and to submit them to the ratification of each separate state. In the case of most of these treaties, provision is made that in the event that not all states desire to become a party to them, they may come into effect between those states that ratify them. The recommendations of the U.N. General Assembly, while not creating binding obligations, have, however, now come to have a practical value beyond their legal force; they must be taken into account in studying the widening scope of international cooperation since the establishment of the United Nations. In like manner the work of the specialized organizations extends far beyond the legal force of the decisions of their governing bodies.

B. THE RELATION BETWEEN ECONOMIC AND POLITICAL INTERESTS

The economic interests of states have become so complex of recent years and have come to bear so important a relation to the national welfare that it is difficult in many cases to find a basis upon which they may be distinguished from the interests commonly designated as *political*. Assigning the term *political* somewhat arbitrarily to the interests that are connected with the position of a state in the community of nations and with the organization and administration of its domestic government, the *economic* interests of a state may be said in general to involve the production of raw materials or access to supplies of them, the manufacture of goods, the protection of patents and copyrights, the sale of goods in domestic and foreign markets, transportation, communication, finance, and the conservation of natural resources. Obviously these interests must form an object of international law, for they have brought into play the most sharply competitive forces of national life, and they have been since the sixteenth century the underlying causes of one war after another. The closing years of the nineteenth century and the opening years of the twentieth witnessed perhaps the climax of that "economic imperialism" which, succeeding the earlier political imperialism, had for its object the exploitation of the economic resources of undeveloped countries and the control of their foreign trade.[2] The decades between the two World Wars witnessed in its most acute form the policy of what is known as "economic nationalism," which sought to develop the economic power of the individual state as an adjunct to its military power, looking only to immediate gains and indifferent to the effect which its measures might have upon the welfare of other states.

---

[2] The situation is well presented in Moon, *Imperialism and World Politics;* Simonds and Emeny, *The Great Powers in World Politics;* Schuman, *Int. Politics;* and see note 7 of this chapter.

C. ECONOMIC COOPERATION BEFORE 1945

Protection of industrial and literary property. There were, however, certain economic interests into which competition did not enter, or in respect to which all states had a common interest in regulation. Prominent among these interests, the first of them indeed, was the development of the facilities of communication, beginning with the General Telegraphic Convention signed at Paris in 1865, followed by the Universal Postal Union of 1878, and followed later by numerous agreements and amendments adopted to take into account new inventions and improvements in the field of communications. The Union for the Protection of Industrial Property of 1883 sought to assure reciprocal national treatment to patent rights throughout the member states; with it was associated the Convention for the Protection of Literary and Artistic Works signed at Bern in 1886.[3]

International communications. In the field of international communications it was early seen that only by international regulation could the benefits of the new instruments and agencies of communication be enjoyed to the fullest degree. Cooperative regulation was first undertaken by the General Telegraphic Convention, signed at Paris in 1865, and subsequently modified and extended. In 1925 the International Telegraph Conference and in 1927 the Radio-Telegraph Conference decided to combine their conventions, and in 1932 at Madrid a new Telecommunication Convention was signed creating the International Telecommunication Union, abrogating the earlier conventions of the two services and creating a single Bureau of the Union at Bern. The General Postal Convention, signed at Bern in 1874, created the General Postal Union, which in 1878 became the Universal Postal Union. Provision was made that for the purposes of the convention the territory of the member states should be regarded as "one single territory." New conventions were adopted from time to time, repeating the terms of earlier conventions, as at London in 1929, at Cairo in 1934, at Buenos Aires in 1939, and at Paris in 1947. In 1884 a Convention for the Protection of Submarine Cables was signed which is still in force.[4]

Navigation and transit. Paralleling the development of international communications were the numerous agreements opening up the great international rivers of Europe to the commerce of the riparian states; these culminated in the Convention on the Regime of Navigable Waterways of International Concern signed at Barcelona in 1921. Freedom of transit across land was secured by a Convention also signed

[3] For the texts of these agreements, see Hudson, *Int. Legislation,* Vols. I-VI, as indexed; Peaslee, *Int. Governmental Organizations,* 2nd ed., as indexed.

[4] For the texts of these agreements, see Hudson, *op. cit.,* and Peaslee, *Int. Gov. Organizations,* as indexed.

at Barcelona in 1921, by a Convention on the International Regime of Railways signed at Geneva in 1923, and by two additional conventions dealing with the transport of passengers and goods. A Convention on Motor Traffic was signed at Paris in 1926, together with a separate Convention on Road Traffic dealing with rules of the road. The Pan American Highway Convention of 1936 expressed the mutual interest of all of the American States in the construction of a highway which was to open up sections of the different states hitherto isolated from one another. In the field of aerial navigation, a Convention on the Regulation of Aerial Navigation was signed at Paris in 1919, followed in 1944 by the Convention on Civil Aviation signed at Chicago by the delegates of fifty-four nations.[5]

Conservation of natural resources. Cooperation was also carried into the field of the conservation of natural resources. The prevention of plant diseases and pests early called for concerted measures, represented by the convention signed at Bern in 1881. A convention for the Protection of Migratory Birds, useful to agriculture, was signed at Washington in 1916; and a convention on the Organization of the Fight against Locusts at Rome in 1920. The protection of fisheries was, as we have seen, an object of special solicitude on the part of the United States, the Pelagic Sealing Convention being signed at Washington in 1911, and the Convention concerning Halibut Fisheries in the North Pacific Ocean in 1923. An agreement for the Regulation of Whaling was signed in London in 1937, which was superseded by a new convention in 1946.[6]

D. UNREGULATED COMMERCIAL RIVALRIES

Important as were the objectives of these measures of international cooperation, however, the statesmen of the times failed to see in them the far more urgent need of control over their competitive economic interests. It is for the historian to recite the long story of the economic lawlessness which, combined with an unstable balance of power, led to the war of 1914. The conflicts between states in extending their overseas commerce began, if a starting point may be fixed, with the simultaneous rounding of the Cape of Good Hope and discovery of the American continent. While the interests involved were limited in earlier days to a small class of the people, the transition from an agricultural economy to an industrial economy that took place within the leading states during the nineteenth century made the development of foreign commerce a matter of vital concern to the entire citizen body. What was formerly a rivalry between great banking and commercial houses, with governments lending in most cases merely their indirect aid, became

---

[5] For the texts, see Hudson, *op. cit.*, and Peaslee, *op. cit.*

[6] Details of these agreements may be found in *Treaties and Conventions,* Vols. III-IV, as indexed; and in Hudson, *Int. Legislation,* Vols. I-VII, as indexed.

a direct rivalry between the governments themselves, and the interests at issue came to be regarded as second only to the great issue of national security, if not part of that security itself.

Competition for supplies of the raw materials of industry. By the middle of the nineteenth century the competition between the leading European powers had become acute, as they sought both sources of supply of raw materials and exclusive markets for the products of industry. Few of the industrial countries possessed within their borders the vital raw materials of iron, copper, and coal in sufficient quantity. Later, new raw materials became equally essential—oil and rubber, manganese, and other ores. How was the industrial state to assure itself of a constant supply of these materials? If it did not control territories in which there were assured deposits, it would be at the mercy of its rivals, who might decide at any time to throttle its industrial life. International control of the supply and distribution of these materials was not believed to be within the range of practical statesmanship. The leading powers shifted for themselves, relying upon their political power to give them the assurance they needed. Smaller industrial states, unable to bring diplomatic pressure to bear to secure special advantages, acquiesced with a greater or less degree of uneasiness in the necessity of living at the commercial mercy of their more formidable rivals.[7]

The struggle for foreign markets. The second great concern of the modern industrial state was to secure foreign markets for the disposal of the surplus products of industry.[8] It was an old problem made acute by labor-saving machinery and standardized production, in consequence of which many of the products of industry were manufactured in excess of domestic consumption. Economists taught that the prosperity of a country depended upon its having a favorable balance of trade. But no economic theory was needed to induce industrial leaders to expand their production and then in turn look to foreign markets to maintain their higher rate of production. The result was a ruthless competition not merely between individual manufacturers but between governments acting in their own interest to obtain a privileged position wherever it could be obtained. If the particular state had political control over a colony or dependency, it sought to reserve the market for itself as far as possible. Where it did not have political control it sought to maintain the policy of the "open door," in accordance with which the foreign

[7] In addition to Moon, *Imperialism and World Politics, op. cit.,* see Staley, *Raw Materials in Peace and War;* Emeny, *Strategy of Raw Materials;* Wallace and Edminster, *International Control of Raw Materials; Raw Materials Problems and Policies,* League of Nations, 1946.

[8] The literature of the subject is extensive. See, in addition to Moon, *op. cit.* Culbertson, *Int. Economic Policies;* Donaldson, *International Economic Relations;* Williams, *The Economic Foreign Policy of the United States;* McClure, *World Prosperity;* Addresses by J. B. Whitton, B. Emeny, W. McClure, *Proceedings,* Am. Soc. Int. Law, 1936, pp. 104 ff.

market was to be accessible to all upon equal terms.[9]

Opportunities for the investment of capital. But the products of industry were not the only goods for which foreign markets were sought. Opportunities had to be found for the investment of surplus capital which, like the excess of goods, resulted from the mechanical inventions that multiplied the productivity of labor. But the investment of capital frequently involved political complications and led at times to the intervention of the Great Powers in the domestic affairs of undeveloped countries. In the case of independent states the rivalry between the leading industrial powers took the form of making loans with special economic advantages in view, securing concessions for the building of railways and the opening of mines and oil wells and the development of public services such as water supply and electric power.[10] In the case of colonies and protectorates, the political control of the empire did not necessarily mean an exclusive monopoly of the investment of capital, but it had as a rule that practical effect.

The partition of Africa followed in a sense the normal course of economic imperialism, marked, however, by the formal Congress at Berlin in 1885 at which the Great Powers delimited their areas of exploitation so as to avoid a conflict of interests. A number of the Near Eastern and Far Eastern states fell in like manner before the advances of political and economic imperialism.[11]

Thus things stood on the eve of the First World War. The Hague Conference of 1907 had met and left untouched not only the regulation of competitive armaments but the regulation of economic rivalries which gave to national armaments part of their justification. To protect its commercial interests in all parts of the world a state must have a powerful army and a powerful navy; it must be able to meet rival states at the conference table with a consciousness on both sides that the failure to meet demands believed to be reasonable would have unfortunate consequences. But powerful armies and navies in turn were a heavy drain upon

---

[9] Compare the note sent by Secretary of State Hay in 1899 to the principal powers of Europe in an effort to check the encroachments of the powers upon China. Latane, *History of American Foreign Policy,* pp. 564 ff.; Bemis, *Diplomatic History of the United States,* p. 484.

[10] During the long presidency of Porfirio Diaz in Mexico, 1876-1911 (with the exception of four years), concessions were freely granted by the Mexican Government to foreign capitalists, with the result that the revolutionary government of Carranza secured the adoption of a new constitution in 1917 which included provisions asserting the ultimate ownership of the nation in all lands and waters, including minerals, salt, mineral fuels, and petroleum in its different forms. Legislation in pursuance of the constitution brought on a series of sharp international controversies. See p. 345. In like manner the exploitation of Persia in pursuance of the Anglo-Russian agreement of 1907 and the exploitation of Morocco in the opening decade of the century led to acute international rivalries. See Moon, *op. cit.,* Chaps. X, XI.

[11] Moon, *op. cit.;* Schuman, *Int. Politics;* Seymour, *Diplomatic Background of the War, 1870-1914.*

national resources; they consumed raw materials that might otherwise have been available to industry and made new sources of supply imperative. The point was now reached where political and economic imperialism were so closely interrelated as to be a single policy, and statesmen had no difficulty in seeing in that policy the vital interest of national defense.

Proposed equality of opportunity.   Among the Fourteen Points set forth by President Wilson in 1918 as the conditions of a permanent peace was: "The removal, as far as possible, of all economic barriers and the establishment of an equality of trade conditions among all the nations consenting to the peace and associating themselves for its maintenance." In accordance with this principle, a provision was included in the Covenant of the League of Nations which aimed at "equal opportunity for trade and commerce of other members of the League" in certain of the territories to be placed under mandate. Two years later, at the close of the Washington Conference of 1921-1922, a general agreement was signed "relating to the principles and policies to be followed in matters concerning China." [12] For half a century China had been subjected to various forms of exploitation by foreign powers. Treaties with individual powers granted leases and concessions, fixed maximum rates that might be imposed upon imports, and pledged certain revenues in payment of public debts.[13] By the "Nine Power Treaty" of 1922 the signatory powers agreed to respect the sovereignty, independence, and territorial and administrative integrity of China and to use their influence to establish and maintain the principle of equal opportunity for commerce and industry of all nations throughout Chinese territory. With the object of making effective the principle of the "open door" in China, the contracting powers agreed not to seek themselves, or to support their respective nationals in seeking, any arrangement which might establish in their favor superior rights with respect to commercial or economic development in any designated region of China or any such monopoly or preference as would deprive the nationals of any other power of the right of undertaking any legitimate trade or industry in China.[14]

Economic nationalism.   But these limited provisions failed to meet the larger problem of the growing "economic nationalism" which succeeded to the economic imperialism of the prewar period. The study by the League of Nations of plans for military disarmament was not accompanied by the study of plans for the "economic disarmament" which

[12] For the text of the treaty, see *Treaties and Conventions*, Vol. III, p. 3120; Hudson, *Int. Legislation*, Vol. II, p. 823.

[13] See Willoughby, *Foreign Rights and Interests in China*; G. A. Finch, "American Diplomacy and the Financing of China," *Am. Journal*, Vol. 16 (1922), p. 25.

[14] The literature of the situation in China at this period is extensive. See, in particular, Goodnow, *China, an Analysis*; Hornbeck, *China Today: Political*; Bau, *Foreign Relations of China; Open Door Doctrine in Relation to China*.

was equally urgent. The economic rivalries of the leading powers became more acute than ever, and they were only intensified by the financial and economic depression which in 1929 spread from one country
to another. The London Conference of 1933 sought to establish basic
principles of international economic relations, in accordance with which
the competitive struggle might have been directed to the general welfare; but the failure of the conference threw the leading industrial states
back upon their own resources. New tariff barriers were erected, quotas
were fixed for imported goods, currencies were "managed" to gain
temporary advantages, barter agreements were entered into, and what
was in effect an economic war for national survival ensued. The international community failed to assert its authority in a field in which economic and political interests went hand in hand.[15]

Trade agreements program. On the part of the United States a special effort was made in 1934 to lower the barriers of trade by the conclusion of a series of "reciprocal trade agreements" in accordance with
which the parties to the agreement sought to develop their foreign
markets by making reciprocal concessions in respect to existing tariff
duties upon specific articles. A significant feature of the agreements was
the provision that the contracting countries should grant each other unconditional and unrestricted most-favored-nation treatment, so that any
advantage or favor granted to a third country should be accorded immediately and without compensation to the other contracting country.[16]
The program was interrupted by the outbreak of the war, but in any
case it was clear that stronger forces were at work in certain states than
could have been checked by minor economic measures.

E. CONSTRUCTIVE MEASURES

The Atlantic Charter. The first announcement of new economic principles came with the Atlantic Charter, subsequently incorporated into
the Declaration by United Nations. The Charter proclaimed the intention
of the signatories to endeavor, with due respect for their eixsting obligations, "to further the enjoyment by all States, great or small, victor or
vanquished, of access, on equal terms, to the trade and to the raw materials of the world which are needed for their economic prosperity";
and it expressed their desire "to bring about the fullest collaboration
between all nations in the economic field with the object of securing,
for all, improved labor standards, economic advancement and social
security." The hope was held out that after the war a peace might be

[15] See Simonds and Emeny, *The Price of Peace;* Inter-American Juridical Committee, "Preliminary Recommendation on Post-War Problems," *Recommendations
and Reports,* 1942-1944, pp. 31 ff.; E. M. Patterson, "Les Bases économiques de la
paix," *Recueil des Cours,* Vol. 37 (1931-III), p. 419.

[16] See Hackworth, *Digest,* Vol. V, pp. 419 ff., where the legal aspects of the trade
agreements are discussed.

established which would not only afford to all nations the means of dwelling in safety within their own boundaries, but which would "afford assurance that all men in all the lands may live out their lives in freedom from fear and want." [17] The objectives of the Atlantic Charter thus aimed not only at "a wider and permanent system of general security" for states as members of the international community, but also at measures of international cooperation for the promotion of the welfare of the individual citizens within the separate states.

Bretton Woods agreements. In July, 1944, a conference met at Bretton Woods, and as a result of its discussions an agreement was reached to create an International Monetary Fund, the chief object of which was to assist states in the stabilization of their currencies and to promote orderly exchange arrangements. The agreement was signed in Washington on December 27, 1945. A Board of Governors was elected and the organization began its activities in September, 1946, with an effort to obtain agreements with its thirty-nine member states in the structure of exchange rates.[18]

A second agreement reached at Bretton Woods was for the establishment of an International Bank for Reconstruction and Development. The purposes of the bank are to assist its member states by facilitating the investment of capital for productive purposes and to supplement private capital by bank loans for urgent projects of national reconstruction.[19]

Economic and Social Council of the United Nations. It was, however, with the adoption of the Charter of the United Nations that the regulation of competitive economic interests was given its greatest impulse. The opening article of the Charter looks beyond the maintenance of the *status quo* to the prevention and removal of threats to the peace. Article 61 creates an Economic and Social Council and calls upon it to make studies and reports in economic, social, and other fields and to enter into agreements with existing specialized agencies. In pursuance of these functions and operating under the authority of the General Assembly, the Council appointed four regional commissions dealing respectively with Europe, Asia and the Far East, Latin America, and Africa, each promoting economic reconstruction, investigating technological problems, and collecting and disseminating information.[20]

Abandonment of colonialism. While the dominant objective in the

---

[17] For the text of the Atlantic Charter, see Appendix C. Compare the "Four Freedoms" message of President Roosevelt to Congress of January 6, 1941: "The third is freedom from want, which, translated into world terms, means economic understandings which will secure to every nation a healthy peacetime life for its inhabitants— everywhere in the world."

[18] For the text of the agreement, see *United Nations Monetary and Financial Conferences, Final Act and Related Documents,* 1944, Dept. of State Publication, No. 2187; Halm, *International Monetary Cooperation;* Peaslee, *op. cit.,* Vol. II, p. 1258.

[19] For the text of the agreement, see Peaslee, *op. cit.,* Vol. II, p. 942.

[20] *Everyman's United Nations,* 1964, pp. 198 ff.; *U.N. Yearbook,* 1962, pp. 270 ff.

abandonment of colonialism has been political rather than economic in character, the effects of the independence of some forty or more Near Eastern, Far Eastern, and African states upon the economic imperialism of colonial days have been far-reaching. As the former colonies and protectorates have one by one obtained recognition of their independence and been admitted to membership of the United Nations, they are taking command of their resources and of their markets and putting an end to special privileges except in so far as an independent state may enter into voluntary agreements believed to be in its own interest.

Promotion of trade and industry. Outstanding among the measures of economic cooperation is the promotion of trade, both as a means of raising standards of living and as an indirect solution for the commercial rivalries of pre-World War II days. In addition to the functions of the World Bank and the Fund, referred to above, an International Finance Corporation was established in 1956 to encourage investment in private enterprises particularly in underdeveloped countries, and an International Development Association was established in 1960 to facilitate loans on more flexible terms than the Bank could make.[21]

Bearing more directly upon the promotion of trade was the proposed International Trade Organization, known as the "Havana Charter," adopted at a Conference on Trade and Employment in 1946, having as its objectives the removal of trade restrictions and discriminations and the establishment of an international body to assist in the observance of the obligations assumed. The failure of this project was followed by the adoption, in 1948, of the General Agreement on Tariffs and Trade (GATT) which directs its activities to the reduction of trade barriers and the settlement of trade disputes.[22]

Closely associated with the promotion of trade have been the efforts, both of the Economic and Social Council of the United Nations and of the corresponding Council of the Organization of American States, to develop local industries in backward countries in order to offset the disparity between the prices of agricultural products and those of manufactured goods.

Navigation and transit. In addition to the conventions providing for the adoption of uniform national legislation and those of 1914 and 1929 on Safety of Life at Sea, the Inter-Governmental Maritime Consultative Organization, established by a Convention that entered into force in 1957, provides for intergovernmental cooperation in maritime

---

[21] Details may be found in Peaslee, *op. cit.*, Vol. II, p. 1172. *World Economic Survey,* 1960, 1961; *U.N. Yearbook,* 1961, pp. 635 ff.; 1962, pp. 594 ff.

[22] The wide scope of the activities of GATT may be seen in *U.N. Yearbook,* 1961, p. 672; 1962, p. 644. For the text of the agreement, see Peaslee, *op. cit.*, Vol. I, p. 688.

navigation and is concerned with standards of safety and efficiency and adequate shipping services.[23]

The International Civil Aviation Organization, established at the Conference at Chicago in 1944, became a specialized agency of the United Nations. It holds regional as well as general air navigation meetings, offering, *inter alia*, technical assistance to undeveloped countries.[24]

Communications and radio broadcasting. By separate agreement with the Economic and Social Council, the International Telecommunication Union (ITU) and the Universal Postal Union (UPU) both became specialized agencies of the United Nations, the membership of both Unions rising with the admission of new members. A new telecommunication convention was signed at Geneva in 1959, and supplementary agreements to the Universal Postal Convention at Ottawa in 1957. The activities of both bodies have now become of vast scope.[25]

F. COOPERATIVE REGULATION OF SOCIAL INTERESTS

In a broad way the term *social* may be applied to certain interests of the state which are connected neither with the political interests of government nor with the economic interests associated with the production and distribution of goods. These interests, as between nations, are on the whole not controversial in character, being in varying degrees common to all states; and they may be conveniently classified under the heads of public health, public safety, public morals, and what has now come to be called "social justice." In some instances, as in the case of public health, the effective promotion of these social interests may be beyond the efforts of the individual states, so that cooperative action by the nations as a body is imperative. In other instances, while individual action and bilateral treaties may be sufficient to bring satisfactory results, cooperative action by the whole community of nations may promote the particular interest to a far greater degree. The various conventions by which states have undertaken to promote their social interests have grown steadily in number, and it will be sufficient here to enumerate their titles and general scope, leaving the details to treatises dealing more particularly with the subject.[26]

Public health. Prior to the establishment of the League of Nations, international cooperation in the field of public health consisted in the

---

[23] Peaslee, *op. cit.*, Vol. I, p. 901; *U.N. Yearbook*, 1961, p. 669.

[24] Peaslee, Vol. II, p. 989; *U.N. Yearbook*, 1962, p. 621.

[25] *U.N. Yearbook*, 1962, pp. 625, 630. See above, pp. 491 ff.

[26] The distinction between social and economic interests is obviously arbitrary in respect to a number of organizations, and the classification here followed is for purposes of convenience only. Note the combination in the Economic and Social Council of the United Nations.

adoption of a series of multipartite conventions, the first of which was the International Sanitary Convention signed at Venice in 1892. This was followed by successive Cholera and Plague Conventions in 1893, 1894, and 1897. A revised sanitary convention was adopted in 1903, which contained elaborate provisions with respect to the enforcement of quarantine measures in ports and frontiers. A convention adopted in 1907 established an International Office of Public Health at Paris. In 1920 the League of Nations established its own Health Organization, creating a separate Health Section in the Secretariat and appointing a Health Committee composed of representatives of the health administrations of the separate states. It was not, however, until the establishment of the United Nations in 1945 that coordination of the various health activities was made effective. A new World Health Organization (WHO) was established at a conference held in New York in 1946, in which sixty-seven states participated. The new WHO came into effect in 1948 when its constitution was ratified by twenty-six members of the United Nations, and it became at the same time a specialized agency of the United Nations.[27] The main organs of WHO, as provided in its Constitution, are the World Health Assembly, the Executive Board, and the Secretariat. At the same time, the Pan American Sanitary (Health) Organization entered into an agreement with the World Health Organization by which it became the regional branch of the World Organization, with its own executive organ, the Pan American Sanitary Bureau.[28]

International Labor Organization. The Constitution of the International Labor Organization, forming Part XIII of the Treaty of Versailles, was based upon the principle that the universal peace which was the object of the League of Nations could be established "only if it is based upon social justice." Section I cited the urgent need of improving the conditions of labor and stated that "the failure of any nation to adopt humane conditions of labour is an obstacle in the way of other nations which desire to improve the conditions in their own countries." Acting in pursuance of this objective of social justice the successive General Conferences of the Organization have adopted a long list of draft conventions and recommendations to be submitted to the member states. The subjects dealt with by these draft conventions and recommendations include the following problems of labor policy: employment; general conditions of labor; the work of women and children; industrial health, safety, and welfare; social insurance; industrial relations; and administration of social legislation. At the meeting of the General Conference of the ILO in 1944, a declaration of the aims and purposes of

[27] See Peaslee, Vol. II, p. 1878. The background of the WHO is also summarized in *U.N. Yearbook*, 1946-1947, pp. 789 ff.; and its present activities in *ibid.*, 1962, p. 588.

[28] See Fenwick, *OAS*, p. 470; *Basic Documents of the Pan American Health Organization*, 3rd ed. (1958).

the organization and of the principles which should inspire the policy of its members was adopted, known as "The Philadelphia Charter." In 1946, the organization adopted an amended constitution, under which it has functioned as a specialized agency of the United Nations.[29]

Protection of fundamental human rights. The Charter of the United Nations contains in its preamble a strong statement of the determination of the peoples of the United Nations "to reaffirm faith in fundamental human rights, in the dignity and worth of the human person, in the equal rights of men and women and of nations large and small"; it is the first treaty in recorded history to look behind the formal organization of governments to the individual human beings who constitute the legal entity that is "the state." Article 1 of the Charter enumerates among its purposes "to achieve international cooperation . . . in promoting and encouraging respect for human rights and for fundamental freedoms for all without distinction as to race, sex, language, or religion." Succeeding articles stress different aspects of the same objective.

In pursuance of the provisions of the Charter, the General Assembly adopted on December 10, 1948, the Universal Declaration of Human Rights, including the traditional rights of freedom of speech, of the press and of assembly, of fair trial, and of the right to vote, together with other rights of more modern character, such as the right to social security and to education.[30]

Supplementing the Declaration are drafts of international covenants on human rights which, when ratified, will create legal obligations. The scope of these proposed conventions is wide, embracing not only political but economic, social, and cultural rights, which, certain members of the General Assembly claim, it would be difficult to enforce.[31] In the special field of the rights of women, where discrimination has prevailed, the General Assembly adopted in 1952 a Convention on the Political Rights of Women, which by 1964 had been ratified by forty states. The Convention provides that women shall be entitled to vote in all elections and shall be eligible for election to public office on terms of equality with men and to exercise public functions in positions established by law.

Of outstanding importance in the protection of human rights are the activities of the two organs of the Convention on Human Rights signed

[29] *U.N. Yearbook,* 1961, p. 598; 1962, p. 571, and previous *Yearbooks* for background material. For the documents, see Peaslee, *I.G.O.,* p. 1230.

[30] The bibliography of the subject has become extensive. See, in particular, Jessup, *A Modern Law of Nations;* Lauterpacht, *International Law and Human Rights.* For the text of the Universal Declaration, see *U.N. Yearbook,* 1947-1948, p. 575; *Am. Journal,* Vol. 43 (1949), Supp., p. 127. It follows in part the American Declaration of the Rights and Duties of Man, adopted at the Ninth International Conference of American States at Bogotá in 1948. The subject is also discussed in connection with the topic, "Position of individuals in international law," see above, p. 152.

[31] *U.N. Yearbook,* 1961, pp. 292 ff.; *U.N. Yearbook on Human Rights.*

at Rome, November 4, 1950. While the Convention is no more than a regional agreement within the circle of the Council of Europe, its influence has spread beyond the regional group, and it gives promise of permanence beyond the life of the Council itself. The European Commission on Human Rights, created by the Convention, handles the applications and complaints submitted under the terms of the Convention, and the European Court on Human Rights hears the cases and decides on their merits.[32]

Public morals. To be included in the program of social cooperation are the various conventions that have been adopted for the suppression of the slave trade and the traffic in dangerous drugs, both of which antedated the measures now being taken by the United Nations. In 1926 a new Convention for the Suppression of the African Slave Trade was adopted, replacing earlier conventions; [33] and in 1921 a new Convention for the Suppression of Traffic in Women and Children was opened for signature at Geneva, designed to suppress more effectively the "White Slave Traffic." [34] In 1919 a Convention on the Liquor Traffic in Africa was adopted which sought to protect the natives of the continent against the dangers of alcoholism.[35] With this convention may be associated the Brussels Act of 1890 regulating the trade in arms and ammunition in Africa which was replaced by the Convention on the Control of the Trade in Arms and Ammunition signed at St. Germain-en-Laye in 1919, and which, remaining unratified by the Great Powers, was in turn replaced by the convention of 1925 which also remained unratified.[36] In 1936 the Convention for the Suppression of the Illicit Traffic in Dangerous Drugs was opened for signature at Geneva, supplementing earlier conventions of 1912, 1925, and 1931.[37] In accordance with Article 23 of the Covenant, the first Assembly of the League of Nations in 1920 created an Advisory Committee on Traffic in Opium and Other Dangerous Drugs.[38] This Advisory Committee was replaced in 1946 by the Commission on Narcotic Drugs established by the Economic and Social Council of the United Nations.[39] In 1923 a Convention on the Suppression of the Circulation of and the Traffic in Obscene Publications

---

[32] See G. L. Weil, "The Evolution of the European Convention on Human Rights," *Am. Journal*, Vol. 57 (1963), p. 804. For the text of the Convention, see Lawson, *International Regional Organizations*, p. 41. *U.N. Yearbooks on Human Rights.*

[33] Hudson, *Int. Legislation*, Vol. III, p. 2010.

[34] *Ibid.*, Vol. I, p. 726. A later convention of 1933 deals with the Suppression of the Traffic in Women of Full Age, *ibid.*, Vol. VI, p. 469.

[35] *Ibid.*, Vol. I, p. 352.

[36] For the text of the unratified convention of 1925, see *ibid.*, Vol. III, p. 1634.

[37] *Ibid.*, Vol. VII, p. 359.

[38] *Ten Years of World Cooperation*, p. 301. B. A. Renborg, "Principles of International Control of Narcotic Drugs," *Am. Journal*, Vol. 37 (1943), p. 436.

[39] *U.N. Yearbook*, 1946-1947, p. 532.

was adopted, replacing the earlier convention of 1910.[40] These and other related problems have now been taken over by commissions of the Economic and Social Council of the United Nations.

Protection of refugees. In 1938 an Intergovernmental Committee on Refugees was formed at Evian, France, for the consideration of aid to refugees from Nazi persecution. Subsequently, during the course of the war, the mandate of the Committee was extended to include all European refugees who were obliged to leave their country of residence because of danger to their lives or liberties on account of race, religion, or political beliefs. On December 15, 1946, the General Assembly of the United Nations adopted the Constitution of the International Refugee Organization (IRO), and the agreement constituting the new specialized agency was opened for signature the following day. The primary task of the organization was the repatriation of refugees and displaced persons, with the secondary task of the resettlement of those who, for valid reasons, could not return to their countries of origin. The organization was liquidated in 1951 in favor of the United Nations High Commissioner for Refugees (UNHCR), appointed by the General Assembly and having offices in Geneva, Switzerland. In 1951 a Convention relating to the Status of Refugees was adopted, which codifies the minimum rights that the parties obligate themselves to give to refugees.[41] The Inter-Governmental Committee for European Migration functions under a constitution adopted October 19, 1953.

Inter-American regional cooperation. Paralleling, and in a degree anticipating, the constructive plans of the international community for the regulation of economic interests have been the successive measures adopted by the American states to regulate and promote inter-American economic and social interests. The protection of industrial and literary property was one of the earliest objectives of inter-American conferences. In the field of communications numerous special congresses and conferences have been held for the improvement of inter-American postal services and telegraph and radio communication. In the field of transportation, in addition to railway, maritime, and aerial committees and commissions, the project of greatest significance has been the development of a Pan American Highway, linking the capital cities of each of the American states. The emergency conditions created by the outbreak of war in 1939 led to the creation of the Inter-American Financial and Economic Advisory Committee, the objective of which was the promotion of closer cooperation in monetary and commercial relations, so as to enable the American states to meet the dislocations caused by the war. The Committee drafted a Convention for the Establishment of an

[40] Hudson, *op. cit.*, Vol. II, p. 1051.
[41] For details of current activities of the IRO, see *U.N. Yearbook*, 1961, p. 331; 1962, p. 354.

Inter-American Bank, created an Inter-American Development Commission, formulated an Inter-American Coffee Agreement to bring about a more equitable distribution of coffee crops, and in other ways sought to promote the "economic mobilization" of the American states. At the Conference on Problems of War and Peace held at Mexico City in 1945 an "Economic Charter of the Americas" was adopted which sought to lay down the principles which might form "a constructive basis for the sound economic development of the Americas."

With the adoption of the Charter of the Organization of American States an additional impulse was given to both economic and social cooperation. The Inter-American Economic and Social Council covers a wide field of cooperative activities, notably the administration of the Alliance for Progress. Problems of production, finance, technical cooperation, transportation, and finance parallel those of the United Nations, varying in details to meet the needs of the regional organization. Close cooperation is maintained with the United Nations Commission for Latin America (ECLA).

Corresponding parallels exist in respect to the problems of social cooperation, the protection of fundamental human rights, the special protection of children, the status of women, the welfare of workers, public health, and public morals. In accordance with the terms of the Charter, the Specialized Organizations are instructed to establish cooperative relations with world agencies of the same character in order to coordinate their activities, although at the same time preserving their identity, as is illustrated in the status of the Pan American Health Organization acting as regional agency of the World Health Organization.[42]

Since the adoption of the Charter of Punta del Este in 1961, the Alliance for Progress has dominated the field of inter-American economic cooperation. Its importance lies in the fact that while its primary objective is economic, its secondary objective is directed to raising standards of living—"a vast effort to bring a better life to the peoples of the Continent," as is proclaimed in the Declaration which precedes the more specific objectives of the Alliance. Thus economic, social, and cultural goals are brought together in a forward-looking synthesis: industrialism, increase of agricultural productivity, stable price levels, and agrarian reform being planned to lead to a fairer distribution of the national income, the elimination of illiteracy, improvement of housing, and the general welfare of the people. The program is highly organized, and it promises to have far-reaching effects upon the political as well as the economic and social life of the continent.

[42] For a survey of these activities, see Fenwick, *OAS*, Chaps. IX-XI. The Alliance for Progress has now come to dominate the field of inter-American economic cooperation, although its objectives are political and social as well.

G. THE PROBLEM OF MORAL DISARMAMENT

The sharp conflicts of national ideologies which came to the front during the decade preceding the Second World War made it clear that both the problem of political disarmament and that of economic disarmament could only be made effective if accompanied by measures which might be described as "moral disarmament." The power of these ideologies lay in the suppression of freedom of speech and of the press and in the control of the several governments over the sources of information and of communication. The result was on the one hand to intensify the spirit of fanatical nationalism, and on the other hand to create suspicion and distrust of other countries. Negative methods of suppression were supplemented by positive measures taken by governments to direct public opinion through control of education and through the use of the new instrumentality of radio broadcasting. Under such conditions of intellectual isolation, cooperation between certain states was dependent not upon the mutual understanding by peoples of their common interests but upon the will of the dictatorship actually in control of the country.[43]

UNESCO. On November 16, 1945, the Constitution of the United Nations Educational, Scientific and Cultural Organization (UNESCO) was signed by the delegates of forty-four states, and was thereupon submitted to the governments for their "acceptance." [44] The Preamble of the Constitution declares that "since wars begin in the minds of men it is in the minds of men that the defenses of peace must be constructed," that the war just ended "was a war made possible by the denial of the democratic principles of the dignity, equality and mutual respect of men"; and that a peace must be founded, if it is not to fail, "upon the intellectual and moral solidarity of mankind"; and that the states parties to the Constitution "are agreed and determined to develop and to increase the means of communication between their peoples and to employ these means for the purpose of mutual understanding and a truer and more perfect knowledge of each other's lives." Article I sets forth the purpose of the organization as being to promote collaboration among the nations through education, science, and culture in order to further universal respect for justice, for the rule of law, and for the human rights and fundamental freedoms affirmed in the Charter of the United Nations.

The Organization became on February 3, 1947, a specialized agency or organization of the United Nations, and it has expanded in member-

[43] See C. G. Fenwick, "The Problem of Moral Disarmament," *Am. Journal*, Vol. 41 (1947), p. 112.

[44] For the text of the Constitution, see Dept. of State *Bulletin*, Vol. XIII, p. 802; Peaslee, *I.G.O.*, Vol. II, p. 1799. *Am. Journal*, Vol. 41 (1947), Official Documents, p. 1.

ship with the admission of new members to the United Nations. It functions through a General Assembly, an Executive Board, and a Secretariat, and its activities cover a wide field, including the "Addis Ababa Plan" of 1961 for the expansion of education in Africa, as well as oceanographic and seismographic studies, research in the field of natural resources, and the promotion of cultural relations.[45]

If law has as its twofold function on the one hand to substitute the collective judgment of the community for the resort to violence by the individual, and on the other hand to promote the general welfare by community measures beyond the reach of the individual, then it would seem that the recent extension of international law into the fields of economic and social cooperation is one of the two features that mark the line between the old law and the new. Perhaps it may be that in time this second feature of the law may, as suggested above, not only come to occupy as significant a place in the foreign relations of states as the adjustment of mutual rights and duties, but perform the even more important role of creating a stronger sense of unity in the international community and making effective the system of collective security which for the time lacks the moral bond which must be its ultimate binding force.

[45] A description of the activities of UNESCO may be found in the *U.N. Yearbooks.* For a critical study, see Laves and Thomson, *UNESCO: Purpose, Progress, Prospects;* Sharp, *The Role of UNESCO: a Critical Evaluation; International Organizations in the Social Sciences,* UNESCO Reports and Papers, No. 13.

PART **IV**

International Procedure
for the Settlement of
Conflicts of Claims

The Pacific Settlement of
International Disputes

A. INTERNATIONAL PROCEDURAL LAW

In the theory of general jurisprudence a distinction is made between the *substantive law* and the *adjective law* or *law of procedure*.[1] The substantive law defines in positive terms the various rights which the law will aid and protect. Accompanying these substantive rights and forming an essential part of them are certain remedial rights, which entitle their possessor to use due and proper means to enforce his primary rights or to obtain redress in case of their violation. *Ubi jus, ibi remedium.* "Where there is a right there is likewise a remedy." A right which has no remedy attached to it is, therefore, in a technical sense, not a right at all; it is merely a claim for which perhaps the fullest moral justification may be advanced, but which can not be made effective by the agencies of the law.

Possessed of a legal right, it is to the *law of procedure* that the holder turns to find what steps he must take to make his right effective. Under municipal law these steps are, as a rule, strictly defined; and the claimant must proceed according to them if he is to obtain the redress to which he is entitled under the law. In all cases the procedure is pacific, and the determination of the redress due under the circumstances is made by designated judicial agencies acting in the name of the state and applying the principles of law laid down for the decision of the particular case. Enforcement of the decision of the court remains, like the determination of the measure of redress, a function of the state, beyond the control of the individual.[2]

In international law the distinction between the substantive law and

[1] See Holland, *The Elements of Jurisprudence,* 8th ed., pp. 78, 147, 347.
[2] See above, pp. 42 ff., where the general nature of international law is discussed.

the law of procedure is a relatively recent development. Writers of the nineteenth century, following the lead of Grotius and Vattel, were content to distinguish between "the law of peace" and "the law of war," without seeking to assert principles of jurisprudence which might appear to make the protection of substantive rights dependent upon a procedure so lacking in juridical character as that of war.[3] The international community was not as yet organized so as to impose upon its members the obligation of pacific settlement. It was only with the development of arbitration at the turn of the century that jurists found it appropriate to mark off the law of procedure from the substantive rights of states, seeking in that indirect way to condemn recourse to war by placing it in contrast with the available alternative of procedure by arbitration.[4]

Arbitration was, however, a procedure of limited scope, as specified in the particular treaty which made provision for it. Hence it came about that the obligation to resort to the procedure of arbitration and the procedure itself were regularly embodied in the same international document. In the first of the important multipartite treaties of arbitration, the Hague Convention of 1899, the articles setting forth the scope of the obligations undertaken by the parties to the treaty were followed by articles describing the procedure to be followed when a case came within the treaty. This combination of substantive and procedural law characterized subsequent multipartite treaties for the peaceful settlement of international disputes, being conspicuous in the General Act of Geneva of 1928, as well as in the Statute of the Permanent Court of International Justice and in that of its successor, the International Court of Justice.[5]

B. NEGOTIATION

The general recognition by nations of reciprocal rights and duties, as well as the drastic nature of war as the ultimate form of self-help, led at an early date to the creation of a legal obligation to negotiate in advance of an appeal to force. The College of Fetials of ancient Rome went through the formality of sending ambassadors or heralds who presented the demands of their state and asked for due redress.[6] The elaborate discussions by the canonists and the theologians and by Grotius and his followers all insist in the clearest terms upon the necessity of negotia-

---

[3] It was common for writers to divide their treatises into two parts, Vol. I, "Peace," Vol. II, "War," and leave it at that.

[4] The name of James Brown Scott stands out prominently in this connection.

[5] This combination of substantive and procedural law was, however, not followed in respect to the laws of war, which, as in the case of the Hague Conventions of 1899 and 1907, were regularly formulated without any reference to the conditions under which resort to war would be justifiable.

[6] See Phillipson, *International Law of Ancient Greece and Rome*, Vol. II, Chap. XXVI.

tion in advance of a decision to resort to force.[7] Even where there was a deliberate purpose of resorting to force, there appears to have been a recognition of the necessity of some pretense of negotiating as a concession to those general standards of morality to which even absolute monarchs usually paid deference. Negotiations, conducted at reasonable length, left open the possibility of a satisfactory concession on the part of the state upon which the demand was made, and at the same time made it possible for third states to intervene as friendly mediators between the parties. By the close of the nineteenth century it had come to be assumed that an exchange of diplomatic notes would precede resort to forcible measures of redress. The Hague Convention for the Pacific Settlement of International Disputes of 1899, in recognizing arbitration as the most effective and equitable means of settlement, referred to disputes "which diplomacy has failed to settle." In like manner the innumerable multilateral and bilateral treaties of arbitration of recent years.[8]

Quite apart, however, from any specific legal obligation to negotiate, this form of peaceful procedure would appear to have been based upon practical expediency in all cases in which states were acting in good faith. The wars even of the nineteenth century involved in most cases too great a risk not to lead the claimant state to make every effort to persuade the opposing party to accept the terms of settlement proposed. Only in rare cases, therefore, of marked disparity in military power have states suddenly broken off negotiations, as if impatient to get ahead with the use of force. In 1911 Italy, doubtless realizing the preposterous character of its demands, abruptly terminated its negotiations with Turkey and sent an ultimatum which was practically equivalent to a declaration to war.[9] Again, in 1914 Austria-Hungary, losing all self-control, sent an ultimatum to Serbia which closed negotiations almost before they had begun.[10] In September, 1931, Japan undertook military operations in Manchuria without so much as a preliminary exchange of notes with China.[11] The Nazi Government of Germany, having prepared the ground for the annexation of Austria and Czechoslovakia, dispensed

---

[7] See the extensive literature relating to a "just war," above, pp. 57 ff. Also, Scott, *Law, the State, and the International Community*, Vol. II, pp. 299 ff.

[8] The General Act of Geneva (see p. 625) is to the same effect. "Disputes . . . which it has not been possible to settle by diplomacy." Art. 1. Hudson, *International Legislation*, Vol. IV, p. 2529. Also, General Treaty of Inter-American Arbitration, *International Conferences*, 1889-1928, p. 458.

[9] For details, see Barclay, *The Turco-Italian War and its Problems;* Garner, *Recent Developments in International Law*, Lecture VI.

[10] For details, see Stowell, *Diplomacy of the War of 1914*, Chap. II.

[11] In this case, however, Japan was careful not to declare war upon China, so that the action taken must be classed under another head. See p. 643. "War" did not actually begin until China declared it formally after the Japanese attack at Pearl Harbor.

with negotiations, but found it expedient to go through the appearance
of negotiations in the case of Poland.[12] On the other hand Japan negotiated at great length with the United States in regard to the conflicts of
interest between the two powers in the Far East, however treacherous
its conduct when the negotiations came to a deadlock.[13]

C. GOOD OFFICES AND MEDIATION

The history of international relations contains numerous instances of
intervention on the part of third states in cases in which the conflict of
rights between two or more states appeared to be beyond the ability of
the parties to settle by peaceful means. In some instances the intervention was by means of armed force, in which case the intervening state
added a new element to the dispute. Such, for example, was the mediation
or intervention of the Great Powers between Greece and Turkey in 1868
in relation to the island of Crete, and again between Turkey and Crete
in 1897.[14] In other cases the intervention was friendly and noncompulsory
in character, undertaken with the object of reconciling the differences
between the opposing parties, and proposed to them for acceptance or
rejection according to their free choice. In 1856 the signatory powers of
the Treaty of Paris obligated themselves, in the event of a dispute between the sultan and one or other of them, to have recourse to the
mediatory action of the whole body of signatories.[15] At the same time
a protocol was adopted in which the obligation to mediate was presented
in the form of a *voeu* to which all states were invited to adhere.[16] While
as many as forty states adhered to the protocol, its restrictive clause,
"as far as circumstances might permit," rendered it practically ineffective.
A similar limited obligation to have recourse to mediation or, if preferable,
arbitration was entered into by the signatory powers of the Berlin treaty
of 1885.[17] In the same year the dispute between Germany and Spain
over the Caroline Islands, which had threatened to result in war, was
settled by mediation of Pope Leo XIII.[18] An instance of mediation with
the object of putting an end to hostilities is to be seen in the mediation
of the United States in 1866 between Spain on the one hand and Peru,
Chile, Bolivia, and Ecuador on the other.[19] The right of either party to

[12] The negotiations are given in summary form in *Events Leading up to World
War II,* pp. 175 ff. In the case of Austria the interview between Hitler and Schuschnigg at Berchtesgaden one month before the occupation of Austria by German
troops had the character rather of an ultimatum than of free negotiations.

[13] See *Peace and War: United States Foreign Policy, 1931-1941,* pp. 118 ff. and
documents accompanying.

[14] See Fauchille, *Droit international,* Nos. 938, 942 (6).

[15] Art. VIII.

[16] Fauchille, *op. cit.,* No. 936.

[17] Art. 12. See *Br. and For. State Papers,* Vol. LXXVI, p. 4.

[18] See Stowell and Munro, *International Cases,* Vol. I, p. 49.

[19] See Moore, *Digest,* Vol. II, § 1067.

refuse an offer of mediation was exemplified in the refusal of the United States in 1898 to accept the tender of good offices made by Great Britain, France, Austria, and the Pope.[20]

Provisions of the Hague Conventions. In 1899 the Hague Peace Conference, being impressed with the advantages of such friendly intervention for the maintenance of the general peace, endeavored to give a qualified legal standing to it as a form of procedure. The convention for the Pacific Settlement of International Disputes provided for a recourse by the disputants themselves, before an appeal to arms, to the good offices or mediation of one or more friendly powers.[21] A further article sanctioned the action of third powers in coming forward upon their own initiative and offering as far as the circumstances allowed their good offices and mediation to the states at variance. This offer might be made even during the course of hostilities, and it could in no case be regarded as an unfriendly act. Succeeding articles, after pointing out the duties of the mediator to act as a friendly compositor, emphasized the right of the contending parties to reject the offer of mediation and the optional character of the advice that might be offered.[22] A special procedure was recommended by which the two parties might each choose a third state, thereupon leaving it to the two mediators to find a solution if possible.[23]

D. COMMISSIONS OF INQUIRY

Provisions of the Hague Conventions. Commissions of Inquiry made their formal appearance as an international institution at the Hague Peace Conference of 1899.[24] Recourse to fact-finding agencies had, however, long been resorted to by states bilaterally for such problems as the delimitation of boundary lines and the adjudication of private claims. The purpose of the Commission which formulated the Convention for the Pacific Settlement of International Disputes was to give a specific character to a procedure which, being limited to the determination of facts, might be resorted to in cases where the parties might not be willing to submit the whole controversy, involving questions of law and of political interest, to the procedure of arbitration. Title III of the Convention, "On International Commissions of Inquiry" made provision that "in disputes of an international nature involving neither honor nor vital interests, and arising from a difference of opinion on points of fact," it was deemed expedient to institute an international commission of

[20] Further instances may be found in Moore, *Digest*, Vol. VII, §§ 1065-1067; Fauchille, *Droit international*, Nos. 937-942.

[21] Art. 2. See *Hague Conventions*, p. 43.

[22] Arts. 4-6.

[23] Art. 8. The procedure of mediation has now in large part become merged in that of "conciliation." See below, p. 624.

[24] See Higgins, *The Hague Peace Conferences*, pp. 107, 167.

inquiry with the object of facilitating a settlement of the dispute by an impartial investigation of the facts.[25] The composition of the commission was to follow the composition of the arbitral tribunals established by the same convention.[26] Provision was further made that, since the report of the commission was limited to a finding of fact, it should have in no way the character of an arbitral award and should leave the parties entire freedom as to the effect to be given to the finding.[27]

The Dogger Bank case. An opportunity for putting into effect the procedure devised by the Hague Conference was presented in 1904 in relation to the disputed facts connected with the Dogger Bank incident. In that year certain Russian warships, on their way to the Far East, fired by mistake upon a fleet of British fishing vessels. An international commission of inquiry was appointed, three of whose members were of neutral nationality, and was empowered to inquire into and report upon all circumstances relating to the North Sea incident, particularly upon the question as to where the responsibility lay and upon the degree of blame attaching to the nationals of the contracting parties or of other countries.[28] In respect to the scope of its jurisdiction, therefore, the North Sea Commission went beyond the provisions of the Hague Convention and exercised what were in fact the functions of an arbitral tribunal.[29] The success of the commission, which met under circumstances of unusual tension between the two states, greatly enhanced the prestige of that method of settling disputes, and led to the introduction at the Second Hague Conference of 1907 of a number of changes in respect to procedure based upon the actual experience of the Dogger Bank case.[30]

E. ARBITRATION

The procedure of arbitration goes back to the earliest days of international law. It was well established in ancient Greece, numerous cases being recorded not only of actual recourse to arbitration but of treaties in which the parties agreed in advance to submit their disputes to that form of settlement. It was well known in ancient Rome as a civil procedure, even if there were few instances in which it was put into practice

[25] Art. 9, conventions of 1899 and 1907.

[26] Art. 11 (1899); Art. 12 (1907). See below, p. 612.

[27] Art. 14 (1899); Art. 35 (1907).

[28] The text of the Russo-British protocol under which the commission was established may be found in *Am. Journal,* Vol. 2 (1908), p. 929. For the report of the commission, see *ibid.,* p. 931. See also Scott, *Hague Court Reports,* p. 404; Hudson, *Cases,* p. 1189.

[29] See Hershey, *International Law and Diplomacy of the Russo-Japanese War,* pp. 240-241.

[30] See Arts. 10-36, Convention for the Pacific Settlement of International Disputes. Also, Higgins, *Hague Peace Conferences,* pp. 167-170.

in the relations of Rome with other states.[31] From time to time during the Christian era disputes between princes and rulers were submitted to the arbitration of the Pope.[32] Vitoria and Suarez both argued in favor of arbitration as a means of settling disputes, and they found that the Pope had a general competence to require that a cause of war be referred to him and to give a judgment which must be obeyed except when manifestly unjust.[33] Grotius found that war might be obviated by arbitration, quoting instances from ancient Greece, and advocating that conferences of Christian powers be held "where those who have no interest at stake may settle the disputes of others, and where, in fact, steps may be taken to compel parties to accept peace on fair terms." [34] Vattel spoke strongly in favor of the procedure.[35] But it was not until the treaty of 1794 between the United States and Great Britain that statesmen began to regard the procedure as a practical means for the adjustment of controversies in cases where there was a general understanding of the principles of law to be applied.[36]

During the course of the nineteenth century the procedure of arbitration grew in prestige and authority as the just and equitable means for the settlement of international disputes, even if its scope was somewhat narrowly limited. The successful arbitration at Geneva of the *Alabama* Claims between the United States and Great Britain in 1872 brought the procedure into the foreground of international relations.[37] The newly established Institute of International Law drew up a body of rules of arbitral procedure in 1875.[38] At the First International Conference of American States, which met in Washington in 1889-1890, a "Plan of Arbitration" of a comprehensive character was elaborated which made arbitration obligatory in all cases except those which, in the judgment of one of the parties to a controversy, might "imperil its independence." [39] Although the plan remained unratified it proved the inspiration for

[31] See Phillipson, *International Law and Custom of Ancient Greece and Rome,* Vol. II, pp. 61 ff.

[32] Nys, *Les Origines,* Chap. V; Moore, *International Arbitrations,* Vol. V, Appendix III, translating from Mérignhac, *Traité théorique et pratique de l'arbitrage international;* G. Goyau, "L'Eglise catholique et le droit des gens," *Recueil des Cours,* Vol. 6 (1925-I), p. 127.

[33] Vitoria, *De Indis,* Sec. II, no. 5; Suarez, *Selections,* "On War," Sec. VI, no. 5.

[34] *De jure belli ac pacis,* Eng. trans., Bk. II, Chap. XXIII, § VIII.

[35] *Droit des gens,* Bk. II, Chap. XVIII, § 329.

[36] For a critical study of the nature and practice of arbitration, see Moore, *International Adjudications,* Vols. I, XV; Mérignhac, *Traité théorique et pratique de l'arbitrage international;* Ralston, *International Arbitration from Athens to Locarno; International Arbitral Law and Procedure;* Stuyt, *Survey of International Arbitrations,* 1794-1938.

[37] See below, pp. 613, 745.

[38] *Annuaire de l'Institut,* Vol. I, pp. 126 ff.

[39] *Int. Conferences of American States,* 1889-1928, p. 40.

numerous bipartite treaties between the American States,[40] while the new Republic of Brazil signalized the growing importance of the subject by entering an arbitral clause into its Constitution of 1891, qualifying the right of Congress to authorize a declaration of war.[41]

The Hague Convention of 1899: free choice of judges. It was at the first Hague Peace Conference of 1899 that arbitration received recognition as a formal international procedure. The Convention for the Pacific Settlement of International Disputes announced that arbitration had for its object "the settlement of differences between States by judges of their own choice and on the basis of respect for law." [42] The definition expressed two of the essential characteristics of arbitration: first, the fact that the tribunal appointed to decide the dispute is formed by the parties themselves. It is the free choice of the arbitrators which distinguishes arbitration from the procedure of "judicial settlement" by a permanent court established in advance of the dispute. There must be a present confidence of the contending parties in the ability of the particular arbitrators to render a just decision of the case submitted to them.[43]

Basis of the arbitral decision. The second characteristic of arbitration expressed in the definition of the Hague Convention was that the decision of the arbitrators was to be "on the basis of respect for law." The phrase recognized that the law applicable to the case might not always be clear, but that the task of the arbitrators was to come as near as possible to a legal decision. Arbitration, therefore, was to proceed on the basis of principles or rules known beforehand to the contending parties and accepted by them as a just basis for the award.[44] On occasion, where the dispute involved questions of fact rather than of principle, as in the controversy between the United States and Great Britain in 1794 with reference to the St. Croix River boundary,[45] and in general in cases relating to the interpretation of treaties, the task of the arbitrators might be limited to the decision of concrete issues and need have no reference to general principles of law other than those bearing upon the interpretation and obligation of treaties. Should, however, the dispute involve

---

[40] See Manning, *Arbitration Treaties among the American Nations.*

[41] Art. 34, section 11: the National Congress has the power ". . . to authorize the Government to declare war, if recourse to arbitration has not taken place or has failed, and to make peace." The phrase, "se não tiver lugar ou malograrse o recurso do arbitramento," was interpreted by Ruy Barbosa, one of the framers of the Constitution, as an obligation on the part of the Government first to seek the settlement of the controversy by arbitration. *Commentários a Constituição Federal Brasileira,* p. 250. For other cases of later date, see Garner, *Recent Developments in International Law,* p. 507.

[42] Art. 15, Convention for the Pacific Settlement of International Disputes, 1899.

[43] See, on this point, Scott, *An International Court of Justice,* pp. 25 ff.

[44] On this characteristic of arbitration, see Hudson, *International Tribunals,* Chap. VIII: "Law Applicable by International Tribunals."

[45] See Moore, *International Arbitrations,* Vol. I, pp. 1-43; *Modern Series,* Vol. II.

claims based upon the violation of alleged rights the validity of which was disputed by the party defendant, the arbitral tribunal might be called upon first to determine what rules of law were in force at the time and then to apply them to the facts presented by the controversy.

Owing to the indefinite character of many of the rules of international law, the contending parties have frequently stipulated in the agreement, or *compromis*,[46] under which the dispute is submitted to arbitration that the decision of the arbitrators must be in accordance with certain defined principles, whether these be rules of law alleged to have been in existence at the time the controversy started or the general principles of equity or special rules intended to hold good only in the particular case. The Treaty of Washington of 1871 between Great Britain and the United States provided that the decision of the arbitral tribunal set up for the settlement of the *Alabama* Claims should be governed by three rules agreed upon by the parties as applicable to the case and by such principles of international law, not inconsistent with those rules, as the arbitrators might determine to have been applicable.[47] While Great Britain was unwilling to assent to the three rules as principles of international law in force at the time the claims arose, it accepted them as a satisfactory basis for the existing case and for future cases.[48]

Obligation to submit to the award. The Hague Convention was specific in laying down the rule that the special agreement between the parties to have recourse to arbitration "implies an engagement to submit loyally to the award." This was a third element of arbitration, by which it differed essentially from the procedures of mediation and commissions of inquiry set forth in the Convention. The terms of the submission of a controversy to arbitration, as well as the personnel of the tribunal might be freely determined by the two states; but once the machinery was set in motion the rule of good faith demanded that the award be loyally carried out. If, however, the decision of the arbitral tribunal were clearly in excess of the terms of the *compromis* under which the dispute was submitted to arbitration, the party unfavorably affected was not regarded as bound by it. On this ground the award rendered in 1831 by the king of Holland in the Northeastern Boundary Dispute be-

---

[46] The part played by the *compromis* in the development of international arbitration has been of the greatest importance, since the decision of the case may turn upon the principles of law laid down in it. See, for critical comment, Wehberg, *The Problem of an International Court of Justice*, pp. 16 ff.

[47] Art. VI. *See Treaties and Conventions*, Vol. I, p. 700; see below, p. 745.

[48] "In order to evince its desire of strengthening the friendly relations between the two countries and of making satisfactory provision for the future," the British Government agreed that in deciding the questions arising out of the said claims "the Arbitrators should assume that Her Majesty's Government had undertaken to act upon the principles set forth in these rules." *Treaties and Conventions*, Vol. I, p. 700. Compare the arbitral provisions of the Jay Treaty of 1794, where existing principles of law were adequate. *Ibid.*, Vol. I, p. 590.

tween Great Britain and the United States was set aside by both parties.[49] Other limitations upon the obligation to carry out the award might arise in the case of fraud or corruption on the part of the tribunal in reaching its award, but as a practical matter the urgency of the need of manifesting good faith has generally taken precedence over the contentions of the losing party.[50] The refusal of Nicaragua to carry out the award of the King of Spain in 1906 in the arbitration involving the boundary between that country and Honduras was alleged to be due to an inadequate examination by the arbitrator of the documents; the controversy remained open until the decision of the International Court of Justice in 1957.[51]

F. THE HAGUE PERMANENT COURT OF ARBITRATION

The outstanding accomplishment, however, of the Hague Conference of 1899 was the creation of the Permanent Court of Arbitration.[52] This "court," in spite of its name, was not a permanent tribunal, but a list of judges nominated in advance by the Signatory Powers to the number of four each. The judges were to be persons of "known competency in questions of international law, of the highest moral reputation, and disposed to accept the duties of arbitrators"; and they were to be available at all times, and were to act, in default of agreement to the contrary between the parties, in accordance with fixed rules of procedure. Upon having recourse to arbitration the parties in controversy were to choose their arbitrators from the general list, that is from the Permanent Court, each party appointing two arbitrators, who together were to choose an umpire. The five arbitrators thus chosen constituted the tribunal which was to decide the controversy.[53]

Limited obligation to arbitrate. What obligation did the signatory powers of the Hague Convention of 1899 assume to submit their disputes to the procedure so carefully elaborated? Here the Conference found itself confronted by the determination of the leading powers to reserve to themselves the decision as to the questions which they might be

[49] See Moore, *Digest,* Vol. VII, § 1082; *International Arbitrations,* Vol. I, pp. 81-161.

[50] Hall's comments upon the practical difficulty of questioning the justice of an arbitral award (*International Law,* § 119) may be compared with Secretary Hughes' sharp comment upon the award of the arbitration tribunal in the controversy between the United States and Norway over the requisition of shipping contracts. See below, p. 732.

[51] See above, p. 415.

[52] On the subject of the Permanent Court of Arbitration, see M. O. Hudson, "The Permanent Court of Arbitration," *Am. Journal,* Vol. 27 (1933), p. 440; *International Tribunals, passim.*

On the part played by the Court in the nomination of the judges of the Permanent Court of International Justice and of the International Court of Justice, see below, p. 622.

[53] Convention for the Pacific Settlement of International Disputes (1899), Arts. 23, 24. *Hague Conventions,* pp. 57 ff.

willing to submit to arbitration. They were not yet ready to abandon the right to be the judges in their own case when matters of grave national interest were at stake. In consequence the Convention went no further than to proclaim in broad terms that "in questions of a legal nature, and especially in the interpretation or application of international conventions, arbitration is recognized by the signatory powers as the most effective, and at the same time the most equitable, means of settling disputes which diplomacy has failed to settle." A pious *voeu*, no more.

Bipartite treaties.   During the period between the two Hague Conferences, of 1899 and of 1907, considerable progress was made in the negotiation of bipartite treaties defining and at times extending the scope of the obligation to arbitrate as between the parties to the agreement. Outstanding among these was the treaty of 1903 between Great Britain and France, which went further than the Hague Convention by accepting a formal obligation to arbitrate in place of a mere recognition of the effectiveness and equitable character of arbitration, but at the same time excluded from the obligation differences which affected the vital interests, the independence or the honor of the contracting states.[54] The British-French Treaty led the United States to reopen negotiations for similar bipartite treaties, and at the same time led to the convention adopted at the second American Conference on International Arbitration at Washington in 1904.

At the second Hague Conference of 1907 an important amendment was made to the Convention adopted in 1899. Provision was made that of the two arbitrators appointed by the parties in controversy from the permanent list "one only can be its national or chosen from among the persons selected by it as members of the Permanent Court." [55] Greater impartiality was thus assured in the composition of the arbitral tribunal and greater facility in selecting the fifth member.

The Hague Conference of 1907.   But the second Hague Conference of 1907 was able to go little further than the first in extending the scope of the obligation to arbitrate. The new Convention for the Pacific Settlement of International Disputes reaffirmed the recognition of arbitration as the most effective and equitable means of settling disputes and added: "Consequently, it would be desirable that, in disputes about the above-mentioned questions, the contracting Powers should, if the case arose, have recourse to arbitration, in so far as circumstances permit." [56] The discussions in committee made it clear that circumstances were not expected to permit the arbitration of matters of vital national interest. Conscious of its failure to go further, the Conference proclaimed in the

---

[54] For the text of this important treaty, see *Br. and For. State Papers*, Vol. XCIV, p. 35. For a discussion of restrictive clauses in arbitration treaties, see H. Wehberg, *Am. Journal*, Vol. 7 (1913), p. 301; A. Cavalcanti, *ibid.*, Vol. 8 (1914), p. 723.

[55] Convention for the Pacific Settlement of International Disputes (1907), Art. 45.

[56] *Ibid.*, Art. 38.

Final Act that it was unanimous in admitting "the principle of compulsory arbitration," and in declaring that certain disputes, in particular those relating to the interpretation and application of the provisions of international agreements, might be submitted to compulsory arbitration without any restriction; adding that although it had not been found feasible to conclude a convention to that effect "nevertheless the divergencies of opinion which have come to light have not exceeded the bounds of judicial controversy," and that the Powers had succeeded in the course of their long collaboration "in evolving a very lofty conception of the common welfare of humanity." [57] The phrases were encouraging, but they registered the failure of the Conference in the most important matter before it.

The arbitration of contract debts. In one specific class of cases, however, the Conference went to the length of imposing an unqualified obligation upon a state to arbitrate as a condition of not being subjected to the use of force by another state. The Convention Respecting the Limitation of the Employment of Force for the Recovery of Contract Debts was adopted, in accordance with which the contracting powers "agree not to have recourse to armed force for the recovery of contract debts claimed from the government of one country by the government of another country as being due to its nationals." The undertaking, however, was not to be applicable "when the debtor State refuses or neglects to reply to an offer of arbitration, or, after accepting the offer, prevents any *compromis* from being agreed on, or, after the arbitration, fails to submit to the award." [58]

G. JUDICIAL SETTLEMENT VERSUS ARBITRATION

Strenuous efforts were made by a number of the delegations to the Hague Conference of 1907 to establish a truly permanent court side by side with the so-called Permanent Court of Arbitration. The theory had come to be widely held that disputes between states would be more readily disposed of if a truly permanent judicial tribunal were established. Such a tribunal, sitting continuously and possessed of "a sense of judicial responsibility," would further the development of international law by building up a system of international jurisprudence in the form of precedents having the force of law. The establishment of a permanent court would, it was said, tend to promote the pacific settlement of international disputes by ensuring, in cases where legal rights were at issue, a decision on the basis of law rather than one on the basis of compromise,

---

[57] *Hague Conventions*, p. 27.

[58] *Ibid.*, p. 89. For the relation of the convention to the problem of the responsibility of the state for the protection of aliens, see above, p. 341.

to which arbitration courts were naturally inclined.[59] The court proposed was to be "freely and easily accessible, composed of judges representing the various judicial systems of the world, and capable of ensuring continuity in arbitral jurisprudence." [60] It was not to displace the arbitration tribunals already provided for but, to supplement arbitration by what had come to be known as "judicial settlement."

The Judicial Arbitration Court.   The establishment of an international court presented two distinct difficulties. The first was that of deciding upon the composition of the court. A court of some forty-five judges, one judge appointed by each of the individual states members of the community of nations, was obviously too unwieldy to be practicable. A smaller court, it was thought by certain delegates, must necessarily favor the larger as against the smaller states. In consequence of the sharp division of opinion upon this point it was found impossible to reach a satisfactory compromise.[61] The conference therefore adopted a "Draft Convention Relative to the Creation of a Judicial Arbitration Court," in which the organization and procedure of the new court were prescribed in detail, but no mention was made of the selection of the judges. In general the judges were to be "chosen from persons of the highest moral reputation, and all fulfilling conditions qualifying them, in their respective countries, to occupy high legal posts, or to be jurists of recognized competence in matters of international law." [62] In the Final Act of the conference a formal *voeu* or wish was expressed in which the conference called the attention of the signatory powers to the advisability of adopting the annexed draft convention for the creation of the Judicial Arbitration Court and of bringing it into force as soon as an agreement had been reached respecting the selection of the judges of the court.[63]

H. EXCEPTIONS TO THE OBLIGATION TO ARBITRATE

The Root Treaties.   Following the second Hague Conference individual governments and jurists continued their efforts to define the

[59] The arguments in favor of "judicial settlement," both those presented to the conference and those subsequently advanced by the chief proponents of that procedure, may be found in J. B. Scott, *An International Court of Justice; The Status of the International Court of Justice; The Hague Peace Conferences,* Vol. I, Chap. IX; H. Wehberg, *The Problem of an International Court of Justice.*

[60] Art. I of the Draft Convention Relative to the Creation of a Judicial Arbitration Court. *Hague Conventions,* p. 31.

[61] For a discussion of the various compromise plans proposed by the advocates of the court, see Higgins, *Hague Peace Conferences,* pp. 514 ff.; Scott, *Hague Peace Conferences of 1899 and 1907,* Vol. I, pp. 437 ff. The Brazilian jurist, Ruy Barbosa, was doubtless the most distinguished opponent of any violation of the principle of the equality of states in the selection of the judges of the court. See Wehberg, *op. cit.,* pp. 185 ff.; Scott, *Reports to the Hague Conferences,* p. 288.

[62] Draft Convention, Art. 2.

[63] *Hague Conventions,* p. 28.

obligation to arbitrate more specifically and to widen the scope of the controversies to which it might be applicable. The Root Treaties of 1908, concluded between the United States and a dozen other powers singly,[64] were typical in providing for the arbitration of "differences which may arise of a legal nature or relating to the interpretation of treaties . . . provided, nevertheless, that they do not affect the vital interests, the independence, or the honor of the two contracting states, and do not concern the interests of third parties." But while these treaties marked a step forward, they contained the serious defect that the cases covered by the proviso were the very ones which experience had shown were likely to lead to serious controversy.[65]

The Taft-Knox Treaties.   In 1911 an effort was made by the United States to draw a more logical distinction between disputes which might and others which might not be submitted to arbitration. Treaties, known as the Taft-Knox Treaties, were negotiated in which the phrase "differences . . . of a legal nature" in the treaties of 1908 was replaced by "differences . . . which are justiciable in their nature," these being defined to be differences "susceptible of decision by the application of the principles of law or equity." [66] At the same time the proviso of the treaties of 1908 was omitted. Moreover, the obligation to arbitrate was greatly strengthened by a provision to the effect that, should the parties disagree as to whether a particular difference was justiciable within the terms of the treaty, the question should be submitted to the impartial decision of a joint high commission of inquiry. This paragraph was stricken out by the United States Senate, and the treaties were amended in other respects, with the result that the President refused ratification on his part.[67]

Treaties for the Advancement of Peace.   A marked advance in the development of procedures of pacific settlement was made in the negotiation by the United States in 1913-1914 of the group of treaties desig-

[64] See, for example, the treaty between the United States and Great Britain. *Treaties and Conventions,* Vol. I, p. 814. For a study of the background of these treaties, and of the part played by the preliminary agreement (*compromis*) in relation to the actual submission of a controversy to arbitration, see *Arbitration and the United States,* World Peace Foundation Pamphlets, Vol. IX, Nos. 6-7, p. 513.

[65] The distinction between "legal" and "political" disputes fills a large place in the literature of international law. With it is associated the question of the scope of the possible competence of international courts as against methods of settlement by mediation and conciliation and, later, by reference to the Council of the League of Nations and the Security Council of the United Nations. The subject is exhaustively treated in Lauterpacht, *The Function of Law in the International Community,* where the argument is made that international law is a "complete" system covering the whole field of the rights and duties of states.

[66] For the text of the treaty with Great Britain, see *Am. Journal,* Vol. 5 (1911), Supp., p. 253.

[67] See *Arbitration and the United States,* pp. 524 ff., where the attitude of the Senate toward the proposal to submit the decision of the justiciability of a dispute to an international commission is set forth.

nated as Treaties for the Advancement of Peace.[68] These treaties must be read in the light of the failure of the United States to negotiate a satisfactory arbitration treaty which would not leave a loophole of escape from the obligation by making it impossible to conclude the necessary *compromis* which must precede the submission of a particular dispute to arbitration, or which would not exclude from the obligation the very disputes about which serious controversies were likely to arise. Subject to variations in phrasing, the treaties provided that:

The High Contracting Parties agree that all disputes between them, of every nature whatsoever, other than disputes the settlement of which is provided for and in fact achieved under existing agreements between the High Contracting Parties, shall, when diplomatic methods of adjustment have failed, be referred for investigation and report to a permanent International Commission, to be constituted in the manner prescribed in the next succeeding article; and they agree not to declare war or begin hostilities during such investigation and before the report is submitted.[69]

By comparison with the arbitration treaties of the period, these treaties, popularly known as "Cooling-off Treaties" because of their provision for delay in the resort to war, were more comprehensive in scope, making no exception of questions affecting honor or vital interests or of non-justiciable disputes, but at the same time not imposing an obligation to abide by the report of the commission. The principle underlying their adoption was that, if it was impossible to secure an unlimited agreement to accept the binding award of an arbitral tribunal, there was nothing to prevent an unlimited agreement at least to consider the report of an impartial body upon all aspects of the case, involving both law and facts alike.[70]

In contrast with the Hague commissions of inquiry, the commissions under the Treaties for the Advancement of Peace were permanent rather than temporary, and they were given jurisdiction not only over the facts of the case but over the whole question submitted.

I. PROVISIONS OF THE COVENANT OF THE LEAGUE OF NATIONS

In the formulation of the Covenant of the League of Nations the effort was made to bring together the various procedures of pacific settlement so as to form a legal basis for the system of collective security. The established procedure of good offices and mediation was extended so as

[68] For the texts of the principal treaties, see Scott, *Treaties for the Advancement of Peace*. Secretary of State, William Jennings Bryan, is accredited as the author of the treaties. Hence the designation, "The Bryan Treaties."

[69] Art. I.

[70] For a discussion of the purpose and scope of the treaties, see Scott, *op. cit.*, Introduction; *Am. Journal*, Vol. 10 (1916), pp. 882-892.

to give to every member of the League "the friendly right" to bring to
the attention of the Assembly or of the Council "any circumstance
whatever" affecting international relations which might threaten to
disturb the peace or the good understanding between nations upon
which peace depended.[71] At the same time the broad principle of the
collective responsibility of the League for the maintenance of peace was
set forth in the provision that "any war, or threat of war, whether immediately affecting any of the Members of the League or not, is hereby
declared to be a matter of concern to the whole League, and the League
shall take any action that may be deemed wise and effectual to safeguard the peace of nations." [72]

The Covenant then pledged the members of the League, in the event
of a dispute arising between them, to submit the matter either to arbitration or to inquiry by the Council.[73] The succeeding article stipulated
that matters suitable for submission to arbitration should be so submitted,
and it enumerated as such disputes involving the interpretation of a
treaty, questions of international law, questions of fact bearing upon the
breach of an international obligation, or the reparation to be made for
such breach.[74] The obligation created by Articles 12 and 13, therefore,
did not go beyond the recognition of a general principle; but in the
event that a particular dispute was not submitted to arbitration it was
agreed that it would be submitted to inquiry by the Council. This procedure of inquiry by the Council was adapted from that of the Treaties
for the Advancement of Peace, and it became the central part of the
machinery of the Covenant for the settlement of disputes. Provision was
made that, whichever procedure was resorted to, the members of the
League would in no case resort to war until three months after the
award by the arbitrators or the report by the Council. Detailed rules
were laid down to be followed in the event that the alternative of submission of the dispute to the Council was chosen.[75] The Council was
given general authority to effect a settlement, so that its function was
not limited to findings of fact. If its report was unanimous, not including the vote of the parties to the dispute, the members of the League
agreed not to go to war with a state which complied with the recommendations of the report. If the report was not unanimous, the members reserved the right to take such action as they might consider necessary for the maintenance of right and justice. Finally, the dispute might

[71] Art. 11, no. 2. See Appendix A.

[72] Art. 11, no. 1. This article was the subject of much discussion, and it was
claimed by a number of jurists that for all practical purposes it closed the gap left
in Art. 15.

[73] Art. 12. By a later amendment to the Covenant "judicial settlement" was included as an alternative to arbitration. See Appendix A.

[74] Art. 13.

[75] Art. 15.

be referred from the Council to the Assembly, whether upon motion of the Council itself or of either party to the dispute, in which case the obligation arising from a unanimous report of the Council was made dependent upon a report concurred in by the representatives of the states that were members of the Council, together with a majority of the other members of the League.[76]

J. THE PERMANENT COURT OF INTERNATIONAL JUSTICE

In addition to making provision for the more effective operation of the existing procedures of pacific settlement the Covenant of the League of Nations called upon the Council to "formulate and submit to the members of the League for adoption, plans for the establishment of a Permanent Court of International Justice." [77] In pursuance of this agreement an Advisory Committee of Jurists met at The Hague in June, 1920, and drew up a Draft Scheme for the Institution of the Permanent Court of International Justice.[78] When presented to the Council and the Assembly of the League of Nations, the draft scheme was amended upon a number of points, particularly in respect to a provision calling for compulsory arbitration within a prescribed field. This provision was rephrased in the form of a conditional obligation calling for separate acceptance through the means of an "Optional Clause," [79] so that states might be free to accept or not to accept the particular obligation. The draft as amended was finally approved by the Assembly on December 13, 1920, and was attached in the form of a "Statute" to the protocol of signature signed December 16, 1920. By December 3, 1942, the protocol had been ratified by fifty-one states, including all of the larger states except the United States.[80] A number of amendments to the Statute were made in 1929, being embodied in a new protocol submitted to the members for ratification.[81]

Composition of the Court.   Under the statute of 1920 the Court con-

---

[76] The "gap" or "gaps" in Article 15 consisted in the right of members, in the event of the failure of the Council to agree upon a unanimous report, to "take such action as they shall consider necessary for the maintenance of right and justice." The obligation not to go to war with a state which complied with the recommendations of the report held only if the report was unanimously agreed to by the members of the Council excluding the members parties to the dispute. For critical comment upon this function of the League of Nations, see Kelsen, *Law and Peace*, pp. 151 ff.

[77] Art. 14. An exhaustive study of the organization, procedure, jurisdiction, and activities of the court may be found in Hudson, *The Permanent Court of International Justice, 1920-1942.* See also, J. Hostie, "The Statute of the Permanent Court of International Justice," *Am. Journal*, Vol. 38 (1944), p. 407; Fachiri, *The Permanent Court of International Justice.*

[78] For the text of the draft scheme, see *Am. Journal*, Vol. 14 (1920), Supp., p. 371.

[79] Technically, the Additional Protocol relating to the Optional Clause.

[80] See table printed in Hudson, *The Permanent Court of International Justice, 1920-1942*, p. 666. For the text of the statute, as revised, see *ibid.*, p. 669.

[81] *Ibid.*, p. 668.

sisted of fifteen members: eleven judges and four deputy judges. One of the amendments of 1929 abolished the deputy judges and raised the number of ordinary judges to fifteen. Members of the Court were placed in nomination by the national groups in the older Court of Arbitration organized by the Hague Conventions of 1899 and 1907. The individual qualifications of the members related to their moral character and juristic ability and excluded reference to their nationality, while a general qualification of the Court as a whole was that it should "represent the main forms of civilization and the principal legal systems of the world." [82] When nominated the members were elected by concurrent action of the Council and the Assembly of the League sitting separately, provision being made for the event of a deadlock. The Statute further made provision for the appointment by the contesting parties in a particular case of judges of their own nationality if there were none already upon the bench.

Jurisdiction of the Court. The jurisdiction of the Court was of two kinds: general, based upon the Statute, and special, derived from treaties and conventions to which particular states were parties.[83] The general jurisdiction of the court was limited to "cases which the parties refer to it," so that it was possible for a state to be a party to the protocol without being under any legal obligation to submit its controversies to the Court. This general jurisdiction was supplemented by an optional compulsory jurisdiction, contained in the so-called "Optional Clause," which was conferred upon the Court by the signature of a separate protocol.[84] This jurisdiction covered four classes of "legal disputes," concerning (1) the interpretation of a treaty, (2) questions of international law, (3) the existence of facts involving a breach of an international obligation, and (4) the reparation to be made for a breach of an international obligation. The Court itself decided whether a particular dispute fell within one of the four classes covered by the Optional Clause. In addition to the jurisdiction of the Court based upon the Statute, there was a special jurisdiction, actually far wider than the general jurisdiction, conferred by separate treaties and conventions, bilateral and multilateral. Some of these treaties and conventions were arbitration treaties proper, in which the parties conferred a specified jurisdiction upon the Court; others, such as the Versailles treaty, the mandates and minorities treaties, and the labor, communications, and transit treaties, related to extraneous matters but contained "arbitration clauses" in accordance with which the parties agreed that any disputes arising in connection with the execution

[82] Statute, Art. 9. See Hudson, *International Tribunals*, Chap. III.

[83] The subject is exhaustively treated in Hudson, *The Permanent Court of International Justice, 1920-1942*, Part IV.

[84] The separate protocol had been signed, up to December 3, 1943, by forty-four states. See Hudson, *op. cit.*, p. 703.

of the treaty should be submitted to the Permanent Court for adjudication.[85]

Advisory functions of the Court.   In addition to the jurisdiction of the Court to render decisions which were "final and without appeal," the Court, responding to the terms of Article 14 of the Covenant of the League of Nations, introduced into its Rules of Court a procedure to be followed when advisory opinions might be asked for by the Council or the Assembly of the League. This procedure was later incorporated into the Statute in the form of an amendment.[86] In general the procedure paralleled that followed when judgments were rendered between two contesting parties.[87] While advisory opinions had no binding force and left the Council or the Assembly free to come to an independent decision, as a matter of practice the Council (the only body to request an advisory opinion) appeared to regard the advisory opinion as definitely settling those legal aspects of the dispute submitted to the Court.[88]

The United States and the Court.   In 1923 the President of the United States requested the Senate to give its advice and consent to the ratification of the Protocol of the Court and suggested several reservations to meet the peculiar situation of the United States. The action of the Senate was delayed until January 27, 1926, at which time a resolution was passed giving the advice and consent of the Senate to the Protocol subject to five reservations.[89] The reservations were to the effect (1) that the adherence of the United States to the Court should not be taken to involve any legal relation to the League of Nations or to the Treaty of Versailles; (2) that the United States should participate upon equal terms in the election of judges; (3) that the United States should pay a fair share of the expenses of the Court; (4) that the United States should be allowed to withdraw from the Court upon due notice given;

---

[85] *Op. cit.* Chap. 20, "Jurisdiction under Special Agreements and under Treaties in Force." See also S. B. Jacoby, "Some Aspects of the Jurisdiction of the Permanent Court of International Justice," *Am. Journal*, Vol. 30 (1936), p. 233.

[86] New Articles, pp. 65-68.

[87] In the much-discussed Eastern Carelia case (Series B, No. 5), the Court established the precedent that it would not rule upon a question submitted to it by the Council when one of the parties (Russia) had repudiated the jurisdiction of the Court and refused to put in an appearance before it. Hudson, *Cases*, p. 1218.

[88] See Fachiri, *op. cit.*, pp. 80 ff. On the general subject of advisory opinions, see Hudson, *The Permanent Court of International Justice, 1920-1942*, Chap. 22; A. D. McNair, "The Council's Request for an Advisory Opinion," *British Year Book*, Vol. VII (1926), p. 1; L. M. Goodrich, "The Nature of the Advisory Opinions of the Permanent Court of International Justice," *Am. Journal*, Vol. 32 (1938), p. 738.

[89] The literature with respect to the reservations entered by the Senate in its resolution of January 27 is extensive. See, in particular, Fleming, *The United States and the World Court;* M. O. Hudson, "The American Reservations and the Permanent Court of International Justice," *Am. Journal*, Vol. 22 (1928), p. 776; Q. Wright, "The United States and the Permanent Court of International Justice," *ibid.*, Vol. 21 (1927), p. 1; Hudson, *The Permanent Court of International Justice, 1920-1942*, pp. 218 ff.

and (5) that advisory opinions should be rendered publicly after public hearing and opportunity for hearing given to the parties concerned; and that the Court should not, without the consent of the United States, "entertain any request for an advisory opinion touching any dispute or question in which the United States has or claims an interest."

A conference of the signatories of the Protocol was held in September, 1926, to consider the effect of the reservations proposed by the United States, and a statement was drawn up suggesting a way in which certain objections which some of the signatories had to the second half of the fifth reservation might be overcome; [90] but no action in reply was taken by the United States. In 1929 a committee of Jurists appointed by the Council of the League drew up a draft protocol containing a plan, known as the "Root formula," by which an agreement might be reached between the United States and the signatory states.[91] At the same time the Statute of the Court was amended so as to incorporate the conditions fixed by the United States in respect to publicity of advisory opinions and the hearing to be accorded to the states concerned. On December 9, 1929, the United States signed the three protocols covering respectively the original Statute, the amendments, and the terms of adherence of the United States. Ratification was never effected.[92]

K. THE PROCEDURE OF CONCILIATION

The decade following the establishment of the League of Nations and of the Permanent Court was marked on the one hand by the negotiation of numerous treaties, bipartite and multipartite, having as their purpose to strengthen the obligation of pacific settlement which had come to be regarded as the primary condition of the success of the League. The obligation of submitting disputes to inquiry by the Council, which the Covenant prescribed as the alternative to arbitration, gave a new impulse to what came to be known as the procedure of "conciliation," which might be defined as the submission of disputes to a previously constituted commission, enjoying the confidence of the states in controversy, whose duty it was to examine all aspects of the dispute and to submit to the parties a solution based upon equity and mutual concession which they were free to accept or to reject.[93] In 1922 the Assembly

[90] For the text of the statement, see *Am. Journal*, Vol. 21 (1927), Supp., p. 1. The reservation amounted to a right of veto without other responsibility in the matter.

[91] See Jessup, "The United States and the World Court," *World Peace Foundation Pamphlets*, Vol. XII (1929), No. 4; Hudson, *op. cit.*, pp. 223 ff.

[92] On January 29, 1935, the Senate voted 52 to 32 in favor of giving its consent, but the necessary two-thirds majority was lacking.

[93] On the subject of conciliation, see Vulcan, *La Conciliation dans le droit international actuel;* Efremoff, *Les Traités internationaux de conciliation;* C. C. Hyde, "The Place of Commissions of Inquiry and Conciliation Treaties in the Peaceful Settlement of International Disputes," *British Year Book*, Vol. X (1929), p. 96; N. L. Hill, "International Commissions of Inquiry and Conciliation," *International Conciliation*, No. 278, March, 1932.

of the League recommended to its members the conclusion of these bilateral treaties, setting up special commissions to which disputes might first be submitted rather than immediately to the Council.[94]

L. THE SYSTEM OF ALTERNATIVE PROCEDURES

Closing the "gaps" in the Covenant. Side by side with these bipartite treaties were others of a multipartite character looking more immediately to the development of the procedures laid down in the Covenant of the League. This "centripetal" tendency, as it was called in contrast to the centrifugal tendency of bipartite treaties, found expression in the unratified Geneva Protocol of 1924, which sought to close the "gaps" in Article 15 of the Covenant and to make resort to peaceful methods obligatory not only as an initial step but as a final settlement of the dispute.[95] Alternative procedures of peaceful settlement were enumerated, offering to the parties in controversy the option of one or other procedure according to the character of the dispute, but in the end making conciliation obligatory. The failure of the Geneva Protocol led to the conclusion of the Locarno Treaties of 1925, by which it was hoped that peace might be secured in the storm-center of Europe.[96] The Locarno Treaties were followed by the important General Act, which was adopted by the Assembly of the League of Nations in 1928 and submitted to the individual states for ratification. The Act was divided into four chapters, the first dealing with conciliation and the second, third, and fourth dealing respectively with judicial settlement, arbitration, and general provisions covering forms of adherence to the act and reservations. Even the General Act, however, did not completely close the "gap" left in Article 15 of the Covenant.[97]

M. THE PACT OF PARIS

Outside the circle of the League of Nations an important step was taken in strengthening the obligation to have recourse to peaceful procedures of settlement by the signature on August 27, 1928, of the Pact of Paris, technically known as the Treaty for the Renunciation of War, and

---

[94] *L. of N., Records of the Third Assembly, Plenary Meetings,* p. 199. For the texts of these treaties and an analysis of their content, see Habicht, *Post-War Treaties for the Pacific Settlement of International Disputes.*

[95] On the subject of the Geneva Protocol, see Miller, *The Geneva Protocol;* H. Wehberg, "Le Protocole de Genève," *Recueil des Cours,* Vol. 7 (1925-II), p. 5.

[96] For the texts of the treaties, see *L. of N. Treaty Series,* LIV; *Am. Journal,* Vol. 20 (1926), Supp., pp. 21 ff. On the important part played temporarily by the Locarno Treaties in strengthening the system of collective security, see Steed, *The British Empire and Locarno;* Beneš, *Les Accords de Locarno;* de Visscher, *La Paix de Locarno au point de vue de droit international.*

[97] For the text of the General Act, see *Am. Journal,* Vol. 25 (1931), Supp., p. 204; Hudson, *International Legislation,* Vol. IV, p. 2529.

popularly known as the Kellogg-Briand Pact.[98] This agreement had its immediate origin in a proposal of the French Foreign Minister, M. Briand, that France and the United States should make a solemn renunciation of war as an instrument of policy between the two nations. Secretary Kellogg made a counter-proposal that the two countries should broaden the agreement and seek general approval for it. The result was that the Pact was signed by the representatives of fifteen states, while other independent states were invited to adhere to it. Ultimately ratified by sixty-five states, the Pact of Paris, in spite of the vagueness of its terms, became the basis of numerous other agreements and declarations looking to the maintenance of the general peace.[99] By Article I of the Pact the contracting parties solemnly declared in the name of their respective peoples that "they condemn recourse to war for the solution of international controversies, and renounce it as an instrument of national policy in their relations with one another." By Article II they agreed "that the settlement or solution of all disputes or conflicts of whatever nature or of whatever origin they may be, which may arise among them, shall never be sought except by pacific means."

Neither the "outlawry" of war, which Article I sought to proclaim, nor the comprehensive agreement of pacific settlement set forth in Article II were as obligatory as they appeared to be at first reading. In an exchange of identic notes the right of self-defense had been reserved in broad terms; [100] while the obligation of pacific settlement was formulated not in concrete terms calling for recourse to specific procedures, but merely in the negative form of *not seeking* a solution except by pacific means. Nevertheless the Pact soon acquired an authority far in excess of its legal force, and its terms entered into one agreement after another during the following decade.[101]

N. THE CHARTER OF THE UNITED NATIONS

It was to be expected that the Charter of the United Nations would definitely close the gaps left open by Articles 12 and 15 of the Covenant and by the successive alternative procedures upon which so much effort

[98] For the text of the Pact of Paris, see *Treaties and Conventions,* IV, p. 5130.

[99] The Pact was the subject of wide discussion, both legal and political. The literature is extensive. See, in particular, Miller, *The Peace Pact of Paris;* Shotwell (who played an active part in the initiation of the Pact), *War as an Instrument of National Policy;* Wehberg, *The Outlawry of War.* See also Department of State publication (No. 468), *Treaty for the Renunciation of War,* containing text of the treaty, notes exchanged, instruments of ratification and of adherence.

[100] Dept. of State publication, *op. cit.,* pp. 56 ff. See above, p. 278.

[101] In view of the dramatic effect of the Pact of Paris upon public opinion and the hopes that came to center around it for the maintenance of peace, efforts were made at Geneva to amend the Covenant of the League of Nations so as to bring it into harmony with the Pact. A committee was appointed to consider the proposed amendments, largely directed toward closing the "gaps" in Articles 12, 13, and 15 of the Covenant. The amendments were not adopted by the Assembly. See 10th Assembly, Plenary Meetings, 168; 12th Assembly, Pl. 111-114; C. P. Anderson, edit. *Am. Journal,* Vol. 27 (1933), p. 105.

had been spent during the succeeding decades. Chapter VI of the Charter, dealing with the pacific settlement of disputes, pledges the parties to have recourse to one or other of the established procedures; and if necessary the Security Council will call upon them to settle the dispute by such means. But in the meantime the Security Council may investigate any dispute and may at any stage of a dispute recommend appropriate procedures; and if it deems that the continuance of the dispute constitutes a danger to the peace, it may recommend terms of settlement, ending, in an extreme case, in measures to meet a threat to the peace. While the inherent right of self-defense is recognized, it exists only until such time as the Security Council has taken the measures necessary to maintain peace.[102]

O. THE INTERNATIONAL COURT OF JUSTICE

The Permanent Court of International Justice had functioned so effectively within its limited jurisdiction that little difficulty was found in securing an agreement to incorporate the new International Court of Justice into the Charter of the United Nations itself. The Dumbarton Oaks Proposals left open the question whether the statute to be incorporated in the Charter would be the existing Statute that had been separately adopted and ratified or a new statute creating a new court of a corresponding character, the decision at San Francisco being in favor of the latter as the easiest means of having Charter and Statute come into effect simultaneously.[103]

The International Court of Justice thus came into existence with the ratification of the Charter of the United Nations. Article 92 of the Charter describes the new Court as "the principal juridical organ of the United Nations," and states that the Court is to function in accordance with the annexed statute "which is based upon the Statute of the Permanent Court of International Justice and forms an integral part of the present Charter." [104] The Court consists of fifteen judges, elected by the General Assembly and the Security Council each acting independently of the other. The judges, as in the case of the Permanent Court, serve for terms of nine years, but instead of a full court being elected every nine years, one-third of the judges are elected every three years, thus assuring that the Court will have at all times a two-thirds membership of judges familiar with pending cases and with the procedure of the court.[105] The method of nominating judges follows the former statute without change.[106]

[102] The Charter thus closes the gaps left open in the Covenant, assuming, however, that there is agreement among the permanent members.

[103] See Stettinius, *Report to the President,* pp. 137 ff. *U.N. Yearbook,* 1946-1947, p. 31.

[104] For the text of the Statute, see Appendix D.

[105] Art. 13.

[106] Arts. 5-7.

The jurisdiction of the Court, like that of its predecessor, "comprises all cases which the parties refer to it and all matters specially provided for in the Charter of the United Nations or in treaties and conventions in force." [107] States parties to the Statute may at any time declare that they "recognize as compulsory *ipso facto* and without special agreement," in relation to any other state accepting the same obligation, the jurisdiction of the Court in all legal disputes concerning: (1) the interpretation of a treaty; (2) any question of international law; (3) the existence of any fact which, if established, would constitute a breach of an international obligation; (4) the nature or extent of the reparation to be made for the breach of an international obligation.[108] In view of the large number of acceptances of the Optional Clause of the Statute of the Permanent Court, provision was made that those which were still in force at the time would be regarded as acceptances of the same compulsory jurisdiction provided for in the new statute.[109] The law to be applied by the Court is set forth in identical terms with those of the former statute.[110]

The Connally Amendment. The acceptance by the United States of compulsory jurisdiction under the Optional Clause of Article 36 of the Statute, in accordance with the Resolution of the Senate of August 2, 1946, was attended by a qualification known as the "Connally Amendment," providing that the jurisdiction of the Court should not apply to "disputes with regard to matters which are essentially within the domestic jurisdiction of the United States of America as determined by the United States of America." [111]

While the Charter provides that "All Members of the United Nations are *ipso facto* parties to the Statute of the International Court of Justice," provision was made that a state which was not a member of the United Nations might become a party to the Statute under conditions to be determined in each case by the General Assembly upon the recommendation of the Security Council. On July 28, 1948, Switzerland became a party to the Statute, Liechtenstein following in 1950, and San Marino in 1954.[112]

[107] Art. 36, no. 1.
[108] The text follows literally that of the Statute of the Permanent Court of International Justice. See above, p. 621.
[109] Art. 36, no. 5.
[110] The first elections to the International Court of Justice were held on February 6, 1946; and the Court held its first regular session on April 18, 1946.
[111] The amendment immediately gave rise to sharp controversy and to appeals from jurists for its elimination from the Resolution as opening the door to evasions of the Statute. See F. Wilcox, "The United States Accepts Compulsory Jurisdiction," *Am. Journal*, Vol. 40 (1946), p. 699; H. Briggs, "Towards the Rule of Law," *ibid.*, Vol. 51 (1957), p. 517; "The United States and the International Court of Justice: A Reexamination," *ibid.*, Vol. 53 (1959), p. 301; *Proceedings*, Am. Soc. of Int. Law, 1954, pp. 128-163.
[112] *U.N. Yearbook*, 1948-1949, 1950, 1954.

The record of the Court over the years since its creation has been impressive, if not as outstanding as might have been desired. Emphasizing the need of having greater recourse to the Court, the General Assembly recommended on November 14, 1947, that the specialized agencies of the United Nations refer points of law arising in their activities to the Court for advisory opinions; it called the attention of its members to the advantage of inserting in treaties arbitration clauses providing for the submission to the Court of disputes concerning the interpretation and application of the treaty. The General Assembly on its part promptly turned to the Court for advisory opinions on matters involving points of law in its own international activities.[113]

It was to be expected that cases would arise in which the jurisdiction of the Court would on occasion be brought into question by the party against whom the suit would be brought. In the Ambatielos Case, brought by Greece in 1951 against Great Britain on behalf of a shipowner, the Court found that it was without jurisdiction to decide on the merits of the claim, although it did have jurisdiction to decide whether the United Kingdom was under an obligation to submit the dispute with Greece to arbitration.[114] In the Anglo-Iranian Oil Co. Case, the Court interpreting a convention of 1933 between the United Kingdom and Iran giving to the oil company certain privileges in the form of exclusive legal remedies, held that it was without jurisdiction to settle the dispute under Article 36 of the Statute, Iran having withdrawn its acceptance of compulsory jurisdiction.[115] In the suit brought by the United States in 1955 against Czechoslovakia for damage done to a United States aircraft, Czechoslovakia refused consent to the jurisdiction of the Court.[116] In the Interhandel Case involving the question of enemy ownership in 1942 of shares of a corporation established in the United States and claimed by Switzerland to be the property of Interhandel, a company registered in Switzerland, the Court first held that the Swiss claims were inadmissible because of nonexhaustion of local remedies, and later because it lacked jurisdiction by reason of the refusal of the United States to submit the case under its interpretation of an earlier treaty of 1931 and under its interpretation of the

---

[113] For a summary of the decisions and advisory opinions of the Court, see the annual *U.N. Yearbooks; Am. Journal*, section on *Judicial Decisions Involving Questions of International Law*. For critical comment, L. Gross, "Some Observations on the International Court of Justice," *Am. Journal*, Vol. 56 (1962), p. 33. During the long period, 1923-1959, Manley O. Hudson presented the jurisprudence first of the Permanent Court and later of the International Court of Justice in successive articles in the *American Journal of International Law*. Upon the death of Judge Hudson the series was taken up by Leo Gross. See "The Jurisprudence of the World Court: Thirty-eighth Year (1959)," *Am. Journal*, Vol. 57 (1963), p. 751.

[114] *I.C.J. Reports*, 1953, p. 10; *Am. Journal*, Vol. 47 (1953), p. 708.

[115] *I.C.J. Reports*, 1952, p. 93; *Am. Journal*, Vol. 46 (1952), p. 737.

[116] *I.C.J. Reports*, 1956, p. 6.

Statute of the International Court as restricted by the Connally Amendment to exclude cases within the domestic jurisdiction of the United States "as determined by the United States." [117]

More important in their practical consequences, perhaps, than in their intrinsic legal merits have been the numerous advisory opinions of the Court. In an advisory opinion on Interpretation of Peace Treaties with Bulgaria, Hungary, and Rumania, given in 1950, the Court held that while the consent of States, parties to a dispute, was the basis of the Court's jurisdiction in contentious cases, the situation was different in regard to advisory opinions which had no binding force.[118] Hence no state might prevent the Court from responding to the request of the United Nations made in order to obtain enlightenment as to its course of action. A significant advisory opinion was rendered in 1949 in Reparation for Injuries Incurred in the Service of the United Nations,[119] and another in the International Status of South West Africa.[120]

P. INTER-AMERICAN REGIONAL AGREEMENTS

From the record of cases settled it would appear that the procedures of pacific settlement developed by the American states in multilateral treaties have played a more significant role in fostering the spirit of continental unity than in the actual settlement of disputes. But for all that they have at the same time helped to emphasize the dominant role of regional security procedures in giving practical application to obligations of peaceful settlement otherwise without sanction.

In 1923, at the Fifth International Conference of American States held at Santiago, the Treaty to Avoid or Prevent Conflicts between the American States, known as the Gondra Treaty,[121] was adopted, in accordance with which all controversies of whatever character not settled by diplomatic negotiation or by submission to arbitration were to be submitted for investigation and report to a Commission of Inquiry, consisting of five members, to be convoked at the time one or other of the parties in controversy might desire to do so. The investigations of the Commission might extend to questions of law as well as questions of fact; but no provision was made for including in the report of the Commission suggestions for a just and equitable settlement of the dispute. This deficiency was made good by the General Convention of Inter-American

[117] *I.C.J. Reports,* 1959, p. 6. *Am. Journal,* Vol. 53 (1959), p. 671; Vol. 52 (1958), p. 320. For critical comment, H. Briggs, "Towards the Rule of Law," *ibid.,* Vol. 51 (1957), p. 517.

[118] *I.C.J. Reports,* 1950, p. 65; *Am. Journal,* Vol. 44 (1950), p. 742.

[119] See above, p. 212.

[120] See above, p. 245.

[121] For the text of the treaty, see *Int. Conferences of American States,* 1889-1928, p. 285. Antokoletz considers the treaty less liberal than the Bryan Treaties, *Tratado de Derecho Int. Público,* Vol. III, p. 345.

Conciliation,[122] negotiated at Washington in 1929, in which the commissions of inquiry of the Gondra Treaty were given "conciliatory functions." Investigation and conciliation thus became parts of a single procedure. As was customary in conciliation treaties, the report of the Commission was not to have the character of a decision or of an arbitral award.

General Treaty of Arbitration. In 1929, at the same Washington Conference, the General Treaty of Inter-American Arbitration was negotiated,[123] incorporating provisions of earlier bipartite agreements and of the Statute of the Permanent Court of International Justice. By Article I, the contracting parties bound themselves to submit to arbitration all differences of an international character which had arisen or might arise between them "by virtue of a claim of right made by one against the other" and which were "juridical in their nature by reason of being susceptible of decision by the application of the principles of law." The article then enumerated as "included among the questions of juridical character" the four classes of legal disputes covered by the Optional Clause of the Permanent Court of International Justice. Two groups of controversies were excepted from the stipulations of the treaty: "(a) those which are within the domestic jurisdiction of any of the Parties to the dispute and are not controlled by international law; and (b) those which affect the interest or refer to the action of a State not a party to this treaty."

Anti-War Treaty of 1933. The Anti-War Treaty of Non-Aggression and Conciliation, signed on October 10, 1933,[124] was a combination of various earlier agreements. Article I condemned wars of aggression and declared that the settlement of controversies of any kind should be effected "only by the pacific means which have the sanction of international law." Succeeding articles proclaimed the doctrine of the non-recognition of territorial arrangements not obtained by pacific means and the principle of "a common and solidary attitude" of neutrality in relation to states failing to comply with the obligations of pacific settlement. A unique feature of the Treaty was the series of limitations that might be entered to the conciliation procedure, which were in sharp contrast with the all-comprehensive scope of the jurisdiction of the commissions provided for in the Gondra Treaty.[125]

---

[122] For the text of the convention, see *Int. Conferences*, 1889-1928, p. 455.

[123] For the text of the treaty, see *Int. Conferences*, 1889-1928, p. 458. See D. P. Myers, "Acceptance of the General Treaty of Inter-American Arbitration," *Am. Journal*, Vol. 30 (1936), p. 57.

[124] For the text of the treaty, see *Int. Conferences*, 1933-1940, p. 496. The treaty is also known by the name of the Argentine Foreign Minister, Saavedra Lamas.

[125] The Anti-War Treaty also changed the method of selecting the commissions of conciliation from that provided in the Gondra Treaty for the commissions of inquiry. But less than three months later the provisions of the Anti-War Treaty were superseded by the Additional Protocol to the General Convention of Inter-American Con-

The Buenos Aires treaties of 1936. Three years later, at the Conference at Buenos Aires in 1936, an effort was made to bring together the existing treaties of pacific settlement and to assist their fulfilment by correlating them with the new procedure of consultation adopted at the Conference. The procedure of consultation might, indeed, be considered as a form of conciliation, in that provision was made for resort to it when other methods of peaceful settlement failed. In the Convention for the Maintenance, Preservation, and Reestablishment of Peace, signed December 23, 1936,[126] the American Republics, signatories of the Treaty of Paris of 1928 or of the Anti-War Treaty of 1933, pledged themselves, in the event of a threat to the peace, to consult together "for the purpose of finding and adopting methods of peaceful cooperation." In the Treaty to Coordinate Existing Treaties [127] it was agreed that the consultation and cooperation provided for should have as their object "to assist, through the tender of friendly good offices and of mediation, the fulfilment by the American Republics of existing obligations of pacific settlement." These obligations were described as "the alternative procedures of mediation, commissions of inquiry, commissions of conciliation, tribunals of arbitration, and courts of justice."

The Pact of Bogotá. Two new procedures were created at the same Conference of 1936. The Treaty on Good Offices and Mediation introduced a simple and informal procedure analogous to what is known in private law as "settlement out of court." [128] The Treaty on the Prevention of Controversies sought by means of mixed Commissions to study the causes of future difficulties and anticipate controversies.[129] But as treaty mounted upon treaty it was realized that coordination of the successive agreements was urgently needed, and the task was assigned to the Inter-American Juridical Committee created by the Meeting of Foreign Ministers at Rio de Janeiro in 1942.[130] The successive drafts

ciliation. *Int. Conferences,* 1933-1940, p. 120. For editorial comment on the treaty, see P. C. Jessup, *Am. Journal,* Vol. 27 (1933), p. 109; Vol. 28 (1934), p. 538. For the critical comments of the Inter-American Juridical Committee, see *Recommendations and Reports,* p. 94.

[126] For the text of the convention, see *Int. Conferences,* 1933-1940, p. 188. For comment, see C. G. Fenwick, "The Inter-American Conference for the Maintenance of Peace," *Am. Journal,* Vol. 31 (1937), p. 201.

[127] *Int. Conferences,* 1933-1940, p. 192. For comment, see Fenwick, *op. cit.,* p. 211.

[128] *Int. Conferences,* 1933-1940, p. 199.

[129] *Ibid.,* p. 197.

[130] At the Eighth International Conference of American States, held at Lima in 1938, a resolution (XVII) was adopted calling attention to the fact that "the juridical measures to prevent war in America are scattered in numerous treaties, conventions, pacts, and declarations, which it is necessary to coördinate into an organized and harmonious unified instrument." In 1943 the Governing Board of the Pan American Union assigned the task to the Inter-American Juridical Committee. For the texts of the two drafts and for comment explaining the documents, see Inter-American Juridical Committee, *Recommendations and Reports,* pp. 53 ff., 81 ff. See Fenwick, "The Coördination of Inter-American Peace Agreements," *Am. Journal,* Vol. 38 (1944), p. 4.

prepared by the Juridical Committee resulted in the Pact of Bogotá, signed in 1948 under the more formal title, American Treaty on Pacific Settlement.[131]

The qualified response to the Pact of Bogotá, set forth in numerous reservations attending its signature, made it clear that the attempt to secure an all-comprehensive system of pacific settlement, including political as well as legal disputes, was simply not a practical approach to the problem. Revision of the Pact was sought at the Conference at Caracas in 1954, but to no avail.[132] But what might have been a serious setback to the progress of peaceful procedures proved to be of little consequence due to the efficient functioning of the procedure of consultation under the Rio Treaty of Reciprocal Assistance. A half century ago, when arbitration was the one hope of preventing recourse to hostilities, it was urgent to close as far as possible the gaps in arbitration treaties. Today, if the controversy should reach an acute stage, a case can readily be made out of a threat to the peace.

[131] *Int. Conferences*, 1942-1954, p. 200.
[132] Fenwick, *OAS*, p. 192.

CHAPTER **XXVII**

Forcible Procedure by Methods
Falling Short of War

A. LEGAL STATUS OF SUCH PROCEDURE

Failing a resort by two contending states to one or other of the pacific methods of settlement available to them, international practice at the opening of the twentieth century recognized a number of methods by which a state might bring physical pressure to bear upon the opposing party without actually resorting to war. Since war itself was an admissible procedure, an alternative remedy, less drastic than war, was preferable where it could accomplish the same purpose. Obviously such a remedy, involving the use of force, could as a rule only be resorted to by stronger powers against weaker ones, the latter not being in a position to take up the challenge by a declaration of war. In general, the methods thus resorted to by stronger powers had little effect upon the interests of third states, so that the latter remained more or less indifferent spectators of the procedure, acquiescing in the results reached, except in the occasional case in which their own interests were directly affected. In consequence international law failed to develop any clear rules governing the use of these methods of coercion; and it is difficult at times to determine whether a particular method falls within one classification or another.[1]

With the adoption of the Charter of the United Nations forcible procedure by methods falling short of war came under the general condemnation of the use of force, as prohibited by Article 2(3,4) of the Charter and, by implication, by Articles 39-40. But inasmuch as Article 51 recognizes the right of individual or collective self-defense it is still possible that a state may, in taking measures of self-defense, resort to the tra-

[1] On the general subject of measures short of war, see Hindmarsh, *Force in Peace,* which sets forth, however, the law as of 1933.

ditional procedures short of war, rather than have recourse to direct hostilities.[2] In any case a survey of these procedures is necessary to throw light upon certain historical incidents that have left their mark upon the development of international law.

B. RUPTURE OF DIPLOMATIC RELATIONS

Before resorting to one or other of the various forms of coercion it was common for governments to break off diplomatic relations with the offending state by recalling their public ministers resident at the foreign capital. This measure was not in itself a form of forcible procedure, since it was not intended to inflict injury upon the offending state, but rather to serve as a warning that the issue between the two states had reached a point where the injured party regarded normal diplomatic relations as no longer compatible with the conduct of the other state, and that sterner measures might possibly follow.[3] Mexico broke relations with the United States following the occupation of Vera Cruz in 1914. The United States broke relations with Germany following the resumption of submarine attacks upon merchant ships in 1917. The American Republics recommended to themselves the breaking of relations with the three countries following the attack by Japan and the declarations of war by Germany and Italy upon the United States in 1941.[4]

C. RETORSION

Although commonly associated with methods of coercion falling short of war, retorsion is not strictly speaking a measure of redress for legal injuries. It consists in retaliation where the acts complained of do not constitute a legal ground of offense but are rather in the nature of unfriendly acts done primarily in pursuance of legitimate state interests but indirectly hurtful to other states. The offense is therefore comparable to an act causing *damnum sine injuria*, a loss where no legal wrong has been done, in municipal law. Vattel cites the action of the elector of Saxony in enforcing the law of escheat only against the subjects of those provinces which subjected the Saxons to it.[5] Resort to retorsion is chiefly

[2] A recent striking instance being the quarantine established by the United States against the shipment of arms to Cuba in October, 1962. See above, pp. 279, 513.

[3] This measure, which assumes the previous existence of normal relations between the two countries, is not to be confused with the refusal to recognize the *de jure* character of a particular government. Recognition once given is not regarded as susceptible of revocation. Hence the withdrawal of diplomatic relations does not affect the *de jure* character of the offending government. See above, pp. 180 ff.

[4] See Hackworth, *Digest*, Vol. VI, p. 148. The recommendation, however, was attended by conditions which made the actual fulfilment of the obligation less than certain. See below, p. 727.

It should be observed that the mere withdrawal of an ambassador in protest against conditions in a foreign state is not equivalent to the withdrawal of diplomatic relations.

[5] *Droit des gens*, Vol. II, § 340.

had in connection with discriminatory tariffs, domestic legislation against aliens, port restrictions, depreciation of currency, and other national legislation not subject to international control.[6] The practice is still within the law, since it does not involve the use of force in the sense prohibited by the Charter of the United Nations.

D. REPRISALS

Earlier forms. The modern procedure of reprisals is a relic of a primitive form of self-help between nations and between their respective citizens. The ancient Athenians were familiar with the practice of androlepsia (ἀνδροληψία), by which compensation for an offense committed upon the person of a citizen by a foreigner might be obtained by the seizure of the person of a fellow countryman of the offender.[7] During the Middle Ages merchants frequently resorted to the practice of obtaining, where necessary, redress for their losses by seizure of both the person and the property of foreigners whose national relationship to the offender made it seem equitable that they should make good his delinquencies.[8] In time this practice came to be regulated by governments to the extent of issuing letters of marque and reprisal to the injured individual, who, armed with this official sanction, made capture of the property of citizens of the state which had wronged him or of fellow countrymen of the individual wrongdoer. These reprisals were known as "special reprisals" and were, in effect, nothing more than private warfare legitimatized by the municipal law of the state.[9]

The modern practice. The procedure of special reprisals was abandoned during the course of the nineteenth century, and such reprisals as were practiced were put into effect by the state itself, acting either in its own interest or in that of its injured citizen. Moreover, the term came to be applied to any form of forcible redress by which a state, without resort to formal war, undertook to bring the offending state to terms. Reprisals differed from retorsion in that they were generally resorted to in consequence of alleged illegal acts on the part of the

[6] While the traditional conception of retorsion is that of retaliation in kind, certain writers include also within the term other forms of coercion, such as a display of force or the actual use of force without a formal declaration of war. See Westlake, *International Law*, 2d ed., Vol. II, pp. 6-11; more recently, Hyde, *International Law*, Vol. II, § 588.

[7] See Phillipson, *International Law and Custom of Ancient Greece and Rome*, Vol. I, p. 361; Grotius, *De jure belli ac pacis*, Bk. III, Chap. II, § 7.

[8] Walker, *History*, pp. 121, 167, 187; Westlake, *International Law*, 2d ed., Vol. II, p. 8; Yves de la Brière, "Evolution de la doctrine et de la pratique en matière de représailles," *Recueil des Cours*, Vol. 22 (1928-II), p. 241. For the origin of the term "reprisal," see Hyde, *International Law*, Vol. II, § 589, no. 5.

[9] The Constitution of the United States recognizes the existence of the custom by enumerating among the powers of Congress that of issuing letters of marque and reprisal. Art. I, Sec. 8, part 11. There appears to be "no example in the history of the United States of authority for special reprisals." Moore, *Digest*, Vol. VII, p. 122.

offending state and in that they were not limited to retaliation in kind but might take any form of coercion which the state believed to be effective to secure redress. In the Naulilaa case, involving reprisals by Germany against Portugal for the death of three German officers who were killed in Portuguese territory by members of a frontier post in Angola, the German-Portuguese Arbitration Tribunal laid emphasis upon the necessity of a preceding illegal action as a justification for reprisals, and not finding it in the instant case the tribunal held Germany responsible for the damage done by way of reprisals.

The tribunal discussed at length the nature and scope of reprisals, observing: "Reprisals are acts of self-help of the injured state, acts in retaliation for unredressed acts contrary to international law on the part of the offending state. In consequence of such measures, the observation [observance] of this or that rule of international law is temporarily suspended. They are limited by considerations of humanity and the rules of good faith." [10] In principle, reprisals of the more drastic character were not to be distinguished from acts of war. Their practical justification, however, lay in the fact that they afforded to the injured state a measure of immediate redress, and at the same time they avoided the necessity of creating a state of hostilities which might result in consequences more serious than the offense in question would justify. In the case of Gray, Administrator v. United States,[11] the Court of Claims held that the reciprocal captures and other acts of hostility between France and the United States from 1791 to 1800 did not constitute "public general war" but only "limited war, in its nature similar to a prolonged series of reprisals." It would appear that reprisals, unlike war, could not be carried so far as to affect the rights of third states. The state seeking redress might indeed declare war; but if it refrained from doing so it could not treat third states as neutrals in respect to commerce with the offending state.[12]

E. EMBARGO

With the disappearance of special reprisals by the beginning of the nineteenth century, a form of general reprisals frequently resorted to by states was that of laying an embargo upon all vessels of the offending state that happened at the time to be in the ports of the state seeking redress. This was not the same as the embargo formerly placed upon ships of the enemy in port at the outbreak of hostilities, which was, in

---

[10] Quoted by Schwarzenberger, *Int. Law*, Vol. I, p. 243. For a summary of the case see *Annual Digest*, 1927-1928, p. 526.

[11] 21 Court of Claims, 340 (1886). Fenwick, *Cases*, p. 722.

[12] See, on this point, Westlake, *Collected Papers*, p. 590, "Reprisals and War." For the past practice of the United States, see Moore, *Digest*, VII, § 1096; Hyde, *International Law*, §§ 590, 591.

law as in fact, an act of war.[13] Embargo by way of reprisal did not contemplate confiscation, except in the event that redress for the injuries suffered should be finally refused. In the case of the *Boedes Lust*,[14] decided in 1803, it was stated by the court that a seizure of Dutch property under the embargo of 1803 was "at first equivocal; and if the matter in dispute had terminated in reconciliation, the seizure would have been converted into a mere civil embargo, and so terminated. . . . On the contrary, if the transaction ended in hostility, the retroactive effect is exactly the other way." In 1807 the Congress of the United States, confronted with illegal seizures of merchant vessels by both Great Britain and France, established a general embargo on all shipping, foreign and domestic, in the ports of the United States, making exception in favor of the departure of foreign ships in ballast.[15]

Seizure of vessels on the high seas.   The practice of laying an embargo upon vessels of the offending state was at times accompanied by the seizure of such vessels on the high seas as were encountered by the armed ships of the state demanding redress. In the case of the reprisals of Great Britain against the Two Sicilies in 1839, undertaken on account of the alleged violation of treaty rights, an embargo was laid upon ships flying the flag of the offending state, and at the same time orders were given to the British navy to seize all Neapolitan and Sicilian ships which might be met with in their national waters. Upon grant by the Two Sicilies of redress, the vessels under detention were restored to their owners.[16] As late as 1908 Holland put into effect reprisals against Venezuela for the seizure of certain Dutch vessels and for the dismissal of the Dutch minister by the capture of two public vessels of the latter country. The vessels were released when a new president of Venezuela made redress.[17]

F. SUSPENSION OF PRIVILEGES

On the border line between retorsion not involving the use of force and reprisals involving the use of force was the practice of suspending the operation of treaties granting privileges to the offending party. In 1780 Holland's repudiation of its treaty obligation to assist Great Britain when attacked was followed by the latter's suspension of the stipulations providing for freedom of navigation and commerce between the two countries.[18] In 1798 the United States Congress, by way of reprisal for

---

[13] See below, p. 701.
[14] 5 C. Rob. 233 (1804). Fenwick, *Cases*, p. 730.
[15] Act of December 22, 1807. 2 *Stat. at Large*, p. 451.
[16] Hall, *International Law*, § 126.
[17] See *U. S. Foreign Relations*, 1909, pp. 630 ff., where the response of the United States to the inquiry of Holland as to the attitude of the former toward coercive measures is given.
[18] Hall, *International Law*, § 120.

the illegal capture of American vessels, passed an act suspending commercial intercourse with France.[19] In 1809, after the failure of the general embargo of 1807, Congress passed a Non-Intercourse Act prohibiting commerce with France, England, and their colonies.[20]

G. BOYCOTTS

The practice of the boycott, by which the citizens of one state undertake to put into effect a concerted suspension of trade and business relations with the citizens of the offending state, is a relatively modern one. So long as the boycott is a purely voluntary act on the part of citizens acting individually or in concert, it would appear that the measure falls outside the scope of international law. But if any element of governmental pressure, or even of governmental persuasion, should enter into the boycott, there would be ground for protest by the foreign government.[21] In 1931 the Japanese Government held that the boycott of Japanese goods conducted by Chinese citizens, being encouraged by the Chinese Government, was in violation of international law. China answered by pointing to conduct of Japan believed to be far more seriously in violation of international law.[22] The Committee of Nineteen appointed by the League of Nations to inquire into the findings of the Lytton Report came to the conclusion that the boycott fell "under the category of reprisals." [23]

H. PACIFIC BLOCKADE

During the second quarter of the nineteenth century the larger states developed the practice of instituting a pacific blockade as a means of putting coercion upon weaker states. Pacific blockade differed from hostile blockade only in respect to the absence of a formal state of war and in respect to the relations of third states to the blockade. When resorted to upon political grounds—that is to say, when the blockading state had no technical ground of offense against the blockaded state but was

[19] Act of June 13, 1798. 1 *Stat. at Large,* p. 565.

[20] Act of March 1, 1809, 2 *Stat. at Large,* p. 528. For the effect of the several acts, see Moore, *Digest,* Vol. VII, § 1099. These acts must be distinguished from such measures as the act of March 14, 1912, by which Congress authorized an embargo upon the shipment to Mexico of arms and ammunition manufactured in the United States, the object of which was not to make reprisals upon Mexico but to maintain better the neutrality of the United States during the civil conflict in Mexico.

[21] The subject is controversial. See C. C. Hyde and L. B. Wehle, "The Boycott in Foreign Affairs," *Am. Journal,* Vol. 27 (1933), p. 1; C. L. Bouvé, "The National Boycott as an International Delinquency," *Am. Journal,* Vol. 28 (1934), pp. 19 ff. For a study of the economic effects of Chinese boycotts, see Remer, *A Study of Chinese Boycotts with Special Reference to their Economic Effectiveness.*

[22] Willoughby, *The Sino-Japanese Controversy and the League of Nations,* pp. 604 ff.

[23] Bouvé, *op. cit.,* p. 42.

acting in pursuance of national interests above the law—pacific blockade was commonly classed as "intervention,"[24] although none the less a form of reprisals. In 1827 Great Britain, France, and Russia, without declaring war upon Turkey, brought pressure to bear upon that state in the interest of the independence of Greece by blockading those parts of the Greek coast in occupation of the Turks.[25] Even the subsequent battle of Navarino was fought without the acknowledgment of a state of formal war. In 1832 Great Britain and France blockaded the coast of Holland with the object of coercing that state to recognize the independence of Belgium.[26] In 1850 Great Britain blockaded the ports of Greece as a means of securing redress for an attack upon the house of an English subject, a native of Gibraltar, known as Don Pacifico.[27] In this case, however, the blockade was generally condemned by authors on the ground that it was resorted to before recourse had been had by Don Pacifico to the Greek courts.[28] In 1886 the Great Powers blockaded the Greek coast to prevent that country from going to war with Turkey; and again in 1897 the Great Powers blockaded the coast of Crete to prevent the island from annexing itself to Greece.[29] In 1902 Great Britain, Germany, and Italy blockaded the coast of Venezuela as a means of coercing that state to settle outstanding claims of their respective citizens; but in this case it was not clear whether the blockading powers were not actually at war with the blockaded state.[30] During the First Balkan War of 1913 the Great Powers blockaded the port of Antivari to prevent Montenegro from annexing Scutari which the blockading powers believed should be attached to Albania.[31] In 1916 the Allied Powers blockaded certain ports of Greece with the object of preventing that state from joining forces with the Central Powers.[32]

Its effect upon the commerce of third states. Although condemned by some publicists as a form of international procedure, such practice gave to pacific blockade some degree of legal standing. As to the effect of a pacific blockade upon the commercial intercourse of third states with the blockaded state, it would appear that the earlier blockades at times included the ships of third states in the restrictions imposed, whereas later blockades, such as that of Greece in 1886, were as a rule applied

[24] See above, p. 285.

[25] For details, see Hogan, *Pacific Blockade,* pp. 73 ff.

[26] For details, see *ibid.,* pp. 80 ff.

[27] For details, see Moore, *Digest,* Vol. VI, p. 852; Vol. VII, p. 132.

[28] See above, p. 338, where the facts of the case are given.

[29] Hogan, *op. cit.,* pp. 126 ff.; Moore, *Digest,* Vol. VII, p. 138.

[30] For details see Moore, *Digest,* Vol. VII, p. 140; *U. S. Foreign Relations,* 1903, pp. 420 ff.; Stowell and Munro, *Cases,* Vol. II, p. 7.

[31] Hayes, *A Political and Social History of Modern Europe,* Vol. II, p. 530.

[32] Hackworth, *Digest,* Vol. VI, p. 158, where, however, the political reasons for the blockade are not assigned. See also Hyde, *Int. Law,* Vol. II, § 592.

only to ships of the blockaded state.[33] In 1902 the United States announced, in anticipation of the blockade of Venezuela, that it refused to acquiesce "in any extension of the doctrine of pacific blockade which may adversely affect the rights of states not parties to the controversy, or discriminate against the commerce of neutral nations." [34] It was in view, however, of the fact that a blockade could be of little value if it did not interfere with the commerce of third states that the British jurist, Hall, argued that blockade was "essentially an incident of war" and that it could not be defended on the basis of general principle.[35] In 1916, when the Entente Powers announced their intention to blockade Greece, the United States declared that it did not concede "the right of a foreign power to interfere with the commercial rights of uninterested countries by the establishment of a blockade in the absence of a state of war.[36] Whether blockade was a useful alternative to war was a question outside the field of strict law. It would appear that it was the protest of third states against the pacific blockade of Formosa in 1885 that led France to declare war upon China, and that Great Britain, Germany, and Italy declared their blockade of Venezuela in 1902 to be a war blockade with the object of enforcing it against the vessels of third states.[37]

Following the First World War the question of the effect of a pacific blockade upon the commerce of third states was widely discussed in connection with collective sanctions of the League of Nations under Article 16 of the Covenant. Obviously a collective blockade undertaken by the League of Nations against a state violating the obligations of the Covenant could not be successful if states not members of the League, especially one of the leading commercial powers, should refuse to permit the interruption of its relations with the offending state. A number of American jurists refused to make any distinction between a pacific blockade of the older type and one conducted by the League of Nations.[38] On the other hand the Secretary-General of the League of Nations, in a

[33] The blockade of Crete in 1897 was exceptional in the restrictions placed upon the commerce of neutral ships. For the protest of the United States see Moore, *Digest*, Vol. VII, p. 139.

[34] *Ibid.*, p. 140. See also Vol. VI, pp. 586-592. For the collateral question as to the preferential treatment accorded to the claims of the blockading powers, see Award of Tribunal of Arbitration, February 22, 1904. Scott, *Hague Court Reports*, p. 56; Wilson, *Hague Arbitration Cases*, p. 34; Fenwick, *Cases*, p. 732.

[35] *International Law*, ed. 1883, § 121. This view was modified in later editions.

[36] Hackworth, *Digest*, Vol. VI, p. 158.

[37] With respect to Formosa, see Hall, *International Law*, § 121, where the protest of Lord Granville against the treatment of third states by France is given. For the case of Venezuela, see Moore, *Digest*, Vol. VII, p. 140.

[38] Hyde, for example, stated that it was "not to be anticipated that the United States would acknowledge that its rights under international law could be diminished by the institution of a pacific blockade by a group of members of the League of Nations acting at the instigation of that body in penalizing a covenant-breaking member." *International Law*, Vol. II, § 592.

report on the subject to the Council of the League, in 1927, observed: "Third states may be led, by their sense of the importance to the whole world of the observance of the methods of pacific settlement laid down by the Covenant, or by sympathy with the League's attitude in the particular case, to acquiesce in the application of the pacific blockade to their own ships." [39]

A striking instance of resort by the United States to pacific blockade as a means of self-defense against Cuba when formal hostilities might have had more far reaching consequences is to be seen in the quarantine established by President Kennedy to prevent the import of war material into Cuba following the dramatic demand upon the Soviet Union on October 22, 1962, to demolish the missile bases and remove the missiles and atomic warheads. In addition to the demands directed to the Soviet Union based upon the general principle of self-defense, the quarantine extended to vessels of other nations and involved the assertion of a right of visit and search. Justification for the quarantine, which doubtless exceeded measures of pacific blockade recognized by the United States in the past, lay in the danger of missile bases so close to the United States as to make defense practically impossible. On November 20, 1962, the quarantine was lifted when it appeared that the conditions calling for it no longer existed. [40]

I. OTHER FORCIBLE MEASURES OF REDRESS

Occupation of Vera Cruz. In addition to pacific blockade, states have at times had recourse to other forcible measures of redress which differed only from acts of war by the absence of formal hostilities. In 1854 an American warship twice bombarded Greytown, Nicaragua, and finally destroyed the town by fire as reprisals for the failure of the authorities to grant the redress demanded. In justification of such exceptional action, President Pierce offered the fact that the community was no more than a "piratical resort of outlaws." [41] In 1858 the United States despatched a naval fleet to the River Plate with the object of making a demonstration which would facilitate the settlement of claims against Paraguay. [42] In 1895 British forces occupied the customhouse and other public buildings in the port of Corinto as a means of coercing Nicaragua to pay the indemnity demanded. [43] A conspicuous instance of reprisals was the occupation by United States naval forces of the city of Vera Cruz in 1914 as a means of compelling the Mexican Government to grant specified redress for the arrest of an American officer and seamen in the port of

[39] *Official Journal*, 1927, p. 839.
[40] See *Am. Journal*, Vol. 57 (1963), pp. 515 ff.; and above, pp. 263, 279, 513.
[41] Moore, *Digest*, Vol. VII, § 1168.
[42] *Ibid.*, § 1092. For other examples of the display of force, see *ibid.*, § 1091.
[43] *Ibid.*, § 1906.

Tampico.[44] The resolution of Congress of April 22, 1914, authorizing the president to use the armed forces of the United States "to enforce his demand for unequivocal amends for certain affronts and indignities committed against the United States" exhibited the paradoxical nature of reprisals in announcing "that the United States disclaims any hostility to the Mexican people or any purpose to make war upon Mexico."

Occupation of Corfu. Following the murder of certain Italian officers engaged in an official expedition on the Greek border, the Italian Government, not satisfied with the reply of Greece to its ultimatum of August 29, 1923, bombarded and seized the island of Corfu on the following day. The occupation of the island was explained as indicating not an intention to go to war but merely a desire to obtain a security which would make it clear to the Greek Government that no trifling would be permitted. The killing of a number of refugees in the fortress was described as unintentional. The island and others adjacent to it were evacuated on September 27.[45] In 1925 Greek troops invaded Bulgaria following the outbreak of local hostilities along the border. In spite of the allegation by Greece that the act had no aggressive or warlike design the Council of the League of Nations decided that Greece should pay compensation to Bulgaria for the loss of life and property.[46]

Japanese hostilities against China. The most extreme case of resort to measures of armed force to obtain redress without declaring formal war were the hostilities carried on by Japan against China during an entire decade, 1931-1941. In 1931 Japan invaded Manchuria, but in doing so it declared that the acts of armed force to which it was resorting were not to be considered as war.[47] Again in 1937 Japan began hostilities against China without considering that it was formally at war.[48] In both cases China, for reasons of its own, preferred to avoid declaring war upon its own account.[49] The United States, taking the hostilities at the value set upon them by the two countries, avoided applying the provisions of the several neutrality acts of 1935-1939, and at the same time

[44] For details, see Hackworth, *Digest,* Vol. I, p. 151; Vol. VI, p. 152. Hyde, *International Law,* Vol. II, § 591. See above, p. 292.

[45] In respect to the legal aspects of this extraordinary affair see M. O. Hudson, "How the League Met the Corfu Crisis," *World Peace Foundation Pamphlets,* Vol. VI (1923); League of Nations, *Official Journal,* 1923, 1924, *passim;* C. Eagleton, "The Responsibility of the State for the Protection of Foreign Officials," *Am. Journal,* Vol. 19 (1925), pp. 293, 303.

[46] *Official Journal,* 1926, pp. 108, 172, 196. See also J. W. Garner, "Settlement of the Greco-Bulgarian Dispute," *Am. Journal,* Vol. 20 (1926), p. 337.

[47] Hindmarsh, *op. cit.,* pp. 128-129.

[48] For a brief survey of the situation, see Sharp and Kirk, *Contemporary International Politics,* pp. 644 ff. For a critical examination of the position taken by Japan, see Willoughby, *Japan's Case Examined.*

[49] A declaration of war by China would have given Japan the right to blockade the coast of China and prevent the carriage of contraband goods, while at the same time bringing into effect restrictions upon American trade resulting from the neutrality laws of the United States.

refused to recognize any right on the part of Japan to exercise the normal rights of a belligerent in respect to neutral vessels entering zones blockaded against Chinese vessels.[50] It was not until two days after the attack by Japan upon the United States at Pearl Harbor that China finally declared war against Japan on December 9, 1941. A more recent instance of meeting force with force was the order given in August, 1962, to United States air and naval units to fire back at destroyers of North Viet Nam in an attack upon United States ships lying in the open sea of the Gulf of Tonkin. The hostilities carried on by the United States against North Viet Nam in 1965 fall within a category of their own.

In view both of the provisions of the Covenant of the League of Nations not to "resort to war" and of the provisions of the Kellogg Pact renouncing "war" as an instrument of national policy, the question was presented whether a state could, by proclaiming that its acts of force were not intended to constitute "acts of war" free itself from its obligations under the two treaties. What limits were there to the use of force by one state against another without having recourse to formal war? Was the existence of a "state of war" to be determined by the intention of one of the parties to engage in "war," or was it to be determined by the facts of the particular case, by the character and scope of the acts of force, whatever designation the parties might apply to them? [51] In 1924 a Special Commission of Jurists, appointed by the Council of the League of Nations in connection with the Italian bombardment of Corfu, found it impossible to formulate a general rule to determine whether measures of coercion which were not meant to constitute acts of war were consistent with the terms of Articles 12-15 of the Covenant, replying that they might or might not be consistent, and that it was for the Council to decide the matter, "having due regard to all the circumstances of the case and to the nature of the measures adopted." [52] The consensus of opinion of scholars saw in the hostilities committed by Japan against China a *de facto* war, whether or not it might be advisable for third states, members of the League of Nations or nonmembers, not

[50] A blockade of a part of the coast of China was declared by Japan, effective August 25, 1937. The United States refused to admit any legal right on the part of Japan even to stop American vessels and verify their nationality. Hackworth, *Digest*, Vol. VII, p. 9. On the application of the Nine Power Treaty to the crisis in China, see C. G. Fenwick, *Am. Journal*, Vol. 31 (1937), p. 671.

[51] For a general discussion of the problem, see Briggs, *The Law of Nations*, pp. 682 ff., 718 ff.; C. Eagleton, "The Attempt to Define War," *Int. Conciliation*, June, 1933, No. 291; A. D. McNair, "The Legal Meaning of War, and the Relation of War to Reprisals," *Transactions of the Grotius Society*, 1926, pp. 29 ff.; Q. Wright, *A Study of War*, Vol. I, p. 8; Vol. II, p. 685; "When does war exist?", *Am. Journal*, Vol. 26 (1932), p. 362; W. J. Ronan, "English and American Courts and the Definition of War," *Am. Journal*, Vol. 31 (1937), p. 642.

[52] *Official Journal*, 1924, pp. 524 ff.; 1926, pp. 597 ff. For comment, see Q. Wright, "Opinion of Commission of Jurists on Janina-Corfu Affair," *Am. Journal*, Vol. 18 (1924), pp. 536 ff.

to recognize it as such for political reasons. The problem was complicated by the question of sanctions, and the desire to limit hostilities which might otherwise extend in scope and intensity.[53]

J. COERCIVE ACTION BY THE UNITED NATIONS

If it should happen that the Security Council of the United Nations should find it necessary to use coercive measures to give effect to its decisions, it is to be expected that the action taken would fall within the traditional classification of procedures short of war. Article 41 provides that the Security Council may decide what measures "not involving the use of armed force" are to be employed to give effect to its decisions. These, it is stated, may include "complete or partial interruption of economic relations and of rail, sea, air, postal, telegraphic, radio, and other means of communication, and the severance of diplomatic relations." Article 42 provides that, if the Security Council should consider that the above measures would be inadequate, "it may take such action by air, sea, or land forces as may be necessary to maintain or restore international peace or security. Such action may include demonstrations, blockade, and other operations by air, sea, or land forces of Members of the United Nations."

The Republic of the Congo had scarcely won its independence from Belgium (June 30, 1960) before serious internal disorders broke out. The situation began as a purely domestic one outside the jurisdiction of the United Nations. But charges of aggression brought by the new state against Belgium soon enabled the Security Council to take action, and an emergency force was sent to the country which, after serious resistance from the Katanga province, finally succeeded in maintaining order. In spite of the actual fighting that took place, the measures taken by the Security Council raised none of the issues incident to war. They might rather be described as the action of an international police force functioning in accordance with treaty provisions.[54]

In 1964 the Island of Cyprus became the scene of rioting and bloodshed between the Greek and Turkish Cypriots. The island had obtained independence on August 16, 1960, in accordance with a treaty of guarantee between the Republic of Cyprus, Greece, the United Kingdom, and Turkey, and in accordance with a treaty of alliance between the Republic of Cyprus, Greece, and Turkey. A constitution was adopted, dividing the government between the two groups: 70 percent Greek Cypriot and 30 percent Turkish, each group voting separately for its own delegates in the House of Representatives. With the outbreak of

[53] See H. Lauterpacht, "Resort to War and the Interpretation of the Covenant during the Manchurian Dispute," Am. Journal, Vol. 28 (1934), pp. 43 ff.

[54] U.N. Yearbook, 1960, pp. 52 ff. Compare the action of the Emergency Force created by the General Assembly in 1956 to secure and supervise the cessation of hostilities between Israel and Egypt in the Suez crisis. U.N. Yearbook, 1956, pp. 19 ff.

disorder which the British could not control from their bases, appeal was made to the United Nations. The Secretary General appointed a "moderator" supported by a peace-keeping force.[55]

K. SANCTIONS UNDER THE RIO TREATY OF RECIPROCAL ASSISTANCE

Corresponding roughly to the forcible procedures short of war which the Security Council is authorized to take under Articles 41 and 42 of the Charter are the procedures set forth in Articles 8 and 10 of the Rio Treaty of Reciprocal Assistance. In 1960 the Sixth Meeting of Foreign Ministers, in response to the evidence submitted by Venezuela that the President of the Dominican Republic had been involved in the attempted assassination of President Betancourt, imposed sanctions in the form of the breaking of relations and partial suspension of trade.[56] In 1964 the Ninth Meeting of Foreign Ministers, in response to evidence of subversive activities of the Cuban Government directed against Venezuela, not only called for the discontinuance of diplomatic and consular relations, but for a complete embargo of commercial trade and suspension of communication by sea.[57]

[55] Whiteman, *Digest,* Vol. 2, p. 149; *U.N. Review,* April, 1964.
[56] Final Act, August 21, 1960. *OAS Official Records,* Ser. C/11.6.
[57] Final Act, July 26, 1964. *OAS Official Records,* Ser. F/11.9.

CHAPTER **XXVIII**

Forcible Procedure by War[1]

A. CHARACTER OF WAR AS A LEGAL REMEDY

The right to make war. The right of a state to make war as an ultimate means of self-help when other measures of obtaining redress for
alleged wrongs were unsuccessful had, until the year 1920, a recognized
place in international law. The community of nations, lacking an effective organization through which conflicting claims might be adjusted,
threats of injury prevented, or the commission of wrongs punished,
recognized the right of the individual state to take the law into its own
hands and prosecute the offender in its own name and in its own interest.
While not all offenses were regarded as of sufficient gravity to warrant
a resort to force to redress them, each state was left to determine for
itself the gravity of the offense and the extent to which its vital national
interests were involved. The sanction of the public opinion of the international community was supposed to see to it that a state should not be
wholly arbitrary in deciding that its national interests justified recourse
to war. But events generally moved too fast for the effective operation
of this sanction, so that when the war came to an end there was nothing
for the international community to do but to accept the results of the
conflict and reconcile itself to the terms imposed by the victor upon the
vanquished. The victor must, of course, be careful not to encroach upon

---

[1] How far the procedure of war, whether in limited or unlimited form, still retains
a legal character under the provisions of the Charter of the United Nations, and what
is the scope of the obligations incumbent upon the parties to a conflict will appear
in the course of a review of the elements involved in the procedure itself. The text
of this chapter is retained largely intact, partly because it describes the international
law of a period of such recent date as to figure prominently in the discussion of
current events, and also because it presents the background against which the controversial issue of a possible revision of the laws of war may be better understood. See
Chap. XXIX, note 1.

the rights of third states, or to impose terms so severe as to make third states feel that they themselves must be on their guard against a similar fate. But short of this the victor was free to decide how far he could safely go.[2]

Jurists abandon the conception of a "just war." It is significant that on the eve of the First World War the principle that there must be a "just cause of war" had practically disappeared from the treatises of jurists. The principle had been the cornerstone of the system built up by Grotius.[3] To the writers of the positive school which dominated the first decade of the twentieth century there was little value in elaborating upon distinctions which could not lead to the precise and definite conclusions called for by "law." National defense was an obvious ground of a "just war"; but it proved difficult, if not impossible, to draw the line between defense which took the form of anticipation of attack and an act of aggression itself.[4] A state had an obvious right to maintain the integrity of its national territory; but in the absence of a method of determining the just title to property it was impossible to distinguish the defense of what was one's own from the taking of what was one's neighbor's.[5] As long as there was no collective judgment of the international community taking precedence of the judgment of the individual claimant, it was impossible to reduce the problem to terms of positive law. The general principle was accepted that a nation must not go to war except for a just cause; but the application of the principle to the concrete case did not get beyond the province of international morality or ethics.[6] Equally significant with the omission of the tests of a just war

[2] It was to be expected that the terms of peace would go beyond the original demands of the victor. The risk of war was not to be taken for nothing. See p. 751.

[3] Grotius compared the sources of war to the sources of actions at law, but the elaborate analogies which he worked out between private and public law advanced the question little beyond the stage of general principles. "Most writers," he said, "state three just causes of war: defense, recovery of property, and punishment of wrong." *De jure belli ac pacis,* Eng. trans., Bk. II, Chap. I, § II. Vattel elaborated upon the same general principles: "We may say, therefore, in general, that the foundation or cause of every just war is an injury, either already received or threatened." His practical analysis of this generalization, however, together with the distinction which he introduced between perfect and imperfect rights (see p. 64), left numerous loopholes for evasion. *Droit des gens,* Eng. trans., Bk. III, § 26. On the general subject, see J. von Elbe, "The Evolution of the Concept of the Just War in International Law," *Am. Journal,* Vol. 33 (1939), p. 665, and references there given.

[4] For the manner in which aggression could disguise itself as defense by way of anticipating the attack of another, see above, pp. 275 ff.

[5] For example, the campaign cry of 1844, "Fifty-four forty or fight," had it resulted in war between the United States and Great Britain would have given voice to a popular conviction on the part of the American people of just defense of property rights. Again, the declaration of war against Mexico in 1846 was based upon alleged defense of national territory.

[6] Hall stated the case succinctly: "It is not therefore possible to frame general rules which shall be of any practical value [in determining the causes for which war may be justly undertaken], and the attempts in this direction, which jurists are in the

from the treatises of the jurists was the fact that the second Hague Peace Conference of 1907 paid no attention whatever to the subject.[7] International jurisprudence had become too practical to deal with mere theories of right. The matter simply appeared to be unsuited for legal determination.

War loses its legal character. With the close of the First World War the old "right to make war" was greatly restricted. The Covenant of the League of Nations created a general, if qualified, guarantee of the political independence and territorial integrity of the members of the League. It proclaimed the principle that any war or threat of war, whether immediately affecting any of the members of the League or not, was thenceforth to be a matter of concern to the whole League, and it authorized the League to take any action that might be deemed wise and effectual to safeguard the peace of nations; and it thus established the principle of the collective responsibility of the members of the League as a group in place of the former principle of neutrality. It limited the right to make war to cases in which the Council might be unable to report unanimously upon a dispute submitted to it, or the Assembly might be unable to reach a majority decision including all of the members of the Council.[8] The Pact of Paris called for the renunciation of war as an instrument of national policy. In consequence war lost much of its former legal character as an instrument of self-help. But due to the defective organization of the League war still remained a practical possibility, and it was taken for granted that if it should come it would give rise to the same legal relations between the belligerents themselves and between belligerents and neutrals that had prevailed during the First World War.[9]

Under the Charter of the United Nations the "right to make war" in the old traditional sense is definitely ruled out. The use of force is the prerogative of the Security Council, or of the General Assembly acting

---

habit of making, result in mere abstract statements of principles, or perhaps of truisms, which it is unnecessary to reproduce." *International Law,* § 16.

"The question of the justice or injustice of war," wrote the Swiss publicist Rivier, "stated as a general and abstract proposition, although much debated in earlier times, is of little practical importance and is impossible of solution. The question can only be put in the concrete with reference to a particular war; and even then the answer will be far from clear." Quoted by Bonfils, *Droit international,* § 1002. Brierly points out how Grotius failed in his great task of securing a distinction between just and unjust war. See *Law of Nations,* p. 25.

[7] The Final Act of the Conference recognized the desirability of arbitrating controversies, but made no effort to define the character of the questions which a state might be justified in refusing to submit to that procedure. See above, p. 614.

[8] See above, pp. 25, 46.

[9] In consequence of the restraints put upon war by the League of Nations and by the Pact of Paris the practice developed of resorting to hostilities without a declaration of war. The problem was then presented of determining when such hostilities amounted to "war" in the technical sense. See above, p. 643.

in default of the Council; and the decision of the Security Council to resort to measures of force under Article 42 of the Charter would be a fundamentally different procedure from war as resorted to under the law of 1907. The same is true of "individual or collective self-defense" under Article 51 of the Charter, which justifies hostilities only until the Security Council has taken action to restore peace.[10]

B. THE "LAWS OF WAR"

Distinct from the question of the right to make war, was the question of the proper conduct of belligerents during the war itself. Grotius was the first to make the distinction in clear terms, and his treatise set the standard for succeeding jurists.[11] The devastation and general misery resulting from the Thirty Years' War forced the nations in 1648 to recognize as fundamental principles the territorial independence and legal equality of the existing members of the family of nations. These principles became the basis of a new and more stable international system, and around them there grew up by degrees a body of substantive rules defining the rights and duties of states within the various fields of international relations. This development of the substantive law was accompanied by a corresponding development of the procedure of war. Statesmen and publicists, unwilling or unable to deny to states in controversy the right to maintain their claims by force, sought to regulate what they could not, or would not, abolish. Thus there grew up a formal body of the "laws of war," being the restrictions and limitations upon what states might do when resorting to war.[12] Where Grotius had appealed to broad principles of moral conduct, jurists now began to appeal legal obligations binding upon nations by reason of established custom or the provisions of treaties.

Substantive and procedural law. Modern international law thus found itself divided into two separate and distinct branches, the one substantive in character, dealing with the normal rights and duties of states, the other procedural in nature, defining the relations between states which had resorted to force to maintain disputed claims. It was common with authors of the early twentieth century to classify the two branches of the law as the "law of peace" and the "law of war," the

[10] As observed later in this work, it is to be assumed that hostilities in self-defense would be conducted in accordance with the applicable Hague Conventions, not as technical legal obligations, but as embodying in large part the customary laws of war. The Charter makes no reference to the problem.

[11] The first two books of his treatise are devoted to a discussion of the substantive rules of law, under the caption of "What constitutes a just war"; the last book discusses lawful methods of warfare. See above, p. 59.

[12] The student will distinguish sharply between the legality of a resort to war and the legality of the ways and means by which war might be prosecuted once it had begun.

latter including not only the relations between the belligerents themselves but the relations between the belligerents and neutral states.[13]

Attitude of the Hague Conferences. It was the tragedy of the time that the attention of statesmen came to be concentrated upon the development of the procedural law of war to the neglect in large part of the substantive law. The Hague Conference of 1907, the greatest gathering of statesmen that the world had yet seen, waived aside the problem of analyzing the causes of war and seeking a constructive solution of the conflicting interests of states. The original objective of disarmament was found no more practicable than in 1899. Of the thirteen conventions elaborated at the Conference, eleven related to the conduct of the next war.[14] The progress of international law was seen to consist not in restrictions upon the right to have recourse to force for the settlement of conflicting claims, but in restrictions upon the way in which force might be used to attain its ends. No voice was raised to suggest that belligerents might not observe the laws of war under stress of difficult conditions; and few called attention to the fact that new conditions might make existing rules inapplicable.

Accepting, then, the legality of war as an ultimate means of self-help and having confidence that the rules they adopted would contribute to the regularization of hostilities and the avoidance of unnecessary suffering and loss of property, the Hague Conference of 1907, like its predecessor in 1899, recognized the belligerents on both sides as being upon an equal footing, having equal rights in the prosecution of the war, both in respect to the measures of force they might use against each other and in respect to the extent to which they might interfere with the commerce between neutral states and the enemy.[15] It was no one's business but that of the two belligerents whether the controversy between them could not have been settled by negotiation or arbitration. However inconvenient the situation might be for third states, they had no choice but to accommodate themselves to it as best they might. The right of the two belligerents to make war simply could not be interfered with.[16]

Sources of the laws of war. In the formulation of the laws of war the Hague Conferences had an elaborate body of customary law to build upon. To some extent this customary law had already been set forth in the works of the leading writers on international law and in such codes

---

[13] See, for example, the treatises of Westlake, Oppenheim, and Lawrence.

[14] The Convention on the Pacific Settlement of International Disputes did, indeed, seek to substitute the procedure of arbitration for that of war. But, as has been seen, it did so within recognized and, it might be said, respectful limitations.

[15] See above, pp. 22 ff.

[16] It was this alleged "right," with all of its destructive effects upon neutral commerce, that provoked President Wilson to declare in 1916 that "the business of neutrality" was over. See below, p. 719.

as that published by President Lincoln in 1863 and that prepared by
the Institute of International Law in 1880.[17] Customary law was obviously binding without the need of an international convention. But, as
has been observed, customary law was an uncertain law. It was difficult
to determine what practices had received the approval of a sufficient
number of states to be regarded as the law of the community of nations
as a whole. Besides, the external conditions of warfare were changing
rapidly, and a number of governments were not prepared to abide by
rules which they believed to be inapplicable under the new circumstances. After all, modern war was not the sport of kings; and while
proclaiming their desire to avoid it, governments wanted to be sure
that the rules of the contest were as much to their advantage as possible,
considering all the elements that entered into the military situation.

The Hague Conventions. At first sight the elaborate conventions
adopted at the Hague Conference of 1907 appeared to have given the
necessary definition to the uncertain rules of the customary law; [18] but
upon closer examination it was seen that their force was greatly weakened, if not altogether nullified, by the provision attached to the particular convention, that it should be binding upon the signatory powers
only if all of the belligerents were parties to the convention. The effect
of these provisions was that if, in a war between a large number of
states, a single belligerent, for example Serbia in 1914, had failed to
sign, or having signed failed to ratify a convention, the entire agreement fell to the ground. Thus the whole conduct of belligerent operations during the First World War must be judged by the standard of
what was obligatory under the customary law at the time the new codes
of 1907 were being drawn up.

Nevertheless the discussions attending the drafting of the several
Hague Conventions threw a valuable light upon the content of the customary law as understood at the time. In many cases their provisions
were little more than a codification of existing rules of customary law.
In consequence jurists and governments continued to refer to the Hague
Conventions as embodying the correct rule to be followed even though
the failure of certain of the belligerents to ratify them deprived them

[17] For collections of documents, see Baker and Crocker, *Laws of Land Warfare;*
Martin and Baker, *Laws of Maritime Warfare;* Baker, *Laws of Neutrality.*

[18] Of the eleven conventions on the laws of war adopted at the Hague in 1907 one
related to the opening of hostilities, a second and comprehensive one to the laws and
customs of war on land, seven to specific conditions of maritime war, and two to the
relations between belligerent and neutral powers. The convention dealing with the
relations between belligerent and neutral powers in maritime war was supplemented
by the Declaration of London of February 26, 1909, which, however, failed of
ratification. It was not until the close of the First World War that an attempt was
made to regulate aerial warfare; but the convention proposed by the jurists who met
at The Hague in 1922, like those which preceded it before the war, remained unratified.

of technical legal validity. Actually they represented what the leading powers, after long debate and with many compromises, were ready to accept as the law, and this gave to them an authority which made the non-ratification of a minor power relatively negligible. Their subsequent failure was due to other reasons.

On the other hand, looking upon the conventions of the Hague Conference as the culmination of the attempt to put legal restraints upon the conduct of belligerents in time of war without at the same time making a parallel attempt to remove the causes of war and to put restraints upon the resort to war, the conflict of opinion manifested in the elaboration of the conventions made it clear, or should have made it clear, that the law was in a state of flux and that there was little hope that many rules alleged to be law would stand the test of a major war. Unfortunately the leading military and naval powers preferred not to anticipate that situation.

Sanctions of the laws of war. The sanctions of the laws of war accepted at the time of the Hague Conference of 1907 corresponded in general to the sanctions applicable to the substantive rules of international law. In so far as concerned the general conduct of the belligerents, respect for the law was maintained by their regard for neutral public opinion, which in time of war was generally more watchful and acute than in time of peace. When, however, one of the belligerents resorted to practices which the other believed to be flagrantly illegal and neutral public opinion was of no avail as a present remedy, the second belligerent might resort to reprisals as a means of bringing pressure upon the offending state to discontinue its illegal conduct.[19] The separate rules dealing with the relations of belligerent and neutral states were specially sanctioned by the active interest which neutral states had in resisting any extensions by the belligerents of their acknowledged right to interfere with neutral commerce; and while belligerents regularly sought to overleap the restrictions placed upon them, they were for the most part restrained by the fear of reprisals and by the possible intervention of neutral states in defense of their rights of commerce.

Status of rebel forces. While the laws of war were strictly applicable only to hostilities between states, international law came in time to regard them as applicable to provinces or colonies in rebellion against the mother country, whenever the insurrection assumed such proportions that third states were directly affected or for other reasons concerned themselves with the conflict. In such cases the rebellious community was said to be "recognized as a belligerent"; and it thereby became entitled to the rights, as well as obligated by the duties of a state engaged in formal war.[20] The problem of the recognition of bel-

[19] For a discussion of the nature and scope of reprisals, see above, p. 636.
[20] See Chap. VII, B, "Recognition of belligerency."

ligerent rights in time of civil war was more difficult. In the case of the American Civil War of 1861-1865, which was rather a sectional and international war than a civil war in the strict sense, there was a tendency at first on the part of the Union to treat the Confederate forces as mere rebels; but the magnitude of the struggle soon brought about recognition of their rights as belligerents. In true civil wars, where the struggle is between insurgents and the *de jure* government for control of the organization of the state, respect for the laws of war has been dependent upon the personal character of the military commanders and upon the extent to which they have been able to enforce discipline. Captured rebels have not always been accorded the status of prisoners of war; and they have themselves at times indulged in acts of vengeance after victory has been won.

C. FUNDAMENTAL PRINCIPLES OF WARFARE

Limits to the use of force. As between two regular belligerents the laws of war consisted, therefore, in the limits or bounds set by international law within which the force required to coerce the enemy must be exercised. What these bounds were was prescribed both in general principles and in concrete rules of warfare. There was the fundamental principle that the procedure of war was a means to an end. It followed that the measures employed must have a direct or indirect relation to the desired coercion of the enemy. In no case might the force used exceed at any time the necessities of the situation or be directed to any other object than the submission of the enemy; and to continue the war after the enemy state had announced its willingness to surrender would be in clear violation of the law.[21]

But this principle, clear enough in the abstract, left room for a wide latitude of interpretation. "Military necessity" technically meant the necessity of using legitimate measures of coercion to attain the desired end.[22] But of its very nature "necessity," translated into terms of overcoming the resistance of a determined enemy, tended to go beyond bounds. During the later years of the nineteenth century certain German

[21] Hall states the case with his usual clarity: "But just as violence in war has at no time of modern European history been in fact exercised without the encumbrance of moral restraint, so theoretically it must always be exercised with due regard to the character of the state as an aggregate composed of moral beings. It is agreed that the use of wanton and gratuitous violence is not consistent with the character of a moral being. When violence is permitted at all, the amount which is permissible is that which is necessary to attain the object proposed," *International Law*, § 17. This was the doctrine of Vitoria, *De jure belli*, no. 15; of Grotius, Bk. III, Ch. I, § 2; and of Vattel, Bk. III, Ch. VIII, §§ 136-138. The most that could be obtained from the jurists assembled at the Hague Conferences of 1899 and 1907 was that "the right of belligerents to adopt means of injuring the enemy is not unlimited." Art. 22, Regulations respecting the Laws and Customs of War on Land.

[22] See, for example, the definition of "military necessity" given by Lieber, *Instructions for the Government of Armies of the United States in the Field*, Nos. 14-16.

writers put forth a theory of "military necessity" (*Kriegsraison*) which included within the term not only the general justification of coercive measures, subject to the restrictions of the law, but the justification of measures in excess of the law when the necessity of the situation called for them.[23] Taken literally, this interpretation of military necessity reduced the entire body of the laws of war to a code of military convenience, having no further sanction than the sense of honor of the individual military commander or chief of staff and no practical effect where the contending forces were sufficiently equal to render the issue doubtful.[24]

The "laws of humanity." Supplementing the principle that the measure of force must not exceed the necessities of the situation were certain "laws of humanity" based, as the name suggests, upon the universal dictates of public morality. These laws of humanity prescribed that belligerents must refrain altogether from certain measures of coercion which by reason of their extreme cruelty or their violation of good faith would destroy the very foundations of human relationships and make the return to peace impossible. Experience had shown that needless cruelty, particularly violence offered to noncombatants, inflicted deeper wounds than defeat upon the field of battle. The object of the war was peace; peace, indeed, upon the terms imposed by the victor, but peace at that. The enemy was not to be annihilated, but to be reduced to submission. "Humane warfare," as it was paradoxically called, while seeking to overcome the resistance of the enemy state, still regarded it as composed of human beings whose general rights of life and security were not wholly forfeited because of their resistance to the forcible measures of redress applied to them. They must be brought to terms, but not in such a way or by such means as to create in them feelings of bitterness and resentment which time would not alleviate.[25]

Conflicting views of "humane conduct." But here again the jurists of the late nineteenth century could not refrain from rationalizing upon a principle which was, indeed, not without its inconsistencies. To attempt to humanize war was, some said, both futile and illogical. On the

[23] See, for citation of German authorities, de Visscher, *La Belgique et les juristes allemands, passim*. Also Westlake, *International Law*, 2d ed., Vol. II, pp. 126-128; Oppenheim, *International Law*, Vol. II, § 69; Garner, *International Law and the World War*, Vol. II, §§ 439-440.

[24] Compare the doctrines laid down in *German War Book* (*Kriegsbrauch im Landkriege*, trans. by Morgan), Introduction, pp. 51-55, where the restrictions upon certain methods of warfare are denied the validity of laws.

[25] The conception of "humane warfare" was perhaps best expressed by Phillimore, as, for example, "Wanton devastation of the enemy's territory, wanton cruelty exercised towards his subjects, are, therefore, according to the principles and practice of Christian nations, unjustifiable and illegal." *Commentaries upon International Law*, Vol. III, 3rd ed., pp. 78 ff. Practice had improved since Grotius' time, although it was soon to degenerate.

one hand it was argued that a sharp and decisive war was more humane
than a prolonged conflict, and that to reach this end means might be
employed which, while seemingly inhumane, in fact brought about a
return of peace with the least amount of general suffering.[26] Others held
that, as modern wars were conducted, it was as important to break
down the moral resistance of the enemy population as to defeat armed
forces in the open field.[27] As the instruments of war became more and
more deadly, many jurists appeared to be unable to decide whether to
attempt to restrict their use or to allow belligerents a free hand in the
hope that they might wear themselves out more quickly. The conception of an organization to prevent war, a system of collective security,
was as yet the dream of impractical pacifists.

Combatants and noncombatants. As a corollary to the principle that
war was a means to an end and that the measures employed might not
be extended beyond their effectiveness to secure the submission of the
enemy was the principle that war was primarily a relation between
states as represented by their armed forces and persons directly associated with them; so that on one hand the noncombatant population
must commit no act of violence toward the invading armies and on the
other hand the invading armies must, apart from the operations of war,
respect the persons and property of unarmed citizens. Certain writers,
beginning with Portalis in 1801, had endeavored to uphold the principle
that war was a relation between states as such, not between individuals,
so that persons included in the fighting forces were enemies only by
accident of their combatant character and other persons not members
of the fighting forces were not to be regarded as enemies.[28] But this
attempt to distinguish between the state and the body of its citizens
was too inconsistent with the traditional practices of nations and too
illogical in itself to obtain wide acceptance. International law had always
made noncombatants the indirect victims of sieges, blockades, and
other military operations and had held them to direct responsibility

[26] Bonfils, for example, held that "in time of war humanity can not claim anything
incompatible with the object of the war. Whatever should go beyond that would be
not only useless, but hurtful. A humanity which sought to obstruct the object of the
war would not be a true humanity. There is a measure of truth in the saying of
Moltke: 'the most vigorous war is at the same time the most humane war.' " *Manuel
de droit international public,* 6e ed., Fauchille; § 1009. Compare *Instructions for the
Government of the Armies of the United States in the Field,* No. 29: "The more
vigorously wars are pursued, the better it is for humanity. Sharp wars are brief." A
more extreme view is to be found in the German *Kriegsbrauch,* where it is laid down
that "certain severities are indispensable in war, nay more, that the only true humanity
very often lies in a ruthless application of them." *German War Book,* Eng. trans. by
Morgan, Introduction, p. 35. See also, *ibid.,* p. 65, with respect to certain instruments
of war, which "just because they attain the object of war as quickly as possible are
on that account to be regarded as indispensable and, when closely considered, the
most human."

[27] See below, pp. 680 ff.

[28] See Hall, *International Law,* § 18, where the subject is discussed in detail.

for the indemnities exacted from the defeated state. Grotius had stated the principle clearly, that the subjects of enemy states were themselves individually enemies; [29] and the numerous efforts made during the nineteenth century, culminating in the conventions of the Hague Conference of 1907, seeking to spare noncombatants as far as possible from the effects of war, all proceeded upon the principle that they were technically enemies in their individual capacity.[30] Unhappily as war became more and more totalitarian the distinction between combatants and noncombatants practically disappeared, armies and civilian populations becoming involved in a common fate.[31]

Absolute and conditional prohibitions. In addition to and derived from these fundamental principles of warfare were numerous specific and concrete rules of conduct. Those originating in custom were known as the "usages of war," representing the practical application of the principle under the conditions of actual warfare. Some were *absolute* prohibitions which forbade the use of certain measures under all circumstances, no matter what the necessity of the situation. In this class were the rules which forbade the poisoning of wells, the killing of prisoners, the misuse of flags of truce.[32] Others were *conditional* prohibitions, which restricted the use of permissible measures under certain circumstances. The condition attached to these prohibitions left a greater or less latitude of interpretation to the individual belligerent, being generally expressed by the phrase, "so far as the conduct of military operations permits." [33]

D. EFFECTS OF THE FIRST WORLD WAR

Such were the "laws of war" on the eve of the First World War, as embodied in custom or explicitly set forth in the conventions drawn up

[29] Book III, § 9; Ch. IV, § 8.

[30] Vattel stated the rule correctly in 1758 in saying that "when the ruler of the State, the sovereign, declares war upon another sovereign, it is understood that the whole Nation is declaring war upon the other Nation; for the sovereign represents the Nation and acts in the name of the whole society, and it is only as a body, as a unit, that one Nation can deal with another." *Droit des gens,* Eng. trans., Bk. III, § 70. Compare *Instructions for the Government of the Armies of the United States in the Field,* No. 20: "Public war is a state of armed hostility between sovereign nations or governments. It is a law and requisite of civilized existence that men live in political, continuous societies, forming organized units, called states or nations, whose constituents bear, enjoy, and suffer, advance and retrograde together, in peace and in war."

[31] See below, pp. 679 ff.

[32] See below, pp. 667 ff.

[33] See, for example, *Instructions,* No. 19, where it is held that "commanders, wherever admissible, inform the enemy of their intention to bombard a place, so that the noncombatants, and especially the women and children, may be removed before the bombardment commences." The rule reappeared as No. 217 of *Rules of Land Warfare,* published by the War Department of the United States, but was qualified almost beyond recognition by Nos. 50-57 of the Rules published in 1940.

at the Hague. That many of them broke down in the presence of new and unforeseen conditions should have been expected. Under stress of desperate conditions a number of rules were set aside on the ground that "necessity knows no law." [34] Other laws were regarded as no longer binding on ground of reprisal for alleged illegal acts of the enemy. Others still were considered inapplicable by reason of the changed conditions of modern warfare. Rules originally possessing a degree of logic or founded upon a compromise of conflicting interests had, it was said, become inconsistent with new situations confronting the belligerents. The invention of more deadly weapons of destruction raised the issue of the feasibility of restricting any method of putting the enemy out of action, particularly in view of the fact that in a war of opposing trenches the mere disabling of the individual soldier did not permanently remove him as an active combatant. Moreover the general participation of the unarmed population in the manufacture of munitions and in other services directly contributory to the support of the armies in the field tended to abolish the distinction between combatants and noncombatants. The result was that few of the rules of the Hague Conventions, assuming them to have represented the formulation of existing custom, survived intact the strain put upon them.[35]

Attempts to revise the laws of war. Nevertheless in spite of the demonstration of the inability of law to restrain belligerents when engaged in what might be called by analogy "mortal combat," and in spite of the system of collective security established by the League of Nations, there were governments and jurists who still believed in the value of revising the laws of war and giving new and more effective sanctions to them.[36] The Washington Conference of 1921-1922 undertook to put more effective restrictions upon the use of poisonous gases and upon submarine warfare, and it made provision for the appointment of a commission of jurists to consider the question whether the existing rules of

---

[34] The outstanding instance during the First World War was the violation of the neutrality of Belgium. See below, p. 127. It is difficult to select the outstanding instance of the Second World War, so many of the smaller states being the victims of alleged acts of necessity.

[35] For details, see further in the present work under each separate item.

[36] The point of view of those favoring a revision of the laws of war is to be found in John Bassett Moore's *International Law and Some Current Illusions*, Introduction and Chaps. I, V. Those who had no faith that nations would keep their promises of collective security somehow had faith that they would observe new rules of warfare by way of compensation. On the other hand the inconsistencies, both logical and moral, of the laws of war led many jurists to denounce the attempt to define or revise them or even to be concerned with their application in the future. In the 1934 edition of this treatise the author confessed that he was "a skeptic with regard to the 'legal' character or practical validity of much that will be included in the following chapters under the 'laws of war.'" In the third edition of 1948 the chapters on war were put in the past tense, although still presented in full detail, as part of recent history.

international law adequately covered new methods of attack and defense resulting from the new agencies of warfare developed since 1907.[37] Learned societies continued to discuss the laws of war in anticipation of another world conflict.[38] But the inconsistency of formulating new laws of war in the presence of the Locarno Treaties, the Briand-Kellogg Pact, and other multipartite treaties looking to the abolition of war and the development of procedures of peaceful settlement prevented the proposed revision of the laws of war from reaching the stage of international agreements. When, during the second decade of the interwar period, the threat of a general conflagration came closer, the governments of the leading powers were too divided to make an agreement possible even if there were any jurists left who had faith that the new rules would be observed when the time came.

Military necessity finds its logical fulfilment. If the laws of war were unequal to their purpose of keeping the belligerents within bounds during the First World War they proved to be even more unequal to their purpose during the Second World War. New instruments of warfare were invented and new methods discovered which broke through the established traditions. Military occupation took on new totalitarian forms in keeping with the political principles of the occupant. If warfare had already become totalitarian in the First World War it became doubly so in the Second; with the result that practically the last vestiges of the distinction between combatants and noncombatants disappeared. The logic of the jurists who, fifty years before, had given a broad interpretation to "military necessity" found its fulfilment.[39]

E. FUTURE OF THE LAWS OF WAR

It was confidently hoped that with the signing of the Charter of the United Nations in 1945 the laws of war, in the older traditional sense, had now ceased to have any application. What the League of Nations had been unable to do would now be done under the new order; and with the elimination of war as an accepted legal status there would be merely the collective action of the United Nations under Article 42 of the Charter as a possible restraint upon the individual state resorting

[37] See Moore, *op. cit.*, Chap. V, for a description of the organization and purposes of the Commission of Jurists appointed in pursuance of a resolution adopted by the conference.

[38] For the sharp conflict of opinion upon the subject expressed at the annual meeting of the American Society of International Law, see *Proceedings*, 1922, pp. 85-92. The failure of the United States to become a member of the League of Nations made the subject of neutrality a particularly attractive topic.

[39] The author ventured to observe many years ago that the only laws of war that would be likely to hold in a future war would be the moral instincts and restraints of the individual commanders. The experience of the Second World War only confirmed this opinion, notwithstanding that individual commanders, put on trial for crimes against laws of war, sought to pass on the responsibility to those "higher up."

to violence. Assuming the necessity on the part of the United Nations of having recourse to armed forces, it was equally to be assumed that the Security Council would hold its military operations within the limits of the traditional laws of war, avoiding the interpretations of military necessity that had marked the two World Wars. Moreover, account had to be taken of the possibility of acts of self-defense under Article 51 of the Charter of the United Nations. But here again it was not to be expected that a nation or collective group of nations, acting under the restraints of the Charter, would fail to keep within the restraints of the customary laws of war, which, by a rough estimate, probably constituted 70 percent of the Hague Conventions. At any rate no provision was entered in the Charter dealing with military operations under two possible situations.[40]

Out of the legal uncertainties resulting from the prohibitions upon the recourse to force imposed by the Charter and the practical possibility of limited wars of individual or collective self-defense, there developed a new procedure described as "non-war hostilities," or a state of armed conflict as distinct from a "state of war." Japan had already found it convenient to declare its hostilities against China in 1937 as not constituting war in order to avoid condemnation under the provisions of the Kellogg-Briand Pact. When hostilities broke out in Korea in 1950 it was clear that the "breach of the peace" and the assistance proposed by the Security Council to "repel the armed attack" did not create the status of formal war. As the hostilities progressed the restraints of the Hague Conventions in respect to measures and instruments of warfare were recognized as applicable, as were the Geneva Conventions of 1949. But the Conventions prescribing the rights and duties of neutrals had lost their meaning. The United Nations Command, while not representing all of the signatories of the Charter, was engaged in a police measure which was not to be embarrassed by issues of contraband and blockade.[41]

In like manner the hostilities in connection with the resistance of Great Britain to the measures taken by Egypt in the Suez Canal zone in 1956 were not regarded as "war" by Great Britain; nor was the extended police action by the United Nations forces in the Congo in 1960, carried

[40] Compare Stone, *Legal Controls of International Conflict*, Chap. XI; and see R. Baxter, "Reciprocity, Self-Research and the Laws of War," *Proceedings*, Am. Soc. Int. Law, 1964; P. C. Jessup, "Political and Humanitarian Approaches to the Limitation of Warfare," *Am. Journal*, Vol. 52 (1958), p. 757; Q. Wright, "The Outlawry of War and the Law of War," *Am. Journal*, Vol. 47 (1953), p. 565; Report of Commission on Study of Legal Problems of the United Nations, "Should the Laws of War Apply to United Nations Enforcement Action?," *Proceedings*, Am. Soc. Int. Law, 1952, p. 216.

[41] See, on this point, H. J. Taubenfeld, "International Actions and Neutrality," *Am. Journal*, Vol. 47 (1953), p. 377. The resolution of the General Assembly of November 17, 1950, was entitled "Duties of States in the Event of the Outbreak of Hostilities."

on in pursuance of resolutions of the Security Council,[42] considered "war" in the traditional sense; nor in like manner the military action carried on by the United States in North Viet Nam in 1965.

In the catastrophic event of a nuclear war between the powers of conflicting ideologies, it could not be expected that the provisions of the Hague Conventions distinguishing between combatants and noncombatants, between military and nonmilitary objectives in bombardment, between permissible and prohibited methods of warfare, would have application, or rather be possible of application, the very instruments themselves being inherently beyond control. The prospect defies the conditions contemplated at The Hague, and all that would remain would be the instinctive reactions of humane conduct where one party or the other might survive outside the devastated areas. To speak of *law* in such circumstances would obviously be a mockery.

[42] See E. M. Miller (O. Schachter), "Legal Aspects of the United Nations Action in the Congo," *Am. Journal,* Vol. 55 (1961), p. 1; Whiteman, *Digest,* Vol. 1, p. 296.

CHAPTER XXIX

The Laws of Land and Aerial Warfare[1]

6 6 4

A. OBLIGATION TO GIVE WARNING BEFORE COMMENCING HOSTILITIES

Derived basically from the rule of good faith, it was one of the oldest and best established rules of international law that a state must not resort to force against an opponent without giving due warning that hostilities were about to commence. A sudden attack by one state upon another, before negotiations looking to a settlement of the controversy had reached the point where the redress demanded was apparently not to be granted, was regarded from the earliest times as an act of brigandage. Among the ancient Greeks and Romans, as apparently among other ancient peoples, the practice prevailed of announcing the

---

[1] As will be observed, the violation during the two world wars of many of the rules set forth in this and succeeding chapters has naturally raised the question whether it is feasible or practical to undertake a revision of the laws of war to meet the new conditions with which the international community is confronted and the "limited hostilities" which are still in progress from time to time.

It is agreed that so long as war, in limited or unlimited form, remains a possibility, it is the part of wisdom to seek to restrain its excesses as far as possible. Professor Kunz has been conspicuous in advocating the revision of the laws of war, believing that there are still fields of limited hostilities in which the traditional rules of warfare must be reaffirmed and given new application in the light of changing conditions. In "The Chaotic Status of the Laws of War and the Urgent Necessity for their Revision," *Am. Journal,* Vol. 45 (1951), p. 37, he criticizes sharply the opponents of revision who take the position that revision is either unnecessary or hopeless. In a later article, "The Laws of War," *Am. Journal,* Vol. 50 (1956), p. 313, while still urging revision in the field of limited hostilities, he recognizes that the possibility of atomic warfare has raised the imperative question whether in the event of such war there would be any law left, whether of war or of peace.

The practical question, moral in its implications, is still to be taken into account, that is, whether a nation which is prepared to violate its solemn obligations under the Charter of the United Nations would be controlled by other legal obligations created by revised laws of war.

commencement of hostilities by a formal declaration of war. The Romans in particular laid stress upon the necessity of a prior demand for reparation (*rerum repetitio*), following which, if redress was not granted, war was formally declared by members of the college of fetials to whom that duty was intrusted. During the Middle Ages the practice of despatching heralds to announce war with due ceremony was revived, doubtless under the influence of the traditions of the Roman Law. In later centuries formal diplomatic announcements were made; but by the eighteenth century, notwithstanding the assertions of publicists that a declaration of war was necessary,[2] the practice of giving formal notice had fallen into disuse. On occasion, as between Great Britain and France in 1756, formal declarations were issued some time after actual hostilities had begun. In 1898 the United States regarded the terms in which Spain replied to the ultimatum contained in the joint resolution of Congress on April 21 as equivalent to a declaration of war and thereupon commenced hostilties without delay. The formal declaration of war, issued on April 25, dated the existence of hostilities back to April 21. A serious charge brought against Japan by Russia in 1904 of treachery in the attack upon the Russian fleet at Port Arthur two days before the declaration of war showed the necessity for a general international agreement upon the subject.

Three years later the subject was brought before the Second Hague Conference, and a rule of treaty law was adopted in the form of a Convention (III) Relative to the Opening of Hostilities. This convention provided that hostilities between the contracting powers "must not commence without previous and explicit warning, in the form either of a reasoned declaration of war or of an ultimatum with conditional declaration of war." [3]

The effect of the provisions of the Hague Convention was, for the powers that ratified it, to fix an unequivocal date for the commencement of war instead of the less certain date of the first act of hostilities. Moreover, it assured a definite statement of the grounds upon which the war was undertaken. It did not, however, preclude the possibility of a surprise attack in case the ultimatum was immediately followed by hostilities. In the case of the Austro-Hungarian forty-eight-hour ultimatum to Serbia in 1914 the violation of good faith lay not in the failure to give warning that hostilities were about to commence, but in the fact that negotiations had not been in progress, and the state against which the ultimatum was directed was not aware that a crisis was at hand.

---

[2] Grotius held that a war to be just must be "publicly decreed." *De jure belli ac pacis*, Eng. trans., Bk. III, Chap. III, § V. Vattel looked upon a declaration of war as "necessary as a last effort to end the dispute without shedding of blood, by making use of fear to bring the enemy to a sense of justice." *Droit des gens*, Eng. trans., Bk. III, § 51.

[3] Art. 1. *Treaties and Conventions*, Vol. II, p. 2259.

War without a declaration: "Pearl Harbor." In 1931 Japan evaded the necessity of a declaration of war against China by pretending that the invasion of Manchuria was not "war";[4] and the same device was resorted to in 1937.[5] In 1935 Italy undertook military operations against Ethiopia without a formal declaration of war,[6] as did Germany against Poland in 1939,[7] although in both cases the failure to observe the Hague Convention occurred under circumstances which indicated the danger of an attack without the explicit warning called for. The attack by Germany upon Russia on June 22, 1941, was, however, not only without a declaration of war or an ultimatum, but even without preliminary negotiations making Russia aware of the danger.[8] On December 7, 1941, Japan attacked the United States at Pearl Harbor without a declaration of war or a formal ultimatum; but in this case negotiations had been in progress long enough to constitute an informal ultimatum. The treachery consisted in commencing hostilities before the explicit warning called for by the Hague Convention had been given.[9]

Action under the United Nations Charter. The Hague Convention may now be regarded as having lost its legal character. In the event of the necessity of collective action by the United Nations, whether to meet acts of aggression under the Charter or in answer to the need of maintaining law and order, the use of force by the United Nations would not be considered as "war" in the technical sense, and there would be under the circumstances no element of surprise. The discussions in the General Assembly preceding the decision of the United Nations to maintain the unity of the Congo obviously disposed of any violation of the Hague Convention even if it had been considered as in effect. Apart from collective action by the United Nations there is still the possibility of a case of self-defense under Article 51 of the Charter, but here again the circumstances would practically preclude a surprise attack.

Is it to be expected that a state in possession of atomic weapons would forego the advantages of a surprise attack if it were determined to

[4] *Events Leading up to World War II*, p. 4. See above, pp. 607, 643, 660, where the distinction between hostilities and technical "war" is pointed out.

[5] *Events*, p. 127; *Documents on Int. Affairs 1937*, p. 659.

[6] Italy appears to have proceeded after the manner of Japanese hostilities in Manchuria in 1931, as if Ethiopia were unworthy of a declaration of war. For the report of the committee of the Council of the League of Nations, holding that the hostilities constituted "war" in the sense of the Covenant, see League of Nations, *Official Journal*, 1935, p. 1223.

[7] See Dept. of State *Bulletin*, Vol. IV, p. 224; *Events Leading up to World War II*, p. 210.

[8] *Bulletin*, Vol. V, p. 556; *Events*, p. 286. In like manner Belgium, Luxemburg, and the Netherlands were invaded without warning on May 9, 1940; Yugoslavia on April 6, 1941. Greece was invaded by Italy after a three-hour ultimatum. Finland was invaded by Russia on November 29, 1939, after a declaration on the 28th that Russia considered itself released from the treaty of nonaggression.

[9] *Events*, pp. 307 ff. For editorial comment upon the act of treachery, see L. H. Woolsey, C. C. Hyde, and E. C. Stowell, *Am. Journal*, Vol. 36 (1942), pp. 77, 83, 87.

press its case to the end? It is estimated that a surprise attack by long-range missiles would, if successful, give an immediate advantage of some 60 percent in the contest. Under existing circumstances, the United States must assume the possibility of a surprise attack and be as prepared for it as every instrument of prevention will permit. The mere suggestion of a declaration of war by the other party would be naive. Strategy would consist in being able to receive the first knock-out blow and be able to rise and deliver an equally devastating blow against the opponent—the high-water mark of the futility of the resort to nuclear weapons, but the low-water mark of the maintenance of an adequate system of defense.

B. LAWFUL COMBATANTS

As late as the seventeenth century no clear distinction was recognized between the regular armed forces of a state and able-bodied citizens who, upon the approach of the enemy, might take up arms to defend their country. As Vattel put it in 1758: "In former times, and especially in small States, as soon as war was declared every man became a soldier; the entire people took up arms and carried on the war." [10] Even those who made no resistance were at times not spared when the discipline of armies became lax and passion ran high.[11] Conditions improved during the succeeding centuries, and it came to be accepted that unarmed citizens were not subject to attack provided they themselves took no part in hostilities. There remained, however, the difficult question whether individual citizens taking up arms independently of the organized forces of their country or groups of citizens rising en masse upon the approach of the enemy were to be allowed the privileges of combatants engaged in lawful warfare.

Levies en masse; guerrillas. The Instructions for the Government of Armies of the United States in the Field issued during the American Civil War made a distinction between "partisans," who were soldiers belonging to a corps detached from the main army and acting under the authority of the commander-in-chief and who were held entitled to be treated as prisoners of war, and on the other hand bodies of men who committed hostilities "without commission, without being part and portion of the organized hostile army, and without sharing continuously in the war," and who were to be treated "summarily as highway robbers or pirates." [12] The Instructions further recognized the right of the population of an invaded territory to rise en masse to resist the invader.[13]

[10] *Droit des gens,* Eng. trans., Bk. III, Chap. II, § 9.

[11] Compare the plea made by Grotius in favor of children, women, and other noncombatants. *De jure belli ac pacis,* Bk. III, Chap. IX, §§ VIII-XII.

[12] No. 82. For the status of the Confederate Partisan Rangers, see Bordwell, *The Law of War between Belligerents,* p. 79.

[13] Nos. 51, 52.

In 1899, at the Hague Peace Conference, an effort was made to reconcile the conflicting points of view of the larger states with regular standing armies and the smaller states which might be obliged to improvise their defense forces. The Regulations attached to the Convention Respecting the Laws and Customs of War on Land laid down conditions under which "the laws, rights, and duties of war" might apply to militia and volunteer corps as well as to the "army" proper; [14] and they also provided that the inhabitants of a territory might upon the approach of the enemy spontaneously take up arms to resist the invading troops and must be regarded as belligerents provided that they conformed to the conditions of carrying arms openly and respecting the laws and customs of war.[15]

The provisions of the Hague Regulations broke down seriously in the First World War and even more seriously in the Second. Once the decision was taken by Germany to violate the neutrality of Belgium in 1914, military necessity made it imperative for the German army to overcome the resistance of the inhabitants both to the passage of troops and to the permanent occupation of the territory. The German interpretation of the legality of levies en masse was applied rigorously,[16] and unauthorized acts of hostility committed upon the approach of the enemy by the inhabitants of towns and villages were punished with great severity. Sniping, whether on the part of individuals or of groups, was repressed not only by the execution of the offenders but by the burning of houses and the execution of hostages taken as a rule from among the older and more important personages of the district.[17] On occasion hostages were used as a screen to protect the column of the enemy as it entered a new village.

During the Second World War the same practice was followed of holding an entire village responsible for the resistance of unauthorized individuals. The speed with which the invading armies moved, the wide area of territory covered by them on some fronts and the mountainous character of the territory on other fronts made resistance by small groups of guerrillas and partisans feasible, and it was to be expected that the invader would not recognize them as lawful combatants.[18] At times, as in the uprising in Warsaw under General Bor in 1944, the status of the

[14] For the text of the convention, see *Treaties and Conventions*, Vol. II, p. 2269; *Hague Conventions*, p. 100.

[15] Art. 2. Compare *Instructions*, No. 51.

[16] See *German War Book*, Morgan's trans., Chap. 1. The German requirements were that levies en masse should be organized in the same manner as volunteer corps and wear a distinctive mark visible at a distance.

[17] For details and references, see Garner, *International Law and the World War*, Vol. I, Chap. XII.

[18] See I. P. Trainin, "Questions of Guerrilla Warfare in the Law of War," and L. Nurick and R. W. Barrett, "Legality of Guerrilla Forces under the Laws of War," *Am. Journal*, Vol. 40 (1946), pp. 534, 563.

forces of resistance would have been difficult to determine even if the invader had had any concern for the legality of his acts. The rules of military occupation entered to complicate the situation, which did not permit in any case the making of fine distinctions between lawful and unlawful combatants. The irony of "laws of war" was illustrated here as well as in other phases of the war where the judgment of individual commanders determined what was lawful and unlawful.

C. INSTRUMENTS OF WARFARE

It is part of the irony of "laws of war" that attempts to prohibit instruments of warfare of a particularly destructive or painful character have been in each case doomed to evasion or open defeat. The prohibition of the use of poison goes back to the Code of Manu, and it entered into the code of the ancient Greeks and Romans as well as that of medieval writers; but practice often failed to conform to principle.[19] The Second Lateran Council, meeting in 1139, issued a prohibition of the use of the crossbow and the arbalist, although the injunction proved ineffective.[20] Again, the harquebus was condemned, but without effect upon international practice.[21] The attempt of chivalry to bar as unworthy of brave men the newer inventions of science failed, apparently on grounds similar to those advanced in more modern times. The Instructions of 1863 forbade the use of poison in any manner, "be it to poison wells or food or arms." It remained, however, an open question whether the pollution of drinking waters by methods which involved no deception, such as the contamination of a well or stream by dead cattle, was in violation of customary law.[22]

Prohibition of explosive bullets. In 1868 a conference of European military delegates met at St. Petersburg to take action with regard to the new explosive bullets, and a declaration was adopted containing both a statement of general principles and a specific agreement forbidding the use of "any projectile of a weight below 400 grammes (about fourteen ounces avoirdupois) which is either explosive or charged with fulminating or inflammable substances." [23] The principles upon which the declaration proceeded were: (1) that the progress of civilization should have the effect of alleviating as much as possible the calamities of war; (2) that the only legitimate object which states should endeavor to accomplish during war was to weaken the military forces of the

[19] See Walker, *History of the Law of Nations*, Vol. I, pp. 42, 56, 72.
[20] *Ibid.*, Vol. I, p. 125, note 1.
[21] The student may be reminded of the classic words of the Chevalier Bayard who, when dying in 1524 of a wound inflicted by a harquebus, thanked God he had never shown mercy to a musketeer.
[22] For a discussion of instances occurring during the American Civil War and the Boer War of 1899-1902, see Spaight, *War Rights on Land*, p. 84.
[23] For the text of the declaration, see Higgins, *Hague Peace Conferences*, p. 5.

enemy; (3) that for that purpose it was sufficient to disable the greatest possible number of men; and (4) that this object would be exceeded by the employment of arms which needlessly aggravated the suffering of disabled men or rendered their death inevitable. The Declaration was obviously open to attack on ground of its logical inconsistencies, and it must be regarded as an effort to prevent certain excesses of cruelty under circumstances which did not admit the prohibition of others. Why, argued the critics, save a man from an explosive bullet only to have him blown to bits by shrapnel from a cannon? [24]

Prohibitions adopted at the Hague Conferences. Further restrictions upon the instruments of warfare were laid down by the First and Second Hague Conferences. Article 23a of the Regulations attached to the Convention Respecting the Laws and Customs of War on Land forbade the employment of poison or poisoned arms.[25] Article 23e forbade the employment of "arms, projectiles or material of a nature to cause superfluous injury." In addition, three declarations were drawn up, although not signed by a sufficient number of states to give them general validity.[26] The first of these, as renewed in 1907, prohibited for a period extending to the close of the Third Peace Conference "the discharge of projectiles and explosives from balloons and by other new methods of a similar nature." France, Germany, Italy, Russia, and Japan refused their signatures when the declaration was renewed in 1907.[27] The second declaration embodied an agreement, without time limit, "to abstain from the use of projectiles the sole object of which is the diffusion of asphyxiating and deleterious gases." The United States delegation refused its signature, Captain Mahan pointing out that the prohibition was being adopted in ignorance of the practical effects of such shells, and that the restriction was inconsistent with other instruments and methods of warfare.[28] A third declaration, also without time limit, contained an agreement, "to abstain from the use of bullets which expand or flatten easily in the human body, such as bullets with a hard envelope which does not entirely

[24] There was, indeed, little logic in the humanitarian sentiment of the period. Statesmen simply could not foresee the practicability of putting restrictions upon war itself.

[25] For the text of the convention, see *Treaties and Conventions,* Vol. II, p. 2269; *Hague Conventions,* p. 100.

[26] For the texts of the declarations, see Higgins, *Hague Peace Conferences,* pp. 484 ff.; *Hague Conventions,* pp. 220 ff.

[27] In explanation of the refusal of his signature in 1907 the French delegate stated that the problem of aerial navigation was progressing so rapidly that it was unwise to "forbid in advance the right to profit by new discoveries" which might be more effective with respect to the legitimate objects of attack without being less humane. *Proceedings,* Vol. III, p. 147. In view of the refusal of so many of the leading powers to ratify the declaration, it can scarcely be regarded as binding even between those that ratified, general ratification being doubtless an implied condition.

[28] Higgins, *op. cit.,* p. 493, gives the argument at length. See also *Proceedings of the Hague Peace Conferences,* Conf. of 1899, pp. 283, 366.

cover the core, or is pierced with incisions." These bullets, known as "dumdum" bullets, after the arsenal near Calcutta where they were first made, were introduced by the British as a means of putting out of action Indians who could not be stopped by the use of ordinary bullets. The declaration was not signed in 1899 by the United States or Great Britain, owing to their preference for a prohibition framed in more general terms; [29] and the United States continued its opposition even after Great Britain had acceded to the declaration in 1907.

During the First World War the only restrictions which obtained legal recognition were those relating to the traditional forms of the use of poison and to dumdum bullets. Accusations were made on both sides of violations of the prohibition against the poisoning of wells and the use of dumdum bullets, but it would appear that they were justified only in exceptional instances.[30] Germany protested against the use of shotguns by the American army, but the United States refused to admit the obligation to abandon them. In the spring of 1915 the German army began using asphyxiating and poisonous gases, and the British and French armies promptly retaliated. With the invention of adequate masks the earlier denunciation of "gas attacks" as illegal [31] was succeeded by competition in the discovery of more deadly gases, and by the close of the war the new instruments of warfare were in regular use.

The Washington treaty of 1922. Upon the return of peace the question of the use of poisonous gases was reconsidered upon its merits, and at the Washington Conference of 1921-1922 a treaty was signed by the powers represented at the conference which declared that "the use in war of asphyxiating, poisonous or other gases, and all analogous liquids, materials or devices, having been justly condemned by the general opinion of the civilized world and a prohibition of such use having been declared in treaties to which a majority of the civilized Powers are parties," the signatory powers assented to the prohibition and invited other nations to adhere to the agreement in order that the prohibition might be "universally accepted as a part of international law." [32] The

[29] For the argument of Captain Crozier in favor of permitting modified dumdum bullets and prohibiting explosive bullets, see *Proceedings of the Hague Peace Conferences,* Conf. of 1899, pp. 79 ff. Hyde, writing in 1922, justified the explosive bullet, "by reason of its potentiality in destroying human life," and condemned expansive bullets as offering "no military advantage commensurate with the harm inflicted." The same position is taken in the edition of 1945, although in modified terms. *Int. Law,* ed. 1922, Vol. II, § 661.

[30] For a review of the controversy, see Garner, *International Law and the World War,* Vol. I, Chap. X.

[31] The question whether the use of gas, by the methods employed, came within the prohibitions of the Hague Convention was reviewed by Garner, *op. cit.,* Chap. X. At this distance of time the distinction between gases spread by the use of projectiles and gases emitted from cylinders and blown toward the enemy by the wind seems somewhat subtle.

[32] Art. V. For the text of the treaty, see *Treaties and Conventions,* Vol. III, p. 3116.

prohibition, however, remained unratified, owing possibly to the fact that the treaty also regulated the use of submarines. On June 17, 1925, the Protocol Prohibiting the Use in War of Asphyxiating, Poisonous or other Gases, and of Bacteriological Methods of Warfare [33] was opened for signature at Geneva, and was ratified by a large number of states. The protocol followed the Washington treaty in reciting the condemnation of gases "and of all analogous liquids, materials or devices" by the general opinion of the civilized world and the prohibition of their use by a majority of states; and it called for the universal acceptance of this prohibition and its extension to the use of bacteriological methods of warfare. The failure, however, of certain important states, notably the United States and Japan, to ratify the agreement made it impossible for other states to rely upon it, so that research work for the discovery of new and more effective gases continued as before.[34]

V-bombs and atomic bombs. During the Second World War two new instruments of warfare were used, both giving rise to controversy as to their legality. Germany used rocket bombs fired from bases on the coast of Holland against London and other British cities, and the United States used the atomic bomb against the Japanese cities of Hiroshima and Nagasaki. The illegality of the V-bomb lay in the fact that of its very nature it could not be aimed with accuracy against its proper target, and that the speed with which it came made it impossible to give warning to the inhabitants of the city to take to shelter.[35] On the other hand the illegality of the atomic bomb consisted in the fact that the range of its action and its destructiveness were so great as to make it impossible to observe the restrictions upon the bombardment of undefended cities.[36]

Control of the atomic bomb. Following the war the General Assembly of the United Nations adopted, on January 24, 1946, a resolution creating a Commission on Atomic Energy, the object of which was to make specific proposals for extending between all nations the exchange of basic scientific information for peaceful ends, for the control of atomic energy to the extent necessary to ensure its use only for peaceful purposes, for the elimination from national armaments of atomic and other

---

[33] For the text of the Protocol, see *L. of N. Treaty Series,* Vol. XC, p. 65; Hudson, *Int. Legislation,* Vol. III, p. 1670.

[34] The vicious circle was obvious, being the result of the necessity of individual self-protection in the absence of an international organization capable of assuring the general peace by the collective action of the community. It appeared to be believed that poisonous gases were too effective a weapon to permit a nation to forego preparations for their use in reliance upon the good faith of a possible opponent.

[35] For a description of the V-bomb and its effects, see N. Tangye, "Flying Bombs and Rockets," *Foreign Affairs,* Vol. 24 (1945-1946), p. 40.

[36] For comment upon the legal aspects of the atomic bomb, see E. Stowell, P. B. Potter, E. Borchard, and E. Turlington, *Am. Journal,* Vol. 39 (1945), pp. 784, 788; Vol. 40 (1946), pp. 161, 165. Secretary of War Stimson's defense of the use of the atomic bomb may be found in "The Decision to Use the Atomic Bomb," *Harpers Magazine,* February, 1947.

weapons adaptable to mass destruction, and for effective safeguards by way of inspection and other means to protect complying states against the hazards of violations and evasions.[37] On its part the United States submitted to the Commission a series of proposals looking to the progressive attainment of the objectives set forth in the resolution of the General Assembly. The Soviet Union countered with a draft international convention by which the contracting parties were to agree to prohibit the production and employment of weapons based on the use of atomic energy, and to destroy existing stocks of such weapons.[38]

The chief obstacle in reaching an agreement lay in the unwillingness of the United States to give up the possession of bombs already made and the continued production of bombs without being given adequate assurances, in the form of international inspection, that the obligations undertaken would be mutually observed; and in the unwillingness of the representative of the Soviet Union to accept the plan of inspection, which, it was alleged, conflicted with the principle of sovereignty. In consequence, the Soviet Union refused to enter into any agreement which would not leave the final decision with the Security Council, so that the veto power could be used to check measures that might be taken by the International Atomic Development Authority proposed by the United States.

The Test Ban Treaty. The succeeding years were marked by a long succession of technical conferences and nuclear test ban negotiations, in which the inability of the United States and the Soviet Union to reach an agreement did not differ substantially from the conflicting attitudes of 1946, distrust of bare promises on the one hand and unwillingness to permit inspection on the other. In the meantime new and more destructive weapons were developed and new bases established, with corresponding tension. With the manufacture of atomic weapons becoming less costly and their manufacture being taken up by new countries it remains an open question whether the danger of their use, inadvertently, has become greater or less great. The test ban treaty signed on October 6, 1963, between the United States and the Soviet Union, and adhered to by numerous other states, was only a limitation upon new inventions and improvements of the atomic bomb; it did not extend to the limitation

[37] For the text of the resolution of the General Assembly and the terms of reference of the Commission, see *The International Control of Atomic Energy*, Dept. of State publication No. 2702, p. 132. For the "principle of trusteeship" on the part of the United States, see *ibid.*, pp. 10, 106. A resolution of the General Assembly, adopted December 13, 1946, urged the Security Council to expedite consideration of a draft convention for the creation of an international system of control and inspection in connection with the general problem of disarmament. The International Atomic Energy Agency is intergovernmental, but not a specialized agency of the United Nations.

[38] The proposals of the United States and the memoranda accompanying them may be found in *The International Control of Atomic Energy*, pp. 138 ff. For the draft convention proposed by the Soviet Union, see *ibid.*, p. 209.

of existing stocks of atomic warheads or methods of long-range bombardment.[39]

Would the use of the atomic bomb be lawful in a future war? The question obviously falls within the prohibition of war itself under the provisions of the Charter of the United Nations. As observed above, it is not to be expected that the United Nations itself, in resorting to force to restrain a state which has had recourse to violence, would go beyond the most moderate measures called for by the situation; and the use of the bomb by the state violating its obligations under the Charter not to have recourse to force would clearly be illegal. In consequence the sole permissible use of the bomb would be in self-defense against a state which has illegally used it; and here we have the paradox of a situation in which a state would be justified in possessing an unlawful instrument of warfare in order to deter another state from using an unlawful instrument, the two negatives making a positive—a precarious situation in view of the possible uncertainty of the source from which the bomb came in case an irresponsible state should come to obtain possession of the instrument and use it in a moment of madness.

D. METHODS OF WARFARE

Obligation to give quarter.   In respect to methods of warfare, as in respect to instruments, the same difficulty arose of determining what conduct was admissible, or legal, under the circumstances of the particular case in hand. Certain general principles were accepted, but their application to concrete situations presented numerous points of dispute. In respect to methods of warfare affecting the combatant armies only, custom as well as convention declared it unlawful "to kill or wound an enemy who, having laid down his arms, no longer having means of defense, has surrendered at discretion." [40] It was likewise forbidden to announce in advance that no quarter would be given. The latter rule presented no difficulties in practice. It negatived the earlier custom of attempting to intimidate the enemy to surrender in cases where a small number held a strategic position from which it would be costly for the larger force to dislodge them.[41]

The rule forbidding the killing of those who have surrendered was more difficult of application. The practical conditions of a frontal attack

[39] For the text of the Test Ban Treaty, see Dept. of State *Bulletin*, August 12, 1963, p. 239. For official comment, *ibid.*, August 26, p. 316; September 2, p. 350; September 23, p. 454. But compare H. J. Morgenthau, "The Four Paradoxes of Nuclear Strategy," *Am. Pol. Science Rev.*, March, 1964, p. 23.

[40] Hague Regulations, Art. 23c.

[41] For a discussion of the former attitude of commanding officers toward besieged towns which presumptuously dared to hold out against superior forces when the capture of the fortress was regarded as certain, see Vattel, *Droit des gens*, Bk. III, § 143. Hall, *International Law*, § 129, note. For a modern instance see Spaight, *War Rights on Land*, p. 99.

frequently made it impossible for the attacking troops to "take prisoners." The necessity of pushing deeper into the enemy's lines, the difficulty of disposing of those who had surrendered without endangering the rear of the attacking troops, and the practical impossibility for officers to restrain themselves or their men when in the heat of action led to numerous violations of the general principle.[42] The American Instructions of 1863 recognized the right of a commander to refuse quarter in cases of imperative necessity, when the presence of prisoners would endanger the safety of the army,[43] and the exception was doubtless consistent with international practice. During both the First and the Second World War there were numerous accusations of refusal to give quarter where the circumstances permitted it, a particular unhappy instance taking place during the counter-offensive of General Rundstedt against the American invasion forces in December, 1944.[44]

Use of deceit. Ruses of war or stratagems were recognized by international law as legitimate means of deceiving the enemy, and their customary use was confirmed by the Hague Regulations.[45] Their use, however, was restricted by the condition that they must not involve a violation of good faith. Hence they might not be resorted to in cases where the enemy had been taken off his guard by any of the recognized signs, such as flags of truce or the Red Cross emblem, of a desire to establish communication or to enjoy immunity from attack. Nor might the agents appointed to enter into a parley with the enemy perform any hostile act under cover of their pacific character. A debatable issue was presented by the use of the uniform of the enemy or of his national flag. The Regulations forbade the "improper" use of these emblems,[46] but the vagueness of the prohibition would seem to have left the question to be settled by the customary law.[47] The customary rule merely prescribed that in such cases the disguise must be dropped before action commenced; but it was pointed out that there was no logic in a rule which permitted a belligerent to lure the enemy to a position by a form of deceit which became unlawful only when it was too late for the enemy

[42] For instances in illustration of the practical problems presented to attacking forces, see Spaight, *op. cit.*, pp. 91 ff.

[43] *Instructions,* No. 60. See, however, *Rules of Land Warfare,* 1914, No. 183. The *Rules* of 1940 merely repeat the Hague Regulations.

[44] See protest of Department of State, released December 29. *Bulletin,* Vol. XI, p. 848. For the orders given to German commanders to refuse the surrender of members of Allied "commando" units, see *Nazi Conspiracy and Aggression,* p. 58.

[45] Art. 24. "Ruses of war and the employment of methods necessary for obtaining information about the enemy and the country are considered lawful."

[46] Art. 23f. It is forbidden "to make improper use of a flag of truce, of the national flag, or of military insignia and uniform of the enemy, as also the distinctive signs of the Geneva Convention." See V. Jobst III, "Is the Wearing of the Enemy's Uniform a Violation of the Laws of War?," *Am. Journal,* Vol. 35 (1941), p. 435.

[47] Compare the discussion of the subject by Grotius, *De jure belli ac pacis,* Bk. III, Chap. I.

to benefit by the removal of the disguise.[48] By an old customary law, confirmed by the Hague Regulations, it is forbidden "to kill or wound treacherously individuals belonging to the hostile nation or army." [49] Apart from the above cases involving bad faith, deceit was widely used in warfare, and under the name of "strategy" it was the deciding factor of many battles.

Spying. The use of spies in time of war was a measure of recognized legality, notwithstanding the severe penalty inflicted upon the spy if caught by the enemy. In international practice, however, difficulties arose from lack of a sharp distinction between spies, scouts, despatch-bearers, and war traitors. The Hague Regulations of 1899 followed the customary law in making the essence of spying consist in acting "clandestinely or on false pretenses" with the object of obtaining information in the zone of operations of a belligerent and of communicating it to the enemy.[50] It was further provided that soldiers not in disguise, properly known as "scouts," might penetrate the enemy's lines to obtain information without being considered spies. So also despatch bearers, whether soldiers or civilians, were not considered spies if they carried out their missions openly. Persons sent in balloons to deliver despatches or maintain communication between different parts of the army or territory came within the same class. Upon the outbreak of the Russo-Japanese War, Russia announced the intention of treating as spies war correspondents who should communicate news to the enemy by wireless telegraphy; but the threat was not carried into effect.[51] The regulations provided for the trial of spies before punishment, and they emphasized the legality of the use of spies by providing that a spy who had escaped and was afterward captured was to be treated as a prisoner of war.[52] The American Rules of Land Warfare emphasized the customary rule that no distinction of sex was made in respect to the penalty inflicted upon spies.[53]

Sieges and bombardments. Possibly the most difficult problem of the "laws of war" was the attempt to regulate sieges and bombardments so as to permit the belligerent to reduce an enemy stronghold and at the same time to spare noncombatants as far as possible and to do no more harm than necessary to public buildings not used for military purposes. From the earliest times sieges figured prominently in wars, and the *Iliad* of Homer has made the seven-year siege of Troy an indelible memory.

[48] See Hall, *International Law*, § 187; Hyde, *International Law*, Vol. II, § 659. For the use of the enemy's flag at sea, see below, p. 700.

[49] Art. 23b. Vattel quotes the classic instance of the rejection by the Roman consuls of the proposal of the physician of Pyrrhus that he should poison his master. Bk. III, § 155.

[50] Art. 29.

[51] See Hershey, *International Law and Diplomacy of the Russo-Japanese War*, pp. 115 ff.

[52] Arts. 30-31.

[53] No. 204. For the case of Edith Cavell, see below, p. 684.

Romantic legends center around the sieges of medieval town-fortresses, and the "relief" of a besieged city, as of Vienna by the Polish king, Sobieski, in 1683, marked at times a turning point in the history of civilization. But with the spread of Christianity the doctors of the Church were hard put to it to determine the limits of the use of force in carrying out the siege of a town or city.[54] Reduction by starvation was a regular method, and it bore upon combatants and noncombatants alike. Must a besieging commander permit the exit from the city of "useless mouths" which consumed supplies without contributing to the defense? Might the water supply of a city be cut off with the result of spreading disease among the people? How could the fire of cannon be directed so as reach military objectives and yet not destroy adjacent churches and monuments? How could the general of an attacking force restrain his troops when taking a city by assault? These and other problems troubled moralists and jurists alike, and no acceptable solution was found for them.[55]

It was not until the meeting of the Hague Conference in 1899 that conventional law came to supplement the uncertain customary law. The Regulations attached to the Convention Respecting the Laws and Customs of War on Land provided that "The attack or bombardment of towns, villages, dwellings, or buildings which are undefended, is prohibited." [56] The Regulations of 1907 went a step further by emphasizing "the attack or bombardment by any means whatever," so as to include bombardment by projectiles from balloons or airships.[57] Before commencing bombardment, except in case of an assault, the commander of the attacking force must do all in his power to warn the authorities.[58] Buildings devoted to religion, art, science, and charity; historic monuments; hospitals, must be spared as far as possible; and it was the duty of the besieged to indicate these buildings by special visible

---

[54] Compare Vitoria, De bello, Art. I; De jure belli, No. 52, in Scott, The Spanish Origin of International Law; Suarez, De bello, in ibid.

[55] Vattel gives what was in his day a progressive interpretation of the obligations of the belligerent. See Droit des gens, Bk. III, Chaps. VIII, IX. For a review of modern practice, see Spaight, op. cit., pp. 174 ff.

[56] Art. 25.

[57] Higgins, op. cit., p. 269. In view of the other loopholes of evasion in the Convention, the amendment added nothing to its actual scope.

[58] Art. 26. The U. S. Rules of Land Warfare, 1914, following the Instructions of 1863, pointed out that "surprise may be a necessity," in which case there is no obligation to give warning (No. 217). The phrase is omitted in the Rules of 1940, but the principle is retained (No. 50). In the case of Coenca Brothers v. Germany, Greco-German Mixed Arbitral Tribunal, Dec. 1, 1927, the tribunal held that Art. 26 of the Hague Regulations, requiring that warning be given by land forces before bombardment, was applicable to aircraft as well, so that the bombardment of Salonika by Germany in 1916, otherwise justifiable because of the occupation of the city by Allied troops, was unlawful and gave rise to a proper claim of damages. See Annual Digest, 1927-1928, p. 570.

signs.[59] The Regulations unfortunately failed to define what constituted a defended as distinct from an undefended town, and in the absence of such a definition the prohibition was of little value.[60]

Aerial raids during the First World War. Doubtless there would have been little left of the prohibitions against bombardment during the First World War even if the development of the airplane as an instrument of combat had not come to give a definition of "defended town" suited to its own purposes. When the German army set up "Big Bertha" at a distance of seventy-five miles from Paris there was little reason to believe that the aim of the monster gun could be accurate. But was not Paris a defended town in the sense that it was surrounded by armies whose chief purpose was to prevent the taking of the city? [61] When the German fleet bombarded Scarborough, Hartlepool, and Whitby, the justification offered by Germany was the presence of troops, barracks, and land batteries.[62] The coroner's jury at Scarborough declared that the victims of the bombardment had met their death as the result of a "murderous attack"; but it would have been difficult to prove the case by the terms of the Hague Convention. Aerial raids were directed against railway terminals, docks, munition factories, and storehouses. Was the presence of these sufficient to convert London from an undefended city into a defended one? On both sides the belligerents insisted that their aviators were instructed to "confine their attacks to points of military importance"; but, assuming every effort on the part of the aviators to obey instructions, the mechanical possibilities of accurate aim at great heights and high speeds made it impossible to carry out the instructions without desisting altogether from the attack. Towns within the zone of the operations of the land forces were obviously subject to direct attack, and in many cases the concentration of troops in such towns before the civilian population could be removed made it impracticable to draw any distinction between combatants and noncombatants as objects of bombardment.[63]

All towns become defended towns. The inevitable loss of life on the part of noncombatants would doubtless have led to charges of violation of the laws of war no matter what the intention of the belligerent governments had been. But reprisals by one belligerent for the alleged excesses

[59] The Regulations obviously failed to anticipate night bombing and blackouts.

[60] The subject was, however, discussed in connection with maritime bombardment, but without result.

[61] An "open town" in the traditional sense was one which the enemy could enter without opposition. But that was before the invention of weapons which could fire over the heads of the intervening forces of defense.

[62] The same problem was presented in maritime war. See below, p. 700.

[63] The subject is discussed at length in Garner, *International Law and the World War*, Vol. I, Chap. XIX. See also, Spaight, *Air Power and War Rights; Air Power and the Cities;* Royse, *Aërial Bombardment and the International Regulation of Warfare.*

of the other soon made the argument from legal obligation meaningless. Before the war closed in 1918 the bombardment of open towns outside the region of military operations had become common practice.[64] A town was now a defended town simply because it was located in the enemy country and was within range of attack by airplanes.

Proposed code of aerial warfare. The experience of the First World War proved conclusively that the necessary regulation of the use of aircraft in war could not be obtained by the mere application to airships of the existing rules applicable to land and maritime warfare, inadequate as were the latter within their own particular sphere. So important had airships become to both armies and navies for scouting and observation service and so effective was their work of destruction that the proposal of restrictions upon their use in war did not seem feasible to the leading air powers at the time of the adoption of the Aerial Navigation Convention in 1919.[65] Article 38 of that agreement expressly left to the parties freedom of action in time of war. The Washington Conference of 1921-1922 likewise found the problem of restrictions too difficult for immediate settlement, and in consequence it adopted on February 4, 1922, a resolution for the appointment of a commission of jurists to consider the question whether the existing rules of international law adequately covered new methods of attack and defense resulting from the "new agencies of warfare" developed since 1907, and, if not, what changes in the existing rules ought to be adopted in consequence.[66] The Commission, consisting of delegates of Great Britain, United States, France, Japan, and the Netherlands, prepared two sets of rules, Part I dealing with the control of radio in time of war and Part II dealing with aerial warfare.[67] While neither set of rules was adopted, the provisions of the aerial code were significant as showing that the framers of the code still had hope that the use of the airplane might be kept within the limits of land and naval warfare.

The question of bombardment. The draft code sought to exclude definitely certain purposes of bombardment, namely, the terrorizing of the civilian population, the destruction of nonmilitary property, the injuring of noncombatants, and the enforcement of requisitions in kind and contributions. It laid down the generalization that "aerial bombard-

[64] See the evidence presented in the *Report of the Commission of Responsibilities,* Appendix I, 1919.

[65] See above, p. 484.

[66] For the text of the resolution, see *Am. Journal,* Vol. 16 (1922), Supp., p. 74.

[67] For the text of the draft code, see *Am. Journal,* Vol. 17 (1923), Supp., p. 245; J. B. Moore, *International Law and Some Current Illusions,* pp. 210 ff., where the General Report may be found. For comment, see W. L. Rodgers, "The Laws of War Concerning Aviation and Radio," *Am. Journal,* Vol. 17 (1923), p. 629; J. W. Garner, *ibid.,* Vol. 18 (1924), p. 56, where the provisions of the code are examined in detail and controversial points discussed.

ment is legitimate only when directed at a military objective," that is, an objective the destruction of which would constitute a "distinct military advantage to the belligerent." Certain legitimate objectives were then enumerated, such as military establishments and munition factories; but even these were excluded when they could not be bombarded without the "indiscriminate bombardment" of the civilian population. The bombardment of cities and villages "not in the immediate neighborhood of the operations of land forces" was prohibited, and it was permitted in the immediate neighborhood of the operations of land forces only when "there exists a reasonable presumption that the military concentration is sufficiently important to justify such bombardment." The usual care to avoid as far as possible bombardment of buildings devoted to public worship, art, science, or charity was enjoined. Finally the code provided that, except in so far as was otherwise stipulated in the code itself or in maritime warfare conventions, the laws of war and neutrality applicable to land troops were applicable to aerial warfare.[68]

The Second World War.   No prophet was needed to foresee that the next war would be fought with no regard for the rules which the several governments were unwilling to adopt, and in the framing of which Germany and Russia had not been consulted. The bombardment of Warsaw and other Polish cities in 1939 was succeeded the following spring by the devastating bombardment of the neutral city of Rotterdam and the following fall by the indiscriminate bombardment of London and other British cities. With the growing power of the British and American air fleets began the equally indiscriminate bombing of German cities, ending in the almost complete destruction of Berlin, Munich, Hamburg, and numerous other centers of military movement and industrial life.[69] The war in the Far East witnessed in like manner the use of the airplane without regard for the lives of noncombatants or for churches and historic monuments. Was it lawful for an American task force to bombard Tokyo under conditions which precluded either warning in advance or accurate aim towards military objectives? The Japanese Government answered with the execution of the crew of planes forced down in combat.[70] Was it lawful to use the atomic bomb against Hiroshima and Nagasaki on August 6 and 9, 1945, without giving due warning of the danger to noncombatants? The devastation wrought by atomic bombs

[68] For comment upon the code and upon the impracticable character of some of its provisions, see Spaight, "Air Bombardment," *British Year Book,* Vol. IV (1923-24), p. 21. See also E. Colby, "Aerial Law and War Targets," *Am. Journal,* Vol. 19 (1925), p. 702; P. W. Williams, "Legitimate Targets in Aerial Bombardment," *ibid.,* Vol. 23 (1929), p. 570.

[69] The question of the legality of these bombardments was complicated by the argument of reprisals which, as in other cases, reduced the laws of war to the vanishing point.

[70] See note 131.

upon those two cities was destined to remain a symbol of what might be expected in future wars.[71]

Accompanying the development of more and more powerful atomic bombs was the establishment of permanent bases from which missiles with nuclear warheads could be fired at predetermined targets with greater accuracy than bombs could be dropped from airplanes. But the development of these new instruments carried with it no suggestion that there would be any return to the former rule of distinguishing between military objectives and churches and historical monuments. Rather the greater power of the missiles only made clearer the impossibility of doing so. Had the missile bases discovered by the United States under process of construction in Cuba in October 1962 been completed, Washington and its suburbs would have been exposed to an attack as devastating as that on Hiroshima. Atlantic Coast towns would have been sitting ducks waiting helplessly, and doubtless uneasily, for the fire of one who had persuaded himself that the United States was responsible for the plight in which his country found itself. The bases would have been too near for any measures of protection to be effective.

Seizure and destruction of property. The laws of war permitted the seizure and destruction of enemy property by a belligerent when military necessity demanded it. The earlier practice of wanton destruction complained of by Grotius [72] had long been formally condemned in principle and was virtually obsolete in practice at the time of the Hague Conferences. The Hague Regulations followed the customary law in forbidding the destruction and seizure of the enemy's property unless it be "imperatively demanded by the necessities of war." [73] The rule was thus a conditional one, and left to the determination of the belligerent army the circumstances under which military necessity demanded such measures. Custom and convention combined to draw a distinction between the right of a commander in the field to seize and destroy enemy property as an incident to offensive or defensive military operations and the limited right of an army of occupation to make use of enemy property as an incident to the effective administration of the country.[74] In the former case the right of the belligerent commander applied equally to

---

[71] See the references cited in note 36 above. The moral aspects of the problem have become almost a matter of daily discussion.

[72] While condemning wanton destruction, Grotius recognized the right of confiscation, going so far as to say that "By the law of nations not merely he who wages war for a just cause, but in a public war also any one at all becomes owner, without limit or restriction, of what he has taken from the enemy." *De jure belli ac pacis,* Eng. trans., Bk. III, Chap. VI, § II. Vattel, in 1758, was scarcely less drastic in his doctrines, including private property in "enemy property" and stating that the belligerent "takes possession, when he can, of the enemy's property, and confiscates it." *Droit des gens,* Eng. trans., Bk. III, §§ 73, 161.

[73] Art. 23f.

[74] Hague Regulations, Arts. 52-53.

public and to private property, and it was regularly exercised in connection with army supplies and storehouses, railways, munition factories, and other property of direct military value to the enemy. The exercise of the right with respect to property of a nonmilitary character was more debatable. Destruction of dwellings lying in the line of fire was common practice. On occasion, as at Atlanta in 1864, whole sections of a city were set on fire as a means of depriving the enemy of resources of food or shelter.[75] On the other hand, the burning of public buildings in Washington by British forces in 1814 was generally condemned.[76] The Hague regulations confirmed customary law in declaring that "the giving up to pillage of a town or place, even when taken by assault, is forbidden." [77] General devastation of property as a means of covering the retreat of an army was, however, a common practice of belligerents.

Devastation for military purposes. A more difficult problem was to determine how far the destruction of enemy property was justified, not in connection with direct hostilities, but as a means of cutting the enemy's lines of communication, eliminating his subsequent sources of supply, or intimidating the civilian population and inducing it to bring pressure upon the government to sue for peace. In 1864 General Sherman devastated a wide area from Atlanta to the sea in pursuance of an interpretation of military necessity which included the objects above mentioned, and shortly afterward the devastation of the Shenandoah Valley was carried out to the same end.[78] Devastation on a broad scale was carried out by Spain in Cuba in 1897. The practice of "concentrating" the civilian population in garrison towns, which accompanied the devastation, led to protests from the United States which ultimately formed part of its grounds of war.[79] In 1901 the British armies in South Africa interned the civilian population in "concentration camps," with the result of serious loss of life. At the same time the country was laid waste far and wide as a means of cutting off the supplies of the guerrilla forces.[80]

During the First World War the fixed lines of battle along the western front resulted in the destruction of entire towns and villages, such as Ypres and Mons, lying in the line of fire. Devastation for military purposes accompanied the retreat of the German armies on the western front in the spring of 1917. On the other hand numerous outrages occurred, such as the burning of the Louvain library and the destruction of the cathedral at Rheims, which were clearly in excess of military necessity, taking that term in its juridical sense.[81]

[75] For details, see Spaight, *War Rights on Land*, pp. 131, 307, 410.
[76] *Ibid.*, p. 112.
[77] Art. 28.
[78] For details, see Spaight, *ibid.*, pp. 133-135.
[79] Moore, *Digest*, Vol. VI, p. 130.
[80] For details, see Spaight, *ibid.*, p. 136.
[81] See J. W. Garner, "Some Questions of International Law in the European War," *Am. Journal*, Vol. 9 (1915), pp. 72, 93.

It remained for the Second World War to witness devastation on a scale which made mockery of the prohibitions of the Hague Conventions. Enemy property of every character was seized without regard to its public or private character. Vast areas in Russia were laid waste in the path of the advancing German armies and even more in the wake of their retreat. Historic monuments were reduced to ruins in the invasion of one country after another. If much of the destruction was unnecessary, much more was the inevitable accompaniment of hostilities on the greatest scale yet known.

Intimidation of the civilian population. Intimidation of the civilian population as a means of bringing about the surrender of the enemy's armies had long been an incident of warfare, although condemned by moralists and impliedly repudiated by the Hague Regulations. Even during the American Civil War, when a higher standard of conduct might have been expected than in other wars, both General Sherman and General Sheridan accepted the necessity of bringing war home to the civilian population as a means of terminating more speedily the military conflict.[82] Intimidation was doubtless the primary motive in the long-range bombardment of Paris during the First World War, and at least a secondary motive in the bombing of London. During the Second World War the technique of the *Blitzkrieg* was doubtless directed as much against the civilian population as against the opposing armies. In any case the wholesale exodus of the population from towns and villages was intended by the enemy to obstruct the movement of troops and thus facilitate conquest. In the unhappy event of an atomic war, whether delivering its warheads from airplanes, from submarines, or from missile bases, it is clear that any distinction between devastation for actual military purposes and devastation for its terroristic effect upon the civilian population would lose all meaning. Property could not be expected to receive more consideration than noncombatant lives. Intimidation of the civilian population would have already been exhausted in the anticipation of resort to such methods; there would be no one left to be intimidated.[83]

E. OCCUPATION OF ENEMY TERRITORY

International law possessed a separate set of rules governing the occupation of enemy territory by a belligerent when the latter had defeated or

---

[82] Bordwell cites General Sherman as saying that he attached "more importance to these deep incisions into the enemy's country, because this war differs from European wars in this particular; we are not only fighting hostile armies, but a hostile people, and must make old and young, rich and poor, feel the hard hand of war, as well as their organized armies." *Law of War*, p. 79. Similar views of General Sheridan are also cited, *ibid.*, p. 78. See Sherman's *Memoirs*, Vol. II, p. 227; Sheridan's *Memoirs*, Vol. I, p. 486.

[83] How total "total war" might become has offered a fertile field for novelists and script writers.

driven out the opposing army and had obtained, for the time being, control over the particular area. At the time Grotius wrote, no distinction was made between the temporary rights of an army of occupation and the permanent rights belonging to a belligerent as the result of conquest. Armies in possession of enemy territory exercised rights of sovereignty over it, and went at times so far as to recruit their forces from among the inhabitants of the country.[84] But by the middle of the seventeenth century a distinction came to be made between the provisional authority exercised by the belligerent army and the final status of the territory as determined by the treaty of peace.[85] The army of occupation was held to exercise temporary legal authority based upon the actual fact of possessing control over the territory. The character and scope of this authority were determined on the one hand by the military necessities of the belligerent army and on the other by the human interests and welfare of the civilian population of the occupied territory. The interaction of these two objectives of military occupation resulted in a series of compromises which formed the modern law.[86]

When occupation began; hostages. A preliminary issue was to determine when occupation began, and the Hague Regulations decided in favor of the rule that "occupation" in the technical sense applied only to the territory where the authority of the hostile army was actually established, that is, the occupant could then demand the obedience and temporary loyalty of the inhabitants. He could not, however, compel them to take an oath of allegiance or to take part in the operations of war. Nor could hostages be taken, although a practice described as "prophylactic reprisals" was on occasion resorted to, in the form of using civilians to test areas suspected of being mined. Private property was to be respected, although this did not interfere with requisitions and contributions. The practice of holding an entire community responsible for acts of sabotage by individuals was prohibited by the Hague Regulations, but the phrasing of the rule left the question of "collective responsibility" uncertain.[87]

Practice during the First World War. The violations of the Hague Convention in respect to military occupation were so general during the First World War that there appeared to be little left of its provisions when the war came to a close. The invading German armies, particularly in their sweep through neutral Belgium, interpreted freely the principle

---

[84] See Westlake, *International Law,* 2d ed., Vol. II, p. 95, where the instance of Frederick the Great is cited.

[85] Vattel, *Droit des gens,* Vol. III, §§ 197-198.

[86] On the general subject, see Conner, *The Development of Belligerent Occupation;* Nys, *L'Occupation de guerre.*

[87] The Hague Regulations were detailed in respect to the duties of the military occupant; but they appear to be almost naïve in the light of the practice of the two world wars.

of the collective responsibility of the community for the illegal acts of individuals. Hostages were taken and in many cases executed; heavy fines were imposed upon towns and villages in punishment of acts committed by individuals; men, and in some cases women, were deported from occupied territory and made to work in factories and mines of the enemy; and the food and other supplies of the occupied territory were drawn upon in excess of and without reference to the needs of the army of occupation.[88] Whether the measures taken were so far in excess of customary law as to constitute violations of the laws of war was never juridically determined.[89] The punishment meted out by German tribunals to a few criminals after the war did not deal with the question comprehensively.

Practice during the Second World War. During the Second World War military occupation, first by the German and later by the Allied armies, covered far wider areas than were covered in the First World War. On the part of the German army, hostages were taken even more freely than in Belgium in 1914; larger numbers of hostages were executed; villages, such as Lidice, were completely wiped out in reprisal for alleged unlawful acts committed within their areas; the deportation of forced labor reached the high figure of more than five million; requisitions went to the limit of available resources, leaving the local populations on the verge of starvation. What remained of "the law" was no more than the personal restraint of individual officers when there was no military gain to be had by further demands.[90]

On the part of the Allied armies military occupation was scarcely established in the enemy country before the war came to a close. What followed after the surrender of the enemy must be judged in the light not of the specific laws of war but of the general principles of justice and equity in respect to the reparations that might be exacted for wrong done. On this matter there were no rules of customary law. The victor exacted what he believed to be his due, with an eye to his future relations with the defeated country.[91]

---

[88] See Garner, *Int. Law and the World War*, Vol. I, § 195 ff.; "Memoire of the Belgian Government," *Am. Journal*, Vol. 11 (1917), Supp., p. 99; *Diplomatic Correspondence between the United States and Belligerent Governments, ibid.*, Vol. 11 (1917), Spec. Supp., pp. 249 ff. For events during the Balkan Wars of 1912 and 1913, see *Report of the International Commission*, Chap. II, "The War and the Non-Combatant Population.

[89] See, however, the *Report of the Commission of Responsibilities*, Appendix I.

[90] For details of the treatment by the German authorities of the civilian population and the pillage of public and private property by the German occupation forces, see *Nazi Conspiracy and Aggression*, pp. 62 ff., 77 ff., and documents accompanying the Nuremberg trials.

For the reaction of the American Republics to the ill-treatment of hostages, see Resolution XXXIII of the Meeting of Foreign Ministers at Rio de Janeiro in 1942, "Humanization of War."

[91] See below, p. 757, where the military occupation of Germany after the war is discussed.

War treason. A difficult problem of military occupation during both World Wars was that presented by what was technically known as "war treason."[92] The Hague Regulations forbade the military occupant to compel the population to "take the oath" to the hostile state. But it was well established by customary law that individual citizens must refrain from communicating in any way with the armies of their own country and from giving them other aid and comfort. Customary law recognized that war traitors might be severely punished, the death penalty being imposed for betraying information concerning the condition or operations of the occupying army.

Case of Edith Cavell. It would appear that the offense committed by the British nurse, Edith Cavell, at Brussels in 1915 was that of war treason, aggravated by the fact that her position as a Red Cross nurse was one of special trust. On the other hand, the aid alleged to have been rendered by her to the enemy appears to have been insignificant in itself, and it bore no relation to the safety of the army of occupation. The penalty of death imposed upon her was, therefore, more severe than usage warranted.[93]

"Underground" resistance. During the Second World War the offense of war treason became even more complicated by the fact that in Norway, France, and other occupied countries the military occupant established national governments which proclaimed their loyalty to the occupant and administered the country under the general control of the occupant. Resistance to these "quisling" governments was widespread, taking the form of underground organizations which carried on a campaign among the people both to maintain their morale and to prepare them for the possible day when they might openly take up arms against the military occupant. Numerous members of these resistance groups were executed; and patriotism fell afoul of traditional laws of war which demanded obedience of a defeated people.[94]

F. TREATMENT OF PRISONERS

The modern rules of international law with respect to the treatment to be accorded to prisoners of war stood in marked contrast with the prevailing practice of earlier times. As Grotius found it, the law of nations authorized the enslavement of prisoners; but the influence of Christianity had moderated the rigor of the law in favor of the alterna-

[92] On the subject of "war treason," see Oppenheim, *Int. Law,* Vol. II, 7th ed., §§ 162, 255.

[93] For details of the case, see Garner, *op. cit.,* Vol. II, §§ 382-386. Doubtless the secrecy attending the trial of Miss Cavell and the general policy of intimidation pursued by the German army of occupation in Belgium during the First World War served to accentuate the severity of the death penalty.

[94] The "underground" must be distinguished from guerrillas (see p. 665), although both were likely to share the same fate.

tive practice of holding prisoners for ransom.[95] This latter practice was encouraged by the rule, later discarded, that prisoners belonged to the individual or to the army corps which captured them, so that the ransom money went directly to the captors.[96] At times the prisoner was allowed to ransom himself by means of a ransom contract, which formed an exception to the rule with respect to the validity of contracts between enemies. The growing tendency during the second half of the nineteenth century toward the "humanizing" of war led to the formulation, at the Brussels Conference in 1874, of elaborate provisions for the improvement of the condition of prisoners.[97] Finally, the First and Second Hague Conferences incorporated these and other proposals into the Regulations annexed to the Convention respecting the Laws and Customs of War on Land.[98]

Provisions of the Hague Regulations. The regulations laid down the two general principles that prisoners of war were "in the power of the hostile government," as distinct from that of the individuals or corps which captured them and that they must be "humanely treated." Further provisions of a most specific character dealt with various aspects of the treatment to be accorded them. The captor government obligated itself to maintain them and accepted as a normal standard of maintenance the food, quarters, and clothing assigned to its own troops. They might be interned in towns or fortresses, and they might be kept in confinement only when the circumstances urgently demanded it. They might, with the exception of officers, be put to labor at tasks not connected with the operations of war, and they must be paid for their services. Provision was made for the establishment by the belligerents of bureaus of information relative to prisoners and for the acceptance of the charitable services of relief societies organized in the country to which the prisoner belonged, both of which agencies were granted special privileges for the performance of their duties. On the whole the prisoner's lot, as the delegates to the Hague Conferences contemplated it, was to be relatively a fortunate one, and he could await the end of the war with the certainty of being rejoined to his family in reasonably good health.[99]

Practice during the First and Second World Wars. But the humanitarian provisions, adopted in such detailed form at The Hague, failed, as in other cases, to take into account the conditions of modern total war. How could Germany, blockaded by Great Britain during the four years of

---

[95] *De jure belli ac pacis*, Bk. III, Chap. VII.

[96] See Walker, *History of the Law of Nations*, pp. 189 ff.

[97] For the text of the Brussels Declaration, see Higgins, *The Hague Peace Conferences*, pp. 273 ff.

[98] Arts. 4-20. See, on the general subject, Flory, *Prisoners of War*; G. Werner, *Recueil des Cours*, Vol. 21 (1928-I), p. 5.

[99] The inability of the delegates to the Hague Conferences to forecast the circumstances of "total war" is nowhere better shown than in the provisions of the Regulations relating to prisoners of war.

the First World War, be expected, even had there been the will to do it, to feed prisoners according to the standard of its own army which had to bear the burden of the war, or even according to the standard of its factory workers whose work was essential to the winning of the war? And if prisoners revolted against the meager fare to which they were subjected, disciplinary punishment appeared to be justified.[100]

The Geneva Convention of 1929. The inadequacy of the provisions of the Hague Conventions was obvious. But the leading powers still had faith in the adoption of new and more specific rules of law. A conference of forty-seven states met at Geneva, and on July 29, 1929, an elaborate convention was adopted, consisting of 97 articles.[101] Provision was made that the new convention should be regarded as complementary to articles 4-20 of the Hague Convention of 1907. The fundamental principles of the Hague Convention were reaffirmed and specific articles were added with the object of protecting prisoners from abuses such as had occurred during the war of 1914-1918. In particular, reprisals were forbidden, including the so-called "prophylactic reprisals." A prisoner might not be sent to an area where he would be "exposed to the fire of the fighting zone," or "employed to render by his presence certain points or areas immune from bombardment." "All forms of corporal punishment, confinement in premises not lighted by daylight, and in general all forms of cruelty whatsoever are prohibited." Collective penalties for the acts of individuals were also prohibited. Work done by prisoners must have "no direct connection" with the operations of the war. The scope of the Hague rules was broadened to include noncombatant members of the armed forces, whether on land, at sea, or in the air.[102]

The provisions of the Geneva Convention did little or nothing to alleviate the lot of prisoners in Germany during the Second World War. Protests made through neutral "protecting governments" were of no avail.[103] At the close of the war numerous German officers and guards were put on trial and punished for inhuman treatment of prisoners exceeding the necessities of the situation.[104] The "death-march" of the American prisoners taken by the Japanese at Bataan and Corregidor in 1942 led to the execution of the general responsible.

Geneva Conventions of 1949. On April 21, 1949, the Swiss Government, under the influence of the International Red Cross, convoked a

[100] In respect to the treatment of prisoners of war during the First World War, see Garner, *op. cit.*, Vol. II, Chaps. XXI-XXII.

[101] For the text of the convention, see Hudson, *International Legislation*, Vol. V, p. 20. The convention entered into effect on June 19, 1931.

[102] Arts. 9, 46, 81.

[103] For the protest of the United States against the refusal of the German Government to allow representatives of the Embassy in Berlin to visit camps in Belgium in 1940, see Hackworth, *Digest*, Vol. VI, p. 285.

[104] See *Nazi Conspiracy and Aggression*, pp. 57 ff. and documents relating to the Nuremberg trials.

Conference at Geneva which adopted on August 12 a series of conventions dealing with the protection of the victims of war. Convention III, dealing with prisoners of war, is a revision of the Convention of 1929, based upon the experience of the Second World War, and extending the protection of prisoners of war not only to war correspondents but to the civilian members of military aircraft crews. With respect to the controversial issue of "partisans," the Convention includes them as prisoners of war when they conform to the conditions fixed for militia and volunteer corps. A new provision requires that the food rations of prisoners shall be sufficient in quantity, quality, and variety to keep prisoners of war in good health, replacing the provision of the 1929 Convention based upon the food rations of the troops of the detaining army, which, the United States argued, was not adequate in Asiatic countries.[105]

In spite of the provisions of the Geneva Convention of 1949, accusations of mistreatment of prisoners during the Korean War were made on both sides. The General Assembly of the United Nations rejected in 1952 a Soviet draft resolution accusing the United States of mass murder in prison camps, and 1953 expressed grave concern at reports of inhuman practices employed against soldiers of the United Nations Command, condemning such acts as a violation of international law and of the basic standards of morality.[106]

A special problem arose when arrangements were being discussed during the Armistice negotiations between the military commanders in Korea for the exchange of prisoners, due to the fact that the United Nations Command was unwilling to return those who would violently resist repatriation. The Armistice Agreement of July 27, 1953, created a United Nations Repatriation Commission and provided that no force or threat of force was to be used against the prisoners.[107]

The sick and the wounded. The adoption of definite international obligations with respect to the care by belligerents of the sick and wounded of the enemy dated from the Geneva Conference of 1864. Prior to that time the practice of states varied widely, being dictated apparently more by the humane instincts of the particular belligerent than by accepted customary rules. The Geneva Convention [108] laid down the broad principle that sick and wounded soldiers should be cared for by

---

[105] Dept. of State Publication No. 3938, August, 1950. For detailed comment, see R. T. Yingling and R. W. Ginnane, "The Geneva Conventions of 1949," *Am. Journal*, Vol. 46 (1952), p. 393; J. S. Pictet, "The New Geneva Conventions for the Protection of War Victims," *Am. Journal*, Vol. 45 (1951), p. 462.

[106] *U.N. Yearbook*, 1952, p. 204; 1953, p. 148.

[107] See J. Mayda, "The Korean Repatriation Problem and International Law," *Am. Journal*, Vol. 47 (1953), p. 414, analyzing the application of the Geneva Convention to the particular situation.

[108] For the text of the convention, see Higgins, *op. cit.*, p. 8.

the belligerent in whose power they were, without distinction of nationality. In addition to elaborate provisions with respect to ambulances and military hospitals and their personnel and equipment, it was agreed to adopt the emblem of the Red Cross as the distinctive sign of the sanitary service. A second conference met in 1906 and drew up a revised convention bringing the earlier provisions more into accord with modern science and modern methods of warfare.[109] This convention was in force during the First World War, but a number of its provisions were difficult of observance, even in cases where the belligerent was willing to observe them. The belligerents were pledged to respect and protect "movable sanitary formations," which accompanied armies in the field, as well as the "fixed establishments" or stationary hospitals behind the lines or at more distant points, and with certain exceptions "convoys of evacuation" transporting the sick or wounded to the rear. This involved, however, a degree of selectivity in the objectives of long-range bombardment which was practically impossible. Numerous accusations of violations of the Red Cross Convention were made, many of which appeared to be well grounded, and some of which took on the character of atrocities.[110]

The Geneva Conference of 1929, which drew up the Convention on the Treatment of Prisoners of War, also adopted a Convention for the Amelioration of the Condition of the Wounded and Sick in Armies in the Field.[111] Particular attention was given to the protection of the mobile medical units and fixed medical establishments. The personnel engaged in the care of the sick and wounded were to be respected under all circumstances and were not to be made prisoners of war. New provisions were adopted relating to medical aircraft, which must be painted white and bear the distinctive emblem of the Red Cross. Elaborate provisions were adopted for the communication by the belligerents of the names and indications of identity not only of the sick and wounded but also of the dead, so as to avoid as far as possible the tragedies connected with the innumerable "missing persons" of the First World War.

During the Second World War the alleged violations of the Geneva Convention equaled those of the First World War, notably the violations of Red Cross convoys and the bombardment of hospitals bearing the Red Cross emblem. The indictment of the Japanese war criminals recited, among the violations of the laws and customs of war, "mistreatment of the sick and wounded, medical personnel, and female nurses," contrary to articles of the Geneva Convention of 1929 and to the Red Cross

[109] For the text of the convention, see *ibid.*, p. 18; *Am. Journal*, Vol. 1 (1907), Supp., pp. 201 ff.

[110] See Garner, *op. cit.*, Vol. I, Chap. XX.

[111] For the text of the convention, commonly referred to as the "Red Cross Convention," see Hudson, *International Legislation*, Vol. V, p. 1.

Convention of the same date.[112] Two of the Conventions adopted at the Geneva Conference of 1949 dealt with the Amelioration of the Condition of the Wounded and Sick of Armed Forces in the Field and of Armed Forces at Sea, being revisions of the earlier conventions in the light of the experience of the Second World War, notable changes being the wider scope of the persons included and the more rigid provisions outlawing the use of the Red Cross emblem for commercial purposes.[113]

G. INTERCOURSE BETWEEN BELLIGERENTS

Communication through neutral states. Owing to the development of modern means of communication, a considerable amount of non-hostile intercourse was carried on between the belligerent governments during the First and Second World Wars through the agency of neutral diplomatic representatives.[114] Each belligerent transmitted to the particular neutral diplomatic representative in charge of its interests such communications as it desired to have forwarded to the other belligerent, and replies were made through the same indirect channel. These communications related to such matters as proposals for new agreements with respect to the conduct of hostilities, the status of alien enemy citizens, and particularly to complaints and protests by one belligerent against the violation of the laws of war by the other belligerent.

Direct intercourse: flags of truce. Direct intercourse between commanders in the field was always an incident of warfare, and from the earliest times such intercourse was surrounded by special sanctions. The personal inviolability of the bearer of a flag of truce ranked, with the good faith of treaties, as one of the oldest and best-recognized rules of international law. The Hague Regulations followed custom in extending the inviolability of the bearer of a flag of truce to "the trumpeter, bugler or drummer, the flag bearer and interpreter who may accompany him." [115] Both custom and convention justified a commander in refusing to receive the bearer of a flag of truce when to do so might endanger the success of pending military operations. The abuse of a flag of truce by an army which sent it, as, for example, the act of firing upon those who came forward to receive it, was an offense of the most serious character, and as a rule gave rise to reprisals.[116]

---

[112] See *Trial of Japanese War Criminals*, Dept. of State Publication, No. 2613, pp. 94, 96.

[113] For details, see references in note 105.

[114] Switzerland, Sweden, and Spain were the chief neutral intermediary governments.

[115] Art. 32.

[116] For cases occurring during the First World War, see *Report of the Commission of Responsibilities*, p. 57.

Passports, or safe-conducts, and safeguards were commonly classed under the heading of "intercourse between belligerents"; but it should be observed that these agree-

Agreements between belligerents: capitulations. Informal agreements frequently took place between belligerents for the adjustment of minor questions relating to the conduct of hostilities, and they were governed by the same rule of good faith applicable to treaties. Formal agreements fell into three general classes: cartels, capitulations, and armistices. *Cartels* were agreements entered into by belligerents for a variety of purposes, the chief of which was the exchange of prisoners of war.[117] *Capitulations* were agreements for the surrender of a town or fortress or surrender of a body of troops operating within a particular district. The Hague Regulations followed custom in requiring that the terms of the capitulation "must take into account the rules of military honor"; that is, they must contain nothing personally degrading to the force which surrendered. Moreover, the terms, once settled, must be "scrupulously observed by both parties." [118]

A special difficulty arose in determining whether the terms of the surrender came within the implied authority of the contracting officers. This difficulty was formerly of great consequence, in view of the impossibility on the part of the commanders of obtaining adequate instructions from their home governments. The term *sponsions* was applied to such capitulations entered into in excess of the authority of the officer making them and upon the mere hope of subsequent ratification. Vattel cites the classic instance of the agreement made by the Roman consul with the Samnites at the Caudine Forks, the terms being later repudiated by the Roman Senate.[119] At the close of the American Civil War General Sherman stipulated in an agreement of surrender with General Johnston that the several State governments should be recognized and that the people of the Confederate States should be guaranteed their political rights and franchises as citizens of the Union.[120] Since these terms were political in their nature and extended beyond the sphere of military operations intrusted to General Sherman, the Government of the United States did not consider itself bound by his act.[121]

Armistices. Agreements between belligerents for the temporary sus-

---

ments were as a rule entered into not between the belligerents themselves, but between one belligerent and citizens of the enemy state. A *passport* or *safe-conduct* entitled the bearer to pass unmolested within the territory occupied by the enemy. A *safeguard* was a notification from a commander to persons lower in command, or to his successor, that certain buildings had been granted special protection. The term was also applied to the guard stationed by a commander to protect particular buildings and houses.

[117] Cartel ships, as they were called, were belligerent vessels specially commissioned for the transport of exchanged prisoners and, on occasion, of official communications.

[118] Art. 35.

[119] *Droit des gens,* Vol. II, § 209.

[120] For details, see Rhodes, *History of the United States,* Vol. V, p. 166.

[121] Compare *U. S. Rules of Land Warfare,* 1940, No. 246.

pension of hostilities figure among the oldest rules of the laws of war, and numerous practical problems arose in connection with their application and interpretation. Usage was not uniform with respect to the terms employed to designate these agreements, but the term *suspension of arms* was more often used to designate agreements between local commanders for a brief suspension of hostilities for such purposes as the removal of the wounded or the burial of the dead, while the terms *armistice* and *truce* were used interchangeably to indicate agreements of longer duration and more comprehensive purpose. All three terms were used to designate both the agreement itself and the period of cessation of hostilities for which it provided. The Hague Regulations distinguished between general and local armistices: "The first suspends the military operations of the belligerent States everywhere; the second only between certain fractions of the belligerent armies and within a fixed radius." [122] The terms of the armistice regularly fixed the precise time at which it was to commence and at which it was to terminate; and the rule of good faith was held to apply with special force to the observance of the spirit as well as the letter of the agreement.

The so-called "armistice" of November 11, 1918, between the Allied Powers and Germany was not technically an armistice, since it imposed terms which made the renewal of hostilities by Germany impossible. Hence it falls more properly under the heading "Termination of War." [123]

H. SANCTIONS FOR THE OBSERVANCE OF THE LAWS OF WAR

Reprisals. A survival in the laws of war of the complete lawlessness of earlier times was to be seen in the practice of *reprisals* or *retaliation* as a sanction to prevent the continuation or recurrence of violations of the law. If a serious offense was committed by one of the belligerents, the other belligerent thereupon ordered that corresponding measures in excess of the law be taken as a means of impressing upon the other party the necessity of observing the law. In its turn the other belligerent, considering that the measures taken by way of retaliation were more severe than were warranted by the circumstances, put into effect still more drastic measures, until the original offense was lost in a vicious circle of charges and countercharges, and every element of law disappeared from the subject.

National war codes generally recognized the necessity of resorting to reprisals.[124] The complete failure of the efforts at the Brussels Conference of 1874 to regulate them made it seem inadvisable at the Hague Conferences of 1899 and 1907 to reopen the question. Customary law

[122] Art. 37.
[123] See below, Chap. XXXV.
[124] See, for example, *Instructions*, Nos. 27, 28; *Rules of Land Warfare*, 1940, No. 358. The Oxford Manual of 1880 offered two brief articles regulating reprisals. See *Resolutions of Institute of International Law*, p. 42.

upon the subject was vague and indefinite. In general it may be said that reprisals were not resorted to as a means of punishment or revenge, but only as a means of securing the observance of the laws of war for the future. Hence the method of retaliation did not need to be identical with that of the offense, although it generally assumed a form approximating the latter in order that the relation between the two acts might be made more apparent. Again, since it was not as a rule possible to reach the guilty parties, retaliation might be carried out against other forces of the enemy who were guilty of no offense themselves.[125] Owing to the grave character of the measures, it was generally prescribed that reprisals might only be ordered by a commanding officer, following a careful investigation of the act complained of.

Reprisals directed against noncombatants. The extent to which reprisals might be put into effect against noncombatants was much debated as a matter of abstract justice, but in point of law it was clear that noncombatants might claim no exemption. The burning of towns and villages was a common form of retaliation.[126] So also was the practice of carrying off hostages, which assumed large proportions during the occupation of Belgium in 1914.[127] A special form of protection against possible unlawful conduct was the practice of "prophylactic reprisals," by which enemy prisoners or noncombatants were made to search for hidden mines or bombs, or to ride on the tender of railway trains, or to stand in the middle of a suspected bridge.[128]

During the First World War the resort to reprisals confused at almost every turn the discussion of the legality of the conduct which gave rise to them. On both sides measures were taken which could only be defended by charging that the enemy had been guilty of other acts equally in excess of the law. Admitting the technical illegality of their acts and justifying themselves on the ground of reprisals the belligerents extended the rules of blockade, destroyed merchant shipping by submarines, used poisonous gases, and bombed undefended cities. There was no legal answer to the problems presented. The inherent lawlessness of war manifested itself to its fullest extent.[129]

During the Second World War the story of the First World War was

[125] Prisoners of war, formerly subject like others to reprisals, were protected against them by Article 2 of the Geneva Convention of 1929. Contrast *Instructions,* No. 59, and practice during the First World War, in Garner, *op. cit.,* Vol. II, §§ 349, 355, 357.

[126] For the reprisals put into effect by the United States and Great Britain in the war of 1812-1814, see Moore, *Digest,* Vol. VII, pp. 183 ff., and Hyde, *Int. Law,* Vol. III, § 657, where reference is made to the denunciation of the reprisals by a British jurist.

[127] For details see Garner, *op. cit.,* §§ 195-201; de Visscher, *Belgium's Case: a Juridical Inquiry.*

[128] For instances, see Spaight, *War Rights on Land,* pp. 462 ff.

[129] See Harvard Research, *Draft Convention on Rights and Duties of Neutral States in Naval and Aerial War,* pp. 392 ff., 403 ff.; Le Fur, *Des représailles en temps de guerre.*

repeated with additional emphasis, if possible, upon the inherent impossibility of determining responsibility. From the beginning the conduct of the German armies was directed by policies which took little account of the traditional laws of war; so that little or no need was felt of justifying particular illegal acts by the doctrine of reprisals.[130] If the order was given to execute commandos and parachute troops it was not in fact because they were believed to be guilty of violations of the laws of war by reason of the secrecy and suddenness of their attacks. The execution of the American airmen whose planes were grounded in Japan after the flight over Tokyo may, however, be taken as a case of reprisals for the alleged illegality of the attack.[131]

[130] See evidence submitted in the Indictment of the Four Powers against the twenty-four defendants at Nuremberg. See below, p. 760.

[131] For a discussion of the executions from the point of view of international law, see C. C. Hyde, "Japanese Executions of American Aviators," Am. Journal, Vol. 37 (1943), p. 480.

CHAPTER **XXX**

The Laws of Maritime Warfare[1]

A. SOURCES OF THE LAW

The laws of maritime warfare followed the general lines of the laws
of war on land. Jurists found it convenient, however, to classify them
separately, owing to the fact that they presented special problems of
their own and contained, in a few striking instances, principles not applied in land warfare. As has been pointed out above, the Hague Conference of 1907 failed to adopt a general convention covering the rules
of maritime warfare, but a number of special conventions were adopted,[2]
and while these were not technically binding, they embodied in many
cases the customary rule of law; and where there was no clear rule
of custom the provisions of the conventions remained as evidence of

---

[1] How much of the impressive code of customary and conventional law of maritime
warfare is still of interest now that formal warfare has come to an end and neutrality
has ceased to be a legal status remains an open question. As in the case of hostilities
on land, if a limited war should break out there might still be some rules that would
find application, assuming that the parties possessed battleships and merchant fleets.
But this would appear to be highly improbable; and in any case the elaborate code of
neutral rights and duties in respect to contraband and blockade would cease to have
application. But, as in the case of warfare on land, the laws of maritime warfare
once played such an important part in the relations between belligerents and neutrals
that the subject deserves brief treatment, if only as a matter of historical interest.

On the general subject of maritime warfare, see Higgins and Colombos, *The Inter-
national Law of the Sea;* Hall, *The Law of Naval Warfare;* Smith, *The Law of the
Sea* and "Le développement moderne des lois de la guerre maritime," *Recueil des
Cours,* Vol. 63 (1938-I), p. 607; Tucker, *The Law of War and Neutrality at Sea.*

[2] These included the Convention Relating to the Conversion of Merchant Ships into
Warships (No. VII), the Convention Relative to the Laying of Automatic Submarine
Contact Mines (No. VIII), the Convention Concerning Bombardment by Naval
Forces in Time of War (No. IX), the Convention for the Adaptation to Maritime
Warfare of the Principles of the Geneva Convention (No. X), and the Convention
Relative to Certain Restrictions with Regard to the Exercise of the Right of Capture
in Naval War (No. XI).

what was regarded by the powers assembled at the Hague as the substantially just rule by inference from general principles.

B. LAWFUL COMBATANTS

Privateers. It was common practice in the early nineteenth century for a belligerent to supplement its public armed ships by accepting the volunteer services of privately owned and privately manned ships. These vessels, when properly commissioned by the state by the issuance of a letter of marque, were known as privateers; they might include vessels owned and manned by citizens of either the belligerent state or neutral states. The prevailing rule of national law which rewarded the privateer by granting it a property right in the prizes taken by it provided the inducement needed. Following the Crimean War, in which the Allied Powers refrained from issuing letters of marque, the Conference at Paris put forth the Declaration of Paris of April 16, 1856, in which, in consideration of the fact that "maritime law, in time of war, has long been the subject of deplorable disputes," the contracting parties agreed, among other things, that "privateering is and remains abolished." [3] The United States, although represented at the conference, was unwilling to sign the agreement in view of the failure of the conference to accept the Marcy Amendment providing for the abolition of the rule permitting a belligerent to capture on the high seas the private property, apart from contraband, of citizens of the belligerent state. The declaration was subsequently acceded to by the majority of states, including all of the European powers. The United States, on its part, refrained from the use of privateers during the Civil War of 1861-1865, and again during the Spanish-American War of 1898. On the latter occasion the American Secretary of State, without waiting to learn the views of the enemy government, announced that the "policy" of the United States would be not to resort to privateering.[4]

Conversion of merchant ships into warships. A new problem arose when governments began entering into agreements with private steamship companies providing for the transfer of their vessels to the government upon the outbreak of war. In consequence, the Hague Conference of 1907 adopted a convention defining the conditions under which the conversion might be effected: the vessel must be under the control of the power whose flag it flies, must bear the external marks of warships, and must observe the laws and customs of war.[5]

[3] Art. I. For the text of the Declaration, see Higgins, *op. cit.*, p. 1.

[4] Moore, *Digest,* Vol. VII, p. 541.

[5] Arts. 2-7. For the text of Convention VII, see *Hague Conventions,* p. 146. The Convention was not signed by the United States on the ground that signature would amount to an implied adhesion to the clause of the Declaration of Paris concerning the abolition of privateering—a step which the United States was prepared to take only on condition of the inviolability of private property on the high seas.

Distinct from the vessel of war, whether such by original construction or by conversion from a merchant ship, was the merchant ship which was armed for self-defense without losing its character as a private commercial vessel and noncombatant. By customary law, originating in the days of privateers and pirates, a merchant ship was permitted to arm itself against attack and might, if it considered it expedient, resist capture on the high seas.[6] Its decision to resist capture would naturally depend upon the circumstances. The penalty of unsuccessful resistance was none other than the injuries sustained in consequence of it and the detention of the master and crew as prisoners of war. The passengers were regarded as innocent bystanders having no ground of complaint for injuries received and not subject to detention as prisoners. It was important, however, that the armed merchant vessel should in no case act as the aggressor. To do so would, in the absence of a commission from its government as a privateer, place it in the class of unlawful combatants subject to the penalties imposed upon freebooters and pirates.

A merchant ship could thus retain its noncombatant character as a merchant ship and at the same time carry defensive armament against privateers no better, or little better, armed than itself. The mere fact that it was armed did not of itself subject it to attack without warning. It must show resistance before it could be treated as a warship and sunk at sight. During the second half of the nineteenth century the disappearance of privateers and the superior armament of warships led to abandonment of the practice of arming merchant ships. Then came the submarine, and with its appearance the question of the status of defensively armed merchant ships gained new importance.

Submarines as lawful combatants. With the coming of the submarine during the First World War, a new situation arose. The submarine was without question itself a lawful combatant, and it could of course be used against enemy warships, taking advantage of its ability to attack unseen, whether upon the high seas or by stealing its way into enemy ports. But the submarine, while secure so long as it operated in secrecy beneath the surface, was vulnerable upon the surface and might readily be engaged by a merchant vessel carrying the defensive armament it was privileged to carry if it chose to resist capture. Must the submarine go through the formality of older days and call upon the merchant ship to submit to capture before attacking it? To do so would deprive the submarine of its most effective means of combat. The war of

---

[6] In the case of the *Nereide* [9 Cranch 388 (1815), Fenwick, *Cases,* 824], the court adverted to the facts that "a belligerent merchant vessel rarely sails unarmed," and that "a belligerent [merchant vessel] has a perfect right to arm in his own defense." The court went too far in adding that such a vessel was "an open and declared belligerent; claiming all the rights, and subject to all the dangers of the belligerent character," for even in that day the armed merchant vessel must not itself attack first, or be attacked without warning.

1914 had not been long in progress before Germany and Great Britain announced their conflicting policies. Germany asserted that armed resistance by merchant vessels to German cruisers was "contrary to international law"; while on its side Great Britain instructed its commanders not merely to resist attack, but to take the offensive against the submarine, in view of the fact that these craft had on previous occasions failed to give warning before launching their torpedoes. The argument thus ran in a circle; and the question of reprisals entered to complicate still further the respective rights of the parties.[7]

Execution of Captain Fryatt. Might an unarmed merchant vessel take advantage of its bulk and ram an approaching submarine without thereby becoming an unlawful combatant? On July 28, 1916, the German Government announced the execution of Captain Fryatt, commander of an unarmed British steamer, the *Brussels*, who, on March 20, 1916, had attempted to ram a submarine which had summoned his vessel to stop and show its flag. Captain Fryatt was subsequently captured and condemned to death on the ground that, since he was not a member of a combatant force, he had committed an act of hostility against a German war vessel and was guilty of the crime of being a *franc-tireur* at sea. The British Government denounced the act as an "atrocious crime against the law of nations and the usages of war," asserting on a later occasion that there was no distinction between the rights of an unarmed and an armed vessel, and that the only restriction upon either was that it "must not seek out an enemy in order to attack him." It was admitted to the German court by Captain Fryatt that he had acted in accordance with the instructions of the British Admiralty.[8]

Case of the *Baralong*. In consequence of the methods pursued by German submarines against British merchant vessels, public opinion in Great Britain freely denounced the submarine as a pirate to which the laws of war no longer applied. This attitude was apparently reflected in the *Baralong* incident. On December 6, 1915, the German Government submitted to the United States Government a memorandum stating that on August 19, 1915, while a German submarine was firing upon the British merchant ship *Nicosian*, from which the entire crew had first been removed, a British cruiser, the *Baralong*, approached in the disguise of an American merchant vessel and upon reaching a strategic position fired upon the submarine, and after sinking it continued to shoot at and kill the officers and crew of the submarine while they were struggling in the water. The German Government, it was said, looked to the British Government to punish the authors of the "terrible deed" and

[7] See *Am. White Book*, Vol. III, pp. 167, 171.

[8] For details of the case and a discussion of its merits, see Garner, *op. cit.*, Vol. I, pp. 407 ff.; Scott, "The Execution of Captain Fryatt," *Am. Journal*, Vol. 10 (1916), p. 865. Compare memorandum of Secretary Lansing, March 25, 1916, Vol. II (11); *Am. White Book*, Vol. III, p. 192.

announced that "should they be disappointed in this expectation, they would consider themselves obligated to take serious decisions as to retribution for the unpunished crime." [9] Reconciliation of the conflicting points of view in the above cases was clearly impossible. Germany was not prepared to relinquish the advantages of the submarine as a commerce destroyer and Great Britain was not prepared to acquiesce in the destruction of merchant ships on the high seas without the traditional right of resistance when resistance was feasible.[10] Nor was Great Britain prepared to turn every noncombatant merchant ship into a warship, in view of the severe limitations imposed upon warships in neutral ports.

C. INSTRUMENTS OF MARITIME WARFARE

Automatic contact mines. During the Russo-Japanese War of 1904-1905 the use by both parties of floating mines raised the question of a restriction upon such instruments, owing to the injury which they were capable of inflicting upon neutral and noncombatant ships.[11] At the Hague Conference of 1907 the Convention Relative to the Laying of Automatic Submarine Contact Mines [12] was adopted, in which the contracting parties, recognizing that "the existing position of affairs" made it impossible to forbid the employment of such mines, sought to restrict and regulate their use both to mitigate the severity of war and to protect, as far as possible, peaceful navigation. A distinction was made by the convention between anchored and unanchored mines. The latter might not be laid "except when they are so constructed as to become harmless one hour at the most after the person who laid them ceases to control them." With this prohibition was included one against using torpedoes "which do not become harmless when they have missed their mark." In the case of anchored mines an absolute prohibition was laid against such as do not "become harmless as soon as they have broken loose from their moorings." Moreover, it was forbidden to lay anchored mines off the coast or ports of the enemy "with the sole object of intercepting commercial shipping." The convention was frankly referred to at the conference as an unsatisfactory compromise and as likely to be of little effect in view of the obvious loopholes in the law which conflicting views made it necessary to leave.

Practice during the First World War. Due to the failure of Russia

[9] For a summary of the correspondence, see Stowell and Munro, *Cases,* Vol. II, pp. 218 ff.

[10] On the general subject, see Higgins, *Defensively Armed Merchant-Ships and Submarine Warfare.*

[11] The Chinese delegate to the Hague Peace Conference of 1907 complained that "from five to six hundred of our countrymen engaged in their peaceful occupations have there met a cruel death in consequence of these dangerous engines of war." Higgins, *The Hague Peace Conferences,* p. 329.

[12] For the text of the convention, see *Treaties and Conventions,* Vol. II, p. 2304.

to sign the convention, the belligerents in the World War were thrown back upon the uncertain customary law. Great Britain early announced that in view of the alleged indiscriminate laying of mines by Germany it might have to adopt similar measures in self-defense. On October 2, 1914, these threatened measures made their appearance, taking the form of a system of minefields in the southern portion of the North Sea, which was later extended over the whole of the North Sea. Germany replied, February 4, 1915, by proclaiming the waters surrounding the United Kingdom a "war zone" in which enemy merchant ships would be destroyed without warning.[13] A further extension by Great Britain of the North Sea area led to protests from the United States; but upon the entrance of the latter into the war an even more elaborate "North Sea barrage" was established, imposing severe restrictions upon neutral shipping. As a result of the measures taken by the several belligerents, numerous neutral and enemy merchant ships were destroyed.[14]

Practice during the Second World War reflected the history of the First World War, except that the use of contact mines was even more indiscriminate, while the use by Germany of the "electro-magnetic mine" added to the dangers of navigation both for belligerent and neutral merchant ships. The use of aircraft for laying mines made control more difficult. War zones and military areas were extended, and little if anything was left of the provisions of the Hague Convention.[15] The experience of the two World Wars does not suggest that the Convention of 1907 would be regarded as of obligation in the future, even if the war were to be of a limited character.

D. METHODS OF MARITIME WARFARE

Obligation to give quarter. In martime warfare, as in land warfare, it was forbidden by customary law to announce that no quarter would be given, or to kill those who had laid down their arms, or to refuse possible aid to those who were defenseless and at the mercy of the sea. But this general rule did not prevent secret attacks, as by torpedoes, which at times made impossible the rescue of the crew of an armed vessel after it had ceased to offer resistance. The elaborate rules in respect to the treatment of prisoners in naval warfare, the provisions with respect to the special protection of hospital ships and the distinguishing marks by which they should be known, culminating in the provisions of the Hague Convention with respect to the sick-wards of warships, went the way of other rules which failed to take into account that the new instruments of warfare, operating at longer range, made

---

[13] See Phillipson, *International Law and the Great War,* Chap. XX. *Am. White Book,* Vol. I, pp. 52 ff.; Vol. II, pp. 21 ff.; Hackworth, *Digest,* Vol. VI, pp. 505 ff.

[14] For a general review of the situation, see Garner, *op. cit.,* Vol. I, Chap. XIV.

[15] See Hackworth, *Digest,* Vol. VI, pp. 509 ff.

the restrictions practically impossible of observance, even had there been greater good faith on the part of the belligerents, which appears to have been at times lacking.[16]

The use of deceit: false flags.   In naval as in land warfare, the use of deceit was an accepted part of strategy. Ruses of any kind not involving perfidy might be resorted to. Usage, more or less general, sanctioned the employment of false flags, whether enemy or neutral, as a stratagem to lead the enemy into action or to escape from him; but customary law definitely required that the national flag must be clearly displayed before actual attack.[17] The disguise of a merchant ship was used at times by men-of-war to take the enemy by surprise, either by erecting false funnels or by masking their batteries behind camouflaged fronts. Attack in secret, whether under cover of darkness or by submersed submarine, was permissible. Signs of distress, as a means of luring the enemy into a position where he might be taken unawares, were, however, condemned, since they involved a degree of perfidy in their urgent appeal for help.[18]

Bombardment of coast towns.   The rules of both customary and conventional law with respect to bombardment by naval forces paralleled, in a general way, the rules of war on land. Certain exceptional conditions of maritime warfare, however, led to the adoption by the Hague Conference of 1907 of the Convention Concerning Bombardment by Naval Forces in Time of War.[19] But here again, as in the case of attempts to regulate the instruments and methods of warfare, the Convention failed to anticipate aerial bombing from carrier ships and the practical impossibility of deciding what constituted a "defended town" or of directing the fire so as to spare churches and other nonmilitary buildings. By the end of the Second World War the provisions of the Convention had lost their meaning.

Blockade of enemy territory.   If by traditional law particular cities could be besieged and the starvation of noncombatants as well as combatants made a ground for surrender, the method might be applied to whole countries as well if a successful blockade could be established. The blockade of the Confederate States by the United States in 1861-1865 affected only military supplies; but the tight blockade of Germany

16 For the text of the Hague Convention of 1907 revising earlier conventions, see *Treaties and Conventions*, Vol. II, p. 2326; *Hague Conventions*, p. 163.

17 Compare the more restricted use of false flags in warfare on land. Hague *Regulations*, Art. 23f, above, p. 673. For the question as to the use by a belligerent of a neutral flag as a means of deceiving the enemy, see *Am. White Book*, Vol. I, p. 55.

18 Vattel cited as a "detestable breach of good faith" the reported case of a British frigate which came within sight of the coast of France and made signals of distress in order to decoy a vessel to come to the rescue "and thereupon seized the boat and made prisoners of the sailors who generously went to its aid." *Droit des gens*, Eng. trans., Bk. III, § 178.

19 For the text of the convention, see *Treaties and Conventions*, Vol. II, p. 2314.

by Great Britain in 1914-1918 caused severe suffering to the civilian population and led Germany to denounce the blockade as unlawful and as justification for reprisals, as in the case of the *Lusitania*. The blockade of 1939-1945 was maintained with equal rigor, but it lost part of its effectiveness by reason of the open front on the east, and no question was raised by Germany of its lawfulness.[20]

E. CAPTURE OF PRIVATE PROPERTY IN MARITIME WAR

One of the many paradoxes of the laws of war was the fact that while in warfare on land the invading armies were expected to respect the private property of enemy individuals, in maritime war the belligerent was free to capture and confiscate the private property, in ships or in cargoes, of enemy subjects found upon the high seas. The survival of this right at sea long after the right in land warfare was abandoned is to be explained chiefly by the fact that the right to destroy the merchant marine and overseas commerce of the enemy was a powerful weapon in the hands of states having formidable navies. The persistent agitation of the United States for the abolition of the right to capture enemy private property on the seas was consistently opposed by Great Britain and was the ground of the refusal of the United States to adhere to the Declaration of Paris and to sign the Convention Relating to the Conversion of Merchant Ships into Warships adopted at the Hague Conference of 1907. At this conference the United States again introduced its proposal of the inviolability of private property at sea, but the proposal met with opposition from Great Britain, whose delegates were supported by those of France, Russia, Japan, and other smaller states, so that under the rules of the conference the proposition, although supported by a majority, could not be considered as adopted.[21]

Exemption of enemy merchantmen in port. Accompanying the rule which permitted a belligerent to capture privately owned enemy merchant ships was a qualified exception in favor of vessels which the belligerent happened to find in its ports at the beginning of the war. By the time of the Crimean War in 1854-1856 the usage had developed of

---

[20] For the British Order-in-Council of November 27, 1939, see *Documents on American Foreign Relations*, Vol. II, p. 705. For the economic objectives of the later Allied blockade, see J. V. Lovitt, "The Allied Blockade," Dept. of State *Bulletin*, Vol. XI, p. 597.

[21] The literature upon the subject of the proposed abolition of the capture of enemy private property on the seas is voluminous. A summary of the position of the United States may be found in the address of Mr. Choate before the Fourth Commission of the Hague Peace Conference, June 28, 1907. See *Proceedings*, Vol. III, pp. 752 ff. An exposition of the political motives influencing the attitude of the different powers toward the question may be found in Hyde, *International Law*, Vol. III, §§ 771-772. The history of the subject is sketched in Quigley, *Immunity of Private Property from Capture at Sea*. Wehberg, *Capture in War on Land and Sea*, argued for the abolition of the law of prize at sea.

permitting privately owned enemy merchant vessels to depart from port within a specified time. Subsequent wars showed an adherence to the same practice, and in 1898 the United States recognized the force of the growing practice by providing that Spanish vessels, either in American ports or having departed from American ports prior to the outbreak of war, were to be permitted to discharge their cargoes and depart "without molestation" within thirty days from the commencement of hostilities. The Hague Conference of 1907 attempted to give statutory force to the existing usage by the adoption of the Convention (VI) Relative to the Status of Enemy Merchant Ships at the Outbreak of Hostilities. The provisions of the convention suggested however, that the powers were not ready to regard the usage as a rule of customary obligation, for the convention merely prescribed that when a merchant ship belonging to one of the belligerent powers was found, at the commencement of hostilities, in an enemy port, it was "desirable" that it should be allowed to depart freely, either immediately or after a certain term of grace. Moreover, the convention permitted the belligerent to detain a merchant vessel without payment of compensation but subject to the obligation of restoring it after the war; or the belligerent might requisition the vessel on payment of compensation. Ships which had left port before hostilities had begun and were encountered on the high seas while still ignorant of the outbreak of hostilities were not subject to confiscation.[22]

Practice during the two world wars. Practice during the First World War was what might have been expected. Technical grounds were found by Great Britain, France, and Germany for taking over vessels found in their ports and for confiscating those found on the high seas after the outbreak of war. Upon the outbreak of war between the United States and Germany in 1917, the United States found itself in possession of a large number of interned German merchant vessels. Congress promptly authorized the President to take them over and to operate them or otherwise put them into service. During the Second World War the United States and other American states found themselves, as neutrals, in possession of numerous German and Italian merchant vessels immobilized in their ports. In accordance with a recommendation of the Inter-American Economic and Financial Advisory Committee, the United States and other governments issued decrees requisitioning more than a hundred of these vessels; so that when war came later, confiscation had been anticipated.[23]

[22] The naivete of many of the decisions of the Conference nowhere appears more obvious. But war was still a gentleman's game, and it was hoped that on certain points governments might be reasonable. There was a degree of hospitality due to foreign vessels in port.

[23] For critical comment, see L. H. Woolsey, "The Taking of Foreign Ships in American Ports," *Am. Journal,* Vol. 35 (1941), p. 497.

Exemption of fishing vessels. By customary law fishing vessels engaged in coast fisheries, as distinct from deep-sea fisheries, were regarded as exempt from the rule of capture of enemy property at sea. The ground of this exemption was stated by the United States Supreme Court in the case of the *Paquete Habana* [24] as being "considerations of humanity to a poor and industrious order of men" and "the mutual convenience of belligerent states." The court reached the conclusion in the above case that "by the general consent of the civilized nations of the world, and independently of any express treaty or other public act," it was an established rule of international law "that coast fishing vessels with their implements and supplies, cargoes and crews, unarmed and honestly pursuing their peaceful calling of catching and bringing in fresh fish, are exempt from capture as prize of war." [25]

At the Hague Conference of 1907 the Convention (XI) Relative to Certain Restrictions with Regard to the Exercise of the Right of Capture in Naval War was adopted. It confirmed the customary rule of exempting from capture coastal fishing vessels and included with them "small boats employed in local trade." In both instances the exemption was made conditional upon the vessels not taking "any part whatever in hostilities." Further, the convention provided that "vessels charged with religious, scientific, or philanthropic missions are likewise exempt from capture," thus confirming another customary rule.[26]

That the rule should have been observed under the stress of total war was not to be expected. Fishing vessels contributed to the food supplies of the enemy; that alone was enough to refuse to exempt them from capture. While it was sheer inhumanity on the part of certain of the belligerents to attack fishing vessels and sink them under conditions which made the death of their crews practically certain, it was not to be expected that noncombatants at sea should be exempt even from capture when noncombatants on land had lost all protection whatever in time of bombardment.

The test of enemy character. Owing to the liability of enemy property to capture at sea, the problem was presented to prize courts, when passing upon the legality of captures, to determine what properly constituted enemy property. The accepted general principle, namely that the property of enemy subjects was enemy property, was qualified by a number of special rules enforced by some of the leading powers although repudiated by others. With respect to the national character of

[24] 175 U.S. 677 (1900). Fenwick, *Cases*, p. 17; Bishop, *Cases*, p. 24; Briggs, *Cases*, p. 30.

[25] In reaching its conclusion the court referred to the historical practice of maritime states, to treaties, judicial decisions, and the evidence presented by jurists and commentators upon international law. It would appear that the recognition by Great Britain of the rule was as one "of courtesy only, and not of legal decision."

[26] *Treaties and Conventions*, Vol. II, p. 2348; *Hague Conventions*, p. 182.

a vessel as distinct from its cargo, the customary rule of international law was that such character, whether enemy or neutral, was determined by the flag the vessel was authorized to fly. In the case of the *Pedro*,[27] the Supreme Court of the United States held that the fact that British citizens were owners of the stock of the company controlling the vessel could not offset the further facts that the company was incorporated under the laws of Spain and that the vessel flew the Spanish flag, thus making her liable to capture. The rule of custom found confirmation in the Declaration of London. The enemy ownership of a vessel, therefore, did not subject it to capture provided it had been duly registered and carried the papers of a neutral state; nor did neutral ownership protect a vessel flying an enemy flag.

Greater difficulty arose in determining the national character of the cargo carried by the vessel, Great Britain and the United States following the rule making the domicile of the owner the test of enemy or neutral character; and France, Germany, and other continental states following the rule which made the test the nationality rather than the residence of the owner. The Declaration of London of 1908 could do no more than evade the issue by providing that the neutral or enemy character of goods found on board an enemy vessel was determined by the neutral or enemy character of the owner.[28]

F. CONDITIONS ATTENDING THE CAPTURE OF MERCHANT VESSELS

Assuming the right of a belligerent to capture enemy merchant vessels on the high seas, under what circumstances could it be exercised? Until the opening of the First World War the traditional practice of maritime states was to subject all merchant vessels encountered on the high seas to visit and search with the object of determining the national character of the vessel and of its cargo.[29] On the part of the merchant ship itself, the right to resist capture, whether by taking to flight or by the use of whatever forcible measures were at its command, was, as has been seen, clearly recognized, although the consequences of its exercise might be disastrous to noncombatant passengers on board. In the absence of resistance the belligerent cruiser was under obligation to effect the capture of the vessel in such manner as to ensure the safety of the passengers and crew, whether by placing upon the vessel a prize crew and sending it into port, or by transferring the passengers and crew to another vessel. Prior to the First World War resistance on the part of

[27] 175 U.S. 354 (1899).

[28] In the report accompanying the declaration the following comment was made: "It can not be concealed that article 58 solves no more than a part of the problem, and that the easier part; it is the neutral or enemy character of the owner which determines the character of the goods, but what is to determine the neutral or enemy character of the owner?" See Higgins, *op. cit.*, pp. 567, 604.

[29] On the general subject of visit and search, see Oppenheim, Vol. II, Chap. IV, "Warfare on Sea."

merchant ships to capture, common in the days of privateers, had practically ceased as a result of the marked inequality between the armament of a warship and that capable of being carried by a merchant ship. In an emergency the merchant ship might be destroyed, subject, however, to the prior removal of the passengers and crew to a place of safety.[30]

Submarines as commerce destroyers. Upon the outbreak of the First World War the German submarine made its appearance on the seas as a man-of-war, lightly armed both for defense and for offense, and relying for its effectiveness upon its ability to approach unseen and launch its torpedoes against an unsuspecting enemy. So far as warships of the enemy were concerned, the submarine was, as has been seen, a lawful combatant. It could also be used as a commerce destroyer, provided it observed the customary law governing the capture of merchant vessels. The question was, however, whether the submarine might claim a modification of the law in view of the fact that it could not operate effectively under the traditional rules. Must Germany forego the advantages of this new weapon simply because of rules framed under completely different conditions? The issue was so acutely argued and had such a decisive effect on the decision of the United States to enter the war that it merits analysis even if not likely to arise again in a possible future war.

Status of unarmed merchant ships. In the case of unarmed merchant ships, the greater speed of the new commercial liners made it possible for them to elude the attack of the submarine if warning had to be given in advance. Even if they were to heed the warning given them, it was, as a practical matter, impossible for the submarine either to put a prize crew on board or to transfer to its own deck so large a number of passengers and crew. Moreover, modern means of communication by wireless telegraph made it imperative that action with respect to the merchant ship be taken promptly, lest enemy warships come to the aid of the merchant ship before it could be disposed of. Besides, argued Germany, these ships, as carriers of food and ammunition, were in reality engaged in hostile service. Why was Great Britain free to blockade and starve Germany, yet Germany could not do the same to Great Britain? The problem of noncombatant passengers could easily be solved by their keeping off such ships.[31]

---

[30] In the case of Great Britain and the United States the practice was followed that the title to property seized as prize changed only as the result of the decision of the national prize court, so that while destruction was permissible in an emergency and when there was no doubt that the vessel was good prize, it was obligatory upon the commander of the belligerent cruiser to send in to the prize court such papers and other evidence of the character of vessel and its cargo as would permit a decree to be duly entered. See *U. S. Naval Instructions,* June 30, 1917. On the general subject, see Sir F. Smith, *The Destruction of Merchant Ships under International Law.*

[31] The argument of the German Government is perhaps most effectively stated in the memorandum of February 4, 1915. *Am. White Book,* Vol. I, p. 53; Savage, *Policy of the United States toward Maritime Commerce in War,* 1914-1918, Vol. II, p. 265.

Status of armed merchant ships. More difficult was the issue in the case of armed merchant vessels. Germany argued that they might be attacked without warning on the ground that their armament, being equal or superior to that of the submarine when upon the surface, practically put them in the class of ships of war, against which it was lawful for the submarine to direct its attack unseen. Moreover, the alleged defensive armament of a merchant ship might immediately be used as offensive armament when the submarine appeared upon the surface of the sea to give the necessary summons to surrender. This argument was strengthened by the fact that instructions were alleged to have been issued by the British Admiralty ordering the officers of merchant ships to attack submarines at sight.[32] As against this position it was argued on the side of Great Britain that the existing law recognized the right of a merchant ship to defend itself if it chose to take the risk, and that the law did not excuse the belligerent submarine from the obligation to give due warning simply because doing so would weaken its strategic position.[33]

Case of the *Lusitania*. The United States, as a neutral, was drawn into the controversy because of its interest in the welfare of its citizens who were passengers on merchant ships of the Allies and because of its obligations of neutrality in respect to the admission of armed merchant ships into its ports. On May 7, 1915, the sinking of the *Lusitania* by a German submarine presented the issue in acute form.[34] In a series of notes addressed to the American Secretary of State the German Government argued that the *Lusitania* was not an "ordinary unarmed merchant vessel" but was in the class of an auxiliary cruiser and was included in the navy list published by the British Admiralty. Moreover, there was reason to believe that the vessel was armed and that it had on previous trips carried Canadian troops and large quantities of ammunition. Further, the general practice of the British Government in arming its merchant ships and instructing them to use neutral flags and to attack the enemy made it impossible to consider them any longer as "undefended territory" in the zone of maritime war. In addition, the unlawful blockade of Germany and the unwarranted extension of the rules of contraband made it necessary to resort to reprisals. As against these arguments the American Government, speaking on behalf of its neutral citizens, waved aside technical arguments and insisted that it

[32] See memorandum of German Foreign Office, February 8, 1916, *Am. White Book*, Vol. III, pp. 167 ff. The allegation appears to have been correct.

[33] See *ibid.*, Vol. III, p. 187. Also, Garner, *op. cit.*, Vol. I, § 252.

[34] The facts attending the sinking of the vessel are reviewed at length in *The Lusitania*, Petition of the Cunard Steamship Company, Limited, 251 Fed. Rep. 715 (1918). Fenwick, *Cases*, p. 752; Briggs, *Cases*, p. 736; Hudson, *Cases*, p. 1255, in which the court held that the petitioner was not liable for the loss of life and property; which, the court held, was due to the "illegal act" of the German Government.

was "contending for nothing less high and sacred than the rights of humanity" and that only the "actual resistance [of the *Lusitania*] to capture or refusal to stop when ordered to do so for the purpose of visit could have afforded the commander of the submarine any justification for so much as putting the lives of those on board the ship in jeopardy." [35]

Position taken by the United States. On January 18, 1916, while the *Lusitania* case was still unsettled, the American Department of State, acting in the interest of neutral rights and obligations, proposed that the Allies agree that merchant ships should thereafter "be prohibited and prevented from carrying any armament whatsoever," on condition that submarines should be made to adhere strictly to the rules of international law in respect to visit and search, the determination of belligerent nationality, and the removal of passengers and crew to a place of safety. The argument in support of the proposal was based upon the fact that the customary right of a merchant ship to go armed was "predicated on the superior defensive strength of ships of war" and the relatively inferior armament of piratical ships and privateers. The use of the submarine had, however, changed these relations, and moreover pirates had been driven from the seas and privateering abolished. Hence the arming of a merchant ship under the existing conditions could be explained only on the ground of a purpose to make the ship superior in force to submarines and to prevent warning and visit and search by them. "Any armament, therefore, on a merchant ship," the Department suggested, "would seem to have the character of an offensive armament." The proposal being unacceptable to Great Britain, the Department reverted to the old rule and in a memorandum of March 25, 1916, took the stand that the mere presence of armament on board a merchant ship was not sufficient ground for a belligerent to consider it a warship and attack it without regard to the rights of persons on board. The status of an armed vessel on the high seas must, it was argued, "be determined only upon conclusive evidence of aggressive purpose, in the absence of which it is to be presumed that the vessel has a private and peaceable character, and it should be so treated by an enemy warship." [36]

Shortly after, on May 4, 1916, the German Government as the culmination of a long exchange of notes, agreed not to sink merchant vessels "without warning and without saving human lives, unless those ships attempt to escape or offer resistance." This agreement was, however, set aside on January 31, 1917, when the German Government announced that the "brutal methods of war" of the Entente Allies and their determination to destroy the Central Powers gave Germany "the freedom of action" which she denied herself in her note of May 4, 1916. Henceforth,

---

[35] *Am. White Book,* Vol. II, pp. 169 ff.

[36] *Am. White Book,* Vol. III, p. 183. For critical comment on this memorandum, see E. Borchard, "Armed Merchantmen," *Am. Journal,* Vol. 34 (1940), p. 107.

all vessels met within the prescribed zone would be sunk.[37] The threat was soon carried into effect, and on April 6, the United States declared war.

G. OUTLAWRY OF SUBMARINES AS COMMERCE DESTROYERS

In view of the suffering and loss of life on the part of noncombatants and of the unwarranted damage to neutral shipping caused by the methods of warfare pursued by the German submarines, the Washington Conference on the Limitation of Armaments in 1921-1922 undertook to lay down specific rules governing the use of the submarine in the future.[38] The British delegation proposed that, since the use of the submarine, while of small value for defensive purposes, inevitably led to violations of the laws of war, "united action should be taken by all nations to forbid their maintenance, construction or employment." To this extreme position the United States delegation was opposed, and it offered as an alternative that laws should be drawn up prescribing the methods of procedure to be followed by submarines against merchant vessels both belligerent and neutral. The decision taken by the conference was incorporated in a treaty signed on February 6, 1922.[39] The treaty applied to the submarine the existing rules, "deemed to be an established part of international law," as regarded the visit and search of merchant vessels, and required that if a submarine could not conform to them it must desist from attack and permit the merchant vessel to proceed unmolested. Further, the contracting powers, recognizing the practical impossibility of using submarines as commerce destroyers without violating the laws of war, prohibited as between themselves the use of submarines for that purpose and called upon other powers to adhere to the prohibition.[40] The London Treaty of April 22, 1930, adopted at the close of the Conference on the Limitation of Armaments, merely contained a restatement of the Washington rules.[41]

H. PRACTICE DURING THE SECOND WORLD WAR

In spite of the efforts made to control the submarine, none of the agreements reached at the several conferences were binding when the

[37] Am. White Book, Vol. III, pp. 302 ff.; ibid., Vol. IV, p. 405. Savage, op. cit., Vol. II, p. 552.

[38] On the Washington Conference, see Buell, The Washington Conference; Hackworth, Digest, Vol. IV, pp. 466 ff.

[39] For the text of the treaty, see Treaties and Conventions, Vol. III, p. 3116; Am. Journal, Vol. 16 (1922), Supp., p. 57.

[40] The treaty remained unratified, mute evidence of the difficulty of securing a limitation of armaments apart from the system of collective security.

[41] Art. 22. For the text of the treaty, see Treaties and Conventions, Vol. IV, p. 4757; Hudson, International Legislation, Vol. V, p. 394.

war began in 1939.[42] So far as the law was concerned, nothing had been settled, and the use of the submarine might be argued to be lawful or unlawful according as it kept reasonably within the traditional rules for the capture of enemy merchant ships, giving the passengers and crew of the vessel opportunity to escape in lifeboats under conditions which assured their safety, if not their convenience. Unhappily the effects of total war were felt here as elsewhere. Sinkings on the high seas, without warning and far from shore, were a regular occurrence; and the crews of merchant ships came to be regarded as no more entitled to protection than the workers in munitions factories in war on land. From time to time ships were sunk under circumstances which left no doubt as to violation of the elementary laws of humanity, and for such acts there was no pretense of justification.[43]

[42] The *Instructions for the Navy of the United States*, 1941, spoke of Art. 22 as in effect, although other provisions of the treaty were not.

At the beginning of the Second World War the Meeting of Foreign Ministers of the American States, held at Panama, adopted a Resolution (VI) on Humanization of War, making a "fervent appeal" to the belligerents to abstain from "(g) sinking merchant vessels without having first placed the passengers, crew and ship's papers in a place of safety." *International Conferences of American States*, 1933-1940, p. 329. The Inter-American Neutrality Committee, acting in pursuance of the General Declaration of Neutrality adopted at the same meeting, recommended, by majority vote, the exclusion of submarines from neutral ports and harbors not only because of the difficulties of regulating their activities but as a means of giving expression "to the universal reprobation" of their use as commerce destroyers. *Am. Journal*, Vol. 34 (1940), Supp., p. 78.

[43] Admiral Raeder, Commander-in-Chief of the German Navy, and Admiral Doenitz were adjudged guilty at Nuremberg of "crimes arising out of sea warfare" and were condemned to prison. For the judgment of the Tribunal in the case of the two Admirals, see *Nazi Conspiracy and Aggression*, pp. 137 ff.

The Nuremberg Tribunal announced that it was not prepared to hold the two admirals guilty for their conduct of submarine warfare against British armed merchant ships because the British Admiralty had ordered its armed merchant ships to ram U-boats if possible.

CHAPTER XXXI

Measures of War Against Enemy Persons and Property Within the Belligerent States

A. MEASURES OF WAR AGAINST RESIDENT ENEMY ALIENS

If the traditional laws of war broke down in the presence of new instruments and new methods of warfare, it was to be expected that they would give way before the modern and complicated commercial relations normally existing between citizens of the belligerents.[1] As far back as the English Magna Charta of 1215 alien merchants were a problem, but the law only detained them until there could be assurance that English merchants were being properly treated by the enemy.[2] Grotius, writing in 1625 and surveying the practice of the past, recognized that persons "caught by their ill-fortune" in the land of the enemy when war had suddenly broken out might be detained while the war lasted "in order to lessen the strength of the enemy," but that they should be released when the war was over.[3] Vattel, writing in 1758, thought that it was a point of good faith on the part of a belligerent not to detain enemy subjects who had entered the state under an implied promise of being able to return in freedom and safety; he found it a general practice to allow merchants full time to wind up their affairs and withdraw from the country.[4] Numerous treaties of the nineteenth century were to the same effect, the treaty of 1794 between the United States and Great Britain providing that merchants and others should have the

[1] The literature of the subject is extensive. See, in particular, McNair, *Legal Effects of War*, 3rd ed.; Baty and Morgan, *War: Its Conduct and Legal Results;* Hyde, *International Law*, Vol. III, §§ 605-637 A, showing chiefly the practice of the United States; Hackworth, *Digest*, Vol. VI, pp. 183 ff.; O. C. Sommerich, "Recent Innovations in Legal and Regulatory Concepts as to the Alien and his Property," *Am. Journal*, Vol. 37 (1943), p. 58.

[2] McNair, *ibid.*, p. 403.

[3] *De jure belli ac pacis*, Book III, Chap. IX, § IV.

[4] *Droit des gens*, Book III, § 63.

privilege of remaining "so long as they behave peaceably and commit no offense against the laws." [5]

By the time of the First World War, however, conditions had changed. Enemy aliens of military age were confined in concentration camps, and severe restrictions were placed upon the activities of other enemy aliens, particularly with respect to communication with the enemy. In like manner, during the Second World War large numbers of "civilian enemy aliens" were interned and strenuous measures were taken to control the subversive activities of unfriendly enemy aliens, a specific measure being those proposed by the Committee of Political Defense set up by the American States at Montevideo in 1942.[6]

Could resident alien enemies bring suit in court to maintain their normal rights? Yes, said the British and United States courts, as did Continental practice; and the right was confirmed by the Hague Convention of 1907, provided there was no trading with the enemy involved.[7]

B. MEASURES OF WAR AGAINST ENEMY PROPERTY

Private property of enemy nationals. During the nineteenth century a distinction was made between the property of resident enemy aliens, which was exempt from confiscation, and the property of nonresident enemy aliens over which the belligerent might happen to have control, as over stocks, securities, copyrights, and patents, about which practice differed. But with the coming of the First World War it was found that the resources of the state were too heavily involved in enemy property, private and corporate, to risk the possibility of its use by enemy alien owners in a manner detrimental to the prosecution of the war. In consequence the Congress of the United States in 1917, following the lead of Great Britain in 1914, passed the Trading with the Enemy Act which provided for the issuance of licenses to resident enemy aliens to continue in business and further authorized the appointment of an

[5] Art. XXVI. *Treaties and Conventions,* Vol. I, p. 590. The provisions were progressive. Vattel had cited the action of the King of England in permitting alien enemies to remain in the country subject to good behavior on their part as exceptional.

[6] On the general subject, see R. M. W. Kempner, "The Enemy Alien Problem in the Present War," *Am. Journal,* Vol. 34 (1940), p. 443; R. R. Wilson, "Treatment of Civilian Enemy Aliens," *ibid.,* Vol. 37 (1943), p. 30; "Recent Developments in the Treatment of Civilian Alien Enemies," *ibid.,* Vol. 38 (1944), p. 397. With respect to the policy of the American States, see Resolution (XVII) of the Meeting of Foreign Ministers at Rio de Janeiro in 1942, on "Subversive Activities," together with attached Memorandum; C. G. Fenwick, "The Third Meeting of Ministers of Foreign Affairs," *Am. Journal,* Vol. 36 (1942), pp. 169, 173. For the work of the Committee of Political Defense in connection with the suppression of subversive activities, see C. B. Spaeth and W. Sanders, "The Emergency Advisory Committee for Political Defense," *Am. Journal,* Vol. 38 (1944), p. 218.

[7] Hague Convention Respecting the Laws and Customs of War on Land, which forbade belligerents to declare abolished, suspended, or inadmissible in a court of law, the rights and actions of the nationals of the hostile party.

alien property custodian with power to receive and hold all money or other property due to alien enemies which might be transferred to him. Subsequent acts authorized the custodian to sell any property in his custody, and a large part of it was disposed of at auction.[8] The ultimate disposal of the proceeds of such sales was not made clear, the primary object of the seizures and sales being to destroy the financial influence of the German owners. By the Treaty of Versailles (Article 297), the Allied and Associated Powers reserved the right to retain and liquidate all property, rights, and interests formerly belonging to German nationals within their territories; the proceeds were to be used for the purpose of compensating their nationals for losses suffered at the hands of the German Government during the war. The United States, however, subsequently sought to undo in large measure the effects of the sequestration, although certain of the "sales" of sequestrated property amounted to practical confiscation.[9] During the Second World War the United States went even further, due in part to the fact that in a number of cases business firms under the direction of enemy aliens had been established with the object of cooperation with the German Government in the event of war.[10] The methods resorted to by the different American republics differed widely, depending upon the special circumstances with which they were confronted.

C. TRADING WITH THE ENEMY

The illogical and at times paradoxical character of warfare in modern times was perhaps nowhere more manifest than in the practice of states

[8] For the text of the act, see *Am. Journal*, Vol. 12 (1918), Supp., p. 33. In the case of United States v. Chemical Foundation, 272 U.S. 1 (1926), involving the disposition of certain German patents seized by the Alien Property Custodian and sold for what price they would bring, the Supreme Court held that the power of Congress to enact the legislation was unrestricted. The enemy alien owners had no rights under the due process of law clause of the Constitution.

[9] The rights of the United States under the Treaty of Versailles were retained in the separate treaty of peace of August 25, 1921. See *Am. Journal*, Vol. 16 (1922), Supp., p. 10. On August 10, 1922, a special executive agreement was entered into between the United States and Germany providing for the creation of a mixed claims commission to determine the amount of Germany's obligations under the treaty of peace. See *ibid.*, Supp., p. 171. On March 4, 1923, Congress passed the Winslow Act, in the form of an amendment to Section 9 of the Trading with the Enemy Act, authorizing the Alien Property Custodian to release to former enemy owners an amount up to $10,000 of their seized property. By act of March 10, 1928, provision was made for the return of the balance of the property except for the temporary retention of 20 percent. For the text of the act, see *Am. Journal*, Vol. 22 (1928), Supp., p. 40.

The practice of the United States was the object of sharp criticism. See in particular E. M. Borchard, *Am. Journal*, Vol. 18 (1924), p. 523; Vol. 22 (1928), pp. 373, 636; Vol. 30 (1936), p. 108; Vol. 31 (1937), p. 675.

[10] See J. P. Bullington, *Proceedings*, Am. Soc. Int. Law, 1943, p. 59; M. B. Carroll, "Legislation on Treatment of Enemy Property," *Am. Journal*, Vol. 37 (1943), p. 611.

in respect to commercial relations between the citizens or resident aliens of the respective belligerents. Here again Anglo-American and Continental practice varied. In the early case of the *Hoop,* the British court condemned a cargo which a neutral vessel had shipped at Rotterdam for the account of certain British merchants, announcing that there was "a general rule of maritime jurisprudence of this country, by which all trading with the public enemy, unless with the permission of the sovereign, is interdicted." [11] In the case of the *Rapid,* the United States Supreme Court condemned a cargo which an American citizen had purchased before the outbreak of war and had deposited upon an island near the boundary line of the United States and which he attempted to bring home after the outbreak of war. The decision, admittedly causing "considerable hardship," rested largely upon a theory of personal hostility between citizens of the enemy states: "In a state of war, nation is known to nation only by their armed exterior; each threatening the other with conquest or annihilation. The individuals who compose the belligerent states exist, as to each other, in a state of utter occlusion. If they meet, it is only in combat." [12] By contrast the states of Continental Europe in general followed the practice of not regarding trade with the enemy as illegal by the mere fact of war, but only in consequence of an express prohibition of the government.

Contracts between enemy citizens. If war immediately cuts short the commercial relations between the citizens of the states at war, it is to be expected that numerous complicated relations will arise with reference to the validity of relations established between them in the normal course of business before the war.[13] What contracts between enemy citizens must be held to be "trading with the enemy?" Contracts entered into *during the war* were declared by British and American courts to be *ipso facto* void, unless entered into under a special license. Contracts entered into before the war were either dissolved, when they were executory and time was material and of the essence of the contract, or else were merely suspended in their operation until the close of the war. In the case of Griswold v. Waddington [14] it was held by a New York court that a business partnership between an American and a

[11] C. Rob. 196 (1799). Fenwick, *Cases,* p. 780.

[12] Cranch 155 (1814). Fenwick, *Cases,* p. 782; Hudson, *Cases,* p. 1297. The Court seems to have been carried away by the force of its theory of personal hostility between citizens of the opposing belligerents. "The whole nation are embarked in one common bottom, and must be reconciled to submit to one common fate. Every individual of one nation must acknowledge every individual of the other nation as his own enemy—because the enemy of his country." But the test of confiscation should rather have been whether the transport of the goods under the circumstances could in any indirect way have been of aid to the enemy, since the purchase took place before the outbreak of war.

[13] On the general subject, see McNair, *Legal Effects of War,* Chaps. 4, 5, 7.

[14] 16 Johnson's Rep. 438 (1819). Fenwick, *Cases,* p. 785.

British citizen was forthwith dissolved by war between the two countries, since a partnership necessarily involved commercial intercourse.
Again, in the case of New York Life Insurance Co. v. Statham [15] the
Supreme Court of the United States held that a life insurance policy
was annulled by reason of the nonpayment of premiums caused by the
existence of a state of war. On the other hand, it was held in Hanger v.
Abbott [16] that since war only suspended debts due to an enemy, the
statute of limitations of Arkansas could not be pleaded against a citizen
of New Hampshire who had been unable owing to war to bring action
within the prescribed period.

Practice during the First World War. Upon the outbreak of the First
World War Great Britain promptly issued a proclamation forbidding
trade "with any person resident, carrying on business, or being in the
German Empire" without permission of the government. This was followed by the Trading with the Enemy Act which put into effect the
traditional policy of the country.[17] On December 23, 1915, however, the
British Government adopted the policy followed by France of proscrib-
ing trade with persons or corporations of enemy nationality doing business in neutral states. A "black-list" was drawn up enumerating the firms
with which trade relations might not be maintained. This action led to
a protest from the United States, under date of July 26, 1916,[18] claiming
that the measure was "inevitably and essentially inconsistent with the
rights of the citizens of all the nations not involved in the war." However, when the United States itself became a belligerent the same policy
toward enemy traders in neutral countries was adopted in the Trading
with the Enemy Act of October 6, 1917, the President being empowered
to extend the term *enemy* to include such persons should he deem it
expedient to do so.[19]

Practice during the Second World War. The British Trading with
the Enemy Act of 1939 followed the general lines of the earlier act. For
the purposes of the act a person was deemed to have traded with the
enemy if he had had any commerce, financial, or other intercourse with
an enemy, supplied goods to an enemy, paid or transmitted any money
or negotiable instrument to an enemy, or performed or discharged any
obligation of an enemy. The term *enemy* included not only an enemy
state, or an individual resident in enemy territory, but any incorporated

[15] 93 U.S. 24 (1876). Hudson, *Cases,* p. 1304; Fenwick, *Cases,* p. 786.

[16] Wallace 532 (1867). Hudson, *Cases,* p. 1317.

[17] For the text, see Baty and Morgan, *War: Its Conduct and Legal Results,* pp.
492 ff.

[18] *Am. White Book,* Vol. IV, p. 85; Savage, *Policy of the United States,* Vol. II,
p. 505; Hackworth, *Digest,* Vol. VI, pp. 333 ff.

[19] See Hackworth, *Digest,* Vol. VI, pp. 338 ff., where an instruction of the Department of State describes the various "lists" into which persons coming under the law
were divided.

or unincorporated body controlled by an enemy or incorporated under the laws of the enemy.[20]

Freezing of assets.   In the United States, even during the period of technical neutrality, measures were taken to "freeze" the assets of the neutral countries invaded by Germany, and the assets of Lithuania, Latvia, and Esthonia, as well as the assets of China and Japan.[21] By Executive Order of June 14, 1941, German and Italian assets were frozen, the purpose of the order being "to prevent the use of the financial facilities of the United States in ways harmful to national defense and other American interests, to prevent the liquidation in the United States of assets looted by duress or conquest, and to curb subversive activities in the United States." [22] On July 17 a proclamation was made authorizing the preparation of what was described as "The Proclaimed List of Certain Blocked Nationals," the object of which was to cut off the exportation of goods to persons who might be acting for the benefit of Germany or Italy either directly or indirectly, whether by transmitting funds or by subversive activities in their behalf.[23] When war came on December 9 it was only necessary to add a supplementary list of Japanese firms and persons affiliated with Japanese enterprises. The earlier Trading with the Enemy Act of 1917 was amended to meet the new conditions, particularly with respect to the transfer of funds.[24]

[20] In the leading case of Daimler Company v. Continental Tire and Rubber Company (1916) 2AC307; Fenwick, *Cases,* p. 194; Hudson, *Cases,* p. 311, it was held that while a company incorporated in the United Kingdom could as such be neither friend nor enemy, yet such a company could only act through its agents and these might assume an enemy character when they were resident in enemy country, or, wherever resident, were adhering to or taking instructions from the enemy. See McNair, *op. cit.,* pp. 62 ff.

[21] See Hackworth, *Digest,* Vol. III, pp. 653 ff.

[22] Dept. of State *Bulletin,* Vol. IV, p. 718. On the general subject, see Domke, *Trading with the Enemy in World War II,* with its Supplement, *The Control of Alien Property.*

[23] Dept. of State *Bulletin,* Vol. V, p. 41.

[24] For the text of the amendments, see *Am. Journal,* Vol. 36 (1942), Supp., p. 56.

CHAPTER **XXXII**

The Relation of Neutral States to Belligerents:
Principles at Issue

A. DEVELOPMENT OF THE STATUS OF NEUTRALITY

Neutrality as understood at the beginning of the twentieth century might be defined as the legal position of a state which remained aloof from a war between two other states or groups of states while maintaining certain rights towards the belligerents and observing certain duties prescribed by customary law or by international conventions or treaties. The status of neutrality was the logical result of an international system in which war was a legal procedure to which individual states might have recourse for the protection of their national interests and in which the community of nations assumed no responsibility for the maintenance of law and order and recognized no obligation to distinguish between the merits of the claims made by the contending parties. Let a war start, and whether third states liked it or not they found themselves in a new legal situation. They could join in the war if they wanted to, but if they decided to stay out of it they found themselves confronted with a new code of rights and duties which they had no choice but to accept.[1]

Grotius' conception of neutrality. The formal status of neutrality was an essentially modern conception. Under the feudal system there was little room for the development of a law of neutrality; and with the break up of the Holy Roman Empire and the development of national states princes preoccupied themselves with obtaining support in their dynastic wars by entering into treaties in anticipation of coming conflicts. The doctors of the Church taught that there were just wars and unjust wars; but the line between the two was more a matter of conscience than of legal rules, and it is significant that neither Vitoria nor

---

[1] On the general conception of neutrality, see *Neutrality, Its History, Economics and Law*, Vols. I-IV; Fenwick, *American Neutrality: Trial and Failure.*

716

Suarez, in their efforts to restrain the new "sovereign states" by appeals to the fundamental principles of moral conduct, felt called upon to discuss the status of neutrality. Grotius, still under the influence of the moral law, devoted only a brief chapter to those whom he described by the expressions "*qui in bello medii sunt; qui extra bellum sunt positi.*" It seemed to him consistent that a state might remain neutral and yet pass upon the justice of the war and modify its conduct accordingly. Whether it was expedient for a particular state to do so was another matter. It need not be restrained by any rigid doctrine of neutrality.[2]

Vattel's contribution. During the century succeeding Grotius the commercial interests of the leading maritime states exercised an important influence upon the development of neutrality. Neutral maritime states, such as Holland and Sweden, began to have a heavy stake in resisting the pretensions of the belligerents to capture vessels and goods on their way to enemy ports.[3] By the time of Vattel's treatise, in 1758, two fundamental principles had come to be accepted: first that belligerents were under an obligation to respect the neutrality of states which chose to remain neutral, and secondly that the status of a neutral carried with it specific obligations of impartiality. Vattel's Swiss origin made him particularly sensitive to the rights and obligations of the neutral state; and while his views were not on all points consistent they had considerable influence outside of the narrow circle in which he wrote.[4]

The nineteenth century. At times neutral states had to prepare to fight for their rights, as in the case of the "Armed Neutralities" of 1780 and 1800.[5] The United States, having proclaimed its neutrality in the war between Great Britain and France in 1793, struggled to maintain its rights against the excessive claims of both belligerents. It came close to war with one of the belligerents in 1798,[6] and after adopting em-

---

[2] "It is the duty of neutrals," he said, "to do nothing to strengthen those who are prosecuting an unjust cause, or which may impede the movements of him who is carrying on a just war. . . . But if the cause is a doubtful one they must manifest an impartial attitude towards both sides, in permitting them to pass through the country, in supplying their troops with provisions, and in not relieving the besieged." Book III, Chap. XVII, p. 3. The expression "Back to Grotius," used by scholars during the period between the two world wars, means "back to the principle of distinguishing between right and wrong in the conduct of nations," away from the later doctrine of Vattel and his successors that one nation could not sit in judgment upon another.

[3] The controversy between Selden and Grotius on the freedom of the seas which took place at the beginning of the seventeenth century was carried on unabated during the succeeding centuries and only found its definitive solution with the abandonment of neutrality. See p. 497. For a study of the effect of international commerce upon neutrality, see *Neutrality, Its History, Economics, and Law,* Vol. I.

[4] See the Introduction by De Lapradelle to the English translation of Vattel's treatise.

[5] See below, p. 733.

[6] See below, p. 733.

bargoes and passing nonintercourse acts was finally drawn into the war against the other belligerent in 1812.[7] But as the century progressed the position of neutral states became more secure. The neutrality of Great Britain during the American Civil War gave to that country an understanding of the position of neutral states which, as mistress of the seas, it had hitherto lacked.[8] By the close of the century neutrality had won an equal position with the claims of belligerency; but its rights and duties were still lacking definition and precision.

The Hague Conventions of 1907; the Declaration of London. The Hague Peace Conference of 1899 made no effort to codify the existing law of neutrality, confining itself to a *voeu* that the subject might be dealt with at a future conference. The second Conference, meeting in 1907, adopted two separate conventions, the one dealing with the rights and duties of neutral states in war on land, the other with the rights and duties of neutral states in naval war.[9] The first of the two conventions offered relatively little difficulty, the fundamental principles of the inviolability of neutral territory and of the corresponding obligations of the neutral state being then well established. The second convention, however, was adopted only after a long struggle between the powers that thought of themselves as probable belligerents in the next war and those that expected to be neutral, with the weight of the United States thrown on the side of the second group. The struggle was complicated by questions of naval power, the size of merchant marines, colonial possessions, and other factors bearing upon the success of maritime warfare.[10] The result was that a number of the controversial issues were left unsettled, notably questions relating to the scope of blockade and the character of contraband goods. The following year a smaller group of the leading maritime powers met at the London Naval Conference; but the compromise agreements there reached, embodied in the Declaration of London, had not yet been ratified when war broke out in 1914.[11] Neutrality was then put to a test such as it had not known before.

B. NEUTRALITY DURING THE FIRST WORLD WAR

The war opened with a series of neutrality proclamations by the states not involved in the issues leading to the conflict, the proclamation of President Wilson announcing in the usual set terms that the United States was "on terms of friendship and amity with the contending

[7] See Latané, *A History of American Foreign Policy*, Chap. VI; Bemis, *A Diplomatic History of the United States*, Chap. IX.

[8] See Bemis, *op. cit.*, Chap. XXI, "The Civil War, 1861-1867."

[9] For the texts of the two conventions, see *Hague Conventions*, pp. 133, 209.

[10] For comment upon the conflicting policies of the leading naval powers, see Higgins, *Hague Peace Conferences*, pp. 457 ff.

[11] For the text of the Declaration, see Higgins, *op. cit.*, p. 540, where the report of the committee is given explaining the compromises reached.

powers." [12] But the war had not progressed far before it was clear that it would be difficult for the United States to remain neutral and yet at the same time defend its traditional rights as a neutral in respect to the "freedom of the seas." Great Britain pressed hard upon the neutral rights of the United States by new extensions of the belligerent rights of blockade and capture of contraband; while Germany pressed even harder, and finally to the breaking point, with submarine warfare which affected both neutral ships and neutral passengers on enemy ships.[13] Harassed by both belligerents President Wilson had come to the conclusion by October 16, 1916, that the "business of neutrality" was over, and that no nation must henceforth be permitted to declare war and set in motion forces so destructive to the normal commerce of peaceful nations.[14] While the dominant issue which led to the entrance of the United States into the war on April 6, 1917, was the renewal of unrestricted submarine warfare by Germany, above and beyond technical neutral rights was the belief of President Wilson that something must be done to put an end to war itself, since by its very nature it put the neutral state in a position where it must either abandon its neutral rights or fight to maintain them.[15]

C. NEUTRALITY BETWEEN TWO WORLD WARS

Effect of the Covenant of the League of Nations. The Covenant of the League of Nations put an end in principle to the traditional law of neutrality. The obligation assumed by the members of the League under Article 10, "to respect and preserve as against external aggression the territorial integrity and existing political independence of all Members of the League" made it impossible for a member of the League to stand aside and take no part in the common defense of the victim of an act of aggression.[16] Article 11 of the Covenant made "any war or threat of war, whether immediately affecting any of the high contracting parties or not," a matter of concern to the whole League and authorized the League to take "any action that may be deemed wise and effectual to safeguard the peace of nations." [17] The members of the League were thus collectively responsible to find ways and means of preserving the peace in the presence of a situation of whatever kind that might threaten it. By Article 16 of the Covenant a member of the League which resorted to war in

---

[12] See p. 746, where President Wilson's appeal to the American people to be "impartial in thought as well as in action" is discussed.

[13] See above, p. 706 and below, pp. 733 ff.

[14] Address to the Senate.

[15] See, on this point, Fenwick, *American Neutrality: Trial and Failure,* pp. 16 ff.

[16] See Whitton, "La neutralité et la Société des Nations," *Recueil des Cours,* Vol. 17 (1927-II), pp. 449 ff.; McNair, "Neutrality and the League of Nations," in Oppenheim, *Int. Law,* 4th ed., §§ 292a-292g.

[17] On the broad scope of Art. 11 of the Covenant, see Kunz, *Die intrasystematische Stellung des Art. XI des Völkerbundpaktes;* Ray, *Commentaire,* pp. 372 ff.

violation of its obligations of peaceful settlement was *ipso facto* held to have committed an act of war against all other members of the League, and the latter were pledged to discontinue trade and financial relations with it.[18]

Technically, however, the Covenant was no more than a multilateral treaty, creating special obligations for the parties to it but leaving the status of nonsignatory states just what it was before the treaty. The failure of the United States and of other states to accept the obligations of the Covenant, however, created a situation in which it was difficult to determine what was left of the old law of neutrality.[19] Suppose that the League should take collective action against a state resorting to war in violation of the provisions of the Covenant, would the United States and other nonmember states be entitled to the full application of their rights as neutrals under the old law? Would they be obliged to acquiesce in measures short of war which the members of the League might find it convenient to resort to if the situation could be adequately met by them?

Effect of the Kellogg-Briand Pact. In 1928 the United States, responding to the suggestion of the French Foreign Minister, Briand, promoted the adoption of the General Pact for the Renunciation of War, known as the Pact of Paris or the Kellogg-Briand Pact.[20] The provisions of the Pact were comprehensive. The contracting parties condemned recourse to war for the solution of international controversies; they renounced war as an instrument of national policy; and they agreed that the settlement of disputes of whatever kind should never be sought except by pacific means. But the Pact made no provision for measures of enforcement in case of the violation of its pledges; it set up no machinery to determine whether a particular act should constitute a violation; and its broad "outlawry of war" was limited and qualified by a covering letter of Secretary Kellogg in which the right of self-defense was reserved in such general terms as to permit escape from the obligations of the Pact even more easily than the terms of Article 15 permitted escape from the obligations of the Covenant.[21] Nevertheless its provisions were regarded by a large number of jurists as definitely restricting the status of neutrality which might otherwise be claimed by states not members of the League of Nations.[22]

The invasion of Manchuria by Japan in the summer of 1931 led the American Secretary of State, Stimson, to issue a statement on January 7,

---

[18] For the "loopholes" in Arts. 12, 13, and 15 which made the obligations of Art. 16 less definitive than the terms appeared to read, see above, p. 621, note 76.

[19] See p. 293.

[20] For the text of the Pact, see *Treaties and Conventions*, IV, 5130.

[21] See p. 278, where the terms of the Pact are discussed in connection with the right of self-defense.

[22] See below, p. 723, note 32.

1932, declaring that the United States could not "admit the legality of any situation *de facto*" nor did it "intend to recognize any situation, treaty or agreement which may be brought about by means contrary to the covenants and obligations of the Pact of Paris." [23] Seven months later, on August 8, Secretary Stimson expressed the opinion that: "Under the former concepts of international law" states not parties to a conflict could only exercise "a strict neutrality alike towards the injured and the aggressor. . . . But now under the covenants of the Briand-Kellogg Pact such a conflict becomes of legal concern to everybody connected with the Treaty." [24] The position thus taken was, however, not put to the test in consequence of the fact that Japan refrained from declaring war against China. In 1934 the International Law Association adopted a series of resolutions proposing measures that might be taken against a state violating the Pact of Paris. These "Budapest Articles of Interpretation" recognized that a state, without entering the war or being guilty of illegal conduct, might modify the traditional laws of neutrality in favor of the victim of an attack in violation of the terms of the Pact.[25]

Legislation to insure neutrality.   In the meantime the threat of war in Europe gave rise to a succession of laws by which the Congress of the United States sought to prevent the country from being drawn into war by any of its citizens who might have a commercial interest in the profits of neutral trade with the belligerents. A resolution had been adopted in May, 1934, giving the President authority to apply an arms embargo against Bolivia and Paraguay if he found that it would contribute to the reestablishment of peace between the two countries.[26] No distinction was made between the two belligerents with respect to responsibility for the war or willingness to discontinue hostilities in accordance with the terms of the commission of mediators. A year later, on August 31, 1935, a joint resolution was passed providing that upon the outbreak or during the progress of war between two or more foreign states the President should proclaim the fact and thereafter it should be unlawful to export arms, ammunition, or implements of war from any place in the United

[23] For the text of the statement, see *International Conciliation*, 1933, p. 413. For editorial comment, see Q. Wright, "The Stimson Note of January 7, 1932," *Am. Journal*, Vol. 26 (1932), p. 342.

[24] For excerpts from the text of the address, see *Int. Conciliation*, 1933, p. 419.

For a discussion of the relation of the Pact of Paris to the status of neutrality, see C. G. Fenwick, "The Implications of Consultation in the Pact of Paris," *Am. Journal*, Vol. 26 (1932), p. 787; Q. Wright, "The Meaning of the Pact of Paris," *ibid.*, Vol. 27 (1933), p. 57; Q. Wright and C. Eagleton, "Neutrality and Neutral Rights Following the Pact of Paris for the Renunciation of War," *Proceedings*, Am. Soc. Int. Law, 1930, pp. 79, 87.

[25] For the text of the Budapest Articles, see International Law Association, *Report of the 38th Conference*, p. 66. For editorial comment, see M. O. Hudson, *Am. Journal*, Vol. 29 (1935), p. 92.

[26] For the text of the resolution, see Deak and Jessup, *A Collection of Neutrality Laws, Regulations and Treaties of Various Countries*, Vol. II, p. 1143.

States to any port of the belligerent states or to any neutral port for transshipment to a belligerent country.[27] A later section of the act made it unlawful for American citizens to travel as passengers on vessels of a belligerent nation if the President should find that the prohibition would serve to maintain peace.[28]

But there were other rights of the neutral state which it was believed must be renounced if the United States was to keep out of the coming war. A law of 1936 made it unlawful to buy or sell the bonds or securities of any belligerent country or to "make any loan or extend any credit to any such government," thus depriving bankers as well as munition-makers of an opportunity of making profits out of a war or of having an interest in the outcome of a war.[29] By a law of May 1, 1937, a "cash and carry" plan was put into effect, by which "certain articles or materials," as determined by the President, must, if bought in the United States, be paid for before leaving the United States and must be transported in the vessels of some other country.[30] The United States had now provided against a repetition of the incidents which had led to its entry into the war in 1917. It had anticipated the possibility that any act or interest of its citizens should lead it into another war. It had announced to the world that it would remain neutral in the coming war, no qualifications or reservations being made as to the possibility of a distinction between the belligerents on ground of the violation of the provisions of the Kellogg-Briand Pact.

Theories of jurists. During the years between the invasion of Manchuria in 1931 and the outbreak of war in Europe in 1939 jurists engaged in a sharp debate with respect to the place of neutrality in a system of international law. European and Latin American jurists, whose countries

[27] For the text of the act, see *ibid.*, Vol. II, p. 1100. For editorial comment on the act, see C. G. Fenwick, P. C. Jessup, *Am. Journal,* Vol. 29 (1935), pp. 663, 665. The Act of 1935, as amended in 1936, was qualified by a provision in favor of an American republic engaged in war against a non-American state.

[28] The law obviously had in mind the case of the *Lusitania,* and other vessels during the First World War. See above, p. 706.

[29] For the text of the law, see *Am. Journal,* Vol. 30 (1936), Supp., p. 109.

[30] For the text of the law, see *Am. Journal,* Vol. 31 (1937), Supp., p. 147.

[31] A survey of the purpose of these various laws may be found in Fenwick, *American Neutrality: Trial and Failure,* § III. Unhappily their general effect was to assure the aggressors that if war came, their enemies, less prepared than themselves, would be denied the traditional right to obtain supplies from the United States as a neutral.

On September 21, 1939, following the outbreak of the war, President Roosevelt urged the repeal of the embargo provisions of the act of 1937 as being "wholly inconsistent with ancient precepts of the law of nations." Repeal of the embargo on arms, he said, would put the country "back on the solid footing of real and traditional neutrality." For the text of the message, see Department of State *Bulletin,* p. 275. In spite of the impartiality suggested in a return to traditional neutrality, it was clear that the purpose of the repeal was to put the states which were resisting the aggression of Germany in a position to make good in part their unpreparedness by purchases of arms in the United States.

were members of the League of Nations, took in general the position that law must henceforth begin with the principle of the collective responsibility of the whole community of nations for the protection of its individual members. Changes in the *status quo*, called for by the principle of justice, must follow, not precede, the prevention of acts of violence.[32] Jurists in the United States were sharply divided. A majority, perhaps, recognized the incompatibility between solemn pledges condemning recourse to war and the unwillingness of their country to agree to take sides against a state violating its pledges and committing an act of aggression. Neutrality, it was said, was fundamentally immoral; for it represented in practice a refusal to distinguish between right and wrong when the principles were at hand for making the distinction feasible.[33] Besides it was clear that in the event of another war belligerents would encroach upon the rights of neutrals as they had done in the past war, so that the neutral state would be put in the position of either abandoning its traditional rights or of fighting to maintain them.[34] As a practical matter the only hope of remaining neutral in another war was to see that there would not be another war.[35]

In contrast with this position other jurists believed that it was still possible to insist upon the observance of the traditional laws of neutrality;

[32] Outstanding among the European proponents of the incompatibility of neutrality with the system of collective security were Politis, *Neutrality and Peace*, to whom neutrality was an anachronism, immoral, and impractical; Ray, *Commentaire du Pacte de la Société des Nations*, who, speaking of cases of violation of the Kellogg Pact, observed that there was no longer the duty nor even the right to treat belligerents in the same way; Le Fur, *Précis de Droit International Public*, who described neutrality in an organized society as an antijuridical notion the product of international anarchy; Fauchille, *Traité de Droit International Public*, 8ème ed. of Bonfils. See also, Cohn, *Neo-Neutrality*, who, while rejecting traditional neutrality, called for a combination of neutrals to suppress illegal warfare; G. Scelle, H. Lauterpacht and others in *Collective Security*, International Studies Conference, 1936.

[33] See, for example, the opinions expressed by Fenwick, Wright, Whitton, Vandenbosh, Graham, Eagleton, and others, *Proceedings*, Am. Soc. Int. Law, 1933, pp. 55, 63, 92, 142, 147, 151, 157, 163.

[34] Compare, on this point, C. Warren, "What Are the Rights of Neutrals Now, in Practice?", *Proceedings*, Am. Soc. Int. Law, 1933, pp. 128 ff., where the speaker suggested that the United States should enter into negotiations with the belligerents at the outset of each war to obtain the utmost concessions for the trade of American citizens, or else to negotiate with belligerents other than the aggressor so as to discourage aggression.

[35] See on this point Fenwick, *American Neutrality: Trial and Failure*, Introduction.

An interesting compromise was reached by the Harvard Research group. Those who were opposed to the codification of the laws of neutrality insisted that the Draft Convention on Rights and Duties of Neutral States in Naval and Aerial War, which a majority of the Advisers believed feasible, should be accompanied by a Draft Convention on Rights and Duties of States in Case of Aggression, which was based upon the principle that a state which violated a specific obligation not to resort to force was not to be given the benefit of the impartial treatment required of neutrals by the traditional law. *Am. Journal*, Vol. 33 (1939), pp. 167, 809. The second draft is accompanied by an elaborate bibliography listing articles both by the opponents of traditional neutrality and by its adherents.

that it was impossible under the existing political conditions to distinguish between right and wrong; and that the only hope for law and order in the world consisted in limiting the range of war as far as possible and in making the neutral states "islands of peace" until such time as the belligerents exhausted their will to fight.[36] Sanctions, it was argued, were nothing more than war in another form. The only method of avoiding war was to call attention to the time-honored methods of peaceful settlement. If these procedures would not work, methods of coercion would not either.[37]

D. NEUTRALITY DURING THE SECOND WORLD WAR

The outbreak of war in 1939 witnessed a temporary revival of the traditional law of neutrality. The League of Nations found it impossible under the circumstances to put into effect the provisions of Article 17 of the Covenant.[38] The President of the United States, in his proclamation of neutrality, announced that the United States was "on terms of friendship and amity with the contending powers and with the persons inhabiting their several dominions." [39] No distinction was made between the belligerents in respect to the restrictions imposed by the law upon acts committed within the jurisdiction of the United States. Proclamations of neutrality were made by other states not involved in the conflict. On their part the belligerents proceeded to enforce the usual restrictions upon neutral trade and to push their measures of attack and defense to the limits of the law as they construed it.

Inter-American defense of neutrality. Acting in accordance with the provisions of the Buenos Aires treaty of 1936 and the Declaration of Lima of 1938, the Government of Panama initiated the procedure of consultation provided for, and a meeting of Foreign Ministers was held

---

[36] See P. C. Jessup, "Is Neutrality Essential?" *Proceedings,* Am. Soc. Int. Law, 1933, p. 134, and remarks by E. M. Borchard, *ibid.,* pp. 61, 160; also E. M. Borchard, *Am. Journal,* Vol. 27 (1933), pp. 114, 293, 518; *Proceedings,* Am. Soc. Int. Law, 1930, pp. 115 ff.

[37] A significant statement of the position in favor of the maintenance of traditional neutrality was made by J. B. Moore, "An Appeal to Reason," *Foreign Affairs,* July, 1933. See also Borchard and Lage, *Neutrality for the United States,* Part III, where the authors argued that the whole conception of "aggressor" was "a delusion and a betrayer of reason in a world such as this. . . . The assumption that you can 'enforce peace' without creating the psychology of war, without inciting to war, is hazardous in the extreme." President Wilson's statement that "Neutrality is no longer possible or desirable when the peace of the world and the liberty of the peoples is at stake" was described as a "summons to world war in the name of peace."

[38] Art. 17 called for an appeal to Germany to accept the obligations of the Covenant, and in the event of its refusal to do so the provisions of Art. 16 were applicable.

[39] Notwithstanding the terms of the Proclamation President Roosevelt promptly sought the repeal by Congress of the prohibition against the sale of arms and munitions of war. See note 31.

at Panama City on September 23, 1939.[40] Measures were promptly taken to carry out the agreement of 1936 in accordance with which the American Republics were to "adopt in their character of neutrals a common and solidary attitude." "Standards of conduct" were adopted which the American Republics proposed to follow "in order to maintain their status as neutral states and fulfil their neutral duties, as well as require the recognition of the rights inherent in such status." [41] An exceptional measure, departing from customary law, was the establishment of a "zone of security" around the American continent, from which belligerent operations were to be excluded.[42] The preamble of this "Declaration of Panama" called attention to the absence of any justification that the interests of belligerents should prevail over the rights of neutrals, and that there was nothing in the nature of the war to warrant any obstruction to inter-American communications. For these reasons the Governments of the American Republics declared that "as a measure of continental self-protection" they were "as of inherent right" entitled to have the waters adjacent to the American continent "free from the commission of any hostile act" by any non-American belligerent nation. The "zone of security" was marked out as beginning at the terminus of the United States-Canada boundary in Passamaquoddy Bay and following east, south, west, and north around the continent to the Pacific terminus of the United States-Canada boundary in the strait of Juan de Fuca.[43]

On what legal basis could the security zone be justified? The assertion in the Declaration of an "inherent right" must be taken as meaning that under the circumstances with which they were confronted the American Republics believed that the new rule they were adopting as a measure of self-defense was essentially reasonable and should be accepted by the

[40] For the proceedings of the Meeting, see *International Conferences,* 1933-1940, pp. 315 ff.

[41] Resolution V, General Declaration of Neutrality of the American Republics. The "standards" set forth in the Declaration follow in general the established rules of neutrality; but definite positions were taken with respect to transfer of flag and the status of armed merchant vessels. The Declaration made provision for the creation of an Inter-American Neutrality Committee, to be composed of seven experts in international law whose duty it should be to study and formulate "recommendations with respect to the problems of neutrality, in the light of experience and changing circumstances." See C. G. Fenwick, "The Inter-American Neutrality Committee," *Am. Journal,* Vol. 35 (1941), p. 12.

[42] For the text of the "Declaration of Panama," see *International Conferences,* 1933-1940, p. 334.

[43] The Declaration provided that compliance with the resolution was to be secured "through joint representation to such belligerents as may now or in the future be engaged in hostilities, . . . without prejudice to the exercise of the individual rights of each State inherent in their sovereignty." This left each state free to use forcible measures if it chose to do so.

Brazil, having a special interest in the protection of its coastal cities, added a supplementary declaration explaining the reasons for its support of the action taken.

belligerents for that very reason. The Declaration of Panama made no reference to the means of securing its enforcement; but it was generally understood that the American Republics were not limiting themselves to the expression of a "pious wish." [44]

Effect of violations of neutrality. The violation by Germany of the neutrality of Norway, Denmark, Holland, Belgium, and Luxemburg in the spring of 1940 had far-reaching effects upon the neutral American states.[45] A meeting of Foreign Ministers was held at Havana, in July, 1940, and a declaration was adopted providing for Reciprocal Assistance and Cooperation for the Defense of the Nations of the Americas, in the event of an act of aggression "by a non-American nation." [46] A convention was signed providing for the provisional administration of European colonies and possessions "in the Americas," and a resolution, designated as the "Act of Habana," was adopted providing for an emergency committee which could take action pending the ratification of the proposed convention.[47] The United States negotiated with Great Britain the exchange of fifty destroyers, described as "out-of-date," for the lease of naval bases on British islands in the Caribbean.[48]

Lend-Lease Act. The following spring, on March 11, 1941, the Lend-Lease Act was passed by the American Congress authorizing the President, through the appropriate executive officer, to manufacture "any defense article for the government of any country whose defense the President deems vital to the defense of the United States" and to sell, exchange, "lease, lend," or otherwise dispose of such defense articles to any such government.[49] The most serious obligations of the neutral state were

[44] In justification of the principle of defense underlying the Declaration of Panama, see Fenwick, *American Neutrality: Trial and Failure*, pp. 129 ff.; P. M. Brown, C. G. Fenwick, Q. Wright, *Am. Journal*, Vol. 34 (1940), pp. 112, 116, 246.

[45] See Dept. of State *Bulletin*, Vol. II, p. 568.

[46] The opening paragraph of the declaration constituted what was practically a wartime alliance: "The Second Meeting of the Ministers of Foreign Affairs of the American Republics declares: That any attempt on the part of a non-American State against the integrity or inviolability of the territory, the sovereignty or the political independence of an American State shall be considered as an act of aggression against the States which sign this declaration." *International Conferences*, 1933-1940, p. 360.

[47] See *ibid.*, pp. 373, 364; Hackworth, *Digest*, Vol. V, pp. 465 ff. For the statement of Secretary Hull concerning the background of the convention, see Dept. of State *Bulletin*, Vol. III, p. 269.

[48] The elaborate justification of the act by the Attorney General and by President Roosevelt on ground of self-defense (see Dept. of State *Bulletin*, Vol. III, p. 199) could not hide the fact that the transaction was contrary to the traditional law of neutrality. International law of the time knew of no halfway status. Acts contrary to strict neutrality which a neutral might do in self-defense were done at the risk of retaliation by the injured belligerent. In this case Germany preferred to overlook the transaction rather than bring the United States into the war.

[49] For the text of the act, see *Am. Journal*, Vol. 35 (1941), Supp. 76. Secs. 3 (a) and 3 (b) of the act are given in Hackworth, *Digest*, Vol. VII, p. 691.

thus set aside on ground of national defense, although the United States still continued technically neutral.[50]

E. THE ABANDONMENT OF NEUTRALITY

Following the entrance of the United States into the war on December 7, 1941, a special consultative meeting of the Ministers of Foreign Affairs of the American Republics was held at Rio de Janeiro in January, 1942, at which the American Republics reaffirmed their declaration at Havana to consider any act of aggression on the part of a non-American state against any one of them as an act of aggression against all, and their determination to cooperate jointly for their mutual protection, and they thereupon recommended the breaking of their diplomatic relations with Japan, Germany, and Italy, "since the first-mentioned state attacked and the other two declared war on an American country." [51] Subsequent resolutions and recommendations of the meeting went into details with respect to the mobilization of the economic resources of the American states for the common defense of the continent.[52]

Provisions of the Charter of the United Nations. It was to be expected that, with the establishment of the "wider and permanent system of general security" contemplated in the Atlantic Charter and the "general international organization" specifically provided for in the Moscow Declaration of October 30, 1943, the existing international law in respect to the rights and duties of neutral states would no longer be regarded as having legal validity. The adoption of the Charter of the United Nations on June 26, 1945, finally marked the end of neutrality as a legal system.[53] No provision was made for a separate neutral status on the part of the states not invited to participate in the framing of the Charter and not subsequently admitted to membership. In as much, however, as action by the Security Council to enforce the terms of the Charter would not be "war" in the technical sense, it was possible to overlook the technical question as to the rights and duties of states not participating in the action of the Security Council.

[50] For an elaborate exposition of the principle of self-defense underlying the act, see address of Attorney General Jackson before the Inter-American Bar Association at Havana, 1941. *Am. Journal,* Vol. 35 (1941), pp. 349 ff. Also statement of Secretary Hull, Hackworth, *Digest,* Vol. VII, p. 687.

[51] For the text of the document, see *Int. Conferences of American States,* 1942-1954, p. 10.

[52] See, in particular, No. II, Production of Strategic Materials, and No. V, Severance of Commercial and Financial Relations. For a study of the specific objectives of the meeting, see C. G. Fenwick, "The Third Meeting of Ministers of Foreign Affairs at Rio de Janeiro," *Am. Journal,* Vol. 36 (1942), p. 169.

[53] See above, p. 219, "Functions of the United Nations," where the collective security provisions of the Charter are discussed. The Charter nowhere mentions the effect of its provisions upon the traditional law of neutrality, but the inconsistency between the new and the old law was too obvious to require specific mention.

"Neutralism" in relation to the "cold war." To be sharply distinguished from neutral states under the old, now antiquated, law of neutrality, are the states that have adopted an attitude of neutrality in respect to the obligations of collective security under the Charter of the United Nations. "Neutralism" appears to describe the position of certain states that are unwilling to take a part in the decisions relating not to war in the traditional sense, but to the "cold war" involving the conflicting policies of the Soviet Union and the Western World which, the new neutrals fear, may at any time involve them in a conflict in respect to which they are not prepared to take sides. Justification for the failure to live up to the obligations of the Charter in respect to collective security appears to lie in the fact that the anticipated collective security system broke down from the start, releasing them from their obligations on the principle *rebus non sic stantibus*.[54]

[54] See "The Legal Aspects of Neutralism," *Am. Journal,* Vol. 51 (1957), p. 71.

CHAPTER XXXIII

Neutral Rights: In Retrospect

Accepting the traditional status of neutrality as definitely terminated upon the adoption of the Charter of the United Nations, the elaborate provisions of the two Hague Conventions and the numerous controversies over their application in the two world wars have no longer any standing in the existing system of international law. But the historic interest attaching to them and the large place they once occupied in the technical treatises and political literature of the period down to 1945 justify a condensed survey of the chief issues involved.

A. INVIOLABILITY OF NEUTRAL TERRITORY

The primary and most vital right of the neutral state was the inviolability of its territory implicit in the conception of sovereignty. No act of hostility might be committed by either of the belligerents within the jurisdiction of the neutral state. But here, as in other branches of the law, belligerents frequently alleged the justification of self-defense when the opportunity presented itself to gain an advantage over the enemy by the violation of neutral territory. Self-defense was alleged by the British Government for the demand made upon Denmark in 1807 for the surrender of the neutral Danish fleet to Great Britain to prevent it from being used by Napoleon against Great Britain. Upon the failure of Denmark to comply with the request, orders were given to seize the fleet.[1] In the case of the Confederate cruiser *Florida*, which in 1864 was captured in Brazilian waters by the United States man-of-war *Wachusett*, the United States admitted that the capture was "an unauthorized, unlawful, and indefensible exercise of the naval force of the United States,

[1] The act has been variously commented upon by writers, some, as Hall and Westlake, excusing it, others condemning it, and again others finding extenuating circumstances. See Stowell, *Intervention in International Law*, pp. 409 ff.

within a foreign country, in defiance of its established and duly recognized government." Due apology was made, the commander of the *Wachusett* was sent before a court-martial, and the crew of the *Florida* were set at liberty.[2]

Alleged justification of self-defense. The First World War opened with the violation of the neutrality of Belgium and of Luxemburg, notwithstanding specific treaties guaranteeing their permanent neutral status.[3] Self-defense was claimed by Germany as justification, the claim being made that it was necessary to anticipate an attack by France from that direction. Great Britain, not accepting the justification and believing its own national interests to be imperiled by the act, declared war. The United States, not being a party to the neutralization treaties, followed the traditions of the time and made no protest.

Airships over neutral territory. Was there a right of innocent passage for belligerent airships through neutral air spaces similar to the right of innocent passage through neutral territorial waters? The question had been debated before 1914, but upon the outbreak of war Holland, as a neutral state, promptly announced that the use of the air space over Dutch territory would be considered a violation of its neutrality and that resistance would be offered by it to the passage of belligerent airships. Consistently with this position, the Dutch Government not only fired upon belligerent airships invading the national air space but was careful to intern the officers and crew of belligerent planes which were forced to descend upon Dutch territory.[4] At the close of the war the position taken by Holland was adopted by the commission of jurists which had been designated by the Washington Conference to prepare a code of aerial warfare; and while the proposed code failed of ratification the rule adopted by Holland came to be accepted as the law of the future.

Violations of neutrality during the Second World War. Shortly after the opening the Second World War, in December, 1939, the German pocket battleship *Graf Spee*, following a battle with three British cruisers, took refuge in the harbor of Montevideo. The Uruguayan Government, intent upon fulfilling its duties as a neutral, ordered the vessel to leave port when the period of seventy-two hours allowed for making necessary repairs had expired. The vessel left the harbor, and after the crew had been transferred by prearrangement to the German merchant ship *Tacoma*, it was scuttled at a point within the river about six or seven miles from shore, still within waters claimed by Uruguay as territorial.[5]

---

[2] Moore, *Digest*, Vol. II, pp. 1090 ff. See also *The Florida*, 101 U.S. 37 (1879). Fenwick, *Cases*, p. 792.

[3] See above, p. 127.

[4] See above, p. 484.

[5] For the facts of the case, see Uruguayan Blue Book; Hackworth, *Digest*, Vol. VII, pp. 450, 509. Query, whether the scuttling of a warship in neutral territorial

The American governments presented a collective protest against the violation of the security zone they had established at Panama three months earlier; but the belligerents on both sides contested the validity of a new rule of neutrality that had been adopted without their agreement. The case of the German transport *Altmark*, attacked by a British cruiser in Norwegian territorial waters on February 16, 1940, was justified by Great Britain on the ground that the British prisoners on board exempted the case from the rule of free passage through territorial waters.[6]

Invasion of neutral states. Little was left of the inviolability of neutral territory as the war proceeded. On April 9, 1940, the German Government invaded neutral Norway, alleging the possession of documentary proof that Great Britain and France intended to cross Norwegian territory; and on the same day neutral Denmark was also invaded.[7] A month later British troops occupied Iceland in order to anticipate a German invasion of the island, and the following year the United States joined in the occupation in order to prevent the island from being used as an air or naval base by Germany.[8] On May 9, alleging that it was in possession of evidence that the Allies were about to attack through Belgium, Luxemburg, and the Netherlands, the German Government invaded the three neutral states without warning.[9] Ten days later a formal protest was made by the twenty-one American republics of the "ruthless violation by Germany of the neutrality and sovereignty of Belgium, Holland, and Luxemburg." [10] On October 28, 1940, Italy, asserting that the neutrality of Greece had become "more and more of a pure fiction" demanded the right to occupy the country for the duration of the war. The demand being refused by Greece, formal war resulted.[11] The attack by the Axis armies upon Yugoslavia on April 6, 1941, was officially explained by the Yugoslav Government as due to its refusal to

---

waters should be regarded as an act of "hostilities" or merely as a trespass upon the territory of the neutral state. After its suicidal act the *Graf Spee* continued to lie in the bed of the river, a menace to local traffic. But the Government of Uruguay did not press a claim on this account, and acquiesced in the sale by the German Government to a local contractor of the right to remove the derelict vessel.

After delivering the officers and the crew of the *Graf Spee* to Argentine vessels, the *Tacoma* returned to Montevideo, where it was itself interned by the Uruguayan Government. The ground of internment was the unneutral act of giving assistance to a belligerent warship. Hackworth, Vol. VII, p. 561.

[6] See Hackworth, *Digest*, Vol. VII, pp. 568 ff.

[7] See "German Invasion of Denmark and Norway," in *Documents on Am. Foreign Relations*, Vol. II, pp. 398 ff.

[8] See Department of State *Bulletin*, pp. 15 ff.

[9] See "German Invasion of Belgium, Luxemburg and the Netherlands," *Documents*, Vol. II, pp. 415 ff.

[10] See Hackworth, *Digest*, Vol. VII, p. 356. For comment upon the situation see C. G. Fenwick, "The Inter-American Neutrality Committee," *Am. Journal*, Vol. 35 (1941), p. 25.

[11] See "Italian Invasion of Greece," *Documents*, Vol. III, pp. 311 ff.

depart from its position of neutrality adopted at the beginning of the war.[12]

Acts short of hostilities.   In addition to formal hostilities the Hague Conventions of 1907 entered into details with respect to acts short of hostilities prohibited to belligerents in neutral territory, such as the transport of munitions of war, the erection of wireless telegraph stations, and the establishment of prize courts. In the case of the *Appam*, a captured British vessel brought in by a German prize crew to be interned in the port of Norfolk, the Court held that the effort "to make of an American port a depository of captured vessels with a view to keeping them there indefinitely" was a breach of neutrality.[13]

B. STATUS OF NEUTRAL PERSONS AND PROPERTY UNDER BELLIGERENT JURISDICTION

It was agreed that neutral persons in belligerent territory must bear the burdens of the war other than being drafted into military service. But could neutral vessels in belligerent ports be seized under an old *right of angary* and made to transport troops and supplies? Could they be requisitioned upon payment of compensation? During the First World War a number of Dutch merchant ships in American ports were taken over by order of the Government as being "necessary for essential purposes connected with the prosecution of the war"; similar action was taken by the British Government. A further question arose: whether vessels under construction in American shipyards for Norwegian neutral subjects might be requisitioned and what would be "just compensation in such cases," the contract price or the value of the ships under the special circumstances of the war? [14]

Of long standing was the question whether neutral goods on enemy vessels captured on the high seas were subject to capture. Did "free ships," *i.e.* neutral ships make "free goods"? In the case of the *Nereide*,[15] Chief Justice Marshall declared in 1815 that it had been "fully and unequivocally recognized by the United States" that "the goods of an enemy found in the vessel of a friend are prize of war, and that the goods of a friend found in the vessel of an enemy are to be restored." The Declaration of Paris of 1856 confirmed the rule, but this was to no avail when the issue arose of submarine warfare in 1917.

---

12 See "Invasion of Yugoslavia," *Documents,* Vol. III, pp. 324 ff.

13 Berg. v. B. and A. Steam Navigation Co., 243 U.S. 124 (1917). Fenwick, *Cases,* p. 794; Hudson, *Cases,* p. 1352. For comment on the *Appam* case, *pro* and *con,* see *Am. Journal,* Vol. 11 (1917), pp. 270, 302.

14 On the general subject of angary, see Hackworth, *Digest,* Vol. VI, p. 638; Phillipson, *International Law and the Great War,* p. 72; Case of the *Zamora,* Fenwick, *Cases,* p. 827; Hudson, *Cases,* p. 1402; *Am. Journal,* Vol. 11 (1917), p. 266; *ibid.,* Vol. 13 (1919), p. 267.

15 9 Cranch 388 (1815). Fenwick, *Cases,* p. 824.

C. NEUTRAL TRADE WITH BELLIGERENTS:
BLOCKADE AND CONTRABAND

More difficult was the issue of the right of the neutral state to protect the trade of its citizens with the belligerents as against the right of the belligerent to starve out the enemy by capturing goods destined to it. The conflict was an old one, and the formation of the Armed Neutralities of 1780 and 1800 showed that the neutrals were prepared to fight for their neutral rights. On the eve of the First World War the Declaration of London succeeded in drawing up a comprehensive code of law. But the interests at issue were too vital to permit ratification of the compromises there reached; and the experience of two World Wars proved conclusively that the interests of belligerents and neutrals were irreconcilable.[16]

Effectiveness of blockade. Could a belligerent, by simply drawing a line around an enemy port and declaring it blockaded, justify the capture of neutral vessels seeking to enter the port? Such "paper blockades" were wholly unjustified, and the United States, protesting the validity of both British and French blockades, finally declared war in 1812 against the worst offender.[17] Suppose, however, that a British vessel, this time neutral in 1861-1865, consigned its cargo to a neutral port nearer to the southern states so that the cargo could later be transshipped to smaller vessels which might succeed in running the blockade; could the first vessel be condemned for breach of blockade? [18] In the leading case of the *Springbok* the Supreme Court held that the voyage from London to the blockaded port was "both in law and in the intent of the parties, one voyage." The Declaration of London of 1907 rejected the rule, but with the coming of the First World War it reappeared in more drastic form than before. Great Britain, finding that Germany, although itself blockaded, could be equally well supplied by importing goods from adjacent neutral states, announced on March 1, 1915, that it was its intention "to detain and take into port ships carrying goods of presumed enemy destination, ownership or origin." The United States protested but was answered by citation of the Civil War precedents.[19] During the

---

[16] See Bentwich, *The Declaration of London;* Garner, *Prize Law,* pp. 160 ff.; Fenwick, *Am. Neutrality: Trial and Failure,* § V; Colombos, *A Treatise on the Law of Prize.*

[17] The paper blockades of the Napoleonic wars fill many pages of the early history of the United States. See, in particular, Bemis, *Diplomatic History of the United States,* Chap. IX; Latané, *History of American Foreign Policy,* Chap. VI.

[18] Wallace 1 (1866). Fenwick, *Cases,* p. 806. For the views of publicists on this famous case, see Briggs, *The Doctrine of Continuous Voyage.*

[19] The documentary history of the negotiations may be found in the *American White Book,* Vols. I-IV; *Papers Relating to the Foreign Relations of the United States,* 1914-1917; or, in more compact form, in Carlton Savage, *Policy of the United States toward Maritime Commerce in War,* Vol. II, pp. 50-51. See also Hackworth, *Digest,* Vol. VII, pp. 114 ff., where the documents of the controversy are summarized.

Second World War a new form of blockade was directed against *exports* from Germany as a means of cutting off the exchange needed to buy goods from neighboring countries.

What blockade could not accomplish belligerents sought to accomplish by the capture of contraband. But what was contraband? Obviously arms and munitions of war, which even in the time of Grotius made the neutral furnishing them become "of the party of the enemy." On the other hand, there were articles that were of no use in war; and the carriage of these was, therefore, not a matter of complaint by the belligerent. But, again, there were objects "useful both in war and out of war, such as money, provisions, ships, and other fittings." These, Grotius stated, might be intercepted by the belligerent according to the circumstances of the war, when their carriage to the enemy would prolong his resistance.[20]

Years passed and controversies multiplied, Great Britain and the United States holding to the threefold classification, and France and other Continental states to a limited list of absolute contraband. Finally the Declaration of London of 1909 succeeded in drawing up three separate lists of *absolute, conditional* contraband, and a "free list" consisting of articles "not susceptible of use in war" which could not be declared contraband. Among other items on this list were raw cotton, wool, hemp, rubber, and metallic ores.[21]

The distinction between absolute and conditional contraband. The elaborate provisions of the Declaration of London showed little ability on the part of the delegates to anticipate the future. The attempt to draw up a definitive free list including cotton, rubber, and metallic ores, when science was announcing the invention of new instruments of warfare and substitutes for existing war materials, was to invite violation of the provisions even if they had been ratified. But more extraordinary was the failure to realize that the traditional distinction between absolute and conditional contraband had lost its meaning. A hundred years earlier prize courts could determine with fair accuracy the destination of goods, whether for military or civilian use.[22] In the case of the *Jonge Margaretha*, decided in 1799, a cargo of Dutch cheeses captured on its way from Amsterdam to Brest, at that time a French port of naval equipment, was condemned by the British court as contraband because destined obviously for the use of the armed forces of the enemy. Had the same cargo been destined to "a general commercial port," said the court, it would have been exempt from capture as being intended for "civil use." There was no

---

[20] *De jure belli ac pacis,* Eng. trans., Bk. III, Chap. I, § V.

[21] The positions taken by the different naval powers with respect to particular articles in dispute naturally reflected the military interest of the particular power in having the article included in or excluded from the list. See Higgins, *op. cit.,* where the famous "Renault Report" is translated in full.

[22] 1 C. Rob 189 (1799). Fenwick, *Cases,* p. 804.

question at this time of inland transportation from a purely commercial port to the armed forces of the enemy operating in the interior of the country. If the goods were not to be used by the military forces at the port of first deposit, they were not to be used by them at all.[23]

Doctrines of "continuous voyage" and "ultimate destination." By the time of the American Civil War, conditions had changed sufficiently to warrant an extension of the traditional rule. The existing doctrine of blockade was, as has been seen, extended to take care of goods which were to be deposited in adjacent neutral ports and subsequently transshipped into smaller and faster vessels which might have a better chance of running the blockade. In like manner, the prize courts of the United States applied the doctrine of *continuous voyage* to the carriage of contraband. In the case of the *Peterhoff*,[24] captured en route to Matamoros, Mexico (opposite Brownsville, Texas), that part of the cargo consisting of military articles whose evident destination was the Confederate States, was condemned; although the vessel itself and its noncontraband cargo were released. This doctrine became known as the doctrine of *ultimate destination,* and it was sharply attacked at the time as an unwarranted innovation. The Declaration of London subsequently affirmed the new doctrine, providing that in the case of absolute contraband "it is immaterial whether the carriage of goods is direct or entails either transshipment or a subsequent transport by land." Even conditional contraband was to be liable to capture when found on board a vessel bound for territory belonging to or occupied by the enemy, except when it was to be discharged at an intervening neutral port.

Practice during the First World War. The innovations of the American Civil War, widely discussed as they were during the years that followed, were as nothing compared to the innovations of the First World War. For a network of railways now spread over Europe, and conditional contraband landed in a neutral port could readily find its way to the armies of the enemy. Great Britain began by transferring articles from the free list of the Declaration of London to the contraband list, and from the list of conditional contraband to that of absolute contraband. Since the Declaration of London was not in force the matter had to be decided on the basis of customary international law. Unwrought copper presented a problem, and Secretary Bryan found "some embarrassment" in dealing with the problem in view of the fact that the United States had in the past placed "all articles from which ammunition is manufactured" on its contraband list. He also found it necessary to yield on the point of having petroleum products proclaimed as contraband, "in view of the

---

[23] During the war between the United States and Great Britain, 1812-1814, a Swedish vessel, the *Commercen,* carrying a cargo of grain to the neutral port of Bilbao, Spain, was captured and its cargo condemned as being destined for the use of the British fleet lying in the harbor. 1 Wheaton 382 (1816).

[24] 5 Wallace 28 (1866). Fenwick, *Cases,* p. 809; Hudson, *Cases,* p. 1375.

absolute necessity of such products to the use of submarines, aeroplanes and motors." Cotton, at first left on the free list, had lost that status by August, 1915. Turpentine and rosin caused a controversy, but the outcome was the same. By October, 1915, specific protests were of no avail, and all that the United States could do was to argue the case on principle and to announce that it had no intention of "waiving any objections" it might entertain as to the inclusion in the British contraband list of "certain articles" which had been so included.[25]

The conflict of views was equally sharp in respect to the distinction between absolute and conditional contraband. Promptly upon the outbreak of war the United States announced that under the rules of international law grain could be shipped to a belligerent country unless it was intended for the use of the army or navy, or destined to a blockaded port or a port occupied by armed forces. A month later it was again insisted that foodstuffs were legitimate articles of commerce, and that mere destination to an enemy port did not justify their seizure or condemnation. But to Great Britain it was of small consequence whether the particular port at which the foodstuffs arrived was or was not occupied by the armed forces of the enemy. Their ultimate use would be determined by other considerations. In the case of the *Kim*[26] and others, a number of Norwegian and Swedish vessels carrying American-owned cargoes of foodstuffs, rubber, and hides were captured en route to Copenhagen; their cargoes were condemned on the ground that they were consigned "to order" and that circumstances indicated that they were ultimately destined to Germany. By April 13, 1916, Great Britain, having tried less effective measures, went to the length of abolishing altogether the distinction between absolute and conditional contraband, offering as justification the fact that so large a proportion of the inhabitants of the enemy country was taking part, directly or indirectly, in the war that the distinction between the armed forces and the civilian population lacked reality. Moreover, the fact that the German Government had taken over the distribution of articles on the list of conditional contraband and was obviously meeting first the needs of the army made the distinction between the two classes of goods meaningless. All that the United States could now do was to notify the British Government of the "reservation of all rights of the United States or its citizens" in respect to any interests that might be adversely affected. The rights reserved were obviously no more than technical ones.[27]

Rationing of neutral countries. The "rationing" of neutral countries followed in order of logic if not of law. As previously applied, the doc-

[25] See Savage, *Policy of the United States toward Maritime Commerce in War,* Vol. II, pp. 247, 390.
[26] Including the *Alfred Nobel,* the *Bjornstjerne Bjornson,* and the *Fridland,* [1915] Probate 215. Fenwick, *Cases,* p. 813; Hudson, *Cases,* p. 1378; Bishop, *Cases,* p. 883.
[27] Savage, *op. cit.,* Vol. II, p. 532. The "reservation" by the United States of its neutral rights was forgotten after it had itself entered the war.

trine of "continuous transports" or the doctrine of "ultimate destination" did not condemn goods which were to be sold in the open market of the neutral port. Yet it soon became clear that even a guarantee from the neutral states adjacent to Germany was not enough to satisfy Great Britain. The larger the volume of foodstuffs and other supplies which neutral merchants could import, the larger the quantity of domestic produce that could be spared for overland shipment to Germany. In consequence Great Britain undertook to determine what were the normal imports of the neutral countries in time of peace and to hold them to the same average quantity in time of war. Whatever was in excess of that amount was presumed to reach Germany by way of substitution.[28] Neutral states adjacent to Germany were thus put on "rations," and what was in effect a complete blockade of Germany was established. It was done, however, not by application of the rules governing blockade, but by an extended operation of the doctrines of contraband. In spite of the protests of the United States while still a neutral against the new application by Great Britain of the doctrine of continuous transports, once the United States itself became a belligerent it set up a plan of licensing trade with neutrals which was to all intents and purposes only another form of the rationing system.

Practice during the Second World War. As in the case of the law of blockade, what little there was left of the law of contraband at the close of the First World War was finally disposed of during the Second World War. The United States had in the years preceding the second war clearly indicated that it had no intention of defending the rights of neutral trade upon which it had insisted so strenuously during the First World War. To do so might involve the risk of being drawn into the war; and it was better, so the dominant opinion in Congress held, to abandon the "freedom of the seas" than to permit the commercial interests of individual traders to become an influence that might favor the cause of one or other of the belligerents. In consequence there were no protests by the United States against the new contraband lists proclaimed by Great Britain in September, 1939, or against the rationing of states adjacent to the Axis Powers. The new form of control transferred the blockade "from the seas to the quays." [29]

---

[28] See British Statement of the Measures Adopted to Intercept the Sea-Borne Commerce of Germany, *Am. Journal*, Vol. 10 (1916), Supp., pp. 87, 96.

[29] While the United States did not protest individually against the British contraband lists, it did join with the other American States in a formal protest. Resolution (VII) on "Contraband of War," adopted at the Meeting of Foreign Ministers at Panama in September, 1939, registered the opposition of the Meeting "to the placing of foodstuffs and clothing intended for civilian populations, not destined directly or indirectly for the use of a belligerent government or its armed forces, on lists of contraband." *Int. Conferences of Am. States*, 1933-1940, p. 330. How the Meeting could have hoped that Great Britain could fail to find in the words "directly or indirectly" sufficient justification, if any was needed, to capture the foodstuffs is difficult to imagine.

Unneutral service. More or less analogous to the offense of carrying contraband was the act of a neutral vessel which transported enemy troops or despatches or which engaged in the service of the enemy. By customary law such a vessel was subject to confiscation irrespective of its destination by reason of the business in which it was engaged. The classic incident was that of the British mail steamer *Trent.* This ship was stopped on its way from Havana to St. Thomas by an American cruiser in 1861, and two of its passengers, Mason and Slidell, Confederate commissioners to Great Britain and France, were forcibly removed. The United States claimed that since despatches were clearly contraband, and that "the bearers or couriers who undertook to carry them fall under the same condemnation," whereas Great Britain held that the character and office of the persons captured did not make them contraband. In consequence, however, of the act of the American captain in removing the commissioners from the vessel rather than bringing the vessel before a prize court, the United States complied with the demand of Great Britain and released the prisoners.[30] At the London Naval Conference elaborate rules were drawn up covering the various forms of unneutral service, but the failure of the parties to ratify the Declaration of London left the law in the uncertain state it was before.

Visit and search. As a means of enforcing the belligerent right to capture neutral vessels for breach of blockade and to confiscate contraband goods, international law recognized the further right of the belligerent to visit and search all merchants vessels encountered on the high seas. Resistance on the part of the neutral vessel to visit and search, or the attempt to escape by flight, subjected it to the same penalties which were inflicted upon belligerent vessels. It was a matter of controversy whether a neutral vessel was exempt from visit and search when sailing under convoy of a warship of its own nationality. In the leading case of the *Maria,*[31] a Swedish merchantman, sailing under convoy of a Swedish man-of-war, was condemned by the British prize court on the ground of sharing impliedly in the resistance offered by the frigate. A hundred years and more later the controversy was settled by the Declaration of London, which held against the British claim; but by that time the British practice had lost its point owing to the better observance of neutrality by belligerents and neutrals alike.

Destruction of neutral prizes. The conflicting points of view at the London Naval Conference with respect to the right claimed by belligerents to destroy neutral prizes when they could not be taken into port for adjudication was settled by a compromise: neutral prizes were, as a general principle, not to be destroyed; but as an exception they might be destroyed if the act of taking them into port "would involve

---

[30] For further details of this important political incident, see Moore, *Digest,* Vol. VII, § 1265.

[31] 1 C. Rob 340 (1799). Fenwick, *Cases,* p. 821.

danger to the warship or to the success of the operations in which she is engaged at the time." This was practically a carte blanche for the German cruisers roaming the high seas at the beginning of the First World War that could not risk attempting to bring their prizes into port. In January, 1915, an American vessel, the *William P. Frye*, sailing from Seattle to Queenstown with a cargo of wheat, was captured by a German cruiser and sunk at sea. The United States protested on the ground that the destruction of the *Frye* was in violation of the treaties of 1799 and 1828. Germany contested the interpretation of the treaties and further defended the capture on the ground that the cargo, being destined to fortified ports, was conditional contraband.[32]

Case of the *Robin Moor*. It was to be expected that the rigor which marked other phases of German warfare would extend to the use of the submarine against neutral shipping, but certain cases appeared to offer no other explanation than open defiance of the law. In May, 1941, the *Robin Moor*, a neutral American vessel, was sunk by a German submarine on the high seas, the passengers and crew being left afloat in small lifeboats. President Roosevelt, in describing the act to Congress, said: "The total disregard shown for the most elementary principles of international law and of humanity brands the sinking of the *Robin Moor* as the act of an international outlaw." [33]

Prize courts. The determination of the legality of the capture by a belligerent of enemy or neutral merchant vessels and of their liability to confiscation rested with the prize courts of the belligerent state. These courts were domestic tribunals, organized and exercising their functions in accordance with the provisions of national legislation. But although the authority and the jurisdiction of prize courts were derived from national law, the rules which they applied to the cases coming before them were the rules of international law, except in so far as special national legislation might have prescribed a particular interpretation of these rules.[34] As a matter of fact, national legislation frequently inter-

---

[32] *Am. White Book,* Vol. II, pp. 185 ff., Vol. III, pp. 311 ff.; Garner, *Prize Law,* pp. 3 ff., 68; Hackworth, *Digest,* Vol. VI, pp. 257, 278; Harvard Draft, Art. 61 and comment.

[33] Dept. of State *Bulletin,* Vol. IV, p. 741. Nevertheless, such are the ways of diplomacy, the payment of the claim submitted was accepted as being "in satisfaction and full settlement" for the losses and damages sustained. Hackworth, *Digest,* Vol. VI, p. 487.

[34] The classic statement of the functions of prize courts is that given in the case of the *Maria,* 1 C. Rob 340 (p. 92): "I trust that it has not escaped my anxious recollection for one moment what it is that the duty of my station calls for from me;— namely, to consider myself as stationed here not to deliver occasional and shifting opinions to serve present purposes of particular national interest, but to administer with indifference that justice which the law of nations holds out, without distinction, to independent states, some happening to be neutral and some to be belligerent. The seat of judicial authority is, indeed, locally here, in the belligerent country, according to the known law and practice of nations; but the law itself has no locality." See Roscoe, *Lord Stowell: His Life and the Development of English Prize Law,* Chaps. IV-VII.

vened to direct the judgment of prize courts, and their decisions must be discounted to that extent when cited as evidence of international law.

The International Prize Court of 1907. Owing to the numerous controversies between belligerents and neutral states arising from the diverse interpretations of international law by belligerent prize courts, as well as from contested points of fact, proposals were made from time to time looking to the creation in time of war of prize courts upon which neutral states as well as both belligerents would be represented. These efforts culminated in the adoption by the Hague Conference of 1907 of the Convention (XII) Relative to the Establishment of an International Prize Court. The convention, although not signed by all the powers and not ratified by any, was widely discussed as a constructive solution of the problem.[35] It provided that, while national courts should continue to exercise original jurisdiction over prize cases, an appeal might be taken in all cases involving the property of neutrals and in certain cases involving enemy property. The law to be applied by the court was, in the absence of treaty provisions, to be "the rules of international law." If no generally recognized rule existed, the court was to give judgment "in accordance with the general principles of justice and equity." It was the uncertainty attaching to the law to be applied by the court that led to the calling of the London Naval Conference and the formulation of the Declaration of London as a definite code of naval warfare.[36]

[35] See, in particular, articles by J. B. Scott and others, *Am. Journal*, Vol. 2 (1908), pp. 21, 458, 476. For the identic note of the United States proposing that the International Prize Court be invested with the functions of a court of arbitral justice, see *ibid.*, Vol. 4 (1910), p. 163, and Supp., p. 102.

[36] See E. Root, "The Real Significance of the Declaration of London," Presidential address, *Proceedings*, Am. Soc. Int. Law, 1912, p. 4.

CHAPTER **XXXIV**

Neutral Duties: In Retrospect

A. DUTY OF ABSTENTION

By contrast with neutral rights, neutral duties represented the conduct which it was the right of the belligerent to demand of the neutral state as the condition of its neutrality. These were of two general classes, duties of abstention and duties of prevention. The duties of abstention were of a negative or passive character deducible from the general obligation of the neutral state to abstain, in its corporate capacity, from participation in the conflict. The duties of prevention were of a positive and active character. The neutral state must not only refrain from giving help to either belligerent by any act of its own, it must also take positive measures to insure that neither the belligerents themselves nor persons acting in their interest make use of its neutral territory in such a manner as to give direct military aid to either party.

Obviously the neutral state must not, as a state, acting through its government, give help of any kind to either of the belligerents. The Hague Convention of 1907 limited its prohibition to warships, ammunition, or war material of any kind; and the prohibition in respect to these applied whether they were supplied directly or sold in the open market under conditions that might permit agents of the belligerent to buy them.[1] What might appear to be forms of indirect assistance were rather situations in which the neutral was not obliged to prevent its citizens from giving assistance.

Policy of the United States during the Second World War. But suppose the neutral state, as happened in 1940, should see that a war was being conducted by one of the belligerents in such a manner that, if it

[1] Art. 6. Convention Respecting the Rights and Duties of Neutral Powers in Naval War.

were victorious, the interests of states that had declared their neutrality when the war began would be endangered? In June, 1940, President Roosevelt transferred to the British Government from the surplus stocks of the United States rifles, machine guns, field artillery, ammunition, and aircraft in large quantities.[2] On September 2, 1940, the Government of the United States transferred fifty overage destroyers to the British Government in exchange for the right to lease naval bases in certain British colonial possessions in the Atlantic.[3] The following spring, in March, 1941, the Lend-Lease Act was approved, in accordance with which the President, acting through the appropriate officer, might sell, lease, or lend defense articles to the government of any country whose defense the President deemed vital to the defense of the United States. As has been said above, all these acts were a departure from traditional neutrality, being based upon the fundamental principle of self-defense. Their technical justification lay in the fact that neutrality itself had lost its traditional meaning and purpose. So far as international law was concerned, the United States might equally well have declared war. Public opinion not being ready for that step, the measures taken went the extreme length "short of war." [4] Neutrality was over, but the Axis Powers chose not to react to it for the time.

B. DUTIES OF PREVENTION

Rigid as was the obligation of the neutral state not to commit acts of hostility itself, there were limits at times to the extent to which the neutral was physically able to prevent them. The nonresistance of Luxemburg to the German armies in 1914 and that of Denmark in 1940 was not an offense on their part.[5] In the case of acts short of hostilities it was recognized by the Hague Convention of 1907 that the neutral state might allow belligerent warships the hospitality of its ports to the extent of a stay of twenty-four hours and might permit the necessary

[2] Hackworth, *Digest*, Vol. VII, p. 690, quotes President Roosevelt's own description of the quantity of goods transferred.

[3] *Ibid.*, Vol. VII, p. 419. The opinion of the Attorney General on that occasion, justifying the transfer of the vessels, was confined to points of constitutional and statutory law. The technical violation of neutral duty was obvious. See p. 726. Compare also the "Ogdensburg Agreement" of August 18, 1940, by which the United States and Canada agreed to set up a Permanent Joint Board on Defense, the purpose of which was clearly directed against the states at war with Canada. For the text, see Dept. of State *Bulletin*, Vol. III, p. 154. The "Hyde Park Declaration" of April 20, 1941, went further and referred not only to the future defense but to present "assistance." *Ibid.*, Vol. IV, p. 494.

[4] See, in explanation of the logical paradox, R. H. Jackson, address read before the Inter-American Bar Association, Havana, March 27, 1941, *Am. Journal*, Vol. 35 (1941), p. 348; Q. Wright, "The Lend-Lease Bill and International Law," *ibid.*, p. 305.

[5] The use of force was, however, justified as a matter of neutral *right*, if the neutral state felt that it could safely have recourse to it. See above, p. 730. Neutral duty did not call for any further risk on the part of the neutral.

repairs to make them seaworthy and might let them take on normal supplies of food and fuel. But what of armed merchant ships? Were they to have the privileges of unlimited stay granted to private ships? [6] The case had not been covered by the provision of the Hague Convention, for the arming of private ships for defense against privateers and pirates had long since been discontinued. But with the coming of the First World War and the advent of the submarine a new problem was presented. The United States at first made a distinction between merchant vessels armed for offense and others armed for defense. But this distinction proving impracticable, new distinctions were proposed, and the problem remained unsolved until the renewal of unlimited submarine warfare made it meaningless. A new rule was adopted in anticipation of the Second World War, but to no effect.

C. ACTS OF INDIVIDUALS IN THE INTEREST OF THE BELLIGERENTS

A more difficult task was imposed upon the neutral state to prevent its individual citizens from compromising its neutrality. Obviously they must not be allowed to give direct military aid, but what of commercial transactions that might be helpful to the belligerent in other ways? A classification of prohibited and permissible acts was recognized, coming down from earlier days when war was of a more limited character and continued long after the circumstances under which it arose had fundamentally changed.[7] That it proved to be a source of controversy between belligerents and neutrals was to be expected.

Neutrality laws. It was agreed that certain acts of individuals must be prevented. The neutral state could not permit its citizens to accept a commission to serve in a foreign army. When in 1793 the French Minister, Citizen Genêt, sought to grant commissions to American citizens to serve in the French Republican army, Secretary Jefferson laid down the rule which later came to be accepted as a fundamental principle: "That it is the *right* of every nation to prohibit acts of sovereignty from being exercised by any other within its limits, and the *duty* of a neutral nation to prohibit such as would injure one of the warring Powers." [8] The United States Neutrality Act of 1794 imposed a penalty upon the citizen who, within the territory or jurisdiction of the United States, should "accept and exercise a commission to serve a foreign prince or state in war by land or sea." In 1794 one Isaac Williams was convicted for accepting a commission under the French Republic and under its authority com-

---

[6] *Am. White Book,* Vol. I, pp. 43, 45; Hackworth, *Digest,* Vol. VII, pp. 490, 494.

[7] The earlier law in this respect may be seen in Hall's treatment of the subject, *International Law,* §§ 19-22.

[8] See Bemis, *Diplomatic History of the United States,* Chap. VI; Moore, *Digest,* Vol. VII, p. 886; Fenwick, *Neutrality Laws of the United States,* Chaps. I, II; Hackworth, *Digest,* Vol. VII, pp. 659 ff.

mitting acts of hostility against Great Britain.[9] In like manner the neutral state was obliged to prevent a belligerent from setting up a recruiting office upon neutral territory. The United States Neutrality Act of 1794 led the way in penalizing "any person," not only citizens, who within the territory or jurisdiction of the United States should "enlist or enter himself, or hire or retain another person to enlist or enter himself" in the service of a foreign prince or state as a soldier or seaman on board a vessel of war.

The Fifth Hague Convention of 1907 embodied existing custom in providing that "corps of combatants can not be formed nor recruiting agencies opened on the territory of a neutral Power to assist the belligerents." [10] The Thirteenth Hague Convention expressly prohibited belligerent warships from making use of neutral ports for "completing their crews." [11] But the law did not call upon the neutral to prevent citizens from leaving its territory with the intention of enlisting in the service of the belligerent; and this was confirmed by the Fifth Hague Convention of 1907, provided, as the United States held in 1914, that they "travel as individuals and not as organized, uniformed, or armed bodies." [12]

Hostile expeditions from neutral ports.   Obviously the neutral state must not permit its ports to be used as a starting point for hostile expeditions in the interest of a belligerent. But what constituted a hostile expedition? In 1793, and again in 1818, the United States Government was chiefly concerned with preventing the fitting out and arming of privateers, which, when equipped with a commission, were to engage in the service of one belligerent to make depredations upon the commerce of the other. The belligerent status of these vessels was beyond dispute. On the other hand, there appeared to be no reason for preventing a citizen who owned a merchant vessel from arming and otherwise equipping it and selling it in the neutral port or sending it abroad for sale to one or other of the belligerents. Such a vessel might be contraband of war and subject to capture on the high seas, but it was not in itself the equivalent of a hostile expedition.[13] Again, it was not thought necessary to prevent citizens or others from building a vessel to the order of a belligerent in a neutral port without any intent on their part other than that of reaping the profits of the industry in which they were adventurously engaged.

[9] The defendant's plea that he had expatriated himself was overruled. Fenwick, *Cases*, p. 178.

[10] Art. 4, Convention Respecting the Rights and Duties of Neutral Powers and Persons in War on Land.

[11] Art. 18, Convention Concerning the Rights and Duties of Neutral Powers in Naval War.

[12] See Secretary Bryan's letter to the chairman of the Senate Committee on Foreign Affairs, January 20, 1915, *Am. White Book*, Vol. II, pp. 58, 62.

[13] See the decision of the Supreme Court of the United States in the case of *Santissima Trinidad*, 7 Wheaton 283 (1822). Fenwick, *Cases*, p. 799.

The *Alabama* controversy. By 1861 conditions had changed. Confederate cruisers, notably the *Alabama,* built to order in British ports and armed after their departure from port, inflicted such heavy losses upon the commerce of the United States that it was seen that the commercial intent of the builders was no excuse for the neutral state in the eyes of the injured belligerent.[14] The United States pressed a claim upon Great Britain for damages. Arbitration was resorted to, and, in view of the dispute as to the question of law involved, it was agreed beforehand, in the Treaty of Washington of 1871, that a neutral state was bound "to use due diligence" to prevent the fitting out, arming, or equipping within its jurisdiction of "any vessel" which it had reasonable ground to believe was intended to carry on war against a power with which it was at peace.[15] This newly formulated rule was in keeping with the fact that vessels of war, even though unarmed at the time of leaving port, had developed such potentialities of inflicting injury upon an enemy as to be equivalent to a hostile expedition in themselves. At the Hague Conference of 1907 the new rule was adopted in substance in the Convention concerning the Rights and Duties of Neutral Powers in Naval War, with the change, however, that the somewhat indefinite phrase "due diligence" was replaced by the phrase "a neutral government is bound to employ the means at its disposal" to prevent the acts in question.

The changing conditions of modern warfare were reflected in the position taken by the United States in 1915, against the protests of Germany, that hydro-aeroplanes were not to be regarded as warships simply because they were "fitted with apparatus to rise from and alight upon the sea." Consequently, it was held, they were no more than conditional contraband of war, which might be freely sold by neutral citizens to the belligerents.[16]

D. PERMISSIBLE ACTS OF INDIVIDUALS

Apart from acts regarded as direct participation in the war, individual neutral citizens were free to maintain business relations with one or other of the belligerents, although such commercial activities might be of far more substantial help than individual enlistments. Here again the methods of war had changed, but old customs were still followed. Why should a war in a far-off country disturb the normal life and commerce of neutral citizens!

Expressions of opinion. Neutral states were under no obligation to

---

[14] The diplomatic history of these vessels is told in summary in Bemis, *op. cit.,* Chap. XXI.

[15] For the text of the "Three Rules of the Treaty of Washington," see Moore, *Digest,* Vol. VII, § 1330; *Treaties and Conventions,* Vol. I, p. 703. For a study of the *Alabama* controversy, see *Papers Relating to the Treaty of Washington;* Moore, *International Arbitrations,* Vol. I, pp. 495 ff.; Fenwick, *Cases,* p. 706; Bishop, *Cases,* p. 864; Briggs, *Cases,* p. 1026.

[16] *Am. White Book,* Vol. II, p. 145.

prevent individuals within their jurisdiction from giving expression to opinions or criticism unfavorable to one or other of the belligerents or favorable to insurgents in revolt against a *de jure* government. No democratic nation felt called upon to attempt to suppress freedom of speech in respect to the justice or injustice of a war between foreign states. When President Wilson appealed to the American people shortly after the neutrality proclamations of 1914 to be "impartial in thought as well as in action" and to put a curb upon "sentiments" as well as upon "every transaction that might be construed as a preference of one party to the struggle before another," he went beyond the requirements of international law.[17] At the opening of the Second World War President Roosevelt was careful not to repeat the mistake, although his forecast was equally bad: "This nation will remain a neutral nation, but I cannot ask that every American remain neutral in thought as well. Even a neutral has a right to take account of facts. Even a neutral cannot be asked to close his mind or his conscience." [18]

Loans to belligerents. Must a neutral state, which could not itself lend money to a belligerent, prevent individuals within its jurisdiction from doing so? Vattel somewhat naively judged the whole matter on the basis of whether or not the loan was a safe investment. A neutral citizen, even the state itself, might loan money to one belligerent and not to another on the basis of confidence or lack of confidence.[19] But this was altogether too subjective a test to become a rule of law. The simpler, more objective rule developed of prohibiting state loans and permitting private loans. Even the latter were of doubtful standing as contracts when it came to suits for their enforcement; and where the loan was made to unrecognized revolutionists engaged in war for their independence they might even be held null and void.

In spite of the condemnation of certain jurists, it was generally agreed on the eve of the First World War that a neutral state had no duty to prevent its citizens from making loans to the belligerents.[20] The Fifth Hague Convention evaded the issue, merely declaring that a national

[17] Statement made to the Senate, August 19, 1914. *Am. White Book*, Vol. II, p. 17. Paragraphs of the address are quoted in Hackworth, *Digest*, Vol. VII, p. 374. So sacred was the conception of "neutrality" at that time that Secretary Bryan went to the extreme point of instructing the American consul in Germany to refrain from making investigation of alleged German atrocities in Belgium, lest the investigation might subject his Government to adverse criticism. *Ibid.*, p. 375.

[18] *Ibid.*, p. 374. Nevertheless traditions were so strong that the Proclamation of Neutrality of September 3, 1939, referred to the United States as being "on terms of friendship and amity with the contending powers." Fenwick, *American Neutrality: Trial and Failure*, p. 153.

[19] *Droit des gens*, Book III, § 110.

[20] The reasoning of the older writers is, however, hard to follow. So acute a jurist as Westlake observed that private loans in a free market were purely commercial acts and did not imply "any intent by those persons as to the use to be made of the money by the governments assisted." *International Law*, Vol. II, pp. 217-218.

of a neutral state should not lose his neutral character in consequence of furnishing supplies or making loans to one of the belligerents. Upon the outbreak of the First World War, the United States Department of State announced that loans by American bankers to belligerents were "inconsistent with the true spirit of neutrality," and in January, 1915, it was stated that there was a "clearly defined difference between a war loan and the purchase of arms and ammunition. *The policy of disapproving of war loans affects all governments alike, so that the disapproval is not an unneutral act.*" [21] The logic of the argument was open to question; but in any case no attempt was made to prevent loans, and they were made in large amounts in the form of credits for the purchase of supplies.

In anticipation of a possible war in Europe the United States Congress, by an act of February 29, 1936, made it unlawful, with certain exceptions, for any person in the United States "to purchase, sell or exchange bonds, securities or other obligations of the government of any belligerent country" issued after the date of the proclamation of a state of war, or to "make any loan or extend any credit to any such government" or person acting on its behalf.[22] This was understood to be in excess of the obligations of neutrality and was intended to put restraints upon bankers who, in order to protect their loans, might lure the country into war. The provisions were carried over into the act of November 4, 1939, which controlled the conduct of American citizens until the entrance of the United States into the war.[23]

Sale of munitions of war. Far more controversial was the question whether the neutral state must prevent the sale of munitions of war by its citizens to the belligerents.[24] Here all the logic of the case, looking at it in the light of modern conditions, would seem to favor prohibition. But in the closing years of the eighteenth century, when the rules of neutrality began to take definite shape, the neutral state saw no reason to restrict the ordinary commercial relations of its citizens with the belligerents, and industry was not so far developed as to make a contribution of decisive importance to the war. In reply to protests from both Great

[21] *Am. White Book,* Vol. II, p. 61; Hackworth, *Digest,* Vol. VII, p. 658; Savage, *Policy of the United States,* Vol. II, p. 255.

[22] For the text of the act, see Deak and Jessup, *A Collection of Neutrality Laws,* Vol. II, p. 1105; *Am. Journal,* Vol. 30 (1936), p. 109.

[23] To make assurance doubly sure, it was made unlawful "to solicit or receive any contribution for or on behalf of any government" named in the president's proclamation of neutrality. Compare with these provisions Resolution VII of the Meeting of Foreign Ministers at Panama by which it was declared that the American republics did not consider contrary to neutrality the granting of credits to belligerents for the purchase of foodstuffs and clothing intended for the civilian populations.

[24] See C. N. Gregory, "Neutrality and the Sale of Arms," *Am. Journal,* Vol. 10 (1916), p. 541; Fenwick, *American Neutrality: Trial and Failure,* p. 122; Hackworth, *Digest,* Vol. VII, p. 853.

Britain and France in 1793, Secretary of State Jefferson made a reply which became classic:

> We have answered that our citizens have always been free to make, vend, and export arms; that it is the constant occupation and livelihood of some of them. To suppress their callings, the only means, perhaps, of their subsistence, because a war exists in foreign and distant countries, in which we have no concern, would scarcely be expected. It would be hard in principle and impossible in practice. The law of nations, therefore, respecting the rights of those at peace, has not required from them such an internal derangement in their occupations. It is satisfied with the external penalty pronounced in the President's proclamation, that of confiscation of such portion of these arms as shall fall into the hands of any of the belligerent Powers on their way to the ports of their enemies.[25]

At the meeting of the Hague Conference of 1907 the customary rule was adopted, without taking into account the changed conditions. The Fifth and the Thirteenth Conventions both laid down the general rule that "a neutral Power is not called upon to prevent the export or transport, on behalf of one or other of the belligerents, of arms, munitions of war, or, in general, of anything which can be of use to an army or a fleet." [26]

Practice during the First World War. During the First World War the situation was presented in which one of the belligerent groups drew heavily upon the United States for its military supplies while the other was, by reason of the superior navy of the enemy, almost entirely cut off from them. Moreover, the trade in arms was maintained not only by the munition factories already in existence at the time the war broke out but by numerous other factories built or reconstructed to meet the unprecedented demand.[27] Under these circumstances the German Government pointed out, on April 4, 1915, that, if it was the will of the American people that there should be "a true neutrality," the United States would find means of preventing this "one-sided supply" or at least of making use of it to force Great Britain to desist from interfering with the legitimate neutral trade with Germany.[28] A similar protest was entered by the Austro-Hungarian Government on June 29, 1915, which pointed out that the arms industry had "soared to unimagined heights" and that the Thirteenth Hague Convention contemplated a change in existing law to meet new conditions.[29]

---

[25] *Am. State Papers, For. Rel.*, Vol. I, p. 147; Moore, *Digest*, Vol. VII, p. 955; Hackworth, *Digest*, Vol. VII, pp. 853 ff.

[26] Art. 7, Fifth Convention; Art. 7, Thirteenth Convention.

[27] This was clearly not the situation which Jefferson had in mind in 1793.

[28] *Am. White Book*, Vol. I, p. 73. For the reply of the United States, see Savage, *op. cit.*, Vol. II, p. 297.

[29] *Am. White Book*, Vol. II, p. 193; Savage, *op. cit.*, Vol. II, p. 347.

While a number of proposals for an embargo on arms were made in Congress, the Department of State of the United States took the position that it would not recognize an obligation to change or modify the rules of international usage to meet the special conditions which deprived the Central Powers of access to the American markets. Moreover, the United States was opposed in principle to the prohibition of the trade in arms and munitions between belligerents and neutrals on the ground that such prohibition would put at a disadvantage the state which, from pacific motives, had neglected to obtain adequate supplies in advance of an attack upon it.[30]

E. MEASURES IN EXCESS OF LEGAL OBLIGATION

United States legislation 1935-1939. The experience of the First World War convinced American public opinion that there was an intimate connection between the making of loans and the sale of munitions of war by citizens of a neutral state and the policy of the government toward the belligerents. The bankers and the munitions makers were said to have been responsible for the propaganda which led the United States to enter the war in 1917. That must not happen again.[31] The result was that in the presence of the impending attack of Italy upon Ethiopia Congress passed a joint resolution, approved August 31, 1935, providing that upon the outbreak or during the progress of a war between foreign states the President should proclaim the fact and it should thereafter be "unlawful to export arms, ammunition, or implements of war" from any place in the United States to any port of the belligerent states or to any neutral port for transshipment to a belligerent country.[32] The prohibition was carried over into the act of May 1, 1937.[33] By the same act of 1937 it was further provided that "certain articles or materials in addition to arms, ammunition, and implements of war" might not be transshipped from the United States to any belligerent state in an American vessel, or in a vessel of any other state "until all right, title and interest" in the articles or materials should be transferred to some foreign government or other non-American purchaser. By this "cash and carry" plan would be eliminated all possibility of personal interest on the part of American

---

[30] Note of August 12, 1915. *Am. White Book*, Vol. II, p. 194; Savage, *op. cit.*, Vol. II, p. 368.

[31] Much of the literature of the propaganda against the sale of arms and munitions of war to belligerents was highly sensational. See Engelbrecht and Hanighen, *Merchants of Death: A Study of the International Armament Industry;* Seldes, *Iron, Blood and Profits: An Exposure of the World Wide Munitions Racket;* Herring, *And So To War;* Tansill, *America Goes to War.*

[32] Section 1. For the text of the act, see Deak and Jessup, *A Collection of Neutrality Laws,* Vol. II, p. 1100; *Am. Journal*, Vol. 30 (1936), Supp., p. 58.

[33] Section 1, a. For the text, see *Am. Journal*, Vol. 31 (1937), Supp., p. 147.

citizens in the losses that might result from the destruction of merchant ships by one or other of the belligerents.[34]

After the outbreak of the war a new neutrality act was passed on November 4, 1939, lifting the embargo on arms and munitions of war, but continuing the "cash and carry" plan of the law of 1937. The preamble of the act called attention to the fact that the United States, desiring to preserve its neutrality and to avoid entanglement in foreign wars, "voluntarily" imposed upon its nationals the restrictions set forth in the act, but that in so doing it waived "none of its own rights or privileges, or those of any of its nationals, under international law." [35] Six months later the whole policy of neutrality came to an end.

[34] The provisions of the successive neutrality laws appear to have taken into account everything that might lead the American people to go to war except one thing, their instinctive sense of the danger latent in the possible victory of a state whose fanatical nationalism might lead it to challenge the United States after it had defeated its more immediate enemies. See Fenwick, *Am. Neutrality: Trial and Failure*, Introduction.

[35] For the text of the act, see *Am. Journal*, Vol. 34 (1940), Supp., p. 44. For comment upon the inconsistencies of the situation, see Q. Wright, "Rights and Duties under International Law as Affected by the United States Neutrality Act and the Resolutions of Panama," *ibid.*, Vol. 34 (1940), p. 238.

CHAPTER XXXV

The Termination of War

A. DIFFERENT METHODS OF TERMINATION

In the long history of international relations in which the use of force by one state against another has played so prominent a part, war has terminated in a wide variety of ways.[1] Conquering armies swept over the territory of neighboring states and at times annihilated them as separate corporate groups. At other times the conquered country was left in some degree intact, but was brought under subjection.[2] Again, at other times the conquerer did no more than overcome the armies of his opponent, impose penalties, and then leave it in possession of its independence and territorial integrity. One thing was clear in all cases: the conquered state had no appeal against the terms imposed upon it by the conqueror. Christian principles succeeded in mitigating at times the rigor of the terms imposed by the conqueror;[3] and modern international law clearly recognized that there must be a relation between the offense

---

[1] On the general subject of the termination of war, see Phillipson, *Termination of War and Treaties of Peace;* Hyde, *International Law,* Vol. III, §§ 904-922.

[2] Such was the practice, in general, of ancient Rome. See Phillipson, *International Law of Ancient Greece and Rome,* Vol. II, Chap. XXIV; McMahon, *Conquest and Modern International Law,* Chap. II. Compare the citations in Grotius, *De jure belli ac pacis,* Book III, Chap. XV, § XII. But at times Rome found it necessary to annihilate: *Cartago delenda est.*

[3] The concept of a "just war," as set forth by the doctors of the Church, carried with it the implication that the terms of peace were to bear a relation to the offense which justified the war. See Regout, *La doctrine de la guerre juste,* pp. 266 ff. Suarez: "In order that war may be justly waged, certain conditions are to be observed, and these may be brought under three heads. First, it must be waged by a legitimate power. Secondly, its cause must be just and right. Thirdly, just methods should be used, that is equity in the beginning of war, in the prosecution of it and in victory." *De legibus,* XII, § I, p. 7.

which caused the war and the penalty imposed.[4] But in each case the
will of the conqueror determined the size of the reparations bill. The
international community was not consulted. If, as in Napoleon's case, the
conqueror went too far in his demands he might arouse the fear of other
members of the community. But this brought into play considerations
of a political character which could not be formulated into rules of law.

Subjugation. Subjugation was the term generally used to describe
the conquest of one belligerent by another, followed by the formal annexation of the territory of the defeated state and the extinction of its
sovereignty and international personality.[5] Few wars of modern times
have terminated in that manner. While the Two Sicilies and other Italian
states were subjugated by Sardinia in 1859 and the Papal States in 1870,
all of the subjugated states became part of a new kingdom of their own
nationality; [6] and while Great Britain annexed the South African Republic and the Orange Free State in 1900, it was only to give them dominion status in the British Empire, with a greater degree of actual political power than they possessed before.[7] However, when in 1936
Abyssinia was conquered by Italy, a royal decree proclaimed that "The
territories and peoples that belonged to the Empire of Ethiopia are
placed under the full and entire sovereignty of the Kingdom of Italy.
The title of Emperor of Ethiopia is assumed for himself and for his successors by the King of Italy." [8] Whether the incorporation of Austria
into Germany in 1938 and the dismemberment of the Czechoslovak Republic in 1939 should be described by the term "subjugation," would
appear to be a question of applying old terms to new methods of conquest. The extinction of the sovereignty of Lithuania, Latvia, and Esthonia in 1940 came about under conditions of disguised coercion to
which the term "subjugation" seems scarcely applicable.

[4] Vattel well describes the best thought of the eighteenth century: "A treaty of
peace can be nothing more than a compromise. . . . The only recourse is to compromise the claims and grievances on both sides, and to put an end to all differences
by as fair an agreement as can be reached." *Droit des gens,* Eng. trans., Book IV,
§ 18.

[5] Heffter, writing as late as 1866, was able to say: "According to the modern laws
of war, the conquering state acquires sovereign and absolute power over the conquered state, but he has no right to dispose of the private rights of the conquered
subjects or of their persons. Ordinarily the conquered territory is united to that of
the conqueror. . . ." *Droit International Public,* ed. 1866, p. 339. But his generalization was already out of date. The principle of the balance of power was at work to
prevent excesses of aggression where principles of justice might have failed.

[6] See Hayes, *A Political and Social History of Modern Europe,* Vol. II, p. 163, "The
Political Unification of Italy."

[7] The annexation of the South African Republic on September 1, 1900, was
premature, but soon confirmed by occupation. The "Terms of Surrender" of the Boer
armies in 1902 were therefore not regarded by Great Britain as a treaty of peace.

[8] *Documents on International Affairs,* 1935, Vol. II, p. 472. Query, whether the
resistance of Haile Selassie and the refusal of many states to recognize the conquest,
not to mention the subsequent restoration of the independence of Abyssinia, did not
make the case one of temporary military occupation.

Simple cessation of hostilities. Prior to the nineteenth century wars occasionally terminated by a simple cessation of hostilities, without the conclusion of a formal treaty of peace. In such cases the date of the termination could not be accurately fixed but was roughly determined by extraneous facts indicating the resumption of friendly relations. As late as 1867 the war between France and Mexico terminated without other formalities than the abandonment by France of its efforts to support Maximilian; [9] and the war between Spain and Chile in 1865-1868 terminated by cessation of the efforts of Spain to enforce its demands.[10] In such cases the problems arising as to ownership of property, real or personal, which had changed hands during the course of the war were generally settled by the application of the rule of *uti possidetis,* by which each belligerent was regarded as legally entitled to such property as was actually in its possession at the time hostilities ceased.[11] Third states were accordingly justified in maintaining relations with the former belligerents on that basis.

Armistices and treaties of peace. Within more modern times wars have generally terminated in formal treaties of peace, preceded as a rule by armistices providing for a temporary cessation of hostilities. On occasion, as between the Allies and Germany in 1918, what was an armistice in name might contain provisions which went much further than a mere suspension of hostilities and might be in fact a preliminary treaty. The historic agreement of November 11, 1918, while designated as an "armistice" was in the substance of its terms a capitulation, containing military conditions which made it practically impossible for Germany to renew hostilities, whatever might be the final terms of peace which Germany might be called upon to sign.[12]

Treaty of Versailles. In the negotiations attending the treaties of peace of 1919 the defeated powers took no part. Their plenipotentiaries were presented with definitive documents, and there was no alternative for them but to sign and accept the terms imposed. In this connection, however, an important question of international law arose, whether the terms of the Treaty of Versailles exceeded in severity the terms of the preliminary agreement or "armistice," which stipulated that the treaty of peace should conform to President Wilson's "Fourteen Points," with the exception of the point relating to the "freedom of the seas," which had been specifically excluded from the list. The vagueness of some of the phrases used in the various points would have made it difficult to

---

[9] See Moore, *Digest,* Vol. VI, § 957.

[10] See *For. Rel. of the United States,* 1866, Part 2, p. 322.

[11] The application of the rule of *uti possidetis* in determining the status of territory and property at the close of hostilities must be distinguished from the same rule in cases of disputed title to territory, as between Ecuador and Peru, see above, p. 414.

[12] For the text of the armistice, see *Am. Journal,* Vol. 13 (1919), Supp., p. 80.

arrive at a legal decision of this question, even if the Allied Powers had been willing to submit the issue to an impartial tribunal.[13]

Treaties of 1947. There were no technical armistices at the close of the hostilities of the Second World War. In all cases the defeated armies surrendered unconditionally.[14] The treaties which brought the war to a legal end were thereupon imposed upon the defeated powers, not negotiated with them. The defeated powers were, however, with the exception of Germany, given an opportunity to plead their cause. On their part the Big Four Powers undertook to make the final decisions, although the other states at war with the Axis Powers were permitted to make recommendations at the Paris Conference with respect to the treaties with the so-called satellite powers. The treaties with these latter powers were signed in Paris on February 10, 1947.[15] The treaties with Germany, Austria, and Japan were not signed by the Big Four Powers until two years after hostilities ceased.

Obligation of treaties of peace. Are treaties of peace imposed upon the defeated belligerent at the close of a war to be regarded as coming within the rule of good faith applicable to other treaties? The question has been discussed above in connection with the law of international treaties in general; it is only necessary to observe here that it is probable that the treaties of 1947 are not likely to be considered as more than temporary agreements, binding not so much under the rule of good faith as under the necessity of the situation. At what point the provisions of the treaties may come to be accepted as a basis upon which the defeated powers will be prepared to maintain permanent relations with other states is a political rather than a legal question, and one which only time can answer. Good faith may be expected to come into effect when the substantial justice of certain treaties is generally recognized and when such amendments have been made to others as equity may obtain when the treaties are seen in better perspective. The worst provisions of the Treaty of Versailles had already lost their force when the fanatical movement began to defy them.

B. EFFECTS OF THE TERMINATION OF WAR

Jus postliminii. In older days, when wars dragged on at times indefinitely and when the negotiation of treaties of peace was more difficult, a number of rules developed with respect to the legal effects of

[13] For the question as to whether the terms of the Treaty of Versailles were consistent with the terms of the armistice of November 11, see L. Rogers, "The Relation of the Armistice and the Treaty of Versailles," *Proceedings*, Am. Soc. Int. Law, 1923, pp. 90-96.

[14] For the surrender of Italy, *Documents on Am. Foreign Relations*, Vol. VI, p. 169. For the surrender of Germany, *Am. Journal*, Vol. 39 (1945), Supp., pp. 169 ff.; and of Japan, Dept. of State *Bulletin*, Vol. XIII, pp. 205, 255.

[15] Dept. of State *Bulletin*, Vol. XVI, p. 1076, where summaries of the treaties with the satellite states are given.

the termination of war where there was no formal treaty of peace or where the treaty of peace failed to make provision for the matter. Among these were the *jus postliminii*. This rule had its origin in ancient Rome, and it operated to restore to their former status both persons who after being held in captivity by a foreign state crossed the boundary (*limen*) and came within Roman territory, as well as property held by the enemy and brought back within the boundaries of the Empire. Grotius relied upon it to explain how persons and property reconquered from the enemy or surrendered by the treaty of peace regained their former legal status. "Postliminy, therefore, is a right which arises from a return to the threshold, that is, to the public boundaries." [16] The abolition of slavery in more modern times restricted the application of the rule to territory and to movable property. At the same time the doctrine was extended to cover not only the revival of rights of territorial sovereignty, but also the revival of the laws of the original sovereign. The rule of *uti possidetis*, leaving to each belligerent such property as might be in his possession at the time hostilities ceased, lost its meaning when treaties of peace became highly elaborate documents going into every detail of the relations between the former enemies.[17]

Enemy aliens and prisoners of war. With the conclusion of the treaty of peace friendly relations between the belligerents were restored.[18] Diplomatic relations were renewed, and commerce and intercourse took place upon the basis of the provisions laid down in the treaty. Nationals of the former enemy states, domiciled in the territory of the other belligerent, were relieved of any legal disabilities to which they might have been subject and regained the normal status of resident aliens. Prisoners of war were released from captivity, subject, however, to such conditions as the captor might fix in order to prevent the indirect effects which their release might have upon the restoration of peace.[19] The Geneva Convention of 1929 made provision that ". . . the repatriation of prisoners shall be effected as soon as possible after the conclusion of

[16] Grotius devotes an entire chapter to the subject, examining with his usual learning the origin of the term *postliminium* and discussing its manifold applications in his time. *De jure belli ac pacis*, Book III, Chap. IX.

[17] The Treaty of Versailles ran to 440 articles. The treaties of 1947 were, however, much shorter.

[18] Like other treaties, a treaty of peace comes to effect upon its ratification by the parties when there is no specification to the contrary. Acts done between the actual conclusion of hostilities and the ratification of the treaty will be judged accordingly. See Advisory Opinion of the Permanent Court of International Justice on the *German Settlers in Poland*, rejecting the Polish contention that leases made by Germany after the Armistice in territories subsequently ceded to Poland were invalid. Also, the judgment of the Court on *German Interests in Polish Upper Silesia*.

[19] The United States *Rules of Land Warfare*, 1914, Art. 99, mention as a reason for delay in the repatriation called for by the Hague Regulations, Art. 20, "Obvious risk to captor State in restoring to the vanquished power troops of which it has been deprived."

peace." Following the Second World War, however, the military occupation of Germany made it impossible to release large numbers of prisoners held by the three principal Allied Powers; and in some cases they were made to work upon various projects in connection with the reconstruction of devastated areas and other national emergencies.

Indemnities and reparations. The payment of indemnities to the victor by the vanquished has a long historical tradition. *Vae victis,* said the barbarian Brennus, as he threw his sword into the scales that weighed out the thousand pounds of gold exacted of Rome as the cost of defeat. Rarely was there any relation between the sum fixed as indemnity and the losses resulting from the conflict. But with the close of the First World War the reparations bill imposed upon Germany was definitely related to such losses.[20] By Article 231 of the Treaty of Versailles the Allied and Associated Governments affirmed and Germany accepted "the responsibility of Germany and her allies for causing all the loss and damage to which the Allied and Associated Governments and their nationals have been subjected as a consequence of the war imposed upon them by the aggression of Germany and her allies." By Article 232 it was recognized that the resources of Germany were not adequate to make "complete reparation for all such loss and damage," but that Germany would make compensation "for all damage done to the civilian population of the Allied and Associated Powers and to their property . . . by such aggression by land, by sea and from the air," and in general all damage as defined in an Annex attached to the articles. In pursuance of the terms of the treaty an inter-Allied commission, known as the "Reparation Commission" was created with the object of determining the amount of compensation payable under the terms of the treaty and of supervising the payment. The reparations originally fixed were successively scaled down and in 1932 they disappeared altogether, too late, however, to undo their psychological effect upon the masses of the German people.[21]

C. MILITARY OCCUPATION FOLLOWING THE TREATY OF PEACE

The general principles of equity and justice which, however indefinite, led both Grotius and Vattel to insist that the penalties imposed upon the defeated state should not be such as to prevent the restoration of friendly relations were, perhaps, too vague to constitute rules of law

[20] The literature on the subject of the reparations imposed upon Germany is extensive. See, in particular, Baruch, *The Making of the Reparation and Economic Sections of the Treaty;* Wheeler-Bennett, *The Wreck of Reparations;* Schacht, *The End of Reparations;* Burnett, *Reparation at the Paris Peace Conference;* Keynes, *The Economic Consequences of the Peace.*

[21] On July 9, 1932, an Agreement concerning German Reparations was signed at Lausanne, which "put an end" to reparations. Hudson, *Int. Legislation,* Vol. VI, p. 73. While the agreement was not ratified, the effect of the agreement was to bring the discussion of reparations to an end.

for writers of the twentieth century, although statesmen might have been expected to take into account the effect of the terms imposed by the peace treaty upon the defeated party. At the close of the First World War, the Allied and Associated Powers imposed upon Germany terms hitherto without precedent, but believed to be justified by the magnitude of the struggle.[22] In addition to reparations and territorial adjustments, the armies of the victorious powers were to occupy the Rhineland for a period of fifteen years, with the object of assuring the fulfillment of the provisions of the treaty. At the same time the Rhineland was demilitarized. But these provisions, while of unique severity, did not involve any effort on the part of the victors to change the internal organization of the defeated state. Once Germany had met President Wilson's condition of setting up a government with which a reliable peace could be made, no further steps were taken to prevent a recurrence of the internal political conditions in that country which were believed to be responsible for the war.[23]

The re-education of states guilty of aggression. At the close of the Second World War it was not believed to be sufficient merely to disarm the aggressors and to take measures to prevent their rearmament in the future. It was thought necessary to eliminate, if possible, the false ideologies which had been in large part responsible for the war. Theories of master races, of a hereditary claim to rule inferior peoples, of an inherent right to expand at the expense of other countries must, it was held, be eradicated in order to ensure that the aggressors would not repeat in the future their acts of aggression.[24] Hence the victors undertook to reorganize the governments of Germany and Japan, to prohibit persons from holding office who had been prominently associated with the previous regime, and to control the press, the radio, and in part the educational system of the country so as to change the mental outlook of the people.

[22] For the text of the Treaty of Versailles, see *Am. Journal*, Vol. 13 (1919), Supp., p. 151.

[23] For the demands made by President Wilson as a condition of signing a peace, see Bemis, *Diplomatic History*, Chap. XXXIII.

[24] For the declaration concerning fascism in Italy, see Dept. of State *Bulletin*, Vol. IX, p. 309. For the statement made at Yalta with respect to Germany, see *ibid.*, Vol. XII, p. 213; and for the Potsdam Declaration, *ibid.*, Vol. XIII, p. 153, *Am. Journal*, Vol. 39 (1945), Supp., p. 245. For the case of Japan, see the Potsdam "Proclamation Defining Terms for Japanese Surrender," *Bulletin*, Vol. XIII, p. 137. McNair is of the opinion that the Allied occupation of Germany went beyond the traditional "Belligerent Occupation." *Legal Effects of War*, 3d ed.

The peace treaty with Italy, Art. 17, pledges Italy not to permit the resurgence on Italian territory of Fascist organizations "whose purpose it is to deprive the people of their democratic rights." A similar pledge was exacted of the satellite states to dissolve all organizations of a Fascist type, and not to permit in the future "the existence and activities of organizations of the nature which have as their aim denial to the people of their democratic rights," in which, however, communist activities were apparently not included.

Paradoxically enough, the terms imposed upon Germany were thrown completely out of gear by the dissensions among the victors themslves. The undoing of fascism in a defeated Germany proved to be as nothing in comparison of the aggressiveness of the victorious Soviet Union.

It would be prophecy rather than a statement of law to attempt to determine how far the practice of the recent past in respect to the termination of war may be reflected in the possible minor or limited wars that may take place *de facto* in the Near Eastern, Far Eastern, or African areas where there have been of late threats of conflict. It is to be expected that the United Nations will intervene in each case, as it did in Korea, to attempt to bring about a peaceful settlement, and will determine in each case whether the parties were acting in self-defense under the provisions of Article 51 of the Charter. In any event, acquisitions of territory would properly be ruled out, reparations would be limited, and treaties would be annulled or modified as the Security Council might find proper. The fact that even in cases of self-defense the action of the Security Council would be in the end decisive would make the older traditions meaningless. In the event of an atomic war of large scale proportions there would doubtless be no legal procedure attending its termination, law having disappeared completely in the conflict itself. *Vae victis;* but in this case both parties would be conquered, each by the other.

D. TRIAL OF WAR CRIMINALS

Prior to the First World War it was the custom for belligerents to insert in their treaties of peace an amnesty clause creating an immunity in relation to each belligerent for all persons who had committed wrongful acts on behalf of or in the service of the other belligerent during the course of the war. Even in the absence of treaty stipulation, an amnesty was one of the legal effects of the termination of war.[25] The immunity granted did not, however, extend to civil suit or criminal prosecution in respect to matters not connected with the war.

Indictment of German ex-Kaiser. By the treaty of Versailles a striking exception to the customary law was made in the clauses providing for the trial and punishment of the German Kaiser and of individual members of the German armed forces.[26] In the case of the Kaiser, the treaty provided that he should be tried "for a supreme offense against international morality and the sanctity of treaties." The offense was thus

[25] On the subject of amnesty, see Phillipson, *Termination of War*, pp. 214 ff. Compare Art. 11, Final Act of the Congress of Vienna: "Il y aura amnistie pleine, générale et particulière, en faveur de tous les individus de quelque rang, sexe ou condition, qu'ils puissent être."

[26] Treaty of Versailles, Part VII, Penalties. For an interpretation of the legal basis upon which the Kaiser was to be tried, see J. W. Garner, *Am. Journal*, Vol. 14 (1920), p. 70.

not one cognizable in accordance with the existing law. A special tribunal, appointed by the five leading powers, was to be constituted to try the accused and was to be guided in its decision "by the highest motives of international policy."

Trial of other offenders. In the case of other offenders, the measures provided for were legal rather than political. The German Government recognized the right of the Allied and Associated Powers "to bring before military tribunals persons accused of having committed acts in violation of the laws and customs of war." Such persons were, if found guilty, to be sentenced to punishments laid down by law. In order to make possible these trials, the German Government on its part agreed to hand over to the Allied and Associated Powers all persons accused of the acts in question. In addition the German Government agreed to furnish the documents and information "necessary to insure the full knowledge of the incriminating acts, the discovery of the offenders and the just appreciation of responsibility."

In both cases, however, the proposed trials had to be abandoned. On the one hand, the Dutch Government refused to accede to the request for the surrender of the ex-Kaiser, who had already been granted asylum in that country. On the other hand, the practical difficulties involved in the demand for the surrender of designated members of the German armed forces, together with the obvious legal difficulty that many of the accused persons had acted in obedience to higher authority, and the general *ex post facto* character of the provisions of the treaty, led the Allied and Associated Powers to yield subsequently to the German request that the accused persons be tried by German judicial tribunals.[27]

New rules of responsibility. While the actual results of the trial of military offenders were negligible, the principle was established that persons guilty of offenses against the laws of war might be brought to trial at the close of the war. The termination of war, therefore, did not automatically result in a general amnesty. On the other hand, in view of the fact that the delegates of two of the five leading powers refused to admit the criminal character of the act of the head of the defeated state in bringing on the war itself, it can not be said that the attempt to try the Kaiser constituted a new principle of responsibility in that respect.[28] At the Washington Conference on the Limitation of Armaments provision was made in the Treaty relating to the Use of Submarines and Noxious Gases in Warfare that any person who in the service of any state should violate any of the rules laid down, "whether or not such person is under orders of a governmental superior," should be deemed to have violated the laws of war and be liable to trial "as if for an act

[27] Allied Note, May 7, 1920. See *Am. Journal,* Vol. 16 (1922), Supp., p. 195.
[28] See United States and Japanese reservations to the Report of the Commission on Responsibilities, *Am. Journal,* Vol. 14 (1920), pp. 127, 151.

of piracy" and might be brought to trial before the civil or military authorities of any power within the jurisdiction of which he might be found.[29] While the new rule was limited to the special offenses set forth in the treaty, it contained the important principle that a person who violated its provisions would not be able to excuse himself on ground of *respondeat superior*.[30]

The Moscow Declaration. At the Tripartite Conference at Moscow in 1943, the three powers, proclaiming that they were speaking in the name of the then thirty-two United Nations, declared their intention to demand that those German officers and men and members of the Nazi party guilty of atrocities should be sent back to the countries in which their crimes were committed in order that they might be judged and punished according to the laws of those countries. The declaration further announced that in the case of those "major criminals" whose offenses had no particular geographical location, punishment would be inflicted by the joint decision of the governments of the Allies.[31]

The Nuremberg trials. On August 8, 1945, an agreement was reached in London between the United States, France, Great Britain, and the Soviet Union making definite provision for the establishment of an International Military Tribunal for the trial of war criminals whose offenses had no particular geographical location.[32] Annexed to the agreement was a "Charter," defining the constitution, jurisdiction, and functions of the tribunal and the crimes for which the defendants might be held individually responsible.[33] Provision was made that at the trial of an individual member of an organization the Tribunal might also declare that the organization itself was a criminal organization.[34] Twenty-two major war criminals were indicted; and on November 20 the trial began.

[29] Art. 3. For the text of the treaty, see Hudson, *Int. Legislation*, Vol. II, p. 794; Buell, *The Washington Conference*, p. 220.

[30] The principle would have been a difficult one to apply if the Washington Treaty had ever been ratified, for it would have meant a choice for the submarine officer of execution by the enemy as a pirate or execution by his own forces for disobedience to military orders. Only in the case of orders contrary to the principles of humanity could the officer be expected to disobey orders. In the case of *The Llandovery Castle* the German Supreme Court held, in the Leipsic Trials, that the defense of superior orders could not justify an act which was manifestly and indisputably contrary to international law, such as the killing of unarmed enemies or of shipwrecked persons taking refuge in life-boats. *Annual Digest*, 1923-1924, Case No. 235.

[31] For the text of the Moscow Declaration on German atrocities, see Dept. of State *Bulletin*, Vol. IX, p. 310.

[32] See Dept of State *Bulletin*, Vol. XIII, p. 222. Nineteen other states adhered to the agreement, without however being represented upon the Tribunal.

[33] *Ibid.*, p. 223. While the Charter determined its jurisdiction, the Tribunal felt called upon to justify certain provisions of the Charter which it recognized might not be regarded by public opinion as in accord with law without further explanation.

[34] Art. 9. These organizations included the Reich Cabinet, the Leadership Corps of the Nazi Party, the "SS" and the "SD" (Schutzstaffeln and Sicherheitsdienst), the "Gestapo" (Geheime Staatspolizei), the "S A" (Sturmabteilungen), and the General Staff and High Command of the German Armed Forces,—all of which were made defendants in the indictment.

The trial lasted 216 days and the Tribunal held 403 open sessions. The hearing of evidence and the speeches of counsel for the accused ended on August 31, 1946.[35] Judgment was given on October 1, 1946. Twelve of the major war criminals were sentenced to death, and others to terms of imprisonment. Three of the defendants were acquitted. The Soviet member of the Tribunal dissented in respect of these acquittals and other parts of the conclusion.[36]

The crimes for which the defendants were indicted were listed in the Charter as (1) crimes against peace; (2) war crimes; and (3) crimes against humanity. The indictment for "crimes against peace" was an innovation in international law; and it included the "planning, preparation, initiation, or waging of a war of aggression, or a war in violation of international treaties, agreements or assurances, or participation in a common plan or conspiracy for the accomplishment of any of the foregoing." The term "war crimes" included violations of the traditional laws or customs of war, a number of which were specifically mentioned. The term "crimes against humanity" included inhumane acts which were "committed in execution of, or in connection with the aggressive war," although they might not be war crimes in the strict sense.[37] Participation in the common plan or conspiracy to commit any of the foregoing crimes formed a separate count in the indictment.

The Tribunal justified at length the indictment of the defendants for crimes against peace, the planning and waging of a war of aggression.[38] Chief reliance was placed upon the Kellogg-Briand Pact, by which the contracting parties condemned recourse to war and renounced it as an instrument of national policy, thus making war an illegal act.[39] The argument that there could be no punishment of crime without a preexisting law, *nulla poena sine lege*, was dismissed as inapplicable to the existing facts, since there could be no doubt that the defendants knew they were acting in defiance of international law.[40] The argument that international law deals only with the acts of sovereign states and not

[35] The text of the indictment and the opening statement by the Chief of Counsel for the United States may be found in *The Case against the Nazi War Criminals*, Vol. 111, p. 3. For the closing address of Mr. Jackson and for his final report to the president, see Dept. of State *Bulletin*, Vol. XV, pp. 364, 771.

[36] For the opinion and judgment of the Tribunal, see *Nazi Conspiracy and Aggression*, Government Printing Office, 1947; *Am. Journal*, Vol. 41 (1947), p. 172.

[37] The distinction made by the Tribunal between war crimes and crimes against humanity is confusing. Under the head of crimes against humanity it was possible to include crimes against German nationals or denationalized persons, such as Jews, which it would not have been possible to include technically under "war crimes." The technical aspects of the indictment of Adolf Eichmann by an Israeli court in 1961 are discussed above, on p. 324.

[38] See *Nazi Conspiracy and Aggression*, pp. 16 ff.

[39] *Ibid.*, pp. 49 ff. For the interpretation of the "right of self-defense" asserted by Germany in connection with the obligations of the Pact, see above, p. 273.

[40] *Ibid.*, pp. 49 ff. A distinction should be made between the maxim *nullum crimen sine lege* and the maxim *nulla poena sine lege*. The first relates to the offense committed; the second to the punishment to be assigned to it.

with acts of individuals was rejected as contrary to established practice
in the case of criminal acts.[41] The argument that the defendants were
acting in pursuance of higher orders and that they might plead *respondeat
superior* was held inapplicable in the case of acts condemned as criminal
by international law, although that fact might be taken into account in
mitigation of the punishment.[42] In respect of the common plan or conspiracy to bring about a war of aggression, the first count in the indictment, the Tribunal applied the principles of municipal criminal law.
While the indictment applied the conspiracy charge to all of the offenses
set forth in the Charter, the Tribunal limited it to the crime of aggressive
war, holding in this connection that the conspiracy "must not be too far
removed from the time of decision and of action" and that it must be
in connection with "a concrete plan" to wage war.

Of the seven organizations listed in the indictment, four were declared
to be criminal organizations and three, the S A (Sturmabteilungen), the
Reich Cabinet, and the General Staff and High Command were declared
not to be such.

The Tokyo trials. The trial of Japanese major war criminals was
carried out upon the same general principles applied in the case of the
German war criminals. The Charter of the International Military Tribunal for the Far East classified the crimes as crimes against peace, conventional war crimes, and crimes against humanity, together with the
separate crime of conspiracy to commit those crimes. The Tribunal consisted of eleven judges representing the states at war with Japan, including members of the British Commonwealth of Nations, India, and the
Philippine Islands. The indictment was drawn up in the form of fifty-
five counts, reciting the various crimes charged against the defendants
and the particular countries against which they had been committed.[43]

Comments of jurists. It was to be expected that jurists would be
divided in their views upon the extension of international law by the
two Tribunals into the field of "crimes against peace." [44] There was little

---

[41] *Nazi Conspiracy and Aggression,* p. 52.

[42] *Ibid.,* p. 53, where Art. 8 of the Charter is discussed.

[43] For the text of the Charter, January 19, 1946, as amended April 26, 1946, see
Dept. of State *Bulletin,* Vol. XIV, pp. 361, 890. The Charter was issued in the form
of a proclamation of the Supreme Commander of the Allied Powers. For the text of
the Indictment, see *Trial of Japanese War Criminals,* p. 45.

[44] The literature of the subject of the trial of war criminals is extensive. See, in
particular, Glueck, *War Criminals, Their Prosecution and Punishment,* opposing the
conception of aggressive war as a crime; *The Nuremberg Trial and Aggressive War,*
holding aggressive war an international crime; G. A. Finch, *Am. Journal,* Vol. 37
(1943), p. 81; Vol. 41 (1947), p. 20; Q. Wright, *ibid.,* Vol. 39 (1945), p. 257; Vol.
40 (1946), p. 398; Vol. 41 (1947), p. 38; H. Lauterpacht, in *British Year Book of
Int. Law,* 1944, p. 58; C. C. Hyde, E. D. Dickinson, C. Warren, and others in *Proceedings,* Am. Soc. Int. Law, 1943, pp. 38 ff.; 1945, pp. 68 ff.; H. Ehard, "The
Nuremberg Trial against the Major War Criminals and the International Law," *Am.
Journal,* Vol. 43 (1949), p. 223; Woetzel, *The Nuremberg Trials in International
Law.*

difficulty in accepting the judgment of the Tribunal in respect to "war crimes" and "crimes against humanity," since international custom had long recognized the right of a victorious army to bring to trial individual members of the enemy armies alleged to be guilty of violations of the laws of war. Whether members of the higher command might be held responsible for the acts of subordinates was merely a question of proof that they knew of and either ordered or acquiesced in the acts committed.[45] The refusal of the Tribunals to accept the plea of *respondeat superior* where crimes as grave as those charged against the defendants were involved was in accord with established practice.[46] The fact that similar crimes committed by members of the armed forces of the victorious army might go unpunished was never regarded as invalidating the trial of members of the defeated army.

With respect to "crimes against peace," the criticism of a number of jurists was directed partly against the attempt to consider aggressive war as in itself a crime apart from illegal acts committed during the course of the hostilities, and partly against the character of the tribunal which gave judgment in the case. It was agreed that the adoption of the Kellogg-Briand Pact might be held to have made aggressive war "illegal"; but it was not clear that such illegality could be transformed into an international "crime" in the sense of making the individuals participating in it personally subject to indictment.[47] The line between aggressive and defensive war was, critics observed, not so clear that aggressive war could be regarded as possessing the specific character required for a criminal offense. There was no general understanding at the time of the adoption of the Pact of Paris that a violation of the obligation of the

[45] The United States *Rules of Land Warfare,* while protecting from punishment individuals of the armed forces for offenses "in case they are committed under the orders or sanction of their government or commanders" go on to provide that: "The commanders ordering the commission of such acts, or under whose authority they are committed by their troops, may be punished by the belligerent into whose hands they may fall." No. 347.

[46] It is not believed that the exemption granted by the U. S. *Rules of Land Warfare,* No. 347, above n. 45, was intended to exempt the commander himself from responsibility by pleading the orders of a single superior, Fuehrer, or president. Nor was it understood as protecting the individual soldier or subordinate officer from responsibility for acts of inhumanity of the character attributed to the defendants at Nuremberg.

[47] The Tribunal itself appears to have had doubts on this point, for it granted that: "In interpreting the words of the pact, it must be remembered that international law is not the product of an international legislature, and that such international agreements as the Pact of Paris have to deal with general principles of law, and not with administrative matters of procedure. The law of war is to be found not only in treaties, but in the customs and practices of states which gradually obtained universal recognition, and from the general principles of justice applied by jurists and practiced by military courts. This law is not static, but by continual adaptation follows the needs of a changing world. Indeed, in many cases treaties do no more than express and define for more accurate reference the principles of law already existing." *Nazi Conspiracy and Aggression,* p. 51.

Pact would carry with it a right on the part of other states to treat the leaders of the offending state as personally guilty of a criminal act.[48]

Could the Nuremberg Tribunal of four members properly be regarded as an "international tribunal"? Should it not at least have included representatives of other states in passing upon the question of the crimes against peace? [49] More pointed, however, was the question whether two of the members of the Tribunal were competent to try the defendants. In the case of the United States member there was the fact that the United States had not only adopted neutrality legislation during the years preceding the war, but in the opening days of the war had issued a proclamation of neutrality in which the United States was said to be "on terms of friendship and amity" with the state of which the indicted officials were leaders.[50] In respect to the qualifications of the member of the Tribunal representing the Soviet Union, it was said that the non-aggression pact signed with Germany on August 23, 1939, was clearly made in anticipation of the act of aggression Germany was about to commit, and that the Soviet Union became thereby an accessory before the fact; while the subsequent partitioning of Poland by the two countries made the Soviet Union an accessory after the fact.[51]

The report of the United States member of the Tribunal pointed out that the significance of the trial would depend upon taking the "next step" of a general codification by the United Nations of offenses against

[48] See, on this point, G. A. Finch, "The Nuremberg Trial and International Law," *Am. Journal,* Vol. 41 (1947), p. 20, who cites Secretary Stimson to the effect that the efficacy of the Pact of Paris depended "solely upon the public opinion of the world and upon the conscience of those nations which sign it," and who points out the persistent refusal of the United States to admit that the Pact made any fundamental change in the relations between belligerents and neutrals.

In defense of the criminal character of war following the Pact of Paris, see Q. Wright, "The Law of the Nuremberg Trial," *Am. Journal,* Vol. 41 (1947), p. 38, where a list of jurists supporting and opposing the criminality of a war of aggression is given.

[49] While the Moscow Declaration of 1943 announced that the major criminals whose offenses had no particular geographic location would be punished "by the joint decision of the Governments of the Allies," the Charter of the Tribunal made provision for only four members. But the fact that nineteen other members of the then "United Nations" accepted the agreement of August 8, 1945, to which the Charter was annexed can be said to have made the Tribunal the spokesman of other states than the four represented on it.

[50] See G. A. Finch, article cited, *Am. Journal,* Vol. 41 (1947), pp. 20, 28, where it is said that, "To maintain retroactively that these invasions were international criminal acts involving personal responsibility is to suggest that the United States officially compounded international crime with international criminals." This is perhaps straining the conception of neutrality. It is suggested that a more correct conclusion would be that the United States member should have withdrawn from the Tribunal when the question of "crimes against peace" was under consideration.

[51] On this point Finch observes: "The terms of that pact, the circumstances under which it was signed, and the conduct of Russia as well as of Germany immediately following its signature lead to a strong presumption that it was made in anticipation of a joint attack on Poland by both signatories." *Op. cit.*

the peace and security of mankind.[52] On its part, the General Assembly first approved the principles set forth in the Charter of the Military Tribunal; and two years later, in 1947, it called upon the International Law Commission to formulate the Nuremberg principles and at the same time to prepare a draft code of offenses against the peace and security of mankind. A first draft of the principles was duly formulated, but no further action was taken. The second, more comprehensive code was submitted to the General Assembly in 1951 and again, in revised form, in succeeding years, awaiting answer to the question of the definition of aggression and other related problems.[53]

E. EFFECT OF WAR UPON TREATIES

The question as to the effect of war upon treaties between the belligerent states gave rise to much controversy. Since treaties varied widely in their intrinsic character, both doctrine and practice agreed in dividing them into groups according to their subject matter and holding some of them to be unaffected by war and others to be suspended or completely abrogated.[54] The first of these groups were treaties which were by their nature final and dispositive in character and thus indicated an intention on the part of the framers of the treaty that their provisions were to survive the outbreak of war. Such, for example, were the provisions of the treaty of 1783 between Great Britain and the United States recognizing the independence of the latter country, a matter that could not by any reasoning be regarded as reopened by the subsequent War of 1812 between the parties. Such also were boundary treaties and treaties providing for the transfer of territory, which clearly contemplated a permanent state of things and were not put at issue by the outbreak of war, although they might be changed by the specific provisions of a treaty of peace.

Treaties creating vested rights. Greater difficulty was presented by treaties, or provisions of treaties, which created vested rights. In the case of the Society for the Propagation of the Gospel v. New Haven,[55] decided in 1823, a foreign corporation brought an action of ejectment to recover lands held by them under the treaty of 1783 between the United States and Great Britain of which they had been deprived by a local law. The court recognized the title of the Society as being a vested right under the treaty and laid down, *obiter,* the broad principle that "where treaties contemplate a permanent arrangement of territorial, and

---

[52] Dept. of State *Bulletin,* Vol. XV, p. 954.

[53] *U.N. Yearbook,* 1951, p. 852; 1957, p. 376; Whiteman, *Digest,* Vol. 1, pp. 201 ff.

[54] On the general subject of the effect of war upon treaties see Baker and McKernan, *Selected Topics Connected with the Laws of Warfare,* pp. 220-269; Phillipson, *Termination of War,* pp. 250-268; A. D. McNair, "Les effets de la guerre sur les traités," *Recueil des Cours,* Vol. 59 (1937-I), pp. 527 ff.; *The Law of Treaties.*

[55] 8 Wheaton, p. 464 (1823). Fenwick, *Cases,* p. 870.

other national rights, or which, in their terms, are meant to provide for
the event of an intervening war, it would be against every principle of
just interpretation to hold them extinguished by the event of war." The
same doctrine was laid down by the British Court of Chancery in 1830
in the case of Sutton v. Sutton,[56] which involved the right of an American alien to hold and convey real estate which had vested in him under
the treaty of 1794, notwithstanding the intervening war of 1812-1814.
The court held that it was "a reasonable construction that it was the
intention of the treaty that the operation of the treaty should be permanent, and not depend upon the continuance of a state of peace."

Executed treaties. Treaties of this final and dispositive character
were said by some writers to be suspended while the war lasted, but
upon the return of peace to revive in their operation without any express
or implied renewal. They were also described as "transitory conventions"
(*pacta transitoria*), and while the term was open to objection,[57] it was
interpreted as indicating the fact that such treaties accomplished their
object by a single act and thereupon ceased to have any further contractual force.[58] A better term might perhaps be "executed treaties,"
following the terminology of the executed contracts of municipal law.

Executory treaties. A second group of treaties were those of an executory character, which looked to the performance of a series of acts or
to the creation of a situation the effects of which were continuously
felt as cases arose that were governed by it. The subject matter of these
treaties clearly indicated that they were not intended by the parties to
set up final and definitive arrangements but merely to provide a temporary basis for the adjustment of conflicting interests or for the promotion of common interests. "Political treaties," as they have been
called, such as treaties of alliance or of arbitration, were necessarily abrogated by war as being incompatible with the existence of hostile relations. Treaties of commerce and navigation were almost uniformly
regarded by states as abrogated by hostilities, although the fact that in
the treaties of peace at the conclusion of wars such treaties were occasionally "confirmed" or "reestablished" led writers to assert that they
were merely suspended during the war.[59] At the close of the Franco-
Prussian War of 1870-1871, and of the Russo-Japanese War of 1904-1905
the commercial relations of the two belligerents were temporarily ad-

[56] 1 R. & M. 663. Court of Chancery, 1830.

[57] See Moore, *Digest*, Vol. V, p. 383.

[58] See Sir Cecil J. B. Hurst, "The Effect of War on Treaties," *British Year Book,
1921-22*, pp. 37, 46. Sir Cecil questions "whether it is the character and nature of
the treaty stipulation which is really the decisive element," and submits "that the
true test as to whether or not a treaty survives an outbreak of war between the
parties is to be found in the intention of the parties at the time when the treaty was
concluded" (pp. 39-40).

[59] For a discussion of opposing points of view, see Hall, *International Law,* § 125;
Moore, *Digest*, Vol. V, § 779.

justed on the basis of "most-favored-nation" treatment until new treaties should be negotiated.[60] At the close of the Spanish-American War in 1898, Spain announced that the war had terminated all agreements, compacts, and conventions between the two countries.[61]

Special concessions. The question of special concessions gave rise to frequent controversies. The treaty of 1783 between Great Britain and the United States on the one hand recognized the independence of the former colonies and defined their boundaries and on the other hand granted certain fishing "liberties" to the United States in the waters of Newfoundland. These latter were claimed by the United States in 1815 as surviving the war of 1812-1814; but the British Government replied with the categorical assertion that it knew of "no exception to the rule that all treaties are put an end to by a subsequent war between the same parties," and the United States was obliged to yield the point.[62]

Nor was there any clear rule of international law with respect to treaties granting a favored status to the citizens of the two states in the country of the other state. In the case of Techt v. Hughes,[63] decided in 1920, the Court of Appeals of New York held that the war between the United States and Austria-Hungary had not necessarily abrogated the provisions of a treaty of 1848 and that, in the absence of action by the political departments of the government, the courts were free to permit the alien plaintiff to acquire property by descent as provided in the treaty. By contrast, in the case of Karnuth v. United States,[64] decided in 1929, the Supreme Court of the United States held that Article 3 of the Jay Treaty of 1794, conferring upon British and United States citizens freedom "to pass and repass" into the respective territories of the two parties, had been abrogated by the subsequent war between them, in as much as the treaty conferred a privilege which was "in no sense a vested right" but "wholly promissory and prospective."

Multipartite conventions. A third group of treaties embraced those general or multipartite conventions to which a large number of states were parties, such as the International Sanitary Convention of 1903, which provided for the administration of matters of common convenience to the international community at large. These treaties continued in force with respect to relations between the belligerents and neutrals; and it would appear that in respect to relations between the belligerents

[60] See Crandall, *Treaties: Their Making and Enforcement*, § 181, where a survey of the leading peace treaties is given.

[61] *Treaties and Conventions*, Vol. II, pp. 1701, 1710. See also Moore, *Digest*, Vol. V, § 779.

[62] For details of the controversy, see Moore, *Digest*, Vol. I, § 163. See above, p. 453.

[63] 229 N.Y. Rep. 222 (1929). Fenwick, *Cases*, p. 874; Bishop, *Cases*, p. 179; Briggs, *Cases*, p. 936; Hudson, *Cases*, p. 904.

[64] 279 U.S. 231 (1929). Fenwick, *Cases*, p. 879; Bishop, *Cases*, p. 179; Hudson, *Cases*, p. 913.

themselves they were merely suspended in so far as their provisions were inconsistent with belligerent operations and the cessation of friendly intercourse.[65]

It is scarcely necessary to observe that treaties entered into in direct contemplation of the possibility of war were not only not abrogated by war between the parties, but came into actual effect in consequence of it. Such, for example, were the general conventions adopted at the Hague Conferences in 1899 and 1907 regulating the conduct of belligerents as between themselves and in their relations with neutral states; and also special treaties such as the treaty of 1839 providing for the neutralization of Belgium.

Provisions of the Treaty of Versailles. The provisions of the Treaty of Versailles in respect to the effect of the World War upon the treaties to which Germany was a party were of an exceptional character and represented rather the imposition of penalties upon the defeated state than the recognition of the legal survival of preexisting treaties. Numerous multilateral treaties of an economic or technical character were enumerated as to be "applied" between Germany and the Allied and Associated Powers parties to them. Other bilateral treaties between individual members of the Allied and Associated Powers and Germany were to be "revived" at the option of the former, provided they were not inconsistent with the provisions of the treaty then being concluded. All such treaties which had not been so notified to Germany within a period of six months, as revived, were to be considered as forthwith abrogated. Specific penalties were imposed upon Germany in the form of the required cancellation of treaties concluded between Germany on the one hand and Austria-Hungary, Bulgaria, Turkey, and Russia on the other.[66]

Provisions of the treaties following the Second World War. The peace treaties imposed upon Italy, Finland, and the three satellite states following the Second World War contain sweeping provisions with respect to the bilateral treaties to which they were separately parties.[67] In identic terms it is provided that each of the Allied or Asociated Powers was to notify Italy and the other states, within a period of six months, which of its prewar bilateral treaties with the particular state it desired to keep in force or revive, with the exception of provisions not in conformity with the present treaty. All such treaties which it was desired to keep in force or revive were to be registered with the Secretariat of the United Nations; and treaties not so notified were to be regarded as abrogated.

[65] See Tobin, *The Termination of Multipartite Treaties*, "Termination in Wartime."

[66] Arts. 282, 289, 290, 292.

[67] Treaty with Italy, Art. 44; with Finland, Art. 12; with Bulgaria, Art. 8; with Hungary, Art. 10; with Rumania, Art. 10.

CHAPTER **XXXVI**

International Law: The Old and the New

A. CONTRASTS OF HALF A CENTURY

The international law of today presents sharp contrasts with the law of half a century and more ago. As law, in the sense of the obligation underlying respect for the rules in force, there is perhaps no substantial change: international law is law not because it is the command of a higher authority, but because it has been accepted as law by the nations that constitute the international community. It is a body of collective obligations which might be described as the recognized conditions of membership in the international community, and which are in fact regularly observed although lacking the sanctions attached to national law.

The contrasts of half a century are marked by changes in the membership of the international community, by changes in the fundamental principle of national security, by the expanding scope of international relations, by new organizations created for economic and social objectives, and by changes in the status of war and neutrality. Whether the new law as it has developed over the years will be able to meet the challenge of the day and control the political and technological forces set in motion by the "revolution of rising expectations" in respect to the satisfaction of human needs and by the new instruments of warfare in the hands of nations of conflicting ideologies is the problem of the future.

B. CONTRASTS OF MEMBERSHIP IN THE INTERNATIONAL COMMUNITY

In half a century the membership of the international community has increased from a limited group of some 50 states of the Western World to a worldwide community of some 115 states of every race, language, and national tradition, Near Eastern, Far Eastern, and African. This has had the effect of challenging the authority of many of the principles and customs recognized and respected at the beginning of the century. The greater part of the rules of the old law have been accepted by the new states without difficulty; but their reactions to certain fundamental principles have introduced elements of controversy; and in two vital areas, among others of lesser importance, ideologies have been proclaimed which strike at the very roots of the established system—the good faith of treaties and the exercise of representative democracy.

On the other hand the emancipation of so many colonies and protectorates has brought the hope of a better life to millions of people hitherto living in subjection and held down to economic and social conditions below their effective resources; and if in the process of emancipation they are in some cases passing through stages of civil strife, the outlook is one of developing qualities of self-government hitherto largely dormant. The fact that the high ideals of the Charter of the United Nations have been accepted, where before only the dictates of the colonial power controlled their destiny, marks an advance in the adoption of the international rule of law, even if the advance is at times halting or temporarily stalled.

C. THE PRINCIPLE OF COLLECTIVE SECURITY

The fundamental change of half a century lies in the new principle of collective security. On the eve of the First World War each nation was the keeper of its own gates; each nation depended upon its own resources for its national defense; and if these resources were inadequate the separate states sought to strengthen their position by formal alliances with friendly powers. Alliance was thus set against alliance to the point where there existed a balance of power, essentially unstable because of changing conditions, but relied upon as restraining any individual member from committing an act of aggression.

There was, however, no element of community organization in the balance of power. When the Austro-Hungarian crisis arose in 1914, no effort was made to call a general conference such as had met in 1907. The time, indeed, was short; but there was lacking the sense of the collective responsibility of the nations as a body for the maintenance of peace, the realization by the other members of the international community that they had a national interest of their own in preventing the outbreak of a major war. War was looked upon as something that came in the normal order of things when states in controversy felt that their vital interests were at stake. Other states, not parties to the controversy, had to accept the situation in spite of whatever adverse effect it might have upon their relations with the belligerents.

Three years later, when the United States was drawn into the war in defense of its rights as a neutral, President Wilson conceived the idea of a general association of nations to put into effect mutual guarantees of political independence and territorial integrity to great and small nations alike. No longer was the protection of a state to depend upon its own resources or those of its allies; the organized community of nations would protect it. But the United States refused to take part in the proposed system of collective defense, and the League of Nations proved unable to enforce its authority against a determined lawbreaker.

Only after the Second World War was the principle of collective security accepted by the United States and incorporated into the Charter of the United Nations. But before it could be said to have become a part of international law the discovery of the atomic bomb undermined its effective application. For the destructive power of the bomb was so great that a single state in possession of it and willing to risk its use could defy the whole community. Collective security thereupon gave way to a "cold war" between the two powers possessing the bomb, in which open conflict was prevented by the knowledge that while each could destroy the other the price would be its own destruction—a new balance of power described as a "balance of terror."

But while collective security, in the sense that the protection of the individual state is assured by the combined force of the community against the aggressor, has not been made effective, it can be said that the provisions of the Charter of the United Nations have established the general principle that all of the members of the international community, acting through the Security Council and the General Assembly, are collectively responsible for the maintenance of peace. Even if the principle has not as yet become an effective rule eliminating the need for individual national defense, it has laid the foundations upon which a system of collective security may in time be built. The day is past when an act of aggression was of no legal concern to states whose national interests were not directly affected by it.

D. PROGRESS IN OTHER FIELDS

But if international law has failed to develop an effective rule of collective security, it has made marked progress in other fields of international relations. Problems of national jurisdiction have been adjusted; the responsibility of the state for the protection of resident aliens has come to be more clearly recognized, although there are still minor areas of disagreement; there is also a clearer recognition of the obligation on the part of a state to prevent acts injurious to other states; the extradition of fugitive criminals has been extended in scope; territorial boundaries have been adjusted or at least prevented from becoming sources of conflict; the law of the sea has been defined in specific fields; and the law of the air and of outer space is being adapted to meet the changing conditions of travel, communication, and exploration.

E. NEW FIELDS OF COOPERATION

More important than these developments in the traditional areas of international law has been the extension of the law into the area of economic and social relations. Here the contrast between the old and the new is most striking. On the eve of the First World War the struggle of the manufacturing countries for foreign markets went on without restraint, accompanied by a corresponding struggle for supplies of the raw materials of industry that were essential to manufacture. In both cases the control of a colony gave to the colonial power a practical monopoly of both supplies and markets. To protect its commercial interests a state had to have a powerful army and a powerful navy, and these in turn made necessary more economic resources, so that political and economic imperialism thus proceeded hand in hand. President Wilson had sought to establish an equality of trade conditions but without success; it was only with the adoption of the Atlantic Charter that it came to be accepted that the "wider and permanent system of general security" contemplated by the Charter could only be attained by measures aiming at the welfare of the individual human being over and above the rivalry of the separate states.

To this end new organizations were created, described in the Charter of the United Nations as "specialized agencies," and they undoubtedly constitute a significant, perhaps the most significant, development of the new international law. While the Economic and Social Council of the United Nations is the central coordinating body of these organizations, the organizations themselves are only associated with the United Nations, not an integral part of it; they thus have a separate institutional character which enables them to develop their own law and functions without being dependent upon the political elements of the Security Council and the General Assembly. Supplementing the work of these specialized organizations are numerous, almost innumerable nongovernmental organizations, NGO's, as they are called, devoted to practically every aspect of human interest cutting across state lines. The far-reaching influence of these official and unofficial organizations results from the fact that they appear to be slowly building up a body of international common interests which may in the course of the years prove to be so close a bond of international unity as to accomplish what the more strictly legal elements of the rule of law may be unable to accomplish. The breakdown of nationalistic barriers in the fields of economic and social relations may be a forerunner of the more difficult breakdown in the political field of collective security. In like manner cooperation within the new regional organizations, such as the Organization of American States, may make easier the transition to the wider universal field.

F. WAR LOSES ITS LEGAL CHARACTER

Lastly, the contrast between the old law and the new is to be seen in the fact that the laws of war and of neutrality, which once constituted so large a part of international law, have now lost their formal character and become part of the history of international law rather than rules of present obligation. Minor wars are still being fought, or rather hostilities that are not bearing the name of "war"; and it is to be hoped that the humanitarian customs antedating the Hague Conventions are being observed. But the Hague Conventions of 1907 have gone by the board: there is little or nothing left of the provisions distinguishing between combatants and noncombatants and between the bombing of defended and undefended towns. The worker in the factory making munitions now shares the lot of the soldier in the field. Churches and monuments can no longer be given special protection while military installations are being bombed. The Geneva Convention of 1949 was adopted to improve the lot of prisoners of war; but their lot can be no better than that of the civilian population. As for the elaborate codes of neutrality adopted in 1907 and 1909, once the Charter of the United Nations put the stamp of illegality upon resort to war as a formal procedure, any suggestion of rules of blockade and contraband would be dismissed as anachronistic.

What of the atomic bomb? Quite obviously it can not be brought under the established laws of war, customary or conventional. For its intrinsic character is such that it could not be used for its obvious purposes except in violation of the law, so that the mere possession of it would be illegal except as a deterrent to a state that might be tempted to use it without legal or moral restraint. To this paradox must be added the fact that the continued production of a weapon which can only be justified as a defense against a state that might be tempted to use it first in violation of the law constitutes a standing menace to the peace, increasingly greater as more and more powers come into possession of the bomb; and the situation might readily occur when it would be difficult to determine from what source the first attack came. The lesson is clear, if only it can be learned in time.

Appendices

Covenant of the League of Nations [1]

THE HIGH CONTRACTING PARTIES

In order to promote international coöperation and to achieve international peace and security

by the acceptance of obligations not to resort to war,

by the prescription of open, just and honorable relations between nations,

by the firm establishment of the understandings of international law as the actual rule of conduct among Governments, and

by the maintenance of justice and a scrupulous respect for all treaty obligations in the dealings of organized peoples with one another.

Agree to this Covenant of the League of Nations.

❋   ❋   ❋   ❋   ❋   ❋

Article 10

The members of the League undertake to respect and preserve as against external aggression the territorial integrity and existing political independence of all Members of the League. In case of any such aggression or in case of any threat or danger of such aggression the Council shall advise upon the means by which this obligation shall be fulfilled.

Article 11

1. Any war or threat of war, whether immediately affecting any of the Members of the League or not, is hereby declared a matter of concern to the whole League, and the League shall take any action that may be deemed wise and effectual to safeguard the peace of nations. In case any such emergency should

---

[1] For the complete text of the Covenant, being Arts. 1-26 of the Treaty of Versailles, see *Am. Journal*, Vol. 13 (1919), Supp., p. 151; *Foreign Relations of the United States*, 1919, Vol. XIII, p. 57.

arise the Secretary-General shall on the request of any Member of the League forthwith summon a meeting of the Council.

2. It is also declared to be the friendly right of each Member of the League to bring to the attention of the Assembly or of the Council any circumstance whatever affecting international relations which threatens to disturb international peace or the good understanding between nations upon which peace depends.

Article 12 [2]

1. The Members of the League agree that if there should arise between them any dispute likely to lead to a rupture they will submit the matter either to arbitration *or judicial settlement* or to enquiry by the Council, and they agree in no case to resort to war until three months after the award by the arbitrators *or the judicial decision* or the report by the Council.

2. In any case under this Article the award of the arbitrators *or the judicial decision* shall be made within a reasonable time, and the report of the Council shall be made within six months after the submission of the dispute.

Article 13 [3]

1. The Members of the League agree that whenever any dispute shall arise between them which they recognise to be suitable for submission to arbitration *or judicial settlement,* and which cannot be satisfactorily settled by diplomacy, they will submit the whole subject-matter to arbitration *or judicial settlement.*

2. Disputes as to the interpretation of a treaty, as to any question of international law, as to the existence of any fact which, if established, would constitute a breach of any international obligation, or as to the extent and nature of the reparation to be made for any such breach, are declared to be among those which are generally suitable for submission to arbitration *or judicial settlement.*

3. *For the consideration of any such dispute, the court to which the case is referred shall be the Permanent Court of International Justice established in accordance with Article 14, or any tribunal agreed on by the parties to the dispute or stipulated in any convention existing between them.*[4]

4. The Members of the League agree that they will carry out in full good faith any award *or decision* that may be rendered, and that they will not resort to war against a Member of the League which complies therewith. In the event of any failure to carry out such an award *or decision*, the Council shall propose what steps should be taken to give effect thereto.

---

[2] The words printed in italics were added as amendments by vote of the Assembly in 1921 and came into force on September 26, 1924.

[3] See Art. 12, note.

[4] This paragraph replaces the following paragraph of the original text:

"For the consideration of any such dispute the court of arbitration to which the case is referred shall be the court agreed on by the parties to the dispute or stipulated in any convention existing between them."

Article 14

The Council shall formulate and submit to the Members of the League for adoption plans for the establishment of a Permanent Court of International Justice. The Court shall be competent to hear and determine any dispute of an international character which the parties thereto submit to it. The Court may also give an advisory opinion upon any dispute or question referred to it by the Council or by the Assembly.

Article 15 [5]

1. If there should arise between Members of the League any dispute likely to lead to a rupture, which is not submitted to arbitration *or judicial settlement* in accordance with Article 13, the Members of the League agree that they will submit the matter to the Council. Any party to the dispute may effect such submission by giving notice of the existence of the dispute to the Secretary-General, who will make all necessary arrangements for a full investigation and consideration thereof.

2. For this purpose the parties to the dispute will communicate to the Secretary-General, as promptly as possible, statements of their case with all the relevant facts and papers, and the Council may forthwith direct the publication thereof.

3. The Council shall endeavor to effect a settlement of the dispute, and if such efforts are successful, a statement shall be made public giving such facts and explanations regarding the dispute and the terms of settlement thereof as the Council may deem appropriate.

4. If the dispute is not thus settled, the Council either unanimously or by a majority vote shall make and publish a report containing a statement of the facts of the dispute and the recommendations which are deemed just and proper in regard thereto.

5. Any Member of the League represented on the Council may make public a statement of the facts of the dispute and of its conclusions regarding the same.

6. If a report by the Council is unanimously agreed to by the Members thereof other than the Representatives of one or more of the parties to the dispute, the Members of the League agree that they will not go to war with any party to the dispute which complies with the recommendations of the report.

7. If the Council fails to reach a report which is unanimously agreed to by the members thereof, other than the Representatives of one or more of the parties to the dispute, the Members of the League reserve to themselves the right to take such action as they shall consider necessary for the maintenance of right and justice.

8. If the dispute between the parties is claimed by one of them, and is found by the Council, to arise out of a matter which by international law is solely within the domestic jurisdiction of that party, the Council shall so report, and shall make no recommendation as to its settlement.

[5] See Art. 12, note 2.

9. The Council may in any case under this Article refer the dispute to the Assembly. The dispute shall be so referred at the request of either party to the dispute provided that such request be made within fourteen days after the submission of the dispute to the Council.

10. In any case referred to the Assembly, all the provisions of this Article and of Article 12 relating to the action and powers of the Council shall apply to the action and powers of the Assembly, provided that a report made by the Assembly, if concurred in by the Representatives of those Members of the League represented on the Council and of a majority of the other Members of the League, exclusive in each case of the Representatives of the parties to the dispute, shall have the same force as a report by the Council concurred in by all the members thereof other than the Representatives of one or more of the parties to the dispute.

Article 16 [6]

1. Should any Member of the League resort to war in disregard of its covenants under Articles 12, 13 or 15, it shall *ipso facto* be deemed to have committed an act of war against all other Members of the League, which hereby undertake immediately to subject it to the severance of all trade or financial relations, the prohibition of all intercourse between their nationals and the nationals of the covenant-breaking State, and the prevention of all financial, commercial or personal intercourse between the nationals of the covenant-breaking State and the nationals of any other State, whether a Member of the League or not.

2. It shall be the duty of the Council in such case to recommend to the several Governments concerned what effective military, naval or air force the Members of the League shall severally contribute to the armed forces to be used to protect the covenants of the League.

3. The Members of the League agree, further, that they will mutually support one another in the financial and economic measures which are taken under this Article, in order to minimize the loss and inconvenience resulting from the above measures, and that they will mutually support one another in resisting any special measures aimed at one of their number by the covenant-breaking State, and that they will take the necessary steps to afford passage through their territory to the forces of any of the Members of the League which are coöperating to protect the covenants of the League.

4. Any Member of the League which has violated any covenant of the League may be declared to be no longer a Member of the League by a vote of the Council concurred in by the Representatives of all the other Members of the League represented thereon.

[6] For amendments proposed by the Assembly in 1921, but not in force in 1933, see Hudson, *International Legislation*, Vol. I, pp. 29 ff.

Great Britain—United States:
Joint Declaration of the President and the Prime Minister
(THE ATLANTIC CHARTER)

[Released to the press by the White House, August 14, 1941.]

The President of the United States and the Prime Minister, Mr. Churchill, representing His Majesty's Government in the United Kingdom, have met at sea.

They have been accompanied by officials of their two Governments, including high-ranking officers of their military, naval, and air services.

The whole problem of the supply of munitions of war, as provided by the Lease-Lend Act, for the armed forces of the United States and for those countries actively engaged in resisting aggression has been further examined.

Lord Beaverbrook, the Minister of Supply of the British Government, has joined in these conferences. He is going to proceed to Washington to discuss further details with appropriate officials of the United States Government. These conferences will also cover the supply problems of the Soviet Union.

The President and the Prime Minister have had several conferences. They have considered the dangers to world civilization arising from the policies of military domination by conquest upon which the Hitlerite government of Germany and other governments associated therewith have embarked, and have made clear the stress which their countries are respectively taking for their safety in the face of these dangers.

They have agreed upon the following joint declaration:

Joint declaration of the President of the United States of America and the Prime Minister, Mr. Churchill, representing His Majesty's Government in the United Kingdom, being met together, deem it right to make known certain common principles in the national policies of their respective countries on which they base their hopes for a better future for the world.

First, their countries seek no aggrandizement, territorial or other;

Second, they desire to see no territorial changes that do not accord with the freely expressed wishes of the peoples concerned;

Third, they respect the right of all peoples to choose the form of government under which they will live; and they wish to see sovereign rights and self-government restored to those who have been forcibly deprived of them;

Fourth, they will endeavor, with due respect for their existing obligations, to further the enjoyment by all states, great or small, victor or vanquished, of access, on equal terms, to the trade and to the raw materials of the world which are needed for their economic prosperity;

Fifth, they desire to bring about the fullest collaboration between all nations in the economic field with the object of securing, for all, improved labor standards, economic advancement, and social security;

Sixth, after the final destruction of the Nazi tyranny, they hope to see established a peace which will afford to all nations the means of dwelling in safety within their own boundaries, and which will afford assurance that all the men in all the lands may live out their lives in freedom from fear and want;

Seventh, such a peace should enable all men to traverse the high seas and oceans without hindrance;

Eighth, they believe that all of the nations of the world, for realistic as well as spiritual reasons, must come to the abandonment of the use of force. Since no future peace can be maintained if land, sea, or air armaments continue to be employed by nations which threaten, or may threaten, aggression outside of their frontiers, they believe, pending the establishment of a wider and permanent system of general security, that the disarmament of such nations is essential. They will likewise aid and encourage all other practicable measures which will lighten for peace-loving peoples the crushing burden of armaments.

FRANKLIN D. ROOSEVELT
WINSTON S. CHURCHILL

ǀ

Charter of the United Nations

WE THE PEOPLES OF THE UNITED NATIONS DETERMINED

to save succeeding generations from the scourge of war, which twice in our lifetime has brought untold sorrow to mankind, and

to reaffirm faith in fundamental human rights, in the dignity and worth of the human person, in the equal rights of men and women and of nations large and small, and

to establish conditions under which justice and respect for the obligations arising from treaties and other sources of international law can be maintained, and

to promote social progress and better standards of life in larger freedom,

AND FOR THESE ENDS

to practice tolerance and live together in peace with one another as good neighbors, and

to unite our strength to maintain international peace and security, and

to ensure, by the acceptance of principles and the institution of methods, that armed force shall not be used, save in the common interest, and

to employ international machinery for the promotion of the economic and social advancement of all peoples,

HAVE RESOLVED TO COMBINE OUR EFFORTS TO ACCOMPLISH THESE AIMS.

Accordingly, our respective Governments, through representatives assembled in the city of San Francisco, who have exhibited their full powers found to be in good and due form, have agreed to the present Charter of the United Nations and do hereby establish an international organization to be known as the United Nations.

Charter I

Purposes and Principles

Article 1

The Purposes of the United Nations are:

1. To maintain international peace and security, and to that end: to take effective collective measures for the prevention and removal of threats to the peace, and for the suppression of acts of aggression or other breaches of the peace, and to bring about by peaceful means, and in conformity with the principles of justice and international law, adjustment or settlement of international disputes or situations which might lead to a breach of the peace;

2. To develop friendly relations among nations based on respect for the principle of equal rights and self-determination of peoples, and to take other appropriate measures to strengthen universal peace;

3. To achieve international cooperation in solving international problems of an economic, social, cultural, or humanitarian character, and in promoting and encouraging respect for human rights and for fundamental freedoms for all without distinction as to race, sex, language, or religion; and

4. To be a center for harmonizing the actions of nations in the attainment of these common ends.

Article 2

The Organization and its Members, in pursuit of the Purposes stated in Article 1 shall act in accordance with the following Principles.

1. The Organization is based on the principle of the sovereign equality of all its Members.

2. All Members, in order to ensure to all of them the rights and benefits resulting from membership, shall fulfil in good faith the obligations assumed by them in accordance with the present Charter.

3. All Members shall settle their international disputes by peaceful means in such a manner that international peace and security, and justice, are not endangered.

4. All Members shall refrain in their international relations from the threat or use of force against the territorial integrity or political independence of any state, or in any other manner inconsistent with the Purposes of the United Nations.

5. All Members shall give the United Nations every assistance in any action it takes in accordance with the present Charter, and shall refrain from giving assistance to any state against which the United Nations is taking preventive or enforcement action.

6. The Organization shall ensure that states which are not Members of the United Nations act in accordance with these Principles so far as may be necessary for the maintenance of international peace and security.

7. Nothing contained in the present Charter shall authorize the United Nations to intervene in matters which are essentially within the domestic juris-

diction of any state or shall require the Members to submit such matters to settlement under the present Charter; but this principle shall not prejudice the application of enforcement measures under Chapter VII.

Chapter II

Membership

Article 3

The original Members of the United Nations shall be the states which, having participated in the United Nations Conference on International Organization at San Francisco, or having previously signed the Declaration by United Nations of January 1, 1942, sign the present Charter and ratify it in accordance with Article 110.

Article 4

1. Membership in the United Nations is open to all other peace-loving states which accept the obligations contained in the present Charter and, in the judgment of the Organization, are able and willing to carry out these obligations.
2. The admission of any such state to membership in the United Nations will be effected by a decision of the General Assembly upon the recommendation of the Security Council.

Article 5

A Member of the United Nations against which preventive or enforcement action has been taken by the Security Council may be suspended from the exercise of the rights and privileges of membership by the General Assembly upon the recommendation of the Security Council. The exercise of these rights and privileges may be restored by the Security Council.

Article 6

A Member of the United Nations which has persistently violated the Principles contained in the present Charter may be expelled from the Organization by the General Assembly upon the recommendation of the Security Council.

Chapter III

Organs

Article 7

1. There are established as the principal organs of the United Nations: a General Assembly, a Security Council, an Economic and Social Council, a Trusteeship Council, an International Court of Justice, and a Secretariat.

2. Such subsidiary organs as may be found necessary may be established in accordance with the present Charter.

Article 8

The United Nations shall place no restrictions on the eligibility of men and women to participate in any capacity and under conditions of equality in its principal and subsidiary organs.

Chapter IV

THE GENERAL ASSEMBLY

COMPOSITION

Article 9

1. The General Assembly shall consist of all the Members of the United Nations.
2. Each member shall have not more than five representatives in the General Assembly.

FUNCTIONS AND POWERS

Article 10

The General Assembly may discuss any questions or any matters within the scope of the present Charter or relating to the powers and functions of any organs provided for in the present Charter, and, except as provided in Article 12, may make recommendations to the Members of the United Nations or to the Security Council or to both on any such questions or matters.

Article 11

1. The General Assembly may consider the general principles of cooperation in the maintenance of international peace and security, including the principles governing disarmament and the regulation of armaments, and may make recommendations with regard to such principles to the Members or to the Security Council or to both.
2. The General Assembly may discuss any questions relating to the maintenance of international peace and security brought before it by any Member of the United Nations, or by the Security Council, or by a state which is not a Member of the United Nations in accordance with Article 35, paragraph 2, and, except as provided in Article 12, may make recommendations with regard to any such questions to the state or states concerned or to the Security Council or to both. Any such question on which action is necessary shall be referred to the Security Council by the General Assembly either before or after discussion.
3. The General Assembly may call the attention of the Security Council to situations which are likely to endanger international peace and security.

4. The powers of the General Assembly set forth in this Article shall not limit the general scope of Article 10.

Article 12

1. While the Security Council is exercising in respect of any dispute or situation the functions assigned to it in the present Charter, the General Assembly shall not make any recommendations with regard to that dispute or situation unless the Security Council so requests.

2. The Secretary-General, with the consent of the Security Council, shall notify the General Assembly at each session of any matters relative to the maintenance of international peace and security which are being dealt with by the Security Council and shall similarly notify the General Assembly, or the Members of the United Nations if the General Assembly is not in session, immediately the Security Council ceases to deal with such matters.

Article 13

1. The General Assembly shall initiate studies and make recommendations for the purpose of:

a. promoting international cooperation in the political field and encouraging the progressive development of international law and its codification;

b. promoting international cooperation in the economic, social, cultural, educational, and health fields, and assisting in the realization of human rights and fundamental freedoms for all without distinction as to race, sex, language, or religion.

2. The further responsibilities, functions, and powers of the General Assembly with respect to matters mentioned in paragraph 1 (b) above are set forth in Chapters IX and X.

Article 14

Subject to the provisions of Article 12, the General Assembly may recommend measures for the peaceful adjustment of any situation, regardless of origin, which it deems likely to impair the general welfare or friendly relations among nations, including situations resulting from a violation of the provisions of the present Charter setting forth the Purposes and Principles of the United Nations.

Article 15

1. The General Assembly shall receive and consider annual and special reports from the Security Council; these reports shall include an account of the measures that the Security Council has decided upon or taken to maintain international peace and security.

2. The General Assembly shall receive and consider reports from the other organs of the United Nations.

Article 16

The General Assembly shall perform such functions with respect to the international trusteeship system as are assigned to it under Chapters XII and XIII, including the approval of the trusteeship agreements for areas not designated as strategic.

Article 17

1. The General Assembly shall consider and approve the budget of the Organization.

2. The expenses of the Organization shall be borne by the Members as apportioned by the General Assembly.

3. The General Assembly shall consider and approve any financial and budgetary arrangements with specialized agencies referred to in Article 57 and shall examine the administrative budgets of such specialized agencies with a view to making recommendations to the agencies concerned.

VOTING

Article 18

1. Each member of the General Assembly shall have one vote.

2. Decisions of the General Assembly on important questions shall be made by a two-thirds majority of the members present and voting. These questions shall include: recommendations with respect to the maintenance of international peace and security, the election of the non-permanent members of the Security Council, the election of the members of the Economic and Social Council, the election of members of the Trusteeship Council in accordance with paragraph 1 (c) of Article 86, the admission of new Members to the United Nations, the suspension of the rights and privileges of membership, the expulsion of Members, questions relating to the operation of the trusteeship system, and budgetary questions.

3. Decisions on other questions, including the determination of additional categories of questions to be decided by a two-thirds majority, shall be made by a majority of the members present and voting.

Article 19

A Member of the United Nations which is in arrears in the payment of its financial contributions to the Organization shall have no vote in the General Assembly if the amount of its arrears equals or exceeds the amount of the contributions due from it for the preceding two full years. The General Assembly may, nevertheless, permit such a member to vote if it is satisfied that the failure to pay is due to conditions beyond the control of the Member.

PROCEDURE

Article 20

The General Assembly shall meet in regular annual sessions and in such special sessions as occasion may require. Special sessions shall be convoked by the Secretary-General at the request of the Security Council or of a majority of the Members of the United Nations.

Article 21

The General Assembly shall adopt its own rules of procedure. It shall elect its President for each session.

Article 22

The General Assembly may establish such subsidiary organs as it deems necessary for the performance of its functions.

Chapter V

THE SECURITY COUNCIL

COMPOSITION

Article 23

1. The Security Council shall consist of eleven Members of the United Nations. The Republic of China, France, the Union of Soviet Socialist Republics, the United Kingdom of Great Britain and Northern Ireland, and the United States of America shall be permanent members of the Security Council. The General Assembly shall elect six other Members of the United Nations to be non-permanent members of the Security Council, due regard being specially paid, in the first instance to the contribution of Members of the United Nations to the maintenance of international peace and security and to the other purposes of the Organization, and also to equitable geographical distribution.

2. The non-permanent members of the Security Council shall be elected for a term of two years. In the first election of the non-permanent members, however, three shall be chosen for a term of one year. A retiring member shall not be eligible for immediate re-election.

3. Each member of the Security Council shall have one representative.

FUNCTIONS AND POWERS

Article 24

1. In order to ensure prompt and effective action by the United Nations, its Members confer on the Security Council primary responsibility for the maintenance of international peace and security, and agree that in carrying out its duties under this responsibility the Security Council acts on their behalf.

2. In discharging these duties the Security Council shall act in accordance with the Purposes and Principles of the United Nations. The specific powers granted to the Security Council for the discharge of these duties are laid down in Chapters VI, VII, VIII, and XII.

3. The Security Council shall submit annual and, when necessary, special reports to the General Assembly for its consideration.

Article 25

The Members of the United Nations agree to accept and carry out the decisions of the Security Council in accordance with the present Charter.

Article 26

In order to promote the establishment and maintenance of international peace and security with the least diversion for armaments of the world's human and economic resources, the Security Council shall be responsible for formulating, with the assistance of the Military Staff Committee referred to in Article 47, plans to be submitted to the Members of the United Nations for the establishment of a system for the regulation of armaments.

VOTING

Article 27

1. Each member of the Security Council shall have one vote.

2. Decisions of the Security Council on procedural matters shall be made by an affirmative vote of seven members.

3. Decisions of the Security Council on all other matters shall be made by an affirmative vote of seven members including the concurring votes of the permanent members; provided that, in decisions under Chapter VI, and under paragraph 3 of Article 52, a party to a dispute shall abstain from voting.

PROCEDURE

Article 28

1. The Security Council shall be so organized as to be able to function continuously. Each member of the Security Council shall for this purpose be represented at all times at the seat of the Organization.

2. The Security Council shall hold periodic meetings at which each of its members may, if it so desires, be represented by a member of the government or by some other specially designated representative.

3. The Security Council may hold meetings at such places other than the seat of the Organization as in its judgment will best facilitate its work.

Article 29

The Security Council may establish such subsidiary organs as it deems necessary for the performance of its functions.

Article 30

The Security Council shall adopt its own rules of procedure, including the method of selecting its President.

Article 31

Any Member of the United Nations which is not a member of the Security Council may participate, without vote, in the discussion of any question brought before the Security Council whenever the latter considers that the interests of that Member are specially affected.

Article 32

Any Member of the United Nations which is not a member of the Security Council or any state which is not a Member of the United Nations, if it is a party to a dispute under consideration by the Security Council, shall be invited to participate, without vote, in the discussion relating to the dispute. The Security Council shall lay down such conditions as it deems just for the participation of a state which is not a Member of the United Nations.

Chapter VI

PACIFIC SETTLEMENT OF DISPUTES

Article 33

1. The parties to any dispute, the continuance of which is likely to endanger the maintenance of international peace and security, shall, first of all, seek a solution by negotiation, enquiry, mediation, conciliation, arbitration, judicial settlement, resort to regional agencies or arrangements, or other peaceful means of their own choice.

2. The Security Council shall, when it deems necessary, call upon the parties to settle their dispute by such means.

Article 34

The Security Council may investigate any dispute, or any situation which might lead to international friction or give rise to a dispute, in order to determine whether the continuance of the dispute or situation is likely to endanger the maintenance of international peace and security.

Article 35

1. Any Member of the United Nations may bring any dispute, or any situation of the nature referred to in Article 34, to the attention of the Security Council or of the General Assembly.

2. A state which is not a Member of the United Nations may bring to the attention of the Security Council or of the General Assembly any dispute to which it is a party if it accepts in advance, for the purposes of the dispute, the obligations of pacific settlement provided in the present Charter.

3. The proceedings of the General Assembly in respect of matters brought to its attention under this Article will be subject to the provisions of Articles 11 and 12.

Article 36

1. The Security Council may, at any stage of a dispute of the nature referred to in Article 33 or of a situation of like nature, recommend appropriate procedures or methods of adjustment.

2. The Security Council should take into consideration any procedures for the settlement of the dispute which have already been adopted by the parties.

3. In making recommendations under this Article the Security Council should also take into consideration that legal disputes should as a general rule be referred by the parties to the International Court of Justice in accordance with the provisions of the Statute of the Court.

Article 37

1. Should the parties to a dispute of the nature referred to in Article 33 fail to settle it by the means indicated in that Article, they shall refer it to the Security Council.

2. If the Security Council deems that the continuance of the dispute is in fact likely to endanger the maintenance of international peace and security, it shall decide whether to take action under Article 36 or to recommend such terms of settlement as it may consider appropriate.

Article 38

Without prejudice to the provisions of Articles 33 to 37, the Security Council may, if all the parties to any dispute so request, make recommendations to the parties with a view to a pacific settlement of the dispute.

Chapter VII

ACTION WITH RESPECT TO THREATS TO THE PEACE, BREACHES OF THE PEACE, AND ACTS OF AGGRESSION

Article 39

The Security Council shall determine the existence of any threat to the peace, breach of the peace, or act of aggression and shall make recommendations, or decide what measures shall be taken in accordance with Articles 41 and 42, to maintain or restore international peace and security.

Article 40

In order to prevent an aggravation of the situation, the Security Council may, before making the recommendations or deciding upon the measures provided for in Article 39, call upon the parties concerned to comply with such provisional measures as it deems necessary or desirable. Such provisional measures shall be without prejudice to the rights, claims, or position of the parties concerned. The Security Council shall duly take account of failure to comply with such provisional measures.

Article 41

The Security Council may decide what measures not involving the use of armed force are to be employed to give effect to its decisions, and it may call upon the Members of the United Nations to apply such measures. These may include complete or partial interruption of economic relations and of rail, sea, air, postal, telegraphic, radio, and other means of communication, and the severance of diplomatic relations.

Article 42

Should the Security Council consider that measures provided for in Article 41 would be inadequate or have proved to be inadequate, it may take such action by air, sea, or land forces as may be necessary to maintain or restore international peace and security. Such action may include demonstrations, blockade, and other operations by air, sea, or land forces of Members of the United Nations.

Article 43

1. All Members of the United Nations, in order to contribute to the maintenance of international peace and security, undertake to make available to the Security Council, on its call and in accordance with a special agreement or agreements, armed forces, assistance, and facilities, including rights of passage, necessary for the purpose of maintaining international peace and security.

2. Such agreement or agreements shall govern the numbers and types of forces, their degree of readiness and general location, and the nature of the facilities and assistance to be provided.

3. The agreement or agreements shall be negotiated as soon as possible on the initiative of the Security Council. They shall be concluded between the Security Council and Members or between the Security Council and groups of Members and shall be subject to ratification by the signatory states in accordance with their respective constitutional processes.

Article 44

When the Security Council has decided to use force it shall, before calling upon a Member not represented on it to provide armed forces in fulfillment of the obligations assumed under Article 43, invite that Member, if the Member so desires, to participate in the decisions of the Security Council concerning the employment of contingents of that Member's armed forces.

Article 45

In order to enable the United Nations to take urgent military measures, Members shall hold immediately available national air-force contingents for combined international enforcement action. The strength and degree of readiness of these contingents and plans for their combined action shall be determined, within the limits laid down in the special agreement or agreements referred to in Article 43, by the Security Council with the assistance of the Military Staff Committee.

Article 46

Plans for the application of armed force shall be made by the Security Council with the assistance of the Military Staff Committee.

Article 47

1. There shall be established a Military Staff Committee to advise and assist the Security Council on all questions relating to the Security Council's military requirements for the maintenance of international peace and security, the employment and command of forces placed at its disposal, the regulation of armaments, and possible disarmament.

2. The Military Staff Committee shall consist of the Chiefs of Staff of the permanent members of the Security Council or their representatives. Any Member of the United Nations not permanently represented on the Committee shall be invited by the Committee to be associated with it when the efficient discharge of the Committee's responsibilities requires the participation of that Member in its work.

3. The Military Staff Committee shall be responsible under the Security Council for the strategic direction of any armed forces placed at the disposal of the Security Council. Questions relating to the command of such forces shall be worked out subsequently.

4. The Military Staff Committee, with the authorization of the Security Council and after consultation with appropriate regional agencies, may establish regional subcommittees.

Article 48

1. The action required to carry out the decisions of the Security Council for the maintenance of international peace and security shall be taken by all the Members of the United Nations or by some of them, as the Security Council may determine.

2. Such decisions shall be carried out by the Members of the United Nations directly and through their action in the appropriate international agencies of which they are members.

Article 49

The Members of the United Nations shall join in affording mutual assistance in carrying out the measures decided upon by the Security Council.

Article 50

If preventive or enforcement measures against any state are taken by the Security Council, any other state, whether a Member of the United Nations or not, which finds itself confronted with special economic problems arising from the carrying out of those measures shall have the right to consult the Security Council with regard to a solution of those problems.

Article 51

Nothing in the present Charter shall impair the inherent right of individual or collective self-defense if an armed attack occurs against a Member of the United Nations, until the Security Council has taken the measures necessary to maintain international peace and security. Measures taken by Members in the exercise of this right of self-defense shall be immediately reported to the Security Council and shall not in any way affect the authority and responsibility of the Security Council under the present Charter to take at any time such action as it deems necessary in order to maintain or restore international peace and security.

Chapter VIII

REGIONAL ARRANGEMENTS

Article 52

1. Nothing in the present Charter precludes the existence of regional arrangements or agencies for dealing with such matters relating to the maintenance of international peace and security as are appropriate for regional action, provided that such arrangements or agencies and their activities are consistent with the Purposes and Principles of the United Nations.

2. The Members of the United Nations entering into such arrangements or constituting such agencies shall make every effort to achieve pacific settlement of local disputes through such regional arrangements or by such regional agencies before referring them to the Security Council.

3. The Security Council shall encourage the development of pacific settlement of local disputes through such regional arrangements or by such regional agencies either on the initiative of the states concerned or by reference from the Security Council.

4. This Article in no way impairs the application of Articles 34 and 35.

Article 53

1. The Security Council shall, where appropriate, utilize such regional arrangements or agencies for enforcement action under its authority. But no enforcement action shall be taken under regional arrangements or by regional agencies without the authorization of the Security Council, with the exception of measures against any enemy state, as defined in paragraph 2 of this Article, provided for pursuant to Article 107 or in regional arrangements directed against renewal of aggressive policy on the part of any such state, until such time as the Organization may, on request of the Governments concerned, be charged with the responsibility for preventing further aggression by such a state.

2. The term enemy state as used in paragraph 1 of this Article applies to any state which during the Second World War has been an enemy of any signatory of the present Charter.

Article 54

The Security Council shall at all times be kept fully informed of activities undertaken or in contemplation under regional arrangements or by regional agencies for the maintenance of international peace and security.

Chapter IX

INTERNATIONAL ECONOMIC AND SOCIAL COOPERATION

Article 55

With a view to the creation of conditions of stability and well-being which are necessary for peaceful and friendly relations among nations based on respect for the principle of equal rights and self-determination of peoples, the United Nations shall promote:

a. higher standards of living, full employment, and conditions of economic and social progress and development;

b. solutions of international economic, social, health, and related problems; and international cultural and educational cooperation; and

c. universal respect for, and observance of, human rights and fundamental freedoms for all without distinction as to race, sex, language, or religion.

Article 56

All Members pledge themselves to take joint and separate action in cooperation with the Organization for the achievement of the purposes set forth in Article 55.

Article 57

1. The various specialized agencies, established by intergovernmental agreement and having wide international responsibilities, as defined in their basic instruments, in economic, social, cultural, educational, health, and related fields, shall be brought into relationship with the United Nations in accordance with the provisions of Article 63.

2. Such agencies thus brought into relationship with the United Nations are hereinafter referred to as specialized agencies.

Article 58

The Organization shall make recommendations for the coordination of the policies and activities of the specialized agencies.

Article 59

The Organization shall, where appropriate, initiate negotiations among the states concerned for the creation of any new specialized agencies required for the accomplishment of the purposes set forth in Article 55.

Article 60

Responsibility for the discharge of the functions of the Organization set forth in this Chapter shall be vested in the General Assembly and, under the authority of the General Assembly, in the Economic and Social Council, which shall have for this purpose the powers set forth in Chapter X.

Chapter X

THE ECONOMIC AND SOCIAL COUNCIL

COMPOSITION

Article 61

1. The Economic and Social Council shall consist of eighteen Members of the United Nations elected by the General Assembly.

2. Subject to the provisions of paragraph 3, six members of the Economic and Social Council shall be elected each year for a term of three years. A retiring member shall be eligible for immediate re-election.

3. At the first election, eighteen members of the Economic and Social Council shall be chosen. The term of office of six members so chosen shall expire at the end of one year, and of six other members at the end of two years, in accordance with arrangements made by the General Assembly.

4. Each member of the Economic and Social Council shall have one representative.

FUNCTIONS AND POWERS

Article 62

1. The Economic and Social Council may make or initiate studies and reports with respect to international economic, social, cultural, educational, health, and related matters and may make recommendations with respect to any such matters to the General Assembly, to the Members of the United Nations, and to the specialized agencies concerned.

2. It may make recommendations for the purpose of promoting respect for, and observance of, human rights and fundamental freedoms for all.

3. It may prepare draft conventions for submission to the General Assembly, with respect to matters falling within its competence.

4. It may call, in accordance with the rules prescribed by the United Nations, international conferences on matters falling within its competence.

Article 63

1. The Economic and Social Council may enter into agreements with any of the agencies referred to in Article 57, defining the terms on which the agency concerned shall be brought into relationship with the United Nations. Such agreements shall be subject to approval by the General Assembly.

2. It may coordinate the activities of the specialized agencies through consultation with and recommendations to such agencies and through recommendations to the General Assembly and to the Members of the United Nations.

Article 64

1. The Economic and Social Council may take appropriate steps to obtain regular reports from the specialized agencies. It may make arrangements with the Members of the United Nations and with the specialized agencies to obtain reports on the steps taken to give effect to its own recommendations and to recommendations on matters falling within its competence made by the General Assembly.

2. It may communicate its observations on these reports to the General Assembly.

Article 65

The Economic and Social Council may furnish information to the Security Council and shall assist the Security Council upon its request.

Article 66

1. The Economic and Social Council shall perform such functions as fall within its competence in connection with the carrying out of the recommendations of the General Assembly.

2. It may, with the approval of the General Assembly, perform services at the request of Members of the United Nations and at the request of specialized agencies.

3. It shall perform such other functions as are specified elsewhere in the present Charter or as may be assigned to it by the General Assembly.

VOTING

Article 67

1. Each member of the Economic and Social Council shall have one vote.

2. Decisions of the Economic and Social Council shall be made by a majority of the members present and voting.

PROCEDURE

Article 68

The Economic and Social Council shall set up commissions in economic and social fields and for the promotion of human rights, and such other commissions as may be required for the performance of its functions.

Article 69

The Economic and Social Council shall invite any Member of the United Nations to participate, without vote, in its deliberations on any matter of particular concern to that Member.

Article 70

The Economic and Social Council may make arrangements for representatives of the specialized agencies to participate, without vote, in its deliberations and in those of the commissions established by it, and for its representatives to participate in the deliberations of the specialized agencies.

Article 71

The Economic and Social Council may make suitable arrangements for consultation with non-governmental organizations which are concerned with matters within its competence. Such arrangements may be made with international organizations and, where appropriate, with national organizations after consultation with the Member of the United Nations concerned.

Article 72

1. The Economic and Social Council shall adopt its own rules of procedure, including the method of selecting its President.
2. The Economic and Social Council shall meet as required in accordance with its rules, which shall include provision for the convening of meetings on the request of a majority of its members.

Chapter XI

DECLARATION REGARDING NON-SELF-GOVERNING TERRITORIES

Article 73

Members of the United Nations which have or assume responsibilities for the administration of territories whose peoples have not yet attained a full measure of self-government recognize the principle that the interests of the inhabitants of these territories are paramount, and accept as a sacred trust the obligation to promote to the utmost, within the system of international peace and security established by the present Charter, the well-being of the inhabitants of these territories, and, to this end:

a. to ensure, with due respect for the culture of the peoples concerned, their political, economic, social, and educational advancement, their just treatment, and their protection against abuses;

b. to develop self-government, to take due account of the political aspirations of the peoples, and to assist them in the progressive development of their free political institutions, according to the particular circumstances of each territory and its peoples and their varying stages of advancement;

c. to further international peace and security;

d. to promote constructive measures of development, to encourage research, and to cooperate with one another and, when and where appropriate, with specialized international bodies with a view to the practical achievement of the social, economic, and scientific purposes set forth in this Article; and

e. to transmit regularly to the Secretary-General for information purposes, subject to such limitation as security and constitutional considerations may require, statistical and other information of a technical nature relating to economic, social, and educational conditions in the territories for which they are respectively responsible other than those territories to which Chapters XII and XIII apply.

Article 74

Members of the United Nations also agree that their policy in respect of the territories to which this Chapter applies, no less than in respect of their metropolitan areas, must be based on the general principle of good-neighborliness, due account being taken of the interests and well-being of the rest of the world, in social, economic, and commercial matters.

Chapter XII

INTERNATIONAL TRUSTEESHIP SYSTEM

Article 75

The United Nations shall establish under its authority an international trusteeship system for the administration and supervision of such territories as may be placed thereunder by subsequent individual agreements. These territories are hereinafter referred to as trust territories.

Article 76

The basic objectives of the trusteeship system, in accordance with the Purposes of the United Nations laid down in Article 1 of the present Charter, shall be:

a. to further international peace and security;

b. to promote the political, economic, social, and educational advancement of the inhabitants of the trust territories, and their progressive development towards self-government or independence as may be appropriate to the particular circumstances of each territory and its peoples and the freely expressed wishes of the peoples concerned, and as may be provided by the terms of each trusteeship agreement;

c. to encourage respect for human rights and for fundamental freedoms for all without distinction as to race, sex, language, or religion, and to encourage recognition of the interdependence of the peoples of the world; and

d. to ensure equal treatment in social, economic, and commercial matters for all Members of the United Nations and their nationals, and also equal treatment for the latter in the administration of justice, without prejudice to the attainment of the foregoing objectives and subject to the provisions of Article 80.

Article 77

1. The trusteeship system shall apply to such territories in the following categories as may be placed thereunder by means of trusteeship agreements:

a. territories now held under mandate;

b. territories which may be detached from enemy states as a result of the Second World War; and

c. territories voluntarily placed under the system by states responsible for their administration.

2. It will be a matter for subsequent agreement as to which territories in the foregoing categories will be brought under the trusteeship system and upon what terms.

Article 78

The trusteeship system shall not apply to territories which have become Members of the United Nations, relationship among which shall be based on respect for the principle of sovereign equality.

Article 79

The terms of trusteeship for each territory to be placed under the trusteeship system, including any alteration or amendment, shall be agreed upon by the states directly concerned, including the mandatory power in the case of territories held under mandate by a Member of the United Nations, and shall be approved as provided for in Articles 83 and 85.

Article 80

1. Except as may be agreed upon in individual trusteeship agreements, made under Articles 77, 79, and 81, placing each territory under the trusteeship system, and until such agreements have been concluded, nothing in this Chapter shall be construed in or of itself to alter in any manner the rights whatsoever of any states or any peoples or the terms of existing international instruments to which Members of the United Nations may respectively be parties.

2. Paragraph 1 of this Article shall not be interpreted as giving grounds for delay or postponement of the negotiation and conclusion of agreements for placing mandated and other territories under the trusteeship system as provided for in Article 77.

Article 81

The trusteeship agreement shall in each case include the terms under which the trust territory will be administered and designate the authority which will exercise the administration of the trust territory. Such authority, hereinafter called the administering authority, may be one or more states or the Organization itself.

Article 82

There may be designated, in any trusteeship agreement, a strategic area or areas which may include part or all of the trust territory to which the agreement applies, without prejudice to any special agreement or agreements made under Article 43.

Article 83

1. All functions of the United Nations relating to strategic areas, including the approval of the terms of the trusteeship agreements and of their alteration or amendment, shall be exercised by the Security Council.

2. The basic objectives set forth in Article 76 shall be applicable to the people of each strategic area.

3. The Security Council shall, subject to the provisions of the trusteeship agreements and without prejudice to security considerations, avail itself of the assistance of the Trusteeship Council to perform those functions of the United Nations under the trusteeship system relating to political, economic, social, and educational matters in the strategic areas.

Article 84

It shall be the duty of the administering authority to ensure that the trust territory shall play its part in the maintenance of international peace and security. To this end the administering authority may make use of volunteer forces, facilities, and assistance from the trust territory in carrying out the obligations towards the Security Council undertaken in this regard by the administering authority, as well as for local defense and the maintenance of law and order within the trust territory.

Article 85

1. The functions of the United Nations with regard to trusteeship agreements for all areas not designated as strategic, including the approval of the terms of the trusteeship agreements and of their alteration or amendment, shall be exercised by the General Assembly.

2. The Trusteeship Council, operating under the authority of the General Assembly, shall assist the General Assembly in carrying out these functions.

Chapter XIII

THE TRUSTEESHIP COUNCIL

COMPOSITION

Article 86

1. The Trusteeship Council shall consist of the following Members of the United Nations:

a. those Members administering trust territories;

b. such of those Members mentioned by name in Article 23 as are not administering trust territories; and

c. as many other Members elected for three-year terms by the General Assembly as may be necessary to ensure that the total number of members of the Trusteeship Council is equally divided between those Members of the United Nations which administer trust territories and those which do not.

2. Each member of the Trusteeship Council shall designate one specially qualified person to represent it therein.

FUNCTIONS AND POWERS

Article 87

The General Assembly and, under its authority, the Trusteeship Council, in carrying out their functions, may:

a. consider reports submitted by the administering authority;

b. accept petitions and examine them in consultation with the administering authority;

c. provide for periodic visits to the respective trust territories at times agreed upon with the administering authority; and

d. take these and other actions in conformity with the terms of the trusteeship agreements.

Article 88

The Trusteeship Council shall formulate a questionnaire on the political, economic, social, and educational advancement of the inhabitants of each trust territory, and the administering authority for each trust territory within the competence of the General Assembly shall make an annual report to the General Assembly upon the basis of such questionnaire.

VOTING

Article 89

1. Each member of the Trusteeship Council shall have one vote.

2. Decisions of the Trusteeship Council shall be made by a majority of the members present and voting.

PROCEDURE

Article 90

1. The Trusteeship Council shall adopt its own rules of procedure, including the method of selecting its President.

2. The Trusteeship Council shall meet as required in accordance with its rules, which shall include provision for the convening of meetings on the request of a majority of its members.

Article 91

The Trusteeship Council shall, when appropriate, avail itself of the assistance of the Economic and Social Council and of the specialized agencies in regard to matters with which they are respectively concerned.

Chapter XIV

THE INTERNATIONAL COURT OF JUSTICE

Article 92

The International Court of Justice shall be the principal judicial organ of the United Nations. It shall function in accordance with the annexed Statute, which is based upon the Statute of the Permanent Court of International Justice and forms an integral part of the present Charter.

Article 93

1. All Members of the United Nations are *ipso facto* parties to the Statute of the International Court of Justice.

2. A state which is not a Member of the United Nations may become a party to the Statute of the International Court of Justice on conditions to be determined in each case by the General Assembly upon the recommendation of the Security Council.

Article 94

1. Each Member of the United Nations undertakes to comply with the decision of the International Court of Justice in any case to which it is a party.

2. If any party to a case fails to perform the obligations incumbent upon it under a judgment rendered by the Court, the other party may have recourse to the Security Council, which may, if it deems necessary, make recommendations or decide upon measures to be taken to give effect to the judgment.

Article 95

Nothing in the present Charter shall prevent Members of the United Nations from entrusting the solution of their differences to other tribunals by virtue of agreements already in existence or which may be concluded in the future.

Article 96

1. The General Assembly or the Security Council may request the International Court of Justice to give an advisory opinion on any legal question.

2. Other organs of the United Nations and specialized agencies, which may at any time be so authorized by the General Assembly, may also request ad-

visory opinions of the Court on legal questions arising within the scope of their activities.

Chapter XV

THE SECRETARIAT

Article 97

The Secretariat shall comprise a Secretary-General and such staff as the Organization may require. The Secretary-General shall be appointed by the General Assembly upon the recommendation of the Security Council. He shall be the chief administrative officer of the Organization.

Article 98

The Secretary-General shall act in that capacity in all meetings of the General Assembly, of the Security Council, of the Economic and Social Council, and of the Trusteeship Council, and shall perform such other functions as are entrusted to him by these organs. The Secretary-General shall make an annual report to the General Assembly on the work of the Organization.

Article 99

The Secretary-General may bring to the attention of the Security Council any matter which in his opinion may threaten the maintenance of international peace and security.

Article 100

1. In the performance of their duties the Secretary-General and the staff shall not seek or receive instructions from any government or from any other authority external to the Organization. They shall refrain from any action which might reflect on their position as international officials responsible only to the Organization.

2. Each Member of the United Nations undertakes to respect the exclusively international character of the responsibilities of the Secretary-General and the staff and not to seek to influence them in the discharge of their responsibilities.

Article 101

1. The staff shall be appointed by the Secretary-General under regulations established by the General Assembly.

2. Appropriate staffs shall be permanently assigned to the Economic and Social Council, the Trusteeship Council, and, as required, to other organs of the United Nations. These staffs shall form a part of the Secretariat.

3. The paramount consideration in the employment of the staff and in the

determination of the conditions of service shall be the necessity of securing the highest standards of efficiency, competence, and integrity. Due regard shall be paid to the importance of recruiting the staff on as wide a geographical basis as possible.

Chapter XVI

MISCELLANEOUS PROVISIONS

Article 102

1. Every treaty and every international agreement entered into by any Member of the United Nations after the present Charter comes into force shall as soon as possible be registered with the Secretariat and published by it.

2. No party to any such treaty or international agreement which has not been registered in accordance with the provisions of paragraph 1 of this Article may invoke that treaty or agreement before any organ of the United Nations.

Article 103

In the event of a conflict between the obligations of the Members of the United Nations under the present Charter and their obligations under any other international agreement, their obligations under the present Charter shall prevail.

Article 104

The Organization shall enjoy in the territory of each of its Members such legal capacity as may be necessary for the exercise of its functions and the fulfillment of its purposes.

Article 105

1. The Organization shall enjoy in the territory of each of its Members such privileges and immunities as are necessary for the fulfillment of its purposes.

2. Representatives of the Members of the United Nations and officials of the Organization shall similarly enjoy such privileges and immunities as are necessary for the independent exercise of their functions in connection with the Organization.

3. The General Assembly may make recommendations with a view to determining the details of the application of paragraphs 1 and 2 of this Article or may propose conventions to the Members of the United Nations for this purpose.

Chapter XVII

Transitional Security Arrangements

Article 106

Pending the coming into force of such special agreements referred to in Article 43 as in the opinion of the Security Council enable it to begin the exercise of its responsibilities under Article 42, the parties to the Four-Nation Declaration, signed at Moscow, October 30, 1943, and France, shall, in accordance with the provisions of paragraph 5 of that Declaration, consult with one another and as occasion requires with other Members of the United Nations with a view to such joint action on behalf of the Organization as may be necessary for the purpose of maintaining international peace and security.

Article 107

Nothing in the present Charter shall invalidate or preclude action, in relation to any state which during the Second World War has been an enemy of any signatory to the present Charter, taken or authorized as a result of that war by the Governments having responsibility for such action.

Chapter XVIII

Amendments

Article 108

Amendments to the present Charter shall come into force for all Members of the United Nations when they have been adopted by a vote of two thirds of the members of the General Assembly and ratified in accordance with their respective constitutional processes by two thirds of the Members of the United Nations, including all the permanent members of the Security Council.

Article 109

1. A General Conference of the Members of the United Nations for the purpose of reviewing the present Charter may be held at a date and place to be fixed by a two-thirds vote of the General Assembly and by a vote of any seven members of the Security Council. Each Member of the United Nations shall have one vote in the conference.

2. Any alteration of the present Charter recommended by a two-thirds vote of the conference shall take effect when ratified in accordance with their respective constitutional processes by two thirds of the Members of the United Nations including all the permanent members of the Security Council.

3. If such a conference has not been held before the tenth annual session of the General Assembly following the coming into force of the present Charter, the proposal to call such a conference shall be placed on the agenda of that

session of the General Assembly, and the conference shall be held if so decided by a majority vote of the members of the General Assembly and by a vote of any seven members of the Security Council.

Chapter XIX

RATIFICATION AND SIGNATURE

Article 110

1. The present Charter shall be ratified by the signatory states in accordance with their respective constitutional processes.

2. The ratifications shall be deposited with the Government of the United States of America, which shall notify all the signatory states of each deposit as well as the Secretary-General of the Organization when he has been appointed.

3. The present Charter shall come into force upon the deposit of ratifications by the Republic of China, France, the Union of Soviet Socialist Republics, the United Kingdom of Great Britain and Northern Ireland, and the United States of America, and by a majority of the other signatory states. A protocol of the ratifications deposited shall thereupon be drawn up by the Government of the United States of America which shall communicate copies thereof to all the signatory states.

4. The states signatory to the present Charter which ratify it after it has come into force will become original Members of the United Nations on the date of the deposit of their respective ratifications.

Article 111

The present Charter, of which the Chinese, French, Russian, English, and Spanish texts are equally authentic, shall remain deposited in the archives of the Government of the United States of America. Duly certified copies thereof shall be transmitted by that Government to the Governments of the other signatory states.

IN FAITH WHEREOF the representatives of the Governments of the United Nations have signed the present Charter.

DONE at the city of San Francisco the twenty-sixth day of June, one thousand nine hundred and forty-five.

[*Here follow the signatures of the delegates.*]

Statute of the International Court of Justice

Article 1

THE INTERNATIONAL COURT OF JUSTICE established by the Charter of the United Nations as the principal judicial organ of the United Nations shall be constituted and shall function in accordance with the provisions of the present Statute.

Chapter I

ORGANIZATION OF THE COURT

Article 2

The Court shall be composed of a body of independent judges, elected regardless of their nationality from among persons of high moral character, who possess the qualifications required in their respective countries for appointment to the highest judicial offices, or are jurisconsults of recognized competence in international law.

Article 3

1. The Court shall consist of fifteen members, no two of whom may be nationals of the same state.

2. A person who for the purposes of membership in the Court could be regarded as a national of more than one state shall be deemed to be a national of the one in which he ordinarily exercises civil and political rights.

Article 4

1. The members of the Court shall be elected by the General Assembly and by the Security Council from a list of persons nominated by the national groups

in the Permanent Court of Arbitration, in accordance with the following provisions.

2. In the case of Members of the United Nations not represented in the Permanent Court of Arbitration, candidates shall be nominated by national groups appointed for this purpose by their governments under the same conditions as those prescribed for members of the Permanent Court of Arbitration by Article 44 of the Convention of The Hague of 1907 for the pacific settlement of international disputes.

3. The conditions under which a state which is a party to the present Statute but is not a Member of the United Nations may participate in electing the members of the Court shall, in the absence of a special agreement, be laid down by the General Assembly upon recommendation of the Security Council.

Article 5

1. At least three months before the date of the election, the Secretary-General of the United Nations shall address a written request to the members of the Permanent Court of Arbitration belonging to the states which are parties to the present Statute, and to the members of the national groups appointed under Article 4, paragraph 2, inviting them to undertake, within a given time, by national groups, the nomination of persons in a position to accept the duties of a member of the Court.

2. No group may nominate more than four persons, not more than two of whom shall be of their own nationality. In no case may the number of candidates nominated by a group be more than double the number of seats to be filled.

Article 6

Before making these nominations, each national group is recommended to consult its highest court of justice, its legal faculties and schools of law, and its national academies and national sections of international academies devoted to the study of law.

Article 7

1. The Secretary-General shall prepare a list in alphabetical order of all the persons thus nominated. Save as provided in Article 12, paragraph 2, these shall be the only persons eligible.

2. The Secretary-General shall submit this list to the General Assembly and to the Security Council.

Article 8

The General Assembly and the Security Council shall proceed independently of one another to elect the members of the Court.

Article 9

At every election, the electors shall bear in mind not only that the persons to be elected should individually possess the qualifications required, but also that in the body as a whole the representation of the main forms of civilization and of the principal legal systems of the world should be assured.

Article 10

1. Those candidates who obtain an absolute majority of votes in the General Assembly and in the Security Council shall be considered as elected.

2. Any vote of the Security Council, whether for the election of judges or for the appointment of members of the conference envisaged in Article 12, shall be taken without any distinction between permanent and non-permanent members of the Security Council.

3. In the event of more than one national of the same state obtaining an absolute majority of the votes both of the General Assembly and of the Security Council, the eldest of these only shall be considered as elected.

Article 11

If, after the first meeting held for the purpose of the election, one or more seats remain to be filled, a second and, if necessary, a third meeting shall take place.

Article 12

1. If, after the third meeting, one or more seats still remain unfilled, a joint conference consisting of six members, three appointed by the General Assembly and three by the Security Council, may be formed at any time at the request of either the General Assembly or the Security Council, for the purpose of choosing by the vote of an absolute majority one name for each seat still vacant, to submit to the General Assembly and the Security Council for their respective acceptance.

2. If the joint conference is unanimously agreed upon any person who fulfils the required conditions, he may be included in its list, even though he was not included in the list of nominations referred to in Article 7.

3. If the joint conference is satisfied that it will not be successful in procuring an election, those members of the Court who have already been elected shall, within a period to be fixed by the Security Council, proceed to fill the vacant seats by selection from among those candidates who have obtained votes either in the General Assembly or in the Security Council.

4. In the event of an equality of votes among the judges, the eldest judge shall have a casting vote.

Article 13

1. The members of the Court shall be elected for nine years and may be re-elected; provided, however, that of the judges elected at the first election, the terms of five judges shall expire at the end of three years and the terms of five more judges shall expire at the end of six years.

2. The judges whose terms are to expire at the end of the above-mentioned initial periods of three and six years shall be chosen by lot to be drawn by the Secretary-General immediately after the first election has been completed.

3. The members of the Court shall continue to discharge their duties until their places have been filled. Though replaced, they shall finish any cases which they may have begun.

4. In the case of the resignation of a member of the Court, the resignation shall be addressed to the President of the Court for transmission to the Secretary-General. This last notification makes the place vacant.

Article 14

Vacancies shall be filled by the same method as that laid down for the first election, subject to the following provision: the Secretary-General shall, within one month of the occurrence of the vacancy, proceed to issue the invitations provided for in Article 5, and the date of the election shall be fixed by the Security Council.

Article 15

A member of the Court elected to replace a member whose term of office has not expired shall hold office for the remainder of his predecessor's term.

Article 16

1. No member of the Court may exercise any political or administrative function, or engage in any other occupation of a professional nature.

2. Any doubt on this point shall be settled by the decision of the Court.

Article 17

1. No member of the Court may act as agent, counsel, or advocate in any case.

2. No member may participate in the decision of any case in which he has previously taken part as agent, counsel, or advocate for one of the parties, or as a member of a national or international court, or of a commission of enquiry, or in any other capacity.

3. Any doubt on this point shall be settled by the decision of the Court.

Article 18

1. No member of the Court can be dismissed unless, in the unanimous opinion of the other members, he has ceased to fulfil the required conditions.

2. Formal notification thereof shall be made to the Secretary-General by the Registrar.

3. This notification makes the place vacant.

Article 19

The members of the Court, when engaged on the business of the Court, shall enjoy diplomatic privileges and immunities.

Article 20

Every member of the Court shall, before taking up his duties, make a solemn declaration in open court that he will exercise his powers impartially and conscientiously.

Article 21

1. The Court shall elect its President and Vice-President for three years; they may be re-elected.

2. The Court shall appoint its Registrar and may provide for the appointment of such other officers as may be necessary.

Article 22

1. The seat of the Court shall be established at The Hague. This, however, shall not prevent the Court from sitting and exercising its functions elsewhere whenever the Court considers it desirable.

2. The President and the Registrar shall reside at the seat of the Court.

Article 23

1. The Court shall remain permanently in session, except during the judicial vacations, the dates and duration of which shall be fixed by the Court.

2. Members of the Court are entitled to periodic leave, the dates and duration of which shall be fixed by the Court, having in mind the distance between The Hague and the home of each judge.

3. Members of the Court shall be bound, unless they are on leave or prevented from attending by illness or other serious reasons duly explained to the President, to hold themselves permanently at the disposal of the Court.

Article 24

1. If, for some special reason, a member of the Court considers that he should not take part in the decision of a particular case, he shall so inform the President.

2. If the President considers that for some special reason one of the members of the Court should not sit in a particular case, he shall give him notice accordingly.

3. If in any such case the member of the Court and the President disagree, the matter shall be settled by the decision of the Court.

Article 25

1. The full Court shall sit except when it is expressly provided otherwise in the present Statute.

2. Subject to the condition that the number of judges available to constitute the Court is not thereby reduced below eleven, the Rules of the Court may provide for allowing one or more judges, according to circumstances and in rotation, to be dispensed from sitting.

3. A quorum of nine judges shall suffice to constitute the Court.

Article 26

1. The Court may from time to time form one or more chambers, composed of three or more judges as the Court may determine, for dealing with particular categories of cases; for example, labor cases and cases relating to transit and communications.

2. The Court may at any time form a chamber for dealing with a particular case. The number of judges to constitute such a chamber shall be determined by the Court with the approval of the parties.

3. Cases shall be heard and determined by the chambers provided for in this Article if the parties so request.

Article 27

A judgment given by any of the chambers provided for in Articles 26 and 29 shall be considered as rendered by the Court.

Article 28

The chambers provided for in Articles 26 and 29 may, with the consent of the parties, sit and exercise their functions elsewhere than at The Hague.

Article 29

With a view to the speedy despatch of business, the Court shall form annually a chamber composed of five judges which, at the request of the parties, may hear and determine cases by summary procedure. In addition, two judges shall be selected for the purpose of replacing judges who find it impossible to sit.

Article 30

1. The Court shall frame rules for carrying out its functions. In particular, it shall lay down rules of procedure.

2. The Rules of the Court may provide for assessors to sit with the Court or with any of its chambers, without the right to vote.

Article 31

1. Judges of the nationality of each of the parties shall retain their right to sit in the case before the Court.

2. If the Court includes upon the Bench a judge of the nationality of one of the parties, any other party may choose a person to sit as judge. Such person shall be chosen preferably from among those persons who have been nominated as candidates as provided in Articles 4 and 5.

3. If the Court includes upon the Bench no judge of the nationality of the parties, each of these parties may proceed to choose a judge as provided in paragraph 2 of this Article.

4. The provisions of this Article shall apply to the case of Articles 26 and 29. In such cases, the President shall request one or, if necessary, two of the members of the Court forming the chamber to give place to the members of the

Court of the nationality of the parties concerned, and, failing such, or if they are unable to be present, to the judges specially chosen by the parties.

5. Should there be several parties in the same interest, they shall, for the purpose of the preceding provisions, be reckoned as one party only. Any doubt upon this point shall be settled by the decision of the Court.

6. Judges chosen as laid down in paragraphs 2, 3, and 4 of this Article shall fulfil the conditions required by Articles 2, 17 (paragraph 2), 20, and 24 of the present Statute. They shall take part in the decision on terms of complete equality with their colleagues.

Article 32

1. Each member of the Court shall receive an annual salary.

2. The President shall receive a special annual allowance.

3. The Vice-President shall receive a special allowance for every day on which he acts as President.

4. The judges chosen under Article 31, other than members of the Court, shall receive compensation for each day on which they exercise their functions.

5. These salaries, allowances, and compensation shall be fixed by the General Assembly. They may not be decreased during the term of office.

6. The salary of the Registrar shall be fixed by the General Assembly on the proposal of the Court.

7. Regulations made by the General Assembly shall fix the conditions under which retirement pensions may be given to members of the Court and to the Registrar, and the conditions under which members of the Court and the Registrar shall have their traveling expenses refunded.

8. The above salaries, allowances, and compensation shall be free of all taxation.

Article 33

The expenses of the Court shall be borne by the United Nations in such a manner as shall be decided by the General Assembly.

Chapter II

Competence of the Court

Article 34

1. Only states may be parties in cases before the Court.

2. The Court, subject to and in conformity with its Rules, may request of public international organizations information relevant to cases before it, and shall receive such information presented by such organizations on their own initiative.

3. Whenever the construction of the constituent instrument of a public international organization or of an international convention adopted thereunder is in question in a case before the Court, the Registrar shall so notify the public

international organization concerned and shall communicate to it copies of all the written proceedings.

Article 35

1. The Court shall be open to the states parties to the present Statute.

2. The conditions under which the Court shall be open to other states shall, subject to the special provisions contained in treaties in force, be laid down by the Security Council, but in no case shall such conditions place the parties in a position of inequality before the Court.

3. When a state which is not a Member of the United Nations is a party to a case, the Court shall fix the amount which that party is to contribute towards the expenses of the Court. This provision shall not apply if such state is bearing a share of the expenses of the Court.

Article 36

1. The jurisdiction of the Court comprises all cases which the parties refer to it and all matters specially provided for in the Charter of the United Nations or in treaties and conventions in force.

2. The states parties to the present Statute may at any time declare that they recognize as compulsory *ipso facto* and without special agreement, in relation to any other state accepting the same obligation, the jurisdiction of the Court in all legal disputes concerning:

a. the interpretation of a treaty;

b. any question of international law;

c. the existence of any fact which, if established, would constitute a breach of an international obligation;

d. the nature or extent of the reparation to be made for the breach of an international obligation.

3. The declarations referred to above may be made unconditionally or on condition of reciprocity on the part of several or certain states, or for a certain time.

4. Such declarations shall be deposited with the Secretary-General of the United Nations, who shall transmit copies thereof to the parties to the Statute and to the Registrar of the Court.

5. Declarations made under Article 36 of the Statute of the Permanent Court of International Justice and which are still in force shall be deemed, as between the parties to the present Statute, to be acceptances of the compulsory jurisdiction of the International Court of Justice for the period which they still have to run and in accordance with their terms.

6. In the event of a dispute as to whether the Court has jurisdiction, the matter shall be settled by the decision of the Court.

Article 37

Whenever a treaty or convention in force provides for reference of a matter to a tribunal to have been instituted by the League of Nations, or to the Permanent Court of International Justice, the matter shall, as between the parties to the present Statute, be referred to the International Court of Justice.

Article 38

1. The Court, whose function is to decide in accordance with international law such disputes as are submitted to it, shall apply:

a. international conventions, whether general or particular, establishing rules expressly recognized by the contesting states;

b. international custom, as evidence of a general practice accepted as law;

c. the general principles of law recognized by civilized nations;

d. subject to the provisions of Article 59, judicial decisions and the teachings of the most highly qualified publicists of the various nations, as subsidiary means for the determination of rules of law.

2. This provision shall not prejudice the power of the Court to decide a case *ex aequo et bono,* if the parties agree thereto.

Chapter III

PROCEDURE

Article 39

1. The official languages of the Court shall be French and English. If the parties agree that the case shall be conducted in French, the judgment shall be delivered in French. If the parties agree that the case shall be conducted in English, the judgment shall be delivered in English.

2. In the absence of an agreement as to which language shall be employed, each party may, in the pleadings, use the language which it prefers; the decision of the Court shall be given in French and English. In this case the Court shall at the same time determine which of the two texts shall be considered as authoritative.

3. The Court shall, at the request of any party, authorize a language other than French or English to be used by that party.

Article 40

1. Cases are brought before the Court, as the case may be, either by the notification of the special agreement or by a written application addressed to the Registrar. In either case the subject of the dispute and the parties shall be indicated.

2. The Registrar shall forthwith communicate the application to all concerned.

3. He shall also notify the Members of the United Nations through the Secretary-General, and also any other states entitled to appear before the Court.

Article 41

1. The Court shall have the power to indicate, if it considers that circumstances so require, any provisional measures which ought to be taken to preserve the respective rights of either party.

2. Pending the final decision, notice of the measures suggested shall forthwith be given to the parties and to the Security Council.

Article 42

1. The parties shall be represented by agents.

2. They may have the assistance of counsel or advocates before the Court.

3. The agents, counsel, and advocates of parties before the Court shall enjoy the privileges and immunities necessary to the independent exercise of their duties.

Article 43

1. The procedure shall consist of two parts: written and oral.

2. The written proceedings shall consist of the communication to the Court and to the parties of memorials, counter-memorials and, if necessary, replies; also all papers and documents in support.

3. These communications shall be made through the Registrar, in the order and within the time fixed by the Court.

4. A certified copy of every document produced by one party shall be communicated to the other party.

5. The oral proceedings shall consist of the hearing by the Court of witnesses, experts, agents, counsel, and advocates.

Article 44

1. For the service of all notices upon persons other than the agents, counsel, and advocates, the Court shall apply direct to the government of the state upon whose territory the notice has to be served.

2. The same provision shall apply whenever steps are to be taken to procure evidence on the spot.

Article 45

The hearing shall be under the control of the President or, if he is unable to preside, of the Vice-President; if neither is able to preside, the senior judge present shall preside.

Article 46

The hearing in Court shall be public, unless the Court shall decide otherwise, or unless the parties demand that the public be not admitted.

Article 47

1. Minutes shall be made at each hearing and signed by the Registrar and the President.

2. These minutes alone shall be authentic.

Article 48

The Court shall make orders for the conduct of the case, shall decide the form and time in which each party must conclude its arguments, and make all arrangements connected with the taking of evidence.

Article 49

The Court may, even before the hearing begins, call upon the agents to produce any document or to supply any explanations. Formal note shall be taken of any refusal.

Article 50

The Court may, at any time, entrust any individual, body, bureau, commission, or other organization that it may select, with the task of carrying out an enquiry or giving an expert opinion.

Article 51

During the hearing any relevant questions are to be put to the witnesses and experts under the conditions laid down by the Court in the rules of procedure referred to in Article 30.

Article 52

After the Court has received the proofs and evidence within the time specified for the purpose, it may refuse to accept any further oral or written evidence that one party may desire to present unless the other side consents.

Article 53

1. Whenever one of the parties does not appear before the Court, or fails to defend its case, the other party may call upon the Court to decide in favor of its claim.

2. The Court must, before doing so, satisfy itself, not only that it has jurisdiction in accordance with Articles 36 and 37, but also that the claim is well founded in fact and law.

Article 54

1. When, subject to the control of the Court, the agents, counsel, and advocates have completed their presentation of the case, the President shall declare the hearing closed.

2. The Court shall withdraw to consider the judgment.

3. The deliberations of the Court shall take place in private and remain secret.

Article 55

1. All questions shall be decided by a majority of the judges present.

2. In the event of an equality of votes, the President or the judge who acts in his place shall have a casting vote.

Article 56

1. The judgment shall state the reasons on which it is based.

2. It shall contain the names of the judges who have taken part in the decision.

Article 57

If the judgment does not represent in whole or in part the unanimous opinion of the judges, any judge shall be entitled to deliver a separate opinion.

Article 58

The judgment shall be signed by the President and by the Registrar. It shall be read in open court, due notice having been given to the agents.

Article 59

The decision of the Court has no binding force except between the parties and in respect of that particular case.

Article 60

The judgment is final and without appeal. In the event of dispute as to the meaning or scope of the judgment, the Court shall construe it upon the request of any party.

Article 61

1. An application for revision of a judgment may be made only when it is based upon the discovery of some fact of such a nature as to be a decisive factor, which fact was, when the judgment was given, unknown to the Court and also to the party claiming revision, always provided that such ignorance was not due to negligence.

2. The proceedings for revision shall be opened by a judgment of the Court expressly recording the existence of the new fact, recognizing that it has such a character as to lay the case open to revision, and declaring the application admissible on this ground.

3. The Court may require previous compliance with the terms of the judgment before it admits proceedings in revision.

4. The application for revision must be made at latest within six months of the discovery of the new fact.

5. No application for revision may be made after the lapse of ten years from the date of the judgment.

Article 62

1. Should a state consider that it has an interest of a legal nature which may be affected by the decision in the case, it may submit a request to the Court to be permitted to intervene.

2. It shall be for the Court to decide upon this request.

Article 63

1. Whenever the construction of a convention to which states other than those concerned in the case are parties is in question, the Registrar shall notify all such states forthwith.

2. Every state so notified has the right to intervene in the proceedings; but if it uses this right, the construction given by the judgment will be equally binding upon it.

Article 64

Unless otherwise decided by the Court, each party shall bear its own costs.

Chapter IV

ADVISORY OPINIONS

Article 65

1. The Court may give an advisory opinion on any legal question at the request of whatever body may be authorized by or in accordance with the Charter of the United Nations to make such a request.

2. Questions upon which the advisory opinion of the Court is asked shall be laid before the Court by means of a written request containing an exact statement of the question upon which an opinion is required, and accompanied by all documents likely to throw light upon the question.

Article 66

1. The Registrar shall forthwith give notice of the request for an advisory opinion to all states entitled to appear before the Court.

2. The Registrar shall also, by means of a special and direct communication, notify any state entitled to appear before the Court or international organization considered by the Court, or, should it not be sitting, by the President, as likely to be able to furnish information on the question, that the Court will be prepared to receive, within a time limit to be fixed by the President, written statements, or to hear, at a public sitting to be held for the purpose, oral statements relating to the question.

3. Should any such state entitled to appear before the Court have failed to

receive the special communication referred to in paragraph 2 of this Article, such state may express a desire to submit a written statement or to be heard; and the Court will decide.

4. States and organizations having presented written or oral statements or both shall be permitted to comment on the statements made by other states or organizations in the form, to the extent, and within the time limits which the Court, or, should it not be sitting, the President, shall decide in each particular case. Accordingly, the Registrar shall in due time communicate any such written statements to states and organizations having submitted similar statements.

Article 67

The Court shall deliver its advisory opinions in open court, notice having been given to the Secretary-General and to the representatives of Members of the United Nations, of other states and of international organizations immediately concerned.

Article 68

In the exercise of its advisory functions the Court shall further be guided by the provisions of the present Statute which apply in contentious cases to the extent to which it recognizes them to be applicable.

Chapter V

Amendment

Article 69

Amendments to the present Statute shall be effected by the same procedure as is provided by the Charter of the United Nations for amendments to that Charter, subject however to any provisions which the General Assembly upon recommendation of the Security Council may adopt concerning the participation of states which are parties to the present Statute but are not Members of the United Nations.

Article 70

The Court shall have power to propose such amendments to the present Statute as it may deem necessary, through written communications to the Secretary-General, for consideration in conformity with the provisions of Article 69.

Inter-American Treaty of Reciprocal Assistance

Signed at the

Inter-American Conference

for the

Maintenance of Continental Peace and Security

Rio de Janeiro

August 15-September 2, 1947

In the name of their Peoples, the Governments represented at the Inter-American Conference for the Maintenance of Continental Peace and Security, desirous of consolidating and strengthening their relations of friendship and good neighborliness, and

Considering:

That Resolution VIII of the Inter-American Conference on Problems of War and Peace, which met in Mexico City, recommended the conclusion of a treaty to prevent and repel threats and acts of aggression against any of the countries of America;

That the High Contracting Parties reiterate their will to remain united in an inter-American system consistent with the purposes and principles of the United Nations, and reaffirm the existence of the agreement which they have concluded concerning those matters relating to the maintenance of international peace and security which are appropriate for regional action;

That the High Contracting Parties reaffirm their adherence to the principles of inter-American solidarity and cooperation, and especially to those set forth in the preamble and declarations of the Act of Chapultepec, all of which should be understood to be accepted as standards of their mutual relations and as the juridical basis of the Inter-American System;

That the American States propose, in order to improve the procedures for the pacific settlement of their controversies, to conclude the treaty concerning the "Inter-American Peace System" envisaged in Resolutions IX and XXXIX of the Inter-American Conference on Problems of War and Peace;

That the obligation of mutual assistance and common defense of the American Republics is essentially related to their democratic ideals and to their will to cooperate permanently in the fulfillment of the principles and purposes of a policy of peace;.

That the American regional community affirms as a manifest truth that juridical organization is a necessary prerequisite of security and peace, and that peace is founded on justice and moral order and, consequently, on the international recognition and protection of human rights and freedoms, on the indispensable well-being of the people, and on the effectiveness of democracy for the international realization of justice and security,

Have resolved, in conformity with the objectives stated above, to conclude the following Treaty, in order to assure peace, through adequate means, to provide for effective reciprocal assistance to meet armed attacks against any American State, and in order to deal with threats of aggression against any of them:

Article 1

The High Contracting Parties formally condemn war and undertake in their international relations not to resort to the threat or the use of force in any manner inconsistent with the provisions of the Charter of the United Nations or of this Treaty.

Article 2

As a consequence of the principles set forth in the preceding Article, the High Contracting Parties undertake to submit every controversy which may arise between them to methods of peaceful settlement and to endeavor to settle any such controversy among themselves by means of the procedures in force in the Inter-American System before referring it to the General Assembly or the Security Council of the United Nations.

Article 3

1. The High Contracting Parties agree that an armed attack by any State against an American State shall be considered as an attack against all the American States and, consequently, each one of the said Contracting Parties undertakes to assist in meeting the attack in the exercise of the inherent right of individual or collective self-defense recognized by Article 51 of the Charter of the United Nations.

2. On the request of the State or States directly attacked and until the decision of the Organ of Consultation of the Inter-American System, each one of the Contracting Parties may determine the immediate measures which it may individually take in fulfillment of the obligation contained in the preceding paragraph and in accordance with the principle of continental solidarity. The Organ of Consultation shall meet without delay for the purpose of examining

those measures and agreeing upon the measures of a collective character that should be taken.

3. The provisions of this Article shall be applied in case of any armed attack which takes place within the region described in Article 4 or within the territory of an American State. When the attack takes place outside of the said areas, the provisions of Article 6 shall be applied.

4. Measures of self-defense provided for under this Article may be taken until the Security Council of the United Nations has taken the measures necessary to maintain international peace and security.

Article 4

The region to which this Treaty refers is bounded as follows: beginning at the North Pole; thence due south to a point 74 degrees north latitude, 10 degrees west longitude; thence by a rhumb line to a point 47 degrees 30 minutes north latitude, 50 degrees west longitude; thence by a rhumb line to a point 35 degrees north latitude, 60 degrees west longitude; thence due south to a point in 20 degrees north latitude; thence by a rhumb line to a point 5 degrees north latitude, 24 degrees west longitude; thence due south to the South Pole; thence due north to a point 30 degrees south latitude, 90 degrees west longitude; thence by a rhumb line to a point on the Equator at 97 degrees west longitude; thence by a rhumb line to a point 15 degrees north latitude, 120 degrees west longitude; thence by a rhumb line to a point 50 degrees north latitude, 170 degrees east longitude; thence due north to a point in 54 degrees north latitude; thence by a rhumb line to a point 65 degrees 30 minutes north latitude, 168 degrees 58 minutes 5 seconds west longitude; thence due north to the North Pole.

Article 5

The High Contracting Parties shall immediately send to the Security Council of the United Nations, in conformity with Articles 51 and 54 of the Charter of the United Nations, complete information concerning the activities undertaken or in contemplation in the exercise of the right of self-defense or for the purpose of maintaining inter-American peace and security.

Article 6

If the inviolability or the integrity of the territory or the sovereignty or political independence of any American State should be affected by an aggression which is not an armed attack or by an extra-continental or intra-continental conflict, or by any other fact or situation that might endanger the peace of America, the Organ of Consultation shall meet immediately in order to agree on the measures which must be taken in case of aggression to assist the victim of the aggression or, in any case, the measures which should be taken for the common defense and for the maintenance of the peace and security of the Continent.

Article 7

In the case of a conflict between two or more American States, without prejudice to the right of self-defense in conformity with Article 51 of the Charter of the United Nations, the High Contracting Parties, meeting in consultation shall call upon the contending States to suspend hostilities and restore matters to the *statu quo ante bellum,* and shall take in addition all other necessary measures to re-establish or maintain inter-American peace and security and for the solution of the conflict by peaceful means. The rejection of the pacifying action will be considered in the determination of the aggressor and in the application of the measures which the consultative meeting may agree upon.

Article 8

For the purposes of this Treaty, the measures on which the Organ of Consultation may agree will comprise one or more of the following: recall of chiefs of diplomatic missions; breaking of diplomatic relations; breaking of consular relations; partial or complete interruption of economic relations or of rail, sea, air, postal, telegraphic, telephonic, and radiotelephonic or radiotelegraphic communications; and use of armed force.

Article 9

In addition to other acts which the Organ of Consultation may characterize as aggression, the following shall be considered as such:

a. Unprovoked armed attack by a State against the territory, the people, or the land, sea or air forces of another State;

b. Invasion, by the armed forces of a State, of the territory of an American State, through the trespassing of boundaries demarcated in accordance with a treaty, judicial decision, or arbitral award, or, in the absence of frontiers thus demarcated, invasion affecting a region which is under the effective jurisdiction of another State.

Article 10

None of the provisions of this Treaty shall be construed as impairing the rights and obligations of the High Contracting Parties under the Charter of the United Nations.

Article 11

The consultations to which this Treaty refers shall be carried out by means of the Meetings of Ministers of Foreign Affairs of the American Republics which have ratified the Treaty, or in the manner or by the organ which in the future may be agreed upon.

Article 12

The Governing Board of the Pan American Union may act provisionally as an organ of consultation until the meeting of the Organ of Consultation referred to in the preceding Article takes place.

Article 13

The consultations shall be initiated at the request addressed to the Governing Board of the Pan American Union by any of the Signatory States which has ratified the Treaty.

Article 14

In the voting referred to in this Treaty only the representatives of the Signatory States which have ratified the Treaty may take part.

Article 15

The Governing Board of the Pan American Union shall act in all matters concerning this Treaty as an organ of liaison among the Signatory States which have ratified this Treaty and between these States and the United Nations.

Article 16

The decisions of the Governing Board of the Pan American Union referred to in Articles 13 and 15 above shall be taken by an absolute majority of the Members entitled to vote.

Article 17

The Organ of Consultation shall take its decisions by a vote of two-thirds of the Signatory States which have ratified the Treaty.

Article 18

In the case of a situation or dispute between American States, the parties directly interested shall be excluded from the voting referred to in the two preceding Articles.

Article 19

To constitute a quorum in all the meetings referred to in the previous Articles, it shall be necessary that the number of States represented shall be at least equal to the number of votes necessary for the taking of the decision.

Article 20

Decisions which require the application of the measures specified in Article 8 shall be binding upon all the Signatory States which have ratified this Treaty, with the sole exception that no State shall be required to use armed force without its consent.

Article 21

The measures agreed upon by the Organ of Consultation shall be executed through the procedures and agencies now existing or those which may in the future be established.

Article 22

This Treaty shall come into effect between the States which ratify it as soon as the ratifications of two-thirds of the Signatory States have been deposited.

Article 23

This Treaty is open for signature by the American States at the city of Rio de Janeiro, and shall be ratified by the Signatory States as soon as possible in accordance with their respective constitutional processes. The ratifications shall be deposited with the Pan American Union, which shall notify the Signatory States of each deposit. Such notification shall be considered as an exchange of ratifications.

Article 24

The present Treaty shall be registered with the Secretariat of the United Nations through the Pan American Union, when two-thirds of the Signatory States have deposited their ratifications.

Article 25

This Treaty shall remain in force indefinitely, but may be denounced by any High Contracting Party by a notification in writing to the Pan American Union, which shall inform all the other High Contracting Parties of each notification of denunciation received. After the expiration of two years from the date of the receipt by the Pan American Union of a notification of denunciation by any High Contracting Party, the present Treaty shall cease to be in force with respect to such State, but shall remain in full force and effect with respect to all the other High Contracting Parties.

Article 26

The principles and fundamental provisions of this Treaty shall be incorporated in the Organic Pact of the Inter-American System.

IN WITNESS WHEREOF, the undersigned Plenipotentiaries, having deposited their full powers found to be in due and proper form, sign this Treaty on behalf of their respective Governments, on the dates appearing opposite their signatures.

Done in the city of Rio de Janeiro, in four texts respectively in the English, French, Portuguese and Spanish languages, on the second of September nineteen hundred forty-seven.

RESERVATION OF HONDURAS:

The Delegation of Honduras, in signing the present Treaty and in connection with Article 9, section (b), does so with the reservation that the boundary between Honduras and Nicaragua is definitively demarcated by the Joint Boundary Commission of nineteen hundred and nineteen hundred and one, starting from a point in the Gulf of Fonseca, in the Pacific Ocean, to Portillo de Teotecacinte and, from this point to the Atlantic, by the line that His Majesty the King of Spain's arbitral award established on the twenty-third of December of nineteen hundred and six.

Index

Judicial decisions and arbitration cases are indexed in bold face type. Names of vessels are in italics.